D1587979

VOLUME SEVEN

LYRIC—PAPUA

THE BRITISH ENCYCLOPEDIA

IN TEN VOLUMES

ILLUSTRATED

THE BRITISH ENCYCLOPEDIA

ILLUSTRATED

With an Introduction by
CYRIL NORWOOD, M.A., D. Litt.,
Headmaster of Harrow

Prepared under the general editorship of J. M. Parrish, M.A. (Oxon.), John R. Crossland, F.R.G.S., and Angelo S. Rappoport, Ph.D., B. ès L., with the specialist assistance and contributions of over 100 experts

VOLUME
SEVEN

ODHAMS PRESS LIMITED
LONDON, W.C. 2

Printed in Great Britain

KEY TO PRONUNCIATION

The method of marking pronunciations here employed is either (1) by marking the syllable on which the accent falls, or (2) by a simple system of transliteration, to which the following is the Key :

VOWELS

ā, as in f*a*te, or in b*a*re.

ä, as in *a*lms, Fr. *â*me, Ger. B*a*hn = á of Indian names.

ȧ, the same sound short or medium, as in Fr. b*a*l, Ger. M*a*nn.

a, as in f*a*t.

ạ, as in f*a*ll.

a, obscure, as in rur*a*l, similar to *u* in b*u*t, ė in her : common in Indian names.

ē, as in me = *i* in mach*i*ne.

e, as in met.

ė, as in her.

ī, as in p*i*ne, or as *ei* in Ger. m*ei*n.

i, as in p*i*n, also used for the short sound corresponding to ē, as in French and Italian words.

eu, a long sound as in Fr. j*eû*ne = Ger. long *ö*, as in S*ö*hne, G*ö*the (Goethe).

eu, corresponding sound short or medium, as in Fr. p*eu* = Ger. *ö* short.

ō, as in note, m*oa*n.

o, as in not, soft—that is, short or medium.

ö, as in m*o*ve, tw*o*.

ū, as in t*u*be.

u, as in t*u*b : similar to ė and also to *a*.

ụ, as in b*u*ll.

ü, as in Sc. ab*u*ne = Fr. *û* as in d*û*, Ger. *ü* long as in gr*ü*n, B*ü*hne.

u̇, the corresponding short or medium sound, as in Fr. b*u*t, Ger. M*ü*ller.

oi, as in *oi*l.

ou, as in p*ou*nd ; or as *au* in Ger. H*au*s.

CONSONANTS

Of the *consonants*, **b, d, f, h, j, k, l, m, n, ng, p, sh, t, v, z, always** have their common English sounds, when used to transliterate foreign words. The letter **c** is not used by itself in re-writing for pronunciation, **s** or **k** being used instead. The only consonantal symbols, therefore, that require explanation are the following :

ch is always as in ri*ch*.

d, nearly as *th* in *th*is = Sp. *d* in Ma*d*ri*d*, etc.

g is always hard, as in *g*o.

h represents the guttural in Scotch lo*ch*, Ger. na*ch*, also other similar gutturals.

ṇ, Fr. nasal *n* as in bo*n*.

r represents both English *r*, and *r* in foreign words, which is generally much more strongly trilled.

s, always as in *s*o.

th, as *th* in *th*in.

th, as *th* in *th*is.

w always consonantal, as in *w*e.

x = ks, which are used instead.

y always consonantal, as in *y*ea (Fr. *ligne* would be re-written lēny).

zh, as *s* in plea*s*ure = Fr. *j*.

THE BRITISH ENCYCLOPEDIA

VOLUME VII

LYRIC POETRY. Originally poetry adapted to the lyre and intended to be sung. The term was afterwards applied to short poems (whether meant to be sung or not), usually divided into stanzas, and directly expressing the poet's own thoughts and sentiments. The earliest recorded use of the expression "lyric poets" is in Puttenham's *Arte of English Poesie* (1589). When the term was first used, it was considered helpful to classify poets and poetry with much accuracy, but the phrase "lyric poetry" has now lost its exactness of meaning and much of its helpfulness. It may now be more accurately defined by saying that all poetry which is not quite definitely epic, dramatic, or didactic is lyric poetry.

Greece was the original home of lyric poetry. Amongst the greatest of the Greek lyric poets are Sappho, Alcæus, Alcman, Simonides, and Pindar. If among names so great it is allowable to pick out the greatest, Sappho and Pindar may be picked out; their work has had and still has a powerful influence upon the development of lyric poetry. Nor was the writing of lyrical poetry confined in Greece to purely lyrical poets. Æschylus's plays are lyrical dramas, and contain some of the noblest lyrical poetry in the world; and the lyrics of Aristophanes, particularly those in the *Birds* and *Clouds*, are unequalled, save by Shelley, for grace and lightness of touch. Among Roman poets Catullus proved himself the equal of Sappho, and Horace adapted the metres of Sappho and Alcæus and reached great heights of poetry in his Roman odes.

To enumerate many of the writers of lyric poetry would be a long task, but a few of the greatest may be mentioned. Shakespeare and many of the other Elizabethan dramatists have written beautiful songs in their plays. Herrick may be mentioned as one of the most delightful of lyric poets; he had many contemporaries only slightly less great. Burns has perhaps the greatest range of any lyric poet. Shelley seems to be an incarnation of the spirit of lyric poetry, and among English poets stands nearest to the Greeks.

The short lyric has a prominent place in modern poetry. Among lyricists the following names are preeminent: John Davidson, A. E. Housman, Robert Bridges, Thomas Hardy, J. E. Flecker, John Masefield, Alfred Noyes, W. B. Yeats, "A. E." (George Russell), Rupert Brooke, Siegfried Sassoon, Julian Grenfell, W. H. Davies, Walter de la Mare, Sir J. C. Squire.

Among lyric poets of other nations may be mentioned Lamartine, V. Hugo, A. de Musset, A. de Vigny, and Verlaine in France; Leopardi and Carducci in Italy; Goethe, Schiller, and Heine in Germany; Pushkin in Russia; and Mickiewicz in Poland. Continental lyricists of to-day include Claussen of Denmark, Cammaerts of Belgium, George of Germany, and Jean Cocteau of France. William Campbell and Robert Service are Canadian lyric writers.—BIBLIOGRAPHY: E. Rhys, *Lyric Poetry* (Channels of English Literature Series); F. Brunetière, *L'Évolution de la Poésie lyrique en France*; G. R. Carpenter, *Outline Guide to the Study of English Lyric Poetry*.

LYS. A river rising in Pas-de-Calais, France, which runs through Belgium, and enters the Schelde at Ghent; length, 120 miles. It formed the line of much fighting during the European War.

LYSAN'DER. An ancient Greek general who was appointed to the command of the Spartan fleet off the coasts of Asia Minor in 407 B.C., during the Peloponnesian War. In 405 B.C. he defeated and captured the Athenian fleet off Ægospotami, and thus put an end to the war.

He was killed in a battle with the Thebans in 395 B.C.

LYS'IAS. An Athenian orator, born about 458 B.C. He studied philosophy and eloquence at Thurii in Magna Græcia, and was there employed in the government. On the defeat of the Athenians in Sicily he

Lysias, the Athenian orator

returned to Athens in 412, but was banished by the thirty tyrants. When the city recovered its freedom he returned in 403, and gave instruction in eloquence, also writing speeches for others to deliver. He died in 378. Only about thirty orations have been preserved.

LYSIM'ACHUS. A general in the army of Alexander the Great, was born in Macedonia 360 B.C., and at the death of the emperor and the division of the empire he became King of Thrace. During the latter years of his reign he was instigated by his wife to kill his son Agathocles. This murder caused his subjects to rebel, and in the war which followed Lysimachus was defeated and slain at Corus in 281 B.C.

LYTHAM ST. ANNE'S. A watering-place of Lancashire, England, on the estuary of the Ribble, 8 miles from Blackpool. The place, which has two piers, promenade and gardens, consists of Lytham and St. Annes, which until 1922 were separate urban districts. Pop. (1931), 25,760.

LYTHRA'CEÆ. The loosestrife tribe, a natural order of polypetalous dicotyledons, containing about thirty genera of herbs, trees, and shrubs, of various habit, often with square branches; the leaves usually are opposite or whorled, entire, and shortly petiolate; the flowers being often large and showy. Henna and tulipwood belong to the order.

LYTHRUM. A genus of plants, the type of the ord. Lythraceæ (q.v.). *L. salicaria*, purple loosestrife, is a tall and handsome British plant. *See* HETEROSTYLISM.

LYTTELTON. A seaport in the Canterbury District, New Zealand, connected by rail with Christchurch (7 miles via tunnel), of which it is the port. There is a good natural harbour and graving-dock. The exports are principally of wool and frozen meat. Pop. 3720.

LYTTELTON, Alfred. English politician and athlete. The youngest son of the fourth Lord Lyttelton, he was born 7th Feb., 1857, and went to Eton and Trinity College, Cambridge. He became a barrister and a K.C., and in 1895, as a Liberal Unionist, was elected M.P. for Warwick and Leamington. In 1902 he went to the Transvaal on public business, and on his return to England in 1903 succeeded J. Chamberlain as Colonial Secretary. He held office until 1905, being chiefly concerned with the question of Chinese labour in the South African mines. In 1906 he lost his seat at Warwick, but was soon elected for St. George's, Hanover Square, and was in the House of Commons until his sudden death, 5th July, 1913. His only son is **Captain Oliver Lyttelton, D.S.O.** His first wife was Laura, a daughter of Sir Charles Tennant, Bart., and sister of the Countess of Oxford; the second was Miss Edith Balfour, who wrote his Life.

Lyttelton was a superb athlete. At cricket he was captain of Eton and Cambridge, and played for England against Australia. He represented Cambridge and England at association football, and he was the amateur racquets champion, 1882 to 1895.

Of Alfred Lyttelton's seven brothers, the most notable perhaps were **Sir Neville Gerald Lyttleton,** the fourth, and **Edward Lyttleton,** the seventh. The former entered the army and held high commands in the South African War (1899-1902). From 1904-12 he was commander-in-chief in Ireland and from 1912 until his death, 6th July, 1931, was governor of Chelsea Hospital.

Edward was captain of the Cambridge cricket eleven. He became a schoolmaster and a clergyman. From 1890 to 1905 he was headmaster of Haileybury and from 1905 to 1916 of Eton.

LYTTON, Edward George Earle Lytton Bulwer-Lytton. Baron, youngest son of General Bulwer of Woodalling and Elizabeth Barbara Lytton of Knebworth, was born 25th May, 1803, died at Torquay 18th Jan.,

1873. He entered Trinity Hall, Cambridge, graduated B.A. in 1826. M.A. in 1835, and gained the chancellor's prize medal for his English poem on *Sculpture.* He published poetry at an early age, but first gained reputation by the novels *Pelham* and *The Disowned* (1828), *Devereux* (1829), and *Paul Clifford* (1830). These were followed by the popular romances of *Eugene Aram, The Pilgrims of the Rhine, The Last Days of Pompeii, Rienzi,* and *Ernest Maltravers* with its sequel *Alice.*

In connection with Macready's management at Covent Garden Bulwer-Lytton produced his *Duchesse de la Vallière,* which proved a failure, but this was retrieved by the instant success of the *Lady of Lyons, Richelieu,* and *Money.* When he had thus shown his quick adaptability of talent he returned to novel-writing, and published in steady succession—*Night and Morning, Zanoni, The Last of the Barons, Lucretia, Harold, The Caxtons, My Novel,* and *What will He Do with It?* In 1845 he published a poetical satire called *The New Timon,* in which he attacked Tennyson, who replied more vigorously than had probably been expected.

He entered Parliament for St. Ives in 1831, and supported the Reform Bill as a Whig; but he changed his opinions and subsequently supported the Conservatives. Under Lord Derby's ministry he was Colonial Secretary, and in 1866 entered the House of Lords as Baron Lytton. He was elected rector of Glasgow University in 1856. His later literary works were *The Coming Race,* published anonymously (1871); *The Parisians* (1872); and *Kenelm Chillingly* (1873). Among his poetic works were the epic *King Arthur*; *The Lost Tales of Miletus*; and *Brutus,* a drama.—BIBLIOGRAPHY: T. H. S. Escott, *Edward Bulwer, first Baron Lytton of Knebworth*; V. A. G. R. Lytton, *The Life of Edward Bulwer, first Lord Lytton*; J. C. Watt, *Great Novelists.*

LYTTON, Edward Robert Bulwer-Lytton. First Earl of, son of the first Baron Lytton, was born in 1831; educated at Harrow and Bonn; entered the diplomatic service in 1849 as attaché at Washington; and successively served in the embassies of Florence, Paris, The Hague, Copenhagen, Athens, Madrid, Vienna, Paris, and Lisbon. He was appointed Viceroy of India by Lord Beaconsfield in 1876, and during his administration the queen was proclaimed Empress of India, and war was waged with Afghanistan. In 1880 he resigned and was created an earl. He attained some reputation as a poet under the pen name of "Owen Meredith"; and wrote *Clytemnestra and other Poems*; *Lucile*; *Tannhäuser, or the Battle of the Bards*; *Fables in Song*; *King Poppy*; and *Glenaveril*; besides prose works. He died in Paris in 1891.

Lord Lytton

Victor Alexander George Robert Lytton, who became the second Earl in 1891, was a grandson. Born 9th Aug., 1876, and educated at Eton and Trinity College, Cambridge, he held positions in the coalition ministry between 1916 and 1921 and from 1922 to 1927 was governor of Bengal. He wrote the *Life* of his grandfather Lord Lytton. In 1932 he went out to Manchuria as head of a mission sent by the League of Nations. Lord Lytton's seat is Knebworth House, Hertfordshire. His eldest son, Viscount Knebworth, a noted athlete, was killed in a flying accident in 1933.

M

M. The thirteenth letter and tenth consonant of the English alphabet. It represents a labial and nasal articulation, the compression of the lips being accompanied with the fall of the uvula so as to allow the voice to form a humming sound through the nose, which constitutes the difference between this letter and *b*.

MAARTENS, Maarten. The pen-name of Joost Marius van der Poorten Schwartz, novelist, born at Amsterdam in 1858, and died in 1915. He was educated in England, at Bonn, and the University of Utrecht. He wrote several novels in English, notably *The Sin of Joost Avelingh* (1890), *God's Fool* (1892), *The Greater Glory* (1894), *My Lady Nobody* (1895), and *Dorothea* (1904).

MAAS. *See* MEUSE.

MAASTRICHT. A town and capital of the Dutch province of Limburg, on the Maas (Meuse), near the Belgian-Dutch frontier. The town has a large river trade, and has breweries and manufactures of earthenware and paper. The church of St. Servatius was founded between A.D. 560 and 569, and is the oldest in the Netherlands; the Stadhuis dates from 1664, and there are quarries (Petersberg) worked by the Romans in the vicinity. The town was plundered by the Spanish under Parma (1579); fell to Louis XIV. (1673), to Marshal Saxe (1749), and to Kléber (1794). It was successfully defended by the Dutch against the Belgians in 1830, Until 1871-8 Maastricht was one of the first fortresses of Europe. Pop. (1932), 61,763.

MACAD'AM, John Loudon. Scottish inventor, was born at Ayr 1756, and died in 1836. In 1815 he was appointed surveyor of the Bristol roads, and was so successful in this that the House of Commons presented him with a sum of £10,000. His system of road-making is still known as Macadamization, and consists in covering the roadway or forming the road-crust with small broken stones to a considerable depth, and consolidating them by rollers, so as to form a hard, firm and smooth surface.

MACA'O. A Portuguese settlement and city of China, on the Island of Macao at the mouth of the Canton River, and forming, with the adjacent islands of Taipa and Colôane, a

Macao : The Cathedral

province. Macao has been a Portuguese colony since 1577, but was not formally recognized as independent of China until 1887. Area, 4 sq. miles; pop. (settlement), 157,175; (town), 83,984.

MACARONIC POEMS. A kind of facetious Latin poems, in which are interspersed words from other languages, with Latin inflections. They were first written (at least with the above designation) by Teofilo Folengo (1491–1544); and were introduced into England in the reign of Henry VII. Drummond of Hawthornden is credited with a macaronic poem, *Polemo-Middinia,* published in 1684. There is good reason, however, to believe that it is later than Drummond's time, and that it is the work of Dr. Pitcairne (1652–1713).

MACAS'SAR. A seaport town of Celebes (q.v.), Dutch East Indies, on Macassar Strait, and second only to Batavia in commercial importance. It was made a free port in Dec., 1846, and now exports spices, Macassar oil, rubber, and valuable woods. Pop. about 20,000.

MACAULAY, Rose. English novelist and essayist. She spent her childhood in Italy and was educated at Oxford. Her publications, which are marked by a lively humour, include *What Not,* 1919; *Potterism,* 1920; *Dangerous Ages,* 1921; *Mystery at Geneva,* 1922; *Told by an Idiot,* 1923; *Orphan Island,* 1924; *Crewe Train,* 1926; *Keeping up Appearances,* 1928; *Staying with Relations,* 1930; two books of verse, 1914 and 1919, *A Casual Commentary,* essays, 1925, and *Some Religious Elements in English Literature,* 1931.

MACAU'LAY, Thomas Babington, Lord. Historian, essayist, and politician, born 1800 at Rothley Temple,

Lord Macaulay

Leicestershire, and died at Kensington 1859. In 1818 he entered Trinity College, Cambridge, where he obtained the chancellor's medal for a poem on *Pompeii,* and a second time for a poem on *Evening*; received a fellowship, and took his M.A. degree in 1825. Before this he began to contribute to Knight's *Quarterly Magazine,* in which appeared his poems of the *Armada, Ivry,* and *The Battle of the League*; and in 1825 he published in the *Edinburgh Review* his article on Milton.

He was called to the Bar at Lincoln's Inn in 1826, and entered Parliament in 1830 as member for Calne. He afterwards became member for Leeds, but resigned his seat and proceeded to Calcutta as legal member of the Supreme Council of India, in which position he prepared a new penal code that was not adopted because of its liberal dealing with the native races. Returning from India, he was elected a member of Parliament for Edinburgh; was made Secretary of War in the Melbourne ministry (1839–41); and when the Whigs returned to power in 1846 he was appointed Paymaster of the Forces. At the election of the same year his Edinburgh constituency refused to re-elect him, but their attitude was reversed in 1852, when he was returned (although he had not presented himself as a candidate).

During his political career Macaulay had continued to write. In 1842 he published his *Lays of Ancient Rome*; and in 1848 appeared the first two of the five volumes of his *History of England,* which covers the period between the accession of James II. and the death of William III. This work, although touched with partisanship and with a tendency to paradox, has attained the position of an English classic. He was created a peer in 1857, and at his death he was buried in Westminster Abbey.—BIBLIOGRAPHY: Sir G. O. Trevelyan, *Life and Letters of Lord Macaulay*; J. A. C. Morison, *Macaulay* (English Men of Letters Series); D. H. Macgregor, *Lord Macaulay.*

MACAW'. The name of beautiful parrots native to tropical America.

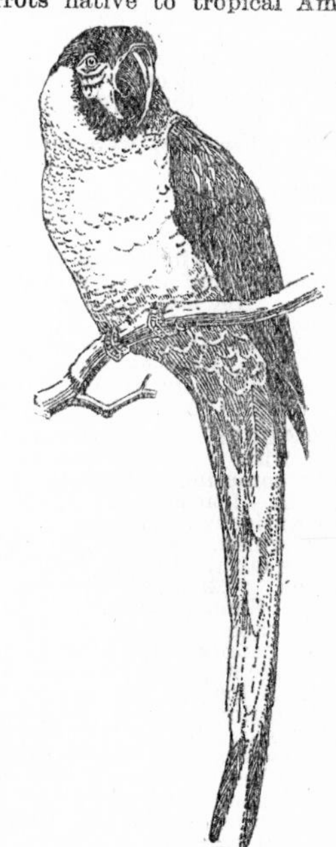

Blue-and-yellow Macaw

The macaws are magnificent birds, distinguished by having their cheeks destitute of feathers, and their tail-feathers long.

Species.—The largest and most splendid in regard to colour is the great scarlet or red-and-blue macaw (*Ara chloroptera*). The great red-and-green macaw (*A. militaris*) and the blue-and-yellow macaw (*A. ararauna*) are somewhat smaller. The hyacinthine macaws (species of Anodorhynchus and Cyanopsittacus) of Brazil are blue.

MACBETH'. Son of Finnlaech and nephew of Malcolm II., a king of Scotland who reigned from 1040 to 1057. He was hereditary *mormœr* of Moray, and slew King Duncan at Bothgowan, near Elgin, in 1040, when he proclaimed himself king. In 1050 he is said to have gone on a pilgrimage to Rome. At the death of their father the sons of Duncan had taken refuge with their uncle Siward, Earl of Northumbria, and with his aid they invaded Scotland in 1054; a battle was fought at Dunsinane, but it was not until 1057 that Macbeth was finally defeated and slain at Lumphanan, in Aberdeen. The legends which gradually gathered round the name of Macbeth were collected by John of Fordun and Hector Boece, and reproduced by Holinshed in his *Chronicle*, where they were found by Shakespeare.

M'BEY, James. Scottish painter and etcher. Born at Newburgh, Aberdeenshire, 23rd Dec., 1883, he entered a bank at fifteen, but studied art privately, and began etching at seventeen. His first exhibition was in London in 1911. He has made etchings of Scotland, Wales, Holland, Spain, Venice, Morocco, and France, and in 1917–18 went as official artist to the Egyptian Expeditionary Force.

MAC'CABEES. A dynasty of ruling Jewish priests of whom the first who came into prominence was Mattathias. During the persecutions of Antiochus Epiphanes he slew a Jew who came to the altar to renounce his faith, and then fled to the mountains with his five sons—Johannes, Simon, Judas, Eleazar, and Jonathan. Being joined by numerous patriotic Jews, they were able to make successful resistance to the national foe and re-establish the ancient religion. When Mattathias died (166 B.C.), his sons Judas and Jonathan became successively leaders of the national movement. The last remaining member of the family was Simon, who now carried forward the national cause to a triumphant issue, reduced "the tower" of Jerusalem, and established the power of the new state. Under his rule trade and agriculture flourished, until (in 135 B.C.) he was treacherously murdered by Ptolemy, his own son-in-law.—Cf. E. Schürer, *History of the Jewish People*.

MACCABEES. Two books associated with the Old Testament, treating of the Jewish history under the Maccabean princes. They are included in the English *Apocrypha*. 1 Maccabees is of historical value.

M'CARDIE, Henry Alfred. British judge. Born in Edgbaston, 18th July, 1869, he was called to the Bar in 1894, and in 1916 became a Bencher of the Middle Temple and a judge of the High Court. His advanced views and outspoken comment on social affairs made the "bachelor judge" a famous figure. He died in 1933.

M'CARTHY, Justin. Novelist, historian, and politician, born at Cork, 1830, died 1912; became connected with the Liverpool press in 1853; joined the staff of *The Morning Star* in 1860, and became its chief editor in 1864. He afterwards was connected with *The Daily News* (1870–85) nected with *The Daily News* (1870–85). His novels are numerous, and his historical writings include *A History of Our Own Times* and *History of the Four Georges*. He was chairman of the Anti-Parnellite section of the Irish National party from the fall of Parnell in 1890 to 1896.

M'CARTHY, Lillah. English actress. She was born at Cheltenham, 22nd Sept., 1875, and educated there. She has played leading parts in England, Australia, and the United States with Wilson Barrett; and in Shaw plays between 1905–8. She assumed management of the Little Theatre in 1911, playing Margaret Knox in *Fanny's First Play*, and later played with Sir Herbert Beerbohm Tree and Sir Martin Harvey. She became manager of the Kingsway Theatre in 1912 and 1919, and produced plays by Eden Phillpotts and Arnold Bennett, afterwards playing with Matheson Lang in *The Wandering Jew*. In 1920 she married Sir F. W. Keeble.

MACCLELLAN, George Brinton. American general, born at Philadelphia 1826, died 1885. In 1855 he was appointed to the Commission reporting upon the condition of European armies, and watched the military operations during the Crimean War. At the outbreak of the Civil War in the United States he superseded M'Dowell after the first battle of Bull Run, and became commander-in-chief on 1st Nov., 1861. In this capacity he organized the raw levies of the North and advanced against Richmond the following spring, but was relieved from supreme command by President Lincoln in 1862, and thenceforth led the army of the Potomac.

When Lee advanced into Maryland, MacClellan fought the battles of South Mountain and Antietam (14th–17th Sept., 1862), and compelled the Confederate forces to retire. The political authorities being dissatisfied with his apparent slackness in following up this victory, MacClellan was relieved from his command and retired from the army. In 1864 he was nominated for the presidency, but was overwhelmingly defeated by Abraham Lincoln.

MACCLESFIELD. A town of Cheshire, England, on the little river Bollin. The staple manufacture is silk. In the vicinity are extensive coal-pits and stone- and slate-quarries. A canal connects the town with the Grand Union system. Pop. (1931) 34,902.

M'CORMACK, John. Irish vocalist. Born at Athlone, 14th June, 1884, he was educated in Dublin, where he sang in the choir of the Roman Catholic cathedral. He then went to Milan for study, and in 1907 appeared for the first time in opera in London. Possessing a beautiful tenor voice, he sang for several seasons at Covent Garden, also in concerts in London, New York, Naples, Melbourne, and elsewhere. His singing of Irish folk-songs was also noteworthy. In 1917 he became an American citizen, and in 1924 the Pope made him a count and an official at the papal court.

MACCULLOCH, or M'CULLOCH, Horatio, R.S.A. One of the most distinguished of Scottish landscape-painters, was born in Glasgow in 1806, died near Edinburgh 1867. From 1831 he was a regular contributor to the exhibitions of the Royal Scottish Academy, Edinburgh. His paintings are nearly all of Scottish scenery. Among the most celebrated are the *Cuchulin Mountains* (Skye), *A Dream of the Highlands, Highland Loch, Views in Cadzow Forest, Loch-an-Eilan, Mist on the Mountains, Loch Achray, Loch Katrine,* and *Loch Lomond.*

MACCUNN, Hamish. Scottish composer. Born at Greenock, 22nd March, 1868, he studied music in London. From 1888-94 he was Professor of Harmony at the Royal Academy of Music, London. His works include the operas *Jeannie Deans* and *Diarmid*, some cantatas, and the popular overture *Land of the Mountain and the Flood.* Maccunn died 2nd Aug., 1916.

MACDONALD, Étienne Jacques Joseph Alexandre. Duke of Taranto and Marshal of France, was born in 1765, and died 1840. He was closely related to Flora Macdonald, and belonged to a Jacobite family exiled for their support of James II. Entering the French army, he served with an Irish regiment, but early espoused the Revolutionary cause, and in 1796, after his capture of the Dutch fleet (1795), he became general of division. Napoleon made him Governor of the Roman States (1798), and in 1809 he broke the Austrian centre at Wagram and was made a duke and marshal on the field. Macdonald was loyal to Napoleon until the last eventful days of abdication and exile, and although he was made a peer by the Bourbons at the Restoration, he refused to take part against Napoleon in the Hundred Days. From 1816 onwards he was Chancellor of the Legion of Honour.

MACDONALD, Flora. Born at Milton, South Uist (Outer Hebrides), in 1720, died 1790. She became celebrated in 1746 for the part she took in assisting Prince Charles Edward to escape the Government pursuit after Culloden, when she conveyed him from South Uist to Skye, disguised and in an open boat. For this she was imprisoned in the Tower of London, but was released in 1747. She married, settled in North Carolina, but afterwards returned to and died in Skye.

MacDONALD, George. Novelist and poet, was born at Huntly 1824, died 1905. He was educated at King's College, Aberdeen, became an Independent minister, but soon retired from this position and adopted literature as a profession. Among his numerous novels are: *David Elginbrod, Alec Forbes, Annals of a Quiet Neighbourhood, Robert Falconer, Malcolm, The Marquis of Lossie,* and *Castle Warlock.* He also published some poetry, and stories for the young.

MACDONALD, James Ramsay. British politician. He was born at Lossiemouth in humble circumstances, 12th Oct., 1866, and educated at the elementary school there. Settling in London, he worked as a clerk and then as a journalist, He became identified with the Fabian Society and the Labour Party, and was soon an influential member of the group that inspired this movement. He edited *The Socialist Review* and wrote a good deal on Socialism. In 1900 he was made

Secretary of the Labour Party, a post he held for twelve years, and for the next twelve he was its treasurer. From 1900 to 1904 he was a member of the London County Council.

In 1895 MacDonald stood for Parliament for Southampton, but failed to secure election, as he did at Leicester in 1901. In 1906 he was returned for Leicester, and he held the seat until 1918 when, owing to his pacifist ideas during the Great War, he was defeated. He was absent from Parliament until 1922, when he was returned for the Aberavon division of Glamorganshire, a seat which he exchanged in 1929 for the Seaham Harbour division of Durham.

Having been from 1906 to 1909 Chairman of the Independent Labour Party, MacDonald was, in 1911, chosen leader of the Labour Party in the House of Commons. He held this position until 1914, and returned to it in 1922, when the Labour Party was the official opposition in Parliament. As leader, he was called upon in Jan., 1924, to form a ministry, and he became the first Labour Prime Minister in Great Britain. He also filled the office of Foreign Secretary until the ministry fell before the end of the year. Having been leader of the Opposition for a period of nearly five years, he was called upon, after the general election of 1929, to form the second Labour Ministry. This was in office under his premiership until a financial crisis led to its break-up in Aug., 1931. With a few colleagues and followers MacDonald acted with the other two political parties, and a National Government was formed, with himself as Premier. This was confirmed in office when the general election of Oct., 1931, sent an immense majority to its support in the House of Commons. In 1932 he underwent two operations on his eyes, but was able to preside over the Lausanne conference in July.

MacDonald has travelled very widely and is a man of considerable culture. His books include *Socialism and Society, Labour and the Empire, The Awakening of India, The Socialist Movement, Parliament and Revolution, Wanderings and Excursions,* and a *Memoir* of his wife. In 1912-14 he was a member of the royal commission that inquired into the public services of India, and he has received numerous academic and other honours.

MacDonald married, in 1896, Margaret Ethel, daughter of J. H. Gladstone, the eminent scientist, a woman of unusual gifts. She died in 1911, leaving five children. One son, Malcolm, was returned as M.P. for the Bassetlaw division in 1929 and again in 1931. In 1931 he was appointed Under-Secretary for the Colonies.

MACDUFF. Burgh, market town, and seaport of Scotland. It stands at the mouth of the river Deveron, 50 miles from Aberdeen, on the L.M.S. Railway. There is a modern harbour for the shipping and the fishing. On the other side of the Deveron is Banff, and a bridge connects the two. The old name of the burgh was Doune. Pop. (1931) 3276.

The eldest son of the Duchess of Fife is called the **Earl of Macduff.**

MACE. A weapon of war in use in Europe as late as the sixteenth

Mace of House of Commons

century. It consisted of a staff about 5 feet long, with a heavy metal head, which assumed a variety of forms, but was frequently in the form of a spiked ball. Another kind of mace is a sort of heavy ornamental staff used as an emblem of authority in universities and courts of law. In the House of Commons it is the symbol of the Speaker's authority, and is removed from its place on the table when the Speaker leaves the chair or the House rises.

MACE. *See* NUTMEG.

MACEDONIA. In ancient geography, a territory lying north of Greece, which first became powerful under its king, Philip, father of Alexander the Great and conqueror of Greece. Alexander added immensely to the Empire of Macedonia and made it mistress of half the ancient world. After his death the empire was partitioned, dominion over Greece was lost, and the battles of Cynoscephalæ (197 B.C.) and Pydna (168 B.C.) reduced the ancient kingdom to a Roman province.

In the fifteenth century Macedonia fell under the sway of the Turks, and, being inhabited by Greeks, Turks, Bulgarians, and Serbians, it was the scene of many revolts. It is now divided among Greece, Bulgaria, and Yugoslavia.

MACEIO (mȧ-sā′i-o). A seaport and, since 1839, capital of the state of Alagôas, Brazil, at a short distance from Jaraguá, its port on the Lagôa do Norte, and connected by rail with Pernambuco. Cotton and machinery are manufactured. Pop. (1930), 103,930.

MACENTA. A territory of West Africa, forming, with others, the colony of French Guinea.

MACERATA (mȧ-che-rä′tȧ). A maritime province of the Marches, Central Italy, traversed by the Roman Apennines and lying around the valleys of the Potenza and Chiente. Area, 1070 sq. miles; pop. (1931), 277,696.

MACERATA. A city of Italy, and capital of Macerata Province, founded with Recanati immediately after the destruction of *Helvia Ricina* by Alaric (408), where there are ruins of an amphitheatre. The State university was founded in 1290. Pop. (1931), 26,432.

M'EVOY, Ambrose. English portrait-painter. Born at Crudwell, Wiltshire, 12th Aug., 1878, he was encouraged by his father to take up art, and entered the Slade School in 1893. He became friendly with Augustus John, and soon gained a reputation for clever portraits in line and wash, and became a fashionable portrait-painter. He was elected A.R.A. in 1924, and died 4th Jan., 1927.

MACFAR′REN, Sir George Alexander. Musical composer, born in London 1813, died 1887. He became a member of the Board of the Academy, and ultimately chairman and principal; was elected professor of music, Cambridge University (1875); and was knighted in 1883. His chief operas are: *The Devil's Opera* (1838), *Don Quixote* (1846), and *Robin Hood* (1860). He also essayed the cantata in *Lenore* (1852) and *The Lady of the Lake* (1870). His oratorios are: *St. John the Baptist* (1873), *The Resurrection* (1876), *Joseph* (1877), and *King David* (1883).

MACGILL, Patrick. Irish novelist and poet. He was born in Donegal in 1870, and was educated at a mountain school. He worked between the ages of twelve and nineteen about the farm and as a navvy, and joined the staff of the *Daily Express* in 1911. He served in the British Army during the Great War. His books include *Songs of a Navvy, Songs of the Dead End, The Great Push, Soldier Songs, Glenmornan, Moleskin Joe* (a play), *Fear*, and *Suspense* (a play produced in London in 1930).

MACGIL′LICUDDY'S REEKS. A mountain range of County Kerry, Ireland, extending for 13½ miles west of Killarney. Carrantuohill, the highest peak, rises 3414 feet above sea-level.

M'GILL UNIVERSITY. A Canadian university, founded in 1821, which originated in an endowment of James McGill (1744-1813), a Scottish merchant in Montreal. There are the McGill, Macdonald, and Royal Victoria Colleges, the last named being for women.

MACHIAVELLI (mȧk-yȧ-vel′lē), **Niccolo.** Italian statesman and historian, born at Florence 1469, died 1527. In 1498 he was appointed secretary to the Ten at Florence, and for more than fourteen years he guided the destinies of the Florentine Republic, undertook embassies, concluded treaties, and jealously conserved the rights and liberties of his native city.

When, by aid of Pope Julius II., the Medici returned to power in 1512, Machiavelli was deprived of his office, and imprisoned for his supposed complicity in a plot to overturn the new authority; but being released after a time, he retired to his country house of San Casciano. Here he devoted himself to literature and produced a *History of Florence*, embracing the period between 1215 and 1492; *Discourses upon the first ten books of Livy*; *The Prince* (Il Principe), by which he is best known; a military treatise entitled *Dell' Arte della Guerra*; and the comedies of *La Mandragola* and *La Clizia*. *The Prince* was first published in 1532 by permission of Pope Clement VII.

Machiavelli

Machiavelli made a clear distinction between ethics and politics, and he has been followed in this conception by numerous statesmen in modern times, who never allow objection on ethical grounds to interfere with their political and diplomatic schemes.—BIBLIOGRAPHY: *Cambridge Modern History* (vol. i.); L. Villari, *Machiavelli and his Times*; J. M. Robertson, *Pioneer Humanists*.

MACHINE DESIGN. Concerns not only the selection of a suitable mechanism to perform any specified mechanical action, but also the determination of the stresses to which the parts are subjected; for these stresses must be known before the dimensions required for safety can be assigned.

When metals are loaded, a change of form takes place gradually and proportionately until the *elastic limit* is reached, when the deformation becomes more marked. After loading to this extent a *permanent set* is shown. In any actual machine the designer must select sections of such proportions as to prevent actions of this character. Even when material is subjected to stresses of a lower value than the elastic limit, either on and off or acting in tension and compression alternately, the material becomes *fatigued*, and rupture takes place after a number of repetitions.

To avoid these possibilities, as well as to allow for any irregularities in the material, a *factor of safety* is introduced into the calculations. It is the ratio of the ultimate strength of the material to the working load it is called upon to bear. The value of the factor of safety varies considerably, according as the load is *dead*, i.e. steady, or *live*, i.e. alternating. In the main calculations for any machine, whether it be a shearing-machine or a steam-engine, the loads on the essential parts can be calculated from the work to be done If these loads act as simple stresses, the cross-sectional areas are obtained by dividing the load by the allowable stress. The stresses to which a machine part is subjected are frequently of a combined character, such as tension and twisting or tension and bending, and in these cases the resultant stress due to both actions must be considered. In many examples the stresses are indeterminate, and former experience then enters largely into the selection of a suitable section.

Common details of machines have been standardized, and the relationship of their dimensions is given in the textbooks in terms of some standard, such as the diameter of a shaft, bolt, or rivet. This simplification of the machine-designer's work is based on a combination of experience of the nature of trial and error, consideration of appearance, and scientific principles. Many empirical equations are used in design work which, as the accumulation of knowledge of stress actions grows, are seen to be based on fundamental principles. —BIBLIOGRAPHY: H. J. Spooner. *Machine Design, Construction, and Drawing*; W. C. Unwin and A. L. Mellanby, *Elements of Machine Design*.

MACHINE-GUN. A small-calibre firearm arranged to fire from a stand, carriage, or tripod, and provided with mechanical devices calculated to produce a very rapid rate of fire. Stands or rests, or even carriages, are necessary, partly on account of the weight and partly to increase the stability required for rapid and continuous fire.

Machine-guns in use in the British army are the "Vickers," the "Hotchkiss," and the "Lewis" (q.v.), of which the first is the machine-gun *par excellence*, the other two being, in some degree, of the nature of automatic rifles. Speaking generally, there are two main classes of machine-guns, i.e. those which depend principally on the shock of discharge or recoil for their action, and those in which the gases generated by the explosion are controlled in such a way as to give the same effect. In both classes a powerful spring is also used to counteract the backward movement caused by recoil or action of gas. The modern Vickers gun is a recoil-action weapon, while the Hotchkiss and Lewis come under the gas-action category.

Historical Survey.—For all practical purposes machine-guns did not exist before 1862, in which year the "Gatling" gun (q.v.) appeared in America. Then, just before the Franco-German War, the French authorities began experimenting with a machine-gun invented by a Belgian (*see* MITRAILLEUSE). In the British service, both naval and military, the first machine-gun to be adopted was the Gatling ·45 calibre, and then came in rapid succession trials of the "Nordenfeldt" and "Gardner" guns. All these guns were of the multi-barrel type, i.e. they were constructed with from two to ten barrels, or even as many as thirty-seven. These guns were worked by a lever or handle. Then, in the early 'eighties, Mr. (afterwards Sir) Hiram Maxim invented a very much superior weapon to any that had previously appeared, a weapon, moreover, which with modifications and improvements held its own for many years, and of which the present Vickers gun is the lineal and improved descendant.

As we have seen, all former guns depended for their action on the elementary idea of turning a handle, and no automatic aids were made use of. Maxim broke new ground, and, instead of ignoring or counteracting the recoil present to a greater or less extent in every gun at the moment of discharge, harnessed it to his will, and made use of it to keep his mechanism running and his gun firing. He also abolished the collection of barrels and used only a single one, which, together with certain portions of its attached mechanism, he made movable. The effect of this was that when a cartridge was fired the barrel and the movable portion attached to it was forced back by the power of the recoil, the "extracting" and "reloading" mechanism being brought into play at the same time. Having reached the farthest limit of recoil, a powerful spring, known as the fusee spring, took charge and forced the movable portion back to its original position, at the same time causing the loading device to complete its work and the firing-pin to reach the new cartridge. Once the gun was loaded and fired, it was only necessary to maintain the pressure on the trigger, by means of a double button, to secure a continuous stream of bullets up to a maximum of 700 a minute. Stoppages did of course occur, but these were soon recognized and provision for their rapid adjustment made, and as the gun was improved these became less frequent. The loading is by means of a belt, in which cartridges are held, passing through a "feed block" operated by the moving portion of the mechanism.

The present Vickers gun resembles the original Maxim in its main features, but embodies many improvements suggested by experience; it is also considerably lighter, which is an additional advantage. In the Vickers, as in the original Maxim, the barrel proper is encased in a water-jacket to counteract the undue and excessive heating of the barrel which inevitably results from the rapid firing of hundreds of rounds. All machine-guns use the ammunition which is used in the ordinary rifles of the army concerned.

The Maxim principle has been adopted by a very large number of countries, including Germany, where the value of the machine-gun was so well recognized that on the outbreak of the European War the German army took the field with thousands of these weapons, whereas in our army the allotment was merely two to a battalion. Now all this has been changed, and each battalion has thirty-two Lewis guns and a proportion of the heavier Vickers, which are also the arms of the separately organized machine-gun battalions.

With regard to the tactical use of machine-guns, it must suffice to say that it has been long recognized that the true rôle of this weapon is not that of artillery. The French in 1871 used them in this way, forming their artillery brigades of two batteries of ordinary guns and one of mitrailleuses, with the inevitable result that the unfortunate machine-guns were out-ranged and smothered by the opposing artillery proper. The rôle of the machine-gun is the rôle of the small-bore arm, in which sphere it is highly efficient, both in taking its own considerable share in an attack and other operations and in providing covering-fire for advancing bodies of troops.

In 1915 a **Machine-Gun Corps** was formed. It was divided into four branches: infantry, cavalry, heavy, and motor. In 1919 a school for training officers was opened at Sleaford, but in 1921 the corps was disbanded. There is a memorial at Folkestone to those of its members who fell in the Great War. Machine gun detachments are now attached to each battalion of infantry. *See* FIRE TACTICS; HOTCHKISS; LEWIS GUN, MITRAILLEUSE.—Cf. Longstaff and Atteridge, *Book of the Machine-gun.*

MACHINES, Theory of. A machine is a combination of parts whose motions relative to one another are restricted to achieve the purpose of transmitting or transforming mechanical energy. The old system of classification of machines subdivided them into the so-called *mechanical powers*—the lever, the wheel and axle, the pulley, the inclined plane, the wedge, and the screw. All these types are better included in the two divisions of levers and inclined planes. The *Principle of Work* states that if friction be neglected the work put into a machine is equal to the work taken out. As work is the product of force and the distance through which it operates, if the force applied to the mechanism is increased to achieve the purpose of the machine, then the distances travelled by the parts in question will be decreased in the same ratio. The *mechanical advantage* is the ratio of the load to the effort.

Higher and Lower Pairs.—Reuleaux introduced the system of discussing machine problems by reference to certain standard combinations of parts or *pairs.* These may be rated as *higher* or *lower* according to their simplicity.

The *lower pairs* are (*a*) *sliding,* as the piston and cylinder; (*b*) *turning,* all pin joints; and (*c*) *screw,* all nuts and screws. *Chains* in the machine sense are made up of three or more *links* consisting of two *pairs.* The slider-crank mechanism is the simplest of all the kinematic chains, and is the essential mechanism of the direct-acting engine. By fixing the different links in turn, although the relation of the parts remains the same, mechanisms which serve different purposes can be obtained. Thus Scott-Russell's straight-line motion and the Whitworth quick-return motion are obtained from the same slider-crank combination as the steam-engine.

The *higher pairs* concern examples of line or point contact, and include spur gearing (*see* GEARING), bevel gearing, friction drives, cams (q.v.), and escapements (q.v.) as *rigid links*; and rope, chain, and belt pulley drives as *flexible links.* The kinematic chains are combinations of lower pairs, as in the crank and screw chains, or of higher and power pairs in pulley, wheel (constant motion), cam (variable motion), or ratchet chains (intermittent motion). The use of such a classification reduces the number of different mechanism problems to a few standard types. In spur- and bevel-gearing pairs the teeth are formed to transmit perfectly uniform motion. To fulfil this condition the normals to all surfaces of contact must pass through the meeting-point of the pitch lines (*see* GEARING).

Friction.—With belt drives there must be a tight and slack side, and the relationship of these tensions is fixed by the coefficient of friction between belt and wheel and the angle embraced by the belt. Much experimental work has been done to determine the laws of friction (q.v.) under different conditions. There is an essential difference between the friction of two dry solids and the same bodies when lubricated. The first type, *solid friction,* varies directly with the pressure, is independent of the surface, and at moderate speeds is independent of the velocity. *Fluid friction* is independent of the pressure, varies directly with the wetted surface and with the velocity raised to a power which increases with the speed. By the introduction of fluid lubricants between bodies in relative motion the friction is changed from the solid to the fluid type, and is considerably reduced in magnitude.

Rolling friction, as in ball and roller bearings, is also less than the simple, solid, sliding type, and is not much diminished by lubrication. Belt drives can be arranged between shafts which are not parallel to one another if the side of the belt advancing towards the pulley is at right angles to the shaft. Where the drive is difficult or impossible otherwise, small jockey or idle pulleys may be introduced with success. Chain driving with pitch chains gives a *positive* drive, with which it is possible to transmit considerable power.

Friction is made use of in all forms of locomotion between the vehicle wheels and the track, in clutches (*see* FRICTION CLUTCH), and in brakes used on winding engines, on vehicles, and in testing. The efficiency of a machine is the ratio of the work got out of it to the input (*see* EFFICIENCY). Frictional losses account for the work loss in a machine, the energy lost for useful purposes being converted into heat.—BIBLIOGRAPHY: John Goodman, *Mechanics applied to Engineering*; S. Dunkerley, *Mechanism*; W. C. Unwin and A. L. Mellanby, *Machine Design.*

MACHINE TOOLS. All machines used in engineering work to shape material, usually iron or steel, into simple geometric forms. The tools used before James Watt's day were few in number and type, simple in construction, and crude in the quality of their work. In one of his letters Watt remarks that several cylinders have been bored "almost without error," and shows what he meant by that expression by going on to say that a cylinder 50 inches in diameter "did not err the thickness of an old shilling."

The development of the steam-engine necessitated improved tools, both for the construction of the engine and for more efficient use of its power. Progress has continued until to-day the number and variety of machine tools is so great as to make classification difficult. In a rough way they may be divided into two groups: those in which the essential motion is rotation, and those in which it is a reciprocating motion, but the border is very indefinite.

Rotary Group. — The earliest machine tool was the simple turning lathe. Great credit is due to Henry Maudslay (1771-1831) for his pioneer work in developing the essential mechanism of the engineer's self-acting lathe. A lathe provides the means of rotating a billet against a fixed tool so that material can be cut from it until it attains the desired size. The headstocks are the parts of the machine between which the billet is held. The slide rest carries the tool holder, and can be moved along the lathe bed by means of the lead screw which runs along the front of the frame. There are screws to move the tool holder in two directions at right angles to one another. A general tool employed for turning, boring, surfacing, and screw-cutting is used in tool-rooms and also in small general engineering works.

Messrs. John Lang & Sons, of Johnstone, Renfrewshire, have evolved a 12½-inch centre-sliding, surfacing, and screw-cutting lathe. The drive from a separate electric motor or from the works shafting is taken to the step cone through a countershaft. The various steps of the cone are used in combination with the gearing to obtain suitable speeds of rotation for the billets. The lathe shown is provided with a gap, so that flat faces of large diameter may be turned. The lead screw is driven by the headstock spindle through change wheels, by changing which the relative speeds of spindle and screw may be varied. In this way threads of various pitches can be cut with the use of one guide screw.

In some lathes there are complete gear boxes fitted so that the removal and replacement of change wheels is unnecessary, the requisite gear change being effected by the simple movement of a lever. Messrs. John Lang & Sons manufacture a variable speed gear for lathe headstocks which consists of two cones on long shaft and spindle. The one pair is driven from the other by the edges of a special belt. The relative speeds of the two shafts are altered by bringing together or separating the cones. The lever system makes one pair close up as the other pair opens out. The simple, non-screw cutting lathe has many varieties. Shafts, gears, pulleys, wheels, tyres, crank shafts, turbine rotors, and motor-car engine pistons all present differences in turning requirements.

Economic and rapid production demands that machines should, almost without exception, be designed for a single purpose. There are thus innumerable varieties of lathe beds, headstocks, chucks, and centres. For instance, a large lathe has been designed for turning steam-turbine rotors. It is about 40 feet long, and has a double slide bed 12 feet across. The face plate is a strong and rigid casting with four heavy forged-steel jaws, moved by screws. This lathe is operated by two motors, a main one of 60 h.p. driving the spindle, and an auxiliary one of 25 h.p. driving the tool saddles.

The production of short articles of a simple form from long bars is standard practice. In this work a lathe is used which has a hollow mandrel and an automatic chuck. It adopts a capstan or turret, a device for holding the various tools, usually five or six, required in the work. These tools are brought into action in turn until the cycle of operations is complete. Automatic machines requiring no attention, except the provision of fresh bars, are used in the manufacture of standard bolts, studs, and other small parts. The capstan is moved by mechanism just after each stage is completed. The finished parts are cut off from the bar by the machine and new material pushed into place. Modifications of the lathe which permits a number of different operations without resetting, such as surfacing, boring, milling, drilling, and tapping, save a considerable amount of time in a machine shop. A machine of this character made by George Richards & Company of Broadheath has two tables; the upper one can be revolved or detached, and the lower one slides on a saddle of considerable length. This system of tables makes possible all the adjustments requisite to carry out a great number of different operations on the work.

The sensitive drill is a tool with which small holes, say up to about 1 inch diameter, are drilled. The drill is driven by belts over jockey or guide pulleys. The term sensitive is used because, the feed being by hand, any unusual difficulty in drilling is felt.

A radial drilling machine is different from a sensitive drill in that the feed motion is given by gears and the drill can be altered in position along the radial arm. In many cases it is easier to adjust the drill to the hole centre than to move a heavy casting back and forward until its proper position for drilling is obtained. If a number of holes in a line are to be drilled, the radial arm can be set parallel to their centres and the drill saddle moved from centre to centre. A machine of this character is provided with a change speed-gear box in which the wheels run in oil. In this machine the elevating arm is of box section, and is adjusted by power. The saddle is carried on rollers. The spindle is driven by gearing through a powerful friction clutch, and can be reversed for tapping.

Milling is the term applied to machining surfaces by means of cylindrical cutters with a number of teeth. The work is fixed to a table and carried under the cutter by motion obtained from the gearing. The milling tool is carried on a shaft which is driven by a headstock at its one end and supported by vertical brackets and arms suspended from the overshaft.

The greatest development in modern engineering practice is found in the use of grinding machinery. Machine parts are now roughly machined and ground to gauged dimensions. Grinding machines are of the lathe form with a driven grinding wheel in place of the ordinary tool. The wheels are made of emery, carborundum, alundum (an aluminium oxide abrasive), and crystolon (carbide of silicon). They are graded according to their hardness, and these different grades suit particular classes of work. The wheels are run at high speeds—5000 to 6000 feet per minute—and these surface speeds should be kept up, as the wheel wears down, by increasing the number of revolutions per minute. In the universal form of this machine almost any type of grinding, internal or external cylindrical and surface can be successfully undertaken. This machine has a grinding length between centres of 24 inches, and the maximum swing over the table is 10 inches.

Reciprocating Group.—In this group of machines the essential operation is a to-and-fro motion. In the planing machine the work is cramped to the table, which is provided with slots to take the necessary bolts. The table moves backwards and forwards under the tools fixed in the holders. Cutting is done on the forward stroke only. Motion is given to the table by changing belts and gear, or alternatively from an electric motor with reversing devices. The cutting speed is low, the return speed usually high. Special electric drive systems providing efficient power transmission with suitable cutting, and high return speeds are in considerable use. Where the piece to be machined is of small dimensions, it is more economical to keep the work fixed and move the tool back and forward, as is the case in the shaping machine. Then the reciprocating motion is usually obtained by a mechanism of the crank connecting-rod type.—BIBLIOGRAPHY: Joseph G. Horner, *Practical Metal Turning*, and *Modern Milling Machines*; Thomas R. Shaw, *Lathes, Screw Machines, Boring and Turning Mills*, and *Machine Tools*; John T. Nicolson and Dempster Smith, *Lathe Design for High and Low Speed Steels*.

MACHPELAH. A place name mentioned in Gen. xxiii. It is a locality of Hebron where, according to tradition, Abraham and other Jewish patriarchs were buried in a double cavern. The modern Haram encloses the place.

MACHYNLLETH. Urban district and market town of Montgomeryshire. It stands near the Dovey, 18 miles from Aberystwyth, on the G.W. Rly. It is visited by tourists and for the fishing. Pop. (1931) 1892.

MACKAIL, John William. British scholar. Born in 1859, he was educated at Balliol College, Oxford, and became an inspector under the Board of Education. His works include a fine verse translation of Homer's *Odyssey*, a valuable primer on *Latin Literature*, *Lectures on Greek Poetry*, and *Lectures on Poetry*. He edited *Select Epigrams from the Greek Anthology*, and wrote lives of William Morris and George Wyndham. He was Professor of Poetry at Oxford, 1906-11. In 1932 he was chosen president of the British Academy.

Mackail married Margaret, daughter of Sir E. Burne-Jones, and their son, **Denis George Mackail,** won fame by his humorous stories. These include *Bill the Bachelor, According to Gibson, Greenery Street, How Amusing. The Square Circle,* and *David's Day.* He was born 3rd June, 1892, and was educated at St. Paul's School and Balliol College, Oxford.

M'KEESPORT. A city of Allegheny county, Pennsylvania, United States, on the Monongahela, near Pittsburgh. It is in the coal and natural gas district, and has large steel- and iron-works. Founded in 1795, it became a city in 1891. Pop. (1930), 54,632.

M'KENNA, Reginald. English financier. Born in London, 6th July, 1863, he was educated at King's College, London, and Trinity Hall, Cambridge. He rowed against Oxford in 1887. He was called to the bar in 1887, but soon turned his attention to politics, and was elected Liberal M.P. for North Monmouthshire in 1895. In 1905 he was appointed Financial Secretary to the Treasury. From 1907-8 he was President of the Board of Education: from 1908-11, First Lord of the Admiralty: from 1911-15, Home Secretary: and in 1915-16, Chancellor of the Exchequer. He introduced the war loan of 1915 and was responsible for the duties on certain imports called the **M'Kenna Duties.** He lost his seat in Parliament in 1918, and in 1919 was made Chairman of the Midland Bank, assisting the Government in an advisory capacity on several occasions.

M'KENNA, Stephen. British novelist. Born 27th Feb., 1888, he was educated at Westminster School and Christ Church, Oxford. From 1915-19 he served in the War Trade Intelligence Department, visiting the U.S.A. in 1917. The first of his many novels, *The Reluctant Lover*, appeared in 1912. Others include *Sonia*, 1917; *Midas & Son*, 1919; *Vindication*, 1923; *An Affair of Honour*, 1925; *The Secretary of State*, 1927; and *The Datchley Inheritance*, 1929. In 1932 appeared *The Way of the Phœnix.*

MACKENNAL, Sir Bertram. Australian sculptor. Born in Melbourne in 1863, he was educated in Australia, afterwards studying art in Paris. His work soon attracted attention, and he was selected to carve several statues of Queen Victoria and later to design the coinage issued after the accession of George V. His other work includes memorials to Edward VII. in St. George's Chapel, Windsor, and elsewhere, and the national memorial to T. Gainsborough. In 1909 MacKennal was made A.R.A., and in 1922 R.A. He was knighted in 1921 and died 10th Oct., 1931.

MACKENSEN, August von. German general, born in Saxony in 1850 of Scots (Mackenzie) ancestry. He entered the army in 1869, served with the Hussars (1870-71), was ennobled by William II. (1899), and on the outbreak of the European War he was in command of the Death's Head Hussars and the 17th Army Corps (Dantzig). In German popularity he rivalled Hindenburg, of whose twelve Army Corps he commanded five during the Russian drive of 1915. By cutting the Lublin-Cholm line (29th July, 1915) Mackensen isolated Warsaw and crushed the Russian centre.

In 1915 he became Field-Marshal, directed the occupation of Serbia, and commanded in the Dobrudja against Rumania (Aug.-Sept., 1916), which he subjugated and controlled until the armistice of 1918, when he was interned in Hungary. In 1919 he was permitted by the Supreme Council to return to Germany. The Mackensen method was crude but effective. An immense artillery concentration on a wide front blasted an avenue for the massed advance of infantry.

MACKEN'ZIE, Sir Alexander. Canadian explorer, born at Inverness, Scotland, 1755, died 1820. In the employment of the North-West Fur Company he explored the great river named after him from the western end of Great Slave Lake to the Arctic Ocean (1789). He made another expedition to the western coast (1792), and was the first white man to cross the Rocky Mountains and reach the Pacific coast. He was knighted on his return to Britain in 1801.

MACKENZIE, Sir Alex. Campbell. Composer, born at Edinburgh 1847; received his musical education partly in Germany. He became principal of the Royal Academy of Music in 1888, and was knighted in 1895. Among his works are the oratorio *The Rose of Sharon* (1884), the operas *Colomba* and *The Troubadour*, cantatas of *The Story of Sayid, The Dream of Jubal, Eve of St. John* (opera); *A Musician's Narrative* (1927).

MACKENZIE, Compton. British author. He was born at West Hartlepool, 17th Jan., 1883, and was educated at St. Paul's School, London, and at Oxford. He served in the South African and Great Wars, and directed the Ægean Intelligence Service with great distinction in 1917.

He has written *The Passionate Elopement*, 1911; *Carnival*, 1912; *Sinister Street*, 1913-14; *Poor Relations*, 1919; *Rich Relatives*, 1921; *Rogues and Vagabonds*, 1927; *Gallipoli Memories*, 1929; *More Athenian Memories*, 1932, and three plays. He was elected Rector of Glasgow University in 1932.

MACKENZIE, Henry. Scottish writer, born 1745, died 1831. Educated in the University of Edinburgh, he became an attorney of the Scottish Court of Exchequer, and in 1771 he published the work by which he is best known—*The Man of Feeling*.

MACKENZIE. A provisional district of the Canadian North-West Territories as from 1st Jan., 1920. It embraces the western part of the North-West Territories, while Keewatin covers the eastern part, and Franklin includes the vast island group in the north. Area, 527,490 sq. miles.

MACKENZIE RIVER. A river of the North-West Territories of Canada, which rises in the Rockies (Mt. Alberta, 13,500 feet) as the Athabasca River, flows into Lake Athabasca (680 miles), and passes as the Slave River into the Great Slave Lake, being joined on its way (20 miles down) by the Peace River. Emerging from the Great Slave Lake as the Mackenzie, it is navigable for 1000 miles to its mouths, which form a wide delta on Mackenzie Bay, within the Arctic Circle. The lower stretches are ice-bound from November to May annually. Total length, 2514 miles.—Cf. E. Stewart, *Down the Mackenzie and up the Yukon*.

MACKEREL (*Scomber scombrus*). One of the spiny-finned fishes (Acanthopteri), a well-known and excellent table fish, which inhabits almost the whole of the European seas.

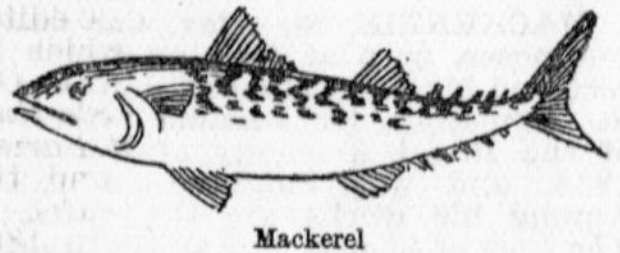

Mackerel

Mackerel, like herring, are caught only when they approach the shore to spawn, nets being chiefly used. Related species are the southern mackerel (*S. pneumatophorus*) and the Spanish mackerel (*S. colias*).

M'KINLEY, William. President of the United States from 1897 to 1901; born at Niles, Ohio, 1843, died in 1901. In 1861, on the outbreak of the Civil War, he enlisted as a private soldier, and served till the end of the war, when he had attained the rank of major. After this he studied law, and started in practice at Canton, Ohio, in 1867. In 1876 he was elected to Congress, where in 1889 he became chairman of the Ways and Means Committee and Republican leader in the House. In 1890 he was associated with the M'Kinley Tariff Bill, a protective measure, and in 1891 was elected Governor of Ohio.

In 1896 M'Kinley was nominated Republican candidate for the presidency, having as his opponent W. J. Bryan, an advocate of free silver coinage, and was elected by a large majority. He was re-elected in 1900, but on 6th Sept., 1901, he was shot by an anarchist at Buffalo, and died eight days later. He was succeeded by Vice-President Roosevelt.

M'KINLEY, Mount. The highest peak of North America, in Alaska, near the Arctic Circle. Height, 20,464 feet. It was first ascended by

Mt. M'Kinley

Archdeacon Stuck in 1913.—BIBLIOGRAPHY: H. C. Parker, *Conquering Mount M'Kinley*; Dr. H. Stuck, *Ascent of Denali*.

MACLAREN, Archibald Campbell. English cricketer. Born in Manchester, 1st Dec., 1871, he was educated at Elstree and Harrow. For four years he played cricket for Harrow against Eton and in 1891 he was made captain of the Lancashire county team. For the next twenty years or so he was one of the outstanding figures in the game, a superb batsman and fieldsman and a captain of unusual discernment. He played many times in test matches in England and Australia and was captain of the English team at home in 1899, 1902, and 1909, and in Australia in 1897-98 and 1901-2. In 1895 he scored 424 runs at Taunton, the highest score in first-class cricket. He wrote *Cricket, Old and New*, 1924.

MACLAREN, Ian. Name taken by the Scottish writer, Rev. John Maclaren Watson. Born at Manningtree, Essex, 3rd Nov., 1850, he was educated at Stirling and in Edinburgh. He became a minister of the Free Church of Scotland in 1874, his first church being in Edinburgh. He was at Logiealmond and in Glasgow before becoming minister of the influential church in Sefton Park, Liverpool, where he was from 1880 until just before his death, 6th May, 1907.

As Ian Maclaren, he wrote in 1894 some sketches of Scottish life called *Beside the Bonnie Brier Bush.* The book had an extraordinary success and was followed by others, including *The Days of Auld Lang Syne* and *Kate Carnegie.* He also wrote *The Mind of the Master,* and other theological books.

MACLAURIN, Colin. Scottish mathematician, born 1698, died 1746. He studied for five years at Glasgow University, and was professor of mathematics at Aberdeen, and afterwards at Edinburgh. As a geometer and analyst he is of the first rank, and he is the only British mathematician of the eighteenth century fit to be placed on a level with the great Continental mathematicians of that period.

His *Treatise on Fluxions* develops Newton's method of presenting the calculus, and contains a famous geometrical treatment of the attraction of ellipsoids. "Maclaurin's method" of tracing a conic is given, as an example of a remarkable theory of curve generation, in *Geometria Organica.* In 1740 Maclaurin divided with Euler and Daniel Bernouilli the prize of the French Academy for an essay on the tides.—Cf. W. W. R. Ball, *A Short History of Mathematics.*

MACLAURIN'S THEOREM. A formula for the expansion of a function in ascending powers of the independent variable, first given by Colin Maclaurin (q.v.). If $f(x)$, or y say, is a function of x, its derivative dy/dx (*see* CALCULUS) may be denoted by $f'(x)$. This derivative has itself a derivative, which is called the second derivative of $f(x)$, and is denoted by d^2y/dx^2, or $f''(x)$. Similarly *the third derivation of* $f(x)$ is d^3y/dx^3, or $f'''(x)$, and so on. The values of $f(x)$ and its *successive derivatives,* as thus defined, for $x=0$ are written $f(0), f'(0), f''(0), \ldots f^{(n)}(0), \ldots$ Maclaurin's Theorem is then

$$f(x)=f(0)+xf'(0)+x^2f''(0)/(1\cdot2)+x^3f'''(0)/(1\cdot2\cdot3)+\ldots,$$

the number of terms in the series being, in general, infinite. Nearly all the expansions of elementary algebra and trigonometry are special cases of this theorem. One of the most important examples is the *Binomial Theorem*

$$(1+x)n=1+nx+n(n-1)x^2/(1\cdot2)+n(n-1)(n-2)x^3/(1\cdot2\cdot3)+\ldots,$$

the series terminating when n is a positive integer, and converging for other values of n when x lies between 1 and −1. Other examples are the expansions quoted in the article *Function. See* TAYLOR'S THEOREM. —BIBLIOGRAPHY: F. F. P. Bisacre, *Applied Calculus*; G. A. Gibson, *Elementary Treatise on the Calculus.*

MACLEAN, Sir Donald. Scottish politician. Born in Tiree, he became a solicitor in London. In 1906 he entered the House of Commons as Liberal M.P. for Bath. From 1910-18 he represented the counties of Peebles and Selkirk and from 1918 to 1922 Peebles and Midlothian. In 1929 and 1931 he was elected for a division of Cornwall. From 1911 to 1916 he was Deputy Chairman of Committees and in 1917 he was knighted. In 1919 Mr. Asquith, having lost his seat, Sir Donald was chosen the leader of the Liberal group in Parliament, a position he retained until 1922. In Aug., 1931, he joined the National Government as President of the Board of Education. He died suddenly, 15th June, 1932.

MACLEOD (ma-kloud'), **Norman.** A minister of the Church of Scotland, born at Campbeltown, Argyllshire, 1812, died at Glasgow 1872. Educated at Glasgow, Edinburgh, and in Germany, he became minister first of Loudon and then of Dalkeith, when he published his first work, entitled *The Earnest Student,* and became editor of the Edinburgh *Christian Instructor.*

In 1851 he became minister of the Barony parish, Glasgow. Besides his untiring interest and labours in connection with the general work of the Church, and in various philanthropic movements, he became editor of *Good Words* in 1860, in which he published his stories of *The Old Lieutenant and his Son, The Starling, Wee Davie,* and *A Highland Parish.* In 1867 he visited India, and the results of this journey appeared in his *Peeps at the Far East.* In 1869 he was elected moderator of the General Assembly of the Church of Scotland.

MACLISE', Daniel. Irish painter, born at Cork 1811, died 1870. In 1833 he established his reputation with his picture *Snap Apple Night.* He became a member of the Royal Academy in 1840. Maclise was commissioned to paint for the new

Houses of Parliament, and produced *The Spirit of Chivalry*, *The Spirit of Religion*, and the two great paintings of *The Meeting of Wellington and Blücher after Waterloo* and *The Death of Nelson* (1858-64).

Among his best-known pictures are: *Merry Christmas in the Baron's Hall*, *The Ordeal of Touch*, *The Marriage of Strongbow and Eva*, *The Play Scene in Hamlet*, *The Banquet Scene in Macbeth*, and *Malvolio and the Countess*. His sketches, book illustrations, humorous drawings, and outline portraits were very numerous. He declined the presidency of the Academy in 1866. The works of Maclise show great fertility of invention, skill in composition, and excellence in drawing, but are not distinguished for colour.

MACMAHON, Marie Edmé Patrice Maurice de. Duc de Magenta, Marshal of France, and President of the French Republic from 1873 to 1879 (*the Septennate*); was born in 1808 of Irish parents exiled for Jacobite sympathies, and died in 1893. Educated at St. Cyr, he served in Algeria: assisted in storming the Malakov (Crimea) in 1855; and, in the campaign of 1859 against Austria, he won (with Napoleon III.) the battle of Magenta (Italy), being created duke and marshal on the field. From 1864 to 1870 he was Governor-General of Algeria.

In the Franco-Prussian War (1870-71) MacMahon took command of the 1st Army Corps; was defeated at Weissenburg and Wörth, and carried out a masterly retreat to Châlons. Reorganizing, he marched to relieve Bazaine and raise the siege of Metz, but was encircled by the Germans in Sedan, wounded in the ensuing battle, and captured before the final surrender. After the armistice he was employed in suppressing the Parisian communists, and succeeded Thiers as President. As a result of political crisis in 1877 and 1879 he resigned office.—**MacMahon** is an Algerian railway town named after the Marshal.—Cf. E. Daudet, *Le Maréchal de MacMahon*.

M'NEILL, James. Irish politician. Born 27th Aug., 1869, in Co. Antrim, he was educated at Blackrock College, Dublin, and at Emmanuel College, Cambridge. In 1890 he won a position in the Indian Civil Service, and he remained in India until 1921. Returning to Ireland he was made Chairman of the Dublin County Council, and took part in drawing up the constitution of the Irish Free State. From 1923 to 1927 M'Neill was High Commissioner for the Free State in London, and from 1928 to 1932 he was Governor-General.

MÂCON. A town and capital of Saône-et-Loire, France, on the River Saône, a centre of trade in Burgundy wine. The cathedral of St. Vincent was destroyed during the Revolution, the ruins being still extant. Mâcon was the Roman *Matisco*, and was a bishopric from the seventh century until suppression in 1790. Prior to 1477 it formed part of the Duchy of Burgundy. Pop. 18,496.

MA'CON. A city of Georgia, United States, county town of Bibb county, on the Ocmulgee River, and almost in the centre of the state. It is an important railway centre, and has cotton manufactures. Pop. (1930), 53,829.

MACPHERSON, James. Scottish author, was born in 1736, and died in 1796. He studied at Aberdeen and Edinburgh; became a school teacher, and afterwards a tutor; and in 1760 published *Fragments of Ancient Poetry*, translated from the Gaelic or Erse language. The success of this venture enabled Macpherson to issue the so-called poems of Ossian in the form of *Fingal, an ancient epic poem in six books* (1762, 4to) and *Temora and other Poems* (1763, 4to). The genuineness of these poems was severely questioned (*see* OSSIAN), but the "editor" maintained his position without submitting the necessary proofs.

Macpherson was afterwards agent to the Nabob of Arcot; had a seat in the House of Commons from 1780 to 1790, and was interred in Westminster Abbey. He was the author of a prose translation of Homer's *Iliad*, and of some other works. Macpherson's poetry had an influence on romantic literature both in England and in Germany.—BIBLIOGRAPHY: J. S. Smart, *James Macpherson: an Episode in Literature*; H. A. Beers, *History of English Romanticism in the Nineteenth Century*.

MACQUARIE. A river of New South Wales, Australia, a tributary of the Darling.

MACQUARIE. A sub-Antarctic island of the Southern Pacific, administered by Tasmania. The habitable island is 20 miles long and approximately 3 miles broad, and abounds in birds and animals. Kerguelen cabbage (q.v.) is found. Sea-elephants averaging about 2 tons in weight abound in the Macquarie waters, and seals were once common. There is a meteorological and wireless station. The two-island clusters north and south of the main island are called Judge and Clerk and Bishop and Clerk respectively.

MACREADY (mak-rē'di), **William Charles.** English tragedian, born in London 1793, died at Cheltenham 1873. His father, the lessee and manager of several provincial theatres, sent him to Rugby and Oxford to be educated, but circumstances compelled him to join his father's company at Birmingham in 1810. Afterwards he played in the provinces with considerable success, and appeared at Covent Garden in 1816. In 1826 he made his first visit to America, and in 1828 played in Paris, with great success in both countries.

William Charles Macready

He undertook the management of Covent Garden in 1837, and Drury Lane in 1842, but although he did much to reform the stage, both in respect of its moral and in respect of the artistic qualities of the representations, and endeavoured to cultivate the public taste for Shakespearean drama in both theatres (he himself taking the leading parts in Shakespeare's plays), his pecuniary losses required him to retire from managership. He finally retired from the stage in 1851. His *Reminiscences* appeared in 1875.—Cf. W. Marston, *Our Recent Actors.*

MACRO'BIUS, Ambrosius Aurelius Theodosius. A Latin author in the reigns of the Emperors Honorius and Theodosius (end of fourth and beginning of fifth century A.D.). He was the author of a work entitled *Saturnalia,* valuable for the light it throws upon the manners and customs of antiquity. He also wrote a commentary on Cicero's *Somnium Scipionis,* and a treatise, *De Differentiis et Societatibus Græci Latinique Verbi.*

MACROCYS'TIS. A genus of marine Algæ, family Laminariaceæ. The *M. pyrifĕra* exceeds all other vegetable productions in the length of its fronds, some of which have been estimated on reasonable ground to attain a length of 700 feet. It is found in the southern temperate zone, and in the Pacific as far north as the Arctic regions.

MACROOM'. A town and urban district of Cork, Ireland, on the Sullane. The castle is said to have been built by King John, and was besieged and burnt on several occasions in the seventeenth century. Macroom is a railway terminal station. Pop. (1926), 2413.

MACROSPORIUM. A genus of parasitic Fungi Imperfecti, section Hyphomycetes. *M. solani* causes a leaf-curl in potato, *M. tomato* the black-rot of tomatoes, and *M. nobile* a spot-disease of carnations. Spraying with sulphide of potash or Bordeaux mixture is the best remedy.

MACWHIRTER, John. Scottish painter, born in 1839, died in 1911. He was educated at Peebles and the School of Design, Edinburgh. In 1864 he was elected A.R.S.A., in 1879 A.R.A., and R.A. in 1893. He is famous chiefly as a landscape-painter, and among his best-known works are: *Loch Coruisk* (1870), *The Lady of the Woods* (1876), *The Three Graces* (1878), *The Vanguard* (1878), *The Valley by the Sea* (1879), and *Crabbed Age and Youth.*

MADAGASCAR. A French island in the Indian Ocean, at least 240 miles from the south-east coast of Africa, from which it is separated by the Mozambique Channel; length, 980 miles; greatest breadth, 360 miles; area, 241,094 sq. miles. Orographically the principal features are the small Northern and the larger Southern Plateaux, connected by a low saddle. Extinct volcanic peaks are numerous; that of Ankaratra (8790 feet) is the highest point in the island. Rivers are numerous, short, and unnavigable. The climate is subtropical, with a wet season from December to April, and the flora and fauna are extensive and varied. Lemurs are numerous. Antanànarìvo (pop. 92,475), in the interior, is the capital; Tamatave (15,022), Majunga (20,000), Diégo Suarez (12,300), and Tuléar (12,300) are the chief ports; Fianarantsoa (12,575), Antsirabe (8300), Mananjary (11,000), Sainte-Marie (7922), and Nosy-Bé (12,000) are also important. (Figures are those of the 1931 census.)

Products, Minerals, etc.—Agriculture and stock-raising are extensive native monopolies, rubber, mulberries, cloves, vanilla, rice, sugar, manioc cacao, cotton, and ground-nuts being produced, and the afforested interior yields teak and other valuable woods. Horses, pigs, sheep, ostriches, and goats are raised. Meat-canning and the preparation of food-stuffs are under European control, and there are canneries at Antanànarìvo, Tamatave, Diégo-Suarez, and Bo-anamary. Among minerals, graphite is exported; gold, copper, lead, silver, manganese, nickel, and coal (lignite) have been worked. Imports are mainly cottons, liquors, machinery, cement, lime, and clothing; and exports, gold-dust, cattle, tanning-bark, rice, and hides—all in order of importance.

Madagascar
Huts in a village of the Mananjary region

Communications.—Internal communications are generally poor, but there is a railway (to be electrified shortly) from Antanànarìvo to Tamatave (229 miles) with several branches in all 430 miles of track (1927). A new line (which will also be electrified) is being constructed from Fianarantsoa to the east coast (105 miles). There is postal communication, and a telephone system, inland telegraphs (total length in 1931, 9207 miles), three Government wireless stations, and cable connections with Mozambique, Mauritius, Réunion, and Aden. An important wireless station was opened at Antanànarìvo in 1924.

People.—The population of Madagascar is varied, and comprises the Malagasy or indigenous inhabitants with their numerous subdivisions, Hindus, Chinese, and French. The census population in 1931 was 3,701,770, 23,077 being French, 13,460 Europeans and other foreigners, and 3,665,234 Malagasy. Of the numerous Malagasy tribes the Hovas (910,000) and the Bétsiléo (520,000 are pre-eminent. The Hovas are of exceptional intelligence, and rapidly acquire the arts of wood- and metal-working, so that, although manufactures do not exist in Madagascar as yet, manufacturing enterprise does not lack potentially efficient labour. Missionary efforts have resulted in a partial conversion of the natives, 450,000 of whom embrace Protestantism, and 150,000 Roman Catholicism. The language is of the Malayo-Polynesian division. Education is compulsory between the ages of eight and fourteen years. A knowledge of the French language is required.

History.—Madagascar was known to Marco Polo (thirteenth century), and in 1506 was visited by Portuguese, who called it St. Lorenzo. Radama I. became King of the Hovas in 1810, and he permitted missionaries to teach in the capital (1820), when the Bible was translated into Malagasy and the language was first reduced to a systematic written form. By a treaty of 1885 Madagascar became a French Protectorate. In 1890 Great Britain recognized the Protectorate to secure French influence in Zanzibar, the transfer of Heligoland to Germany being contemporaneous.

Queen Rànavàlona III. confirmed the treaty in 1895, and in 1896 Madagascar was declared a colony of France, the native government being retained. A rebellion caused the deposition of the queen, her exile to Réunion and afterwards Algeria, and the government of the island is now in the hands of a Consultative Council of Administration, sitting at Antanànarìvo. Madagascar is divided into twenty-four provinces and seventy-five districts, supervised by officials of the Council, who are usually natives. The Comoro Islands (q.v.) form one of the Madagascar provinces. The island is not represented in the French Parliament.—BIBLIOGRAPHY: W. E. Cousins, *Madagascar of To-day*; E. W. Dawson, *Madagascar: its Capabilities and Resources*; G. Gravier, *Madagascar*.

MADANG. Chief town of the Territory of New Guinea.

MADDALENA. An Italian island on the northern seaboard of Sardinia, which with the adjacent islands forms a naval and torpedo station.

MADDALONI. A town of Caserta, Italy, 15 miles north-east of Naples. Nearby is the famous Ponté della Valle, a three-storied aqueduct,

215 feet high and 25 miles long. Weaving and quarrying are the main industries. Pop. 21,380.

MADDEN, Sir Charles Edward. British admiral. Fourth Sea Lord of the Admiralty (1910–11), he served in the Battle of Jutland in 1916, and was mentioned in despatches. He was Admiral of the Fleet in 1924, and First Sea Lord of the Admiralty (1927 30), retiring in 1930. He was created a baronet in 1919, and awarded the O.M. in 1931. He also holds many foreign decorations.

MADDER. A dye-plant, *Rubia tinctorum*, nat. ord. Rubiaceæ. It is a climbing perennial, with whorls of dark-green leaves, and small yellowish cross-shaped flowers. The prepared root is used as a red dye-stuff. It yields colours of the greatest permanence, and is employed for dyeing both linen and cotton. Two kinds of it are fixed upon cotton; one is simply called *madder-red*, and the other, which possesses a much higher degree of lustre and fixity, is called *Turkey* or *Adrianople red*, because it was for a long time obtained entirely from the Levant, where it was called *alizara*.

The colouring principle of madder is termed *alizarine*, and as this can now be obtained artificially from coal-tar, the use of madder in dyeing is almost entirely superseded by that of artificial alizarine.

MADEIRA. A group of Portuguese islands, in the Atlantic, off the coast of Africa, the chief being Madeira and Porto Santo. Area, 314 sq. miles; pop. (1930), 210,220.

Madeira, Camara de Lobos

Madeira proper derives its name from the dense primeval forest that once enwrapped it. (Port. *madeira*, timber; Lat. *materia*). It is roughly 35 miles long by 11 to 12 miles broad, of volcanic origin and mountainous, culminating in Pico Ruiva (6056 feet) and Pico Grande (5391 feet). The climate is mild and equable, and Madeira has consequently become a health-resort for Europeans.

Products.—The northern part of the island is irrigated, and produces cereals and vegetables; the lowlands abound in orange, coffee, banana, lemon, and many other varieties of fruit-trees. Madeira wine, a product similar to sherry, but of exceptional flavour and bouquet, is made from Madeira-grown grapes, and was first produced in 1485. Wicker goods, sugar, grapes, wine, arrowroot, and lace are exported. Funchal on the south coast is the capital. In Porto Santo water is scarce, and wines and grain are the only products.

History.—Madeira was colonized by Portugal in 1419, held by Spain between 1580 and 1640, and was in British hands from 1807 to 1814. A line regiment of Portuguese infantry forms the normal garrison of the group. The Habsburg family arrived at Funchal on 19th Nov., 1921, where they were exiled by the Supreme Council, and where Karl, "the last of the Habsburgs," died of pneumonia on 1st April, 1922.—Cf. C. A. Power, *Tourists' Guide to the Island of Madeira.*

MADEIRA. The principal tributary river of the Amazon, South America. It is formed by the union of the Beni and Mamoré on the Brazil-Bolivian frontiers, and flows through Amazonas to the Amazon, which it enters near Serpa, 78 miles below Manaos. The total length is about 2000 miles, and the drainage area about 400,000 sq. miles. The Madeira is navigable for ocean steamers as far as Porto Velho, 1500 miles from the sea, a wireless station, and the base of the wonderful Madeira-Mamoré forest railway. *See* MAMORE.

MADERO, Francisco. President of Mexico, born 1873, died 1913. He was the National Democratic party's candidate for the presidential election of 1910, but was arrested, imprisoned for a time, and finally compelled to flee to the United States. Returning, he led a revolt, and replaced Diaz as President on 1st Oct., 1911. On 9th Feb., 1913, he was captured by insurgents, and subsequently murdered.

MADISON. A city and capital of Wisconsin, United States, lies between Lakes Mendota and Monona in a district famous for its scenery. The State university was established in 1848, and introduced a system of correspondence instruction in 1911. Trade is mostly in agricultural goods. Pop. (1930), 57,899.

MADRAS. A maritime city, capital of Madras Presidency, and third city of India, on the Coromandel coast. It has no natural harbour, but has become the first seaport of the Deccan, and the fifth of India, by the construction of an artificial harbourage.

Madras is the headquarters of the Government during the cool season. It has railway communication by four systems with Calcutta, Calicut, Bombay, and Tuticorin. The native and business quarter of the town, on the foreshore, was formerly called Black Town, but since 1905 has been called George Town; it is still densely peopled, and forms the commercial centre. Triplicane is also a squalid native quarter, abounding in Hindu temples. Madras University was founded in 1857, and the Scots Kirk dates from 1821. There is a Supreme High Court with twelve judges (1920). Unlike other great Indian seaports, the town has no exporting monopoly of a specific commodity, and there are few manufactures.

History.—Madras was founded in 1639 by the East India Company, who were granted a site close to the Portuguese settlement, St. Thomé (founded 1504), by the Rajah of Chandrgiri. The city gradually grew up around the citadel and fort of St. George (which still exists as a barracks and as Government offices). In 1702 it was successfully defended against Aurangzib's army under Daood Khan. After an attack by the Mahrattas in 1741 Madras was taken by the French under Labourdonnais (1746), but was restored in 1748 (Treaty of Aix-la-Chapelle). It was ineffectually besieged by the French under Lally-Tollendal (1758-59). Pop. 526,911.

MADRAS, Presidency of. One of the fifteen administrations of British India; area, 142,260 sq. miles, including native states. The three chief rivers, Godavari, Kistna or Krishna (with the Tungabhadra), and Cauvery, rise in the Western Ghāts and enter the Bay of Bengal. The Eastern and Western Ghāts form its chief surface features. The climate is varied; in the Nilgiri Hills it is temperate, on the Malabar coast the monsoon brings an excessive rainfall, while in the central tableland the rainfall is low and the heat almost unendurable. The soil is sandy along the coast, but there are many fertile districts; while iron, copper, lead, and coal are found in considerable quantities. There are extensive forests yielding teak, ebony, and other valuable timber trees. The total afforested area under the State Forest Department is about 20,000 sq. miles; the output of timber in 1931 was 85,580 tons.

Products.—The principal products are rice, millet, maize, and other grains; sugar-cane, cotton, oil-seeds, indigo, tea, coffee, tobacco, plantain, tamarind, jack-fruit, mango, melons, coco-nuts, ginger, turmeric, and pepper. About 32,000,000 acres are cropped annually, of which 7,573,043 acres were irrigated. About 22,000,000 acres are unavailable agriculturally. The actual area under tea is generally about 30,000 acres. The wild animals comprise the elephant, tiger, cheetah, jackal, and wild hog.

Social Conditions.—The administration of Madras is now regulated by the Government of India Act, 1919, which came into force in 1921 (*see* INDIA). The revenue, which considerably exceeds the expenditure, is over £10,000,000 annually. The pop. is 46,748,644, 89 per cent. being Hindus; the native protected states have a pop. of 4,190,322. The chief languages spoken are the Dravidian, namely, Tamil, Telugu (which are spoken by the great majority of the inhabitants), Canarese and Malayalam, while Hindustani is the language spoken by the Mahommedans.—Cf. E. Thurston, *The Madras Presidency*.

MADRE-DE-DIOS (Sp., "Mother of God"), the eastermost department of Peru, created in 1912. It is to a large extent an impenetrable forest inhabited by savages (unconquered tribes of the Mashos and Campas). The principal communication is by the Cuzco-Arequipa-Mollendo Railway. Mineral and other natural resources are undeveloped. Maldonado, at the junction of the Tambopata and Madre-de-Dios Rivers, is nominally the seat of government. Area, 58,827 sq. miles; pop. estimated at 5000. The River Madre-de-Dios (native, Quichua Amaru-Mayu) is the principal navigable tributary of the Beni (q.v.); length, about 950 miles.

MAD'REPORE. A coral-building polyp of the genus Madrepŏra, the type of the family Madreporidæ, forming coral of stony hardness and

Madrepore Corals

of a spreading or branching form, hence called *tree-coral.* Madrepore coral is of a white colour, wrinkled on the surface and full of little cavities, in each of which an individual polyp was lodged. These polyps raise up walls and reefs of coral rocks with astonishing rapidity in tropical climates. The term is often applied also to other branching corals.

MADRID (må-*drid'*). The capital of Spain, on the Manzanares, near the centre of the Iberian Peninsula. Situated upon a high treeless plateau, 2109 feet above the sea, wind-swept

Madrid : The Toledo Bridge

from the snowy Guadarrama, with unhealthy daily and seasonal extremes of temperature, the city has no climatic advantages.

Ten streets converge on the Puerta del Sol, the busiest and brightest square of the city. The royal palace (1764) is in the form of a quadrangle enclosing a court, and is 500 feet long and from 80 to 165 feet high. It occupies the site of a palace which succeeded the Moorish Alcazar, and was burned in 1734. The Bull-Ring (Plaza de Toros) seats 12,000 spectators. The Boulevard del Prado is a magnificent thoroughfare 2½ miles in length. Founded in 1892, the Biblioteca Nacional houses the National Library (upwards of 700,000 volumes) and several museums.

Tobacco, soap, cork, jewellery, furniture, and perfumes are a few of the productions of Madrid, and books and publishing are of importance.

The University of Madrid, transferred from Alcala de Henares in 1836, has faculties of philosophy and letters, sciences, law, medicine, and pharmacy.

Madrid is first mentioned about A.D. 930-933. Philip II. definitely made it the capital (1560). Cervantes lived in Madrid from 1609 till his death, and during this period he produced the latter half of *Don Quixote.* Until the middle of the eighteenth century Madrid was reputed to be "the dirtiest capital in Europe." Pop. (1931), 896,511.—Cf. A. F. Calvert, *Madrid.*

MAD'RIGAL (Fr. *madrigal* ; It. *madrigale*), a short amorous poem, consisting of not less than three or four stanzas or strophes. The madrigal was first cultivated in Italy, and those of Petrarch and Tasso are among the finest specimens of Italian poetry. Several English poets of the time of Elizabeth and the Charleses wrote madrigals of notable grace and elegance, the chief names being Lodge, Wither, Carew, and Suckling.

The term is also applied to an elaborate vocal composition now commonly of two or more movements, and in five or six parts. The musical madrigal was at first a simple song, but afterwards was suited to an instrumental accompaniment. Famous English composers of musical madrigals are: Morley, Bennett, Ward, Gibbons, Dowland, and Ford.

MADURA'. A district of Madras Presidency, India ; a plateau drained by the Vaigai River. It is an irrigated agricultural area, producing cotton and subtropical grains. Area, 4907 sq. miles ; pop. 2,007,082.

The capital is Madura, on the Vaigai, once the religious and political capital of Southern India, and renowned for its Great Temple of Siva. Pop. 182,007.

MADU'RA. An island of the Dutch East Indies, north-east of Java, of which it forms a Residency, and from which it is separated by the broad Strait of Madura. The Madurese are mainly Mahommedan, and have a national language. Cattle-raising, agriculture, and fishing are the staple occupations. Area, 1770 sq. miles ; pop. 1,632,000.

MÆCE'NAS, Gaius Cilnius. A distinguished Roman born between 73 and 63 B.C., died 8 B.C. He was the companion of the Emperor Augustus in nearly all his campaigns, and his most trustworthy counsellor in political matters. For the three years 18-15 B.C. he was invested with the government of Italy. He is chiefly famous, however, as a patron of learning, and the friend of Virgil and Horace (q.v.).

MAELSTRÖM ("grinding stream"). An ocean current between the Norwegian islands Moskenæs and Mosken, in the Lófodens. It is formed by the pouring of the tide through a narrow strait, and assumes a formidable appearance during a "nor'-wester," when the wind blows against the current.

MAESTEG. An urban district of South Wales, in Mid-Glamorganshire, on the River Llyfnu. There are collieries and ironworks in the neighbourhood which, like Maesteg, owe their existence to the South Wales coal-field. Pop. (1931), 25,552.

MAETERLINCK (mä'-ter-lingk), **Maurice.** Belgian author, born at Ghent in 1862, studied there, adopted the law as a profession, but latterly has lived as a literary man in Paris. His first publication was *Serres Chaudes*, a volume of verse (1889); but he is best known as a dramatist. Among his plays are *La Princesse Maleine, Les Aveugles, Pélléas et Mélisande, Aglavaine et Sélysette, Monna Vanna, Mary Magdalene, The Blue Bird, The Betrothal, The Burgomaster of Stilemonde, The Miracle of St. Anthony, Mountain Paths, The Cloud that Lifted*, and *The Power of the Dead.* Most of his plays have been translated into English. He is also known as an essayist and writer of works of a philosophic character, his works in this field including *Le Trésor des Humbles, La Vie des Abeilles*, and *La Vie des Termites*, all of which have been translated into English. In 1911 he received the Nobel Prize for literature. Among his more recent works are *The Life of Space* (1927) and *The Magic of the Stars* (1930).

MAFEKING. A town of Bechuanaland, Cape Province, the administrative centre of the Bechuanaland Protectorate, and an important railway station. It was the starting-point of the Jameson Raid (1895), and was defended by Baden-Powell against the Boers from 12th Oct. 1899, to 17th May, 1900. Pop. (Europeans), 2313.—Cf. J. A. Hamilton, *Siege of Mafeking.*

MAFI'A. A Sicilian secret society similar to the Neapolitan Camorra, but much more powerful. Its organized lawlessness has baffled all attempts of the Government to suppress it. Its members are bound never to carry their suits to the regular courts nor to give evidence before them. Murder and robbery, though discountenanced under ordinary conditions, are resorted to without hesitation in the case of informers or specially obnoxious persons. Blackmail is levied from landowners, who are required to employ none but *mafiosi* in certain occupations, and the society further makes its power felt by means of the *vendetta* and an extreme form of boycotting. Criminals are protected and elections controlled by this infamous association, whose authority is greater than that of the law among the lower classes in Sicily.

MAFRA. A town of Estremadura, Portugal, famous for its convent, built (1717) by John V. It consists of a church, a monastery, and a palace; and there were also barracks. The entire building forms a quadrangle 820 feet long by 720 feet wide.

MAGADHA. An ancient kingdom of India which lay about the modern Bihar, south of the Middle Ganges. Pataliputra, now Patna, was the capital. Magadha was the nucleus of the first Indian Empire, destroyed in 184 B.C.

MAGALLANES. A territory of Southern Chile extending from lat. 47° S. to Cape Horn. The territory embraces half of Tierra del Fuego. The mainland is wild and afforested, and deeply indented with fjords of a Norwegian type, and the innumerable islands on its coasts are separated by deep, narrow channels. Punta Arenas is the principal settlement. Area, 52,054 sq. miles; pop. (1930), 37,913.

MAGDALA. A town and fortress of Abyssinia (q.v.). Pop. about 3000.

MAGDALEN (or **MAGDALENE**), **Mary** (i.e. Mary of Magdăla). A woman mentioned in the New Testament as having had seven devils cast out of her, as watching the crucifixion, and as having come early to the sepulchre on resurrection morning. She was erroneously identified with "the woman who was a sinner" (Luke vii. 37); hence the term Magdalen became synonymous with penitent harlot.—Cf. Luke viii. 2.

MAGDALENA. The principal river of Colombia, South America, rising in the central Cordillera of the Andes, in Ecuador, and flowing northwards through Colombia to the Caribbean; course, 950 miles; drainage area, about 90,000 sq. miles. The Magdalena is navigable for 600 miles up-stream to Honda.

Magdalena Bay is an opening of the Pacific Ocean on the coast of Mexico. It forms one of the finest natural harbours in the world.

MAGDALENA. A department of Colombia, South America, facing the Caribbean Sea, and bounded by the Magdalena on the west. Gold and coal are mined; coffee, sugar, and maize are produced, with some valuable woods and live-stock. Santa Marta is the capital. Area, 21,916 sq. miles; pop. 302,031.

MAGDALEN COLLEGE. College of the University of Oxford. It was founded in 1458 by William of Waynflete and has a fine pile of buildings in the High Street. Its tower is a landmark and its chapel is noted for its choir. The grounds are

Magdalen College, Oxford

extensive and include a deer park. The hall is worthy of mention, as are the cloisters. The head is the president and the scholars are called demis. The college includes Magdalen Hall. Notable members include Addison and the Prince of Wales.

MAGDALENE COLLEGE, Cambridge, was founded in 1519 by Thomas, Baron Audley of Walden. The buildings are in Magdalene Street, and the head is the master. The college is famous for its connection with Pepys; the manuscript of his *Diary* belongs to it.

MAGDALENIAN. Uppermost stage of the palæolithic period in Europe. Named from La Madeleine rock-shelter near Les Eyzies, Dordogne, where many engraved bone and horn implements were found, it exhibits man in association with the reindeer under subarctic conditions, and developing prehistoric art to its highest. It extended from south Britain to Russia.

MAGDEBURG. A city of Germany, and capital of Magdeburg district, Prussian Saxony, on the Elbe, which here divides into three arms. The Dom or cathedral dates from the thirteenth century. Machinery, castings, sugar, tobacco, fertilizers, chemicals, pottery, alcohol, cotton, and leather are among the manufactures. Magdeburg is the most important beet-sugar centre of Germany.

Historically the town is of great interest. Charlemagne granted it definite privileges (803); the Benedictine monastery (founded 937) became an archbishopric (968); and Magdeburg was placed under the ban of the Empire and taken by Maurice of Saxony in 1551. During the Thirty Years' War the city was unsuccessfully besieged by Wallenstein (1629), but the Swedish garrison surrendered to Tilly in May, 1631, when Magdeburg was sacked and thousands of unarmed citizens were put to the sword. In 1648 the archiepiscopal lands were erected into a duchy, and passed to Brandenburg in 1680. Marshal Ney captured Magdeburg in 1806, and from 1807 to 1813 it formed part of the Kingdom of Westphalia. Pop. (1925), 291,151.

MAGELLAN, Ferdinand (Port. *Fernão de Magalhães*), Portuguese navigator, born about 1470, died about 1521. He served under Albuquerque in the East Indies; distinguished himself at the taking of Malacca; and in 1519 Charles V. of Spain appointed him to command five ships, in which he discovered the strait that bears his name and also the Pacific Ocean. Eventually he reached the Philippines, but was killed in a skirmish with the natives of Mactan. His expedition doubled the Cape of Good Hope and returned to Seville, having circumnavigated the world.

MAGELLAN, Strait of. The channel, connecting the Atlantic with the Pacific, which lies between Tierra del Fuego and the Chilian mainland. The greatest length is about 360 miles, and it varies in breadth from 2½ miles to 17 miles. Between 1826 and 1836 the *Beagle* explored and charted the strait, upon which the only port is Punta Arenas, the most southerly town in the world.

MAGELLAN'IC CLOUDS. Two oval-shaped cloudlike masses of light in the southern hemisphere near the pole, consisting of swarms of stars, clusters, and nebulæ of every description. They cover spaces in the heavens of 42 and 10 square degrees respectively, and look much like detached portions of the Milky Way.

MAGENTA. A town of Milan, Italy, where, on 4th June, 1859 (Franco-Austrian War), the French and Sardinians under Napoleon III. and Marshal MacMahon gained a decisive victory over the Austrians. Pop. 8600.

MAGGIORE, Lago. A lake partly in Northern Italy and partly in the canton of Ticino, Switzerland, where it is called *Locarno*. It is the *Lacus Verbanus* of the Romans, and nestles

Lake Maggiore

in an amphitheatre of hills 600 feet above sea-level. Maggiore is 39 miles long, from ½ to 5½ miles broad, and 1100 feet deep in parts. The Borromean Islands (q.v.) lie directly opposite Pallanza.

MAGI (mā'ji). The hereditary priests among the Medes and Persians, set apart to manage the sacred rites, and preserve and propagate the sacred traditions, acting also as diviners and astrologers. The connection of the magi with astrology and enchantment in time brought it about that they acquired unbounded influence both in public and private life. They were entrusted with the education of youthful princes, and became the trusted companions of the sovereign. Their order was reformed by Zoroaster. The name came also to be applied to holy men or sages in the East.

MAGIC. The art or pretended art or practice of producing wonderful effects by the aid of superhuman beings or of departed spirits or the occult powers of nature. The word is used to include a mass of beliefs and practices which bear on matters beyond the ordinary known actions of cause and effect. A large proportion of magical rites are connected with the religious beliefs of those using them, their efficacy being ascribed to supernatural beings. There is, however, a non-spiritual element in magic which depends on certain imagined powers and correspondences in nature, that can be utilized in various ways. (*See* ALCHEMY; ASTROLOGY; CHARM; DIVINATION; WITCHCRAFT.)

In savage countries the native magician is often sorcerer and priest, and sometimes chief of the tribe. Among the ancient Egyptians magic was worked into an elaborate system and ritual, and it was regularly practised among the Babylonians and Assyrians, as well as in Greece and Rome. Alexandria, from the second to the fourth century, became the headquarters of theurgic magic, in which invocations, sacrifices, diagrams, talismans, etc., were systematically employed. This system, influenced by Jewish magical speculation, has a strong hold in mediæval Europe.

The name *natural magic* has been given to the art of applying natural causes to produce surprising effects. It includes the art of performing tricks and exhibiting illusions by means of apparatus.—BIBLIOGRAPHY: Andrew Lang, *Magic and Religion*; Sir J. G. Frazer, *The Golden Bough*; Lynn Thorndike, *The Place of Magic in the Intellectual History of Europe*; A. C. Haddon, *Magic and Fetishism*.

4	9	5	16
14	7	11	2
15	6	10	3
1	12	8	13

2	7	6
9	5	8
4	3	1

Magic Squares

MAGIC SQUARE. A term applied to a series of numbers in arithmetical progression, arranged in equal and parallel rows and columns, in such a manner that the vertical, horizontal, and diagonal columns when added shall give the same sums. There are also **Magic Circles, Magic Cubes, Magic Cylinders, Magic Spheres,** etc., in all of which the same result is brought about by various arrangements of the terms of an arithmetical series.

MAGINN (ma-gin'), **William.** Born at Cork 1793, died at Walton-on-Thames 1842. He was educated at Trinity College, Dublin, and established himself as a literary man in London. He was for long a regular contributor to *Blackwood's Magazine*, and was successively editor of *The Standard*, of *Fraser's Magazine*, and other publications. His *Homeric Ballads* and *Shakespeare Papers* were collected and published after his death.

MAGISTRATE. A public civil officer invested with the executive government or some branch of it. In this sense a king is the highest or first magistrate in a monarchy, as is the president in a republic. But the word is more particularly applied to subordinate officers, to whom the executive power of the law is committed, either wholly or in part, as governors, intendants, prefects, mayors, justices of the peace, and the like. In England the term is usually restricted to justices of peace in the country, and to police and stipendiary magistrates in London and the larger towns; and in Scotland to the provost and bailies in burghs.

MAGMA. In geology, the molten mass from which an igneous rock develops, whether as a glass, through rapid cooling, or as an assemblage of crystals of various mineral species.

MAGNA CHARTA LIBERTA'TUM. The Great Charter of Liberties, a document forming part of the English Constitution, and regarded as one of the mainstays of English liberty, extorted from King John at Runnymede in 1215 by the confederated barons.

Articles provide that no freeman shall be taken, or imprisoned, or proceeded against except by the lawful judgment of his peers or by the law of the land; and that no scutage or aid shall be imposed in the kingdom (except certain feudal dues from tenants of the Crown), unless by the common council of the kingdom. The remaining and greater part of the charter is directed against abuses of the king's power as feudal superior. It originally contained sixty-three clauses; subsequent confirmations altered the number of these till 1225, when it took its final and accepted legal form with thirty-seven clauses.

The most accurate and complete copy of the original charter is that preserved in Lincoln Cathedral. The Board of Commissioners on the public records ordered a facsimile of it to be engraved, and it has been frequently translated into English.—Cf. W. S. M'Kechnie, *Magna Charta.*

MAGNA GRÆCIA. The collective name given to the Greek cities and settlements in Southern Italy mostly founded in the eighth century B.C. by different Greek peoples. The Chalcidians founded Rhegium about 730 B.C.; and subsequently Croton, Sybaris (by the Achæans), Tarentum (by Laconian Dorians), Metapontum (by the Achæans), etc., were founded. These colonies and their offshoots reached a great pitch of wealth and power in the seventh and sixth centuries B.C. Mutual discord, however, gradually weakened them, and their independent existence came to an end in the third century B.C., when they were conquered by the Romans.

MAGNALIUM. The name given to alloys consisting mainly of aluminium, with magnesium and small quantities of other metals. Those found on the market at the present time contain only 1 to 2 per cent. of magnesium as a rule, together with similar quantities of one or more of the metals, copper, nickel, and tin. The alloys are light, their specific gravities differing little from that of aluminium, but they are superior to aluminium in strength and ease of working. They have been used extensively instead of brass for parts of scientific instruments, &c.

MAGNE'SIA. The name of two ancient cities of Asia Minor.

Magnesia ad Mæandrum was a city of Ionia, on the Lethæus, a tributary of the Mæander. It was an Æolian city, was destroyed by the Cimmerians, and rebuilt by the Milesians or Ephesians.

Magnesia ad Sipylum is the modern *Manisa*, a large city on the railway from Smyrna, and the junction of a line to Panderma, on the Sea of Marmara. Cotton is manufactured. Manisa was the capital of the thirteenth-century Byzantine government, and was the residence of Murad II. after his exile. It was anciently a city of Lydia.

MAGNE'SIA. A white, tasteless, earthy substance, possessing alkaline properties, the oxide of magnesium (q.v.). It is absorbent, antacid, mildly cathartic, and almost insoluble. It is found native as periclase, and exists as a component part of several minerals. In commerce pure magnesia is generally distinguished by the term *calcined magnesia*. It is readily obtained by exposing the hydrated carbonate to a red heat. The commercial *magnesia alba* is a basic carbonate. The chief use of magnesia and its carbonate is in medicine.

MAGNESIAN LIMESTONE. A yellowish rock composed of carbonates of lime and magnesia, as the joint mineral carbonate, dolomite, but usually with some excess of calcium carbonate as calcite. There are several varieties, more or less useful for building or ornamental purposes, which are included under the generic rock-name dolomite. This rock is very largely developed in the Permian system of North-East England.

MAGNESITE. Native magnesium carbonate, $MgCO_3$, a mineral occurring in white compact masses, or sometimes as crystals. It is used for the lining of furnaces, where a high temperature is essential, and in the manufacture of cement for floors; as a source of magnesia; as a substitute for plaster of Paris, &c. Formerly the supply came mostly from Greece; but the great demand has led to a large development in the United States.

MAGNE'SIUM. A metal; symbol Mg; atomic weight, 24·32. It is usually prepared by the electrolysis of the fused chloride or of carnallite. It has a silver-white colour, a high metallic lustre, and low specific gravity. It is usually met with in the form of ribbon or powder. When heated in oxygen or air, it burns with a brilliant white light rich in actinic rays, and is used for pyrotechnics and also as a flash-light in photography. The product formed when it burns is a white ash, magnesia, MgO (q.v.). The chief salts are the carbonate, the chloride, the sulphate (Epsom salts), the phosphates and the silicates, among which are the hydrous mineral silicates talc, meerschaum, and a large number of silicates of magnesium with iron, calcium, &c.

MAGNETISM. The science which treats of the properties of magnets, also the name of the thing which is the cause of these properties. All substances may, by the use of very intense magnetic forces, be shown to have magnetic properties, but these properties are possessed, in a notable degree, only by iron, steel, nickel, cobalt, loadstone, and Heusler's alloy, an alloy composed of three unmagnetic metals, copper, manganese, and aluminium. These substances are classed as *ferromagnetic*; others in which the property is feeble are *paramagnetic*; whilst those which appear to be less magnetic than air are *diamagnetic* (q.v.).

Loadstone was first found as a natural magnet in Magnesia, Asia Minor, from which place the name "magnet" is derived. Loadstone or magnetite (*see* IRON) is composed of ferroso-ferric oxide, Fe_3O_4; it exhibits certain properties common to magnets which may be shortly stated.

A magnet possesses polarity, i.e. the magnetism appears, so far as external action shows, to be concentrated near the ends of the magnet at two points called the *poles* of the magnet; these two poles are unlike. The magnetism, in reality, permeates the magnet from end to end, since, if a magnet is broken, two magnets are produced, each having opposite poles. Two magnets react on each other in such a way that like poles repel, and unlike poles attract. A suspended magnet, free to move horizontally, comes to rest in a position which lies nearly north and south. The pole which is towards the north is called a north-seeking pole, the other a south-seeking pole.

Magnetic material may be hard, like steel, or soft, like pure iron. Hard steel is difficult to magnetize, but when magnetized it retains its magnetism, and is as difficult to demagnetize. Such material is used for making permanent magnets. Soft iron, on the other hand, is easily magnetized, but when the magnetic force is withdrawn, the iron also loses its magnetism. This kind of material is required for the cores of electromagnets and transformers.

Unit Pole, Pole Strength.—Regarding the magnetism as being concentrated at the poles, *unit pole* is that quantity which, when placed 1 cm. distant from an equal similar pole, repels it with a force of 1 dyne. The line joining the two poles of a magnet is the *magnetic axis*, and the quantity of magnetism resident in each pole is the *pole strength*. The product of the pole strength and the distance between the poles is the *moment* of the magnet; for bar magnets the pole distance may be taken roughly as five-sixths of the length of the bar. The force between two poles of strengths m and m' at distance d cm. is mm'/d^2 dynes (Coulomb's Law).

Magnetic Field.—The space round the bar in which the magnetic effect of the bar is perceptible is known as the *magnetic field*, at any point of which the bar exerts a magnetic force in a definite direction. A *line of force* in a magnetic field is such that a tangent to the line at any point on it denotes the direction in which a small compass-needle would set itself under the action of the field. The field round a magnet may be supposed to be filled with lines of force; these may extend from one pole to the other, or to neighbouring magnetic material; their distribution may be made out by means of iron filings on paper, or by following out the direction in which a small needle points when moved over the paper. Where the magnetic force is strong, the lines are crowded, and in regions of weak force the lines are farther apart. The *field intensity* at a point may thus be expressed by the number of lines of force passing through a unit of area taken perpendicular to the lines.

Magnetic Induction.—When a bar of unmagnetized material is subjected to an increasing magnetic force, the magnetism acquired by the bar increases at first slowly, then more rapidly, and finally attains a state of *saturation* in which it is incapable of becoming more strongly magnetized, however intense the magnetic field may be. At any stage in the process the pole strength of the bar, divided by its sectional area, measures the *intensity of magnetization* of the bar; this quantity depends on the material of which the bar is composed, and the ratio of the magnetization to the magnetizing force is called the *susceptibility* of the material. If we imagine the bar to be crowded with lines from end to end, these lines will be due partly to the applied magnetic field, but mostly to the magnetization of the bar. The total number of lines passing through a unit of sectional area is called the *magnetic induction*, and the ratio of the induction to the intensity of the applied field is known as the *permeability* of the bar. The permeability increases with the induction, attains a maximum value, and then falls off to a very small value at high inductions. Its value is of importance in choosing magnetic material for dynamo iron, and the magnetic qualities of materials are tested by processes based on two fundamental methods, known respectively as the magnetometric and ballistic methods.

Hysteresis Cycle.—In these methods the material is subjected to a cyclic change of magnetic field, under which the magnetization of the body lags behind the magnetizing force—an effect known as *hysteresis* (q.v.). In the course of a complete cycle of magnetization the field is increased from zero until the specimen is saturated, then diminished to zero, reversed, and increased to the same high negative value, again diminished to zero, again reversed, and finally increased to the maximum again. During a complete cycle a certain amount of work is done in magnetization and demagnetization which appears in the form of heat in the body under test, and which, when expressed in ergs per cubic centimetre is called the *hysteresis loss*. In the course of the cycle the intensity of magnetization when the field is zero is known as the *remanent magnetism*, and the magnetic force required to make the specimen part with its remanent magnetism is the *coercive force*. Material used for permanent magnets requires to possess a high coercive force as well as high remanent magnetism.

Permanent Magnets.—The best available material for permanent magnets consists of a tungsten steel with 5 to 7 per cent. of tungsten and ½ per cent. of carbon. Honda, in Japan, has brought out a new steel, KS steel, which also contains cobalt, and which is in several respects superior to the above tungsten steel.

Heat Treatment.—A magnet is found to be stronger, and also more retentive, if it is heated to about 900° C., and then cooled or quenched rapidly in water, oil, or brine. It is thereby made mechanically hard, and at the same time its coercive force is much increased.

Maturing.—The remanent magnetism is the maximum amount which a magnet retains after saturation, and this amount is subject to loss caused by internal change with time, fluctuations of temperature, and mechanical shock. The magnet loses strength most rapidly immediately after magnetization, and the rate of loss diminishes with time, the magnet ultimately reaching a constant state. To attain this constant condition rapidly, the steel is matured before magnetization by boiling or steaming for ten or twelve hours.

Magnetization.—This is most efficiently done by means of a magnetizing coil, through which a strong electric current is passed for a short time. It may also be done by rubbing with another magnet, or by placing the bar between the poles of an electromagnet (*see* ELECTROMAGNETISM). The magnet is then demagnetized by an amount depending on its shape and dimensions, generally from 5 to 10 per cent.

Effect of Temperature.—When a rod of magnetic material is raised in temperature, its magnetic properties change. The permeability of iron in a weak field increases rapidly as the iron approaches a *critical temperature* at 785° C.; on passing through the critical temperature the iron loses its magnetic properties, but regains them on cooling. The magnetic change is comparatively sudden, and is caused by a change in the molecular constitution of the iron. Nickel loses its magnetic properties about 340° C., cobalt at about 1070° C., and magnetite at 580° C. When a piece of steel is cooling down through a dull red heat, it suddenly glows more brightly and then continues to cool; this is known as *recalescence*, and is due to the liberation of latent heat while undergoing internal transformation. Recalescence takes place in steel at a temperature of about 680° C.

The Magnetic Circuit.—Magnetic lines of force form a circuit whose path, in an iron ring, lies entirely within the iron, but in a bar magnet, lies partly in the steel and partly through the air. By analogy with the electric circuit carrying a current, the total number of magnetic lines is known as the *magnetic flux*; that which gives rise to the flux, e.g. a current of c amperes flowing through n windings of a magnetizing coil, possesses a *magnetomotive force* of value $0{\cdot}4\pi nc$, and the different parts of the circuit have the property of *reluctance*, measured by $l/\mu A$, where l is the length of the medium, μ its permeability, and A its sectional area. The magnetic flux is equal to the quotient magnetomotive force ÷ reluctance.—BIBLIOGRAPHY: Sir J. A. Ewing, *Magnetic Induction in Iron and other Metals*; S. P. Thompson, *Magnetism of Permanent Magnets* (Journal of the Institute of Electrical Engineers, 1913); S. S. Richardson, *Magnetism and Electricity*.

MAGNETITE. An important ore of iron, the oxide Fe_3O_4, crystallizing in the cubic system as octahedra, but more commonly massive. Magnetite is black and cannot be scratched by a knife. *See* IRON; LOADSTONE.

MAGNETO. A type of combined dynamo and transformer used to generate electrical pressures sufficient to jump the gap between the points of a plug by a spark. The invention is due to two Germans, Simms and Bosch, and at the beginning of the European War the magneto industry was practically entirely in foreign hands, but the British magneto-makers by their research work and its application to practical design have produced instruments superior to all.

The magneto has a permanent magnet field system, and in the air-gap an armature rotates which has two coils wound on it. The first coil is the primary one, and in this coil an electromotive force is generated. The flow of current on the primary coil is interrupted by the contact breaker. At these moments a high electrical pressure is generated in the secondary coil, which is wound on the same core. This secondary supply is conducted to each plug by the distributor, the return being by the frame of the machine. The magnetic field must be sufficiently strong to ensure the generation of a high electromotive force when running slow or in starting, and to ensure certainty in action at high speeds when working under adverse conditions.

The plug referred to has the centre-pin insulated. The side-pins or ring are in metallic connection with the threaded part which screws into the engine cylinder. The condenser is connected across the contact breaker to reduce the sparking. A safety spark-gap is usually provided on the magneto to allow any exceptionally high voltage current to pass across to earth.

MAGNETOM'ETER. An instrument or apparatus used in determining the horizontal component of the earth's magnetic force. The experiment consists of two parts: in the deflection experiment a bar magnet of moment M and pole distance $2l$ is placed with its axis east and west, and its centre at a distance r to the east or west of a delicately suspended magnetic needle, causing the latter to be deflected through an angle θ from the magnetic meridian. If the earth's field has an intensity H at the position of the needle, it may be shown that $M/H = (r^2 - l^2)^2 \tan\theta/2r$. In the second operation the bar magnet is suspended horizontally in the place previously occupied by the needle, and caused to vibrate, like a compass-needle, through a small angle under the action of the earth's horizontal force. Its period T, or time of one complete vibration, is measured, also I the moment of inertia of the bar. These are related by the formula $MH = 4\pi^2 I/T^2$. Knowing the values of M/H and MH from the two experiments, both M and H may be found. For accurate work the effects of temperature, induction, and torsion of the suspending system require to be allowed for.

The Kew Observatory type of magnetometer may also be employed to measure the declination, or angle between the geographical and magnetic meridians. In observatories the changes of the magnetic elements are automatically recorded by an instrument called a magnetograph. The magnetometer is used for field-work during magnetic surveys; another type has also been employed in which a magnetic field of known value is set up by means of a current flowing in a Helmholtz coil, and the value of H is found from the observed deflection of the needle.—BIBLIOGRAPHY: Stewart and Gee, *Practical Physics* (vol. ii.); A. Gray, *Absolute Measurements in Electricity and Magnetism.*

MAGNO'LIA. A genus of trees and shrubs, type of the nat. ord. Magnoliaceæ; named from *Pierre Magnol*, a French botanist of the seventeenth century. The species, which chiefly inhabit North America, Northern India, China, Japan, and other parts of Asia, are trees much admired on account of the beauty of their flowers and foliage, and are in great request in gardens. In their native countries some of them attain great height, and have flowers 10 inches across.

The bark of the root of *M. glauca*, or the beaver tree, is an important tonic. *M. tripetăla*, or umbrella tree, has also tonic properties. *M. grandiflōra*, or big-laurel, and *M. conspicua* or *Yulan*, the yulan or Chinese magnolia, grow well in the south of England, and are splendid ornamental trees. The yulan is remarkable in that it flowers in spring before the leaves expand.

MAGNOLIA METAL. Largely used for bearings, for which purpose the alloy should contain a hard and a soft constituent, the function of the former being to resist wear and to provide a surface with a low coefficient of friction, and that of the latter to allow of a uniform distribution of the load and so prevent local heating and seizing. Magnolia metal generally contains 78 to 80 of lead, 15 to 16 of antimony, 5 to 6 of tin, and about 0·25 per cent. of bismuth.

MAGPIE. A bird of the genus Pica or related genera, belonging to the Corvidæ or crow family. The common European magpie (*P. rustica*), which ranges eastward to Formosa, and is also found in North America, is about 18 inches in length; the plumage is black and white, the black glossed with green and purple; the bill is stout, and the tail is very long. The magpies continue in pairs throughout the year, and prey on a variety of food, chiefly animal. They are determined robbers of other birds' nests, destroying the eggs and young birds. In captivity they are celebrated for their crafty instincts, their power of imitating words, and their propensity to purloin and secrete glittering articles.

Two related species (*P. mauritanica* and *P. nuttalli*) are native, respectively, to North Africa and California. Blue magpies are found in South Spain (*Cyanopica cooki*) and East Asia (*C. cyana*).

MAHĀBHĀRATA (literally the great history of the descendants of Bharata). An ancient Indian epic of about 400,000 verses, and divided into eighteen books. The groundwork of the poem is the Kaurava-Pandava War (24,000 verses). In Bharata two brothers established rival thrones: Dhritarashtra, the elder, had a hundred sons, called the Kaurava, the powers of evil; the Pandava, the powers of good, were the five sons of Pandu, the younger brother, by his two wives. Both the Kaurava and the Pandava were related to Krishna, Pritha, mother of three of the Pandava, being aunt of Krishna.

The *Mahábhárata* form an encyclopædia of Hindu mythology, legendary history, and philosophy. To Vyâsa, "the arranger," is attributed the authorship, but this simply means that at one time the fragmentary pieces were welded together in a definite order and sequence to form a complete work.—BIBLIOGRAPHY: E. W. Hopkins, *The Great Epic of India: its Character and Origin;* S. Sorensen, *Index to the Names in the Mahábhárata*; V. Vaidya, *The Mahábhárata*; *The Mahábhárata* (in Everyman's Library).

MAHAFFY, Sir John Pentland. Born in Switzerland 1839, died 1919. He was educated in Germany, and in 1856 entered Trinity College,

Magpie

Dublin, where he became a Fellow in 1864. He was appointed professor of ancient history in 1871, and he was knighted (G.B.E.) in 1918. He wrote: *Lectures on Primitive Civilization, Social Life in Greece from Homer to Menander, History of Classical Greek Literature, Rambles and Studies in Greece,* and *Alexander's Empire.*

MAHÂNADI, or **MAHANUDDY.** A river of India, rising near Raipur, Central Provinces, and flowing hence through Orissa to the Bay of Bengal, which it enters by several mouths, 120 miles south-west of the Ganges sunderbunds. It is navigable as far as Sambalpur, and a dam at Cuttack supplies the Orissa canal system. The Mahânadi has a course length of about 520 miles, and drains an area of 53,000 sq. miles.

MAHARAJPUR. A village of Gwalior, India, the scene of a desperate battle during the Gwalior War, when the Mahrattas under Bhagerat Rao Scindhia were defeated by the British under Sir Hugh Gough (29th Dec., 1843). During the Indian Mutiny Havelock, on the march to Cawnpore, defeated Nana Sahib here (16th July, 1857), and entered Cawnpore on the following day.

MAHATMA. Sanskrit word, "great-souled," applied by modern Western theosophists to men said to be endowed with preternatural powers acquired by ascetic or astral means. The word became associated by the Indian populace with the Hindu nationalist leader, Mohandas Gandhi (q.v.), because of his asceticism.

MAHDI (mä'dē; Ar., the Guided One). A name assumed by some of the successors of Mahomet, particularly applied to the twelfth imam, the lineal descendant of Mahomet, born A.D. 868. He mysteriously disappeared, being probably murdered by a rival, and the belief was that he would remain hidden until the "last days," when he would reappear, and at the head of the faithful spread Mahommedanism over the world.

Many professed Mahdis have appeared from time to time in Africa as well as Asia, the chief being Mahomet Ahmed, the leader of the Sudanese insurrection (1883-85). He was born at Dongola in 1843, died at Omdurman 1885. He studied Mahommedan theology at Khartoum and Berber, and at twenty-five years of age he retired to the Island of Aba in the White Nile, where he lived in solitude for fifteen years. At the age of forty his short victorious career as a prophet began. *See* EGYPT; SUDAN.

MAHÉ. A French settlement on the Malabar coast, Madras, India, at the mouth of a small river of the same name. The settlement is administered by Pondicherry. Pop. 11,572.

MAHÉ. The principal island of the Seychelles.

MAH JONGG. Chinese gambling game. It is played with 136 counters or tiles, not unlike dominoes. Four players usually take part, but it can be played by two. The tiles are divided into three suits, and there are four sets of each. Each player plays for himself and tries to secure the tiles representing the highest score.

Mahmud II.

MAHMUD (mä'mud). Sultan of Ghazni, the founder of the Mahommedan Empire in India, born at Ghazni about 970, died 1030. His father, Sabaktagin, Governor of Ghazni, owned a nominal allegiance to Persia, but was really independent. On his death Mahmud put aside his elder brother, formed an alliance against the Persian monarch, overthrew his kingdom, and laid the foundation of an extensive empire in Central Asia (999). He then turned his attention to India, and in a series of twelve invasions secured a great amount of treasure, and vastly extended his power. He was a patron of literature, and brought many men of learning about his court, among whom was the poet Firdusi (q.v.). He established large educational institutions at Ghazni, and spent vast sums on public works.

MAHMUD I. Sultan of Turkey, born 1696; reigned 1730-50.—**Mahmud II.**, Sultan of Turkey, born 1785, died 1839; placed on the throne by the Janizaries after the murder of his predecessor (1808). The chief events of his reign are the war with Russia from 1808 to 1812, which cost him Bessarabia and the provinces of Serbia, Moldavia, and Wallachia, as settled by the Treaty of Bucharest; the war of Greek independence, which ended in the separation of that country, and the destruction of the Turkish fleet at Navarino, 1820-28; the extermination of the Janizaries, 1826; the Treaty of Adrianople with the Russians, who were on the point of entering Constantinople, 1829; the independence of Egypt under Mehemet Ali, and the new Treaty of Unkiar-Skelessi with the Russians, 1832-33.

MAHOG'ANY. The wood of the *Swietenia mahogăni*, a lofty and beautiful tree, indigenous to Central America and the West Indies, belonging to the nat. ord. Meliaceæ. It grows most abundantly, and attains its greatest development between 10° N. lat. and the Tropic of Cancer. It reaches maturity in about 200 years, and grows to a height of 40 to 50 feet, diameter 6 to 12 feet.

The wood is hard, compact, reddish-brown, and susceptible of a brilliant polish. It is one of the best and most ornamental woods known, and is of universal use in the making of furniture. It is imported chiefly from Mexico and British Honduras. That which is imported from the West Indies is called "Spanish" mahogany, and is the most valued. *African mahogany* is the wood of *Khaya senegalensis*, and is brought from Sierra Leone. *Indian mahogany* is the wood of *Soymida febrifuga* found in mountainous districts of India. *Ceylon mahogany* is the *Artocarpus integrifolia*, widely cultivated throughout the warm parts of Asia. *Australian mahogany* is the red gum (*Eucalyptus rostrata*).

MAHOMET, or **MOHAM'MED,** or more correctly **MUHAMMAD.** The founder of Islam, an Arabian by birth, of the tribe of the Kuraish, and was born of poor parents in A.D. 571 in Mecca. His parents died early, and he was brought up by his uncle Abu Talib, who trained him to commerce, and with whom he journeyed through Arabia and Syria. In his twenty-fifth year his uncle recommended him as agent to a rich widow, named Chadidja, and he acquitted himself so much to her satisfaction that she married him, and thus placed him in easy circumstances. She was fifteen years older than he, but he lived with her in happy and faithful wedlock. He seems to have had from his youth a propensity to religious contemplation, for he was every year accustomed, in the month Ramadan (q.v.), to retire to a cave in Mount Hara, near Mecca, and dwell there in solitude.

Mahomet began his mission in the fortieth year of his age by announcing his apostleship to his own family. His wife was one of the first to believe in him, and among other members of his family who acknowledged his mission was his cousin Ali, the son of Abu Talib. Of great importance was the accession of Abu Bekr, a man of estimable character, who stood in high respect, and persuaded ten of the most considerable citizens of Mecca to join the believers in the new apostle. They were all instructed by Mahomet in the doctrines of *Islam*, as the new religion was styled, which were promulgated as the gradual revelations of the divine will, through the angel Gabriel, and were collected in the *Koran* (q.v.).

After three years Mahomet made a more public announcement of his doctrine, but his followers were few for years. In 621 Mahomet lost his wife, and the death of Abu Talib took place about the same time. Deprived of their assistance, he was compelled to retire for a time to the city of Taïf. On the other hand, he was readily received by the pilgrims who visited the Kaaba (q.v.), and gained numerous adherents among the families in the neighbourhood.

Mahomet now adopted the resolution of encountering his enemies with force. Only the more exasperated at this, they formed a conspiracy to murder him; warned of the imminent danger, he left Mecca, accompanied by Abu Bekr alone, and concealed himself in a cave not far distant. Here he spent three days undiscovered, after which he arrived safely at Medina, but not without danger (A.D. 622). This event, from which the Mahommedans commence their era, is known under the name of *Hijra*, which signifies flight.

In Medina Mahomet was well received; thither he was followed by many of his adherents. He now assumed the sacerdotal and regal dignity, married Ayesha, daughter of Abu Bekr, and as the number of the faithful continued to increase, declared his resolution of propagating his doctrines with the sword. In the battle of Bedr (623), the first of the long series of battles by which Islamism was established over a large portion of the earth, he defeated Abu Sofian, the chief of the Kuraish. He in turn was defeated by them at Ohod, near Medina, soon after, and in 625 they unsuccessfully besieged Medina, and a truce of ten years was agreed on.

Wars with the Jewish tribes followed, many Arabian tribes submitted themselves, and in 630 he took possession of Mecca as prince and prophet. The idols of the Kaaba were demolished, but the sacred touch of the prophet made the black stone again the object of the deepest veneration, and the magnet that attracts hosts of pilgrims to the holy city of Mecca.

The whole of Arabia was soon after conquered, and a summons to embrace the new revelation of the divine law was sent to the Emperor Heraclius at Constantinople, the King of Persia, and the King of Abyssinia. Preparations for the conquest of Syria and for war with the Roman Empire were begun, when Mahomet died at Medina (632). His body was buried in the house of Ayesha, where he died, and which afterwards became part of the adjoining mosque, and a place of pilgrimage for the faithful in all time to come. Of all his wives, the first alone bore him children, of whom only his daughter Fatima, wife of Ali, survived him.

There is no doubt that Mahomet was a man of extraordinary insight and deep reflection. Though without book-learning, he had a deep knowledge of man, was familiar with Bible narratives and Eastern legends, and possessed a grasp of the eternal ground of all religion, though tinged and modified by his vivid poetic imagination. *See* KORAN; MAHOMMEDANISM. — BIBLIOGRAPHY: W. Muir, *Life of Mahomet*; D. S. Margoliouth, *Mohammed and the Rise of Islam*; E. Sell, *The Life of Mohammed*; *The Cambridge Mediæval History* (vol. ii.).

MAHOMMEDANISM. The name commonly given in Christian countries to the creed established by Mahomet. His followers call their creed *Islam* (entire submission to the decrees of God), and their common formula of faith is, "There is no god but Allah, and Mahomet is his prophet."

Dogma.—The dogmatic or theoretical part of Mahommedanism embraces the following points: (1) Belief in God, who is without beginning or end, the sole Creator and Lord of the universe, having absolute power, knowledge, glory, and perfection. (2) Belief in His angels, who are impeccable beings, created of light. (3) Belief in good and evil jinn (genii), who are created of smokeless fire, and are subject to death. (4) Belief in the Holy Scriptures, which are His uncreated word revealed to the prophets. Of these there now exist, but in a greatly corrupted form, the Pentateuch, the Psalms, and the Gospels; and in an uncorrupted and incorruptible state the *Koran*, which abrogates and surpasses all preceding revelations (*see* KORAN). (5) Belief in God's prophets and apostles, the most distinguished of whom are Adam, Noah, Abraham, Moses, Jesus, and Mahomet. Mahomet is the greatest of them all, the last of the prophets and the most excellent of the creatures of God. (6) Belief in a general resurrection and final judgment, and in future rewards and punishments, chiefly of a physical nature. (7) The belief, even to the extent of fatalism, of God's absolute fore-knowledge and predestination of all events both good and evil.

Duties.—The practical part of Mahommedanism inculcates certain observances or duties, of which four are most important. The first is prayer, including preparatory purifications. Prayer must be engaged in at five stated periods each day. On each of these occasions the Moslem has to offer up certain prayers held to be ordained by God, and others ordained by His prophet. During prayer it is necessary that the face of the worshipper be turned towards the *kebla*, that is, in the direction of Mecca. Prayers may be said in any clean place, but on Friday they must be said in the mosque. Second in importance to prayer stands the duty of giving alms. Next comes the duty of fasting. The Moslem must abstain from eating and drinking, and from every indulgence of the senses, every day during the month of Ramadan, from the first appearance of daybreak until sunset, unless physically incapacitated. The fourth paramount religious duty of the Moslem is the performance at least once in his life, if possible, of the pilgrimage (*el-Hajj*) to Mecca and the Hill of Arafat, after which he becomes a *Hajji*.

Circumcision is general among the Mahommedans, but is not absolutely obligatory. The distinctions of clean and unclean meats are nearly the same as in the Mosaic code. Wine and all intoxicating liquors are strictly forbidden. Music, games of chance, and usury are condemned. Images and pictures of living creatures are contrary to law.

Charity, probity in all transactions, veracity (except in a few cases), and modesty are indispensable virtues.

After Mahomet's death Abu Bekr, his father-in-law, became his successor, but disputes immediately arose, a party holding that Ali, the son-in-law of Mahomet, was by right entitled to be his immediate successor. This led to the division of the Mahommedans into the two sects known as Shiites and Sunnites. The former, the believers in the right of Ali to be considered the first successor, constitute at present the majority of the Mussulmans of Persia and India; the latter, considered as the orthodox Mahommedans, are dominant in Turkey, Arabia, Turkestan, and Africa. The total Mahommedan population of the world is estimated at fully 200,020,000. *See* CALIPH; SHIITES; SUNNITES; MUEZZIN.

MAHON'Y, Francis Sylvester. Known as "Father Prout," born at Cork 1804, died at Paris 1866. About 1834 he began the contribution of an amusing series of articles known as the *Prout Papers* to *Fraser's Magazine.* In 1846 he became Roman correspondent to *The Daily News,* his letters being afterwards republished under the title of *Facts and Figures from Italy.* For the last twelve or fifteen years of his life he was Paris correspondent for *The Globe. Reliques of Father Prout* were published in 1836 and 1860, and *Final Reliques* in 1876.

MAIA. In Greek mythology, one of the Pleiades, the daughter of Atlas and Pleione, and the mother of Hermes (Mercury).

MAIDEN CASTLE. Earthwork just outside Dorchester, Dorset. It was formed in the Neolithic Age, and covers 16 acres, being perhaps the largest of its kind in the country. The hill is 430 feet high, and is protected by concentric ramparts of earth.

MAIDENHAIR. The name given to the *Adiantum Capillus-venĕris,* a fern with a creeping scaly rhizome, and bipinnate fronds, the leaflets of which are between rhomboidal and wedge-shaped, margined with oblong sori, and more or less deeply lobed. It is found growing on rocks and walls in some parts of Britain, and possesses demulcent and mucilaginous properties.

MAIDENHAIR TREE. *See* GINKGO.

MAIDENHEAD. A municipal borough of Berkshire, England. Its first charter dates from the reign of Edward III. A popular boating centre on the Thames, it is 26¼ miles, on the G.W. Railway. The industries include brewing. Pop. (1931), 17,520.

MAIDSTONE. A municipal borough, market town, and county town of Kent, on the Medway. The church of All Saints was formerly attached to a college of that name built by Archbishop Courtenay in the reign of Richard II., and suppressed by Edward VI. The archepiscopal palace was also built by Courtenay. Fairfax took the town and suppressed a Royalist rising in 1648. Maidstone "adopted" Montauban, France, in 1921. The town is in the hop-field area, but has also manufactures of paper, cement, beer, and agricultural implements. It is also a military centre. Pop. (1931), 42,259.

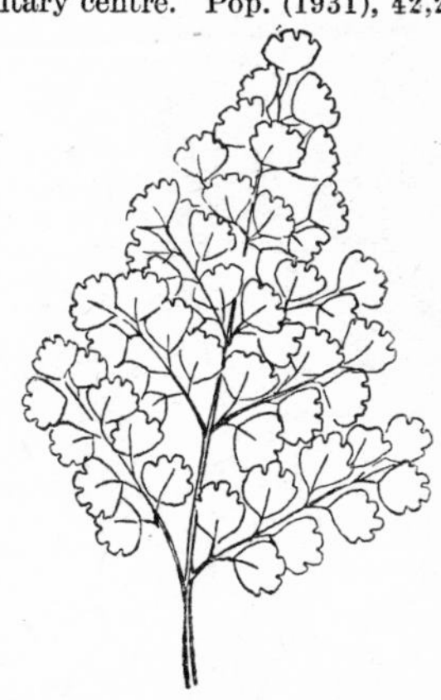

Maidenhair

MAIMANSINGH. A district of the Dacca division of Eastern Bengal, better known as Nasirábád (q.v.). Area 6287 sq. miles; pop. 3,915,000.

MAIMONIDES (mī-mon'i-dēz), properly **MOSES BEN MAIMON BEN JOSEPH.** Jewish scholar, born at Cordova about 1131-39, died about 1201-9. He received an excellent education, studied Jewish and Arabic literature and Greek philosophy, attended the lectures of the Arabic philosophers, and studied medicine. He systematized the whole mass of Jewish tradition, and demonstrated the principles on which Judaism is based. His books were widely circulated in Europe by means of Latin translations.

His best writings in Arabic are: *The Guide of the Perplexed,* an exposition of Judaism; a *Compendium* of *Logic*; a *Commentary on the Mishna*; an *Exposition of the 613 Laws of Moses*; &c. He wrote in Hebrew a complete system of the Talmudic Judaism.—BIBLIOGRAPHY: H. Graetz, *History of the Jews*; D. Yellin and I. Abrahams, *Maimonides*; see also M. Friedländer, *The Guide of the Perplexed.*

MAIN (mīn). A river of Germany, which rises in the Fichtelgebirge, flows in a generally westerly direction for a distance of 310 miles, and

Main: Frankfort-on-the-Main

joins the Rhine a little above the town of Mainz. It is navigable for about 240 miles, and has been improved so as to admit the largest Rhine steamers (vessels of 1000 tons) to Frankfort.

MAINE, Sir Henry James Sumner. English jurist, born 1822, died 1888. From Christ's Hospital he went to Pembroke College, Cambridge, where he graduated in 1844. He was appointed regius professor of civil law in the same university, 1847, and reader in jurisprudence at the Middle Temple, 1854. From 1862 to 1869 he was law member of the Supreme Council of India, and on his return home he was elected Corpus professor of jurisprudence at Oxford. In 1877 he became master of Trinity Hall, Cambridge.

His chief works are: *Ancient Law in Connection with the Early History of Society, and its Relation to Modern Ideas*; *Village Communities in the East and West*; *The Early History of Institutions*; *Dissertations on Early Law and Custom*; *The Whewell Lectures on International Law*, delivered before the University of Cambridge, 1887. His works place him in the very front rank of modern philosophical jurists.

MAINE. A north-eastern maritime state of the United States, bordering New Brunswick and Quebec, Canada, with its seaboard of 2500 miles on the Gulf of Maine. In the north the country is hilly (Mount Katahdin, 5385 feet), and an elaborate lake system is the result of erosion by the Laurentian glacier. The island-studded coast is deeply indented, and the state is traversed by several navigable rivers, principally the Penobscot and Kennebec, but all of them are harnessed for power.

Lumbering is important in the afforested northern district; agriculture, quarrying, and fisheries are generally the principal occupations. Oats, maize, buckwheat, potatoes, and hay are the chief agricultural products. There are few minerals, felspar being the only one of any commercial importance.

The State university (founded 1868) is located at Orono, and there are also colleges at Brunswick (founded 1794) and Lewiston. Augusta (q.v.) is the State capital, but Portland, the seaport, is by far the largest city. Maine covers an area of 33,040 sq. miles (land area, 29,895 sq. miles), and has a pop. of (1930) 797,423.

History and Constitution.—Maine was founded in 1622 by Sir Ferdinando Gorges, who, with John Mason, was granted land by the Government of New England. Eventually the state became part of Massachusetts (1692), but at last was made an independent state and admitted into the Union (3rd March, 1820). The present Government comprises a legislature of two Houses, the Senate (51 members), and the House of Representatives (151 members), both sitting for a limited period of two years, but for local government the state is divided into sixteen counties, subdivided into towns, cities, and some unincorporated places.—BIBLIOGRAPHY: H. S. Burrage, *Beginnings of Colonial Maine*; H. E. Holmes, *Makers of Maine.*

MAINE. A pre-Revolutionary province of France, lying immediately south of Normandy, and comprising the modern departments of Sarthe and Mayenne with parts of Orne and Eure-et-Loir. Le Mans was the capital. When Henry II. ascended the throne of England in 1154, Maine passed to him from the Plantagenets. It was wrested from John by Philip Augustus in 1204.

MAINE DE BIRAN (mān-dė-bērāṇ), **François Pierre Gonthier.** French philosopher, born 1766, died 1824. His chief philosophical essays are:

Influence de l'habitude, Sur la décomposition de la pensée, Sur l'aperception immédiate, and *Rapports du physique et du moral.* Maine de Biran's importance as a philosopher is chiefly due to his giving the direction to philosophic speculation afterwards developed in the school founded by Victor Cousin.

MAINE-ET-LOIRE. A north-western department of France, part of pre-Revolutionary Anjou; area, 2811 sq. miles; Pop. (1931), 475,991. It is generally hilly, and is traversed centrally from east to west by the Loire, which receives within the department the Maine, comprising the united streams Loir, Sarthe, and Mayenne. Other rivers are the Authion and Layon. Quarrying (slate, freestone, and granite) is an extensive industry, slate being confined to the district around the capital, Angers (q.v.). Agriculturally the department produces flax, beet, wheat, and oats; the vine is also cultivated. Angers is the chief town and railway centre; Baugé, Saumur, Cholet, and Segre are of importance.

MAINTENANCE. In law, an unlawful intermeddling in a suit, by assisting either party with money, or otherwise, to prosecute or defend it. This is prohibited by the English law. A man may, however, maintain the suit of his near kinsman, servant, or poor neighbour with impunity, and any suits in which he has an actual interest. The law seeks to prevent only harsh and vexatious intermeddling.

MAINTENON, Françoise d'Aubigné, Marquise de. Second wife of Louis XIV., was born in 1635, and died in 1719. She returned to France from Martinique in 1645, and promptly married (1651) the aged and deformed but celebrated wit and poet Scarron. On his death in 1660 she was left in straitened circumstances, and although aided by Anne of Austria, the "widow Scarron," as she was contemptuously called by her enemies, was glad to accept the post of *gouvernante* to the children of Louis XIV. and Madame de Montespan (1669). Maintenon played her cards well; beloved by her charges and admired no less for her wit than for her beauty, she was created Marquise in 1678, and from that time was known as "Madame" de Maintenon.

In 1680 Louis discarded Montespan, his mistress, and upon the death of the queen he was secretly married to Maintenon (1685), who became his adviser, and was indispensable to him. She was a devout, bigoted *pro-clerical,* ambitious and resolute, and the period of her influence coincides with an unfortunate increase in religious persecution.—Cf. C. C. Dyson, *Madame de Maintenon: Her Life and Times.*

MAINZ (Fr. *Mayence*). A town of Germany, in the Republic of Hesse, on the Rhine opposite the mouth of the Main. The Rhine is bridged, and Mainz is connected with Kastel (*Castellum Mattiacorum* of the Romans), on the opposite bank. The town has a lively shipping and general river trade, and is an important railway junction. Mainz Cathedral was founded in A.D. 978, but has been many times burned and restored; it has three choirs and six towers. The ancient castle of the Electors, built between 1627 and 1678, houses both Roman and Germanic antiquities, and the Gutenberg Museum (1901).

History.—Mainz was the Roman *Moguntiacum,* and was founded by Drusus (13 B.C.), to whom a concrete tower, called the Eigelstein, which stands in the citadel and on the site of the ancient Roman camp, is said to have been erected. In 747 the town was made an archbishopric under Saint Boniface, and Mainz was long the first ecclesiastical city of Germany, of which its Archbishop-elector ranked as the premier prince. Mainz was ceded to France in 1801 (Peace of Lunéville), and in 1803 the archbishopric was abolished. In 1814 the town was retaken and definitely incorporated in the Grand-Duchy of Hesse (1816). Once highly fortified, Mainz is one of the German fortress towns dismantled under the Treaty of Versailles. Pop. (1925), 130,915.

MAITLAND, Sir Richard (Lord Lethington). Scottish poet, lawyer, and statesman, born 1496, died 1586. He studied at St. Andrews and in France. In 1551 he took his seat on the Bench as an extraordinary Lord of Session. In 1560 he became blind. In 1561 he was appointed an ordinary Lord of Session, and assumed the title of Lord Lethington. From 1562 to 1567 he held the office of Lord Privy Seal. He made a celebrated collection of early Scottish poetry. *Ancient Scottish Poems,* selections from Maitland's collection, were published by John Pinkerton in 1786. The Maitland Club, named after him, published a volume of his own poems in 1830.

MAITLAND, William. Commonly known as Secretary Lethington, a Scottish statesman, eldest son of Sir Richard Maitland, born about 1528, died 1573. In 1558 he was appointed Secretary of State by Mary of Guise, the Queen-Regent. In the following year he joined the Lords of the Congregation. On Queen Mary's arrival in Scotland he was chosen one of her principal ministers. After Darnley's murder he conspired to effect Mary's escape from Lochleven. He fought against her at Langside, but the Regent Moray, suspecting his good faith, had him arrested in

Sir William Maitland

1569 as an accessory to Darnley's murder. After the assassination of Moray he became the life and soul of the queen's party. In 1571 he joined Kirkcaldy in Edinburgh Castle; was proclaimed a traitor by the Parliament, and attainted with his two brothers. He died in prison in Leith.—Cf. E. Russell, *Maitland of Lethington: a Study of his Life and Times.*

MAITLAND. A town of New South Wales, 95 miles north of Sydney, on the Hunter River. It comprises two distinct municipalities, East Maitland and West Maitland, connected by rail and tram. It was situated in a very fertile agricultural district, which is now devoted to coal-mining. Total pop. (1931), 11,940.

MAIZE (Sp. *maiz*, from Haytian *mahiz*, the native name of the plant). Indian corn, a genus of plants commonly cultivated in the warmer parts of the world, where it answers a purpose similar to that of wheat in more northern countries. The common maize or Indian corn is the *Zea Mays* of botanists, a monœcious grass, of vigorous growth, with stems not more than 2 feet high in some varieties, and reaching the height of 8 or even 10 feet in others. The grains are large, compressed and packed closely in regular parallel rows along the sides of a receptacle many inches long. In large varieties the ear or *cob* is often 1 foot long and 2 or 3 inches in thickness.

Maize is extensively cultivated in America, where it forms almost the only bread eaten by many of the people. Its flour, though exceedingly nourishing, is not glutinous, and must accordingly be mixed with wheat, rye, or other flour before it can be baked. In America large quantities of unripe grain are roasted till they split, and are then eaten under the name of *pop-corn.* From the green stems a syrup is expressed, which is fermented and converted into a kind of spirits. Paper has been made from maize fibres.

It is also cultivated throughout a great part of Asia and Africa, and in several countries of the south of Europe, as Spain and Italy. The green stems and leaves form nutritious food for cattle, and in Great Britain it is sown and cut green for this purpose. *Z. Curagua,* a smaller species, is the Chile maize or Valparaiso corn.

MAJESTY (Lat. *majestas*). A title belonging to kings and queens. In England Henry VIII. first adopted the title, and at present all emperors and kings are addressed as "your majesty." The former kings of France were addressed as "most Christian majesty," the kings of Spain as "most Catholic majesty," the former kings of Portugal as "most faithful majesty," and the former kings of Hungary as "apostolic majesty." The former emperors of Germany and Austro-Hungary had the title of "imperial-royal majesty." In England the full title is: *His most Gracious Majesty.*

MAJOR. In the British service, the commissioned rank next below that of lieutenant-colonel; the junior grade of field-officer. The origin of the word is curious and is as follows. In the Middle Ages, when fighting was a profession of some profit, and troops were raised as required for a particular service, the commander of any given body was invariably a knight, and the rank and file (if a modern expression be permitted) were engaged to serve him personally. Out of these personal retainers the knight, for convenience of command, selected certain men as his assistants or "servientes" (sergeants), to whom he issued his orders. In course of time a superior rank of "serviente" or sergeant, known as the sergeant-major, grew up, who acted as the link between the knight or commander and his subordinates, the sergeants; in other words, the sergeant-major became the second-in-command of the unit. In time the prefix sergeant was dropped, and the second-in-command became the major. (The present-day sergeant-major is a warrant-officer, and as such senior to all non-commissioned officers.)

MAJOR. In music, designates in general a larger in contradistinction to a smaller interval of the same denomination, called a *minor* interval; thus a *major tone* is the interval between two tones having the proportion to each other in number of vibrations of 8 : 9; a *minor tone* the interval between two tones in the ratio of 9 : 10; a *major third* is an interval of two tones (major and minor); a *minor third* an interval of a tone and semitone. The *major mode* is one of the two recognized modern modes (or forms of the scale), in which the first third in the scale is a major third, in contradistinction to the *minor mode*, in which the first third is a minor third.

MAJOR'CA (Sp. *Mallorca*). The ancient *Balearis Major*, a Spanish Mediterranean island, the largest of the Balearic group; area, 1325 sq. miles. Divided by a mountain chain running from north-east to south-west, the island rises steeply from the sea on the west and north; elsewhere the coasts are low and shelving. The climate is temperate, and, since the drainage of the malarial Albufera Morass at Alcudia, the island has been fairly healthy. Oranges, figs, wine, and subtropical cereals are produced; coal is mined, slate and marble are quarried, and precious stones are found. There are many wonderful stalactite caves. Palma, the capital, is in railway communication with Manacor, Inca, La Puebla, Alcudia, and Felanitx. Pop. 260,150. *See* BALEARIC ISLANDS.

MAKÔ. A town and capital of the province of Csanád, Hungary, near the Maros River, on the frontier line of Hungary, Yugoslavia, and Rumania, 19 miles east by south of Szegedin (Szeged). Pop. 35,814.

MALABAR'. A maritime district of Madras, India, on the west coast; area, 5795 sq. miles. A great portion is comparatively low, intersected by narrow ravines, covered with forests and jungle, and watered by innumerable streams. The annual rainfall is over 100 inches. Rice, coffee, rubber, and coco-nuts are produced. The principal towns are Calicut (the largest), Cananor, and Tellicherry. Pop. about 3,000,000. The name Malabar is often applied to the whole extent of coast country as far north as Bombay. Malayalam is the language of the coast. It is Dravidian, and an offshoot from Tamil, dating back to the ninth century.

MALABAR PLUM. *See* ROSE-APPLE.

MALAC'CA. A British maritime territory in the Straits Settlements, lying between Singapore and Penang and extending for 42 miles along the shores of Malacca Strait, the channel separating the Malay Peninsula from Sumatra. Area, 637 sq. miles. The seaboard is low-lying, and the annual rainfall is heavy. Rubber is the staple product. Pop. (1932), 191,335.

MALACCA. Capital of the above territory, lies on Malacca River, and has a railway connection with Tampin and the Federated Malay lines. The town is one of the oldest European settlements in the East. It was taken by the Portuguese in 1511, held by the Dutch from 1641 until taken by the British in 1795, and restored to Holland in 1818. It was regained by Britain in 1824. Pop. *c.* 20,000.

MALACHI (mal'a-ki). The twelfth and last of the minor prophets. Nothing is known of his history, and it is even doubtful if Malachi (Messenger of Jehovah) be a proper name or an assumed epithet. The book evidently belongs to the latter part of the governorship of Nehemiah, about 420 B.C. It contains denunciations of the sins of the Israelites, and predicts the coming of the Messiah and the conversion of the Gentiles.

MALACHITE (mal'a-kit). A carbonate and hydroxide of copper, $CuCO_3 . Cu(OH)_2$, of an emerald-green colour, and of a laminated,

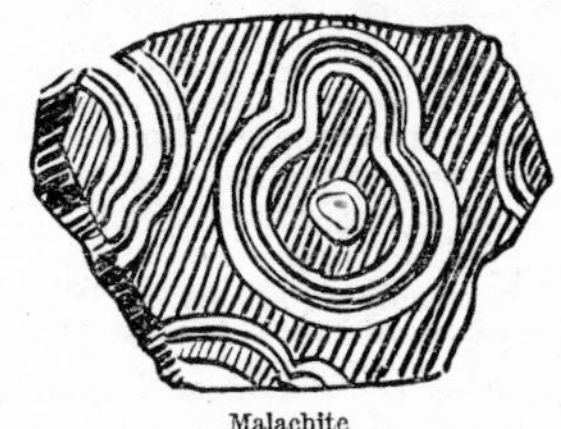

Malachite

fibrous, or massive structure. The finest specimens are obtained from Siberia, but it is found in many places all over the world, and in films in nearly all copper-mines. Fibrous malachite, when finely pulverized, is used as a paint; massive malachite is made into boxes, knife-handles, table-slabs, and other ornamental articles, and is susceptible of a beautiful polish. The allied mineral azurite contains a larger proportion of copper carbonate, and is blue; the two minerals are sometimes associated in alternating zones.

MALACOP'TERI, or **MALACOPTERYGII** (-tėr-ij'i-ī). A name given to those osseous fishes which are distinguished by all the rays of the fins being soft (except in a few individuals), exhibiting minute articulations, and often divided into small fibres at their extremities. They are divided into two sub-orders, the Malacopteri (proper) and the Anacanthini. They include the carp, salmon, pike, herring, cod, turbot and other flat-fish, and the eels. *See* ICHTHYOLOGY.

MALACOS'TRACA. A sub-class of crustaceans divided into two primary groups, sessile-eyed and stalk-eyed, the latter including the shrimps, lobsters, crabs, etc., and the former the wood-lice, sandhoppers, etc.

MAL'AGA. A maritime province of Southern Spain, on the shores of the Mediterranean, and a part of the ancient Kingdom of Granada. It is traversed in all directions by spurs of the Sierra Nevada, and is therefore exceedingly hilly; but the climate is warm and equable, and cereals, muscatel grapes, oranges, figs, almonds, lemons, and sugar-beet are abundant in the well-watered valleys. Iron and lead are found, and there is a large coastal fishery business. Area, 2812 sq. miles; pop. (1931), 619,045.

MALAGA. Capital of above province; a seaport at the mouth of the Guadal Medina, and on Malaga Bay, an arm of the Mediterranean. The Guadal Medina (Ar., "river of the city") dries up in summer, but is a raging torrent during the winter months. Oranges, figs, almonds, melons, pomegranates, and lemons abound in the vicinity, and with raisins and wine are exported from the commodious, mole-protected harbour.

Of immemorial antiquity, Malaga is the oldest and most famous seaport on the Mediterranean. It was founded by the Phœnicians, and was the ancient *Malaca*. Scipio made it a *municipium*; Leovigild, King of the Visigoths, took it from the Byzantines in A.D. 571; and Tarik with his Berbers conquered it in 711. Malaga was one of the finest seaports of Granada in the thirteenth century. Ferdinand and Isabella captured it after an obstinate siege in 1487 (war of Granada). Pop. (1931), 191,611.

MALAR. Lake of Sweden. Just outside Stockholm, it covers 650 sq. miles, and its waters are carried to the Baltic. There are over 1000 islands on the lake, which is the centre of magnificent scenery.

MALARIA (ague, remittent fever, jungle fever). A specific fever of protozoal origin, the infection of which is transmitted by the anopheline mosquito. It is characterized by the periodicity of the attacks, enlargement of the spleen, and the rapid response to quinine treatment. It has been known since early times, and reference is made in old Indian medicine to fever spread by mosquitoes, while Hippocrates and other ancient writers have described several types of the fever and emphasized the relationship between malaria and marshy districts.

The bite of an anopheline mosquito, infected by the parasite, causes malaria in persons otherwise unexposed to the disease, and, once infected, a person may have recurring attacks for an indefinite period.

The disease is widely distributed all over the tropics and subtropical regions, and is also found in many parts of the temperate zones. The incubation period is generally eight to ten days, but may vary considerably. The patient may feel out of sorts for a few days before an attack, or there may be no prodromal symptoms. He suddenly feels very cold and soon begins to shiver, with chattering teeth, blue lips, and coldness of the extremities. This "cold" stage lasts from ten to thirty minutes, and gradually the chill diminishes, to be replaced by a feeling of warmth, which soon becomes a burning heat with much discomfort. This "warm" stage lasts from four to five hours, and is followed by profuse sweating and considerable prostration.

In the tertian type of the disease, at the end of forty-eight hours another attack develops similar to the first, and in the quartan type the second attack occurs on the fourth day. In the malignant type the feverish period lasts about twenty-four hours, and is more severe, while it may reappear after only twenty-four hours' remission.

Various atypical forms are described, in some of which the patient is comatose, in others delirious, while almost any organ of the body may be specially affected, and the symptoms vary accordingly.

Nearly all cases respond rapidly to suitable quinine treatment, and the drug should be continued in decreasing doses for at least three months after the last attack of fever. Beyond the administration of quinine, suitable nursing and dietetic treatment are indicated, and any of the special symptoms that may arise should be treated. Prevention is primarily anti-mosquito measures, and secondarily the preventive administration of quinine. All the pools and ponds near houses, camps, etc., should be oiled with crude petroleum in order to destroy the larvæ, and mosquito-nets and masks should be used in dwelling-houses. The preventive use of quinine is not so important as the anti-mosquito measures, but the two should be carried out together to ensure the effective control of the disease.

MALATIA (ancient **Melitēnē**). A town of Kurdistan, Asiatic Turkey, noted for its vineyards. Pop. 27,737.

MALAYA. The political nomenclature applied to the Malay Peninsula and Archipelago generally, but technically denoting only those parts which have come to be known as British Malaya. The **Malay Archipelago** separates the Indian and the Pacific Oceans south and west of the Malay Peninsula. Most of the islands are Dutch (*see* DUTCH EAST INDIES; JAVA; SUMATRA, etc.), except part of Timor (q.v.) and of Borneo (q.v.).

The **Malay Peninsula** lies in South-Eastern Asia, and stretches 700 miles southward from the Isthmus of Kra to Singapore. It therefore includes part of Siam as well as British Malaya. There is a heavily forested mountain backbone, but the coast-lands are low and often swampy. Rivers are numerous but small, and the climate, though enervating, is, with due care, healthy.

British Malaya consists of the following divisions (1931):

	Area in Sq. Miles.	Population.
Straits Settlements	1,535	1,114,012
Federated Malay States	27,500	1,713,096
Unfederated States	22,855	1,477,135
TOTAL	51,890	4,304,243

Communications.—All the railways in the Straits Settlements form part of the Federated Malay States Railway system; the last trade route between Pahang and Siam was opened in 1932. In 1929 there were 1049 miles of roads. There are also wireless stations at Paya Lebar and Penaga. In the Federated Malay States, in 1931, were 2840 miles of metalled roads, unsurpassed for motoring; also 1771 miles of bridle roads, in addition to numerous other roads. The railway system joins with the Siamese railways in the north, the total mileage open for traffic being 1073 miles. A causeway has been built from Singapore to the Peninsula across Johore Strait.

Tin is one of the main products of Malaya, and tungsten, iron ore, and coal (in Selangor) are also mined. Rubber (2,500,000 acres planted) is the chief agricultural product, while coconut palms (for copra and coconut oil) occupy 450,000 acres. The output of rubber for 1931 was 434,857 tons. Palm oil, pineapples, tapioca, spices, fibres, various kinds of nuts (for oils), etc., are also produced. The forests of ebony, teak, sandal-wood, etc., are not exploited, the only commercial forest products being rattans, damars (resins), and gutta-percha (including jelutong).

Singapore and Georgetown (Penang) are the chief ports. They both stand on islands, but Singapore is connected with the mainland by rail causeway. Port Swettenham has a good trade. The total value of British Malayan exports in 1931 was £46,835,000 (rubber, £13,806,000; tin, £9,739,000; motor spirit, £6,309,000; copra, £1,914,000), and of imports £52,897,000. The currency unit is the Singapore dollar (standardized at 2*s.* 4*d.*). The population includes Malays (49 per cent.), Chinese (35 per cent.), Hindus (14 per cent.), and 14,954 Europeans.

Education is compulsory for Malays. There is the King Edward VII. College of Medicine, also Raffles College, opened in 1929.

The Straits Settlements.—Singapore (including Labuan, off Borneo, Christmas Island, and the Cocos or Keeling Islands, all of which see), Penang (including Province Wellesley and the Dindings, all of which see), and Malacca—form a Crown Colony under a Governor, who is also High Commissioner for the Federated and Unfederated States and for Brunei, and British Agent for North Borneo and Sarawak (all of which see). In 1826 Singapore, Penang, and Malacca were incorporated under one government, the Cocos Islands were added in 1886, and Christmas Island in 1889. In 1907 the boundaries of the Colony were extended to include Labuan.

The Federated Malay States are Perak, Selangor, Negri-Sembilan, and

British Malaya

Pahang (all of which see). They form a British protectorate under a Commissioner (see above). A Federal Council legislates for the federation as a whole, but each state has a resident who advises the sultan and a State Council which legislates for itself and controls its own finance. Railways and postal affairs are under federal control, but there is no common purse. The capital is Kuala Lumpur in Selangor, and Port Swettenham is the port. The Treaty of Federation was entered into in 1895.

The Unfederated States are Perlis, Kedah, Kelantan, Trengganu, and Johore (all of which see). Each one is a British protectorate governed by its own ruler under control of a British Resident—BIBLIOGRAPHY: *Colonial Office List*; Publications of Malay States Information Agency; R. O. Winstedt, *Malaya*.

MALAYS. A race of people inhabiting Malaya and the whole Asiatic Archipelago from Madagascar to the Philippines, numbering upwards of 50,000,000. They are of Mongoloid stock.

MALCOLM. The name of four kings of Scotland: Malcolm I.

Malcolm I.

(943-954), Malcolm II. (1005-1034), Malcolm III. (1058-1093), Malcolm IV. (1153-1165).

MALDEN. A parish of Surrey, England, near Kingston. Close at hand is New Malden. The two are part of the urban district of the Maldens and Coombe. Pop. (1931), 23,412.

MALDEN. A city of Massachusetts, United States. It stands on Malden River, and is a suburb of Boston. Pop. (1930), 58,036.

MALDEN ISLAND. A British island in the Pacific (4° S. lat., 155° W. long.), of coralline structure, with valuable guano deposits. It is under the High Commissioner of the Western Pacific. Area, 35 sq. miles; pop. 168.

MALDIVE ISLANDS. A chain of nineteen (politically thirteen) coral islets in the Indian Ocean, 400 miles west of Ceylon, to which island their Sultan pays tribute. The Sultanate is elective, and the administrative centre is Malé Island. The larger atolls are richly clad with coconut palms, and produce copra, millet, fruit, edible roots, and nuts, and the waters abound in *bonito* fish. The natives are mainly engaged in fishing and trading. Mahommedanism is the recognized religion. Pop. 70,000.

MALDON. A municipal borough market town, and river-port of Essex, England, on the Blackwater estuary. The industries include shipping, engineering works, brewing, and milling. During the Danish invasions Maldon was a Saxon stronghold, and was twice taken (921 and 993). Pop. (1931), 6559.

MALDONADO. A maritime dedepartment of Uruguay facing the La Plata estuary. Area, 1587 sq. miles; pop. (1932), 58,745.—**Maldonado,** on the coast, east of Monte Video, is capital of the department. It possesses a fine harbour.

MALEBRANCHE (mál-bräṇsh), **Nicolas.** A French philosopher, born in 1638, died 1715. In 1673 he published his treatise *De la recherche de la vérité.* The doctrines of this work are founded upon Cartesian principles, and are in some particulars Platonic, Malebranche conceiving ideas to be the immediate objects of perception. Among his other writings are: *Conversations métaphysiques et chrétiennes, Traité de la nature et de la grâce, Méditations métaphysiques et chrétiennes,* and *Traité de morale.*—Cf. H. Joly, *Malebranche.*

MALESHERBES (mál-zerb), **Chrétien Guillaume de Lamoignon de.** French statesman, the son of Guillaume de Lamoignon, Chancellor of France, was born at Paris in 1721, died 1794. Aided by Tronchet and Desèze, he acted as leading counsel for Louis XVI. at his trial before the Convention. Acts of loyalty far less decided were in that day the sure road to destruction. He was condemned to death and guillotined,

MALHERBE (mál-erb), **François de.** French poet, born at Caen 1555, died 1628. He was the protégé of Henry IV.; wrote light lyrics, odes, and epigrams; and so far as form is concerned he may be considered the father of French classical poetry.

MALIBRAN (má-lē-bräṇ), **Maria Felicita.** One of the greatest singers of the nineteenth century, born at Paris 1808, died in 1836. She made her début in 1825 at the opera in London. Among the operas in which she played were *Othello, The Barber of Seville, Don Juan,* and *Romeo and Juliet.* She excelled both in tragic and comic parts, and was no less accomplished as an actress than she was as a singer.

MALIC ACID ($C_4H_6O_5$). A dibasic acid found in many fruits, particularly in the apple; hence the name, from Lat, *malum.* It is most easily obtained from the fruit of *Pyrus Aucuparia* (mountain-ash or rowan tree), immediately after it has turned red, but while still unripe.

MALICE. In law, has two meanings: (1) wilful and deliberate wrongdoing "without just cause or excuse," (2) an act done from an improper motive, i.e. a motive which the law considers improper. It need not necessarily amount to spite. *Malicious damage* is an instance under (1). It is the committing of an injury to public or private property from sheer wantonness or malice. This offence is punishable with great severity. A *malicious prosecution*, an instance of (2), is a prosecution brought against a person from an improper motive and without reasonable and probable cause. From the mere want of reasonable and probable cause malice may be inferred.

MALINDI. A harbour of Kenya, East Africa, 66 miles N.E. of Mombasa. Pop. 5000.

MALINES, or **MECHLIN** (the mediæval **Machlina**). A town of Antwerp, Belgium, on the Dyle, with large railway workshops and some manufactures, notably of lace. It is an important railway junction. In 1546 the town was made an archbishopric, the holder being primate of the Netherlands, and at the present time Malines is the ecclesiastical capital of Belgium. The cathedral of St. Rombold (1312, rebuilt fourteenth to fifteenth century) and the Cloth Hall (1320) are the most important historical buildings. During the European War Malines was bombarded by the Germans on three distinct occasions (Aug.-Sept., 1914) and greatly damaged. Pop. (1931), 60,506.

MALLEABILITY. The property of being susceptible of extension by rolling or beating; almost restricted to metals. The following is the order of malleability of the metals: gold, silver, aluminium, copper, tin, platinum, lead, zinc, iron, nickel. Ductility and malleability are nearly allied, but they are seldom possessed in the same proportion by the same metal.

MALLECO. Formerly an inland province of Chile, now forming part of the provinces of Bio-Bio and Cautin. It is an agricultural and stock-raising district, but lumbering is also extensive. Angol is the capital. Area, 3303 sq. miles; pop. 121,429.

MALLOW (Malva). A genus of plants of the nat. ord. Malvaceæ. *M. sylvestris* (the common mallow) is a common and widely diffused species. When fresh the flowers are reddish-purple, but on drying they become blue. The mucilaginous and demulcent properties of the plant make it useful in pharmacy.

The dwarf mallow (*M. rotundifolia*) is also a native of Britain. Its stems are short and simple, spreading widely from a long, deeply buried root. Its leaves are of a handsome, round, heart-shaped form, somewhat lobed and crenate on their edges; the flowers white, violet-white, or purplish.

The musk mallow (*M. moschāta*) is also found in Britain; it has handsome, deeply cut leaves, which diffuse a pleasant musky odour, and large rose-coloured flowers. The fibre of *M. crispa* is sufficiently tenacious to be used in making cordage.

MALLOW. A town of County Cork, Irish Free State, on the Blackwater. Remains of the ancient stronghold of the Earls of Desmond (destroyed 1641) are still extant. It is a railway junction and agricultural centre. Pop. (1926), 4562.

MALMÉDY. A district and town of Belgium, formerly in Rhenish Prussia, on the Warche, in a basin surrounded by hills. The district was ceded to Belgium in accordance with the Treaty of Versailles (1919). Pop. of district, 37,000.

MALMESBURY (mämz'be-ri). A municipal borough and market town of England, county of Wilts, on an eminence, 28 miles N.E. of Bristol. It is well built, and has the remains of an abbey founded in the sixth century. To-day an agricultural and brewing centre, Malmesbury was once a centre of cloth manufacture. It was a parliamentary borough till 1885. Pop. (1931), 2334.

MALMESBURY, William of. An English historian, born probably in Somersetshire about the year 1075, died about 1143. He received his education at the Benedictine Abbey of Malmesbury, and subsequently became librarian and precentor of the abbey. His *De Gestis Regum Anglorum* is a general history of England from the arrival of the Saxons in 449 to 1128; he also wrote a history from that year to 1143; *De Gestis Pontificum Anglorum*; and *Antiquities of Glastonbury*.

MALMÖ (mål'meu). A seaport and third town of Sweden, situated on The Sound opposite Copenhagen (16 miles distant). Malmö was the chief commercial town on The Sound in mediæval times, but declined in the sixteenth-seventeenth century owing to the failure of the herring fishery and the growing importance of Copenhagen. The foundation of the new harbour (1775-78) restored the town to its former commercial importance. Pop. (1932), 129,927.—The län of **Malmöhus** is the southernmost county (län) of Sweden. Malmö is the capital. Area, 1871 sq. miles; pop. (1931), 512,366.

MALONE′, Edmund. A commentator and editor of Shakespeare, was born at Dublin in 1741, died 1812. He published an edition of Shakespeare with notes in 1790, *Remarks on the Rowley* (*Chatterton*) *Controversy*, and an *Inquiry into the Ireland Shakespearean Forgeries*.

MAL′ORY, Sir Thomas. Born probably about 1430. His compilation, the *Morte d'Arthur*, was first printed by Caxton in 1485. Malory is supposed to have been a Welshman, but all that is known of him is that he was a knight, and finished the book about 1470.

MALPIGHI (mȧl-pē′gē), **Marcello.** Italian physician and anatomist, born 1628, died 1694. He was successively professor of medicine at Bologna, Pisa, and Messina. In 1691 he became physician to Pope Innocent XII. His works relate to anatomy, physiology, and vegetable anatomy.

MALPIGHIACEÆ. A considerable natural order of polypetalous dicotyledons consisting of tropical shrubs, trees, and climbers. Glandular sepals, clawed petals, and a trilocular ovary with oblique symmetry are among their distinctive features. The type-genus is Malpighia; the fruits of *M. urens* (Barbados cherry) are eaten in the West Indies.

MALPLAQUET (mȧl-plȧ-kā). A village in the French department of Nord, on the Belgian frontier, 26 miles S.E. of Valenciennes, celebrated for the defeat of the French under Villars by the allied British and Austrian troops under Marlborough and Prince Eugene, 11th Sept., 1709.

MALT. Grain, usually barley, steeped in water and made to germinate, the starch of the grain being thus converted into saccharine matter, after which it is dried in a kiln, and then used in the brewing of porter, ale, or beer, and in whisky distilling. One hundred parts of barley yield about ninety-two parts of air-dried malt. *See* BREWING.

MALTA (ancient **Melita**). A British Mediterranean island, some 58 miles south of Sicily and 180 miles from the coast of Africa, forming with the adjacent islands of Gozo (ancient *Gaulos*) and Comino (area 1 sq. mile) a Crown colony. Malta proper is 17·4 miles long; area, 95 sq. miles. Gozo has an area of 26 sq. miles. The total area of the colony is 122 sq. miles, and the population 241,621.

For Britain Malta's chief value is strategic. About 9000 troops are constantly in garrison. It is a naval base, a coaling-station, and a fortress. The chief town is Valetta, which a railway 8 miles long connects to the old capital, Citta Vecchia.

The Maltese are of mixed extraction, and their language (*lingua Maltese*) is a corrupted jargon of Arabic intermixed with Italian. English is the official language of the colony, but Maltese is permitted in elementary schools, and Italian is the *lingua franca* of the law courts. The Maltese are invariably bilingual or polyglot. The staple industry of Malta is agriculture, and upon a thin soil on a mere rock rising steeply from the sea oranges, lemons, mandarins, onions, cumin-seed, corn, and cotton are produced in profusion. The temperature varies from 61° F. in January to 95° F. in August. Lace, cotton, filigree, and cigarettes are manufactured. There is a State university at Valetta, a Roman Catholic institution under Government control.

History.—Malta was colonized successively by the Phœnicians, Greeks (736 B.C.), and Carthaginians (400 B.C.), from whom it was taken in 218 B.C. by the Romans. In A.D. 61 St. Paul was shipwrecked on the north coast of Melita (Acts xxviii. 1-11). Malta was in turn conquered by the Vandals (454), Goths (464), Belisarius (533), Moors (870), and Count Roger of Sicily (1090). The Emperor Charles V. in 1530 presented it to the Knights of St. John, then expelled from Rhodes. The knights defended it against the Sultan Suleiman II. from 19th May to 11th Sept., 1565. Napoleon took Malta (17th June, 1798) on his way to Egypt. It was recaptured by the British in Sept., 1800, and definitely allocated to Great Britain in 1814 (Treaty of Paris).

In 1921 a constitution was given to Malta. This provided for a legislature of two houses, the members of the lower house being elected. Matters of imperial concern, such as defence, trade and coinage are under the control of the governor, who is assisted by two councils. English is the official language and British coins are the legal tender, but the islanders have their own tongue, a Semitic one, which is in general use. The island has an order of nobility consisting of 29 families, and there is a university.

In 1929 there was a serious dispute between the State, represented by Lord Strickland, and the Church of Rome, to which most of the people belong. The interference of the priests in secular matters led to a crisis, and after negotiations for a settlement had failed, the constitution was suspended on 26th June, 1929. A royal commission visited the island to inquire into the matter in 1931, and in 1932 the constitution was restored and an election held.—BIBLIOGRAPHY: R. H. Bradley, *Malta and the Mediterranean Race*; T. A. Keble, *Malta: its Charm and Worth*.

MALTA FEVER. Variety of fever found in the Mediterranean countries; also in other parts of the world. It takes very much the same course as other fevers, but the illness lasts longer than in most of them, sometimes as long as six months. It is caused by a parasite which is conveyed by the milk of goats.

MALTESE TERRIER. Breed of dog. It is an ancient form of lapdog, traceable for 2000 years; the inaccurate name terrier is becoming obsolete. It resembles a toy Skye terrier, averaging 5 to 6 lb., dark-eyed, black-nosed, with long, white, silky coat and thickly-haired tail curling over the back. It is intelligent, affectionate and good-tempered.

MALTHUS, Thomas Robert. English political economist, born 1766, died 1834. He studied at Jesus College, Cambridge, became Fellow of his college, took orders and held a small living in Surrey. In 1805 he was appointed professor of history and political economy in the East India Company's college at Haileybury, an office which he held till his death.

In 1798 he first published the views with which his name is associated in his *Essay on the Principle of Population as it Affects the Future Improvement of Society*. It was improved in subsequent editions. His leading principle is that population, when unchecked, goes on increasing in a higher ratio than the means of subsistence can, under the most favourable circumstances, be made to increase; that the great natural checks to excessive increase of population are vice, misery, and moral restraint; and the great business of the enlightened legislator is to diminish the first two and give every encouragement to the last.—Cf. J. Bonar, *Malthus and his Work*.

MALVA'CEÆ. The mallows, a large natural order of polypetalous dicotyledons, having monadelphous stamens, unilocular anthers, valvate estivation, and often an external calyx (epicalyx) or involucre. A large proportion of the order consists of herbaceous or annual plants, inhabiting all the milder parts of the world, but found most plentifully in hot countries. Several species are of essential service to man. As emollients they are well known in medical practice. The hairy covering of the seeds of the various species of Gossypium forms raw cotton. The inner bark of many species yields fibre of considerable value. Many species of Althæa, Sida, and Hibiscus are splendid flowering plants. *See* MALLOW.

MALVERN, Great. A fashionable watering-place and health-resort of England, county of Worcester, on the eastern side of the Malvern Hills, embracing **Malvern, Malvern Link,** and **Malvern Wells.** It has many mansions, large hydropathic establishments, several mineral springs, a church once part of an eleventh-century Benedictine priory, and Malvern College, one of the great public schools. Pop. (1931), 15,632.

MALVERN HILLS. A range of England, on the borders of Worcester and Hereford shires, which extends north and south for about 9 miles, and attains an altitude of 1395 feet. Some part of the region is national property, and in 1930–31 steps were taken to protect the hills from disfiguration by quarrying. The district was once a hunting ground and was called **Malvern Chase.**

MALWA. A group of native states, in the Central India Agency, producing wheat, hemp, sugar, some opium, and native cereal foodstuffs. Area, 2704 sq. miles; pop. about 383,156.

MAM'ELUKES. The former mounted soldiery of Egypt, consisting originally of Circassian slaves. As early as 1254 they became so powerful that they made one of their own number Sultan, this dynasty continuing till 1517, when it was overthrown by Selim I. They still continued to be virtual masters of the country, however. They suffered severely in opposing the French at the end of the eighteenth century, and in 1811 Mehemet Ali caused a general massacre of them throughout Egypt.

MAMETZ. A village of France, in the department of Somme, near Albert. During the European War, Mametz-Fricourt formed a strongly, organized position taken by the British (7th division), 1st July, 1916. The wood, occupying about 220 acres and traversed partially by a German light railway, was captured on 10th-12th July, 1916. In the German offensive of March, 1918, the positions were again lost, but were eventually retaken. Mametz was "adopted" by Llandudno.

MAMMA'LIA (Lat. *mamma*, a breast). The highest class at once of the Vertebrata and of the animal kingdom, including those warm-blooded animals we familiarly term "quadrupeds," the whales and other fish-like forms, and man himself. Their distinctive characteristic is that the female suckles the young on a secretion peculiar to the class, furnished by the mammary glands of the mother, and known as milk. Teats are present except in Monotremes. The skin is always more or less covered with hairs, which are found in many forms, from the finest wool or silky down to large coarse bristles and even spines. The cavity of the thorax or chest is bounded by the ribs, which vary greatly in number, but generally correspond to that of the thoracic vertebræ.

The skull forms a single piece composed of bones immovably united together, to which is articulated the lower jaw, composed of two halves (rami) joined at the chin. The skull is articulated to the vertebral column by means of two condyles which fit into the ring-like first cervical vertebra (atlas). The second cervical vertebra (axis) possesses a peg (odontoid process) on which the head and atlas can rotate.

The front limbs are invariably present, but in cetaceans and such allied forms as the dugongs and manatees the hinder limbs are either completely suppressed or present only in a rudimentary state. The limbs are generally well developed, and are most commonly adapted for terrestrial progression; some are suited for burrowing, others for climbing, those of the cetaceans and seals for swimming, while some (the bats) have the fore limbs developed into a kind of wing.

Teeth are present in most mammals; but they are only represented in the embryo in the whale-bone whales, and are entirely absent in the ant-eater, pangolin, and echidna. The teeth are lodged in *alveŏli* or sockets, and are not fused with the jaw-bones as in reptiles and amphibia. Mammals which have only a single set of teeth throughout life are termed *monophyodont*; those which have the first set of teeth (milk or deciduous teeth) replaced by a second set of permanent teeth are called *diphyodont*. The permanent or second set of teeth are referable to four groups, which differ in form, position, and function: *incisors*, *canines*, *premolars*, and *molars*.

The chest or thorax is separated from the abdominal cavity by a complete *diaphragm* or "midriff," which constitutes a great muscular partition with a central tendon between these cavities, and also forms the most important agent in effecting the movements of breathing. Within the thorax the heart and lungs are contained; whilst the abdomen and its lesser pelvic cavity contain the organs relating generally to digestion, excretion, and reproduction. The stomach, generally simple, may, as in some monkeys, in the kangaroos, and most of all in the ruminants, exhibit a division into compartments. A liver and pancreas are present in all Mammalia. The lungs agree in essential structure with those of man, as also does the heart with its four chambers—right and left auricles and right and left ventricles. The red corpuscles of the blood are *non-nucleated*, and are circular in shape except in the case of the camels.

All mammals with the exception of the monotremes are viviparous, but there are considerable differences in the relations subsisting between mother and young before birth. (*See* PLACENTA.) All mammals possess mammary or milk glands, which, however, may differ in number and position throughout the class. (*See* MAMMARY GLANDS.)

In the *classification* of this important group the following orders are usually distinguished: Man, Apes, Monkeys, and Lemurs (Primates); the Bats (Chiroptera); the Insect-eaters (Insectivora); the Flesh-eaters (Carnivora); the Whales and Dolphins (Cetacea); the Sea-cows (Sirenia); the Hoofed Mammals (Ungulata); the Gnawers or Rodents (Rodentia); the Edentates (Edentata); the Marsupials or Pouch-bearing Mammals (Marsupialia); and the Monotremes (Monotremata).—BIBLIOGRAPHY: Flower and Lydekker, *Introduction to the Study of Mammals*; Beddard, *Mammals* (*Cambridge Natural History*); Aflalo, *Natural History* (*Vertebrates*) *of the British Isles*; British Museum, (*Natural History*); various *Guides* and *Monographs*.

MAMMARY GLANDS. The milk-producing organs, the distinctive mark of the mammals. These structures present in man an essentially *lobular* structure. The lobes are divisible into smaller *lobules*, which consist ultimately of groups of vesicles which open into minute ducts converging into larger channels which lead to the milk reservoirs at the nipple. The nipple itself is composed of unstriped muscular fibres and areolar tissue. It also possesses erectile powers, and blood-vessels are in consequence freely distributed to it. These glands, save in exceptional instances, remain in a rudimentary condition in the male. They are always in pairs on some part of the ventral surface of the body, but in number and position they vary much in the various groups.

MAMMEE' TREE, or **WEST INDIA APRICOT** (*Mammēa americāna*), nat. ord. Guttiferæ. A tall, handsome tree bearing a fruit about the size of a coco-nut. This has two rinds enclosing the pulp, which is firm, bright-yellow, and has a pleasant taste and smell. The seeds, which are large, are used as anthelmintics, and a gum distilled from the bark is used to destroy chigoes.

MAMMON. A Syriac word used in Matt. vi. 24 as a personation of riches or worldliness. In Luke xvi. 9-11 it is used literally for riches. There does not appear to have been any idol in the East receiving divine honours under this name.

MAMMOTH. A species of extinct elephant, the fossil remains of which are found in European, Asiatic, and

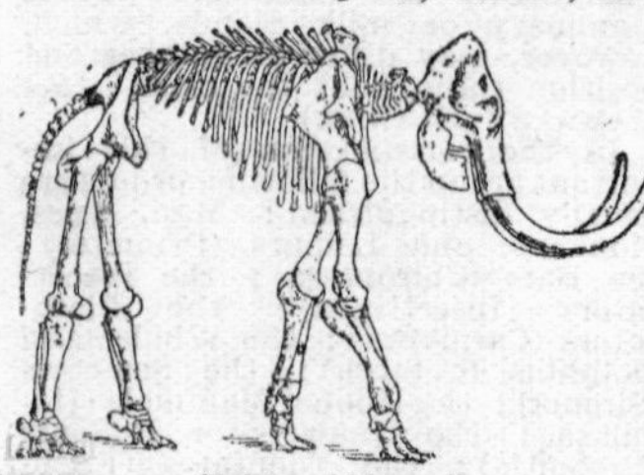

Skeleton of Mammoth
(*Elephas primigenius*)

North American formations. Geologically speaking, the mammoth, or *Elephas primigenius*, dates from the Post-pliocene period. It survived the glacial epoch, and lived into the earlier portion of the human period, its remains having been frequently found associated with relics of man's activities, and carvings represent it with its curved tusks and its covering of hair. It appears to have been widely distributed over the northern hemisphere, as far south, at any rate, as Spain and Italy, and future discoveries may extend our knowledge of its range. The bones and tusks have been found in great abundance in Siberia, and are exported as ivory.

An entire carcass, which had been preserved in the ice and thawed out, was discovered near the end of the eighteenth century on the banks of the River Lena, in such a perfect state that the flesh was eaten by dogs, wolves, and bears. Its skin was perfectly preserved, and was seen to be clothed with a furry wool of reddish colour, interspersed with black hairs. The skeleton and other parts of this animal are preserved in the Petrograd Museum. Similar finds have been made at later dates in the frozen soils of the Asiatic tundra. The mammoth crossed from England to Ireland at a time when our islands were connected with other European areas by the delta of the Rhine.

MAMMOTH CAVE. An enormous cave in Kentucky, near Green River, about 80 miles S.S.W. of Louisville. It is one of a large series of vast caverns here formed in the limestone rock, and found over a very wide area of Kentucky, Tennessee, and Indiana. It has been penetrated along tortuous passages for many miles, and these ramifying waterways of ancient times have been for the most part mapped. The walls and floor are mostly dry, and the remains of its stalactite and stalagmite formations are dusty and dilapidated ; consequently it is more remarkable for its extent, the size of its halls, and height of its domes, than for the variety or beauty of its scenery.

It contains several small lakes or rivers, the largest, Echo River, being more than half a mile long. It rises and falls according as Green River is in flood or otherwise, there being an underground connection between them. The animals of the cave include blind wingless grasshoppers, beetles, rats, etc., and the viviparous blind fish Amblyopsis.

MAMMOTH TREE. *See* SEQUOIA.

MAMORÉ. A river of Bolivia, rising in the Cochabamba Mountains as the Rio Grande, and uniting with the Beni at Villa Bella to form the Madeira. The Madeira - Mamoré forest railway was opened for traffic on 15th July, 1912. It runs from São Antonio, on the Madeira River, to Gujara Mérim on the Mamoré, and was constructed by Brazil under the terms of the Treaty of Petropolis (1903).

MAN. The most highly organized member of the animal world. The endeavour has often been made in classification to separate man from the brute creation. One system expressing a vast gap between the Quadrumana and man, classifies man in the order Bimana (" two-handed "), the highest division of the Mammalian class ; and relegates the monkeys and apes to the lower and distinct order—that of the Quadrumana (" four-handed "). The more recent arrangements, however, classify man and the monkeys in one order, making man the highest family or group of this order. From the purely anatomical point of view the differences which separate the anthropoid apes from man are in some respects less than those which separate these higher apes from apes lower in the scale. But the mental or psychical endowments of man oblige us to remove him far above the highest Quadrumana; and even the characters by which he is anatomically separated from the highest apes form a very distinct and appreciable series.

Characteristics.—The first grand characteristic of man is his *erect position* and bipedal progression. The lower limbs, with the feet broad and plantigrade and the well-developed heel, are devoted exclusively to progression and supporting the weight of the body; while the upper limbs have nothing to do with progression, but subserve prehension entirely. The bones of the face in man do not project forwards, whilst they are elongated in a downward direction; and the face and forehead are in the more civilized races situated nearly in the same plane, so that the face immediately underlies the brain. Similarly the development of a distinct chin is also a peculiarly human feature, and one which in the highest varieties of mankind becomes most marked.

The great *cranial* capacity of man, or the greater size of the cranial or brain portion as compared with the facial portion of the skull, forms another noteworthy and distinctive character of the human form. The brain convolutions also are more numerous and complex than is the case with any other mammal. The teeth of man are arranged in a continuous series, and without any *diastema* or interval. The development of hair too is very partial.

The gorilla presents of all the apes the nearest approach to the human type taken in its entirety; but it differs in the relative number of vertebræ (13 dorsal and 4 lumbar, to 12 and 5 respectively in man), in the order of dental succession and in the presence of the interval or diastema, in the less prominent muscular development of the buttocks and calves, and in other minor differences. The orangs most closely approach man's structure in the number of ribs and in the form of the cerebrum, whilst they exhibit the greatest differences from him in the relative length of the limbs. The chimpanzees are most anthropoid in the shape of the cranium, in the arrangement and succession of the teeth, and in the length of the arms as compared with that of the legs. Of the higher apes the gibbons are those furthest removed from the human type of structure.

Chief among the psychical features, or rather among the results of the operation of the principle of *mind*, we note the possession of a well-developed moral *sense of right and wrong*. The possession of an articulate language, by which he can communicate his thoughts, is also the exclusive possession of man, and draws a sharp line of separation between him and all other animals.

Origin of Man.—With regard to the geological history of man, the earliest traces yet discovered belong to the Post-pliocene deposits in conjunction with existing species of shells and some extinct species of mammals. Man's advent upon the earth is consequently referred to a period much anterior to that which former limits and theological ideas prescribed. Among the modern theories regarding the origin of man may be noted those of (1) Darwin: that man is directly descended from an extinct form of anthropoid ape, with a tail and pointed ears, arboreal in its habits and an inhabitant of the Old World; further, that man has diverged into different races or sub-species, but that all the races agree in so many unimportant details of structure, and in so many mental peculiarities, that they can be accounted for only through inheritance from a common progenitor. (2) Wallace also affirms the original unity of man, and places him apart as not only the head and culminating point of the grand series of organic nature, but as, in some degree, a new and distinct order of being; maintaining that a superior intelligence has guided the development of man in a definite direction and for a special purpose, just as man guides the development of many animal and vegetable forms. (3) Carl Vogt holds a plurality of the race; adopts Darwin's idea of natural selection accounting for the origin an endowments of man, but rejects Wallace's idea of the higher controlling intelligence. (4) Mivart propounds a theory of a natural evolution of man as to his body, combined with a supernatural creation as to his soul. *See also* ETHNOLOGY; ANTHROPOLOGY; ANTHROPOMETRY, etc.

MAN, Isle of. An island of the Irish Sea; greatest length, 33 miles; maximum breadth, 12 miles; area, 221 sq. miles. The Calf of Man (800 acres) lies just off the main island, of which it forms a part. A range of hills extends throughout almost the entire length of the island (Snaefell, 2034 feet).

Dairy-farming is practised; wheat, oats, and barley or bere are raised, and lead, zinc, clay, gravel, sand, and limestone are produced. The herring fisheries were formerly of considerable importance. Manufactures are comparatively rare.

Manx, the native Celtic dialect, akin to Scots and Irish Gaelic, is practically extinct. The chief towns and their approximate populations in 1931, were: Douglas (capital, 19,265), Ramsey (4198), Peel (2462), and Castletown (1712).

The Isle of Man generally, and Douglas in particular, is annually the playground of a vast number of pleasure-seekers, and the entire island is practically laid out to attract visitors. Customs dues are

Isle of Man: Peel Castle

mainly responsible for the revenue, which in 1931-32 amounted to £401,381; the expenditure was £390,503. There are 25 miles of electric and 46½ miles of steam railway lines converging on Douglas. Pop. (1931), 49,338, varying as the season.

History.—The Isle of Man was known to Cæsar as *Mona*, and, occupied by the Welsh (517), it was taken by the Norsemen (1098), ceded by Magnus II. to Alexander III. of Scotland (1266), and eventually passed to England (1344). It was held as a feudal sovereignty by the Stanley family, Earls of Derby from 1406 (Henry IV.) until 1736, when the direct male line became extinct and Man passed to the Dukes of Atholl, from whom it was purchased for the British Crown in 1764, and, finally, in 1829 the duke's remaining privileges were ceded by purchase for £417,000. The island is not bound by Acts of the Imperial Parliament unless specially mentioned, and is governed by a Lieutenant-Governor and "Tynwald," comprising a Legislative Council and the House of Keys (twenty-four members).

MANAAR. A gulf and island between India and Ceylon. Pearl-fishing is important.

MANA'GUA. A lake of Nicaragua.

MANAGUA. Capital of Nicaragua, on Lake Managua. In 1931 it was almost completely destroyed by earthquake, but is being rebuilt. It is a great coffee market. The Pan-American Airway connects Managua with Central America and the United States. It has also a wireless station. Pop. 32,536.

MAN'AKIN. The name given to small perching birds forming the family Pipridæ. They are generally of bright plumage, and are mostly confined to South America, a few species being found in Central America and Mexico.

MANA'MEH. Commercial capital of the Bahrein Islands in the Persian Gulf, on Bahrein, the chief island.

MANA'OS. A modern city and capital of Amazonas state, Brazil, on the Rio Negro near its confluence with the Amazon, and 1000 miles from the Atlantic. It has a university. The harbour is modern, and is an important call for ocean-going liners from United States and Europe. The town is a centre of the rubber industry. Pop. (1930), 83,736.

MANAS'SEH. (1) Eldest son of Joseph, born in Egypt. His descendants formed a tribe, which, in the Promised Land, was settled half east of the Jordan and half to the west of this river. (2) King of Judah, son of Hezekiah, whom he succeeded at twelve years of age, 697 B.C. He became an open idolater; was taken captive to Babylon; ultimately repented and was restored to his kingdom. He reigned for fifty-five years.

MANATEE'. The sea-cow or lamantin, a gregarious aquatic mammal of the genus Manātus, ord. Sirenia, found on the Atlantic coasts of South America and Africa. They generally frequent the mouths of rivers and estuaries, and feed on Algæ and such littoral land vegetation as they can reach at high tide. Their anterior limbs or swimming-paddles are furnished with nails, by means of which they drag themselves along the shore. They are large awkward animals, attaining a length of 8 to 10 feet as a rule, but sometimes growing to 20 feet. The skin is of a greyish colour, sparsely covered with hairs. Their flesh is excellent, and they furnish a soft clear oil which does not become rancid.

There are several species, the principal being the American manatee (*M. americānus*), which inhabits the shallow waters of the east coast of South America, and the African, manatee (*M. senegalensis*). The dugong (q.v.) belongs to the same order.

MANCHA, La. An ancient province of Spain, now included mainly in Ciudad Real; the Don Quixote country.

MANCHE. A maritime department of Northern France, with its coast-line on the English Channel (Fr. *La Manche*); part of pre-Revolutionary Normandy. The surface is hilly and well-watered (Rivers Vire, Douve, Selune, etc.); pears, flax, hemp, cereals, and cider apples are grown, and horses are raised. Granite is extensively worked. St. Lô (capital) and Cherbourg are the principal towns. Area, 2475 sq. miles; pop. (1931), 433,473.

MANCHESTER. A city and county of a city, municipal, county, and parliamentary borough of Lancashire, 183½ miles N.N.W. of London. The major part of the town stands on a level plain with rising ground on the north side. The dark, viscous waters of the River Irwell divide the city from Salford, a royal borough, which, although it possesses a separate municipal entity, is really part of the same town. The river is spanned by a number of bridges in its progress to join the River Mersey.

Transport facilities are essential to a community depending so largely on export trade, and, in addition to its connections with the western group of railways, Manchester has its Ship Canal (*see* MANCHESTER SHIP CANAL), making the city a port in touch, through its lines of steamships, with the seaports and trading centres of the world.

The old town has Market Street, perhaps the most congested street in Europe, as its centre-line. No attempt was made in old Manchester to follow a regular scheme of street-planning, but every endeavour has been made in modern times to remedy this by opening up through traffic-relieving streets parallel to the main thoroughfares. The centre of the city is entirely occupied by business premises and places of amusement. The factories and workshops are mainly on the eastern side of the town and in Trafford Park, where an industrial area of considerable importance has been developed beside the Ship Canal.

The south side is the most favoured residential district, and villadom is extending towards the boundary of Cheshire, in which county there are many residential towns. Manchester has a very cosmopolitan population, with colonies of nationals of every European country, Jews, and Armenians. The surroundings of the city are not devoid of rural beauty.

There are many public buildings of note. The town hall, an example in the Gothic style of the work of Alfred Waterhouse, was finished in 1877 at a total cost of £1,062,000. In 1932 arrangements were made to build a new City Hall. The cathedral was built as a parish church in 1422, and was raised to its present status in 1847, when the bishopric was established with James P. Lee as the first bishop.

Manchester Ship Canal

The Royal Exchange was built in 1869, and greatly enlarged, at a cost of £800,000, in 1921, when it was reopened by King George V. The university buildings, with the Manchester Museum, Whitworth Hall, and Christie Library, are in Oxford Street. The university was founded with £100,000 left by John Owens in 1846. The Municipal College of Technology, in Sackville Street, perhaps the largest and best-equipped institution of its character in the country, is a constituent college of the university. The city is famous as a musical centre, with a Royal College of Music, and the fine Hallé Orchestra.

The Rylands Library was gifted to the city, with a permanent income of £13,000, by Mrs. John Rylands as a memorial to her husband. The library contains many historical manuscripts and early editions, including the Althorp Collection purchased from Earl Spencer. The Art Galleries contain a large and representative collection in a building which is totally inadequate in size.

Chetham's Hospital was founded by the will of Humfrey Chetham in 1653 for the education of poor boys. There are numerous denominational colleges, many of which are associated in the faculty of divinity of the university.

The Free Library, established in 1851, has, since the old building in King Street was sold many years ago, been housed in temporary wooden buildings on the corner of a vacant plot in Piccadilly. There are numerous scientific, literary, musical, and philosophical societies, some of them of considerable standing.

There are many public parks, of which the chief are Heaton Park (692 acres), Platt Fields, Whitworth, Alexandra, and Queen's Parks, in some of which there are museums and art galleries. Peel Park, Salford, has an excellent museum and technical institute within its bounds. Among the public monuments, the Albert Memorial in front of the town hall, and that of Queen Victoria in Piccadilly are the most noteworthy. The leading newspaper, the *Manchester Guardian*, is known throughout the civilised world.

The textile industry centres in Manchester, but there are also chemical-, engineering-, leather-, and rubber-works. Gas- and electricity-supply are municipal enterprises. The water-supply is brought by the corporation from the Longendale Valley and Thirlmere. The electric tramways and the extensive markets of the city are also under the corporation. The history of the town is depicted in a series of frescoes by Ford Madox Brown in the town hall.

Manchester is the *Mancunium* of the Romans. Its history is legendary down to the tenth century, when it was devastated by the Danes. In the twelfth century the woollen manufactures began to develop, and in 1301 it received municipal liberties and privileges. During the Civil War the town suffered much at the hands of both parties. The introduction of machinery in cotton-spinning towards the end of the eighteenth century gave power and direction to the trade of modern Manchester, and its progress since has been extraordinarily rapid. It has played an important part in the political history of the country, especially in connection with the agitation for parliamentary reform and the establishment of free trade. A temporary check resulted from the Civil War in America, which led to a cotton famine in 1862, causing the deepest distress in South Lancashire.

Since 1918 Manchester returns ten members to Parliament, while Salford has three members. There is an aerodrome on Chat Moss. It has two broadcasting stations, North Regional (480 M., 50 kW.) and North National (301.5 M., 50 kW.). Pop. of Manchester (1931), 766,333, of Salford, 223,442.—Cf. G. E. B. Saintsbury, *Manchester: a Concise History*.

MANCHESTER. The largest city in New Hampshire, U.S.A. Pop. 78,384.

MANCHESTER, The Victoria University of. *See* VICTORIA UNIVERSITY.

MANCHESTER COLLEGE. A theological institution established in 1786 at Manchester, subsequently removed to York, then back to Manchester, next up to London, and in 1889 to Oxford. Its main object is the teaching of theology apart from the doctrines of any particular sect. It has mainly been supported by Unitarians.

MANCHESTER PARTY, or SCHOOL. The name given to an English political party whose exertions were particularly directed to the development and carrying out of the principles of free-trade and *laissez-faire*. The immediate object of attack was the Corn Laws, and the Anti-Corn Law League was established in 1839. It had its chief seat in Manchester, and Cobden and Bright were the principal leaders. From its advocating non-intervention in foreign affairs, and arbitration instead of war, it was sometimes called the "peace-at-any-price" party.

MANCHESTER SHIP CANAL. Has a length of 35½ miles, the seaward end being at Eastham on the south side of the Mersey estuary, where three large locks have been constructed. Locks were also made at four other places, namely, Latchford, Irlam, Barton, and Mode Wheel, Manchester being 60 feet above the sea-level. The canal has converted this inland town to the third largest British seaport. The barge canals of England and all the railway systems have connections to the Ship Canal.

The average width of the canal at the top is 172 feet, while the minimum depth is 28 feet. There are large docks at Manchester and Salford, of 71 and 33½ acres area respectively. The canal was opened by Queen Victoria in 1894, and altogether cost about £20,000,000, the Manchester corporation being large shareholders, with representation on the board of directors. The opening of the canal has had a large influence on the industrial development of the town, the use of Trafford Park as an industrial estate with over one hundred works, some giving employment to thousands of men, being a natural consequence.

The tonnage and revenue have shown continuous increases since the opening date. It is interesting to note that the first navigable acqueduct, that at Barton, constructed by James Brindley, had to be converted to the first swing aqueduct by Sir E. Leader Williams, the engineer who designed the Ship Canal.

MANCHURIA. A Chinese territory occupying the north-east corner of the republic and abutting on Siberia and Korea. It is divided into three provinces: Liaoning (Shengking or Fengtien), Kirin, and Heilung-chiang or the Amur Province; area, 363,610 sq. miles. The chief towns are: Mukden, the capital (pop. 250,000), Newchang (65,600), Antung (72,500), Tatungkou, Tiehling, Tung-chiangtzu, Fakumen, and the port of Ying-k'ou. In the province of Kirin is Kirin, the capital, and Chang-chun (pop. 80,000). Tsitsihar (Heilung Hsien) is the capital of Heilung-chiang (pop. 30,000).

Manchuria is one of the richest agricultural districts of Eastern Asia, 81,718,945 acres being under cultivation. The principal food-crops are millet, wheat, and rice; about 7,000,000 acres were cultivated for soya beans in 1930; minerals are abundant. The Trans-Siberian Railway runs to Harbin, where it forks for Vladivostok and Mukden.

In 1900, after the Boxer outbreak Russia occupied Manchuria. By the Manchurian Convention (1902) she was expected to evacuate the occupied territory, but failed to do so, and war ensued between Russia and Japan (Feb., 1904), which resulted in the restoration of Manchuria to China. In 1931 there was war in Manchuria between China and Japan. In 1932 Manchuria was proclaimed an independent state under Japanese protection. The name was changed to Manchowko, Changchun became the capital, and Hsuan Tung (Mr. Henry Pu Yi), former Emperor of China, was appointed Head of State. A Commission appointed by the League of Nations, and under the chairmanship of Lord Lytton, investigated the situation in Manchuria in 1932 and found that Japan had far exceeded her rights. When the League adopted the report in 1933, the Japanese delegates left the Assembly, and war once more broke out in Manchuria. Pop. of the territory, probably 24,520,661, but variously estimated at from 5 to 30 million.—Cf. A. Hosie, *Manchuria: its People, Resources, and Recent History.*

MANDÆANS, NASORÆANS, SABIANS, or **ST. JOHN'S CHRISTIANS.** A religious sect which existed in Babylonia and Mesopotamia from the beginning of the Christian era. Known as Sabians (from *sabba*, to baptize), and as *Mandaye* (gnostikoi), they are the only gnostic sect whose sacred writings are still extant. Their religion is a form of gnosticism with elements of Judaism, and Hindu and Parsee philosophy.

About fifty years ago (in 1880) the number of Mandæans was estimated at about 4000, but at present the followers of the Mandæan faith are but few, and may be found in some cities on the Lower Euphrates and the Lower Tigris, near Basra and in Khuzistan.—BIBLIOGRAPHY: W. Brandt, *Die mandäische Religion*; and article in Hastings' *Encyclopædia of Ethics and Religion.*

MANDALAY. A city and capital of Upper Burma; a river-port on the Irrawaddy, 400 miles north of Rangoon. From 1857 Mandalay was capital of Burma, but in 1885 King Theebaw was deposed by the British and his dominions annexed to Burma. In 1892 the old city was partly destroyed by fire; a new one was built, and the ancient, square-built, walled, and towered city is now known as Fort Dufferin. Theebaw's palace and the pagodas of the Temple of Kuthodaw are unique. Pop. (1931), 147,932.

MANDARIN DUCK. A beautiful species of duck (*Aix galericulata*)

Mandarin Duck

from Eastern Asia, the males of which exhibit a highly variegated plumage of green, purple, white, and chestnut, the females being coloured a more sober brown. The male loses his fine plumage in summer.

MANDATED TERRITORIES. Former German and Turkish colonies and territories which, after the European War, ceased to be under the sovereignty of these states, and which, being unfit for self-government, were mandated by the League of Nations to other countries. The League defines the degree of authority and control to be exercised by the Mandatories, and each country holding a mandate has to render an annual account to the League Council. The system of mandates is dealt with in the Covenant of the League of Nations (Art. 22) and in the Treaty of Versailles (Art. 22).

Mandated Territories are of three classes (A, B, and C), class A consisting of those parts detached from the Ottoman Empire which, being sufficiently developed, can exist independently with such advice and assistance from the mandatory power as occasion may demand, class B consisting of the former German colonies in Central and East Africa which are to be treated as protected states, and class C consisting of territories which can best be administered under the laws of the mandatory as integral parts of it. The mandates and mandatory powers are:

A MANDATES.—'Iraq (Mesopotamia) and Palestine with Transjordania to *Great Britain*; Syria and Lebanon to *France*.

B MANDATES.—Part of Togoland and the Cameroons to *France*; remainder of Togoland and the Cameroons, and Tanganyika Territory to *Great Britain*; part of former German East Africa to *Belgium*.

C MANDATES.—Former German South Pacific possessions to *Australia*; Samoa to *New Zealand*; Nauru to *Australia, New Zealand*, and *Great Britain*; former German North Pacific possessions to *Japan*; former German South-West Africa to the *Union of South Africa*.

'Iraq is now an independent kingdom. *See* 'IRAQ.

MAN'DEVILLE, Bernard de. Poet and philosophical writer, born in Holland about 1670, died in 1733. His most celebrated production is *The Fable of the Bees, or Private Vices Public Benefits*, the first part of which appeared in 1723, and the second in 1728. It created quite a sensation, and called forth replies from Bishop Berkeley, William Law, sand others. Among his other work are: *Free Thoughts on Religion* (1720) and *Origin of Honour* (1732).

MANDEVILLE, Sir John de. The name assumed by the author of a famous book of travels, *The Voiage and Travaile of Sir John Maundevile, knight*, which was originally written in French between 1357 and 1371. The *Travels* is perhaps the most wonderful literary forgery in the world. The book enjoyed a world-wide fame for five centuries before it was discovered that Sir John never lived, and that the author of the *Travels* never travelled, but sat in his well-stocked library and drew his materials from innumerable sources some as old as Pliny if not as old as Homer.

According to the *Travels*, Mandeville was born at St. Albans about 1300, started on his travels in 1322, returned in 1357 owing to an attack of arthritic gout, and settled at Liége, where he wrote his book to pass the time during attacks of his malady, and where he eventually died and was buried. The real author of the book is not known with complete certainty, but strong cumulative evidence points to one Jean d'Outremeuse, a voluminous writer who lived at Liége, the supposed site of Sir John's death and burial.

The authors from whom "Mandeville" borrowed most are Albert of Aix, who wrote an account of the first Crusade, William of Boldensele, and, above all, the travels of a Franciscan missionary, Friar Odoric of Prodenone (1330). *Mandeville's Travels* is quite one of the most delightful of the books of the Middle Ages; it was one of the earliest books to be written with no other aim than that of entertainment.

Many well-known stories and legends owe their origin to "Mandeville." Prester John and the Great Cham, the Earthly Paradise, the loadstone mountains, the fountain of youth—these and such like are the subjects of his marvellous tales. The English translation, charming in its *naïveté*, is one of the best specimens of prose of its time.

MANDING'OES. *See* BAMBROK; BARRA.

MAN'DOLINE (It. mandolina, dim. of *mandola*), a musical instrument of the guitar kind. There are several varieties, each with different tunings. The Neapolitan has four strings tuned like those of the violin, G. D. A. E; the Milanese has five double strings (each pair in unison) tuned G, C, A, D, E. A plectrum is used in the right hand, the fingers of the left stopping the strings on the fretted finger-board.

MANDRAKE. The popular name of plants of the genus Mandragŏra, nat. ord. Solanaceæ, natives of south and east of Europe and Western Asia, and not uncommon in British gardens. *M. officinarum* has large tap-roots; the leaves radical, sessile, ovate, entire, and waved. There is no stem; but the flowers, which are white with a bell-shaped corolla, stand upon simple stalks. The fruit is a large two-celled berry of an orange colour, containing many kidney-shaped seeds.

The root possesses narcotic qualities, and from its occasional resemblance to the human figure was formerly supposed to possess an inferior kind of animal life, and to shriek when torn up. It was believed to have many magical virtues, and to be an aphrodisiac and a cure for barrenness (Gen. xxx. 14, 16).

MANDRILL. A species of baboon (*Cynocephălys mormon*), which is distinguished by the short tail, by the elongated dog-like muzzle, and by the presence of buttock callosities which are generally brightly coloured.

Mandrill (*Cynocephalus mormon*)

Mandrills are natives of Western Africa, where they associate in large troops. Full-grown males measure about 5 feet; they are exceedingly strong and muscular, and fierce in disposition. They have cheek protuberances coloured with stripes of brilliant red and blue.

MA'NES. Among the Romans, the souls or ghosts of the dead, to whom were presented oblations of victims, wine, milk, garlands of flowers, &c. The offerings were made at funerals, and at the *Parentalia*, or *Feralia*, commemorative ceremonies held by the Romans in February. A similar worship of ghosts or ancestral spirits prevails among many races.—Cf. W. W. Fowler, *Roman Festivals*.

MAN'ETHO. An Egyptian priest and historian, who belonged to the town of Sebennytus, in Lower Egypt, and lived in the reign of Ptolemy Soter, about the beginning of the third century B.C. His history was divided into three books, and beginning with the fabulous or mythological history of Egypt, ended with the 30th dynasty, when Egypt fell under the rule of Alexander the Great. The history itself is lost, but the lists of the dynasties are preserved in Julius Africanus and Eusebius, and in the work of George Syncellus of Byzantium (A.D. 792), and some fragments of the work are to be found in Josephus (*Against Apion*).

MANFREDONIA. A seaport of Foggia, Italy, on the Gulf of Manfredonia, an arm of the Adriatic. The town lies south of Monte Gargano (3460 feet). The fisheries occupy the inhabitants; figs and almonds are exported. Manfredonia was founded by King Manfred (1231-66) about 1263, was destroyed by the Turks (1620), and subsequently rebuilt. Two miles west of the town is the cathedral of S. Maria di Siponto, forming part of the remains of Roman *Sipontum*, founded 194 B.C. Pop. 15,000.

MANGALORE. A seaport and headquarters of the South Kanara district, Madras, India, on an open roadstead suitable for small craft. There is a Jesuit college affiliated with the University of Madras, and a Jesuit mission (founded 1880). Coffee, tiles, salted fish, and spices are the principal exports. The town was taken by Tippoo Sultan (Sahib) after a siege lasting from 19th May, 1783, to 23rd Jan., 1784. It became British in 1799. Pop. 53,877.

MAN'GANESE (symbol, Mn; atomic weight, 54·93), a metal of a reddish-white colour; it has a high metallic lustre, is harder than iron, and melts at 1260° C. It does not readily tarnish, does not decompose water, but reacts readily with most dilute acids. The common ore is a dioxide, black oxide, or peroxide (MnO_2), the pyrolusite of mineralogists, a substance largely employed in the preparation of chlorine for the manufacture of bleaching-powder or chloride of lime. It is employed in the manufacture of plate-glass, to correct the yellow colour which oxide of iron is apt to impart to the glass. It is also used in making the black enamel of pottery.

Other oxides are the protoxide (MnO), sesquioxide (Mn_2O_3), the red oxide (Mn_3O_4), and permanganic anhydride (Mn_2O_7). From the last is derived the well-known compound potassium permanganate ($K_2Mn_2O_8$). Metallic manganese is obtained by reduction of the oxide by means of aluminium powder. It resembles iron in appearance and properties; its salts are contained in many mineral waters, and are employed in medicine.

In steel manufacture it is used in certain proportions with advantage as regards the ductility of the steel and ability to withstand forging, and in other manufacturing operations it forms an important element. It is added to steel in the form of spiegeleisen, an alloy of iron containing about 20 per cent. of managanese made in blast-furnaces, or as ferro-manganese, an alloy containing about 80 per cent. made in blast- or electric-furnaces.

MANGANESE BRONZE. Copper-zinc alloys which contain a small quantity of manganese, and which have exceptional qualities in the way of strength, hardness, toughness, &c. Various qualities are manufactured, each suited for certain special purposes. The usual alloys contain copper, 58 to 60; zinc, 39 to 41; manganese, traces to 2 per cent., and often about 1 per cent. of tin, iron, and aluminium.

The manganese is added to the copper-zinc alloy in the form of cupro-manganese or as ferro-manganese. The alloys are strong, and remain strong at high temperatures, and are suitable for steam-valves, &c. They resist the action of sea-water, and are used for propellers, rudders, &c.

MANGANITE. A black prismatic mineral, one of the ores of manganese, MnO(OH), that is, Mn_2O_3,H_2O. It is also called *Grey Manganese-ore*, and is used as a decolorizer in the manufacture of glass.

MANGE. A parasitic skin disease affecting horses, cattle, and dogs; known as *scab* in the case of sheep. Two mites cause body-mange (sarcoptic and psoroptic), which are contagious and notifiable diseases; chorioptic, symbiotic or leg mange chiefly affects horses, and is not notifiable. Treatment is difficult, but a preliminary scrubbing with hot water, soap, and soda removes dirt and scales, and prepares for washing in a solution of coal-tar disinfectant (second day). Sulphur, 1 part, and train-oil, 6 parts, should be applied on the third day. Disinfection and isolation are essential.

MANGEL-WURZEL (Mangold). A large-rooted species of beet (*Beta vulgāris macrorhīza*) extensively cultivated in Britain and on the Continent for feeding cattle. It requires a sunny climate and liberally manured generous soil, which in favourable circumstances may grow from 70 to 80 tons per acre.

MANGO. The fruit of the mango tree (*Mangifĕra indica*), nat. ord. Anacardiaceæ, a native of tropical Asia, but now widely cultivated throughout the tropics. Fine varieties produce a luscious, slightly acid, and resinous fruit much prized for dessert. The large flat kernel of the fruit is nutritious, and has been cooked for food in times of scarcity. The fruit forms a fleshy drupe about the size of a hen's egg or larger, somewhat kidney-shaped and yellowish or reddish in colour, spotted with black on the outside. The fruit is

Mango (*Mangifera indica*)

much used for making pickles, chutneys, and curries. Dried, it forms a considerable article of commerce.

It yields by distillation a spirit said to be not unlike whisky in flavour. The tree grows to a considerable size, with an erect trunk, and yields a timber that is used for purposes for which fine timber is not required, as for packing-boxes, country carts, rough furniture, and house carpentry.

MANGOSTEEN'. A tree of the East Indies, *Garcinia Mangostāna*, nat. ord. Guttiferæ. The tree grows to the height of 18 feet, and the fruit is about the size of an orange, and contains a juicy white pulp of a delicate, sweet, sub-acid flavour. It is esteemed one of the most delicious and wholesome of all known fruits. The thick fleshy rind has astringent properties, and hence is used medicinally in diarrhœa and dysentery.

MANGROVE (Rhizophŏra). A genus of plants (type of the family Rhizophoraceæ) consisting of trees or shrubs which grow in tropical countries along the muddy beaches of low coasts, where they form impenetrable barriers for long distances. They throw out numerous roots from the lower part of the stem, and also send down long slender roots from the branches, like the Indian banyan tree. The seeds germinate in the seed-vessel, the young seedling ultimately falling root foremost and thus planting itself in the mud. By retaining mud and vegetable matter among their roots, mangroves often help in the gaining of land from the sea.

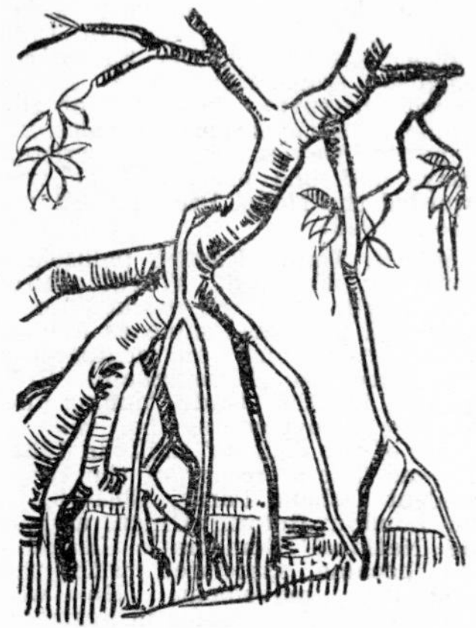

Mangrove

The wood of *R. Mangle* is dark-red, hard, and durable, and the bark is used for tanning. The fruit is said to be sweet and edible, and the fermented juice is made into a kind of light wine. The name is also given to the genus Avicennia of the verbena family, which occupies large tracts of shore in tropical countries, extending as far south as New Zealand and Tasmania.

MANHATTAN ISLAND. *See* NEW YORK.

MANICHÆANS (man-i-kē´anz), or **MANICHEES.** An Oriental religious sect founded by Manichæus, Manes, or Mani, a Persian of the third century after Christ, educated in the religion of Zoroaster. His object was to incorporate Zoroastrian dualism with Christianity. (*See* ZOROASTER.) In the fervour of his fanaticism he gave himself out to be the Paraclete promised in the Gospel of John, by which he understood, not the Holy Ghost, as many had erroneously imagined, but a teacher commissioned to diffuse and perfect Christianity, and free it from the vile corruptions of the evil genius Ahriman (q.v.).

Manes appeared as a religious teacher under Sapor I. As a man of multifarious accomplishment he attracted great attention; but the hostility of the magi forced him to a speedy exile. He wandered into distant countries, still pursuing his mission, and in the East his contact with Buddhism gave new shape and tinge to his eclectic views. On his return to Persia Hormisdas received him with welcome; but under his successor Varanes, Manes was apprehended and flayed alive, while his skin was stuffed and hung up in public.

MANICURE. Term applied to the treatment of the finger nails to preserve their healthy condition and appearance. The nails are cleaned in soapy water and shaped with a flexible steel file. Orange wood sticks are used for pressing back the cuticle, the loose portions of which are removed by a cuticle knife or fine scissors.

MANIHIKI. One of the Cook Islands, an atoll in the Pacific Ocean, 650 miles N. of Raratonga. Area, 30 sq. miles; pop. 429.

MANI´LA. A city, chief seaport, and capital of the Philippines, on the south-west coast of Luzon and on Manila Bay, an arm of the China Sea, forming the finest harbour in the Far East. The city is divided into a northern and a southern half by the River Pasig, at the mouth of which it stands, the southern being enclosed by a sixteenth-century wall, and the northern forming the modern suburbs.

There is a cathedral, and a university (St. Thomas) founded by the Dominicans and Jesuits through an authorization granted by Philip II. of Spain in 1585. The modern university dates from 1857, and is conducted on American lines, with faculties of medicine, pharmacy, engineering, law, philosophy, and arts. A mint is established in Manila, where the Philippine coinage is produced. Cigars, cigarettes, tobacco, and Manila hemp, ships and boats, and textiles are manufactured, and copra, sugar, tobacco, and hemp are exported.

Manila was founded by Spain (1571), was in British occupation 1762-64), and was annexed by the United States during the Spanish-American War (1898), when Admiral Dewey destroyed the Spanish fleet under Montijo in Manila Bay (1st May, 1898). Pop. (1932), 341,034.

MAN'IPLE. In the Roman Catholic and some other Churches, one of the sacred vestments, being an ornament worn by the priest above the left wrist at the celebration of the Eucharist. It is now of the same width and colour as the stole and the vestment or chasuble, fringed at the ends, and generally about 1¼ yards in length.

MANIPUR (-pör'). A native state of North-Eastern India, in Assam. The Indian Government, which put down a rising here in 1891, receives tribute from the state, and has some control over its affairs. Area, 8456 sq. miles; pop. 384,016; capital, Imphal.

MANITOBA. The most easterly of the three prairie-provinces of Canada; area, 251,832 sq. miles (27,055 sq. miles are water). It is an extensive plain traversed by the Nelson, Assiniboine, Hayes, and Red Rivers, and containing Lakes Winnipeg (9398 sq. miles), Winnipegosis (2086 sq. miles), and Manitoba (1820 sq. miles). Among towns are Winnipeg (the capital), Brandon, Portage la Prairie, St. Boniface, Pas, Churchill, and Port Nelson.

Manitoba is essentially agricultural, producing wheat (Manitoba "No. 1 Hard" is the world's standard), oats, barley, flax, rye, and potatoes. Live-stock and dairy-farming are popular (dairy products value 20,000,000 dollars annually); fishing and lumbering are carried on, and vast deposits of gold and copper have been found.

Winnipeg is the focus of all the Canadian Transcontinental Railway systems, and the province is traversed by 4420 miles of track (1930). The capital also contains the Provincial Agricultural College and Manitoba University.

The nucleus of Manitoba was the Red River Settlement, founded by Lord Selkirk in 1812, and annexed to the dominion in 1870. In 1912 the provincial boundaries were extended to Hudson Bay at the expense of Keewatin.

A Lieutenant-Governor is assisted in local government by a Legislative Assembly of fifty-five members, elected every five years. The province sends six members to the Senate and seventeen to the Commons of the Dominion Parliament (Ottawa). The Crown lands of the Province, hitherto under the Dominion Government, were handed over to the Province in 1930. Pop. (1931), 700,139, mixed, but mainly of British descent.—Cf. H. T. Boom and A. G. Brown, *The Prairie Provinces of Canada.*

MANIZALES. A city of Colombia, South America, capital of the department of Caldas (lat. 5° 5′ N., long. 75° 36′ W.); altitude, 7000 feet. It is a trading centre exporting gold, coffee, and cocoa. Pop. 81,091. Caldas has an area of 5459 sq. miles, and a pop. of 624,201.

MANN, Thomas. German writer. Born at Lübeck, 6th June, 1875; at the age of nineteen his family removed to Munich, and while working in insurance, he devoted himself to literature. He published *Buddenbrooks* in 1903, a massive story of a family of Lübeck merchants such as his own. He wrote short stories and a novel, and in 1925 another long novel, *Der Zauberberg* (English translation, *The Magic Mountain*, 1926), the story of the people in a tubercular convalescent home in Davos. He has written essays and one play, and he was awarded the Nobel Prize for Literature in 1929.

MANN, Tom. English politician. Born at Foleshill, Warwickshire, 15th April, 1856, he worked on a farm and in a coal mine as a boy. Later he became an engineering apprentice in Birmingham. Prominent in the trade union and Socialist movements, he was a leader of the dockers' strike in 1889. He was first secretary of the Independent Labour Party, 1894-96, of the London Reform Union, and of the National Democratic League; and became associated with the syndicalist movement. He was active as a Labour leader in Australia between 1902 and 1908, and in South Africa. In 1918-21 he was general secretary of the Amalgamated Society of Engineers. He has written *A Socialist's View of Religion*, *Russia in 1921*, *Tom Mann's Memoirs*, and *What I Saw in China, 1927.*

MANNA. The sweet concrete juice which is obtained by incisions made in the stem of a species of ash, *Fraxinus Ornus*, a native of Sicily, Calabria, and other parts of the south of Europe. The manna of commerce is collected in Sicily, where the manna-ash is cultivated for the purpose in regular plantations.

The best manna is in oblong pieces, or flakes of a whitish or pale-yellow colour, light, friable, and somewhat transparent. It has a slight peculiar odour, and a sweetish taste mixed with a slight degree of bitterness, and is employed as a gentle laxative. Other sweetish secretions exuded by some other plants growing in warm and dry climates, as the *Eucalyptus mannifĕra* of Australia, the *Tamarix mannifĕra* or *gallica* of

Arabia and Syria, are considered to be kinds of manna.

Small quantities of manna, known under the name of *Briançon manna*, are obtained from the common larch. In Scripture we are told that a substance called manna was miraculously furnished as food for the Israelites in their journey through the wilderness of Arabia. Some identify it with the saccharine substance yielded by the *Tamarix mannifĕra.*

MANNHEIM (mån'hīm). A town and river-port of Baden, Germany, on the Rhine. It is surrounded by a promenade on the site of the ancient ramparts, and is connected by a bridge with Ludwigshafen (Bavaria) on the opposite bank of the Rhine. It has extensive harbours, and is the chief commercial town on the Upper Rhine. Machinery, sugar, chemicals, and tobacco are manufactured.

The palace was built by the Elector Palatine Charles Philip, 1720-29. Mannheim was founded in 1606 by the Elector Palatine Frederick IV., was destroyed in the Thirty Years' War, and passed from Bavaria to Baden in 1802. Pop. (1925), 247,486.

MANNING, Henry Edward. Cardinal, born at Totteridge, Hertfordshire, 1808, died 1892. He was educated at Harrow and Balliol College, Oxford; rector of Lavington and Graffham, Sussex (1834-40); Archdeacon of Chichester (1840-51). He took an active part in the Tractarian movement, and in 1851 joined the Church of Rome and was ordained priest. On the death of Cardinal Wiseman he succeeded him as Archbishop of Westminster (1865), and ten years after he was made cardinal.

Social and philanthropic questions received much of his attention; he was an ardent supporter of total abstinence, and he was a member of commissions on the housing of the poor and on education. Besides sermons, he wrote: *The Temporal Power of the Pope, The True Story of the Vatican Council,* and *The Four Great Evils of the Day.*—Cf. S. Leslie, *Henry Edward Manning: his Life and Labours.*

MANNITE, or **MANNITOL** ($C_6H_{14}O_6$). A hexa-hydric alcohol closely related to the sugars. It occurs in many plants and in some fermented juices, e.g. beet-root juice. It may be obtained from manna by extracting with alcohol, from which it crystallizes in colourless needles of melting-point 166° C. It is readily soluble in cold water, insoluble in ether, has a sweet taste, and on oxidation yields the sugar mannose, $C_6H_{12}O_6$.

MANŒUVRES. A series of exercises performed by fleets or large bodies of troops of all arms as a means of providing combined tactical training for war. In war, however, no restrictions exist as to the use of ground other than those which can be imposed by enemy agency, while, under manœuvre conditions, rules and restrictions as to where troops may pass or may not pass are endless and vexatious. As a rule, all private property is "out of bounds," and is so marked on the manœuvre maps, causing much confusion to troops operating in that particular neighbourhood, and adding considerably to the difficulties of the directing staff.

Of course the chief dissimilarity between manœuvres and war, and the one which above all tends to make such operations unreal, is the absence of bullets. The British soldier—incomparable in war—does not take kindly to the make-believe variety, and, from his point of view, it must be admitted that it would require a very highly developed sense of duty to cause Mr. Atkins—or for the matter of that a junior regimental officer—to carry out movements and actions required of him in the same manner and with the same expenditure of physical energy he would use in war, knowing full well that failure to do so would in no case cause him any actual physical hurt or injury. But when we come to consider the staff—both general and administrative—the position is quite different.

The staff is concerned either with the moving of the troops, as one moves pieces on the chess-board, or with their supply and administration before, during, and after movement, and the absence of bullets and other missiles in the enemy's guns and rifles does not so much affect the questions to be dealt with. It is therefore open to question whether, from the point of view of actual tactical training, manœuvres are not of more value to staff and senior regimental officers than to junior officers and rank and file. These last two categories do no doubt gain some experience in the A B C of active service conditions, and as far as it goes this is of value.

It is probable that when manœuvres on a scale such as was planned for the autumn of 1914 again take place in England, many of the methods developed during the European War will be simulated; this will tend towards realism, and will make the operations more interesting to the rank and file of the army, and incidentally may help to solve the difficulties of the directing and umpire staff in dealing with prohibited areas.

Umpires are a necessary evil on manœuvres; they are presumed to represent the controlling influence that in war would be the province of the bullets and shells of the enemy, and, in order to permit of this being done, they are vested with authority to control movements of troops in actual contact; occasionally, also, they serve to give away the position to be attacked by appearing on the sky-line.

MANOM'ETER. An instrument used to measure fluid pressures. In its simplest form it consists of a simple U-tube in which the pressure is balanced by a column of water or mercury acting with or against the atmospheric pressure. A tube similar but with a closed arm is another form, the compression of the enclosed air being used to obtain the pressure. A barometer is also a type of manometer.

MAN'OR (Fr. *manoir*; Lat. *manerium*, a dwelling-place, from *manere*, to dwell), originally a piece of territory held by a lord or great personage, who occupied a part of it, as much as was necessary for the use of his own immediate family, and granted or leased the remainder to tenants for stipulated rents or services.

Manors were also called baronies, as they still are lordships, and the lord was empowered to hold a domestic court called the *court baron* for punishing misdemeanours, settling disputes, etc., within the manor. No manors, with all their incidents and franchises, have been granted in England since the reign of Edward III.

MANRE'SA. An ancient city of Barcelona, Spain; the Roman *Munorisa*, capital of the *Jacetani*; on the Cardoner, which is spanned by a Roman bridge. The city is 40 miles N.N.W. of Barcelona by rail, and is a railway junction. Cotton, woollens, and paper are manufactured. There is a Dominican convent, and a church associated with Loyola. Pop. 27,000.

MANSARD, or MANSART (mȧn̦-sär), **François.** French architect, born in Paris 1598, died there 1666. Among his principal works are part of the château of Blois, and the château of Maisons. Based on the study of classical antiquity, his buildings show a characteristic dignity, elegance, and logic in construction. His nephew, Jules Hardouin, who assumed his name (1645-1708), was less great as an artist, but achieved much worldly success. The Palais de Versailles, the Hôtel des Invalides and the Place Vendôme in Paris, and other works of the reign of Louis XIV., are from his designs.

MANSE. In Scotland, the dwelling-house of a parish minister of a rural parish. Every minister of a rural parish (*quoad omnia*) is entitled to have a manse erected and upheld by the heritors, but the ministers of royal burghs have properly no such right, unless where there is a landward district belonging to the parish in which the burgh lies. The term is sometimes loosely applied to the dwelling-house of dissenting ministers.

MANSEL, Henry Longueville. A logician and theologian, born at Cosgrove, Northamptonshire, 1820, died in London 1871. He became professor of moral and metaphysical philosophy at Oxford in 1859; professor of ecclesiastical history 1867; and Dean of St. Paul's, London, 1868. He was the chief exponent of the philosophy of Sir William Hamilton, and collaborated with Professor Veitch in editing Hamilton's Lectures. Among his publications are: *The Philosophy of Kant* (1856); *The Limits of Religious Thought, being the Bampton Lectures for* 1858; and *Metaphysics, or the Philosophy of Consciousness* (1860).—Cf. A. W. Benn, *History of Rationalism.*

MANSFIELD, William Murray, Earl of. The fourth son of David, Lord Stormont, was born at Scone, in Scotland, 2nd March, 1705, died 20th March, 1793. Educated at Westminster School and at Oxford, he entered Lincoln's Inn and was called to the Bar in 1731. In 1742 he was appointed Solicitor-General, and obtained a seat in Parliament about the same time. In 1754 he was Attorney-General, and in 1756 he was appointed Chief Justice of the King's Bench, and made Baron Mansfield. In 1776 he was advanced to the dignity of earl.

On the trial of Woodfall for publishing *The Letters of Junius*, and on some other occasions, he showed himself the zealous supporter of the Government, and gave offence to the popular party. During the riots of 1780 his house in London was burned down by the mob. In 1788 he resigned his office of Chief Justice, and the remainder of his life was spent in retirement.

He was a great lawyer, not merely in a technical sense, but as one who could direct the practice of the courts towards broad principles of jurisprudence. Many departments in the mercantile law of England and Scotland were created by him, and among others the law of marine insurance was made and systematized by his decisions.

MANSFIELD. A borough and market town of Nottinghamshire, England, on the Maud, served by the L.M.S. and L.N.E. Railways. There are collieries in the vicinity. Thread, hosiery, lace, and boots are manufactured. The town has a technical school for the mining industry. The Courts for Sherwood Forest were held at Mansfield till 1715. Pop. (1931), 46,075.

MANSFIELD COLLEGE. A theological college established at Oxford for the education of men for the Nonconformist ministry, and opened in 1889. The college is not incorporated with the university. Its students must be graduates of some recognized university, or undergraduates of Oxford who have passed Moderations.

MANSION HOUSE. The nomenclature applied to the official residence of the Lord Mayor of London, and frequently used in describing other mayoral residences, e.g. at Dublin. The London building stands opposite the Bank of England. It was erected by George Dance between Oct., 1739 and 1753, and was restored and extensively improved in 1930–31, when a fine roof garden was added. The principal room is the Egyptian Hall, where banquets and balls are given, and which is a reproduction of the Egyptian Hall described by Vitruvius. The City police-court is held in the basement.

MANSLAUGHTER. The crime of unlawfully killing a human being without malice aforethought. It is essential that there should be want of premeditation to kill. Unlawful premeditated killing is the graver crime of murder (q.v.). There may, however, be premeditation in the eyes of the law though there was no real intent to kill, e.g. when death is caused by any one while committing a felony, or when an act is done in the knowledge that death will probably ensue and it does.

Manslaughter may vary from cases in which negligence alone is the cause of death, as when one, driving negligently, runs down and kills another, to cases nearly approaching murder, as when one kills another in sudden passion under great provocation. Manslaughter is punishable by penal servitude, imprisonment, or fine, according to the degree of culpability. *See* HOMICIDE.

MANS, Le (lė mȧn). A town and capital of Sarthe, France; the Roman *Cenomani*; on the Sarthe. The cathedral of St. Julien (partly eleventh and twelfth centuries) and the church of Notre Dame de la Couture (twelfth to fourteenth centuries) are historically interesting. Le Mans was the birthplace of Henry II., first Plantagenet king of England; it witnessed the final dispersion of the Vendean insurgents by Marceau (1793), and the defeat of the French army under Chanzy by the Germans under Prince Frederick Charles, Jan., 1871. Pop. 76,868.

MANSÛ'RA. A city of Lower Egypt, at the junction of the Nile (Damietta branch) and a canal running to Lake Menzala. It is a commercial centre in the Delta cotton district. Mansûra was founded in 1222, and was attacked by the Crusaders under Louis IX. in 1250. Louis was captured and his army defeated. Pop. (1927), 63,676.

MANTEGNA (mȧn-ten'yȧ), **Andrea.** Early Italian painter, born at Padua 1431, died at Mantua 1506. About 1459 he went to Verona, where he painted a magnificent altar-piece in the church of St. Zeno. About 1466 he removed to Mantua, and the rest of his life was passed there, with the exception of two years at Rome. At Mantua he opened a school, and painted among other important works the *Triumph of Julius Cæsar*, now at Hampton Court.

One of the latest and best of this artist's works is the *Madonna della Vittoria*, now in the Louvre at Paris. There are others of his works in the Louvre, in particular *Wisdom vanquishing Vice*, and a mythological work, *Parnassus*. Mantegna excelled in perspective, which was then a rare merit; he also excelled in engraving, and introduced the art of engraving on copper into Upper Italy.

MANTINE'A (Gr. *Mantineia*). A city of Arcadia, ancient Greece, the scene of the victory and death of Epaminondas (Theban victory over the Spartans, 362 B.C.).

MANTIS. A genus of orthopterous insects. They frequent various plants, and the forms and colours of their bodies and wings are so like the leaves, twigs, and flowers which surround them as to make them very inconspicuous. (*See* MIMICRY.) The *M. religiōsa*, or praying-mantis, has received its name from the peculiar position of the anterior pair of legs, resembling that of a person's hands at prayer. In their habits they are very voracious, killing insects and cutting them to pieces. They are natives chiefly of tropical regions, but are also found in France, Spain, and the warmer parts of Europe. They are very pugnacious, and are kept by the Chinese for the purpose of watching them fight.

MAN'TUA (It. *Mantŏvo*). A province of Lombardy, Italy, traversed by the Po, Mincio, and Oglio. It is low-lying, level, and produces rice, silk, vines, and cereals. Area, 903 sq. miles; pop. (1931), 397,686.—**Mantua,** the provincial capital, is a fortress city on the Mincio; with Legagno, Verona, and Peschiera it formed the Austrian *Quadrilateral.* The church of S. Andrea, begun 1472, was designed by Alberti, and contains the tomb of Mantegna.

The twelfth-century cathedral (S. Pietro) and the ducal palace of the Gonzagas (1302) are historical. Founded by the Etruscans, Mantua (*Andes* or *Pietole* near by) was the birthplace of Virgil. From 1328 to 1708 the House of Gonzaga (q.v.) held sovereign power over Mantua, first as captains, or marquesses, and afterwards as dukes. Stormed and sacked by the Austrians (1630), Mantua was forfeited to the Empire (1703). It suffered during the Napoleonic campaigns, and was ceded to Italy in 1866. Pop. (1931), 42,939.

MANURES. *See* SOILS AND MANURES.

MANUSCRIPTS (Lat. *manuscriptus*, written by the hand) are writings of any kind, whether on paper or other material, in distinction to printed matter and inscriptions. Previous to the introduction of printing all literature was contained in manuscripts, and the deciphering and proper use of these form an important part in the science of palæography.

All the existing ancient manuscripts are written on parchment, vellum, leather, papyrus, or paper. The most common ink is the black, which is very old. Red ink of dazzling beauty is also found in ancient manuscripts. With it were written the initial letters, the first lines, and the titles, which were thence called *rubrics* (Lat. *ruber*, red). Blue, green, and yellow inks were more rarely used.

On rare occasions gold and silver inks were used, though from their cost they are oftenest confined to initial letters. With respect to external form, manuscripts are divided into rolls (*volumina*), and into stitched books or volumes (*codices*). Among the ancients the writers of manuscripts were mainly freedmen or slaves.

At a later period the monks were largely engaged in the production of manuscripts. In all the principal monasteries was a *scriptorium,* in which the *scriptor* or scribe could pursue his work in quiet, generally assisted by a *dictator,* who read aloud the text to be copied; the manuscript was then revised by a *corrector,* anf afterwards handed to the *miniator,* who added the ornamental capitals and artistic designs.

The most ancient manuscripts still preserved are those written on papyrus, and found in Egyptian tombs. A number of these are of date long before the Christian era, and one in Egyptian writing dates from perhaps 2500 B.C. Valuable MSS. of Greek writings, have been found in Egypt, some of them containing works supposed to have been entirely lost. They go back to about 300 B.C. Next to them in point of age are the Latin manuscripts found at Herculaneum.

Among manuscripts of the imperial era of Rome are the *Vatican Terence* and *Septuagint* (fourth century), and the *Codex Alexandrinus* of the British Museum. Few Biblical manuscripts are as old as the third century, one of the most famous being the *Codex Sinaiticus,* discovered in a Sinai convent and belonging to the fourth century. Among those of Latin authors may be noted that of Virgil (fourth century), in the Laurentian Library at Florence, and a Livy (fifth century) in the Imperial Library of Vienna.

The characters used in the older manuscripts were generally of large size, often what we should call capital letters, these and other large letters being called *majuscules* and *uncials,* as contrasted with *minuscules* or small letters. It was common in the Middle Ages to erase writings on parchment, and to re-use the material, manuscripts so treated being called *palimpsests.*

The art of illuminating manuscripts dates from the remotest antiquity. The Egyptian papyri were ornamented with vignettes or miniatures attached to the chapters, either designed in black outlines or painted in primary colours in distemper. The oldest ornamented Greek and Roman manuscripts that have survived are the Dioscorides of Vienna and the Virgil of the Vatican, both of the fourth century, and having vignettes or pictures in a Byzantine style of art.

From the eighth to the eleventh century the initial letters in use were composed of figures of men, quadrupeds, fishes, birds, etc. The initials of the twelfth century are made up of masses of conventional foliage interspersed with the animal figures of the preceding centuries. Continuous borders, with vignettes, tail-pieces, etc., were also prevalent in later times, and some manuscripts are ornamented with very artistic designs.

In the sixteenth century the art of illumination became extinct. Some attempts have been made to revive it by adorning paper, parchment, and vellum with designs in colours or metals.—BIBLIOGRAPHY: T. J. Wise, *Reference Catalogue of British and Foreign Autographs and Manuscripts*; J. H. Middleton, *Illuminated Classical and Mediæval MSS.*

MANU'TIUS, Aldus, or **ALDO MANUZIO.** Italian printer, born about 1447, died 1515. In 1488 he established himself as a printer at Venice, but the first work which he finished was not published till 1494. In the course of the ensuing twenty years he printed the works of the extant Latin and Greek authors, as well as those of his contemporaries. He was the inventor of the italic or cursive character, hence called *Aldine*. His business was continued by his son Paolo Manuzio, born 1512, died 1574, a man distinguished as a classical scholar no less than as a printer; and by his grandson Aldo, born 1547, died 1597. *See* ALDINE EDITIONS.

MANZO'NI, Alessandro. An Italian poet and novelist, born 1785, died 1873. His chief works are the *Inni Sacri*, a series of sacred lyrics; *Il Cinque Maggio*, a powerful ode on the death of Napoleon; the tragedies *Il Conte di Carmagnola* and *Adelchi*; and his great novel *I Promessi Sposi* (The Betrothed).

Manzoni strove earnestly to make the Florentine dialect universal in Italy. As a poet he outrivalled all his contemporaries, and his novel is one of the finest works of its kind in the language.

MAP, or MAPES, Walter. Scholar and poet of the twelfth century, a native of the Welsh Marches, is supposed to have been born in Herefordshire about 1140, and to have died about 1210. He was the author of a curious book, *De Nugis Curialium*, a notebook of the events of the day and of court gossip; and to him is attributed a collection of rhymed Latin verse, in which the abuses of the Church are hit off with vigour and humour.

Among the most remarkable of these are the satirical *Apocalypse* and the *Confession of Bishop Golias*, which contains the famous drinking-song beginning with *Meum est propositum in taberna mori*.

MAP. A representation of the features of one surface on another. The most important use of the word is in application to the earth. In a map of the earth, the system on which the meridians and parallels (*see* LATITUDE; LONGITUDE) are drawn, or the rule connecting position on the map with position on the earth, is called the *projection*. If the earth were a *developable* surface,

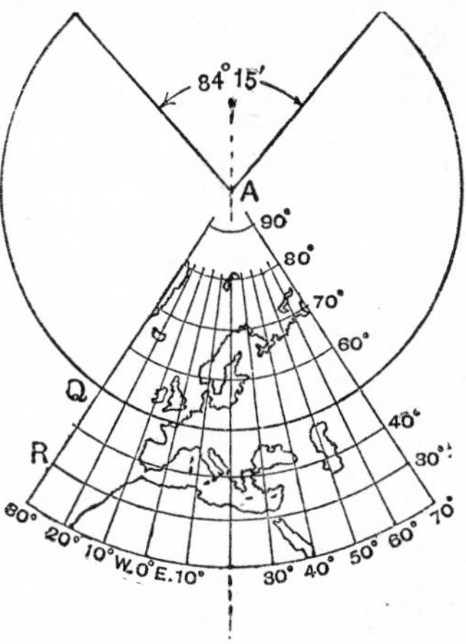

Map of Europe on simple Conical Projection, with one standard parallel. Scale 1/250,000,000. Radius of standard parallel (50° N.) 0.84″; distance apart of meridians on standard parallel, 0.11″; distance apart of parallels, 0.17″–0.175″.

so that like a cylinder or cone it could be unrolled upon a plane, map-making would be an easy matter.

A map would simply be a copy of the unrolled surface on a reduced scale. The map would be *orthomorphic*, i.e. a small area would retain its shape, or the scale of length would be the same in all directions round a point; it would also be *equal-area*, i.e. the scale of areas would be the same all over the map.

With the earth as it is, a map may have either of those valuable qualities at our discretion, but it cannot have both, and in some important projections it has neither. Of orthomorphic projections the best known is *Mercator's projection*, in which meridians and parallels are straight lines at right angles to each other, the meridians being correctly spaced at their equatorial distances.

Every parallel is of the same length, so that the scale is much exaggerated in high latitudes, and the map is useless near the poles. A straight line on the map represents a *rhumb line*, i.e. a line cutting the meridians at a constant angle. A ship keeping a constant course must therefore follow a straight line on the map. On account of this convenient property, Mercator's projection is still universally used at sea.

Another important orthomorphic projection is the *stereographic*. This is a true projection in the geometrical sense (*see* GEOMETRY), the centre of projection being a point on the surface, and the plane of projection the tangent plane at the antipodal point. In a *conical projection*, meridians are represented by straight lines converging to a centre, and parallels by the concentric circles at right angles to these lines. In the *simple conical* projection, the scale is correct along every meridian, and also along one standard parallel.

This projection can be made nearly true to scale over a fairly wide region, and it has been used a great deal for atlas maps. *Bonne's projection* is a modification, in which the parallels are concentric circles, all divided truly, and the meridians are curves formed by joining up corresponding points on the parallels. This projection is equal-area, and has been used in official surveys in France, Scotland, and Ireland.

Another modified conical projection is the orthomorphic with two standard parallels, usually called *Lambert's second projection.* The maps used by the Allies in France in the later stages of the European War were of this type.

The *zenithal*, or *azimuthal projection* is a conical projection in which distances from the centre are given to scale, and angles between central radii are shown of their true size, whereas in conical projections in general the complete area round the pole is shown as a sector of a circle. A zenithal projection may have its centre or zenith at any point, not necessarily at the north or south pole as in conical projections in general.

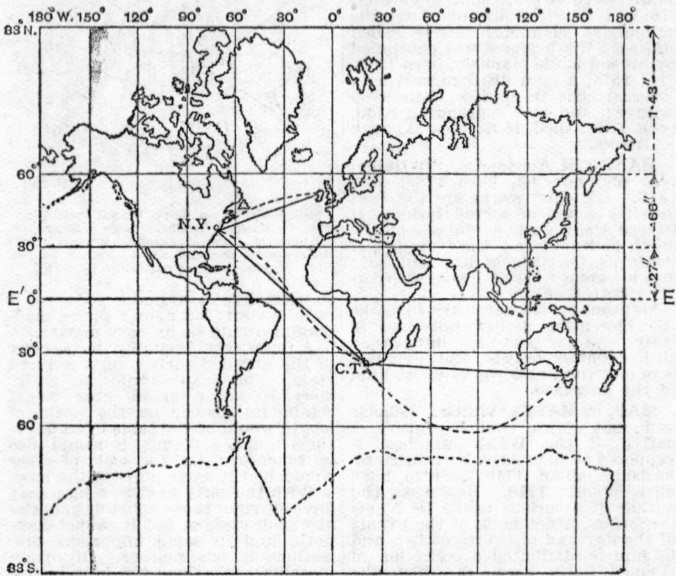

The World on Mercator's Projection

Scale, 1/500,000,000. On left, distances of parallel on map from Equator. Broken lines are great circles. Straight lines are rhumb lines.

The choice of a projection depends on the purpose of the map. If distribution statistics are to be illustrated, an equal-area map is obviously the one to choose. If distances and bearings from a certain point are wanted, a zenithal map with that point as centre is best. For areas of no great extent, however, the results given by the ordinary projections are hardly distinguishable from each other.

The International Map Committee, London, 1909, recommended for the projected map of the world, on the scale 1/1,000,000, the *polyconic* projection, in which the central meridian is divided truly, and the parallels are circles also divided truly, not concentric, but with the radius of each a certain simple function of the latitude.

It has been calculated that on this projection the maximum error of scale of a meridian is 1/1270, and of a parallel 1/3200; and that the greatest alteration in azimuth is six minutes of arc. For the early history of map-making, with illustrations, *see* GEOGRAPHY. *See also* NAVIGATION; SURVEYING.—BIBLIOGRAPHY: A. Germain, *Traité des projections des cartes géographiques*; E. A. Reeves, *Maps and Map-making*; A. R. Hinks, *Map Projections*; Mary Adams, *A Little Book on Map Projection*; A. Stevens, *Applied Geography*.

MA'PLE. A name for trees of the genus Acer, nat, ord. Aceraceæ or Sapindaceæ, peculiar to the northern and temperate parts of the globe. About fifty species are known, distributed through Europe, North America, and different parts of Asia. They are small or large trees, with a sweetish, rarely milky, sap, opposite, deciduous, simple, usually lobed leaves, and axillary and terminal racemes or corymbs of small greenish flowers.

Two species are common in Britain, the great maple, often miscalled sycamore (*A. Pseudo-platănus*), and the common maple (*A. campestre*). The wood of the former is valuable for various purposes, as for carving, turnery, musical instruments, wooden dishes, etc. Another well-known species is the Norway maple (*A. platanoides*), often planted in Britain as an ornamental tree.

The wood of several American species is also applied to various uses. The sugar or rock maple (*A. saccharinum*) is the most important species; this yields maple-sugar, which in many parts of North America is an important article of manufacture. A tree of ordinary size will yield from 15 to 30 gall. of sap yearly, from which are made from 2 to 4 lb. of sugar. The knotted parts of the sugar-maple furnish the pretty *bird's-eye maple* of cabinet-makers.

Some other American species are the white maple (*A. dasycarpum*), the red or swamp maple (*A. rubrum*), the striped maple or moose wood (*A. pennsylvanicum*), the mountain maple (*A. spicatum*), the vine maple (*A. circinatum*), and the large-leaved maple (*A. macrophyllum*).

MÂQUIS (Fr.), or **MACCHIA** (It.). A kind of dense, low, scrubby forest, composed of a great variety of shrubs and small trees with leathery, usually entire, evergreen leaves, characteristic of the Mediterranean lands with cool, moist winters, and hot, dry summers. It is seen to perfection in Corsica. The same sort of vegetation recurs in other countries with a similar climate, such as the Cape, California ("chapparal"), Chile, and Western Australia.

MAR, Earl of. Scottish title held by the family of Erskine. Mar is a district in Aberdeenshire and in early times was under one of the seven Scottish earls, but the line became extinct in the fifteenth century. In 1565 the title was given to John Erskine, but his descendant lost his lands and titles for siding with the Pretender in 1715. In 1824 the earldom was revived for a member of the Erskine family, who, in 1835, became also Earl of Kellie. In 1866 he died, and there was a long dispute about the title. It was given in 1875 to the Earl of Kellie, and its holder is now known as the Earl of Mar and Kellie. His eldest son is called Lord Erskine.

In 1885 the title of Earl of Mar was given to J. F. Goodeve-Erskine, and his descendant still holds it. Owing to this unusual procedure there are two Earls of Mar. The one held by the family of Goodeve Erskine was given precedence from 1405; the earl's eldest son is called Lord Garioch (pron. Gherry).

MAR'ABOU-STORK. The name given to two species of storks, the delicate white feathers beneath the wing and tail of which form the beautiful and ornamental marabou-feathers. One species is a native of West Africa (*Leptoptilus crumenifer*); another is common in India, where it is generally called the *adjutant* ((q.v.).

MAR'ABOUTS, or **MARABUTS.** Among the Berbers of Northern Africa a sort of saints or sorcerers, who are held in high estimation, and who exercise in some villages a despotic authority. They distribute amulets, affect to work miracles, and are thought to exercise the gift of prophecy. Among the Rifi more than among the more Arabicized Berbers (Jebala) the Koranic doctrine and precepts are only nominally embraced, and there is a multitudinous array of marabouts. —The name Marabouts is also used as equivalent to Almoravides (q.v.).

MARACAIBO. The chief seaport of Venezuela, provincial capital of Zulia, on the strait uniting the *lago* and Gulf of Maracaibo. The harbour is small and bad between October and April. Coffee, rubber, cocoa, and sugar, with some timber, hides, and ores, are exported. There is a wireless station. Population, 74,767.

The **gran lago de Maracaibo** is a large Venezuelan freshwater lagoon 130 miles long, connected by a strait with the Gulf of Maracaibo (or Venezuela), an arm of the Caribbean. The gulf was discovered by Ojeda in 1499, and, from the houses of the indigenous population being built on piles, he named the district Venezuela (Little Venice).

MARACHESTI. Town of Rumania. It is in Moldavia, 12 miles from Focsani, on the River Sereth, and is an important railway junction. It has two broadcasting stations (76 and 48·95 metres).

In Aug., 1916, an army of Austrians and Germans, then invading Rumania, was met by a defending army near this town. A battle began on Aug. 13 and continued for some days. A succession of German attacks continued until the 19th, when the battle ceased without decisive result, but the Germans did not advance farther into the country.

MARAJO, or **JOHANNES.** An island of Pará, Brazil, formed by the estuaries of the Amazon and Pará (Tocantins); length, 180 miles; breadth, 125 miles. Rubber is yielded.

MARANHÃO. A maritime state of North-Eastern Brazil, bounded by the Rivers Gurupy, Parnahyba, and the Middle Pará (Tocantins). It is partly afforested, well watered, and produces vanilla, tobacco, cotton, sugar, timber, copper, and gold. São Luiz is the capital. Area, 177,515 sq. miles; pop. 1,140,635.

MARANTA'CEÆ. An order of endogenous plants, growing in tropical countries; called also *Cannaceæ.* They are perennial herbs with fibrous roots or fleshy creeping rhizomes, alternate simple leaves with sheathing footstalks, and irregular racemose or panicled flowers. The type-genus is Maranta (arrowroot).

MARAT (mȧ-rä), **Jean Paul.** One of the most radical leaders of the French Revolution, born near Neufchâtel 1744, died 1793. He studied medicine at Paris, and previous to 1 89 had spent many years in travel, visiting London, Edinburgh, Dublin, Amsterdam. The first breath of the Revolution, however, brought him to the front, and when Danton instituted the club of the Cordeliers, Marat became the editor of the *Publiciste Parisien*, better known under its later title *L'Ami du Peuple*, which was again changed to the *Journal de la République Française*,

Jean Paul Marat

a journal which was the organ of that society, and soon became the oracle of the mob.

It early advocated the most extreme measures, and the tone became more furious as Marat was inflamed by the prosecutions of the authorities. His paper was issued from various places of concealment until 10th Aug., 1792, after which he took his seat at the Commune, and played a leading part in the assassinations of Sept., 1792. He was a member of the Committee of Public Safety, and of the Convention, where General Dumouriez and the Girondists, who endeavoured at first to prevent his taking his seat, were the special objects of his attack.

The establishment of the revolutionary tribunal, and of the committee for arresting the suspected, was adopted on his motions. On the approach of 31st May, as president of the Jacobin Club he signed an address instigating the people to an insurrection, and to massacre all traitors. For this Marat was delivered over to the revolutionary tribunal, which acquitted him; and the people received him in triumph and covered him with wreaths. He was assassinated shortly after by Charlotte Corday. His remains were deposited in the Pantheon with national honours, but were subsequently removed.—Cf. E. B. Bax, *Jean Paul Marat: the People's Friend.*

MARĀTHI (ma-rät′hē). A language of India, closely allied to Sanskrit and written in the Sanskrit character. It is the vernacular of some sixteen millions of people, mostly in the North-West Deccan. It is divided into two great groups, the Konkani, and the Dakhani, and comprises several dialects. *See* INDIA.

MAR′ATHON. A village of ancient Greece, in Attica, about 20 miles north-east of Athens. It was situated (probably on the site of the modern Vrana) on a plain which extends for about 6 miles along the seashore, with a breadth of from 1½ to 3 miles. It is famous for the overthrow of the Persians by the Athenians under Miltiades, 490 B.C.

MARATTIACEÆ. The principal family of Eusporangiate Ferns (q.v.), comprising about twenty-five species of tropical ferns, with stout, fleshy stems, and large, leathery, usually pinnate leaves. The sporangia, generally united into groups, are bulky and numerous, and the prothallus is also stouter and longer lived than that of ordinary ferns Chief genera: Angiopteris, Danæa, Marattia, Psaronius (fossil).

MARAZION. Market town and seaport of Cornwall, also called Market Jew. It stands on Mounts Bay, 4 miles from Penzance, on the G.W. Railway, and the chief industry is fishing. Until 1835 Marazion had its own mayor and corporation. There is a causeway from here to St. Michael's Mount, and in the Middle Ages the town was much visited by pilgrims. Pop. 1200.

MARBLE. The name given to certain varieties of limestone which show ornamental characters when polished, and which, both from their durability and the beauty of the tints of many of them, have at all periods of the world been greatly in request for purposes of art or ornament. White statuary marble is a mass of pure granular crystals of calcite.

Marbles have been divided into many varieties, such as *marbles of a uniform colour,* comprehending solely those which are either white or black; *variegated marbles,* in which the spots and veins are interlaced and disposed without regularity; *shell marbles,* in which the fossil shells provide an ornamental feature; *cipollino marbles,* which are veined with mica; and *breccia marbles,* which are formed of angular fragments of various marbles united by a cement of some different colour.

Black marbles are coloured by a small percentage of carbon; red by iron hydroxide; and green by chlorite, green mica, or, in some handsome examples, by serpentine. By *antique marbles* is understood those kinds made use of by the ancients, the quarries of which have in several cases been reopened by modern enterprise. These include Parian marble, Pentelic marble, Carrara marble, *rooso antico, giallo antico, verde antico,* etc.

MARBLE ARCH. Gateway near the north entrance to Hyde Park. A copy of a Roman arch, it was designed by George Nash in 1828 as an entrance to Buckingham Palace. In 1851 it was removed to its present site. In 1930-31 new buildings made great changes near the Arch, which gives its name to a station on the Central London Tube Railway.

MARBURG. A town of Hesse-Nassau, Prussia, Germany, on the Lahn. Among its buildings are the thirteenth-century castle of the Landgraves of Hesse, the university (1527), and the church of St. Elizabeth, built by the Teutonic Knights. Pop. 23,299.

MARBURG. *See* MARIBOR.

MAR′CASITE. Orthorhombic iron pyrites or bisulphide of iron. It is of a paler colour than ordinary iron pyrites, the cubic pyrite being nearly of the colour of tin, as is seen when it is cleaned with hydrochloric acid. It decomposes on exposure to the atmosphere more readily than pyrite, and fossil remains replaced or infilled by it commonly go to pieces in collections.

MARCELLUS, Marcus Claudius. A Roman general, five times consul (222, 215, 214, 210, and 208 B.C.); the first Roman who successfully encountered Hannibal in the second Punic War; and the conqueror of Syracuse (212 B.C.). He was killed in a skirmish with the Carthaginians in 208 B.C.

MARCH. Originally the first month of the Roman year. Till the adoption of the new style in England (1752), the 25th of March was the first day of the legal year; hence January, February, and the first twenty-four days of March have frequently two years appended, as 1st January, 1701½, or 1701-2. Scotland adopted January as the first month of the year in 1599.

MARCH. Market town and urban district of Cambridgeshire, 30 miles from Cambridge on the L.N.E. Railway. The chief industry is engineering. Pop. (1931), 11,276.

MARCHANTIALES. A family of Liverworts, distinguished by the flat, lobed thallus, usually fleshy and with complicated internal structure, and the sessile or shortly-stalked capsule, which bursts irregularly. The type-genus is Marchantia; *M. polymorpha* is a very common plant.

MARCHES. The frontiers or boundaries of a territory. The term is most familiar as applied to the boundaries between England and Wales, and England and Scotland. The latter were divided into three portions, the western, the eastern, and the middle marches, each of which had courts peculiar to itself, and a kind of president or governor, who was called Warden of the Marches.

What is known as *riding the marches* is a practice still observed occasionally in some of the burghs of Scotland, the original object being to preserve in the memory of the inhabitants the limits of their property. In observing this practice the magistrates and chief men of the town, mounted on horseback, ride in procession along the boundaries of the town property, and perform various ceremonies.

MARCHES. A maritime compartimento of North-Eastern Italy, lying between the Apennines and the Adriatic, and comprising the provinces of Pesaro e Urbino, Ancona, Macerata, and Ascoli Piceno. Formerly a Papal possession, Marches was annexed to Italy by Victor Emmanuel (1860). Area, 3741 sq. miles; pop. (1931), 1,217,746.

MAR'CION. The founder of an ascetic Gnostic sect, called after him Marcionites, was born at Sinope about the beginning of the second century of our era, his father being Bishop of Sinope. He went to Rome about A.D. 140, and founded a system which assumed the existence of three original principles—the supreme and invisible, whom Marcion called the Good; the visible God, the Creator; and the Devil, or perhaps matter, the source of evil. Marcion could not perceive in nature, or in the Old Testament, the same love which was in the Gospel of Christ.

He accordingly made the Creator, the God of the Old Testament, the author of suffering. Jesus was not the Messiah promised by this being, but the Son of the unseen God, who took the form, but not the substance, of man. Marcion denied the resurrection of the body; he condemned marriage, thinking it wrong to increase a race born in subjection to the harsh rule of the Creator. He was vigorously attacked by Tertullian and others, but his sect lasted for several centuries.

MARCOMAN'NI, or **MARKOMANNI.** The name of an ancient German tribe or tribal league, apparently originally marchmen or borderers on the Rhenish frontier. They subsequently migrated east, displaced the Boii from their territory (the modern Bohemia), and under their king, Maroboduus, formed a great Marcomannic confederacy to hinder the extension of the Roman power beyond Pannonia. Being defeated, however, by a rival confederacy composed of the Cherusci and their allies, they entered into more or less friendly relations with Rome until the time of Domitian, whom they defeated. In A.D. 166 they invaded Pannonia, and commenced the long *Marcomannic War.* In the reign of Aurelian they even threatened Rome itself. After that, however, they practically pass out of history.

MARCO'NI, Guglielmo. Inventor of a practical system of wireless

Guglielmo Marconi

telegraphy, was born at Bologna 1874, his mother being an Irishwoman, and was educated at Leghorn and at Bologna University. After experimenting at Bologna, in 1899 he established wireless communication across the Channel, between England and France. In 1901 he established communication between Cornwall and St. John's, Newfoundland (2100 miles), in 1902 between England and Canada, and in the same year between England and the United States.

In 1910 Marconi received messages at Buenos Aires from Clifden in Ireland. In 1918 he sent the first wireless messages from England to Australia. During the European War Marconi served in the Italian army and navy. He was Italian plenipotentiary at the Peace Conference in Paris in 1919. In 1909 he shared the Nobel Prize for physics, and was nominated by the King of Italy to be a member of the Italian Senate. For further details of the early history and later developments of wireless communication see the article WIRELESS TELEGRAPHY.

MARDIN'. A town of Kurdistan, Turkey, 50 miles S.S.E. of Diarbekr, on the slopes of a castle-crowned hill. It has bazaars and khans. Pop. 23,252.

MAREE. A loch of Scotland, county of Ross and Cromarty. It is 13½ miles long.

MAREMMA. A coastal marsh area of Tuscany, Italy, extending along the Tyrrhenian seaboard from Cecina to Orbetello, and inland for 15 to 20 miles. Anciently it was drained by underground channels which fell into disrepair.

MARENGO. A village of Alessandria, North Italy, where Napoleon defeated the Austrians under Melas, 14th June, 1800. As a consequence North Italy was ceded to France.

MARE'S TAIL (Hippūris). A genus of plants with whorled narrow leaves and small inconspicuous flowers set in their axils. They are aquatic or marsh plants. *H. vulgaris* is common in Great Britain.

MARGAM. District of the borough of Port Talbot, Glamorganshire, Wales, a coal-mining centre, near Aberavon. The chief building is the restored church once a Cistercian abbey, of which some ruins, including the chapter house, remain. Near is Margam Abbey, long the seat of the Mansel and Talbot families. The estate was sold in 1921.

MARGARET. Queen of Denmark, Norway, and Sweden, the daughter of Waldemar IV., King of Denmark, born at Copenhagen in 1353, died in 1412. She was married to Haakon VI., King of Norway, in 1363. The death of her husband in 1380 placed Norway in her hands; that of her son Olaf in 1387 enabled her to secure the throne of Denmark, to which she had previously brought about his election; and after defeating Albert, the Swedish king, she also obtained possession of the throne of Sweden.

She endeavoured to place the union of the three kingdoms on a permanent basis by the celebrated Act of Union, or Treaty of Kalmar (1397), and raised herself to a degree of power then unequalled in Europe since the time of Charlemagne.

MARGARET. The daughter of Edward and elder sister of Eadgar Ætheling; after the Norman Conquest took refuge with her brother at the court of Malcolm Canmore of Scotland, whom she shortly afterwards married. She is said to have introduced into Scotland the higher culture of the English court, and to have effected many reforms in the Scottish Church. She died in 1093. Her daughter Matilda married Henry I.

MARGARET. Known as **Margaret of Angoulême,** sister to Francis I. of France, was born at Angoulême in 1492, died in 1549. She was brought up at the court of Louis XII., and married the duc d'Alençon in 1509, became a widow in 1525, and in 1527 was espoused to Henri d'Albret, comte de Béarn and titular king of Navarre. From this time she resided at Béarn, assisting in the development of the resources of the small kingdom, and making it a centre of liberal influence. Many Protestants took refuge in her territories; and her name is closely linked with those of Rabelais, Dolet, Marot, and the leading men of the period.

She herself possessed no ordinary culture, being credited with a knowledge of six languages and the authorship of several works, of which the chief were: *Le Miroir de l'âme pécheresse,* printed in 1553 and condemned by the Sorbonne its Protestant tendencies; the for *Heptaméron,* a collection of tales in imitation of the *Decameron* of Boccaccio, and first printed in 1559; and a collection of poems published in 1547 under the title of *Marguerites de la Marguerite des princesses.* She left one child, Jeanne d'Albret, afterwards mother of Henry IV.—Cf. M. G. Fawcett, *Five Famous Frenchwomen.*

MARGARET OF ANJOU. Daughter of René of Anjou and Provence, titular king of Sicily, was born in Lorraine in 1430, and died in 1482. She married Henry VII. of England in 1445. The king's weakness gave scope for her ambition, and her power being contested by the Duke of York, a claimant of the throne by an elder line, the protracted Wars of the Roses commenced.

At first victorious, she was afterwards compelled to flee to Scotland, but raising an army in the north, she secured, by the battles of Wakefield (1460) and St. Albans (1461), the death of York and the release of the king. Her army, however, was soon afterwards annihilated at Towton (1461), and Edward (IV.), son of the late Duke of York, was declared king.

She succeeded in obtaining assistance from Louis XI. of France, but was once more defeated, and took refuge in France. Warwick then became embroiled with the young king, and determined to replace Henry on the throne. Edward was in turn obliged to escape to the Continent, but, obtaining assistance from the Duke of Burgundy, returned and defeated Warwick at Barnet (1471).

Margaret, collecting her partisans, fought the battle of Tewkesbury (1471), but was totally defeated. She and her son were made prisoners, and the latter was killed. Henry soon after died or was murdered in the Tower, and Margaret remained in prison four years. Louis XI. ransomed her for 50,000 crowns.

MAR'GARINE. Oleomargarine, or margarine, is used as a substitute for normal dairy butter. The better varieties usually have " oleo oil " as their base, and form a food of very good quality.

Butter fat is a mixture of the glycerides of oleic, stearic, palmitic, lauric, and other acids. (A glyceride is a chemical combination of a fatty acid and glycerol.) Since the same glycerides are present in other fats and fatty oils, a product can be made closely resembling butter, physically, chemically, and in flavour, from substances outside the province of the dairy.

The best fat is removed from newly killed oxen or sheep, washed to remove blood, etc., chilled quickly in ice-water, finely shredded and rendered, i.e. melted with a little water and sodium carbonate at the lowest possible temperature, usually between 65° to 66° C. The product, called *Premier Jus,* is allowed to solidify for twenty-four hours, when it is hydraulically pressed, and the soft oil obtained is " oleo oil " or " oleopalmitin," the yield being 50 to 60 per cent. on the fat. Oil-refining can be so carried out that a colourless and tasteless oil is obtained, which may therefore be easily coloured and flavoured as desired.

Twenty-four gallons of separated pasteurized milk containing a butter " starter," which is a culture carefully prepared in the bacteriological laboratory, is mixed with enough eleo oil to give one thousand pounds of margarine. For the highest qualities, 10 per cent. creamery butter, or cream, may be added. Churning takes one hour, and is done at a temperature of 20° to 45° C., the lower temperature preserving the flavour and thus giving a better product.

In this way the " oil " is given the smell and taste of butter. According to the grade desired, neutral lard, coco-nut oil (the substitute for butter used by vegetarians), cottonseed, earth-nut, palm kernel, sesame, or other oils may be added, the proportions depending upon the destination of the product—more oleo oil for a warm climate, more neutral lard for a cold climate. For preparing lard, the perfectly fresh leaf of the pig is rendered between 40° to 50° C., producing best quality neutral lard with about 0·25 per cent. free fatty acid. This lard is incorporated with the oleo oil, milk, etc.

During the churning, casein and milk-sugar may be added to confer the properties of browning and frothing, as butter does when melted. " Elaine," a product from yolk of egg, may also be added. The churned mixture is run in a very thin stream between two large drums revolving in the same direction, set close together, and internally cooled to −10° C. In this way all ingredients are retained, the margarine is set, and a uniform flavour and texture is obtained.

The margarine is scraped from the drums, allowed to ripen, kneaded to get rid of excess water and obtain uniformity. At an earlier stage, salt and colouring matter may or may not have been added. These help to give the product the flavour and appearance of butter. The same colouring matter as that used by dairymen for butter is employed, viz. annatto dissolved in vegetable oil, extract of carrot or marigold, turmeric and alum, etc. Sometimes an azo dye is used, but a vegetable dye is considered better. The margarine is then moulded and packed for market.

As a food, some hold that margarine is scarcely inferior to butter; but others deny this, insisting on the paramount importance of the vitamines which are present in normal butter fat but not in margarine.

MARGARI'TA. A Caribbean island, separated by the Strait of Margarita from Venezuela, to which it belongs. It is mountainous (Macanao, 4484 feet). The Margarita littoral is a Caribbean pearl-fishery. La Asunción (pop. 3000) is the capital, but the harbour and town are in great part ruinous. Pampatar is the chief port. Margarita was discovered by Columbus (1498), and is now the main constituent of the insular state of Neuva Esparta (q.v.). Pop. about 50,000.

MAR'GATE. A municipal borough and watering-place, Isle of Thanet, Kent, England, served by the Southern Railway and in steamboat communication with London, for whose inhabitants it forms a favourite resort. It has a curious grotto, discovered in 1837, and many amusements. The eastern part is known as Cliftonville. In 1931 a new general hospital was opened. Margate was much damaged by German air-craft during the European War. Pop. (1931), 31,312.

MAR'GAY. An American animal of the cat kind, the *Felis tigrina*, which ranges from Mexico to Paraguay. It is about the size of the domestic cat, is of a pale-fawn colour, with black bands on the fore-parts, and leopard-like spots on the hind-parts and on the long bushy tail. It has been domesticated and made very useful in rat-killing.

MARGHILAN. A town of Turkistan, Russian Central Asia. Silk and woollen goods are manufactured. Marghilan is the traditional burial-place of Alexander the Great. Pop. 49,318.—Nine miles south is **Novo Marghilan,** a European-style city, and nominal capital of the former province of Ferghana. Pop. about 12,000.

MAR'GRAVE (Ger. *markgraf*, count of the mark). Originally a commander entrusted with the protection of a *mark*, or country on the frontier. The margraves acquired the rank of princes in the former German Empire.

MARIANNE ISLANDS. *See* LADRONES.

MARIA THERESA. Queen of Hungary and Bohemia, Archduchess of Austria, and Empress of Germany, daughter of the Emperor Charles VI., was born at Vienna 1717, and died 1780. In 1736 she married Francis Stephen, duc de Lorraine. On the death of her father in 1740 she ascended the throne of Hungary, Bohemia, and Austria, and a little later declared her husband joint ruler. Her accession was in accordance with the Pragmatic Sanction, but her claims were at once contested. *See* AUSTRIA-HUNGARY.

During the time of peace which followed the Treaty of Aix-la-Chapelle (1748), Maria Theresa, with the aid of her husband and the minister Kaunitz, made great financial reforms; agriculture, manufactures, and commerce flourished, the national revenue greatly increased, and the burdens were diminished. The Seven Years' War once again reduced Austria to a state of great exhaustion and destitution. Of the sixteen children which she bore to the emperor ten survived her, one of whom was the unfortunate Marie Antoinette.—BIBLIOGRAPHY: M. Moffatt, *Maria Theresa*; J. F. Bright, *Maria Theresa.*

MARIBOR. A town of Styria, Yugoslavia, on the Drave. There is a sixteenth-century cathedral, and a bishop's palace. Railway rolling-stock and boots are manufactured; trade is good in wine and agricultural produce. Pop. (1931), 33,149.

MARIE ANTOINETTE (ån-twå-net; **MARIE ANTOINETTE JOSEPH JEANNE DE LORRAINE**). Archduchess of Austria and Queen of France, the youngest daughter of the Emperor Francis I. and of Maria Theresa, was born at Vienna 2nd Nov., 1755; guillotined at Paris 16th Oct., 1793. Married at the age of fifteen to the Dauphin, afterwards Louis XVI., her manners were ill-suited to the French court, and she made many powerful enemies by her contempt for its ceremonies.

The affair of the diamond necklace, in which the Cardinal Louis de Rohan, Joseph Balsamo, comte de Cagliostro and the comtesse de Lamotte (q.v.) were the chief actors, cast a stigma on her, and the *canaille* subsequently laid every public disaster to her charge. There is no doubt she had great influence over the king, and that she constantly opposed all measures of reform.

The enthusiastic reception given her at the guards' ball at Versailles on 1st Oct., 1789, raised the general indignation to the highest pitch, and was followed in a few days by the insurrection of women, and the attack on Versailles. When practically a prisoner in the Tuileries, it was the queen who advised the disastrous flight of the royal family (June, 1791). On 10th Aug., 1792, she heard her husband's deposition pronounced by the Legislative Assembly, and accompanied him to the Temple Prison, where in Jan., 1793, they were parted after Louis's condemnation by the Convention.

In August she was removed to the Conciergerie; and in October she was charged before the revolutionary tribunal with having dissipated the finances, exhausted the Treasury, corresponded with the foreign enemies of France, and favoured the domestic foes of the country. She defended herself vigorously, and heard the sentence of death pronounced with a calmness born of hopeless resignation, which did not forsake her when the sentence was carried out the following morning.—BIBLIOGRAPHY: The best modern books are Pierre de Nolhac's *Marie-Antoinette Dauphine* and *La Reine Marie-Antoinette*. (The author is conservator at Versailles.)

MARIE DE MEDICI (må-rē dė med'i-chē). The daughter of Francis II. of Tuscany, was born in 1573, and died in 1642. She married in 1600 Henry IV. of France. On the assassination of Henry she became

Marie de Medici

regent, but proved utterly incompetent to rule. Her partiality for unworthy favourites caused her deposition and imprisonment. She escaped, and after wandering through several countries died in misery at Cologne.

MARIE GALANTE. A French West Indian island, one of the five dependencies of Guadeloupe. It produces sugar, coffee, tobacco, indigo, and cotton. The name Marie Galante is that of the ship of Columbus who discovered the island (1493). Area, 55 sq. miles; pop. about 18,000.

MARIE LOUISE. Second wife of Napoleon I., born in 1791, died 1847, eldest daughter of the Emperor Francis I. of Austria. Her marriage with Napoleon took place in 1810 after the divorce of Josephine, and in 1811 she bore him a son. After his overthrow she received in 1816 the Duchies of Parma, Piacenza, and Guastalla, which she governed till her death. At Napoleon's death she made a morganatic marriage with her chamberlain, Count Neipperg.

MARIENBAD, or **MARIANSKE LAZNE.** Since 1808 an inland watering-place, formerly of Bohemia, Austria, but now of Czechoslovakia. It was often visited by King Edward VII. It became known in the nineteenth century owing to the curative properties of its mineral springs for gout and diabetes. Pop. about 7000.

MARIENBURG. A town of Germany in East Prussia, on the Nogat. There are saw-, cotton-, and flour-mills. Marienburg was the seat of the

The Marientor, Marienburg

Grand Master of the Teutonic Order from 1309. The town passed to Poland in 1457. The enormous castle of the

Knights is still extant. Pop. about 21,039.

MAR'IGOLD. A name of several composite plants. The common marigold (*Calendŭla officinālis*) is a native of France and of the more southern parts of Europe. It is an annual, from 1 to 2 feet high, with large deep-yellow flowers. It is as prolific as any weed, and was formerly used in broths and soups, partly to give colour and partly as an aromatic seasoning. It had also many medicinal virtues assigned to it.

A number of species of this genus are indigenous to the Cape of Good Hope. The so-called African marigold and French marigold, common in flower borders, are both Mexican species, and have brilliant flowers. They belong to the genus Tagētes. The corn-marigold is *Chrysanthĕmum segĕtum*; the fig-marigold is a species of *Mesembryanthemum*; the marsh-marigold is *Caltha palustris*.

MARINDUQUE. One of the Philippine islands, directly south of Luzon, and a division of the province of Tabayas. Copra, rice, hemp, and coco-nuts, with some tobacco, are produced, and cattle are raised. It is well wooded. Boac is the chief town. Area, 352 sq. miles; pop. 53,000.

MARINES. The name used to designate certain bodies of troops raised and organized for the dual purpose of serving either on shore or afloat on His Majesty's ships. In the days when troops were raised as required for special campaigns or undertakings it did not much matter whether they fought on land or at sea; in either case it was largely a matter of hand-to-hand encounters, and bodies of troops were used indiscriminately either on land or on board ship.

The first record of a body of troops being raised especially for the sea service is in 1664, when Charles II.—no doubt with the idea of somewhat increasing his standing army, while at the same time hoodwinking the Parliament by calling it a sea-regiment—gave orders for the embodiment of "The Duke of York and Albany's Maritime Regiment of Foot," to consist of 1200 "land soldiers."

This maritime regiment was first dressed in yellow coats with scarlet breeches and stockings, but this uniform was very soon changed to scarlet coats, lined yellow, with dark grey breeches.

For the next ninety years the fate of the maritime regiments was identical with that of most other regiments of the period; that is to say, they were raised, disbanded, transferred to the line, or raised again as necessity arose. The present 1st East Lancashire, 1st East Surrey, and 1st Duke of Cornwall's Light Infantry all started life as marine or maritime regiments. Then in 1755 it was decided to raise a permanent force of marines, which was to consist of fifty companies formed into three divisions, with headquarters at Chatham, Portsmouth, and Plymouth. The uniform was red with white facings.

Thereafter, wherever there was fighting or naval activity, the marines held their own, and in 1802, in recognition of their services, were designated "Royal" and their facings altered from white to blue, remaining so to the present day.

In the following year certain artillery companies provided by the Royal Artillery were attached to the corps, and in the 'fifties of last century these were definitely incorporated in the Royal Marines, which became separated into two distinct divisions, known as the Royal Marine Artillery and the Royal Marine Light Infantry. And so they remained till 1923, the uniform being blue in the first and scarlet in the second, in each case with the Royal Marine badge, the "globe and laurel," and the motto *Per Mare per Terram.*

The Royal Marines are administered by the Admiralty, and the expense of the force is a charge against the Admiralty vote. Men enlist for twelve years, with power to re-engage to complete twenty-one. When serving ashore the Royal Marines are subject to the Army Act, when afloat to the Naval Discipline Act. In Oct., 1923, the Royal Marine Artillery and the Royal Marine Light Infantry were amalgamated.

MARIO, Giuseppe (Marquis di Candia). A famous tenor, born at Turin in 1808, died 1883. In Paris in 1838, under the assumed name of Mario, he accepted an appointment as first tenor of the opera, and a year later was secured for the Théâtre Italien. In 1839 he made his first appearance in London, and for many seasons subsequently divided his time between London, Paris, and Russia. He took farewell of the London stage in 1871, and retired to Paris, afterwards to Rome; but subsequently lost his large fortune by speculation.

MARIOTTE, Edme. A French mathematician and natural philosopher, born in Burgundy 1620, died in 1684. He made many important discoveries in hydrostatics and hydraulics.

MARIŞK. An autonomous region of the Russian Socialist Federal Republic, in Central Asia, immediately north-west of the Tatar Republic; area, 54,263 sq. miles; pop. 482,519. Krasmokokshaisk is the capital.

MARITIME PROVINCE. The geographical nomenclature indicating proximity to the sea or ocean, e.g. the Maritime Provinces of Canada—Nova Scotia, New Brunswick, and Prince Edward Island. The name (Russ. *Primorskaya Oblast*) is particularly applied to the narrow Siberian coastal belt extending northwards to Ayan from the Korea-Manchurian frontiers.

MARIT'SA (ancient **Hebrus**). A river rising in the Rhodope Mountains (Bulgaria) and flowing through Eastern Roumelia, south-east to Edirne (Adrianople), where it bends to the south-west, and falls into the Ægean Sea by the Gulf of Enos. It is over 300 miles long, and navigable to Edirne, about 100 miles from its mouth.

MARIUPOL. A seaport of Yekaterinoslav, Southern Russia, on the Sea of Azov; the terminus of a branch of the Kharkov-Taganrog Railway. Cereals, coal, and linseed are exported. Pop. 54,528, mainly Greeks.

MA'RIUS, Gaius. A Roman general, born 157 B.C., of obscure parents, at the village of Cereatæ, near Arpinum, died in 86 B.C. He served with distinction at Numantia in 134 B.C. under Scipio Africanus; was made tribune of the people in 119, and acquired much popularity by his opposition to the nobles. In 115 B.C. he was appointed prætor, and a year later proprætor of Spain, which he cleared of bandits; he also increased his influence by his marriage with Julia, the aunt of Julius Cæsar.

In 109 B.C. he accompanied the Consul Q. Cæcilius Metellus as his lieutenant to the Jugurthine War. He brought this war and the war in Transalpine Gaul against the Teutons to a victorious close; and was chosen consul six times. On the outbreak of the war against Mithridates, Marius, who had long been jealous of Sulla, endeavoured to deprive him of his command, and in the struggle which followed was compelled to flee from Italy. After hairbreadth escapes he landed in Africa amid the ruins of Carthage, and remained there until recalled by Cinna, who had headed a successful movement in his favour.

In company with Cinna he marched against Rome, which was obliged to yield, the entry of Marius and his followers being attended with the massacre of most of his chief opponents. On the completion of the term of Cinna's consulship he declared himself and Marius consuls, but the latter died seventeen days later at the age of seventy.—Cf. A. H. J. Greenidge, *History of Rome.*

MARIVAUX (mà-rē-vō), **Pierre Carlet de Chamblain de.** French dramatic writer and novelist, born at Paris 4th Feb., 1688, died 12th Feb., 1763. After writing three or four novels and a series of articles of the *Spectator* type, from 1720 onwards he produced a large number of plays, the best being the *Surprise de l'Amour* (1722), the *Jeu de l'Amour et du Hasard* (1730), and *Les Fausses Confidences* (1737). They were characterized by a certain skilfully embroidered phrasing which gave rise to the term *marivaudage.* Two uncompleted novels, *Marianne* and the *Paysan Parvenu*, contain much excellent work. He was made an Academician in 1736.—Cf. Jean Fleury, *Marivaux et le Marivaudage.*

MAR'JORAM (Origănum). A genus of plants of the nat. ord. Labiatæ. The common marjoram (*Origănum vulgāre*) a native of Britain, is a perennial under-shrub, growing among copse-wood in calcareous soils. The leaves are small and acute; the flowers reddish, in clustered spikes. Sweet marjoram (*O. Majorāna*) is a biennial, cultivated in gardens. As soon as it blossoms it is cut and dried for culinary use, being employed as a seasoning.

MARK (A.-Sax. *marc*; Ger. *mark*). A term formerly used in England for a money of account, and in some other countries for a coin. The English mark was two-thirds of £1 sterling, or 13*s.* 4*d.*; and the Scottish mark, or *merk*, was two-thirds of £1 Scots, or 13⅓*d.* sterling.

In the coinage of Germany the *mark* was, before the European War, a coin of nearly the same value as the English shilling. After the War its value depreciated, until in 1922 it was worth only a fraction of a penny. In 1924 a new mark, called the Reichsmark, was introduced and given the value the mark had before the War (about 11¾*d.*). It is coined in silver and is issued in notes for 10 marks, 20 marks, and other denominations. In 1932 the rate of exchange on London varied from about 14 to 16 marks to the £. A *mark banco* used to be a money of account in Hamburg equal to nearly 1*s.* 6*d.*

MARK, St., the Evangelist. According to the old ecclesiastical writers, the person known in the Acts of the Apostles as "John, whose surname was Mark" (Acts xii. 12, 25), for many years the companion of Paul and Peter on their journeys. His mother, Mary, was generally in the train of Jesus, and Mark was himself present at a part of the events which he relates in his gospel, and received his information partly from eye-witnesses.

A cousin of Barnabas (Col. iv. 10), he accompanied Paul and the former to Antioch, Cyprus, and Perga in Pamphylia. He returned to Jerusalem, whence he afterwards went to Cyprus, and thence to Rome. He was the cause of the memorable "sharp contention" between Paul and Barnabas. Of the close of his career nothing is known; and it is by no means certain even that the various passages, on which the Church has based the biographical notes already cited, uniformly refer to the same individual.

MARKET BOSWORTH. A town of Leicestershire, England. There is an old grammar school, and the town has an agricultural trade. Near is the field where the battle was fought in which Richard III. was killed, 22nd Aug., 1485. Pop. (1931, rural district), 23,543.

MARKHAM, Sir Clements Robert. English geographer and traveller, born 1830, died 1916. Educated at Westminster School, he was in the navy from 1844 to 1851, after which he travelled in Peru, and published *Cuzco and Lima* (1856). In 1865-66 he visited Ceylon and India, and in 1867-68 accompanied the Abyssinian expedition, an account of which he wrote. He was made K.C.B. in 1896, and held several Government appointments. Other works of his are: *Life of The Great Lord Fairfax*, *Sketch of the History of Persia*, *Peruvian Bark*, *The War between Peru and Chile*, and a *Life of Columbus*.

MARL. A natural earthy substance, such as the "chalk marl," essentially composed of calcium carbonate and clay in various proportions. In some marls the argillaceous ingredient is comparatively small, while in others it abounds, and furnishes the predominant characters. The most general use of marl is to improve soils; the calcareous matter serves to lighten heavy clays, while the argillaceous matter may be useful in rendering sands more retentive of water. The quicker action and fine division of slaked lime, which passes promptly into calcium carbonate in the soil, has now generally led to its substitution for marl as a lightener of soils, and for other purposes for which calcium carbonate is required.

MARLBOROUGH, John Churchill, Duke of. English general and statesman, second son of Sir Winston Churchill, born at Ashe, in Devonshire, in 1650, died 16th June, 1722. At the age of twelve he became page to the Duke of York (afterwards James II.), by whom at sixteen he was appointed an ensign. He was present at the siege of Tangiers, and soon after his return rose to the rank of captain. In 1672 he accompanied

Marlborough

the Duke of Monmouth to assist Turenne against the Dutch.

At the siege of Maestricht he distinguished himself so highly as to obtain the public thanks of the King of France. On his return to England he was made lieutenant-colonel, and through the influence of his sister Arabella, mistress of the Duke of York, his advancement was rapid.

He had a regiment of dragoons presented to him, and strengthened his influence at court by his marriage with Sarah Jennings, an attendant upon the princess afterwards Queen Anne. In 1682 he obtained the title of Lord Churchill of Eyemouth, and a colonelcy in the guards. On the accession of James II. he was appointed Ambassador to France, and soon after his return was created Baron Churchill of Sundridge, and raised to the rank of general. The same year he suppressed the rebellion of the Duke of Monmouth. On the arrival of the Prince of Orange he joined him at Axminster, and was rewarded by the earldom of Marlborough, and the appointment of commander-in-chief of the English army in the Low Countries.

The following year he served in

Ireland, where he reduced Cork, Kinsale, and other places. In 1691 he was suddenly dismissed from all his employments and committed to the Tower on the charge of high treason, but soon obtained his release; though it appears that the suspicions against him were not without foundation.

On the death of Queen Mary he was made a Privy Councillor, and appointed governor to the young Duke of Gloucester; and in 1701 was created by King William commander-in-chief of the English forces in Holland, and also Ambassador Plenipotentiary to the States-General.

Still greater honours awaited him on the accession of Queen Anne in 1702, when he was created captain-general of all the forces at home and abroad, and sent as plenipotentiary to The Hague, where he was also made captain-general by the States. In the campaign of the same year he drove the French out of Spanish Guelders, and took Liége and other towns, for which he was created Duke of Marlborough.

In 1704 he stormed the French and Bavarian lines at Donauwörth, and in the same year, in conjunction with Prince Eugène, gained the victory of Blenheim over the French and Bavarians, headed by Marshal Tallard and the Elector of Bavaria. The nation testified its gratitude by the gifts of the honour of Woodstock and hundred of Wotton, and erected Blenheim Palace for him, one of the finest seats in the kingdom.

During the year 1705 he conducted successful negotiations at the courts of Berlin, Hanover, and Venice, and the new emperor, Joseph, presented him with the principality of Mindelheim. On the victory of Ramillies, 1706, a Bill was passed to settle his honours upon the male and female issue of his daughters.

In the campaign of 1707 his antagonist was the famous duc de Vendôme, over whom he gained no advantage, and on his return, found that his popularity at court was on the decline. In 1708, in conjunction with Prince Eugène, he gained the battle of Oudenarde. In 1709 he defeated Marshal Villars at Malplaquet, though at a cost ill repaid by the capture of Mons. On the next visit of the duke to England he found that the duchess, by her great arrogance, had so disgusted the queen that a total breach had ensued.

Early in 1710 he returned to the army, and with Prince Eugène gained another victory over Villars. During his absence a new ministry, hostile to himself, was chosen, and on his return his command was taken from him, and a prosecution commenced against him for applying the public money to private purposes.

He repaired in disgust to the Low Countries in 1712, but returned a short time before the queen's death, and on the accesssion of George I. was reinstated in the supreme military command. Retiring from all public employments, his mental faculties gradually decayed, and he died at Windsor Lodge, leaving four daughters, who married into families of the first distinction.

His duchess, Sarah Jennings, born 1660, died 1744, has been almost equally celebrated for her boundless ambition and avarice. The only son of the Duke and Duchess of Marlborough having died while young, the title fell to the descendants of one of their daughters, the wife of Charles Spencer, Earl of Sunderland, who have assumed the name of Churchill.—BIBLIOGRAPHY: William Coxe, *Memoirs of the Duke of Marlborough*; G. E. B. Saintsbury, *Marlborough*; S. J. Reid, *John and Sarah, Duke and Duchess of Marlborough*; J. W. Fortescue, *The Briitsh Army.*

MARLBOROUGH. A municipal borough of Wiltshire, England, on the Kennet, served by the Great Western Railway. Marlborough College (1845) occupies the site of a castle built in the reign of Henry I. The town was a royal demesne at the time of the Domesday survey. There is an agricultural trade. Pop. (1931), 3492.

The hills near Marlborough are known as the **Marlborough Downs,** and are famous for their sheep.

MARLBOROUGH. A north-eastern maritime district of South Island, New Zealand, drained by the navigable Wairau River and traversed by the Kaikouras (Mount Tapuae-nuku, 9462 feet). Sheep-farming is extensive; wool, timber, tallow, and hides are exported. Picton, on an arm of Queen Charlotte Sound, and Blenheim are the chief towns. Area, 4220 sq. miles; pop. (1932), 18,700.

MARLBOROUGH HOUSE, London. Royal residence, in a garden of 4 acres extent, on the south side of Pall Mall; erected by Sir Christopher Wren between 1709 and 1710 for the first Duke of Marlborough. The house was purchased by the Government in 1817 as a residence for the Princess Charlotte and Prince Leopold (1817–31), passed to Queen Adelaide (widow of William IV.) in 1837, and was successively the residence of both Edward VII. and George V. when Princes of Wales. In 1910 Queen Alexandra took up her residence there.

MARLOWE, Christopher. English dramatist and poet, was born in Canterbury on 6th Feb., 1564, and was killed in May, 1593. His father was a shoemaker by trade. He was educated at the King's School, Canterbury, which he entered in 1578, and at Benet College, Cambridge (now Corpus Christi). He matriculated in 1581, took his B.A. degree in 1584, and his M.A. in 1588. Francis Kett, the mystic, who was burnt for heresy in 1589, was a Fellow and tutor of Benet College, and may perhaps have helped to develop Marlowe's attitude towards religion, an attitude often described as atheistical, but probably merely unconventional.

It is likely that Marlowe went to London in 1586, and that soon after his arrival there he joined the Lord Admiral's Company of Players. His career as a dramatist must have begun soon after his career as an actor. Nothing definite is known about his life in London; it was rumoured that he was wild and licentious. Certainly he worked hard, for in six years he wrote six plays, four of which were great successes on the stage.

He was criticized by Nash, and attacked by Greene and Gabriel Harvey; he numbered Sir Walter Raleigh and Thomas Walsingham among his friends. He was killed at Deptford late in May, 1593. In 1925 an American scholar, Dr. Hotson, brought to light in his *Death of Christopher Marlowe* some valuable information.

Marlowe was killed by one Ingram Frizer, and the official cause of the quarrel was the reckoning. The exact truth of the story of Marlowe's death is not yet ascertained, but various exaggerated accounts of it were used by Puritanical writers to point a moral.

Marlowe's earliest extant play is *Tamburlaine the Great,* which was probably produced in 1587. It is in two parts, but is virtually one play in ten acts. At the outset of the play Marlowe with superb self-confidence proclaims himself an innovator:

> From jigging veins of rhyming mother-wits,
> And such conceits as clownage keeps in pay,
> We'll lead you to the stately tent of war,
> Where you shall hear the Scythian Tamburlaine
> Threatening the world with high astounding terms.

With all its faults of violence and bombast, *Tamburlaine* was incomparably the best tragedy that had as yet been produced on the English stage. It is important not only for its intrinsic merits, which are considerable, but also as a piece of pioneer work. It is the first play to be written in blank verse, as distinguished from mere unrhymed decasyllabic lines.

Marlowe's verse, while dignified and majestic, is much more supple and infinitely less monotonous than that of any of his predecessors. *Tamburlaine* is obviously a young man's work, but its exaggeration contributed to its success, and its influence on English tragedy was very great.

The Tragical History of Doctor Faustus was produced in 1588. It is not a well-constructed play, being a series of disconnected scenes rather than a connected whole. Its text is not in a satisfactory condition, and the comic scenes, which contain extremely poor fooling, are, it is believed or hoped, by another hand. Yet *Doctor Faustus* is a memorable play; the speech of Faustus, addressed to Helen, and the concluding scenes of the play and soliloquies of Faustus are among the best things not only in Marlowe, but in all English drama.

Goethe said of this: "How greatly it is all planned!" and thought of translating it. In the great work of his life he extended and embroidered the Faust legend almost beyond recognition; but it may be doubted if he wrote anything that arouses so much pity and terror as the conclusion of Marlowe's play.

The Famous Tragedy of the Rich Jew of Malta was produced in 1589. It is a play of very unequal merits; the first two acts are written in Marlowe's best style, and the last three are feeble and melodramatic. Barrabas is scarcely a more life-like figure than Mr. Punch, whom he resembles in his taste for atrocities. He finally perishes by means of "something lingering with boiling oil in it" which he had prepared for someone else. In spite of some absurdities, this play has many passages of noble poetry in it, notably the opening soliloquy of the Jew.

Edward II., which was produced about 1590, is the most flawless of Marlowe's plays, though not the most magnificent. It is his greatest work as a dramatist, but not as a poet. It is obvious that Shakespeare had this play in mind when he was writing *Richard II.*, but he did not improve on the earlier play. The death-scene in Marlowe's play is one of the most moving scenes in all drama, ancient or modern.

Marlowe's other two plays are of comparatively small importance. Both have been preserved in a mutilated and mangled state. *The Massacre at Paris* is notable for little except its strong anti-Catholic tendencies. In *Dido, Queen of Carthage*, in which Nash collaborated, Marlowe failed mainly because he adhered too closely to Virgil, regardless of the different medium in which he was working.

As a poet Marlowe stands almost higher than as a dramatist. His versions of Ovid's *Amores* and of the first book of Lucan's *Pharsalia* are commonplace, but in his *Hero and Leander*, which is a recasting rather than a paraphrase of the poem of Musæus, he has written what may claim to be the greatest as well as the most influential of Elizabethan poems. *Venus and Adonis*, clearly an imitation of it, is pale and colourless in comparison. Among Marlowe's shorter poems *Come live with me and be my love* is, as Walton called it, "choicely good."

Marlowe, although he died so young, was great not merely in promise but in performance. He created blank verse, founded English tragedy, and wrote some of the finest passages of dramatic poetry in the language. He is incomparably the greatest of Shakespeare's predecessors, being as much above Greene, Kyd, and Peele as Shakespeare is above Jonson and Beaumont and Fletcher.

Less than three months older than Shakespeare in actual age, he was years older in development. He was Shakespeare's master, and Shakespeare does not pay any other contemporary a compliment like that paid to Marlowe in *As You Like It*, iii. 5, 82. To no pioneer do English poetry and drama owe so much.—BIBLIOGRAPHY: J. A. Symonds, *Shakspere's Predecessors*; F. S. Boas, *Shakespeare and his Predecessors*; J. H. Ingram, *Christopher Marlowe and his Associates*; A. W. Verity, *Influence of Christopher Marlowe on Shakespeare's Earlier Style.*

MAR'MARA, or **MARMORA, Sea of** (ancient **Propontis**). The sea separating Asia Minor from Europe. It communicates with the Black Sea by the Bosporus, and with the Ægean and Mediterranean by the Dardanelles; length, about 170 miles; breadth, 50 miles; area, 4500 sq. miles. The name is derived from Marmara (ancient *Proconnesus*), the largest island, noted for its marble and alabaster. The Treaty of Lausanne (1923) placed the control of the Sea of Marmara under an Allied Commission.

MARMONT (mår-mōŋ), **Auguste Fréderic Louis Viesse de.** Duc de Ragusa and Marshal of France, was born 1774, and died in 1852. He became acquainted with Bonaparte, who chose him for his aide-de-camp. In Italy he greatly distinguished himself, and after the battle of Marengo attained the rank of general of division. He obtained the title of duc de Ragusa for his defence of Ragusan territory against the Russians and Montenegrins, was present at Wagram, and after the truce of Znaim was made field-marshal.

He afterwards governed the Illyrian Provinces till 1811, when he succeeded Masséna as commander in Portugal. In conjunction with Soult he raised the siege of Badajoz, but was ultimately badly beaten at Salamanca by Wellington. In the campaign of 1813 he held the command of an army corps in Germany, and fought in the battles of Lützen Bautzen, and Dresden. In 1814 he fought a final battle under the walls of Paris, but, opposition appearing fruitless, he surrendered to the Allies.

MARMOSE. A marsupial quadruped resembling the opossum, but smaller, being about 6 inches in length exclusive of the tail; the *Didelphys murīna* of Cayenne, *D. dorsigĕra* of Surinam. It carries its young about with it on its back.

MAR'MOSET, or **OUISTITI.** A name of several small Central and South American monkeys, the smallest of the monkey tribe. They are agile in their movements, possess long, non-prehensile tails, and have a thick woolly fur. They bear a close resemblance to squirrels in general appearance, feed upon fruit and insects, and occasionally upon the smaller birds and their eggs.

The marmoset family (Hapalidæ) is generally divided into two genera, Hapălē and Midas, of which the most familiar species are the common marmoset (*Hapale Jacchus*) with its varieties *H. penicillāta, H. vulgāris*, etc., and the common or negro tamarin (*Midās ursulus*).

MARMOT. A burrowing rodent mammal of the genus Arctŏmys, belonging to the squirrel family. They are thick-bodied, have short tails and short legs, and live in burrows, which are generally excavated in mountainous situations, and consist of a series of galleries in which whole communities reside. During the winter they lie dormant. The marmots inhabit Europe, Northern Asia, and North America. The Alpine or European Marmot (*Arctŏmys marmotta*) is found in plenty on the Alps, and is about the size of a rabbit. The Siberian marmot (*A. bobac*) ranges into Eastern Europe.

One of the four North American species is the woodchuck (*A. monax*) of the middle states. A close relative of the marmots is the prairie-dog, prairie-marmot, or wistonwish, of North America (*Cynŏmys Ludoviciānus*). Rattlesnakes and ground-owls (*Speotyto cunicularis*) live in the burrows of this animal.

MARNE (ancient **Matrŏna**). A river of France, tributary of the Seine, rises in the Plateau de Langres (Haute-Marne), and joins the Seine at Charenton, 2 miles S E. of Paris; length, 328 miles. Its tributaries are the Ourcq, Saulx, and Ornain on the right, and the Grand Morin and Petit Morin on the left. Navigable to Dizier, it forms part of the Marne-Rhine Canal system. The Haute-Marne Canal from Donjeux connects the Marne with the Saône.

MARNE. A department of France, part of the pre-Revolutionary province of Champagne, traversed by the River Marne and by the Aisne-Marne, Marne-Rhine Canals. It is a wine-growing (Champagne) district, with some manufactures of marble and chalk-quarries. Châlons-sur-Marne is the capital; Rheims, Ste Menehould, and Épernay are important. Area, 3167 sq. miles; pop. (1931), 412,156.

MARNE, Battles of. *See* EUROPEAN WAR.

MARNE, HAUTE-. A department of France, part of the pre-Revolutionary province of Champagne. The Marne rises in the hilly region, and traverses the department. Cereals are raised, and the vine is extensively cultivated. Chaumont is the capital; Langres, St. Dizier, Nogent, and Bourbonne-les-Bains (watering-place) are important. Area, 2420 sq. miles; pop. (1931), 189,791.

MAR'ONITES. A sect of Eastern Christians, whose origin was a consequence of the Monothelite controversy. (*See* MONOTHELITES.) On the condemnation of the Monothelites by Anastasius, early in the eighth century, the remnant of this party survived in the *Maronites*—so named from their founder Maron—a society of monks in Syria, about Mount Lebanon, which is mentioned as early as the sixth century. They became a warlike mountain people, who defended their political and religious independence boldly against the Mahommedans.

Their political constitution is that of a military commonwealth. Since the twelfth century they have several times submitted to the Pope and joined the Roman Catholic Church, without giving up their own peculiarities.

Their head is called the *Patriarch of Antioch*, although his residence is in the monastery of Kanobin, upon Mount Lebanon; and he gives an account every ten years to the Pope of the condition of the Maronite Church. Since 1584 there has been a Maronite College established at Rome for the education of clergymen. At present the Maronites are supposed to number about 150,000.—Cf. F. J. Bliss, *The Religions of Modern Syria and Palestine.*

MAROS-VASARHELY. *See* OSORREI.

MAROT (må-rō), **Clement.** A French epigrammatist and writer of light lyrical pieces, born at Cahors 1495, died in 1544. He wrote *L'Enfer*, a satire; and a modernized edition of the *Romance of the Rose*. His translation of the Psalms, made in conjunction with Beza, was long used in the Protestant churches in France, though his own life was marked by complete religious indifference. The combination of satirical humour, naïveté, and delicacy exhibited in his works is known as the *Style Marotique*, of which La Fontaine furnishes the best subsequent examples.

MARQUESAS. A French island-group in the Southern Pacific, north of the Paumotu, and administered by Tahiti. There are thirteen islands; seven are inhabited; Nukahiva and Hiva-oa are the largest. The interiors are hilly, and the coasts rise steeply from the sea. Copra and pearl-shell are the chief products. The Marquesas were discovered partly by Medaña (1595) and partly by Ingraham (1791), who named them the Washington Islands. They were annexed to France in 1842. Total area, 480 sq. miles; pop. 3424.

MARQUESS, or **MARQUIS** (Fr. *marquis*; It. *marchese*; Ger. *markgraf*). A title of honour next in dignity to that of duke, first given to those who commanded on the marches or frontiers of countries. The title was first introduced into England by King Richard II. in the year 1387, but fell into disuse until the reign of Edward VI., who created the Marquessate of Winchester in 1551.

MAR'QUETRY (Fr. *marqueterie*). Inlaid cabinet-work in which thin slices of different-coloured wood, sometimes of ivory, pearl, shell, or metal, are inlaid on a ground usually of oak or fir, well seasoned to prevent warping. At one time figures and landscapes were represented by means of marquetry, but it is now chiefly disposed in regular geometrical figures.

MARRIAGE. Necessarily the basis of social organization. Whether or not the original practice among mankind was sexual promiscuity or a monogamous association of a more or less permanent kind is a problem which has been hotly disputed for many years. But, although the evidence for coming to a definite conclusion in this matter is not available, the facts revealed by primitive human societies, as well as comparison with the sexual habits of anthropoid apes, seem to suggest that monogamy may have been the original form of marriage.

Descent was originally matrilineal, not merely because of the mother's function of feeding and controlling her children, but also because the facts of paternity were not appreciated until a relatively recent period in man's history, when he acquired the physiological knowledge of his share in the production of offspring. Until this fact was demonstrated women were regarded as the obvious parents, and all descent was reckoned matrilineally.

Whether originally marriage was monogamous or not, the peculiarities in the usage of family names among primitive peoples suggest that a condition of sexual communism was a very early and widespread custom. In accordance with this system sexual relations were regarded as orthodox and proper between all the men of one social group and all the women of another social group, without any particular woman being regarded as the wife of a given man.

Perhaps as an outcome of this system a widespread practice grew up of regarding it as improper for a man to take to wife any woman of his own clan or social group; he had to obtain a wife from another group, to which in many cases he transferred his allegiance and that of his children. The practice is known as *exogamy*. In communities where such marriage customs prevail it is often regarded as incestuous, and as such strictly tabooed, to marry within one's clan.

But among other peoples the orthodox form of marriage is *endogamous*, i.e. within the clan. Many varied forms of marriage custom are found among different peoples: *polygamy*, or plurality of wives; *polyandry*, where a woman has several husbands, usually brothers, at the same time; and *cross-cousin marriage*, where the orthodox union is for a man to marry the daughter of his mother's brother or of his father's sister, being some of the most widely recognized varieties.

In some regions marriages are regarded as proper which in other places are regarded as incestuous and most strictly forbidden. Not only so, but in some places it was considered imperative for kings to enter into alliances, say, with their own sisters or daughters, which were forbidden to other members of the community.

The most diverse views are held by different peoples respecting chastity in a bride before marriage. Among some peoples, like the Arabs, lack of the evidence of virginity at marriage is a sufficient ground for nullification. Other people regard sexual gratification on the part of unmarried girls not merely as a natural procedure, but even as a necessary preliminary to marriage. For an account of the intimate relationship of these varied forms of marriage to sociology, see W. H. R. Rivers, *Kinship and Social Organization* (1914); for an encyclopædic discourse on the manifold aspects of the subject, see E. Westermarck, *The History of Marriage* (1921).

MARRIAGE LAWS. Marriage is the "voluntary union for life of one man and one woman to the exclusion of all others." As a rule such union to be valid must be entered into according to the law of the place where it is contracted, and, generally, a marriage contracted in a foreign country in accordance with the forms prevailing there is valid in England if it does not contravene English law. Marriage is a contract, and with some special exceptions the rules applicable to contract apply. But it cannot be entered into or dissolved at pleasure, and during its subsistence the personal rights and duties of the spouses are regulated by law.

By English law a marriage cannot be contracted by a male under fourteen years or a female under twelve, and until majority the consent of parent or guardian is required. (Contrast Scots law, under which a minor (q.v.) may marry without such consent, and French law, under which the parents' consent is necessary though the parties are of full age.)

Neither party must be bound by a subsisting legal marriage, be physically incapable of consummating the marriage, or be insane, but a marriage entered into during a lucid interval is not invalid. Lastly, the parties must not be within the prohibited relationships, namely, ascendants and descendants *ad infinitum*, brothers and sisters, and collaterals where one stands *in loco parentis* to the other (e.g. uncle and niece), half-blood relationships, and the corresponding relationships by affinity (excepting, by recent enactments, the case of marriage with a deceased wife's sister or a deceased husband's brother) being prohibited equally with the full-blood.

A marriage may be invalidated by duress or fraud, but, generally, not by misrepresentation as to character, circumstances, or position. Specific performance of a promise of marriage will not be ordered by the court, but damages may be awarded for the breach.

Certain preliminary procedure is required by law before a marriage can take place: (1) publication of banns for three successive Sundays at divine service in the parish (or in each of the two parishes) in which the parties have resided for the preceding fifteen days, the marriage taking place in church within three months of the last publication; or (2) notice to the superintendent registrar of the district in which each party has resided for the preceding seven days, a certificate being issued twenty-one days later and the marriage taking place in church (with consent of the clergyman) or dissenting place of worship or registrar's office within three months; or (3) issue of an ordinary bishop's licence after application by one party, who must have resided in the parish for fifteen days, the marriage taking place in church within three months; or (4) issue of a special licence by the Archbishop of Canterbury, no previous residence being necessary, and the marriage being celebrated at any time and place; or (5) issue of a licence by the superintendent registrar after twenty-four hours' notice, the applicant having fifteen days' residence in the district and the marriage taking place in a dissenting place of worship or registrar's office.

In Scotland a marriage may be "regular" or "irregular." A regular marriage is one celebrated by a clergyman before two witnesses after proclamation of banns or notice to the registrar. Fifteen days' residence of at least one party when the procedure is by proclamation of banns, and of both parties when it is by notice, is necessary.

An irregular marriage, constituted by present interchange of consent, by promise *subsequente copula*, or by cohabitation with habit and repute of marriage, without any ceremony, is equally binding, but the first-mentioned form requires at least twenty-one days' previous residence of one of the parties.

In the United States and Canada a licence is necessary as a rule, and the marriage must take place before a minister of religion or (in United States) a magistrate. *See* DIVORCE; HUSBAND AND WIFE; JUDICIAL SEPARATION; etc.

MAR'RYAT, Frederick. English novelist and naval officer, born 1792, died at Langham, Norfolk, 1848. In 1808 he entered the navy as midshipman on board the *Impérieuse* commanded by Cochrane, afterwards Lord Dundonald, and, having served with distinction and attained the rank of captain, he retired in 1830. His first attempt in literature was made in 1829, by the publication of *Frank Mildmay*. Its success led to an extensive series of works of the like kind, including: *The King's Own*, *Peter Simple*, *Jacob Faithful*, *Japhet in Search of a Father*, *Newton Forster*, *Midshipman Easy*, *The Pacha of Many Tales*, *The Poacher*, *The Phantom Ship*, *Snarley-Yow or the Dog Fiend*, *Percival Keene*, *Masterman Ready*, *Poor Jack*, and others.

Frederick Marryat

He was also the author of a *Code of Signals for the Merchant Service* (1837). Captain Marryat's novels are remarkable for broad humour and fidelity of description as regards sea-life, but he cannot be said to be a great master of plot.

MARS. The Roman god of war, at an early period identified with the Greek *Arēs*, a deity of similar attributes. Like Jupiter he was designated *father*, and was regarded in particular as the father of the Roman people, Romulus and Remus being the fruit of his intercourse with Rhea Sylvia. Several temples at Rome were dedicated to him. His service was celebrated not only by particular *flamines* devoted to him, but by the College of the Salii, or priests of Mars.

The month of March, the first month of the Roman year, was sacred to him. As the tutelary deity of Rome he was called *Quirinus*, in his character as the god of war *Gradīvus* (the striding). Arēs, the Greek god of war, was the son of Zeus (Jupiter) and Hera (Juno).

He is represented as terrible in battle, but not as invulnerable, since he was wounded at various times by Heracles, Diomedes, and Athena. He is represented as a youthful warrior of strong frame, either naked or clothed with the chlamys. The chief seats of the worship of Arēs were in Thrace and Scythia.

MARS. Of the superior planets that which lies nearest the sun, or next beyond the orbit of the earth. It moves round the sun in 686·95 of our mean solar days, at the average distance of 141,500,000 miles, its greatest and least distances being 154,700,000 and 128,300,000 miles; its orbit is inclined to the ecliptic at an angle of 1° 51′ 5″; its distance from the earth varies from about 35,000,000 to 244,000,000 miles; it rotates on its axis in 24 hours 37 minutes 22 seconds; the inclination of its axis, or the angle between its equator and its orbit, is 23°; its diameter is about 4200 miles.

Mars shines with a reddish light, due to the fact that most of its surface has an ochre hue, and doubtless is in an arid condition resembling our deserts. Considerable portions, however, have a bluish-green colour, and vary decidedly in tint with the seasons. There seems much reason to suppose that such changes are caused, in part at least, by recurrent growth and decay of vegetation. The polar regions exhibit white caps, probably of snow, which melt in the summer season of the respective hemispheres, and extend in the winter.

At times snowfalls appear to occur suddenly over vast areas. Lines seen traversing the surface have been termed *canals*, and by some authorities have been supposed to be the work of intelligent beings, and designed to irrigate the planet's surface by tapping the polar snows. The inferring of such artificial origin is, however, mere conjecture.

In 1877 two satellites, both very small bodies, were discovered by Professor Hall of the Naval Observatory, Washington. The outer one, 14,500 miles distant from the centre of Mars, revolves round the planet in a period of 30 hours 18 minutes; the inner one, 5800 miles from the centre of Mars, has a period of 7 hours 39 minutes.

MARSA'LA (ancient **Lilybæum**). A seaport of Trapani, Sicily. The name is of Saracenic origin, i.e. *Marsa-Ali*, the harbour of Ali. Marsala is the centre of the wine-growing district which produces Marsala, a light-coloured wine of the sherry type. Garibaldi landed at Marsala 11th May, 1860, and inaugurated the campaign that liberated Sicily from the Bourbons. Pop. 30,788.

MARSEILLAIS HYMN (mȧr-se-lāz′). The war-song of the French Republic. The words and, as is generally believed, the music were written in 1792 by Rouget de Lisle, an officer in garrison at Strasbourg, on the occasion of a body of volunteers leaving that city for the war against Austria and Prussia, and the poem was entitled by him *Chant de guerre de l'armée du Rhin* (War-song of the Army of the Rhine). It was called Marseillaise because first sung in Paris by volunteers from Marseilles. The song was suppressed under the First Empire and the Bourbons, but the Revolution of 1830 called it up anew, and, after being suppressed under the Second Empire, it is now again the recognized national hymn of France.

MARSEILLES (ancient **Massilia**). Second city and chief seaport of France, capital of the department of Bouches-du-Rhône. It stands on the Bay of Marseilles (Gulf of Lions), and lies in the form of an amphitheatre round a natural harbourage known as the Old Harbour. The principal thoroughfare, la Cannebière, is considered one of the finest in Europe. Although of ancient foundation, the town is comparatively modern, and includes no buildings of genuine antiquity or architectural rarity.

Soap, soda and chemical products, oils, sugar, machinery, candles, glass, and earthenware are manufactured, and there is a large transit trade in soap, oil, hides, grain, tobacco, wool, iron, and cotton. The port was entered and cleared by 13,582,621 and 12,719,565 tons respectively in 1932. It comprises a series of docks extending along the shore and protected by a mole, and is strongly fortified. Sheltered by the Île Ratonneau is the Château d'If, immortalized by Dumas in *Monte-Cristo*. Pop. (1931), 800,881.

Marseilles was founded by Phocæon

colonists (600 B.C.), who called it Massilia. It espoused the cause of Pompey, and was taken by Cæsar (49 B.C.). On the decline of the Roman Empire the town fell successively to the Goths, Burgundians, and Franks, was sacked by the Saracens in A.D. 735, and, having been taken by Charles of Anjou in 1256, it was united to France (with Provençe) in 1481. All its ancient privileges were abolished by Louis XIV. (1660). During the European War (1914-18) Marseilles was the principal centre of Mediterranean communications, forming a convenient base for Indian troops in France and for Allied troops in the Near East.

MARSHAL (Fr. *Maréchal*). A word of German origin signifying originally a man appointed to take care of horses. A similar term is the French *connétable* or constable, from Latin *comes stabuli* (count or master of the stable). He had to superintend the ceremonies at the coronation of the emperor, and on other high occasions. Until the Revolution of 1918 there was a marshal at the head of the households of German sovereigns.

In France *maréchal de France* is the highest military honour. In Germany *general-field-marshal* is the highest military honour. In Great Britain *field-marshal* is the highest military rank. The *air-marshal* is an officer of the Royal Air Force, and the third in rank in the service. The post was created in Aug., 1919, and is equivalent to the rank of vice-admiral in the navy and lieutenant-general in the army.

Another English title is *earl-marshal*. (*See* FIELD-MARSHAL, EARL-MARSHAL.) Marshal also signifies a person who regulates the ceremonies on certain solemn celebrations. In the United States a marshal is an executive officer (resembling the sheriff) connected with the United States courts.

MARSHALL ISLANDS. A Pacific archipelago, in Micronesia, comprising two chains of lagoon islands—Radak (13 islands) on the east, and Ralik (11 islands) on the west; total area, 158 sq. miles. There are plantations of coconut-palm; phosphates and copra are exported. The Marshall group belonged to Germany from 1885 until it was occupied by an Australian force, 12th Sept., 1914. It is administered by Japan under a League of Nations mandate. Jaluit is the administrative centre and chief island. Majeru (pop. 2600) is the most populous. Pop. 9,708, of which 198 are Japanese and 13 Europeans.

MARSH-HARRIER (*Circus æruginosus*). A nearly exterminated British bird of prey about 2 feet

Marsh-Harrier

in length, frequenting marshes, and living on water-birds, mice, rats, water-rats, frogs, and fish. It is sometimes called the *Moor-buzzard*.

MARSH-MALLOW (*Althæa officinālis*). A common European plant, growing in marshes, especially near the sea, in great abundance. It is perennial, and has a white, fleshy, carrot-shaped root, which may be used as food. The stem is from 2 to 3 feet high, both leaves and stem being covered with a soft down. The flowers are flesh-coloured. The hollyhock (*A. rosea*) is another species.

MARSH-MARIGOLD (*Caltha palustris*). A plant of the nat. ord. Ranunculaceæ, a common British plant found in meadows and by the sides of wet ditches. It has kidney-shaped, shining leaves, and large yellow flowers, and like the other plants of the same order it is bitter to taste.

MARSH-SAMPHIRE. A leafless, much-branched, jointed, succulent plant, *Salicornia herbacea*, found on muddy or moist sandy shores, and frequent in England and Ireland. It is eaten by cattle, and makes a good pickle. It is also named *Glasswort* and *Saltwort*.

MARSILIACEÆ. A family of Water-ferns or Hydropterideæ (q.v.), allied to Schizæaceæ. The only genera are Marsilia and Pilularia. Both have thin creeping stems, but whereas Pilularia (Pillwort) has quill-shaped leaves, those of Marsilia resemble a four-leaved clover. The sporangia (of two kinds) are enclosed in roundish pod-like structures (sporocarps).

MARSIPOBRANCHII (Gr. *marsipos*, a pouch, and *branchia*, gills). The group of vertebrates comprising the hag-fishes and lampreys, with pouch-like gills. The organization of these animals is of a very low grade, as indicated chiefly by the persistent notochord, the absence of any traces of limbs, the absence of a mandible and of ribs, and the structure of the gills.

MARSTON, John. English dramatist and satirist, was born in 1575 or 1576, and died in 1634. His father was a lecturer of the Middle Temple, and his mother was the daughter of an Italian physician. Marston's Italian blood explains some of the peculiarities of his temperament; for, although he does not completely illustrate the proverb "Inglese Italianato è un diavolo incarnato," his youth was a wild and unbridled one. He was educated at Brasenose College, Oxford, where he graduated B.A. in 1594.

He began his literary career as a satirist, and then took to the composition of plays. He did not write anything for the stage after 1607, and at some unknown date, probably about 1608 or 1609, he took holy orders. In 1616 he was presented to the living of Christchurch, in Hampshire, which he resigned in 1631. His works were published in 1633, and he died in the following year. *The Metamorphosis of Pygmalion's Image*, a satire, appeared in 1598. Archbishop Whitgift ordered it to be burnt.

Another satire, *The Scourge of Villany*, appeared in the same year. *Antonio and Mellida*, an ill-constructed and bombastic tragedy in two parts, was published in 1602. *The Malcontent*, a better but far from perfect play, appeared in 1604. It was dedicated to Ben Jonson, and was probably intended as a peace-offering after one of the many quarrels between the two dramatists.

The Dutch Courtezan (1605) is a coarse but lively play. *Eastward Ho* (1605), in which Jonson and Chapman collaborated, is a splendid play, and contains one of the best pictures of city life in all Elizabethan drama. Marston's exact share in it is unknown and unknowable. It nearly got its authors into serious trouble (*see* JONSON). *Parasitaster, or the Fawn* (1606) is a good comedy; *Sophonisba* (1606), a tragedy on the theme immortalized by Jemmy Thomson in 1730, is a feeble and melodramatic play.

What You Will (1607) borrowed its title from the sub-title of *Twelfth Night*. Other plays in which Marston had a share are: *The Insatiate Countess* (probably in part the work of William Barksteed), *Jack Drum's Entertainment*, and *Histriomastix*.

Marston can hardly be classed among the greater Elizabethan dramatists. He had, without doubt, very great abilities, but he did not make the most of them. Fustian language and uncertainty of taste mar much of his work, though now and again short passages and single lines occur that completely disarm the most querulous critic. Marston had no high opinion of his own work, and said of it: "He that thinks worse of my rhymes than myself, I scorn him, for he cannot; he that thinks better is a foole."

He dedicated his early satires "To everlasting oblivion," and "To his most esteemed and best beloved Selfe." In leaving the stage for the pulpit he showed that the days of his youth were over, and that his true bent did not lie in dramatic composition.—BIBLIOGRAPHY: J. H. Penniman, *The War of the Theatres*; R. A. Small, *The Stage-Quarrel between Ben Jonson and the so-called Poetasters*; A. C. Swinburne, *The Age of Shakespeare*.

MARSTON, Philip Bourke. English poet, son of Westland Marston, born in London 1850, died 1887. He became blind in his fourth year, and to this the introspective and morbid character of much of his work must be attributed. His poems were collected at various times in the volumes entitled *Song-tide* (1870), *All in All* (1875), and *Wind Voices* (1883).

MARSTON MOOR. In Yorkshire, near York, a locality celebrated for the battle between the Royalists under Prince Rupert and the troops of the Parliament under Fairfax and Cromwell (2nd July, 1644), in which the latter were victorious.

MARSUPIALIA, or **MARSUPIALS** (Lat. *marsupium*, a pouch). An extensive order of mammals distinguished by the possession of a pouch, in which the teats are situated, and which serves as a shelter for the young, these being born in a very imperfect state. The order is intermediate between the primitive egg-laying mammals (Prototheria or Monotremata) and the higher forms (Eutheria), which include the great majority of the class.

The opossums and opossum-rat (Cænolestes) are American, but all other living marsupials are native to the Australian region, where, in the absence of competition, they have evolved along many different lines, occupying places in the economy of nature elsewhere filled by members of the higher orders. There are two sub-orders, divided into various families as follows:

Sub-order I. — Polyprotodontia, chiefly flesh- or insect-eating species:

(1) Dasyuridæ, the dasyures; (2) Didelphyidæ, the opossums; (3) Peramelidæ, the bandicoots; (4) Notoryctidæ, the pouched mole. Suborder II.—Diprotodontia, herbivorous species: (1) Macropodidæ, kangaroos and wallabies; (2) Phalangeridæ, the phalangers; (3) Epanorthidæ, opossum rats of Colombia and Ecuador.—BIBLIOGRAPHY: F. G. Aflalo, *Natural History of Australia*; Oldfield Thomas, *British Museum Catalogue of Marsupialia*; F. E. Beddard, *Mammals* (in *The Cambridge Natural History*).

MARTABAN, Gulf of. A Burmese arm of the Bay of Bengal. The city of Martaban was for centuries the capital of the Kingdom of Pegu. It is now a small town, and was taken by the British in 1824 and 1852.

MARTEN. The name of several carnivorous mammals of the genus Mustēla, family Mustelidæ (weasels). The body of the marten, like that of the weasel, is elongated and slender. The legs are short, the feet being provided with five toes, armed with sharp claws. In habit the martens differ from the weasels in being arboreal, these forms

Beech-marten (*Mustēla foina*)

climbing trees with great ease. The pine-marten (*M. abietum*), which has a wide range in the northern hemisphere, is the only species indigenous to Britain. The beech-marten (*M. foina*) is closely related to this.

Martens feed on the smaller wild animals, such as rats, mice, etc., but also attack birds and devour eggs. The pine-marten possesses a yellowish mark on the throat, and its fur is largely used for trimmings. It burrows in the ground. The famous sable marten (*M. zibellina*), which furnishes the valuable sable fur, is nearly allied to the pine-marten. It inhabits Siberia. The American sable is furnished by the *M. americana*; and Pennant's marten (*M. pennanti*), or the *fisher*, as it is popularly called, is another well-known species.

MARTIAL (Marcus Valerius Martialis). Roman epigrammatist, was born between A.D. 38 and 41, and died about A.D. 102 or 103. His home was at Augusta Bilbilis, in Spain, and he became acquainted with his fellow-countrymen Seneca and Lucan. They were more or less his patrons, and he followed them to Rome in the year A.D. 64. In the following year Lucan and Seneca were implicated in the conspiracy of the Pisos, and compelled to commit suicide.

Martial was left to his own devices, and for almost thirty-five years he followed the precarious career of a man of letters at Rome. He relied for his livelihood mainly upon his high-born patrons, though when his reputation was established he had a certain income from booksellers. He had first a flat and then a house in Rome, and a small country house at Nomentum.

He returned to his native town in A.D. 98, and soon after was presented with a small estate by a lady named Marcella, thus securing independence for his declining years. In Rome he had cherished a theoretical love for the country, but at Bilbilis he felt a keen regret for the bustle and pleasures of the capital.

Martial's works consist of fifteen books of epigrams. The earliest of his extant works is usually incorrectly called *Liber spectaculorum*, and is a collection of epigrams upon the shows provided by Titus and Domitian, especially those given in the Colosseum. This book was published in A.D. 81. The two books of epigrams called *Xenia* and *Apophoreta*, and numbered xiii. and xiv. by editors, were published at Christmas A.D. 84.

All the epigrams in these books are distichs intended to accompany Christmas presents. They have no more literary value than modern cracker-mottoes have. Martial's reputation rests upon his twelve books of miscellaneous epigrams, the first of which was published in A.D. 86, and the last of which was sent from Spain to Rome, and published soon before Martial's death. These twelve books contain over eleven hundred epigrams.

There are some features in Martial that are repellent to modern readers. Some of his epigrams are outrageously indecent. They are, however, gross rather than prurient, Rabelais rather than Ovid. About seven-eighths of his work is free from this fault, which may be due to a literary convention as much as to any depravity in Martial.

What offends some readers almost more is Martial's gross flattery of Domitian. This can also be forgiven if we judge Martial by the standards of his time. Customs have changed, but not so long ago. Some of Ben Jonson's epigrams and the Dedication of the Authorized Version of the Bible are just as offensive as Martial in this respect.

It is more profitable to consider Martial's good points. He was a good friend and companion, and was fond of children. He had a real gift for occasional verse, and in some of his epigrams he has managed to write charming poems. He has drawn a splendid picture of Rome during a reign of terror. He has given the reverse of Juvenal's picture, and shown that there was a Rome where the comedy of life could still be played. R. L. Stevenson has well said of him: "Martial is a poet of no good repute, and it gives a man new thoughts to read his works dispassionately, and find in this unseemly jester's serious passages the image of a kind, wise, and self-respecting gentleman.

"It is customary, I suppose, in reading Martial, to leave out these pleasant verses; I never heard of them, at least, until I found them for myself; and this partiality is one among a thousand things that help to build up our distorted and hysterical conception of the great Roman Empire" (*Books which have influenced me*).—BIBLIOGRAPHY: W. M. Lindsay, *The Ancient Editions of Martial*; R. T. Bridge and E. D. C. Lake, *Select Epigrams of Martial*; L. Friedländer, *Sittengeschichte Roms*.

MARTIAL LAW. This must not be confused with military law (q.v.), being, as it is, of an entirely different nature. The term may commonly be used in two senses: (*a*) the method of governing an occupied enemy country by the will of the conqueror, known to English practice as military government; (*b*) the government (total or partial) of any portion of the Home Country or Dominions by armed force in times of expected invasion, riot, or insurrection. In case (*a*) the right so to govern an occupied country is given to the conqueror by the laws of war, and this officer may, in order to preserve tranquillity and to protect his troops, give such orders as he may consider necessary, that is, he may abolish the native courts entirely, or he may curtail or increase their powers. In case (*b*) there are two varieties differing somewhat the one from the other. According to the strictest and most accurate interpretation of the term, it means the entire suspension of the ordinary law of the land and its supersession by military government; in such a sense martial law could be put in force only by an Act of Parliament. In the second and more usual variety the power of invoking martial law is based on the common-law right of every Government to meet force by force. This power will probably be taken by Government by means of a "proclamation," which is merely a statement on the part of the Government of its intention to avail itself of its legally constituted forces to assist the civil power in keeping the peace in case of riot or insurrection, or of enforcing military precautions in case of invasion. In either case no greater area of country than is necessary will be placed under martial law, and the boundaries of such an area will be defined in the proclamation; further, all reasonable acts done by officers and soldiers in carrying out their duties will be covered by a subsequent "Act of Indemnity."

MARTIN. A name applied to several birds belonging to the swallow family. The one best known is the *Chelidon urbica*, or house-martin, a familiar British bird, which builds a rounded mud-nest under the eaves of houses, or in the upper angles of windows. In habits it resembles the chimney-swallow, but its tail is less markedly forked and the throat is white, while its nest also differs, that of the chimney-swallow being cup-shaped. The lighter-backed sand-martin (*Cotile riparia*) excavates a burrow in the face of a cliff or bank, and makes a loose nest of grass and feathers. *See* SWALLOW.

MARTIN, ST., or ST. MARTIN OF TOURS. Born of heathen parents in Pannonia about the year A.D. 316. He served under Constantius and Julian, and went to Gaul. Among other virtuous and benevolent acts, he divided his cloak with a poor man whom he met at the gates of Amiens (Ambianum). The legend says that Christ appeared to him in the following night covered with the half of this cloak. Soon after this vision Martin was baptized, in 337.

After living many years in retirement he visited his native place, and converted his mother. About the year 375 he was chosen against his will Bishop of Tours. In order to withdraw himself from the world he built the famous convent of Marmoutiers, and is said to have died about the year 400. He was the first saint to whom the Roman Church offered public adoration. His festival takes place on the 11th of November.—Cf. J. G. Cazenove, *St. Hilary of Poitiers and St. Martin of Tours.*

MARTIN, St. One of the Leeward Islands, lying close to Anguilla, and divided between France and Holland, the inhabitants speaking English. The Dutch (south) portion has an area of 17 sq. miles; pop. 2312. It is included in the colony of Curaçao (q.v.). The French (north) portion is a dependency of Guadeloupe (q.v.).

MARTINEAU (mar'ti-nō), **Harriet.** English authoress, of French Huguenot descent, born at Norwich 1802, died at Ambleside 1876. Her works include: *Deerbrook*; *The Hour and the Man*; *Eastern Life, Past and Present*; and a *History of England during the Thirty Years' Peace.*—Cf. F. F. Miller, *Harriet Martineau.*

MARTINEAU, James. Unitarian minister and philosophical writer, a younger brother of Harriet Martineau, was born at Norwich 1805, died 1900. He was educated at the Norwich Grammar School, Dr. Lant Carpenter's school at Bristol, and Manchester New College, York. After holding ministerial appointments in Dublin and Liverpool, he became in 1841 professor of mental and moral philosophy in Manchester New College.

In 1857 he removed to London, and was minister of Little Portland Street Chapel from 1859 to 1872. From 1869 to 1885 he held the principalship of Manchester New College (which from 1857 had been in London). Among his works are: *The Rationale of Religious Inquiry* (1836), *Endeavours after the Christian Life* (2 vols., 1843-47), *Miscellanies* (1852), *Studies of Christianity* (1858), *Essays Philosophical and Theological* (1868), *Modern Materialism* (1876), *Hours of Thought on Sacred Things* (2 vols., 1876-80), *A Study of Spinoza* (1882), *Types of Ethical Theory* (1885), *A Study of Religion* (2 vols., 1887), etc. —Cf. J. H. Hertz, *The Ethical System of James Martineau.*

MARTIN - HARVEY, Sir John. English actor-manager. He was born at Wyvenhoe in Essex on 22nd June, 1867. Educated at King's College School, London, and intended for a naval architect, he later studied for the stage and made his first appearance in 1881 at the Court Theatre. He was with Henry Irving's company for fourteen years. In 1897 he began work under his own management, and was knighted in 1921.

He has played in Shakespeare, *The Only Way* (achieving remarkable success in the character part of Sydney Carton), *The Corsican Brothers*, *Pelleas and Melisande*, *The Cigarette Maker's Romance*, *The King's Messenger*, etc.

MARTINIQUE. A French island of the Windward group, West Indies; area, 385 sq. miles. It is of volcanic origin, culminating in Mont Pelée (4430 feet), other volcanic peaks being Pitons de Carbet (3963 feet) and Vauclin (1656 feet). Sugar, rum, and cocoa, with some coffee, tobacco, and cotton, are the chief productions and exports. There are one hundred and twenty-six rum distilleries and fifteen sugar-works on the island. The former commercial capital, St. Pierre, was destroyed by an eruption of Mont Pelée (May, 1902), and Fort-de-France (pop. 43,338) has taken its place. There is a law school at Fort-de-France and a lycée for boys. Pop. (1931), 234,695.

Martinique was the birthplace of Joséphine, and the home for a time of Mme. de Maintenon. It was discovered by Spaniards on St. Martin's Day (1493), being then peopled by Caribs. In 1635 it was settled by the French, who exterminated the Caribs. It was twice taken and held by the British (1794-1802, 1809-14). The present Government comprises a Governor, a General Council, and elective municipal councils, and the colony is represented in Paris by a Senator and two Deputies.—Cf. H. Monet, *La Martinique.*

MARTOS (ancient **Colonia Augusta Gemella**). A town of Jaen province, Andalusia, Spain, with a trade in grain, oil, and wine. It was taken from the Moors by Ferdinand III. (1225). Pop. 20,000.

MARTYRS (Gr. for "witnesses"). A name applied by the Christian Church to those persons in particular who, in the early ages of Christianity and during the great persecutions, suffered ignominy and death rather than renounce their faith.

Festivals in honour of the martyrs seem to have been observed as early as the second century. The Christians offered prayers at the tombs of the martyrs, and thanked God for the example which they had given to the world. The rite was concluded with the sacrament of the Lord's Supper and the distribution of alms. Eulogies were also delivered, and accounts of the lives and actions of the deceased read.

MAR'VELL, Andrew. A political and miscellaneous writer, born at Hull in 1621, died in London 1678. In 1635 he went to Trinity College, Cambridge. After travelling for four years on the Continent, he was appointed assistant to Milton in his office of Latin secretary. In 1660 he was chosen member of Parliament for his native place, which he represented to the end of his life. Besides a small handful of finely musical poems, he composed much humorous and satirical verse, and was the writer of several political pamphlets.

MARX, Karl Heinrich. German economist and founder of a school of Socialism, born at Trèves (Trier) 1818, died in London 1883. He studied history and philosophy at the Universities of Bonn and Berlin. After living at Cologne and Paris, in

Karl Marx

1845 he proceeded to Brussels, where he wrote his *Misère de la Philosophie.* In 1847 he drew up, in conjunction with Engels, whose acquaintance he had made in Paris, the famous *Communist Manifesto*, a document which embodies the creeds of the Socialist-revolutionaries. He took part in the Revolution of 1848 in the Rhine country, and in 1849 he settled permanently in London.

In 1864 he was at last able to realize his plan of organizing the working-men of the civilized world, and on 28th Sept., at a meeting in St. Martin's Hall, he outlined his scheme and founded the International Working-Men's Association. The first volume of his great work *Das Kapital* appeared in 1867; the second volume was completed by Engels and published in 1885; and the third volume appeared in 1895.

As an economist, Marx carefully analysed the "theory of value" and the nature of capitalistic production. The measure of the value of an article is, according to Marx, the amount of labour necessary to produce it. The labourers, however, produce more than they consume, but under the capitalistic régime they lose the surplus value, i.e. of what they produce over and above their wages. The capitalist is therefore the enemy of the labourer, and it is in the latter's interest to emancipate himself from the régime of the former.

He also traced the growth of the working-classes, or the proletariat, and maintained that "the emancipation of the working-classes must be accomplished through the working-classes themselves." BIBLIOGRAPHY: B. Croce, *Historical Materialism and the Economics of Marx*; J. Spargo, *Karl Marx: his Life and Doctrine*; E. B. Aveling, *The Student's Marx.*

MARY, The Virgin. The mother of Jesus, according to tradition embodied in the apocryphal gospels the daughter of Joachim and Anna (cf. Luke ii. 36). The story of her life so far as it is given in the New Testament begins with her betrothal to Joseph (Luke i.), and the narrative of the birth of Christ. She is thrice mentioned during Christ's public ministry (John ii.; Matt. xii. 47; John xix. 25-27), and once after his death (Acts i. 14). A tradition asserts that she lived and died at Jerusalem under the care of John; another that she died at Ephesus, to which she and John had retired from the siege of Jerusalem.

A later tradition asserts that on her grave being opened three days after her burial only the grave-clothes were found in it. The devotion or adoration paid by Roman Catholics and others to the Virgin Mary is condemned by Protestants in general, who stigmatize it as *Mariolatry.*

The title of Mary to adoration did not become a tenet in the orthodox Latin Church till the sixth century, when the Christian Church began to celebrate festivals in her honour, of which the Purification, the Annunciation, and the Visitation (the visit of Mary to Elizabeth) are still retained in Protestant countries.

The Greek and Roman Catholics,

and the schismatic Churches in the East, observe several feasts besides the above in honour of the Virgin; for instance the birth of Mary, and her death and reception into heaven (by the Roman Catholics called the *Assumption*). The festival of the Immaculate Conception is celebrated only by the Roman Catholic Church. —Cf. J. S. Northcote, *Mary in the Gospels*.

MARY I. Queen of England, daughter of Henry VIII. by Catherine of Aragon, born in 1516, died 1558. After her mother's death she was declared illegitimate, but was restored to her rights when the succession was finally settled in 1544. She was brought up by her mother in the Roman Catholic faith, on which account she was treated with rigour under Edward VI. She ascended the throne in 1553, after an abortive attempt to set her aside in favour of Lady Jane Grey.

One of her first measures was the reinstatement of the Roman Catholic prelates who had been superseded in the late reign. Her marriage to Philip II. of Spain, united as it was with a complete restoration of the Catholic worship, produced much discontent.

Insurrections broke out under Cave in Devonshire, and Wyat in Kent, which, although suppressed, formed sufficient excuses for the imprisonment of the Princess Elizabeth in the Tower, and the execution of Lady Jane Grey and her husband, Lord Guildford Dudley. England was now formally declared to be reconciled to the Pope; the sanguinary laws against heretics were revived, and nearly 300 perished at the stake, including Cranmer, Latimer, and Ridley.

Under Philip's influence a war began with France, which ended in the loss of Calais in 1558, after it had been held by England for above 200 years. This disgrace told acutely upon Mary's disordered health, and she died shortly afterwards.

MARY II. Queen of England, born in 1662, died 1694. She was the elder daughter of James, Duke of York, afterwards James II., by his wife Anne Hyde, daughter of Lord Clarendon. Married in 1677 to William, Prince of Orange, when the Revolution dethroned her father, she was declared joint-possessor of the throne with William, on whom all the administration of the government devolved. During the absence of William in Ireland in 1690, and during his various visits to the Continent, Mary managed at home with extreme prudence. She was strongly attached to the Protestant religion and the Church of England. *See* WILLIAM III.

MARY. Queen Consort of King George V., born at Kensington Palace 26th May, 1867, daughter of the Duke of Teck. Queen Mary's baptismal names were Victoria Mary Augusta Louisa Olga Pauline Claudine Agnes. On the death of the Duke of Clarence (14th Jan., 1892), to whom she was betrothed, she became engaged to (3rd May, 1893), and married his brother, the Duke of York, second son of King Edward VII. (6th July, 1893). The Duke of York, created Prince of Wales in 1901, ascended the throne with his consort on 6th May, 1910, and on 22nd June, 1911, they were crowned in Westminster Abbey. During the period of War and after, Queen Mary filled with great dignity, constant industry, and unfailing courtesy the high position of first Lady of the Land. Her solicitude for the troops was notable. During the King's illness, 1928-29, she acted as President of the Council of State. Of their six children, the youngest, John, died in 1919. The others are the Prince of Wales, the Dukes of York and Gloucester, Prince George, and Mary, Princess Royal.

MARYBOROUGH. A port of Queensland, Australia, 140 miles N. of Brisbane, on the railway line from Brisbane to Rockhampton. It is the trading centre for a district. Gold and coal are mined, and sugar is grown. Pop. (1931), 12,000.

MARYLAND. A maritime state of the United States, one of the thirteen original states. It lies around Chesapeake Bay, occupying part of the peninsula formed by the Chesapeake and Delaware Bays, and extending inland to West Virginia, bounded on the south by the Potomac and on the north by Pennsylvania. It has about 35 miles of seaboard on the Atlantic, the bulk of the natural Atlantic coast-line being occupied by Delaware in the north and by a detached portion of Virginia in the south. Maryland is divided into twenty-three counties and Baltimore City.

Baltimore is the principal seaport and commercial centre (pop. in 1930, 804,874), but Annapolis is the capital (pop. 12,531). Other towns and their populations (1930) are: Cumberland (37,747), Hagerstown (30,861), Frederick (14,434), Salisbury (10,997). Agriculture is the principal industry, and wheat the main crop, but maize, potatoes, vegetables, fruit, and tobacco are also raised. Dairying and sheep-farming are extensive. Coal and clay are worked, and some slate is quarried. The oyster fisheries are the most important in the United States.

Maryland is the eighth state in manufacturing importance; first in canning and in fertilizer manufacture, eighth in tobacco production, second in iron and shipbuilding, and third in clothing manufactures. There are two universities and an agricultural college, and other institutions for music and art. State area, 12,300 sq. miles (2430 water, Chesapeake Bay alone occupying 1203 sq. miles); pop. (1931), 1,631,526.

Maryland was founded (1632) by Leonard Calvert, acting on behalf of Lord Baltimore, his brother, and the name is commemorative of Henrietta Maria, Queen of Charles I. The state is now governed by a General Assembly consisting of a Senate (29 members), and a House of Delegates (118 members). Senators serve for four years, one half being re-elected every two years: delegates are elected for two years. Two Senators and six Representatives are sent to Congress.—Cf. W. H. Browne, *Maryland* (American Commonwealth Series).

MARYLEBONE, St. A metropolitan borough of the county of London. It contains the Middlesex Hospital, Bedford College, Philharmonic and Queen's Halls, Lord's Cricket Ground, and Madame Tussaud's Waxwork; and its area embraces St. John's Wood district, most of Regent's Park, Cavendish and Portman Squares, Wimpole Street, as well as the railway stations of Marylebone and Baker Street, and Harley Street. The name of the borough means St. Mary's on the brook, the brook being the Tyburn. Much of the land forms the Portland estate, now the property of Lord Howard de Walden. Pop. (1931), 97,620.

MARYPORT. A seaport of Cumberland, England, at the mouth of the Ellen, and on the Solway Firth; served by the Maryport and Carlisle Railway. There are coal and iron mines in the vicinity, for which Maryport is the shipping outlet. The main industries are shipbuilding, saw-milling, and iron-founding. Maryport (formerly Ellenfoot) was so named in 1750 because Mary Queen of Scots landed there in 1568. Pop. (1931), 10,182.

MARY STEWART. Queen of Scots, was born at Linlithgow Palace in 1542, beheaded 8th Feb., 1587. She was the daughter of James V. by his queen, Mary of Lorraine, a princess of the family of Guise. Her father dying when she was a few days old, the regency was, after some dispute, vested in the Earl of Arran. In 1558 she was married to the dauphin, afterwards Francis II. He died seventeen months after his accession to the crown, in Dec., 1560, and in Aug., 1561, the widowed queen returned to Scotland.

Mary was a Roman Catholic, but when she returned to Scotland she found that the influence of the Presbyterians was paramount in her kingdom. Though inclined to have Roman Catholicism again set up in Scotland, after a vain attempt to influence Knox she resigned herself to circumstances, quietly allowed her half-brother, the Protestant Earl

Mary, Queen of Scots

of Moray, to assume the position of first minister, surrounded herself with a number of other Protestant advisers, and dismissed the greater part of her train of French courtiers.

She even gave these ministers her active support in various measures that had the effect of strengthening the Presbyterian party; but she still continued to have the mass performed in her own private chapel at Holyrood. At first her subjects were quiet, she herself was popular, and her court was one of the most brilliant in Europe.

The calamities of Mary began with her marriage to her cousin, Lord Darnley (29th July, 1565). Darnley was a Roman Catholic, and immediately after the marriage the Earl of Moray and others of the Protestant lords combined against the new order of things. They were compelled to take refuge in England, and the popularity of Mary began to decline. In addition to this, Darnley proved a weak and worthless profligate, and almost entirely alienated the queen by his complicity in the murder of Rizzio (9th March, 1566), though a reconciliation seemed to be effected between them about the time of the birth of their son, afterwards James VI. of Scotland and I. of England (19th June, 1566).

About the close of the same year, however, Darnley withdrew from the court, and in the meantime the Earl of Bothwell had risen high in the queen's favour. When the young prince James was baptized at Stirling Castle, on the 7th of Dec., 1566, Bothwell did the honours of the occasion, and Darnley, the father of the prince, was not even present. Once more, however, an apparent reconciliation took place between the king and queen. Darnley had fallen ill, and was lying at Glasgow under the care of his father. Mary visited him, and took measures for his removal to Edinburgh, where he was lodged in a house called Kirk-of-Field, close to the city wall.

He was there tended by the queen herself; but during the absence of Mary at a masque at Holyrood the house in which Darnley lay was blown up by gunpowder, and he himself was afterwards found dead with marks of violence on his person (9th Feb., 1567). The circumstances attending this crime were very imperfectly investigated, but popular suspicion unequivocally pointed to Bothwell as the ringleader in the outrage, and the queen herself was suspected, suspicion becoming still stronger when she was carried off by Bothwell, with little show of resistance, to his castle of Dunbar, and married to him on the 15th of May.

A number of the nobles now banded together against Bothwell, who succeeded in collecting a force; but on Carberry Hill, where the armies met on the 15th June, his army melted away. The queen was forced to surrender herself to her insurgent nobles, Bothwell making his escape to Dunbar, then to the Orkney Islands, and finally to Denmark. The confederates first conveyed the queen to Edinburgh, and thence to Loch Leven Castle, where she was placed in the custody of Lady Douglas, mother of the Earl of Moray.

A few days after, on the 20th of June, a casket containing eight letters and some poetry, all said to be in the handwriting of the queen, fell into the hands of the confederates. The letters, which have come down to us only in the form of a translation appended to Buchanan's *Detection*, clearly show, if they are genuine, that the writer was herself a party to the murder of Darnley.

They were held by the confederates to afford unmistakable evidence of the queen's guilt, and on the 24th of July she was forced to sign a document renouncing the crown of Scotland in favour of her infant son, and appointing the Earl of Moray regent during her son's minority.

After remaining nearly a year in captivity Mary succeeded in making her escape from Loch Leven (2nd May, 1568), and, assisted by the few friends who still remained attached to her, made an effort for the recovery of her power. Defeated by the Regent's forces at the battle of Langside (13th May, 1568), she fled to England, and wrote to Elizabeth entreating protection and a personal interview; but this the latter refused to grant until Mary should have cleared herself from the charges laid against her by her subjects.

For one reason or another Elizabeth never granted Mary an interview, but kept her in more or less close captivity in England, where her life was passed in a succession of intrigues for accomplishing her deliverance. For more than eighteen years she continued to be the prisoner of Elizabeth, and in that time the place of her imprisonment was frequently changed, her final prison being Fotheringhay Castle, Northamptonshire.

She was at last accused of being implicated in a plot by one Babington against Elizabeth's life, and having been tried by a court of Elizabeth's appointing, was on the 25th of Oct., 1586, condemned to be executed. There was a long delay before Elizabeth signed the warrant, but this was at last done on the 1st of Feb., 1587. Mary received the news with great serenity, and was beheaded a week later, on 8th Feb., 1587, in the castle of Fotheringhay. Authorities are more agreed as to the attractions, talents, and accomplishments of Mary Stewart than as to her character.

Contemporary writers who saw her unite in testifying to the beauty of her person, and the fascination of her manners and address. She was witty in conversation, and ready in dispute. In her trial for alleged complicity in Babington's plot she held her ground against the ablest statesmen and lawyers of England.—BIBLIOGRAPHY: Agnes Strickland, *Life of Mary, Queen of Scots*; H. G. Bell, *Life of Mary, Queen of Scots.*

MASACCIO (mȧ-sȧt'chō), properly **TOMMASO GUIDI.** One of the oldest painters of the Florentine school, said to have been born about 1401, died at Rome about 1428. In the church dei Carmine, at Florence, are some excellent paintings of his. Baldinucci and Vasari place Masaccio among the first painters by whom the harshness and difficulty of the art was diminished, and life and expression given to it. His *Madonna and Child* is in the National Gallery, London.

MASAI. An African nomad people mainly found in Kenya Colony and Uganda.

MASARYK, Thomas Garrigue. President of the Czecho-Slovak Republic. Born 7th March, 1850, in Moravia, a coachman's son, he was first a blacksmith. After study at Vienna and Leipzig Universities he took to teaching, and at twenty-nine became lecturer on philosophy and professor at Prague. He was a member of the Austrian parliament, 1891-93. Re-elected in 1907 he opposed the encroachment of Germany on Austria and the aggressive policy of Austria in the Balkans. While lecturing at King's College, London, during the War, he organised the Czecho-Slovakian Movement for Independence. He is the author of *The New Europe*, 1918, and *The Making of a State*, 1925. He was made President of Czecho-Slovakia in 1918, re-elected in 1920, and again in 1927.

MASBATÉ. An island of the Philippine group, south of Luzon, forming, with adjacent islands, the province of Masbaté. The capital is Masbaté. Area, 1255 sq. miles; pop. 108,800.

MASCARA. A town of Algeria, about 90 miles S.E. of Oran. Pop. (1931), 31,449.

MASCARENE ISLANDS. The collective name for Réunion, Mauritius, and Rodriguez, so called from the discovery of Réunion (Bourbon Island) by the Portuguese navigator Mascarenhas (1545).

MASEFIELD, John Edward. English poet. Born at Ledbury, 1st June, 1878, the son of a solicitor, he was educated at King's School, Warwick, and trained as a seaman. After a voyage to Chile as an apprentice he became an officer in the merchant service. He left the sea after a few years and spent some time in New York before returning to England. In 1902 he published *Salt Water Ballads*, and in 1911, *The Everlasting Mercy*. Henceforward he took high rank among the poets of the day. Other notable poems include, *The Widow in the Bye Street* and *The Daffodil Fields*. In 1930 he was appointed Poet Laureate.

Masefield has also written dramas and a good deal of prose. His dramas include *Pompey the Great, The Faithful, Good Friday, The Trial of Jesus*, and *The Coming of Christ*. Among his novels are *Captain Margaret, Multitude and Solitude, Sard Harker*, and *The Hawbucks*. Other books are *The Old Front Line* and *Gallipoli* (dealing with the World War) and a study of Shakespeare. He also edited *The Voyages of Captain William Dampier*. At his home at Boar's Hill, near Oxford, he constructed a private theatre.

MASHONALAND. The country south of the Zambezi (South Africa), now comprising, with Matabeleland, Southern Rhodesia. Salisbury is the chief town. *See* RHODESIA.

MASK. A covering for the face, often shaped so as to form a rude representation of the human features. Masks have been in use from the most ancient times. Among the Greeks they were used particularly in the processions and ceremonies attending the worship of Dionysus (Bacchus). As the origin of Grecian tragedy was closely connected with the worship of Dionysus, masks were used in it even in its early days.

The ancient masks usually covered the whole head, and accordingly represented the features, head, hair, and eyes. They had mostly very large open mouths, and seem to have had some effect in strengthening the voice of the speaker, this being required by the immense size of the ancient theatres. The Roman theatre differed little from the Grecian in the use of the mask, which the Italian popular theatre, called Commedia dell' Arte, closely resembling the old Roman mime and pantomime, still retains. The mask used at masked balls or masquerades is a covering for the head and face made from a light stuff, a common form being the half-mask covering eyes and nose only.

MASKINONGY (*Esox nobilior*). A fine North American freshwater fish of the pike genus, inhabiting the St. Lawrence basin, and twice the size of the common kind.

MASON-BEES. A name given to solitary bees of the genus Chalicodoma, which construct their nests with sand or gravel, agglutinated together by means of a viscid saliva, and fix them on the side of walls.

MASON-SPIDER (Cteniza). A spider more commonly known as a "Trap-door Spider" (q.v.).

MASON-WASP. A name given to certain solitary wasps, especially species of Eumenes and Odynerus, the former making curved clay-nests, and the latter burrowing in sand.

MASO'RA, or **MASSO'RAH.** A Hebrew word signifying "tradition," the name of a collection of notes referring to the Hebrew text of the Old Testament, and written in Chaldee chiefly on the margin of Hebrew MSS. These notes are various in their character, critical, grammatical, and explanatory, and include an indication of the vowel-points and accentuation of the Hebrew text according to the Jewish tradition.

At what time the accumulation of these notes was commenced cannot be ascertained. According to some Jewish writers they were begun in the time of Ezra. A large part of them were compiled in the Jewish schools of Tiberias subsequent to the third century, and the collection was not completed till the eighth century at the earliest.—Cf. C. D. Ginsburg, *The Massorah*.

MASPERO, Sir Gaston Camille Charles. French Egyptologist. Born at Paris, 23rd June, 1846; in 1874 he became Professor of Egyptology at the College de France. He was for many years the keeper and director of the museum at Bulak, and carried out notable excavations at Memphis, Carnac, Sakkara, etc. He was the author of several works on the history of Egypt. He was awarded the K.C.M.G. in 1909, and died in Paris, 30th June, 1916.

MASQUE. A form of entertainment popular at court and among the nobility in England during the reigns of Elizabeth, James I., and Charles I. The history of the English masque is inseparably connected with the name of Ben Jonson, who wrote about half of all the extant masques. The pre-Jonsonian masque was spectacular and of no literary importance. Typical specimens will be found in *Timon of Athens*, i. 2, and in *Henry VIII.*, i. 4. Jonson's earliest masques were embedded in *Cynthia's Revels* (1600), and followed the old tradition.

His first court masque was *The Masque of Blackness* (1605), other notable ones being *The Masque of Queens* (1609), *Love Restored* (1612), *News from the New World discovered in the Moon* (1621), and the last of his masques, *Chloridia* (1631). Other famous writers of masques were Fletcher (none of whose masques has been preserved), Beaumont, Campion, Daniel, and Davenant, who wrote the last of all the masques, *Salmacida Spolia* (1640). The Civil War put an end to the masque, as it did to many of the amenities of life in England.

The masque has sometimes been defined as a kind of miniature drama, but it is not a drama and is not subject to the laws of dramatic criticism. It always had for its central feature a dance or series of dances. The dancing-master, who was paid £50 for his services, was more important than the librettist or even the designer of scenery, who were paid £40 a-piece.

The masquers were eight, twelve, or sixteen in number. They were noble lords and ladies as a rule, the king and queen sometimes taking part themselves. Their sole duty was to look imposing and to dance; they did not speak or sing. Their costumes were elaborate and costly, and they represented mythological or heroic characters. Every masquer was accompanied by a torch-bearer. The masquers danced the following dances, first the Entry or Descent, then the Main Dance; then they chose partners from among the audience and danced the Revels, quick lively dances performed without rehearsal. Finally they danced their going-out dance.

It became customary to introduce each masque by means of an anti-masque, which Jonson defined as "a foil or false masque . . . not unaptly consorting with the current and whole fall of the device." It is chiefly Jonson's skill in writing anti-masques that gives his work the pre-eminence; some of his anti-masques (e.g. in *Love Restored*) contain excellent dialogue. The actors in the anti-masque and those who spoke or sang in the masque proper were frequently professionals. Masques were almost always performed at Christmas time, often on Twelfth Night, or else at Shrovetide.

They were almost all performed in the Banqueting House at Whitehall. The scenery, machinery, and dresses were usually designed by Inigo Jones, the music was written by Alfonso Ferrabosco and by Nicholas Lanier. The masque was the spoilt child of the arts—poetry, painting, and music were lavished upon it. It was a costly toy; *The Masque of Blackness* cost £3000, and *The Masque of Queens* £4000—immense sums of money in those days.—BIBLIOGRAPHY: P. Reyher, *Les Masques anglais*; H. A. Evans, *English Masques*; M. Sullivan, *Court Masques of James I.*; E. K. Chambers, *The Mediæval Stage*.

MASS. In the Roman Catholic Church, the prayers and ceremonies which accompany the consecration of the eucharist. The word is used generally for all that part of the Catholic service in which the eucharist is offered. At present the mass consists of four chief parts: (1) the introduction; (2) the *offertorium*, or sacrifice; (3) the consecration; (4) the communion. These four chief parts, of which the three last are considered the most essential, are composed of several smaller parts, each having its proper denomination.

They consist of prayers, hymns, shorter and longer passages of the Holy Scriptures, and a number of ceremonies, which, as the essential point of the mass is the sacrifice of the Lord, consist partly of symbolical ceremonies commemorative of important circumstances in the Saviour's life, or signs of devotion and homage paid to the presence of the Lord in the host. The order of these ceremonies, and of the whole celebration of the mass, is given in the missal or mass-book.

The masses are modified according to many circumstances, e.g. according to the saint in honour of whom the mass is celebrated, or the seasons of the year connected with different events in the Saviour's life, or the purpose for which the mass is said, as the *missa pro defunctis* (mass for the dead).

Votive mass is an extraordinary mass, instead of that of the day, rehearsed on some special occasion. *Low mass* is the ordinary mass performed by the priest, without music. *High mass* is celebrated by the priest, assisted by a deacon and sub-deacon or other clergy, and sung by the choristers, accompanied by the organ and other musical instruments. Besides these there are different masses according to the different rites; the *Greek mass*, the *Latin mass*, the *Roman* and *Gregorian mass*, etc.—BIBLIOGRAPHY: L. Duchesne, *Origines du Culte chrétien*; C. H. H. Wright, *The Service of the Mass in the Greek and Roman Churches*; H. Lucas, *Holy Mass*; A. G. Mortimer, *Catholic Faith and Practice*.

MASSACHU'SETTS. A maritime state of New England, United States, one of the original thirteen states. It has a large coast-line on the Atlantic, and is traversed by the Connecticut and other rivers; the coastal plain rises gradually to the east, where the Berkshire Hills run from north to south. The most important railways are the Boston and Albany, Boston and Maine, and the New York, New Haven, and Hartford Railway, all of which have termini in Boston, the state capital. There is a Boston-Cambridge elevated track, and a total electric mileage of 1893, the steam railway mileage, main and branch (1931), being 2014.

The state is divided into 14 counties and contains 39 cities and 316 towns. Although it has been transformed from a rural to an industrial community, Massachusetts still has some agriculture, dairy- and sheep-farming, potatoes (1,950,000 bushels in 1932), maize, and tobacco being produced.

Among manufactures are boots, leather, cottons, woollens, machinery, and paper; stock-yards, abattoirs, and canneries are prominent. A large foreign trade is carried on through Boston and eight associated minor ports, collectively called Massachusetts Customs District.

The cities whose population in 1930 exceeded 100,000 were Boston, Worcester, Springfield, Fall River, Cambridge, New Bedford, Somerville, Lynn, and Lowell.

There are 31 colleges and universities (including Harvard), 3 of which are sectarian (2 Roman Catholic, 1 Methodist), and 7 devoted exclusively to women; a State Department of Education exercises a general control. State area (including Atlantic islands of Nantucket and Martha's Vineyard) 8266 sq. miles, 227 sq. miles being water; pop. (1930), 4,249,614.

Massachusetts is supposed to have been visited by the Norsemen about A.D. 1000, but it was not permanently settled until the Pilgrim Fathers founded Plymouth (Dec., 1620). Other Puritans settled Salem (1628), subsequently called Massachusetts Bay Colony. Boston was settled in 1630. In 1692 the two original colonies were definitely merged.

The government now consists of the General Court of Massachusetts, comprising a Senate (40 members elected annually from the 40 State Senatorial districts), and a House of Representatives (240 members elected from 159 districts, each returning a quota based on population). Two Senators and 15 Representatives are sent to Federal Congress.—Cf. L. A. Frothingham, *A Brief Outline of the Constitution and Government of Massachusetts*.

MASS ACTION, The law of. A principle in physical chemistry discovered in Christiania by Guldberg and Waage. Some chemical reactions take place much more quickly than others, the speed depending upon the strengths of the reacting substances. Guldberg and Waage found that the velocity at which a reaction proceeds is proportional to the product of the strengths of the reacting substances; thus if a substance A unites with a substance B to form a substance C, the speed at which the substance C is produced is proportional to the product of the "strength" of the substance A by that of the substance B.

The strength is technically called "the concentration" and is usually measured in *mols* per litre, or, in other words, by the number of grammes of the substance present per litre, divided by the molecular weight of the substance. This law enables a definite mathematical equation to be written down expressing the rate at which the new substance is formed, in terms of the concentrations of the reacting substances, and the solution of this equation gives the complete history of the chemical change from its start till the moment of its completion.

On the other hand, the progress of the chemical change can often be studied experimentally, and by comparing experiment with theory it is possible to determine the mechanism of the reaction. For instance, when arsine (AsH_3) decomposes into arsenic and hydrogen, one might suppose that, since $2AsH_3=2As+3H_2$, the reaction proceeds by the union of a pair of molecules of arsine, with the formation of metallic arsenic and three molecules of hydrogen.

The progress of this reaction can be easily studied, because 1 c.c. of arsine gives 1·5 c.c. of hydrogen, and hence, if the reaction proceeds at constant volume and temperature, the pressure must rise, and the rate of rise of pressure is clearly a measure of the rate at which the reaction proceeds.

A curve can thus be plotted showing the amount of hydrogen present, in terms of the time. This curve can also be found by the law of mass action. If the reaction were $AsH_3+AsH_3 \rightarrow 2As+3H_2$, the rate at which the hydrogen is formed would depend on the square of the concentration of the arsine, for it is proportional, by the Law of Mass Action, to the concentration of arsine multiplied by the concentration of arsine.

On the other hand, if it were a monomolecular reaction, due to the splitting up of the individual AsH_3 molecules, the velocity of reaction would be simply proportional to the concentration of arsine (not to the square of it). The curve giving the amount of hydrogen in terms of time on the latter assumption agrees with the experimental curve, and hence we conclude that the reaction is monomolecular.

In this way the law affords valuable information as to the mechanism of chemical changes. In particular the law plays a most important part in the study of radio-activity, the various laws of decay of the activity of the radio-active substances being calculated by its aid and checked by experiment.—BIBLIOGRAPHY: W. C. McC. Lewis, *A System of Physical Chemistry* (vol. i.); J. H. Van't Hoff, *Lectures on Theoretical and Physical Chemistry*; R. A. Lehfeldt, *Text-Book of Physical Chemistry*; F. F. P. Bisacre, *Applied Calculus.*

MASSA-E-CARRARA. A province of Tuscany, North Italy. The chief product is Carrara marble. Massa, near Marina di Massa, its seaport, is the joint capital with Carrara. The pop. of Massa (commune) was, in 1931, 39,841. Area of province, 446 sq. miles; pop. (1931), 189,678.

MASSAGE. *See* REMEDIAL EXERCISES AND MASSAGE.

MASSAGETÆ (mas-saj'e-tē). A collective name given by the ancients to the nomadic tribes of Central Asia who dwelt to the east and north-east of the Caspian Sea. Cyrus is supposed to have lost his life in fighting against them.

MASSAWA. The chief port of Eritrea, on an atoll in the Red Sea, and joined to the mainland by a causeway. It is a pearl-fishing centre, and has a large transit trade. A railway runs from Massawah to Asmara, the seat of government (75 miles), with extensions to Cheren (65 miles) and Agordat (53 miles); the line from Agordat to Tessenei is still under construction. There is a wireless station at Massawah, ensuring communication between Coltano (Italy) and Italian Somaliland. Pop. 4154 (654 European, mainly Italian).—The *commissariat* (district) of Massawah has an area of 5106 sq. miles; pop. 42,406. Asmara (altitude, 7765 feet) has a pop. of 21,601 (3101 Europeans).

MASSÉNA (mȧs-ā-nȧ), **André.** Marshal of France, born in 1756 at Nice, died 1817. In 1775 he entered the French army and became sous-officier-adjudant. During the Revolution he entered a battalion of volunteers, was elected chief of his battalion in 1792, and in 1793 made general of brigade. In 1794 he was appointed general of division, and took command of the right wing of the French army in Italy.

In 1799 he defeated the Austrian and Russian forces at Zürich, and in 1800, by his defence of Genoa for three months, gave Bonaparte time to strike successfully at Marengo. In 1804 he was created marshal of the Empire. In 1805 he received the chief command in Italy. In 1807 he was given the command of the right wing of the French army

André Masséna

in Poland, and soon after received the title of duc de Rivoli.

In 1809 he distinguished himself against the Austrians, and at Esslingen his constancy and firmness saved the French army from total destruction. Napoleon rewarded him with the dignity of Prince of Esslingen. In 1810 he took command of the army in Portugal, and forced Wellington within the lines of Torres Vedras, till want of provisions compelled Masséna to retire.

Napoleon recalled him from Spain, and in 1812 left him without a command. In 1814 he was made a peer by Louis XVIII., and though on the return of the emperor he acknowledged his authority, he took no active part in the events of the Hundred Days.

MASSENET (màs-nā), **Jules.** French composer, born in 1842, died 1912. He studied at the Paris Conservatoire, of which in 1878 he became a professor. He composed several operas, of which the best known are *Herodias, Don César de Bazan,* and *Manon Lescaut.* His *Scènes Pittoresques* are also well known, and there is a long list of works by him, including the choral works *Maria Magdalene, Eva, La Vierge,* etc.

MASSINGER, Philip. English dramatist, was born at Salisbury 1583, and died in London in 1640. His father was a member of Parliament, and was attached to the household of the second Earl of Pembroke. He was educated at St. Alban's Hall, Oxford, which he entered in 1602 and left, without taking a degree, in 1606. The third Earl of Pembroke (often identified wlth Mr. W. H. of Shakespeare's *Sonnets*) was not a patron of Massinger's, and this has been explained by supposing that the dramatist became a Roman Catholic. The evidence is not conclusive, but there are indications in three plays which support this theory.

The Renegado is a dramatized treatise on Christian evidences, *The Virgin Martyr* is a chronicle of Christian martyrdom, and *The Maid of Honour* ends with Camiola taking the veil. Almost all that we know about Massinger's life apart from his plays is that he was often short of money. In his early days he almost invariably collaborated, sometimes with Dekker, oftener with Fletcher. Of the so-called Beaumont and Fletcher plays, at least eighteen are believed to contain the work of Massinger.

When Massinger died, he was buried in the same grave as Fletcher. There are nineteen plays extant which are Massinger's in their entirety. Eight other plays were extant in manuscript until the middle of the eighteenth century, when they were used for pie-covers by Betsy Baker, the cook of John Warburton, F.R.S., who had got possession of them.

Among Massinger's plays may be mentioned : *The Duke of Milan,* a fine tragedy ; *The Great Duke of Florence* (1627), a masterpiece of dramatic construction ; *The Picture* ; *The City Madam* (1632) ; and his best-known play, *A New Way to pay Old Debts* (1633). The last-named play has long been a favourite, and has kept the stage for a long time. This is mainly on account of its leading character, Sir Giles Overreach, who was drawn from the infamous extortioner Sir Giles Mompesson, banished and degraded from knighthood in 1620. This character gives a leading actor a great opportunity.

Massinger's excellent play *The Fatal Dowry* was shamelessly plagiarized by Nicholas Rowe, poet laureate and Shakespearean editor, in his *Fair Penitent* (1703), a play to which we owe the expression "a gay Lothario."

Massinger is perhaps the least

poetical of all the early dramatists. Not only can he not write lyrics; his blank verse is pedestrian and undistinguished. If, however, he stands low as a poet, as a dramatist he stands among the first. He is a masterly constructor of plots, far surpassing Fletcher, Jonson, or Webster in this respect. He was a man of a far more serious cast of mind than most of his fellow playwrights.

Some of his plays are as interesting as a novel, others as solid as a treatise on political philosophy. The drama was declining when he was writing, but he did not hasten, though he failed to delay its decline. He must be placed at the head of Caroline dramatists.—BIBLIOGRAPHY: Sir A. W. Ward, *History of English Dramatic Literature*; Sir Leslie Stephen, *Hours in a Library*; A. C. Swinburne, *Philip Massinger* (*Fortnightly Review*, July, 1889).

MASSINIS'SA. King of ancient Numidia. By the help of the Romans in the Second Punic War he added Western Numidia to his own kingdom of Eastern Numidia, having defeated Syphax, taking him prisoner with his wife Sophonisba, who had been promised to Massinissa. Massinissa now made her his wife, but Scipio Africanus, fearful of her influence, claimed her as a prisoner of Rome. Unable to resist, Massinissa sent her a poisoned chalice, of which she voluntarily drank.

Massinissa commanded the Roman cavalry on the right wing at the battle of Zama, which ended the Second Punic War (201 B.C.). His acquisition of a number of Carthaginian provinces led to the Third Punic War, in the second year of which he died (148 B.C.), aged about a hundred years. His grandson was Jugurtha.

MASSON, David. Critical and biographical writer, born at Aberdeen 2nd Dec., 1822, died at Edinburgh 6th Oct., 1907. In 1852 he was appointed to the chair of English language and literature at University College, London, and from 1865 to 1895 he occupied the chair of rhetoric and English literature in the University of Edinburgh. His works include an elaborate and comprehensive study of *Milton's Life and Times* (6 vols., 1858-80), *British Novelists and their Styles* (1859), *Recent British Philosophy* (1865), *Drummond of Hawthornden* (1873), *The Three Devils* (1874), an edition of *Milton's Poems* (1877), a *Life of De Quincey* (1878), and *Edinburgh Sketches and Memories* (1892).

MASSEY, William Ferguson. New Zealand statesman. Born at Limavady, Ireland, 26th March, 1856, he went to New Zealand in 1870 and became a farmer. In 1894 he entered Parliament and in 1903 became leader of the Conservative opposition. In 1912 he became Prime Minister, and his character and ability enabled him to lead New Zealand with success throughout the World War. A member of the Imperial War Cabinet in 1917-18 he represented his country at the Peace Conference in Paris, 1919, and attended the Imperial Conference in London in 1921. He was defeated at the general election in 1922 and died 10th May, 1925.

MASTER AND SERVANT. In legal acceptation a servant is one who owes his services to another for a limited period. Servants consist of two classes, namely, those who engage to perform certain duties for certain wages, and apprentices who may receive something by way of wages, but who have to be taught a trade. The chief classes of servants are: agricultural labourers, operatives or skilled labourers, and menials or domestic servants.

In England, if the contract for service is for more than a year, it must be drawn up in writing; if for a year or less, or for an indefinite period, it may be verbal. If the contract is for a year, and if the servant is discharged without just cause during the year, he may claim wages up to the end of the year; on the other hand, if he leave without cause before the time, he can claim no wages at all. If he happen within the year to fall sick, or be hurt or disabled in the service of his master, the master cannot, apart from agreement, put him away or abate any part of his wages for that time. But the illness of the servant may so go to the root of the consideration as to entitle the master to rescind the contract.

In the case of a yearly hiring, the hiring usually cannot be terminated by either party before the end of the year. It is sometimes agreed in a contract of service that in the event of a breach by the servant the master shall be allowed to retain as damages the accrued wages of the servant to the date of the breach. If there is no such agreement, the servant is entitled to his wages to the date of the month, but he has no right to claim part of his wages to the date of the breach if none have accrued at the date of the breach.

If a domestic servant be engaged

under no special contract, a month's warning or payment of a month's wages is all that is necessary. Operatives may be discharged or may leave at a week, a fortnight, or a month's notice, according to the recognized local or trade usage. The grounds on which a servant may be legally discharged without warning are: wilful disobedience of lawful commands within the sphere of the service for which he is engaged, gross immorality, habitual negligence, or even an isolated case of neglect if attended by serious consequences, dishonesty, permanent disability from illness, conduct incompatible with the due performance of his duties, e.g. if he takes secret commissions, and incompetence.

A servant is liable to an action for gross neglect of his master's property, and may even be indicted therefor, as when the duty involved a duty to the public also, e.g. the captain of a ship who navigates so negligently as to cause the death of a person, and also for fraud and misfeasance. In general, if a servant refuse to enter service after engagement, or leave it without sufficient cause, he is liable merely to an action for breach of contract.

A master has no right to chastise a servant, whatever the servant's age may be, but has the right of moderately correcting an apprentice under age. The master is held liable in cases where his servant, in the ordinary course of his duty and acting within the scope of implied or expressed orders, injures a third party.

A master can turn a domestic servant out of his house at a moment's warning without notice and without cause on payment of wages for the full term of the engagement, or for one month if there is no special contrary agreement.

The death of the master discharges the contract; but in Scotland the servant can claim wages for the whole of the contracted period, though he is bound in that case to serve the master's executors. In case of the bankruptcy of the master the servant, if a labourer or workman, is a privileged debtor for wages due and unpaid for two months, but not exceeding £25, and ranks as an ordinary creditor for the balance; if he is a clerk, shopman, etc., the period is four months, and the preferential limit £50; but a labourer in husbandry, paid his wages in a lump sum at the end of his year of hiring, may be entitled to payment in full. In Scotland farm and domestic servants have a preference for their full wages for the current term.

MASTER OF THE HORSE. The third chief officer in the royal household of Britain, whose duty it is to superintend the royal stables and all horses belonging to the king. He has the privilege of using the royal horses, pages, and servants, and rides next to the king on all State occasions. His tenure of office (annual salary £2000) is dependent upon the existence of his political party in power.

MASTER OF THE ROLLS. One of the judges of the Chancery Division of the High Court of Justice, the keeper of the rolls of all patents and grants that pass the Great Seal, and of all records of the Court of Chancery. He is the third member of the Supreme Court of Judicature in England, and ranks after the Lord Chief Justice of England. The salary attached to the office is £6000 a year. Before the Judicature Act of 1873 the Master of the Rolls was permitted to sit in the House of Commons.

MASTER-SINGERS (Ger. *Meistersinger*), the name of a literary guild or association which flourished in Mainz, Strasbourg, Augsburg, Nürnberg, and various other German cities, in the fourteenth and fifteenth centuries. It represented the poetical efflorescence of burgher life as the Minne-singers had represented that of the feudal chivalry. The members of the guild met and criticized one another's productions in accordance with a remarkable series of canons dealing with literary form.

Victory in their own competitions carried with it the right to take apprentices in song-craft, who at the expiry of their term, and after singing for some time with proficiency were themselves admitted as full masters. Among the most famous master-singers were Hans Sachs, Henry of Meissen (Frauenlob), Regenbogen, Hadlaub, and Muscatblut. The development of artificial canons in the search for novelty ultimately reduced the whole scheme to utter absurdity.

MASTERTON. A town of North Island, New Zealand. It is 60 miles N. of Wellington, with which it is connected by rail. The town is the centre of a large sheep-rearing district. It was damaged by the earthquake of Feb., 1931. Pop. 8525.

MASTIC, or MASTICH. A resin exuding from the mastic tree (*Pistacia Lentiscus*), a native of Southern Europe, North Africa, and Western Asia. It is principally produced in the Levant.

MASTIFF. A race of large dogs found under various names from Tibet to England. The English mastiff is a noble-looking dog with a large head, a broad muzzle, lips thick and pendulous on each side of the mouth, hanging ears, and

Mastiff

smooth hair, the height at the shoulder usually ranging from 25 to 29 inches. The old English breed was brindled, but the usual colour to-day is some shade of buff with dark muzzle and ears. The Tibet mastiff, which is also a fine animal is common in Tibet and in Bhutan, as a house dog.

MASTIFF-BAT. A name given to tropical and subtropical American bats of the genus Molossus, from a supposed resemblance of the head to that of a mastiff.

MAS'TODON. An extinct genus of Proboscidea or elephants, the fossil remains of which first occur in the Miocene rocks of the Tertiary era, and which persist through the Pliocene and Post-pliocene periods

Mastodon

also. In general structure the mastodons bear a close resemblance to the existing species of elephants. Their chief peculiarities consist in the dentition and structure of the teeth; the generic name is derived (Gr. *mastos*, breast), from the prominent mammillations on the molar teeth.

The geographical range of the mastodons included America, Europe, and Asia—one species, *Mastodon longirostris*, having inhabited England, Germany, France, and Italy. A specimen, almost entire, of *Mastodon turicensis*, from the Pliocene deposits of Piedmont, measured 17 feet from the tusks to the tail; and an American specimen measured 18 feet in length and 11 feet 5 inches in height. *Mastodon angustidens* of the European Upper Miocene developed tusks in both jaws.

MATABELELAND. *See* RHODESIA.

MATADI. A seaport of the Belgian Congo, about 90 miles up the Congo. Pop. 15,000.

MATAGALPA. A department of Central Nicaragua, traversed by the Rio Grande. It is mountainous; sugar, tobacco, and coffee are produced. Matagalpa (pop. 10,271) is the capital.

MATANZAS. A province of Cuba, hilly in the interior, and a swamp at the coast. Sugar, bananas, rice, and tobacco are produced. Area, 3256 sq. miles; population (1930), 359,562. — The capital, **Matanzas**, is the second seaport of the island, on Matanzas Bay, 55 miles by rail east of Havana. Vessels lie off in the roadstead. Sugar, rum, and molasses are exported. Pop. 70,000.

MATCHES. Prior to the early part of the nineteenth century, the principal method of producing fire was by means of the tinder-box. In 1805 Chancel invented the lucifer match, which began to supersede tinder, flint, and steel about 1820. In 1827 matches known as "Congreves" came into use. These contained the dangerous yellow phosphorus, but the red non-poisonous variety was discovered in 1845, and was afterwards used in Sweden for "safety" matches.

In all types of matches ignition is due to a chemical reaction between oxidizing and reducing substances, with the resulting formation of a flame, the act of striking being sufficient to start the reaction. Potassium, chlorate, nitre, manganese dioxide, potassium bichromate, and red oxide of lead are used as oxidizing agents.

The reducing agents (oxidizable substances) comprise yellow and red phosphorus, phosphorus sesquisulphide, antimony sulphide, sulphur, and certain thiosulphates and sulphocyanides. In addition, binding materials, such as glue, gum, and dextrine are added, also inert substances like powdered glass, sand,

and whiting, to increase friction and moderate the reaction.

Matches at present in use may be divided into two classes: those which will strike on any surface, and those if the "safety" type, which require a specially prepared surface for ignition. In the former class, the most satisfactory result is still obtained by the incorporation of a small quantity of yellow phosphorus in the mixture, but other materials are now largely employed.

In 1898 the Belgian Government offered a prize for the best substitute for yellow phosphorus, which resulted in the use of phosphorus sesquisulphide. This substance is now largely used in France, where the manufacture of matches is a Government monopoly, and also to a certain extent in this country for the production of wooden matches. These, however, require a considerable amount of striking; for this reason the substance is not very satisfactory for the manufacture of wax vestas, which are too fragile to stand more than a slight amount of friction.

Safety matches are tipped with a mixture of which the following is a typical example: 50 per cent. potassium chlorate, 5 per cent. potassium chromate, 5 per cent. powdered sulphur, 15 per cent glue and gum, and 25 per cent. of filling and colouring matter. Those materials are carefully ground and mixed together with water to form a paste. The friction surface on the box is made of about 50 per cent. red phosphorus, 10 per cent. antimony sulphide, 25 per cent. gum or glue, and 15 per cent. lamp-black or brown pigment as filling and colouring materials. *Fusees*, for outdoor use in winds, are coated with a large, black head containing charcoal and nitre, the extreme tip only consisting of an ordinary ignition paste.

Manufacture.—Enormous quantities of matches are made annually. The industry exists chiefly in countries where timber is readily available, e.g. Norway and Sweden, England, France, United States, Belgium, Germany, and Austria import the timber and have large factories. The wood employed must be very straight-grained, and is used in the green state; the varieties most commonly employed are white and yellow pine and aspen.

In this country the timber is sawn into rectangular pieces about 4½ inches long, which are split so as to yield splints equal in length to two matches. In other countries a continuous band or veneer as thick as a match is turned off the rotating log and cut transversely and longitudinally into match-sticks. All these operations are performed by ingenious machines of special design, which are capable of turning out millions of splints per day.

The match-sticks are then dried, sifted, and, in the most modern factories, fed on to a running belt at regular intervals, the belt being afterwards coiled so as to produce a bunch of splints, each one being thus separated from its neighbour. Both sides of the coil are dipped in paraffin and then in the ignition paste, after which they are placed in the drying-room. When the head is thoroughly dry the matches are cut in half and automatically packed.

MATÉ, or YERBA MATÉ. The plant that yields Paraguay tea, the *Ilex Paraguayensis*, a kind of holly, nat. ord. Aquifoliaceæ. It has smooth, ovate-lanceolate, unequally serrated leaves, much branched racemes of flowers, the subdivisions of which are somewhat umbellate. In Brazil and other parts of South America the leaves are extensively used as a substitute for tea, the name *Maté* having been transferred to the plant from the gourd or calabash in which the leaves are infused.

Boiling water is poured upon the powdered leaves, then a lump of burned sugar and sometimes a few drops of lemon juice are added. Usually the infusion is sucked through a tube, sometimes of silver, having a perforated bulb to act as a strainer at the lower end. It contains theine, and acts as a slight aperient and diuretic.

MATERIALISM. In philosophy, the theory which, whilst conceiving the world as a unity, maintains that matter is at the basis of everything. Nothing but matter exists, and all mental phenomena are only the effects of matter. Mind, or what we call mind, is a product of matter, one of its manifestations, or one of the forms which ever-changing matter assumes.

All psychical phenomena are functions of one of our organs—the brain. Just as digestion is the function of the stomach, and the secretion of bile a function of the liver, thought is a function of the brain; it is a motion of matter, vanishing with it.

The brain is one of the most delicately constructed organs, and neither will nor emotions can exist without some corresponding brain manifestation, but an injured brain results in the derangement of mental functions.

The materialist, however, does not consider matter as an inert lifeless mass, into which a superior force infuses life and motion, but maintains, on the contrary, that it is ever-active. Force and motion are inherent in matter, manifesting themselves in various transformations, and life and thought are the result of a complex combination of the molecules of matter. Matter is infinite and imperishable, and its laws are immutable. Life and thought, as Buechner said, " are not what matter *is*, but what matter *does*."

All existence, including consciousness, is thus reduced to a modification of matter. Materialism denies the existence of a Divine Creator and of an immortal soul, although some Materialists, like Dr. Priestley, were deists. The latter denied the existence of a soul, but not that of a God.

Materialism is the first philosophical attempt to conceive the world as a unity, and is found in Buddhism, as well as in the religious systems of the Chinese and the Egyptians. The clearest exposition of materialism, however, is that of the Atomists, and especially of Leucippus and Democritus of Abdera, who explained matter as an aggregation of atoms, endowed with motion. They formulated the great principles of the indestructibility of matter and of the conservation of force. The theory was taken up by the Epicureans and defended by Lucretius in his poem *De Rerum Natura*. Nothing comes from nothing, and nothing is lost, neither an atom, nor a molecule, but only changes its form :

> Imperious Cæsar, dead and turned to clay,
> Might stop a hole to keep the wind away.

During the Middle Ages philosophers either adopted Aristotle's view distinguishing between matter and form, or adhered to the " charcoal burner's simple and blind creed," as taught by the dogma of religion. But the doctrine of materialism was revived in England by Hobbes, and later on in France, when La Mettrie and Holbach, Helvetius, and Cabanis were its apostles.

In Germany materialism followed as a reaction against the idealistic systems of Fichte, Schelling, and Hegel, and the revival of natural science gave a new stimulus to the materialistic doctrine. Its exponents were Feuerbach, Moleschott, Buechner, Vogt, and Haeckel, who adduced a mass of new scientific facts in favour of his materialistic views.

In England, Spencer and Huxley taught that, whilst mental phenomena can be resolved into physical, the latter are also resolvable into mental, and that both were the manifestations of an unknown and unknowable reality (Agnosticism).

It cannot be said, however, that any of the systems of materialism are satisfactory. Mind and matter are certainly inseparably united within the sphere of the animal kingdom, but the Materialists rely too much upon conjecture, and can never explain satisfactorily either the ultimate nature of the atoms or the phenomena of consciousness by means of motion and atoms.

In the course of evolution consciousness grows, develops, and becomes more complex. It is a principal factor in the evolution of man, and consequently cannot be a product of matter, or one of its manifestations.—BIBLIOGRAPHY : F. A. Lange, *History of Materialism* ; Janet and Séailles, *History of the Problems of Philosophy* ; E. Haeckel, *The Riddle of the Universe* ; J. G. Hibben, *The Problems of Philosophy* : W. F. Wilkinson, *Modern Materialism*; A. S. Rappoport, *A Primer of Philosophy*.

MATHEMATICS (Gr. *manthanein*, to learn). That branch of knowledge which deals with number and magnitude. *Pure mathematics*, so called, concerns itself with the logical development of a small number of fundamental abstract ideas, by the aid of appropriate symbols.

Every deductive science must be based on certain undefined concepts and postulates, and in the history of mathematics, since the time of the Greek mathematicians, there have been two contrasting *motifs*, on the one hand towards the continual elaboration of the consequences deducible from the fundamental ideas and their application to the problems of natural philosophy and the arts, and on the other towards scrutinizing the basic concepts and postulates, and reducing them to the simplest and fewest.

The extent to which the elaboration of mathematics has been carried out is reflected in such works as the *Encyklopädie der Mathematischen Wissenschaften*, which aims at giving a comprehensive yet concise summary of the present state of mathematics, its contributors being leading mathematicians throughout the world ; or the *Revue semestrielle*, which gives each half-year, in about one hundred and fifty closely printed pages, a short description, or the title only, of the mathematical memoirs and articles appearing in about one hundred and fifty periodicals (mathematical journals and published transactions of learned societies).

Pure mathematics may be classified under two heads, analysis and geometry, the former embracing arithmetic and algebra and their developments, including the calculus. Arithmetic, with its basic concept of the series of natural numbers, or integers, and the four fundamental operations of addition, subtraction, multiplication, and division (the *rational* operations), has been extended to apply to fractional, negative, irrational, complex, and other more abstruse types of numbers, and to include the theory of powers and logarithms.

Common algebra, furnishing a set of symbols for undetermined numbers and for the arithmetical operations, enormously facilitates arithmetical reasoning, and again has given rise to other systems of algebra, such as Boole's Algebra of Logic, and the Algebra of Quaternions.

Other branches of analysis are: trigonometry (in which arithmetic and algebra are applied to geometrical calculations), theory of series, theory of equations, the theories of combinations and permutations, of sets, of invariants, of determinants, of functions (*a*) of a real variable, (*b*) of a complex variable, (*c*) of several variables, and in particular the theories of algebraic, of exponential, of elliptic and hyper-elliptic, of spherical harmonic, of Bessel's, and many other special functions.

The *calculus* is founded on the notion of a *limit* (q.v.), and includes differential and integral calculus, differential equations and calculus of variations. The calculus of finite differences belongs rather to algebra proper than to "the calculus," with which, however, it is interrelated.

A theory which has lately become prominent is that of integral equations, an integral equation being one which involves an unknown function under the sign of integration. Special examples were discussed by Laplace, Fourier, Cauchy, Abel, and Schlömilch, and the method was successfully applied to the solution of differential equations by Liouville. The recent great advances are chiefly due to Fredholm, Hilbert, and Volterra (cf. Whittaker and Watson, *Modern Analysis*).

While analysis may be considered as a development of arithmetic, which is based on the operation of "counting," i.e. placing any assemblage of things in one-to-one correspondence with the natural numbers 1, 2, 3, etc., geometry is based on the idea of extension or space, and the operation of *superposition* of one figure upon another takes the place of "counting" as the fundamental operation.

Objection has been raised to the logical validity of this use of superposition, on the ground that the existence of ideal *rigid* figures which can be moved in space without change is inadmissible until *rigidity* has been defined, and that no definition of rigidity is possible that does not involve the fallacy of "reasoning in a circle." This logical difficulty is avoided if, as suggested in the article *Geometry*, we take the co-ordinates as fundamental concepts, and treat geometry simply as a branch of analysis.

There is, however, one very fundamental branch of geometry which is independent of metrical and projective properties and co-ordinates, that which has been variously named calculus of situation, topology, topics; examples of which are L. Euler's famous theorem $F + V = E + 2$, where F, V, E, are respectively the number of faces, of vertices, and of edges of a simple polyhedron, and J. B. Listing's very comprehensive generalization of it; also P. G. Tait's researches on the "Topics" of knots.

In modern times, since Descartes, geometry has undergone enormous development chiefly by the aid of co-ordinate systems and analysis, and, in turn, analysis has had much light thrown upon its problems by geometrical considerations. In many practical applications of mathematics only a certain degree of approximation is required. In such cases graphical (i.e. geometric) methods are often employed where arithmetical or analytical methods would be inapplicable, or inconvenient from complexity (*see* GRAPH; NOMOGRAPHY).

Mechanical aids to calculation (Amsler's and other planimeters, the integraph, Napier's slide rule, equation-solving machines, etc.) supplement graphical methods of approximate calculation, and arithmetical machines of various types are available for adding, multiplying, etc.

The widest field for *Applied Mathematics* is in connection with the various branches of natural philosophy, viz. dynamics and hydrodynamics, the theories of heat, light, sound, electricity, and magnetism, the constitution of matter, and astronomy. Engineering calculations by analysis and by graphic methods also form an important branch of applied mathematics. The theory of probabilities is a branch of applied analysis which has more special applications to statistics and actuarial science.

For further information the reader may consult the articles on the various mathematical topics referred to above. The student of mathematics will find in the *Royal Society Catalogue* a complete list of mathematical publications up to the year 1900, and for later mathematical literature he may consult the *International Catalogue of Scientific Literature*, which includes a section for pure mathematics, as well as sections for mechanics, for physics, and for astronomy, which cover the most important part of applied mathematics, all classified both according to author and according to subject. —BIBLIOGRAPHY: *Encyklopädie der Mathematischen Wissenschaften* (nearly complete, a French edition in progress); E. Pascal, *Repertorio di Matematiche Superiori* (translated into various languages, an excellent, comprehensive, yet concise résumé of all the important theorems of mathematics); G. S. Carr, *Synopsis of Mathematics*; H. Weber and J. Wellstein, *Encyklopädie der elementaren Mathematik*; M. Cantor, *Geschichte der Mathematik*; W. W. R. Ball, *Short History of Mathematics*; F. Cajori, *History of Mathematics*; B. Russell, *The Principles of Mathematics*; A. N. Whitehead, *Introduction to Mathematics*; *Revue semestrielle des publications mathématiques*; *Fortschritte der Mathematik*.

MATHER, Cotton. American writer, the eldest son of Increase Mather (1639-1723), one of the early presidents of Harvard College, born in Boston 1663, died 1728. He graduated at Harvard College in 1678, and in 1684 was ordained minister in Boston, as colleague of his father. In 1685 he published his *Memorable Providences relating to Witchcraft and Possessions*, which was used as an authority in the persecution and condemnation of nineteen victims burned for witchcraft at Salem in 1692.

He left the reputation of having been the greatest scholar and author that America had then produced, his publications, some of huge dimensions, amounting to 382. Credulity, pedantry, quaintness, and eccentricity are blended in most of his works with great erudition.

MATHEW, Theobald. Popularly known as *Father Mathew*, Irish apostle of temperance, was born 1790, died 1856. He is chiefly famous for his celebrated temperance crusade, which was so successful that in a few months he had 150,000 converts in County Cork alone. A similar success attended his work in many Irish and English towns.

MATHEWS, Charles. English comedian, born in London 1776, died 1835. He made his debut at Richmond in 1793, and after ten years' acting in the provinces appeared in London in 1803. After playing with success at various theatres, he instituted, in 1818, a species of entertainment in the form of a monologue, which, under the title *Mathews at Home*, for five successive seasons drew crowded audiences to the English Opera House.

He continued his entertainments for upwards of ten years, appearing at intervals in the regular drama. His powers of mimicry have perhaps never been surpassed on the stage, while his personal qualities won him the friendship of Coleridge, Lamb, and many other eminent men.

MATHEWS, Charles James. Son of the preceding, born in 1803, died in 1878, long held a prominent place as a light comedian. He excelled in light eccentric comedies. Many of the plays in which he acted were written by himself.

MATLOCKS, The. Urban district and inland watering-place of Derbyshire. It consists of Matlock Bridge, Matlock Bath and Matlock Bank, which until 1927 were separate areas. It stands on the Derwent, and is served by the L.M.S. Railway; is 144 miles from London and 17 from Derby. There are some industries, but the place is chiefly a pleasure and health resort. There are medicinal springs at Matlock Bath. Near Matlock is some of the most beautiful of the Derbyshire scenery, including the High Tor and the Heights of Abraham. Matlock Bath is famous for its caves and its petrifying wells. Pop. (1931), 10,599.

MATONIACEÆ. A small family of primitive Leptosporangiate Ferns, section Simplices. The only living forms are *M. pectinata*, with large fan-shaped leaves, and *M. sarmentosa*, both rare Malayan ferns; but in Mesozoic times the family was very prominent.

MATSUMOTO. An inland town of Honshiu, Japan, on the Central Railway, west of Tokyo. It has a raw-silk trade and is a tourist centre. Pop. (1925), 63,427.

MATSUSHIMA. A group of about 800 islands on the east coast of Honshiu, Japan.

MATSUYAMA. A town of Shikoku, Japan, about 4 miles from Mitsu, its port on the Inland Sea. Pop. 82,479.

MATSYS, METZYS, or **MASSYS, Quintin.** Flemish painter, was born at Antwerp before 1460, and died there between 13th July and 16th Sept., 1530. He became a member of the Antwerp guild in 1491, and was a friend of Erasmus and Dürer. He painted chiefly life-size figures, which are much admired for their clear flesh tints. Among his works are: a *Triptych with Pietà* (1508-11, at Antwerp), *The Money-changer and his Wife* (1518, Louvre), *Christ and the Virgin* (National Gallery), and *Advocate and Clients* (Dresden).

MATTER, Atomic and molecular theories of. An atomic theory of matter is one which holds that material bodies are not infinitely divisible, but are made up of indivisible atoms, which are usually regarded as discrete and separated from each other by vacuous spaces. Such a theory was maintained by Democritus (q.v.) in opposition to Aristotle and celebrated in the magnificent poetry of Lucretius (q.v.). But it had little in common with the modern atomic theory, for it was applied primarily to philosophical problems and not to the explanation of experimental laws.

Again, an atomic rather than a continuous theory of matter has always been adopted in speculations on the nature of compressibility and solution; but the definite conceptions which underlie modern chemistry and physics first appear in the explanation of chemical combination which was put forward by John Dalton in 1803.

Dalton supposed that any substance recognized in chemistry as an element (q.v.) was composed of a multitude of atoms, all having the same weight characteristic of the element. In a chemical combination resulting in the formation of a compound of the elements A, B, C, . . ., *a* atoms of A, *b* of B, . . ., unite with each other to form the ultimate particle of the compound, indivisible by physical processes and divisible only when the chemical combination is reversed.

a, b, c . . . are small numbers (the greatest value assumed by Dalton was 3) and are characteristic of the compound; different compounds of the same elements differ only in the values of *a, b, c*. . . . By this theory could be explained very simply the laws of "constant," "multiple," and "reciprocal" proportions, which govern the proportions by weight in which elements enter into combination with each other; and by examining those proportions, values (known as atomic weights) could be assigned to the ratio of the weights of the atoms of other elements to that of the atom of hydrogen (*see* CHEMISTRY).

Further, as was natural, Dalton applied his theory to physics as well as to chemistry, and supposed that the discrete particles of which gases had long been supposed to consist were identical with the ultimate chemical particles—atoms in elements and the chemically combined groups of atoms in compounds. Dalton's theory has undergone no essential change.

His conclusions concerning the values of *a, b, c*, . . . in various compounds have been corrected, and the limitation to small numbers removed. The theory has been extended by supposing that compounds may differ in the geometrical arrangement of the constituent atoms as well as in their number (*see* STEREOCHEMISTRY). His physical theory is also retained with minor modifications.

Avogadro showed that the densities of various gases were on the whole concordant with the assumption that equal volumes of gases at the same temperature and pressure contain the same number of ultimate particles; but discrepancies appear which make it necessary to modify the simplicity of Dalton's scheme if the rule is to be maintained.

Nowadays the rule is accepted (for "perfect" gases), and it is therefore concluded that the "molecules" of gases (as the ultimate discrete particles are called) may consist of two or more atoms chemically combined, even when the gas is an element and all the atoms similar, and in compounds may consist of a multiple of the least number of atoms required by the chemical constitution.

It had long been suspected, e.g. by Bernouilli, (1738) and Clausius (1857), that the molecules of gases were in motion, that the kinetic energy of the molecules represented the thermal energy of the gas, and that their impact on the walls of the containing vessel produced the pressure. But the conceptions of this dynamical or kinetic theory (q.v.) of gases were first made definite by Clerk Maxwell (1860), who calculated the motions of such molecules on the assumption that, like elastic spheres, they exercised forces on each other only at collisions.

He deduced the distribution of the velocities of the molecules about the mean, and showed that, in a mixture of two gases with molecules of different weights, the mean kinetic energy of a molecule of one kind must be equal to that of the other kind. Since both gases in such a mixture must be at the same temperature, it follows that the temperature is determined by the mean kinetic energy of the molecule.

Further, from the experimental laws of Avogadro, Boyle, and Gay-Lussac, it follows that the absolute temperature must be proportional to this kinetic energy. Maxwell's theory explained these laws (as did the earlier theories) and deduced from them the absolute value of the mean speed of a molecule; for hydrogen at 0° C. it is 1840 metres per second. But it gave also an adequate account of the viscosity and thermal conductivity of gases and evaluated from these the number (and therefore weight) and size of the molecules.

The values obtained agree well with those found by more modern methods (which depend on the study of molecules when they are electrically charged), but there are unavoidable sources of error.

Thus the size deduced for the molecule depends on its unknown shape, and all values are somewhat changed if it is assumed (more plausibly) that the molecules are not hard spheres, but more complex systems exerting forces on each other even when they are not in contact. The following are the best determinations: No. of mols. in 1 c.c. of perfect gas at 0° C. and 760 mm. pressure $=2{\cdot}7\times10^{19}$; mass of hydrogen mol. (2 atoms) $=3{\cdot}32\times10^{-24}$ gm.; diameter of hydrogen mol. $=2\times10^{-8}$ cm.

The kinetic theory has received striking confirmation in recent years by the observation that when particles, very small but individually visible, are suspended in a fluid, they are continually in irregular motion (Brownian motion) with mean kinetic energies equal to that of the hypothetical and invisible molecules and with velocities distributed in accordance with Maxwell's law.

No theory as simple and complete as that for gases has been put forward for liquids or solids. In these states of matter the molecules (or possibly the atoms which compose them) exert forces on each other continually; even if the forces were known (and they are only just becoming known in very simple cases) the calculation of the motion and of the properties which depend on it would be very complex.

Much progress has been made in recent years in our knowledge of the structure of crystalline solids (*see* QUANTUM THEORY and X-RAY SPECTRA), from which it appears that the principles so successfully applied to gases may have to be modified considerably in their application to more concentrated forms of matter; but there is no doubt that all forms are atomic in the most general sense.

Meanwhile attempts to explain the properties of atoms in terms of a structure of particles yet more ultimate have been much more successful. A bare reference will suffice to attempts to represent atoms as singularities in a primordial continuous medium, usually identified with the *Ether* (q.v.); for while such theories might explain the indestructibility of atoms, they could throw no light on the remarkable relations between the properties of different atoms which gave rise to Prout's hypothesis (*see* ISOTOPES) and are made still more striking by the Periodic Table (q.v.). These relations inevitably suggest that the atoms of different elements are built up of common constituents; the discovery of the electron (q.v.), which is such a common constituent, produced at once theories of the structure of the atom.

Electrons bear charges of negative electricity, while normal atoms are electrically neutral. Accordingly the atom must contain, besides electrons, some portion positively charged. All electronic theories of the atom represent its structure as determined by electrostatic (or, if the parts of the atom are in relative motion, electrodynamic) forces between the electrons and the positive part.

Of the nature of the positive portion there was at first no evidence; the earliest electronic theories, following that of J. J. Thomson, represented it as a uniformly charged sphere throughout which the electrons were distributed. This choice, which is less plausible *a priori* than that of a positive particle, was dictated partly by mathematical tractability, partly by the need of introducing some quantity (e.g. the radius of the positive sphere) other than the number and charges of the particles, if the size of the atom was to be determinate.

It had to be abandoned when Rutherford (1911) showed from experiments on the passage of α-rays (*see* RADIO-ACTIVITY) through atoms that, in accordance with a suggestion previously put forward by Nagaoka, the positive portion of the atom must be a particle of radius very small compared with that of the atom.

The difficulty of indeterminateness was overcome by Bohr (1913), who suggested that the electrostatic laws were to be supplemented by quantum relations (*see* QUANTUM THEORY) and the additional quantity supplied by Planck's constant *h*.

It is now known that the positive portion or "nucleus" of the atom is a particle about 10^{-12} cm. in diameter, in which resides almost all the mass of the atom. It carries a charge equal and opposite to that on N electrons, where N is an integer characteristic of the atom and called by Moseley the "atomic number." N is the ordinal number of the element in a series arranged in the order of increasing atomic weights, corrected in a few instances to remove the anomalies of the Periodic Table: for hydrogen it is 1, for helium 2, for lithium 3, and so on. The mass thus increases generally, but irregularly, with the atomic number.

The nucleus is itself complex, and is decomposed spontaneously in radio-active disintegration, or artificially (in some cases at least) by the impact of α-rays; no circumstances are known at present in which this process is reversed. The constituents of the nucleus of the heavier atoms include hydrogen and helium nuclei together with "cementing" electrons; it is possible that the helium nucleus is itself built of hydrogen nuclei. Plausible suggestions can be made concerning the exact composition of the various nuclei, but not of their arrangement or of the principles which determine it.

In its normal state (which is not necessarily that of most frequent occurrence) the nucleus is surrounded by N electrons, but in suitable circumstances a few of these electrons can be detached or a few others added. On the number and distribution of these electrons depend all the properties of the atom other than its weight, radio-active change, and effect upon α- or β-rays; in particular, chemical and mechanical properties and optical and X-ray spectra so depend.

Since the distribution of the electrons is determined wholly by the charge on the nucleus, these properties depend only on the atomic number and but very slightly on the mass (*see* ISOTOPES). When chemical combination takes place, the electrons normally surrounding the combining nuclei are redistributed, and the nuclei are held apart by their repulsion, counteracted by their common attraction for the electrons.

It will be observed that the nucleus is the only permanent and characteristic part of the atom; the electrons can be transferred from one to another, and loss or gain of electrons does not change the element. On the other hand, a change in the nucleus is that from one element to another.

The general problem of the distribution of the electrons about the nuclei is not yet solved. According to Bohr's theory (*see* SPECTRA, THEORY OF), the electrons revolve round the nucleus in orbits which are special members of the class of those possible according to classical electrostatics and mechanics, but are selected by certain quantum relations.

Owing to mathematical difficulties this principle can be applied with certainty only in the simplest cases, namely, when there is only one electron, or when the electrons are so close to a nucleus of large atomic number that the forces due to other electrons are insignificant compared with those due to the nucleus. In other words, the theory can predict only the structure of the hydrogen and positively charged helium atom, and the distribution of those electrons which, in atoms of greater atomic number, are involved in the X-ray spectrum.

A theory of a different type, and to some extent inconsistent with this, has been proposed by Lewis and developed by Langmuir. Here the electrons are supposed to be distributed on shells surrounding each nucleus which contain, proceeding outwards, 2, 8, 8, 18, 18, 32, . . . electrons. The inner shells are filled first, so that an atom with N = 19 (say), would have shells of 2, 8, 8, 1 electrons.

When two atoms combine chemically, the electrons arrange themselves so as to complete as far as possible the shells round the nuclei, and those compounds are most stable in which there are just enough electrons to fill all the shells, some electrons being common to the outer shells of two or more nuclei.

The theory accounts well for many of the simpler chemical compounds, but is attended with difficulties in explaining the more complex. No reason is alleged why the electrons should be so distributed. *See* WAVE MECHANICS.—BIBLIOGRAPHY: J. W. Mellor, *Inorganic Chemistry*; J. Perrin, *Les Atomes*; O. E. Meyer, *Kinetic Theory of Gases*; J. H. Jeans, *Dynamical Theory of Gases*; A. Sommerfeld, *Atombau and Spectrallinien*.

MATTERHORN. *See* CERVIN, MONT.

MATTHEW, St. Evangelist and apostle, son of Alpheus; previous to his call a publican or officer of the Roman customs, and, according to tradition, a native of Nazareth. After the ascension of Christ we find him at Jerusalem with the other apostles, but this is the last notice of him in Scripture. Tradition represents him as preaching fifteen years in Jerusalem, then visiting the Ethiopians, Macedonians, Persians, and Syrians, and finally suffering martyrdom in Persia.

His Gospel has been supposed by some critics to have been originally written in Hebrew, or rather Aramaic, but it is only found in Greek. The chief aim of this Gospel is evidently to prove the Messianic character of Jesus. *See* GOSPEL.

MATTHEW OF WESTMINSTER. The name of the fictitious author of a chronicle entitled *Flores Historiarum*, written or compiled in the fourteenth century by monks of St. Albans and Westminster. Luard's edition of 1890 (3 vols.) is the most important, and in it the true character of the chronicle, which ends with 1325, was first established.

MATTHI'AS CORVI'NUS. King of Hungary, second son of John Hunyadi, born in 1443, died in 1490. The enemies of his father kept him imprisoned in Bohemia, but in 1458, at the age of sixteen years, he was called to the throne of Hungary.

He maintained his position against Frederick III., repelled the invading Turks, and between 1468 and 1478 conquered Silesia, Moravia, and Lusatia; he was also victorious over the Poles, and took the greater part of Austria, including Vienna, from Frederick, and held all his extensive conquests till his death. He encouraged science and scholarship, and collected a great library (afterwards destroyed by the Turks) at Buda.

MATISSE, Henri. French artist. Born 31st Dec., 1860, he studied in Paris and his work soon attracted attention. He was one of the original Fauvists and his style is noted for its simplicity, its rather violent colouring, and its vigorous calligraphic manner of brushwork. With Picasso he came to be acknowledged as the leader of the more mature art movement of Paris. Matisse, who lived for a time in Morocco, is represented in several European galleries, and among his pictures are *Toilet* and *The Sisters*.

MATTO GROSSO (Port., dense forest). The largest state of Brazil after Amazonas, entirely inland, and mainly an elevated plain drained by a complex river-system. Gold, silver, lead, salt, diamonds, and precious stones are found. Rubber trees abound in its vast forests. Sugar, yerba-maté (Paraguayan tea), and tobacco are cultivated, and stock-raising is important. Cuyábá is the capital; Corumba is commercially important. Area, 532,210 sq. miles; pop. (1929), 349,857.

MAUBEUGE. A frontier fortress and town of Nord, France, on the Sambre. Metal goods, porcelain, and machine tools are manufactured. Maubeuge is the junction of five railway lines opening upon the Franco-Belgian coal-fields, and as such the town became of enormous strategic value early in the European War. It was defended by General Fournier and 30,000 French troops, and was partially invested on 25th Aug., 1914; Fournier capitulated on 7th Sept., 1914. *See* EUROPEAN WAR (RETREAT FROM MONS). Pop. 20,000.

MAUDE, Sir Frederick Stanley. British soldier, born 1864, died 1917. The son of General Sir F. Maude, V.C., he came of a famous fighting family, and early joined the Coldstream Guards (1884), with which he served in the Sudan (1885). On passing Staff College he became brigade-major, Brigade of Guards (1897-9), served in South Africa with Lord Methuen and the Transvaal Force (1899-1900), was military secretary to the Governor-General of Canada (1901-4), and Assistant-Director of the Territorial Forces (1909-12).

In 1914 Maude proceeded to France with the 5th Divisional Staff, was severely wounded, and, on recovery, was posted to command the 13th Division at Gallipoli (with which he remained at the evacuation), in Egypt, and in Mesopotamia until his appointment as commander-in-chief there in Aug., 1916. Kut had fallen, and until that time the British Mesopotamian campaign had been a failure. In Dec., 1916, Maude advanced, captured Kut, and led his victorious army into Bagdad, 11th March, 1917. At Bagdad he died of cholera.

MAUI. One of the Hawaiian Islands. Area, 728 sq. miles; pop. (1930), 48,756.

MAULE. A maritime province of Central Chile, drained by the River Maule and its affluents. Cauquenes is the capital, and the seaport (former capital) is Constitucio. Area, 5937 sq. miles; pop. (1930), 197,468.—Maule City is in the province of Talca.

MAUMBURY RINGS. Spot near Dorchester, Dorset. It is believed to have been in Roman times the site of an amphitheatre which held 12,000 spectators.

MAUNDY-THURSDAY. The Thursday in Holy Week, on which *maundy-money* is given in London by the sovereign to as many poor men and women as the years of his age. Pennies, twopennies, threepennies, and fourpennies in silver are coined for this purpose. It used to be the custom for sovereigns to wash the feet of poor persons and make them presents on this day. The name is derived from the Lat. *mandatum*, a commandment, the words *mandatum novum* occurring in the Gospel according to St. John xiii. 34.

MAUPASSANT (mō-pās-sāṉ), **Henri René Albert Guy de.** French novelist, born in 1850, died 1893. He began his career as a clerk in the navy department, and served in the army during the Franco-Prussian War. Trained by Flaubert, whom he took as a model in the art of composition, he practised the art of story writing for years, destroying numerous MSS. before publishing his *Boule de Suif* in *Les Soirées de Médan* (1880).

He then continued to cultivate the short story, and was soon rightly considered one of the greatest writers of short stories in the nineteenth century. Maupassant belongs to the realistic school, and, like Gorky and many other artists of this school, he studied life as an observer. He is never didactic, but faithfully portrays the reality of life. His style is sharp, clear, and precise, his delineation of character sure, brief, and exact. In a few terse lines he portrays a scene or a character.

His stories, at once tragic and comic, even grim in their irony, reveal human meanness and selfishness, sordid brutality and cruelty. Besides his short stories he also wrote six long novels : *Pierre et Jean* (1888), in the preface to which he summarized the counsels of Flaubert and explained his theories on the aim of the novelist; *Une Vie* (1883); *Bel-ami* (1885); *Mont-Oriol* (1887); *Fort comme la Mort* (1889); and *Notre Cœur* (1890). The last two were evidently written under the influence of Bourget. — BIBLIOGRAPHY : A. Symons, *Studies in Prose and Verse* ; R. Doumic, *Écrivains d'Aujourd'hui* ; H. James, *Partial Portraits*.

MAUPERTUIS (mo-pār-twē), **Pierre Louis Moreau.** French mathematician, born 1698, died 1759. The geodetic expedition to Lapland in 1738 excited much interest, and Maupertuis as chief of the party acquired an extraordinary reputation. In 1746 Frederick II. appointed him president of the Royal Academy of Sciences at Berlin. His conduct as president appears to have been more of a hindrance than a help to the eminent men, such as Euler, over whom he was set in authority. Maupertuis is usually, though on slight grounds, cited as the author of the *Principle of Least Action* in dynamics. In his later years he quarrelled with Voltaire who, somewhat unjustly, denounced him as a charlatan.

MAURICE, John Frederick Denison. A leader of the Broad Church party, son of a Unitarian minister, was born in 1805 at Normanston, Suffolk, died in 1872. He took orders in 1835, and in 1836 he was appointed chaplain to Guy's Hospital. In 1840 he became professor of modern history and English literature in King's College, London, and in 1846 professor of ecclesiastical history, but in 1853 the publication by him of an essay on future punishment necessitated his resignation of both chairs. In 1866 he became professor of moral philosophy at Cambridge, a position which he held until his death.

MAURICE OF NASSAU. Prince of Orange, stadtholder of the Netherlands, the youngest son of William the Silent, was born 1567, died at The Hague in 1625. He was elected stadtholder of the provinces of Zeeland and Holland on the assassination of his father in 1585, and subsequently of Utrecht, Overyssel, and Gelderland ; and as commander of the army of the Netherlands he carried on war against the Spaniards with extraordinary success, driving them entirely out of the United Provinces. Previous to the truce of twelve years, concluded in 1609, when Spain was compelled to acknowledge the United Provinces as a free republic, about forty towns and several fortresses had fallen into his hands. He had defeated the Spaniards in three pitched battles, besides the naval victories which were gained by the vice-admirals of the republic on the coasts of Spain and Flanders. In 1621 the war with Spain was renewed, but the superior force under Spinola compelled Maurice to act upon the defensive only. He was succeeded by his brother Frederick Henry.

MAURITANIA. A French colony in North-West Africa, with a coastline on the Atlantic, bounded north by Rio de Oro (Spanish) and south by Senegal (French). It was acquired by France in 1893, became a Protectorate in May, 1903, a "Civilian Territory" in Oct., 1904, and a Colony in 1921. Area, 322,335 sq. miles; pop. (1931), 323,819, of which 321 were Europeans and the remainder Moorish Mussulmans.

The Roman **Mauritania** extended

across modern Morocco to Western Algeria, and was bounded in the south by the Atlas range. From A.D. 40 it was a Roman province, and was held by the Vandals from A.D. 429 to 534, passing to the Arabs in A.D. 650.

Mauritanian Native

MAURITIUS. An island and British Crown Colony of the Indian Ocean, 500 miles east of Madagascar. It is surrounded by coral reefs, and is mountainous, two peaks reaching 2600 feet and 2700 feet altitude respectively. The annual rainfall is heavy and the climate hot. Port Louis (pop. in 1931, 54,290), fortified and garrisoned, is the capital and seaport. The bulk of the inhabitants are of Indian descent and embrace Hinduism, but the Protestant and Roman Catholic Churches are State aided.

French is the prevailing language; English is used in the law courts; the Government debates are bilingual. The standard of coinage is the Indian rupee; weights and measures are on the metric system. Among exports are sugar (mainly to the United Kingdom), aloe fibre, coco-nut oil, and hemp; manures, coal, machinery, and cotton goods are imported from the United Kingdom. Exports and imports for 1931 amounted to £1,787,688 and £2,405,407 respectively; taking £1 = 13·33 rupees. Education is free but not compulsory, and there is a subsidized Royal College. Area, about 720, sq. miles; census pop. (1931), 393,418 (265,000 Indians and 6820 Chinese).

Mauritius was discovered by the Portuguese in 1505, abandoned and re-occupied by the Dutch (1598) who named it after Prince Maurice of Orange-Nassau. In 1710 the Dutch left, and about 1715 the French took possession, naming it Ile de France. It fell to the British in 1810, and became a British possession in 1814 (Treaty of Paris). The Government consists of a Governor and Executive Council with a Council of Government (Governor and 27 members, 10 elected under a moderate franchise, 8 ex-officio, and 9 nominated by the Governor). The Chagos Islands (q.v.), Rodriguez (q.v.), Farquhar Island, Trois Frères, Six Islands, Solomon Islands, Agalega, and the St. Brandon group are dependencies of Mauritius. Total pop. (including Rodriguez) is 9659.—BIBLIOGRAPHY: A. Walter, *The Sugar Industry of Mauritius*; A. Macmillan, *Mauritius Illustrated.*

MAUROIS, André. French author. He was born in 1885, and educated at Rouen. Many of his books have been translated into English. Among them are *The Silences of Colonel Bramble,* dealing with the War, a *Life of Disraeli*, *Ariel*, an imaginative biography of Shelley, and *Don Juan*, a similar work on Lord Byron. He has written a book on Marshal Lyautey. In 1931 he lectured in London.

MAUSOLE'UM (Gr. *mausoleion*). A sepulchral monument, so named from Mausōlus, a king of Caria, to whom his wife Artemisia erected a monument which became so famous as to be esteemed the seventh wonder of the world, and to give a generic name to all superb sepulchres. From Pliny we learn that its height was 140 feet. In modern times the term is applied generally to a sepulchral edifice erected for the reception of a monument, or to contain tombs.

MAWSON, Sir Douglas. British explorer. Born at Bradford in 1882, and educated at Sydney University, he was appointed to the scientific staff of the Shackleton Antarctic Expedition in 1907. He was also on the staff of the Everest Expedition and the Magnetic Pole journey in 1908. He was leader of the Australasian Antarctic Expedition of 1911-14, when he discovered radium ore at Mount Painter, and of the British Australian and New Zealand Antarctic Expedition of 1929. Since 1920 he has been Professor of Geology and Mineralogy in Adelaide University. He was knighted in 1914 and wrote *The Home of the Blizzard.*

MAXEN'TIUS, M. Aurelius Valerius. A Roman emperor, A.D. 306-312, son of Maximianus, and son-in-law of Galerius, whom he deposed. He reigned along with his father for a short time; was defeated by Constantine in 312, and in the retreat drowned in the Tiber.

MAXIL'LA (Lat. *maxilla*, a jaw). The term applied in comparative anatomy to the upper jaw-bones of Vertebrates, in contradistinction to the mandible or lower jaw; and in Invertebrata to the second or lesser pair or pairs of jaws. Thus in insects, spiders, crustaceans, etc., the maxillæ form definite and important organs in the trituration and division of food.

MAXIMA AND MINIMA. A magnitude which varies with the time is, at a moment taken at random, either increasing or decreasing, but at certain special moments may be stationary. If it has just ceased to increase, and is just about to decrease, the magnitude is said to have a *maximum* value; a *minimum* value if it has just ceased to decrease, and is just about to increase. In a similar way, a function y of any independent variable x is, for a value of x not specially chosen, either increasing or decreasing as x increases, but may be a maximum or minimum for certain values of x.

Now, if y is increasing with x when $x=a$, then dy/dx (*see* CALCULUS) is positive for $x=a$; if y is decreasing, dy/dx is negative. Hence, if y is a maximum or minimum when $x=a$, dy/dx must be 0 for $x=a$; the values of x corresponding to maximum or minimum values of y are therefore found by solving the equation $dy/dx=0$.

To discriminate between maxima and minima, we may consider the behaviour of dy/dx in respect of sign as x increases through a. For a maximum, the sign of dy/dx must change from + (when $x<a$) to −(when $x>a$); dy/dx must therefore be decreasing as x increases through a; this will be ensured if d^2y/dx^2 (*see* MACLAURIN'S THEOREM) is negative for $x=a$. Similar conditions hold for a minimum. *Example:* Let $y=32x-x^4$. Then $dy/dx=32-4x^3$, and $d^2y/dx^2=-12x^2$. For a maximum or minimum, $32-4x^3=0$, or $x=2$; also d^2y/dx^2 is negative for this value of x, so that y is a maximum for $x=2$.

In questions on this subject, the graph (q.v.) of a function is always helpful and sometimes indispensable; on the other hand, for functions given by a formula, knowledge of the maxima and minima is of great use in tracing the graph.—Cf. F. F. P. Bisacre, *Applied Calculus.*

MAXIMIA'NUS, Marcus Aurelius Valerius Herculius. A Roman emperor, who became colleague of Diocletian in the empire A.D. 286. He endeavoured to murder his rival Constantine, to whom he had given his daughter Faustina in marriage, and being frustrated by the fidelity of the latter, strangled himself in 310. He was the father of Maxentius.

MAXIMIL'IAN I. Emperor of Germany, son of the Emperor Frederick III. and Eleonora of Portugal, was born at Wiener Neustadt 1459, died 1519. In 1486 he was elected king of the Romans, and emperor in 1493. He first became an independent prince by his marriage with Mary of Burgundy, the daughter of Charles the Bold, who was killed in 1477. This match involved him in a war with Louis XI., King of France, in which he was successful, though he was defeated at a later period by the Milanese. He was succeeded by his grandson, Charles V. *See* GERMANY.

MAXIMILIAN II. Emperor of Germany, born 1527, died 1576. He succeeded his father, Ferdinand I., in 1564; was tolerant of the Reformation, but did not join the Protestant Church.

MAXIMILIAN. Emperor of Mexico, known in his earlier life as *Ferdinand Maximilian Joseph,* Archduke of Austria, born at Vienna 1832, died 19th June, 1867. He was the younger brother of Francis Joseph I. of Austria. In 1863 he was induced by the Emperor Napoleon, and also by a deputation of Mexicans, to accept the throne of Mexico. With this intention he entered Mexico in June 1864. Maximilian was at first extremely popular; yet he failed to conciliate either the Church party or the Republicans, and the latter, under Juarez, rose in revolt.

Having become involved in financial and political difficulties, Maximilian, with the approval of Napoleon, resolved to abdicate (1866), and he had proceeded to Orizaba when he was induced to return by the Conservative party in the state. The fighting which followed culminated in the capture and execution of the emperor and two of his chief generals. —BIBLIOGRAPHY: P. F. Martin, *Maximilian in Mexico*; J. M. Taylor, *Maximilian and Carlotta.*

MAXIMILIAN JOSEPH. King of Bavaria, born 1756, died 1825. He married his daughter to Eugene Beauharnais, son of Napoleon's wife Josephine, and had his duchy raised to a kingdom in 1806. In 1813 he joined the League against France.

MAXIMI'NUS, Gaius Julius Verus. Roman emperor, the son of a peasant of Thrace. He entered the Roman army under Septimus Severus before

210, and gradually rose in rank until, on the death of Alexander Severus, he caused himself to be proclaimed emperor, A.D. 235. He was successful in his German campaigns, but his acts of barbarity and tyranny provoked an insurrection, in the attempt to quell which he was assassinated by his own soldiery, A.D. 238. The emperor is represented as being of immense stature and strength.

MAXWELL, James Clerk. Physicist, born 1831, died 1879. He was educated at the academy and university of his native town, Edinburgh, and afterwards at Peterhouse and Trinity College, Cambridge. He was professor of natural philosophy at Aberdeen (1856-60), and in King's College, London (1860-65). In 1871 he was appointed to the chair of experimental physics at Cambridge, and organized the now famous Cavendish laboratory. Next to Kelvin, Maxwell was the greatest physicist of the second half of the nineteenth century. He revolutionized electrical theory, and the experiments which led to the discovery of electric waves were directly inspired by his electromagnetic theory of light (*see* ETHER; LIGHT). Maxwell wrote some admirable textbooks, and his *Treatise on Electricity and Magnetism*, *Theory of Heat*, and *Matter and Motion* are still widely read.—Cf. L. Campbell and W. Garnett, *James Clerk Maxwell*.

MAXWELLTOWN. With Dumfries a burgh of Kirkcudbrightshire. It stands on the Nith, on the L.M.S. Railway. It has an observatory and a museum. Three bridges connect it with Dumfries. Tweeds are manufactured. The old name of the place was Bridgend; it was renamed in 1810 after the Maxwell family.

MAY. Fifth month in the year, but third in the old Roman calendar. The Romans regarded it as unlucky to contract marriages during its course—a superstition still prevalent in some parts of Europe. On the 1st of May the old Celtic peoples held a festival called Beltane (q.v.). In former days outdoor sports and pastimes on the 1st of May were very common, and are not yet entirely given up. They included the erection of a *May-pole* decorated with flowers and foliage, round which young men and maidens danced, one of the latter being chosen for her good looks as queen of the festival, or "Queen of the May."

MAY. An island in the Firth of Forth, Scotland, in Fifeshire. Area, 2 sq. miles. It has a lighthouse.

MAY-APPLE. A plant, *Podophyllum peltātum*, nat. ord. Berberidaceæ (barberries). It is a native of North America, and its creeping root-stalk affords an active cathartic medicine known as *podophyllin*. The yellowish pulpy fruit, of the size of a pigeon's egg, is slightly acid, and is sometimes eaten.

MAYAS. A race of Indians inhabiting Yucatan and the adjacent regions of Mexico and Central America, believed to be the descendants of those who built the great ruined cities of these parts. In ancient times, and especially from the third to the tenth centuries A.D. the Maya people were the most highly civilized people in America; and the culture of the rest of America in Pre-Columbian times was derived directly or indirectly from them.

MAYBOLE. A police burgh and market town of Ayrshire, Scotland, on the L.M.S. Railway. It was the capital of Carrick, and is closely associated with the Kennedys, now represented by the Marquess of Ailsa, whose seat, Culzean Castle, is near Maidens, in the vicinity. Boots and agricultural implements are manufactured. Pop. (1931), 4210.

MAYENNE. A department of North-Western France formed from parts of the pre-Revolutionary provinces of Maine and Anjou. It is traversed north to south by the Mayenne, which rises in the department of Orne and falls with its affluents, the Jouanne, Colmont, and Oudon, into the Sarthe (tributary of the Maine) near Angers. Stock and cereals are raised; cider apples are produced. Laval is the capital; Mayenne (pop. 9960), once (1573) a seat of Charles, duc de Mayenne, son of the duc de Guise, is important. Area of department, 1986 sq. miles; pop. (1931), 254,479.

MAYFAIR. District of London. It lies between Piccadilly and Oxford Street with Park Lane to the west and Bond Street to the east. It is a fashionable residential district, and there are many large houses in its streets and squares. It owes its name to a fair which was held here every year until 1708. Much of the land belongs to the Duke of Westminster,

MAYMYO. A Burmese hill-station 60 miles N.E. of Mandalay. Pop. 6000.

MAYNOOTH. A village of Kildare, Irish Free State, 15 miles N.W of Dublin, on the Great Southern Railways. There are ruins of the ancient stronghold of the Geraldines of Kildare, probably built by Maurice Fitzgerald (1176). The College of Maynooth, founded in 1795, exists for the education of candidates for the Roman Catholic priesthood. From its inception until 1869 it was State subsidized. The splendid part of Carton, seat of the Dukes of Leinster, is near Maynooth.

MAYO. A large maritime county of Connaught, Irish Free State, with a long, irregular, island-studded coast-line on the Atlantic. It is drained by the Moy, Owenmore, and other rivers, and contains Loughs Mask, Conn, and Carrowmore. The western side is mountainous (Slieve Cor, 2369 feet; Nephin, 2646 feet; Muilrea, 2688 feet).

The Great Southern Railways traverse the county. Stock, oats, and potatoes are raised, and there is some fishing. Castlebar is the county town; Westport, Newport, and Ballina are others. After the English conquest Mayo was the property of the Bourke (Burgh) family. Area, 1,333,941 acres; pop. (1926), 172,690.

MAYOR (Lat. *major*, greater). The chief magistrate of a city or corporate town in England, Ireland, the British colonies, and the United States; in Scotland called *provost*. The mayor is elected by the aldermen or councillors, and holds office for a year, but he may be re-elected. The Mayors of London, York, Dublin. and other cities are called "lord mayor"; the Lord Mayor of London having also the title of "right honourable," first allowed in 1354 by Edward III. Mayors are *ex officio* justices of the peace during both their year of mayoralty and the following one. *See* MANSION HOUSE.

MAYOTTE′, or MAYOT′TA. An island in the Indian Ocean, one of the Comoros, at the north-east entrance of the Mozambique Channel, and forming with the Comoro Islands a French Colony. In the valleys the soil is fertile. The chief exports are sugar and rum. Area, 140 sq. miles; pop. (1931), 12,690.

MAYURBHANJ. A hill state, Bihar and Orissa, India. Area, 4243 sq. miles; pop. *c.* 730,000.

MAZANDERAN, or MAZENDERAN. A province of Persia, bounded on the north by the Caspian. Along the Caspian Sea the land is flat and fertile, but southward it rises rapidly into the spurs of the Elburz Mountains. Sugar-cane, rice, cotton, and mulberry trees grow luxuriantly. The capital is Sari, but Barfurush is the largest town. The population of the province is estimated at 200,000. Area, 10,640 sq. miles.

MAZARIN (mâ-zâ-raṇ), **Jules, or GIULIO MAZARINI**, First minister of Louis XIV. and cardinal, an Italian by origin, born 14th July, 1602, died 9th March, 1661. He was educated at Rome by the Jesuits, thence proceeded to the University of Alcala in Spain; entered the Pope's military service, and distinguished himself by diplomatic ability, for which he was rewarded with two canonries, and the appointment of nuncio to the court of France (1634-36).

Here he gained the favour of Richelieu; accepted service from the king, and became a naturalized citizen of France; was made a cardinal in recognition of his diplomatic services in Savoy; and in 1642, when Richelieu died, Mazarin promptly succeeded him. On the death of Louis XIII. the queen, Anne of Austria, became regent for her young son, Louis XIV., and it was thought that Mazarin would be dismissed; but instead he gained over the queen-regent, and made himself master of the nation.

Two parties in the State rebelled against this usurpation of supreme power by the cardinal. The Parliament of Paris denounced his increasing taxation, while the nobility dreaded his supremacy, and the combination of these malcontents resulted in the civil war of the Fronde (q.v.). As the immediate result of the conflict, Mazarin had to go into exile, but by the means of intrigue he formed a powerful royal party in the State, gained Marshal Turenne to his cause, and finally returned to his position at court in 1653. During the succeeding eight years he remained all-powerful in France; pursued the policy of Richelieu in foreign affairs; made an alliance with Cromwell; brought the Rhine provinces under the headship of France; and in the Treaty of the Pyrenees humiliated Spain, and gained much of French Flanders. Just as his foreign policy was successful, so was his home policy disastrous. He did nothing for the people but increase their taxes to fill an impoverished exchequer. Yet when he died Mazarin left an enormous fortune to his nieces, whom he had married into the most powerful families of Italy and France.—BIBLIOGRAPHY: Arthur Hassall, *Mazarin*; Mrs. Colquhoun Grant, *Queen and Cardinal*.

MAZEP′PA, Ivan Stephanovitsh. Hetman of the Cossacks, born about 1645, died in 1709. He became page to the King of Poland, and being detected in an intrigue with a Polish lady of high rank, Mazeppa was bound naked upon an untamed horse and cast loose. He was found and released by some peasants, and afterwards joined the Cossacks, where his skill, sagacity, and strength procured him the position of hetman in 1687.

He gained the confidence of Peter the Great, who made him Prince of the Ukraine; but having entered into a treasonable intrigue with Charles XII., he suffered defeat with the Swedish monarch at Poltava, and fled to Bender, where he died. He is the hero of a poem by Byron, and a drama by Pushkin.

MAZZINI (måt-sē'nē), **Giuseppe.** Italian patriot, born at Genoa 1805, died at Pisa 1872. His father was a physician and a professor in the university, and Mazzini studied with a view to following this profession, but afterwards took a new bent and graduated (1826) in law. While he was an advocate he turned his attention to literature, his first significant essay being *Dante's Love of Country*.

As his writings grew more distinctly liberal in their politics the Government suppressed the *Indicatore Genovese* and *Indicatore Livornese*, the papers in which they appeared. He afterwards joined the Carbonari, and was imprisoned in Savona for some months. On his release (1832) he was exiled to Marseilles, but was compelled by the French Government to retire into Switzerland. During the following five years he planned and organized various unsuccessful revolutionary movements, until, in 1837, he was expelled by the Swiss authorities and sought refuge in London.

During the revolutionary movements of 1848 he proceeded to Italy; served for a time under Garibaldi; and when the Pope fled from Rome he became president of its short-lived republic, and made a heroic defence of the capital against the French until compelled to surrender. From that time he continued to organize various risings in Italy, and the successful Sicilian expedition of Garibaldi in 1860 was due largely to his labours. For some time Mazzini was associated with Karl Marx in the first Socialist International organization.

When Italian unity was accomplished under a monarchy, Mazzini accepted the results with reserve. The latter part of his life was spent chiefly between London and Lugano. Mazzini was a man of great and varied acquirements, and wrote both in French and English with elegance and facility. He was buried at Genoa.—BIBLIOGRAPHY: E. A. Venturi, *Joseph Mazzini: a Memoir*; Linton, *Recollections of Mazzini and his Friends*; Bolton King, *Life of Mazzini*.

MAZZOLA (måt-sō'lå), or **MAZZUOLI** (måt-sụ-ō'lē), **Girolamo Francesco Maria** (called *Il Parmigiano*, the Parmesan). A painter of the Lombard school, born at Parma 1503, died 1540. His earliest works were in the style of Correggio, but in his twentieth year he went to Rome, where he came under the influence of Raphael and Michael Angelo, and was patronized by Clement VII. After the sack of Rome in 1527 he went to Bologna. His paintings are numerous, both fresco and easel, among the best known being the *Virgin and Child with Saints* (of which there are several repetitions), *Vision of St. Jerome, Cupid making a Bow, Baptism of Christ, Moses breaking the Tables of the Law* (fresco), etc. He was the earliest Italian etcher.

MBABANE. Seat of administration of Swaziland.

MEADOW - SWEET. A well-known British plant, *Spiræa Ulmaria*, nat. ord. Rosaceæ. It grows on the banks of streams and in damp places, has pinnate leaves, and stems 2 feet high bearing corymbs of white fragrant flowers.

MEASLES (Morbilli; Rubeola). An acute contagious disease characterized by catarrh of the upper respiratory passages and a blotchy irregular rash. It is the commonest of all infectious diseases, and is widely distributed throughout the world. It is more prevalent in towns than in the country, and, though it may occur at any age, is much more common in childhood. It is estimated that by the age of fifteen at least 95 per cent. of the population have been attacked.

The incubation period is about fourteen days, and the principal symptoms are first catarrhal signs with rise of temperature, followed in three or four days by the rash, at first behind the ears and on the neck, and later spreading to the face and all over the body. Along with the appearance of the rash there is an aggravation of the catarrhal symptoms and increased fever. There is always a certain amount of bronchitis present and in severe cases it is marked, causing considerable respiratory distress. The most serious complication is broncho-pneumonia, which occurs most frequently in children under three, and accounts for 70 per cent. of the deaths from measles.

Next to broncho-pneumonia the most serious complication is diarrhœa due to enteritis, and this usually arises in debilitated and weakly infants. Other complications are tonsillitis, laryngitis, gastritis, but none of these is nearly so frequent or so serious as broncho-pneumonia and enteritis. Throughout the illness great care should be given to treatment of the eyes and ears, as neglect of this may lead to weakened eyesight or chronic ear disease and deafness.

MEASUREMENT IN ENGINEERING. *See* TOLERANCE.

MEATH. A county of Leinster, Irish Free State, with a short coastline to the Irish Sea. It is traversed by the Boyne and the Blackwater, and is largely flat country. The Midland Great Western and Great Northern Railway systems serve the county. Trim is the county town; Navan and Kells are important. Cattle and sheep are raised; oats and potatoes are grown. Area, 577,816 acres; pop. (1926), 62,969. Meath was one of the kingdoms of Ireland, and included Meath, Longford, West Meath, and parts of other counties. It was divided up in the sixteenth century.

MEATH, Earl of. Irish title held by the family of Brabazon. In 1616 Sir Edward Brabazon, M.P., was made Baron Ardee. His son, William, the second baron, was made an earl in 1627. Reginald, the twelfth earl, was known as a philanthropist and for his efforts to make Empire Day a national holiday. He died on 11th Oct., 1929. His son, the thirteenth earl, when Lord Ardee, commanded a battalion of the Irish Guards in the Great War.

MEAUX. A town of Seine-et-Marne, France, on the Marne. The cathedral of S. Étienne is notable. Meaux was besieged by the English in 1520. During the European War the Germans reached Meaux (Sept., 1914)—their nearest approach to Paris. Pop. 14,000.

MECCA. A city of Arabia, capital of the Kingdom of Hejaz, and, as the birthplace of Mahomet, the holiest of all Mahommedan cities. It lies 70 miles E. of Jeddah, its port on the Red Sea. Thousands of pilgrims annually perform the *hajj* (pilgrimage to Mecca), encompassing the Kaaba (q.v.), running seven times between the hills of Safa and Merwa, and listening to a sermon on the hill of Arafat in order to attain the dignity of a *hajji.* To non-Muslims the city is closed. It was captured in 1924 by Idn Saud, Sultan of Nejd. Pop. estimated at 85,000, but rising during the *hajj.* *See* ARABIA; HEJAZ.

MECHANICAL DRAWING. The system of orthographic projection of plans, elevations, and sections used in engineering-works to show the exact construction of any machine or structure. The number of views required is reduced by the use of the conventions of showing the hidden parts in dotted or broken lines, and portions of views in section. Detail drawings are made full size or to some large scale. General drawings are made to scales of from about ⅛ inch to 1 inch to a foot. Standard parts can, to some extent, be used in a range of machines, in which case they are shown in detail in the drawings, but reference is made to their identification and store numbers in a table at the side.

A number of conventions are used, such as showing bolt threads by thick and thin parallel lines; rivets, bolts, and studs by their centres only; and toothed wheels by their pitch circles. All drawings should be fully dimensioned, and over-all figures should always be given as a check to the others.

Long details, such as columns, are usually not shown in full, but broken; and thin sections, such as boiler plate and girder sections, are blacked in. The views usually shown are plan, elevation, end elevation, and sections, which may be parts of the other views. Where the parts are to be fitted to some scale of limits, a letter is placed after the dimension on the drawing to indicate the class of fit required; running, push, etc. (*see* TOLERANCE).

Certain conventional shadings and tints are used to indicate the materials of construction. Tracings are made in Indian ink on cloth or paper. Photo-copying from tracings was introduced by Sir John Herschel, who used ferro-prussiate paper in 1840. Photographic blue or white prints are made from the tracings for use in the workshop. The tracing is placed against the glass of the printing-frame, commonly cylindrical, and the sensitized paper behind the tracing is acted on by the light from a rising and falling arc lamp. After the printing is complete, the print is developed in water and dried.

MECHANICS, Applied. Deals with the application of the principles of dynamics and kinematics to engineering problems. It may be divided into strength of materials (q.v.), theory of machines (*see* MACHINES, THEORY OF), theory of structures (*see* STRUCTURES, THEORY OF), and hydraulics (*see* HYDRAULICS AND HYDRAULIC MACHINERY). The units employed by engineers are not always those used in pure science. The main difference is found in the unit of force.

The weight of one pound is the engineer's definition, and consequently it differs in magnitude according to the latitude and the height of the place of observation. The variation is not of great significance, and in many ways the unit is a useful one. All units dependent on force are dealt with in the same way, pressures being gauged in pounds per square inch, and work in foot-pounds.

MECHITARISTS (me-kit'a-rists). A society or sect of Armenian Christians acknowledging the authority of the Pope, but retaining their own ritual with a few alterations. They have printed the best editions of Armenian classics. The name originated from *Mechitar* Da Petro, who founded a religious society at Constantinople for the purpose of disseminating a knowledge of the old Armenian language and literature.

MECHLIN. Flemish name of Malines (q.v.).

MECKLENBURG - SCHWERIN. Formerly a grand-duchy, and since 1918 a republic of Germany. It is bounded on the north by the Baltic Sea; area, 5068 sq. miles; capital, Schwerin (pop. 48,157). The surface is flat, except where a ridge of low hills forms the watershed between the Elbe and the Baltic. The sea-coast is indented by several inlets, and lakes are very numerous. The streams flow partly to the Elbe, partly to the Baltic.

The chief products are corn, peas, beans, potatoes, beet, and turnips. Both horses and cattle are exported. Distilling is largely carried on. Mecklenburg was proclaimed a republic in Nov., 1918, and the Constitution was promulgated on 17th March, 1920. Pop. (1925), 674,045. *See* WISMAR.

MECKLENBURG - STRELITZ. Formerly a grand-duchy, and since 1918 a republic of Germany; capital, Neu-Strelitz (pop. 12,260). It consists of two larger and several smaller districts; the former separated by the interposition of Mecklenburg-Schwerin, and the latter existing in separate patches. The whole area is estimated at 1131 sq. miles. Pop. (1926), 110,269.

MECON'IC ACID ($C_7H_4O_7$). An acid with which morphia is combined in opium. When pure, it forms small white crystals. Its aqueous solution gives a deep red colour with ferric chloride, and a bright yellow colour with silver nitrate, to which a drop of ammonia has been added.

MECONOPSIS. A genus of Papaveraceæ, natives of temperate mountains. *M. cambrica* is the Welsh poppy; *M. wallichii* is a beautiful blue-flowered poppy of the Himalaya.

MEDAL. A piece of metal, generally in the shape of a coin, struck or cast to commemorate some person or event. It should be distinguished from a *medallion*, the term usually applied to a circular bas-relief in sculpture; and fr m a *plaquette*, a small piece of metal decorated on one side only, for application as ornament. The history of the medal is closely bound up with that of

Medal commemorating the defeat of the Spanish Armada

coinage, but at certain periods it has had an independent life of its own.

It differs from a coin in that the metal used is chosen from the artistic point of view, the baser metals, such as bronze and lead, in fact providing the best material; and, not being intended for circulation, size and the amount of relief can be greater than in a coin.

Almost invariably a medal is decorated on both sides, the *obverse* bearing a portrait, the *reverse* a historical or heraldic design. The latter was usually the case in Germany, while the Italians favoured a personal device known as an *impresa*, which form a kind of bastard heraldry whose meaning is often obscure.

The great age of the medal as an artistic product is the Renaissance; and it admirably reflects the assertion of human personality characteristic of that period. In the fifteenth century, Italy was the chief centre of production, and Antonio Pisano (1380 to about 1456) known as Pisanello was the most celebrated medallist. His medals made for Leonello d'Este of Ferrara and for the Malatesti of Rimini are unsurpassed in any age.

Notable contemporary or slightly later medallists are Matteo de' Pasti of Verona Sperandio of Mantua, Giovanni Boldù of Venice, Caradossa Foppa of Milan, Cristoforo di Geremia of Mantua, who worked mainly at Rome, and Nicolo Fiorentino of Florence. Early medals were cast from a preliminary design made in wax or similar material, whose character helped the artist to secure both unity and delicacy of detail.

In the sixteenth century striking from dies became the usual practice, a method much used by Benvenuto Cellini, and by his contemporary Leone Leoni of Milan. This introduction of a mechanical element, and the difficulty of making the die, combined with mannered imitation of Greek and Roman coins to cause a decline in the art of the medal. Italian influence soon spread to Northern Europe.

The most independent school was that of Germany, where in method of production and final result, the medal represented the art of the goldsmith rather than of the sculptor. The chief centre was Nuremberg, where Dürer designed, if he did not make, several medals. In France the Italian tradition found more congenial soil. In the fifteenth and sixteenth centuries some remarkable medals were produced at Lyons, Vienne and Tours, to commemorate royal visits to these towns; and, in the seventeenth century, Guillaume, Dupré and Jean and Claude Warin are notable for their technical skill.

In England no native school developed until the seventeenth century when Abraham Simon and his more famous brother Thomas were at work. In later centuries medals were produced in large quantities, especially in France for Louis XIV., Louis XV., and Louis XVI., and for Napoleon I.; but their artistic value is small. Of late years there has been somewhat of a revival in the medal, wherein France has played a leading part.—BIBLIOGRAPHY: Hill, *Pisanello* and *Medals of the Renaissance*; Forrer, *Biographical Dictionary of Medallists*.

MEDAL. An honourable distinction conferred by the sovereign or the State on those who have taken part in a naval or military capacity in a given campaign, and a record of services performed. The custom of granting medals as rewards is a very ancient one, dating back as far as the Roman era; then, many hundred years later, it was revived in England by Queen Elizabeth, who, as an outward sign of approval, conferred a jewel and badge on Sir Walter Raleigh, while in the next century Charles I. decorated one R. Welch with a gold medal for gallantry in action at the battle of Edgehill.

These and others were given for individual acts which, no doubt, closely concerned the sovereign, and it was left to Oliver Cromwell, after the battle of Dunbar in 1650 to make the first general issue of medals to all the Republican troops engaged in the battle, irrespective of rank or individual merit. After the Restoration the matter of medals again retired into the background, and no further general issue to troops was made till after the battle of Waterloo, 165 years later. This, the Waterloo Medal, was issued in 1817 to all troops engaged, and was worn with a red ribbon with blue edges, the ribbon being practically the same as that selected seventy years later for the Distinguished Service Order.

Waterloo, though the last battle of the Napoleonic wars, was the only one for which a separate medal was awarded to officers and men alike, though, in accordance with the custom of the times a number of gold medals had been presented to high commanders from time to time, and it was not till 1848 that it was decided to issue a medal designed to cover the whole period of the wars from 1793 to 1814. This medal, known as the Military General Service Medal, and worn with the Waterloo ribbon, was accordingly issued to any survivors who could be found, and was provided with "clasps" or "bars" bearing the names of the different engagements commemorated; at the same time a Naval General Service Medal was issued, with a blue and white ribbon.

It may be here convenient to explain very briefly the meaning of the words "clasps" or "bars" in connection with medals. From 1817, in the case of medals awarded by the sovereign, and from a good many years earlier in the case of those issued by the Honourable East India Company in India, it had been the custom to strike a separate medal for each battle selected for commemoration, quite regardless of the fact that two or more battles might have been incidents in the same campaign; consequently the number of medals and incidentally the expense increased alarmingly, e.g. in India alone something like two dozen medals had been issued between 1795 and 1843, of which four were awarded for the first Afghan War.

When, therefore, it was decided to commemorate the Napoleonic wars posthumously, the plan was adapted of making one medal do for the whole set of campaigns, and of marking individual battles and expeditions by a bar suitably inscribed and intended to be worn across the ribbon in the form of a brooch or clasp, and this arrangement has been continued ever since.

In the case of a group of campaigns more or less connected and extending over a considerable number of years, the medal is termed a "General Service Medal," e.g. "India General Service," 1854-95 (ribbon three red and two blue perpendicular stripes); "India General Service" 1908 onwards (ribbon blue and green). When the campaigns are unconnected with any others, a separate medal and clasps are given, e.g. 'Afghanistan," 1878-80 (ribbon red and green); "China," 1900 (red and yellow); "Queen's South Africa," 1899-1902 (red, blue, and yellow).

In the European War four medals and stars have been given, of which three can have been earned by any one man. They are: the 1914 Star; the 1914-15 Star (ribbon, red, white, and blue, watered); the British War Medal (blue, black, white, and orange); and the Victory Medal, with ribbon of watered silk. Of these four over 7,000,000 were issued between July 1919, and Sept. 1921.

No description of medals can be complete without mention of the Victoria Cross. This, though strictly speaking more in the nature of a decoration than a medal, is, as is well known, given simply and solely as a reward for an outstanding act of gallantry in face of the enemy. Other medals coming more under the head of decorations are the Military Medal and the Distinguished Conduct Medal, for the rank and file of the army, and the Conspicuous Gallantry Medal and the Distinguished Service Medal, for the navy.

In uniform the actual medals are only worn in full dress on the left breast; on all other occasions the ribbons only are worn, the one exception being that officers in mess-dress wear miniature medals and decorations. Medals and decorations granted by foreign powers are worn in uniform by His Majesty's permission only; the medal of the Royal Humane Society (ribbon dark blue) is worn by military or naval recipients on the right breast.

MEDE'A. In Greek mythology, daughter of Æetes, King of Colchis. She enabled Jason to obtain the celebrated golden fleece, and lived with him for ten years, until he discarded her in favour of Glauce or Creusa, daughter of King Creon. In revenge she sent Glauce a bridal robe which enveloped her in consuming flame, and thereafter she slew her own children by Jason. The tragedies of the name of *Medea* by Æschylus and Ovid have perished, but the *Medeas* of Euripides and Seneca are extant. The story has also been treated by Corneille and by Grillparzer, and is the subject of an opera by Cherubini. *See* JASON; ARGONAUTS.

MEDELLIN. The second largest town of Colombia, capital of the department of Antioquia; altitude, 4900 feet. There is a University, founded in 1822, also the School of Mines. It is a centre for the gold mines (Antioquia), has a transit trade, and is the seat of an archbishop. There is a wireless, telephone, and telegraph station here. Pop. 120,044.

MEDIA. An ancient country in Western Asia, formerly the seat of a powerful kingdom, corresponding nearly to the north-western portion of modern Persia. According to the Greek historians, Deioces, 708-655 B.C., was the first native king, but the true founder of the great Medean monarchy was Cyaxares, 633-593 B.C. He extended his dominion over the highlands of Southern Armenia and Asia Minor as far as the Halys, overthrew the Assyrian monarchy, and in conjunction with Nabopolassar, King of Babylon, destroyed Nineveh in 607 or 606 B.C.

Astyages, the successor of Cyaxares and the last king, reigned for thirty-five years, 593 to 558 B.C., when he was overthrown or deposed by Cyrus. Media henceforward formed part of the Persian Empire, and shared its fate. Cyrus is supposed by some authorities to be the Darius the Mede mentioned in the Book of Daniel as reigning over Babylon after its conquest by the Persians.

MEDICAL ACT. An Act for the registration of medical practitioners, passed 2nd Aug., 1858, and amended by subsequent Acts. The Act establishes a general council for the United Kingdom, with branch councils for England, Scotland, and Ireland. The members are appointed by the Crown, the medical and surgical corporations, and the universities. They are appointed for a term of five years, and are eligible for re-election.

The chief function of the councils is to register such persons as are qualified to practise medicine or surgery in the three kingdoms; and any fellow, licentiate, or extra-licentiate of any of the medical bodies named in the Act, or possessing any of the qualifications scheduled in the Act, is entitled to be registered on payment of a fee of £5.

The general council has power to remove the name from the register of any person who has been guilty of crime or of malpractices in his profession. Further, any person who obtains registration by false statements is liable to be imprisoned for twelve months, and any one falsely claiming to have been registered is liable to be fined £20.

The registrar of the general council publishes annually *The Medical Register*, containing the names of all persons appearing on the general register on 1st Jan. in each year. Registered persons are entitled to practise medicine and recover medical fees in all parts of the United Kingdom. The council also publish *The British Pharmacopœia*, a list of medicines and compounds and the manner of preparing them.

MEDICAL JURISPRUDENCE. The application of medical knowledge to questions of civil and criminal law. The evidence obtainable from medical practitioners is frequently the most significant in the whole case. The questions involved in this subject are those of injuries to the person, and the civil and social rights of individuals. Assaults of all characters, fatal or not fatal, raise legal questions very difficult of solution.

In the case of death it is commonly difficult to decide whether the wounds were self-inflicted, and medical testimony and deductions from the position of the body, the common capabilities of movement of hand and arm, the position and line of the wounds, and the effects upon the internal organs are the matters on which the decision is based. Great cunning has been shown by some murderers in making the death appear the result of natural causes or due to suicide. In poisoning cases it is necessary to know the properties of the poison used and its actions upon the human body.

The court has frequently to decide whether the poison could be taken in mistake for some other substance due to faulty labelling or other negligence. The cause of death is determined by post-mortem examination, and chemical analysis of the contents of the various organs. If little or nothing is known of the properties of the poison used, experiments upon animals must be resorted to for information.

Bodies are found in water in which they have been placed after death. The post-mortem examination provides evidence as to whether the case is one of drowning or not, by the characteristic actions upon the lungs and other organs. In questions relating to criminal responsibility, validity of contracts and the identification of a living being or corpse the knowledge of the characteristic development of the human frame is of great value.

Statistical records of longevity, and the prevalence of and mortality due to specific diseases are treated in this subject, and also form the basis of the estimates of insurance risks. The identification of persons long absent from their homes, perhaps exposed to hardships, wounds, and foreign climates, is of importance in settling claims of succession to titles and estates.

Marriage and parentage provide complicated cases of rights to estates in which medical evidence, though it can never be exact, provides a guide that is equitable.

Deviations from a recognized normal state have been acknowledged in test-case decisions, and have thus established the degree of variation in human functions which may be considered reasonable. The detection of malingering among claimants from insurance companies and public funds, recognition of maladies exempting people from public duties, and of the signs of insanity, form important sections of this subject.—Cf. J. Glaister, *A Text-book of Medical Jurisprudence and Toxicology*.

MEDICI (mā′di-chē). A Florentine family which rose to wealth and influence by successful commerce, and whose members combined the career of merchants and bankers with the exercise of political power, a princely display of private munificence, and a liberal patronage of literature and art. The Medici were associated with the history of the Florentine Republic from an early period, but they first became prominent in the person of Salvestro, who became gonfalonier in 1378. Giovanni de' Medici (1360-1429) amassed great riches by trade, rendered great services to the city, and in 1421 became gonfalonier.

He was succeeded by his son Cosmo (the elder, 1389-1464), surnamed the *father of his country*. Cosmo acquired immense wealth and influence, and laid the foundation of his reputation by his munificent patronage of art and letters, and the conjunction of consummate statesmanship with his commercial enterprise. He was for thirty-four years the sole arbitrator of the Re public and the adviser of the sovereign houses of Italy.

His grandson Lorenzo the Magnificent (1449-92) was the second great man of the House of Medici. He governed the state in conjunction with his brother Giuliano (1453-78) till the latter was assassinated by the Pazzi, a rival Florentine family. Escaping from this massacre, he sustained a war with Ferdinand of Naples, with whom he signed a definitive peace in 1480. The rest of Lorenzo's reign was passed in peace, and in those acts of profuse liberality and munificent patronage of arts and sciences in which he rivalled or excelled his grandfather.

He left three sons—Piero (1471-1503), Giovanni (afterwards Pope Leo X.), and Giuliano, Duke of Nemours. Piero succeeded his father, but was deprived of his estates when the French invaded Italy in 1494. He finished his career in the service of France. His eldest son Lorenzo came to power after the abdication of his uncle Giuliano, who became Duke of Urbino. He died in 1519, leaving a daughter, the famous Catherine de' Medici, Queen of France.

After several reverses in the family, Alessandro, an illegitimate son of the last named Lorenzo, was restored to Florence by the troops of Charles V., and by an imperial decree he was declared head of the Republic, and afterwards Duke of Florence. The next name of importance in the family is that of Cosmo "the great," in 1537 proclaimed Duke of Florence and afterwards Grand-Duke of Tuscany.

A learned man himself, he was a great patron of learning and art, a collector of paintings and antiquities. He died in 1574. Francisco Maria, his son, obtained from the Emperor Maximilian II., whose daughter Joanna he had married, the confirmation of his title of grand-duke in 1575, which continued in his family until it became extinct in 1737 on the death of Giovanni Gasto, who was succeeded by Francis, Duke of Lorraine. *See* TUSCANY; CATHERINE DE' MEDICI; MARIE DE' MEDICI.—BIBLIOGRAPHY: W. H. O. Smeaton, *The Medici and the Italian Renaissance*; Janet Ross, *Lives of the Early Medici as told in their Correspondence*; *Cambridge Modern History* (vols. i. ii.); Ch. Yriarte, *Florence.*

MEDICINE. From earliest times in all nations there has been some method of treating disease, and wherever the art of writing was practised records of these methods have been preserved in some kind of system of medicine. In primitive societies the priest, the magician, and the medicine-man were one and the same. Black magic produced drought, famine, disease, and death; white magic averted these. In its origin, medicine was a form of white magic.

Naturally medicine did not progress very far so long as it was under the sway of the supernatural, but as the savage advanced a little further in the knowledge gained by experience, special talent was developed in herb-doctoring, bone-setting, and rude surgery, and this was employed as a means of livelihood by certain individuals.

A knowledge of herbs and some surgical skill were possessed by the medicine-man of these primitive tribes, and further development of such methods, along with belief in the supernatural and its effects, were largely the basis of the medical principles and practices of the ancient civilizations of Egypt, Persia, Mesopotamia, India, and China. It is not until we come to the medicine of the Greeks that we find a fundamental change of principle, which removed the study of medicine from mere folk-lore, and brought about the foundations of medical principles as they are understood to-day.

In contrast to these ancient systems, which were based on a belief in the supernatural, the Greeks based their study of medicine on observation of the signs and symptoms of disease. The earliest Greek medical school was that of Cnidos, a Lacedæmonian colony, and its origin reaches back to 700 B.C., while a later school began on the Island of Cos about 600 B.C., and flourished for several centuries. Out of this latter school came Hippocrates, known as the "Father of Medicine."

His period of greatest activity was about 400 B.C., and he led a somewhat wandering life throughout Greece, teaching in various centres and leaving many pupils to carry on his methods and traditions. His methods have been preserved in the *Hippocratic Corpus*, a collection of about seventy separate books, which gives the principles and spirit of his system.

The method of the Hippocratic writers is that known to-day as the inductive, and the greatness of the man is made evident when we consider his patient observation of fact, his scepticism concerning the mar-

Some Members of the Medici Family

A, Cosmo (1389-1464). *B*, Giuliano (1453-1478). *C*, Ferdinand (1610-1670). *D*, Lorenzo (1449-1492).

vellous, his hesitation to theorize beyond data, and, on the other hand, his ability to generalize from actual observation, and his faithful and effective treatment of the sick.

His spirit is well shown in the famous "Hippocratic oath," still the ideal of the profession of medicine, and respected by all civilized peoples to-day. The history of Greek medicine did not end with Hippocrates, but continued active for more than five centuries. Various schools of thought arose, and, finally, though Greek intellect was as creative as before, a decay of the spirit was reflected in the medical, as in the literary, products of the time.

In the second century of the Christian era this great period came to an end, but not before its influence had spread westward, for it was in Rome that the second great figure of ancient medicine, Galen, began to practise, but he early retired to devote himself to study, travel, and teaching. His energies were many-sided, and his works are an encyclopædia of the knowledge of his time. Along with his widespread knowledge and wonderful observation, however, went a dogmatic nature and a tendency to find plausible explanations for every phenomenon, which resulted in the simple observation and interpretation of facts by Hippocrates being replaced by an elaborate system of medical philosophy.

The effect of Galen's dogmatism and infallibility upon Europe in the centuries to follow has been extraordinary, and it may be said that medicine remained practically stationary for fourteen centuries after his death. With the decay of the Roman Empire and the stagnation of Greek thought the progress of medicine came to a standstill, and it remained in a state of stagnation through most of the Middle Ages. The Byzantine period added little to medical knowledge, nor was the period of conquest and conversion by the Moslems productive of medical advance.

Though many of the European universities were formed in the twelfth, thirteenth, and fourteenth centuries, and despite the growth of the Christian virtue of compassion, resulting in many hospitals being raised and the sick nursed, medical science made but slight advance through the Middle Ages, chiefly for two reasons.

The first is that the strife of intellects was of a kind that tended to the suppression of all experimental science, and the second that, by the scholastic type of mind, craftsmanship was held in low esteem; hence surgery was separated from medicine and the physician ranked as a man of learning; the surgeon as a barber.

This separation delayed progress, and it is not until the nineteenth century that we find the two ranked as equal. With the Renaissance the study of medicine shared in the general freedom from accepted authority, and progress began once more.

Four men stand out in the sixteenth century on account of their influence. Paracelsus, a Swiss, was an original medical thinker, and the precursor of chemical pharmacology and therapeutics. Vesalius, the most striking figure in European medicine after Galen and before Harvey, was of Flemish birth, but did most of his work in Italy, and laid the foundation of modern anatomy. Paré, a French surgeon, shares with Hunter and Lister the credit of raising surgery to its present level. Leonardo da Vinci, the artist, was also the greatest scientist of the Renaissance in Italy.

Medical practice during the Renaissance was still largely a combination of superstition, herb-doctoring, and quackery, and the influence of the great masters was seen more in the following seventeenth century, when there was considerable improvement in the practice of medicine, and also great advance by individual scientific endeavour.

It was an age of great writers and great scientists, but the greatest name in seventeenth-century medicine is William Harvey. Born in Kent, he studied for four years in Padua, then returned to England, where, after years of study combined with practice, he discovered the circulation of the blood—the most important medical event since the days of Galen.

Throughout the seventeenth century all medical science advanced, but special advance was made in anatomy, physiology, chemistry, and ophthalmology. In the latter half of the century English medicine was dominated by Sydenham, the reviver of the Hippocratic methods, and a man of great personality and high personal honour.

Following the advances of the seventeenth century, the eighteenth century appears as a period of calm, and as in other things so in medicine there was a tendency to formalism. It was an age of theories and of systems, and there were fewer great original workers. Of these the most notable were: Linnæus, the great Swedish botanist; Galvani and Volta, who were the first workers in electricity; Priestley and Lavoisier, the two foremost chemists; John Hunter, the greatest surgeon of the century; and Jenner, his pupil, who introduced preventive inoculation against smallpox.

During the two previous centuries medicine owed much to the great scientists, and in the nineteenth century this is equally evident. Foremost among these are Darwin, Helmholtz, and Virchow, whose works have had far-reaching effect on medical advance since their day.

In the second half of the nineteenth century surgical practice made rapid strides, due to the discovery of anæsthetics—first widely used by Simpson, of Edinburgh—and to the antiseptic principles of Lister, who applied the work of Pasteur, the founder of modern bacteriology. The discovery of X-rays toward the end of the century had immediate effect in greater accuracy, and opened up lines of treatment not yet fully developed.

The outstanding feature of twentieth-century medicine is the rapid development of its preventive side. There has been great increase in laws relating to public health, sanitation, the health of the industrial worker, and the widespread establishment of clinics to control tuberculosis and venereal disease, and for maternity, and child welfare. The Insurance Act of Great Britain in 1911 has given greater opportunity for early treatment of the worker, and is the first step toward a national medical service.

In line with these, much work has been done in regard to medical statistics, and in bacteriological research in the production of preventive inoculation, while of late years the study of medical psychology has been widely developed. The discovery of radium by Madame Curie in the beginning of the century has opened up a new era which may prove as far-reaching in medical science as in chemistry.—BIBLIOGRAPHY: F. H. Garrison, *History of Medicine*; R. W. Livingstone, *Legacy of Greece*; W. Osler, *Medicine*.

MEDICINE AS A CAREER. The main careers open to members of the medical profession may be listed as follows:

(1) General Practice.
(2) Government Medical Services at Home and Abroad.
(3) Public Health Work.
(4) Poor-Law Medical Service.
(5) Psychological Medicine.
(6) Scientific Research or Teaching.
(7) Consultants and Specialists.
(8) Certain other Careers (as Ship Surgeoncies).

It will be seen that the scope is very wide for the qualified doctor, and the opportunities especially in branches other than General Practice, are increasing.

Since the Act of 1876, which rendered women eligible to obtain degrees and diplomas, more and more women's names have appeared on the Register of the General Medical Council. The disfavour with which women doctors were originally looked upon, both by their male colleagues and by the public, is rapidly disappearing, and generally speaking, women are regarded as eligible for nearly all kinds of medical work, excluding the Services of the Crown.

The two main spheres of work in which they are especially finding opportunities are general practice and posts as Maternity and Child Welfare and School Medical Officers under the local authorities. There is a special organisation for Women's Medical Service in India.

Before medical practice can begin it is necessary under law for the student to have his or her name entered on the Register of the General Medical Council, and for this certain medical degrees or other recognised qualifications are necessary. (It is advisable also for a student after the preliminary examinations have been taken, to have his or her name entered on the Students' Register: a copy of the regulations can be obtained from the G.M.C., 44 Hallam Street, London, W. 1.)

The work necessary for a recognised medical degree or qualification falls into three periods:

(1) A period of about two years at a public or secondary school devoted to the study of Chemistry, Physics, and often Biology.
(2) A period of two years in the dissecting room and laboratories of a university or medical school.
(3) A period of three years of clinical study in a hospital.

This is the minimum time taken—illness or failure at examination frequently extends the period.

After the general degree or diploma has been taken, specialised courses for further degrees or special diplomas may be taken.

The Medical Course is therefore a long one, and it requires a considerable financial outlay in fees and maintenance before recognised qualifications are obtained. It is advisable to obtain full particulars as early as possible from the G.M.C. or from the British Medical Association

(B.M.A. House, 19B Tavistock Square, London, W.C. 1). The regulations, examination syllabuses and fees of the particular university or medical school it is proposed to enter should also be studied before the first examinations are taken.

The prospects before the qualified medical practitioner are good. The doctor in general practice has a high social standing, and although a good practice must be developed—or capital must be available to purchase a partnership in one—the remuneration is steady and adequate. Thus an income of £1000 per annum may be expected from an established practice.

The specialist can, of course, command higher fees, and the salaries scale in most of the public services extends above this figure. Full particulars of these salaries scales are available.

MEDICINE HAT. A town of Alberta, Canada, 180 miles E. of Calgary. There are some manufactures and railway shops, and the city is the distributing and trading centre for a large district. It is rich in natural gas. Pop. (1931), 10,300.

MEDINA. A city of Arabia, the terminus of the Hejaz Railway, and, as the burial-place of Mahomet, the second holiest of Mahommedan cities. It is about 125 miles N.E. of Yembo, its port on the Red Sea. The principal attraction is the magnificent mosque containing the tomb of the Prophet. Medina was the scene of the Prophet's labours after the *Hejira* (Friday, 16th July, 622). Pop. 10,000, rising during the *Hajj*.

MEDINET-EL-FAIYUM. A city of Egypt, 25 miles from Cairo. Pop. (1927), 52,372.

MEDITERRANEAN SEA (Lat. *Mare Internum*). The inland sea between Europe, Asia, and Africa, about 2200 miles long and 1200 miles in extreme breadth. It communicates on the west with the Atlantic Ocean by the Strait of Gibraltar, and on the north-east with the Black Sea through the Dardanelles, the Sea of Marmara, and the Bosporus. It is divided, near its centre, into two distinct and not very unequal portions, an eastern and a western, the latter lying west of Italy, Sicily, and Cape Bon in Africa. The other important subdivisions are the Adriatic Sea and the Ægean Sea.

The most important islands are Sardinia, Sicily, Corsica, and the Balearic Isles, in the west division; and Cyprus, Rhodes, Crete, the Ionian Isles, and Malta, in the east division. The principal rivers which discharge themselves directly into the Mediterranean are the Ebro, Rhone, Po, and Nile.

Its greatest ascertained depth is about 14,000 feet, sounded between Malta and Crete. Owing to the very narrow channel which connects the Mediterranean with the main ocean, there is very little tide. The Mediterranean abounds with fish, and also furnishes coral and sponges.

MEDLAR. A tree of the genus Mespĭlus, the *M. germanica,* found wild in several parts of Central Europe, and cultivated for its fruit, which is remarkable for its acerbity when first gathered. It loses this acerbity after a few weeks' keeping.

MÉDOC. A wine-growing district of Western France, in the department of Gironde, producing some of the best varieties of red Bordeaux.

MEDUL'LA, or MARROW. In animals, the highly vascular connective tissue, interspersed with adipose or fat-cells, which fills up the hollow shafts or *medullary canals* of long bones, and is the chief blood-forming tissue of the body. It is responsible for the production of all the red corpuscles of the blood in the adult, and it also gives rise to some of the white blood corpuscles. In the shafts of the long bones the marrow is of the white or yellow variety; whereas in the extremities of these bones and in such bones as the ribs the marrow is red and rich in blood-forming elements. The *medulla oblongāta* is the upper enlarged continuation of the spinal cord, while the *medulla spinālis* is the spinal cord itself. In vegetable physiology the *medulla* is otherwise known as the *pith.* *See* BOTANY.

MEDULLARY RAYS. In botany, plates of parenchymatous tissue running inwards and outwards from the cambium through wood and bast. They form an important part of the living tissue of the wood, and also serve for storage. The "silver grain" of oak and other wood is due to their presence.

MEDU'SIDÆ. The jelly-fishes or sea-nettles, a name given to cœlenterate animals of the class Hydrozoa, being free and oceanic forms, the most typical of which consist of a single *medusa* or swimming-bell, shaped like an umbrella with a straight handle. The mouth is situated at the end of the handle, and leads into a cavity communicating with a system of canals. The umbrella is fringed with tentacles, and bears other sense-organs. A number of the medusæ formerly believed to be distinct species have been shown to be really the free, generative buds of other Hydrozoa.

See HYDROZOA; SCYPHOZOA; SIPHONOPHORA.

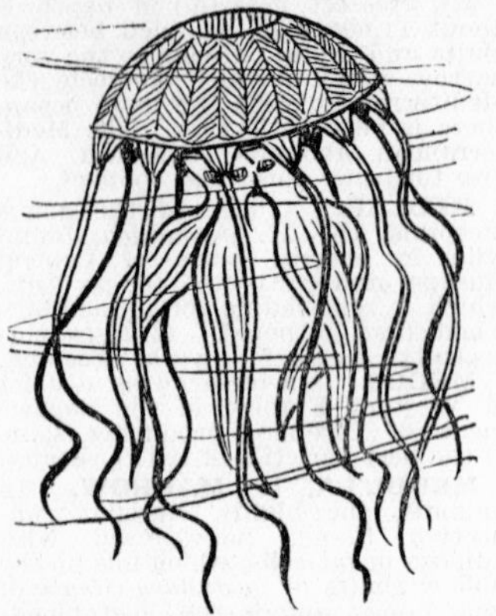

Medusidæ—Medusa

MED'WAY. A river of England, which flows in a winding course across Kent, past Tunbridge and Maidstone to Rochester and Chatham, where it spreads out into a broad estuary, joining that of the Thames. It is navigable to Maidstone; length 70 miles.

MEERANE (mā'rȧ-ne). A town of Germany in Saxony, with manufactures of woollens and textiles. Pop. 24,094.

MEERSCHAUM (mēr'shum). A hydrous silicate of magnesium, consisting of about 61 per cent. silica, 28 magnesia, and 11 water, occurring as a fine white compact clay, commonly in lumps. It is found in Europe, but more abundantly in Asia Minor, especially in the alluvium of Eski-Shehr in the province of Brusa, where it is associated with magnesite. It is manufactured into tobacco-pipes.

MEERUT. A division and district of the United Provinces, India. The division has an area of 11,194 sq. miles; pop. about 5,800,000. District area, 2344 sq. miles; pop. 1,499,074. Wheat, barley, and the sugar-cane are cultivated; about a quarter of the area is irrigated.

MEERUT. A city of the United Provinces, India, between the Ganges and the Jumna. It was the scene of the first great outbreak among the sepoys (1857). Pop. (1931), 136,709.

MEGALICHTHYS (-ik'this). A genus of fossil ganoid fishes found in the British coal-measures, characterized by smooth, but minutely punctured, enamelled scales, some of which have been found as large as 5 inches in diameter. The fish was about 4 feet long.

MEGALO'NYX. A genus of large fossil edentate mammals, allied to the sloth, but adapted for a terrestrial instead of an arboreal life, found in the Pleistocene of North America.

MEGALOSAU'RUS. A fossil dinosaurian reptile found in Jurassic and Cretaceous strata. Its length has been estimated at between 40 and 50 feet. Its powerful, pointed, and trenchant teeth indicate its carnivorous habits, and it must have been one of the most formidable saurians. Its remains were first known from England, but it has now been traced into India and North America. The American Allosaurus is a closely related genus. The anterior limbs of the Megalosaurs were much reduced, and they walked habitually on the posterior pair only.

MEGAPO'DIUS. A genus of gallinaceous birds, type of the family Megapodiidæ, the best-known species of which is the Australian brush-turkey (*Catheturus lathami*), a large bird remarkable for erecting large mounds, composed of earth, grass, and decayed leaves, in the centre of which it deposits its eggs, leaving them to be hatched by the heat of the fermenting vegetable mass. There are fifteen species of the type-genus indigenous to Australia and some of the islands of the Pacific, and possessing similar nesting habits.

MEG'ARIS. A small district or state of ancient Greece, partly in Northern Greece, partly on the Corinthian Isthmus. The only important town was Megara, situated a mile from the sea. It contained a Pelasgian citadel, called Caria, on a hill north-west of the city, with a temple to Demeter, called Megaron, from which the name of the town is supposed to be derived. Megaris had flourishing colonies at an early period, but afterwards became annexed to Attica.

MEGASPORE. *See* HETEROSPORY.

MEGATHE'RIUM. A fossil genus of edentate mammals, allied to the sloths, but having feet adapted for walking on the ground, found in the Pleistocene Pampas deposits of South America. It was about 8 feet high, and its body 12 to 18 feet long. Its teeth prove that it lived on vegetables, and its fore-feet, about a yard in length and armed with gigantic claws, show that roots were its chief food. Its remains are found throughout a very large part of

South America, and it penetrated the southern part of North America.

MEGIDDO. A place in Palestine, in the plain of Esdraelon (q.v.). It has been identified with the Armageddon which is mentioned in Rev. xvi. 16, as the site of the battle of the great day of God. During the European War it was captured by the British, 19th Sept., 1918.

MEHEM'ET ALI. Viceroy of Egypt, born at Kavala, in Macedonia, in 1769, died 1849. He entered the Turkish army, and served in Egypt against the French; rose rapidly in military and political importance; became pasha of Cairo, Alexandria, and subsequently of all Egypt. In 1811 he massacred the Mamelukes to the number of 470 in Cairo, and about 1200 over the country. He then commenced, by the orders of the Porte, a war of six years' duration against the Wahabites of Arabia, which was brought to a successful conclusion by his son Ibrahim, and secured him the possession of Hejaz.

Ibrahim also aided in bringing a large part of the Sudan under Egyptian rule. By means of a vigorous domestic policy Mehemet reduced the finances to order; organized an army and a navy; stimulated agriculture, and encouraged manufactures. From 1824 to 1827 he assisted the Sultan in endeavouring to reduce the Morea, which led to the destruction of his fleet by the allied European powers at Navarino (1827).

Subsequently he turned his arms against the Sultan, and in his efforts to secure dominion over Syria by armed invasion, he was so far successful (*see* IBRAHIM PASHA) that the European powers had to interfere and compel him to sign a treaty in 1839, which gave him the hereditary pashalic of Egypt in lieu of Syria, Candia, and Hejaz.—Cf. Sir C. A. Murray, *A Short Memoir of Mohammed Ali*.

MEIGHEN, Arthur. Canadian politician. Born in Ontario, 16th June, 1874, he was educated at the University of Toronto. For a time he was a teacher, but later became a barrister in Manitoba. In 1908 he was elected to the House of Commons at Ottawa, and in 1913 was made Solicitor-General in the Conservative ministry. In 1917 he became Secretary of State, and a little later Minister of the Interior. In July, 1920, on the resignation of Sir Robert Borden, he succeeded as Premier, but he resigned on his party's defeat in 1921. He was again Premier for a few months in 1926, having in the meantime been leader of the opposition. On leaving office he took up an important business appointment.

MEININGEN (mī'ning-en). A town of Germany, Republic of Thuringia, formerly the capital of the Duchy of Saxe-Meiningen; on the Werra. The castle of the former duke is of antiquarian interest. Pop. 18,221.

MEISSEN (mī'sen). An ancient town of Saxony, founded by Henry I. between 922 and 933, 14 miles W.N.W. of Dresden, at the influx of the Triebisch into the Elbe. On a height above the town stands a Gothic cathedral, erected between 1260 and 1450, and an extensive castle in the late Gothic style, belonging to the fifteenth century, restored and decorated with frescoes. Porcelain (in the porcelain factory near the town) is the staple manufacture. Meissen is the see of an archbishop. Pop. (1925), 45,485.

MEISSONIER (mā-son-yā), **Jean Louis Ernest.** French painter, born in Lyons 1815, died in Paris 1891. He went to Paris in 1830; worked in the studio of Cogniet, and exhibited his first picture, *The Visitors*, in 1834. Great accuracy of draughtsmanship, keen observation, and the sharp accentuation of the important note in the picture distinguish all his works. Amongst his pictures may be mentioned: *The Smoker* (1839); *La Partie des Boules* (1848); *Napoleon III. at Solferino* (1864); *The Cavalry Charge* (1867), sold for 150,000 francs; the picture entitled *1807* (1875), representing Napoleon I. in the battle of Friedland, sold for 300,000 francs; *Le Guide* (1883); and *Jena* (1889).

MEKNES. A city of Morocco, in the French sphere of influence. Pop. (1931), 56,770.

MEKONG, or CAMBODIA. The longest of all the Indo-Chinese rivers, rises in East Tibet, flows through Western China, touches Burma, separates Siam from French territory, and after intersecting the latter enters the China Sea by several mouths; length, 2700 miles.

MELA, Pomponius. A Roman geographer who flourished during the first century after Christ, and is the author of a treatise, *De Situ Orbis*.

MELAMPSORA. A genus of parasitic Fungi, family Uredineæ (rusts), mainly infesting trees, especially conifers, poplars, and willows; most are heterœcious.—Cf. W. B. Grove. *British Rust-fungi*.

MELANCHTHON (me-langk'thon; Ger. me-lang*h*'ton), **Philipp.** German reformer, born at Bretten, in the

Palatinate, 16th Feb., 1497, died at Wittenberg 19th April, 1560. His father was an armourer, and his original German name was Schwarzerd, which he Grecized into Melanchthon, or Melanthon. Both names denote "black earth." After having studied at Pforzheim he removed to Heidelberg University, where he took his Bachelor's degree, and afterwards to Tübingen University, where he attained the degree of Master, and became a lecturer.

In 1518, at the instigation of Luther and Reuchlin, he was invited by Frederick, Elector of Saxony, to fill the chair of Greek in the recently founded University of Wittenberg. In 1519 he accompanied Luther to Leipzig, in order to dispute with Dr. Eck, and in 1521 he published his famous *Loci Communes*, an exposition of Protestant dogmatics, which ran through some sixty editions in his lifetime, and was followed by other influential writings, such as the *Epitome Doctrinæ Christianæ* (1524).

There is no doubt that many of the plans carried out by the reformers were the result of Melanchthon's wise suggestions. His Greek scholarship was also of inestimable advantage to Luther in his work of translating the Bible. In 1530 Melanchthon was appointed to draw up the general *Confession* which was presented to the emperor at Augsburg (hence known as the *Augsburg Confession*), and he also wrote the *Apology* for it.

Before Luther's death, in 1546, a certain difference of view developed itself between the two reformers, and after that event Melanchthon lost in some measure the confidence of a section of the Protestants, and was involved in painful controversies, being accused by one party of a too great leaning to Calvinism, by another of a similar leaning to Romanism.—BIBLIOGRAPHY: A. Harnack, *Philipp Melanchthon*; G. Wilson, *Philipp Melanchthon*.

MELANCONIALES. A section of Fungi Imperfecti (*see* FUNGI), distinguished by having their conidium-bearing branches (conidiophores) massed in layers but not enclosed in cavities. Representative genus: Pestalozzia.

MELANE'SIA. A division of Oceania (q.v.).

MEL'ANITE. A lime-iron variety of garnet, the more ferriferous type of andradite, of a velvet-black or greyish-black, occurring always in crystals of a dodecahedral form. *See* GARNET.

MEL'APHYRE. A compact black or blackish-grey igneous rock, now recognized as resulting from the alteration of andesite or basalt through the hydration of the mineral silicates and general decay under processes of weathering.

MELASTOMACEÆ. A large natural order of tropical and subtropical polypetalous dicotyledons, mostly shrubs or trees, easily recognizable by the three or five prominent veins in each leaf, and the peculiar horned stamens opening by apical pores.

MELBA, Dame Nellie. Name taken from her birthplace, Melbourne, by the Australian singer, Helen Porter Mitchell. A daughter of David Mitchell, she was born 19th May, 1859. In 1882 she married Charles Armstrong. Having shown exceptional talent as a singer, she studied in Paris and became a professional. Her first appearance was in Brussels in 1887, and for the next thirty years she was one of the world's leading singers. In 1918 she was made D.B.E. In 1925 she published *Melodies and Memories*. She died 23rd Feb., 1931.

MELBOURNE, William Lamb, Viscount. English statesman, born 15th March, 1779, died 24th Nov., 1848. Educated at Eton and Cambridge, he became a barrister, but relinquished the law and became member of Parliament for Leominster. During the ministry of Canning he was Secretary for Ireland; in 1830 he became Home Secretary in the Grey administration, and succeeded to the premiership when it was overthrown in 1834 on the Irish question. He continued to lead the Whig party with varying success until 1841, when he resigned and retired from public affairs. He is chiefly known for the tactful way in which he advised Queen Victoria on her accession in 1837.

MELCHETT, Alfred Moritz Mond, Baron. British politician and industrial magnate. Born at Farnworth, Lancashire, 23rd Oct., 1868, the son of Dr. Ludwig Mond, F.R.S., he was educated at Cheltenham College, St. John's College, Cambridge, and Edinburgh University. Called to the bar in 1894 he entered his father's firm of Brunner, Mond & Co., chemical manufacturers, and became identified with a number of other important industrial concerns, later forming the great Imperial Chemical Industries. His writings on industrial and political problems were re-issued in *Questions of To-day and To-morrow*, 1912. As a politician he was Liberal M.P. for

Chester, 1906-10 ; Swansea, 1910-22 ; he lost his seat in 1923, but was returned for Carmarthen it 1924. He seceded over the land policy of 1926, and became Conservative. He was First Commissioner of Works in the Lloyd George Ministry, 1916, and Minister of Health, 1921-22. Made a baronet in 1910, a privy councillor in 1913, and a baron in 1928, and F.R.S. He died 27th Dec., 1930.

MELBOURNE. A city of Australia, capital of Victoria, on the River Yarra. The city and its suburbs occupy an extensive area, which is mostly hilly or undulating, with the Yarra winding through it, the city proper, on the north bank of the Yarra, being the central and most important business part of the whole. Beyond the city proper are the far more extensive suburbs, such as Collingwood, North Melbourne, Fitzroy, Carlton, Brunswick, Prahran, Richmond, Hawthorn, St. Kilda, etc.

Among the public buildings are the Houses of Parliament, Government house, the treasury, the law-courts, the free library, containing over 300,000 volumes; the mint, the university, with an admirable museum attached; the Ormond Presbyterian College, and the Anglican and Roman Catholic cathedrals. There are several public parks a botanical garden, and race-courses, including that of Flemington (Melbourne Cup). There is access to the centre of the city for vessels of considerable size by means of the River Yarra.

The shipping trade is large, both in exports and imports, the chief of the former being wool, of the latter manufactured goods. By its railway systems Melbourne is connected with all the principal towns of the Australian continent.

The chief industrial products are leather, clothing, furniture, flour, ales, cigars, ironware, and woollens. The first settlements on the site of Melbourne were made in 1835 ; it was incorporated in 1842, and became capital of Victoria in 1851.

A Centennial International Exhibition was held in 1888 in celebration of the founding in 1788 of the Australian Colonies. The ground set apart for the Exhibition covered 43¾ acres, and the buildings 35½ acres. The first Parliament of the Commonwealth of Australia was opened in the Exhibition building by the present king (George V.), then Duke of Cornwall and York, on 5th May, 1901. Population of city, inclusive of suburbs (1931), 1,030,750.

MELEA'GER. Greek poet and anthologist, flourished about 60 B.C. The exact dates of his birth and death are unknown. He was born in Gadara, in Syria, the scene of the casting out of the legion of devils. He was educated at Tyre, and eventually settled in the Island of Cos, where he died at a great age. The famous anthology which he collected and named *Stephanos* (Garland) contains one hundred and thirty-four poems of his own. Meleager's epigrams are beautifully finished and polished, but, owing to his Asiatic origin, they are exotic and fantastic rather than Greek.

They are almost all love-poems, many of them being addressed to Heliodora. The epigram on her death is one of the most graceful of Greek epigrams. In his introductory poem Meleager calls his own poems, wit exquisite aptness, " early white violets." His *Stephanos*, which is the basis of the *Greek Anthology*, includes epigrams of all periods. He mentions forty-eight poets by name as being represented in it ; the work of many others, whom he does not name, is also there.

MELEAGER. In Greek mythology, the son of Œneus, King of Calydon. He distinguished himself in the Argonautic expedition and more particularly at the Calydonian hunt, killed the boar, and gave its skin as the highest token of regard to his beloved Atalanta. A celebrated marble statue of Meleager, found in 1500, is in the Vatican.

ME'LIA. A small genus of trees, type of the nat. ord. Meliaceæ, natives of tropical Asia and Australia. *M. Azadirachta*, the neem tree or margosa, is a native of the East Indies. Its bark yields a bitter used as a tonic, its seeds yield a valuable oil, and its trunk a tenacious gum. *M. Azedarach*, sometimes called *Persian lilac*, *pride of India*, and *bead tree*, is a native of the north of India, now cultivated in the United States as well as in Southern Europe.

MELIACEÆ. A natural order of polypetalous dicotyledons, distinguished by their stamens being united into a tube.

MELILITE. A mineral calcium magnesium iron silicate, allied to idocrase, occurring in small tetragonal prisms in some exceptional types of igneous lavas poor in silica.

MELILLA. A Spanish seaport on the Mediterranean seaboard of Morocco ; the main entry to the Rif country. It is a Spanish " military command," and has a military wireless station on the Telefunken system; range, 320 miles. Extensive harbour works and narrow-gauge railways have been constructed. Melilla passed to Spain in 1490. During a hill fight in July, 1921, the tribesmen inflicted a severe defeat on the Spanish troops. Melilla was the military and air-force base of the Spanish troops operating against Raisuli during the 1922 campaign. Pop. 60,580.

MEL'ILOT (Melilōtus). A genus of leguminous plants, sub-ord. Papilionaceæ, differing from the clovers in having racemose flowers. The common yellow melilot (*M. officinālis*) grows wild in woods, hedges, and neglected fields in Britain and most parts of Europe. White melilot (*M. vulgāris* or *leucantha*), common in some parts of Europe, has become naturalized in Britain. It has been recommended as a fodder plant under the names of *Cabul* and *Bokhara clover*.

MELLITE, or MELLILITE. Honey-stone, a mineral of a honey-yellow or brownish colour, occurring in brown coal. It has the composition mellitic acid 45, alumina 15, and water 40 per cent.

MELOBESIA. A genus of Red Algæ, family Corallinaceæ. The thallus is heavily encrusted with lime, and forms stony or coral-like concretions on rocks, etc.

MELOCAC'TUS. A genus of plants, nat. ord. Cactaceæ, characterized by the flowers being produced in a hemispherical or cylindrical head at the top of the plant. The plants themselves consist of simple fleshy stems of a globular or conical form, with numerous prominent ribs armed with fascicles of stiff spines placed at regular distances.

MELODRAMA (Gr. *melos*, song, and *drama*, play), a stage-play into which songs were introduced, and in which the action was accompanied by appropriate orchestral music. The word was first used in the opening decade of the nineteenth century. Originally a melodrama was an extension of the principle that "nothing introduces you a heroine like soft music." The emotional effect of music was used to obscure the deficiencies of plot and dialogue. In later use the term melodrama was applied to a play characterized by sensational incidents and violent appeals to the emotion.

Tragedy has been defined as a sequence of incidents or events so presented as to emphasize with seriousness their causal relationship. Melodrama is inadequately motivated tragedy, which stops at nothing to gain its effect. Melodrama stands to tragedy as farce stands to comedy. It is usually what Stevenson calls "a delicate study in snow and ink." It has as a rule a painfully virtuous heroine, a strong, silent hero, and a determined villain with a blue chin and an overgrown cigar. Virtue invariably triumphs after many vicissitudes. There is very often a scene which involves elaborate stage-devices, such as an explosion or a railway accident. Examples of melodrama are *The Lyons Mail*, produced by Henry Irving, *The Silver King*, played by Wilson Barrett, and *The Sign of the Cross*.

Melodrama in its palmy days was often spoken of as "transpontine," because the London theatres which specialized in this form of entertainment were situated on the Surrey side of the Thames. An extremely clever skit upon transpontine melodrama is to be found in the Gilbert and Sullivan opera *Ruddigore, or the Witch's Curse*, which, like its model, errs gravely in the direction of unnecessary extravagance.

MELON (*Cucŭmis Melo*). A well-known plant and fruit of the nat. ord. Cucurbitaceæ or gourds. It is an herbaceous, succulent, climbing or trailing annual, cultivated for its fruit in hot Eastern countries from time immemorial. There are many varieties, as the Canteloup, which is reckoned the best, Egyptian, Salonica, Persian, etc.

In Britain the melon, to be raised to perfection, requires the aid of artificial heat and glass throughout every stage of its culture. The *water-melon* (*C. Citrullus*) is much cultivated in the warmer parts of the world on account of its refreshing juice, which, however, is less sweet than that of the common melon. The *musk-melon* is a variety of *Cucŭmis Melo*.

MELPOMENE (mel-pom'e-nē). The muse who presides over tragedy, daughter of Zeus and Mnemosyne. She is generally represented as a young woman, with vine leaves surrounding her head, and holding in her hand a tragic mask.

MEL'ROSE. A town of Roxburghshire, Scotland, on the Tweed. Melrose Abbey, founded by David I. in 1136, destroyed by Edward II. (1322), and rebuilt by Bruce (1326), was partly demolished by the English in 1545. Sir Walter Scott describes it in imperishable lines in his *Lay of the Last Minstrel*.

Abbotsford, his home, is about 3 miles from Melrose Abbey. In 1918 the abbey was presented to the nation by the Duke of Buccleuch; a heart found in a leaden casket during excavations (1921) is believed to be that of Robert the Bruce. Pop. (1931), 2052.

MELTING-POINT. The temperature at which a solid becomes liquid. This temperature may be determined by the ordinary mercury thermometer when it lies within the range of the instrument. For a wide range of temperatures the thermo-electric pyrometer is convenient; this consists of a platinum and platinum-iridium thermocouple electrically connected to a moving-coil galvanometer which has been calibrated to read temperatures by the use of standard fixed points or melting-point temperatures which have been determined by means of the gas thermometer. For very high temperatures the radiation pyrometer has been employed. *See* FREEZING; PYROMETER.

MELTON-MOWBRAY. A town of Leicestershire, England, at the junction of the Eye and Wreak Rivers; served by the London, Midland and Scottish Railway. It is famous for pork-pies and Stilton cheese, and is a hunting centre. Pop. (1931), 10,437.

MELVILLE, Andrew. A Scottish reformer, born near Montrose 1545, died at Sedan 1622. He was educated at St. Andrews; studied at the University of Paris, 1564-66; became a professor at Poitiers, and afterwards at Geneva; returned to Scotland in 1574, where he was appointed successively principal of Glasgow and of St. Andrews Universities.

After doing much to give Scottish presbyterianism its special character, he was accused of sedition and contempt of court, but escaped prison by going into England (1584). Returning in 1585, he resumed his duties at St. Andrews, and became Moderator of the General Assembly in 1587, 1589, 1594. In 1606 he was summoned to London by the king to confer on Church matters, but because of his outspokenness he was committed to the Tower, and there remained until 1611. He then retired to France, and became professor in the University of Sedan.

MELVILLE, Hermann. American author and novelist. Born 1st Aug., 1819, in New York City, he went to sea when seventeen, in a whaler, deserted twice, was captured by cannibals in the South Seas, and eventually joined a man-of-war, and after serving, returned to Boston in 1844 and began writing. He published *Typee* (1846) and *Omoo* (1847), tales of life among the cannibals. In 1850 came *White Jacket*, embodying his experience as a sailor, and by its force, largely abolishing corporeal punishment in the navy. In 1851 he published his masterpiece, *Moby Dick*, a tale of the sea and whaling. He died 27th Sept., 1891.

MEMBRANE. In anatomy, a texture of the animal body, arranged in the form of laminæ, which covers organs, lines the interior of cavities, or takes part in the formation of the walls of canals or tubes. Membrane is generally divided into three kinds, mucous, serous, and fibrous. The lining of the nose, trachea, œsophagus, stomach, and intestines is of the first kind; the serous membranes form the lining of the sacs or closed cavities, as of the chest, abdomen, etc.; the fibrous membranes are tough, inelastic, and tendinous, such as the dura mater, the pericardium, and the capsules of joints.

MEMEL, now **KLAIPEDA.** A Baltic seaport and territory on the Kurisches Haff, formerly German, but ceded to the Allies by the Treaty of Versailles. It became Lithuanian in 1923, but Poland has the right to use the port. Trade is the source of its prosperity, timber, grain, and fish being shipped. Shipbuilding and allied trades are carried on. Memel was founded by the Teutonic Order in 1252, became a member of the Hanseatic League, and has been sacked frequently by Russians and Swedes. The area of the territory is estimated at 943 sq. miles. Pop. 146,000. Pop. of the seaport, 37,400.

MEMLING, or **MEMLINC, Hans.** A distinguished Flemish painter, born probably about 1430, died probably in 1495. He lived at Bruges, of which town he was a prosperous citizen, but little is known of his life. He was especially famous as a religious painter, and his works display a singular tenderness, ideality, and elevation. They are generally extremely well preserved.

MEMNON. A Greek hero mentioned in the Homeric poems as the beautiful son of Eōs (the morning), and in the post-Homeric accounts as the son of Tithōnus and nephew of Priam, whom he assisted at the siege of Troy. He slew Antilochus, but was himself slain by Achilles. His mother was filled with grief at his death, which Zeus endeavoured to soothe by making her son immortal. The name of Memnon was afterwards connected with Egypt, and was attached to a statue still standing at Thebes, being one of two known from their size as "the Colossi."

This statue, known as "the vocal Memnon," was celebrated in antiquity as emitting a sound every morning at the rising of the sun—perhaps through the craft of the priests, though some think it was owing to expansion caused by heat. Both statues seem originally to have been about 70 feet high.

MEMORY. A convenient word used to indicate collectively the mental processes involved in the recollection and presentation of past experience. The function of memorization is performed by the mind, and the theory of a *memory* as a separate faculty or department of the mind has long been discredited. It is in connection with the improvement of memory that the inquirer who is not a psychologist is most generally concerned, and such a faculty being non-existent, efficient memorization is dependent wholly upon improved methods of learning and of systematic remembering.

A fundamental principle of memorization in any subject is that it must be understood, while the pre-existence within the mind of other associated past experiences, an organized body of learning, is of material assistance in a rapid and effectual assimilation of the new matter, and aids in fixing it as a part of the mental organization. Concentration or attention is essential to rapid memorization, and the ability to concentrate improves greatly with practice, although enthusiasm for the object of study or a mere interest in learning frequently provides all the external stimulus that is required.

Improvement in memory is synonymous with improved methods of learning. A common example of faulty method is that known as the *part* method of learning—for instance, a lengthy passage from Shakespeare, whereby the selected passage is divided into sections, each being mastered at one sitting, and combined with the other sections as they are memorized.

Empirical psychology has proved the inutility of this method, and it has fully been demonstrated that an easier and more effectual method of memorizing lengthy passages consists in the repetition of the entire passage from beginning to end until it shall have been completely mastered. *See* ASSOCIATION OF IDEAS; MNEMONICS.—Cf. H. J. Watts, *The Economy and Training of Memory.*

MEMPHIS. An ancient city of Egypt, on the left bank of the Nile, some 20 miles S. of Cairo, said to have been founded by Menes, the first king of Egypt. It was a large, rich, splendid city, and after the fall of Thebes, the capital of Egypt. At the time of the conquest of Egypt by Cambyses (524 B.C.) it was the chief commercial centre of the country,

Sphinx at Memphis

and was connected by canals with the Lakes of Mœris and Mareotis. With the rise of Alexandria the importance of Memphis declined, and it was finally destroyed by the Arabs in the seventh century. The pyramids of Sakkara and the colossal statue of Rameses II., now mutilated and thrown down, are the chief objects of antiquarian interest on the site.

MEMPHIS. The largest and most important commercial city of Tennessee, United States; county seat of Shelby county, and a river-port on the Mississippi. It is a distributing-point for cotton and live-stock, and has manufactures of cotton-seed oil and cotton-cake, flour, and tobacco. The town was settled in 1819 on the site of a fort built in 1739. It became a city in 1849. Pop. (1930), 253,143.

MENAI STRAIT. The channel separating Anglesey from the mainland (Caernarvonshire). It is 14 miles long and from ½ to 2 miles wide. *See* BRIDGE.

MENAM'. The chief river of Siam, rising in the Laos country, and flowing generally southward to enter the Gulf of Siam 25 miles below Bangkok; length, about 900 miles.

MENAN'DER. Greek comic dramatist, was born in 342 B.C., and died in 291 B.C. His parents were rich, and, as far as we know, Menander lived the life of a man of fashion in Athens. He was a friend of Theophrastus, and was patronized by Ptolemy Sōtēr. According to a scholium on Ovid's *Ibis*, he was drowned while bathing.

Menander is said to have written over a hundred comedies, and to have gained the prize only eight times. He became the favourite writer of antiquity, and it is not uncommon to find critics of the ancient world (e.g. Plutarch) speaking of him in terms that we would reserve for Shakespeare alone. He added many maxims and quotations to everyday speech, such as "Whom the gods love die young" and "Evil communications corrupt good manners" (quoted by St. Paul, 1 Cor. xv. 33). To his sententiousness and quotability he probably owed a considerable amount of his fame.

Until the end of last century we only possessed about 1650 fragments of Menander, mostly single lines or parts of single lines. These lines were mostly of a gnomic nature. However, in 1897 we got eighty lines of his *Farmer*, in 1899 and 1906 and later some three hundred lines of his *Lady with the Shorn Locks*, and in 1906 three hundred and forty lines of *The Samian Woman*, and five hundred lines of *The Litigants*. While there is something unsatisfactory about fragments, it is good to have even these scanty remains, and we have sufficient to enable us to form some idea of Menander's gifts as a comic writer.

His great reputation, as far as we can tell, seems somewhat undeserved. The characters are all stock types, the situations conventional, and the plots of a highly unoriginal nature. Menander must have shone less as a dramatist than as a stylist; in his pure and elegant diction he must have stood high. In the plays of Terence, whom Julius Cæsar called "half a Menander," we get some idea of the New Comedy as written by Menander.

MENCIUS. The Latinized name of Meng-tse, a Chinese teacher, who was born about 370 B.C., and died about 288 B.C. He was educated by his mother with such success that the approbation contained in the phrase, "the mother of Meng" has become proverbial. Mencius was one of the greatest of the early Confucians. Man's nature, according to Mencius, is good, although it may appear otherwise. Propriety, righteousness, and kindness are as natural to man as his four limbs.

MENDEL, Gregor Johann. Austrian biologist, born 1822, died 1884. He became an inmate of the Augustinian monastery at Brünn in 1843, and abbot in 1860. He carried out experiments in his cloister garden on the laws of heredity in plants, and published an account of his results in 1866, but his work lay neglected until 1900, when several distinguished botanists independently called attention to its importance.

Mendelism (q.v.) is the name given to the theory of heredity (q.v.) suggested by Mendel's work; its influence on present-day research and speculation in biology is hardly second even to that of Darwinism.

MENDELÉEV (men-del-e-yef'), **Dmitri Ivanovitsh.** Russian chemist, born in 1834, became professor of chemistry at St. Petersburg (Petrograd) University in 1866, died in 1907, and was especially noted for his researches in the subject of the Periodic Law. His works include *Principles of Chemistry*, written in 1868-70, and translated into several languages. *See* CHEMISTRY.

MENDELISM. A theory of heredity (*see* MENDEL; HEREDITY). Mendel's most important work was carried out with the edible pea (*Pisum sativum*), which is self-fertilizing, and exists in a number of distinct strains that breed true to type. He artificially crossed these strains, not in a haphazard way, but with the idea of studying the inheritance of obvious characters.

For example, he crossed a tall strain (6 to 7 feet high) with a short strain ($\frac{3}{4}$ to $1\frac{1}{2}$ feet high), giving a first filial or hybrid generation (F_1), the further filial generations (F_2, F_3, etc.) being allowed to propagate themselves by selfing in the normal way. The results were as follows:

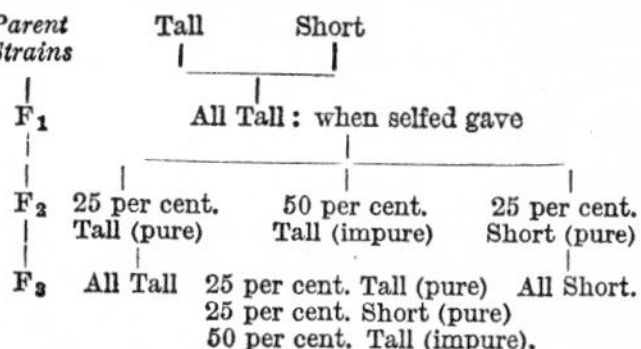

It will be seen that of the two opposing characters (Mendelian characters), tallness and shortness, the former was possessed by all the offspring of the first cross (F_1), and this was called the *dominant* character, the other being termed *recessive*. The members of the next generation can therefore be described as 25 per cent. *pure dominants* (D) breeding true, 25 per cent. *pure recessives* (R) also breeding true, and 50 per cent. *impure dominants* (D(R)), in which the recessive character is present but masked.

To explain these remarkable facts Mendel proposed a theory, known as the *segregation of pure gametes*, which is the essential part of Mendelism. Gametes are sex-cells, male and female, and a new individual (zygote) results from the fusion of a male gamete with a female gamete. A particular character, such as tallness or shortness, is supposed to be carried by a something (factor) present in a gamete, and according to the above theory any given gamete is "pure," containing in this case either a tall factor or a short factor, but not both. When the first filial generation (F_1) is selfed, it is presumed that half the male gametes and half the female gametes are "tall," and the other half "short," and the chances of pairing between a male or female gamete with one of the same or different kind are equal, the possibilities being

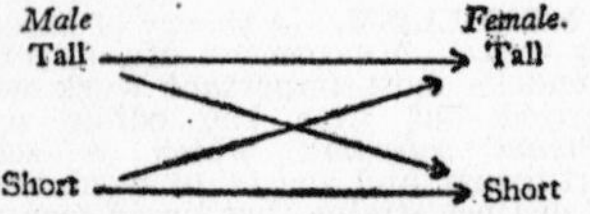

uniting to give zygotes, which may be called tall-tall, short-tall, tall-short, and short-short. The first and last (25 per cent. each) are *pure dominant* and *pure recessive* respectively, the two others (together 50 per cent.) *impure dominant*. The zygotes that breed true are known as *homozygotes*, and those with a mixture of factors, which do not breed true, are termed *heterozygotes*. Opposed pairs of Mendelian characters, such as tallness and shortness, are conveniently designated *allelomorphs*.

So far we have considered *monohybrids*, or crosses with reference to one pair of allelomorphs, but Mendel also produced *dihybrids* by crossing strains differing in two ways. He found that in the seeds of pea roundness is dominant to wrinkledness, and yellow dominant to green, and that when a round green strain is crossed with a wrinkled yellow one, a shuffling of characters takes place, and an entirely new strain is produced, wrinkled green, that breeds true. It is also possible to work with three or more opposing pairs of opposed characters.

Examples of allelomorphs among plants are :—

	Dominant.	*Recessive*
Wheat	Absence of "beard" or awn,	Presence of awn.
	Rough chaff,	Smooth chaff.
	Red chaff,	White chaff.
	Keeled glumes,	Rounded glumes.
	Flinty endosperm,	Floury endosperm.
	Susceptibility to rust,	Immunity to rust.
Barley	Two-rowed ears,	Six-rowed ears.

The Mendelian theory also applies to animals, but here presents greater difficulties. The following are a few pairs of allelomorphs :

	Dominant.	*Recessive.*
Mice . . .	Coloured coat,	Albino coat.
Rabbit . . .	Coloured coat,	Albino coat.
Poultry . .	Rose comb,	Single comb.
Cattle . . .	Hornlessness,	Horns.
Snails . . .	Bandless shell,	Banded shell.

It must not be supposed that all characters of plants and animals are due to the presence of single factors, for there is good evidence to show that some of them are brought about by the combined action of two or more factors. Among fowls, for example, there are various kinds of comb. The *rose comb* has a broad irregular surface with a pointed projection at the back, while the small *pea comb* has two well-marked side ridges with a lower one between them. When a rose-combed breed is crossed with a pea-combed one, the offspring possess a *walnut comb*, shaped like half a walnut, and unlike either the pea or the rose.

We have seen that when tall and short peas are crossed, the 50 per cent. impure dominant (heterozygous) talls exactly resemble the 25 per cent. pure dominant (homozygous) talls in appearance, and only reveal their nature when they are allowed to breed. There are cases, however, where impure dominants can at once be recognized, the recessive character being less completely masked. The classical case is afforded by Andalusian poultry. When black Andalusians are crossed with splashed whites, the F_1 generation is blue, and in the next, or F_2 generation, we get 25 per cent. pure black dominants, 25 per cent. pure splashed white recessives, and 50 per cent. impure dominants, which are blue in colour. This explains why fanciers have never been able to raise a pure-breeding strain of blue Andalusians, for these are of mongrel constitution.

Mendelism has thrown much light on the phenomena of reversion, variation, and sex. As to the last, Bridges has shown that special sex chromosomes (*see* HEREDITY; MITOSIS) exist, and that sex inheritance follows Mendelian laws. A series of brilliant researches have lately been carried out by Morgan and his colleagues in America—more particularly on the fruit-fly (*Drosophila ampelophila*)—in the endeavour to discover the physical basis of Mendelian "factors," and a *chromosome theory* has been formulated as the result. According to this, a chromosome is a linear chain of factors, like a string of beads, and this gives a plausible explanation of the fact that characters are inherited in groups of varying size. Chromosomes are arranged in pairs, and it appears probable that the members of a pair can exchange one or more factors (*crossing-over* or *linkage*), which renders a further series of facts intelligible.—BIBLIOGRAPHY: W. Bateson, *Mendel's Principles of Heredity*; R. C. Punnett, *Mendelism* E. S. Goodrich, *The Evolution of Living Organisms*.

MENDEL'S LAW. *See* MENDELISM; HEREDITY.

MENDELSSOHN (men'delz - zōn), **Moses.** German philosopher, born of Jewish parents 1729, died 1786. In 1754 he formed a friendship with Lessing, who made him the hero of

Moses Mendelssohn, German Philosopher

his *Nathan the Wise*, while he in turn defended his friend from the attacks of Jacobi, who accused Lessing of being a Spinozist. The chief works of Mendelssohn are a *Treatise on Metaphysics*; *Phædon*, a dialogue on immortality (1767); *Jerusalem* (1783); and *Morgenstunden* (1785).

MENDELSSOHN - BARTHOLDY, Felix. Distinguished composer, born at Hamburg 3rd Feb., 1809, died at Leipzig 4th Nov., 1847. He was the son of a wealthy Jew, who, recognizing his son's talent for music, had him carefully trained. In his ninth year he publicly appeared in Berlin, and before he was eighteen years old produced the well-known overture to the *Midsummer Night's Dream*.

In 1829 he began an extensive tour in England, Scotland, France, and Italy, and on his return to Germany he became musical director in Düsseldorf. Here he tried to establish a theatre but without success; and when he left that city in 1835 he became conductor of the famous concerts in the Gewandhaus of Leipzig—a position which he maintained with several slight interruptions until his death.

In 1841 he was appointed musical director to the King of Saxony; was afterwards summoned to Berlin by the King of Prussia to become director of music at the Academy of Arts; journeyed repeatedly to England, where he conducted his own music at London and Birmingham. Of his musical compositions the best known are the oratorios *Elijah* and *St. Paul*; the overture to *Ruy Blas*; and his *Songs without Words*. He left unfinished the oratorio of *Christus* and the opera of *Lorelei*.—Cf. J. C. Hadden, *Life of Mendelssohn*.

MENDÈS (mȧṇ-dās), **Catulle.** French poet, novelist, and dramatist, born at Bordeaux, of Jewish parents, in 1841, died in 1909. He began his literary career in 1859, when at the age of eighteen he founded the *Revue Fantaisiste*. Among his poems may be mentioned: *Philomela* (1864), *Hesperus* (1869), *La Colère d'un franc-tireur* (1871), and *Poésies* (1885); among his novels, *Les Folies amoureuses* (1877), *Le Roi vierge* (1880), and *Le Chemin du cœur* (1896); whilst he has also written some historical works and several plays, including *La Part du Roi* (1872), *Justice* (1878), and *La Reine Fiammette* (1898).

MENDO'ZA, Don Diego Hurtado de. A Spanish author, general, and politician, born 1503, died 1575. He wrote an account of the Moorish insurrection in the Alpujarras Mountains, and is generally but erroneously considered to have been the author of the *Life of Lazarillo de Tormes*, the first of a class of novels descriptive of the life of clever rogues.

MENDOZA. A western province of the Argentine Republic, traversed by the Andes on the west, but elsewhere a plain. Cattle, cereals, hides and wool, maize, fruit, and olives are raised and produced; gold, silver, lead, coal, copper, and petroleum are found. Area, 5 ,445 sq. miles; pop. (1932), 445 492. The capital, Mendoza, is the link town on the Transandine railway system. It was destroyed by earthquake (1861), and rebuilt a mile nearer the mountains. Pop. (1930), 76,780.

MENELA'US. In Greek mythology, son of Atreus, brother of Agamemnon, and husband of the beauteous Helen, with whom he received the kingdom of Sparta or Lacedæmon. His wife having been abducted by Paris, son of Priam, King of Troy, he summoned the Greek princes to avenge the affront, and himself led sixty ships to the siege of Troy. After its conquest he returned with Helen to his native land in a devious voyage which led him to Cypria, Phœnicia, Egypt, and Libya during a period of eight years.

MENELIK, or **MENELEK II.** *Negus* or Emperor of Abyssinia (officially styled *negus negusti*, king of kings), born at Shoa 18th Aug., 1844, died at Addis Ábaba 12th Dec., 1913. The son of the Crown Prince of Shoa, he claimed King Solomon and the Queen of Sheba as his ancestors. He established himself as King of Shoa in 1865, and ultimately became King of Abyssinia. In 1885 Italy threatened his independence, and in consequence of the Treaty of Ucciali in 1889 claimed a protectorate over Abyssinia. Menelik protested in 1893, and in 1896, by the victory of Adowa, he forced Italy to sign the peace of Addis Ábaba. Italy received the colony of Eritrea, but Abyssinian independence was saved.

MENHA'DEN. An American salt-water fish (*Alōsa menhāden*). It belongs to the herring family (Clupeidæ), and abounds on the shores of New England. It yields quantities of oil, the waste being used as manure. It is also preserved in the same way as the sardine.

MENIN (mė-naṇ). A town of Belgium, province of West Flanders, on the Lys, with manufactures of lace and cotton. The town was captured by the Germans in Oct., 1914, and recovered by the Allies four years later (Oct., 1918). Pop. 19,723.

The **Menin Gate** is a memorial on the Menin Road at Ypres to the British who fell in the European War. Designed by Sir Reginald Blomfield, it is in the form of a Roman arch. It was unveiled on 24th July, 1927.

Menin Gate

MENINGITIS. An inflammation of the membranes of the brain or spinal cord, due to infection by germs.

Four different types are recognized, and of these epidemic cerebro-spinal meningitis is described under cerebro-spinal meningitis (q.v.).

The remaining three are: (1) septic meningitis, which arises from infection of wounds of the cranium, or through the nasal passages, or more rarely through the blood-stream from a septic focus in another organ of the body. The earliest symptoms are headache and general prostration, followed by feverishness. Vomiting and constipation are present at first, but later incontinence. The pulse is rapid, and the respirations are irregular (known as the cerebral type of breathing), while the mind is early clouded; this is followed by complete unconsciousness. Marked retraction of the neck, convulsions, spasms, and squint are frequently present. Septic meningitis is very fatal and recovery rare.

(2) Serous mengitis, due to serous inflammation within the membranes, as a result of some septic focus outside the skull. The symptoms are similar to those of septic meningitis, but less severe, and they may subside if the septic focus is located and removed.

(3) Tuberculous meningitis arises from infection of the membranes, due to tuberculous disease in a gland or bone. It is most frequent in young children, and has a slow and insidious onset. The child is listless, complains of headache, and soon vomiting begins. After being drowsy for about two weeks the child gradually becomes comatose. The disease lasts from six to eight weeks, and is nearly always fatal.

MENISPERMA'CEÆ. An extensive natural order of polypetalous dicotyledons, consisting of twining, often scrambling and slender, shrubby plants, with alternate leaves without stipules, and small greenish or white unisexual flowers. They are common in the tropical parts of Asia and America, and are usually bitter and tonic plants, the seeds of some of them having narcotic properties. One species yields cocculus indicus.

MENNO, Simons. The founder of the sect known as the Mennonites, was born in Friesland, 1496, died 1561. He was educated for the Church, and became a Roman Catholic priest; but about 1530 he joined the Anabaptists. He founded a sect of his own and there are still a number of congregations in Holland, Germany, and Russia who pass under the name of Mennonites. These do not believe in original sin, and object to taking oaths, making war, or going to law. The Mennonites are also found in the United States. *See* ANABAPTISTS.

MENOBRAN'CHUS. *See* NECTURUS.

MEN'OPOME, or MENOPO'MA. A tailed amphibian, the "hellbender" (*Menopōma alleghaniensis*), peculiar to the fresh waters of North

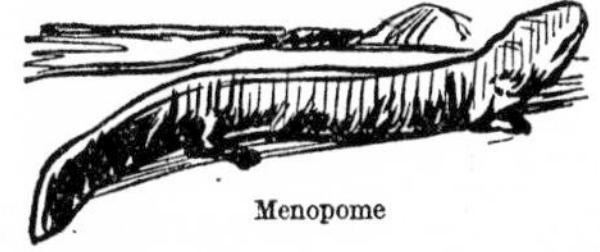

Menopome

America, which seems to form a connecting link between the perennibranchiate amphibians and the salamander. The Giant Salamander (*Cryptobranchus japonicus*) of China and Japan is closely related.

MENSTRUATION, or MENSES. The periodical discharge of blood-stained material from the generative organs of the human or Simian female. As an ovum ripens, the mucous membrane lining the womb grows rapidly to provide a fresh bed of new cells in which the ovum, if it becomes fertilized, can become implanted. If the ovum is not fertilized, the overgrown mucous membrane is shed together with a certain amount of blood that escapes from the severed blood essels. The period at which menstruation begins is usually between the fourteenth and sixteenth year; it recurs at monthly intervals, lasting for four to six days and thus continues until from the forty-fifth to the fiftieth year; the discharge at each period is from 6 to 8 oz. All these conditions, however, vary with each individual. A discontinuance of this discharge is one of the first signs of conception, and the cessation usually continues during the period of pregnancy and lactation.

MENSURATION. The branch of mathematics which deals with the measurement of lengths, areas, and volumes. The following are the more important formulæ. Area of triangle $= \frac{1}{2}$ base × height; or $= \sqrt{\{s(s-a)(s-b)(s-c)\}}$, where a, b, c are the sides, and $s = \frac{1}{2}(a+b+c)$; or $= \frac{1}{2}bc \sin A$. Area of parallelogram = base × height $= bc \sin A$. Area of trapezium $= \frac{1}{2}$ sum of parallel sides × perpendicular distance between them. Circle (q.v.): circumference $= 2\pi r$; area $= \pi r^2$; area of sector $= \frac{1}{2}\theta r^2$, where θ = angle of sector, r = radius. Area of ellipse $= \pi ab$, where a, b are the semi-axes. Cylinder or prism: volume = area of base × height; surface = perimeter of base × height + area of ends. Cone or pyramid: volume $= \frac{1}{3}$ area of base × height; curved surface of cone $= \frac{1}{2}$ perimeter of base × slant side. Sphere: volume $= \frac{4}{3}\pi r^3$; surface $= 4\pi r^2$; surface of any zone $= 2\pi r \times$ height of zone; volume of zone between a great circle and a parallel small circle $= \pi(r^2 z - \frac{1}{3}z^3)$, where z = height of zone. The general problem of finding lengths, areas, and volumes belongs to the integral calculus (*see* CALCULUS). For a very useful approximate method, *see* SIMPSON'S RULE. For mechanical methods, *see* PLANIMETER.

MENTHOL ($C_{10}H_{20}O$). Peppermint camphor, a white crystalline substance obtained from mint (genus Mentha), of which it smells strongly; used externally in cases of nervous headache.

MENTONE (Fr. Menton). A Riviera town and winter-resort, Alpes-Maritimes, France, on the Mediterranean. The climate is equable and very mild. In the neighbourhood there are many groves of oranges and lemons. The town was purchased by France from the Prince of Monaco in 1861. Pop. about 18,000.

MENZALEH, or MENZALA. A lagoon of Egypt extending from the Damietta branch of the Nile to the Suez Canal, which traverses its eastern side. It runs parallel with the Mediterranean, from which it is separated by a narrow sandpit pierced by three openings, and containing several villages and Port Saïd. It provides fish and salt. Area, about 450 sq. miles.

MEPHISTOPH'ELES (older forms **Mephistophilus, Mephistophilis**). The name of a demon in the old puppet-days, adopted and developed by Marlowe in his tragical history of

Dr. Faustus; and more especially by Goethe in the first part of *Faust*, where he becomes the cultured personification of evil rather than the Satan of popular belief.

MEQUINEZ, or **MEKNÈS.** A city of Morocco, on the Atlantic slopes of the Atlas range, in the French zone of influence, and a military area of the Sherifian army. There are vineyards in the vicinity. Pop. (1919) 37,247 (2202 Europeans).

MERCANTILE LAW. In England, the law regulating dealings between merchants, i.e. commercial law (Lat. *merx*, merchandise). It is built up in greater part of the customs and usages of traders (the law merchant), and includes the law of negotiable instruments, the sale of goods, partnership, agency (brokers, factors, warehousemen, and others), carriage (charter-parties, bills of lading, etc.), insurance, patents, trade-marks, etc. Any custom which is against commercial morality is not binding and cannot be founded on.

MERCANTILE MARINE. The British merchant service had its origin in the fleet built by King Alfred to protect England from the ravages of Danish pirates. He copied but improved on the Danish ships, and at first manned his vessels with sea-rovers of Frisia; but ultimately his own Englishmen learned the art of seamanship, and, having become proficient navigators by necessity, they saw no reason why they should not continue to be seamen when that necessity had been removed. In this manner the mercantile marine was founded, and with it the nation's prosperity, of which British supremacy at sea is still the basis.

The following table gives the losses of the Allies from enemy action during the European War, 1914-18:

Britain .	. 2197	vessels,	7,638,020	tons.
France .	. 238	„	698,845	„
Italy .	. 230	„	742,365	„
Japan .	. 29	„	120,176	„
United States	80	„	341,512	„

On 30th June, 1932, there were 10,518 vessels over 100 tons showing the British flag, including 9772 steam- and motor-vessels of 22,531,941 tons, and 746 sail-vessels of 252,442 tons. The world's total showed steam- and motor-vessels, 68,368,141 tons, and sail-vessels, 1,366,169 tons. In 1914 there were 295,652 seamen employed in British ships, including fishing-craft, but exclusive of river and inland navigation vessels. 212,640 of the total were British, 31,396 were European foreigners, and 51,616 were Lascars and Asiatics. Among European foreigners employed were: Germans, 5000; Swedes, 3600; Norwegians, 2150; Russians, 2000. Much information regarding officers, men, and tonnage will be found under SHIPPING.

The Mercantile Marine in Great Britain is controlled by the Board of Trade which administers the laws that deal with it. The Board has a mercantile marine consultative branch at Great George Street, London, S.W. 1. To unite the service there is a master of the Merchant Navy, an office created in 1928, and held by the Prince of Wales.

THE MERCHANT NAVY. As a career the training of a Navigating Officer normally takes place either partly in a recognized Training Ship or Nautical Training College, or by apprenticeship wholly at sea.

In the former case training may begin at thirteen years or earlier, and continued until sixteen or seventeen. Evidence of a satisfactory standard of education is required on entry, and after a minimum period of two years' training a certificate is granted to the successful candidate carrying exemption from one of the four years required for the Second Mate's Certificate. Application should be made as below for admission as an apprentice. The fees payable vary, but are of the order of £100 to £170 per annum.

In the latter case the boy should continue his general education until sixteen or seventeen, and apply to be admitted as an apprentice to the shipping companies selected or to the Shipping Federation Ltd., 52 Leadenhall Street, E.C. 3, through which body a number of the companies customarily recruit. No written examination is required—inquiries take the form of personal interview. It should be remembered that some physical defects, especially defective eyesight, will definitely disqualify a boy when he comes to take the Second Mate's Certificate.

The Board of Trade issues a model form of indenture for apprenticeship. Full particulars of the examinations necessary for Board of Trade Certificates during and after the period of apprenticeship may be obtained from the B.O.T. Regulations (Examination of Masters and Mates).

The prospects may be studied from the rates of pay which will be supplied in detail by the General Secretary of the National Maritime Board, 3-4 Clement's Inn, London, W.C. 2, from The Shipping Federation, or from firms of shipowners. Most officers continue at sea for the whole of their professional life, but there are a few shore appointments, with salaries ranging up to £1500 per annum.

Although a seafaring life may not offer a fortune, it does offer opportunity for saving, a good life, and prospects of seeing something of the world, while modern conditions for apprentices are very different from those of the old exacting days of sailing-ships. There is little home life, of course, and at present the supply of Officer and Deck ratings is rather more than equal to the demand—with resulting unemployment

MERCATOR, Gerard. Mathematician and geographer, born at Rupelmonde, in Flanders, 1512, died 1594. He studied at Louvain; became a lecturer on geography and astronomy; entered the service of Charles V., for whose use he made a celestial

Gerard Mercator

and a terrestrial globe; and in 1552 retired to Duisburg, on being appointed cosmographer to the Duke of Juliers (1559). He is the author of a method of projection called by his name, the principles of which were applied practically by Edward Wright in 1599. He is also the author of *Tabulæ Geographicæ*.

MERCATOR'S PROJECTION. *See* MAPS.

MERCHANDISE MARKS ACT. Passed in 1887, it provides that all goods of foreign manufacture bearing any name or trade-mark of any manufacturer, dealer, or trader in the United Kingdom (unless such goods are accompanied by a definite declaration of the country in which they were produced) are prohibited under penalties from being imported into the United Kingdom; while under an Amending Act of 1911 the importer of such goods may be required to give all particulars of the goods to the person whose name or trade-mark has been infringed. All such goods are forfeitable.

Under the Act of 1887 it is an offence to forge any trade-mark or so to mark or describe goods as to mislead the buyer. Any one purporting falsely to be a maker of goods for the King or Government is liable to a penalty of £20. By the Merchandise Marks Act of 1926 no imported goods may lawfully be sold in the United Kingdom to which there is applied the name or trade-mark of any manufacturer or trader, or the name of any place or district in the United Kingdom, unless accompanied by indication of origin, that is, by giving conspicuously the word "foreign" or "empire" or the country of manufacture or production. Nor may such goods be offered for sale by sample in the United Kingdom.

MERCHANT SHIPPING ACTS. *See* SHIPPING.

MERCIA. The largest of the Anglo-Saxon kingdoms, comprehended all the middle counties of England, and was founded by Crida in 585. In 827 it was conquered by Egbert, who united the different kingdoms of England into one. After this time it was repeatedly overrun by the Danes. *See* ENGLAND.

MERCIER, Désiré Joseph. Belgian prelate. Born 21st Nov., 1851, he was educated in Malines and ordained in 1874, afterwards studying at Louvain and Paris. Professor of Philosophy in the University of Louvain, 1882-1906, he was then made Archbishop of Malines and Primate of Belgium. In 1907 he was created a cardinal. When the Germans entered Belgium in Aug., 1914, Mercier boldly upheld the rights of his country. He took a leading part in the conferences with representatives of the Church of England held in Malines between 1920 and 1923, and died in Brussels, 23rd Jan., 1926. A noted philosopher, Mercier edited until 1906 *La Revue Néoscholastique*, and in his writings sought to adapt the philosophy of St. Thomas Aquinas to the conditions of the modern world. He published his *War Memories* in 1920.

MERCURY. In mythology, the name of a Roman god, identified in later times with the Greek Hermēs. As representing Hermēs he was regarded as the son of Jupiter and Maia, and was looked upon as the god of eloquence, of commerce, and of robbers. He was also the messenger, herald, and ambassador of Jupiter. As a Roman god he was

Mercury

merely the patron of commerce and gain

MERCURY. In astronomy, the planet nearest the sun. It moves round the sun in 87·9693 of our mean solar days, at a mean distance of 35,960,000 miles; its eccentricity of orbit is 0·205618; the inclination of its orbit to the ecliptic is 7° 0′ 8″; its diameter is about 3050 miles. The period of its axial rotation is uncertain, but is believed by many astronomers to be the same as that of its revolution round the sun. The volume is about $\frac{1}{17}$ that of the earth; the density about $\frac{1}{8}$ less than the earth's. Mercury is most conveniently placed for observation by the naked eye when an evening star in spring or when a morning star in autumn. Transits of the planet across the sun's disc are not infrequent. They can occur only near 7th May or 9th Nov., on account of the position of the nodes of the orbit.

MERCURY. Called also **QUICKSILVER,** symbol Hg, atomic weight 200·6 (*see* ISOTOPES). A metal whose specific gravity is greater than that of any other metal, except the platinum metals, gold, and tungsten, being 13·56, or thirteen and a half times as heavy as water. It is the only metal which is liquid at common temperatures. It freezes at −38·8° C. and boils at 356·7° C. When heated in the presence of air it is gradually converted into a red oxide.

Mercury is used in barometers to ascertain the pressure of the atmosphere, and in thermometers used to determine temperature, for which purpose it is well adapted by its expansibility and the extensive range between its freezing- and boiling-point. Preparations of this metal are among the most powerful poisons, and are extensively used as medicines. The preparation called calomel or mercurous chloride (HgCl) is a most efficacious deobstruent. Another valuable preparation is corrosive sublimate or mercuric chloride ($HgCl_2$). Mercury combines with or dissolves other metals, e.g. gold, silver, tin, forming amalgams; and these metals should therefore not be brought into contact with it. Amalgams are, however, largely used in certain industries, and especially by dentists for stopping teeth.

Mercury is chiefly found in the state of sulphide, *cinnabar* (HgS), but it is also found native. The chief mines are in Spain, Italy, California, Mexico, and Peru. The metal is readily extracted from its ores by simply roasting them in suitable furnaces. During this roasting operation the sulphur is eliminated as sulphur dioxide gas, and the metallic mercury, being at a temperature above its boiling-point, is distilled off and passes forward with the furnace gases, from which it is condensed and collected by passing through suitable coolers. This process, or a modification of it, has been in use at the great Almaden mines in Spain for hundreds of years.

MEREDITH, George. British novelist and poet, was born 12th Feb., 1828, and died 18th May, 1909. His father, a naval outfitter at Portsmouth, was of Welsh extraction, and his mother had a strain of Irish blood in her. Meredith went as a day boy to St. Paul's Church school,

George Meredith

Southsea, and at the age of fifteen he was sent to the Moravian school at Neuwied, on the Rhine, where he remained nearly two years. On his return he was articled to a solicitor, and made many friends among literary people. Among them was Thomas Love Peacock (q.v.), whose widowed daughter, Mrs. Nicolls.

Meredith married in 1849. He then abandoned law, and turned to journalism and literature for a livelihood. He wrote for *The Ipswich Journal*, *Once a Week*, and *The Morning Post*. His first published volume, *Poems*, appeared in 1851. His career as a novelist began with *The Shaving of Shagpat* (1856).

His first marriage was a failure; his wife left him in 1858, and died in 1861. In 1864 he married Marie Vulliamy, with whom he had twenty-one years of happy married life. In 1862 he became literary adviser to Messrs. Chapman & Hall, and continued his connection with that publishing house for more than thirty years. *Erewhon* and *East Lynne* were among the books upon which he reported adversely. During the Austro-Italian War of 1866 he acted as special correspondent for *The Morning Post*. There is little to record in the incidents of his life apart from the appearance of his novels. In 1865 he took up his residence at Flint Cottage, Box Hill, and remained there until his death.

Novels.—*The Shaving of Shagpat* (1856) and *Farina* (1857) were Meredith's two earliest novels. The former, which is decidedly the more successful, is based upon *The Arabian Nights*, and the latter, which is a legend of Cologne, upon the mediæval and romantic tale. Both these books contain a strong burlesque element; the latter was somewhat influenced by Meredith's father-in-law, Peacock. *The Ordeal of Richard Feverel* (1859) and *Evan Harrington* both contained richly farcical scenes in their original form. They were ruthlessly revised (and not improved) for later editions in 1878 and 1897. The revision made *Evan Harrington*, which was an excellent farce centring round some thinly disguised members of the novelist's own family, a somewhat ill-proportioned comedy.

Emilia in England (1864), afterwards re-christened *Sandra Belloni*, and its sequel *Vittoria* (1867) are written in his best manner, but were not well received. *Rhoda Fleming* (1865), a powerful story, deals with the yeoman class. *The Adventures of Harry Richmond* (1871) is a brilliant first-person romance; *Beauchamp's Career* (1874) was its author's favourite among all the novels. *The Egoist* (1879) is by many considered Meredith's masterpiece; he certainly wrote it primarily to please himself, and it therefore contains the quintessence of his philosophy of life. *The Tragic Comedians* (1880) is a much less elaborate novel founded on fact. *Diana of the Crossways* (1885) was the first of his novels to be widely read by the general public. Its popularity was largely due to the fact that its heroine was modelled upon Caroline Sheridan, the Hon. Mrs. Norton, and its central incident was based upon a widespread but erroneous story that Mrs. Norton had betrayed a Cabinet secret to *The Times*. *One of Our Conquerors* (1891) is one of the most obscure of the series, and was called by its author "a strong dose of my most indigestible production." *Lord Ormont and his Aminta* (1894) and *The Amazing Marriage* (1895) were the last of his novels. *Celt and Saxon*, an unfinished early novel, was posthumously published in 1910.

Appreciation.—About Meredith's position as a novelist there can be no two opinions. He stands in the front rank, with one or two others. Yet he has never been widely popular, but remains the favourite of "an honourable minority." His enemies have charged him with fantastic foppery of expression, with sham profundity, and with having an oracular air of superiority. His novels are certainly not always easy reading, but their difficulty has been much exaggerated. Some of his obscurity was due to the spirit of mischief. When he chose, he could write crisply and clearly. He is not liked by those who read novels merely for the plot. It is in character-drawing, especially in portraying women, and in describing the manifold variety of nature that he excels. He is the most intellectual of the Victorians.

Much light is thrown on his theory of art by his *Essay on Comedy and the Uses of the Comic Spirit*, which was a lecture delivered at the London Institution, 1st Feb., 1877. There he dwells on the uses of the Comic Spirit, which arouses thoughtful laughter, prevents us from taking ourselves too seriously, and destroys the bugbear of sentimentalism.

As a poet Meredith does not rank so high, though *Love in the Valley*, *Modern Love*, and some of his shorter poems are haunting and melodious, in spite of their occasional obscurity.

During the last years of his life Meredith was generally recognized as the most prominent man-of-letters in England. He was chosen to succeed Tennyson as president of the Author's Society; he held the gold medal of the Royal Society of Literature; and he was given the Order of Merit in 1905.—BIBLIOGRAPHY: R. Le Gallienne, *George Meredith; some Characteristics*; G. M. Trevelyan, *The Poetry and Philosophy of George Meredith*; J. Moffatt, *George Meredith: a Primer to the Novels*; C. Photiades, *George Mere-*

dith: his Life, Genius, and Teaching (translated by A. Price); S. M. Ellis, *George Meredith: his Life and Friends in Relation to his Work.*

MERGAN'SER. A genus of aquatic birds belonging to the duck family. The red-breasted merganser (*Mergus serrator*) and the goosander (*M. merganser*) are the commonest British

Red-breasted Merganser (*Mergus serrator*)

species, which range from the Bermudas to China and Japan. The smew (*M. albellus*) is native to the northern part of the Old World, wintering in Britain, the Mediterranean, Northern India, China, and Japan. There are two North American species, *M. americanus* and the hooded merganser (*Lophodytes cucullatus*). Mergansers inhabit lakes and the sea-coast, migrate southward in winter, lay from eight to fourteen eggs, and are gregarious in habit.

MÉRIDA (ancient **Augusta Emerita**). A dilapidated city of Badajoz, Spain, on the Guadiana. Founded by the Romans (23 B.C.), Augusta Emerita became capital of Lusitania. It fell to the Moors under Mûsa (713), and was retaken by Alfonso IX. of Leon in 1228. The Roman remains (forum, bridge built by Trajan, amphitheatre, circus, and aqueduct) are outside the modern town, and are the most important in Spain.

MÉRIDA. Capital city of Yucatan, Mexico, 25 miles inland from the port of Progreso, on the Mexican Gulf, with which it is connected by railway. It was founded in 1542; the cathedral dates from 1598. Pop. (1930), 91,139.

MÉRIDA. A state of Venezuela, created in 1901. Area, 4000 sq. miles; pop. (1926), 150,128. The state capital is Mérida (founded 1558), on the Chama. It is the seat of the University of Los Andes. Pop. 16,000.

MERIDEN. A town of Connecticut, United States, in New Haven county. Silver-ware, glass, and fire-arms are among its manufactures. Pop. (1930), 38,481.

MERIDIAN. A line imagined as described upon the earth's surface so as to pass through a given place and the two poles. It is therefore one-half of a great circle, if we assume that the earth is spherical. The plane of a meridian will evidently pass through the earth's axis, and be perpendicular to the equator. This plane, extended outwards from the earth, will intersect the imaginary celestial sphere which astronomers picture as surrounding the earth, the intersection constituting the celestial meridian. The celestial meridian of a place thus passes through the zenith of the place, and the north and south points of the horizon. Each star, as well as the sun, crosses the meridian twice daily, though, except for the *circumpolar stars*, one transit occurs beneath the horizon. We say that the body crosses the meridian. At the moment of upper transit it is either due south or due north, unless exactly overhead. In reality, of course, it is the moving plane of the meridian that crosses the sun's or star's disc, being carried round by the earth's rotation.

The name meridian is derived from Latin *meridianus* (from *medius*, middle, and *dies*, day), because the sun's crossing the meridian marks midday. All places situated on the same meridian have the same local time, and midday at the same instant, but the times of sunrise and sunset, and consequently the lengths of the day, differ with the latitudes of the places, except at the vernal and autumnal equinoxes. *See* DAY; LATITUDE; LONGITUDE.

MERIDIAN CIRCLE. *See* TRANSIT CIRCLE.

MÉRIMÉE (mā-ri-mā), **Prosper.** French poet and prose writer, born 28th Sept., 1803, died 23rd Sept., 1870. He studied law and passed advocate; but employed himself more with literature, and first came prominently forward in 1825 with eight comedies professedly translated from the Spanish of "Clara Gazul." He contributed to the *Revue de Paris* and the *Revue des Deux Mondes*; became inspector of historical monuments, in which capacity he travelled through France, and wrote several archæological works. He continued to publish romantic tales, such as *Arsène Guillot*, *Carmen*, *Colombo*, *Mateo Falcone*, etc.; was made a Senator in 1853, and grand officer of the Legion of Honour in 1866.

Among his writings are: *The History of Don Pedro I. of Castile*

(1843), *Poetry of Modern Greece* (1855), *Lettres à une inconnue* (1873), and *Travels in various parts of France*. —Cf. G. Saintsbury, *Writings of Prosper Mérimée*.

MERINO (me-rē′nō). A short fine-stapled wool, very rank and wavy, and derives its name from a type of Spanish sheep. Very fine wools from other countries often receive the same name, which always indicates a wool of very good quality, and from which high counts (very thin yarns) can be spun. Botany wool, the original of which came from Australia, and was shipped from Botany Bay, is of the same quality.

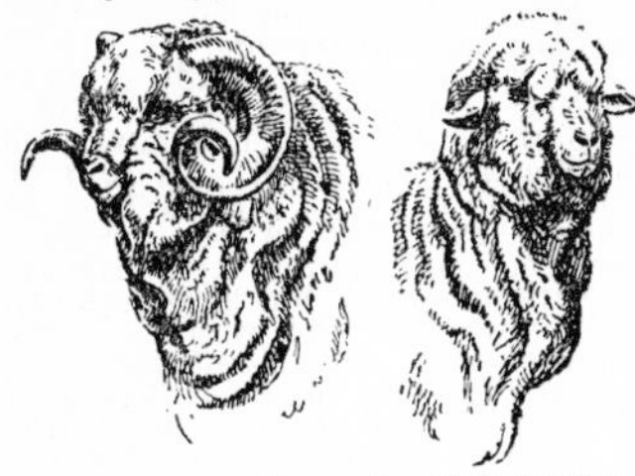

Australian Merino Ram Spanish Merino Ewe

The term merino is also applied to high-grade fabrics made from merino or Botany yarns. French merinos, for example, were at one time largely made from such fine wools, woven with twill weave, dyed in all shades, and used extensively for ladies' dresses. The chief British seat for these goods is Bradford, Yorkshire, but they are also made in several other districts in the United Kingdom.

MERIONETH, or **MERIONETHSHIRE.** A maritime county of North Wales, served by the Great Western and L.M.S. Railways. The coast-line is broken and rugged; the surface of the county mountainous (Aran Mawddwy, 2970 feet; Cader Idris, 2929 feet); the chief rivers the Dee, the Mawddach, the Dovey; and the largest lake Legid or Bala Lake (largest in Wales). Slate, limestone, and manganese are worked. The soil is for the most part poor, oats being the chief grain crop; cattle, sheep, and small hardy ponies are reared. Merioneth returns one member to Parliament. Chief town, Dolgelly. Area 422,372 acres; pop. (1931), 43,198.

MERISTEM. A group, layer, or mass of cells capable of continued division. The principal types are: (1) primary meristems, such as the mass of embryonic cells forming the apex ("growing-point") of root and shoot in seed-plants; these produce all the cells that subsequently by growth and differentiation give rise to the various "permanent" tissues; (2) secondary meristems, such as the *cambium* and *phellogen* (q.v.).

MERIT, Order of. British order. Founded in 1902, its membership is limited to 24, but it gives neither title nor precedence. The letters O.M. signify membership. An Indian order of merit was founded in 1837 for native officers and soldiers, and there are similar orders in several European countries.

MERLE D'AUBIGNÉ (merl dō-bēn-yā), **Jean Henri.** Historian and theologian, born at Geneva 1794, died 1872. His education, commenced at Geneva, was completed at Berlin. He became pastor at Hamburg to a French congregation, and removed afterwards to Brussels. Returning to his native city in 1830, he became professor of Church history in the theological school founded by the Genevan Evangelical Society. Besides his well-known *History of the Reformation in the Sixteenth Century* (1835-53), he published a supplementary history to the time of Calvin (Paris, 1862-68); *The Protector* (Cromwell), 1847; and the *Recollections of a Swiss Minister*.

MERLIN. A legendary Welsh prophet and magician, who is said to have lived in the fifth century. He is said to have been the offspring of a demon and a Welsh princess, and became adviser to the English kings Vortigern, Ambrosius, Uther-pendragon, and Arthur. There was also a prophet connected with the ancient kingdom of Strathclyde called *Merlin the Wild*, or *Merlinus Caledonius*, who is said to have lived in the sixth century. His prophecies, containing also those ascribed to the Welsh Merlin, were published at Edinburgh in 1615.

MERLIN, or **STONE FALCON** (*Æsalon regulus*). The smallest of the

Merlin

British falcons, being only about the size of a blackbird, but very bold. It was formerly used in hawking quails, partridges, larks, and such small game, and is even yet occasionally trained. It is of a bluish-ash colour above, reddish-yellow on the breast and belly, with longitudinal dark spots; the throat of the adult male is white. It builds its nest on the ground.

MERMAID'S PURSE. A name given to the horny egg-case of the skate, spotted dog-fish (q.v.), etc., which is often thrown up on the shore.

MER'OË. A city and state of ancient Ethopia, in the north-eastern part of Africa, corresponding mainly with the district between the Nile and Atbara, north of Abyssinia. Meroë was the centre of the caravan trade between Ethiopia, Egypt, Arabia, Northern Africa, and India. There are pyramids at the site of ancient Meroë, and a small town of same name on the Nile.

MEROSTOMATA. A group of arthropods, represented by the living king-crab, the extinct members of which are important in the fauna of late Silurian, and especially of Devonian times. The division Eurypterida includes forms up to 6 feet long, and their remains are well known in the Scottish Old Red Sandstone.

MEROVINGIANS. The first dynasty of Frankish kings which ruled in the northern part of Gaul from 496 to 752, when they were supplanted by the Carlovingians. They derived their name from Merwig or Merowig (Merovæus), the grandfather of Clovis.

MERRIMAC. A river of the United States flowing through New Hampshire and Massachusetts. The immense water-power furnished by its falls has created the towns of Lowell and Lawrence in Massachusetts, and of Nashua and Manchester in New Hampshire.

MERRIMAN, Henry Seton. Name taken by the English novelist, Hugh Stowell Scott. He was born at Newcastle-on-Tyne, 9th May, 1862, and educated at Loretto. He entered business life in London, but soon gave his whole time to literature, and died 19th Nov., 1903.

Among his books are *With Edged Tools*, *The Sowers*, *Roden's Corner*, *Barlasch of the Guard*, *The Isle of Unrest* and *In Kedar's Tents*.

MERSEBURG (mer'zė-burh). A town of Prussian Saxony, on the Saale. It is walled, has a seventeenth-century castle used as Government offices, and a cathedral dating from the eleventh century. Pop. 21,000.

MERSEY. A river and commercial highway of England, has its origin in Derbyshire by the junction of the Goyt and Etherow; receives as affluents the Tame, Irwell, Bollin, and Weaver; expands into an estuary 18 miles from its mouth at Runcorn; entire length, 70 miles. The Manchester Ship Canal is entered at Eastham on the Mersey estuary.

MERSEY, Viscount. English lawyer. Born in Liverpool, 3rd Aug., 1840, John Charles Bigham was educated there and abroad. He became a barrister and soon won a reputation by his skill in conducting commercial cases. From 1895 97 he represented a Liverpool division in Parliament. In 1897 he was made a judge, and in 1909 he became President of the probate, divorce, and admiralty division. In 1910 he retired, but he was chosen to inquire into the wrecks of the *Titanic* and the *Lusitania*, and served the State in other directions. In 1910 he was made a baron and in 1916 a viscount. He died 3rd Sept., 1920.

MERTHYR-TYDVIL, or **TYDFIL.** A parliamentary borough of South Wales, county of Glamorgan, on the Taff. The borough includes Dowlais, Plymouth, and Cyfarthfa. The town owes its prosperity to its situation near the centre of the coal- and mineral-field of South Wales. Pop. (1931), 71,099.

MERTON COLLEGE, Oxford. First founded at Maldon, in Surrey, in 1264 by Walter de Merton, Bishop of Rochester and Lord High Chancellor of England, was removed to Oxford before 1274.

MERU. A mountain of Tanganyika Territory, Africa, west of Kilimanjaro. Altitude, 14,955 feet.

MERV (ancient **Antiochia Margiana**). A town and oasis of Turkmenistan, Russian Central Asia, in the Transcaspian province, and in an extensive oasis producing wheat, barley, rice, cotton, and melons. Merv stands on the Murghat, and is on the Transcaspian Railway, on the road to Herat. Carpets, silks, and silver-ware are manufactured. Merv is mentioned in the *Zendavesta*, was refounded by Alexander the Great, and was successively in Arab, Seljuk, Turk, and Mongol hands before occupation by the Russians in 1883. Pop. about 100,000.

MESHED. A town of Persia, capital of the province of Khorassan and a sacred city of Shiah Mahommedanism, containing the tomb of Imâm Ruza, son of Ali and grandson of Mahomet. Swords, velvets, silks, cottons, and jewellery are manufactured, but Meshed owes its prosperity to the annual influx of about 100,000 pilgrims. Pop. about 85,000. During the European War Meshed was occupied by the British (1918) to guard the Transcaspian Railway from the Bolshevists.

MESMER, Friedrich Anton. German physician, founder of the doctrine of mesmerism or animal magnetism, was born in 1733, died in 1815. He professed to cure diseases by stroking with magnets,

Friedrich Anton Mesmer

but about 1776 he renounced their use, and declared that his operations were conducted solely by means of the magnetism peculiar to animal bodies. He went to Paris in 1778, where he achieved considerable success and fame and made many converts to his views, but was regarded by the medical faculty as a charlatan. The Government at length appointed a committee of physicians and members of the Academy of Sciences to investigate his pretensions. The report was unfavourable, and the system fell into disrepute. Mesmer retired to Swabia, where he died.

MESMERISM. *See* HYPNOTISM.

MESNE (mēn). In law, middle or intervening; as, a *mesne* lord, that is, a lord who holds land of a superior but grants a part of it to another person. In this case he is a *tenant* to the superior, but *lord* or superior to the second grantee. Mesne profits are the rents and profits of land accrued while the land is in the possession of an occupier not lawfully entitled thereto. The action brought by the true owner to recover such profits is known as an action of mesne profits.

MESOPHYTES. Plants adapted to grow under average conditions of water-supply, such as the vegetation of meadows, also most cultivated crops of temperate countries. *See* HYGROPHYTES; XEROPHYTES.

MESOPOTA'MIA, literally "the land between the rivers." A name given by the Greeks to the extensive region enclosed by the Tigris and Euphrates, anciently associated with the Assyrian and Babylonian monarchies. Its Old Testament name is *Aram Naharaim* (Gen xxiv. 10), or *Padan Aram.* Mesopotamia was formerly a part of the Turkish Empire, and was composed as follows:

Vilayet.	Area. Sq. Miles.	Population.
Baghdad . . .	113,867	1,360,304
Basrah . . .	27,070	785,600
Mosûl . . .	36,211	703,378
Mesopotamia . .	177,148	2,849,282

During the European War the country was conquered by British troops, and was erected into an independent state under Article 22 of the Covenant of the League of Nations, a mandate being authorized. By the Treaties of Sèvres and Lausanne Turkey confirmed this agreement, Britain acting as mandatory. On 23rd Aug., 1921, Emir Faisal, third son of the King of the Hejaz and ally of Britain in Mesopotamia, was proclaimed King of Iraq and crowned at Baghdad. The prevailing religions of Mesopotamia are Shiah and Sunnite Mahommedanism, with some Jewish and Christian sects.

Among industries agriculture, carried on by the help of irrigation, is important, wheat, barley, cotton, dates, and ground-nuts being produced. Some asphalt deposits are worked at Hit, on the Euphrates. Oil, however, is the chief product; petroleum wells are worked at Mandali, near Baghdad, at Gazara, near Mosul, and recently in the Transferred Territories near the Persian frontier. Imports are mainly of cotton goods and sugar; staple exports are grain and carpets. The Baghdad Railway (European 4-foot-8½-inch gauge) traverses the country, with a line between Baghdad and Samara and other offshoots. The total railway mileage open in 1932 was about 753 miles, with 170 miles of siding. Air mail communication is maintained by means of the Imperial Airways Ltd.; there is also communication with Persia and Syria. Basra has a Strowager Automatic Telephone Exchange. Part of Al ul Bait University was opened in 1926. *See* 'IRAQ. — BIBLIOGRAPHY: E. Bevan, *The Land of the Two Rivers* L. J. Hall, *The Inland Water Transport in Mesopotamia.*

MESOPOTAMIA COMMISSION. A Committee appointed in Aug., 1916, to inquire into the British campaign in Mesopotamia during the European War, and the disaster of General Townshend beyond Kut. The Commission consisted of Lord George Hamilton (chairman), Lord Hugh Cecil, Admiral Sir Cyprian Bridge, General Sir Neville Lyttleton, Sir Archibald Williamson, M.P., Mr. John Hodge, M.P., and Commander Josiah Wedgwood, M.P.

The report of the Committee was published in June, 1917, strongly censured both the India Office and the Indian Government, and made them responsible for the ill-advised policy and the defects of execution which resulted in Townshend's disaster. All the commissioners signed the Report, with the exception of Commander Wedgwood, who made a separate report. Mr. Chamberlain resigned the Secretaryship of India, being succeeded by the Right Hon. Edwin Montagu (resigned 9th March, 1922).

MESOZO'IC (from Gr. *mesos*, middle, and *zoē*, life), the term applied by geologists to the era and group of stratigraphical systems between the Palæozoic and the Cainozoic. The Mesozoic group is coextensive with the Secondary formations, and includes the rocks of the Triassic, Jurassic, and Cretaceous systems.

MESQUITE (*Prosōpis glandulōsa*). A small tree allied to the acacia, common in Mexico, Texas, and other parts of western North America. It yields a gum not much inferior to gum arabic; its seeds are eaten and a drink is prepared from the mucilage of its pods. Another species (*P. pubescens*) has pods that are eaten by the Indians, being rich in saccharine matter. They are of a twisted form, hence the name "screw bean."

MESS. A word derived from the Latin and French, and meaning "those who take their food at the same table." At the present day the word is used almost exclusively in naval and military circles. On His Majesty's ships the principal officers' mess is known as the "ward-room," while that for the junior officers is the "gun-room," in both cases the word "mess" being understood.

In the army every regiment, battalion, or similar unit has its officers' mess and sergeants' mess, both conducted by a committee of officers or non-commissioned officers for the benefit of the members, partly according to certain well-defined rules, and partly according to ancient custom and unwritten laws of the service. To a regimental officer the mess, under which name is included all the rooms set apart for general use, such as the dining- or mess-room, the sitting- or ante-room, and the billiard-room, fulfils the dual purposes of a home and a club for as long as he remains in the regiment. All officers of a unit are necessarily members of the mess, while the unmarried officers are what is known as "dining members," *i.e.* they must live and eat and generally have their being in the mess. Married officers use it more as a club. All, married or single, pay a certain fixed monthly subscription towards the upkeep of the mess, while the "dining members" pay in addition a daily sum for their food or "messing."

The mess dinner is a parade for all "dining members," and any one wishing to be absent on a given occasion is expected to obtain permission as from a parade. In practice this is done by merely writing one's name in a book kept for the purpose. This custom of treating the mess dinner as a parade is said to have originated—as did messes themselves—in 1745, when the Young Pretender was active in Scotland. In those days there were many Jacobite sympathizers in the English Royal army, and, it being the custom for officers to feed as and when they liked, there was little to prevent such sympathizers from attending treasonable meetings under cover of darkness. The order consequently went forth that for the future all officers of a regiment would dine together and in uniform, the underlying idea being no doubt that, in those days of hard drinking, the conviviality inseparable from such a form of communal dinner would keep the treasonably inclined ones occupied till they were too sleepy to think of anything else but getting to bed.

From these hot-blooded three-bottle days descend also some of the unwritten laws of a present-day mess, e.g. the rule against drawing a sword in a mess or that prohibiting the mention of a lady's name. The necessity for these rules can easily be seen when one remembers that duels took place with considerable frequency, and often on the very flimsiest pretexts, as late as the 'forties of the last century.

In all officers' messes the king's health is drunk usually once a week, all officers standing. The usual procedure is that the president rises and proposes the toast in the words "Mr. Vice—The King." The vice-president replies "Gentleman —The King." The band plays a part or the whole of the National Anthem, after which all officers repeat the words "The King" and drink. The late King Edward, in conformity with the spirit of the times, issued an order that the sovereign's health might, according to the taste of the individual, be drunk in water. In the navy the loyal toast is drunk sitting, for obvious reasons.

MESSALINA, Valeria. Wife of the Roman Emperor Claudius. She was noted for her avarice, cruelty, and lust. While the emperor was away she publicly married one of her favourites, and eventually Claudius had her executed in A.D. 48.

MESSENIA. A department of modern Greece. Pop., about 219,000. In ancient Greece Messenia was a country located in the southern part of the Peloponnesus. Its capital was Messēnē. Messenia struggled long in defence of her liberty against the Lacedæmonians, with whom she waged three wars between 743-724 B.C., 685-668 B.C., and 464-456 B.C.

MESSI'AH (Gr. form, *Messias*; Heb. *Mashiach*), corresponding to the Greek *Christos* of the New Testament, that is, "anointed," has in the Old Testament several applications, as to the whole Jewish people, to the priests, to the kings ("the Lord's Anointed"), and even to Gentile kings, as persons who had been anointed with holy oil.

The designation, however, owes its special importance to the application of it in the prophetic books of the Old Testament to an ideal holy king and deliverer whose advent they foretold. The whole of the prophetic pictures agreed in placing Jehovah in the central place of the desired kingship. These prophecies, which are called the Messianic prophecies, had at the time of our Lord come to be applied by the Jews to a temporal king who should free them from foreign oppression. They are affirmed by Jesus Christ and His apostles to apply to and be fulfilled in Him; and this is the belief of the Christian Church, by which He is called "The Messiah." The rationalistic school of theologians assert that Jesus laid claim to the dignity either to meet the preconceptions of His countrymen, or because He felt that the truth which He taught was the real kingdom never to be destroyed which the God of Heaven was to set up.—BIBLIOGRAPHY: M. Vernes, *Histoire des idées messianiques*; W. V. Stanton, *The Jewish and the Christian Messiah*; J. Drummond, *The Jewish Messiah.*

MESSINA. A maritime province of Sicily, traversed by mountain ranges (Monte Sori, 6055 feet) falling east and north to the sea; railways are confined to the coastline. Copper, sulphur, flax, corn, fruit, oils, and wine are produced. Messina is the capital. Area, 1254 sq. miles; pop. (1931), 600,092.

MESSINA (ancient Gr. *Zancle*; Rom. *Messana*), a seaport city of Sicily, capital of the province of Messina, on the Strait of Messina. The harbour is celebrated. Messina was destroyed by earthquake on 28th Dec., 1908, when 70,000 people perished. Oranges, liquorice, pumice stone, wine, and oils are exported. The population is 182,508 (commune).

MESSINA, Strait of. The channel separating Italy from Sicily, and connecting the Tyrrhenian with the Ionian Sea; length, 20 miles; breadth, from 2 to 14·15 miles. It is deep and the current is strong; and it is almost certain that the Scylla and Charybdis of the *Odyssey* were situated here. Anciently the strait was called *Mamertinum Fretum* or *Fretum Siculum.*

MES'SUAGE. In English law, is the term used for a dwelling-house with a piece of land adjoining assigned to the use thereof. In Scottish law it denotes the principal dwelling-house of a barony, being synonymous with the English *manor-house.*

MESTROVIC, Ivan. Croatian sculptor. Born in Dalmatia in 1883, he started life as an apprentice to a master mason at Spalato. He studied art at Vienna and soon attracted attention by his sculptures, first exhibited in 1902. In 1906 and 1915-17 works by him were on view in London and there is a torso by him in the Victoria and Albert Museum, South Kensington. Other works include portraits of Pius XI. and President Hoover.

META. An intendency and river of Colombia, South America. The intendency has an area of 32,692 sq. miles. Population, 19,320, 1587 being Indians. Villavicencio is the capital. The river rises in the Cordillera Oriental, and flows through Colombia to join the Orinoco, of which it is the chief tributary; length, about 650 miles.

METABOLISM (Gr. *mĕtabolē*, change), in biology, the cycle of chemical changes which continually goes on in living organisms, and consists of constructive processes (anabolism or assimilation), resulting in the gradual building up of living matter (protoplasm), and destructive processes (katabolism), whereby complex substances are resolved into simpler ones, with the ultimate formation of waste products (water, carbon dioxide, and nitrogenous compounds), and the conversion of potential into kinetic energy.

In green plants the first step in anabolism is the synthesis of water and carbon dioxide (photo-synthesis) into formic aldehyde. This is rendered possible by the presence of a green pigment (chlorophyll) which possesses the power to use the kinetic energy of sunlight for this purpose. Animals, however, require complex foodstuffs, derived from other organisms, and the soluble substances formed by the digestion of these constitute the building materials for constructive purposes. Colourless plants (fungi, yeasts) also require complex organic food, but the necessary nitrogen can be derived from tartrates, which are much simpler than the proteins required by animals.

MET'ACENTRE. *See* Stability of Ships.

METALLOG'RAPHY. A branch of metallurgy dealing with the internal structure of metals and alloys, and its relation to their composition and to their physical and mechanical properties. It is closely related to physical chemistry, since the internal structure depends on the physical and chemical conditions under which the solid metal or alloy is formed. Metallography also takes into account the mechanical arrangement of the component particles of metals and alloys, and is thus intimately connected with crystallography.

The word *metallography* was formerly used to signify the description of metals and their properties, but in this sense it is now obsolete. It was reintroduced by Osmond in 1892 to designate the microscopic structure of metals and alloys, but its meaning has gradually been extended to cover the results of other methods of examination, and now includes the complete physical study of metals and alloys.

The most important methods of examination used in the study of metallography are pyrometric, in which complete records are made of the rate of solidification and cooling of alloys; and microscopic, in which prepared sections of the alloys are highly polished, treated with suitable etching reagents, and examined by the microscope. By these means exact knowledge of the constitution of alloys is obtained, and in the case of iron and steel certain constituents have been named, the best known being ferrite, cementite, austenite, martensite, troostite, sorbite, and pearlite.—Bibliography: C. H. Desch, *Metallography*; J. W. Mellor, *The Crystallization of Iron and Steel*; W. Rosenhain, *An Introduction to the Study of Physical Metallurgy.*

METALLURGY. The art of extracting metals from their ores and adapting them for use in the metal industries. The art comprises the whole of the processes involved in the separation of the minerals containing the metals from other matters associated in the ore, smelting or treatment of the minerals for the separation of the metals, refining the metals thus produced, and casting them into suitable forms; and generally includes preliminary mechanical work for the production of shapes and sizes suited to particular branches of the metal industries.

The success of the art of metallurgy depends on a large number of facts concerning the metals; the determination of these facts and their application to the requirements of the metallurgist may be said to constitute the science of metallurgy. A complete study of the various branches of metallurgy requires a knowledge of many other branches of science. Geology and mineralogy must be studied in connection with the occurrence and distribution of the ores and minerals in nature. Not only is an accurate knowledge of the properties and values of the metallic minerals required, but also a knowledge of the effect of impurities on these properties, and also the effect of associated minerals, rocks, etc. A knowledge of chemistry is of vital importance to the metallurgist, and, in fact, metallurgy is frequently considered as a specialized branch of chemistry. The analysis and valuation of ores and minerals requires a knowledge of analytical chemistry, and practically all the methods used in the extraction of the metals are based on chemical reactions.

A good knowledge of physics is becoming of more and more importance to the modern metallurgist, not only as regards the application of heat and electricity to the extraction of metals, but also with reference to the properties of the metals as applied in the arts, and especially in connection with the study of the constitution and properties of alloys, a branch of the work now known as metallography (q.v.). A knowledge of mechanics is also essential to the metallurgist in connection with the study of mechanical properties of metals and alloys, such as strength, hardness, etc., and also in the design of the plant necessary for successfully carrying out on a commercial and profitable scale the various operations necessary in the practice of metallurgy.

The workers in the various chemical, electrical, and engineering institutions undertaking research work soon find that for the solution of their problems they must have materials with such combinations of properties as have not been found before, or that a common substance could be used for a certain purpose if an obnoxious property could be removed. Corrosion troubles in chemical plant and steam-condenser tubes; the growth, and ultimate breakdown of the structure, of cast iron when used in plant using superheated steam; the peculiar wear that takes place in the cylinders and piston rings of certain internal-combustion engines, all present problems of a metallurgical character. In fact in almost every field of industrial activity an essential requirement is a thorough knowledge of metallurgy.

Extraction of Metals.—For the extraction of the metals widely different processes are used, depending on the nature of the occurrence of the metal and on its chemical and physical properties. After the mineral matter has been obtained from its deposit in the earth's crust by the miner, it is frequently submitted to crushing, sizing, washing, and concentrating operations in order to fit it better for subsequent treatment; these operations are sometimes considered as falling within the domain of the mining engineer, but are frequently regarded as part of the duty of the metallurgist.

The metals sometimes occur in the free or native condition, as in gold, silver, copper, etc.; they are found more frequently as oxides (iron, copper, tin, etc.), and as sulphides (copper, lead, zinc, etc.); and occasionally as other chemical compounds, such as silicates, carbonates, sulphates, arsenides, etc. Very often, especially where the ores occur in large masses of uniform composition, as in the case of iron ores, the only preliminary treatment is one of crushing and sizing. In other cases there is a considerable difference between the specific gravities of the valuable mineral and the worthless minerals associated with it in the deposit, and by crushing to a suitable size and washing with water the waste minerals may be washed away, and the heavier valuable mineral may thus be concentrated into smaller bulk for treatment. This process of water concentration is largely used in the treatment of tin ores, lead ores, etc.

The magnetic properties of some minerals render them capable of easy separation from non-magnetic minerals, so that magnetic concentration of minerals is of some importance. The use of oil in assisting certain mineral particles to float on water has become of great importance during recent years, and at the present time vast quantities of mineral are treated by some form of oil flotation concentration process (*see* FLOTATION OF MINERALS).

The methods applied for the actual extraction of the metal may be divided into dry or smelting methods, and wet or solution methods; but before either type of method is used, the ore is frequently submitted to an operation of calcination or roasting which may result in an alteration of physical properties; for example, a dense close ore may be made comparatively porous, or certain chemical changes may take place, with the result that sulphides are converted into sulphates and oxides, carbonates into oxides, etc. The operation of smelting has for its objects the extraction of the body sought for, either as metal or as a concentrated compound of a metal, such as sulphide (known as *matte*) or arsenide (known as *speiss*), from which the metal may be recovered as such; and the separation of the associated non-metallic mineral matter as a slag. The formation of this slag is generally assisted by the inclusion of a flux in the smelting mixture. Iron is obtained in the form of pig-iron direct by the smelting of oxide ores in blast-furnaces; tin is obtained by smelting tin ores in reverberatory furnaces.

When smelting methods are to be undertaken, there are two important matters which have to be taken into account, viz. the fuel used as a source of heat, and the refractory materials to be used in the construction of the furnaces. For metallurgical purposes the fuel may be either solid (e.g. coal, coke, charcoal), liquid (e.g. various varieties of mineral and distilled oils), or gaseous (e.g. coal-gas and producer-gas). The kind of fuel which is best suited to any particular smelting operation will depend on the temperature required for the operation and the type of furnace best suited for the reactions. The selection of suitable refractory materials for the erection and lining of metallurgical furnaces is obviously of great importance, as the vessels or structures used must be able to resist a higher temperature than that required for the reactions. Within recent years various metallurgical smelting processes have been introduced in which electric current is used as the source of heat instead of fuel; these are generally known as electro-thermic processes.

In wet processes the ore is submitted to the action of some solvent which is capable of dissolving out the valuable constituents, leaving the barren mineral mass behind. Generally speaking, wet methods are not so efficient as smelting methods, but there are several exceptions to this rule, the most important occurring in the case of gold, in the extraction of which the finely crushed ore is lixiviated with a solution of sodium or potassium cyanide, which dissolves the gold readily. In wet processes means must be provided not only for the solution of the metal, but also for the recovery or precipitation of the metal from solution. This is generally carried out either by a chemical process or by electrical deposition. As examples of the former method may be mentioned the precipitation of gold from cyanide solutions by means of metallic zinc, and the precipitation of metallic copper on iron from solutions of sulphate or chloride of copper. As examples of electro-deposition methods may be mentioned the recovery of copper from sulphate solutions, and the recovery of zinc from zinc sulphate solutions, the latter process having become of very considerable importance during recent years.

Refining.—Metals as extracted by smelting or wet methods, with the exception of those which are electro-deposited, are generally impure, and require an operation of refining before they are fit for industrial uses. The commonest processes are fire-refining, used in the case of copper, tin, lead, etc.; and electro-refining, used in the case of copper, lead, gold, etc. In fire-refining the metal is generally melted down, and the impurities present are oxidized by atmospheric oxygen. Electro-refining is very similar in operation to electro-plating or depositing, a suitable bath beng used in which anodes of the crude metal are placed together with cathodes consisting of thin plates of the pure metal. By the use of suitable current the metal is dissolved at the anode and deposited at the cathode, the impurities being either left as an insoluble residue at the anode or passed into solution where they accumulate. The manufacture of the various classes of iron and steel from pig-iron may be considered as refining operations, although something more than mere refining is required in these cases.

Comparatively few of the metals are used in the industries in the pure state, and a very important matter to the metallurgist is the influence of the presence of very small quantities of other elements on the properties of the metals. In some cases these small quantities have a very deleterious action; the admixture of a little bismuth with copper, for example, renders the copper brittle and quite unfit for many industrial purposes; on the other hand, all the valuable properties of ordinary steel depend on the presence of quite small quantities of carbon.

In the industries comparatively few metals are used in the pure state, as more useful properties are obtained by an association of metals with each other in the form of alloys; for example, pure gold is too soft for use as jewellery or for coinage, but by the addition of copper, silver, etc., the hardness is increased and the wearing properties improved. Copper, again, when associated with zinc in the form of brass, or with tin in the form of bronze, is of greater service for most purposes than pure copper.

To indicate the enormous scale on which the metallurgist works, the following figures are given to show the estimated world production of some of the non-ferrous metals in 1931: copper, 1,430,000 tons; gold, 22,000,000 ounces; lead, 1,400,000 tons; silver, 195,000,000 ounces; tin, 145,000 tons; zinc, 1,000,000 tons.—BIBLIOGRAPHY: A. H. Sexton and C. O. Bannister, *An Elementary Textbook of Metallurgy*; Sir W. Roberts-Austen, *An Introduction to the Study of Metallurgy*; W. Gowland, *The Metallurgy of the Non-Ferrous Metals*; L. S. Austin, *The Metallurgy of the Common Metals.*

METALS. Elementary substances have been divided by chemists into two classes, *metals* and *non-metals*, but these merge into each other by gradations so imperceptible that it is impossible to frame a definition which will not either include some non-metallic bodies or exclude some metallic. Intermediate elements, such as arsenic and antimony, are sometimes called *metalloids*. The term metal is an ideal type, and is applied to those elements which approximate closely to the type as regards their general physical and chemical properties.

Characteristics.—The following are some of the chief characteristics of metals. They are opaque, having a peculiar lustre connected with their opacity called *metallic*; fusible by heat; good conductors of heat and electricity; capable, when in the state of an oxide, of reacting with acids and forming salts, i.e. their common oxides are basic oxides; and have the property, when their compounds are submitted to electrolysis, of generally appearing at the negative pole of the battery. Many of the metals are also malleable, or susceptible of being beaten or rolled out into sheets or leaves, and some of them are extremely ductile or capable of being drawn out into wires of great fineness. They are sometimes found native or pure, but more generally combined with oxygen, sulphur, and some other elements, constituting *ores*. The great difference in the malleability of the metals gave rise to the old distinction of *metals* and *semi-metals*, which is now disregarded.

Principal Metals.—The following—sixty-eight in number—are the principal substances usually regarded as metals: actinium, aluminium, antimony, arsenic, barium, beryllium or glucinum, bismuth, cadmium, cæsium calcium, cerium, chromium, cobalt, columbium or niobium, copper, dysprosium, erbium, europium, gadolinium, gallium, germanium, gold, holmium, indium, iridium, iron, keltium, lanthanum, lead, lithium, lutecium, magnesium, manganese, mercury, molybdenum, neodymium, nickel, osmium, palladium, platinum, polonium, potassium, praseodymium, radium, rhodium, rubidium, ruthenium, samarium, scandium, selenium, silver, sodium, strontium, tantalum, tellurium, terbium, thallium, thorium thulium, tin, titanium, tungsten, uranium, vanadium, ytterbium, yttrium, zinc, zirconium. Of these gold, silver, copper, tin, lead, zinc, platinum, and iron are the most malleable; gold, which possesses the quality in the greatest degree, can be hammered into leaves $\frac{1}{10000}$ of a millimetre in thickness. The following, given in the order of their ductility, are the most ductile: gold, silver, platinum, iron, nickel, copper, aluminium, zinc, tin, lead; platinum wire has been obtained of not more than $\frac{1}{1200}$ of a millimetre in diameter.

The majority of the useful metals are between seven and eight times as heavy as an equal bulk of water; platinum, osmium, and iridium are more than twenty times as heavy; while lithium, potassium, and sodium are lighter. The metals become liquid, or change their physical state, at widely varying temperatures: platinum is only fusible at the high temperature of 1755° C., iron melts at 1530° C., and silver at 960° C., while potassium melts below the boiling-point of water, and becomes vapour at a red heat, and it and sodium may be moulded like wax at 16° C. Mercury is liquid at ordinary temperatures, and freezes only at 38·8° C. below zero.

Osmium and tellurium are regarded by some as non-metals. All the metals, without exception, combine with oxygen, sulphur, and chlorine, forming *oxides*, *sulphides*, and *chlorides*, and many of them also combine with bromine, iodine, and fluorine. Several of the later discovered metals exist in exceedingly minute quantities, and were detected only by spectrum analysis, and there is every likelihood that research in this direction will add to the present list of metals.

METAM'ERISM. In chemistry, a particular form of isomerism used to characterize certain substances having the same molecular weight and containing the same elements in the same proportion, but which have totally different properties. The term is not much used now, the wider term *position isomerism* taking its place. Thus ethyl alcohol (CH_3CH_2OH) and methyl ether (CH_3OCH_3) are spoken of as being metameric, and methyl formate ($HCOOCH_3$) and acetic acid (CH_3COOH) are also metameric.

METAMOR'PHIC ROCKS. In geology, stratified or unstratified rocks of any age whose original texture has been altered and rendered less or more crystalline by subterranean heat, pressure, or both, accompanied usually by chemical changes. Metamorphic rocks are naturally best represented among the lowest and azoic, or non-fossiliferous masses, consisting of crystalline schists, and embracing granitoid schist, gneiss, quartzite mica-schist, and clay-slate. Many of these rocks were originally deposited from water and became crystallized by subsequent agencies. They exhibit for the most part cleavage, crumpling, and foliation, and lines of original stratification are often indistinct or obliterated. The metamorphic gneisses are commonly altered granites, that is, of igneous origin in the first instance. Hornblende and chlorite schists are usually altered igneous rocks of basic character.

METAMOR'PHOSIS. Any marked change of form, shape, or structure. In ancient mythology the term is applied to the transformations of

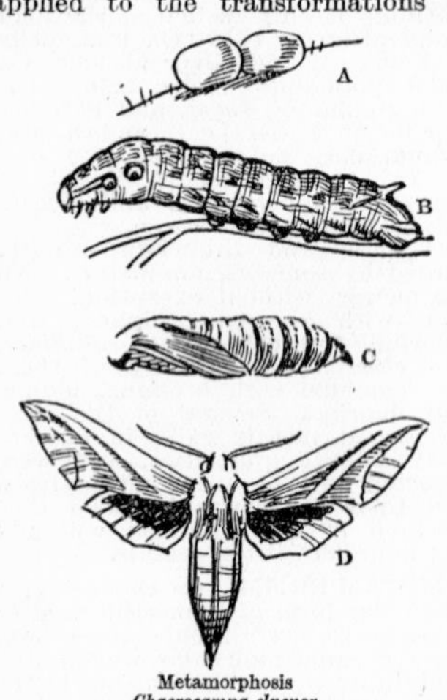

Metamorphosis
Chaerocampa elpenor
(Elephant Hawk Moth)
A, Ova; B, larva; C, pupa; D, Imago.

human beings into inanimate objects, with which ancient fable abounds.

In zoology it includes the alterations which an animal undergoes after its exclusion from the egg or ovum, and which greatly modify the general form and life of the individual. In a butterfly, for example, the egg hatches out into a worm-like actively feeding caterpillar (larva), which passes into a motionless chrysalis (pupa), from which the adult (imago) emerges. Insects which undergo a complete metamorphosis of this kind are known as *Heteromorphous* or *Holometabolic* insects. These are also termed the *Endopterygota*, from the fact that the wings develop from internal rudiments. Other insects, such as the grasshoppers, locusts, bugs, dragon-flies, etc., undergo a less perfect series of changes, and are termed *Hemimetabolic* or *Homomorphous* insects. The name *Exopterygota*, also applied to them, refers to the fact that the wing rudiments project externally.

The occurrence of metamorphosis is by no means confined to the lowest groups of the animal series, for we find the amphibian Vertebrates—as in the case of frogs, newts, and their allies—exemplifying these phenomena in a very striking manner; as also do many fishes, lampreys, lancelets, and tunicates. The metamorphoses of some Invertebrates, however, including the insects, crustaceans, worms, etc., are among the most marked and familiar with which we are acquainted.

MET'APHOR. A figure of speech founded on the resemblance which one object is supposed to bear, in some respect, to another, and by which a word is transferred from an object to which it properly belongs to another in such a manner that a comparison is implied, though not formally expressed. It may be called a simile without any word expressing comparison. Thus, "that man is a fox," is a metaphor; but "that man is like a fox," is a simile. So we say, a man *bridles* his anger; beauty *awakens* love or tender passions; opposition *fires* courage.

METAPHYSICS. A branch of philosophy which deals with ultimate reality, with the problem of unity, or the fundamental principle animating the universe. Each science, in its own domain, employs certain conceptions as its tools and instruments. It investigates the forms and changes of things and the manifestations of matter; it deals with the laws and facts of the material world as it is revealed to our senses. Science, however, does not question the value of the conceptions, such as space, time, cause, effect, matter, and form, of which it avails itself. The cause of a fact is another fact, the cause of a movement another movement. The sphere of science is limited by the boundary-line of the finite, by facts based on experience. It does not inquire *why* matter is, nor does it deal with the ultimate grounds of *being* and the attributes which belong to it as such.

The human spirit, however, in its inquisitiveness, is not satisfied with this knowledge. There must be something permanent and eternal, some hidden energy, something everlasting and absolute, which is the cause of all reality. There should therefore be a science which takes as the object of its investigations the very conceptions of which other sciences avail themselves, but which they have become accustomed to consider as needing no explanation. This science is metaphysics. Not content with a knowledge of things, as they *appear* to our senses, possibly so as to seem different from what they really are, metaphysics deals with the very essence of things, searches for ultimate reasons, and endeavours to know what is *behind* or *beyond* the natural phenomena. It investigates the ultimate principles that underlie and are presupposed in all *being* and *knowledge*.

The term metaphysics is due to a simple literary accident. The friends and followers of Aristotle, having placed his writings dealing with the question of the essence of things and bearing the title of *First Philosophy* after that part which he described as physics, called these writings metaphysics, i.e. *after* physics. Aristotle's own formal definition of First Philosophy was that of "a descriptive definition of Being as Being." Since then metaphysics has been variously defined, and much difference of opinion has prevailed as to its character and function, and even its utility.

It has been said that the metaphysician is a poet who has lost his vocation, or that "metaphysics constituted the romance of mind." Kant defined metaphysics as the science of *a priori* laws of thought in their relation to objects; Wolff styled it ontology; Ed. von Hartmann called it the philosophy of the unconscious, whilst Bergson defines it as being "a science which claims to dispense with symbols." Throughout the eighteenth and nineteenth centuries the term metaphysics was applied to inquiries concerning mind and matter, and divided into *ontology*, dealing with being, and *epistemology*, dealing with the nature and limits of human knowledge.

To sum up, metaphysics is the science of the first cause, of a cause which has no other causes behind it, or the science of ultimate principles independent of other principles. It deals with appearance and reality, with unity and diversity, with activity and passivity, mingled in the universe and revealed to our observations. It deals with the relations of cause and effect, investigates the true nature of such conceptions as space and time, and discusses the question whether reality is given in experience.

The Problems of Metaphysics.— The problems with which metaphysics deals existed long before the term, based on a literary incident, was applied to them. They were treated before Aristotle by the Ionian philosophers and by Plato. Among the numerous questions which man, seized with a feeling of wonder and anxious to solve the riddle of the universe, had been asking himself were the following: What is? What exists? What do I know? The man of an ordinary, unreflective mind readily replied: "All that surrounds me, all that I grasp and touch." The philosopher, however, endeavoured to find the fundamental principle which lies behind existence, and from which all things proceed. He asked himself: "What is the common essence of all substances amidst the various forms of manifestation?" He had noticed the existence of a plurality of things and of the apparently contradictory principles of activity, or movement, and passivity, the principles of mind and matter, and he investigated the cause of these contradictions, apparent or real, and the nature of their interrelations.

Various answers have been given to these questions by different philosophers. Some admitted only one principle, or cause, as the essence of all things—this theory is called *monism* (Gr. *monos*, alone)—whilst others maintained that there were two principles (*dualism*), or a plurality of principles (*pluralism*). The *monists* again differed in opinion. "There is nothing but spirit," said some of these philosophers, whilst "there is nothing but matters" taught others. The theory of the latter is termed *materialism* (q.v.), that of the former *spiritualism* (or *idealism*). In contradistinction to *monism*, *dualism* is the theory which admits the existence of two substances, material and immaterial, mind and matter.

Some thinkers, however, as has been pointed out, include in metaphysics not only the question of the real or apparent relation between mind and matter, but also the question of knowledge itself and the relation between a known subject and the knowing mind. Metaphysics is thus supposed to deal not only with the essence and origin of being, but also with knowledge, its essence and limitation. Faced by the philosophical problem as to whether it is at all possible for the human mind to solve the questions concerning the nature and origin of being, philosophers investigated the very nature of knowledge and its possibility. They asked themselves: "Is the human mind capable of obtaining certitude?"

Again various answers have been given to this question. *Dogmatism* affirms the harmony of thought and its object, thought being the natural connection between mind and matter. *Scepticism*, on the contrary, denies the possibility of knowledge. The human mind, it maintains, may strive to know the nature of the thing or object, but can never really reach it. Some philosophers think that knowledge is the exact copy and representation in our mind of reality. Things are exactly so in reality as they appear to us through the medium of our perceptive faculties. Appearance and reality are absolutely identical, and knowledge is the perception of things as they really are. In sense-perception we thus have a guarantee of the reality of existence. This theory is called *realism*.

In contradistinction to this doctrine, *idealism* derives the object of knowledge from the knowing mind itself. It maintains that perceptions of "things in themselves" and "existence," or "reality," are widely different. Knowledge is an inner, psychical process, and there could be no similarity between it and the things "without." Knowledge is therefore not at all the perception of things as they *really* are, but as they *appear* to us. The world around us is only the product of our mind. In other words, "the only reality of the external world in its perceptibility," and all that we know of the world around is only imagination, the product of our own mind. (*See* IDEALISM.)

Such are briefly the problems of metaphysics, which thinkers and philosophers of all ages, "a thousand poor and perspiring heads of us mortals" have tried to solve, although the modern materialist is inclined to relegate the labours of the metaphysician to the lumber-room of useless objects.—BIBLIOGRAPHY: J. M. Baldwin, *Dictionary of Philosophy and Psychology*; P. Janet and G. Séailles, *A History of the Problems of Philosophy*; G. S. Fullerton, *A System of Metaphysics*; P. Deussen, *Elements of Metaphysics*; E. Vacherot, *La Métaphysique et la Science*; A. S. Rappoport, *A Primer of Philosophy*.

METASTASIO, Pietro Buonaventura. Italian poet, born at Assisi 1698, died at Vienna 1782. His true name was Trapassi. He produced many operas, commencing with the *Didone Abbandonata* in 1724. His success was such that Charles VI. invited him to Vienna in 1729, and appointed him Poet Laureate with a pension of 4000 guilders. Metastasio may be said to be the father of the modern Italian opera. His works, while not possessing the highest literary merit, were eminently fitted for musical effect.—Cf. Vernon Lee, *Studies of the Eighteenth Century in Italy*.

METAY'ER. A cultivator who tills the soil for a landowner on condition of receiving a share, generally a half of its produce, the owner furnishing the whole or part of the stock, tools, etc. The phrase *metayage system* is applied to that mode of land cultivation, practised chiefly in France and Italy, in which the land is cultivated by metayers.

ME'TEOR. A name originally given to any atmospheric phenomenon; it is now more usually applied to the phenomena known as shooting-stars, falling-stars, fireballs or bolides, aerolites, meteorolites, meteoric stones, etc. It is now generally believed that these phenomena are all of the same nature, and are due to the existence of a great number of bodies, most of them extremely minute, revolving round the sun, which, when they happen to enter the earth's atmosphere, are heated by friction and become luminous. Under certain circumstances portions of these bodies reach the earth's surface, and these are known as meteorites or meteoric stones. They are composed of chemical elements found terrestrially, and are mostly of a stony nature, but a few are almost pure iron, alloyed with nickel.

Many showers of meteors are associated with particular dates in the year, when they appear to diverge from a point in the sky known as the radiant. Well-known showers are the *Perseids* of August, and the *Leonids* and *Andromedids* of November. As to the connection of meteors with comets, *see* COMETS.

METEROIC STONES. *See* METEOR.

METEOROLOGY. Literally the study of meteors. The term meteors signifies things elevated above the earth, and was originally applied to luminous appearances of any kind in or supposed to be in the air. Astronomy and meteorology are now pretty sharply differentiated, and meteorology is concerned not only with appearances of a luminous order, but undertakes investigation of the entire phenomena and conditions of the atmosphere, of climate, and of weather. On the other hand, it has practically nothing to do with meteors in the modern sense of the term, the consideration of these bodies, which arrive from inter-

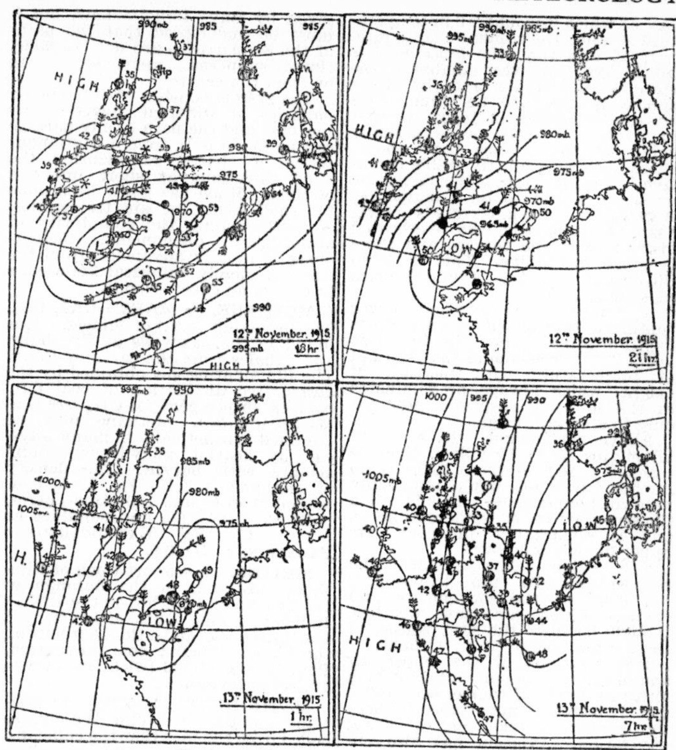

Passage of a Depression across the British Isles

planetary space, coming within the province of astronomy.

The atmosphere is an ocean of gases, which surrounds the globe, pressing upon the solid land and liquid oceans which form its exterior. At the sea-level the normal atmospheric pressure is nearly 15 lb. per square inch, or equal to that given by a column of mercury some 30 inches high. If the density were the same throughout, this pressure would be produced by a height of atmosphere of about 5 miles, which is called the height of the homogeneous atmosphere. But air being a compressible fluid, its density diminishes upwards. At about 3½ miles height the pressure is reduced by a half.

Above 50 miles or so the atmosphere can hardly have any appreciable density, but observations made on meteoric trails and auroral streamers show that it extends in extremely rarefied condition to 200 miles or more. The atmosphere is in constant motion, the movements being largely due to alterations of its temperature by solar heat, direct or reflected, by its own radiation into space, by convection between it and the land or sea surface, by evaporaton and precipitation. The pressure changes from time to time, and from place to place, and a study of these changes, their causes and results, forms an important part of meteorology.

In the lowest parts of the atmosphere temperature generally diminishes with altitude. If a given mass of air were to rise, without any gain of heat from, or loss to, the surrounding air, it would expand through reduction of pressure, and thereby fall in temperature. The rate at which it would fall in temperature is called the adiabatic lapse rate.

If at any time the lapse rate is much less than the adiabatic, the state is very stable, and the atmosphere is likely to be calm. This frequently occurs in foggy weather in winter. If the air is actually colder at the surface than above, there is an exceedingly stable condition. The lapse rate is then negative, or there is said to be a temporary inversion. If the lapse rate is greater than the adiabatic, the overheated lower strata tend to rise, and there is great instability. This is often illustrated in the thunderstorms of summer.

A temperature inversion never continues throughout a very great depth of atmosphere. But in recent years it has been found that the fall of temperature with increase of height, which always predominates in the lower atmosphere, proceeds only to a certain height.

Above this height, viz. 8 to 12 kilometres (5 to 7½ miles), there is reached a region where there is no further falling off, but a practically uniform temperature. This is called the stratosphere, or isothermal layer, and is remarkably quiescent. Its upper limit is unknown.

The region below is called the troposphere. To the troposphere are confined the movements and changes which constitute weather, though possibly the first causes of these often operate from without.

Investigations of the upper air and of the currents prevailing at high altitudes have, of course, acquired a greatly increased importance through the modern development of aerial navigation. Aviation has also enabled the study of clouds to be much extended. Electrical and magnetic investigations are now regularly made at many stations.

The older forms of meteorological work, which still retain their importance, include observation of atmospheric pressure by the barometer, temperature by the thermometer, humidity by the hygrometer, intensity of insolation and terrestrial radiation by the aid of the black-bulb and the grass thermometer, rainfall by the rain-gauge, bright sunshine by the sunshine recorder, wind direction and force by the wind vane and anemometer.

The weather phenomena of countries situated like our own are much more complex in general than those of lower latitudes. Their elucidation depends largely on the study of the moving pressure systems known as cyclones and anti-cyclones. The directions of the wind in these are given by Buys Ballot's Law, but it must be understood that the paths of the air particles are not, as sometimes supposed, mere spirals to or from the centre.

The system consists of different air particles at different stages of its journey, and the path of any particle can be found only from a continuous series of charts, representing the wind directions at short intervals of time. Much has lately been done by such study of air trajectories. Notwithstanding the complexity of atmospheric phenomena, meteorology is rapidly advancing from the stage of merely empirical knowledge to that of an exact science.

METHANE, or MARSH-GAS, CH_4. The fire-damp (q.v.) of miners. It is found in the gas-wells at Pittsburg, and exhales from the earth at Baku. The illuminating gas obtained by the destructive distillation of coal may contain 40 per cent. of CH_4 (*see* GAS MANUFACTURE). Methane may be obtained synthetically in many ways, e.g. by heating anhydrous sodium acetate with baryta. The density of methane is 8(H = 1). It is condensed at 0° C. and 140 atmospheres, boils at −164° C., and solidifies at −186° C. *See* HYDROCARBONS; PARAFFINS; DAMPS.

METHIL. A seaport town of Fifeshire, Scotland, in the borough of Buckhaven and Methil, on the L.N.E. Railway, 1 mile south of Leven. It has three docks and a tidal harbour on the Firth of Forth; coal is exported. Pop. (1931), 17,643 (with Buckhaven and Innerleven).

METHODISTS. A society of Christians founded by John Wesley, so called from the fact that the name was applied to Wesley and his companions by their fellow-students at Oxford. The religious movement which resulted in the foundation of this society began at Oxford in 1729, the chief leaders besides John Wesley being his brother, Charles, and George Whitefield.

The first general conference of the Methodists was held in 1744, and the Methodists were constituted a legally corporate body in 1784. Their doctrines are substantially those of the Church of England. The appointment of a minister of the body to any circuit is annual, but the limit of a minister's term of service in one circuit varies in the different Methodist bodies. In the Wesleyan Church the usual period is three years. The body is governed by an annual conference, having at its head a president and secretary, whose term of office lasts but for a year.

The District Meeting, or Synod, is

an important feature of Methodist polity. The several chairmen are appointed either by Conference, as with the Wesleyans, or by the vote of the Synod, as with other Methodist bodies. There are also quarterly circuit meetings of ministers and lay officers. The supreme legislative and judicial power is vested in the Conference, to which the half-yearly and quarterly district and circuit meetings are subordinated.

The number of members at Wesley's death was 76,968; in 1931 there were in different parts of the world about 32,000,000 adherents. Various secessions have from time to time taken place from the original body. The chief of these are: the Calvinistic Methodists, which originated in a difference between Wesley and Whitefield regarding the Calvinistic doctrines; the Methodist New Connexion, founded in 1797-98; Primitive Methodists (1808); Bible Christians; the Wesleyan Reform Union, and the United Methodist Free Churches, originating in the Wesleyan Methodist Association of 1836, with the subsequent additions of the Protestant Methodists of 1828, and the Reformers, who seceded from the parent connection in 1849-52.

The New Connexion, the United Methodist Free Church, and the Bible Christians united in 1907 to form the United Methodist Church. On 20th Sept., 1932, the three Methodist Churches of Great Britain —Wesleyan, Primitive, and United Methodist—were united. The first United Conference met in 1933. The Methodists are especially numerous in North America, forming numerically the leading denomination in the United States. The Methodist Episcopal Church is the oldest and leading Methodist body in America. In 1845 the Methodists of the Southern States formed the Methodist Episcopal Church, South.—BIBLIOGRAPHY: A. Stevens, *History of Methodism*; J. R. Gregory, *History of Methodism*; Green, *Mission of Methodism*; Townsend, Workman, and Eayrs, *The New History of Methodism* (2 vols.).

METH'YL (CH_3). The name given to the organic radicle CH_3 present in many compounds and behaving like a single element, as in methyl sulphate, $(CH_3)_2SO_4$; methyl alcohol, CH_3OH; and methyl chloride, CH_3Cl.

METHYLATED SPIRIT. Rectified spirit of wine (ethyl alcohol, $CH_3{\cdot}CH_2OH$) "denatured" by the addition of 10 per cent. of wood naphtha, which contains a large proportion of methyl alcohol, $(CH_3{\cdot}OH)$. The naphtha gives a disagreeable taste to the spirit and renders it undrinkable; for this reason it may be sold, under restrictions, duty free. It is largely used in the manufacture of varnishes, as a source of heat when burnt in spirit-lamps, and as a solvent for many purposes in the chemical industry.

METONIC CYCLE, or **METONIC YEAR.** The cycle of the moon, or period of nineteen years, in which the lunations of the moon return to the same days of the month; discovered in 432 B.C. by Meton, an Athenian mathematician. This cycle contains 235 lunations. It is still employed for determining the date of the Easter Full Moon, which regulates the ecclesiastical calendar.

METRIC SYSTEM. A decimal system of weights and measures based on the metre as the unit of length. The system originated in France at the time of the Revolution. Its use is now compulsory in most countries, and optional in some others, such as the United States, Japan, and (since 1897) Britain. *See* WEIGHTS AND MEASURES.

MET'RONOME. An instrument consisting of a weighted pendulum

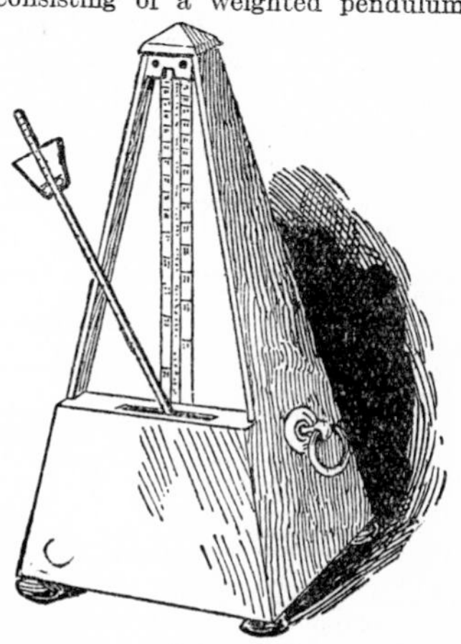

Metronome

moving on a pivot and set in motion by clock-work; invented about 1814, for the purpose of determining, by its vibrations, the quickness or slowness with which musical compositions are to be executed, so as to mark the time exactly. There is a sliding weight attached to the pendulum rod, by the shifting of which up or down the vibrations may be made slower or quicker. A scale indicates the number of audible beats given per minute, and this must be made to agree with the number attached to the music by its composer.

METROSIDE'ROS. A genus of trees and shrubs, nat. ord. Myrtaceæ. *M. vera,* known as ironwood, is a tree, a native of Java and Amboyna. Of the wood of this tree the Chinese and Japanese make rudders, anchors, etc. *M. robusta* is the rata of New Zealand, where it is employed in shipbuilding and in other ways. The trees of this genus have thick opposite, entire leaves, and heads of showy red or white flowers.

METSHNIKOV, Ilya. Russian biologist, born in the province of Kharkov 1845, died at Paris 1916. Metshnikov gained a reputation by his investigation of the white blood corpuscles, but the subject to which he devoted most attention was that of the prolongation of life. He maintained the therapeutic value of lactic ferments, both as a preventive and a remedy in intestinal putrefaction.

In 1909 he put forth the theory that soured milk contained bacilli which retard or counteract the intestinal putrefaction, responsible for senility. According to his belief, persons who had no organic disease could live to the age of 150. In 1908 he shared the Nobel Prize for medicine with Paul Ehrlich. His works include: *Leçons sur la pathologie comparée de l'inflammation* (1894), *L'Immunité dans les maladies infectieuses* (1901), *Étude sur la matière humaine* (1903), and *La Vieillesse* (1904).

METTERNICH (met'tėr-ni*h*), **Clemens Lothar Wenzel, Prince von Metternich.** Austrian statesman, born at Coblenz 1773, died at Vienna 1859. Entering the Austrian diplomatic service in 1794, he represented Austria as ambassador at various European courts between 1801 and 1809.

In the latter year he became Minister of Foreign Affairs. In this capacity he negotiated the marriage of the Archduchess Marie Louise with Napoleon, and conducted her to Paris. In 1813, after the French reverses in Russia, Austria gave in her adhesion to the other allied powers, and declared war against France. From this period the policy, not only of Austria, but in a great measure that also of the leading Continental powers, was shaped by Metternich.

He was one of the plenipotentiaries who signed the Treaty of Paris, and he presided at the Congress of Vienna (1814). The object of his policy was to arrest the progress of what were called revolutionary principles. With this view he formed the scheme known as the Holy Alliance.—BIBLIOGRAPHY: G. A. C. Sandeman, *Metternich: Life and Career*; G. B. Malleson, *Life of Prince Metternich.*

METZ (mes). A town of France, capital of the department of Moselle, on the Moselle. The major part of the town stands on a height within the fortifications, outside of which there is a series of strong detached forts. The cathedral is a late Gothic structure, surmounted by a spire of open work 397 feet high. The manufactures consist of woollens, cottons, hosiery, hats, muslin, glue, and leather. A battle was fought under its walls between the Germans and French in Aug., 1870.

The Germans subsequently invested it, and, being reduced to a state of famine, on 28th Oct. it capitulated with 180,000 officers and men under the command of Marshal Bazaine. It was included in the cession of territory to Germany at the peace of 1871, but was restored to France by the Treaty of Versailles (1919). Pop. (1931), 78,767.

MEU, or **BALD-MONEY** (*Meum athamanticum*). An umbelliferous herb with very finely divided foliage, common at high levels in Britain.

MEUNG, MEUN, or **MEHUN** (meuṇ), **Jean de.** A French poet, surnamed from his lameness *Clopinel,* was born at Meung sur Loire about 1250, died about 1322. He lived at the court of Philippe le Bel, and enjoyed a high reputation as a scholar, a poet, and a satirist. His principal work was his continuation of the *Roman de la rose,* which Guillaume de Lorris had left unfinished in 1237. To the 4000 verses of his predecessor Meung added about 18,000. In respect of quality, however, his work is less poetical than that of Lorris.

MEURTHE (meu*r*t). A river of France, which rises in the Vosges, and joins the Moselle near Nancy; total course, about 100 miles.

MEURTHE-ET-MOSELLE (meu*r*t-ė-mo-zel). A department of North-East France, formed in 1871 by uniting portions of the old departments of Meurthe and Moselle, in consequence of the cession by France to Prussia of a portion of her territory on the east under the Treaty of Frankfort (10th May, 1871); area, 2036 sq. miles. The chief river is the Moselle. Wheat, oats, barley, and fruit are raised; wine-growing is extensive, iron ore and salt are produced. Among manufactures are machinery, woollens and cottons, glass, paper, earthenware, and leather. The capital is Nancy. Pop. (1931), 592,632.

MEUSE (me*u*z; Du *Maas*). A river of Western Europe, rising in France, in the south of the department of Haute-Marne, and flowing through France, Belgium, and Holland. Its principal affluents are the Sambre, which joins it on the left at Namur, and the Ourthe, which joins it on the right at Liége. At Gorkum it joins the Waal, one of the arms of the Rhine, and gives its name to the united streams.

Meuse at Dinant

It is divided near Dordrecht into two great rivers, the one of which bends round to the north and reaches Rotterdam; the other branch continues west; and shortly after the two branches again unite and discharge themselves into the North Sea. Its length is 575 miles, of which 305 are in France and 120 in Belgium. It is navigable for about 460 miles. The principal towns on its banks are Namur, Huy, Seraing, Liége, Maestricht, Rotterdam, Schiedam, and Vlardingen.

MEUSE. A north-east department of France, drained by the Meuse; area, 2408 sq. miles. Iron is extensively worked; cereals and beetroot are raised; horse-breeding is important. A large area is afforested. The department was prominent in the European War, a large area being completely devastated, particularly around Verdun. Bar-le-Duc is the capital. Pop. (1931), 215,819.

MEXBOROUGH. A town of the West Riding of Yorkshire, England, on the Don; served by the L.M.S. and L.N.E. Railways. Ironworks and potteries are the main manufacturing industries. Coal-mines are located nearby. Pop. (1931), 15,856.

MEXICO. A republic in the southern part of the North American continent, bounded by the United States and Central America, and with an extensive coast-line on both the Pacific (2000 miles) and the Atlantic (1500 miles, on the Gulf of Mexico); area estimated at 767,198 sq. miles. Nearly one-half of this territory lies within the torrid zone, but the peculiar geological structure of the republic, that of an elevated plateau rising into volcanic peaks, supported by the two branches of the Mexican Cordilleras, the North-East and North-West, causes the greatest diversity of climate.

The principal summits, all of volcanic origin, are Popocatepetl (Smoking Mountain), 17,888 feet; Orizaba, or Citlaltepetl (Star Mountain), 18,208 feet; and Ixtaccihuatl (White Lady), 17,323 feet. All these are above the limit of perpetual snow, which is here about 15,000 feet. The largest river is the Rio Grande del Norte, forming part of the boundary with the United States; most of the others are rather insignificant. Among lakes are Chapala, at an altitude of 6000 feet (area, 1500 sq. miles), and Parras in Coahuila, on the headwaters of the River Nazas.

Agriculture.—Mexico is a country of great natural resources, and its three distinct zones of climate—that of the hot coast-lands, the temperate zone, and the "cold" country of the elevated plateaux—permit the cultivation of almost all the plants of the world. The principal agricultural products are maize (1,929,502 tons in 1931), maguey (*agave*, from which *pulque*, the national beverage of the Mexicans, is produced), cotton, henequen, wheat (420,000 tons in 1931), coffee, beans, chicle (raw chewing-gum), and rubber; most of the crops are grown on irrigated land. Banana production has been started near Tampico, in the Gulf Coast district. Large irrigation schemes have been carried out at Nuevo Leon, Aguascalientes, and Tecamachalco.

Sugar and molasses to an annual value of about £2,500,000 are also produced. Timber and fine wood are found in the southern states and on the coast, and include numerous dyewoods, ebony, mahogany, sandalwood, rosewood, oak, and pine. The vine flourishes in the north, and a fair quality wine is produced.

Mining.—Mining, the principal industry, is carried on all over Mexico as far south as the state of Oaxaca, and great sources of mineral wealth are so far undeveloped, chiefly through bad transport facilities and political unrest. Gold, silver, copper, lead, zinc, mercury, antimony, graphite, tungsten, tin, arsenic, manganese, and molybdenum are all actively worked. Coal is extensively worked in the State of Coahuila, and almost 1,000,000 tons are mined annually.

Oil.—Mexico is one of the world's greatest oil-producing countries, and the Constitution of 1917 makes the Government control over oil deposits absolute (Article 27). The principal oilfields are near Tampico, in the Elbano district; others exist in the Panuco, Tuxpan, and Huastica districts. The potential production is about 1,250,000 barrels daily. There are over 343 wells.

Towns.—Mexico City is the state capital. Vera Cruz and Tampico, both on the Gulf of Mexico, are the principal seaports, but much oil is exported through the Port of Tuxpan.

Communications and Shipping.—The National Railways of Mexico owned 14,680 miles of track in 1931 and controlled an additional 322 miles. There were also in the same year 3439 miles belonging to the various States. There is a State airplane service, also a service to South and Central America. The Merchant Navy have been assisted since 1930 by subsidies from the Government.

Administration, etc.—The republic is divided into twenty-eight states, two territories, and what is called the Federal District, which comprises Mexico, the capital of the republic, and a small portion of adjoining territory consisting of eleven villages. The population in 1910 was 15,063,207, and by the census of 1930 was 16,404,030. The Creoles are naturally the dominant race, and the Spanish language is generally spread over Mexico.

Religion.—Roman Catholicism is the prevailing religion, but under the Constitution of 1917 Church and State are separate and toleration of all other religions is guaranteed, but no religious body can own landed property. In 1926 all foreign priests were expelled, and all Church property was declared to belong to the State. An agreement was made between the Government and the Church in 1929, but in 1931 the dispute broke out afresh, resulting in that year in the expulsion of the Papal delegate.

Education and Justice.—Primary education is free, compulsory, and secular, but the law is not strictly enforced. There are three universities at Mexico City, Mérida, and Guadalajara. In 1930 the death penalty was abolished, except for the army.

Constitution and Government.—The present form of government is that of a Federative Republic, divided into states, each with Governor, legislature, and judicial officers, similar to those of the Federation. The supreme executive power is vested in a President, who has powers very similar to those of the President of the United States. The legislative power is vested in a Congress, comprising a Senate and a House of Representatives. The President is nominally elected for four years by direct popular vote.

History.—Prior to 1521 Mexico was inhabited by an Aztec race and ruled by native emperors. (*See* AZTECS.) This race had attained a remarkable degree of civilization, and interesting remains of their architecture are existent in the teocallis or pyramids of Cholula, Pueblo, and Papantla. In 1521 Mexico fell into the hands of the Spaniards under Hernando Cortez. Cortez called it *New Spain*, and was created captain-general, but in 1535 was displaced by a viceroy. From that date till 1821 the country was one of the viceroyalties of Spanish America, and governed by a series of viceroys possessed of almost absolute power.

The spirit of discontent engendered by the selfishness of the Spanish rule manifested itself in open rebellion, when in 1808 the deposition of King Ferdinand by Napoleon and the unsettled state of affairs in Spain afforded an opportunity. This rebellion, begun by a priest, Hidalgo, and continued with more or less vigour till 1821, secured in that year the independence of Mexico.

After an unsuccessful attempt to secure a Bourbon prince for the throne, General Augustin Iturbide, the chief of the insurgents, caused himself to be proclaimed emperor, 18th May, 1822, under the title of Augustin I., but was forced to abdicate, March, 1823. The republic was proclaimed in 1824. The republican form of government has been interrupted by civil war, numerous dictatorships, and by the brief rule of the Austrian Archduke Ferdinand Maximilian as emperor from 1864 till his execution in 1867, when Benito Juarez assumed power. General Porfirio Diaz (died 2nd July, 1915) ruled the country from 1876 until 25th May, 1911 (excepting 1880–84), General Manuel Gonzalez, when he resigned.

Francisco I. Madero became President until 23rd Feb., 1913, when he was murdered, and General Victoriano Huerta became President. Civil war broke out in April, 1913, and Carranza became President on the fall of Huerta. A resumption of civil war in April, 1920, resulted in the death of Carranza and the election of General Adolfo de la Huerta (May, 1920), until (Sept., 1920) the popular election returned General Alvero Obregon. He was succeeded in 1924 by Plutarco Elias Calles, but was re-elected in 1928 and was assassinated about a fortnight later.

Two years later a revolution broke out, beginning in the army and led by General Aguirre. Calles became War Minster, and with the sympathy and practical support of the U.S.A., who supplied the Federal Government with arms and ammunition, endeavoured to suppress the rebels. After severe fighting, notably at Reforma, near Jiminez, he succeeded; General Aguirre was captured and executed, and the revolution subsided.

President Portes Gil, who followed Calles, enjoyed a less eventful term of office, and was succeeded in the following year by Pascual Ortiz Rubio, the Revolutionary candidate, who polled an overwhelming number of votes at the elections.—BIBLIOGRAPHY: J. H. Smith, *The War with Mexico*; P. H. Middleton, *Industrial Mexico*, 1919; *Facts and Figures*; A. H. Prescott, *History of the Conquest of Mexico*.

MEXICO. Capital of the Republic of Mexico, is situated within the state of Mexico in the Federal District, about 7400 feet above the level of the sea. It is located at about an equal distance from Vera Cruz on the Mexican Gulf and Acapulco on the Pacific, and is built on the site of the ancient city of Tenochtitlan, which was destroyed by the Spaniards in 1521. It is connected with the United States by rail. The cathedral, forming one of the sides of the central square, was founded in 1572 and completed in 1791. The Palace of Government, the National University, and the National Museum are also important. The manufactures are comparatively limited. It has two broadcasting stations (49·8 and 48·65 M.). Pop. (1930), 960,905.

MEXICO. An inland state of the Mexican Republic. It lies in the south of Mexico, and forms an elevated region (Nev. de Toluca, 15,168 feet), one of the best cultivated and most thickly peopled parts of the republic. It embraces within its boundaries, but outside its administrative sphere, the city and Federal District (587 sq. miles; pop. 763,500) of Mexico. Toluca (pop. 30,000) is the capital. Area, 9230 sq. miles; pop. (1930), 978,412.

MEXICO, Gulf of. A large bay or gulf of the Atlantic, oval in form, and nearly surrounded by a continuous coast-line 3000 miles in length, of the United States and Mexico; estimated area, 800,000 sq. miles. It gives name to the Gulf Stream, which issues from it by the Strait of Florida.

MEYERBEER (mī′ėr-bār), **Giacomo.** Musical composer, born in Berlin 1791, died at Paris 1864. His first two operas, *Jephtha's Vow* (1813) and *Abimelek*, the one produced at Munich and the other at Vienna, having failed, he went to Italy. There he rapidly composed a series of operas in the Italian style, which were generally well received. In 1826 he went to Paris. There he produced *Robert le Diable* (1831), *Les Huguenots* (Paris, 1836), *Le Prophète* (1849), *Pierre le Grand* (*L'Étoile du Nord*, 1854), *Le Pardon de Ploermel* (*Dinorah*, 1858), and *L'Africaine* (1865). In these Parisian operas he ceased to be an imitator of the Italians, and it is upon them that his fame as a composer is founded.—Cf. A. Hervey, *Meyerbeer*.

MEZE'REON (*Daphne Mezereum*). A well-known shrub grown in gardens, having fragrant pink flowers that appear in spring before the leaves, and are followed by red and poisonous berries. The bark is exceedingly acrid, and has been used in medicine.

MÉZIÈRES (mā-zyār). A town of France, capital of the department of Ardennes, on the Meuse. Captured by the Germans during the European War (Sept., 1914), it was retaken by the Allies in Nov., 1918, but destroyed before and bombarded for twenty-four hours after the German evacuation. It was "adopted" by Manchester. Pop. about 10,000.

MEZZOTINT. A method of engraving in which a copper plate is first covered with a series of fine indentations, each having a burr, by means of a *rocker* with a curved and serrated edge. From this surface, which would print black, the engraver removes the burr with a *scraper*, in proportion to the degree of lightness required; thus reversing the other engraving processes, and working from dark to light. When combined with other processes, such as etching or aquatint, mezzotint is known as mixed mezzotint.

Its inventor was Ludwig van Siegen (1609 to after 1676), and the process was practised by Prince Rupert. In their day the engraver left untouched the parts of the plate which were to print light, and roughened only the darks; but W. Vaillant (a Frenchman, said to have been an assistant to Prince Rupert) appears sometimes to have used the rocker, which was systematically used by Abraham Blooteling (1640-90). In the eighteenth century the art became very popular, especially in England, and for reproductive purposes.

The most prominent figures of the period are James M'Ardell (1729-65), one of the first engravers to work to a considerable extent after Reynolds; Richard Earlom (1743-1822), whose 200 plates in etching and mezzotint after Claude's *Liber Veritatis* are a forerunner of Turner's *Liber Studiorum*; Valentine Green (1739-1815); Thomas Watson (1743-81); and John Raphael Smith (1752-1812).

In the early nineteenth century, the work of William and James Ward, Charles Turner, and S. W. Reynolds is important; and David Lucas (1802-81) produced a series of masterly plates after John Constable. The development of photogravure has largely killed mezzotint; but among modern artists, Sir Frank Short has produced some remarkable plates.—Cf. A. M. Hind, *Short History of Engraving and Etching*.

MIAUTSE, or MIAO-TSE. A race of people found in the provinces of Yunnan, Kweichow, Kwang-tse, and Kwang-tung in China. They are one of the aboriginal tribes of the country, and number several millions. Some of the tribes are under Chinese rule, but others retain their independence.

MICA. A group of common mineral silicates crystallizing in six-sided plates of the monoclinic system, with a perfect basal cleavage, so that they split easily into thin flexible laminæ, having a shining, pearly, and almost metallic lustre. The magnesium-micas are optically almost uniaxial, and were on this account long regarded as belonging to the hexagonal system. The platy crystals are often large, having been found 9 feet across in Canada, and they are employed in Russia for window-panes, and in that state are called *muscovy-glass*.

The micas are mostly developed in igneous rocks, such as granite and diorite, or by the metamorphism of argillaceous masses, as in mica-schist. They are also found in many sedimentary rocks, as shales and sandstones, giving them their laminated texture. In the latter case the mica is derived from the disintegration of the crystalline rocks.

The micas are essentially hydrous aluminium potassium silicates. The common colourless species *muscovite* is free from magnesium and iron; but these are important constituents in the darker mica *biotite*, which frequently decomposes into chlorite. The flexibility and elasticity of cleaved plates of muscovite cause it to be used for lamp-chimneys and shades. Mica is also worked up into non-conducting boards for electrical apparatus, and is employed to give lustre to wallpapers.

MICAH.—The sixth of the minor prophets, a member of the tribe of Judah. He prophesied in the reigns of Jotham, Ahaz, and Hezekiah, and was a contemporary of Isaiah. His style is pure and correct, his images bold and vivid.

MICA-SCHIST, or MICA-SLATE. Probably the commonest of metamorphic rocks, composed of mica and quartz; it is highly fissile and passes by insensible gradations into clay-slate. It is a product of the alteration of shale by heat, or pressure, or both, acting together in the earth's crust. The mica is usually muscovite, but biotite-schists occur, weathering to a golden brown on their surfaces of parting. Almost all mica schists include almandine garnet, developed during the metamorphism of the original sediments. The foliation very often records the bedding of the shales; but in other cases it has developed parallel to surfaces of shear.

MICHAEL, St. (Heb., "he who is equal to God"), in Jewish theosophy, the greatest of the angels (Dan. x. 13, 21; xii. 1), one of the seven archangels. In the New Testament he is spoken of as the guardian angel of the Church (Jude, ver. 9; Rev. xii. 7). There is a festival of St. Michael and All Angels in the Western Church, held on 29th Sept.

MICHAELMAS. The feast of St. Michael the Archangel. It falls on the 29th of Sept., and is supposed to have been established towards the close of the fifth century, in consequence of an apparition of the archangel which took place on Monte Gargano in Apulia in 493. In England, Michaelmas is one of the regular terms for settling rents.

MICHELANGELO (Michelangiolo Buonarroti), a descendant of the ancient family of the Counts of Canossa, born at Caprese, in Tuscany, 1475, died at Rome 1563; a distinguished Italian painter, sculptor, architect, and poet. He studied drawing under Domenico Ghirlandaio, and sculpture under Bertoldo at Florence, and having attracted the notice of Lorenzo de' Medici, was for several years an inmate of his household.

Having distinguished himself both in sculpture and painting, he was commissioned (together with Leonardo da Vinci) to decorate the Senate-hall at Florence with an historical design, but before it was finished, in 1505, he was induced by Pope Julius II. to settle in Rome.

Here he sculptured the monument of the pontiff (there are seven statues belonging to it) now in the church of

Michelangelo

St. Pietro in Vincoli; and painted the dome of the Sistine Chapel, his frescoes representing the creation and the principal events of sacred history. In 1530 he took a leading part in the defence of Florence against Charles V. Three years later he began his great picture in the Sistine Chapel, *The Last Judgment,* which occupied him eight years. His last considerable works in painting were two large pictures: *The Conversion of St. Paul* and *The Crucifixion of St. Peter* in the Pauline Chapel. His *Madonna and Saints* and *The Entombment of Christ* are in the National Gallery.

In sculpture he executed *The Descent of Christ from the Cross,* four figures in one piece of marble. His statue of *Bacchus* was thought by Raphael to possess equal perfection with the masterpieces of Phidias and Praxiteles. As late as 1546 he was obliged to undertake the continuation of the building of St. Peter's, and planned and built the dome, but he did not live long enough to see his plan finished, in which many alterations were made after his death. Besides this, he undertook the building of the Piazza del Campidoglio (Capitol), of the Farnese Palace, and of many other edifices.

His style in architecture is distinguished by grandeur and boldness, and in his ornaments the untamed character of his imagination frequently appears, preferring the uncommon to the simple and graceful. His poems, which he considered merely as pastimes, contain, likewise, convincing proofs of his great genius. The chief inspirer of his poetry was the pious and accomplished lady Vittoria Colonna, widow of the Marquis Pescara. His prose works consist of lectures and speeches.—Cf. J. A. Symonds, *The Life of Michelangelo.*

MICHELET (mēsh-lā), **Jules.** A French historian and miscellaneous writer, was born in Paris in 1798, died at Hyères in 1874. In 1821 he was called to the chair of history in the Collège Rollin, where he was also professor of ancient languages and of philosophy till 1826. After the Revolution of 1830 he was appointed chief of the historical section of the archives of France, and in 1838 became professor of history at the Collège de France. He lost all his offices at the *coup d'état* in 1851. His principal historical works are: *Histoire de France* (18 vols., 1833-66), *Histoire de la Révolution française* (7 vols., 1847-53), *Histoire romaine, Précis de l'histoire moderne, Précis de l'histoire de France jusqu'à la révolution,* and *Origines du droit français.*

MICHIGAN. The "peninsula state," a north-central state of the United States, divided by Lake Michigan into two separate peninsulas, one projecting eastwards from Wisconsin, and the other projecting northwards from Indiana and Ohio to their common meeting-point. Mackinac Strait. The state is drained by the Kalamazoo and other rivers, which are generally tapped for water-power. Lansing (pop. 1930, 78,397) is the state capital; but Detroit, fourth city of the United States (pop. 1930, 1,568,662) is the largest town. Others are Grand Rapids (1930, 168,592), Flint (1930, 156,492), and Saginaw (1930, 80,715). The inhabitants are mainly white, with some negroes and Asiatics. There is an Indian Reserve; area (1931), 191 acres; pop. 1080.

Production and Industry.—Michigan is largely an agricultural state, producing oats (34,101,000 bushels in 1932), corn, wheat, hay, potatoes, beans, and sugar-beets. Dairying (butter and cheese production) is extensive, and sheep-farming is progressive. The state ranks sixth in mineral wealth, iron ore and copper (Lake Superior region), silver, salt, clay, coal, graphite, gypsum, and a small quantity of petroleum being produced. Fisheries on the Great Lakes are valuable (25,000,000 lb. average annual catch). Among manufactures are machinery and automobiles (of which Michigan manufactures about 75 per cent. of the total American output); abattoirs and canneries are prominent.

Communications.—8020 miles of steam and 326 miles of electric railroad track traverse the state (1931), and St. Mary's Falls Ship Canal ("Soo" Canal) provides inter-lake communication.

Education.—Education is free and compulsory between seven and sixteen years of age. The University of Michigan (founded 1841) is located at Ann Arbor, the State Agricultural College (founded 1857) at Lansing, and at Houghton there is a College of Mines (founded 1886). Area, 57,980 sq. miles (500 sq. miles of water); additional areas of 16,653 sq. miles on Lake Superior, 12,982 sq. miles on Lake Michigan, 9925 sq. miles on Lake Heron, and 460 sq. miles on Lakes St. Clair and Erie are technically included in Michigan; pop. (1930), 4,842,325.

Government.—Michigan was settled in 1668 by French colonists of Marquette's Jesuit Mission (Sault de Ste Marie), and remained under French control until 1760-1, when it fell to the British. In 1805 it became a separate territory, and was admitted to the Union as a state, 26th Jan., 1837. The present Government comprises a Governor (elected for two years), a Senate (32 members elected by counties or county groups for two years), and a House of Representatives (100 members). The electoral districts are redistributed every ten years on a population basis. Two Senators and seventeen Representatives are sent to Congress. For local government there are eighty-three counties, each a corporate body with a Board of Supervisors in administrative power.—BIBLIOGRAPHY: L. H. Wood, *Physical, Industrial, and Sectional Geography of Michigan*; H. M. Dilla, *The Politics of Michigan.*

MICHIGAN, Lake. The second largest of the great lakes of North America. It is wholly within the United States. On the north-east it communicates with Lake Huron by the narrow strait of Mackinac. It is over 320 miles long, and on an average 60 miles broad; area, estimated at 22,500 sq. miles. The lake is 580 feet above sea-level; the greatest depth is 865 feet.

MICHIGAN CITY. A city of Indiana, United States, on the south shore of Lake Michigan. It has a large timber trade. Pop. 26,735.

MICHOACÁAN. A maritime state of Central Mexico, on the Pacific coast. It is mountainous (Patamban, 12,300 feet; Tancitaro, 12,661 feet), and is watered by the Rio de las Balsas and its tributary the Tepalcatepec. Cereals, sugar, coffee, and tobacco are raised; gold, coal, silver, and lead are mined. Morelia is the capital. Area, 22,621 sq. miles; pop. (1930), 1,014,020.

MICROCLINE. A potassium felspar of the same composition and general characters as orthoclase, but crystallizing in the triclinic system. A great deal of what was formerly regarded as orthoclase in granite is now known to be microcline.

MICRO-FARAD. The practical unit of electrical capacity, being the millionth part of a farad (q.v.).

MICROMETER. *See* TOLERANCE.

MICRONESIA. A division of Oceania (q.v.).

MICROPHONE. An instrument invented by Hughes in 1878, and employed in the electrical transmission of sound. It consists, in its original and simplest form, of a rod of carbon loosely pivoted between two blocks of carbon provided with sockets to hold the pointed ends of the rod. The carbon blocks are fixed on a sounding-board or box, and are connected to a small battery and a telephone receiver. When sounds are produced in the neighbourhood of the microphone, they set up vibrations which disturb the state of the electrical contacts at the ends of the rod. The movement of the rod causes changes of resistance of the microphone, and the current undergoes equally rapid variations in strength, with the result that the sound made near the microphone is reproduced more or less distinctly by the telephone. Hughes also discovered that the microphone was sensitive to electrical impulses, and detected electrical waves by means of his instrument up to a distance of about 500 yards. The imperfect-contact detector of electrical waves was reinvented by Branly under the name of the coherer. The microphone is employed as a transmitter of speech in the telephone service; in the Hunnings transmitter a quantity of granulated coke carbon is held loosely between two metal or carbon surfaces situated behind the mouthpiece. *See* WIRELESS TELEGRAPHY AND TELEPHONY.

MICROSCOPE. An optical instrument for producing and observing magnified images of small objects. In its simplest form it consists of a single convex lens, near which the object to be examined is placed (*see* LENS). The single lens is, however, subject to the defects of spherical and chromatic aberration, which cause respectively distortion and colouring of the image, but these errors were largely obviated by using two or three weaker lenses at a distance apart. Wollaston's *doublet* (1829) consisted of two plano-convex lenses, one three times as strong as the other, with their plane sides towards the object, and the weaker lens next the eye. Doublets and triplets were devised by Chevalier, Brücke, Herschel, and others, magnifications from 10 to 70 being obtained with these developments of the simple microscope. The *compound microscope* contains two lenses or systems of lenses, viz. an object-glass or *objective*, and an *eyepiece* or ocular. The object is placed on the *stage* at a distance from the objective greater than the focal length of the latter, and a real, inverted, and magnified image is formed in the focal plane of the eyepiece, which forms a virtual and magnified image of the first image. When a negative or Huygenian eyepiece is used, the rays proceeding from the objective converge to form an image behind the field lens of the eyepiece, which is adapted to focus converging rays. The improvements of the compound microscope date from the beginning of the nineteenth century. Chromatic aberration was reduced by placing in contact a diverging lens of flint glass and a converging lens of crown glass. Spherical aberration was also removed by the correct relative placing of the achromatic elements of the objective according to principles given by Lister (1830). *Aplanatic* objectives were thus realized, i.e. objectives which bring all the rays to one focus. Later, much progress was made by improvements in the manufacture of glass. In the earlier forms of achromatic combination referred to, it was only possible with two lenses to achromatize two colours, owing to the different dispersive powers of flint and crown glass. But Abbe of Jena, in conjunction with Schott and Zeiss, produced a series of new varieties of glass from which it was possible to form combinations of lenses which gave images almost entirely free from colour. The new objectives made from these glasses were termed *apochromatic* objectives. The eyepiece generally supplied with a microscope is of the Huygenian type, as it is nearly free from spherical and chromatic error. When measurements of an object are to be made, a Ramsden eyepiece is used with a fine scale in its focal plane. With high magnifications, optical improvement is obtained by using the method of *oil immersion*. A drop of cedar oil is placed between the coverglass of the slide and the lower plane surface of the objective, thus giving an optically homogeneous medium between object and objective. The oil has the same refractive index as the glass, and its use results in an increase of the effective aperture of the objective; the method is termed one of homogeneous immersion. The magnifications employed vary from 12 to 1200. The tendency in recent years is to concentrate on obtaining as perfect an image as possible with the object-glass, and to leave a greater share of the magnification to be provided by the eyepiece. To secure such perfect images it must be possible to bring the objective exceedingly close to the object, so as to obtain high effective aperture. The homogeneous immersion system secures this very efficiently. For this reason the old $\frac{1}{60}$-inch air objective has given place to the $\frac{1}{12}$-inch oil-immersion lens, with better results and a great reduction in price.—BIBLIOGRAPHY: W. B. Carpenter, *The Microscope*; E. J. Spitta, *Microscopy*.

MICROSPORE. *See* HETEROSPORY.

MIDAS. In Greek mythology, the son of Gordius and Cybele, and King of Phrygia, whose request that whatsoever he touched should turn to gold was granted by the god Dionysus (Bacchus). In this way even his food became gold, and it was not until he had bathed in the Pactolus that the fatal gift was transferred to the river.

MIDDELBURG. A town of the Netherlands, capital of the province of Zeeland, near the middle of the Island of Walcheren. It is an ancient place, and was taken by the Dutch from the Spaniards in 1574. Pop. 18,389.

MIDDELBURG. A town of Cape Province, South Africa, 165 miles north of Port Elizabeth. It is an agricultural centre. Pop. 5016 (2178 white).

MIDDLE AGES. The term used sometimes for the whole period between the fall of the Roman Empire in the west (for which A.D. 476 is usually taken as a convenient date) and the Renaissance of the end of the fifteenth century, and sometimes for the later portion of that period, the years from the end of the fifth to about the middle of the tenth century being described as the Dark Ages. An outline of the political history of both the Dark Ages and the Middle Ages (in the narrower sense) will be found under *History*. The most notable event in the social history of the Dark Ages was the rise of the Empire of Charles the Great (768-814), which put an end to a long era of barbaric warfare, and introduced new ideals of government and civilization. The break-up of the Carolingian Empire in the ninth century was followed by a reversion to barbarism. Weak kings failed to maintain the administrative machinery created by Charles the Great, the lawless rule of greedy and merciless nobles was the source of widespread oppression and misery, the Church was corrupt and degenerate, and fresh hordes of barbarian invaders—Norsemen in the north-west of Europe, Saracens in the south, Slavs and Magyars in Central Europe—attacked what had been the Empire. The barbarians were ultimately defeated, but their defeat was accomplished by the feudal nobility which was itself the greatest obstacle to internal good government, and it was followed by the establishment of the feudal system all over Europe. Society between the tenth and the twelfth century came to be based on a system of land tenure, largely military in origin, which profoundly influenced every department of administrative life, and involved the complete dependence of the lower classes of the community upon the owners of the lands which they held, or on which they worked as serfs. Coincidently with this development there came the division of Europe into separate states, and, as the conception of the state progressed, each country experienced a struggle between the central power and the feudal barons, whose aim was decentralization or anarchy. The conflict went on through the Middle Ages, and the victory of the principle of centralization was not complete at their close, for international warfare, the struggle between the Papacy and the Empire, and the Crusades all tended to preserve the power of barons who commanded their own fighting forces. In England the monarchy was powerful enough to bring the barons into subjection long before a similar result was attained in France, while in Germany feudalism crystallized into a series of small dominions uncontrolled by any central power. The growth of commerce led to the establishment of independent municipal states, the most important of which were the Free Towns of the Empire and the cities of the north of Italy. Serfdom survived the Middle Ages alike in England, France, and Germany, though it had disappeared in Scotland.

In religious history the period witnessed many important movements. At the beginning of the Dark Ages only a small portion of Europe had been converted to Christianity, and the process of conversion forms a large part of the history of the time. It was completed by the expansion of German influence in the east of Europe in the eleventh and twelfth centuries. Contemporaneously with the growth of Christianity, the Dark Ages witnessed the rise of Islam, which is dated from the flight of Mahomet to Medina in A.D. 622, after which Mahommedanism spread with amazing rapidity. In the Christian Church there was a succession of religious revivals, beginning with the reformation of monastic life by St. Benedict in the early sixth century, which gave an immense impetus to the foundation of monasteries. These deeply affected not only religious but also social and economic life by the provision which they made for the poor and by their enterprise in agriculture and even in commerce. There was another revival in the tenth century, associated with the monastery of Cluny (near Macon, in Burgundy), and in the eleventh century the Cluniac movement led to a general Reformation in the Church all over Europe, accompanied by an advance in the power of the Papacy. A third revival dates from the thirteenth century, when St. Francis of Assisi and St. Dominic founded orders of mendicant friars whose aim was not contemplative life in monastic seclusion, but the care of the sick and the preaching of the Gospel to the poor. The appearance of the friars in the thirteenth century gave to conservative religious opinion much the same shock as the Wesleyan preachers did in the eighteenth or the Salvation Army in the nineteenth century. The influence of the Church decreased towards the end of the Middle Ages, owing to the degeneration of the monastic orders and of the friars, and also through a series of schisms in the Papacy and its subordination to French policy during the residence of the Popes at Avignon (known as the "Babylonish Captivity," 1305-78). The Great Schism began in 1378, and was closed by the Council of Constance in 1415.

The intellectual life of the Middle Ages was marked by two great revivals of learning. The first of these was connected with the court of Charles the Great, who, like Alfred of England about a century later, was a patron of scholars, whom he gathered round him and to whose discussions he listened. The second was the classical renaissance in the twelfth century, with which is connected the rise of European universities. Intellectual life is also illustrated by a large number of mediæval poems in all languages, by treatises on the problems of religion and philosophy, and by advances in ecclesiastical and domestic architecture, in the methods and aims of commerce, and in the art of war. Archery was brought to perfection by the English, and gunpowder was invented in the early fourteenth century, and was freely used in warfare before the end of the Middle Ages. There was also a considerable development in shipbuilding (especially in the size of vessels), and in the use of water-ways for internal communications. Canals were introduced in Holland and Belgium in the twelfth century, and rivers, as means of communication, were much more important than the ill-made tracks which served as roads. Above all, the Middle Ages were a great period in the history of painting. Perhaps the best general characterization of Europe in the later Middle Ages is that given by the late Professor York Powell: "A knot of states whose commerce, regulated by self-governing guilds, flowed westward from the great Italian trading republics, through the fairs of France and Germany, to the marts of Flanders and the ports of England and Gascony . . . and the Baltic. Europe was a set of kingdoms governed by curious half-feudal, half-free, half-despotic constitutions, in which local feelings were everywhere strong, but centralization everywhere welcome. . . . In these states dwelt a succession of generations who invented no single tool, implement, or art, who with rarest exceptions were wholly ignorant of the sciences of the past, and disliked the very dreams of the sciences that were to come, but who could . . . show, amid squalor, dirt, and misery, a true and unfailing taste in every article of daily life. A state of society ignorant, cruel, and superstitious . . . but withal a state of society in which men were earnest, dutiful, and hardworking, and which could display such noble types of character as the untiring and unselfish Francis, the friend of the poor and helpless, . . . and the saintly King Louis."—BIBLIOGRAPHY: Sir C. W. C. Oman, *The Dark Ages*; T. F. Tout, *The Empire and the Papacy*; *Cambridge Mediæval History*.

MIDDLE CONGO. A colony of French Equatorial Africa. The area is 172,411 sq. miles; and the population (1931), 661,909.

MIDDLESBROUGH. A river-port, municipal and county borough of England, on the Tees and in the North Riding of Yorkshire. A transporter bridge crosses the river here. It is served by the London and North Eastern Railway. There are numerous blast-furnaces and rolling-mills, foundries, engineering works and shipyards. Salt is extensively worked. There is an extensive harbour. The borough was incorporated in 1853, and returns two members. Pop. (1931), 138,489.

MIDDLESEX. The metropolitan county of England, formerly containing the greater portion of London (now a county by itself); area, 148,691 acres. Brentford is the county town. The district is almost entirely covered with urban districts and towns, all suburbs of London. Pop. (1911), 1,126,694; (1931), 1,638,728.

MIDDLETON, Thomas. English dramatist, was born about 1570, and died in 1627. Very little is known about his life. He was City Chronologer from 1620 until his death, when he was succeeded by Ben Jonson, who in 1618 had mentioned him to Drummond of Hawthornden as "a base fellow." This is almost all that is known about him. He frequently collaborated with other dramatists, especially with Rowley and Dekker. His earliest printed play was *Blurt, Master Constable* (1602), a light comedy. Two interesting prose tracts, *Father Hubbard's Tale* and *The Black Book*, appeared in 1604. Amongst Middleton's plays may be mentioned the following: *The Phœnix*; *Michaelmas Term* (1607); *A Trick to catch the Old One* (1607); *The Family of Love*, a weak satire on the Puritans (1608); *Your Five Gallants*; *A Mad World, my Masters*; *The Roaring Girl* (written with Dekker, 1611); *A Chaste Maid in Cheapside*; *The Witch*; *The Mayor* of *Quinborough*; *The Changeling*; *The Spanish Gipsy*; and *A Game at Chesse.* It is unlikely that Middleton wrote a highly incompetent paraphrase of *The Wisdom of Solomon. Microcynicon, Six Snarling Satires* (1599) may be his work. Middleton wrote with much fluency, and his plays were written under the uncomfortable necessity of having to get them finished by a fixed date. Yet much of his work is memorable and some supremely good. *The Changeling* is perhaps his masterpiece, and in one scene (the conversation between De Flores and Beatrice after the murder of Alonzo) he surpasses Webster and Tourneur, and is momentarily on a level with Shakespeare. *The Witch* is interesting on account of its resemblances to *Macbeth*, which was probably written earlier; some of the songs

Thomas Middleton

from Middleton's play were interpolated into *Macbeth* by the players. *A Game at Chesse* is an altogether excellent play, and is perhaps the most Aristophanic comedy in English. Under the thin disguise of pieces and pawns, the characters of the play were those English and Spanish personages who were involved in the matter of the Spanish marriage. Gondomar, the Spanish Ambassador, who was satirized as the Black Knight, got a stop put to this play after a run of nine days. The play was an instant success, and in spite of its short run it brought in £1500, an immense sum for those days. Middleton was fined and perhaps also imprisoned. In this play, which is a criticism not of city manners and customs, but of diplomacy and international politics, Middleton reaches a height to which he never before attained in comedy.—BIBLIOGRAPHY: A. C. Swinburne, *The Age of Shakespeare*; P. G. Wiggin, *An Enquiry into the Authorship of the Middleton-Rowley Plays*; Sir A. W. Ward, *History of English Dramatic Literature.*

MIDDLETON. A borough of England, Lancashire, served by the L.M. & S. Railway. Extensive cotton, silk, engineering, and chemical works give employment. Pop. (1931), 29,189.

MIDGE. The ordinary English name given to numerous minute species of flies, resembling the common gnat, but constituting a special family (Chironomidæ). The eggs are deposited in water, where they undergo metamorphosis.

MIDIANITES. An Arabian tribe, represented in the Old Testament as the descendants of Midian, son of Abraham by Keturah (Gen. xxv. 2), and described as engaged at an early period in a commerce with Egypt. They dwelt in the land of Moab (Arabia Petræa), to the south-east of Canaan.

MIDLOTHIAN. *See* EDINBURGH, COUNTY OF.

MIDNAPUR. An administrative district and town of Bengal, forming the most southern part of the Bardwán division, bounded on the east by the River Hugli, and with an area of 5055 sq. miles. Pop. (district), 2,822,000; (town), 28,965.

MIDRASH. The general name given among the Jews to the exposition of the hidden meaning of the Scriptures. It includes any and every ancient exposition on the law, psalms, and prophets. The *Midrash* is divided into the *Halacha*, or the authoritative law laid down in the *Talmud*; and the *Haggada*, or poetical homiletics on the whole body of the Old Testament. The term midrash is generally applied to the latter branch of rabbinical literature.

MIDSHIPMAN. A junior officer in the Royal Navy, ranking between a cadet and a sub-lieutenant. The midshipman's time is principally occupied in receiving instruction, both literary and professional, and his professional duties are continued as a sub-lieutenant. Midshipmen carry a dirk instead of a sword, wear white tabs on the jacket lapel, and mess in the gun-room. The title is derived from their former quarters, amidships on the lower deck.

MIDSUMMER DAY. The feast-day of the nativity of St. John the Baptist, and is commonly reckoned the 24th of June. On midsummer eve, or the eve of the Feast of St. John, it was the custom in former times to kindle fires (called St. John's fires) upon hills in celebration of the summer solstice. It is also the second quarter-day in England for the payment of rent.

MIDWIFERY. *See* OBSTETRICS.

MIGNONETTE (min'yon-et ; *Resēda odorātā*). A well-known fragrant annual plant of the nat. ord. Resedaceæ, a native of North Africa. It is largely cultivated in gardens, also in flower-pots, in apartments, and in the boxes which are placed outside windows. There is also a subbiennial variety, called *tree mignonette*. Weld or dyers' weed, a native of Britain, belongs to the same genus.

MIGRATION OF ANIMALS. The phenomenon of certain animals moving, either periodically or at irregular times and seasons, from one locality or region to another, sometimes far distant. Migration has been observed in mammals, birds, fishes, and insects, but it probably occurs in other groups of the animal world, the observation of which is less easy than that of the higher forms. The buffaloes or bisons of North America used to migrate in herds between Canada and Mexico. Many fishes (for example, salmon, lampreys, etc.) make periodical journeys from the sea towards freshwater streams and rivers for the purpose of depositing their eggs ; eels descend rivers to breed in the deep sea, from which the young eels (elvers) travel back. The migratory habits of locusts, and those of certain species of ants, etc., exemplify migration among insects ; but amongst the birds we meet with the best-marked instances of migration. With sea-birds (for example, puffins) the day of arrival or that on which they appear in certain localities may be prognosticated with perfect safety ; and similarly, the day of departure appears in some birds (for example, swifts) to be almost as accurately timed. Storks have been known to return regularly to their old nests, and the same has been observed of swallows. The mode in which birds migrate varies greatly even in the same species of bird. The swallows migrate in bodies comprising vast numbers, and so also do cranes, wild ducks, geese, and many other forms. The migratory flight is generally made against the wind ; but certain species of birds, as quails for instance, appear to wait for favouring winds, and to delay their flight by resting on islands when the wind is unfavourable. Regarding the causes of migration, science cannot at present definitely pronounce. Probably a combination of causes, or different causes in different cases, as scarcity or plenty of food-supply, the powerful influences of temperature, and the influence of the breeding-season, may contribute to the migratory "instinct." It has been further suggested by A. R. Wallace that this migratory habit or instinct has gradually been acquired since a time when the breeding- and feeding-grounds of the animals were coincident, these having been gradually separated by climatic and geological changes.

MIL'AN (It. *Milano*). An inland province of Lombardy, Northern Italy. It is mainly a canal-irrigated plain, and produces rice, flax, corn, wine, oil, and mulberry trees (for silk-worms). Dairying (production of butter and cheese) is progressive. Milan is the capital. Area, 1060 sq. miles ; pop. (1931), 2,001,875.

MILAN (It. *Milano* ; Lat. *Mediolānum*). Capital city of Milan, Lombardy, and the second city of Italy, on the Olona, in the middle of the

Milan
Basilica of San Ambrogio

Lombard Plain between the Adda and Ticino. Among the public edifices the first place belongs to the Duomo or cathedral, dedicated to the Virgin, a magnificent structure, inferior only in size to St. Peter's at Rome and the cathedral of Seville. In its present form it was begun in 1387, and was finished between 1805 and 1815 by order of Napoleon. Among other buildings are the Palazzo di Brera or Delle Scienze, Lettere ed Arte, containing the picture-gallery and the library of the academy (300,000 vols.) ; and the Ambrosian Library, the earliest, and still one of the most valuable public libraries in Europe. There is also a valuable museum of natural history, a conservatory of music, a military college, and a theological seminary. The Galleria Vittoria Emanuele, a covered street, connects the Piazza del Duomo with the Piazza of La Scala Theatre. The chief theatre is La Scala (*Teatro della Scala*), accommodating 3600 spectators. The manufactures include silks, cottons, lace, carpets, hats, earthenware, machinery and metal goods, and jewellery.

The first distinct notice of Milan occurs in 221 B.C., when it was subdued by the Romans. In the third century after Christ it ranked next to Rome. It became a republic in 1101, and, having refused to submit to the Emperor Frederick I., it was destroyed by him in 1162. It was soon rebuilt, but long continued to be torn by internal factions, headed by the leading nobility, among whom the Visconti and the Sforzas were the most prominent. It afterwards belonged with Lombardy to Austria, until 1859, when by the Peace of Villafranca Lombardy was ceded to Piedmont and incorporated in Italy. Pop. (1931), 992,036.—Cf. Ella Noyes, *Story of Milan*.

MILAZZO (mi-låt′zō). A seaport of Messina, Sicily, where Garibaldi defeated the Neapolitan troops in his Sicilian campaign of 1860. Pop. 16,540.

MILDEW. A name given to various minute Fungi, but properly pertaining only to the parasitic Erysiphales and Peronosporinea (q.v.).

MILE. A measure of length or distance, used in almost all countries of Europe. The English statute mile contains 8 furlongs, each 40 poles or perches, of 5½ yards. The statute mile is therefore 1760 yards, or 5280 feet. It is also 80 surveying chains, of 22 yards each. The square mile is 6400 square chains, or 640 acres. The Roman mile was about 1620 English yards. The ancient Scottish mile was 1984 yards = 1·127 English miles; the Irish mile, 2240 yards = 1·273 English miles. The geographical or nautical mile is the sixtieth part of a degree of latitude, or 6080 feet.

MILE′TUS. An ancient city of Ionia, Asia Minor, situated near the mouth of the Meander, one of the chief Greek cities of Asia Minor, birthplace of Thales, Anaximander, Anaximenes, and Aspasia. It had upwards of seventy-five colonies, most of which were on the coasts of the Euxine. The most flourishing period was before its destruction by the Persians, 494 B.C., though it again rose to be a place of some importance.

MILFOIL, or **YARROW.** The common name of *Achillea millefolium*, nat. ord. Compositæ, a plant which grows commonly on banks, by roadsides, and on dry pastures. It has numerous very finely divided leaves, and corymbs of small, white or sometimes rose-coloured flowers.

MILFORD, or **MILFORD HAVEN.** A seaport and urban district of Pembrokeshire, Wales, on the north shore of the inlet called Milford Haven; served by the Great Western Railway. There are docks capable of accommodating the largest vessels, and trade is with Ireland principally. Milford Haven, an opening of the Atlantic Ocean, is one of the finest natural harbours in Britain. Pop. (1931), 10,116.

MILITARY DISCIPLINE. Military discipline—and in this connection the word military is used in its broader sense to include all armed forces of the Crown—demands respect for the authority which men recognize when taking service under the State; it demands instant and exact obedience to all orders given by that authority; it requires a mode of life according to certain rules made for the greatest good of the greatest number; and it assumes as an axiom the obvious fact that in any corporate body of men banded together for a definite purpose there must be one head whose word is law and must be obeyed. With regard to the armed forces of Great Britain and Ulster, this head is the king, whose authority, though not exercised directly and constitutionally delegated to the responsible minister of the Crown, descends through officers of various grades holding His Majesty's commission, and through these officers to other subordinates not holding commissions, i.e. non-commissioned officers. This gives the chain of command, in which each link owes obedience to the one above it, and exerts its authority according to well-defined rules over the ones below. In addition to this principle, military discipline takes to itself the power of punishment provided by the Army Act (*see* MILITARY LAW), and calls to its aid the sentiment known as *esprit de corps*.

Discipline, like faith, is the better for outward and visible signs, and it is on the necessity for these that untrained opinion is likely to differ. Take as an example the question of "saluting," than which no outward and visible sign has ever caused more heart-burning. Every free and independent modern man is inclined to argue: "Why should I salute (and by so doing own myself inferior) another who is merely a man like myself, though he may possibly wear a more expensive uniform?" It is in this last word, uniform, that the answer to the question is to be found; it is the uniform which is saluted, or, more correctly, the king's commission borne by the wearer of the uniform, and not the individual man. The act exemplifies subjection to control, and is the sign of that respect for authority which we all admit. In discussing this question it is well to remember the early days of the Russian Revolution, when one of the first changes made was the abolition of all saluting in the army; this led by natural stages to the lessening of respect for authority, the final disappearance of all discipline, and—chaos.

Discipline to be effective must be strict and exact, though it need not be repressive; there can be no two ways of doing things, and no "to-morrow"; obedience must be instant and without argument, and must be given cheerfully in the firm conviction that the particular order in question is either directly or indirectly for the general good. Our form of discipline, whatever may be the case in other countries, is not based on fear; rather is it founded on expediency and enforced with sympathy and the human touch, the power of punishment being kept in the background for use if required. Normally we depend very largely for our discipline on an appreciation of the facts, and on a good understanding between officers and men. It is an unwritten law in the services that one of an officer's first duties is to his men; he is their leader in time of emergency; and how can he better qualify himself for their leadership than by knowing his men, by watching over their comforts and little privileges, and by helping them in their troubles? For such an officer men will do anything, and there will be small necessity to call on the powers given by the Army Act to maintain discipline. Example among the officers and the feeling of *esprit de corps* among all ranks will go further towards building up a satisfactory state of discipline in a unit than any amount of punishment. A very fair idea of the discipline of a given corps may be obtained by watching the behaviour of a junior non-commissioned officer marching off a small party of men when no officer is present. If every movement is slack, and the whole performance is a "go-as-you-please" affair, then it is ten chances to one that the discipline of that corps is unsatisfactory. If, on the other hand, orders are given and the necessary movements performed in exactly the same manner as they would be on a parade of the battalion, then it may safely be concluded that the discipline is of the best. *See* ARMY; DRILL; MILITARY LAW.

MILITARY LAW. That form of the statute law of England to which all officers and soldiers are amenable both in peace and war. It is administered by military courts, which have no jurisdiction whatever over any person who is not either an officer or a soldier. There is one exception to this general rule, i.e. in time of war any civilians who may accompany the army become, in virtue of a pass issued to them by the commander-in-chief, subject to military law, either as officers or soldiers, during the period they remain with the army (Army Act, sec. 175–6). Broadly speaking, the following are subject to military law: officers, both regular, militia, and territorial, and regular soldiers at all times; militia and territorial soldiers when embodied or called out for training. An individual becomes subject to military law immediately he enters into military service, but he does not in consequence divest himself of his obligation as a citizen to obey the civil law. During his service he remains amenable to both codes, and can be tried and punished for an offence against ordinary criminal law as if he were not a soldier. English military law is contained in the Army Act, Rules of Procedure, and King's Regulations.

MILITIA. The old constitutional military force of England, now, after a period of oblivion under the name of the Special Reserve, once more resuscitated under its old title. The militia is the lineal descendant, through the Train Bands of the seventeenth century, of the old feudal and general levy of the kingdom, and became generally known under that designation about the time of the Restoration. In 1660 the feudal levy or knight service (*see* ARMY) was finally abolished, but the general levy, in which was included the Train Bands, was taken in hand and, in the course of the next few years, reorganized on a county basis, while retaining the principle of obligatory service customary with the general levy. As to the method of raising, in course of time, and after various changes had been made, it became much as follows: the county authorities and parishes were informed of the number or quota required from them; each authority was then at liberty to raise its quota in any way considered suitable, i.e. either by ballot or by offering bounties for volunteers. In the event of the number obtained falling short of the requirements, the defaulting authority was fined; substitutes for those balloted were allowed, and the age limit was between eighteen and fifty.

In the course of years it became the custom to depend less on the ballot than on voluntary enlistment, and since 1852 this has been the principle invariably followed, though the power to ballot was retained for use in emergency.

By the Reserve Forces Act, 1907, power was taken by the king in council to transfer any specified number of battalions of existing militia to the Special Reserve; such transferred battalions henceforward became the third (or subsequent number) battalions of the county regiments, under the general heading of "Regular and Special Reserve Battalions."

MILK. The product of the mammary gland found in all female mammals. Cows' milk is most generally used in Europe and North America for human consumption. It has a specific gravity ranging between 1·028 and 1·034 (average 1·032), and is produced by the cow for a period of forty-two weeks, or about three hundred days, after parturition. This period is technically known as a lactation. The quality of milk is dependent entirely upon the condition, quality, and activity of the milk-producing organs, and upon the nature of the blood, from which it is derived by a process involving the building up and breaking down of minute cells contained within the udder. Many variants affect composition, and it has been found that even vitamines may be absent if cows are fed on a diet from which they are either absent or present in insufficient quantity. Quantity is dependent upon mammary development and the pedigree of the animal. The following table is the result of the analysis of a great many samples, and may be accepted as representative of the great bulk of all cow's milk:

Fat	3·75	per cent.
Casein	3·00	"
Albumen	0·40	"
Lactose	4·75	"
Ash	0·75	"
Water	87·35	"

The fat is the most variable constituent, and exists in milk as an emulsion in the form of tiny globules averaging $\frac{1}{2500}$ inch in diameter. It consists of glycerol in combination with certain fatty acids. Lactose is second in order of variability. It is the milk-sugar of commerce, and is technically known as $C_{12}H_{22}O_{11}$. Lactose exists in milk in solution. It is readily attacked by the lactic bacteria, which decompose it with formation of lactic acid (*see* STARTER). Casein and ash are practically constant, and the albumen varies only in *colostrum*, the first milk yielded after calving, which may contain as high as 15 per cent., and is unfit for human consumption either raw or as butter or cheese.

Legal Standards.—In Great Britain whole milk must contain not less than 3 per cent. butter-fat, and not less than 8·5 per cent. solids-non-fat. Skim, or separated milk, must contain not less than 8·7 per cent. total solids. Grade "A" milk is produced from tuberculin-tested, disease-free cows, specially milked. The milk is refrigerated and sold in hermetically sealed bottles. It must conform to certain bacteriological standards, and a high price may be demanded for it. Few dairies possess grade "A" licences in Great Britain. In Great Britain there is no standard of bacterial or sedimentary content, although such laws have been in existence in the United States for some considerable time.

Cream is that portion of milk which rises to the surface and forms a clearly defined layer when milk is set (allowed to stand). Commercially it is obtained by means of the cream separator (q.v.), which yields cream of any desired consistency by a slight alteration of the regulating screw. In America there are cream standards; in Britain there are none. The specific gravity of cream varies as the percentage of fat it contains: 5 per cent. cream = 1·031 approximately; but 40 per cent. cream has a specific gravity of less than ·94.

Bacteria is fully dealt with under PASTEURIZATION and STARTER. **Fermented Milks** are treated under YOGHURT. *See* TESTING OF MILK; SEPARATED MILK; RENNET; LACTOMETER; WESTPHAL BALANCE; KOUMISS.—BIBLIOGRAPHY.: R. H. Leitch, *Buttermaking on the Farm*; G. S. Thomson, *British and Colonial Dairying*; H. Droop Richmond, *Dairy Chemistry*; W. A. Stocking, *Manual of Milk Products*; H. A. Macewen, *The Milk Supply*; *Standard Cyclopædia of Agriculture* (Gresham Publishing Company).

MILK-FEVER. At one time this condition was supposed to occur in women after childbirth, when the milk was being secreted in the breasts. It is now recognized that the symptoms of feverishness, when they do arise at such a time, are due to the absorption of infective material in some part of the female genital tract directly following parturition. The condition requires treatment, and should never be looked upon as a natural process.

MILKING-MACHINES. Although the idea of a mechanical apparatus to facilitate the milking of cows was discussed as far back as 1819, it is only within comparatively recent years that an efficient and economical milking-machine has been evolved, chiefly through the genius and untiring effort of two Scotsmen, a dairyman named Robert Kennedy, and an engineer named Lawrence, who subsequently gave their conjoined names to the *Lawrence-Kennedy Milking-machine.* They were followed by Messrs. Wallace of Castle-Douglas (about 1907), who adopted the "L.-K." principle, but applied miniature pulsating mechanism to the base of each teat-cup. At the present day there are many types of machine on the market, some borne by the cow and the others resting upon the ground, the cow carrying the teat-cups only, but the general principles are identical in all cases.

The Lawrence-Kennedy-Wallace idea was to construct a teat-cup capable of imitating closely the action of the suckling calf, and a system has been evolved whereby the teat is pressed by a rubber pad, a little suction being exerted,[1] and the milk is drawn by a vacuum into the milk-pail.

General Principles.—A modern milking installation, consists essentially of a vacuum-producing apparatus, a double-action pump actuated by a 2- to 3-h.p. engine, and connected to a 50-gallon, galvanised-iron, vacuum storage-tank. From the tank a system of piping runs through the byre, carrying taps above each stall. These taps are in turn connected by means of rubber tubing with the milk receptacles, so that, when the tap is turned on, the vacuum is transferred to the interior of the receptacle. From each can, or receptacle, lengths of rubber tubing end in the teat-cups, of which there may be two sets to a can, so that two cows may be milked simultaneously. Inspection glasses are fitted to the tubing, and on a cessation of the milk-flow from any cause, natural or accidental, this may be observed by the operator, who takes action accordingly. The vacuum in each set of teat-cups is regulated by an inlet air-valve, and a gauge is placed in the byre to indicate the degree of vacuum in the tubes as a whole. The efficiency of any machine, everything else being equal, depends almost wholly upon the pulsator and on the skill of the operator.

Machine Milking.—It has been found that most cows take kindly to good milking-machines, and soon become familiar with the rhythmical beating of the pulsator; but those trained from their first calving, and accustomed to little else but mechanical milking, invariably show better results than animals brought to the machine after, say, a third or fourth calving. On the introduction of the "L.-K." machine it was expected that, by drawing the milk directly from the cow's teat to closed, sterilized milk-cans, without allowing it to come in contact with the air or exposing it to other forms of contamination, a very pure milk should be produced, but a bacteriological count has proved a disappointment. Milking by machine does not by any means eliminate the personal element, and all operators must be trained, intelligent, experienced, and scrupulously clean both in person and in habits.

The air of every cow-shed invariably teems with bacteria (micro-organisms) of useful and, more frequently, of dangerous types. Care must therefore be taken in cleaning the machine, and teat-cups must not be allowed to fall from the teats during milking (a quite frequent occurrence), permitting dust and organisms from the floor and surroundings to be sucked into the milk-pail.

Good hand-milking and expert machine-milking are about equal as regards efficiency, but the latter is preferable in extreme cases, such as obtained during the European War, when wages were prohibitive and labour was exceedingly scarce. —BIBLIOGRAPHY: *Standard Cyclopædia of Agriculture* (Gresham Publishing Company); N. A. Macewen, *The Milk Supply.*

MILKWORT. A British plant, *Polygăla vulgāris*, ord. Polygalaceæ, abounding in a milky juice, and believed by the ignorant to promote the flow of milk in cows.

MILL, James. Born at Logie Pert, Forfarshire, Scotland, 6th April, 1773, died 23rd June, 1836. He was educated at the grammar-school of Montrose and the University of

1 Continuous suction causes a congestion in the udder of the cow, and a consequent decrease in productivity, etc., so that an *intermittent suction* is now provided by means of the *pulsator.*

Edinburgh; accompanied Sir John Stuart to London and became tutor in his family; edited the *Literary Journal*, and contributed articles to the *Edinburgh*, *British*, *Eclectic*, and *Monthly Reviews*; began his *History of British India* in 1806, and published it in 1817-18. In consequence of the knowledge which his researches had given him of Indian affairs, he was appointed assistant-examiner of correspondence by the East India Company, and soon afterwards became chief-examiner. He was a frequent contributor to the *Westminster Review*; wrote articles on social and political subjects for the *Encyclopædia Britannica*; and published a treatise on the *Elements of Political Economy* (1821-22), and an *Analysis of the Phenomena of the Human Mind* (1829). In philosophy Mill was a follower of the school of Hobbes and Bentham.

MILL, John Stuart. Son of James Mill, was born in London 1806, died at Avignon 1873. He was trained under the immediate influence of his father. His fifteenth year was spent in France; on his return he studied law for a time, and in 1823 he obtained a clerkship in the East India House, remaining in the Company's employment till it was supplanted by the Crown in 1858. In 1823 the *Westminster Review* was begun by the followers of Bentham, and young Mill was one of its earliest contributors, while from 1835 to 1840 he was its principal conductor. In his twenty-first year he edited Bentham's work *On Evidence.* In 1843 appeared the first of his two chief works, *A System of Logic, Ratiocinative and Inductive*, the second being *Principles of Political Economy* (1848). To these he afterwards added his work *On Liberty* (1859), *Thoughts on Parliamentary Reform* (1861), *Utilitarianism* (1862), the *Examination of Sir William Hamilton's Philosophy*, and a *Study of Auguste Comte and Positivism* (1865). In this last year he was returned to Parliament as member for Westminster, where he advocated a measure to admit women to the suffrage, and took part in the Reform Bill debates. At the election of 1868 he was defeated and retired to Avignon. Besides the works already mentioned, he published *Considerations on Representative Government* (1861), *The Subjection of Women* (1869), and *The Irish Land Question* (1870). His *Autobiography* was published in 1873, and the three essays, *Nature, The Unity of Religion*, and *Theism*, in 1874. Mill's works on logic and political economy are standard textbooks. In the former he placed the system of inductive logic on a firm basis. As a politician Mill belonged to the school of philosophical radicals, adopting a combination of democratic and conservative ideas. As an economist he was an exponent of the principles of the Utilitarian school, but he was not an unquestioning adherent of this doctrine.—BIBLIOGRAPHY: W. L. Courtney, *Life of J. S. Mill*; C. Douglas, *John Stuart Mill: a Study of his Philosophy*; A. S. Pringle-Pattison, *English Philosophers and Schools of Philosophy.*

MILLAIS (mil'ās), **Sir John Everett, Bart., R.A.** Born at Southampton 1829, died in London 1896. He exhibited his first picture, *Pizarro*

Sir John Everett Millais, Bart., R.A.

seizing the Inca of Peru, in 1846; and received the gold medal for an historical painting, *The Tribe of Benjamin seizing the Daughters of Shiloh*, in 1848. In his earlier days he was a leader of the Pre-Raphaelite school, but on attaining maturity in art he abandoned the peculiarities for which that school was noted. As the result of this new departure Millais painted such pictures as *Ferdinand lured by Ariel*, *Mariana in the Moated Grange*, *The Huguenot Lovers*, *The Black Brunswicker*, and *Ophelia*, while its influence was also apparent in his landscapes of *Chill October* and *The Fringe of the Moor.* Among his later works are: *The North-West Passage*, *The Princes in the Tower*, *Effie Deans*, *Cinderella*, and *Mercy—St. Bartholomew's Day*, 1572. In portraiture he holds the foremost rank, and he painted many of the most distinguished men of the day. He was made a baronet in 1885. In Jan., 1896, he was elected P.R.A., but died the following August. Many of his works are well known by engravings.—Cf. J. E. Reid, *Sir J. E. Millais.*

MILLAU (ancient **Æmilianum**). A town of Southern France, department of Aveyron, on the Tarn. It is in a coal-producing area, and manufactures gloves and wool. In mediæval times Millau was a fortress town. The fortifications were destroyed by Richelieu (1620).

MILLEN'NIUM (Lat. *mille*, thousand, and *annus*, year), a period of one thousand years. The term is applied to the reign of peace preceding the Last Judgment, and supposed to last one thousand years. The Millennarians believe that at the end of time Christ will return, gather together the just, resuscitate the dead saints, and establish His glorious earthly kingdom. This fervent expectation of and belief in an earthly Messianic kingdom, a sort of interregnum preceding the Last Judgment, is mentioned in the apocalyptic books of Enoch, Baruch, and 2 Esdras. Nowhere, however, is the duration fixed at one thousand years. In the New Testament the doctrine of the Millennium is clearly taught in Rev. xx., where it is said that Satan would be put in chains, and the martyrs of faith, raised from the dead, would participate in the glorious reign of Christ. Under the influence of Alexandrinian philosophy the belief was abandoned for some time, but was again revived during the Reformation and cherished by the Anabaptists. Cromwell's Fifth Monarchy men were all Millennarians, and at present millennial hopes are entertained by several religious sects, and the doctrine has many adherents in this country and in the United States.

MILLEPEDE, or **MILLIPEDE** (Lat. *mille*, a thousand; *pes, pedis*, a foot), a name common to animals resembling centipedes, of the phylum Myriapoda, from the number of their feet.

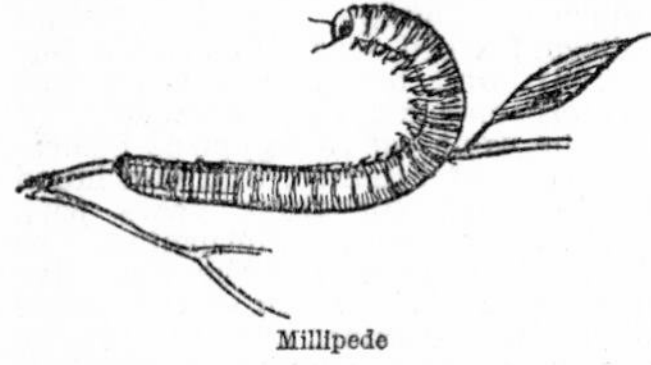

Millipede

The most common is the *Iūlus sabulōsus*, about 1¼ inches long. The young when hatched have only three pairs of legs, the remainder being gradually acquired till the number is complete, which is usually about 120 pairs. *See* MYRIAPODA.

MILLER, Hugh. Geologist, was born at Cromarty in 1802, and died 1856. He became a stone-mason, and while working at his trade he studied literature, wrote a great deal, and in particular became an expert geologist. His first publication appeared in 1829, under the title of *Poems Written in the Leisure Hours of a Journeyman Mason*, and this was followed in 1835 by the prose volume of *Scenes and Legends of Cromarty*. He was then appointed to a post in a bank at Cromarty, and while employed in this capacity took an active part in the religious controversy that ended in the Disruption. In 1840 he went to Edinburgh as editor of *The Witness* newspaper, after 1843 the chief organ of the Free Church. In this paper he printed the work subsequently published under the title of *The Old Red Sandstone*, which attracted the immediate attention of the scientific world and established his reputation as a geologist. This was followed by *First Impressions of England and its People*; *Footsteps of the Creator*; *My Schools and Schoolmasters*, a charming account of his earlier life; and *The Testimony of the Rocks*, in which he tried to reconcile the Mosaic account of creation with the teachings of geology. His *Schools and Schoolmasters* was supplemented by the *Life and Letters*, published in 1871.—Cf. W. K. Leask, *Hugh Miller*.

MILLER, Joseph. English actor, better known as Joe Miller, was born in 1684, it is supposed in London, and was a favourite low comedian. He died in 1738. The jests which have immortalized his name were collected in 1739 by John Mottley (1692-1750). A lithographic facsimile of the first edition, which is very rare, was published in 1861.

MILLERAND, Alexandre. President of the French Republic, born 1859. Admitted to the Bar (1881) and elected Deputy for Paris (1885), he became the leader of the Socialist Left, and afterwards an independent Socialist. He was editor successively of *La Voix*, *La Petite République* (until 1896), and *La Lanterne*, in which he was associated with Aristide Briand and René Viviani. He was Minister for Commerce in the Waldeck-Rousseau Cabinet, and became Minister of Public Works in 1909. On 25th Aug., 1914, he returned to the Ministry of War, which he had occupied between 1912 and 1913, and remained there until the resignation of the Viviani Cabinet in 1915. Elected to the Academy of Moral and Political Sciences (1917), he became Administrator of Alsace Lorraine (1920), followed Clemenceau as Premier, and succeeded Paul Deschanel (died, 29th April, 1922) as President, 3rd Sept., 1920, relinquishing office in 1924. He was a member of the Senate 1925-27, and again from 1927. Among his works are *Travail et Travailleurs* (1906), and *La Guerre liberatrice* (1918).

MILLET. A common name for various species of cereals yielding abundance of small seeds, more particularly *Pamicum miliaceum* and *P. miliare*, cultivated in the East Indies, China, Arabia, Syria, Egypt, etc., where it is used as human food. The leaves and panicles are given both green and dried as fodder to cattle. *German millet* (*Setaria germanica*) is cultivated on account of its seeds, which are used as food for cage-birds. *Italian millet* (*Setaria italica*) is a closely allied species.

MILLET (mi-lā), **Jean François.** French artist, born at Gruchy, near Cherbourg, 1814, died 1875. He worked with his peasant father in the fields; studied drawing at the academy of Cherbourg; from thence passed with an allowance from this town to the atelier of Delaroche in Paris, and exhibited at the Salon in 1840. As a student and until the death of his first wife in 1844 he was frequently in the greatest poverty, and his life subsequently was by no means free from difficulty. In 1849 he left Paris and settled among the peasants of Barbizon, on the edge of Fontainebleau Forest, and devoted himself to transferring their simple everyday life to his canvases, which he did with great truth and charm. Of his paintings may be mentioned: *The Sheep-shearers, The Gleaners, The Sower, The Shepherdess with her Flock*, and *The Angelus*. The last was sold by auction in Paris in 1889 for about £23,000.—BIBLIOGRAPHY: J. C. Ady, *Jean François Millet: his Life and Letters*; R. Muther, *Jean François Millet*; Edgcumb Staley, *J. F. Millet.*

MILLING-MACHINE. An important machine used in the fulling department of woollen-mills. After the cloth has been well washed, scoured, and hydro-extracted, it is taken to the milling-machine, where it is threaded through one of the holes of a knock-off board, then through a kind of spout and trough, down the curved bed of the back of the machine, and again led up to the knock-off board. This cycle is repeated three or four times, but each time the cloth is passed through a different hole in the knock-off board. The latter is attached to the control pulleys and adapted, when lifted, to stop the machine if the lengths of cloth get entangled. Pressure is applied to the cloth in the spout, and occasionally the required amount of soap is fed automatically. All parts are enclosed, and a certain degree of heat is obtained during the operation. The combined action of the various parts causes the fibres of the cloth to become more or less interlocked with each other, the ultimate result being a decreased length and width, and a consequent increase in solidity and thickness.

MILLOM. A market town and urban district of Cumberland, England, 9 miles N.W. of Barrow, with iron-mines and blast-furnaces. Pop. (1931), 7406.

MILLPORT. A burgh and watering-place of Buteshire, Scotland, on the island of Great Cumbrae. There is a marine biological station and a mineral well. Here is the cathedral for the Roman Catholic diocese of Argyll and the Isles. The population at the census of 1931 was returned at 2083.

MILMAN, Henry Hart. Born 1791, died 1868. In 1812 he received the Newdigate prize for an English poem on the *Apollo Belvidere*; published *Fazio*, a tragedy, which was performed at Covent Garden Theatre; and in 1815 was appointed vicar of St. Mary's, Reading. He became professor of poetry at Oxford 1821-31; appointed rector of St. Margaret's, Westminster, in 1835, and dean of St. Paul's in 1849. His principal works are: *Samor*, a legendary poem (1818); *The Fall of Jerusalem* (1820); *The Martyr of Antioch* (1821); *History of the Jews* (1829); *History of Christianity to the Abolition of Paganism* (1840); and *History of Latin Christianity* (1855).

MILNER, Alfred, Viscount. Born in 1854; he was educated at King's College, London, and Balliol College, Oxford, was called to the Bar in 1881, and for several years was actively engaged in journalism. In 1889 he went out to Egypt as Under-Secretary of Finance, and continued in this post for three years with marked success. Returning to England in 1892, for the next five years he was chairman of the Board of Inland Revenue, and in 1897 he was appointed Governor of Cape Colony and High Commissioner of South Africa. Sir Alfred, who had been created K.C.B. in 1895, undertook the duties of this office at a most critical period, arriving as he did while the Jameson raid was still fresh in the minds of the Dutch population. He played a prominent part in the complicated negotiations with the Transvaal, which were followed by the outbreak in Oct., 1899, of the South African War. After the annexation of the Boer territories he was appointed Governor of the Transvaal and Orange River Colonies in 1901, retaining at the same time the post of High Commissioner, but resigning that of Governor of Cape Colony. In May, 1901, he paid a short visit to England, and was created a baron, returning to South Africa the same year. In 1902 he was raised to a viscountcy. He resigned his offices in 1905 and returned home, being succeeded in South Africa by the Earl of Selborne. In 1916 he became a member of the War Cabinet, and was appointed Secretary for War in 1918. From 1919 to 1921 he was Colonial Secretary. He died 13th May, 1925.

MILTI'ADES (dēz). An Athenian general of the fifth century B.C. When Greece was invaded by the Persians, he was elected one of the ten generals, and drew up the army on the field of Marathon, where, 490 B.C., he gained a memorable victory. Next year he persuaded the Greeks to entrust him with a fleet of seventy vessels, in order to follow up his success. With this, to gratify a private revenge, he attacked the Island of Paros, but was repulsed, and dangerously wounded. On his return to Athens he was impeached, and condemned to pay a fine of fifty talents. Being unable to pay, he was thrown into prison, where he soon after died of his wound.

MILTON, John. English poet, the son of John Milton, scrivener, London, was born in the metropolis 9th Dec., 1608, died there 8th Nov., 1674. His father had him carefully educated, and at the age of seventeen he entered Christ's College, Cambridge, where he resided for seven years, took his B.A. and M.A. degrees, and excelled in Latin verse and English composition. It had been intended by his parents that he should enter the Church, but their puritanical beliefs and his own scruples regarding the oaths decided otherwise. During this period were written: *On the Death of a Fair Infant* (1625-26), *On the Morning of Christ's Nativity* (1629), *On Shakespeare* (1630), *On Arriving at the Age of Twenty-three* (1631), and the *Epitaph on the Marchioness of Winchester*.

Leaving the university, he went to reside with his father, who had retired to Horton, in Buckinghamshire, and here he remained for the following six years. In this leisured retreat he studied classical literature, philosophy, mathematics, and music. To this period belong his Latin hexameters *Ad patrem*, the fragment called *Arcades*, *L'Allegro*, and *Il Penseroso*; the beautiful monody of *Lycidas*, occasioned by the death of his college friend Edward King, and the pastoral masque of *Comus*, played before the Earl of Bridgewater at Ludlow Castle in 1634.

In 1637, on the death of his mother, he made a Continental journey, in which he visited Paris, where he was introduced to Grotius; Florence, where he met Galileo; Rome, and Naples. After remaining abroad for fifteen months he returned to England. His Italian sonnets and some other pieces were written during this journey.

John Milton

The home at Horton having been broken up, Milton settled in the Metropolis, and undertook the education of his two nephews, the sons of his sister, Mrs. Phillips, and to these, betimes, were added the sons of a few personal friends, who boarded or received daily lessons at his house in Aldergate Street. While settled here his *Paradise Lost* was partially sketched out, but the immediate fruits of his pen were (1641-42) vigorous polemical treatises entitled, *Of Reformation touching Church Discipline in England*, *Of Prelatical Episcopacy*, *Animadversions against Smectymnuus*, and *The Reason of Church Government*.

In the summer of 1643 Milton married Mary Powell, the daughter of a Royalist family. Divided from her kinsfolk by politics, he was also dissimilar to his wife in age—she being little more than seventeen, while he was thirty-five. Moreover, she found his habits austere and his house dull, with the result that she returned to her father about a month after marriage. Milton quickly made his private trouble a plea for public protest against the marriage laws in his pamphlets on *The Doctrine of Divorce, The Judgment of Martin Bucer, Tetrachordon,* and *Colasterion.* In the end, however, his wife returned in 1645, bore him three daughters, and continued to live with him until her death in 1653.

Besides his pamphleteering, he was at this time occupied in publishing the first edition of his *Minor Poems* in Latin and English (1645), with no apparent recognition of his claims as a poet. In connection with his divorce pamphlets he was prosecuted by the Stationer's Company for having published them without licence or registration. His answer to this was the famous *Areopagitica,* a speech for the liberty of unlicensed printing, which he addressed to the Parliament of England.

When in 1649 Charles I. was executed and a republic established, Milton avowed his adherence to it in his pamphlet *Tenure of Kings and Magistrates,* and was appointed Foreign (Latin) Secretary to the Commonwealth. While occupying this position he wrote in 1649 *Eikonoklastes* (Image-breaker) in answer to the *Eikon Basilikē* (q.v.), and his *Pro Populo Anglicano Defensio* (Defence of the People of England), the latter in answer to Salmasius of Leyden, who had vindicated the memory of the late king. In this literary task his eyesight suffered so much that in 1652 he became totally blind. Nevertheless he continued Latin Secretary with the assistance of Andrew Marvell, and dictated some of Cromwell's most important dispatches. Upon the death of the latter, and in the confusion which resulted, Milton in 1659 wrote his *Ready and Easy Way to Establish a Free Commonwealth.* But when Charles II. was restored a few months later, the blind politician remained in hiding, his books were burned by the common hangman, and he himself narrowly escaped the scaffold.

He had married a second wife in 1656, who fifteen months after had died in childbirth. In 1663 he married a third time, and began the writing of *Paradise Lost.* This was published in 1667, the publisher agreeing to pay the author £5 down and a further £5 after the sale of each edition of 1300 copies. The published price was three shillings, and the poem was at first in ten books. In two years a second edition, now arranged into twelve books, was printed, and Milton's position as the greatest poet of his time was established.

In 1670 there appeared his *History of Great Britain to the Norman Conquest,* and in the following year the continued vigour of his poetic faculty was shown in *Paradise Regained* and *Samson Agonistes.* In 1674, the last year of his life, he printed his *Epistolæ Familiares* and *Prolusiones Oratoriæ.* His death took place at his house in Bunhill, and he was buried in the church of St. Giles, Cripplegate. Professor David Masson's *Life* of the poet is the most complete history we have of the man in relation to his times.—BIBLIOGRAPHY: D. Masson, *Life of John Milton*; M. Pattison, *Milton* (English Men of Letters Series); R. Garnett, *Milton* (Great Writers Series); R. Bridges, *Milton's Prosody.*

MILWAU'KEE. Chief city and port of Wisconsin, United States, on the west shore of Lake Michigan; served by the Chicago & North-Western Railway, etc. Part of the town occupies a high bluff overlooking the lake, and among the chief buildings of the city are the court-house, post office, two cathedrals, free library, and museum. The main element in the prosperity of Milwaukee is its vast trade in grain, and extensive industrial establishments connected with iron, flour, leather, lager beer, agricultural implements, etc. It has rapidly advanced from a population in 1840 of 1700 to one in 1930 of 578,249.

MIME. A kind of dramatic performance common among the ancient Greeks and Romans. Mimes appear to have originated among the Greek colonists of Southern Italy, and consisted first of extemporary representations at festivals of ludicrous incidents of common life, but afterwards developed into dialogues intended for reading, not acting. The inventor of the original mime was Sophron, whose work influenced that of Plato. The literary mime is preserved in the works of Herodas (q.v.).

MIMICRY. A more or less close resemblance between two non-related animal species. One of these, the "model," exhibits warning coloration, marking the presence of characters helping to protect it from the attacks of carnivorous forms. The "mimic" superficially resembles the model, but does not possess its special protective characters. Bees, for example, are mimicked by clear-wing moths and drone-flies. A well-known North American butterfly, the

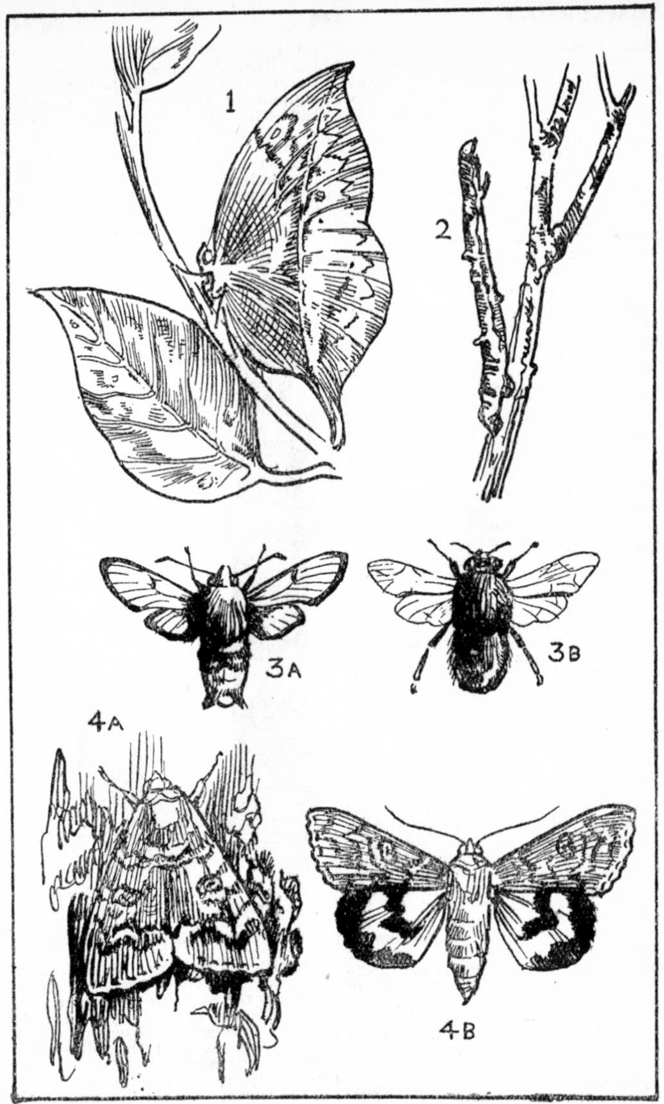

MIMICRY

1, *Kallima Inachis* (Indian Leaf Butterfly) mimicking dead leaf. 2, Larva of *Ennomos Autumnaria* (Large-thorn Moth) which closely resembles a twig. 3A, *Hemaris Tityus* (narrow-bordered Bee Hawk Moth), and 3B, The Bee which it mimics. 4A, *Catocola Nupta* (Red Underwing Moth) at rest on tree trunk, and 4B, with wings expanded.

Black-veined Brown (*Anosia crippus*), is unconsciously imitated by an edible species (*Limenitis misippus*). One of the most remarkable instances is that of a South African Swallow-tail Butterfly (*Papilio merope*), in which the male is protectively coloured, while there are three kinds of female, that mimic three distinct species of butterflies found in the same area, and known to be unpalatable to insectivorous animals. Other cases have been described among birds, reptiles, and spiders; while instances of plant mimicry have also been noticed.

MIMNER'MUS. An ancient Greek poet and musician, who was probably born at Smyrna, and flourished from about 630 to 586 B.C. His poems chiefly consisted of love elegies, and only a few fragments have come down to us. They form an epoch in the history of elegiac poetry, having first diverted it from warlike and convivial to plaintive, amatory, and mournful strains.

MIMO'SA. A genus of leguminous plants, type of the subdivision Mimoseæ. The stigma is irritable, the two lobes folding together quickly when touched, a condition which favours cross-pollination. *See* SENSITIVE PLANTS.

MIM'ULUS. A genus of plants, nat. ord. Scrophulariaceæ. There are about forty species, natives of extra-tropical and mountainous regions of Asia, Africa, Australia, and America. They have often handsome red, yellow, or violet flowers. *M. luteus* has become naturalized in Britain on the banks of streams, etc. *M. moschātus* is the musk plant of gardens. Others are favourite flowers.

MIN'ARET. A slender lofty turret rising by different stages or stories, surrounded by one or more projecting balconies, commonly attached to mosques in Mahommedan countries, and frequently of very graceful design. Minarets are used by the muezzin for summoning from the balconies the people to prayers at stated times of the day; so that they answer the purpose of belfries in Christian churches. The minarets of Egypt, Spain, Syria, India, and Persia, built between the thirteenth and sixteenth centuries, are among the most graceful works of Eastern architecture. *See* MUEZZIN.

MINAS. A town of Uruguay, capital of the department of Lavalleja It is 80 miles N.N.E. of Montevideo by rail. Pop. about 9000.

MINAS GERAES. An inland state of Brazil, an afforested plateau (altitude 1500-3000 feet), watered by the São Francisco and Parahyba River systems. Bello Horizonte supplanted Auro Preto as capital in 1894-95. There is a railway system of 4046 miles. Foreign "colonies," maintained by the Union, are located at João Pinheiro (1910) and Inconfidentes (1910). Much coffee is produced, with some yerba maté; manganese ore is worked. Area, 221,894 sq. miles; pop. 7,442,243.

Minaret of the Mosque of Sultan Hassan, Cairo

MIND. A term used in philosophy to designate that form of reality which is the opposite of matter; i.e. the principle of activity and order in the universe. Observation and experience revealed to philosophers two fundamentally distinct and contradictory principles of reality in the world. On the one hand there was matter, occupying space and possessed of inertia and passivity. On the other there was the principle of movement, harmony, and order, of consciousness and design. The question consequently arose whether these two forms of being were quite distinct from each other, or merely two phases of one substratum, and to this question philosophers have endeavoured to find an answer. In psychology the term *mind* is applied to the cognitive faculty of man, the thinking part of the individual, his will and self-conscious intelligence, thus covering all our mental processes. In a narrower psychological sense mind has been distinguished from soul, or the emotional and volitional faculties of man. Mind thus forms the subject-matter both of metaphysics and psychology, which may be defined as the philosophy of the mind. This science inquires into the operations of the human mind, and gives an account of the phenomena of developed consciousness as it manifests itself in man. Psychology treats of mental life, intellectual or affective, and of consciousness in all its aspects. It analyses the powers of perception, memory, retention, volition, and freedom of will, and also the relation existing between the human mind and the human body (*see* PSYCHOLOGY). In metaphysics the problem of mind has occupied philosophers of all ages, from Anaxagoras to Bergson. Struck by the apparent contradiction of activity and passivity in the world, and, above all, by the intellectual life pervading the universe, of consciousness, design, and order, philosophers tried to define and explain the efficient cause of movement, order, and harmony. They also formulated answers to the question connected with the inter-relation of mind and non-mind. These answers have ranged from the assumption that non-mind, or matter, is a manifestation or mode of mind, to the opposite view which holds that mind itself is only a product of matter. Three distinct theories have been formulated in answer to the question concerning the relation of mind and matter.

Idealism (or spiritualism) maintains that mind is the only reality of being, everything else is derived from mind, or is only appearance. The real essence of things is an immaterial force, self-conscious and endowed with the sense of personality. Matter, physical and unconscious, cannot think, and, as a French poet expressed it—

Je pense que la pensée, éclatante lumière,
Ne peut pas sortir du sein de l'épaisse matière.

The essence of being therefore, working behind appearances, is of a spiritual, immaterial nature, i.e. mind. The first philosopher who clearly made a distinction between the material and the spiritual, between matter and mind, was Anaxagoras (q.v.), who introduced the idea of *nous*, intelligence, or the organizing and governing principle. He assumed the existence of an intelligent cause of motion, endowed with activity, force, and consciousness, and producing movement and life in the universe. Socrates praised this doctrine of the *nous*, and Aristotle said of Anaxagoras that "he was like a sober man among drunken people who speak at random." *Materialism* (q.v.) denies the existence of mind, and looks upon all mental phenomena as the result of matter. *Dualism* again admits the existence of both matter and mind. Mind is unextended, and active, whilst matter is extended and soulless. "We can neither conceive mind," says Sir W. Hamilton, "without consciousness, nor body without extension." The two great philosophers of antiquity, Plato and Aristotle, are dualists, but the founder of Dualism in modern philosophy is Descartes. The dualists consider mind and matter as two separate substances, existing side by side and independently of each other. Dualism, or the existence of both mind and matter, is also at the basis of the purer religious systems, especially of the three most important forms of monotheism, Christianity, Judaism, and Mahommedanism. (For "Human Mind," *see* PSYCHOLOGY).—BIBLIOGRAPHY: P. Janet and G. Séailles, *A History of the Problems of Philosophy*; A. S. Rappoport, *A Primer of Philosophy*.

MINDEN. A city of Westphalia, Germany, on the Weser. In the Middle Ages the town was a strongly fortified commercial centre and a member of the Hanseatic League. The Bishop of Minden ruled the diocese as a principality, but his temporal power was transferred to Brandenburg in 1648, and with that electorate contributed to the rise of Prussia. In 1759 the French were defeated at Minden by an Anglo-Hanoverian army (Seven Years' War). Pop. 27,139.

MINE. In a military or naval sense, means an arrangement by which a certain road, locality, or area of sea is prepared with explosives in order to deny its use to an enemy. On land such an arrangement is known as a "land-mine" or "fougasse" (q.v.), while at sea the word is used without prefix. Land-mines are of two main sorts: the one designed to work automatically on being subjected to the weight of troops or vehicles crossing it (contact mine), the other intended to be exploded electrically from an observation-point. In the European War, during the period of trench warfare, mines were largely used as an aid to assault, i.e. tunnels were driven under the enemy lines, and a mine laid and exploded at the hour fixed for the commencement of the operations.

Mines used at sea are, in these days, almost invariably of the contact variety, i.e. they are huge metal containers of a suitable shape filled with a great quantity of high explosive, and fitted with strikers (or horns) similar to the buffers on a railway carriage. The horns, when struck heavily, as by a moving ship, cause the mine to explode. Such mines are usually grouped together in minefields of greater or less extent, and are anchored by a contrivance which keeps the top of the mine, bearing the strikers, at a suitable distance below the surface of the water to intercept the particular class of ship it is meant to guard against. The use of both land- and sea-mines is permitted by the laws of war, but the intentional laying of floating or loose mines is not allowed.

MINE INSPECTION. First instituted in 1850 under the provisions of a Bill for the Better Regulation of Coal-mining in the United Kingdom. Amending Acts were passed in 1860 and 1872, but all previous legislation was amended and consolidated in the Coal Mines Regulation Act, 1887. Between that date and 1911 minor changes were introduced by various Acts. These Acts are in the main repealed by the Coal Mines Act, 1911. Under the last-mentioned Act provision is made for the better inspection of locked safety-lamps, the use of explosives in blasting, the ventilating of shafts, roads, and workings, the fencing of shafts and entrances, provision of shafts, outlets, and refuge holes, support of roofs and sides, prevention of coal dust, provision of baths, the regulation and the upkeep of machinery. In the case of an accident which has caused injury of person or loss of life, notice must be sent to the mine-inspector for the district, so that he may report the same to the Home Secretary, who shall provide for a formal investigation should he think fit. It is the duty of the inspector to see that boys under fourteen years and women and girls of any age do not work below ground in the mine, and that the conditions and hours of their employment above ground are strictly observed. It is also enacted that every mine shall be under the supervision of a certificated manager, and must be visited and inspected daily. Wages are to be paid weekly if the majority of employees so desire, and they must not be paid in a public-house or other house of entertainment. The mine-inspector is permitted to inspect the books, plans, and documents which the law prescribes shall be kept by the mine-owner, and he is also entitled to receive all special rules and annual returns. The Mining Industry Act, 1920, established a department of the Board of Trade (to be known as the Mines Department) for, *inter alia*, securing the safety and welfare of the workers, and provides for pit committees, whose functions are to discuss and make recommendations with respect to, *inter alia*, the safety, health, and welfare of the workers, and the reports of inspections made on their behalf. The Mines Department is also responsible for the administration of the Miners' Welfare Fund.

MINERALOGY. The scientific study and description of minerals, was originally bound up with the study of rocks, and many bodies of composite mineral constitution, now treated as rocks, found their place in mineral classfication. It is well, then, to limit the science at the outset by defining a *mineral* as a natural body of inorganic origin, which has a definite chemical composition, and which, under favourable conditions, can assume a characteristic crystalline form. This definition excludes a number of substances popularly classed as minerals, such as mineral oil, obsidian, and common potter's clay; these must go over to the rocks which are aggregates of mineral particles but which cannot assume a crystalline form. Their constituents may separate out, or be already separated out, as distinct minerals; but a rock-mass is of composite structure, and commonly contains examples of more than one mineral species. Coal is excluded from minerals as a mixture of hydrocarbons, and it is, moreover, of organic origin.

The determination of the chemical constitution of the more complex minerals is beset with difficulties, owing to possibilities of change and decay during their long life-history, and of inclusion of other substances during their original growth. Here synthesis is of great value, and a number of minerals have been artificially reproduced from pure chemicals under suitable conditions. The element of geological time is, however, lacking in our laboratory experiments, and we are commonly ignorant of the environment of minerals at the epoch of their birth, including the presence of catalyzers that have now disappeared, but which promoted deposition and co-ordination of the particles in the arrangement that we style crystalline. Chemical composition, moreover, does not always define a mineral species, since this may be the same in two or more species which differ in physical characters and crystal-form. Measurement of crystals by the goniometer, and the consequent assignment of them to this or that crystallographic system and class (*see* CRYSTALLOGRAPHY), afford the surest means of determining mineral species.

Short of these delicate investigations, materia for which may rarely be obtainable, a consensus of evidence drawn from a number of characters will commonly serve to identify a mineral specimen. The specific gravity and hardness of crystalline examples are particularly helpful. Among metallic ores, colour is important, though it is of little value among ordinary translucent or transparent minerals, where it may be due to trivial stainings, or even to a response to external radiations. While, for instance, pyrite, cubic iron disulphide is always brass-yellow, and nickel ne, nickel arsenide, is always coppery red, both ruby and sapphire are differently coloured varieties of the mineral corundum, crystallized aluminium ox'de, while fluorspar, calcium fluoride in a mineral condition, is noted for a range of colour from purple, green, and yellow, down to rusty red. In such cases colourless varieties may be rare; but their occurrence indicates a character of the pure mineral.

Simple chemical tests, especially when aided by an expert use of the mouth blowpipe, are of immense service in identifying mineral species, provided that other characters than those due to chemical response are at the same time taken into consideration. During the last hundred years the determination of the optical characters of minerals has been immensely extended, and even minute crystals may now be identified in thin sections of rocks under the polarizing microscope. Early studies on polarized light were made by using the mineral calcite, and the development of theoretical optics has depended largely on the observed behaviour of light-rays in traversing minerals and on emergence from them. The application of these observations to determinative mineralogy has received great impetus from the requirements of modern petrology. The use of "angles of extinction" in the felspars, and in the pyroxene-amphibole group, and of the optic axial angle in the micas, may be cited as examples.

The study of mineralogy from early times had two aspects, economic and æsthetic. Sometimes this led to the destruction of fine specimens on account of the value of their constituents; and even the æsthetic use, as illustrated in the cutting of gems, and in the strewing of cinnabar, the vermilion ore of mercury, on the floor of a Roman amphitheatre, may bring regret to the mineralogist, who is a student of natural things. Yet the search for minerals of economic importance has enriched the science by the opening up of veins that are veritable treasure-houses of new species, or of known species in their habit as they lived, exquisitely preserved from the destructive influences that attack them on the surface of the earth. It is no wonder that interest in mineralogy mainly developed in regions of mining activity, such as southern Saxony and Cornwall, and in later days Colorado and South Africa.

The founders of the science were men who collected and correlated facts from the whole range of natural history. Even J. B. Romé de l'Isle, the crystal-measurer, owed much to his sojourn as a prisoner of war amid the natural attractions of the Indies. The elder Pliny, Linné, and Buffon were, in varied measure, mineralogists. The wealthy travellers of the close of the eighteenth century, men of literary rather than scientific culture, often formed collections of minerals, as a record of things strange and beautiful, for the adornment of their spacious homes. The specialized mineralogists who arose in the same epoch looked on such men as their patrons, and gradually great national collections were built up, such as those of London, Leningrad, and Vienna, where minerals were classified on scientific lines. The importance and the charm of mineralogy have been to some extent overshadowed by the wide growth of geology, and it must be admitted that university curricula do not always recognize the subject as fundamental for the geologist, and as the natural history branch of chemistry.—BIBLIOGRAPHY: J. D. Dana, *Textbook of Mineralogy*; H. A. Miers, *Mineralogy*; T. Crook, *Economic Mineralogy*; G. J. Brush and S. L. Penfield, *Manual of Determinative Mineralogy*.

MINERAL TALLOW, or HATCHETTITE. A mineral hydrocarbon

found in the coal measures of South Wales and Belgium. It is a yellow, odourless, waxy substance, transparent when found, but turning opaque on exposure to the air.

MINERAL WATERS. The term commonly applied to the spring-waters that contain an unusual quantity of such substances as sodium, magnesia, iron, carbonic acid, and sulphur; but it cannot be used in any absolute fashion. The most popular European springs are those of Aix-la-Chapelle, Wiesbaden, Baden-Baden, Carlsbad, Ahrweiler (Apollinaris), Friedrichshall, Buda-pest (Hunyadi-Janos), Vichy, and Bath. The waters are usually drunk at an early hour before breakfast, and the curative effects are greatly aided by early rising, moderate exercise, mental relaxation, and complete freedom from all kinds of excess. It has not been found practical or useful to classify mineral waters under their chemical elements, but the attempt has been made, as where the springs are described as—salt, earthy, sulphur, iron, alkaline, and alkaline-saline. Besides the substances which these terms indicate, the waters are frequently impregnated with carbonic acid gas, which is found to aid digestion while giving a pleasant stimulus to the general system.

MINERAL WOOL (also known as **SLAG-WOOL** or **SILICATE COTTON**). A substance which is produced from the vitreous liquid slag of a blast-furnace drawn out into fine fibres under pressure of steam. The slag, when in a molten condition running from the furnace, is driven by the steam through a crescent-shaped aperture, and suddenly cools into long fibrous filaments. The thin, glassy, thread-like substance thus produced is useful

Minerva

Temple of Minerva

as a non-conductor of heat, and it has, therefore, been largely employed as a covering for boilers and steam-pipes, to prevent loss of heat by radiation, and also as a covering for water-pipes, etc., to prevent freezing.

MINERVA. A daughter of Jupiter, and one of the great divinities of the ancient Romans. She was looked upon as the patroness of all arts and trades, and her annual festival, called Quinquatrus, lasted from the 19th to the 23rd of March inclusive. This goddess was believed to protect warriors in battle, and to her was ascribed the invention of numbers, and of musical instruments, especially wind instruments. At Rome a temple was built for Minerva by Tarquin on the Capitol, where she was worshipped along with Jupiter and Juno; and there was also a temple on the Aventine dedicated to herself alone. This deity is supposed to be of Etruscan origin, and her character has much in common with the Greek goddess Athena (q.v.).—Cf. A. Fairbanks, *The Mythology of Greece and Rome.*

MINGRE'LIA. A district of the Georgian S.S.R.; area, 2400 sq. miles. It was annexed by Russia in 1867. The Mingrelians are closely related to the Georgians. The country is mountainous, but cereals, wine, and oil are raised; gold and manganese are found.

MINIATURE. A term derived from the Lat. *minium* (red lead), used to describe the illustrations in illuminated manuscripts (*see* ILLUMINATION), and thence applied to any paintings on a small scale, especially portraits. In its latter sense, the miniature has found its chief home in England, and reflects the same passion to express individual personality which produced the Renaissance medal. Oil paint and enamel, on copper, have been used for miniatures; but the most usual medium has been transparent or opaque water-colour on vellum or thin card, or (since the end of the seventeenth century) on ivory.

The earliest miniatures date from the sixteenth century, and in delicacy of execution, and decorative use of colour and gold, show their kinship to the illuminated manuscript. They include examples ascribed on good grounds to Holbein, and the work of Nicholas Hilliard (1547-1619), miniaturist to Queen Elizabeth. Similar in type are several delicate and refined portraits, approximating to the miniature, produced in France by members of the Clouet group. Isaac and Peter Oliver, employed by James I. and Charles I., mark the tendency of the miniature to become an easel portrait on a small scale, in a greater use of modelling, and occasional use of realistic backgrounds. During the Commonwealth, John Hoskins occupies an important place; but he was eclipsed by his nephew Samuel Cooper, whose unfinished portrait of Oliver Cromwell (in the collection of the Duke of Buccleuch) shows the breadth of handling and strong characterization which mark all his work.

In France, meanwhile, there flourished a number of skilful miniature painters in enamel, including Leonard Limousin (1505-77); Jean Petitot (1607-91), a Swiss who worked in France and England; and the members of the Toutin family. Their work, however, is a technical *tour de force* in dealing with refractory material, rather than an artistic achievement.

Prominent during the earlier eighteenth century in England were Lawrence Crosse, Gervase Spencer, and Bernard Lens. A later and more famous group includes Richard Cosway (1742-1821), whose brilliant and facile, though empty and mannered, work marks some return to the decorative tradition, and won him great reputation; Cosway's pupils, Andrew and Nathaniel Plimer; his rival, George Engleheart (1750-1829), dryer and more severe, but equally mannered; John Smart (1741-1811), in power of characterization the best miniaturist of his time; and Henry Bone (1755-1839), an accomplished painter of enamel portraits.

On the Continent, contemporary miniaturists include Pierre Adolf Hall, a Swede working in Paris; Dumont; and Füger, known as the Cosway of Vienna. Fragonard produced a few miniatures eagerly sought for by collectors. Later, J. B. Isabey (1767-1855) painted, during the Imperial and Restoration epochs, a series of skilful miniatures, whose importance is personal and historical rather than artistic. With the eighteenth century, the art of the miniature virtually died. Spasmodic attempts at its revival have been made; but the development of photography has prevented their success.—BIBLIOGRAPHY: G. C. Williamson, *History of Portrait Miniatures*; J. J. Foster, *British Miniature Painters.*

MINICOY. An isolated atoll of the Indian Ocean, between the Andaman and Laccadive groups, and included in the latter.

MINIM FRIARS, or **MINIMS** (from Lat. *minimus*, least). An order of reformed Franciscans, founded by St. Francis of Paola in Calabria in 1473. The order was confirmed by the Pope in 1474. The dress of the Minim Friars is black, and, like that of the Franciscans, they were provided with a scourge. They belong to the mendicant orders, and possessed, in the eighteenth century, 450 convents in thirty provinces.

MINIMUM WAGE. In economics, a term applied to the lowest level of earnings and wages fixed by law; wages which enable the worker and his family to live in social decency. The movement to secure a minimum wage, which arose in the nineteenth century, when the idea of State interference gradually began to supersede that of *laissez-faire*, is due to the efforts of social reformers and labourers to force less highly paid trades to pay their workers a living wage. The first minimum wage legislation was enacted in New Zealand (1894), and a similar legislation was enacted in New South Wales in 1901, and in Australia in 1904. In the United Kingdom the first Act establishing trade-boards, with power to fix minimum rates of wages, was enacted in 1909 (Trade Boards Act). This Act at first applied to four trades, but in 1913 wage-boards were established in four additional trades. Its scope was again widened in 1918, and by the beginning of 1921 forty-nine additional trade boards, covering

3,500,000 persons, had been established. At the present time (1933) there are forty-five Boards in operation.

MINING. A term which embraces all the processes necessary for the extraction of minerals from the crust of the earth. The art of mining is very ancient, and is referred to in the Book of Job. There is a considerable amount of literature on the subject, and a systematic account of mining operations was published in Latin as early as 1556 by Agricola. The two principal methods of obtaining minerals are by open workings, known in this country as "quarries," and underground workings, known as mines. The principal substances obtained as a result of the labour of the miners are coal, the minerals from which the metals are obtained, such as iron ore, lead ore, etc., building materials, salt, gems, etc. The method adopted in the mining of any particular mineral will depend largely on the mode of occurrence of the material in the earth's crust, the most important modes being the following: (1) Beds or seams, which are individual members of groups of stratified rocks, and have been formed as a layer at the bottom of a sea, lake, river, etc. (2) Veins or lodes which have been formed subsequently to the rocks which enclose them, probably by the filling in of fissures formed in the original rock. (3) Masses which comprise mineral deposits which cannot be classified as beds or veins.

Before a mine can actually produce mineral, much preliminary work is necessary. The actual discovery of the deposit may have been accidental or the result of prospecting work; after discovery, and before mining proper is attempted, a large amount of preliminary or exploratory work is necessary to ascertain the probable extent of the deposit and its thickness, in order to calculate the amount of mineral available. During this work samples are obtained from which to determine the value of the deposit, and to ascertain variations in quality existing at different parts, and at the same time information is collected on the nature of the deposit as regards its effect on the mode and cost of working. This exploratory work may be carried out by boring operations supplemented by underground exploration. The actual excavation of the mineral may be made by hand or by machinery, the motive power in the latter case being steam, water, compressed air, or electricity. Blasting by means of explosives is very commonly used as a method of excavation in hard deposits, and is also largely used in the case of softer minerals such as coal. In modern mining, a large amount of the heavy work, at one time done by hand labour, is performed by means of machines, such, for example, as rock drills used for boring holes for blasting purposes, etc., and cutting machines used for cutting out coal, etc. Excavations made in hard rock are sometimes safe without support, but, generally speaking, the miner has to arrange support for the roofs and sides of his shafts, levels, and working places, and for this purpose timber is most largely used, although masonry and steel are also employed.

In underground workings, the deposits are reached by shafts which are vertical or steeply inclined passages, by inclines which are sloping passages or tunnels, or by means of adits which are nearly horizontal passages running into the deposit from the side of a mountain, etc. The decision as to which of the methods is used depends largely on the contour of the country and the depth of the deposit. Several methods are used for the actual working or removal of the mineral, of which the two following are the most important. (1) Chambers and permanent pillar method, in which the deposit is not completely removed, part of it being left as supporting pillars. This method is adopted with minerals of low intrinsic value, when the pillars left behind may be of less value than the cost of putting in the artificial supports, which would be necessary were the whole deposit removed. (2) Subsidence of roof or caving method, in which the removal of the mineral is carried out as completely as possible with subsidence of the roof. This method is chiefly used in the mining of coal and iron ore. Two important modifications of this process may be described here, viz. the pillar and stall method, and the longwall method. The pillar and stall method consists in cutting passages in the coal towards the boundaries of the deposit, but leaving a considerable quantity in the form of large pillars; the result at this stage being that the coal is blocked out into large rectangular masses with passages all round. Then the attack on the pillars commences at the boundaries, only sufficient of each block being left to keep out the rubbish and to prevent the too early fall of the roof. In the longwall method of working coal, the mineral is removed in one operation by the aid of long working faces on the seam; these faces may be half a mile long or even more. The roof near the working place is timbered, and, as the face is gradually worked away, the props behind are removed, and the roof is allowed to fall. The roadways up to the working face are protected by timbering. In some cases waste material is filled in to take the place of the mineral removed.

After the actual breaking down and excavation of the mineral, it is conveyed in suitable mine cars to the hoisting shaft and is then drawn up this shaft to the pit bank. The removal of the material from the working place to the shaft is known as haulage, and the raising to the surface as hoisting or winding. The efficient drainage and ventilation of mines are matters of the utmost importance, and require the constant attention of the engineer in charge. As regards drainage, a mine which is worked on a hillside by means of an adit drains itself as far as the workings situated above the adit are concerned. In all cases care should be taken to prevent the percolation of surface water into the mine by efficient surface drainage, and underground inflows of water should also be shut off by suitable means. In cases where the quantity of water is not excessive, it is often removed by special buckets lowered and raised by the winding machinery, but the principal method of removing the water is by means of pumps. In certain districts, drainage is effected by co-operative pumping agencies, a good example in this country being the coal-fields of South Staffordshire and East Worcestershire, which are drained by the South Staffordshire Mines Drainage Commission.

Of equal importance with drainage is the efficient ventilation of the mines, as the mine air is subject to various influences which are constantly rendering it less fit for supporting life. Various noxious gases escaping from the rocks into the workings, respiration of miners and animals in the pits, combustion products of candles and lamps used for the illumination of the working places, explosions of gunpowder, etc., used for blasting, all vitiate the atmosphere to a considerable extent; and in addition to these causes there may be underground fires, explosions of fire-damp and coal dust, and the effects of the decay of timber. The most important gases which issue from the rocks are; (1) methane (q.v.), an inflammable gas which forms explosive mixtures with air and is the chief constituent of "fire-damp" (q.v.); (2) carbonic acid gas, which is non-combustible, and is the chief constituent of "black-damp." Carbonic acid gas also results from the breathing of animals and from underground fires, explosions, etc. Two systems are used for the ventilation of mines, viz. natural and artificial. In the former methods, currents of air are set up by natural differences of temperature, but these are often inconstant, and the artificial method is mostly used. In this method the movement of the currents of air is assisted, either by artificial heat or by mechanical means. By placing a furnace at the bottom of one of the shafts, the temperature of the air in this shaft may be raised, thus rendering it lighter than the air in a second similar shaft in communication with the first, so that a current of air is produced, descending by the second or cold shaft, traversing the workings, and ascending the heated shaft. In modern mines, the furnace or heating method of ventilation has been largely replaced by ventilating fans, which are arranged as exhausters, that is they suck air out of the mine, its place being immediately taken by fresh air entering at one of the shafts.

In underground workings, artificial light is a necessity during the whole of the working hours, and the methods of illumination vary considerably in different mines. Candles, generally of the "common dip" or tallow kind, are largely used, being held in lumps of clay. Open lamps of various kinds burning oil are frequently used, but not to a great extent in English and Welsh mines. Miners' safety lamps have to be used in certain coal-mines, as they are constructed in such a manner as to be incapable of igniting fire-damp. Electric lamps have more recently been introduced on a considerabe scale in modern mines.

The mining industry differs appreciably from most other industries in being regulated by special statutes. Owing to the dangers to life and health involved in mining occupations, all operations are subject to rigorous inspection by Government Inspectors of Mines (*see* Mine Inspection). To indicate the enormous quantities of minerals which are mined during the course of a year, the following figures are given in connection with the two chief minerals, viz. coal and iron. In 1931, 219,458,951 tons of coal were produced in the United Kingdom, 118,640,113 tons in Germany, and

378,110,000 tons in the United States; in the same year 7,625,860 tons of iron ore were produced in the United Kingdom, 38,476,000 tons in France, and 31,131,502 tons in the United States.—BIBLIOGRAPHY: Robert Peele, *Mining Engineers' Handbook*; G. J. Young, *Elements of Mining*; Sir C. Le Neve Foster, *The Elements of Mining and Quarrying*, and *Ore and Stone Mining*; H. C. Hoover, *The Principles of Mining*; Arthur J. Hoskin, *The Business of Mining*; T. H. Cockin, *Coal Mining*; H. W Hughes, *Textbook of Coal Mining*.

MINISTRY OF AGRICULTURE AND FISHERIES, see under AGRICULTURE.

MIN'IUM. The red oxide of lead, often designated *red lead*, and commonly used as a pigment for ordinary purposes. *See* LEAD.

MIN'IVER. The Siberian squirrel, a variety of the common European species (*Sciurus vulgāris*), with grey or white fur; also the fur itself.

MINK. The name of North American, Siberian, and European mammals, allied to the polecat. They are semi-aquatic, burrowing on the banks of rivers and ponds, living on frogs, crayfishes, and fishes, which they pursue in the water. They exhale a strong odour of musk, and their fur is in considerable request.

MINNEAP'OLIS. A city of Minnesota, United States, county seat of Hennepin county; on the Mississippi at the Falls of St. Anthony; and served by the Chicago, Milwaukee and St. Paul, and other railways. The public buildings include the University of Minnesota (founded 1868), and a school of arts. The principal industries are the manufacture of flour, engines, boilers, agricultural implements, carriages, wagons, and pork-packing. Minneapolis is an important centre of the grain trade. The city owns a territory of about 33 sq. miles, with the celebrated Falls of Minnehaha and several fine lakes. Pop. (1910), 301,408; (1930), 464,356.

MINNESINGERS, or **MINNESÄNGER** (O. Ger. *minne*, love). A class of German lyric poets of the twelfth and thirteenth centuries, so called from love being the chief theme of their verse. They were knights, or at least men of good family, who, after the fashion of the Provençal troubadours, engaged in poetical contests for the gratification of princes and ladies of the court. The most prominent names among the minnesingers are those of Wolfram von Eschenbach, Gottfried von Strassburg, Hartmann von der Aue, and Walther von der Vogelweide. They sang their lyrics to the accompaniment of the viol, generally in honour of high-born ladies. The songs, chiefly in the Swabian dialect, were seldom written down by their authors, and the manuscripts which contain their verse are mostly the result of oral traditions and repetitions. The largest collection of their songs was compiled by Rüdiger von Manesse, burgomaster of Zürich in the early part of the fourteenth century, and a good selection was published by Bartsch, entitled *Deutsche Liederdichter* (Leipzig, 1864). This remarkable poetical movement gradually merged into that other class of German lyric poets called Meistersingers. *See* MASTERSINGERS.—Cf. F. Grimm, *Geschichte der Minnesinger*.

MINNESOTA. A west-north-central state of the United States, bounded on the north by Manitoba-Ontario, with a coast-line on Lake Superior, to the west of which it lies. It is traversed by the Red and Minnesota Rivers, and by the headwaters of the Mississippi, which rises within the state in Lake Itasca. The state capital is St. Paul (pop. in 1930, 271,606), but Minneapolis is the largest town; others are Duluth (pop. 101,463), an important port on Lake Superior; St. Cloud (pop. 21,000); Winona (pop. 20,850), and Rochester (pop. 20,621). There is an Indian Reserve of 868 sq. miles (1931); pop. 15,700.

Production and Industry.—Minnesota is mainly an agricultural area, producing corn (176,916.000 bushels in 1932), wheat (14,445,000 bushels), oats (164,700,000 bushels), barley, and flax-seed. Dairying and sheep-farming are progressive. 1,171,000 acres are afforested (1932). Iron ores (mostly red hematite) are worked in the Mesaba and Vermilion ranges, west of Lake Superior; granite, limestone, and sandstone are also produced. Manufactures are principally of leathers, clothing, and machinery.

Education, etc.—Higher education is provided by the State university at Minneapolis; Hamelin University, St. Paul; St. John's (R.C.) University, Collegeville (founded 1857); Carleton College, and St. Olaf College at Northfield. Area, 84,682 sq. miles, of which 3824 sq. miles are water; an additional area of 2514 sq. miles on Lake Superior is technically included in Minnesota. In 1931 there were 9285 miles of steam and 660 miles of electric railways.

Government.—Minnesota was explored in 1766, and was admitted to the Union on 11th May, 1858. It is divided into eighty-seven counties, and the administration comprises a Governor, Senate (67 members, elected for four years), and a House of Representatives (131 members, elected for two years). Two Senators and nine Representatives are sent to Congress. Cf. W. W. Folwell. *Minnesota* (in American Commonwealth Series).

MINNOW (*Leuciscus phoxinus*, or *Phoxinus aphya*), a species of fresh-water fish belonging to the carp family. They swim in shoals, seldom exceed 3 inches in length, and make excellent bait for trout. They are distributed throughout Europe (except Spain and Portugal), Russian Turkestan, and Siberia. In America various small fish receive this name.

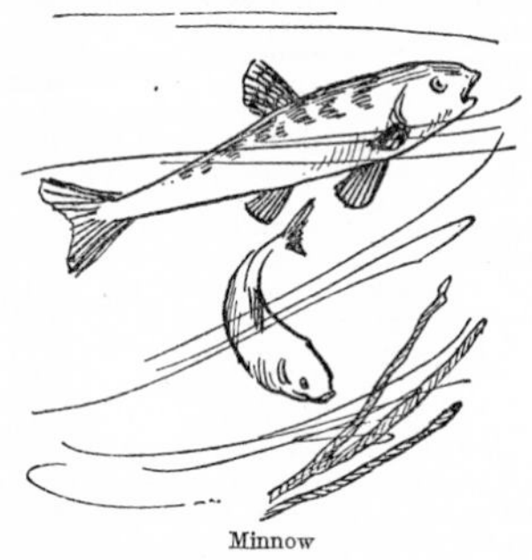

Minnow

MINOR. Generally a person under age and therefore under certain legal disabilities (*see* AGE). In Scotland boys between fourteen and twenty-one and girls between twelve and twenty-one are minors. If such a person has a curator his contracts are valid only if the curator concurs. If he has no curator he has ordinary powers. But he cannot gratuitously dispose of heritage. His contracts during minority are voidable until he becomes twenty-five on proof of minority and lesion, i.e. serious injury to his estate, e.g. where the minor has made a gift or discharged a debt for an inadequate sum. The plea of minority and lesion is excluded if the minor was reasonably believed to be of full age, or if he was in trade and the contract was connected with that trade, or if after majority he with full knowledge ratifies the contract. Besides being curator to the minor's estate the father has a vague authority over a minor personally, terminating at majority or earlier if the minor has set up for himself. *See* CHILD and CURATOR.

MINORCA (Sp. *Menorca*). The second largest island of the Balearic group, in the Mediterranean. It is separated from the largest island, Majorca, by a strait 27 miles broad. The surface is hilly. Port Mahon, a naval station and seaport, is the capital. It has a wireless station. Minorca was ceded to Spain by Britain in 1802 (Peace of Amiens). Area, 293 sq. miles; pop. 42,000.

MINOS. In Greek mythology, a ruler of Crete, said to have been the son of Zeus and Europa, and a brother of Rhadamanthus. During his lifetime he was celebrated as a wise lawgiver and a strict lover of justice, and after his death he was made, with Æacus and Rhadamanthus, one of the judges of the infernal world. The story evidently contains reminiscences of Cretan supremacy in the Ægean. This theory is supported by recent discoveries, which tend to prove the existence of a powerful kingdom of Crete during the Mycenæan Age.

MIN'OTAUR. In Greek mythology a monster fabled to have had the body of a man with the head of a bull, and to have fed on human flesh, on which account Minos shut him up in the labyrinth of Dædalus, and at first exposed to him criminals, but afterwards youths and maidens yearly sent from Athens as a tribute. He was slain by Theseus.

MINSK. A town of U.S.S.R., capital of the white Russian S.S.R., on the Svislotch. It has some manufactures and a considerable general trade. Fighting took place at Minsk during the European War, and in 1920 between the Bolshevik army and the Poles. Pop. (1926), 153,500.

MINSK. A former government of Russia, now included in the white Russian S.S.R. It has extensive forests and great stretches of marsh or swamp. Area, 35,290 sq. miles; pop. 3,070,900.

MINSTREL. A singer and musical performer on instruments. In the Middle Ages minstrels were a class of men who subsisted by the arts of poetry and music, and sang to the harp or other instrument verses composed by themselves or others. The name was introduced into England by the Normans. The person of the minstrel was sacred; his profession was a passport; he was "high placed in hall, a welcome guest." So long as the spirit of chivalry existed the minstrels were protected, but they afterwards sank to so low a level as to be classed, in the reign of Queen Elizabeth, with beggars and vagabonds.

MINT. The name given to several herbaceous aromatic plants of the genus Metha, nat. ord. Labiatæ. They are nearly all perennial, having square stems which bear opposite and simple leaves; they are widely distributed throughout temperate regions, and they abound in resinous dots which contain an essential oil. Mint has an agreeable odour, and partakes in the highest degree of tonic and stimulating properties. Spearmint (*M. viridis*) is generally used, mixed with vinegar and sugar, in sauce. Peppermint (*M. piperita*) yields the well-known stimulating oil of the same name. Pennyroyal (*M. Pulegium*) is used for the same purposes as peppermint.

MINT. The place where a country's coinage is made and issued under special regulations and with public authority. In England there was formerly a mint in almost every county; the sovereign, barons, bishops, and principal monasteries exercised the right of coining; and it was not till the reign of William III. that all the provincial mints were abolished. The present mint on Tower Hill, in London, was erected between the years 1810 and 1815. In former times the coinage was made by contract at a fixed price. The English mint is the centre of supply for the British Empire, but Australia has branch mints at Sydney, Melbourne, and Perth. In the United States there are several mints, the chief being at Philadelphia. In France, as in England, the number of mints was at one time considerable. *See* COINING.

MIN'UET. A slow, graceful dance said to have been invented in Poitou, in France, about the middle of the seventeenth century, performed in ¾ or ⅜ time.

MINYA. A town of Upper Egypt. Pop. (1927), 44,325.

MI'OCENE (Gr. *meiōn*, less, *kainos*, recent). In geology (q.v.), the name given by Sir Charles Lyell to a subdivision of the Tertiary strata. The Miocene strata contain fossil plants and shells which indicate a warm uniform climate. The mammals are important, and foreshadow the animal life of the present day. No strata of Miocene age occur in the British Isles; but the system is excellently represented in Central Europe (Vienna basin) and elsewhere, and by freshwater and terrestrial beds, with some marine zones, in Switzerland and Northern France. The great *Alpine* mountain-building movements, which affected the whole globe, culminated in the last epoch of the Miocene period.

MIÖSEN (my*eu*'sen). The largest lake in Norway, about 40 miles N.E. of Oslo. It is 62 miles long and about 9½ miles in greatest breadth, and its waters are carried by the Vormen to the Glommen.

MIQUELON. An island of North America, in the Atlantic, close to the south coast of Newfoundland; a French possession. The southern part is known as Little Miquelon, and was until 1783 a separate island. It is now connected with Great Miquelon by a sandspit. Fishing is the only industry of economic importance. Area, 83 sq. miles; pop. 544. *See* ST. PIERRE.

MIRABEAU (mē-rȧ-bō), **Gabriel Honoré Riquetti, Comte de.** French statesman, son of Victor Riquetti, marquis de Mirabeau, born in 1749 at Bignon, near Nemours, died at Paris 1791. At an early age he manifested extraordinary intelligence; but his youth was a stormy one, so much so that on several occasions he was imprisoned by his father under a *lettre de cachet*. It was during an imprisonment at Vincennes, which lasted three years and a half, that he wrote his *Lettres à Sophie*, *Lettres de Cachet*, and *L'Espion Dévalisé*. On his release from this prison he lived for some time in Holland and England, returning to France in 1785. On the assembling of the States-General, Mirabeau, elected for Aix, soon became prominent. When the king required the *tiers état* to vote apart from the other two orders, it was Mirabeau who counselled resistance, demanded the withdrawal of the troops, consolidated the National Assembly, and defied the king's orders. For some months he continued to lead, but he soon found that the members of the Assembly were mostly unpractical and inexperienced men, whose chief function was to discuss an ideal Constitution. As a practical statesman Mirabeau desired action, and for this reason he attempted to form alliances with Lafayette, the duc d'Orleans, Necker, and finally with the queen. Correspondence with the latter was maintained through La Marck, and he received a subsidy from the royal party. No practical result followed from this secret alliance, for the queen rejected Mirabeau's counsel and suspected his methods of government. Whether he might ultimately have been able to guide the Revolution into peaceful ways has always been a matter of conjecture to historians, but this possibility was prevented by his death in 1791. This was regarded as almost a national calamity, and the people buried him with splendid pomp in the Pantheon. —BIBLIOGRAPHY: A. J. T. Mézières, *Vie de Mirabeau*; L. Barthou, *Mirabeau*; W. R. H. Trowbridge, *Mirabeau, the Demi-god.*

MIRAB'ILIS. A genus of plants, nat. ord. Nyctagineæ, one species of which, *M. jalāpa,* is well known in gardens as the marvel of Pēru. It is a native of South America.

MIRABILITE. A mineral sodium sulphate, $Na_2SO_4.10H_2O$, common as a product of desiccating lakes.

MIRACLE (Lat. *miraculum,* a wonder, a prodigy; in the original Greek *sēmeion,* a sign, *teras,* a wonder or prodigy). A suspension of, or deviation from, the known laws of nature, brought about by the direct interference of a supreme supernatural Being. It is in its nature, as the term implies, an occurrence which is strange, marvellous, inexplicable, and is usually connected with some ulterior moral purpose. By the elder theologians a miracle was conceived to be the triumph of the Divine Will over the work of His hands and the laws of His making. In modern exegesis, however, the miraculous element is not considered to give evidence of opposing forces. On the contrary, a miracle is explained as a manifestation of the Divine Power working through laws and by methods unknown to us, and which, upon a higher plane, are altogether natural and orderly.

MIRACLE PLAYS. *See* DRAMA.

MIRAGE. An optical illusion caused by the curving of the rays of light in an atmosphere of varying density. As a rule, this curving is slight, and merely shifts objects, as seen, more or less out of their true position. The phenomena of *looming,* and of the *Fata Morgana,* are caused in that way. In looming, objects appear magnified and somewhat dim in their outlines; in the *Fata Morgana,* as seen especially in the Straits of Messina, objects on the shore appear much elongated in the vertical direction. Sometimes, however, and especially over hot desert sand, or over an Arctic ice-field, the bending is much greater, and may have a much more extraordinary effect. In the desert a ray passing from the top of a tree towards the ground is gradually bent upwards, and may be bent so much that it seems to come from a point underneath the level of the ground, so that the tree seems to be reflected in a lake. Over ice, an upward ray may be so bent downward that an inverted image of the object is seen in the sky. Whale-fishers quite often discover the presence of another ship in their neighbourhood by a reflection of this sort. Captain Scoresby, when sailing in Greenland waters in 1822, found out unexpectedly that his father was not far off, by recognizing the image of his ship in the sky.

MIRAMICHI (mi-ra-mi-shē'). A bay and river of New Brunswick, Canada. The bay is 20 miles wide at its entrance and runs 21 miles inland. The river falls into the bay after a north-east course of about 220 miles, of which 40 are navigable for large vessels.

MIRANDA. A northern maritime state of Venezuela, on the Caribbean. It is mountainous in parts, but is one of the most fertile of Venezuelan coffee areas. Ocumare is the capital. Area, 3000 sq. miles; pop. 189,572.

MIRAN'DOLA, Giovanni Pico della. Surnamed the *Phœnix,* born 29th Feb., 1463, died 17th Nov., 1494. He was the youngest son of Gianfrancesco della Mirandolla, of the princely family of Mirandolla. He studied at Bologna and at different towns of Italy and France, attending the most celebrated schools and most distinguished professors. He had few rivals as a finished scholar, and challenged disputation on abstruse subjects in many of the universities. He endeavoured to harmonize the doctrines of Aristotle and Plato.

MIRFIELD. A town of England, West Riding of Yorkshire, on the Calder, near Huddersfield. It is served by the L.M.S. Railway. There are coal-mines in the vicinity; cotton and woollen goods are manufactured. Mirfield is the headquarters of the community of the Resurrection, a religious order in the Church of England, founded by Charles Gore in 1892. Pop. (1931), 12,099.

MIRROR. A highly polished sheet of metal, which may be very thin; a mere film, in fact, protected by a sheet of glass. Light reaching the surface is largely reflected, and mirrors are used for that purpose and for the production of reflected images of objects facing them. The mirrors of the ancient Greeks and Romans consisted of thin discs of metal made slightly convex. The Japanese magic mirrors have the peculiar property, when a strong beam of light is reflected from them, of showing an image of the relief design on the back. This is due to the reflecting surface not being uniform, but pressed to the shape on the back in the process of polishing with the back against a hard surface. Until the middle of the nineteenth century glass mirrors were made with a tin amalgam backing, but in 1835 von Liebig discovered how metallic silver could be deposited from ammoniacal solutions of silver nitrate by the use of reducing agents. In the hot process the reduction is effected with tartaric acid at a temperature of about 40° C. Sugar is used for the same purpose in the cold process. The yellowish colour is removed by treating the deposit with cyanide of mercury, which makes the film more adherent. The silver is protected with shellac or copal varnish and a coat or two of red lead or electrically deposited copper. *See* REFLECTION.

MIRZAPUR. A city of India, in the Benares division of the United Provinces, on the Ganges. Pop. 54,994.—The Mirzapur district has an area of 4368 sq. miles. Pop. 724,183.

MISAPPROPRIATION. In English law, is the wrongful appropriation by any person, to his own use, of money or property entrusted to him. It is dealt with under the Larceny Acts. In order to prevent a servant from pretending to have given to his master's horse or other animal corn or other food which he has appropriated to his own purposes, the Misappropriation by Servants Act, 1863, provides that any servant who, contrary to orders, gives his master's corn, etc., to any animal belonging to his master, shall be liable to a penalty not exceeding £5.

MISDEMEANOUR. An offence of a less serious nature than a felony, including generally all indictable offences which do not amount to felony, as perjury, libels, conspiracies, and assaults. *See* FELONY.

MISHNA (Heb., teaching). A collection or digest of Jewish traditions and explanations of Scripture, preserved by tradition among the doctors of the synagogue, till Rabbi Jehudah, surnamed the *holy*, reduced it to writing about the end of the second century. The *Mishna* is divided into six parts: the first relates to agriculture; the second regulates the manner of observing festivals; the third treats of women and matrimonial cases; the fourth of losses in trade, etc.; the fifth is on oblations, sacrifices, etc.; and the sixth treats of the several sorts of purification. *See* TALMUD.

MISIO'NES. A territory of the Argentine Republic, stretching as an arm between Paraguay and Brazil. The territory is hilly and afforested, but stock is raised, and sugar, timber, tobacco, and verba maté are produced. Posadas, on the Parana, is the chief town. Area, 11,749 sq. miles; pop. (1932), 86,790.

MISKOLCZ. A town of Hungary, on the Sajo, and connected by rail (116 miles) with Budapest. The wheat and cattle trade and flour milling are important. Pop. (1930), 61,559.

MISPICKEL. Arsenical pyrites, FeAsS, an ore of arsenic, containing this metal in combination with sulphur and iron, sometimes found in orthorhombic crystals, but more often massive. It is grey, with metallic lustre, and not scratched by a knife.

MISPRISION. In law, any high offence under the degree of capital, but nearly bordering thereon. Misprision is contained in every treason and felony. *Misprision of felony* is the mere concealment of felony. *Misprision of treason* consists in a bare knowledge and concealment of treason, without assenting to it. Maladministration in offices of high public trust is a *positive misprision.*

MISREPRESENTATION. In law, a false statement of fact. Any party who has been induced to enter into a contract by the material misrepresentation, however innocent, of the other party may repudiate the contract and be restored to the same position as before, that is to say, the contract is voidable. But unless the statement was knowingly false, or made recklessly without due regard to the truth, or warranted, the injured party cannot claim damages. In contracts of insurance, where the utmost good faith is necessary, non-disclosure of any material circumstance which would influence a prudent insurer in accepting or rejecting the risk or in fixing the rates of premium is misrepresentation rendering the contract voidable. If the statements made are warranted, any misrepresentation, though not material to the risk, may render the contract void.

MISSAL. In the Roman Catholic liturgy, the book which contains the prayers and ceremonies of the Mass. The greater part of these prayers and ceremonies are very ancient, and some of them have come down from the times of the Popes Gelasius I, (end of fifth century) and Gregory the Great (end of sixth century); some are even older. The *Missal* was revised by the Council of Trent, its adoption by the whole Catholic Church demanded by Pius V. in 1570, and in this form it is still retained. In England before the Reformation there were missals of the Sarum use, Lincoln use, Bangor use, etc. Before the invention of printing the writing of missals ornamented with illuminated ornaments, initials, miniatures, etc., was a branch of art raised to high excellence in the monasteries.

MISSING QUANTITY. A term used by engineers to denote the difference in quantity of steam used by an engine, as shown by the indicator diagram (*see* INDICATOR), and actually as obtained by condensing and measurement. The question of how this steam passes through the engine has been the subject of considerable dogmatic assertion based on assumptions, denied by the evidence of analogous physical actions and by actual steam-engine research. It has been assumed, in the *initial condensation theory*, that the metal wall of an engine cylinder goes through the same temperature cycle as the steam, and that steam is condensed on entering, of which a part is re-evaporated later in the cycle. The difference between this condensation and re-evaporation is taken to account for the missing quantity. Professor J. H. Cotterill, as early as 1872, in his book *The Steam Engine*, pointed out that these suppositions would account for a missing quantity many times that ever found. Professors H. L. Callendar and John T. Nicolson, at the M'Gill University, Montreal, in 1895, actually tested the temperature cycles in the metal wall of a steam-engine cylinder, and found the exceedingly small temperature range it was subjected to, and also discovered the means of determining the actual condensation and re-evaporation. They found that the major part of the missing quantity was due to leakage past the moving valves, and investigated the nature of this action (*see* LAW OF CONDENSATION OF STEAM, Proc. Inst. Civil Eng., vol. cxxxi.). Professor A. L. Mellanby (see Proc. Inst. Mech. Eng., June, 1905) continued this work by investigating the effects of steam jacketing on the missing quantity. His work confirmed that of Callendar and Nicolson, and extended considerably the knowledge we have of the temperature actions in engine cylinders and at valve seats. It is interesting to note that whenever a gain in economy is obtained by the use of superheated steam, compounding, increasing the speed of running, or other similar change, the gain is mainly produced by a reduction in the missing quantity.

MISSIONS. Christianity claimed to be a world-religion and not merely the faith of a single race, and from the first was missionary in its aim and methods. The earliest Church was a missionary Church, and by the end of the fifth century the larger part of the civilized world had been Christianized. With the declension of spiritual life missionary activity practically ceased, leaving the field open for the conquests of Mahommedanism. Mediæval effort was restricted in scope and meagre in results, but with geographical discovery the zeal of the Church reawakened, and much was accomplished by the Jesuits, though their policy was chiefly to convert by compulsion. To this day traces of their influence can be found in East Central Africa and along the West Coast. The Reformation brought no increase of interest in the missionary enterprise; the eighteenth century saw tentative measures being taken; but it was not until the beginning of the nineteenth century that Christendom shook itself free from a parochial conception of the Gospel and—largely through societies independent of the Churches—inaugurated the modern era of missions. The view prevalent then was that non-Christian peoples were outside the divine pale, and the missionary appeal was based on vivid pictures of multitudes of lost souls perishing every moment. At first, therefore, the object of the missionaries was simply conversion. It was recognized, however, that evangelism was not enough, that little progress could be made until converts were able to read and write, and elementary schools were the result. These were followed, as the need arose, by institutions of a higher grade. It was also realized that the people had to be taught to use their hands in order to improve their social environment and economic status, and industrial and agricultural training was added to preaching and teaching; and, in countries where the caste system prevailed, farm colonies and co-operative banks were formed to provide self-contained communities where the converts could live in security and peace.

Medical work was also inevitable; every missionary found himself besieged by the sick and diseased, who had absolute faith in his healing power, and dispensaries and hospitals came naturally to be indispensable adjuncts of all important missions. There was no co-ordination in the policy or the activities of the missionaries, but in the course of time their united efforts began to tell: intelligence, ambition, and habits of industry were developed, and gradually a new social order was established in the regions under their influence. Unconsciously they made mistakes; they failed to recognize that the great race-religions contained elements of good. Instead of realizing that each race had innate qualities capable of utilization in the interests of Christianity, they adopted the attitude of superior beings bringing a superior religion to replace what they considered to be pure superstition and idolatry. The tendency was to impose their own ways of thought and life on the natives. In this way Christianity everywhere came to be regarded as the white man's religion, and was associated with a change to foreign dress and customs—it was accompanied not only by social disintegration, but by a process of denationalization. The effect was not at first appreciated by the missionaries. Their work continued, along with the material agencies of Governments, to foster the moral and mental enlightenment of backward peoples until the European War revealed the remarkable extent to which race-consciousness and national dignity and aspiration had, largely by their efforts, been evolved. Missionaries, and British missionaries in particular, were faced with an entirely new set of problems. The general desire for self-determination and self-government extended to the mission communities, and the local Churches pressed for a fuller measure of responsibility. In India the political and religious questions were intermixed, but the anti-British movement was directed not so much against Christian ideals as against the ideas and methods of Western civilization.

Underlying the African attitude was resentment on the part of educated natives at the manner in which they were treated by the white population. This race assertion on the part of their wards proved disconcerting to missionaries, although it was the natural outcome of their work, and they were divided in their view as to the measure of freedom it would be wise to give. But since each race might have a distinctive contribution to bring to the evolution of Christianity and the enrichment of the moral force of the world, it was generally agreed that foreign influence and authority should gradually decrease, and that the native Christian Church should be allowed to develop autonomously along the line of its own genius. The enterprise in the field still consists of a multitude of isolated and unrelated activities, but at the home base there is a certain amount of unified effort, while the subject of missions is treated in a more scientific spirit, and the literature connected with it is becoming more attractive and readable. Women are also taking a larger share in the enterprise, both in the sphere of administration and in every department of the work abroad. The actual results in the various fields, and as a whole, are extremely difficult to estimate; statistics are incomplete and unreliable, and they do not indicate the extent of the indirect influence wielded by the missions. In some areas the accessions to the Christian community outnumber the natural increase of population; in others they exceed it. The idea that the world can be evangelized, with existing forces, in a generation or two is not now entertained, and a more sober view is taken of the situation, though the possibility of mass movements is not ignored. The hope for the future lies in the multiplication of native evangelists, and the tendency is to concentrate missionaries at central stations and use them chiefly for teaching and training these agents. Interest in the work on the part of the general public is growing, in the belief that it is the only certain means of bringing about world brotherhood and peace.

MISSISSIP'PI ("Great Water"). The principal river of North America, and one of the largest rivers in the world. It has its source in Lake Itasca, state of Minnesota, whence it issues about 12 feet wide and 2 feet deep; from thence it trends southward through a number of lakes and over a series of rapids until the Falls of St. Anthony are reached; below this it receives the Iowa, the Illinois, and the Missouri as tributaries, but the latter is really the main stream, having a length of 2908 miles before the rivers unite, while that of the Mississippi is only 1330 miles. From St. Louis, a little below their confluence, the Mississippi becomes a broad, rapid, muddy river, liable to overflow its banks; lower down it receives in succession the Ohio, Arkansas, and Red Rivers, and it finally enters the Gulf of Mexico through a large delta with several "passes," some distance below New Orleans. The combined lengths of the Missouri and Mississippi are about 4200 miles; the whole area drained by the Mississippi is 1,246,000 sq. miles; the maximum flood volume reaches 1,400,000 cubic feet per second below the Ohio; and the sediment transported to the gulf annually would make a solid block 1 mile square and 260 feet high. Above its junction with the Ohio at Cairo the river enters upon a large alluvial basin, bounded on both sides by high bluffs, and through this plain the river winds for about 1150 miles. The volume is usually smallest in October and greatest in April, and the low-lying lands are subject to terrible floodings during the spring freshets. At many places attempts have been made to secure the river within its banks and save the country from loss and suffering by building dikes, or *levees* as they are called. The sediment carried down, however, is continually raising the bed of the river, and thus breaks are frequently made in these levees. The most important towns on the river banks are St. Paul, St. Louis, Cairo, Memphis, Vicksburg, Natchez, and New Orleans.

MISSISSIPPI. An east-south-central state of the United States, with a coast-line of 85 miles on the Gulf of Mexico (Mississippi Sound). The Mississippi forms the western boundary for 530 miles. Near the Gulf of Mexico the country is low and swampy; the central part is hilly and mainly prairie-land; a large area in the north-east is afforested. 7000 sq. miles along the Mississippi and in the Yazoo delta consist of rich bottom-lands. The climate is subtropical. Jackson (pop. 1930, 48,282) is the state capital, Meridian (31,954), Vicksburg (22,943), Hattiesburg (18,601), and Laurel (18,017) are other towns. Of religions, one-half of the state population is Baptist and one-third is Methodist.

Production and Industry.—The state is mainly devoted to agriculture, cotton (1,150,000 bales in 1932), maize (32,589,000 bushels, 1932) rice, wheat, oats, and potatoes being produced. There is some dairying and sheep-farming. Among minerals are coal and gypsum, but the mining industry is undeveloped.

Communications.—4,170 miles of steam and 47 miles of electric railway track traverse the state (1932), the principal lines being the Yazoo & Mississippi Valley; Illinois Central; Mobile & Jackson & Kansas City; Southern; and the Mobile & Ohio Railways.

Education, etc.—Attendance at school is compulsory; the colour-line is rigid, and black children are kept strictly separate from white. There are twenty universities and colleges, including an Agricultural and Mechanical College for negro youths, and an Industrial Institute-College, devoted to young women. Area, 46,865 sq. miles, 503 sq. miles being water; pop. (1930), 2,009,821.

Government.—Mississippi was first permanently settled as part of Louisiana in 1716, when some Frenchmen founded Natchez, then called Fort Rosalie. The territory was admitted to the Union as a state on 10th Dec., 1817. It is divided into eighty-two counties, and the administration is controlled by a Governor and a Legislature, comprising Senate and House of Representatives, both elected for four years. Two Senators and seven Representatives are sent to Congress.—Cf. *Encyclopædia of Mississippi History* (*1540-1907*) (2 vols.).

MISSOLONGHI (mis-o-lon'gē). A town of Greece, capital of the nomarchy of Acarnania and Ætolia, near the Gulf of Patras. It is notable for its gallant resistance in 1821 and in 1825-26 to a large Turkish army. Lord Byron died there in 1824, and a cenotaph has been erected to his memory. Pop. 9270.

MISSOURI (mi-sö'rē). A river of North America, which is formed in the Rocky Mountains, in Montana, winds circuitously along the base of the mountains, then east till it reaches the western boundary of North Dakota, and receives the Yellowstone. Here it begins to flow south-eastwards through North and South Dakota, then forms the eastern boundary of Nebraska, separating it from Iowa and Missouri; separates for a short distance Kansas from Missouri, then strikes eastwards across the latter state, and joins the Mississippi after a course of 2908 miles. It is navigable 2500 miles from the Mississippi. Its affluents are very numerous on both banks, but by far the most important of them are the Yellowstone, the Nebraska or Platte, and the Kansas, all from the west.

MISSOURI. A west-north-central state of the United States, between Iowa (north) and Arkansas (south), bounded by the Mississippi (east), and traversed from east to west by the Missouri. Jefferson City (pop. 1930, 21,596) is the state capital; other towns are St. Louis (821,960), Kansas City (399,746), St. Joseph (80,935), and Springfield (57,527).

Production and Industry.—Missouri is mainly devoted to agriculture, and produces maize (186,721,000 bushels in 1932), wheat (14,851,000 bushels in 1932), oats, potatoes, and sorghum. In the south-eastern lowlands cotton (285,000 bales, 1932) and flax-seed are produced. Tobacco (7,175,000 lb., 1932) and fruit are also cultivated; dairying and sheep-farming are progressive. Stock-raising, and particularly the breeding of hogs, is important. Among minerals, copper, limestone, sandstone, granite, and red and brown hematite iron are worked; the coal-fields occupy 14,000 sq. miles (estimated). Missouri is the greatest zinc- and lead-producing state of the Union, the ores at Mine Lamotte containing also cobalt and nickel.

Communications. — About 7970 miles of railway and 861 miles (1932) of electric track traverse the state, the principal railways being the Missouri Pacific; Atchison, Topeka, & Santa Fé; St. Louis South-Western, and the St. Louis & San Francisco systems. An additional 15,248 miles of state highways are being constructed. There is also a heavy traffic of river steamers between St. Louis and the Gulf of Mexico.

Education, etc.—Education is free and compulsory between the ages of seven and fourteen years. Higher education is provided by the State university (Columbia), founded in 1839; by Washington University, founded in 1857; by the St. Louis University (R.C.), founded in 1818; and by many other colleges. Area, 69,420 sq. miles, of which 693 sq. miles are water; pop. (1930), 3,629,367.

Government.—Missouri originally formed a part of Louisiana, and the district was bought by the United States in 1803, a territory being created in 1812. On 2nd March, 1821, it was admitted as a state to the Union. There are 114 counties, and the City of St. Louis. The administration comprises a Governor, Senate (34 members, elected for four years, one-half seeking re-election every two years), and a House of Representatives (150 members, elected for two years). Two Senators and thirteen Representatives are sent to Congress. — Cf. MISSOURI (in American Commonwealth Series).

MISTAS'SINI. A large lake of Quebec, Canada, drained to Hudson Bay by the Rupert River. A chain of small islands divides it into two distinct basins. Length, about 100 miles; breadth, 15 to 22 miles; depth (average), 400 feet.

MISTI, El. A snow-capped, extinct volcanic peak of Peru, in the department and overlooking the town of Arequipa. Altitude, about 19,000 feet.

MISTLETOE. The *Viscum album* of botanists, nat. ord. Loranthaceæ, a European plant growing parasitically on various trees, and celebrated on account of the religious purposes to which it was consecrated by the ancient Celtic nations of Europe, being held in great veneration by the Druids, particularly when it was found growing on the oak. It is a small shrub, with sessile, oblong, entire, somewhat leathery leaves, and small, yellowish-green flowers, the whole forming a pendent bush, covered in winter with small white berries, which contain a glutinous substance. It is common enough on certain species of trees, such as apple and pear trees, hawthorn, maple, lime, and other similar trees, but is very seldom found on the oak. Its roots penetrate into the substance of the tree on which it grows, and eventually it kills the branch supporting it.

MISTRAL, Frédéric. Provençal poet, the leader of the modern Provençal revival in France, was born at Maillane in 1830, died in 1914. His first important work was the epic poem *Mirèio* (popular as the opera *Mireille*, with music by Gounod), which appeared in 1859. Another epic, *Calendou*, came out in 1867; a volume of poems, *Lis Isclo d'Or*, in 1876; *Lou Trésor dóu Félibrige*, a dictionary of modern Provençal, in 1878-86. In 1906 appeared *Mes origines, mémoires et récits*; in 1910 a Provençal translation of Genesis; and in 1913 a collection of his poems, entitled *Oulivado*. In 1904 Mistral shared the Nobel Prize for Literature.

MISTRAL. A violent, cold north-west wind experienced in Provençe and other neighbouring districts bordering on the Mediterranean. It blows with greatest violence in autumn, winter, and early spring.

MITAU. *See* SELGAVA.

MITE. A name common to numerous small, in some cases microscopic, animals, of the class Arachnida (spiders) and ord. Acarina. The two pairs of jaws (chelicerae and pedipalpi) are variously modified for sucking, piercing, and biting. Some are of a wandering character, and are found under stones, leaves, and the bark of trees; or in provisions, as meal, cheese, pepper, etc.; others are plant parasites; and many are parasitic on or in the skin of various animals, sometimes proving of serious injury to them. The following are common species: black currant gall-mite (*Eriophyes ribis*), the cause of "big bud"; itch-mites (Sarcoptes); cheese-mites (Tyroglyphus); red "spider" (*Tetranychus telarius*); harvest-mites (Trombidium), of which the minute larvæ are known as harvest "bugs."

MITFORD, Mary Russell. English authoress, daughter of a physician at Alresford, Hampshire, and born there 1787, died 1855. Her best-known work is *Our Village*, a series of prose sketches descriptive of English country life and scenery, drawn from the village of Three Mile Cross, near Reading. A subsequent work, *Belford Regis, or Sketches of a Country Town*, was nearly equally popular.

MITFORD, William. English historian, born 1744, died 1827. He studied at Queen's College, Oxford, and entered the Middle Temple, but early quitted the profession of law, and obtained a commission in the Hampshire Militia, of which he became colonel. His early fondness for Greek led him to undertake a *History of Greece*. The first volume appeared in 1784; the fifth and last, bringing the narrative down to the death of Alexander the Great, was published in 1818. Despite its strong anti-democratic prejudices, until the appearance of the works of Thirlwall and Grote his history was considered the standard.

MITHRAS. The Mitra of the Rig Veda, the Sun, or the genius of the Sun, with the Persians, which was worshipped as a deity at a later period also in Rome. Mithras stands as mediator between Ormuzd and the world. The cultus of Mithras found its way into all parts of Europe visited by the Roman legions. In Germany many tokens of its former existence are still to be found, such as the monuments at Hedernheim, near Frankfort-on-the-Main.

MITHRIDA′TES, or MITHRADA′TES. King of Pontus, on the southern shore of the Black Sea, surnamed the *Great*. His father was murdered 120 B.C., and Mithridates ascended the throne at the age of thirteen. Soon after attaining his majority he commenced his career of conquest, which made him master of nearly all Asia Minor, besides Greece, and brought him into conflict with Rome. In 88 B.C. Sulla led a Roman army into Greece, and restored the Roman power in that country. For four years Mithridates disputed possession of Asia, but was at last compelled to succumb, 84 B.C., and to confine himself to his hereditary dominions, though he soon again began the war. After the death of Sulla, which occurred in 78 B.C., Mithridates levied another army with a determination to expel the Romans from Asia. Being defeated by Lucullus, who was appointed consul 74 B.C., he was followed by the victorious Romans into his own states, and driven to seek a refuge in Armenia, then ruled by Tigranes, who refused to deliver him up. Here Mithridates raised a third great army, and in 67 B.C. completely defeated the Romans under Triarius, the lieutenant of Lucullus, who had been recalled; and, following up his success, rapidly recovered the larger part of his dominions. The Romans now invested Pompey with absolute power in the East, and by him, in 66 B.C., the forces of Mithridates were completely routed near the Euphrates. The king retired to Bosporus (the Crimea), where his troops, headed by his son Pharnaces, broke out in mutiny, and Mithridates killed himself, 63 B.C.

MITO′SIS, or KARYOKINESIS. Indirect cell division, in which remarkable changes take place in the nucleus. The deeply staining substance (chromatin), which this contains, becomes a convoluted thread, that breaks up into a number (constant for a given species) of minute curved pieces, the chromosomes. At the same time the nuclear membrane disappears, and a spindle-shaped aggregate of delicate fibres comes into existence. The chromosomes collect together at the equator of the spindle, each divides longitudinally into halves, and these travel away from each other to the poles of the spindle. In animal cells this process appears to be directed by a minute body, the centrosphere, usually placed just outside the nucleus. This divides into two, each half travelling to one pole of the spindle. Simultaneously with the changes described, the extra-nuclear protoplasm (cytoplasm) divides, so that in the end the original cell is divided into two daughter cells. Chromosomes are believed to be linear aggregates of minute particles serving as the bearers of hereditary characters, and the complex process just outlined secures qualitative as well as quantitative halving of the chromatin between the two daughter cells. In the maturation of sex-cells "reducing" division takes place, so that a mature ovum or sperm contains only half the normal number of chromosomes. When, in fertilization, a sperm fuses with an ovum the full number is restored. Sex is perhaps determined by an extra or "odd" chromosome that has been described in a number of cases.—BIBLIOGRAPHY: E. B. Wilson, *The Cell*; W. E. Agar, *Cytology*; L. Doncaster, *Textbook of Cytology*.

MITRAILLEUSE. The name by which machine-guns are known in the French army. The word is derived from *mitraille*, meaning grape-shot, and was originally given to the first machine-gun used in the French

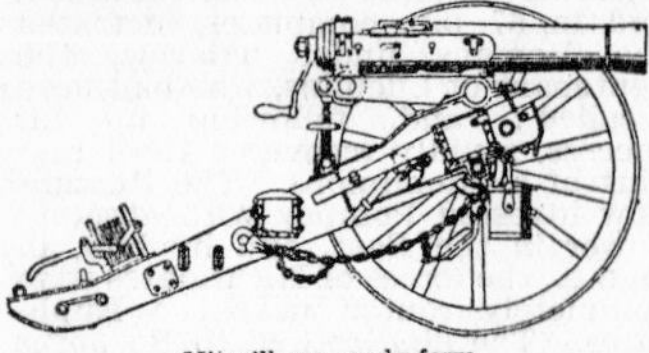

Mitrailleuse, early form

army in 1870, i.e. the thrower or distributor of grape-shot. It is still used in France as the general name for machine-guns, though the original type has long since given place to an improved Hotchkiss gun.

When originally invented, the mitrailleuse consisted of thirty-seven barrels enclosed in a cylinder or tube, looking, when mounted on a gun-carriage, much like an ordinary field-gun. The gun was loaded by means of a steel disc or plate, which, after the cartridges had been inserted, was dropped into grooves in the breech-block. The breech was then closed by means of a lever, the same motion preparing the gun for firing. Each round could be fired separately or so quickly as to be almost instantaneous, one complete revolution of the firing-handle only being necessary. The breech was then opened, and the disc with the fired cases removed and replaced by another. *See* MACHINE-GUN ; HOTCHKISS GUN.

MITRE (Lat. *mitra* ; Gr. *mitra*, mitre, fillet, belt), a sacerdotal ornament worn on the head by bishops and archbishops (including the Pope), cardinals, and in some instances by abbots, upon solemn occasions, or by a Jewish high-priest. It is a sort of

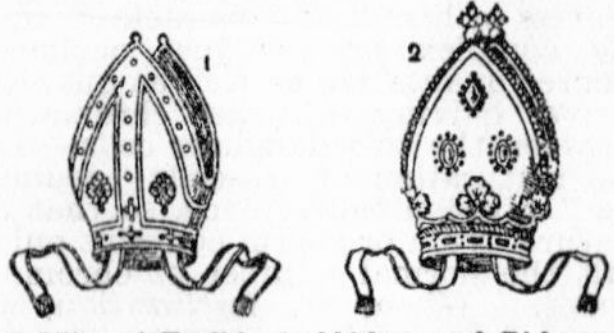

1, Mitre of English Archbishops and Bishops.
2, Mitre of Bishop of Durham.

cap pointed and cleft at the top, this form being supposed to symbolize the " cloven tongues " of the day of Pentecost. The Pope has four mitres, which are more or less rich according to the solemnity of the feast-days on which they are to be worn.

MITRE (Mitra). A name of many sea-snails possessing an elegant turreted shell. The shells exhibit a great variety of patterns, and are variegated with every kind of colour. They abound in the seas of hot climates.

MIVART, St. George. Naturalist and scientist, born 1827, died 1900. He was educated at Harrow ; King's College, London ; and the Roman Catholic College at Oscott. Among his works are : *The Genesis of the Species* (combating the Darwinian " natural selection "), *Man and Apes*, *Contemporary Evolution*, *The Cat*, *Nature and Thought*, *Origin of Human Reason*, and *Types of Animal Life*.

MNEMONICS (nē-mon'iks). The collective term employed to designate " memory systems " which make use of the device of connecting unfamiliar with familiar ideas as an aid to recollection. All such systems are more or less arbitrary. The art is of remote antiquity, Simonides, the Greek poet (500 B.C.), having devised a system. *See* MEMORY.

MNEMOSYNE (nē-mos'i-nē ; Gr., " Memory "). In the Greek mythology, daughter of Urănus (Heaven) and Gaia (Earth), and by Zeus the mother of the nine Muses.

MNIUM. A large genus of broad-leaved mosses. *M. punctatum*, with roundish, and *M. undulatum*, with strap-shaped leaves, are abundant in moist woods and glens.

MOA. An extinct bird of New Zealand. *See* DINORNIS.

MOAB. The land of the Moabites, a tribe dwelling in the mountainous region east of the Dead Sea. According to the Mosaic account (Gen. xix. 37) the Moabites were descended from Moab, the son of Lot by his eldest daughter. In the time of the judges they were for eighteen years masters of the Hebrews, but in the time of David were rendered tributaries to them. After the Babylonish captivity they lost their separate national existence.

MOABITE STONE. A monument of black basaltic granite about 3 feet 5 inches high and 1 foot 9 inches wide and thick, with rounded top but square base, on which there is an inscription of thirty-four lines in Hebrew-Phœnician characters, discovered by F. A. Klein in 1868 at Dhiban in the ancient Moab. It was unfortunately broken by the natives. The larger pieces were secured for the Louvre by Clermont-Ganneau, who had obtained a paper impression of the inscription before the stone was broken. The inscription dates about 900 B.C., and is the oldest known in the Hebrew-Phœnician form of writing. It was erected by Mesha, King of Moab, and is a record of his wars with Omri, King of Israel, and his successors.

MOBILE (mo-bēl'). A city and port of entry of Alabama, United States, on the Mobile, at its entrance into Mobile Bay. It has an important export trade, and next to New Orleans is one of the greatest cotton marts of the south. A channel 33 miles long is maintained by dredging to allow the approach of tolerably large vessels to the harbour; but from 1911 to 1914 large harbour improvements were made. It is also a fishing port and has some manufactures. Pop. (1930), 68,202.

MOBILE. A river of the United States, in Alabama, formed by the union of the Alabama and the Tombigbee, which unite about 45 miles above the town of Mobile. It enters Mobile Bay by two mouths.

MOBILE BAY. An estuary of the Gulf of Mexico, from 8 to 18 miles wide, and about 35 miles in length, north to south, the general depth being 12 to 14 feet.

MOC'CASIN SNAKE, or **COPPERHEAD.** A very venomous serpent (*Ancistrŏdon contortrix*) of the rattlesnake kind, frequenting swamps in many of the warmer parts of the United States. It is about a yard in length, with dark-brown or red markings above, and grey below.

MOCHA (mok'a), or **MOKHA.** An Arabian fortified seaport in the Yemen, on the Red Sea, formerly the chief port and emporium of trade in this region, but now little more than a heap of ruins. Pop. about 5000.

MOCHA-STONE. *See* MOSS-AGATE.

MOCKING-BIRD. An American bird of the thrush family (*Mimus polyglottus*). It is of an ashy-brown colour above, lighter below, and is much sought for on account of its wonderful faculty of imitating the cries or notes of almost every species of animal, as well as many noises that are produced artificially. Its own notes form a beautiful and varied strain. It inhabits North America chiefly, being a constant resident of the Southern States, and but rare and migratory in the northern parts of the continent. It is also found in the West Indian Islands.

Mocking-bird (*Mimus polyglottus*)

MOCK-ORANGE (*Philadelphus coronarius*). A large bushy shrub, ord. Saxifragaceæ, common in cottage gardens and shrubberies, and remarkable in early summer for its terminal tufts of creamy-white flowers having a powerful odour, which at a distance resembles that of orange-flowers. Also called *Syringa*.

MOD'ENA (ancient **Mutĭna**). A town of North Italy, capital of the province of Modena, situated in a somewhat low but fertile plain, between the Secchia and the Panaro. The most interesting buildings are the cathedral; the campanile; the ducal, now the royal palace; and the university. The manufactures and trade are unimportant. Pop. (1931), 92,757.—**Modena** was formerly an independent duchy bordering on Tuscany, Lucca, Bologna, Mantua, and Parma. It is now divided into the provinces of Modena (1043 sq. miles; pop. in 1931, 448,429), Massa-Carrara, and Reggio. Previous to 1859 Modena was governed by a branch of the House of Este.

MODERATES. A party in the Church of Scotland which arose early in the eighteenth century, and claimed the character of moderation in doctrine, discipline, and church government. It differed from the Evangelical party more particularly on the question of patronage. The difference of opinion between the two parties led to the Disruption in the Church of Scotland in 1843.

MODERNISM. The term modernism is sometimes applied in theology to designate the modern movement in general, which may be described as a movement towards freedom from the bonds of ecclesiastical authority. But the term is specially, and was indeed originally, applied in designation of a movement of reform within the Roman Catholic Church belonging chiefly to the last decade of the nineteenth century and the first decade of the twentieth. Among the representatives of the movement may be named Alfred Loisy, Lucien Laberthonnière, and Édouard le Roy in

France; Antonio Fogazzaro and Romolo Murri in Italy; George Tyrrell and Friedrich von Hügel in England; and Hermann Schell and Joseph Schnitzer in Germany. Modernism was in fact a complex of movements initially independent of each other, yet united in the end by a common sympathy and in a common condemnation, having been condemned together in the encyclical *Pascendi Dominici gregis* issued by Pope Pius X. on 8th Sept., 1907. Modernism, ideally regarded, has been defined by George Tyrrel (*Letters*, p. 119), perhaps the most prominent leader in the movement, as "a synthesis of Catholicism and Science." So defined, modernism may have a future before it, although so soon suppressed in the Roman Church. Of course the terms here used, Catholicism and Science, are to be widely interpreted. If Catholicism spells Roman Catholicism, or Ultramontanism, then the attempted synthesis would be in vain, judging from the fate of the historical movement. Or again, unless Science includes in its scope historical research and philosophical reflection, then the attempted synthesis would not be so broadly based as the historical movement. For characteristic of modernism were its critical investigations of the Bible and of the history of Church and dogma, its studies in the philosophy of religion, and its use of a new philosophical apologetic, not to speak of its deep interest in ecclesiastical and social reform.—Cf. A. L. Lilley, article *Modernism* in Hastings's *Encyclopædia of Religion and Ethics*.

MOD'ICA. A town of Sicily, in the province of Syracuse. It trades in grain, oil, wine, cheese, and cattle. Pop. 55,924.

MÖEN. A Danish island in the Baltic, between Zeeland and Falster. It is very picturesque. Farming and fishing are staple industries. The capital is Stege, a seaport on the west coast. Pop. about 14,200.

MŒRITHERIUM. A small ancestor of the elephants, without tusks, and probably with no trunk, occurring in the Oligocene beds of Lower Egypt.

MOFFAT, Robert. Scottish missionary traveller, born 1795, died 1883. He began missionary work in South Africa in 1813, and in 1818 made a long exploratory tour in the Damara country. He received the degree of D.D. from Edinburgh University, and in 1873 he was presented with a public testimonial (£5800). One of his daughters became the wife of Dr. Livingstone.

MOFFAT. A burgh of Scotland, in the county of Dumfries, situated in an amphitheatre of rounded hills in the valley of Annan. It has mineral springs, and is much frequented by visitors in summer. Pop. (1931), 2006.

MOGADOR'. A seaport of Morocco, about 110 miles west by south of the city of Marrakesh. It is fortified, and has a good harbour, improved greatly during 1922. The exports are wool, gum, wax, hides, skins, honey, ostrich feathers, and grain. Pop. (1931), 14,423.

MOGUL', or **MUGHAL.** A word which is the same as *Mongol*, but is applied particularly to the sovereigns of Mongolian origin, called Great or Grand Moguls, descendants of Tamerlane, who ruled in India from the sixteenth century downwards, the first of them being the conqueror Baber.

MOHAIR. The outer covering of a well-known type of animal from the Middle East, of which, perhaps, the chief centre is Angora—hence the name Angora goat. The staple of mohair is pure white, soft, and long, and, being comparatively straight (the typical feature of hair) is exceedingly lustrous. It is used extensively in the manufacture of yarns for dress mantles and other garments for ladies, constitutes the pile yarn for several types of plush fabrics, and is also utilized in the manufacture of braid of various kinds for the ornamentation of dresses, hats, and the like. Artificial silk yarns now enter largely into competition with mohair and similar fibres for this trade.

MO'HAWKS. A tribe of North American Indians, belonging to the confederacy of the Five (afterwards Six) Nations. They originally inhabited the valley of the Mohawk River. With the rest of the confederacy they adhered to the British interest during the War of the Revolution, and left the country on its termination for Canada, where lands were assigned them on the Grand River. Their language has been committed to writing.

MOHIC'ANS, or more correctly **MAHICANS.** A tribe of Indians formerly occupying the country now forming the south-western parts of New England and that portion of New York state east of the Hudson. The Mohegans are an allied tribe.

MO'HILEV. A town in white Russia, U.S.S.R., capital of a former government of the same name, on both banks of the Dnieper, 212 miles W.S.W. of Moscow. It has spacious streets and a large octagonal square occupied by the principal buildings, among others the palace of the Greek archbishop and the bazaar. The staple manufacture is tobacco; and before the European War the trade with Riga, Memel, Danzig, and Odessa was very extensive. Pop. 47,000.

MOHURRUM. *See* MUHARRAM.

MOIDORE (from the Portuguese, *moeda d'ouro*, literally, coin of gold). A gold coin formerly used in Portugal (from 1690-1722), of the value of 4800 reis, or £1, 7*s.* sterling.

MOIRÉ (mwa'rā). The French name given to silks figured by a process called "watering." The silks for this purpose are of a substantial structure, and are first damped and folded lengthwise if wide fabrics, or two narrow pieces are placed face to face. They are then subjected to a very high pressure, and the air in trying to escape drives the small quantity of moisture before it, and, in addition, the pressure between the various parts of the face-to-face cloths varies because of the relative positions of the two; this joint action results in some parts being crushed or flattened more than others, and hence the permanent water-marks which appear in waved lines. The finest kinds of watered silks are known as *moirés antiques*. A very similar appearance is often obtained on linen fabrics by damping and beetling. An open-net fabric placed on a more compact fabric yields the same effect without any special finishing operation. *Moirette* is similar to moiré or moreen, but made from dyed yarns instead of being piece-dyed.

MOJI. A seaport of Japan, island of Kiushiu, on the Strait of, and opposite to Shimonoseki, at the entrance to the Inland Sea. A railway tunnel below the Strait connects Moji and Shimonoseki. Pop. (1930), 108,130.

MOKANNA (*Al-Moqanna*, "the veiled"). The assumed name of Hashim-Ibn-Hakim, a fuller of Gheze, in the district of Merv, who proclaimed his divine mission as a prophet, headed a revolt in Khorasan against Caliph Mahdi, and held out for five years (until A.D. 779), when he poisoned and burned his family, and then burned himself. His followers continued to pay him divine honours after his demise.

MOLA-DI-BARI. A seaport of Italy, on the Adriatic, in the province of Bari. Pop. 14,650.

MOLASSES. The uncrystallized syrup produced in the manufacture of sugar. It differs from treacle, as molasses comes from sugar in the process of making, treacle in the process of refining. Rum is a fermented product of molasses.

MOLD. County town and urban district of Flintshire, North Wales. There are some manufactures, and around are coal- and lead-mines. Pop. (1931), 5133.

MOLDAVIA. A district of Rumania, west of Bessarabia. The capital is Iasi (Jassy). Area, 14,700 sq. miles; pop. 2,500,000.

MOLDAVIA. An Autonomous Socialist Soviet Republic, included in the Ukrainian S.S.R. It is on the left bank of the Dniester, and became a separate republic in 1924. The chief industry is agriculture. Tiraspol is the capital. Area, 3315 sq. miles; pop. (1931), 613,900.

MOLDE. A summer resort of Norway, 30 miles S.W. of Christiansund. Pop. 1820.

MOLE. A name given to small insectivorous mammals, mostly belonging to the family Talpidæ, which,

Common Mole (*Talpa europæa*)

in search of worms or insect larvæ, form burrows just under the surface of the ground, throwing up the excavated soil into ridges and hillocks. The common mole (*Talpa europæa*) is found all over Europe, except Ireland, and the extreme south and north; and ranges through Asia north of the Himálaya to Japan. It is from 5 to 6 inches long; its head is large, without any external ears; and its eyes are very minute, and concealed by its fur, which is short and soft. Its fore-legs are very short and strong, and its snout slender, strong, and tendinous. It is the only British representative of the family. The "star-nosed moles" of North America (Condylūra) are so named from a star-shaped appendage on the snout. The web-footed moles (Scalops) are also North American. The golden moles (Chrysochlōris), native to

Africa south of the equator, and representing a distinct family, are remarkable for the metallic appearance of their fur, due to the presence

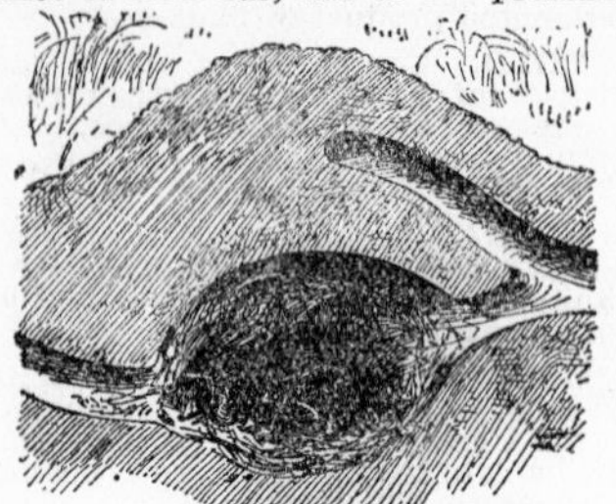

Section of Molehill

of iridescent hairs. The pouched mole (*Notoryctes typhlops*), native to the deserts of South Australia, constitutes a distinct family of the Marsupialia.

MOLE. *See* JETTY.

MOLE-CRICKET. A name given to certain orthopterous insects from the peculiar similarity of the anterior extremities of the species, and from the resemblance in their habits, to those of the mole. The best-known species (*Gryllotalpa vulgāris*), not uncommon in England, is about 1½ inches long and of a brown colour. In making its burrows it cuts through the roots of plants and commits great devastation in gardens.

MOLECULAR WEIGHTS. The distinction between a *molecule* and an *atom* has been explained under CHEMISTRY (*see also* MATTER). The molecular weight of any elementary or compound substance is a number expressing, in terms of a chosen unit, the sum of the weights of the atoms which make up the molecule of the substance. Atomic and molecular weights were formerly expressed in terms of the weight of an atom of hydrogen as the unit (H = 1); the unit now almost universally used is defined to be one-sixteenth of the weight of an atom of oxygen (O = 16, H = 1·008). According to Avogadro's Law, the molecular weight of a substance in the gaseous state is proportional to its density. *See* GASES, PROPERTIES OF.

MOLE-RAT. A name given to rodents of the genus Spalax, family Spalacidæ. They are dumpish, stout-bodied rodents, with short, strong limbs, a short tail or scarcely any, and minute or rudimentary eyes and ears. They make tunnels and throw up hillocks like the mole, but their food appears to consist wholly of vegetable substances. All the species belong to the Old World, *S. typhlus*, inhabiting the south of Russia, some parts of Asia, and Egypt.

MOLESKIN. A strong, twilled, cotton fabric of the fustian type of weave, cropped or shorn before dyeing. In reality it is a cloth of the type known as velveteen, but uncut instead of cut, in which there may be from 200 to 400 weft threads per inch. It receives its name from being soft and having a resemblance to the skin of the mole, and the cloth is much used for workmen's clothing.

MOLFETTA. An Italian seaport on the Adriatic, in the province of Bari. The church of S. Corato at Molfetta was formerly a cathedral. There are manufactures of linen and saltpetre, and a good trade. Pop. 46,000.

MOLIÈRE (mol-yār). The *nom de théâtre* of Jean Baptiste Poquelin, the greatest of French writers, and the greatest of modern dramatists after Shakespeare. Almost every fact and date in Molière's life is the subject of a more or less acrimonious controversy; many of even the minutest details have called forth elaborate monographs. The short sketch of his life here given follows the majority of competent authorities. Molière was born in Paris, and was baptized on 15th Jan., 1622. His father was an upholsterer, who became *valet tapissier* to the king, a lucrative position of some importance. He was educated at the Jesuit Collège de Clermont, which he left in 1641. He became a pupil of Gassendi, and made a complete translation (not preserved) of the *De Rerum Natura* of Lucretius. It is probable that he was called to the Bar. In 1643 he hired a tennis-court, and began therein his career as an actor, along with various members of the Béjart family. They took the name of L'Illustre Théâtre. After three years of varying success in Paris, they were obliged to tour the provinces from 1646 to 1658, when they were able to return in triumph to the scene of their former failure. While travelling in the provinces Molière got practice in writing for the stage; two of his early farces, *La Jalousie du Barbouillé* and *Le Médecin volant*, have been preserved. Some of his more elaborate pieces existed in whole or in part before he returned to Paris, but his career as dramatist may practically be said to commence with *Les Précieuses ridicules* (1659); it ended with his death in 1673. During these fourteen busy years Molière was not merely a playwright, he was also principal actor and stage-manager. Some time early in 1662 Molière married Armande Béjart, an actress in his own company, probably about twenty years his junior, and a sister of his friend Madeleine Béjart. The marriage was not a happy one, and caused much scandal at the time, scandal which was originally spread abroad by Molière's enemies, but which has since been propagated by many of his admirers and biographers, mainly his own countrymen. There are three degrees of scandal about Molière's marriage: the positive says that Madeleine had been Molière's mistress in her younger days; the comparative says that Armande was not the sister but the daughter of Madeleine; and the superlative says that Molière was the father of his own wife. This crowning scandal, which was the impudent invention of Molière's rival Montfleury, has supplied several learned gentlemen with material for a dissertation. There is no proper evidence of the truth of any of these calumnies. It is certain that Molière was a jealous husband; it is probable that Armande was a flighty, if not an unfaithful wife. These two things would not be worth recording were it not that so many lies about Molière's married life are solemnly set down as facts. In 1665 the king adopted Molière's troupe as his own servants. In 1667 Molière showed symptoms of lung disease, which placed him in the hands of the physicians, whom he ridiculed and mistrusted. On 17th Feb., 1673, after acting the principal part in *Le Malade imaginaire*, Molière, a genuine sick man, burst a blood-vessel while coughing, and died soon after. Molière's plays are as follows: *L'Étourdi* (1655), *Le Dépit amoureux* (1658), *Les Précieuses ridicules* (1659), *Sganarelle* (1660), *Don Garcie de Navarre* (1661), *L'École des maris* (1662), *Les Fâcheux* (1662), *L'École des femmes* (1662), *La Critique de l'école des femmes* (1663), *Impromptu de Versailles* (1663), *Le Mariage forcé* (1664), *La Princesse d'Élide* (1664), *Le Festin de Pierre* (*Don Juan*) 1665, *L'Amour médecin* (1665), *Le Misanthrope* (1666), *Le Médecin malgré lui* (1666), *Mélicerte* (1666), *Le Sicilien* (1666), *Amphitryon* (1668), *George Dandin* (1668), *L'Avare* (1668), *Tartuffe* (1669; the first three acts were performed in 1664, and the whole play was performed in 1667, but stopped after the first night), *Monsieur de Pourceaugnac* (1669), *Les Amants magnifiques* (1671), *Le Bourgeois gentilhomme* (1671), *Les Fourberies de Scapin* (1671), *La Comtesse d'Escarbagnas* (1672), *Les Femmes savantes* (1672), *Le Malade imaginaire* (1673). All of Molière's plays, even the most hastily composed of his farces, contain passages of characteristic brilliancy; some stand out as masterpieces unequalled and unapproached. The early *Précieuses ridicules* and *Les Femmes savantes*, dealing with the affectation of learning by the ignorant, are excellent, the maturer play being, as is natural, the more effective. *Don Juan* is a masterpiece of another kind, a play which is terrible and romantic as well as comic. *George Dandin*, a farce based on a story at least as old as Boccaccio, is raised to the dignity of a satiric comedy by the De Sotenvilles. Another excellent farce is *Le Médecin malgré lui*, which is founded on an old *fabliau*. Even better is *Le Bourgeois gentilhomme*, which deals with the social aspirations of the newly enriched, and *Monsieur de Pourceaugnac*, which describes some of the difficulties of a provincial lawyer in the capital. *L'Avare* and *Amphitryon* are both founded upon Plautus, and are wholly admirable. *Tartuffe* stands even higher than any of the plays hitherto mentioned, and is a masterly exposure of hypocrisy. It raised a storm of criticism, and was not produced in full until five years had elapsed since its composition. When its hostile reception was contrasted by the king with the favourable reception of a worthless farce *Scaramouche*, it was wittily said that "*Scaramouche* only ridicules God and religion, about which these people care nothing, while Molière's piece ridicules themselves." *Le Misanthrope* has been acclaimed by many as the greatest of all the plays; certainly it is that which contains most of the quintessence of the comic spirit of Molière. This play has little action, but is one of the most delicate satires ever penned. Its original sub-title was *L'Atrabiliaire amoureux*, a fine description of its leading character. Like all great comic writers, Molière has a vein of seriousness in him. His muse is not only eminently witty but extraordinarily wise. His plays are a corrective to much of the humbug of modern life. He teaches many lessons, not obtrusively as, for example, Ben Jonson does, but by means of stimulating thoughtful laughter, a sense of humour, and its companion quality, a sense of proportion. He stands among the greatest of comic writers beside

Aristophanes and Shakespeare, and in France he occupies a similar position to that held by the latter in England.—BIBLIOGRAPHY: A. A. Tilley, *Molière*; E. Faguet, *En lisant Molière*; E. Rigal, *Molière*; E. Soulié, *Recherches sur Molière et sur sa famille*; P. Lacroix, *Bibliographie molièresque.*

MOLI'NA, Luis. A Jesuit and professor of theology at the Portuguese University of Evora, was born at Cuenca, in New Castile, in 1535, and died in 1601 at Madrid. He has become known by his theory of grace. In order to reconcile man's free-will with the Augustinian doctrine of grace, he published a work in which he undertook to reconcile the free-will of man with the foreknowledge of God and predestination. It caused lengthened discussion, and passed subsequently into the Jansenist controversy. Molina was attacked by Pascal in the *Provincial Letters.*

MOLINE (mo-lēn'). A manufacturing city of Illinois, United States, on the Mississippi, served by the Chicago, Milwaukee and St. Paul, and other railways, and by the Hennepin canal. Pop. (1930), 32,236.

MOLI'NOS, Miguel. A Spanish mystic and theologian, born 1628, died 1696. In 1675 he published the *Spiritual Guide,* an ascetical treatise, which promulgated the new religious doctrine known as *Quietism.* In 1685 he was cited before the Holy Office, and in 1687 the Inquisition condemned his works. He spent the rest of his days as a prisoner in a convent of the Dominicans.

MOLLASSE. A soft greenish or yellowish sandstone series which occupies the country between the Alps and the Jura, and is of Oligocene and the Miocene age.

MOLLENDO. A seaport and railway terminal station of Southern Peru, capital of the province of Islay, in the department of Arequipa. It is situated between the valleys of Tambo and Camara and the rivers bearing these names, and stands on the top of cliffs, the surroundings being barren, sandy, and rocky. Mollendo has no manufactures, and is, like Liverpool in Great Britain, entirely devoted to transport. Imports are mainly earthenware, cottons, machinery, iron and steel, automobiles, and foodstuffs, part of which are in transit for Bolivia. Wood, hides and skins, quinine, coca leaves, tin, copper, and antimony are exported for Bolivia; Peruvian exports comprise merino and sheep's wool, alpaca and vicuña wool, gold, silver, copper, lead and antimony ores, a little rubber, and some sugar and cocoa. Prior to 1873, when it was made the starting-point of the Southern Railway, Mollendo was merely a fishing-village. Shipping work is carried on by lighters, ships anchoring in the open roadstead about one mile off-shore. Mollendo is an oil-fuel depot. Pop. 10,000.

MOLLUS'CA. A phylum of animals including such common shellfish as snails and slugs; oysters, cockles, and other bivalves; and the soft-bodied cuttle-fishes and octopuses, to which the name (Lat. *mollis,* soft) was originally applied. Molluscs are unsegmented, *i.e.* the body is not divided into successive rings or segments, and in most cases the body-wall is drawn out into a sort of flap, the *mantle,* that helps to bound a cavity sheltering the breathing organs, which in aquatic types are usually plume-like gills. The blood, which is purified by these, passes into a heart situated near the upper or dorsal side of the body, and is thence pumped to the various organs. A muscular thickening, or *foot,* developed on the under or ventral side of the body, is the organ of locomotion, as may be seen in a crawling snail. The central nervous system consists of a nerve-ring surrounding the front end of the digestive tube, and thickened into swellings known as ganglia.

Most molluscs possess a distinct head, bearing tentacles and eyes; and a curious rasping organ (*odontophore*), consisting of a projection on the floor of the mouth, over which is stretched from front to back a horny tooth-studded ribbon, the *radula,* often miscalled "palate" or "tongue." The body is generally protected by a hard calcareous shell, which may be in one piece (*univalve*), two pieces (*bivalve*), or, more rarely, several pieces (*multivalve*). Sometimes the shell is internal.

Five classes are recognized: (1) Cephalopoda (q.v.), head-footed molluscs, all marine. (2) Gasteropoda (q.v.), snails and slugs. (3) Lamellibranchia (q.v.) or Pelecypoda, bivalve molluscs. (4) Scaphopoda, tusk-shells. Small marine forms with reduced head and a curved tubular shell open at both ends. (5) Amphineura, primitive molluscs. —BIBLIOGRAPHY: Sir E. Ray Lankester, *Treatise on Zoology* (Part v., by P. Pelseneer); A. H. Cooke, *Molluscs* (*Cambridge Natural History*) Forbes and Hanley, *British Mollusca*; M. S. Lovell. *Edible Mollusca of Great*

Britain and Ireland; Woodward and Tate, *Manual of the Mollusca*; Zittel and Eastman, *Text-book of Palæontology*.

MOLLWITZ. A village of Silesia. Frederick the Great seized Austria from Maria Theresa, and the Austrians marched against him in 1741. On 10th April, 1741, a battle was fought near Mollwitz.

MOLLY MAGUIRES. The name assumed by members of a secret illegal association in Ireland, afterwards reorganized in the anthracite coal-mining district of Pennsylvania. The organization was guilty of many outrages, and was broken up in 1876, twenty members being hanged for murder.

MOLOCH (*Molech*, or *Molach*, lord, or king). The chief god of the Phœnicians, frequently mentioned in Scripture as the god of the Ammonites, whose worship consisted chiefly of human sacrifices, ordeals by fire, mutilation, etc. These sacrifices were offered chiefly in the valley of Hinnom, to the east of Jerusalem. King Solomon built a temple to Moloch on the Mount of Olives.

MOLOCH LIZARD (*Moloch horridus*). A species of lizard found in the arid parts of South and West Australia. It is one of the most ferocious-looking, though at the same time one of the most harmless of reptiles, the horns on the head and the numerous spines on the body giving it a most formidable and exceedingly repulsive appearance.

MOLOKAI. An island of the Hawaiian group. It is noted for its settlement of lepers, all persons on the islands found to be affected with the disease being sent by Government to Molokai, and kept entirely isolated from the healthy part of the community. Pop. 2581.

MOLTKE (molt'ke), **Helmuth Carl Bernard, Count von.** German field-marshal, born near Mecklenburg 1800, died 1891. He entered the Danish army in 1819; left that service for the Prussian in 1822, and became a staff-officer in 1832. In 1835 he superintended the Turkish military reforms, and he was present during the Syrian campaign against Mehemet Ali in 1839. He returned to Prussia and became colonel of the staff in 1851, and equerry to the Crown Prince in 1855. In 1858, as provisional director of the general staff, he acted in unison with von Roon and Bismarck in the vast plans of military reorganization soon after carried out. The conduct of the Danish War (1864) was attributable to his strategy, as was also the success of the Austro-Prussian War of 1866, and the Franco-Prussian War of 1870-71. In the latter year he was made field-marshal, and became count in 1872. He retired from the position of chief of the general staff in 1888.—Cf. W. Bigge, *Feldmarschall Graf Moltke*.

MOLUCCA ARCHIPELAGO, or **SPICE ISLANDS.** An island-group forming part of the Dutch East Indies. It is divided into the provinces of Amboina (18,914 sq. miles), Ternate (12,796 sq. miles), and New Guinea (160,692 sq. miles, created a province in 1920). The total population in 1930 was 893,030. The Moluccas were discovered by Serrano and D'Abren in 1512, and were in Portuguese possession from 1521. Dutch possession dates from 1613, since when the islands have twice been temporarily occupied by Great Britain.

MOLYBDENITE. Mineral molybdenum sulphide, occurring as steel-grey platy six-sided crystals, commonly in granitic rocks. It is the source of molybdenum, for use in the production of hard steel.

MOLYBDE'NUM. One of the less well-known metals, of a white silvery colour, harder than topaz, and having a specific gravity of 8·6 to 9·0; atomic weight, 96. It is unaltered in the air at ordinary temperatures, but is oxidized when heated. By special means it can be sintered into rods which may be drawn into wire. It is largely used in the manufacture of special steels.

MOMBA'SA. Chief port of Kenya Colony, East Africa, on a fertile coral island off the east coast of Africa, in lat. 4° 4′ S. It has two harbours, one on the Kilindibi side, and another on the north-east (*see* KENYA COLONY). A short railway connects it with the mainland, and it is a terminal station of the Uganda Railway. The chief exports are ivory, grain, rubber, copra, and hides; and among the imports are piece-goods, provisions, rice, grain, building materials, and hardware. Pop. 57,000 (1200 white).

MOMENT OF INERTIA. *See* INERTIA, MOMENT OF.

MOMMSEN, Theodor. German scholar and historian, born 1817, died 1903. He was appointed professor of jurisprudence at Leipzig in 1848, professor of Roman law at Zürich in 1852; obtained a similar chair at Breslau in 1854; in 1858 went to Berlin as professor of ancient history. His best-known work is a *History of Rome*, which has been translated into English; but he also published many other works on Roman history, law, and antiquities. He also edited the great *Corpus Inscriptionum Latinarum.*

MOMPOX'. A town of Colombia. on the Magdalena. Founded in 1538, it was at one time of considerable commercial importance, but the capricious changes of the river's course have seriously injured its prosperity. Pop. 16,000.

MOMUS. The god of mockery and censure among the ancients, was the son of Night. Aphrodite herself was exposed to his satire; and when he could find no fault with her person, he observed that the noise of her footfalls was too loud for the goddess of beauty. He was expelled from heaven for his free criticism of the gods. Momus is generally represented raising a mask from his face and holding a small figure in his hand.

MONA. The ancient name of the Isle of Anglesey. The Isle of Man is also referred to as Mona, principally by Cæsar, but it is called *Monapia* by Pliny, and *Monarina* or *Monacæda* by Ptolemy.

MONA (*Cercopithēcus mona*). A West African monkey, sometimes called the *variegated monkey*, because its fur is varied with grey, red, brown, and green. It is frequently brought to Europe and is easily tamed.

MONACO. A principality on the Mediterranean, surrounded since 1860 by the French department of Alpes-Maritimes, except on the side facing the sea. The capital is Monaco (pop. 2085), a sea-bathing resort and the seat of an international hydrographic bureau established in 1921. Below La Condamine (pop. 11,787), and a mile to the east, is Monte Carlo (pop. 11,055), a collection of hotels and villas, with a casino established in 1860. Commerce is relatively unimportant, coal and wine being imported; olive oil, oranges, perfumes, and citrons are exported. The revenue is mainly derived from the gaming-tables, the concession for which brought in £80,000 (1917), and £90,000 in 1927, and will provide £100,000 in 1937. Area, 370 acres; pop. (1928), 24,927.

Monaco belonged to the Grimaldi family from A.D. 968. The reigning prince was dispossessed in 1792 (French Revolution). The principality was not re-established until 1814, being then placed under the protection of the Kingdom of Sardinia (Treaty of Vienna, 1815). Mentone and Rocabruna revolted in 1848, and were ceded to France in 1861. Until 7th Jan., 1911, the prince was absolute, but a Constitution granted on that date provides for a National Council elected by universal suffrage and *scrutin de liste.* The reigning prince, Louis II., who succeeded in 1922 on the death of his father Prince Albert, dissolved the elected bodies of the Principality in 1930, and suspended a few of the constitutional guarantees. The territory is divided into three communes. The coinage of the principality (100 franc pieces) has been current (since 1876) in all states of the Latin Union. There are special postage stamps and a national flag. Since 1887 there has been a Roman Catholic bishop.—Cf. A. Smith, *Monaco and Monte Carlo.*

MONAD (Gr. *monas*, unit). In philosophy, an imaginary entity in the philosophy of Leibnitz, according to whom monads are simple substances, of which the whole universe is composed, each differing from every other, but all agreeing in having no extension, but in being possessed of life, the source of all motion and activity. Every monad, according to Leibnitz, is a soul, and a human soul is only a monad of elevated rank.

MONAD. A name formerly applied to extremely minute unicellular animals (Protozoa) common in putrefying liquids, and swimming by the undulations of one or more slender protoplasmic filaments (*flagella*).

MON'AGHAN. A county of the Irish Free State; area, 318,985 acres. The surface is hilly, and abounds with small lakes and bogs. Flax, oats, and potatoes are produced, but linen manufacturing forms the chief employment. Monaghan is the county town. Pop. (1926), 65,131.—The town of **Monaghan** is 70 miles N.N.W. of Dublin, on the Ulster Canal. It is an old place, and had a charter from James I. Pop. (1926), 4643.

MONARCHY (Gr. *monarchia*, sole power), is a state or government in which the supreme power is either actually or nominally vested for life in a single person, by whatsoever name he may be distinguished. A monarchy in which the subjects have no right or powers as against the monarch is termed *despotic* or *absolute*; when the legislative power is wholly in the hands of a monarch, who, however, is himself subject to the law, it is termed *autocratic*; but when the monarch shares the power of enacting laws with representatives of the people, the monarchy is *limited* or *constitutional.* In ancient

Greece a monarchy in which the ruler either obtained or administered his power in violation of the Constitution was termed a *tyranny*, however beneficent and mild the rule might be. Monarchies are either *hereditary* or *elective*.

MONASTICISM. The monastic system in Western Europe dates from the time of St. Benedict (about 480 to 544), but the impulse towards a life of religious seclusion is much older and goes back to pre-Christian times, where it is found in India as well as in Judea and in Egypt. Christian monasticism is generally regarded as having originated with St. Anthony (born in Egypt about 250), who lived as a hermit and attracted other hermits to the neighbourhood of his cell. His followers were not organized into a community or Order, and the first monastic Order, governed by a strict and detailed rule of life, was that of St. Pachomius (292-346), who also lived in Egypt. From Egypt both forms of monastic life spread into Syria (where the exaggeration of the eremitic form is illustrated by St. Simeon Stylites, who lived for thirty years on the top of a pillar from which he never descended), into Asia Minor, and into Western Europe. The eremitic life, with its extreme austerities, attracted votaries in Western Europe from the middle of the fourth century, but lack of organization prevented it from exercising any widespread influence. The creator of the historical European monasticism was St. Benedict of Nursia (in Umbria), who established the cenobitic or community life, and devised a Rule which was the model of subsequent founders. The Rule of St. Benedict was distinguished by its abandonment of the austerities which had been introduced from the East, and by its adaptation of the monastic ideal to the climate and circumstances of Italy, and it was less severe than the slightly later Irish Rule of St. Columbanus, which had for a time some vogue on the Continent. The Benedictines or Black monks (so called from their official habit) were to live in separate communities, each under the government of its abbot, who, however, was bound to consult the whole community when important questions arose for settlement. Their day was divided between religious services, reading, and work. The work done might be of almost any nature—manual and agricultural, literary, or educational—and the monks played a great part in the evangelization of Northern Europe, in the introduction of the arts and of civilization, and in the preservation and extension of learning. They came to be known as "regulars," because they lived under a "regula" or Rule, and were thus distinguished from the "secular" clergy, who lived in the world. They were also known as "religious," and "to enter religion" meant, in the Middle Ages, to become an inmate of a monastery. Monks were "clerks" in the wide sense of the term, and had the legal privileges of the clergy, but it was not contemplated that they should all receive holy orders.

Degeneration from the Benedictine ideal led to successive reforms or revivals, the most famous of which was the Cluniac Order, founded at the Abbey of Cluny, in Burgundy (910). This offshoot of the Benedictines exercised a profound influence upon the Church and the Papacy in the tenth and eleventh centuries. Other independent offshoots from the Benedictines subsequently arose, the most important of which was the Cistercians (the Grey or White monks), founded in the end of the eleventh century by St. Robert at Cîteaux, near Dijon. The greatness of the new Order, which aimed at restoring the Rule of St Benedict in its entirety followed the accession of St. Bernard, who in 1115 became abbot of the daughter House of Clairvaux. The Cistercians laid great stress upon manual labour; they became expert farmers, and the English Cistercians contributed much to the English wool trade in the Middle Ages. The example of Cluny led to modifications among the Benedictines proper, and they imitated the Cluniacs in adopting an organization to form a bond of union among the separate monasteries in each ecclesiastical province.

Other Rules grew up from about the middle of the tenth century, the followers of which, though "regulars" or "religious," were not, strictly speaking, monks, that is, the sole aim of the Order was not simply to live a religious life within a monastery which was normally, their permanent home. The Canons Regular, or Austin Canons, founded in the latter part of the eleventh century, lived under what is known as the Rule of St. Augustine. They formed communities and took vows of poverty, obedience, and chastity, as the monks did, but they undertook the cure of souls and were responsible for parochial work. The Austin Canons gave rise, in turn, to the Premonstratensians, whose Rule was more austere than that of the parent body, and, in England, to the Gilbertines, a Double Order, in which the men were Austin Canons, and the women followed the Cistercian Rule. The two communities lived in adjoining buildings, and the canons performed spiritual offices for the nuns. A much greater departure from the monastic ideal came with the establishment of the Mendicant Orders or Friars—Franciscans or Grey Friars (1210), Dominicans or Black Frairs (1215), and Carmelites or White Friars (1245). The friars were sharply distinguished from the monks by belonging not to any particular House and having no permanent home. Unlike the monks, they did not, at first, desire to possess great buildings, and their obedience was due not to the head of an individual House, but to the Order itself or to the authorities of their own province. Their ideal was not contemplative nor connected with the performance of manual labour, and they wandered about the country, begging for their subsistence and paying special attention to the poor, and assisting the regular clergy. The care of the poor and sick was the special duty of the Franciscans, and the Dominicans were distinguished by their zeal for preaching; both Orders made important contributions to learning. All these Orders, both of monks and friars, were cenobitic. The most important foundation suggestive of eremitic monasticism was that of the Carthusians, founded by St. Bruno at Chartreuse, near Grenoble, in 1084. Their Rule was very austere, and though they lived in a Charterhouse, most of their time was passed in separate hermitages. The number of Charterhouses was small, but there were several in England, and one in Scotland—at Perth, founded by James I. Most of the great Orders, including the Benedictines, the Franciscans, and the Dominicans, had branches for women, and separate Orders of nuns, like the Brigittines and the Ursulines, were founded.

By the period of the Reformation, the religious Orders had degenerated all over Europe, and that event led to their disappearance from Protestant countries. During the counter-Reformation, some new Orders were founded—the Society of Jesus (1540) being the most important—and there was a new development in the creation of communities of secular priests bound by temporary vows—the Oratorians (1570) and the Oblates of St. Charles (1578).

Monachism, however, as belonging to the older system of things, was regarded with hostility by the spirit of rationalism and liberalism which found decisive expression in the French Revolution; and during the eighteenth century the monastic Orders were obliged, as the Papal power diminished, to submit to many restrictions imposed upon them by Catholic princes, or to purchase immunity at a high price. In 1781 the houses of some Orders were wholly abolished by the Emperor Joseph II. In France the abolition of all Orders and monasteries was decreed in 1789, and the example was followed by all the states incorporated with France under the protection of Napoleon I. In the nineteenth century, under Napoleon III. and in the early years of the Republic, monachism prospered in France; but restrictions were later imposed, and since 1901 many monasteries have been dissolved. In Germany all Orders except those engaged in tending the sick were abolished in 1875. The unification of Italy was followed by a series of decrees pronouncing all monastic Orders illegal. In Portugal monasteries were abolished by decree in 1834, and in Spain in 1837. In the Roman Catholic states of South America the same policy of abolition has been adopted; whereas in the United States and Canada several Orders have made considerable progress. Protestantism has never favoured monachism as found in the Roman Church, but in the Episcopal Churches of England and America "sisterhoods" and "brotherhoods" (especially the former) have been formed at various times, generally with some philanthropic or charitable object. In the Eastern or Greek Church all nuns and the great majority of monks belong to the Basilian Order. Some monasteries, including the famous monastery of Mount Sinai, obey the Rule of St. Anthony. — BIBLIOGRAPHY: J. O. Hannay, *Spirit and Origin of Christian Monasticism*; F. A. Gasquet, *English Monastic Life*; F. M. Steele, *Monasteries and Religious Houses of Great Britain and Ireland*; T. Carlyle, *Past and Present*.

MONAS'TIR, now **BITOLYE**. A city of Yugoslavia, in Serbia, formerly belonging to Turkey, but ceded to Serbia in 1913. It was captured by the Bulgarians on 2nd Dec., 1915, and retaken by the Allies on 19th Nov., 1916 (European War). At noon on 19th April, 1922, the explosion occurred of a truck of explosives, belonging to a consignment of 400 trucks of war munitions which also exploded, destroying most of the city and surrounding villages.

with great loss of life. Pop. (1931), 32,982.

MONAZITE. A mineral cerium thorium phosphate, occurring in granitoid rocks, and much sought for in the alluvia arising from their decay. It is one of the main sources of thorium for the incandescent gas-mantle trade.

MONCTON. A seaport city of New Brunswick, Canada, on the Petitcodiac, between the Bay of Fundy and Northumberland Strait. It is an important divisional headquarters of the Canadian National Railway. Its situation makes it a most important distributing point for New Brunswick and Nova Scotia. Pop. (1931), 20,617.

MOND, Ludwig. Technological chemist, was born at Cassel, in Germony, in 1839, died in London in 1909. In 1864 he took up his residence in England, where he introduced a process for recovering sulphur from alkali waste. In 1893 he entered into partnership with Sir J. T. Brunner, and founded the great alkali works of Brunner, Mond & Co., near Northwich, Cheshire, the success of this enterprise being due largely to Mond's improvements on the Solvay process of alkali manufacture. He also introduced new processes in other departments of chemical industry, such as the manufacture of chlorine in connection with the ammonia-soda process, the manufacture of gas for heating ("Mond gas"), and a new process for producing pure nickel.

MONDOVI (ancient **Mons Vici**). A city of Italy, in the province of Cuneo, Piedmont, on the Ellero. The sixteenth-century citadel and the bishop's palace and cathedral are notable. Mons Regalis printing press was established here in 1472. Pop. 19,260.

MONET, Claude. French painter, born at Paris 1840. One of the leaders of the Impressionist Movement, which took its name from the picture *Impression*, exhibited by him at the Salon des Refusés in 1863. He was first influenced by Boudin at Boulogne, and then studied in Paris under Gleyre.

In 1871 a visit to London brought him under the influence of Turner's work, which largely helped to form his characteristic style. This is based upon modern scientific discoveries with regard to light, and consists in the use of a palette limited to white and the seven spectral colours, the keying up of shadows to their pitch in nature, and the use of a broken touch to give luminosity, the aim of the painter being not to paint objects but the light they reflect to the eye. Among Monet's most

Claude Monet

notable works are a series of *Haystacks* and of *Rouen Cathedral*, the same view being painted several times under different conditions of light. He died in 1926.

MONEY. This may be defined as anything that passes readilyfrom hand to hand as a means of purchasing. Its use replaces barter or payment in kind, processes involving much inconvenience owing to the difficulty of equating the values of the things exchanged, and of both parties to an exchange being willing to accept what the other can offer. By facilitating exchange, money assists the specialization and division of labour, which are the bases of large-scale production. The breakdown of a monetary system, as in Central Europe to-day, is a severe hindrance to the economic development of a country.

Money may consist of any substance, or take any form dictated by law or custom, but an essential characteristic is that it should be readily and widely acceptable. In primitive communities such articles as cattle, shells, rice, and tea have been used, but modern civilized states invariably employ metal or paper. These, in the form of coin or notes, possess most of the qualities desirable in a money material, viz. portability, durability, homogeneity in quality, and cognizability. The metals chiefly used are gold, silver, copper, and nickel, this last on the continent of Europe and in the United States. Iron, once used in Sparta, is now being used in Germany.

Notes are issued on many different systems. They may either be redeemable on demand, as in the case of Bank of England and Treasury notes, or irredeemable, as are the local currency notes now circulating in France. In the case of redeemable notes, a reserve must be held against them, usually partly in securities and partly in standard money (see later). An issue of notes against securities or without a reserve is called *fiduciary.* Besides acting as a medium of exchange, money serves as a measure of value, thereby enabling values to be compared; as a standard for measuring deferred payments, such as debts; and as a store of value.

An important distinction is between standard money and token money. The former is composed of the standard of value, i.e. any commodity with which other things are compared to measure their value. Before the European War gold was (and nominally still is) the standard of value in all European countries and their colonies, and in America. In the United Kingdom this was embodied in the sovereign and half-sovereign, in the Latin Monetary Union (which includes France, Belgium, Italy, Switzerland, and Greece) in the gold napoleon. Since the European War the sovereign and similar coins have ceased to be true standard money, since their value as metal is now greater than their value as coins.

The value of standard money depends on the value of the material in it; but token money, as in the case of notes, derives its value from law or custom, without regard to its intrinsic value. A country's money may consist entirely of token money, no standard money being in circulation. In India there is virtually a gold standard, but there is practically no gold in circulation. When money whose value depends on its material is in circulation, the famous *Gresham's Law,* "that bad money drives out good," may operate. The tendency is for the better coins to be melted down, hoarded, or exported, while light-weight coins remain in circulation.

Money of Account, in which accounts are kept and prices expressed, may differ from the coins actually in use. Such money is the guinea and pound sterling in the United Kingdom, the franc in France, the mark in Germany. Another distinction is between *legal tender,* which creditors are bound by law to receive in payment of a debt, and other money. In the United Kingdom the sovereign is legal tender to any amount; while certain early issues of Treasury notes are no longer legal tender.

It is important clearly to understand that money is simply one among many commodities. Just as the value of other goods is expressed in terms of money and known as their price, so the value of money may be expressed in terms of anything else. This value is determined by the demand for and the supply of money. Thus, if there is a large supply of money relative to the amount required (which depends on the size and number of transactions involving money, and the rapidity with which money circulates), the value of money in terms of goods falls, i.e. prices rise; while if the supply of money relative to the demand for it falls off, the converse is the case. This conception of money explains why token money has a value though its material contents are comparatively worthless; and why the famous *assignats* issued by the French Republic (1789-94), and the rouble notes recently issued in Russia, fell to a nominal value because of an enormous over-issue. Similarly, the great discoveries of gold during the nineteenth century, by diminishing the value of gold, caused a large rise of prices in gold-standard countries. In consequence of this, *bimetallists* proposed to use as a standard both gold and silver, which for currency purposes were to be made interchangeable at a fixed rate.

A proposal of more practical interest to-day is to use an index number (q.v.) to show how money contracts must be varied so as to make the purchasing power of money constant. Cheques, bills of exchange, and similar credit instruments are sometimes regarded as money; but though they form a most important part of the mechanism of exchange, they lack the characteristic of circulating readily from hand to hand. They really only transfer the right to money, and so economize and dispense with the use of money itself. Thus, an extension or restriction of their use, if no other change takes place, has the same effect as an increase or decrease in the supply of money.

When the supply of money, from whatever cause, is greater than is required, *inflation* takes place. To this, as a result of credit expansion and excessive note issue, is largely due the rise of prices during and after the European War. *See* CREDIT.—

Cf W. S. Jevons, *Money and the Mechanism of Exchange.*

MONEY-LENDERS ACT. An Act which came into force on 1st Nov., 1900. Its main purpose is to prevent the extortion of excessive interest by money-lenders, the Act giving courts power to alter money-lending agreements where there is sufficient reason for so doing. The expression "money-lender" does not include pawnbrokers, friendly societies, building societies, bankers, and certain other specified persons or institutions. Money-lenders within the meaning of the Act had to register themselves in accordance with its provisions. Heavy penalties are also attached to deception and fraudulent statements by money-lenders or those employed by them.

A further Act was passed in 1911. By it money-lenders are prohibited from carrying on business under any name containing the word "bank" or implying a banking business, and from issuing circulars, letters, etc., containing any expressions which might reasonably be construed as implying a banking business.

This was repealed and re-enacted, by the Act of 1927. The Money-lenders Act, 1927, provided that a money-lender shall take out a licence before he may practise, which licence is to be obtained only on the production of a certificate of fitness granted by a petty sessional court; no circulars may be sent (except by request) containing an invitation to borrow, nor may canvassers be employed; money-lending contracts must be evidenced by writing; the rate of interest when expressed must not be higher than 48 per cent., and directions are given as to the calculation of interest when it is not expressed in a given rate; the charging by the money-lender of preliminary expenses is forbidden; actions in respect of loans must be brought by the money-lenders within twelve months of the money becoming due.

MONEYWORT. A plant, the *Lysimachia nummularia*, very often given the names Creeping Loosestrife and Creeping Jenny.

MONGE, Gaspard. French mathematician, born 1746, died 1818. He is remembered chiefly for his invention of descriptive geometry. He took a prominent part in the foundation of the normal and polytechnic schools in Paris, and was professor of descriptive geometry in both of these. Monge supported Napoleon, and was deprived of his offices and honours after Waterloo.

MONGHYR. A district and town of Bihar and Orissa, India. The district lies in the valley of the Ganges, and generally yields two annual crops of tobacco, rice, and maize. Area, 3927 sq. miles; pop. 2,140,000. The town stands on the Ganges, 80 miles E. of Patna. Pop. 46,825.

MONGOLIA. An outlying region of North-Eastern China, partly traversed by the Altai and Khangai Mountains, and by the desert of Gobi. It comprises three areas: *Inner Mongolia*, which is still part of China; *Outer Mongolia*, and *Tannu Tuva* (between the Sayansk and Tannu Ola Mountains in the north-west of Outer Mongolia). Urga, renamed Ulan-Bator-Hoto (Town of the Red Knight), is the chief town and trading-centre, and exports wool, skins, furs, hides, and horns. It has a wireless station.

Mongolia was formerly under the suzerainty of China, and by the Treaty of Kiakhta (1915) Outer Mongolia was given a kind of autonomy. The whole country is now, however, a self-governing republic under the protection of Soviet Russia. The indigenous inhabitants are Kalmucks and Mongols of nomadic tendency. Lamaism (Buddhist) is the prevailing religion. The area is about 1,875,000 sq. miles; and the population about 2,600,000.

MONGOLO-BURYAT REPUBLIC, or BURIAT-MONGOL REPUBLIC. An autonomous Asiatic republic of the R.S.F.S.R. (*see* RUSSIA), lying between the River Vitim and Mongolia and between Transbaikalia and Lake Baikal (west shore); area 389,100 sq. km.; pop. (1931), 575,000. The capital is Verkhne-Udinsk, which in 1926 had a population of 29,271.

MONGOLS. A race of people in the north-east of Asia, whose original seat has been supposed by some writers (but without evidence) to

Mongol

have been in the north of the present Mongolia, and in Siberia to the south-east of Lake Baikal.

Their first great advance was due to Genghis Khan, who, in 1206, conceived the bold plan of conquering the whole earth. After the death of Genghis Khan, in 1227, his sons and grandsons pursued his conquests, subjugated all China, subverted the caliphate of Baghdad (1263), and made the Seljuk sultans of Iconium tributary. In 1237 a Mongol army invaded Russia, and devastated the country with the most horrible cruelty.

The empire of the Mongols was at the summit of its power during the reigns of Mangu Khan (1252-59) and Khubilai or Kûblai Khan (1259-94), the patron of Marco Polo. At that time it extended from the Chinese Sea and from India far into the interior of Siberia, and to the frontiers of Poland. The principal seat of the *khakan* or great khan was transferred by Khubilai from Karakorum to China; the other countries were governed by subordinate khans, all of whom were descended from Genghis, and several of whom succeeded in making themselves independent.

This division of the empire was the cause of the gradual decay of the power and consequence of the Mongols in the fourteenth century. The adoption of new religions (Buddhism in the east and Mahommedanism in the west) also contributed to their fall. The eastern Mongols were finally subdued by the Manchu conquerors of China.

Of the western Mongols the most powerful were the Kipchaks or Golden Horde, who lived on the Volga, and the khanate founded in Bukhâra, on the Oxus, by Jagatai, the eldest son of Genghis Khan. The former gradually fell under the power of the Russians; but among the latter there appeared a second formidable warrior, Timurlenk (Tamerlane), called also Timur Beg. In 1369 he chose the city of Samarkand for the seat of his new government. The other Mongol tribes, with Persia, Central Asia, and Hindustan, were successively subjugated by him. In 1402, at Ancyra (Angora), in Asia Minor, he defeated and captured the Sultan Bajazet I.

After Timur's death, in 1405, his empire barely held together until 1468, when it was again divided. Baber (Babur), a descendant of Timur, founded in India, in 1519, the empire of the Great Mogul, which existed in name till 1857, though its power ended in 1739.

After the commencement of the sixteenth century the Mongols lost all importance in the history of the world, became split up into a number of separate khanates and tribes, and fell under the power of the neighbouring peoples. Their name still lingers in the Chinese province of Mongolia, but Mongolian tribes are found far beyond its boundaries. The term Mongolians is to some extent used by anthropologists to signify a very large division of the races of men (*see* ETHNOLOGY), of which the Mongols proper were considered typical. This use of the name, which includes Tartars, Chinese, and Japanese, is to be carefully distinguished from the historical use.—BIBLIOGRAPHY: J. Curtin, *The Mongols: a History*; H. H. Howorth, *History of the Mongols*.

MONGOOSE. The name of small African or Oriental carnivores of the civet family (Viverridæ), belonging to Herpestes and other genera. The well-known Egyptian mongoose is *H. ichneumon*. The commonest Indian species (*H. mungo*) is easily

Mongoose (*Herpestes griseus*)

domesticated, and is kept in many houses in India to rid them of reptiles and other vermin, as rats, mice, etc. It has been said that it neutralizes the poison of snakes, which it fearlessly attacks, by eating during its contests with them the *Ophiorhiza mungos*, or snake-root; but its immunity is really due to the extreme celerity of its movements. It is of a grey colour flecked with black, and about the size of a large rat.

MON'ICA, St. Mother of St. Augustine, was born in Africa, of Christian parents, in A.D. 332. The grief of her life was the worldliness and long heresy of her great son; but she was miraculously assured by a dream of his conversion, and was informed by an aged bishop that "the child of so many tears could not be lost." With her other son, Navigus, she followed Augustine to Italy, where she died 4th May, 387, at Ostia. Her festival is 4th May.

MONILIA. A genus of Fungi Imperfecti, section Hyphomycetes. *M. fructigena* causes the brown-rot of apples, plums, and other orchard fruits. The best remedies are burning of diseased fruit, and spraying of the trees with copperas or Bordeaux mixture.

MONISM. A philosophical doctrine, which holds that in the universe there is only one form of substance and of activity, and which refers everything to one central and all-pervading principle. It is opposed to dualism, which regards spirit and matter as two distinct things. The term *monism* was first used by Christian Wolf (1679-1754). For a long period it was used only in epistemology.

MONITOR. The type of a family of Old-World lizards (Varanidæ). They are the largest of the order, some species, such as the *Varanus niloticus* of the Nile and Egypt, attaining a length of 6 feet. They generally inhabit the neighbourhood of rivers and lakes, and prey upon all sorts of small animals and eggs of various kinds. Some of the species are used as food. The name is due to the erroneous belief formerly entertained that these lizards gave warning of the approach of crocodiles. It is called in Arabic, *ouaran*, meaning simply lizard, not warning lizard.

MONITOR. The popular name for a class of very shallow, heavily-armed iron-clad steam-vessels, invented by Ericsson, carrying on their open decks either one or two revolving turrets, each containing one or more heavy guns, and designed to combine the maximum of gun-power with the minimum of exposure. Monitors were so called from the name of the first vessel of the kind, built by the Federals during the American Civil War, which proved its superiority in a famous engagement with the Confederate ship *Merrimac* in 1862.

During the European War (1914-18) monitors were considerably developed, their light draught rendering them suitable for short-range coastal bombardments in the shallow waters of the Belgian littoral. The first monitors used in these operations were originally built for the Brazilian navy. Among others H.M.S. *General Wolfe* had an 18-inch armament; other conspicuous ships were the *Mersey*, *Humber*, *Abercrombie*, and *Severn*. The *Mersey*, with the *Severn*, assisted in the destruction of the German cruiser *Königsberg* in the Rufiji River (East Africa) during July 1915. The *Severn* was completed (1913) as the *Solimoes*, and was intended for the Amazon service of the Brazilian Government. Her displacement was 1260 tons; length, 265 feet; beam, 49 feet; armament, three 6-inch, two 4·7-inch, four 3-pounders, and six machine-guns; speed, 11½ knots. The sides were heavily "blistered" against submarine attack.

MONK, George. Duke of Albemarle, an English general, famous for the prominent part he took in the restoration of Charles II., was born in 1608, and died in 1670. At the age of seventeen he volunteered as a private soldier in the expedition to Cadiz. In 1628 he served at the Island of Rhé, and from 1629 till 1638 in the Netherlands, where his soldierly qualities gained him a captaincy.

In the struggle betwixt Charles I. and the Parliament Monk at first joined the Royalists; but in Jan., 1644, he was taken prisoner at the siege of Nantwich, and after a short delay he was committed to the Tower. After the capture of the king Monk took the Covenant and regained his liberty in 1646. Under the Parliament he served in Ireland, and subsequently with Cromwell in Scotland, and in 1650 he reduced that country to obedience within a few weeks. In 1653 he assisted Admiral Dean in inflicting two severe naval defeats on the Dutch under Van Tromp the elder.

Monk had always been regarded with hope by the Royalist party, and he seems to have decided at once upon the Restoration. The coming over of Charles II. was arranged with Monk, and the king rewarded his restorer with the dukedom of Albemarle, the Order of the Garter, and with a pension of £7000 a year. Monk now fell into comparative obscurity. In 1666, however, he once more served against the Dutch at sea, defeating Van Tromp the younger and De Ruyter.—Cf. C. H. Firth, *Scotland and the Commonwealth*.

MONKEY PUZZLE. The popular name of a coniferous tree, *Araucaria imbricata*, a native of the mountains of Chile, but commonly grown in this country, where it thrives even in suburban gardens. The name refers to the prickly nature of the broad rigid leaves.

MONKEYS. The popular name applied to members of the mammalian ord. Primates, exclusive of the lowest and highest types, i.e. lemurs and men. It is sometimes limited to tailed forms, to the exclusion of the apes and baboons. The hallux or great toe is opposable to the other digits of the foot, so that the feet become converted into "hands." The pollex or thumb may be absent, but when developed it is generally opposable to the other fingers; and the animals thus come to possess "four hands," or are "quadrumanous," to use an old-fashioned term.

The monkeys may all be divided into a lower and a higher group. The higher is that of the Catarrhina (Gr. *kata*, downwards, and *rhines*, nostrils) or Old-World monkeys. The catarrhine monkeys are distinguished by their obliquely-set nostrils, which are placed close together, the nasal septum being narrow, and face downwards. Opposable thumbs and great toes exist in nearly all. The tail may be rudimentary or wanting, but in no case is it prehensile. Cheek-pouches, which are used as receptacles for food preparatory to its mastication, are present in many; and the skin covering the prominences of the buttocks is frequently destitute of hair, becomes hardened, and thus constitutes the so-called *ischial callosities*. The catarrhine monkeys inhabit Asia and Africa. They include the anthropoid or man-like apes (gibbons, orang, chimpanzee, and gorilla), the baboons and mandrills, the sacred monkey of the Hindus, the proboscis monkey, the Diana monkey, the mona, the wanderoo, etc.

The lower section of monkeys consists of the *Platyrrhina* (Gr. *platys*, broad, *rhines*, nostrils), or New-World monkeys, which are entirely confined to South America. They have the nostrils widely separated, the septum or partition between being broad, hence the name. Another peculiarity consists in their prehensile tails; and there are none of the cheek-pouches or hard callosities on the rump so characteristic of Old-World monkeys. The diet is especially of a vegetable nature. This section includes the marmosets, the spider-monkeys, the capuchin monkeys, the squirrel-monkeys, the howling monkeys, etc. *See* APE; BABOONS; etc.

MONMOUTH, James Scott, Duke of. The natural son of Lucy Walters, one of the mistresses of Charles II., was born at Rotterdam in 1649, died 1685. He was always acknowledged by Charles as his natural son, though there were doubts of his paternity. After the Restoration he was created Duke of Orkney and Duke of Monmouth (1663), married the daughter and heiress of the Earl of Buccleuch, and received the Garter. He became extremely popular, especially among Protestants, who wished him rather than the Duke of York (afterwards James II.) to succeed to the throne, and who started a groundless rumour that he was legitimate.

In 1679 Monmouth was entrusted with a command in Scotland, and defeated the Covenanters at the battle of Bothwell Bridge, 22nd June, but was soon afterwards sent beyond seas at the instigation of his uncle. A few months afterwards he returned without leave, and became the centre of the popular movement in which the lives of Lord William Russell and Algernon Sidney were sacrificed. The result to Monmouth was his exile in Holland.

On the accession of James II. he was induced to attempt an invasion of England. He arrived at Lyme Regis with less than a hundred followers (11th June, 1685); but his numbers were soon increased. He proclaimed James the poisoner of the late king, and asserted the legitimacy of his own birth; but from the first there was no likelihood of his success. His small body of undisciplined troops was totally defeated at Sedgmoor, and the duke himself was captured and beheaded after abject appeals to the king for mercy.—Cf. Allan Fea, *King Monmouth*.

MONMOUTH (W. *Mynwy*). A municipal borough, and the county town of Monmouthshire, England, situated at the confluence of the Monnow and Wye; served by the Great Western Railway. The Monnow is spanned by an ancient stone bridge, and the Wye by a modern one. Monmouth has malleable iron and tin-plate works, and paper- and corn-mills. It possesses a collection of Nelson relics. The castle, of which only fragments remain, was a favourite residence of John of Gaunt, and the birthplace of Henry V. The borough includes Troy. Pop. (1931), 4731.

MONMOUTH. A county bounded by the counties of Hereford, Gloucester, Brecknock, and Glamorgan, and the estuary of the Severn; area, 349,569 acres. A considerable portion of the surface is mountainous and rocky, the remainder consisting

Fortified Bridge, Monmouth

of fertile valleys and gentle slopes. The chief rivers are the Wye, the Monnow, the Usk, the Ebbw, and the Rhymney. The production of coal and iron is extensive. Pontypool, Blaenavon, Tredegar, Ebbw Vale, and Rhymney are the headquarters of the coal and iron industries. The manufacture of tin-plate is also extensively carried on. Among the antiquities of the county are remains of Llanthony and Tintern Abbeys, and the fine Norman castle of Chepstow. Monmouth returns five members to Parliament. Pop. (1931), 434,821.

MONOBLEPHARIDACEÆ. A small family of saprophytic Fungi, group Oömycetes, unique among Fungi in having motile male gametes (spermatozoids). They are insignificant plants growing on dead twigs in water.

MON'OCHORD. An instrument with one string, much employed by the ancients in musical training, and for the determination of pitch. The string, stretched over a board or sounding-box, emits a musical note on being caused to vibrate. The pitch of the note varies in a definite way with the length of the vibrating portion of the string (*see* HARMONICS); this length may be altered at will by means of a movable bridge. The instrument is still used by lecturers on physics. *See* SONOMETER.

MONOCOTYLE'DONOUS PLANTS. Monocotyledons, the smaller of the two main classes into which Angiosperms are subdivided. As the name implies, they are characterized by the presence in the embryo of a single cotyledon, which is placed directly opposite to the radicle, the plumule being lateral in origin. Other differences from dicotyledons (q.v.) are the scattered arrangement of the vascular bundles in the stem, the absence of a cambium, the parallel-veined leaves, and the number of the floral parts, which are usually in threes or multiples of three. As a rule the leaves are large in relation to the axis (e.g. palms, aroids, banana), and arborescent types are rare, except among palms. A great number of monocotyledons are bulbous plants, or provided with rhizomes, corms, etc. (geophytes); the grass-type prevails in a number of families (Gramineæ, Cyperaceæ, etc.).

MONODEL'PHIA. One of the three sub-classes into which mammals were divided by de Blainville in 1816 in accordance with the nature of their female reproductive organs, the other two classes being Ornithodelphia and Didelphia. The Monodelphia are characterized by the fact that the female passage or vagina is single. This sub-class includes all the Mammalia except monotremes and marsupials. But de Blainville's names are now usually replaced by the terms Prototheria, Metatheria, and Eutheria, proposed by Huxley.

MONOMA'NIA. A popular expression often employed under the belief that there is a form of insanity in which the mind of the patient is absorbed by one morbid idea or impulse, and the person seems to be insane only in one direction. Dipsomania and kleptomania are regarded as two varieties of monomania.

MONOMETALLISM. *See* BIMETALLISM.

MONOPH'YSITES. Those who maintained that there was but one nature in the incarnate Christ, that is, that the divine and human natures were so united as to form but one *nature*, yet without any change, confusion, or mixture of the two natures. They were condemned as heretics by the Council of Chalcedon in 451.

The Monophysites split into several sects. In Egypt, Syria, and Mesopotamia the congregations remained the strongest, had patriarchs at Alexandria and Antioch, existing, without interruption, by the side of the imperial orthodox patriarchs, and after Jacob Baradæus had, about 570, established their religious Constitution, formed the independent Churches of the Jacobites and Armenians, which have maintained themselves ever since. The Coptic Christians of Egypt and the Abyssinian Church are also Monophysites in doctrine.

MONOPLANE. Type of aeroplane in which there is only one set of planes or supporting surfaces. The well-known Fokker three-engined aeroplanes are of this type, also the Dornier flying-boats, Junkers, and the British Fairey postal aeroplane. *See* AEROPLANE.

MONOP'OLI (ancient **Minopolis**). An Adriatic seaport of Apulia, South Italy, in the province of Bari. The castle dates from 1552, when it was founded by Charles V. There is also a cathedral. Oils and wines are exported; there are manufactures of woollen and cotton goods. Pop. about 24,000.

MONOP'OLY. An exclusive right, conferred by authority on one or more persons, to carry on some branch of trade or manufacture. The entire trade and industry of the Middle Ages was characterized by attempts to erect and maintain monopolies, as evidenced by the trade-guilds and such associations as the Hanseatic League. The discovery of the New World only provided a fresh sphere for the same system ; for not only did every Government endeavour to monopolize the trade of its colonies, but in nearly every case the new countries were opened up by privileged " adventurers " and jealous monopoly companies.

The granting of monopolies has at all times been opposed to the spirit of English common law. Notwithstanding the reluctance of the Crown to surrender what was considered one of its most valuable prerogatives, the Statute of Monopolies (21 James I. cap. iii.) was passed in 1623, abolishing all licences, monopolies, etc., with some exceptions. This Act is (with amendments) still in force ; and its excepting clauses are the basis of the present laws relating to patents and copyrights.

Both in Great Britain and other countries there are certain Government monopolies maintained on various grounds of public policy. Examples : the postal and telegraph service, and the tobacco monopoly in France. There are also numerous quasi-monopolies, such as those enjoyed by railway, water, and gas companies, and similar semi-public organizations. *See* TRUSTS.

MON'OTHEISM. The belief in, and worship of, a single, personal God ; opposed to polytheism and distinct also from pantheism. It was at one time the received opinion that monotheism was the primeval intuitive form of religion, but most recent authorities now hold that it was everywhere posterior to polytheism, whence it was gradually evolved.

Henotheism would form an intermediate step, this being the belief in one God as superior to others or as the particular deity of a family, tribe, or people, the existence of other deities being not denied, or indeed fully admitted. Some see this stage in the Jehovah of early Jewish belief.

The three great modern monotheistic religions are Judaism, Christianity, and Mahommedanism. The Jewish prophets had a firm persuasion of one God, the Father and Judge of all ; but they are continually upbraiding the people for lapsing into polytheism. After the Babylonish captivity the people became fixed in their belief. Christian monotheism is, of course, historically a development of Hebrew monotheism ; and Mahomet probably borrowed the doctrine from the same source. Both Jew and Mahommedan regard the Trinitarian conception of the Detiy as a deviation from the pure doctrine of monotheism.—Cf. A. Lang, *The Making of Religion.*

MONOTH'ELITES. A sect of heretics who maintained that Christ had but *one will* (Gr. *monos*, single, *thelein*, to will). Their doctrine was the logical extension of the heresy of the Monophysites, who were all Monothelites. The sect rose into prominence in the seventh century, but the heresy gradually became extinct except in the Monophysite churches.

MONOTRE'MATA. *See* ECHIDNA.

MONOTYPE. A machine for setting up type. Each letter is cast and set as required through the intermediary of a roll of punctured paper. The roll of paper is punctured in a machine resembling a large typewriter, which is called the keyboard, and the roll of paper is then transferred to the casting-machine, where it controls, by means of compressed air, the position of an assemblage of letter-moulds known as a matrix case. The matrix is made to occupy a definite position for any given letter, so that the mould for the letter in question is exactly opposite a small jet through which molten type-metal is squirted. (*See* illustration on p. 225).

MONREALE (mon-re-ä'lā). A city of Sicily, in the province of Palermo. It originally sprang up around the church and monastic establishment founded here in 1174 by the Norman prince William II. Monreale is the see of an archbishop. The old church became the metropolitan cathedral of Sicily in 1182. Pop. about 24,000.

MONRO, Sir Charles Carmichael. First Baronet. British soldier. Born 15th June, 1860, he joined the army in 1879. He served in South Africa and was later commandant of the Musketry School at Hythe. During the Great War he served on the Western front as commander of the 1st Army Corps, and later of the 3rd Army.

As commander-in-chief of the Mediterranean Expeditionary Force he saved the situation in the Dardanelles by carrying out the evacuation of Gallipoli. He was commander-in-chief in India in 1916 and Governor of Gibraltar, 1923-28. He was created a baronet in 1921. He died 7th Dec., 1929.

MONROE (mon-rō'), **James.** Fifth President of the United States of America, was born in 1758 in Westmoreland county, Virginia, died at New York in 1831. He was educated at William and Mary College, and from 1776 till 1778 served in the Revolutionary army. He then de-

MONOTYPE

1, The Keyboard. 2, The Casting Machine. 3, Matrices. 4, The Matrix Case, containing 225 separate matrices.

voted himself to the study of law. In 1782 and in 1787 he was elected a member of the Virginia Assembly, and from 1783 till 1786 he represented Virginia in Congress. In 1788 as a member of the Convention of Virginia he strenuously opposed the ratification of the new Federal Constitution. In 1790 he was elected to the Senate of the United States, and from 1794 to 1796 he was Minister Plenipotentiary to France. From 1799 till 1802 he was Governor of Virginia, and in 1803 he returned as Envoy-extraordinary to France on a mission which resulted in the acquisition of Louisiana for 15,000,000 dollars.

In 1816 the Democratic Republican party elected him to the presidency of the United States. In 1820 he was re-elected, only one vote being cast against him. This he owed chiefly to his having procured the cession of Florida by Spain, and to the settlement of the vexed question of the extension of slavery by the Missouri compromise. Mexico and the emancipated states of South America were formally recognized by the American Government during Monroe's second term; but the leading event in it was the promulgation of the "Monroe doctrine."

MONROE DOCTRINE, The. A principle in international politics, corresponding in America to the balance of power in Europe, was formulated in President Monroe's message of 2nd Dec., 1823, in the statement that the United States would consider any attempt to extend the European political system to any portion of America as dangerous to their peace and safety. At the same time the American continents were declared to be no longer subjects for colonization by any European power. The doctrine has several times been asserted, notably in the attitude of the United States towards Napoleon III. during his Mexican undertaking, and in connection with the Panama Canal and the Venezuela-Guiana boundary question. It has all the force of a first principle in the United States. At the first Hague Conference in 1899 the delegates of the United States stated distinctly that the Monroe Doctrine was the settled policy of their country.—Cf. W. H. Taft, *The United States and Peace.*

MONRO'VIA. The seaport-capital of the West African Republic of Liberia, founded in 1824, and named after President Monroe. Pop. 10,000.

MONS (mons; Fl. *Bergen*). A town of Belgium, capital of the province of Hainault, on the Trouille. It was until 1862 one of the strongest fortresses of Europe, but the fortifications were then demolished and their site occupied by a fine boulevard. The principal buildings are the church of Ste Waudru, built between 1450 and 1589 and the town hall (founded 1458). Among manufactures are linen, woollen, and cotton fabrics, fire-arms, cutlery, and soap. Coal is extensively mined in the vicinity. In 804 Mons, which occupies the site of one of Cæsar's forts, was made the capital of Hainault by Charlemagne. It has figured much in history. The town was occupied by the Germans, and regained by Canadian troops on 11th Nov., 1918. *See* EUROPEAN WAR. Pop. 27,930.

MON'SOON. An alternating wind which blows for one-half of the year in one direction, and for the other half in the opposite direction, contrasting in this respect with a trade-wind, which blows in the same diretion all the year round. Monsoons, like ordinary land and sea breezes, are caused by variations in the relative temperature of ocean and land. The relation between the mean daily temperature of land and sea depends partly on the latitude, and partly on the season of the year. At the equator the ocean mean is always the lower, but as the latitude becomes higher it approaches and ultimately surpasses the mean temperature of the land.

The reversal of sign of relative temperature with change of latitude is very marked in winter, so that it may happen, as it does in Asia, that the ocean acts as the warm (and therefore low-pressure) region in winter, and as the cold (high-pressure) region in summer. Thus in winter the north-east monsoon blows over the China Sea, Cochin-China, and the Indian Ocean. In summer, on the other hand, the monsoon over the Indian Ocean blows strongly from the south-west, with heavy rainfall. Monsoons of slighter intensity occur in Australia, Spain, and the south-eastern part of the United States.

MONSTER, or **MONSTROSITY.** A term applied in anatomy and physiology to living beings which exhibit from birth onwards some important abnormal features in structure, or present notable deviations from the normal type of their kind. The science which investigates such abnormal forms is known as *teratology*.

Monsters present very wide variations in the characters and degrees of the malformations, ranging from an almost imperceptible to an almost total deviation from the normal type. But there are definite types of monstrosities, distinguished by distinct anatomical characters, just as there are definite types of normal structure; and the former may be classified by considering the fœtus or embryo. The anatomist may at once detect all fictitious cases of monstrosities by noting that they present characters perfectly incompatible with any known type of abnormal development. Tales of monsters occurring both in man and in beasts are met with in the writings of the older anatomists and naturalists; but such accounts, if not entirely destitute of truth, owe most of their interest to the liberal embellishment with which they have been recorded.

Old writers have argued for the production of such ideal monsters by the intercourse of demons and women, of brutes and men; and witchcraft, magic, spell, divine vengeance—and, more lately, the effect upon the mother's mind of fright, terror, dreams, etc.—have each and all been credited, but equally erroneously, with causing malformations and abnormalities in the yet unborn child or embryo.

Teratology can explain most, if not all, malformations as results of interference with the normal development of the organism, and as caused by some physical or chemical disturbance. These so-called "*freaks* of nature" are in truth the results of morbid actions and operations in the living organism, as well defined, but not yet so well known, as are those of the healthy and normal body.

Among the prominent or primary causes in the production of monstrosities in the human embryo are the following: Deficiencies or deformations in the reproductive organs and materials of the father and mother, or of both parents; diseases or malpositions of the placenta or after-birth, or of the fœtal membranes; retardation in the development of the fœtus itself, arising from pressure, injuries, or actual disease either originating from the germ itself or communicated from the mother; and the presence of actual or potential disease in either or both parents. Injuries to the mother may also to some extent affect the embryo, though most authorities are doubtful on the point. Malformations and monstrosities are frequently met with in the lower animals, and particularly in those which are domesticated by man. In the plant world monstrosities also occur.

MON'STRANCE, or **REMONSTRANCE** (called also *ostensorium* or *expositorium*. The sacred vessel in which, in the Roman Catholic Church, the host is shown to the people at benedictions, processions, and other solemnities. Its use probably dates from the establishment of the festival of Corpus Christi in 1264 by Pope Urban IV. The earliest monstrances known date from the fourteenth century, and are made in the form of a Gothic tower. The most common form now consists of a chalice-footed stand of some precious metal, and a circular repository, usually a transparent pyx, surrounded by sunlike rays. In the Greek Church the monstrance is shaped like a coffin.

MONTAGNARDS (moṇ-tân-yär), or **LA MONTAGNE,** "the Mountain." A popular name in French history, given to the extreme democratic party in the Convention, because they occupied the higher rows of benches in the hall where it met. The chiefs of "the Mountain" were Danton, Marat, and Robespierre, the men who introduced the "Reign of Terror." The Mountain rose to the height of its power in June, 1793, and for more than a year it was sufficiently formidable to stifle all opposition. Soon after the fall of Robespierre (28th July, 1794) the names of "Montagnard" and "Montagne" gradually disappeared from party nomenclature.

MON'TAGU, Lady Mary Wortley. English writer, was born in 1689, and died in 1762. She was the eldest daughter of Evelyn Pierrepont, afterwards Duke of Kingston. In 1712 she made a runaway match with Edward Wortley Montagu, a wealthy Whig scholar, who had quarrelled with her father.

In 1716 Montagu was appointed Ambassador to the Porte, and Lady Mary accompanied him to Constantinople, where they remained from Jan., 1717, to May, 1718. It was during this period that Lady Mary's famous *Turkish Letters* were written. Lady Mary remained abroad, living chiefly in Italy, from 1739 until her husband's death in 1761; but soon after her return to England she herself died of cancer in the breast. Her letters are marked by great vivacity and graphic power, together with keen observation and independent judgment.—Cf. G. Paston, *Lady Mary Worthley Montagu and her Times.*

MONTAIGNE (mon-tān'; Fr. pron. mon-tayny), **Michel Eyquem de.** French essayist, was born in 1533 at the castle of Montaigne, in Périgord, died in 1592. He learned Latin conversationally before he could speak French, and Greek was also an early acquisition. At the age of six he became a pupil at the Collège de Guienne at Bordeaux, and at thirteen he began to study law. Little is known of his youth and early manhood.

In 1571 he retired to his ancestral château, and devoted himself to peaceful study and meditation. In 1580 he published the first two books of his *Essais*, and immediately afterwards set out on a journey through Germany, Switzerland, and Italy to restore his health, which had been shattered by the attacks of a hereditary disease. In 1582 and 1584 he was chosen Mayor of Bordeaux. In 1588 he republished his *Essais*, with the addition of a third book. After a last visit to Paris (in the course of which he was thrown into the Bastille for a short time by the Leaguers) Montaigne seems to have dwelt quietly in his château.

Montaigne's *Essais* has at all times been one of the most popular books in the French language. They embrace an extraordinary variety of topics, which are touched upon in a lively, entertaining manner, with all the raciness of strong native good sense, careless of system or regularity. Sentences and anecdotes from the ancients are interspersed with his own remarks and opinions, and with stories of himself in a pleasant strain of egotism, and with an occasional licence, to which severer moralists can with some difficulty reconcile themselves. His *Voyages*, a diary of his journeys in 1580-82, the MS. of which was discovered 180 years after his death, was published in 1774. There are two English translations of the *Essais*, one by Charles Cotton, and an earlier one by John Florio.—BIBLIOGRAPHY: W. L. Collins, *Montaigne*; E. Dowden, *Michel de Montaigne*; E. Sichel, *Michel de Montaigne*; V. Giraud, *Les Époques de la pensée de Montaigne*.

MONTALEMBERT (moṇ-tà-làṇ-bãr), **Charles Forbes René, Comte de.** French publicist, politician, historian, and theologian, born in London 1810, died at Paris 1870. Of his very numerous writings the chief is *Les Moines d'occident depuis St. Benoît jusqu'à St. Bernard* (English translation 1861-68). Others are *Vie de Ste Élisabeth de Hongrie* (1836) and *L'Avenir politique d'Angleterre* (1855).

MONTANA. A state in the mountain division of the United States, bounded by Canada in the north, and traversed by the Rocky Mountains in the west. The Missouri has its source in and traverses Montana; the Milk and Yellowstone Rivers, affluents of the Missouri, are also important.

Production and Industry. — In sheep-farming and wool-production Montana holds premier place among the United States, the clip in 1932 yielding 30,728,000 lb. of wool. Agriculture, dependent in a degre upon efficient irrigation, produces wheat (55,010,000 bushels in 1932), oats, barley, flax-seed, potatoes, hay, and some silage; but agricultural resources are not yet fully developed. Stock-raising is very important, and some fruit is grown. In 1920 public lands, unappropriated and unreserved, amounting to 5,973,741 acres, were available for grant in 160-acre lots to prospective farmer-settlers. In 1930 there were 47,495 farms with a total acreage of 44,659,152 acres; of this 11,399,000 acres were under crops. There is an extensive lumbering industry, the afforested area covering (1932) 13,439,000 acres.

Minerals, etc.—Minerals resources are large and almost untapped. Coal, copper, gold, silver, lead, tungsten, zinc, corundum, grindstones, and sapphires being found. Manufactures are principally confined to copper, i.e. smelting and refining. Railway mileage was 5212 in 1932, with an additional 109 miles of electric track.

People.—The inhabitants are of mixed origin, and include large numbers of Canadians, Irish, and Germans. An Indian Reserve of 1183 sq. miles (1930) had a pop. of 14,238.

Towns, Education, etc.—Helena (pop. 1930, 11,813) is the state capital, other towns being Butte (39,532), Great Falls (28,822), Billings (16,380), Anaconda (12,494), and Missoula (14,657). The University of Montana comprises a College of Agriculture and Mechanical Arts at Bozeman, a School of Mines at Butte, a Normal School at Dillon, and the State University (founded 1895) at Missoula. Area, 147,182 sq. miles (796 water); pop. (1930), 537,606.

Government.—Montana was admitted to the Union on 22nd Feb., 1889. The present Government comprises a Governor, Senate (56 members, elected for four years, one-half seeking biennial re-election), and House of Representatives (102 members, sitting for two years). Two Senators and two Representatives are sent to Congress. For local government the state is divided into 56 counties and 20 judicial districts.

MONTA'NUS. The founder of a Christian sect, appeared about the middle of the second century in Phrygia as a new Christian prophet, advocating an ascetic code of morals and behaviour, fasting, celibacy, and willing submission to martyrdom. He sought to establish a community of all true believers at Pepuza, in Phrygia, there to await the second Advent. The Montanists were forced to withdraw from the Catholic Church and form themselves into a separate sect in Phrygia about 180. In North Africa they flourished for some time, but by the fourth century they seem everywhere to have disappeared.

MONTARGIS (moŋ-târ-zhē). A town of France, department of Loiret, on the Loing. It is the junction of the three canals of the Loing, Orléans, and Briare, and is a railway junction with an important trade. Pop. 29,981.

MONTAUBAN (moŋ-tō-bāŋ). Chief town of the department of Tarn-et-Garonne, France; on the Tarn. Silk, wool, etc., are manufactured. Montauban was a stronghold of the Huguenots, and is still a Protestant centre. Pop. 29,981

Montauban is also the name of a village in France, department of Somme, which became prominent during the European War (battles of the Somme, and battle of Bapaume).

MONTBÉLIARD (moŋ-bā-li-är). A town of France, in the department of Doubs. It is situated at the confluence of the Allaine and Lisaine, and is on the Rhône-Rhine Canal. Pop. 10,500.

MONT BLANC (that is, "White Mountain"). The loftiest mountain of Europe, belonging to the Pennine chain of the Alps, and rising 15,781 feet above the sea-level, is situated on the frontiers of France and Italy, and near that of Switzerland. The main portion of the mountain and the highest summit are in France (Haute-Savoie).

Mont Blanc

The huge mountain mass (30 miles long by 10 miles wide) is almost entirely granitic. It has numerous peaks, some rounded, some sharp (aiguilles). On the south-east its face is steep; on the north-west lateral chains are sent off, among which about thirty glaciers are counted. The chief are the glaciers Des Bossons, Bois, Argentière, and Mer de Glace. The summit was first reached in June, 1786, by the guide Jacques Balmat. The ice-summit of Mont Blanc slipped from its place in Nov., 1920.

MONTCALM, Louis Joseph, Marquis de. French soldier. Born 29th Feb., 1712, he was in command of the French troops in Canada and captured the British posts of Oswego and Fort William Henry. After the French had lost Louisburg and Fort Duquesne, Montcalm moved to Quebec and was finally routed in battle by Wolfe on the Plains of Abraham. After trying vainly to rally his forces he was wounded and died the next day, 14th Sept., 1759.

MONTDIDIER. A town of France, department of Somme, 23 miles from Compiègne. It was occupied by the Prussians in 1870, and became prominent during the European War (battles of the Somme). Captured by the Germans in March, 1918, it was retaken by the French on 10th Aug.

MONT-DORE-LES-BAINS. A town of France, department of Puy-de-Dôme. It has mineral springs which attract many people suffering from pulmonary complaints. Pop. 1200.

MONTE CARLO. A Riviera town in the Principality of Monaco, adjoining the town of that name. It stands on the Bay of Monaco, and is much frequented on account of its magnificent casino. Pop. 11,055.

MONTE CASINO (or **CASSINO**). An Italian monastery near Cassino, in the north of Campania, Italy. It was founded in A.D. 529 by St. Benedict, and was the first monastery of the Benedictine Order. As a monastery it was dissolved in 1866, but it continues to exist in the form of an educational establishment.

MONTE CATINI. A health resort and spa of Italy, 15 miles E. of Lucca. Pop. 8748.

MONTE CRISTO (the ancient **Oglasa**). A small island 6 miles in circumference belonging to Italy, 25 miles S. of Elba, the seat of a penal colony. It has been immortalized in the masterpiece of Dumas père, to which he gave the title *Le Comte de Monte-Cristo.*

MONTECU'CULI, or, more correctly, **MONTECU'COLI, Raimondo.** Prince of the Empire and Duke of Melfi, military commander, born 1608, died 1680. In 1664 he gained a great victory over the Turks after having driven them out of Transylvania. In 1673 he was placed at the head of the imperial troops, and checked the progress of Louis XIV. by the capture of Bonn, and by forming a junction with the Prince of Orange in spite of Turenne and Condé. Montecuculi's subsequent advance into Alsace was repulsed by the Prince of Condé. His last military exploit was the siege of Philipsburg.

MONTEFIORE (mon-te-fi-ō'rā), **Sir Moses.** Jewish philanthropist, was born 1784, died 1885. His benevolence to Jews throughout the world was unbounded; and he visited Palestine seven times, the last when in his ninety-second year.

MONTE GRAPPA, The Battles of. Fought during the European War (q.v.).

MONTÉLIMAR (moŋ-tā-li-mär; the ancient **Acusium**). A town of France, department of Drôme, formerly a stronghold of the Huguenots, and capital of Valdaine in mediæval times. It has manufactures of silk and nougat. Pop. 14,000.

MONTENE'GRO (native *Tzrnagora,* Turk. *Karadagh,* "Black Mountain"). Formerly an independent kingdom in Europe, now a province of Yugoslavia. The surface is everywhere mountainous, being covered by an extension of the Dinaric Alps, rising to the height of 8850 feet. The principal river is the Moratcha. Forests of beech, pine, chestnuts, and other valuable timber cover many of the mountain sides. Maize and some tobacco, barley, and oats are produced, and cattle are reared in great numbers. The almond, vine, and pomegranate are cultivated in the more sheltered valleys. Peasant ownership of land is generally in force. The chief occupations of the Montenegrins are agriculture and fishing. The chief towns (in reality little more than villages) are Cettinje and Jakova. The Montenegrins are pure Serbs and speak a Serbian dialect. In religion they are of the Greek Orthodox Church. Montenegro has an area of 3733 sq. miles, and a population of 100,000.

Montenegro, first appearing as a principality under the name of Zeta in the fourteenth century, was subject to the great Serbian kingdom till 1389, when the Serbians were defeated at Kossovo, and the Montenegrins founded a prince-bishopric in the mountains under the protection of a Russian alliance. The dignity was inherited through brothers and nephews, and after 1697 became hereditary in the family of Petrovitch Njegos.

The history of Montenegro for many years is a record of deadly struggles with the Turks, and of a slowly growing civilization among its inhabitants. In 1852 Danilo II. became vladika (prince-bishop), but in 1855 he married, threw off his ecclesiastical character, assuming the title of Hospodar or prince, and transformed his land into a secular principality, the independence of which was soon recognized by Russia. Danilo was assassinated in 1860, and Nicholas I. Petrovitch became Hospodar. In 1861-62 he engaged in a not altogether successful war against Turkey; but in 1876 he joined Serbia and in 1877-78 Russia against his hereditary foe, with the result that 1900 sq. miles were added to his territory by the Treaty of Berlin. He assumed the rank of king in 1910.

During the European War Montenegro was on the side of the Allies. In Nov., 1918, King Nicholas was deposed and Montenegro was united with Yugoslavia.—BIBLIOGRAPHY: F. S. Stephenson, *A History of Montenegro*; C. Stoyanovitch, *The Kingdom of the Serbians, Croatians, and Slovenes.*

MONTEREY, or **MONTERREY.** A city and capital of the state of Nuevo Leon, Mexico. It lies at an altitude of 1625 feet in a spur of the Sierra Madre, about 100 miles from the Texan frontier, and is a railway junction on the direct lines from Tampico and the United States. It is the seat of a bishop. The industries are varied. Monterey was founded in 1560 as Leon, the name being changed in 1599 when it became a city. There is a wireless station. Pop. (1930), 129,748.

MONTESPAN (moŋ-tes-päŋ), **Françoise Athenais, Marquise de.** Mistress of Louis XIV., born in 1641, died in 1707. She was the second daughter of the duc de Mortemart, and was in 1663 married to the Marquis de Montespan. To the most fascinating beauty she added a natural liveliness and wit, and a highly cultivated mind. Soon after her appearance at court she attracted the king's attention, and from 1668 till 1674 she shared his favour with Louise de la Vallière. The latter, however, withdrew in 1674; M. de Montespan had already been ordered to retire to his estate.

Mme de Montespan bore eight children to the king, four of whom died in infancy. The others were entrusted to the care of "the widow Scarron" (later Mme de Maintenon). The influence of the favourite mistress was often exercised in public affairs, and her empire over the king continued until about 1679, when a growing attachment to Mme de Maintenon finally estranged his affections from Mme de Montespan. In 1691 Mme de Montespan quitted the court, and devoted her last years to religious exercises and penitence.

MONTESQUIEU (moŋ-tes-ky*eu*), **Charles Louis de Secondat, Baron de la Brède et de.** Born 1689 at the château of La Brède, near Bordeaux, died at Paris 1755. He studied law; in 1714 became a counsellor of the Parliament of Bordeaux; and in 1716, on the death of his uncle, parliamentary president and Baron de Montesquieu.

The *Lettres Persanes*, the first of the three great works on which his fame principally rests, appeared in 1721. Purporting to consist of the correspondence of two Persians travelling in France, this book is a lively satire upon the manners and customs, and the political and ecclesiastical institutions of the author's age and country. Other works of less importance followed; and in 1728 Montesquieu was admitted to the French Academy. He gave up his president's office in 1726, and then visited Germany, Hungary, Italy, Holland, and England. In England he stayed for eighteen months, and imbibed a deep admiration for its social and political institutions. He returned to France in 1731, and in 1734 he published his *Considérations sur les causes de la grandeur et la décadence des Romains*.

In 1748 *L'Esprit des Lois*, the result of twenty years of labour, was published, and at once placed its author among the greatest writers of his country. The scope of the work is perhaps best indicated by the sub-title of the original edition, which describes it as a treatise on the relation which ought to exist between the laws and the Constitution, manners, climate, religion, commerce, etc., of each country. Among his lesser works are: *Dialogue de Sylla et d'Eucrate*, *Le Voyage de Paphos*, *Essai sur le goût* (unfinished), *Arsace et Isménie* (probably a work of his youth), and *Lettres familières*.—BIBLIOGRAPHY: Sir C. P. Ilbert, *Montesquieu*; L. Vian, *Histoire de Montesquieu: sa vie et ses œuvres*; Sorel, *Montesquieu*.

MONTESSORI, Maria. Italian educationist, was born at Rome in 1870. She took the degree of doctor of medicine in 1894, and from 1898 to 1900 was director of a school for mentally defective children. She lectured in the United States, in 1913, and in England in 1919. Several of her works on education have been translated into English. For the "Montessori Method," *see* EDUCATION.

MONTEVID'EO. A maritime department, forming the most densely peopled area of Uruguay, at the mouth of the Rio de la Plata. It is a wine-growing district, with a hilly surface suited for stock-raising. Area, 256 sq. miles; pop. (1932), 489,685 (or 1912·8 people per square mile).

MONTEVIDEO. A seaport city of Uruguay, the state capital and capital of the department of Montevideo, on the Bay of Montevideo and the Rio de la Plata, of which the bay forms an arm. Montevideo is the principal seaport of Uruguay, and is the terminus of the Central and North-Eastern Railway lines. It is laid out on modern transatlantic lines, and claims to be the finest-built city in America. There are two racecourses and a bull-ring near the city, which abounds in clubs and hotels. As the seat of a bishop and two bishops suffragan there is a fine cathedral (completed 1905). It contains the University of the Republic. The climate is fairly healthy, but it is very hot in summer.

As a port Montevideo's enormous harbour offers insecure protection to shipping from gales and storms, but nevertheless a great transit trade is carried on in live-stock, canned meat, and meat products in general. The town was founded in 1706, and became capital of Uruguay in 1828. Pop. (1932), 655,972.

MONTEZU'MA. Aztec emperor of Mexico when Cortez invaded the country in 1519. Influenced by an ancient prophecy, he at first welcomed the Spaniards; but when he discovered that they were no supernatural beings, he secretly took measures for their destruction. Cortez on learning this seized Montezuma, and compelled him to recognize the supremacy of Spain. The Aztecs immediately rose in revolt, and refused to be quieted by the appearance of Montezuma. While urging them to submission, he was struck on the temple with a stone and fell to the ground. Cut to the heart by his humiliation, he refused all nourishment, tore off his bandages, and soon after expired.

MONTFORT, Simon de. Earl of Leicester, English statesman and soldier, was born in France between 1195 and 1200, died 1265. The youngest son of Simon de Montfort, Earl of Leicester, the "scourge of the Albigenses," he won the favour of Henry III., and married Eleanor, Countess-Dowager of Pembroke, and sister of the king.

After spending some years in France, on his return to England in 1254 he took a prominent part in the disputes between the Crown and the barons. He was conspicuous among those who extorted the *Provisions of Oxford* from the king in the "Mad Parliament" in 1258; and he was the leader of the barons in the so-called "Barons' War" that followed.

In 1264 he agreed to submit the question of the king's right to repudiate the *Provisions* to Louis XI. of France; but when the latter, by the Mise of Amiens, decided in favour of Henry, De Montfort refused to be bound by the decision. Both sides took up arms, and at the battle of Lewes (14th May, 1264) the king was defeated and taken prisoner.

The Mise of Lewes, to which Henry III. agreed, contained the outlines of a new Constitution, in which the principle of representative government was recognized; but this principle was carried a step further in the famous Parliament of De Montfort, which was summoned to meet at Westminster on 20th Jan., 1265. The distinctive feature of the new Parliament was the fact that, for the first time, writs were issued for the election of members from cities and boroughs as well as from the counties. For this reason Simon de Montfort is sometimes spoken of as the "founder of the House of Commons"; though the regular representation of cities and boroughs in Parliament did not really begin till 1295. The king accepted the Constitution on 14th Feb., 1265; but Prince Edward and the Mortimers raised the standard of revolt. At the battle of Evesham De Montfort was defeated and slain. His memory was long revered by the people as that of a martyr for popular liberty.

MONTGOLFIER, Joseph Michel (1740-1810) and **Jacques Étienne** (1745-99). Joint-inventors of the balloon, were born at Vidalon-lès-Annonay, in the department of Ardèche, in France. Their first balloon, inflated with rarefied atmospheric air, descended from Annonay in 1782, and the invention soon brought them fame and honours. Joseph was also the inventor of the water-ram.

MONTGOM'ERY, Alexander. A Scottish poet who flourished during the latter half of the sixteenth century, was born at Hazelhead Castle, in Ayrshire, died probably between 1605 and 1610. His principal poem, the allegory of the *Cherrie and the Slae*, was first published in 1597. Many of his sonnets and miscellaneous pieces were written much earlier and circulated in manuscript.

MONTGOMERY, James. Minor poet and journalist, was born in 1771, and died in 1854. *Prison Amusements*, his first volume of verse, came out in 1797. In 1806 appeared his *Wanderer of Switzerland*, the first effort of his which gained the approbation of the public. It was followed in 1809 by *The West Indies*; in 1813 by *The World before the Flood*; in 1819 by *Greenland*, a missionary poem; and in 1827 by *The Pelican Island*, perhaps his best work. He also wrote a number of hymns and other small pieces, which were published along with his longer poems.

MONTGOMERY, or MONTGOMERYSHIRE. An inland county of North Wales, has an area of 510,110 acres, consisting mostly of wild, rugged, and sterile mountains, varying from 1000 to 2000 feet in height. It contains, however, some fine and fertile valleys, the most extensive and fruitful of which is that of the Severn, the principal river. The county is almost entirely occupied by the slate-rocks which overspread so large a portion of Wales. Some lead is obtained, as well as slate and limestone.

Agriculture is carried on chiefly in the narrow valleys, and on the east side of the county, bordering on Salop, where oats with some wheat and fruit are produced. In the hilly districts sheep-farming is much practised; cattle and small and hardy ponies, commonly called *merlins*, are reared. Flannels are manufactured to some extent. Montgomery is the county town, but the largest town is Welshpool. Pop. (1931), 48,462.

MONTGOMERY. County town of Montgomeryshire, a mere village, with a fine old church and ruined castle, belongs to the Montgomery district of boroughs, which includes also Newton, Welshpool, etc. Pop. (1931), 918.

MONTGOMERY. A city of Alabama, United States, county seat of Montgomery county, on the Alabama River, and on the Louisville and Nashville Railway. The Alabama is navigable for ocean-going steamers as far as Montgomery, which is in direct communication with Europe, Panama, and New York. It is one of the great centres of the United States cotton trade, and has extensive manufactures. Montgomery was settled in 1814, and superseded Tuscaloosa as state capital in 1847. It was the administrative centre of the Confederacy between Feb. and May, 1861, and was taken by the Federals on 12th April, 1865. Pop. (1930), 66,079.

MONTH. A period of time derived from the motion of the moon; generally one of the 12 parts of the calendar year. The calendar months have from 28 to 31 days each, February having 28, April, June, September, and November 30, the rest 31. Month originally meant the time of one revolution of the moon, but as that may be determined in reference to several celestial objects there are several lunar periods known by distinctive names. Thus the *anomalistic month* is a revolution of the moon from perigee to perigee, average 27 days 13 hours 19 minutes; the *sidereal month*, the interval between two successive conjunctions of the moon with the same fixed star, average 27 days 7 hours 43 minutes; the *synodical*, or *proper lunar month*, the time that elapses between new moon and new moon, average 29 days 12 hours 44 minutes. The *solar month* is the twelfth part of one solar year, or 30 days 10 hours 29 minutes.

MONTMÉDY. A town of France, department of Meuse, on the Chiers. It was occupied by the Prussians in 1870, and by the Germans during the European War. It was retaken by the Allies in Nov., 1918. Pop. 3000.

MONTPELLIER. A town of France, capital of the department of Hérault, a railway junction and the headquarters of an army corps. The university was first founded in 1289, and is associated with such names as Petrarch (a student) and Casaubon, who was a professor; the medical school was founded by Moorish physicians. The botanical garden, founded in 1593 by Henry IV., is the oldest in France. There are many manufactures, and a trade in corn, wine, and silk is maintained through the port of Cette (Gulf of Lions).

Montpellier had a charter in 1141 and became a Huguenot centre, being taken by Louis XIII. in 1622. The Edict of Montpellier (20th Oct., 1622) confirmed the Edict of Nantes. The town was capital of pre-Revolutionary Languedoc. Pop. (1931), 86,924.

MONTREAL. The largest city and the commercial and financial metropolis of Canada, on the Island of Montreal, province of Quebec, and at the head of ocean navigation on the St. Lawrence River, 1000 miles from the Atlantic. It has a complete system of river, canal, and

Montreal—Notre Dame

railway connection with the interior, and although only open for about seven months each year (usually between 24th April and 1st Dec.), Montreal is in importance the second port of the two Americas and seventh of the world.

The harbour includes both sides of the St. Lawrence River, and extends for a distance of about 17 miles between Verdun and Bout de L'Ille, vessels entering from the Great Lakes at the east end of the Lachine Canal, and those from the Atlantic using the dredged ship channel above Quebec. There is berthage for twenty ocean-going vessels of 500 feet in length, drawing 28 to 30 feet, and a total wharfage of about 8¼ miles. The floating dock has a length of 500 feet with a width of 100 feet, a docking draught of 30 feet, and a lifting capacity of 25,000 tons. There are stationary and floating grain-elevators, by which eleven ships may be loaded simultaneously at the rate of 15,000 bushels per hour.

Communications.—Montreal is the headquarters of the Canadian Pacific and dissolved Grand Trunk Railways, the former having workshops in the vicinity; the city is served by the Canadian Pacific, Canadian National (with Northern and Grand Trunk lines), Rutland, and the Delaware, Hudson, and Central Vermont Railways. Hydro-electric power is derived from the Shawinigan Falls and Lachine Rapids, and from rapids at Chambly. It has wireless "beam" stations for communication with Great Britain and Australia.

Buildings.—Among buildings are the M'Gill and Laval Universities, and a museum (Château de Ramenzay) situated in the residence of the former French Governors. There are Anglican and Roman Catholic cathedrals.

People.—Montreal shows a marked mixture of races and interests, and although the better classes are largely English, a considerable proportion of the inhabitants are French and Irish Roman Catholics.

Industries.—Industries include boots and shoes, clothing, sugar-refining, flour-milling, cement, tobacco, rubber, iron and steel, machinery, tools, silks, cottons, woollens, paints, furniture, carriages, electric goods, and confectionery.

Montreal stretches back to the wooded slopes of Mont Réal (Mount Royal), from which the city derives its name. It originated on the site of the old Indian town of Hochelaga as a stockaded enclosure, seldom free from attack by the Iroquois, and was a centre of the fur trade. Pop. (1931), 818,577.

MONTREAUX. A parish and series of villages in the canton of Vaud, and on the north-east shore of the Lake of Geneva (Lac Léman). Montreux is a tourish-resort. Pop. (estimated), 17,000.

MONTROSE′, James Graham, Marquess of. Son of the fourth Earl of Montrose, was born at Montrose in 1612, died in 1650. He studied at St. Andrews, and afterwards made a prolonged stay on the Continent. In 1637 Montrose joined the Covenanters in their resistance to episcopacy, and was sent to crush the opposition to the popular cause which arose in and around Aberdeen.

In 1639 he was one of the leaders who were appointed to confer with Charles I., after which he went over to the Royalist side, was created a marquess, and made commander of the royal forces in Scotland. With an army partly composed of Irish and Highlanders he gained in rapid succession the battles of Tippermuir and Bridge of Dee (1644), Inverlochy, Auldearn, Alford, and Kilsyth (1645). Deserted by his Highlanders, however, he was defeated at Philiphaugh by Leslie, and fled to Norway in 1646.

In March, 1650, he returned, landing in Orkney with a small body of followers. He failed, however, in raising an army, and a month later was surprised and captured in Ross-shire, and was conveyed to Edinburgh, where he was hanged and quartered.—Cf. John Buchan, *The Marquis of Montrose.*

MONTROSE. A seaport town of Forfarshire, Scotland, at the mouth of the South Esk, which widens out into a shallow expanse behind the town, known as Montrose Basin; served by the L.M.S. and L.N.E. Railways. The river is crossed by a suspension-bridge, and by a railway bridge. Between the town and the sea are extensive "links." Montrose is a well-built and fairly prosperous provincial town. with the usual public buildings and institutions, including two public libraries and one of the largest parish churches in Scotland.

The principal manufacturing industry is flax-spinning. Shipbuilding, fish-curing, etc., are also carried on, and there are extensive sawmills. The foreign trade, which is largely in timber, flax, etc., is chiefly with the Baltic and Canada. Montrose is also the centre of a fishery-district. It is one of the Montrose district of burghs, which includes Arbroath, Brechin, Forfar, and Bervie. Pop. (1931), 10,196.

MONTSERRAT. An island and one of five presidencies of the Leeward group, British West Indies. It has been described as "a heap of craters smothered in verdure," and it is fairly mountainous, rising in the Soufrière Peak to over 3000 feet, its hills and even its mountains being covered with forests. The island produces lime-juice, cotton, sugar, cotton-seed, cattle, and papain (*see* PAPAW.) About 2000 acres are laid down in lime trees and 3425 in cotton. Citrate of lime is manufactured. Plymouth is the capital. A wireless station was set up in 1925. The Government consists of a nominated Executive and Legislative Councils. Area, 32½ sq. miles; pop. 12,350.

MONZA (ancient **Modicia**). A city of Milan, Italy, on the Lambro, and connected by rail and tram with Milan. The cathedral was founded in A.D. 595 by Queen Theodelinda, and contains the iron crown of Lombardy with which Charlemagne (774) and Napoleon (1805) were crowned. The present building dates from the fourteenth century. Monza was the capital of ancient Lombardy. Pop. 43,750.

MOODY, Dwight Lyman. American evangelist, born in 1837, died in 1899. He began his religious and missionary career in 1855 at Boston, where he was a shop-assistant, and in 1856 he continued it at Chicago, where his influence became widespread. In 1873, in company with I. D. Sankey, he came to Great Britain, and the successful series of meetings held during the visit made the pair at once famous. Subsequent visits were made in 1881, 1883, and 1899, but the bulk of his work was done in the United States.

MOON, The. One of the secondary planets and the satellite of the earth, revolves round the latter in an elliptic orbit, in one sidereal month (*see* MONTH), at a mean distance of 238,840 miles, her greatest and least distances being 252,972 and 221,614 miles. Her mean diameter is 2159 miles. Her surface is about $\frac{1}{13}$ (14,600,000 sq. miles) of that of the earth; her volume $\frac{1}{49}$; her mass about $\frac{1}{81}$; and her mean density a little more than $\frac{1}{2}$. A mass weighing 1 lb. on the earth's surface would weigh about 2·64 oz. on the moon's surface.

For every revolution in her orbit, the moon rotates once on her axis, so that the same portion of her surface is constantly turned towards the earth; but in virtue of an apparent oscillatory motion, known as libration (q.v.), about $\frac{4}{7}$ of her surface is presented at one time or another to terrestrial observers. If the moon's orbit were in the plane of the ecliptic, solar and lunar eclipses would occur monthly. Her orbit is, however, inclined 5° 8′ 48″ to the ecliptic, so that her meridian altitude has a range of 57°, and she occults in course of time every star within 5° 24′ 30″ of the ecliptic. An eclipse of the moon occurs when she passes into the earth's shadow; when she passes exactly between the earth and sun there is an eclipse of the sun. (*See* ECLIPSE.)

Phases.—The changes in the appearance of the moon, described by the words waxing and waning, are known as *phases*. The four chief phases, occurring at intervals of 90° in the lunar orbit, are New Moon, when she is between the earth and sun (i.e. in conjunction with the sun), and so turns an unilluminated side to the earth; First Quarter, when one-half of her illuminated disc (i.e. one-quarter of the entire lunar surface) is visible; Full Moon, when her whole illuminated disc is presented to the earth; and Last Quarter, when once more only half of her disc is visibly illuminated. Between new moon and full moon the moon is said to *wax*; on the rest of her course she *wanes*. When more than a semicircle is visible, she is said to be *gibbous*; when less than a semicircle, to be in *crescent* phase.

On the visible portion of the lunar surface there is either no atmosphere or an exceedingly rare one, and it was long the general belief that organic life was impossible. Some astronomers, however, believe that there are evidences of traces of atmosphere and moisture, and that a low form of vegetation may exist. As each portion is alternately in sunlight and in shade for a fortnight at a time, and any atmosphere is of excessive tenuity, it is conjectured that the lunar extremes of heat and cold far exceed the greatest terrestrial extremes.

Surface.—The surface of the moon is mainly occupied by mountains, most of which are named after eminent scientific men. They are sometimes detached as precipitous peaks, more frequently they form vast continuous ranges, but the most prevalent form is that of crater-mountains, many 8 to 10 miles in diameter, and giving evident traces of volcanic action. Certain crater-like formations, which have still greater diameters, ranging to 60 or even 100 miles, are generally spoken of as "walled plains." Larger still are the "grey plains," which were at one time taken for seas, before the absence of water from the lunar surface was demonstrated. They are thought by some to be the floors of former seas. Some of the mountains have been estimated to be over 24,000 feet in height, from observation of their shadows. Very peculiar ridges of comparatively small elevation extend for great distances, connecting different ranges or craters.

The so-called "rilles" or "clefts" are huge straight furrows of great length (18 to 90 miles), which, it has been suggested, were produced by fracture in a shrinking surface. There are also valleys of various sizes, and "faults," or closed cracks, sometimes of considerable length. In reading descriptions of the visible peculiarities of the moon, it should be remembered that the highest telescopic power applied to that planet is only equivalent to bringing it within about 40 miles of the naked eye.

The attraction of the sun for the earth and the moon tends to diminish in effect their mutual action, and produce what is called the *moon's variation,* which, on the whole, is such that in each lunation the moon's velocity is greatest when she is in syzygy, that is, at new or full, and least when nearly in quadrature, when the line from the earth to the moon is at right angles to the line from the earth to the sun.—BIBLIOGRAPHY: Treatises on the Moon by Nasmyth and Carpenter, Neison, Proctor, W. A. Pickering, Webb.

MOORE, George. Irish novelist. Born in Ireland in 1852, he first studied art in Paris, but turned to literature, beginning with verse, *Flowers of Passion* (1878). His three great novels are *Esther Waters* (1894), *Evelyn Innes* (1898), and *Sister Theresa* (1901). In these he imitated the French philosophical novel and "restored in England the Fielding tradition." *Hail and Farewell*, dialogue of an autobiographical character, *The Brook Kerith* and *Heloise and Abelard* are other outstanding works. He turned later to drama with *The Coming of Gabrielle* (1920), and the successful *Making of an Immortal* (1928). Other works are *The Passing of the Essenes* (1930) and *Aphrodite in Aulis* (1931). He died in 1933.

MOORE, Sir John. British soldier, was born at Glasgow in 1761, killed at Corunna in 1809. Having obtained an ensign's commission in the 51st Regiment, he served at Minorca, in the American War, as brigadier-general in the West Indies (1795), in Ireland during the rebellion of 1798, in Holland in 1799, and in Egypt in 1801, where he was severely wounded in the battle which cost Sir Ralph Abercrombie his life. Moore was now regarded as the greatest living British general, and in 1805 he was knighted.

In 1808 he was appointed commander-in-chief of the British army in Portugal to operate against Napoleon. He advanced to Salamanca in spite of the gravest difficulties, but was finally compelled to retreat to Corunna, a distance of 200 miles, in face of a superior force. This he accomplished in a masterly manner; but the absence of the fleet to receive his army forced him to a battle against Marshal Soult, in which Moore fell, mortally wounded, in the hour of victory (16th Jan., 1809).

MOORE, Thomas. Irish poet, was born in 1779 in Dublin, where his father was a grocer, died near Devizes in 1852. From Trinity College, Dublin, he passed in 1799 to the Middle Temple in London, nominally to study law; but he almost immediately entered fashionable society, and in 1800 he was permitted to dedicate his *Translation of the Odes of Anacreon* to the Prince of Wales. His next venture, the *Poetical Works of the late Thomas Little,* though partly written in a licentious vein, which he afterwards regretted, increased his reputation.

In 1807 Moore agreed to write words for a number of Irish national airs, arranged by Sir John Stevenson. In these *Irish Melodies,* which were not finished till 1834, he found the work for which his genius was peculiarly fitted.

With *The Intercepted Letters, or the Twopenny Post Bag, by Thomas Brown the Younger* (1812), Moore entered upon the field of political and social satire, in which his wit and playfulness found good account; other works of this kind are the *Fudge Family in Paris* (1818), *Rhymes on the Road* (1823), *Memoirs of Captain Rock* (1824), etc. His most ambitious work, the Eastern romance of *Lalla Rookh,* was published in 1817, and brought its author £3000. The *Life of Sheridan* was produced in 1825, and *The Epicurean,* a prose romance, in 1827. Next came the *Life of Lord Byron,* for which he received nearly £5000, and the *Life of Lord Edward Fitzgerald.*

His remaining works include: *The Summer Fête,* a poem; *Travels of an Irish Gentleman in search of a Religion,* a serious apology for Roman Catholicism; and (in 1834) a *History of Ireland* for *Lardner's Cyclopædia,* an uncongenial task-work, never finished.—BIBLIOGRAPHY: S. Gwynne, *Thomas Moore*; Charles Kent, *Poetical Works of Moore*; J. P. Gunning, *Thomas Moore, Poet and Patriot*; Earl Russell (editor), *Memoirs, Journal, and Correspondence of Moore.*

MOORISH ARCHITECTURE. A form of Saracenic architecture which was developed by the Moslem conquerors of Spain in building their mosques and palaces. Its main characteristics are: the horse-shoe arch, varied by the trefoil, cinquefoil, and other forms of arch; profuse decoration of interiors by elaborately designed arabesques in low relief, enriched by colours and gilding, as well as by geometrical designs worked in mosaics of glazed tiles; the slenderness of the columns in proportion to the supported weight; and the curious stalactitic pendentives by which the transition is effected from the rectangular ground plan to the arched or domed roof.

An important specimen of this style is the mosque of Cordova, now the cathedral, which was begun by Caliph Abd-el-Rahman (A.D. 786), completed by his son, and subsequently much altered. It consisted originally of eleven aisles, and the eight aisles which were afterwards added (976–1001) made it one of the largest buildings in Europe, but the effect of its great extent (420 feet by 375 feet) is marred by its height, which is only about 30 feet to the roof. Another notable specimen of Moorish architecture is the Giralda or cathedral-tower of Seville. It is supposed to have been built by Abú Yusúf Yakúb (A.D. 1171) as a tower of victory, and was used by the Moslems as a minaret or muezzin-tower. The base is a square of about 50 feet, from which the tower rises straight for 185 feet, and is now crowned by a belfry added in the sixteenth century. The lower part of this tower is nearly plain, but from about one-third of its height upwards it is enriched by sunk panels filled with ornamentation in relief,

The Giralda

Moorish Decoration
Court of the Alhambra

which give lightness and grace to the structure without affecting its general massiveness.

The most characteristic Moorish palace in existence is the Alhambra in Granada, an immense structure of simple and rather forbidding exterior, but within gorgeous almost beyond description. (*See* ALHAMBRA.) In this palace are found to perfection the distinctive characteristics of Moorish architecture.

MOORS. A Mahommedan, Arabic-speaking race of mixed descent, forming part of the population of Barbary, and deriving their name from the Mauri, the ancient inhabitants of Mauritania, whose pure lineal descendants are, however, the Amazirgh, a branch of the Berbers. The modern Moors have sprung from a union of the ancient inhabitants of this region with their Arab conquerors, who appeared in the seventh century.

As the Mahommedan conquerors of the Visigoths in Spain (711–713) came from North Africa, the name Moor was also applied to them by Spanish chroniclers, and in that connection is synonymous with *Arab* and *Saracen.* These Moors pushed northwards into France, and finally settled in Spain south of the Ebro and the Sierra Guadarrama. Here, for centuries, art, science, literature, and chivalry flourished amongst them, whilst the rest of Europe was still sunk in the gloom of the Dark Ages. Before the close of the thirteenth century their possessions were limited to the Kingdom of Granada, which was finally subdued by Ferdinand the Catholic in 1492. Great numbers of the Moors emigrated to Africa, but the remainder, under the name of *Moriscos,* assuming in great part a semblance of Christianity, submitted to the Spaniards. They were, however, expelled from Spain by Philip II. and Philip III.

Between 1492 and 1610 about 3,000,000 Moriscos are estimated to have left Spain. The expelled Moors, settling in the north of Africa, founded cities from which to harass the Spanish coasts, and finally developed into the piratical states of Barbary, whose depredations were a source of irritation to the civilized Christian powers even till well into the nineteenth century.

MOOSE JAW. A city of Saskatchewan, Canada, midway between Winnipeg and Calgary. It is an agricultural centre. Pop. (1931), 21,299.

MOQUEGUA. A maritime province of Southern Peru, traversed by the Andes. A considerable trade is carried on in wines, spirits, olives, and oil with Bolivia, via the adjacent department of Puno. Borax is produced, the deposits of Salinas being operated by a London company. Moquegua is the capital; Pacocha or Ilo is the southernmost port of Peru near the Ilo Valley, and is famous for olives. Area, 5549 sq. miles; pop. about 42,390.

MOQUEGUA. A town and capital of the above province, is of great antiquity, and of reputed pre-Inca origin. It stands on the River Moquegua at an altitude of 1367 metres, and in a valley of the same name. A State-owned railway connects it with Pacocha (98 kilometres). Formerly Moquegua wines were renowned throughout Peru, but the rapid drying up of the river has reduced the wine-growing industry to poverty. Wines, spirits, and fruit are still traded. Pop. between 5000 and 6000.

MORA. A game known to the ancients, and still in vogue in the south of Europe. The two players simultaneously present each a hand, with some of the fingers extended, at the same moment endeavouring to guess the aggregate number of fingers so extended. An accurate guess counts one; five is game.

MORACEÆ. A family of apetalous dicotyledons, sometimes united with Urticaceæ. It includes many important plants, such as the breadfruit, fig, hemp, hop, mulberry, etc.

MORADABAD. A town of India, in Rohilkhand, in the United Provinces, on the Ramganga. It is noted for its metal-work, and is a centre of local trade. Pop. (1931), 110,562.—The district has an area of 2285 sq. miles. Pop. 1,260,000.

MORALES (mo-rä'lās), **Luis de.** A Spanish painter, surnamed *El Divino,* probably because he painted sacred subjects almost exclusively, was born at Badajoz in 1509, died there 1586. His *Mater Dolorosa,* at Madrid, is considered his masterpiece.

MORALITY PLAY. *See* DRAMA.

MORAT (mo-rä; Ger. *Murten*). A town in the Swiss canton of Freiburg, on the Lake of Morat. Here, on the 22nd of June, 1476, the Swiss Confederacy met and defeated the forces of Charles the Bold, Duke of Burgundy, who was killed during the battle. Pop. about 2400.

MORATORIUM (Lat. *mora,* delay). A period during which the payment of debts cannot be enforced. A moratorium is generally declared by the Government of a state in times of great financial stress (as in France in 1870, and in Britain in 1914), when panic is feared and delay for the restoration of public confidence essential. Commercially, the term is applied to the extension of time given by a creditor to his debtor for payment of a bill of exchange. During the depression of 1930–32 some public companies secured a moratorium for the payment of their debenture interest.

MORAVIA (the Austro-Hungarian **Mähren**). A province of Czechoslovakia, formerly in the Austrian Empire; area, 8616 sq. miles. Brno or Brünn (q.v.) is the capital and the seat of the Supreme Court of Justice of Czechoslovakia. The minerals are of considerable importance, and include iron, coal, graphite, and slate. The chief agricultural crops are rye, oats, barley, potatoes, beetroot, and flax. Before the European War Moravia was the most important manufacturing province in Austria-Hungary. Its woollen industries are of world-wide fame, and linen and cotton, beet-sugar, iron and steel goods, machinery, beer (Pilsener), and spirits are also turned out in large quantities.

In 1029 Moravia was united to the Kingdom of Bohemia, with which it passed to Austria in 1526, and became a part of Czechoslovakia (q.v.) on 28th Oct., 1918. It forms a political divison with W. Silesia. Total area, 10,324 sq. miles; pop. (1930), 3,563,157.

MORAVIAN BRETHREN, also called **UNITED BRETHREN, HERRNHUTER,** and officially **UNITAS FRATRUM** (Unity of Brethren). A Protestant sect or Church which originally sprang up in Bohemia after the death of John Huss. After the sanguinary religious wars which prevailed in Bohemia until 1627 they were everywhere almost annihilated. Their doctrines were still, however, secretly cherished in Moravia, and in 1722 a colony emigrated thence, and were invited by the Lutheran Count Zinzendorf to settle on his estate near Berthelsdorf, in Saxony, where they built the town of Herrnhut, still the headquarters of the Church. The doctrines of the brethren had hitherto been more in harmony with the Calvinistic than with the Lutheran form of Protestantism, but under the influence of Count Zinzendorf, who himself became a bishop, they attached themselves to the Lutheran Church.

The Moravian Brethren have always distinguished themselves as missionaries, and maintain stations in North and Central America, South Africa, Australia, and Tibet. They are distinguished for the puritanical simplicity of their life and manners, and for their earnest, if somewhat narrow and austere piety. The practice of living in exclusive communities or villages still obtains in Germany. Moravian schools deservedly enjoy a high reputation even among those who are not members of the community. The Moravian Church in Britain at the present time is estimated to number over 3500 adherents.

MORAY, or MURRAY, James Stuart, Earl of. Half-brother of Mary Queen of Scots, natural son of James V. of Scotland and Margaret Erskine, born about 1533, shot in 1570. In 1558 he joined the Lords of the Congregation, and was soon recognized as the head of the reformers' party. On Mary's return from France Moray became her favoured adviser, but her marriage with Darnley and subsequent events caused a breach between them which constantly widened.

On the deposition of Mary he was appointed regent, defeated her forces at Langside on her escape from Lochleven (1568), and appeared as evidence against her at her trial in England. He consequently incurred the bitter hatred of the queen's party, but earned from the people the title of "Good Regent." He was snot in the streets of Linlithgow by Hamilton of Bothwellhaugh, who was actuated by private grievances.

MORAY. An ancient division of the Kingdom of Scotland, corresponding approximately to the modern counties of Moray (Elgin), Nairn, Banff, and part of Inverness.

MORAY FIRTH. An arm of the North Sea, on the north-east coast of Scotland, containing at its widest extent the area between Duncansby Head in Caithness and Kinnaird Head in Aberdeenshire, a distance of 78 miles; but in a restricted sense that portion which lies between Tarbat Ness and either Burghead or Lossiemouth, and which extends into the Cromarty and Beauly Firths.

MORAYSHIRE. *See* ELGIN.

MORBIHAN (mor-bi-āṇ). A north-western department of France, on the Bay of Biscay, forming part of pre-Revolutionary Brittany. The northern part is hilly, but the rest is low and level, especially along the coast, which is deeply indented and island-studded. The Canal de Brest traverses the department, which has also a good river system. The fisheries, especially of sardines, are important; rye, wheat, and potatoes are grown under the worst possible natural soil conditions; mineral wealth is represented by iron and slate. The chief town is Vannes; others are Lorient, Quiberon, Ploërmel, and Pontivy. Area, 2738 sq. miles; pop. (1931), 537,528.

MORDVINS. A race of people inhabiting European Russia, and belonging to the Bulgaric or Volgaic group of the Finnish family of peoples. They are found chiefly in the governments of Penza, Simbirsk, Saratov, Samara, Nishegorod, and Tambov. Their numbers are estimated at 1,000,000.

MORE, Sir Thomas. A Chancellor of England, only son of Sir John More, a judge of the Court of King's Bench, born in London in 1480, beheaded 1535. A portion of his youth was spent in the family of Cardinal Morton, Archbishop of Canterbury, and Chancellor; and he was then sent to Oxford, and afterwards entered at Lincoln's Inn. He had already formed an intimate and lasting friendship with Erasmus. About 1502 he became a member of Parliament, and immediately made for himself a place in history by upholding the privileges of the House of Commons to treat all questions of supply as their own exclusive business.

On the accession of Henry VIII. he was made Under-Sheriff of London. In 1514 he was Envoy to the Low Countries, soon after was made a Privy Councillor, and in 1521 was knighted. He appears to have ere this time considerably enriched himself by practice, and with his wife, a daughter of a gentleman of Essex named Colt, he kept up a noble hospitality. In 1523 he became Speaker of the House of Commons, and in 1529 succeeded Wolsey in the chancellorship.

When Henry began his attacks on the Papal supremacy, More at once took up the position which his conscience dictated as a supporter of the old system. Henry marked him out for vengeance as an opponent of his matrimonial views, and More endeavoured to shield himself by retiring from office. He was requested to take the oath to maintain the lawfulness of the marriage with Anne Boleyn. His refusal to do so led to his committal to the Tower, trial for misprision of treason, and execution. His chief work is the *Utopia* (in Latin), a philosophical romance describing an ideal commonwealth.—BIBLIOGRAPHY: W. H. Hutton, *Sir Thomas More*; Sir S. Lee, *Great Englishmen of the Sixteenth Century*; T. E. Bridgett, *Life of Sir Thomas More*.

MÖRE. One of the eighteen *fylker* (counties) of Norway, with a long, fiord-indented coast-line on the Atlantic. Aalesund, Christiansund, and Molde are the chief towns. Fishing is the principal industry. Area, 5811·7 sq. miles; pop. (1930), 165,064.

MOREAU (mo-rō), **Jean Victor.** French general, born at Morlaix, in Bretagne, in 1763, died 1813. Bred to the law, he early displayed a predilection for the military profession, and in 1789 he joined the army of the north at the head of a battalion of volunteers. He so distinguished himself that he was named commander-in-chief of the army of the Rhine and Moselle in 1796, destined to threaten Vienna simultaneously with the invasion of Italy by Bonaparte. In 1799 he was in command of the army of Italy, and next year had the command of the armies of the Danube and the Rhine.

Being found guilty of participation in the conspiracy of Pichegru and Cadoudal against Napoleon (1804), he had to go into exile, and purchased an estate in Pennsylvania, where he resided for some years. He was subsequently induced to aid in the direction of the allied armies against his own country, but was mortally wounded in the battle before Dresden in 1813, and died a few days later.

MORECAMBE. A municipal borough and watering-place of Lancashire, England, on Morecambe Bay; served by the L.M.S. Railway. It is situated near Heysham, a Midland Railway port, whence steamers sail for Belfast, Dublin, and Douglas (Isle of Man). Fishing is the chief occupation. Pop. with Heysham (1931), 24,586.

MOREEN′. A woollen, woollen and cotton, or all cotton fabric of a warp-rib character, made in imitation of moiré (that is, having a watered appearance). It is used for dresses, curtains, hangings, etc.

MO′REL. A genus of edible Fungi, group Discomycetes (Morchella), applied specifically to *Morchella esculenta.* This is plentiful in

Common Morel

some parts of Britain, and common in Germany. It is much used to flavour gravies, and is sometimes employed instead of the common mushroom to make ketchup.

MORE′LIA. A city and capital of the state of Michoacáan, Mexico, 6400 feet above sea-level; served by a branch of the National Railway. There is a cathedral and the oldest college in Mexico (San Nicolas de Hidalgo College). Cheese, cigars, cottons, woollens, and *pulque* are manufactured. Morelia was founded as Valladolid in 1541, and became state capital in 1582. As the birthplace of General Morelos the town received its new designation (Morelia) in 1828. Pop. (1930), 34,000.

MORELOS. An inland state of Mexico, immediately south of the Federal district. In the north it is mountainous (Popocatepetl, 17,784 feet). The first sugar-cane plantations were established by Cortez in Morelos. Silver, copper, and zinc are worked. The capital is Guernavaca. Area, 1895 sq. miles; pop. (1930), 132,582.

MORETON BAY CHESTNUT. *See* CHESTNUT.

MORGAN, John Pierpont. American financier and banker. Born at Hartford, Connecticut, on 17th April, 1837, he was the son of a banker and entered the family firm in 1864. This later became the firm of J. P. Morgan & Company, and, largely through his financial ability, became one of the most powerful banking houses in the world. It organized the Steel Trust, formed an Atlantic Shipping Combine, controlled railways, etc. He was a yachtsman, collector, and philanthropist, and died a multi-millionaire on 31st March, 1913, in Rome. His son, **John Pierpont,** placed contracts and raised loans for the British Government during the War.

MORGANAT'IC MARRIAGE. In some European countries, one in which it is stipulated that the wife (who is inferior in birth to the husband) and her children shall not enjoy the privileges of his rank nor inherit his possessions. It is a perfect marriage from the ecclesiastical point of view, and also from certain legal points of view. The morganatic marriage is not recognized in Great Britain.

MORGARTEN. A place in Switzerland, canton of Zug, where a small body of Swiss in 1315 totally defeated a large force of the Austrians.

MORHANGE. A town of France, department of Moselle (formerly Lorraine), which gives name to a battle of the European War. On 14th Aug., 1914, the French armies of Dubail and Castelnau advanced into Lorraine, the advance culminating on the Morhange-Sarrebourg line, which formed the first trench system of the war, complete with concrete gun-emplacements and barbed-wire entanglements, and thoroughly surveyed and ranged for artillery by the German staff. On 20th Aug. the French armies were driven back in confusion, but were saved from annihilation by the support of Foch's 20th Corps on the extreme right. A stand was made astride the Meurthe, and positions were eventually taken up at the Grand Couronné (23rd Aug.), when one of the most decisive battles of the war turned defeat into victory.

MORIER, James. English novelist, born in 1780, died in 1849. In 1812 and in 1818 he published accounts of two *Journeys through Persia to Constantinople*, but he was best known by his *Adventures of Hajji Baba of Ispahan* (1824), *Adventures of Hajji Baba in England* (1828), *Zohrab the Hostage* (1832), and *Ayesha the Maid of Kars* (1834). *See* PICARESQUE NOVEL.

MORLANCOURT. A village of France, in the department of the Somme, taken by the Germans in March, 1918, during the thrust for Amiens. There was much sanguinary struggling around the village in May and August, and it was definitively recaptured on 8th Aug. It has been "adopted" by Folkestone.

MORLAND, George. Painter, the son of a painter, born in London 1763, died 1804. His work deals with rustic and homely life, and the best of it is now highly prized by connoisseurs. He had extraordinary popularity during his lifetime, and about 250 of his pictures are said to have been engraved. *The Interior of a Stable*, now in the National Gallery, is perhaps his masterpiece.

MORLEY, John. First Viscount Morley, author and politician, born at Blackburn, Lancashire, 24th Dec., 1838. He was educated at Cheltenham and at Lincoln College, Oxford; was called to the Bar in 1873; was for some time editor of the *Literary Gazette*, conducted the *Fortnightly Review* from 1867 to 1882, and edited the *Pall Mall Gazette* for three years (1880-83), and *Macmillan's Magazine* for two years (1883–85). He also edited the English Men of Letters Series, to which he contributed the volume on Burke. He was the author of *Critical Miscellanies, Voltaire, Rousseau, Walpole, Life of Gladstone,* and *Recollections*.

He represented Newcastle from 1883 to 1895; and in 1896 became member for the Montrose burghs. Radical and Home Ruler, he was Chief Secretary for Ireland in 1886 and 1892–95, Indian Secretary from 1905 to 1910, Lord President of the Council from 1910 to 1914, and resigned from the Cabinet when Great Britain decided to enter the European War. One of the original holders of the Order of Merit (1902), he was made a peer in 1908. His *Collected Works* (in 15 vols.) appeared in 1920. He died in September 1923.

MORLEY. A municipal borough of Yorkshire (West Riding), England; served by the L.N.E. Railway. It is mentioned in *Domesday Book*. The place is a centre of the woollen manufacture, and machinery is made. Pop. (1931), 23,397.

MORMONS. A sect founded in 1830 by Joseph Smith, a native of the United States. The distinguishing peculiarities of the sect are—the belief in a continual divine revelation through the inspired medium of the prophet at the head of their Church, the belief in polygamy, and a complete hierarchial organization. The supreme power, spiritual and temporal, rests with the president or prophet (elected by the whole body of the Church), who alone works miracles and receives revelations.

Book of Mormon.—The Mormons accept both the Bible and the *Book of Mormon* as divine revelations, but hold them equally subject to the explanation and correction of the prophet. The latter-mentioned book (in large part a kind of historical romance written by one Solomon Spaulding in 1812) pretends to be a history of America from the first settlement of the continent after the destruction of the Tower of Babel up to the end of the fourth century of our era, at which time flourished the legendary prophet Mormon, its reputed author. It was said to have been written on gold plates, and concealed until its hiding-place was revealed to Smith by an angel. The name given to it was evidently owing to the important part which Spaulding had assigned to Mormon and his son Moroni in his novel; but Smith and his coadjutors, instead of confining themselves to the original manuscript, had clumsily engrafted upon it a number of maxims, prophecies, etc., evidently garbled from the sacred volume, and interpolated in such a manner as to involve anachronisms and contradictions.

Doctrine.—The doctrine of the Mormons is a mixture of materialism and millenarianism, and their most distinctive feature, polygamy, which, though originally condemned in the *Book of Mormon*, was introduced under a theory of "spiritual wives," and a mysterious system of unrestricted marriage called "sealing."

History.—The Mormons first appeared at Manchester, New York, whence they were compelled by the persevering hostility of their neighbours to flee, first to Kirtland in Ohio (1831), then to Nauvoo, the "City of Beauty," in Illinois (1838), and finally to the Salt Lake in Utah (1848). In 1844 the founder, Joseph Smith, was shot by a mob in Carthage prison, where his lawless behaviour had brought him.

The advance made by Mormonism seems to have been due far more to the abilities of Brigham Young, the successor of Smith, than to the founder himself, who was little better than a dissipated and immoral scamp. Under Young's direction large tracts of land at Salt Lake were brought under cultivation, an emigration fund was established, and a skilful system of propagandism set on foot, by which large numbers of converts were brought from Europe, especially from Great Britain. A state was organized under the name of Deseret. Congress refused to recognize it, but erected Utah into a territory, and Brigham Young was appointed Governor of it. He was soon removed by the United States authorities, but after a time the Mormons were left pretty much to themselves. In 1870 Congress passed a Bill to compel them to renounce polygamy, or quit the United States. A prosecution was instituted against Brigham Young, who was sentenced to fine and imprisonment.

In 1877 Young died, and was succeeded by John Taylor, an Englishman, who in turn was succeeded as president by Wilford Woodruff in 1887. In 1890 he proclaimed that polygamy was no longer taught as a doctrine of Mormonism. Woodruff was succeeded by Joseph Fielding Smith as president of the Church, and on the latter's death, in 1918, Heber J. Grant became president. Both Smith and Grant were polygamists. In 1922 Mormon emissaries were busy in London spreading their doctrine and enticing many young women to join the Mormon Church and to travel to Salt Lake. The Mormon Church numbers about 500,000 adherents. In 1933 polygamy was prohibited by the Mormon authorities, excommunication being the punishment for disobedience.—

BIBLIOGRAPHY: W. A. Linn, *The Story of the Mormons*; E. W. Tullidge, *History of Salt Lake City*; B. H. Roberts, *Joseph Smith, the Prophet Teacher*; S. Martin, *The Mystery of Mormonism*; L. A. Wilson, *Outlines of Mormon Philosophy*.

MORNING-GLORY. A name given to several climbing plants of the convolvulus family, having handsome purple or white, sometimes pink or pale-blue, funnel-shaped flowers.

MORNY, Charles Auguste Louis Joseph, Comte de. French politician, said to have been a half-brother of Louis Napoleon, born at Paris 1811, died 1865. He took a prominent part in the *coup d'état* of 1851, and was a prominent figure under the Second Empire.

MOROBE. A town of New Guinea (formerly German, now British). It stands on a bay in the east of the island and is one of the chief ports.

MOROCCO. The extreme north-western country of Africa, bounded by Algeria, Rio de Oro, the Atlantic, and the Mediterranean. Physically it falls into two distinct regions divided by the Atlas Mountains, the one, on the Atlantic and Mediterranean, being temperate and European, the other being exposed to the scorching Saharan winds and being torrid and rainless. Africa proper begins behind the Atlas Mountains on the fringe of the Sahara. The northern Atlas ranges are a continuation of the Sierra Nevada of Spain, and were formerly continued across the Strait between Sicily and Tunisia, and by the fold mountains of Sicily into the Apennines of Italy. Malta is one of the last fragments of the connecting link between the Atlas and the Alpine system.

The indigenous inhabitants are Caucasian and mainly Arabicized Berbers. There are a few pure negroes. Morocco was conquered by Arabs in the eighth century, and being seized by the Sa'dian Shereef during 1519-20 passed to the Shereefian family. The sultan is called the Emir-el-Mumenin (Prince of the Faithful), and is the direct descendant of Ali, son-in-law of the prophet. French, Spanish, and Arabic are spoken, and Sunnite Mahommedanism is prevalent. Education is well provided for in the French Zone, and there are Moslem colleges at Fez and Rabat. The total area of the empire is 213,350 sq. miles, the native population is *c.* 6,051,000, and there are *c.* 49,000 whites.

Though nominally independent the empire is divided into the French Zone (200,000 sq. miles); the Spanish Zone consisting of the North Spanish Zone, the South Spanish Zone, and Ifni (total area, 13,125 sq. miles), and the Tangier Zone (225 sq. miles). The country is largely undeveloped, but agriculture is the chief industry, barley, wheat, maize, and fruits (olives, grapes, figs, dates, etc.) being produced. There are rich deposits of copper, iron, lead, antimony, phosphates (in French Zone), and petroleum. There are large forests of cork-oak, pine, argan, etc. Sardine and tunny fishing are important all along the coast.

French Zone.—The Sultan of Morocco accepted the French Protectorate in 1912 (for events leading

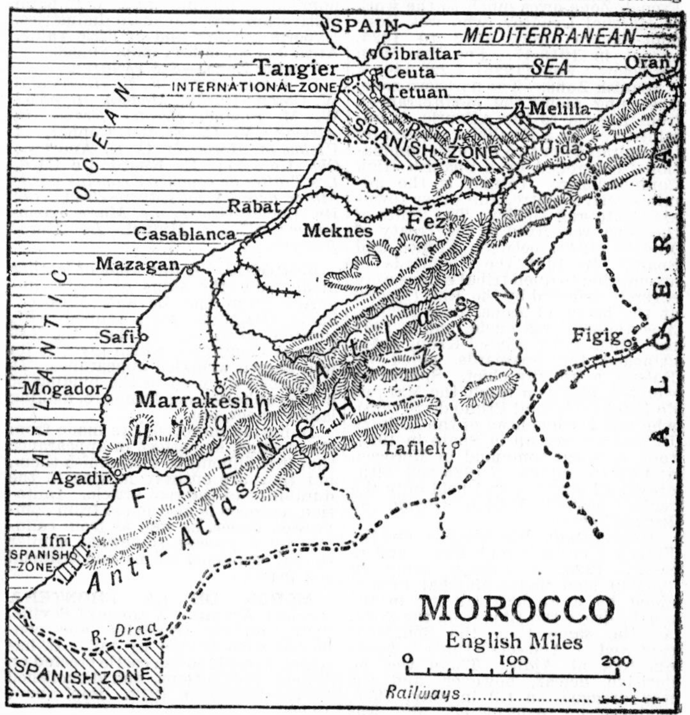

up to this *see* FRANCE), and now follows the advice of the French Resident-General (who is also Foreign Minister) in all matters. The French commander-in-chief is Minister for War, and there are six Shereefian Viziers (Justice, Instruction, etc.). The capitals are Fez, Meknes, Marrakesh, and Rabat, which is the seat of administration. Ports are Agadir, Mogador, Casablanca (the most important), and Rabat.

The value of exports (cereals, eggs, almonds, etc.) was £30,322,511, and of imports *c.* £82,463,642. Agriculture is the main industry in all territories. A great irrigation scheme was begun in 1927. There were in 1931, 1440 kilometres of railway track and 2235 miles of high-roads. The army in 1931-32 comprised 58,614 N.C.O.'s, 2650 officers, and 12,498 irregulars. The currency unit is the gold Moroccan franc which in 1928 was put on the same gold basis as the French franc. The prosperity of the French Zone owes much to the work of Marshal Lyautey, who was Resident-General from 1912 to 1925, except in 1916-17. For RIF WAR see below. Pop. (1926), 4,229,146.

Spanish Zone.—The northern zone, stretching along the Mediterranean from Algeria to the Atlantic, is administered by a Khalipha (chosen by the Sultan from two Spanish nominations) controlled by a Spanish High Commissioner. Tetuan is the administrative centre, and other towns are Ceuta and Melilla. The limits of the zone were fixed in the Treaty of Madrid (1912) between France and Spain. In 1921 the Spaniards in attempting to quell tribal risings were severely defeated by the Rîfis (Moors) at the battle of Anual near Melilla. A settlement was made, but in 1923 the Rîfis, under Abd-el-Krim, again attacked the Spaniards, aided by Raisuli, a friendly chief. Spain was worsted, and as a result the Marquis de Estella (General Primo de Rivera), who had become head of the Military Directorate set up in Spain in 1923, took personal command in Morocco, and by the middle of 1925 had withdrawn all outposts and held only the region around Tetuan (Primo de Rivera line).

Intermittent Rîf attacks on the French Zone also took place, and in Sept., 1925, a French army of 100,000 men under Marshal Petain, aided by a Spanish landing in the north, drove the Rîfis from the Zone. At the same time the Spaniards captured Abd-el-Krim's headquarters at Ajdir. There was no decisive defeat, however, and the war dragged on till in May, 1926, Abd-el-Krim capitulated, and was exiled in Réunion. The Tangier Zone, declared neutral and non-military by an agreement signed by France, Britain, and Spain in 1925, and a later (1928) Protocol signed by these countries and Italy, is governed by an administrator and three assistants, and an international assembly of 27 members. In 1933 the administrator and assistant administrators were respectively French, British, Spanish, and Italian. There are railways from Nadir to Tistutin, from Larache to Alcazar, from Ceuta to Tetuan, and part of the line from Tangier to Fez. The army in 1932 numbered 49,000, all ranks. The southern zone around Cape Juby is of little importance politically, or in any other way, and is usually considered as part of Rio de Oro.

Ifni.—A small maritime territory in the south of the French Zone. It was ceded to Spain by Morocco in 1860, but the occupation is purely nominal. Fishing and date-palm cultivation are the main industries. Exports are few and of little value. Area, 965 sq. miles ; pop. 20,000.

Tangier Zone.—*See* TANGIER.

BIBLIOGRAPHY : W. B. Harris and W. Cozens-Hardy, *Modern Morocco* ; W. M. Sloane, *Greater France in Africa* ; V. C. Scott-O'Connor, *A Vision of Morocco* ; C. E. Andrews, *Old Morocco* ; E. Ruard De Card, *Les Traités de commerce conclus par le Maroc avec les puissances étrangères* ; Dr. Lucien-Graux, *Le Maroc économique* ; Roger Miquel, *Le Maroc français.*

MOROCCO. A fine kind of leather made from the skins of goats, imported from the Levant, Morocco, Spain, Belgium, etc., tanned with sumach, dyed, and grained, the last process being that which gives it its well-known wrinkled appearance. It is extensively used in the binding of books, upholstering furniture, making ladies' shoes, etc.

Imitation moroccos are made from sheep-skins, so perfect in appearance that it is difficult to distinguish them, but they are entirely lacking in the durability of the real article. Imitation morocco is also made from compressed paper, as well as from cellulose by a process somewhat similar to that employed for making artificial silk fabrics.

MORON DE LA FRONTERA (ancient **Arumi**). A town of Seville, Spain, on the Guadaira, and connected with Seville by rail. It has remains of a Moorish castle erected on Roman foundations, and demolished by the French in 1812. Pop. about 19,000.

MOROXITE. A greenish-blue variety of the mineral apatite.

MORPETH. A municipal borough of Northumberland, England, on the Wansbeck. It is served by the L.N.E. Railway, and is a railway junction. An abbey was founded at Newminster, near by, in the twelfth century; the church of St. Mary dates from the fourteenth century. The industries include brewing and malting; and extensive collieries are located in the vicinity. Pop. (1931), 7390.

MORPHEUS. In Greek mythology the son of sleep, and god of dreams.

MOR'PHIA, or MORPHINE. The narcotic principle of opium, is a vegetable alkaloid of bitter taste, which was first isolated from opium, in which it exists in the form of two soluble salts, about 1807. Morphine itself is only soluble in water or ether, but dissolves readily in acids. Its salts, especially the hydrochloride, acetate, and sulphate, are widely used in medicine for the relief of pain. It is most commonly given by hypodermic injection, as by this means more accurate dosage and greater control over the administration are obtained. In small doses it is a powerful sedative, and ensures sleep even when pain of a severe character is present, while in large doses it is a narcotic poison.

Great care has to be taken in regard to its continued use, as the morphia habit (morphomania) may be easily established, so that self-administration of the drug is always unwise. Larger and larger doses can be tolerated by continuous use, and the morphia habit is, among Western races, a serious danger. It occurs most frequently in people suffering from some painful chronic disease, and in over-wrought brain-workers.

MORPHOLOGY, A branch of biology which deals with the structure and *form* of animals and plants, and their different organs, from those of the lowest to those of the highest type. It includes: (1) external morphology; (2) anatomy; (3) histology, or minute anatomy, of which cytology is a branch dealing with the cell. In morphology questions of *homology* and *analogy* (*see* ANALOGUE) are frequently of the greatest importance, and comparative morphology may be said to lie at the foundation of all true systems of classification and arrangement.

MORRIS, Sir Lewis. English poet, born near Caermarthen in 1833, died in 1907. Educated at Oxford, where he graduated first class in classics in 1855, he was called to the Bar, and practised from 1861 to 1881. His poems have been widely popular. They include *Songs of Two Worlds, Epic of Hades, Gwen, Ode of Life, Songs Unsung, Songs of Britain,* etc. His Jubilee and Coronation poems were rewarded with medals. He was knighted in 1895.

MORRIS, William. Poet, artist, designer, and Socialist, was born on the 24th March, 1834, and died 3rd Oct., 1896. He was educated at Marlborough, and at Exeter College, Oxford, where he read for a pass-degree. At Oxford he met Burne-Jones, whose friendship was an important factor in his life. He abandoned his original intention of going into the Church, and chose to follow the profession of painter. He was of independent means, having an income of £900 a year after he came of age. In 1857 he helped Rossetti to decorate the Oxford Union; the work was done too rapidly and too soon, and did not last.

Morris married in 1859, and, desiring an ideal home, he commissioned his friend Philip Webb to build him a house (The Red House) at Upton, in Kent. The building and decoration of this house, the smallest detail of the furniture of which was specially designed, led to the foundation in 1861 of Morris, Marshall, Faulkner, & Co., a firm of decorators and manufacturers. Morris was the senior partner and the moving spirit, and he did more than any one else to exorcise the spirit of drab ugliness from Victorian houses.

In 1858 he published his *Defence of Guinevere*; his *Life and Death of Jason* appeared in 1867, and his *Earthly Paradise* from 1868-70. His poems, good in themselves, did much to widen the outlook of readers of poetry, showing them that there were other civilizations besides that of Victorian England. He became keenly interested in the art of illuminating manuscripts. He translated the *Æneid* (1875) and the *Odyssey* (1887), as well as a number of Icelandic sagas. His epic *Sigurd the Volsung* appeared in 1876.

In 1883 Morris became an ardent Socialist, and managed and financed a Socialist paper, *Commonweal.* He was not altogether trusted by the Socialist party, and finally broke with the anarchistic wing of it. His interest in the movement gradually waned.

In 1890 he started the Kelmscott Press at Hammersmith. It issued in all fifty-three books. The *Kelmscott Chaucer,* issued in 1896, is considered by many the finest printed book ever produced.

Morris was a man of the most forceful personality, and his interests and enthusiasms were manifold. He practised many arts, because according to his conception all art was one. He wished to go back to the Middle Ages, not because he was retrogressive, but because he thought civilization had taken the wrong turning, and that to regain the right path it was necessary to go back to where the ways had parted. His influence both on poetry and house decoration was profound and salutary.—BIBLIOGRAPHY: J. W. Mackail, *Life and Letters of William Morris*; A. Clutton Brock, *William Morris: his Work and Influence*; A. Vallance, *W. Morris: his Art, his Writings, and his Public Life.*

MORRIS-DANCE (that is, *Moorish-dance*). A dance supposed to have been derived from the Moriscos in Spain, formerly danced at puppet-shows, May-games, etc., in England. Bells were fastened to the feet of the performers, which jingled in time with the music, while the dancers clashed their staves or swords. In the reigns of Henry VII. and VIII. it was a principal feature in the popular festivals.

MORRISON, Mt., or NIITAKA-YAMA. A peak of Taiwan (Formosa), the highest in the Japanese Empire, and the culminating point of the Niitaka range to the south of the island. Altitude, about 14,000 feet.

MORRISON, Herbert Stanley. English politician. Born 3rd Jan., 1888, he worked in a shop as a telephone operator. Later he became connected with the newspaper industry and came to the front as a Socialist politician. He was elected to the London County Council and rose to be the leader of his party there. In 1923-24 and in 1929-31 he was M.P. for South Hackney, and from 1929-31 he was Minister of Transport. He conducted the Road Act of 1930 through the House of Commons, and was regarded as one of the most successful of the Labour ministers. He lost his seat at the General Election of 1931. In 1920 Morrison was Mayor of Hackney, and in 1928-29 chairman of the Labour Party.

MORSE, Samuel Finley Breese. Inventor of the electric telegraph in its first practicable form, born at Charlestown, Mass., 1791, died at New York 1872. He was educated at Yale College, and in 1811 went to England to study painting under West. In 1813 he was awarded the gold medal of the Royal Academy for his model of the *Dying Hercules.*

In 1829 he went to Europe for three years, and during the return voyage worked out roughly a plan for employing electro-magnetism in telegraphy. It was not until 1835, however, that he was able to exhibit an instrument that was found to work well. By July, 1837, this instrument was perfected, and ultimately in 1843 Congress granted him means to construct an experimental line between Washington and Baltimore. From that time Morse's instrument came into general use in America and Europe. In 1857 the representatives of ten countries met at Paris, and voted him 400,000 francs.

MORTALITY, Law of. A type of question of great importance to insurance offices is: Of 100,000 men who reach their twentieth birthday, how many will survive till they are fifty? Numerical tables which enable answers to be given to questions of this kind are called *mortality tables*, and the rule or law which they embody, the *law of mortality*. At one time the only statistics available in England were abstracts of parish registers, called *bills of mortality*, and the earliest tables were based on very inadequate data.

The *Northampton Table* was constructed by Richard Price in 1780 from certain records of baptisms in Northampton during the years from 1735 to 1780. In the *Carlisle Table* Joshua Milne adopted the correct method of tabulating the number of deaths occurring within each year of age, and comparing this number with the number of people alive at that age. The Institute of Actuaries in 1869 published tables based on the experience of twenty insurance companies; these tables are still largely used, though many companies work on statistics compiled from their own experience.

Attempts have been made to find a mathematical formula embodying the empirical data of the tables. Demoivre, for instance, proposed the very simple law that out of every 86 children born alive 1 dies every year. This rule gives approximately correct results about middle life, but is far too crude for the purposes of the actuary. Formulæ of much greater value have been suggested by Gompertz and by Makeham; these are useful in calculations of annuities on joint lives.

The annexed table is condensed

from the *English Life Table No. 3* (1864), one of a series of tables based on English census returns, and therefore representative of *average* lives. Insurance companies for the most part use tables applicable to *selected* lives; important examples are the HM (healthy males) and HF (healthy females) tables of the Institute of Actuaries.

Age.	Number Alive at each Age.	Number Dying in the following Year.
0	5117	837
1	4280	275
2	4005	142
3	3863	92
4	3771	67
5	3704	50
10	3530	20
15	3443	18
20	3336	28
25	3194	29
30	3045	31
35	2889	33
40	2721	35
45	2537	39
50	2332	44
55	2095	51
60	1824	59
65	1508	69
70	1144	77
75	758	75
80	411	58
85	169	33
90	48	13
95	8	3
100	1	—

The table, or the graph, supplies the means of answering some interesting questions. If we ask, for example, what chance a man entering upon age thirty has of surviving till he is sixty, we see from the table that, out of 3045 men of just thirty, 1824 reach sixty. The chance of a particular individual surviving is $\frac{1824}{3045}$, or about $\frac{3}{5}$; the chance of his not surviving is therefore $\frac{2}{5}$, so that, in the ordinary phraseology, the odds are 6 to 4 in favour of his being alive at sixty. Again, the table shows that 1508 live to sixty-five; sixty-five is therefore the age which it is an even chance that a man of thirty will reach.

The *expectation of life* at a given age is an important number in calculations of life contingencies. It is the average number of years lived by a person after entering upon the given age, and may be found by calculating the total number of years lived by all the persons on the table after they enter upon that age, and dividing the sum by the number so entering. Take, e.g., the expectation of life of a man who has just reached thirty. Of 3045 who do so, 2889 live five years at least, 2721 other five years at least, and so on. Hence, neglecting small corrections, the total number of years lived by the 3045 men after thirty is found by adding the figures in the "number alive" column from 2889 to the end, multiplying the sum by 5, and dividing the result by 3045. We thus find that the average number of years lived, i.e. the expectation of life at thirty, is thirty-one years nearly. It is easy to see that the exact value of this expectation may be obtained by finding the area under the graph between the age axis and the ordinate at age thirty, and dividing the area by this ordinate.

The *rate of mortality* at a particular age is found roughly by dividing the number who die at that age by the number who enter upon it; the number who die at a particular age is got at once from the table by a simple subtraction. It will be seen that the graph has points of inflexion at ages thirteen and seventy-two. These features have an interesting interpretation. Thus, beginning with 5117 boys at age nothing, we see that 837 die before they are a year old, then fewer and and fewer every year till at age thirteen only 17 die; afterwards the yearly mortality increases till age seventy-two, when 78 die; it then decreases steadily to the end.

To a company doing life-insurance and annuity business, life tables are of course indispensable. Exceptional risks may be undertaken at exceptional terms, but in ordinary business the proposal is treated as if it were concerned with an average life. A man of thirty, let us say, wishes to take out a whole-life policy. A company working on the above table considers what would happen if 3045 men insured at thirty. The table shows the number and the dates of the payments that would be made on both sides. The question is removed from the region of speculation, and becomes one for the exact calculations of the actuary. *See* ANNUITIES.

MORTAR. A mixture of sand with slaked lime and water, used as a cement for uniting stones and bricks in walls. The proportions vary from $1\frac{1}{2}$ parts of sand and 1 part of lime to 4 or 5 parts sand and 1 of lime. When exposed to the action of the air, this mixture absorbs carbon dioxide and "sets," forming a hard, compact mass.

Hydraulic mortars, which harden under water, and are used for piers, submerged walls, etc., are formed from so-called *hydraulic lime,* containing considerable portions of silica and alumina. *See* HYDRAULIC CEMENT.

MORTGAGE. In law, is a pledge of land or other immovable property or chattels or choses in actions, e.g. book debts as a security for debt, on condition that if the debt be not repaid in the time and manner specified in the transaction, the pledge shall be fortified.

Mortgages in England may be either legal or equitable. A legal mortgage must be by deed. Formerly it vested the legal estate in the mortgagee. Since the Law of Property Act, 1925, came into force a legal mortgage of land held in fee-simple is made by (*a*) lease of the land for a term of years (usually 3000), with a provision that the term shall cease on the redemption of the mortgage; a second mortgage by a term one day longer than that of the first; a third mortgage longer than that of the second, etc.; or by (*b*) a charge on the land by deed expressed to be by way of legal mortgage. A mortgagee has the same rights as before. If the mortgagee by either (*a*) or (*b*) gets an order for foreclosure, the legal estate in fee-simple is vested in the mortgagee. Mortgage of leaseholds must be made by sublease less by one or more days than the term vested in the mortgagor; or by (*b*).

An equitable mortgage may be constituted by a deposit of title-deeds. It in fact constitutes an acknowledgment of a grant of security for advances, and implies an engagement to execute a legal mortgage if required. Such a deposit will cover advances made subsequently to it. Joint-stock shares may also be mortgaged in this way. If the mortgagor fail to redeem the mortgage, the mortgagee acquires by law the absolute title to the property. Equity, however, overrules this condition of the common law, and gives the mortgagor a right of regaining his property on condition of subsequent payment of his debt or obligation with interest. This is called his *equity of redemption.* It may be exercised within twelve years of the mortgagee's entry on the estate or of his last-written acknowledgment of the mortgagor's interest in it. The mortgagor may be compelled to redeem his pledge, or forfeit his equity of redemption (now his property), by the process of *foreclosure,* but the equity court gives every indulgence to a mortgagor before allowing the mortgage to be absolutely foreclosed, and will prolong the period several times if there is any prospect of the debtor being able to pay. Instead of foreclosing the mortgagee may, in the absence of any stipulation to the contrary in the mortgage-deed, enter into possession of the mortgaged property even though there has been no default on the part of the mortgagor. This is rare because a mortgagee is liable for "an account on the footing of wilful default," i.e. not only for profit he actually receives but also those he might have received; further courts of equity discouraged this practice.

During and since the European War the Courts (Emergency Powers) Acts and the Rent and Mortgage Interest Restriction Acts imposed restrictions on the rights of mortgagees to enter into possession, sell or foreclose, or to increase the rate of interest.

In Scotland a mortgage is called an heritable bond. A mortgage of chattels is by Bill of Sale (q.v.).

MORTMAIN (Fr. *mort,* dead; *main,* hand), in law, possession of lands or tenements in dead hands, or hands that cannot alienate, as those of a corporation.

Alienation in mortmain is an alienation of lands or tenements to any corporation, sole or aggregate, ecclesiastical or temporal, particularly to religious houses. Such conveyances were forbidden by Magna Charta, and have been restrained and interdicted by subsequent statutes. By 7 and 8 Wm. III. xxxvii., and 51 and 52 Vict. xlii. (1888) a licence from the Crown dispenses from the statutes of mortmain, but in many cases a special charter or statute renders such licence unnecessary.

MOSAIC. Consists of small pieces of coloured glass, marble, stone, or similar material fitted together to form a pattern or picture, and is frequently employed to decorate walls, vaulted ceilings, pavements, or architectural details. In classic times its use for these purposes was widespread, especially in dwelling-houses.

The Romans distinguished several varieties: *opus tessellatum,* cubes of marble for pavements; *opus vermiculatum,* coloured marble for pictorial purposes; *opus musivum,* glass or enamel for wall decoration; and *opus sectile,* marble marquetry for walls and pavements. Common motives in design were the human figure, animals, fish, or geometrical patterns. Examples from Pompeii and Rome are in the British Museum; and fine Roman pavements can be seen at York, Cirencester, Dorchester, and other Roman settlements in England.

In the earlier Middle Ages mosaic played an important part in church decoration. The artists of the Byzantine Empire especially developed its use, and mainly under their influence important schools developed in Spain and Italy. The finest work was produced from the fourth to the eighth centuries A.D., and after a period in which quality declined a revival took place, especially in Italy. This lasted until the fourteenth century, when it was almost entirely replaced by fresco. Small glass cubes were the material almost invariably employed, decoration being applied to the apse, the spaces between arches, and sometimes to the whole interior wall surface, as at St. Mark's, Venice, and the Capella Palatina at Palermo. The effect of the rich colour, modified by the comparatively dim light of the Byzantine or Basilican churches, is one of great splendour. In the earliest examples the background is blue; but this was soon superseded by gold, which was also freely used in other parts of the mosaic, such as the drapery. In the figures there is no attempt at naturalism, formalized and hieratic types being used which usually have singular dignity and decorative quality.

Classic influence is strong both in the subject and treatment of the earlier mosaics; for example, *The Good Shepherd* (Christ within a circle of sheep) is an adaptation of the pagan *Orpheus charming the Beasts*. Later, the most frequent subjects are a *Majesty*, an immense figure of Christ surrounded by saints, Christ as a lamb with the Apostles as sheep, the Virgin and Saints, and the Last Judgment.

Among the best existing mosaics are those of Ravenna (fifth to seventh centuries); St. Mark's, Venice (eleventh to thirteenth centuries); St. Sophia, Constantinople (sixth, ninth, and eleventh centuries), and of Salonika (fifth to eleventh centuries). In modern times mosaic has rarely been employed with success. Examples of its use are the interior of the dome of St. Paul's Cathedral, and the side chapels of Westminster Cathedral. An important application of mosaic to the decoration of pulpits, tombs, and architectural details was made in Italy by the Cosmati family and others during the thirteenth century. Examples can be seen in Westminster Abbey in the tomb of Henry III. and the shrine of the Confessor.—BIBLIOGRAPHY: Dalton, *Byzantine Art*; Ruhter, *Golden Age of Christian Art.*

MOSAIC GOLD. An alloy of copper and zinc, called also *ormolu*; also a sulphide of tin, the *aurum musivum* of the ancients.

MOSASAURUS. A gigantic extinct marine reptile occurring in the calcareous freestone which forms the most recent deposit of the Cretaceous formation in Northern Europe. It was about 25 feet long. Various allied genera are now known, from Kansas and elsewhere, and are styled collectively mosasaurs.

MOSCHELES (mō'she-les), **Ignaz.** A pianist and composer, born at Prague 1794, and died in 1870. He toured successfully in Germany, and caused a great sensation in Paris and London. He then settled in London, and became professor of music at the Royal Academy in 1825. Mendelssohn in Berlin and Thalberg in London were among his pupils, and at Mendelssohn's request Moscheles gave up his London professorship and took a similar post at Leipzig in 1848.

MOSCHUS. A Greek pastoral poet, a native of Syracuse. The time when he flourished is not accurately known, some making him a pupil of Bion, who is supposed to have lived under Ptolemy Philadelphus (third century B.C.), while others suppose him a contemporary of Ptolemy Philomētor (160 B.C.). Four idylls form the whole of the remains of Moschus, of which the most beautiful is the fine lament for Bion.

MOSCOW. A former Government of Central Russia, between the governments of Tver (north) and Kaluga (south), drained by the Volga (which traverses the northern boundary), Oka, Moskva, and Sestra. Moscow (*Moskva*) is the capital. About 39 per cent. of the entire area is afforested, and, although the district is largely unsuitable for agriculture, oats, rye, barley, potatoes, and some flax are produced. It is best known as the great entrepôt of trade and the most densely inhabited area in pre-Revolutionary Russia. Area, 12,847 sq. miles (subdivided into thirteen districts); pop. 3,662,900 (or a density of 285 per sq. mile).

MOSCOW. The ancient capital of Imperial Russia, and since 1918 the capital of the Russian Union of Socialist Society Republics. It stands on the Moskva (which is the Russian for Moscow), a tributary of the Oka, and, like Rome, it is built upon seven hills.

The Kremlin.—The pre-eminent feature of Moscow is the *Kreml*, or Kremlin, an ancient fort surrounded by embattlemented walls 40 feet in height, triangular in shape, and enclosing an area of from 80 to 100 acres. It has five gates and nineteen towers, and contains the

Cathedral of St. Basil, Moscow

Cathedral of the Assumption (Uspenskiy Cathedral ; 1474-79), in the Lombardo-Byzantine style, where Tsars were crowned and their accession proclaimed by the ringing of Ivan Veliky (Big John), a gigantic bell in an isolated cross-surmounted campanile, 318 feet high, erected by Boris Godunov in 1600. Beneath the tower stands on a pedestal the Tsar Kolokol (King of Bells), 65 feet in circumference (rim), 19 feet high, and nearly 200 tons in weight—the largest bell in the world. It was cast in 1735, and cracked in the foundry during the fire of 1737 without having sounded a note.

Commerce.—Moscow has been since the early fourteenth century an important commercial city, and in immediately pre-Revolutionary times it was the hub of the railway and inland-transport systems of European Russia, being the starting-point of the Trans-Siberian Railway, and had an enormous transit trade in hemp, oils, cereals, food-stuffs, textiles, paper, tobacco, and chemicals. There was also a considerable manufacturing industry in sugar-refining, etc It has nine broadcasting stations. The two most powerful operate on 1481 m., 100 kW., and 1304 m., 100 kW. Pop. in June, 1933, 3,546,000.

History.—Moscow is first mentioned in history in 1147. It was a dependency of the Princes of Vladimir during the Mongol conquests of 1237 and 1293. In 1325 the Metropolitan Peter established himself at Moscow, and the city became the centre of Russian life. From *Moskva* comes the name *Muscovy*, " a name which historically describes the growth of the second Russian power." Moscow was to Russia what Paris was to France ; it was from Moscow as the nucleus that the germ of Russian power found its early expansion.

In 1367 the Kremlin was walled ; Moscow was sacked by the Mongols in 1382, and on the accession of Ivan III. (1462-1505), Prince of Moscow, he proclaimed himself Tsar of All Russia. The Tartars burned the city in 1571, when 170,000 people are reputed to have perished in the flames. Peter the Great, desirous of building up a great military empire, mistrusted by the people and face to face with innumerable conspiracies, retired from Moscow in 1703 and founded St. Petersburg (now Leningrad). In 1812, a week after the battle of Borodine, French troops entered the Kremlin, and the Russian army retired. By an accident the city was set on fire ; the inhabitants fled, and the French and Russian soldiers looted the commercial and wealthy quarters. However, the peasants rose in revolt, and Napoleon was forced to evacuate (19th Oct., 1812) after unsuccessful attempts to blow up the Kremlin. The city was rebuilt in 1813.

During the Revolution of 1905 the streets of Moscow were drenched in blood. Kerensky's short-lived régime terminated in the city in Aug., 1917, and Moscow became the Soviet capital on 14th March, 1918.

MOSELEY, Henry Gwyn Jeffreys. English physicist, killed in action in Gallipoli on 10th Aug., 1915, at the age of twenty-seven. His premature death was widely deplored as an irreparable loss to science. His great discovery of the relationship between X-ray spectra (q.v.) and atomic number (*see* MATTER ; NUMBER, ATOMIC) threw a flood of light on the organization of the under-world of electrons, atoms, and molecules. An account of his life and work is given by Lord Rutherford, in *Nature* 9th Sept., 1915.

MOSELLE. A frontier department of North-Eastern France, formed by the district of Lorraine, ceded by Germany under the Peace Treaty of 28th June, 1919. Area, 2403 sq. miles ; pop. (1931), 693,408.

MOSES. Leader, prophet, and legislator of the Israelites, the son of Amram and Jochebed, was born in Egypt about 1600 B.C., during the time of the oppression of the Hebrews. His mother placed him in a basket of bulrushes on the river border, where he was found by the daughter of the Egyptian king as she went to bathe. She adopted him as her son, and in all probability had him educated for the duties of the priesthood. His expedition into Ethiopia in his fortieth year, as leader of the Egyptians, when he subdued the city of Saba (Meroe), won the affections of the conquered Princess Tharbis, and married her, rests only on the tradition preserved by Josephus.

An outrage committed by an Egyptian on a Hebrew excited his anger, and he secretly slew the Egyptian. The deed became known, and he escaped the vengeance of the king only by a hasty flight into Arabia. Here he took refuge with Jethro, a Midianitish prince and a priest, and espoused his daughter Zipporah.

The promises of God that his race would become a great nation occupied much of his thoughts, and at last God appointed him the chosen deliverer from the bondage in Egypt. Being slow of speech, and possessing none of the arts of an orator, God therefore gave him power to prove his mission by miracles, and joined to him his elder brother Aaron, a man of little energy, but of considerable eloquence. Thus prepared, Moses returned to Egypt at the age of eighty years to undertake the work.

At first he had the greatest obstacles to overcome, but after the visitation of ten destructive plagues upon the land, Pharaoh suffered the Hebrews to depart. Moses conveyed them safely through the Red Sea, in which Pharaoh, who pursued them, was drowned with his army. At Mount Sinai he received the Ten Commandments and the laws for the regulation of the lives of the Israelites. When they were already near the end of their journey towards Canaan, Moses saw himself compelled, in consequence of new evidences of discontent, to lead them back into the desert, for forty years more of toilsome wandering. He was not himself permitted, however, to see the Israelites settled in their new country on account of a murmur which, in the midst of his distresses, he allowed to escape against his God.

After appointing Joshua to be the leader of the Hebrews he ascended a mountain beyond Jordan, from which he surveyed the land of promise, and so ended his life in his 120th year. All superstitious reverence for his bones or his place of sepulture was prevented by the secrecy of his burial, and its effectual concealment from the people.—BIBLIOGRAPHY: H. L. Taylor, *The Story of Moses*; T. K. Cheyne, *Encyclopædia Biblica*; S. R. Driver, *Authority and Archæology*.

MOSLEY, Sir Oswald Ernald. English politician. Born 16th Nov., 1896, a son of Sir Oswald Mosley he was educated at Winchester and Sandhurst, and entered the army. Having served in France, he was elected Unionist M.P. for Harrow in 1918. In 1924 he joined the Labour Party. In 1926 he was elected M.P. for Smethwick. In 1929 he became Chancellor of the Duchy of Lancaster in the Labour ministry, but differed from his colleagues and resigned. In 1931 he formed the New Party, but at the General Election of that year he and his colleagues failed to secure election. For a short time he controlled a paper called *Action*. In 1928 he succeeded to the baronetcy. In 1920 Mosley married Cynthia, daughter of the Marquess Curzon. She was M.P. for Stoke-on-Trent in the Labour interest, 1929-31. She died on the 16th May, 1933.

MOSQUE. A Mahommedan church or house of prayer. These buildings are constructed in the Saracenic style of architecture, and often astonish by their extent and the

The Blue Mosque, Cairo

grandeur and height of their cupolas or domes. In these Mahommedan places of worship there are neither altars, paintings, nor images, but a great quantity of lamps of various kinds, arabesques which form the principal interior ornament, and extracts from the *Koran* adorning the walls. Every mosque has its minaret or minarets. The buildings are often quadrangular in plan, with an open interior court, where are fountains for ablutions. The floor is generally covered with carpets, but there are no seats. Facing in the direction of Mecca is the *mihrab*, a recess in the wall to direct the worshippers where to turn their eyes in prayer, and near this is the *mimbar* or pulpit. The buildings may embrace accommodation for educational purposes, etc., besides the temple proper.

MOSQUITO (mos-kē'to). A term synonymous with gnat, and more particularly applied to those species of the gnat family (Culicidæ) whose blood-sucking habits render them a serious pest, especially in the tropical and Arctic regions. The female possesses a proboscis made up of the piercing and sucking mouth-parts. The eggs are laid in stagnant water, and hatch out into wriggling worm-like larvæ that ultimately pass into a resting or pupal stage, from which the adult emerges.

The malarial diseases (including yellow fever) which seriously interfere with colonization in tropical regions are caused by microscopic animal blood parasites which spend part of their lives in the bodies of mosquitoes, and are introduced by their bites into human beings. These disease-carriers are, except in the case of yellow fever, species of Anopheles, distinguished by their bodies being disposed in a straight line when in the resting position, and usually by their spotted wings. The yellow-fever mosquito (*Stegomyia fasciata*) is marked with transverse black and white bands, and there is a characteristic lyre-shaped white mark on the thorax.

Adult mosquitoes are destroyed by means of various sprays, containing formalin and other substances; are kept from sleepers by mosquito curtains; and repelled by smearing exposed parts of the skin with preparations containing essential oils. But the only really effective measures are those directed to abolition of breeding-places by thorough drainage, and the destruction of larvæ. For the latter purpose small fishes ("millions") can be introduced into the stagnant water where they live; various larvicides are employed; or the surface of the water is oiled with petroleum. *See* CULICIDÆ; GNAT MALARIA.

MOSQUITO TERRITORY, or **BLUEFIELDS.** A maritime division of Nicaragua, on the Caribbean, along which it extends for 225 miles; average width inland, 40 miles. The Misskito Indians, Zambos, and Jamaica negroes form the bulk of the population. Bluefields (pop. 5000 is the seaport-capital. Bananas are exported.

The Mosquito Reserve was discovered by Columbus (1502), passed to Spain, and from 1655 to 1850 was a British Protectorate. In 1860 (Treaty of Managua) the territory was ceded to Nicaragua, and was formally incorporated in the Republic (as Zelaya) on 24th Nov., 1894.

MOSS-AGATE, also called **MOCHA-STONE.** Agate including brownish or greenish dendritic forms of some other mineral, which are often taken for traces of vegetation.

MOSSAMEDES. A port on the south of Angola, Portuguese West Africa.

MOSSEL BAY. A seaport of Cape Province, South Africa, 320 miles E. of Cape Town. Pop. 5702 (2856 white).

MOSSES, or **MUSCI.** One of the two main subdivisions of the Bryophyta. They are all small plants found chiefly in cool, moist situations. They have leafy shoots, but no genuine roots, the place of these organs being taken by thread-like rhizoids which are produced in great profusion. The internal structure of Mosses is simple, though rudimentary conducting tissues may be present, especially in the larger forms, such as Polytrichum.

Vegetative propagation takes place abundantly from any detached portions, or by means of special buds (*gemmæ*). The sexual organs are *antheridia* and *archegonia*, similar in principle to the corresponding structures in ferns though somewhat larger. The fertilized egg-cell (zygote) develops into a stalked capsule or *sporogonium*, differing from that of Liverworts mainly in the mode of dehiscence, which is typically by means of an apical pore, fringed by a single or double set of teeth forming the *peristome*; this is a hygroscopic structure, which closes over the pore in damp air, but allows the spores to escape freely during dry weather. The presence of a *calyptra* (q.v.) is another difference from Liverworts. The spore develops into a branched, filamentous, alga-like thallus, the *protonema*, from which one or more leafy moss-plants arise later as lateral outgrowths.

The classification of Mosses is difficult, depending mainly on minute characters of the peristome and the detailed structure of the leaves.

MOSSLEY. A municipal borough of Lancashire, England, on the Tame. There are cotton, woollen, and engineering manufactures. Pop. (1931), 12,041.

MOSTAGANEM. A seaport of Algeria (33° 55′ N. lat., 0° 10′ E. long.). It is connected with Oran direct by rail via Arzeu. There is a large trade, but the port is exposed. Alfalfa is the principal export; flour-milling and tanning are progressive; earthenware is manufactured. Pop. (1931), 28,357.

MOSUL′. A city of 'Iraq, on the Tigris, opposite the remains of the ancient Nineveh. Besides numerous mosques there are churches of the Nestorians, Jacobites, and other Christians. It has a transit trade between Baghdad, Syria, Kurdistan, and Istanbul. The principal manufactures are cotton-stuffs. It was formerly celebrated also for its muslins, the name being derived from the town. Mosul was occupied by a British force on 3rd Nov., 1918. Pop. about 80,000.

MOTET′. In music, a name applied to two different forms of composition: (1) a sacred cantata, consisting of a number of unconnected movements, as solos, duets, trios, quartettes, choruses, fugues, etc. (2) A choral composition, usually of a sacred character, beginning with an introductory song, followed by several fugal subjects, the whole ending with the exposition of the last subject, a repetition of the introduction, or a special final subject.

MOTH. The popular name of a numerous and beautiful division of lepidopterous insects, readily distinguished from butterflies by their antennæ either being plumose or tapering to a point instead of terminating in a knob, by their wings being horizontal when resting, and by their being seldom seen on the wing except in the evening or at night (though some moths fly by day); hence the terms crepuscular and nocturnal lepidoptera applied to them. Amongst the more notable of the moths are the "feather" or "plume-moths," the death's-head moth, the "clothes-moths," and the "silk-moth" (*Bombyx mori*).

MOTHER-OF-PEARL, or **NACRE.** The hard, silvery, brilliant internal or nacreous layer of several kinds of

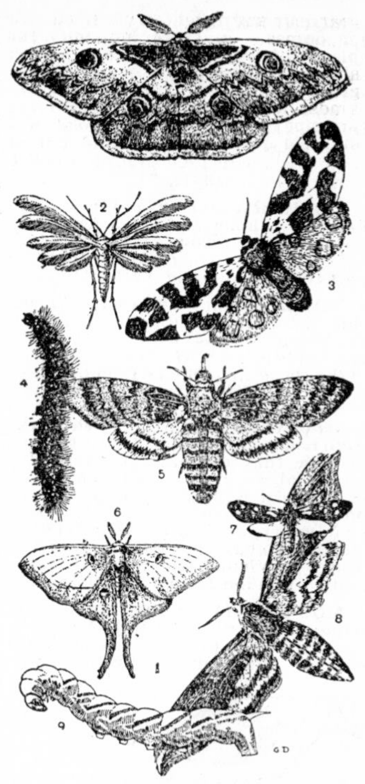

Moths

1, Great Peacock (*Saturnia pyri*), half natural size. 2, Plume (*Pterophorus pentadactylus*), natural size. 3, Tiger-mouth (*Chelonia caja*), natural size. 4, Larva. 5, Death's Head (*Acherontia atropos*), half natural size. 6, Luna (*Actias luna*), quarter natural size. 7, Six-spotted Burnet (*Zygæna filipendula*), two-thirds natural size. 8, Privet Hawk moth (*Sphinx ligustri*), three-quarter natural size. 9, Larva.

shells, particularly of the oyster family, often variegated with changing purple and azure colours. It is destitute of colouring-matter, but is composed of a series of minute and slightly imbricated layers or ridges, the rays reflected from which interfere with each other and produce beautiful iridescent hues. The large oysters of the tropical seas alone secrete this coat of sufficient thickness to render their shells available for the purposes of manufacture. Mother-of-pearl is extensively used in the arts, particularly in inlaid work, and in the manufacture of handles for knives, buttons, toys, etc.

MOTHERWELL. A town of Lanarkshire, Scotland, touching the Clyde on the south-west, and 13 miles from Glasgow by the L.M.S. Railway. It lies in the middle of extensive coal-fields, and has a large iron and steel industry, and engineering works. Motherwell was united with Wishaw in 1920 to form a police burgh. Pop. (1931), 64,708.

MOTHERWORT (*Leonūrus cardiăca*). A labiate plant, 3 feet high, flowers in crowded whorls, white with a reddish tinge, found in some parts of England and North America.

MOTLEY, John Lothrop. American historian and diplomatist, born in Massachusetts 1814, died 1877. He published his *History of the Rise of the Dutch Republic* in 1856 (3 vols.), a work which was further developed in the *History of the United Netherlands* (4 vols., 1860-68). Both works were received with the utmost favour, because they combined capacity for historical research with much power of pictorial representation. A work on a kindred subject was the *Life and Death of John of Barneveld* (1874). He was Ambassador from the United States to Vienna from 1861 to 1867, and to London from 1869 to 1870.

MOT-MOT (Momotus, etc.). The name given to beautiful American birds related to rollers and kingfishers, and ranging from South

Mot-Mot

Mexico and the West Indies to Paraguay. They are about the size of a jay, with a long tail, the two middle feathers of which are destitute of vanes. The name suggests the character of their note.

MOTOR-CAR ENGINE. It is customary to regard the motor-car as a modern invention, but in the eighteenth century Symington and Murdock constructed working models of steam-driven carriages for road locomotion. James Watt looked on Murdock's endeavours as a pure waste of time, and with his partner Boulton endeavoured to turn the young investigator from his folly. Other engineers, notable Trevithick, continued their investigations, and about the time that the first passenger train service was started, an English engineer, Walter Hancock, built a steam-driven car which ran for hire between Stratford and London.

Gottlieb Daimler was the pioneer of the motor-car engine as known today. In 1886 he constructed a twin-cylinder engine which was used to drive a launch. Demonstrations of this boat were made on the Seine

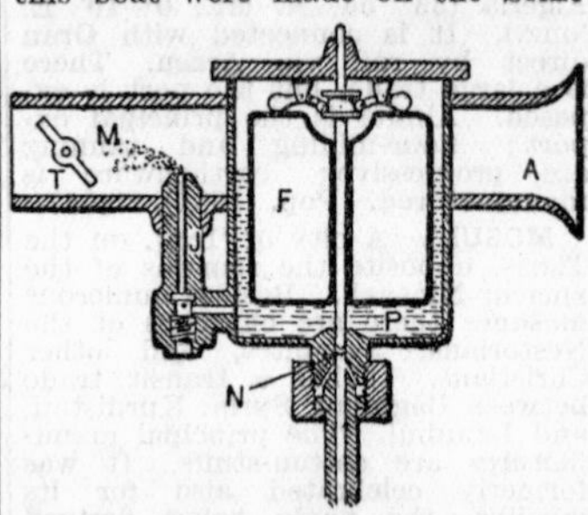

Section of Carburettor

F, Float; A, Air inlet; P, petrol; J, jet; T, throttle; N, needle valve; M, mixture to cylinder.

at the Paris Exhibition of 1887. The next year Daimler sold his patent rights, which were ultimately acquired by M. Levassor, a French engineer, who, in association with his partner M. Panhard, devised the motor-car transmission gear which is used to this day, though its place is now being taken by the pre-selective or "self-changing" gear-box.

Experiments have been made with many fuels: benzol, alcohol, acetylene, coal-gas, and producer gas, but the great majority of engines still use petrol. The motor-car engine is a type of internal-combustion engine (q.v.), and derives its power from a burning mixture of petrol-vapour and air. The engine cylinder is provided with two valves (sometimes four), one to admit and the other to exhaust the gases. Before the petrol enters the engine it is passed through a carburettor where it is completely converted into gas.

A simple type of carburettor is shown in the illustration. The petrol falls from the tank through a pipe to the float chamber. As the float, usually an air-tight copper vessel, rises, the needle-valve passing through the central sleeve is forced to its seat and prevents further petrol entering. The float is of sufficient weight to allow the petrol

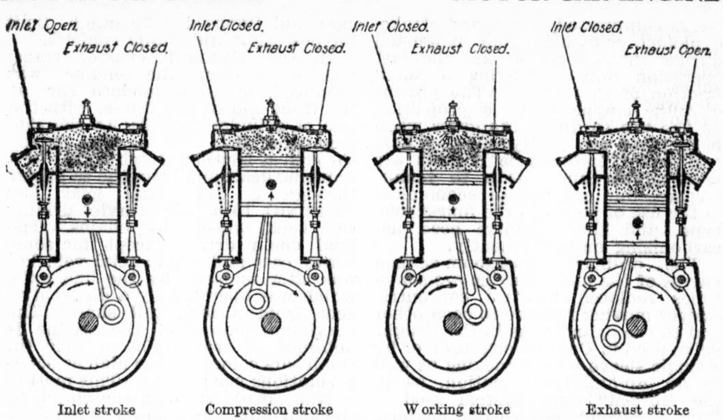

Diagrams showing the Working of an Internal-combustion Engine

level to be high enough to maintain a small drop or " bead " of petrol on the top of the jet. This drop of petrol evaporates, and the gas is taken along with the air passing to the engine cylinder. Whenever the petrol level in the float chamber falls, the needle-valve opens and more petrol flows in. The level necessary to maintain efficient vaporization is thus maintained continuously. The throttle-valve controls the passage of the mixture to the engine inlet-valve.

The engine usually works on the four-stroke cycle. The four sectional views of the engine cylinder show the various actions in the cycle. The inlet-valve opens just as the piston begins to move downward in the cylinder, and the space left behind the moving piston is filled by the indrawn petrol-vapour and air. The second stage is the compression of this explosive mixture into small bulk before exploding it. The use of compression increases the efficiency of the engine. In the third stroke, that is, the second downward one, the mixture is ignited by an electric spark at the plug. The pressure in the cylinder rises abruptly, and then, as the piston moves in its stroke, the burnt gases fill the continuously increasing volume, and their pressure decreases. When the fourth stroke starts, the exhaust-valve opens, and the moving piston sweeps the residue out of the cylinder. The cycle of operations then recommences. Each cycle takes two revolutions for its complete performance. Only during the third stroke is there any useful energy transformation; the other strokes are required to prepare the gas and air for power-producing combustiōn, and to drive away the spent gas.

In motor-cycles, engines working on this cycle are most common, but a large number, especially of the light-weight type, have two-stroke engines, in which case the piston acts as a valve by uncovering ports in the cylinder. The mixture of petrol-vapour and air is compressed slightly in the crank chamber, and enters the cylinder under this small pressure, sweeping the burnt gases out. The

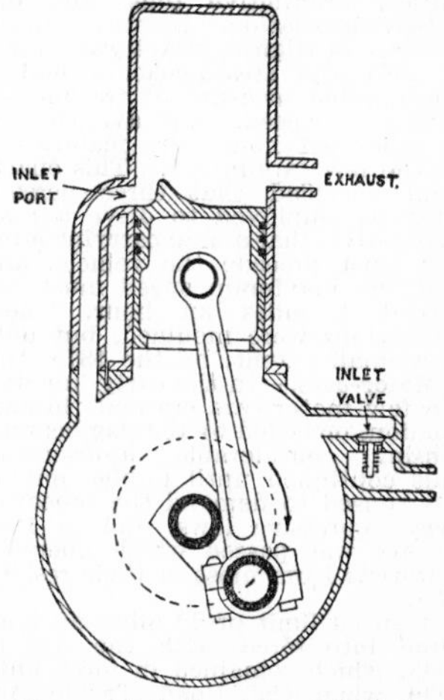

Diagrammatic Section of Two-stroke Engine

gas is compressed in the first stroke, exploded, expanded, and exhausted during the second stroke, the last operation only occupying a small fraction of the stroke. The pistons of these engines have a projection on the top to direct the gases when both ports are partly open. These two-stroke motor-cycle engines are very simple and cheap to manufacture, but are not so economical in the use of petrol as the four-stroke type, and the cylinders need decarbonizing more frequently.

The ordinary mushroom-shaped valves of the motor-engine are sometimes replaced by two concentric sleeves moving relative to each other and to the cylinder, as in the Knight valve used in Daimler engines ; or by a single sleeve with a rocking as well as an up-and-down motion, as in the Burt-M'Cullum system used in Barr & Stroud motor-cycle engines, and Kelvin motor-boat engines. This type of valve is stated to be more silent in action than the mushroom form, and to give a greater and quicker opening, but is not used generally.—BIBLIOGRAPHY: *The Motor Manual* (The Temple Press) ; F. Strickland, *A Manual of Petrol Motors and Motor Cars* ; A. W. Judge, *Automobile* and *Air-craft Engines* ; F. J. Kean, *The Petrol Engine.*

MOTOR VEHICLE. The early history of motor vehicles is the story of a war against engineering difficulties, prohibitive tolls, and oppressive legislation. Before the Locomotives on Highways Act was passed in 1861 the steam-coaches had a considerable measure of freedom in regard to speed, and averages of 10 miles per hour were maintained by the few cars in use. This enactment specified that three persons must be employed to drive a road locomotive, that a man carrying a red flag must precede the vehicle, and that the maximum speed must not exceed 4 miles an hour. These restrictions were modified, but only to a small extent, by the 1878 Act.

Motor-cars.—In the early 'nineties the few motor-cars crawled through London, preceded by red-flag bearers, causing considerable amusement. This continued until public opinion was roused to demand the repeal of these repressive laws, and in 1896 an Act was passed which liberated motorists from most of their restriction.

A speed limit of 20 miles an hour came into force with the Act of 1903, which remained in force until 1930 when the Road Traffic Act removed the speed limit for private cars and imposed a 30 m.p.h. limit for passenger and goods vehicles.

In the Panhard-Levassor transmission system the engine was mounted, as in a modern car, at the front end of the frame, with the line of cylinders parallel to the side members. The drive was taken through a friction clutch (q.v.) to a reducing gear, and from the tail shaft through a differential gear (*see* GEARING), to a pair of axles driving the back wheels by chains. The final chain drive, except for some heavy cars and commercial vehicles, was later replaced by the line axle, which was operated by a differential gear from a long tail shaft. The maximum power of the engine is obtained at from 1500 to 4500 (in small cars sometimes as high as 6500) revolutions per minute. This motion is transmitted through the clutch to the gear-box. Full power is required from the engine when the road wheels are to turn slowly, as when climbing a hill.

Gears must be introduced to reduce the speed of rotation. The lowest gear should be such that the power of the engine would be sufficient to drive the car up the steepest gradient at the speed it gives. Usually there are four gears. The shaft transmitting the power from the gear-box to the back axle has universal joints at its ends. This is called a cardan shaft, after Geronimo Cardano (q.v.), the inventor of this system of power transmission between shafts that are not parallel. In a motor-car the tail shaft is at a different angle to the engine shaft every instant. Differential gearing on the back axle drive is required, because the wheels may have to run at different speeds, as in turning a corner.

Motor-racing, introduced in 1894 by the proprietors of *Le Petit Journal,* who offered a prize for a race between Paris and Rouen, was useful to engineers who were endeavouring to improve the design and construction of motor-car mechanism. In 1902 S. F. Edge won the Gordon-Bennett Cup with his 50-h.p. Napier in the race from Paris to Vienna.

In the British Isles motor-racing on highways is not allowed, except in Ireland and the Isle of Man, where the race for the Tourist Trophy was instituted in 1905. The Brooklands racing-track, near Weybridge, Surrey, was opened in 1907. The track circuit is 2 miles 5½ furlongs round the inner edge. The banking rises 28½ feet.

The early reliability trials organized by the Royal Automobile Club and the Royal Scottish Automobile Club demonstrated the weakness in design of cars intended for touring. The famous races on the International Calendar are the Italian 1000 miles, Monaco Grand Prix, French, German, and Italian Grands Prix; Le Mans 24-hour race; Ulster "T.T.,"; Isle of Man "T.T." (motor-cycle), and Douglas car races, International Trophy, Empire Trophy, 500-miles race, and Indianapolis Grand Prix (U.S.).

The motor-car engine and its cycles of operation are dealt with in the articles *Motor-car Engines* and *Internal-combustion Engines.*

Modern-cars are provided with electric starters, each consisting of a small electric motor supplied with electricity from a battery, and used to turn the engine crank shaft by means of gear-wheels. After the engine is started the electric apparatus is used as a generator, which charges the battery and supplies electricity for lighting.

One of the greatest advances with regard to brakes which has been made was the introduction of the four-wheel braking system. In this system brakes are fitted to the front wheels as well as to the back wheels, and the operating system is so arranged that the four brakes can be applied simultaneously, sometimes through the agency of a servo-motor or friction relay driven from the gear-box.

Steel-spoked wheels of the detachable variety are used on the greater number of cars on the British market to-day. The disc wheel is of cheap construction, and allows central-pivot steering to be used. At the present time on the majority of cars, semi-elliptic laminated-leaf springs are used both back and front.

Although practically every car on the road to-day has a frame consisting of pressed steel channel-section side members braced together laterally with cross members, there is a good deal of difference of opinion as regards the amount of stiffness necessary in the construction. A rigid frame gives a vastly better support for the coach-work, but, on the other hand, a rigid frame may react against the suppleness of the car on its springs. It is noticeable, however, that there is a growing tendency to stiffen up frames laterally, and on several cars cross members consisting of very massive tubes are being fitted.

After the European War, when production costs were high, many motor manufacturers devoted themselves to the production of light cars which could be sold at a reasonable price. This development took many different lines, from that of manufacturers of high-powered expensive cars undertaking the production of a lighter and lower-powered model, to that of others who contented themselves with the production of three- or four-wheeled motor-cycles. From this type of vehicle was developed the modern "baby" car.

Motor-cycles.—The motor-tricycle was invented in 1885 by Butler, and it was developed up to 1901, when the bicycle took its place. The engine may be of the two- or four-stroke type (see MOTOR-CAR ENGINE), and drives the back wheel by chain, through a reducing gear. The comfort of the rider depends largely on the nature of the springing, both of the frame and of the saddle.

A typical 4-h.p. model has an engine cylinder of 85-mm. bore and 97-mm. stroke, a four-speed gear, and a multiple plate clutch. A pressed-steel frame, with a welded petrol-tank replacing the two top tubes of the usual frame, is used by some makers. Cantilever springing is also a distinctive feature of a number of machines. Light-weight cycles with engines of 1¼ h.p. are very popular as solo machines. When a side-car is used, more power is desirable. The bigger machines, with two-cylinder V-type engines, have such a reserve of power that almost any tour in Britain could be made without changing to the low gears. Good design of components of substantial dimensions, and engines of proven reliability, have been characteristic of the British motor-cycles, generally regarded as the best in the world. The annual "T.T." motor-cycle races have never been won by a foreign-built machine. In 1933 the most successful machine was the Norton, winning first three places in both Senior and Junior events.

The commercial motor vehicle is more used in Britain than in any other European country. The carriage of goods by horse-haulage has diminished enormously as the knowledge of the cheapness and convenience of motor-traction extended. There are two main classes of work for which such vehicles are used: first, the transport of heavy goods, either within an industrial area or over long distances; and second, the direct delivery of very light articles from general stores to suburban houses.

Commercial vehicles range from the small three-wheeled van, costing less then £90, up to the eight-wheeled mammoth lorry, between these two extremes being a series of vehicles suitable for every transport purpose. Petrol-driven lorries and buses are gradually giving way to Diesel-engined vehicles, Diesel fuel (" crude oil ") not only being about one-third the cost of petrol, but also increasing the mileage per gallon of from two to three times.

The formidable competition of road transport for both goods and passengers has seriously affected railway and tramcar operators.—BIBLIOGRAPHY.—*The Autocar Handbook* (Messrs. Iliffe & Sons); H. E. Wimperis, *The Principles of the Application of Power to Road Transport*; H. J. Spooner, *Motors and Motoring*.

MOTTRAM, Ralph Hale. English author. He was born in 1883. As a result of his war experiences, he produced the *Spanish Farm* trilogy, which brought him immediate fame. He has written since then *Our Mr. Dormer*, *The English Miss*, *A History of Financial Speculation*, *Europa's Beast*, and *Castle Island*.

MOUFFLON, or MOUFLON. The *Ovis musimon*, a wild sheep inhabiting the mountainous parts of Corsica. It is covered with short hair, generally of a reddish-brown colour, and the male has a powerful pair of horns. It is hunted for its flesh, and is difficult of approach. Another species (*O. ophion*) is peculiar to Cyprus. The name is also given to allied forms, such as the argalis, native to Mongolia (*O. ammon*) and Tibet (*O. nahura* and *O. hodgsoni*).

MOUKDEN. *See* MUKDEN.

MOULD. A name given to various saprophytic Fungi, especially to those which develop on stale comestibles (bread, jam, etc.), on damp leather, paper, and the like. The black moulds are species of Mucor (q.v.) and allied genera. The green mould is Eurotium; the blue, Penicillium.

MOULINS. A city and capital of the department of Allier, France, a railway junction, on the River Allier. Wool, cutlery, hats, and glass are manufactured. The cathedral of Notre Dame was founded in the fifteenth century, and the remains of a castle of the ducs de Bourbon contains a Bible of date 1115. Moulins became the capital of the Bourbonnais in the fifteenth century. Pop. (1931), 38,381.

MOULMEIN. A seaport in the Amherst district of the Tenasserim division, Lower Burma, on the Gulf of Martaban, to leeward of Pelew Gewen (Bilugyun) Island, and connected by rail with Rangoon and Pegu. Moulmein is the second port of Burma, and has large exports of teak and rice. Pop. about 61,301.

MOUNTAIN ASH (W. *Aberpennar*). A market town and urban district of Glamorganshire, South Wales, near Aberdare, on the Cynon, a tributary of the Taff, and served by the Great Western Railway. Coal-mining is important and almost the only industry. The district includes, in addition to Mountain Ash, Aberpennar, Cwmpennar, and Abercynon. Pop. (1931), 38,381.

MOUNTAIN AVENS. An Arctic or Alpine tufted rosaceous plant (*Dryas octopetala*), with simple petioled leaves and white and yellow solitary flowers. They are sometimes cultivated in rock gardens.

MOUNTAIN - LIMESTONE. A series of marine limestone strata, whose geological position is immediately below the Upper Carboniferous zones and above the Old Red Sandstone in England.

MOUNTBATTEN. *See* BATTENBERG.

MOUNT EVEREST EXPEDITIONS. Mount Everest, the highest mountain in the world, standing on the frontier between Nepal and Tibet, was triangulated in 1849. It was then known to the Survey of India as Peak XV. It was not until some years later that the figures of its triangulation were worked out and the Bengali chief computer came into the Surveyor-General's office to announce that his calculations had established the pre-eminence of this peak, 29,002 feet high. It was agreed that it should be called after Sir George Everest, the Surveyor-General responsible for the triangulation of 1849. The Tibetan name is *Chomo-Lungma*, which is interpreted as "The Goddess Mother of the World."

The idea of exploring the mountain first took definite shape in 1893, when the Hon. C. G. Bruce, then a captain in the Indian army, and Sir Francis Younghusband, second in command at Chitral, intended to travel across Tibet to Tingri, 45 miles N.W. of Mount Everest. But political difficulties were in the way then, as always afterwards whenever a plan was suggested, until 1920. Tibet and Nepal alike were closed to travellers.

Meanwhile Dr. Kellas, in the course of his ubiquitous mountaineering in Sikhim, had sent coolies over into Tibet and found out much about the eastern approaches; he made plans by which he hoped to outwit the Tibetan authorities. Captain Noel, too, had been to Tashirak in Tibet, 45 miles E. of the mountain, and was in hopes of reaching a pass where, it was reported, the lamas of a local monastery used to go to worship Chomo-Lungma; but the local Governor came along with his guards, and Captain Noel was forced to retire without seeing his view.

He related these adventures to the Royal Geographical Society in 1919; and in the discussion following his paper a plan was made in conjunction with the Alpine Club. The Indian Government was approached; Lord Chelmsford was favourable to the enterprise, and at last the Dalai Lama gave permission for a limited number of Englishmen to pass through Tibet. A committee was formed and the party was selected, Colonel Howard Bury to be chief, and Dr. Kellas, Messrs. Raeburn, Leigh-Mallory, and Bullock to be the climbing party. To these were to be added two members of the Survey of India, Major Morshead and Captain Wheeler; and Dr. Heron of the Geological Survey.

The party left Darjeeling on 18th May, and followed the trade route to Lhasa as far as Phari Dzong. In the bleak country of pitiless wind between there and Kampa Dzong they fared ill. Dr. Kellas, after being carried five days in some sort of litter rigged up for the occasion, died on the last march coming over a high pass to Kampa Dzong; and Mr. Raeburn was too ill to go farther. On 20th June the expedition reached Tingri Dzong, which was to be used as a base for the northern approach, as General Bruce had intended twenty-eight years before. Messrs. Bullock and Mallory, the only remaining representatives of the Alpine Club, now found their way to the Rongbuk Valley, at the head of which stands Mount Everest. It was a small party, with only sixteen coolies, a sirdar, and a cook, besides the two sahibs. But the coolies were men of a fine stock, from the tribe of Sher Pa Bhotias, who inhabit a part of Nepal not far from Everest itself; about forty of these men had volunteered for the expedition, and the sixteen had been selected from them. Accustomed as they are to carry loads over all sorts of rough ground, sturdy and extraordinarily enduring in both cold and heat, probably no better men could be found for the exacting work of mountaineering porters.

The reconnaissance had three aims: to examine the approaches to various sides of the mountain, to determine its form in every particular so far as possible, and to find out its vulnerable places and that one which should offer the best line of attack.

Mount Everest may be described as consisting primarily of three great ridges set at a wide angle and meeting at the summit. Of these the south ridge, after descending about 1500 feet, goes up to another great peak 28,000 feet high, Lhotse (South Peak), and there divides, sending out one arm which curves round to the south-east, and another which curves round to north-west. The other two ridges are simple: the north-east goes down only 1000 feet in half a mile to a conspicuous rocky shoulder, and then plunges more steeply down to 21,000 feet; the north-west ridge descends very steeply for about 4000 feet, then very gently for 2000 feet, making an immensely long structure like the nave of a cathedral with its roof covered by snow, until it plunges down suddenly to a pass at 19,000 feet. It may be gathered that none of these ridges encourages the idea of conquering the summit. And the faces are no better.

The south face between the two arms of the south ridge has not been explored; but a distant photograph shows it to be a series of rocky precipices; the east face is glaciated in its upper half, and the steep rocks lower down must be continually bombarded by the broken ice-cliffs in which the hanging glacier ends; the west face cannot be used for an ascent for reasons which will appear later; and the north presents itself as a prodigious precipice 10,000 feet high. But here lies a complication. It is not a single mountain-side facing north. Some distance to the east of the summit it is bent back so that the whole is divided by a wide-angled ridge coming down from the north-east shoulder and ending in a snow col at 23,000 feet. This snow col, Chang La (North Col), is a link connecting Mount Everest with a whole series of mountains to the north. And though the lower part of the north face can nowhere be climbed, the upper slopes are not so steep; by climbing first to Chang La it is possible to reach them; the wide dividing ridge is almost certainly accessible, and the angle of the north-east ridge above the shoulder is so gentle as to give some hopes that the highest mountain may one day be climbed by this route.

It was the achievement of the reconnaissance party of 1921 to establish this possibility. They spent a month exploring the north and west sides from the Rongbuk Valley, and found many difficulties to contend with. Not the least was the sun's power. The latitude of Mount Everest is only 28° north, and the sun is able to melt the surface of a glacier into spires of white ice 40 and 50 feet high, or enormous waves and troughs where it is covered with stones. Travelling over such ground was extremely laborious, and the glare from snow and ice had the effect of increasing the feeling of lassitude from which men constantly suffer when exerting themselves strenuously at high altitudes.

On 7th July the monsoon broke in earnest, and from that date onwards it was the general rule that clouds should come up even on the finest days, perhaps an hour after sunrise, to obscure the mountains until evening. Under these circumstances the party suffered many disappointments, and the western side of the mountain long remained a mystery. But camps were pushed up, the coolies were taught the necessity of early starts at 2 or 3 a.m., and eventually, by reaching a high pass at sunrise, it was established that a deep combe exists between the north-west ridge of Everest, the South Peak, and its north-west arm; a glacier flowing from it descends into Nepal, and it would be impossible to use it without organizing an expedition in that country; in any case, it is so steep that it could hardly be used for bringing up camps; and from what they saw the explorers conjectured that little but impracticable precipices would be found on this western side—so that on all counts it must be ruled out for the purpose of climbing the mountain. Other expeditions up to the head of the Rongbuk Glacier under the north face yielded views of the west side of Chang La (North Col), and it was decided that this place was impracticable.

In the last week of July the expedition base was moved round to Kharta for the reconnaissance of the east side. In striking contrast with the barren northern valley, this country was green with pastures and barley. Kharta is situated on the west bank of the Arm River, which cuts through the Himálaya and flows through Nepal into the plain of India. The monsoon pushes its way up as far as Kharta, and to some extent also up the eastern valleys, in the lower parts of which was found a wealth of vegetation.

From Kharta the Kama Valley, leading up to the east face of Mount Everest, was first explored. For magnificence of scenery it is probably unequalled. Besides Everest itself and Lhotse at the head of it, Makalu overlooks it from the south-east, the fifth highest summit in the world and one of the most glorious of mountains.

But from the climbing point of view the result was negative. From a peak of over 21,000 feet, the Kartse, it was easily established that no reasonable line of attack could be chosen on either the east face or north-east arête. It was a further object to find the glacier which must approach the eastern side of Chang

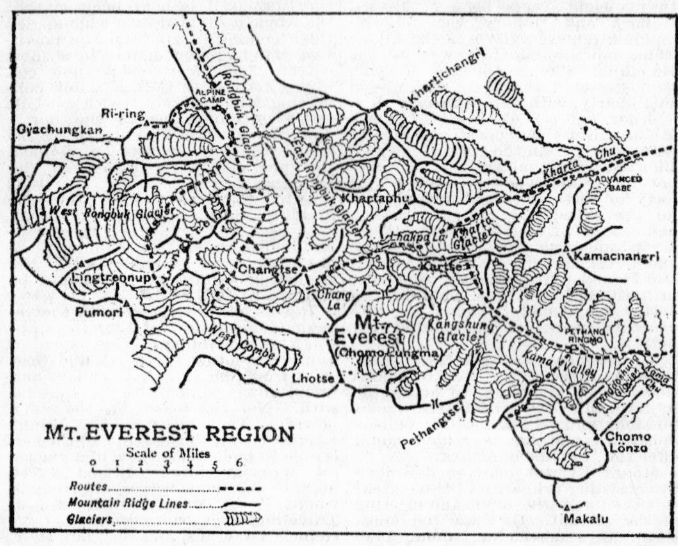

La. It was conjectured that this glacier would flow eastwards; but in reality it flows northwards. The next glacier north of the Kama Valley and flowing east, the Kharta Glacier, ends under a high pass at 22,500 feet, Lhakpa La (Windy Gap), which looks down across the head of the East Rongbuk Glacier to Chang La. This pass was reached on 18th Aug. after the most exhausting efforts; but clouds obscured the view so that the wall under Chang La could not be seen.

With this uncertainty remaining, the assault was planned for September, to bring the party if possible to Chang La and a considerable distance up the mountain above it. In the normal course the monsoon is spent by the beginning of September and fine weather sets in. The issue depended on the snow's hardening; the coolies could not be expected to carry their loads in soft snow over Lhakpa La. The weather cleared on 17th Sept., and on the 20th Lhakpa La was reached again with the beginning of a camp, but not without great difficulty; the season was now too late, and the snow melted very little above 21,000 feet. However, it was possible, once the tracks had been made, to establish the whole party on Lhakpa La two days later—Colonel Howard Bury, A. F. R. Wollaston (medical officer-naturalist), and the two surveyors, besides Messrs. Bullock and Mallory.

On the 22nd it was found that of twenty-three coolies all but ten were *hors de combat*; only three sahibs could go on with the limited transport, and Major Wheeler of the Canadian Alpine Club was added to the climbing party. The way forward was easy to the foot of the wall under Chang La, where a further camp was made. This wall, a formidable obstacle, was climbed on the 24th, and the three sahibs with three coolies reached Chang La (about 23,100 feet). But they were met there by a terrific wind from the north-west blowing up the snow, so that a further advance was impossible either on this or subsequent days.

General Bruce took out a climbing party the following year. This party approached Everest from the East Rongbuk Glacier in Tibet. Three members reached 26,800 feet without oxygen, and two members and a Gurkha, using oxygen, attained a height of 27,200 feet.

In 1924 General Bruce again took an expedition to attempt the assault. The route followed was practically the same as in 1922. Two members, Norton and Somervell, reached 28,000 feet without oxygen, and a few days later G. H. Leigh-Mallory and A. C. Irvine set out to make the final effort to reach the summit. They had oxygen, and were last observed at a height of over 28,200 feet. They failed to return, and such search as was possible showed no traces of them. Whether they reached the top or not is a matter of speculation—that it ultimately will be reached is a matter of certainty. In 1933, after elaborate preparations, another expedition set out. A flight was made over Mount Everest by the Houston Mount Everest Flight Expedition, led by Air Commodore Fellowes and the Marquis of Douglas and Clydesdale, and about the same time the Ruttledge Expedition attempted the climbing of the mountain. —BIBLIOGRAPHY: Lt.-Col. C. K. Howard Bury, D.S.O., *Mount Everest: The Reconnaissance*, 1921; Sir Francis Younghusband, *The Epic of Mount Everest*; J. B. L. Noel, *Through Tibet to Everest.*

MOUNT VERNON. A city of New York, United States, in Westchester county, and on Bronx River; served by the New York, New Haven, & Hartford and other railways. It was founded in 1852, became a city in 1892, and is a north residential suburb of New York City. Pop. (1930), 61,499.

MOURNE MOUNTAINS. A mountain range of Ireland, in the south of County Down, extending for 15 miles in a north-easterly direction between Carlingford Lough and Dundrum Bay; Slieve Donard reaches an altitude of 2796 feet.

MOURNING. As the outward expression of grief, it has greatly varied at different times and among different nations. Thus the Eastern nations and the Greeks cut off their hair, while the Romans allowed the beard and hair to grow; and as an evidence of mourning the ancient Egyptians wore yellow; the Ethiopians, grey; the Roman and Spartan women, white, which is still the colour of grief in China, Japan, and Siam; in Turkey, blue and violet; and in the other European countries black is used for this purpose. The Jews, in sign of grief at the loss of their relatives, rent their garments, tore out their hair, and wore coarse garments of a dark colour; and with the Greeks and Romans it was the custom to lay aside all ornaments of dress, to abstain from the bath and other indulgences.

MOURZOUK. *See* MURZUQ.

MOUSE. The name of a number of small rodents of which the most familiar is the domestic mouse (*Mus* *muscŭlus*), too well known to need description. The harvest-mouse (*Mus messorius* or *minūtus*), the smallest British quadruped, is a hibernating mammal, and constructs a little nest of grass, etc., entwined round and supported by the stalks of the corn or wheat.

The common field-mouse (*M. sylvaticus*) is a dusky brown, with a darker strip along the middle of the back, whilst the tail is of a white colour beneath. The short-tailed field-mouse, or "meadow-mouse," is not a true mouse, but one of the voles (Arvicŏla). It is of a reddish-brown colour, inclining to grey, the under parts are lighter, or ashy-brown, and the tail and feet are of a dusky-grey colour. The dormouse also is of a different family from the true mice.

MOUSE-EAR CHICKWEED (Cerastium). A genus of plants, nat. ord. Caryophyllaceæ, consisting of many pubescent herbs with small leaves and white flowers, forming common weeds in all temperate and cold regions. Nine species of the genus are found in Britain.

MOUSQUETAIRES. A pre-Revolutionary body of French Household Cavalry, comprising two companies, the "Grey" and the "Black.' The first was formed by Louis XIII. in 1622. Charles de Batz, comte d'Artagnan (1621-72), a real personage, immortalized by Dumas père (*Trois Mousquetaires*), was their most celebrated captain. The Mousquetaires were definitely suppressed in 1815.

MOUTH. The aperture in the head of an animal through which food is received. It is central in radially symmetrical animals, such as starfishes and polyps; or generally the anterior opening of the alimentary canal. In the higher animals the use of the mouth is for mastication, the emission of sound or voice, deglutition, and taste. In many animals of a low type of structure there is no distinct mouth. Thus in the simpler Protozoa (e.g. Amœba) the food is taken into the interior of the body by a process of ingestion, any portion of the surface being chosen for this purpose, and acting as an extemporaneous mouth, which closes up again when the particle of food has been received into the body. Some parasites, such as tapeworms, are devoid of mouth or special digestive organs.

MOVILLE. A seaport of Donegal, Irish Free State, on Lough Foyle, a port of call for Transatlantic mail steamers. Pop. 1016.

MOVING PLANT, or **TELEGRAPH PLANT** (*Desmodium gyrans*, nat. ord. Leguminosæ). A native of India, often cultivated in Europe in stoves, having violet flowers, remarkable for the motions of its leaflets.

MOYNIHAN, Lord. English surgeon. Berkeley George Andrew Moynihan was born in Malta, 2nd Oct., 1865, and, having trained as a doctor, began to practise in Leeds. He was appointed professor at the university there and made a great reputation. He served with the R.A.M.C. throughout the Great War, and in 1922 was made a baronet, becoming a baron in 1929. He has written several books on surgical subjects.

MOZAMBIQUE, Province of. *See* PORTUGUESE EAST AFRICA.

MOZAMBIQUE, San Sebastian de. A seaport city of Portuguese East Africa, on an island 3 miles off the Mosuril Bay coast. It has fortifications, erected by the Portuguese in 1508, and a number of other antiquated erections. As a port and former capital of the province of Mozambique it has declined mainly through the rise of Lourenço Marques. Pop. estimated at 7000.

MOZAMBIQUE CHANNEL. The passage between the east coast of Africa and the Island of Madagascar. In its north part lie the Comoro Islands.

MOZAR'ABS. A name applied by the Moorish Mahommedans in Spain to the Christians among them who retained their own religion. The Mozarabic liturgy which they used was suppressed, but was revived at Toledo and at Salamanca, where it is still preserved.

MOZART (mo-zârt'; Germ pron. mō'tsârt), **Johann Chrysostomus Wolfgang Amadeus.** German composer, was born at Salzburg 27th Jan., 1756, and died at Vienna 5th Dec., 1791. At the age of four years his father, Leopold Mozart, a violinist of repute, began to teach him some minuets and other small pieces on the harpsichord. From this period he made rapid progress, and a concerto for the harpsichord, which he wrote in his fifth year, was so difficult that only the most practised performer could play it.

In his sixth year Mozart was taken by his father, along with his sister, to Munich and Vienna, where the little artists were received at court with great favour. In 1763 the family made a journey to Paris, where Mozart published his first sonatas for the harpsichord; and in the following year they proceeded to England, where the child-musician performed before the court the most difficult compositions of Bach and Handel.

In 1767 the family returned to Salzburg, and in 1769 Mozart, who had been made master of the concerts at the court orchestra at Salzburg, commenced a journey to Italy in company with his father. In Rome he wrote down, on hearing it, the famous *Miserere*, annually sung in the Sistine Chapel during the holy week. At Milan in 1770 he composed, in his fourteenth year, his first opera, *Mithridates*, which was performed more than twenty times in succession.

Henceforth he resided chiefly in Salzburg, but also visited Paris,

Mozart

Munich, and finally Vienna. In the last-named city, although he was appointed composer to the court, he found it necessary to maintain himself by giving lessons in music and writing waltzes. Notwithstanding this poverty, it was here that most of his best work, such as his famous operas *Le Nozze di Figaro* (The Marriage of Figaro), *Don Giovanni*, *La Clemenza di Tito* (Clemency of Titus), *Die Zauberflöte* (The Magic Flute), and his last work the *Requiem*, were written. It was here also that the best pianist and greatest composer of his time—perhaps of the world—died in obscurity and was buried in a pauper's grave.

The extent of work done by Mozart during his short life is almost incredible, and in every department of composition, whether vocal or instrumental, he excelled. In the history of music he stands most prominently forward as an operatic composer, his *Don Giovanni*, *Magic Flute*, and *Marriage of Figaro* being works previously unequalled and never since surpassed. In his character he was kind-hearted, guileless, cheerful, void of envy, almost boyish to the last.—BIBLIOGRAPHY: E. Holmes, *Life of Mozart, including his Correspondence*; F. H. Cowen, *Mozart and his Music*; E. J. Dent, *Mozart's Operas: a Critical Study.*

MUCILAGE. A solution of some gummy substance in water, having a certain degree of viscosity. Gum-arabic, dextrine (British gum), and gum-tragacanth are the ingredients most commonly employed. Gum-acacia, the purest form of gum-arabic, dissolves completely in hot water. It is used as an adhesive, with the addition of a small quantity of glycerine or sugar to prevent it from hardening and cracking when dry. Dextrine is best dissolved in cold water; it is the adhesive commonly used on stamps, labels, envelopes, etc., and also for thickening colours used in calico-printing.

Gum-tragacanth does not completely dissolve, but absorbs fifty times its own weight of water to form a thick mucilage which is the basis of many hair-creams and other toilet preparations. In medicine it is used to suspend insoluble substances, and is also applied to irritated mucous membranes. Other mucilages are made from the cherry-tree gum, starch, sassafras pith, elm gum, linseed, barley, etc.

MU'CIUS SCÆVOLA (sē'vo-la). The hero of a Roman legend to the effect that, having attempted to assassinate Porsenna, King of Etruria, Mucius was ordered to be burned alive, but he won the king's favour and pardon by fearlessly holding his hand in the fire.

MUCOR. A genus of saprophytic Fungi, group Zygomycetes, easily recognized by their pin-shaped erect reproductive branches (*sporangiophores*), each ending in a black sporangium. Animal excreta form the natural medium of most species, but several grow readily on stale bread, decaying fruit, etc., especially *M. mucedo* and *M. stolonifer* (*Rhizopus nigricans*), which are the familiar black moulds.

MUCUS. A viscid fluid secreted by the mucous membrane of animals, which it serves to moisten and defend. It covers the lining membranes of all the cavities which open externally, such as those of the mouth, nose, lungs, intestinal canal, urinary passages, etc. It is transparent, glutinous, thready, and of a saline taste; it contains a great deal of water, chloride of potassium and sodium, lactate of sodium and of calcium, and phosphate of calcium. Mucus forms a layer of greater or less thickness on the surface of the mucous membranes, and it is renewed with more or less rapidity. Besides keeping these membranes in a moist and flexible condition, it also protects them against the action of the air, of the aliment, the different glandular fluids, and agencies that might otherwise irritate and inflame.

MUDAR. The Indian name of *Calotrŏpis gigantea*, a shrub or small tree of the nat. ord. Asclepiadaceæ, and also given to a substance used medicinally in India with great alleged effect in cutaneous diseases, and obtained from this and another species (*C. procēra*). The inner bark of *C. gigantea* also yields a valuable fibre.

MUD FEVER. In horses, an ailment similar to cracked heels, involving an inflamed condition of the skin of those parts of the horse most spattered in wet weather, as the back of the front legs, the front of the hind ones, the thighs, belly, and chest. Hunters are the chief victims. Washing with warm water provokes mud fever, and allowing mud to dry on horses whose legs have not been clipped confers a large degree of immunity. Considerable inflammation, swelling of the legs, symptoms of fever, and stiffness characterize the disease. Much hair is lost.

A soothing application of glycerinated water (5-10 per cent.) should be applied warm and thoroughly dried off, followed by a weak coal-tar disinfectant and further drying. An ointment of 1 part of red oxide of mercury to 7 parts of vaseline or lanoline may be used, and is best applied by smearing it on tow or cotton-wool, followed by bandaging of the parts affected. A few cooling saline doses facilitate recovery, which in simple cases generally takes place in about a week.

MUDIE, Charles Edward. English publisher and founder of Mudie's Lending Library. Born on 18th Oct., 1818, the son of a second-hand bookseller, he started a stationery and book-selling business in Bloomsbury, London, and in 1842 began to lend books. This innovation proved so successful that in 1852 he transferred his "select library" to larger premises in New Oxford Street, and branches were also established elsewhere in 1860. In 1864 Mudie's became a limited company. He died on 28th Oct., 1890.

MUDROS. A town and bay on the south coast of the Ægean Island of Lemnos, where the armistice was signed between the Allies and Turkey on 30th Oct., 1918 (European War). Throughout the Gallipoli campaign the extensive landlocked harbour of Mudros formed a naval base (H.M.S. *Europa*, depot ship). The town and adjacent plain were packed with French, British, European, and coloured troops throughout the operations.

MUDSTONE. A term originally applied to certain dark-grey fine-grained shales of early Palæozoic age, but now extended to all similar shales in whatever formation they may occur.

MUEZ'ZIN (Ar. *mu'addin*, from *addana*, to proclaim), a crier in Mahommedan countries who calls the faithful to prayer five times a day—at dawn, noon, 4 p.m., sunset, and midnight, as prescribed by the Prophet. The call is usually made from a minaret or from a roof-top, and takes the traditional form of "God is great" (thrice), "There is no God but God" (twice), "Mahomet is the Prophet of God" (twice), "Come ye to Prayer" (twice), "God is great" (twice), "And there is no one like unto Him." The muezzin is appointed by the imam of the mosque, and a seat in Paradise is reserved for him *ex officio*.

MUFFLE. In metallurgy, an arched fire-brick furnace heated by gas, coke, or electric current. It is used in various metallurgical operations, such as the roasting of certain sulphide ores where it is desirable to keep the sulphur dioxide free from the gaseous products of combustion of the fuel used. Various forms are also used in the heat treatment of metals and alloys for operations such as hardening, annealing, etc., and in the assay laboratory for such operations as scorification and cupellation.

MUFTI. Literally (in Mahommedan countries) an expounder of the law in accordance with Koranic precept and traditional practice. Generally, a cadi approaches a mufti for a ruling upon some definite point of the canon law, and his decision takes the form of a *fetwa* (document) by which the general decision is applied by the cadi to meet a particular case. In Turkey there is a grand mufti, styled the Sheikh-ul-Islam, appointed by the Sultan, who can dismiss him, but who can also be deposed by *fetwa* of the Sheikh, as in the case of Abdul Hamid.

MUGGLETONIANS. A sect that arose in England about the middle of the seventeenth century (1651), of which the founders were John Reeve and Ludovic Muggleton, who claimed to have the spirit of prophecy. They affirmed themselves to be the "two witnesses" of Rev. xi. 3. The sect lasted until the middle of the eighteenth century.

MUHARRAM. A religious festival and the first month of the Mahommedan year. Broadly speaking, Mahommedans are divided into two main sects, known as Sunnites and Shiites. The former acknowledge all the successors of Mahomet, while the latter reject many of them and pin their faith on Ali—the son-in-law of Mahomet—and his two martyred sons, Hassan and Hussein. It is the murder of these two which is commemorated at the Muharram.

In India, where the Mahommedan population is almost exclusively Sunni, and as such might be expected to ignore the deaths of the saints of a rival sect, both classes join wholeheartedly in the Muharram celebrations, which are often made the excuse for falling foul of the Hindus. Numerous acts, such as killing a cow in front of a Hindu temple, are occasionally perpetrated, and acknowledged in kind by the offended Hindus. As a rule these disturbances take place only in the larger towns, though they have been known in country districts; but more often than not the Muharram celebrations, consisting of the immersion of the *taziya* or bier of the martyred brothers, passes off quietly, without any physical exposition of the hatred felt by all good Mahommedans towards all good Hindus, and *vice versa.*

MÜHLHAUSEN. A town of Prussian Saxony, on the Unstrut. It has two fourteenth-century churches and a mediæval town house. Woollen and cotton cloth, leather, and sewing machines are made. Mühlhausen was originally in Thuringia, became a free city until 1802, and was incorporated in Prussia in 1815. Pop. 36,755.

MUIR, John. A Sanskrit scholar, born at Glasgow in 1810, died 1882. He was educated at the university of his native city, and joined (1828) the East India Company's Civil Service, filling various offices until his retiral in 1853. His chief works are: *A Sketch of the Argument for Christianity against Hinduism, in Sanskrit Verse* (1839); and *Original Sanskrit Texts on the Origin and History of the People of India, their Religion and Institutions* (5 vols., 1858-70).

MUIR, Sir William. Arabic scholar and brother of the above, was born at Glasgow in 1819, died in 1905. He was made Principal of Edinburgh University in 1885. His writings include: *The Life of Mahomet* (1858-61), *Annals of the Early Caliphate* (1883), *The Corân* (1877), and *Mahomet and Islam* (1884).

MUIRKIRK. A town of Ayrshire, Scotland, on the L.M.S. Railway. It has coal- and iron-mines. Pop. (parish, 1931), 4358.

MUKDEN, or FENG-TIEN. A city and capital of Feng-Tien province, Manchuria (of which it is also the capital), on the Peiping-Mukden and South Manchurian Railways. The tombs of the imperial Manchu family are near by. Mukden was opened to foreign trade in 1903. It is surrounded by outer and inner walls, and has a university. 800,000 men were engaged in a terrific battle around Mukden during the Russo-Japanese War (19th Feb. to 11th March, 1905), when the Japanese were victorious.

During the Chinese Civil War of 1922 Mukden was the base of Marshal Chang-Tso-lin's pro-Japanese army (known as the Fengtien army). In the Changsintien (near Peking) sector General Wu-Pei-fu's Chihli army engaged the Fengtien forces, and a tremendous battle ensued (3rd to 5th May) when the flank of the "Mukden war-lord's" army was turned, their losses being estimated at 5000 dead, and 20,000 wounded or captured. Pop. 250,000.

MULAI HAFID. Sultan of Morocco, born in 1875. He ascended the throne in 1906, but was forced to abdicate in favour of his brother, Mulai Yusef, on 11th Aug., 1912.

MULBERRY. A fruit tree of the genus Morus, nat. ord. Moraceæ, akin to the Urticacæ or nettles. The black or common mulberry (*Morus nigra*) is the only species worthy of being cultivated as a fruit-tree. The fruit is used at dessert, and also preserved in the form of a syrup. The juice of the berries mixed with that of apples forms a beverage of a deep port-wine colour, called mulberry cider.

The tree thrives in England, but is probably not originally a native of Europe. The white mulberry (*M. alba*) is the most interesting of the genus, on account of its leaves being used for food by silk-worms. It grows to the height of 40 or 50 feet, with a trunk 2 or more feet in diameter. It came probably from China. The red mulberry (*M. rubra*) has fruit of a deep-red colour, and is a valuable American tree. The paper mulberry (*Broussonetia papyrifĕra*) is a distinct genus, belonging originally to Japan, and now much cultivated in Europe. In Japan its bark is used in making paper, and its wood is highly valued for ornamental work.

MULE. The name applied to any animal produced by the crossing of different species, but specifically denoting the hybrid generated between an ass and a mare. The head of the mule is long and thin, its tail is bushy, and its mane short. (*See* HINNY.)

The mule is employed as a beast of burden in Spain, Portugal, Italy, in the East, and in Spanish America. It unites the speed of the horse with the dogged perseverance of the ass, and was extensively employed by the British during the European War. Zebroids are mules produced by crossing the zebra and horse.

MULE. A spinning-machine invented by Samuel Crompton in 1775, and so called from being a combination of the drawing-rollers by Arkwright and the spinning-jenny by Hargreaves. Condenser bobbins for wool, or rovings for cotton, are supported in suitable bearings behind the mule, and are capable of rotating to give off the rove when drawn by the rollers. The rollers rotate intermittently, and the spindles are supported by bearings in the carriage. The carriage, on wheels, moves on rails outwards, or away from the rollers, to a distance of about 6 feet, and then returns. The rollers rotate to give off the rove while the carriage is moving outwards for half its distance and then both stop; for the remainder of the outward travel the rove is drawn out, or attenuated, to a smaller diameter (to that required for the yarn in work). The spindles rotate rapidly to impart the necessary twist, but, as the carriage is moving in towards the rollers, each length of spun yarn (approximately 6 feet), and there may be several hundreds, is wound on to its spindle by the rotation of the latter, and simultaneously shaped by the fuller wires to the well-known cop form. In each cycle the speed of the spindles varies for different functions.

MÜLHEIM-AM-RHEIN. A German river-port, in the Rhine province of Prussia, facing Cologne. There is a good harbour; tobacco, machinery, electrical goods, and chemicals are manufactured. It became a corporate town in 1322. Pop. 53,000.

MÜLHEIM-AN-DER-RUHR. A German river-port, in the Rhine province of Prussia, on the Ruhr, and in the Westphalian coal- and iron-field. Coal is shipped from the harbour; glass, leather, zinc, and machinery are representative manufactures. Pop. 128,830.

MULHOUSE (Ger. *Mülhausen*). A town of France, department of Haut-Rhin, on the Ill, and served by the Rhine-Rhône Canal. It is a cotton-manufacturing town, but has also industries of woollens, chemicals, hardware, and machinery. There is a mediæval town hall. Mulhouse became a free city in 1198, and fell to France in 1797. In 1871 it passed to Germany, and although occupied by the French in Aug., 1914 (European War), it was recaptured by the Germans and held by them until the conclusion of peace. Pop. (1931), 99,534.

MULL. An island of the Hebrides, in Argyllshire, Scotland, separated from the Argyllshire coast by the Sound of Mull and the Firth of Lorne. It is mountainous (Ben More, 3185 feet), with several lochs, and a deeply indented coast-line. Sheep and cattle are raised; granite is quarried and exported. Tobermory is the principal town. Pop. (1931), 3138.

MULLAH. A Mahommedan teacher, or one learned in both canon and civil law. In India the term is applied to a schoolmaster. Fanatical

Mullah

Mullahs ("Mad" Mullahs) have in recent times preached "jehads" in India and Somaliland, and in the latter country British punitive expeditions were undertaken between 1901 and 1905.

MULLEIN (mul'en). The common English name for the plant *Verbascum Thapsus*, nat. ord. Scrophulariaceæ.

Mullein

The common mullein grows in old fields, at road-sides, etc., and is a tall, rough plant. The flowers are yellow, almost sessile, and are disposed in a long cylindrical spike.

MÜLLER (mül'ėr), **Friedrich Max.** A German philologist, son of the German poet Wilhelm Müller, was born at Dessau in 1823, died at Oxford in 1900. In 1846 he came to England and established himself at Oxford, where he was appointed successively Taylorian professor of modern languages (1854), assistant, and ultimately sub-librarian at the Bodleian library (1865), and professor of comparative philology (1868). His numerous writings include an edition of the *Rig-Veda* (6 vols., 1849-74), *History of Sanskrit Literature* (1859), *Lectures on the Science of Language*, *Chips from a German Workshop*, and *On the Origin and Growth of Religion* (1878).

MÜLLER, Hermann. German politician. He was born 18th May, 1876. A strong socialist, he was made editor of a socialist newspaper in Silesia, and in 1906 was chosen one of the leaders of the Socialist party in Germany. In July, 1914, he visited Paris and Brussels in the interests of peace, but his efforts were futile, and he gave his support, somewhat reluctantly, to the war policy of Germany. He undertook the editorship of *Vorwarts*, and in 1917 was made an Under-Secretary of State.

In June, 1919, when Germany was enraged by the terms of the Peace Treaty, he joined the Cabinet founded by Gustav Bauer as Minister for Foreign Affairs and as such signed the Treaty at Versailles. This made him very unpopular, but he held on his way and in 1920 was elected for the first time to the Reichstag. In January of that year he had succeeded Bauer as Chancellor, and during the next few months he carried out hurriedly some important social reforms. In June, 1920, however, he was forced to resign, and for the next eight years he led the Sociality Party in the Reichstag. In May, 1928, he again became Chancellor, with Stresemann as his Foreign Secretary, and he remained in power until March, 1930. He died 20th March, 1931.

MULLET. A name common to two groups of spiny-finned fishes, viz. the family Mugilidæ, or grey mullets; and the family Mullidæ, or red mullets. Naturalists, however, generally restrict the name to the former, designating the red mullets as surmullets.

Of the true mullets the best known is the common or thin-lipped grey mullet (*Mugil capito*), which ranges from Scandinavia to the Cape, found round the shores of the British Islands, and in particular abundance in the Mediterranean. It grows to the length of 18 to 20 inches, and will sometimes weigh

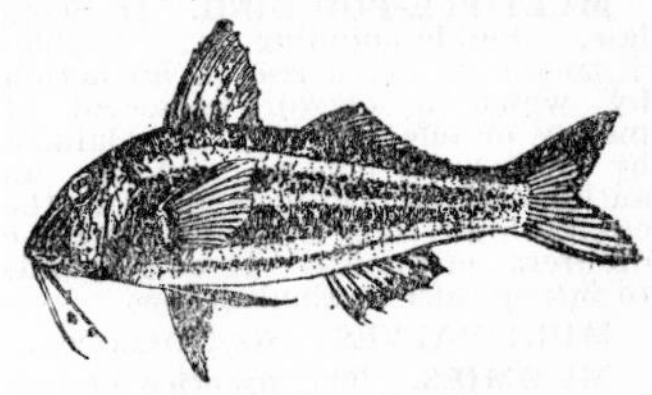

Striped Mullet or Surmullet

from 12 to 15 lb. It has the habit of rooting in the mud or sand in search of food. Another species, also called grey mullet (*M. cephalus*), a native of the Mediterranean, is distinguished by having its eyes half covered by an adipose membrane. It weighs usually from 10 to 12 lb., and is the most delicate of all the mullets. A smaller species, the thick-lipped grey mullet (*M. chelo*), is common on the British coasts. Many other species, natives of India and Africa, are much esteemed as food.

MULREADY, William. Born at Ennis, Ireland, 1786, died 1863. He became a student of the Royal Academy about 1800; exhibited *The Rattle* (1808); *The Music Lesson* (1809), at the Royal Academy; and his *Idle Boys* (1815) secured his election as an associate of the Academy, while the following year he was elected as Academician. Among the most popular of his numerous pictures after this time were: *The Wolf and the Lamb* (1820), *The Last In* (1835), *The Seven Ages of Shakespeare* (1838), *The Sonnet* (1839), illustrations to *The Vicar of Wakefield* (1840), *The Historian Controversy* (1844), *Choosing the Wedding Gown* (1845), *Burchell and Sophia* (1847), *Women Bathing* (1849), and *The Toyseller* (1861).

MULTAN′, or MOOLTAN′. A division of the Punjab, India. The people are mainly Mahommedan. Wheat and cotton are produced. Area, 31,218 sq. miles; pop. 3,821,000.

MULTAN, or MOOLTAN. A city of India, in the Punjab, the chief city and capital of a district of the same name, is situated 4 miles from the Chenab. The streets are mostly narrow and tortuous. It is one of the most ancient cities in India, and is the centre of a large trade. Pop. 119,457.

The district of Multan comprises the south of the Bari Doab. Wheat is produced by the use of irrigation. Area, 5939 sq. miles; pop. 815,000.

MULTIPLE-POINDING. In Scots law, double-poinding or double-distress. It gives rise to an action by which a person possessed of money or effects which are claimed by different persons obtains an authoritative arrangement for the equitable division thereof among the different claimants. It corresponds to *interpleader* in English law.

MULTIVALVES. *See* MOLLUSCA.

MUMMIES. The practice of embalming the dead was probably invented by the ancient Egyptians about 3500 B.C.; and the idea of attempting so remarkable a procedure was probably suggested by the fact that bodies buried in the sand of Egypt were often preserved as the result of a natural process of desiccation, and the idea developed that for the continuance of existence after death the preservation of the body from corruption was essential. The most important ingredient of the preservatives used was common salt, but from the earliest times various resins were also employed, and the body was wrapped in great quantities of linen bandages, sometimes as much as 300 yards being used.

The earliest-known mummy belonged to the time of the Second Dynasty; but the only early mummy that was strong enough to be moved is probably to be referred to the time of the great Pyramids (Fifth Dynasty); it is now in the Museum of the Royal College of Surgeons in London. Many mummies of the Middle Kingdom (about 2000 B.C.) have been found from time to time; but most of them were so extremely fragile that it was impossible to move them.

Mummy Head of Rameses II.

Several mummies of queens of the Middle Kingdom have recently been found in the course of excavations at Thebes on behalf of the Metropolitan Museum of New York. They are remarkable in many respects, not merely for their exceptionally good preservation and toughness, but also because they were not embalmed in the manner that was customary in Egypt. The organs of the body had not been removed, as was the rule, through an incision in the flank; but some resinous material had been injected into the bowel, and in all probability also applied to the surface of the corpse and its wrappings.

It was not until about 1500 B.C.

that the art of embalming had reached so high a pitch of excellence that it became possible to preserve the body with stone-like hardness. One of the factors in the rapid progress of the embalmer's art during the time of the New Empire was the expulsion of the Hyksos kings and the freer intercourse with and conquest of Syria, which enabled the Egyptians to obtain resins, balsams, and aromatic woods in much greater quantities and varieties than before.

The recovery, about forty years ago, of the royal mummies of the Eighteenth to the Twenty-second Dynasties, which had been hidden for more than twenty-eight centuries in a cave at Thebes, provided archæologists not only with the actual bodies of some of the most famous kings and queens in the world's history and enabled people of the present day to gaze upon the actual faces of the men and women who dominated the civilized world thirty centuries ago, but also with the accurately dated material for studying the evolution of the embalmer's art during the six centuries of its most significant development. Altogether about fifty of these royal mummies are now in the Cairo Museum, including such famous Pharaohs as Thothmes III., Amenophis III., Seti I., Ramses II., and Menephtah, who, according to an ancient Alexandrian (but probably untrue legend), was the Pharaoh of the Exodus. Although the mummy of the most romantic of all the royal consorts of Egypt, Queen Tiy's, has never been recovered, those of her parents, Yua and Thua, her husband, Amenophis III., and son, the famous heretic King Akhenaten, have been found.

One of the most remarkable phases in the history of the practice of mummification was the devising of measures (at the time of the Twenty-first Dynasty) for restoring the form and features of the body and making it as complete a reproduction of the living body as possible. The complexity and difficulty of the technique inevitably led to many failures, and as a result the art of embalming rapidly deteriorated during the six centuries before the Christian era. Far more attention was then lavished upon the wrappings and the external decoration of the swathed mummy than upon the body itself. Moreover, the introduction of the use of bitumen from Palestine as a preservative represented a further degradation of the art of mummification.

With the coming of Christianity to Egypt the practice of embalming was not abandoned, in spite of repeated protests by the early bishops of the Christian Church against the continuance of so heathen a custom. In fact, the custom of preserving the body, by packing it in large quantities of salt, was generally observed throughout Egypt until the seventh century, when the coming of Islam is supposed finally to have destroyed this remarkable custom after more than forty centuries of use. But although it was thus abandoned in the land of its birth, it has been retained in other parts of the world,

Mummy Case

to which different phases of the Egyptian method have from time to time been transmitted.

Early methods of embalming spread south up the Nile to the heart of Africa; later on the methods of the New Empire period, and especially the peculiarly distinctive procedures of the Twenty-first Dynasty, were diffused across equatorial Africa to Nigeria, and to the east to India Indonesia, Melanesia, and Polynesia and eventually in a modified form to Peru and Central America. Later methods in late pre-Christian and early Christian times spread far and wide in the Mediterranean area, Europe, and Western Asia.

Apart from the very positive and

precise evidence it affords of the diffusion of ancient culture throughout the world at different epochs, and especially from 900 B.C. onwards, the art of embalming is of general interest from the influence it exerted on the practices and the ritual procedures of most religions, of the part it played in the development of the art and science of medicine, and for its intimate genetic relationship to the development of funerary monuments, from which the crafts of the carpenter and the stone-mason had their origin, as well as the art of architecture.—BIBLIOGRAPHY: G. Elliot Smith, *The Royal Mummies*; *The Migrations of Early Culture*; *The Evolution of the Dragon.*

MUMPS, or **EPIDEMIC PAROTITIS.** An acute contagious disease, characterized by an inflammation of the parotid and, to a less extent, the other salivary glands. The disease is spread by direct contact, and is not conveyed through the air for any distance. The incubation period is usually from eighteen to twenty-one days, and the first symptom is a slight fullness of the parotid gland, just in front and below the level of the ear. The swelling increases rapidly, and leads to much enlargement of the cheeks, and there is usually also some swelling of the glands in the neck. Both sides of the face are as a rule affected, and there is considerable pain, most marked when the jaws are moved. Various complications may arise, but the most frequent is pain and swelling of the testicle, known as orchitis, in the male; much less commonly in women there is similar affection of the female genital organs. The disease is most common between five and fifteen years, and not infrequent in early adult life.

MÜNCHHAUSEN (mün*h*'hou-zn), **Karl Friedrich Hieronymus, Baron von.** A German officer, born in Hanover in 1720, died 1797. He was a passionate lover of horses and hounds, of which, and of his adventures among the Turks, he told the most extravagant stories; and his imagination finally so completely got the better of his memory that he really believed his most improbable and impossible fictions.

Baron Münchhausen's Narrative, a small book of forty-eight pages, appeared in London in 1785. Two years after it was translated into German by Bürger, who naturally passed in Germany for the writer. The real author was Rudolf Erich Raspe (1737-94), a native of Hanover who took refuge in England from a charge of theft. The book was afterwards enlarged by additional stories, many of them very old.

MUNGO. A remanufactured fibre, obtained by submitting milled woollen material, such as cast-off clothing, tailors' cuttings, and the like, to the action of the teeth of a rag-grinding machine, which tears up the felted cloth into shreds. The torn-up material undergoes other treatment before it is ready for spinning, either alone or in conjunction with other waste materials or new fibres, or both. Seams, buttonholes, linings, etc., which contain cotton threads, are clipped from the cast-off clothing, or else the garments are carbonized (subjected to the action of HCl in liquid or fumes) to burn out the vegetable material. Briefly, mungo is a remanufactured substance obtained from heavily-milled cuttings, whereas shoddy (q.v.) is obtained from loose, unmilled articles.

MUNGO, St., or **KENTIGERN.** The patron saint of Glasgow, an early apostle of the Christian faith in Britain, was the son of Owen, king of Strathclyde, and Princess (St.) Theneu, and was born at Culross about A.D. 514, and brought up by St. Serf, the head of a monastery there, whose favourite pupil he became. His name, Kentigern, was exchanged by the brethren of the monastery for *Mungo*, the beloved, on account of the affection they bore him.

On leaving Culross Kentigern founded a monastery on the banks of a small stream flowing into the Clyde, subsequently the site of Glasgow Cathedral. Having some troubles with the king of the Strathclyde Britons, he afterwards took refuge with St. David in Wales, and while in that country he founded a religious establishment under a follower named Asaph, which afterwards became the seat of the bishopric of St. Asaph. He returned to Glasgow, where he acquired a character of great sanctity, and died about 603. Numerous miracles were ascribed to him, and several legendary biographies are preserved.—Cf. A. P. Forbes, *The Historians of Scotland.*

MUNICH (Ger. *München*). The fourth largest city of Germany, capital of the Republic of Bavaria, on the Isar, some 1700 feet above sea-level. The new town, extending to the north and west, is essentially modern and imposing, and altogether Munich is one of the most attractive of European cities.

Buildings.—The former Royal Palace comprises a series of three buildings, the Alte Residenz (1600-16), the Festsaalbau (1832-42), and the Königsbau (1826-33), the latter an imitation of the Pitti Palace at Florence. Among other buildings are the National Theatre; the Library (1832-42), with over a million volumes and forty thousand MSS.; the university, founded at Ingolstadt (1472), transferred to Landshut (1800), and eventually to Munich (1826); and, among many churches, the building dedicated to St. Peter (1170), but frequently restored. It is an important art centre, the Peria

Munich : Frauenkirchen

Rothen and the Glyptothek containing fine collections of paintings and sculpture.

Industries.—The principal industry is brewing, but rifles, scientific instruments, and technical apparatus are manufactured, and photography, engraving, and the applied arts are in general extensively practised.

Jugend, *Simplicissimus*, and other famous periodicals are published in Munich, which is the seat of innumerable literary, scientific, and geographical societies and institutions. It is the centre of the South Bavarian Railway system, and has a broadcasting station (533 M., 1.5 kW.).

History.—Munich was founded by Henry the Lion (1158) on land traditionally the property of the Benedictine monks of Schäftslarn (i.e. *Forum ad Monachos*, whence the name *Munich*). Ludwig the Bavarian rebuilt the city after a fire in 1837, and it was successively under the patronage of Albert V. and the Elector Maximilian I., to whom the present museums and palaces are indirectly due. Ludwig I., during his reign, raised the city to pre-eminent rank as a centre of culture in Germany. The city took a great part in the Revolution of Nov., 1918. Pop. (1925), 680,036.

MUNKACSY (mŭn'kăch-i), **Mihaly,** real name **Michael Lieb.** Hungarian genre and historical painter, born at Munkacs 1846, died in 1900. Among his best-known pictures are: *Last Day of a Condemned Man, Milton dictating Paradise Lost, Christ before Pilate*, and *Last Moments of Mozart.*

MUNRO, Hugh Andrew Johnstone. Classical scholar, was born at Elgin in 1819, died at Rome in 1885. He was educated at Shrewsbury School and at Trinity College, Cambridge, graduating in 1842 as second classic and first chancellor's medallist. In 1843 he was elected a Fellow of his college, where later he became lecturer in classics. From 1869 to 1872 he was Kennedy professor of Latin in his university.

His most notable contribution to scholarship was his great edition of Lucretius, of which he published a text, with critical introduction, in 1860, and an improved text, with a commentary and translation, in 1864 (2 vols.). This work, of which the fourth and final edition in 3 vols. appeared in 1886, forms a landmark in the history of English classical scholarship during the last century. Other works of his include: *The Pronunciation of Latin*, a pamphlet (1871); *Criticisms and Elucidations of Catullus* (1878); and *Translations into Latin and Greek Verse.*

MUNSTER. The southernmost and largest of the four provinces of Ireland (q.v.), wholly within the Irish Free State, comprising the six counties of Clare, Cork, Kerry, Limerick, Tipperary, and Waterford. It is mountainous. The principal rivers are the Shannon, Bandon, Blackwater, Lee, and Suir. At the time of the English conquest Munster, one of the old Irish kingdoms, was divided into two principalities, viz. Desmond in the south and Thomond in the north. During the reign of Elizabeth it was divided into counties. Area, 5,962,803 acres; pop. (1926), 971,033.

MÜNSTER. A town of Westphalia, Germany, on the Aa and Dortmund-Ems Canal. There is a thirteenth-century cathedral, the churches of St. Lambert and Our Lady, erected during the fourteenth century, and an ancient monastery. Administrative offices are accommodated in the ancient castle of the prince-bishops; the university, founded in 1786 and suppressed in 1818, was reorganized in 1902, with faculties of theology, philosophy, and law. Among manufactures are linen and cotton textiles, leathers, beer, Westphalian hams, and paper goods.

Münster is first mentioned as the seat of a Saxon bishopric founded by Charlemagne about A.D. 805, and within it was subsequently established by John of Leyden, leader of the Anabaptists, "the Kingdom of the New Zion," which came to an end in 1535. The bishops were made princes of the empire in the twelfth century. Their lands (2500 sq. miles) were secularized in 1803, and apportioned among Hanover, Prussia, and Brandenburg. Pop. (1925), 106,418.

MUNTJAC. A small species of deer, the *Cervŭlus muntjac*, found in British India, the Malay Peninsula,

Muntjac

Sumatra, Java, and Borneo, about 26 inches high at the shoulder. They are of solitary habits; the male has short horns, and they use their teeth effectually in self-defence.

MUNTZ'S METAL (from G. F. Muntz of Birmingham, the inventor). an alloy of 60 parts copper and 40 parts zinc, used for the construction of bolts, nuts, pump plungers, etc., which come into contact with sea water. It possesses considerable strength and the capacity of being forged.

MÜNZER (mŭnt′sėr), **Thomas.** A German fanatic, born about 1490, executed 1525. He held a mystical belief in continuous divine revelation through dreams and visions, and promulgated the doctrine of community of goods. He collected a large number of peasant followers, who committed many outrages, but in 1525 were totally defeated, when Münzer was taken and executed.

MURAD V. Sultan of Turkey, born 1840, died in 1904. Son of Abdul-Medjid, he succeeded to the throne on the forcible deposition of Abdul Aziz in 1876, but was deposed in the course of the same year on account of insanity, and was succeeded by his younger brother, Abdul Hamid.

MURÆ′NA. A genus of soft-finned fishes, type of the family Murænidæ, closely related to that including ordinary eels. They have no pectoral fins, and the dorsal and anal fins are very low and are united. The *M. helena*, or murry, is found in the Mediterranean; it grows to the length of between 4 and 5 feet, and even more, and is excellent eating.

MURAL CIRCLE. An astronomical instrument consisting of a telescope attached to a vertical brass circle which turns upon an axis passing through a stone pier. The brass circle revolves exactly in the plane of the meridian, and is carefully divided into degrees and smaller angular units. Attached to the stone pier, and at equal distances apart, are six microscopes for the purpose of viewing the graduated circle and determining exactly its position and consequently that of the telescope.

This was formerly a principal instrument in observatories, but is now practically superseded by the transit circle. Its chief use is to measure angular distances in the meridian, and so to determine the declination of a star, or its distance from the celestial equator. The right ascension of a star being given by the transit instrument (q.v.), and its declination by this, its exact position is determined.

MURAL DECORATION. The earliest mural paintings were those executed in Egypt, about 4000 B.C., in some form of tempera on a thin stucco of lime upon brick. Figure subjects, generally arranged in horizontal bands and treated in profile, were the rule. The representation of animals was tolerably naturalistic, but human beings were conventionalized in form and colour.

The influence of Egyptian painting seems to have spread throughout Mesopotamia and to Crete, where mural painting was extensively practised, as recent excavations at Knossos show. Thence it passed to Greece, where progress was rapid and continuous from the archaisms of the sixth to the achievements of the fourth century B.C. No examples survive; but contemporary descriptions and the paintings on vases show that in the earlier periods figures were represented in one plane without landscape, while, later, space was suggested by various means. A celebrated early work was the *Battle of Marathon,* painted 450 B.C. by Polygnotus and Micon. Among their successors, Apelles and Zeuxis were the most famous.

Of Roman mural painting our knowledge is for the greater part derived from late Pompeian and Roman work, which is mainly by workmen who produced versions of Greek originals. On walls coloured deep red, black, or yellow were placed panels of figure subjects (usually taken from mythology), still-life, or conventional ornament, painted in tempera on stucco, with a plain dado below and an ornamental frieze above.

In the Christian era mosaic for a time largely replaced mural painting. Such painting as there was followed the stiff conventional style of the mosaics, until the freer, more naturalistic school of the thirteenth century developed. Prominent in this are Cimabue, his greater pupil Giotto, and Duccio of Siena. They and their contemporaries worked either in *fresco a secco* (dry fresco) or in *buon' fresco,* in which the artist paints on the plaster while still wet (*see* FRESCO), and were chiefly employed in the decoration of churches, whose architectural style of extensive wall-spaces and small window-openings was peculiarly suitable for mural painting. Examples of their work may be seen in Florence, Assisi, Padua, Siena, and Perugia.

A century later this Gothic style of mural painting was superseded by that of the Renaissance, of which the earliest complete expressions are the frescoes by Masaccio in the Church of the Carmine, Florence; and whose greatest achievements include the Sixtine Chapel at Rome by Michelangelo, and the Stanze and Loggie of the Vatican by Raphael. *Buon' fresco* now becomes the almost invariable medium.

During the fifteenth and sixteenth centuries elaborate mural paintings were also carried out in public buildings and the palaces of the nobility, notable examples being the work of Mantegna at Mantua, Cosimo Rossalli at Florence, Pinturicchio at Siena, and of Titian, Tintoretto, and Paul Veronese in Venice.

Since the development of painting in oil in the sixteenth century the medium chiefly used for mural painting has come to be oil on canvas, wax being mixed with the oil to give a non-shiny surface. The canvas is then attached to the wall, usually by a *marouflage* of white lead, oil, and copal varnish. This method is particularly suitable for cool and damp climates; but if the painting is to last, additional precautions, such as damp-proof courses and double walls, are advisable.

Since the seventeenth century France has been the chief centre

Egyptian Wall-painting from the Tomb atThebes, about 1580-1350 B.C.; now in British Museum. The painting depicts the counting and inspection of geese on a farm.

of mural decoration. In Holland the absence of a court, a nobility, and the Roman Catholic Church limited the demand for big decorative canvases to that of the guilds and civic bodies; in England the extensive use of panelling and tapestry in interior decoration checked the development of mural painting.

In France there succeeded to the group of artists employed by Francis I. to decorate his castle at Fontainebleau, the group employed by Louis XIV. at Versailles, the Louvre, Marly, and other residences, of which Charles Le Brun was the leading figure. This in turn was followed by the eighteenth-century decorators, such as François Boucher and J. B. Oudry, whose work is less imposing and grandiose, but better adapted to the smaller rooms which were becoming the rule.

In the nineteenth century little mural painting of genuine distinction was produced. The most important work is that of Puvis de Chavannes, who is represented at the Sorbonne and the Hôtel de Ville in Paris, and at Amiens, by work of great dignity and refinement.

Among contemporary mural painters, Albert Besnard in France, and Frank Brangwyn in England, occupy a leading place. Mention may be made of Brangwyn's panel, "Modern Commerce," in the Royal Exchange, London, and his panels designed for the Royal Gallery in the House of Lords. The latter, commissioned by Lord Iveagh at a cost of £20,000 and offered to the nation, were begun in 1925. Five of the panels were completed and actually placed in the Gallery when in 1930 the House of Lords decided to reject the gift. Another modern exponent of mural decoration is Rex Whistler, whose brilliant and significant art also expresses itself in other decorative forms. *See* MOSAIC; TAPESTRY.—BIBLIOGRAPHY: A. P. Laurie, *Materials of the Painter's Craft*; J. Ward, *History of Mural Decoration*; H. J. Westlake, *History of Mural Decoration.*

MURAT (mü-rä), **Joachim.** French marshal, and for some time King of Italy, the son of an innkeeper at Cahors, born in 1771, died 1815. He served in the constitutional guard of Louis XVI.; then entered the 12th Regiment of mounted chasseurs; rose by his zealous Jacobinism to the rank of lieutenant-colonel; was afterwards removed as a terrorist, and remained without employment till his fate placed him in connection with Bonaparte whom he followed to Italy and Egypt, becoming general of division in 1799. In 1800 he married Caroline, the youngest sister of Bonaparte.

He was present at the battle of Marengo, and in 1804 was made marshal of the empire, grand-admiral, and prince of the imperial House. His services in the campaign of 1805 against Austria, in which he entered Vienna at the head of the army, were rewarded in 1806 with the Grand-Duchy of Cleves and Berg. In the war of 1806 with Prussia, and of 1807 with Russia, he commanded the cavalry, and in 1808 he commanded the French army which occupied Madrid. He anticipated receiving the crown of Spain, Charles IV. having invested him with royal authority; but Napoleon, who destined Spain for his brother Joseph, placed him on the throne of Naples, 15th July, 1808. Murat then took the title of *Joachim Napoleon.*

He shared the reverses of the Russian campaign of 1812, and in 1813 again fought for Napoleon, whose cause he deserted after the battle of Leipzig. He took up arms again in 1815 for Napoleon; but being defeated by Generals Neipperg and Bianchi near Tolentino, 2nd and 3rd May, he was forced to leave Italy, and took refuge in Toulon. After the overthrow of Napoleon he escaped to Corsica, and set sail for the Neapolitan territory with a view to recover his kingdom. He landed at Pizzo on 8th Oct., but was immediately captured, tried by a court-martial, and shot.—Cf. A. H. Atteridge, *Joachim Murat.*

MURATO'RI, Ludovico Antonio. Italian historian, born 1672, died 1750. He was successively librarian at Milan and ducal archivist and librarian at Modena. He made many valuable contributions to Italian history, notably *Rerum Italicarum Scriptores ab Anno* 500 *ad* 1500 (27 vols. folio, 1723-51), *Antiquitates Italicæ Medii Ævi* (6 vols., 1738-42), and *Annali d'Italia.*

MURCHISON (mėr'chi-sun), **Sir Roderick Impey.** Scottish geologist, born at Tarradale, in Ross-shire, 1792, died 1871. He studied at the military college, Great Marlow, and at Edinburgh University; joined the army, and served in thePeninsular War (1807-8). Murchison was one of the most prominent geologists of his time.

In 1831-32, and again in 1842-43, he was elected president of the Geological Society. He was a founder and an active member of the British Association for the Advancement of Science, and he presided over the meeting of that association at Southampton in 1846. In 1855 he was appointed director of the Geological Survey and of the Royal School of Mines. He was several times elected president of the Royal Geographical Society. Among his works are *Siluria* and *The Geology of Russia.*

MURCIA. A maritime province of South-Eastern Spain, on the Mediterranean, traversed towards the north-west by the Sierra de Espuña, but elsewhere comparatively flat. It is well watered (Segura and tributaries); the climate is hot and dry; oranges, maize, vines, and cereals are produced, and the mulberry tree is tended for silk-worm breeding. Zinc, lead, and sulphur are worked. The capital is Murcia; Cartagena is the port.

The modern provinces of Murcia and Albacete correspond with the ancient Moorish Kingdom of Murcia (1224-43), which followed the Carthaginian and Roman settlements. It was taken by Castile in 1240. Area, 4453 sq. miles; pop. (1931) 643,025.

MURCIA (Ar. *Medînát Mursiya*). A city of Spain, capital of the province of Murcia, on the Segura River (ancient *Tader*; Ar. *Skehura*), 50 miles by rail north-north-west of Cartagena. The cathedral of Santa Maria (founded in 1358 on the site of a mosque) possesses a tower 480 feet high (1522-1766). It is a large manufacturing and trading centre. Near the city are the celebrated gardens of Murcia, where vines, olives, mulberries, etc., grow in great profusion. After the fall of the Caliphate of Cordova the town was capital of the Kingdom of Murcia, and was taken (1243) by Ferdinand of Castile. Pop. (1931), 160,478.

MURDER. The act of unlawfully killing a human being with premeditated malice, the person committing the act being of sound mind and discretion, and the victim dying within a year and a day after the cause of death administered. In Britain it is the law that every person convicted of murder shall suffer death as a felon. In the United States of America the law recognizes degrees in murder, and in France and some other nations "extenuating circumstances" are recognized. *See* CAPITAL PUNISHMENT; CRIMINALITY; HOMICIDE.

MUREX. A genus of sea-snails resembling the whelk; shell spiral, rough, with three or more rows of spines simple or branched. Murices are remarkable for the beauty and variety of their spines. They were in high esteem from the earliest ages on account of the purple dye that some of them yielded.

MURGER (mür-zhār), **Henri.** Born at Paris 1822, died 1861. He lived a life of extreme privation; formed an informal club or society of unconventional young artists and authors similarly situated, which was named "Bohemia," and the associates "Bohemians"—a name famous in general literary history.

He made a reputation by his *Scènes de la vie de Bohême,* which is the source of Puccini's famous opera *La Bohême* (1898). He also published two volumes of poetry, *Ballades et fantaisies* and *Les Nuits d'hiver*; and wrote dramas for the Luxembourg theatre, and tales, etc., for the *Revue des Deux Mondes.*

MURGHAB. A river of Asia, which rises in the mountains of Northern Afghanistan, and after a course of 400 miles loses itself in the sands surrounding the oasis of Merv.

MURILLO (mu-rēl'yō), **Bartolome Esteban.** Spanish painter, born at Seville 1618, died there 1682. He first studied under Juan del Castillo,

Bartolome Esteban Murillo

and visited Madrid in 1641, where he worked in the Royal Picture Gallery and was befriended by Velasquez. On his return to Seville in 1645 he painted a group of pictures for the convent of S. Francesco, these being in his first or cold (*frio*) manner, with firm outline and strong chiaroscuro derived from Ribera and Caravaggio. One of these, the *S. Diego,* is in the Louvre.

In 1648 he married a lady of fortune, which, combined with many commissions, enabled him to found the Academy of Seville, of which he became joint president with Herrera. To 1648 belongs his *Flight into Egypt*, after which he adopted his second or warm (*calido*) style, in which are painted *S. Isidoro* and *S. Leandro*, both in Seville Cathedral; the *Dream of Pope Liberius*, at Madrid; and the *Immaculate Conception*, in the Louvre.

He then adopted a third, or *sfumato* (smoky) manner, an unsuccessful compromise between the strong chiaroscuro used by most of his contemporaries and the pattern in colour used by earlier painters. In this last style are *The Charity of S. Juan de Dios*, at Seville; the *Holy Family*, in the National Gallery; and a group of pictures in the Wallace Collection.

In early life he painted many pictures of beggars and working-class life, strongly realistic in treatment, examples of which are in the Dulwich Gallery. Later in life he concentrated on large religious pictures, into which he introduced idealized and sentimental types. He was also a competent portrait-painter.

MURMAN. A name applied to the Kola Peninsula (North Russia), but properly applicable to the coast only, extending between the White Sea and Kola Bay. It is the only ice-free coast of European Russia north of the Crimea. Murmansk, on Kola Bay, was founded in 1915, and is the terminus of the Arctic Railway.

In February to March, 1918 (European War), an Allied army was sent to Murmansk to protect the "Eastern Front" after the breakdown of Russia, and to avoid encroachment by the pro-German state of Finland, who had arranged with the Bolsheviki to extend their territory in this direction. In June, 1918, British, French, and American troops occupied Murmansk, Alexandrovsk, the Russian end of the cable from Peterhead, Scotland, and adjacent territory. The Murman Soviet supported the Allies throughout, and on 11th April the Bolsheviki were defeated at Urosozero, and the Allies advanced to the shores of Lake Onega, where a British expedition captured two lake steamers and took the port of Talvuiski (2nd Aug.). During September a rapid Allied advance was made on Petrozavodsk, the Bolshevik base, but, Germany having collapsed, the need for Allied military action in Russia had disappeared, and troops were operating in North Russia without any clearly defined policy. Hence, at the end of 1919, Murmansk was evacuated.

MUROM. A town of Russia, in the government of Vladimir, on the Oka, and served by the Kovrov-Murom Railway. Murom was of commercial importance as early as the tenth century. It has various manufactures; its industries include milling, distilling, and smelting. Pop. 23,000.

MURRAY, Sir David. Scottish painter. Born at Glasgow, 1849, he was elected A.R.A. in 1891, and R.A. in 1905. In 1917 he was made President of the Royal Institution of Painters in Water Colours, and was knighted in the following year. Among his finest pictures are *In the Country of Constable*, *Young Wheat*, *River Road*, *Marigolds*, *Hampshire*, and *Gorse*.

MURRAY, George Gilbert Aimé. English scholar. Born in Sydney, 2nd June, 1866, he had a remarkable career as a classical scholar at Oxford. He was made a fellow of New College, Oxford, and in 1889 Professor of Greek at Glasgow. In 1908 he returned to Oxford as Professor of Greek. To scholars Murray is known as the author of *A History of Ancient Greek Literature*, *The Origin of Tragedy*, *The Rise of the Greek Epic*, and other books, and to a wider public for his translations of the plays of Euripides. He is one of the leading supporters of the League of Nations. He became Chairman of the League of Nations Union in 1923 and President of the International Committee of Intellectual Co-operation in 1928.

MURRAY, Sir James Augustus Henry. Philologist and lexicographer, was born near Hawick, Roxburghshire, in 1837, died 1915. He was educated at Minto and Edinburgh, and graduated B.A. of London University. After acting as schoolmaster in Hawick, he became master at Mill Hill School, near London, in 1870, remaining there till his removal to Oxford in 1885. He was knighted in 1908. From 1879 until his death Sir James Murray was editor of the *New English Dictionary on Historical Principles*, the great work which has been issued from the Clarendon Press. His writings include: *Dialect of the Southern Counties of Scotland* (1873), and the article "English Language" in the *Encyclopædia Britannica* (9th edition).

MURRAY, John. The name of a firm of eminent London publishers. It was established by John MacMurray in 1768. John Murray (1778-1843) began business when quite young, early attained success, and became the friend of as well as publisher for some of the chief writers of the day, including Byron, Moore, Rogers, Campbell, Crabbe,

Washington Irving, etc. He started the *Quarterly Review* in 1809. The well-known *Handbooks for Travellers* were originated by his son.

MURRAY, Sir John. Biologist and oceanographer, born at Coburg, Ontario, in 1841, died 1914. He was chief naturalist to and edited the scientific reports of the *Challenger* Expedition (1872-76), and carried on special research work in the Clyde area between 1892 and 1894, establishing a marine biological station at Millport. He carried out a bathymetrical survey of the freshwater lochs of Scotland.

MURRAY, Lindley. Grammarian, born in Pennsylvania, of Quaker parents, in 1745, died 1826. About the age of twenty-one he was called to the Bar, and acquired an extensive practice. In 1784 he went to England, and passed the remainder of his life near York. He wrote an *English Grammar* (1795).

MURRAY. The largest river in Australia, rises in the Australian Alps about 36° 40′ S. and 147° E., its sources being partly in New South Wales, partly in Victoria; flows westward, forming the boundary between the two colonies for 1200 miles; then passes into South Australia, and falls into the sea through a large shallow sheet of water called Lake Alexandrina. It is navigable as far as Albury; length, about 1250 miles. Its chief tributaries are the Murrumbidgee, the Darling, and the Lachlan on the right bank, and the Goulburn, Campaspe, and Loddon on the left. The whole system has been manipulated for irrigation and hydroelectric purposes.

MURREE. A hill station of India, on the Punjab, 40 miles from Rawalpindi.

MÜRREN. A winter sport resort in the Bernese Oberland, Switzerland, below the Jungfrau.

MURRUMBID′GEE. A river of New South Wales, rising in the Australian Alps, and entering the Murray after a westward course of about 1300 miles; chief tributary, the Lachlan.

MURSHIDABAD′. A city of India, Bengal, capital of a district of the same name, on the Bhagirathi. It was the capital of Bengal till 1772. The Nawab Bahadur of Murshidabad is the premier noble of Bengal. The industries include the embroidery of fancy articles with gold and silver lace, ivory carving, and the making of musical instruments. Pop. 11,000.

MURZUK. The chief town of Fezzan, in the hinterland of Italian Libya. It was founded in 1310, and is an important oasis on the caravan route from Tripolitania to the Western Sudan. Pop. about 4000.

MUSA′CEÆ. A natural order of monocotyledons, of which Musa is the typical genus. It includes the abaca or manilla hemp, the banana and the plantain.

MUSÆ′US. A legendary Greek poet, said by some to be the son of Eumolpus and Selēnē; by others, of Linus or Orpheus. He is credited with the mystic and oracular verses of the Eleusinian and other mysteries. The ancients attribute to him many works, of which some verses only have come down to us as quotations in Pausanias, Plato, Aristotle, etc.

Mürren

A later Musæus, who probably lived four or five centuries after Christ, is the author of a poem entitled *Hero and Leander*, discovered in the thirteenth century and published in 1494 by Aldus Manutius. It was paraphrased by Marlowe.

MUSÄUS (mu̥-zā′u̥s), **Johann Karl August.** German author, born 1735, died 1787. Among his writings are: *Der Deutsche Grandison*, *Volksmärchen der Deutschen*, and a series of tales under the title *Straussfedern* (Ostrich feathers).

MUSCA. A genus of two-winged insects, including the common housefly (*M. domestica*). It is the type of a family (Muscidæ).

MUSCAT. The capital of Omán, South-Eastern Arabia, a seaport on the Indian Ocean (Gulf of Omán). The town is one of the hottest places in the world. It is an important centre of trade, exporting pearls, mother-of-pearl, dye-stuffs, drugs, dates, and coffee, and importing rice, sugar, and piece-goods. In recent years much of its trade has passed to Matrah. Muscat was occupied by the Portuguese in 1508, and became the capital of a native Sultanate in 1741. British troops occupied Muscat in 1915 on behalf of the Sultan (apart from the European War), and a British Political Agent and Consul has now his headquarters there. Pop. 26,000.

MUSCHELKALK (mush'el-kålk). A compact hard limestone of a greyish colour found in Germany. It is interposed between the Bunter sandstone, on which it rests, and the Keuper variegated marls, which lie over it, and with which at the junction it alternates, thus forming the middle member of the Triassic system as it occurs in Germany. In England the Keuper type of strata rests immediately on the Bunter. It abounds in marine organic remains, its chief fossils being encrinites, the ammonite ceratites, and bivalve molluscs. Its palæontological importance was greatly reduced by the exploration of the extensive series of marine Triassic deposits in the Eastern Alps.

MUS'CIDÆ. A family of two-winged flies, of which the common house-fly (*Musca domestica*) is a familiar example. Here also belong the blue-bottles (flesh flies) and green-bottles; also, among biting forms, stable-flies (Stomoxys) and tsetse-flies (Glossina).

MUSCLE AND MUSCULAR MOTION. The name *muscle* is applied to those structural elements or organs in animals which are devoted to the production of movements, either of a part of the body or of the body as a whole. They consist of fibres or bundles of fibres, susceptible of contraction and relaxation, enclosed in a thin cellular membrane. Muscles are composed of fleshy and tendinous fibres, occasionally intermixed, but the tendinous fibres generally prevail at the extremities of the muscle, and the fleshy ones in the belly or middle part of it. When the fibres of a muscle are placed parallel to each other, it is called a *simple* or *rectilinear* muscle; when they intersect and cross each other, they are called *compound.*

Muscles are divided into *voluntary* and *involuntary*, the former being those whose movements proceed from an immediate exertion of the will, as in raising or depressing the arm, bending the knee, moving the tongue, etc., while the latter are beyond this control, being the agents in the contraction of the heart, arteries, veins, stomach, intestines, bladder, womb, etc. When examined under the microscope, the fibres of the voluntary muscles (as also those of the heart) are seen to be marked by minute transverse bars or stripes, while those of the involuntary are smooth and regular in appearance. The former is therefore called *striped* or *striated* muscle, the latter *unstriped*, *nonstriated*, or *smooth* muscle.

The great property of muscular tissue is the power of responding when irritated. The response is in the form of contraction, that is, when

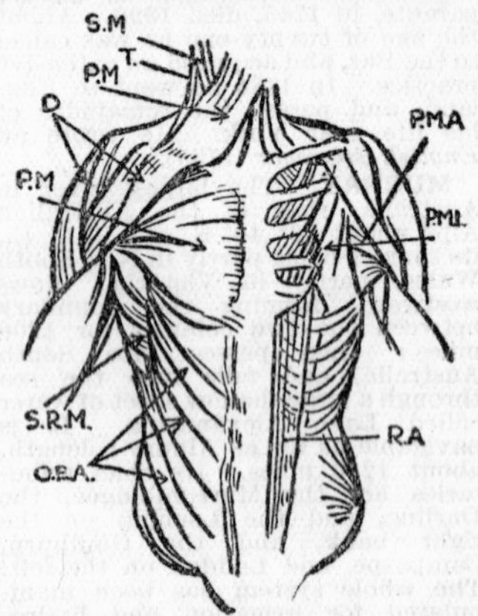

Muscles of Chest and Abdomen

S.M., Sterno mastoid. P.M., Platysma myoides. D., Deltoid. P., Pectoralis major. R.A., Rectus abdominis. O.E.A., Obliquus externus abdominis. P.M.I., Pectoralis minor. T., Trapezius. P.M.A., Pectoralis major (cut). S.R.M., Serratus magnus.

the muscle is irritated or stimulated it responds by shortening itself, so that its ends are brought nearer and it becomes thicker in the middle, its inherent elasticity making it capable of returning to its previous length when the stimulation is withdrawn. By these contractions the muscles are able to do work. Stimulation is by nervous action (*see* NERVOUS SYSTEM), but mechanical means, such as pinching, pricking, etc., electricity, heat, and chemicals also cause irritation.

All the muscles are connected with bones not directly but through the medium of tendons. A tendon presents the appearance of a white glistening cord, sometimes flat, but often cylindrical and of considerable thickness. The mass of flesh composing the muscle is called the *belly* of the muscle. One end is usually attached to a bone more or less fixed, and is called the *origin* of the muscle. The other end is attached to the bone meant to be moved by the contraction of the muscle, and is called the *insertion* of the muscle. Involuntary muscle consists of spindle-shaped cells having an elongated nucleus in the centre. They are united in ribbon-shaped bands, and respond much less rapidly than the voluntary to irritations, and the wave of contraction passes over them more slowly.

There are several hundreds of separate muscles in the human body, and they are broadly grouped into muscles of the head, face, and neck; muscles of the back; muscles of the chest; muscles of the upper extremity, the shoulder, arm, forearm, and hand; muscles of the abdomen; and muscles of the lower extremity, the thigh, leg, and foot.

MUSES (Gr. *Mousa*). In the Greek mythology, the daughters of Zeus and Mnemosynē, who were, according to the earliest writers, the inspiring goddesses of song, and according to later ideas divinities presiding over the different kinds of poetry, and over the sciences and arts. Their original number appears to have been three, but afterwards they are always spoken of as nine in number, viz. *Clio*, the muse of history; *Euterpē*, the muse of lyric poetry; *Thalīa*, the muse of comedy, and of merry or idyllic poetry; *Melpomĕnē*, the muse of tragedy; *Terpsichŏrē*, the muse of choral dance and song; *Erăto*, the muse of erotic poetry and mimicry; *Polymnia* or *Polyhymnia*, the muse of the sublime hymn; *Urania*, the muse of astronomy; and *Calliŏpē*, the muse of epic poetry.

MUSE'UM. *See* BRITISH MUSEUM; KENSINGTON (SOUTH) MUSEUM; PARIS. Other references are given in the index.

MUSHROOMS. The common name of numerous Fungi. Some of them are edible, others poisonous. The species of mushroom usually cultivated is the *Agaricus campestris*, or eatable agaric, well known for its excellence as an ingredient in sauces, especially ketchup. (*See* AGARIC.) Mushrooms are found in all parts of the world, and are usually of very rapid growth. In some cases they form a staple article of food. In Tierra del Fuego the natives live almost entirely on a mushroom-like Ascomycete, *Cyttaria Darwinii*; in Australia many species of Bolētus are used by the natives, and the *Mylitta australis* is commonly called native bread. *Mushroom spawn* is a term applied to the mycelium of the mushroom.

Mushroom. Common edible

MUSIC. History.—It is not customary outside the ranks of serious musicians to regard music as a science, but it is one nevertheless, and the history of music is simply a record of man's study of sound as he found it in nature, his gradual understanding of its physical properties, and its possibilities for artistic pleasure, and finally his slow discovery of the appropriate conditions under which these possibilities could be most completely realized. Music, therefore, is not only one of the most uplifting of human pleasures but also one of man's greatest intellectual triumphs. References to music are found among the earliest literary records, and at no period of which anything is known does the world seem to have been without it. It is therefore remarkable that music, as we know it to-day, is the growth and development of only a few centuries. It is the infant among the arts, younger than painting, and very much younger than literature and sculpture.

Of the nature of the music practised by the ancient civilized nations not much is known, but it would seem to be the case that the Egyptians were the most advanced musically in the earliest days of civilization, and that in their solemn religious ceremonies in particular music played an important part. We gather from the bas-reliefs of ancient Egypt that harps of many kinds, flutes, tambourines, trumpets, and other instruments, were in constant use, and that they were often combined into small orchestras; and the suggestion has been made that these combinations of musicians and of instruments argue the possession of a well-developed art, which, with so much else relating to the early times of the world, has been lost beyond recovery. While the point is not open to proof or disproof, the probability is that the music enjoyed by the Egyptians of early times did not attain to such a degree of expressiveness as would come near to satisfying the modern music-lover.

It is practically certain that the Egyptians brought the beginnings of their musical system from Ethiopia, the country of their origin, and in due time developed it to a considerable degree. The Children of Israel during their sojourn in Egypt would receive into the ready soil of their genuinely musical nature many seeds which they afterwards cultivated so assiduously as to become the most finely developed, musically, of all the ancient nations. The Greeks also borrowed their musical ideas from the same source, and these two peoples form the link between the music of the ancient world and that of to-day.

The influence of the Hebrews has been exerted only in a general way, but the Greeks played a very direct part in laying the foundations of modern music. This they did through the agency of the Romans, who had adopted the Greek system of scales, which in the first centuries of the Christian era exerted a controlling influence on the music of the early Church.

During the decline of the Roman Empire, music, like the other arts, suffered greatly, and almost no progress was made. Indeed what little had been achieved was seriously threatened by the materialistic tendencies of the time. It was at this period (towards the end of the fourth century) that Ambrose, by authorizing for Church use four of the Greek scales and a few traditional melodies, laid the sub-structure on which all subsequent music has been built. His achievements were sufficiently satisfying to hold good for about 200 years, and were capable of producing music of sufficient eloquence to bring about the conversion of St. Augustine.

A further extension of the musical system was introduced by Pope Gregory the Great, who derived four additional scales from those already in use, and introduced some new Church melodies. The music of the Church was now much less indefinite than it had been as regards time values of the notes, and derived the name *cantus planus*, or plain chant, from the regularity of its movement.

By about the end of the ninth century musicians were coming to realize that music had grown too elaborate for the very imperfect notation of the time. This consisted of variously shaped signs called *neumes*, which were only of value as an aid to memory for those who knew their music by heart. By the introduction of first one horizontal line and then others, the actual pitch of more and more notes was definitely shown, and from this gradually developed the five-line stave as we know it.

Necessity also brought about the invention by Franco of Cologne of a set of signs to represent notes of the various time values. These derived their shape from the early neumes, and were in their turn modified till they finally assumed the form of the notes in our modern notation. Music after many centuries of patient waiting was now ready to advance, having found at last that essential thing without which progress was impossible, namely, the power to record musical thoughts on paper, so that all musicians could recreate them exactly. (It is just the absence of any sign of definite schemes of notation, in connection with the music of the early races, which makes it difficult to believe that they had any highly developed art.)

The first step in advance had been taken in the early Middle Ages, when musicians introduced organum or diaphony, which was the first form of harmony. It consisted of parallel versions of the plain song, sung with it at distances of a fourth or fifth, and would sound crude enough to modern ears. A slight improvement was made musically when the transition was gradually brought about from diaphony to descant. This newer and freer style of writing may have arisen in part from the attempts of singers to improvise embroideries to the bald successions of fourths or fifths, and so vary the monotony which as performers they would no doubt strongly feel, though there were not wanting men of insight here and there who boldly advanced the claims of thirds and sixths to be admitted into the company of accepted musical intervals.

Later on, musicians grew bolder still, and devised what were called motets. These were the first attempts at an elaborate musical texture, but the method adopted was rather ingenuous. It consisted of the singing of several tunes at once just as they were, excepting that some slight modifications were generally made when the results were too distressing. It is easy for us of to-day to smile at the crudity of these early attempts at music-making, but an endeavour should be made to place ourselves in the musical world of that time. We would then realize that these attempts were prompted by just such a high curiosity and pioneer daring as actuated Columbus when he set out to sail round the world.

The definite advance of music, after the long period of "marking time," began in Paris in the twelfth century, where, however, little was achieved, probably owing to the unsettled state of the time. About two centuries later England was the leading country in music, and John Dunstable, her leading musician, was regarded as the greatest composer in Europe. Later the supremacy passed to the Netherlands, which held it for a century and a half. Finally it passed to Italy, which witnessed in the wonderful output of Palestrina and many others of several nationalities and almost equal genius the culmination of the great choral epoch. This was in the latter half of the sixteenth century, Palestrina dying in 1594.

In the same year the first opera was produced in Florence. This was the outcome of an attempt on the part of some members of the Florentine nobility, in association with musical enthusiasts, mainly amateur, to revive the style of performance of the ancient Greek dramas. They did not succeed in doing so, but instead achieved something very much greater, something which may fairly be called a musical revolution. Their desire was to find if possible some means of writing music for solo voice with instrumental accompaniment which should be truly dramatic, and not formal in the idiom of the contrapuntal school of composition.

Their early attempts were not anything more than varyingly successful examples of recitative, but they laid the foundations of modern music. They liberated musicians from the all-powerful domination of the great choral epoch by turning their thoughts towards free and direct expression of human aspirations and emotions. This effort towards naturalness in musical expression affected also the sphere of sacred music, and gave rise to oratorio, which, born at the same time and from the same source as opera, has had a very similar story of development.

The new technical requirements of composers included a greater definition of musical phrases, and a more regularly balanced sequence of phrase lengths than had been necessary under the choral dispensation, and in their search for these requirements the Florentine pioneers received invaluable aid from folk-music. The music of the people had been going its own way during the centuries, and had developed to excellent purpose. Free from the restraining influences that surrounded the music of the schools, it knew no laws but those dictated by the instinctive aspirations of its devotees, and under this inspiring guidance had chosen from among the various modes in general use one for special cultivation. The mode so honoured corresponded to our major scale, and the significance of the choice lay in this, that of all the modes it was the one most essential for the era of harmonic development, which was just about to displace the era of counterpoint.

Further, folk-music was either music for folk-dances or was directly descended from it, and in the second case it retained all the elements of rhythmic balance and regularity which are so essential in all dance music. The pioneers of the "Nuove Musiche," as it was called, were therefore very well served indeed by folk-music, and under its steadying influence their somewhat wandering attempts at composition gradually gained definition. This period marks the beginning of modern music, which is therefore directly founded on the music of the people.

From this point onwards the evolution of music made steady progress, and it is possible for the student to trace every step of the way which leads from the folk-dances and folk-songs of the sixteenth century to the symphonic poems of to-day. Some features of this long development will be dealt with in the succeeding sections of this article. For a detailed account recourse must be had to the various standard histories of music.

Theory of Music.—Throughout the history of music theory and practice have been continually at variance. Every great composer has broken the rules which held good in his time, and theory, after a period of vexation and even anger, has toiled panting after to explain it all. The regularity with which this has occurred has given rise to a false idea regarding musical theory which is very widespread, namely, that the study of it tends to cramp and sometimes entirely destroys the artistic individuality of the student. A little reading of musical history would dispel this idea, and show the astonished reader that the great composers were almost without exception hard-working students in this very sphere, and gained from their theoretical studies a confirming and strengthening of their whole musical nature. There is no doubt that the subject has been on the whole badly taught in the past, but the tendency nowadays is towards an increasing use of enlightened methods, which, while teaching the facts of theory, relate them immediately and always to practice.

The student of the rudiments of music is not perhaps in a position to benefit greatly from modern methods of teaching. His subject, with all its intricacies and ramifications, is only the elaborate alphabet of music, and the study of it resolves itself into the acquiring of a definite number of hard facts.

The study of harmony and counterpoint is on a different plane, for actual music-making is here, or should be, the goal of all endeavour. In recent times this is becoming increasingly realized, and the days of exclusive concentration on the working of "figured-basses" are now over. The modern teacher of counterpoint is also shaking off the pedantry which had encrusted the study of this valuable branch of musical knowledge, and is founding his practice more and more, not on the laws of the pedagogues, but on the music of Palestrina, the acknowledged head of the contrapuntal school.

The study of form in music, which has for its object the understanding of the principles of structure as applied to composition, has also been too exclusively concerned in the past with the letter of the law, but the extension of the boundaries of musical form which is always going on has compelled in recent times a little more attention to the spirit, since only by this means could the latest developments be duly accounted for.

In all departments of theoretical study the proper training of the listening faculty, or what is more commonly known as "the ear," is at last being seriously and systematically undertaken, and the power to read music at sight is also being generally cultivated. It is on these two points that theoretical study of music should have been based from the beginning, but the increasing recognition of their vital importance is one of the most hopeful signs for the future.

Choral Music.—It was natural that choral composition should be the first branch of the art to reach maturity. Music as a consciously cultivated thing was in the hands of the Church till almost the close of the sixteenth century, and the voice was the only instrument for music-making that man found ready to his hand. These two facts in combination brought about the great choral era, the early stages of which have been briefly referred to in the opening section of this article.

From the periods of organum and descant progress had been slow but uninterrupted, and about the beginning of the fifteenth century a considerable degree of smoothness of style had been attained by the best composers. The compositions of those days were entirely contrapuntal in their texture, that is, they were wrought by the simultaneous sounding of three or more melodious parts, and the point of view of the composer was entirely horizontal. This was a legitimate development from the time when musicians harnessed together a number of actual melodies without any regard for their powers of mutual agreement, and forced them to run abreast, calling the cacophony which resulted a motet. In the development of this early idea composers contented themselves with selecting one melody only as a basis for their compositions. This they allotted to one of the sections of the choir, generally tenor, expressing it in equal notes of long time-value, and while the tenor "held on" (hence the name) to the long notes of this *cantus firmus*, the other sections of the choir decorated it, both above and below, with melodious embroideries, under the controlling guidance of certain laws of progression. To relate these embroideries to each other by means of imitation, so imparting a family likeness to all of the accompanying parts, was a natural and worthy development of the power to make them graceful and flowing.

Unfortunately the joy of devising imitative phrases soon took complete possession of the minds of composers, and dexterity in the manipulation of musical themes was cultivated for its own sake, particularly in the form of *canons*, which in time reached an absurd degree of complexity at the cost of all that makes music a great art. At the close of this period of arid cleverness music came for the first time into its kingdom, and within a century of that misguided period had found the power to express through the medium of unaccompanied choral music some of the highest and most beautiful thoughts of man. Among the great names associated with this first climax in musical evolution are: Josquin des Près (born about 1450), Orlando di Lasso (1520-94), Palestrina (1525?-94), and Orlando Gibbons (1583-1625).

With the beginning of the harmonic era, which dates from about 1600, the treatment of voices naturally underwent a change in conformity with the new musical outlook. Under the earlier contrapuntal system of composition the various independent melodic parts of the chorus had made harmony among themselves as they moved along together, but the harmonies so created were incidental, not deliberately purposed. In the new era which was just dawning composers were going to write from the harmonic point of view; and any musical interest, which the various parts of the chorus might find allotted to them as individual parts, would be there not from design but rather as a fortunate accident. It must not be thought that there was in this, more than in any other evolutionary process, a clear dividing line between the two periods. In the compositions of the whole of the sixteenth century the approach of the harmonic era is foretold, being manifested with growing clearness as the century advances. Palestrina provides many examples of it, and these not the least beautiful portions of his works, where the voices give up their independence for a time and consent to move in blocks of harmony, such as are found in our hymns and simple part-songs.

Similarly there were many composers in the seventeenth century who remained, from first to last, entirely out of sympathy with the new movement, and showed their loyalty to tradition by writing on in the contrapuntal style. Probably they cherished as their constant companion the hope that the new methods of the musical revolutionaries might come to naught, but the harmonic style was going to remain, and was to be regarded in the fullness of the time as the most important development in the history of the art.

There is no doubt that in giving up the contrapuntal outlook in favour of the harmonic a real artistic sacrifice was made. Under the former system the melody or chief part was placed in an inside voice, and the surrounding parts, while their function was that of accompanists, were nevertheless directly interesting on their own account. Indeed in the earlier works of this school they were often more so than the *cantus firmus*, which was generally laid out in long sustained notes, the precursors of that " row of fat semibreves " which, in its association with the present-day study of strict counterpoint, has aroused the ire of some musicians.

The first effects of writing in the harmonic style were the total abolition of all melodic interest from the inside parts of a composition, and the substitution of dull successions of notes whose sole function was to assist in providing blocks of harmony on which the melody might rest. The melody was now transferred to the top part where it reigned supreme, with the lowest part, as a kind of chief minister, and the inner parts in a state of complete servility. Thus the ideally perfect equality, which existed among the various voices in the best examples of the contrapuntal school, was replaced by a melodic autocracy of the most emphatic kind.

Traces of this undesirable state of things still linger at the present day in the less worthy departments of musical composition, and settings may be found in any of our hymnbooks in which alto or tenor is condemned to sing through an entire tune on only two notes. The glees and earlier part-songs of the English school are also examples, though less terrible, of the dangers of this facile method of writing to the uncritical composer. But the best writers of the seventeenth century, having consolidated the new system of composition, lost no time in improving the quality of their harmonic writing, and learned that the best way to do this was to revert to the methods of the previous school and write contrapuntally, but on a harmonic basis. By so doing, the melody might still remain of first importance, and the harmonic scheme be still the musical support for it, while the underlying parts were redeemed from the dull monotony which had been so characteristic of the first attempts. The possibilities of this combination of harmony and melodic interest of the parts have not even now been exhausted.

As examples of choral compositions in which the contrapuntal element predominates the great fugal choruses of Bach and Handel may be cited, while the harmonizations by Bach of the chorales in his Passion music are wonderful examples of the great beauty and eloquence which may be expressed by purely harmonic methods. Recent composers have sought to extend the range of choral music by increasing the number of parts, and especially by a thoughtful use of the varying tone-qualities that are characteristic of the different registers of the various voices. Among the most successful in this connection may be cited Sir Edward Elgar and Mr. Granville Bantock, who have shown much originality in their choral works. There is also considerable use at the present time of humming effects in choral accompaniment, and the employment of vowel sounds as tonal colour is on the increase. In this manner voices have been introduced in orchestral schemes, as in the *Sirènes* of Debussy.

The Song.—It may safely be assumed that rhythm was the first element of music to be appreciated in the infancy of man, and it is probable that melody, the other essential element, began very early to shape itself out of the inarticulate cries of our prehistoric forbears. A study of the savage races of our own day shows them capable of devising short melodic figures, sometimes of only a few notes, which they are inclined to croon in continuous repetition for a few hours on end, and it is reasonable to suppose that our ancestors in their time did what these are doing now. These early melodic figures were the beginning of song, which is thus the oldest form of music-making. The first occasion on which words were allied to vocal melody is lost in the dimness of the past, but song had existed before that time, and the present dawning tendency to use voices without words would seem to indicate that song may return in the future to its first condition of unalloyed vocal melody. Meantime a definition of song which did not include words as an essential feature would hardly gain acceptance.

The history of the song as it is known to-day may be said to begin with the Troubadours, who date from the latter half of the eleventh century. The tunes composed by them, and the other branches of this great fraternity down to the time of the Minnesingers, are of much value in the history of song, but their musical interest for the people of to-day is mainly historical. There can, however, be no doubt that they influenced and in turn were influenced by the folk-songs of the common people, largely through the instrumentality of the Jongleurs, who were the connecting link between the people and the Troubadours, and the last-named are thereby linked up with the modern " art " song. It is a direct development of the folk-song, which they helped in some degree to bring to its perfect state.

An essential feature of folk-song is the simplicity of the musical means employed. It requires no accompaniment, and the same melody does duty as an expression of the varying sentiments of the different verses of the poem. No doubt folk-songs were as often as not sung to some kind of instrumental accompaniment, and in no way ceased on that account to be folk-songs ; but the first occasion on which an instrumental prelude or a symphony between the verses was introduced as a component part of the song may fairly be taken as the beginning of the evolution of the modern vocal solo.

Very early in the harmonic era composers occupied themselves with the writing of songs, imitating the simplicity of their model by using the same melody for all the verses of the poem. These compositions, the work of trained composers, had, of course, an accompaniment and sometimes interludes that were an essential part of the song. This, the simplest form of the " art " product, may be found frequently in the works of Schubert and Franz and many others. Indeed Schubert's output as a song-writer is remarkable not only as regards quantity and quality, but from the fact that the 600 or more specimens he has left include examples of all kinds of song, many being of the simple nature described above. One of his songs, *Who is Sylvia ?* affords an admirable illustration of the next step in advance. Here there is again a melody which does duty without change for the three verses of the poem, but there are two features that cannot be associated with folk-song. These are, first, the delightful accompaniment, which, while retaining all the simplicity which rightly attaches to a secondary interest, has an importance of its own derived from the independent rhythmic figure in the bass ; second, the interrupting of the course of the melody on two occasions to allow of the interpolation of a short echoing phrase of one bar.

From the time when composers first extended the simple scheme of the folk-song the process of development went steadily on, keeping pace with the developing powers of music itself. The accompaniments became more interesting, the scope and eloquence of the vocal part were extended, and an exact musical counterpart of the poem in all its changes of mood was more and more sought after. The logical outcome of this tendency was the *durchcomponiertes Lied*, or the song composed " right through." Schubert supplied some of the earliest examples of this in such songs as the *Erl King*, and all the best songs of modern times are on the same plan, the present tendency being to seek truth of expression as the first and last essential.

The simple accompaniment has grown to something so intimately associated with the voice part that it is now of equal importance with it, and the true designation of the modern product should be a duet for voice and accompaniment. More recently a further significant advance has been made by scoring the accompaniment for a string quartet or some rarer chamber-music combination in place of the simple piano or organ which had formerly sufficed.

Before leaving the subject of song, mention must be made of the "royalty ballad," which flourishes exceedingly in this country, and furnishes almost the sole musical pabulum of many thousands of people. It is a purely commercial department of our musical activities, and the cause of true music and the artistic welfare of our nation would be better served by its total extinction.

Instrumental.—For the purposes of this article musical composition for instruments may be roughly divided into two great periods, the contrapuntal and the harmonic. This is the same classification that was found convenient in connection with choral music, and the change of style in the instrumental sphere began only slightly later than in the sphere of choral composition. It is interesting to consider the reason for the later appearance in instrumental composition of the harmonic style.

The voice, the only instrument required for unaccompanied choral singing, is also the only instrument which nature has given to man. It has always been a perfect instrument, and the composer has always had an instinctive knowledge of its possibilities, its limitations, and its proper method of treatment in composition. He had therefore no experimental stage through which he must pass before he could acquire certainty of touch in its use. With instruments the case was very different. In the first period of instrumental composition the composer's idiom was contrapuntal, and exactly akin to that of choral music. The instruments themselves were of the kind now only to be found in museums and private collections, comprising the various viols and lutes, and the harpsichord and clavichord, forerunners of the modern pianoforte. So closely did the style of composition for instruments and voices correspond that the common legend on all English publications of the period was "Apt for voices or viols," signifying that the music might equally well be performed in either medium.

With the advent of the harmonic style the position as regards voices was unaltered. By their power of sustaining and varying the tone they could still give to the newer music all the eloquence that it was capable of expressing. But the gentle-toned instruments of the period found their best musical efforts quite ineffective in the absence of that continuous movement and imitative "conversation" of the parts, which was the distinguishing feature of the contrapuntal style. Further, the coming remarkable development in the making of violins was just about due (the great Amati was born in 1596 and Stradivarius and Guarnerius about half a century later), and the transition to the newer class of instruments would further tend to delay the time of adopting the new harmonic style.

But the chief reason for delay was that composers did not know at first how to adapt the harmonic idiom to instrumental requirements. Like every other forward move in the evolution of music, this one of discovering how to make the new style effective in instrumental composition had to be worked out by laborious thought and patient experiment. The idea of the presentation of instrumental harmonies by means of arpeggios and decorative passage-work is so familiar to the present generation that it is difficult to realize that such a seemingly obvious method of procedure had to be discovered. But such was the case.

The overlapping of the old and new methods which has been referred to in connection with choral music was also a feature of the change in the instrumental sphere. The great example of adherence to the contrapuntal methods is J. S. Bach, who, though he lived till 1750 and wrote a large amount of music for keyboard instruments and strings, made only a very limited use of the purely harmonic idiom. The great Italian school of violinists includes followers of both styles. Corelli, who was the first of the school and died in 1713, was a worker in counterpoint, but the many brilliant players who immediately succeeded him, and who were mainly his pupils, belonged for the most part to the new school of composition, and based their creative work on harmonic principles.

Something must now be said regarding the vital part played by these harmonic principles in the development of music. Under the contrapuntal methods of writing music it was not possible to extend the duration of any composition beyond a certain time, which never amounted to more than a few minutes. This was solely because the contrapuntal idiom did not contain within itself the germ of any considerable musical development. This great lack was supplied by giving music a harmonic basis, though it is not probable that the early workers in this new medium could foresee that on this foundation it would be possible in the not distant future to raise such mighty sound-fabrics as the symphonies of Beethoven and the operas of Wagner.

What made such achievements possible was the principle of key relationship. In the melodic methods of the contrapuntal school certain melodic formulæ had been universally accepted as appropriate for use in bringing a phrase or a composition to a close, and in adapting the same principle to the new harmonic conditions a like effect of partial or complete finality was obtained by the use of certain harmonic formulæ called cadences. As a cadence, when presented harmonically, clearly defined the key to which it belonged and excluded all other keys, it was possible by means of it to convey a very definite sense of tonality. Further, by the use at appropriate points of different cadences, it was possible to give the listener a very clear sense of different keys. On this element of key contrast the fabric of modern music has been raised, and the growth and development of the various kinds of musical form made possible.

The simplest application of the principle of key contrast is exemplified by ternary, or three-part form. This consists of an opening section in a certain key, an episode or middle section in a contrasted key, and a third section which gives in the original key a more or less faithful repetition of the opening part. This simple scheme may be seen in its simplest manifestation in many of our folk-songs, and in its most imposing form in all the great overtures, symphonies, and works in chamber music. Everything indeed in modern music will be found to be based on the simple fact of key contrast, and it is the glory of the harmonic period of instrumental development that it has achieved the wonder of the great and ever-satisfying musical forms.

The Orchestra.—It is only in comparatively recent times that the term "full orchestra" has taken on a definite meaning, and suggests to the musical mind a fairly standardized collection of instruments. In the sixteenth century a composer would seem to have employed in his instrumental accompaniments any and every instrument that might be available, and this heterogeneous collection of tone colours was used without any seeming desire to make the best of it. The most important musician of that epoch, so far as the modern orchestra is concerned, was Monteverde, who, by greatly increasing the number of stringed instruments played with a bow, made the first step of real advance. The string department of the orchestra, which he thus brought into being, still to-day supplies the foundation tone.

In the time of Bach and Handel not a great deal of progress had been made. The writing for instruments was naturally much more mature, but there was no sign of any desire to use the tone colours with sensitive artistry. The ideas of suitable orchestration got no further than the general use of the string band for practically all purposes, and the application of colour by the addition to the score of an oboe d'amore or a flute, which seldom had anything distinctive or characteristic to play, but rather followed the first violin part in the most slavish fashion. For full effects and massive choral accompaniments trumpets and drums would be used, and in the orchestra of Handel's day the tutti would include large masses of oboes and bassoons, the former being sometimes as numerous as the first violins.

With the beginnings of the symphony a change came, and the possibilities of artistic instrumental combination and subtlety of tone-colour effects began to dawn on the minds of composers. Haydn and Mozart were among the first to use the forces of the orchestra on the lines to which the audiences of to-day are accustomed, treating the wind instruments, for example, with an independence and an appreciation of their tonal qualities that was quite new. The clarinets were introduced to the orchestra by them but were only used occasionally. Since their day every great composer has added to the orchestral resources till the full modern orchestra has become so large as to be almost overgrown.

A natural reaction from this situation is evident in the tendency to write for orchestra on chamber-music lines, getting effects, not so much by a massed use of the instruments, as by a more sparing and more subtle arrangement of the colour scheme. The earliest example of this manner of writing for orchestra was provided by Wagner in his *Siegfried Idyll*, and the present movement in emulation of its delicate beauties is one that seems to hold promise for the future.

In recent years Jazz Music, introduced from America in 1924, has had an almost universal vogue in this country. It is based on negro rythms, and its most unvarying feature is syncopation emphasised by noisy percussive effects. For its full expression it has required an elaborate modification of the orchestra and its instruments ("jazz band"), and an equally elaborate modification of the principles of orchestral scoring. It is, in fact, the response to the modern demand for a stronger and cruder stimulus than the more classical forms can supply. Its tendency, unfortunately, is to spoil the palate for the finer vintages. Among the more ambitious composers of jazz music are George Gershwin (*Lady, be Good, Tell Me More,* etc.), Arnost Krenek, the Czecho-Slovakian composer, and Constant Lambert.—BIBLIOGRAPHY: *Grove's Dictionary of Music and Musicians*; *Oxford History of Music*; C. H. Parry, *The Evolution of the Art of Music, Studies of Great Composers*; E. Walker, *History of Music in England* (1907).

MUSIC AS A CAREER. Though an overcrowded profession, music, which now comprises so many branches, still offers considerable scope for performers and teachers of real talent and personality. Success in either capacity, however, is by no means easy to achieve, and requires many years of training.

Orchestral players for broadcasting theatres, cinemas, dancing, etc., should be steadily in demand, and have fixed rates of pay. Organists, with city or cinema appointments, may obtain as much as £500 per annum, and whole-time cathedral posts are worth about £300-£500 with a house, as well as allowing opportunity for pupils to be taken.

The Royal Academy of Music and the Royal College of Music in London are the most famous centres of study for all branches of the profession, the fees being fourteen guineas a term at the former and twelve at the latter. Other well-known training schools are the Royal Manchester College of Music, the Guildhall School, Trinity College, and London Academy of Music.

For MUSIC TEACHERS, courses are provided at the Royal Academy of Music, York Gate, Marylebone Road, N.W.1.; the Royal College of Music, Exhibition Road, South Kensington; Trinity College of Music, Mandeville Place, W.1; and the Guildhall School of Music, John Carpenter Street, E.C.4. Courses are also provided at certain reputable institutions in the provinces.

MUSK. A substance used in perfumery and medicine, and obtained from several species of deer. (*See* MUSK-DEER.) A perfume of similar character is also obtained from one or two other animals (*see* MUSK-RAT); and various animals and plants are noted for emitting a strong musky smell.

MUSK-DEER. A genus of deer, forming the type of a sub-family (Moschinæ) of the Cervidæ, or deer family. Their chief habitat is Asia and the islands of the Eastern Archipelago, though one species is found on the west coast of Africa.

Musk-Deer (*Moschus moschiferus*)

The typical species of the family is the *Moschus moschiferus*, found chiefly in the elevated tablelands of Central Asia, and particularly of Tibet. These animals attain the size of a young roe deer, and the upper jaw bears prominent canine teeth. The males alone yield the *musk*, which is secreted by an abdominal gland of about the size of a hen's egg. The Tibet musk is most in repute, that known as Russian or Siberian being inferior in quality. Besides its familiar use as a scent, musk is employed medicinally as an antispasmodic.

MUSK-DUCK. A species of duck, often erroneously called the Muscovy-

Musk Duck

duck (*Cairina moschāta*), a native of America, but now domesticated in Britain. It has a musky smell, and is larger and more prolific than the common duck.

MUSKE'GON. A city of Michigan, United States, county seat of Muskegon county, on the Muskegon Lake; served by the Père Marquette and Grand Trunk Railways, and by lake steamers. There is a good harbour; lumber and fruit are exported. Manufactures include pianos, refrigerators, and furniture. Muskegon was settled in 1834, incorporated in 1861, and became a city in 1870. Pop. (1930), 41,390.

MUSKET. A hand-gun with which infantry soldiers were formerly armed. When first introduced, early in the sixteenth century, as a development of the culverin and arquebus, it was discharged by means of a lighted match (hence the name *matchlock* given to it), and was so heavy that it had to be laid across a staff or *rest* to be fired. To make use of it the soldier required to carry a slow-burning match with him, which was apt to be extinguished in wet weather. The wheel-lock followed (sixteenth century), the chief feature of which was a wheel made to revolve by means of a spring, and to cause sparks by friction against a flint. The next improvement was the flint-lock proper (about 1625), in which sparks were produced by the impact of a piece of flint on the steel above the priming powder.

Musketeers were soon introduced into all armies, and in the beginning of the seventeenth century infantry consisted of pikemen and musketeers, and all changes in regard to the relative proportion of the two arms were always in favour of the latter. The flint-lock musket was introduced into the British army towards the end of the seventeenth century, and was the British musket of the days of the Peninsular War and Waterloo, known familiarly as "Brown Bess." It was superseded by the percussion musket in 1842, this musket being in turn superseded by the rifle. *See* RIFLE.

MUSKETRY.—A term used to describe all forms of training and practice in the mechanism, care, theory, and practical use of all military small-arms. Time was when the whole art of musketry began and ended in the ability of the soldier to load and fire his piece without damage to himself and with problematical danger to his enemy, and in those days, when drill (q.v.) was everything and practical training—in view of the nature and conditions of war—a secondary considerations, and when, moreover, eighteen separate motions were considered necessary before a musket could be fired, this standard would appear to have met the case.

It is, however, of some interest to note that as far back as the first few years of the nineteenth century, and many years before musketry *per se* received any recognition, the author of a military drill-book in very general use comments on the entire absence of instruction in these words. Under the heading of "Firings," to which he dedicates only ten pages out of a total of 250, he says: "There is no doubt, too, that the fire of the musketry may be reduced to a theory; but far from that being the case, the soldier has no principle given him, for, let the distance or situation be what they may, he fires at random. It is principally owing to the exercise of the target being so little practised that this ignorance and deficiency of principle is so severely felt." Admirable sentiments, no doubt, but it was many years before they were recognized to any extent. When the art of musketry did at last begin to be practised, it was at best a perfunctory sort of performance, and at one period if a soldier could even hit the target—a large one—he was allowed to go home, and was not required to fire again till the following year.

Then, following the improvement in fire-arms, considerable interest began to be taken in target shooting, i.e. firing at a large square iron target painted white with a black bull's-eye. Up to about the time of the South African War this was the principal item of musketry training; there were, indeed, practices dignified by the name of "field" practices, but they took place either on the range from measured firing-points, or on some convenient area of country, the one and only idea being to get as many hits as possible, the targets being of a suitable size and shape to ensure this. In short, the aim of all musketry training was to make the soldier a good individual shot at known distances, under easy conditions, and with ample time allowed for each shot; when combined fire effect was thought of at all, it was considered sufficient if a section of twenty men could fire a volley at the command of their leader, by far the greater importance being laid on the simultaneous discharge of the rifles than on the question as to whether the rifles were being aimed at the desired mark, or even whether the individual knew what he was expected to fire at.

Now all this is altered, and musketry does not mean merely the ability to make "bull's-eyes" at 800 yards or "possibles" at 500 yards; in fact the regulations go so far as to point out in quite unmistakable language that the one aim and object of rifle shooting is not "pot-hunting." Instead, "The purpose of musketry training is to render the individual soldier proficient in the use of small-arms, to make him acquainted with the capabilities of the weapon with which he is armed, and to give him confidence in its power and accuracy; and to qualify officers and non-commissioned officers to direct and control fire under service conditions."

These requirements are met by a system of gradual training throughout a soldier's service, particular stress being laid on the necessity of combining musketry training with other tactical exercises, and this perhaps will best be explained by a brief description of the training favoured by the British army. This course is divided into two separate and distinct portions, the first known as the Recruits' Course, and the second as the Trained Soldiers' Course.

As the name implies, the Recruits' Course is an elementary one, in which the young soldier is given a thorough grounding in the use of the rifle, its mechanism, and the names and uses of its various component parts. He is then given instruction on the important matter of how to look after and keep in good working order the weapon on which some day he may have to depend for his own life and the lives of his comrades. Having been taught these preliminaries in a very thorough manner, he is then taken on to the elements of the "theory of rifle fire," and given practical instruction in aiming and firing a rifle without ammunition. During this period he is shown at intervals how to improve his power of perception of objects at a distance, how to recognize objects described by his immediate commander, and how to determine by eye the distance of such various objects. Then, after some preliminary practice on miniature ranges (with the miniature rifle) and on 30-yard ranges (with special ammunition), both being designed to accustom him in some measure to the discharge of the rifle, he is given his first introduction to the open rifle-range, where he fires with service ammunition, and at ranges varying from 100 to 600 yards.

The normal amount of ammunition to be expended on the range by a recruit is 200 rounds, but, as it is very necessary to give a young soldier a thorough grounding in this most important part of his training, additional ammunition is allowed to permit of certain instructional practices being repeated till a satisfactory standard is reached. Targets used in this course are either a 4-foot square white target with an 8-inch bull's-eye, known as an elementary target, or a figure target 4 or 6 feet square covered with two neutral shades of paper, on which is applied a small figure 12 or 18 inches high, made of brown paper. From this description it may be seen that in the earlier stages of the course the recruit has a well-defined mark to aim at in the black bull's-eye on a white ground, while, as the course progresses, he is given the same or even a larger-sized target, but of a much less distinct nature.

It is impossible in the scope of this article to enter into any great detail on each separate item of a soldier's training, but a brief explanation of the different kinds of range practices fired by a recruit will show how detailed is this training. The course is divided into six parts, four of which are termed instructional, while the remaining two consist of individual and collective field practices.

In the instructional parts the soldier fires certain practices known as "grouping," which are intended to discover faults either in rifle or man; with this end in view the whole series of shots is fired with exactly the same sighting and aiming-point, and the result is not known till the last shot has been fired. Other practices are known as "application," and in these the result of each shot is signalled, and the soldier corrects or alters his sighting or aim as necessary. All "grouping" and some "application" are fired at bull's-eye targets, but most of the "application" practice and all "rapid" and "snap-shooting" ones which follow are fired at figure targets as above. As for the position of the firer, lying, either with or without a rest, is the normal one, though a few practices are fired kneeling behind cover. In "field practices" the soldier is able to apply the knowledge he has gained on the range by firing at targets arranged to represent to some extent what he *might* see in war.

Having satisfactorily completed this course, the soldier ceases to be a "recruit" and becomes a "trained soldier," and for the rest of his service will fire annually a more elaborate and more searching course, designed to keep up his musketry sense and to fit him to pull his weight as one member of a fire unit in war

In musketry, as in many other crafts, an ounce of practice is worth a pound of theory, yet a considerable knowledge of elementary theory is, as has already been said, expected of the soldier. "A knowledge of the theory of rifle fire is of great importance . . . but it is of equal importance that such knowledge should be correctly applied."

Theory—sufficient for the purpose—is taught to the recruit by means of short lectures and explanations, by diagrams, by practical demonstrations when such are possible, or by mechanical means. The instruction begins by the young soldier being given various definitions relating to rifle fire which are necessary for his purpose. Among such are: "lines of fire—a line joining the muzzle of the rifle and the target," "line of sight—a line passing through the sights and the point aimed at," "trajectory—the path the bullet takes on its journey from the muzzle to the target." Then, in order to explain why these do not all mean the same thing, a description of the forces which act on the bullet (q.v.), leading to a dissertation on "elevation" and "sighting," has to be given.

The recruit thus learns why somewhat complicated sights are fixed on to his rifle, what would happen if the rifle were fired without their aid, and the why and the wherefore of the continual practice in adjusting his sights which he receives daily, and which on a cold morning he finds most unpleasant. Then, later on, the effect of winds on a bullet is dealt with, and the reasons for alteration of aim in order to counteract it deduced, and the influence of ground in relation to fire-effect dealt with.

In conclusion it should clearly be understood that the mere outline of a soldier's musketry training given above is simply a means to an end. In the words of the Regulations ". . . the soldier should attain a high standard of skill in shooting at known distances, under easy conditions and in various positions . . . he should have confirmed in practice the lessons learned in preliminary training, and be thoroughly acquainted with the peculiarities of his rifle . . . he has fired in the open and from behind cover . . . and should have learned the rate of fire which in his own case best combines volume with accuracy . . . he has been brought to realize the necessity for rapid alignment of sights and the value of time in taking advantage of targets exposed under service conditions. . . . Range practices are in no sense a final training, and it is essential that further practice should take place under service conditions."

This further practice takes the form of the already-mentioned "field practices," which, fired off the usual rifle ranges on any ground which can be made available, are carried out in as near an approximation to active-service conditions as may be. Field practices are both "individual" and "collective." In the former, which are fired at ranges under 600 yards, men work in pairs, a target of sorts being provided for each; while one man fires the other assists by observing the effect of the shot. "Collective field practices," on the other hand, are carried out by "fire units" or sections acting under the orders of the commander, and, this being so, "the value of the fire will depend almost entirely on his ability to apply the fire to the target." In other words, the efficiency of the section or fire unit commander is, in this form of firing, of the utmost importance.

Collective firing means firing with others at a probably ill-defined mark selected and described by a commander, who at the same time observes (if he can) the results of the fire and modifies his orders accordingly. Unless, therefore, the section commander is well trained in giving clear and concise orders, in describing the required aiming-point unmistakably, in estimating the range, and in controlling and regulating the rate and volume of fire under the conditions of active service, the collective fire of his section will be little better than a waste of ammunition. All this is no doubt somewhat in the nature of a child's demand for the moon, as active service conditions are not and never can be comparable with those of peacetime "field practices"; yet, on the principle that "Rome was not built in a day," the army goes on with its musketry training in the certain knowledge that some at least of the principles inculcated in peacetime will hold good when tried in the furnace of war. In any case, we have advanced far beyond the ideals contemplated by the old writer whose words are quoted at the beginning of this article. *See* FIRE TACTICS. Cf. *Musketry Regulations, Part I. and Part II.*

MUSK-MALLOW (*Malva moschāta*). A British perennial plant, so named from the peculiar musky odour thrown off by all parts of the plant.

MUSK-OX (*Ovibos moschātus*). An animal intermediate between the ox and sheep. Resembling in general appearance a large goat-like sheep, its body is covered with a coat of tufted hair, brownish in colour and of great length. The hair about the neck and shoulders is so thick as to give the animal a "humped" appearance; on the rest of the body it is very long, smooth, and flowing, while interspersed among its fibres is a layer of lighter-coloured wool.

The musk-ox is active and agile, and climbs mountainous places with ease and dexterity. The horns, broad at the base and covering the forehead and crown, curve downwards between the eye and the ear, and then upwards and slightly backwards. The horns of the female are smaller than those of the male, and their bases do not touch. The ears are short, the head large and broad, the muzzle blunted. The average size of the male is that of a small domestic ox. Gregarious in habits, each herd numbers from twenty to thirty members. The female brings forth one calf in May or June. The food consists of grass, lichens, etc.

Musk-Ox (*Ovibos moschātus*)

The musk-ox inhabits the Arctic regions of America north of the 60th degree of latitude. The flesh is pleasant to the taste, though it smells strongly of musk, the odour of which is also diffused from the living animal.

MUSK-PLANT. A little yellow-flowered musky-smelling plant of the genus Mimulus (*M. moschātus*), a native of Oregon, but now a common garden plant in Britain.

MUSK-RAT (*Fiber zibethicus*). An American rodent allied to the beaver, and the only known species of the genus. It is about the size of a small rabbit, and has a flattened lanceolate tail, covered with small scales and a few scattered hairs. Its toes are separate, and provided with a stiff fringe of hair. In summer it has a smell of musk, which it loses in winter. The odour is due to a whitish fluid deposited in certain glands near the origin of the tail. Of considerable commercial importance on account of its fur, the musk-rat, or *musquash*, as it is popularly called in America, from its Indian name, is taken in large quantities, the skins of from 400,000 to 500,000 being annually imported into Britain. Very common in

Musk-Rat

North America, the musk-rat lives along the margins of streams, in the banks of which it makes its nest.

The musk-rats of Europe, or desmans (*Myogălē moschāta* and *M. pyrenaica*), are aquatic insectivorous animals allied to the shrews and moles, having a long flexible nose, and a double row of glands near the tail secreting a substance of a strong musky smell; found in Southern Russia and the Pyrenees. The musk-shrews (Crœidura) comprise about eighty species inhabiting South and Central Europe, Africa, and South Asia.

MUSK TREE, or MUSK WOOD. The names of trees and wood that smell strongly of musk. The musk wood of Guiana and the West Indies is *Guarea trichilioides*; the musk tree of Tasmania, *Eurybia argyrophylla.*

MUSLIN. A fine thin fabric, usually made from cotton yarns, but occasionally made from silk or worsted yarns; it is supposed to have been first made at Mosul or Moussul (whence the name), afterwards in India (Madras muslin), and first imported into England about 1670. About twenty years afterwards it was manufactured in considerable quantities both in France and Britain, and there are now many different kinds made, as *book, mull, jaconet, leno, foundation,* etc. The chief centre of manufacture in this country is Glasgow.

These fabrics are extensively used for window decoration, and compete, more or less successfully, with lace curtains. Some Indian muslins, e.g. Dacca muslin, are of extraordinary fineness, and attempts to rival them are very rare. Figured muslins are now very common, and were probably first made to imitate *tamboured* muslins, or muslins embroidered by hand. Lappet fabrics are somewhat similar in structure to muslins, but are made in an entirely different loom. Moreover, they are not so elaborately figured as the modern muslin curtains.

MUSSEL. A term popularly given to several bivalve molluscs, section Asiphonida, or those in which "siphons," or tubes admitting water to the gills, are absent. The common mussel (*Mytĭlus edūlis*) forms a typical example of the family Mytilidæ, the shells of which family are equivalve, and have a hinge destitute of teeth. It has a "byssus" or "beard," by means of which the mussels attach themselves to fixed objects. The mussel is extensively employed in Scotland by deep-sea fishermen as bait; and in some districts it is used as an article of food, the best mussels approaching nearly to the oyster in flavour, though occasionally found to be unwholesome. It is cultivated as an article of diet on the European continent, the "mussel-farms" of the Bay of Aiguillon, near Rochelle in France, forming the most notable example.

Species.—The family Unionidæ includes the freshwater or river mussels (Unio) and the swan or pond mussels (Anodonta). The Unionidæ inhabit fresh water exclusively. The pond mussels, of which many species are known, are found in the rivers and lakes both of Europe and America. The hinges of the shell in the genus Anodon are destitute of teeth, in the genus Unio toothed. The *Unio pictorum* is a familiar species. The *Unio margaritifĕrus*, or pearl-mussel, has attained a reputation from the fact that it has yielded pearls of considerable value in the Don, Tay, Doon, Forth, Spey, and other British streams.

MUSSELBURGH. A municipal police burgh of Scotland, in Midlothian, 5¾ miles east of Edinburgh by the L.N.E. Railway; on the Firth of Forth, at the mouth of the Esk, which divides it into two parts, ancient Musselburgh and Fisherrow. It has a bridge, believed to be of Roman erection; and a curious old tolbooth. Here is Loretto School There is a race-course and annual race-meetings, golf-links, and some sea-bathing. Fishing is the principal industry. The battle of Pinkie (1547) was fought in the vicinity. Pop. (1931), 16,996.

MUSSET (mu-sā), **Louis Charles Alfred de.** French poet, novelist, and dramatist, born at Paris in 1810, died there in 1857. After trying various professions he gave himself up wholly to literature, and in 1829 published a volume of poems called *Contes d'Espagne et d'Italie*, which had an immediate and striking success. In 1831 appeared *Poésies diverses*, and in 1833 *Un spectacle dans un fauteuil*, in which the two chief pieces are a comedy of a light and delicate grace called *A quoi rêvent les jeunes filles*, and a poem entitled *Namouna*, written after the manner of Byron. In 1833 he travelled in George Sand's (Amandine Dudevant) company, but their intimacy soon came to an end.

In 1836 was published his *Confession d'un enfant du siècle*, a gloomy novel, containing the analysis of a diseased state of mind, all the phases of which the author had studied in himself. The same settled melancholy also distingusihes his *Rolla*, *Une bonne fortune*, *Lucie*, *Les Nuits*, *Une Lettre à Lamartine*, *Stances à Madame Malibran*, *L'Espoir en Dieu*, and other poems. Among his light and sparkling dramatic pieces are: *On ne badine pas avec l'amour*, *Les Caprices de Marianne*, *Il ne faut pas jurer de rien*, etc.

In 1848 Musset was deprived by the Revolution of the situation of librarian to the Ministry of the Interior, a sinecure which he had obtained through the favour of the duc d'Orléans; but he was restored to this post under the Empire, and was in addition appointed reader to the empress. In 1852 he was admitted a member of the French Academy.

De Musset was one of the most distinctive, and, in a certain sense, original of modern French writers. At a time when the battle between the Classicists and Romanticists was at its height he took sides with neither, but made for himself a style combining the excellences of the two schools. His elder brother Paul was also a writer of some ability, but always overshadowed by the brilliance of Louis.—Cf. E. Dowden, *Studies in Literature*.

MUSSOLINI, Benito. Italian statesman. Born at Varano di Costa, Dovia, in the province of Forli, 29th July, 1883. The son of a Socialist blacksmith, he attended an elementary school, and later a boarding-school at Faenza, and gained a teacher's certificate at Forlimpopoli, after which he taught for a year at Gualteri, Reggio Emilia. He went to Switzerland in 1902, and while doing manual abour, studied French at Lausanne University, read widely, made speeches, organized unions and strikes, and was expelled from one canton after another.

In 1905 he carried out his military service with the Bersaglieri. He became secretary of the Socialist Society at Trento in 1908, and joined the staff of the local Socialist paper, *L'Avvenire*, but later went over to the *Popolo*, in which his

Benito Mussolini

Irredentist writings attracted the attention of the Austrian authorities, and led to his expulsion from the country. On his return to Italy, he became an active force in the Socialist movement. He founded the weekly paper, *La Lotta di Classe*, in 1910 at Forli, and was imprisoned for his articles. In 1912 he became editor of the Milan Socialist paper, *Avanti*, from which he resigned after the outbreak of the war in 1914. When the war broke out he supported Italy's announcement of her intention to remain neutral, but as the sentiment in favour of her intervention grew he identified himself with it, and founded *Il Popolo d'Italia*. When Italy entered the war in 1915, he was called up for military service as a private soldier in the Bersaglieri. He fought in the trenches until 22nd Feb. 1917, when he was seriously wounded by the explosion of a mortar.

The following September he again became editor of *Il Popolo*, now preaching against pacifism and Socialism. He was, in fact, at that time more in sympathy with the Italian syndicalists than with the Socialists, and gave a qualified support to the seizure of the factories by the workpeople at the end of 1920. Not until the Communists gained control of this movement did he convert the organisation he created, Fascio di Combattimento (esttablished in Milan on 23rd March 1919) into the centre of the anti-communist reaction. (*See* FASCISM.)

Mussolini's policy, at that stage, was directed mainly against the older political parties. His organisation entered politics in the general election of May, 1921, when he and thirty-seven other Fascist candidates were returned, and in November of that year, the Fascists were reorganised as a political party. At first his aim was a coalition with other parties, and he even offered co-operation with his former friends, the Socialists, now his bitter enemies. But by the middle of 1922 he felt himself strong enough to make a bid for the Government himself, and in the late autumn of that year he organised the march of the Fascists on Rome, which led to the downfall of the Facta Government. Mussolini frustrated the attempt to form a coalition government under Salandra by refusing his co-operation, and thereupon the King gave Mussolini the commission to form a government himself.

His government was from its inception a personal dictatorship. In the course of the first few months, beginning with the portfolios of Foreign Affairs and the Interior he concentrated most of the government departments in his own hands. Gradually he built up a new State system by the creation of National Corporations. In this Corporative State his personal will, as head of the State, is the final authority.

No less remarkable was his achievement in 1929 of the treaty which finally settled the Roman Question.

Mussolini's foreign policy has been directed to maintaining the influence of Italy in the Mediterranean and strengthening her position as a European power. In 1924 he negotiated a settlement with Yugoslavia in which the Italian claim to Fiume was recognized. In 1926 he placed Italian relations with Greece on a friendly footing, and vigorously supported the independence of Albania. Italian influence in North Africa has also been maintained. Mussolini's policy with regard to disarmament, reparations, and war debts has been in harmony with that of England. He has consistently advocated disarmament by stages. In respect of reparations, he has urged the cancellation of war debts as a necessary preliminary to the economic restoration of Europe.

The use in Germany of a similar movement to Fascism in Italy has given Mussolini a considerable increase of influence in European politics and diplomacy. Between Hitler (q.v.) and him there are many points of difference on matters of policy; but Mussolini was adroit enough in the early days of Hitlerism to make the European statesmen's fears of the new German Nationalism, and the deadlock on the question of Disarmament at the Geneva Conference, the basis for his project of the Four-Power Pact, which represents his first important essay in international diplomacy.

MUSSOO'REE. A hill station in Dehra Dun district, United Provinces of India, in a picturesque situation among the Himalaya at the height of 7533 feet. Summer pop. about 12,000.

MUSTARD. The common name of plants of the genus Sinăpis, nat. ord. Cruciferæ. The seeds of the *S. alba* and *S. nigra* (white and common mustard), when ground and freed from husks, form the well-known condiment of the shops. The plant is an annual, with stems 3 to 4 feet in height, lower leaves lyrate, upper lanceolate and entire, flowers small and yellow. The preparation from the seeds, when mixed with warm water and taken in large quantities, acts as an emetic. The tender leaves are used as a salad, and the seeds of *S. nigra* are used in the well-known form of poultice, being applied to various parts of the skin as a rubefacient. *Wild mustard* or *charlock* (*S. arvensis*) is a troublesome weed in cornfields, often making them yellow with its flowers. Its seeds are said to have yielded the first Durham mustard, and they are still gathered to mix with those of the cultivated species.—*Oil of mustard* is an essential oil obtained from the seeds of *S. nigra.* It is very pungent to the taste and smell, and when applied to the skin speedily raises a blister.

MUTINY. Resistance by soldiers or sailors to the authority of their officers. In the British army it was formerly dealt with under the Mutiny Act, which was passed annually up to 1879, but has since 1881 been superseded by the Army Act. Joining in, inciting to, or conniving at mutiny is punishable with death, whether the troops are on active service or not; on active service the same sentence may follow treachery or cowardice, deserting a post, etc. Special Reserve and Territorial troops are subject to the Mutiny Act. The government of the Royal Navy is regulated by an Act of 1866, which contains an enumeration of nearly every possible offence, and annexes a certain punishment.

MUTTRA. A town of the Agra division, United Provinces, India, on the Jumna, and an important railway junction. It is an old Hindu city, one of the most artistic and interesting in India, being regarded as the birthplace of Krishna. Pop. 52,840.—The Muttra district has an area of 1450 sq. miles; pop. 765,000.

MUZAFFARGARH. A town of India, in the Multan division of the Punjab, on the Chenab, around a fort built by Nawab Muzaffar Khan. Pop. 4500.—The district has an area of 3422 sq. miles; pop. about 405,600.

MUZAFFARNAGAR. A district of India, in the Meerut division of the United Provinces. Area, 1700 sq. miles; pop. 800,000. The capital is Muzaffarnagar, founded by Muzaffar Khan, about 1633. It has railway connections with Meerut and Delhi. Pop. 23,937.

MUZAFFARPUR. A district of India in the Girhut division of Bihar and Orissa. Area, 3000 sq. miles; pop. 3,000,000. The capital is Muzaffarpur on a former bed of the Little Gandhak River, a centre of the indigo industry, and a divisional headquarters. Pop. 32,755..

MWANZA. A province of Tanganyika Territory, East Africa, lying around Lake Victoria and between Kenya Colony and Bukoba, with the boundary line passing through Lake Eyasi. Mwanza, a wireless station and port on Lake Victoria, is the administrative centre. It was captured by General Crewe and a British force advancing on Tabora on 14th July, 1916 (European War). Pop. of town, 4000.

MWERU. A lake of Central Africa, on the Belgian Congo-Northern Rhodesian frontier, fed by the Luapula River. The Mweru Marsh is a big game preserve and elephant breeding-ground. Mweru was discovered by Livingstone (1867), and was formerly of much greater extent. Length, about 68 miles; average breadth, 24 miles.

MYCE'LIUM. The name given to the characteristic thallus of Fungi. It consists of whitish, richly branched filaments (hyphæ) which spread like a network through the substances on which the Fungi grow. *See* FUNGI.

MYCE'NÆ. An ancient city of Argolis, in the Peloponnesus. It is said to have been founded by Perseus, and before the Trojan War to have been the residence of Agamemnon, in whose reign it was regarded as the leading city in Greece. Its ruins are extremely interesting from their antiquity and grandeur.

Remains at Mycenæ

They were investigated by French archæologists in 1822. Among them are the Lion Gate, and the vaulted building of enormous stones called the *Treasury of Atreus*, etc. In 1876 Schliemann carried out excavations here with valuable and interesting results. The researches were continued by the Greek Archæological Society. New researches were made at Mycenæ in 1920.

MYCORHIZA. A peculiar state of coalition between a fungus and one of the Higher Plants, in which both parties derive benefit from the association. It is commonest among the Flowering Plants. All the so-called saprophytic Angiosperms are of this type (e.g. bird's nest orchid), but also many others, such as heather, orchids generally, Scots pine, oak, and many other forest trees.—Cf. F. O. Bower, *Botany of the Living Plant* (chap. xi.).

MYELI'TIS. An inflammation of the spinal cord. The disease may take several forms, but the most common is acute transverse myelitis. This is usually syphilitic in origin. The onset is characterized by numbness and tingling of the feet and legs, followed by loss of power, while sensation is soon lost and retention of urine appears. The skin becomes dry, and as the condition advances bed-sores develop. The limbs are at first flaccid, but afterwards become rigid.

MYELITIS. In cattle, inflammation of the spinal cord. The disease comes from a variety of causes, and generally results in paralysis. Symptoms include an unsteady gait, coldness of the affected limbs, convulsions perhaps at first, and tenderness along the spine.

The treatment includes bleeding and purging, 1 oz. of chloral hydrate being administered with the purgative, and the dose repeated if necessary. A counter-irritant, such as turpentine and oil, along the spine has a good effect after a day or so. Some unpromising cases frequently recover, and slaughter should only be resorted to as a last resource. Subjects that are unable to rise should occasionally be turned over and given a dry bed.

MYG'ALĒ. A genus of spiders, the type of the family Mygalidæ, furnished with four lung sacs and spiracles, four spinnerets, eight eyes, and hairy legs. Their nests, constructed of silk, are built in clefts of rock, trees, etc., and in the ground. The bird-catching spider of Surinam belongs to this species; other larger species frequently prey on small vertebrate animals, not by laying snares for them, but by regularly hunting them. They envelop their eggs in a kind of cocoon.

MYLAB'RIS. A genus of beetles nearly allied to the Cantharides (q.v.), noteworthy because of the use made of some species as a blister-fly.

MY'LODON. A genus of extinct edentate Mammalia, allied to and ancestor of Megatherium. Its remains have been found in the Miocene, Pliocene, and Pleistocene strata of South America. *Mylodon robustus*—the most familiar species—attained a length in some instances of 11 feet. Of terrestrial habits, Mylodon obtained the vegetable food upon which it subsisted chiefly by uprooting trees. Mylodon reached North America in Pleistocene times.

MYOGALE. *See* MUSK-RAT.

MYOSO'TIS. A genus of plants belonging to the Boraginaceæ, and comprising numerous European and Northern Asiatic, a few North American, and three or four Australian species. The *M. palustris* is the well-known forget-me-not. Other species are popularly known as scorpion-grass.

MYRIAP'ODA (Gr. *myrioi*, ten thousand, and *pous*, *podos*, foot), the lowest class of the higher annulose or arthropodous animals, represented by the centipedes, millepedes, and their allies, and resembling the Annelids in the lengthened form and the numerous segments of the body, each segment being provided with one or two pairs of ambulatory feet, whence the name. They have a distinct head, but no division of the body into thorax and abdomen, as in insects. They are therefore of a lower structural type than insects, which in general organization they resemble. No wings are developed. They respire through minute spiracles or pores along the whole length of the body, and are invested with a hard chitinous or horny covering or exoskeleton.

This class is divided into two orders, the Chilognatha or Diplopoda, in which the fusion of two rings gives apparently two pairs of feet on each ring; and the Chilopoda, which have two pairs of foot-jaws or maxillipeds, and not more than one pair of feet on each segment.

MYRICA. A genus of apetalous Dicotyledons, forming the ord. Myricaceæ, allied to the walnuts. They are shrubs with glandular aromatic foliage, natives of temperate regions and tropical mountains. *M. Gale* is the sweet gale, common in the Scottish Highlands; *M. cerifera* is the candleberry.

MYRIS'TICA. The only genus of the nat. ord. Myristicaceæ. *M. fragrans*, a native of the Moluccas, yields the nutmeg of the shops.

MYRMECOPHILOUS PLANTS. Those which have ants living permanently on them in preformed cavities of the stem or leaf; usually nutriment in the shape of special glands (food-bodies) or extra-floral nectaries is provided as well as lodging. In return for these benefits the ants are believed to afford protection against leaf-cutting ants, browsing animals, etc., but the evidence for this is not conclusive in many cases. *See* BULL'S HORN THORN; CECROPIA; CLERODENDRON.

MYR'MIDONS. An ancient Greek people of Thessaly, who accompanied Achilles to the Trojan War. They are said to have emigrated into Thessaly under the leadership of Peleus. The term has come to signify the followers of a daring and unscrupulous leader, or the harsh and unfeeling agents of a tyrannical power.

MYROBALAN (mī-rob'a-lan). A dried fruit of various species of trees, brought from the East Indies, all slightly purgative and astringent. Myrobalans are used by the Hindus in calico-printing and medicine, and are imported into Britain for dyers and tanners, especially the latter. They are the produce of several species of Terminalia (ord. Combretaceæ), the chief of which are the belleric myrobalan (*T. Bellerica*) and the chebulic (*T. Chebulica*).

MY'RON. One of the chief sculptors of the older Attic school, who flourished in the middle of the fifth century B.C. He excelled in the representation of action, and was famous as a sculptor of animals. No examples from his own hand have survived, but the Lancelotti *Discobolus* (or Disc-thrower) at Rome, and the small bronze *Marsyas* in the British Museum, are accepted as antique copies of his work. In his manner are the *Idolino*, at Florence, and the bust of *Pericles*, in the British Museum. *See* SCULPTURE.

MYRRH. The name given to a gum resin which exudes from a shrub growing in Arabia and Abyssinia, called *Balsamodendron Myrrha.* It was much esteemed as an unguent and perfume by the ancients, who used it also for embalming and for incense. It is still used as a perfume and for incense, as also medicinally. By distillation with water myrrh yields a viscid, brownish-green, volatile oil. Myrrh of the best quality is known as Turkey myrrh; that of an inferior kind goes under the name of East Indian, being exported from Bombay.

MYRTA'CEÆ. The myrtle tribe, an extensive and important natural order of polypetalous exogens, mostly inhabiting warm countries, and in all cases either shrubs or trees. They have simple entire leaves, often dotted with resinous pellucid glands and regular, axillary and solitary, or spiked, corymbose, or panicled white, pink, or yellow (never blue) flowers, with numerous stamens. Some yield useful products, such as guavas, cloves, pimento, and cajeput oil. The eucalypts or gum trees are characteristic of Australia.

MYRTLE (Myrtus). A genus of plants, nat. ord. Myrtaceæ, consisting of aromatic trees or shrubs, with simple opposite leaves sprinkled with pellucid glandular points, and having axillary or terminal white or rose-coloured flowers. One species, the common myrtle, is a native of the south of Europe and other countries bordering on the Mediterranean. It has been celebrated from remote antiquity on account of its fragrance and the beauty of its evergreen foliage, and by different nations was consecrated to various religious purposes. With the moderns it has always been a favourite ornamental plant. In the British Islands the myrtle flourishes in the open air only in the southern counties of England and Ireland. Farther north it must be treated as an exotic.

MYS'IA. In ancient geography, a country in the extreme north-easterly corner of Asia Minor, on the modern Ægean, Dardanelles, and Sea of Marmora. The Mysi were a Thracian people who migrated into Asia. Their country fell to Crœsus, King of Lydia, in the sixth century B.C., passed to the Persian Empire, fell to Syria (323 B.C.), and became part of the Roman Empire in 133.

MY'SIS. The opossum-shrimps, a genus of crustaceans belonging to the ord. Stomapoda. They are the chief crustaceans of the Arctic Ocean, and constitute the principal food of the whalebone whale.

MYSORE'. A native state of Southern India. It is enclosed east and west by the Eastern and Western Ghâts, and on the south by the Nilgiri Hills, and consists of table-lands about 2000 feet above the level of the sea. The only river of importance is the Kaveri. Irrigation is extensive, sagi, a native millet, cotton, sugar-cane, and rice being produced. Gold and manganese are worked. Mysore is the capital; Bangalore is the British headquarters and the largest town.

The misgovernment of the Hindu dynasty, which the British had restored to Mysore, caused its deposition in 1831. The territory continued under British administration till 1881, when it was handed over to a Hindu Maharajah. Area, 29,475 sq. miles; pop. 6,557,871.

MYSORE. The capital of the state of the same name, at an elevation of 2450 feet above sea-level, connected with Bangalore by rail. The fort, separated from the town by an esplanade, is built in the European style. It contains the palace of the Maharajah. Pop. 83,951.

MYSTERIES (Gr. *mysterion*, from *muo*, to close the lips). Among the ancient Greeks, and afterwards also among the Romans, secret religious assemblies which no uninitiated person was permitted to approach. They originated at a very early period, and seem to have had a double object—first, that of handing down the traditions relating to the divinities in whose honour they were celebrated; and secondly, that of teaching and practising religious rites.

The most important Greek mysteries were: (1) The Eleusinian Mysteries (q.v.). (2) The Samothracian, celebrated in honour of the Cabiri (q.v.). (3) The Dionysia, which were celebrated in honour of Bacchus or Dionysus. These were of so licentious a character that they were finally forbidden as prejudicial to the public peace and morals. This was likewise done in Italy by a decree of the Roman Senate in 166 B.C. (4) The Orphic, founded by some who called themselves followers of Orpheus. *See* ORPHISM.—BIBLIOGRAPHY: A. Lang, *Myth, Ritual, and Religion*; L. R. Farnell, *The Cults of the Greek States.*

MYSTERY PLAYS. *See* DRAMA.

MYS'TICISM. A word of very vague signification, applied sometimes to views or tendencies in religion which aspire towards a more direct communication between man and his Maker through the inward perception of the mind, than that which is afforded through revelation, or to efforts and inclinations by some special and extraordinary means to hold intercourse with divine powers or the inhabitants of higher worlds.

Edward Caird defined mysticism as " religion in its most concentrated and exclusive form." According to John Stuart Mill, " whether in the *Vedas*, in the Platonists, or in the Hegelians, *mysticism* is neither more nor less than ascribing objective existence to the subjective creations of our own faculties, to ideas or feelings of the mind, and believing that, by watching and contemplating these ideas of its own making, it can read in them what takes place in the world without."

The tendency towards mysticism seems naturally implanted in some natures, and has been observed in all ages. It is an attitude of mind that appears among all races and at different periods whenever the relation of the soul to the invisible occupies the attention and thoughts of men. It is a characteristic feature of the great Asiatic religions, Brahmanism and Buddhism. In the Neo-Platonic philosophy it is an important element, as represented by Plotinus (A.D. 204-269).

Christianity, in consequence of its special tendency to practical good, as well as of its submission to a system of doctrine expressly revealed, would seem to have afforded little scope for the extravagances of mysticism. It soon, however, made its appearance, being intermingled with paganism, and reached its extreme in the writings of the so-called Dionysius the Areopagite.

This pseudo-Dionysius obtained an extensive influence, especially through Hugo St. Victor, in the twelfth century, and was everywhere held in high respect until the time of the Reformation. In opposition to scholasticism, which laboured in the construction of a systematic and almost demonstrative theology, this system embodied a theology of feeling and immediate illumination, which attached very little importance to intellectual effort, and laid so much the more weight on purification of heart and ascetic morality. Of the most notable of the German mystics in the Middle Ages were Eckhart (died 1381), and Tauler (died 1361).

In the philosophy of the fifteenth and sixteenth centuries, in Paracelsus, Bruno, and others, mysticism took a direction which at a later period gave rise, on the one side, to the alchemists and Rosicrucians, and on the other side to a number of religious sects, of which such men as Jacob Boehme and Swedenborg may be considered the representatives. The Quietism of Madame Guyon and her adherents (such as Fénelon) in France in the eighteenth century was a product of the same nature.

Among English mystics we may mention George Fox (1624-91), the founder of the Quakers; the Cambridge Platonists, Cudworth and More, and especially William Law (1686-1771). Among English poets, Wordsworth, Coleridge, Tennyson, and Browning, and, above all, William Blake (1757-1827) were distinctly mystical. Vladimir Solovjov in Russia (1853-90) was a mystic, and the works of Tolstoy are pervaded by a strain of mysticism.—BIBLIOGRAPHY: R. M. Jones, *Studies in Mystical Religion*; F. von Hügel, *The Mystical Element of Religion*; A. B. Sharpe, *Mysticism: its True Nature and Value.*

MYTHOLOGY. The word myth (Gr. *muthos*) originally simply meant speech, then, in a narrower sense, a tale or tradition, particularly one handed down from prehistoric times giving, in the form of a story about a god or hero, some ancient belief regarding the processes of nature, customs, or problems of cosmogony.

Mythology means, in the first place, the whole body of the myths of a particular country, or circling round a particular figure, as when we talk of Greek or Norse mythology; in the second place, mythology is the scientific study of myths, their analysis, and explanation. While mythology deals largely with questions of gods and the origins of things, religion is only one aspect of it. The mythologies of many lands, for example, contain a story of a deluge, but it has not always a religious significance, and is often simply cosmogonic, that is, purely scientific or even historical. The religious view of the Homeric Zeus, as the chief of the immortals who dwelt on Olympus, is very different from the mythological view, which has also to account for the stories of his amours in the form of animals, and many other myths which one is surprised to find in circulation among so cultured a people as the ancient Greeks.

Myths are largely answers to questions propounded by uncivilized man. They ask themselves: Who made the world? Who was the first man? What is the origin of night and day, and the sun and the stars? Who invented fire? What is the origin of this or that custom? How did a certain place get its name? Whence came the mountains and valleys? The answer to these questions constitute the myths of a nation or tribe. The questions asked are in a way scientific ones, and the mythology of primitive man may be said to be his science. While the answers may be quasi-scientific, it must not be forgotten that they may be quite fictitious, due to the mere love of story-telling in the case of an imaginative race.

Origin of the World.—All peoples seem to have speculated on the origin of the world and of man. The Norse story is typical. In the beginning of time there was nothing but chaos and the giant Ymir; then the world was raised out of the sea and the gods came. The gods killed Ymir and created water and sea from his blood, the earth from his flesh, mountains from his bones, the sky from his skull, etc. Similarly in the Indian legend the gods create the world out of the body of a primeval giant Purusha. This myth assumes the eternity of matter.

Origin of Man.—As to the origin of man, we find very widely spread the belief that he is descended from some animal. There is an evolution theory, like the Greek story of the Myrmidons, and a creation theory, like the Greek story mentioned by Pausanias that Prometheus made man by giving life to clay figures. The story of Prometheus stealing fire from heaven is another common story, and is even found in Australia.

The Origin of Death.—Myths explaining the origin of death are universal. Man was at first meant to be immortal. Stories are told to show that death is a punishment for disobedience to a god; sometimes it is unmerited, the result of a curse. Among the myths relating to death, there is a class of stories of almost successful efforts to bring some one back to the land of the living again, as in the story of Baldr, when Hel, the goddess of the living, agreed to restore him if all creatures will weep for him; all do except one old woman (Loki in disguise), and Baldr is lost.

Heroes.—A large class of myth is that which deals with the heroes of a race. Such as the stories of Perseus, Siegfried, Beowulf, etc. Certain features are found to be common to all these hero-legends of different countries. There we find a hero vulnerable only on a particular spot, like the heel of Achilles, or with a particular weapon, as in the case of Baldr. The latter is an interesting case. Baldr in the oldest story is killed by a magic sword called Mistilteinn; which later being interpreted as mistletoe give rise to the well-known myth. The story of Cupid and Psyche is another common form of hero-myth, exactly parallel to that of Urvasi and Pururavas in the Indian Brahmanas. Very common also are the stories of attempts to avoid a fate or prophecy, as in the case of Œdipus, or the "Sleeping Beauty." Another common motif is that of the queen who is said to give birth to animals, which is familiar alike from the *Arabian Nights* and Grimm's *Fairy Tales*.

A well-known myth is that of the hero who slays a dragon or other monster which guards a treasure, as in the case of Beowulf and Siegfried, or to save a maiden, as in the case of Perseus. It is possible that this wide-spread tale has its prototype in Vedic mythology, where Indra slays the dragon who has imprisoned the cows. Here the thunderstorm is described in mythological language. The cows are the waters which are released when the clouds are burst by Indra's lightning.

The Deluge.—The Chinese story of the deluge is generally recognized to be a memory of an unusually disastrous inundation by the Huang-Ho, which in historic times has frequently done great devastation. The deluge myths of other countries are in many cases of similar origin. The tradition is generally elaborated as it is handed down, its features are exaggerated until they become quite mythical, and in its final form we have a universal catastrophe instead of a local flood. Deluge myths may also be due to primitive scientific curiosity. The story is told to explain the origin of sea and land or of lakes. It also provided the primitive mind with a very rational explanation of the presence of fossils in rocks.

The Indian story of the deluge has several curious features. Manu, the first man, is warned by a fish that there will be a flood, and that this fish is destined to save him. He keeps the fish till it grows to a huge size. The flood then comes, and the fish tows Manu about in a boat till the waters begin to subside, when he ties his boat to a mountain-top and descends from it as the water falls. From him all men are descended.

The Greek story relates that Zeus determined to destroy all men of the Age of Copper. Warned by Prometheus, his father, Deukalion and his wife Pyrrha made a chest and stocked it with provisions. A heavy rain came, and all men were drowned unless they escaped to the mountain-tops. Deukalion and his wife floated about in the chest for nine days till the flood subsided. Then they prayed to Zeus for children, and he told them to throw stones over their shoulders. Those which Deukalion threw became men, and those which his wife threw became women. As in the Indian story we have here a creation myth, possibly not entirely uninfluenced by a false etymology connecting *laos* (people) with *laas* (stone).

Mythology as a scientific study is by no means modern. Men early began to ask themselves how certain stories of their gods could be reconciled with the respect in which they held them as objects of worship. With the advance of civilization much was seen to be monstrous and irrational in a nation's myths; the stories of the origins of the world seemed absurd or childish. The gods were seen to be mortal in many stories, and addicted to all sorts of vices. At quite an early date rationalistic explanations were given of Greek mythology. The story of the battle of the gods, in which the younger generation, led by Zeus, overthrew the older, was said to be an allegory of the strife of the elements.

In the fourth century B.C. Euhemerus propounded his theory that myths were really forgotten history. The gods, he said, were once men whose exploits had been elaborated and glorified in the telling from generation to generation, until they appeared impossible of achievement by mere men. This theory in some ways anticipates that of Herbert Spencer: that the worship of gods arose through the worship of the ghosts of ancestors. It is, however, always possible that stories of men might in time come to be told of gods, and the legends of heroes show figures not yet gods, but more than men.

The scientific study of mythology only became possible in the nineteenth century, when the ancient Egyptian and Assyrian literatures and religions were revealed to the Western world. Still more important for comparative purposes was the opening up of ancient Sanskrit literature, as contained in the hymns of the Rig-Veda, and the prose of the Brahmanas and Puranas. The latter showed that many myths were common to all the Indo-Germanic peoples, and suggested that, like their languages, they might have a common origin.

The study of anthropology and folk-lore has carried this comparative study still further, and shown that the same myths are very widely distributed. When we find that in the ancient hymns of the Rig-Veda the god Indra has the strength-giving soma-juice brought to him by an eagle from the highest heaven, that in Greece nectar is brought to Zeus from the west by an eagle, and in Scandinavian mythology Odin in the form of an eagle carries to the gods the mysterious potion which gives wisdom, one may suspect that these stories have all a common origin.

The comparative study of mythology received a great impetus from the philological researches of Max Müller, following lines laid down by Kuhn and the brothers Grimm in Germany. The task of mythology, according to Max Müller, is to explain the savage and senseless element in mythology—why a people with such a sense of beauty and moderation in all their artistic conception as the Greeks should relate stories of their gods which would make a Red Indian shudder. He held that comparative mythology, by recovering the original meaning of the name of a god, could explain its original significance. This theory he developed to a great extent, led away by the fact that the earliest Indian mythology is undoubtedly largely nature-poetry, and by many etymological comparisons which have not stood the more rigid tests of later scholarship. The Greek name *Zeus*, for example, and the Germanic *Tiw* have no obvious etymology in Greek or Teutonic, but comparative philology shows they are the same word as the Sanskrit *Dyaus*, which means the sky. Hence we conclude that Zeus is originally the sky, and that all that is told of Zeus was originally told of the sky. Similarly other names were to be traced back to natural phenomena, and all mythology could be explained as descriptions of the sun, dawn, twilight, thunder, etc. Its development was a "disease of language"; when it was forgotten, for example, that Zeus was the sky, much of the inherited phraseology was no longer understood, and wrong explanations were given of myths.

This theory is more true of Indian than of other mythologies. In the Vedas, for example, Indra is the god of the thunderstorm, who slays the demon of drought, and brings refreshing waters to man. Almost all the stories told of him are variants of this theme. Agni is clearly the personification of fire. He is called the "son of strength," because of the force necessary to generate him from rubbing the two fire-sticks who are called his parents. In course of time the real meaning of once obvious epithets like "son of strength" becomes forgotten, and stories were told to explain its meaning. Similarly we find names originally used as epithets of gods coming to be used as names of gods. Thus, Prajapati, "lord of creatures," originally an epithet of Soma, comes to be a distinct deity, a creator. Dhatr (creator), an epithet of Indra, becomes an independent creator of the firmament. We even find the word *Ka* (who) becoming a god, from a misunderstanding of a Vedic hymn with the refrain "Whom should we worship with our offerings?"

Max Müller's theory does not allow for the transfer of legends from one deity to another, but the main objection to it is raised by the anthropological school, which points out that the same myths are world-wide, and must therefore be due to primitive man thinking in the same way in different parts of the globe.

We may here briefly mention Herbert Spencer's theory regarding man's habit of personifying all phenomena. He presupposes a process somewhat the reverse of Max Müller's. According to him the Vedic hymns to Dawn, for example, are originally addressed to the spirit of a real maiden whose name was Dawn, and there is nothing remarkable in a person in a primitive state of society bearing a name like Dawn or Cloud, etc. In time it was forgotten that there had been a real maiden named Dawn, and the hymns were explained as being addressed to a goddess "Dawn." Similarly he would explain the common story of tribes being descended from some animal as a memory of an ancestor who did, as is common among savages, bear the name of an animal. In course of time this ancestor was forgotten, and the tribe said it was descended from a real wolf or whatever the animal was. Ancestor worship he holds to be the earliest form of religion, and nature worship is due to the fact that it was forgotten that Sun and Dawn, etc., were originally the names of ancestors, and not the sun or dawn.

This theory has found little acceptance, except in so far as it is generally recognized that ghost or ancestor worship and the belief in spirits does contribute its share to the formation of mythology. It seems unlikely that even the most primitive man, while calling his son Black Bear, should think that his ancestor of the same name really was a black bear. It is unlikely, also, that primitive man had a longer memory than the modern savage—or civilized man for that matter—who does not know who his great-grandfather was.

The folk-lore theory propounded by Tylor, Andrew Lang, and other anthropologists seeks to explain mythology by reasoning from the lower status of civilization to the higher. Just as comparative philology showed that much was common to the mythology of the Indo-Germanic nations, for example, so folk-lore has shown that the same myth is found among widely separated peoples, and it is argued that primitive man thinks in the same way all the world over. This theory explains the savage element in the mythology of a civilized race as a survival from the beliefs of more primitive ancestors. In Greece, for example, we find human sacrifices and the worship of stones surviving long into historic times. These are features which can be paralleled among all primitive peoples, and are to be explained as survivals from more barbaric times.

All the irrational elements in mythology are relics of a stage of society when they seemed quite reasonable to the child-like mind of primitive man. The changing of men into animals, for example, which is common in myths, is accepted as quite reasonable by the savage mind, as it is by a child on hearing a fairy story. Investigation of the mythologies of primitive tribes of the present day seems to show that they are puzzled by the same questions as are answered in older mythologies, and explain them in much the same way.

It is important, however, to remember, as Max Müller emphasized, that primitive man neither thinks like a civilized man nor thinks what we suppose he ought to have thought. He endows all natural phenomena with personalities. Civilized man may think it difficult to imagine the wind as a person, for example, yet Boreas is prominent in Greek mythology, and he can be paralleled in other countries. Primitive man naturally thinks of all the forces of nature as endowed with personality, and as many of these forces are superhuman, he thinks of them as gods. It must be remembered, however, that he can only think of them as savages like himself, and therefore their adventures and manners are savage. Other myth-making factors among savage tribes are the belief in spirits of the dead and intercourse with them—by medicine-men at least—and belief in magic.

The folk-lore explanation is not in itself sufficient. It does not explain everything in mythology. For one thing, much mythology must be due to sheer fancy—to the love of the primitive man for stories. It takes too little note of the philological side of the question. Max Müller is right in saying that many myths are due to a disease of language, and owe their origin to false etymologies. To take as an example the well-known Greek myth of the origin of the Myrmidons. According to this, Zeus transformed ants into men to people Thessaly for his son Æacus to rule over. The philologist says this story owes its origin to an etymology which connects *Murmidones* with *murmēkes*, ants. The anthropologist says the story of the descent from ants only means that the ant was the totem of the Myrmidons, and quotes numerous parallels, or he may say it is a common creation myth, and quote the parallel of the Bushman's god who peopled the earth by turning snakes into men.

According to the theory expounded by Sir J. G. Frazer in *The Golden Bough*, magic is the source of religion and mythology, particularly magic intended to produce rich crops and numerous herds. In all parts of the earth magic rites are practised to stimulate the growth of crops, and Frazer's theory is that out of the representatives in these rites of the spirit of corn, of summer, etc., there have developed the gods with myths explaining the rites. While it is true that the magic is a source of mythology, it seems impossible to prove that all mythical beings were vegetation spirits in their origin. This theory tends to the multiplication of examples in which superficial similarities are noticed, and serious differences not noted. The greatest care must be exercised in explaining a myth of a civilized race like the ancient Greeks from a custom of present-day savages. It may not be true that primitive or savage man is the same everywhere and in all time. If he were, it is difficult to account for the widely differing characteristic traits of the nations.

So far no completely satisfactory explanation of mythology has been propounded. The philologist must contribute his share and so must the anthropologist. Neither should forget that imagination and the mere love of story-telling will play its part in the formation of myths. The fundamental question, however, why —as distinct from how—does man invent such stories? is like the problem of the origin of religion, one not for the philologist or anthropologist, but for the philosopher.—

BIBLIOGRAPHY: G. W. Cox, *Mythology of the Aryan Nations*; F. Max Müller, *Contributions to the Science of Mythology*; *Anthropological Religion*; *The Science of Religion*; Herbert Spencer, *Principles of Sociology*; E. B. Tylor, *Primitive Culture*; Andrew Lang, *Custom and Myth*; *The Making of Religion*; *Myth, Ritual, and Religion*; Sir J. G. Frazer, *The Golden Bough*; W. Mannhardt, *Mythologische Forschungen.*

MYTILENE. *See* LESBOS.

MÝTO VYSOKÉ. A district and town of Bohemia, Czechoslovakia. Pop. of town, about 10,000.

MYXIN'IDÆ. The name applied to the hag-fishes, one of the two families included in the class Cyclostomata of the Vertebrata. The best-known species is the common or glutinous hag (*Myxiné glutinōsa*), which eats its way into various fishes. *See* HAG.

MYXOMYCETES (mix-o-mi-se'tēz), or **MYCETOZO'A.** An order of Fungi (sometimes claimed as Protozoa), growing in moist situations on various substances, such as decaying leaves or rotten wood, over which they spread in the form of a network of naked protoplasmic filaments of a soft creamy consistence, and usually of a yellow colour. The spore-cases are ofteng hihly coloured.

N

N. The fourteenth letter and eleventh consonant of the English alphabet. It is classed as a nasal, a lingual, and liquid or semi-vowel. In English and most other languages *n* has a pure nasal sound; in French and Portuguese, after a vowel in the same syllable, as *on*, *un*, etc., it has the effect of giving a semi-nasal sound to the vowel preceding. At the end of words after *m*, as in *hymn*, or *solemn*, it is mute. The Spanish alphabet has a character *ñ*, called *n* with the *tilde*, as in *España*, pronounced like *ni* in *onion*, *minion*; *gn* in Italian is pronounced in the same way.

NAAS. A town of Kildare, Irish Free State, on the Great Southern Railways and the Grand Canal, about 20 miles from Dublin. Naas was an ancient borough, and had its sovereign and corporation. Near by is Punchestown race-course, famous for its steeplechases. Pop. (1926), 3443.

NABATHÆ'ANS. A Semitic people who from the fourth century B.C. to about A.D. 100 held a position of importance in Arabia Petræa and the adjacent regions. They were ruled by kings; their capital was Sela (later Petra), and they carried on a great caravan trade.

NABEUL. A city of Tunisia, on the north-eastern seaboard, famous for its essences. Oranges, lemons, and flowers are grown in the vicinity for the European markets. Pop. about 11,500.

NÁBHA (näb'h*a*). One of the Punjab native states, India, having British protection, with an area of 928 sq. miles, and a population of 248,887. The chief town is Nábha, which has a pop. of 17,300.

NABLUS (ancient **Shechem**). A town of Palestine, capital of Samaria, 30 miles N. of Jerusalem. It is beautifully situated among gardens, orchards, and fertile fields, along the base of Mount Gerizim. It is the principal residence of the descendants of the ancient Samaritans, and has some manufactures and a considerable trade. The chief objects of attraction to pilgrims are the tombs of Joshua and Joseph, and Jacob's Well, near Gerizim. The town, which was fortified by the Turks during the European War, was taken by Lord Allenby in Sept., 1918. Pop. (1931), 17,171.

NACELLE. In aeronautics, the cabin or accommodation for crew and passengers, as opposed to the fuselage, etc. The word, taken literally, means *skiff* (i.e. Lat. *navicella*, diminutive of *navis*, ship).

NACHTIGAL (nȧ*h*'ti-gȧl), **Gustav.** German explorer, born in 1834, died in 1885 off Cape Palmas. In 1869 he was commissioned by the King of Prussia to carry some gifts to the Sultan of Bornu. He journeyed to Kuka, the capital of Bornu, by way of Fezzan and Tibesti, visited Borgu and Bagirmi, returning by way of Wadai, Durfur, and Kordofan, and finally reaching Khartoum towards the end of 1874. This journey is described in his *Sahara und Sudan* (3 vols., 1879-89). He was afterwards Consul-General at Tunis, remaining there till 1884, when he was sent to the west coast of Africa, and took possession of Togoland for Germany.

NADIR SHAH. King of Persia, a famous conqueror and usurper, was born in 1688, assassinated in 1747. Having distinguished himself against the Afghans and Turks, he acquired the chief power in Persia in 1732, seized the shah, confined and deposed him, and proclaiming his son Abbas, then an infant, in his stead, assumed the title of regent. The young king dying in 1736, he seated himself on the throne as shah.

Being invited by some conspirators about the person of the Great Mogul to undertake the conquest of India, he began his march at the head of 120,000 men, and with little resistance reached Delhi in March, 1739. Being exasperated by some tumults on the part of the inhabitants, he caused a general massacre, in which upwards of 100,000 persons perished. After this barbarity the victor concluded a peace with the Mogul, whose daughter he married, receiving with her, as a dowry, some of the finest provinces of his empire contiguous to Persia. His dominions subsequently stretched from the Indus and the Oxus to the Euphrates and the Caspian. A conspiracy, however, was formed against him, and he was assassinated in his tent, his nephew, Ali Kuli, succeeding to the throne.

NADIYÁ, or **NUDIA.** A district and town of Bengal, India. The Padma or Ganges flows along its north-eastern boundary. The chief town is Nadiyá, on the Bhagirathi. Area of district, 2790 sq. miles; pop. of district, 1,618,000; of town, 14,500.

NÆVIUS, Gnæus. An early Roman poet, born in Campania between 274 and 264 B.C., died 204 or 202 B.C. He wrote tragedies and comedies after the model of the Greek, and an epic poem upon the Punic War. By the introduction of some of the Roman nobility into his comedies he provoked their anger, was banished from the city, and retired to Utica. Fragments only of his works have come down to us.

NÆVUS, or **"MOTHER'S MARK."** A disfigurement which occurs most frequently on the head and trunk, but may also appear on the extremities. It consists essentially of an enlargement of the minute veins, or venous capillaries, which are dilated, and anastomose or unite among themselves to form a vascular patch generally of a deep-red colour. The familiar name of "mother's mark," or "longing mark," is applied from the popular belief that the disfigurement was the result of fear, fright, unnatural longing, or some such irritation acting upon the mother's constitution, and communicating its effects to the unborn child in the shape of this mark.

NAGA HILLS. A district of Assam. It consists largely of unexplored mountain and jungle inhabited by the Naga tribe. Area, 3070 sq. miles; pop. 150,000.

NAGASA'KI. A seaport and eighth city of Japan, on Kiushiu, in a natural harbour 3 miles from open sea. It is connected by rail and sea with other Japanese centres, and contains the shipbuilding-yards of the Mitsubishi Company, constructors for the Japanese navy. There are extensive ironworks; coal is mined near by. Pop. (1930), 204,626.

NAGOYA. The third city of Japan, on Honshiu, connected by rail with Tokyo and Osaka, from which it is about equidistant. It contains one of the greatest Shinto shrines of Japan. Pop. (1930), 907,404.

NAGPUR, or **NAGPORE.** A town in India, capital of the Central Provinces, and of the division of Nagpur (area 23,520 sq. miles; pop. 3,110,000), 440 miles E.N.E. of Bombay, with which and with Calcutta it is connected by railway. The municipal area includes Sitabaldi Hill and Sitabaldi suburb, where the British Residency, Government offices, cantonments, etc., are situated. The manufactures include cotton and woollen cloths, and utensils of copper, brass, etc. There is a large trade, more especially in cotton. There are important educational institutions, libraries, printing-presses, and some handsome Hindu temples. Nagpur was formerly the seat of a line of rajahs which became extinct in 1853, when their territory was annexed to the British dominions. Pop. (1931), 215,165.

NAGY-KANIZSA. A town of Hungary, 20 miles from the western end of Lake Balaton. Pop. 30,936.

NAHUEL-HUAPI, or **TIGER LAKE.** A lake of Argentina, in the territory of Neuquén, in the Andes. Area, 110 sq. miles.

NAHUM. One of the twelve minor prophets, the author of a book of prophecies included in the Old Testament. His prophecies relate to the destruction of Nineveh, which he describes in vivid colours. The period in which he lived is, however, uncertain, probably 700-600 B.C.

NA'IADÆ. A natural order of monocotyledons, consisting of plants living in fresh or salt water in most parts of the world, having inconspicuous hermaphrodite or unisexual flowers. *Zostera marina* (the grass-wrack) is the most familiar example.

NAÏD'IDÆ, or **NAIDOMORPHA.** A family or group of small water-worms, some of them of common occurrence in the mud of ponds and streams. They multiply by transverse division (fission) as well as sexually.

NAILS (OF ANIMALS). Like hairs, are appendages which belong to the category of the exoskeletal elements of the animal frame, or are parts of the skin, of the outer layer of which they are modified appendages. A nail, in fact, is a specialized arrangement of the cells of the epidermis. In man the nails do not enclose the ends of the digits; but in the horse, and "hoofed" or ungulate quadrupeds generally, the nails assume the form of protective coverings to the digits, and are then known as "hoofs." Nails may be produced to form "claws," as in birds and carnivorous mammals, while in the sloths they assume a large relative size, and are used as a means of arboreal progression. In the Amphibia—as in some toads, efts, etc.—the nails appear as mere thickenings of the skin at the extremities of the digits. The nails appear about the fifth month of fœtal or embryonic life.

NAILS. Of many different lengths and shapes. *Brads* used for nailing floors and ceilings have the head only on one side; the small sharp nails with round flat heads, used by saddlers and upholsterers, are called *tacks*; the small sharp taper nails without heads, used by shoemakers, are called *sprigs*; a variety in which the head is large and the spike small has the name *hobnails*; very large nails are called *spikes*.

In early days every kind of nail was produced by hand labour alone, each nail being separately forged from a thin rod of iron. In 1810 a machine was contrived by which nails could be cut from an iron sheet and headed at one operation, at the rate of 100 per minute. Since that time great improvements have been made in nail-making machinery, and the method commonly adopted is to cut nails out of sheet iron of the required thickness, an operation which, by the improved processes, is carried on with great rapidity. The quantity produced in this way is astounding, some mills turning out at the rate of 10 miles of nail-rods an hour.

NAIN. An ancient village of Galilee, 8 miles S.E. of Nazareth, at the foot of Mount Hermon, celebrated as the scene of the raising of the widow's son (Luke vii. 11).

NAINI TAL. A hill-station and district in the Kumaon division of the United Provinces, India. The town is on the banks of a small lake at an altitude of 6409 feet, among the spurs of the Himálaya. It is reached by road from the railway terminus at Holdwani, and is the hot season headquarters of the administration of the United Provinces. The district is not greatly cultivated. District area, 2721 sq. miles; pop. 324,000; town pop. 9750.

NAIRN. A maritime county in the north-east of Scotland, on the Moray Firth, served by the Highland Railway. The south part of the county is hilly (Carn Glas, 2162 feet). The principal rivers are the Findhorn and the Nairn. Agriculture and sheep-farming are the principal occupations. Nairn is the county town; Cawdor and Kilravock with their castles are of historical interest.

Nairn was included in Moray district in ancient Scotland, and in 1891 detached portions of the county were absorbed by Ross, Inverness, and Moray. Area, 104,252 acres; pop. (1931), 8,294.

NAIRN. The county town of above county, is a royal burgh, seaport, and watering-place near the mouth of the River Nairn and on the L.M.S. Railway. Its harbour is accessible only to small vessels. Fishing is important. Nairn, then Invernairn, became a royal burgh in the twelfth century. Pop. (1931), 4201.

NAIRNE, Caroline Oliphant, Baroness. Scottish poet, belonging to the Oliphants of Gask, born in 1766, died in 1845. She married William Murray Nairne, who in 1824 became Baron Nairne. She was the authoress of some exceedingly popular songs, including *The Laird o' Cockpen, The Land o' the Leal,* and *The Auld Hoose.*

NAIROBI. The capital and administrative headquarters of Kenya Colony, on a plateau (altitude, 5450 feet). It is on the Uganda Railway. The climate is excellent, and many Europeans visit the town as a starting point for expeditions into the colony. It has a broadcasting station (49.5 M.). Pop. 85,722 (including 7164 Europeans and 10,000 Indians). In the Nairobi district there are about 50,000 to 60,000 natives and 4000 Europeans. The Thika Railway runs from Nairobi to Fort Hall, and by extension to Mount Kenya. Along this line a papyrus swamp subsided (April, 1922), carrying away main road and railway bridges, and cutting off Nairobi from Kenya Province by the creation of a new valley and a rushing river 60 feet in depth.

NAIRS. A Hindu people of South-West India, belonging to the Sudra caste, most numerous in Malabar and Travancore, where they were formerly dominant. They retain matrilineal customs, following the rule of female descent; and a man's heirs are not his own, but his sister's children. Polyandry was also formerly a recognized institution, but is now dying out.

NAIVASHA. An inland province of Kenya Colony, extending between Lake Rudolf and the Tanganyika frontier. It is mountainous in the central regions, and contains Lakes Naivasha, Elmenteita, and Nakura. The Uganda Railway traverses the province. Naivasha, east of the lake and on the railway, is the provincial capital. Around Nakura agriculture is extensively practised. The estimated pop. is 140,000 (about 2000 Europeans).

NAJA. A genus of venomous snakes. The best-known examples are *N. tripudians,* the cobra de capello of India, and the *N. haje* of Africa, which is tamed by native jugglers, and is identified by many writers with the asp employed by Cleopatra to bring about her death. The king cobra (*N. bungarus*), which feeds on other snakes, ranges from India to the Philippines.

Naja

Other closely related forms are: the Indian krait (*Bungarus cœruleus*), the Australian black snake (*Pseudechis porphyraceus*), tiger snake (*Notechis scutatus*), and death adder (*Acanthophis antarcticus*), and the coral snake (*Elaps corallinus*) of tropical America and the West Indies. *See* COBRA; ASP.

NAKHICHEVAN (ná-*h*ich'e-ván). The name of two towns in Russia. The first is situated on the right bank of the Don, in the Azerbaijan S.S.R., 7 miles E. of Rostov. Pop. 54,000.—(2) A town in the government of Erivan, in Transcaucasia, 175 miles S. of Tiflis, regularly and substantially built. Pop. 9000.

NAMANGAN. A town in Russian Turkestan, in the valley of the Sir Darya, 50 miles from Khoqand. Pop. (1931), 8294.

NAMAQ'UAS. The European name for the Hottentot tribes inhabiting the Namaqualand district. *See* HOTTENTOTS.

NAMES, Personal. It is probable that at first all names were significant. Old Testament names are almost all original, that is, given in the first instance to the individual bearing them, and either originated in some circumstance of birth or expressed some religious sentiment, thus—Jacob (supplanter), Isaiah (salvation of Jehovah), Hannah (favour), Deborah (bee), etc.

Neither the Hebrews, Egyptians, Assyrians, Babylonians, Persians, nor Greeks had surnames; and in the earliest period of their history the same may be said of the Romans. In course of time, however, every Roman citizen had three, the *prænomen* or personal name, the *nomen* or name of the gens or clan, lastly, the *cognomen* or family name, as Publius Cornelius Scipio. Conquerors were occasionally complimented by the addition of a fourth name or *agnomen*, commemorative of their conquests, as Publius Cornelius Scipio *Africanus*. Greek names refer to the personal appearance or character; and were often supplemented by the occupation, place of birth, or a nickname. Times of great public excitement have had a very considerable influence in modifying the fashion in names.

It is impossible to state with any degree of certainty when the modern system of personal nomenclature became general. Surnames were introduced by the Norman adventurers, but were for centuries confined to the upper classes. They became general in Scotland about the twelfth century. In some of the wilder districts of Wales they can hardly be said to have been adopted even yet. The principal sources from which surnames are derived are personal characteristics (Black, Long, Short), rank, profession, or occupation (Bishop, Knight, Miller), localities, or natural objects (Hill, Dale, Stone), and patronymics (Johnson, Wilson, Andrews). The Hebrews had no surnames proper, but to distinguish two men of the same name they used the form Solomon ben David (Solomon son of David). The Welsh use the word ap in the same way: Evan ap Richard (John son of Richard =Prichard).

In Britain and most Continental nations the wife changes her surname on marriage to that of her husband; in Spain, however, she retains it, while the son may adopt either the paternal or maternal name. In Great Britain a man may now change his Christian name and surname without an Act of Parliament, royal licence, or even public advertisement; but there is no law to compel third parties to use the new name.

NAMUR. A southern province of Belgium, on the French frontier, traversed by the Meuse and Sambre and by the combined streams (Maas). The surface is generally hilly and afforested in the south-east. The north is the agricultural area; the industrial area is the Sambre Valley. Namur is the capital. Area, 1413 sq. miles; pop. (1931), 356,120.

NAMUR (Fl. *Namen*). A town of Belgium, capital of the province of

Namur

Namur; a railway junction at the confluence of the Sambre and Meuse. The cathedral of St. Aubin (1751-67) contains the heart of Don John of Austria (died 1578), the conqueror of Lepanto. There are several museums, and the church of St. Loup (1621-53), built in the baroque style, is interesting.

History.—Namur was the capital of a countship that fell to Burgundy in 1420. It has been an episcopal see since 1559. It was invested by the French under Vauban (1692) and by William III. (1695), and a circle of nine detached forts (350 guns) was constructed by Brialmont in 1888 as a link in the Meuse Valley defences. On 19th Aug., 1914 (European War), forces of Bülow's Second Army (German) appeared before Namur, and the town was besieged by General Gallwitz. The bombardment began on 21st Aug., 1914, and with the retreat of de Lanrezac from the Sambre, on the 23rd, the Belgian field troops retired and Namur fell. The Germans lost 12,000 men in the attack, and subsequently gave the town over to a reign of terror. Pop. (1931), 31,611. *See* EUROPEAN WAR.

NANAIMO. A seaport-town of British Columbia, on Vancouver Island, Canada. It is 73 miles from Victoria, and is served by a branch of the Canadian Pacific (Esquimault and Nanaimo) Railway. Coal is exported from the neighbouring mines, chiefly to San Francisco. Pop. (1931), 10,000.

NANA SAHIB. The infamous leader of the sepoys in the Indian Mutiny. He was born in 1825, and adopted by the ruler of the state of Bithoor. On the death of the latter the British refused to recognize Nana as his successor. In May, 1857, Nana placed himself at the head of the mutineers at Cawnpore. The Europeans there capitulated on a promise that they should be sent away in safety. But the men were shot down and the women and children massacred. (*See* CAWNPORE.) Nana was defeated by Sir H. Havelock, and was driven across the frontier into Nepál, and there all knowledge of him ceases.—Cf. J. Burgess, *The Chronology of Modern India.*

NANCOWRY. An island of the Nicobars (q.v.), in the central group of four, the others being Camorta, Trinkat, and Katchall. There is a Government agency at Nancowry (Camorta), but the island is chiefly famous for its magnificent landlocked harbour. A British penal settlement was maintained on the island for nineteen years, but was abandoned in 1888.

The Nancowry group was for long the seat of a gang of Kanaka pirates under one, Worthington, a deserter from the British navy, whose policy was to wait until a vessel entered Nancowry, board her as a trader or inhabitant, and in due course to murder the whole crew, and to plunder and scuttle the ship. They were never suspected until their vigilance was somewhat relaxed on the retirement of Worthington from business.

NANCY. A city of France, capital Moselle, on the Meurthe. It is an important railway junction. The church of Notre Dame, and the cathedral (1742), were erected by Stanislas Leszcinski, King of Poland, who became duc de Lorraine on his abdication in 1736, and there is an old ducal palace. Nancy was, until

Nancy : Porte de la Graffe

1870, the capital of Lorraine. The university was founded in 1572. The town is famous for its cambric and embroideries. Muslin, iron, cottons, and woollens are manufactured. Pop (1931), 120,578.

History.—At Nancy (1477) was fought the great battle between the Swiss under Réné, duc de Lorraine, and Charles the Bold of Burgundy, who was defeated and slain. During the European War the battle of Nancy was fought between the French and Germans (25th Aug. to 12th Sept., 1914). After the defeat at Morhange (q.v.) Castelnau and Dubail (Second and First Armies) fell back upon the gap of Charmes, and a terrific battle ensued until 9th Sept., when the exhausted German armies received a truce to bury their dead. On 12th Sept. a general German retreat began, and on the 16th the victorious French 16th Corps entered Lunéville.

NANDA DEVI. A peak of the Himálaya, in the north of the United Provinces of India ; altitude, 25,665 feet.

NANDGAON. A feudatory state of the Central Provinces, India. Wheat, cotton, and rice are produced. Raj Nandgaon, on the Nagpur-Raipur Railway line, is the capital. Area, 871 sq. miles ; pop. 147,906.

NANKING. City and capital of China, on the Yangtse-kiang, which is navigable at all seasons to Nanking. It is surrounded by a wall generally above 40 feet high. Nanking gives its name to nankeen cloth. There is an arsenal, mint, and small-arms factory ; a university, naval college, and agricultural experiment station. Connection by railway is afforded with Shanghai and Pukow, for the Tientsin-Pukow Railway.

It was at one time the capital of the Chinese Empire ; but the seat of government was transferred to Peking (now Peiping) in 1403 ; in 1928, however, with the setting up of a national government, it again became the nation's metropolis. It was at Nanking that the Chinese-British treaty was signed in 1842. The city was held from the spring of 1853 to July, 1864, by the Raipings, who made it their capital. The famous porcelain tower of nine stories and 200 feet in height, completed in 1432, was destroyed during the Taiping rebellion. Near is an avenue of gigantic statues, leading to the tombs of the Ming dynasty. Pop. (1931), 633,452.

NANSEN, Fridtjof. Norwegian explorer, born in 1861, studied at Christiania University, and in 1882 made an Arctic voyage in a sealing-vessel. In 1888 he crossed Greenland a little north of latitude 64°, as told in his *Across Greenland* (1890). In 1893 he sailed on board a specially built steamer (the *Fram*), expecting that, entering the Polar ice near the New Siberian Islands, he would be drifted by a current over the Pole to Greenland. After being carried so far he left the *Fram*, and with a single companion, and with sledges, dogs, and kayaks, took the ice. In this way he reached the highest latitude till then attained, 86° 14′ (April, 1895), and next proceeded to Franz Josef Land, where he spent the winter of 1895-96 and met Frederick Jackson, leader of an expedition sent from England, with whom he returned, followed soon after by the *Fram*. This great journey he described in his *Farthest North* (1897). He was professor of zoology at Christiania, and Norwegian Minister in London, 1906 to 1908. At the end of the war he devoted himself to the work of repatriating prisoners of war, and as Commissioner of the League of Nations, assisted by the International Red Cross, he repatriated over half a million from Siberia, China, and other countries. In 1921 he was requested by an international conference sitting at Geneva to undertake the task of organizing relief for the famine-stricken parts of Russia, and did it on a gigantic scale. He followed this by equally diligent and successful relief work for refugees. He was awarded the Nobel Peace Prize in 1922, and was elected Lord Rector of the University of St. Andrews in 1925. He was instrumental in securing the entry of Germany into the League.

His works include *Eskimo Life*, *In Northern Mists*, and *Russia and the Peace*. He died 13th May, 1930.

NANTES (nänt). A seaport-city of France, capital of the department of Loire-Inférieure, on several islands formed by the Loire, 35 miles from its mouth. The principal buildings are the castle of the ducs de Bretagne, where the Edict of Nantes (q.v.) was signed, and the cathedral (1434). A serious fire occurred in the castle in 1921. Nantes is a shipbuilding centre, and ships reach the town by ship canal (27 miles) from St. Nazaire. It exports slate and machinery, pit-props and soaps, and imports coal, petroleum, sugar and grain. Pop. (1931), 187,343.

History.—Before the Roman conquest of Gaul, Nantes was the capital of the Gallic tribe of the Namnetes. In 1499 it passed from the ducs de

Nantes Cathedral

Bretagne by the marriage of Anne of Brittany with Louis XII. of France. John Knox was a galley slave at Nantes (1547-49), and Jules Verne was born in the town (1828). During the Revolution Carrier organized at Nantes the wholesale massacres known as the *noyades* or " republican marriages."

NANTES, Edict of. Signed by Henri IV. in that city, 30th April, 1598. It allowed the Protestants the free exercise of their religion, and threw open to them all offices of State. This edict was formally revoked by Louis XIV. on 20th Oct., 1685. As a consequence of this fatal act for France, about 400,000 Protestants, forming the most intelligent and industrious section of the people, emigrated to Britain, Holland, and other Protestant countries, much to the benefit of their adopted homes.

NANTUCK'ET. An island of Massachusetts, 18 miles S. of Cape Cod, 15 miles long, and from 3 to 4 miles wide. Agriculture and pisciculture are the staple industries. The town of Nantucket is situated on the north side of the island, and is the county seat of Nantucket county, comprising the island proper and adjacent islands. Pop. 3678.

NANT'WICH. A market town of Cheshire, England, on the Weaver, 4 miles from Crewe; served by the Great Western and the London, Midland and Scottish Railways. The cruciform church of St. Mary and St. Nicholas is the principal attraction. Nantwich was once famous for its saltworks, but at present its staple manufacture is boots and shoes. Pop. (1931), 7132.

NAP. A card game which at one time was referred to as Napoleon, after whom the game is called, because the chief player in it becomes for the time an Ishmaelite whose " hand " is against every man's. It is a good game for three, four, or five players, the only requirements being an ordinary pack of cards, a little intelligence, and some coppers. Each player receives five cards, dealt singly round the table—or its substitute. In turn calls are made of the number of tricks each thinks he can make if he is permitted to lead the first card and settle which suit is " trump " by leading it. A certain sum changes hands for each value of call, the direction of passage being determined by the success or future of the caller.

NAPH'TALI (Heb., " my wrestling "). The sixth son of Jacob, and the head of one of the twelve tribes. The tribe had its full share in repelling the incursions of the Canaanites during the first centuries of the conquest, but disappears from history when Tiglath-pileser overran the north of Israel and bore away the whole of the population to Assyria. Under the title of Galilee the district occupied by the tribe became in New Testament times more famous than it had ever been before.

NAPHTHA. A term applied to liquid hydrocarbons of low boiling-point obtained in the fractional distillation of petroleum, shale-oil, and coal-tar. They are all highly inflammable liquids, which are used for burning purposes, as a source of fuel in internal-combustion engines, and as solvents for fats, resins, india-rubber, etc.

Mineral or petroleum naphtha consists mainly of paraffins and naphthenes, and is obtained chiefly from the Caspian Sea district, Roumania, the United States, Persia, Burmah, and other countries. The naphtha from shale-oil contains olefines as well as paraffins, whilst coal-tar naphtha consists mainly of xylene and other hydrocarbons of the benezene series. Wood naphtha or wood spirit is the crude spirit obtained by the distillation of wood, and consists chiefly of methyl alcohol and acetone. It is used as a solvent, and also for denaturing alcohol to be sold as methylated spirit.

NAPHTHALENE. A crystalline hydrocarbon with an odour of coal-gas, and is occasionally deposited in gas-pipes in cold weather. It has the formula $C_{10}H_8$, and is commonly obtained by subjecting certain carbon compounds to high temperatures, e.g. when marsh-gas or the vapours of alcohol, ether, or benzene are passed through a red-hot tube. It is a constituent of all coal-tars, the usual amount being 4 to 6 per cent. It is prepared by distilling the tar, collecting the oil which passes over between 210° and 240° C. This is known as carbolic oil, and as it cools deposits solid naphthalene, which is purified by filtration, subsequent pressing, and treatment with various chemical reagents, e.g. dilute caustic soda, sulphuric acid, and ultimately sublimed.

Naphthalene gives rise to numerous derivatives, which resemble those of benzene. They are largely used in the manufacture of dyes. Among its derivatives are the naphthylamines which correspond with aniline, and the naphthols which correspond with phenol.

NAPHTHYL, or DINAPHTHYL, $C_{20}H_{14}$. A hydrocarbon obtained, together with other products, by heating naphthalene with a mixture of manganese dioxide and sulphuric acid diluted with twice its weight of water.

NAPIER, Admiral Sir Charles. British naval commander, cousin of Sir Charles James and Sir William Napier, was born in 1786, died in 1860. He entered the navy as midshipman in 1799, was promoted lieutenant in 1805, and sent to the West Indies, where he served in the operations against the French. He was promoted commander by Admiral Cochrane in Aug., 1809, and in 1811 was employed in Portugal and along the coast of Southern Italy. In 1813 he was attached to the North American squadron, and in August of the following year he led the expedition up the Potomac River. At the conclusion of the war he was made a C.B.

In 1833 he accepted the command of the Portuguese Constitutional fleet, and effected the establishment of Donna Maria on the throne. Returning to England, he was appointed in 1839 to the command of the *Powerful*, and ordered to the Mediterranean, where, on the outbreak of the war between Mehemet Ali and the Porte, and the co-operation of Britain with Russia and Austria on behalf of the latter power, Sir Charles Napier performed some of his most gallant exploits, including the storming of Sidon and the capture of Acre. Having blockaded Alexandria, he concluded on his own responsibility a convention with Mehemet Ali, by which the latter and his family were guaranteed in the hereditary sovereignty of Egypt on resigning all claim to Syria. On his return to England he was created K.C.B

In 1841 he was elected member for Marylebone. In 1847 he received the command of the Channel fleet as rear-admiral; and in 1854, on the commencement of the Russian War, he was nominated to the command of the Baltic fleet, being now a rear-admiral. In this capacity he accomplished little beyond the capture of Bomarsund. He sat in Parliament as member for Southwark from 1855 till his death. He published a series of *Letters to Lord Melville on the State of the Navy*, an *Account of the War in Portugal and of the War in Syria*, and numerous contributions to the *United Service Magazine*. —Cf. General Elers Napier, *The Life and Correspondence of Admiral Sir Charles Napier*.

NAPIER (nā'pi-ėr), **Sir Charles James.** British soldier and administrator, born in 1782, died in 1853.

Sir Charles Napier

He entered the army in 1794, served in Ireland and Portugal, was wounded at Coruña, and taken prisoner in 1809. In 1811, when again at liberty, he returned to the Peninsula, and served through the war. He missed the battle of Waterloo, which took place three days before he reached the scene of action. In 1837 he was made major-general; in 1838 K.C.B.

In 1841 he was appointed to the chief command in the Presidency of Bombay, with the rank of major-general, and was shortly afterwards called to Scinde. Here he gained the splendid victories of Meanee and

Hyderabad, and was afterwards made Governor of Scinde, which he administered till 1847. He had quarrelled with the directors of the East India Company, but during a panic caused by the want of anticipated success in the war with the Sikhs in 1849 his services were again required, and he sailed once more for the East, as commander-in-chief of all the forces in India. Before he arrived Lord Gough had brought the Sikh War to a triumphant termination, and no special work remained for Sir Charles Napier to perform.—Cf. W. N. Bruce, *Life of General Sir Charles Napier.*

NAPIER, John. Laird of Merchiston, near Edinburgh, the inventor of logarithms, was born 1550, died 1617. He was educated at St. Andrews, travelled on the Continent, and ultimately settled down at the family seats of Merchiston, near Edinburgh, and Gartness, in Stirlingshire, as a recluse student.

In 1614 he published his book of logarithms (*Logarithmorum Canonis Descriptio*; Edinburgh, 4to). The invention was very soon known over all Europe, and was everywhere hailed with admiration by men of science. Napier followed it up, in 1617, by publishing a small treatise, giving an account of a method of performing the operations of multiplication and division by means of a number of small rods. These materials for calculation maintained for many years a place in science, and are known as Napier's Bones.

NAPIER, Robert Cornelius. Baron Napier of Magdala, born in Ceylon 6th Dec., 1810, and died in 1890. He entered the Royal Engineers in 1826, and served in the Sutlej campaign in 1845-46, where he was severely wounded. In 1848-49 he served in the Punjab, and was chief engineer at the siege of Multan. He was chief of staff to Sir J. Outram in 1857, and was prominent in the relief of Lucknow at the beginning of the Indian Mutiny. In the Chinese War of 1860 he commanded a division with the local rank of major-general. In Oct., 1867, he was entrusted with the command of the Abyssinian expedition, and captured Magdala, 13th April, 1868. He was then made Baron Magdala and G.C.B. In 1870 he was made commander-in-chief in India, with the rank of general, became Governor of Gibraltar in 1876, was made field-marshal in 1883, and Constable of the Tower in 1887.

NAPIER, Sir William Francis Patrick. British soldier, brother of Sir Charles James Napier, the conqueror of Scinde, was born in 1785, died in 1860. At the age of fourteen he entered the army, served at the siege of Copenhagen, and with his brothers Charles and George took a distinguished part in the Peninsular campaigns, became lieutenant-colonel in 1813, and colonel in 1830.

Some years after the conclusion of peace he commenced his celebrated *History of the Peninsular War*, the publication of which began in 1828, and extended over the intermediate period till 1840. In 1841 Colonel Napier was advanced to the rank of major-general; he was appointed Lieutenant-Governor of Guernsey the following year, and in 1848 created a K.C.B. He also wrote: *History of the Conquest of Scinde, History of the Administration of Scinde,* and a *Life of Sir Charles James Napier.*

NAPIER (nā'pi-ėr). A seaport-town of North Island, New Zealand, exporting much wool and mutton from the adjacent grazing-lands. It was devastated by an earthquake in Feb., 1931. Pop. (1932), 19,300.

NAPLES (nā'plz; It. *Nap'oli*). A maritime province of Campania, Italy, on the Tyrrhenian Sea. It includes the islands of Capri, Procida, and Ischia. Generally it is mountainous (Vesuvius, 4000 feet), but is fertile in the north. Area, 1203 sq. miles; pop. (1931), 2,084,960.

NAPLES (It. *Napoli*). The largest city of Italy, in Campania, capital of the province of Naples. It is situated on the northern shore of the beautiful Bay of Naples, about 160 miles from Rome. Its site is magnificent, being on the side of a nearly semicircular bay, partly along the shore, and partly climbing the adjacent slopes, bounded on the one side by the picturesque heights of Posilipo, and on the other by the lofty mass of Vesuvius.

The city is divided into two unequal parts by a steep ridge proceeding from the height on which stands

Naples: Bay and Vesuvius

the castle of St. Elmo, and terminated by a rocky islet surmounted by the Castello dell' Ovo. The largest and most ancient part of Naples, to the east of these heights, now forms the business quarter. The western and more modern part of the city is the fashionable quarter. After the cholera epidemic of 1884 extensive slum clearance was carried out, and the city was largely reconstructed. There are few remains of historical or antiquarian interest, but there are two castles, Castello dell' Ovo and Castello Sant' Elmo, and four gates of mediæval construction.

Buildings.—The cathedral dates from 1272. It was erected on the site of two temples dedicated to Neptune and Apollo respectively. It possesses two vessels which contain the blood of St. Januarius, Bishop of Benevento, who suffered martyrdom under Diocletian in A.D. 305. Other edifices are the Palazzo Reale (Royal Palace); the palace of Capo di Monte; the old palace, where the courts of justice now hold their sittings; the Palazzo dei Publici Studj, formerly occupied by the university, but now converted into the Museo Nazionale, a museum containing not only a valuable library of 350,000 volumes and many rare manuscripts, but also the older and more recent collections belonging to the Crown, and the Farnese Collection of paintings and sculpture from Rome and Parma; numerous theatres, of which that of San Carlo is one of the largest in existence. Naples has the largest university in Italy. It dates from 1224.

Manufactures and Exports.—The manufactures, which are numerous but individually unimportant, include macaroni, woollens, and cottons, silks known as *gros de Naples*, glass, china, musical instruments, flowers and ornaments, perfumery, soap, and chemicals. The exports consist chiefly of bones, cream of tartar, hoops, linseed, hemp, wheat, figs, oil, wine, wool, tallow, rags, and silk, raw, dyed, and manufactured.

Environs.—In the environs are situated the tomb of Virgil, the ancient ruined cities of Herculaneum and Pompeii, the remains of Roman temples, villas, palaces, and tombs, together with the physical phenomena of Vesuvius. The city has a broadcasting station (319 M., 1.5 kW.). Pop. (1931), 839,390.

History.—*Neapolis* ("New City") was founded by a Greek colony from the town of *Cumæ* many centuries before Christ. It took the name of Neapolis to distinguish it from a still older Greek city adjoining called *Parthenŏpē*. It passed to the Romans in 290 B.C. It was taken by Belisarius (A.D. 536), by Totila (542), and by Robert Guiscard (1130), who united the south of Italy and the adjacent Island of Sicily into one political entity, and from that period the history of Naples ceases to be the history of a city, but becomes the history of a kingdom forming part of the Kingdom of the Two Sicilies, Naples being recognized as the metropolis.

In the year 1189 the kingdom passed from the Norman to the Swabian race. In 1266 Charles I. of Anjou was crowned king of the Two Sicilies, and the kingdom was ruled by this dynasty until 1441, when it came under the dominion of the princes of Aragon.

In the early part of the sixteenth century it came into the possession of Spain, and under the rule of the Spanish viceroys broke out the famous insurrection under Masaniello in 1647. It was governed by Austria until 1735, when it was erected into an independent monarchy in favour of Charles of Bourbon. In 1798 the French Republicans entered Naples, which became a republic; but a Loyalist rising led to the return of the king.

In 1806 Napoleon succeeded in placing first his brother Joseph, and on Joseph's removal to Spain his brother-in-law Murat, on the throne of Naples. After the fall of Napoleon the Bourbons again ruled in Naples, but in the Revolution that broke out in 1860 under the guidance of Garibaldi, Francis II. was deposed, and Naples and Sicily were added to the Kingdom of Italy. — BIBLIOGRAPHY: E. A. Freeman, *History of Sicily from the Earliest Times*; S. R. Forbes, *Rambles in Naples: Archæological and Historical Guide*; A. H. Norway, *Naples, Past and Present*; E. Hutton, *Naples and Southern Italy*.

NAPLES, Bay of (anciently **Crater Sinus**). On the west coast of Italy, in the Mediterranean, extending for about 20 miles from the Capo di Miseno, its north-west boundary, to the Punta della Campanella, its south-east limit. It is separated from the open sea by the Islands of Procida, Ischia, and Capri.

NAPOLEON. Napoleon Bonaparte was born at Ajaccio on 15th Aug., 1769, of a family which originally belonged to Tuscany, but which had been settled in Corsica for 250 years. In the summer of his birth France completed her conquest of Corsica, and Bonaparte from the age of nine was educated in France, and entered the French army in 1785.

He at first regarded the French Revolution as an opportunity for delivering Corsica from the yoke of France, but was satisfied by its recognition as a department under the constitutional monarchy which was the earliest outcome of the Revolution, and in 1793 the Bonaparte family had to flee from Corsica to Toulon, which in the same year adopted the cause of Louis XVII. and received a British fleet.

Bonaparte was commander of the artillery of the Republican army at the siege of Toulon, and for his distinguished services in the capture of the town was made a brigadier-general. In 1795 he suppressed a rebellion against the Convention in Paris and was entrusted with the invasion of Italy, which he carried out in 1796-97 under the new government known as the Directory. After a series of brilliant operations he concluded in Oct., 1797, the Treaty of Campo-Formio with Austria, the last (except Great Britain) of the European powers which had opposed the French Republic.

Returning to Paris in December, he decided that an invasion of the British Islands was meanwhile beyond the capabilities of the French navy, and organized an expedition to Egypt as a blow to British influence in the East. In July, 1798, he occupied Alexandria, and by the battle of the Pyramids became the master of Egypt, but his designs in the East were rendered impracticable by Nelson's victory in the battle of the Nile (1st Aug.) and by the help given to the Turks by Sir Sidney Smith in the defence of Acre (May, 1799), the capture of which was necessary for Bonaparte's plan of using Syria as a base for an invasion of India or the conquest of Constantinople. He afterwards declared that Smith had come between him and his destiny.

Leaving his army in Egypt, Bonaparte made his way back to France, which was threatened by a second European coalition. He put an end to the Directory and established a new Constitution, by which, as First Consul, he became the ruler of France (Nov., 1799). In the summer of 1800 he defeated the Austrians at Marengo, and, after a second disaster at Hohenlinden in December, Austria was compelled to make the Treaty of Lunéville. Russia had already deserted the second coalition, and peace was made with Great Britain by the Treaty of Amiens (1802).

War was renewed in 1803, and for two years the aim of the First Consul was an invasion of England. It was ultimately rendered impossible by the battle of Trafalgar (Oct., 1805), but before that date he had begun a new continental war. In 1804 he had become hereditary Emperor of the French, taking the title of Napoleon I., and in 1805 he broke the Treaty of Lunéville by accepting the title of King of Italy. Russia and Austria joined Great Britain in a coalition against him, but he defeated an Austrian and Russian army at Austerlitz (Dec., 1805) and compelled the Austrians to submit. In the following year he destroyed the Prussian army in the battles of Auerstadt and Jena and entered Berlin, and in 1807 he made the Treaty of Tilsit with

Napoleon Bonaparte

Russia, and attempted to bring Great Britain to its knees by declaring a blockade and forbidding countries dependent on or allied with France to trade with the British.

An occupation of Portugal (which refused to acknowledge this blockade) followed in the same year, and in 1808 he found a pretext for the invasion of Spain, which led to British intervention in the Spanish Peninsula (*see* WELLINGTON). The years 1810-11 witnessed the height of his power. He was supreme in France, and it was impossible to walk from Rome to Hamburg without passing through any country that did not acknowledge French authority. He divorced his first wife (*see* JOSÉPHINE), who had borne him no children, and was received into the circles of European royalty by his marriage with Marie Louise, a daughter of the Austrian Emperor (1810).

A quarrel with the Tsar led to an invasion of Russia in 1812, the most notable events of which were the French victory at Borodino and the capture of Moscow, which was burned by the Russians. He had to return among the winter snows, with vast losses to his army, of which less than a tenth survived the campaign, while the conflict in the Spanish Peninsula was constantly draining his resources in men. The Prussians took up arms and were joined by the Austrians, and an army of Russians, Prussians, and Austrians defeated Napoleon at Leipzig (Oct., 1813).

In the following winter he declined terms offered by his enemies, but his empire was falling to pieces. In March, 1814, the Allies entered Paris, and in April Napoleon abdicated. He was given the sovereignty of the small island of Elba, whence he escaped in March, 1815, and was received with enthusiasm in France. The Allies prepared to meet him, and he was defeated at Waterloo (18th June), and gave himself up to the captain of H.M.S. *Bellerophon* in July. He was sent as a prisoner to St. Helena, where he died in May, 1821. He employed his time at St. Helena in creating the "Napoleonic Legend"—a belief that he had been inspired by ideals of liberty, and this belief, aided by Bourbon misgovernment, led to the restoration of his dynasty thirty years after his death.

Napoleon was scarcely less great as a legislator than as a soldier; the Code Napoléon is still the basis of French law, and his statesmanship had a profound influence upon Italy and upon portions of Germany. In spite of his consummate intellectual powers, he failed because (in the words of Mr. Herbert Fisher) he "took glory as his end, and found it in conquest, and was too often prone to measure it by destruction," and he "remains the great modern example of that reckless and defiant insolence which formed the matter of ancient tragedy and is at war with the harmonies of human life."—BIBLIOGRAPHY: J. Holland Rose, *Life of Napoleon*; J. R. Seeley, *Life of Napoleon*; R. M. Johnston, *The Corsican*; H. A. L. Fisher, *Napoleon* (Home University Library); Lord Rosebery, *Napoleon: the Last Phase.*

NAPOLEON II., Napoleon François Joseph Charles Bonaparte. Only son of the preceding, was born in Paris 1811, died at Schönbrunn 1832. In his cradle he was proclaimed King of Rome. On the first abdication of the emperor he accompanied his mother, Marie Louise of Austria, to Vienna. His title there was Duke of Reichstadt. He never assumed the title of Napoleon II.; but on the accession of his cousin Louis Napoleon in 1852, some title being necessary, the late emperor took that of Napoleon III., which, being recognized by the Governments of Europe, implied the recognition of the former title.

NAPOLEON III., Charles Louis Napoleon Bonaparte. Emperor of the French, was born at Paris 20th April, 1808, died at Chislehurst, England, 9th Jan., 1873. He was the youngest son of Louis Bonaparte, brother of Napoleon I. and King of Holland, and of Hortense de Beauharnais. His early life was spent chiefly in Switzerland and Germany.

By the death of his cousin the Duke of Reichstadt (Napoleon II.) he became the recognized head of the

Napoleon III.

Bonaparte family, and from this time forward his whole life was devoted to the realization of a fixed idea that he was destined to occupy his uncle's imperial throne. In 1836 an attempt was made to secure the garrison of Strasbourg, but the affair turned out a ludicrous failure. The prince was taken prisoner and conveyed to Paris, and the Government of Louis Philippe shipped him off to the United States. The death of his mother brought him back to Europe, and for some years he was resident in England.

In 1840 he made a foolish and theatrical descent on Boulogne, was captured, tried, and sentenced to perpetual confinement in the fortress of Ham. After remaining six years in prison he escaped and returned to England. On the outbreak of the Revolution of 1848 he hastened to Paris, and, securing a seat in the National Assembly, he at once commenced his candidature for the presidency. On the day of the election, 10th Dec., it was found that out of 7,500,000 votes Louis Napoleon had obtained 5,434,226; Cavaignac, who followed second, had but 1,448,107.

On the 20th the Prince-President, as he was now called, took the oath of allegiance to the Republic. He looked forward to a higher position still, however, and pressed for an increase of the Civil List from 600,000 francs first to 3,000,000, then to 6,000,000, with his term of office extended to ten years, and a residence in the Tuileries. At last, on the evening of the 2nd Dec., 1851, the President declared Paris in a state of siege, a decree was issued dissolving the Assembly, 180 of the members were placed under arrest, and the people who exhibited any disposition to take their part were shot down in the streets by the soldiers. Another decree was published at the same time ordering the re-establishment of universal suffrage, and the election of a President for ten years. When the vote was taken, 7,439,216 suffrages were in favour of his retaining office for ten years, while only 640,737 were against it.

As soon as Louis Napoleon found himself firmly seated, he began to prepare for the restoration of the empire. In Jan., 1852, the National Guard was revived, a new Constitution adopted, and new orders of nobility issued; and at last, on the 1st Dec., Louis Napoleon Bonaparte was proclaimed emperor under the title of Napoleon III. On the 29th Jan., 1853, the new sovereign married Eugénie Marie de Montijo, Comtesse de Teba; their son, Napoleon-Louis, was born 16th March, 1856.

In March, 1854, Napoleon III., in conjunction with England, declared war in the interest of Turkey against Russia. (*See* CRIMEAN WAR.) In April, 1859, war was declared between Austria and Sardinia, and Napoleon took up arms in favour of his Italian ally, Victor Emanuel. The Allies defeated the Austrians at Montebello, Magenta, Marignano, and Solferino. By the terms of the Peace of Villafranca, Austria ceded Lombardy to Italy, and the provinces of Savoy and Nice were given to France in recognition of her powerful assistance (10th March, 1860). In 1860 the emperor sent out an expedition to China to act in concert with the British; and in 1861 France, England, and Spain agreed to dispatch a joint expedition to Mexico, the result of which was the appointment of Maximilian, Archduke of Austria, as Emperor of Mexico.

On the conclusion of the Austro-Prussian War of 1866, Napoleon, jealous of the growing power of Prussia, demanded a reconstruction of frontier, which was peremptorily refused. The ill-feeling between the two nations was increased by various causes, and in 1870, on the Spanish crown being offered to Leopold of Hohenzollern, Napoleon demanded that the King of Prussia should compel that prince to refuse it. Notwithstanding the subsequent renunciation of the crown by Leopold, war was declared by France (19th July). (*See* FRANCO-GERMAN WAR.) On the 28th July Napoleon set out to take the chief command, and on 2nd Sept. the army with which he was present was compelled to surrender at Sedan.

One of the immediate consequences of this disaster was a revolution in Paris. The empress and her son secretly quitted the French capital and repaired to England, where they took up their residence at Camden House, Chislehurst. Here they were rejoined by the emperor (who had been kept a prisoner of war for a short time) in March, 1871, and here he remained till his death. His only child, the Prince Imperial, who had joined the British army in South Africa as a volunteer, was killed by the Zulus, 2nd June, 1879.—BIBLIOGRAPHY: Sir W. A. Fraser, *Napoleon III.*; A. Forbes, *Life of Napoleon III.*; F. A. Simpson, *The Rise of Louis Napoleon*; G. Ollivier, *L'Empire libéral.*

NARBADA. A river of the Deccan, India.

NARBONNE (Lat. *Narbo Martius*). A city of France, department of Aude, connected with the Mediterranean by canal (5 miles). It has a fine church (S. Just) founded in 1272, and formerly a cathedral. The honey of Narbonne is celebrated. Narbonne was the first colony which the Romans founded beyond the Alps (118 B.C.). It was the capital of Gallia Narbonensis. Pop. 31,909.

NARCIS'SUS. According to Greek mythology, the son of the river-god Cephissus. The young Narcissus was of surpassing beauty, but excessively vain and inaccessible to the feeling of love. Echo pined away to a mere voice because her love for him found no return. Nemesis determined to punish him for his coldness of heart, and caused him to drink at a certain fountain, wherein he saw his own image, and was seized with a passion for himself of which he pined away. The gods transformed him into the flower which still bears his name.—Cf. Ovid, *Metamorphoses*, iii. 341-510.

NARCISSUS. An extensive genus of bulbous plants, mostly natives of Europe, nat. ord. Amaryllidaceæ. The species are numerous, and from their hardiness, delicate shape, gay yellow or white flowers, and smell, have long been favourite objects of

Narcissus

cultivation, especially the daffodil (*N. pseudonarcissus*), the jonquil (*N. jonquilla*), polyanthus narcissus (*N. tazetta*), and white narcissus (*N. poeticus*). The daffodil is completely naturalized in many parts of England, growing in meadows and woods and under hedges.

NARCOT′IC. Derived from a Greek term signifying numbness or torpor, is the name given to a large class of substances which, in small doses, diminish the sensitivity of the nerves. Most narcotics are stimulating when given in moderate doses; in larger doses they produce sleep; and in poisonous doses they bring on stupor, coma, convulsions, and even death. Opium, hemlock, henbane, belladonna, aconite, camphor, digitalis, tobacco, alcohol, leopard's-bane, and a variety of other substances are narcotics.

NARCOTINE. An alkaloid contained in opium to the amount of 6 or 8 per cent. It is poisonous in large doses, about 45 grains being sufficient to kill a cat.

NARDOO (*Marsilia macrŏpus*). A clover-like water-fern of Australia, occupying extensive tracts of inundated land. Its dried spore-cases are eaten by the natives.

NARDUS. A genus of grasses. *N. stricta*, nard or mat-grass, is abundant on moors in Britain, but has little feeding value.

NARES, Sir George Strong. English Arctic explorer, born 1831, died in 1915. He entered the navy and took part in the Arctic expedition of 1852-54. From 1872 to 1874 he commanded the *Challenger* during her scientific expedition, and in 1875 was first in command of a North Polar expedition. He wrote: *Seamanship*, *Reports on Ocean Soundings*, and *Voyage to the Polar Sea*.

NARES, Owen Ramsay. English actor. Born 11th Aug., 1888, he trained with Miss Rosina Filippe, and first appeared in *Her Father*, at the Haymarket Theatre, in 1909. After touring provincially for two years, he played in London for eleven. In 1926 he toured in South Africa. His best known parts have been Julian Beauclerk in *Diplomacy*, Philip in *The Boy Comes Home*, Peter Beavans in *The Charm School*, Mark Sabre in *If Winter Comes*, Cary Liston in *Two White Arms*, and Garry Anson in *The Calendar*.

NARIÑO. A department of Southern Colombia, South America, traversed by the Cordillera Central, and producing gold from over 2000 mines. Sugar, cocoa, potatoes, cereals, and rice are also raised. Pasto is the capital. Area, 12,150 sq. miles; pop. 411,763.

NARSES. The companion-in-arms of Belisarius, and one of the most successful generals of the Emperor Justinian, was an Asiatic slave and eunuch whom the latter had taken into favour and appointed to a command in A.D. 538. Between that period and 552 he put an end to the dominion of the Goths in Italy, and in 553 was himself appointed exarch, and fixed his court at Ravenna. He was deposed under the Emperor Justinus II. in 565, and died at Rome in 568.

NARSINGHGARH. A native state of the Bhopal Agency, Central India, on the slopes of the Vindhya Mountains. Narsinghgarh is the town. Area, 734 sq. miles; pop. 101,426.

NARSINGHPUR. A native state of Bihar and Orissa, India, feudatory to Orissa. The seat of the rajah is at Narsinghpur. Area, 199 sq. miles; pop. of state, 40,000.

NARTHECIUM. A small genus of herbs, ord. Liliaceæ. *N. ossifragum*, the bog asphodel, is common on wet moors; it has a creeping stem, a tuft of sword-shaped leaves, and bright yellow starry flowers with hairy stems.

NARVAEZ (når-vä′eth), **Ramon Maria.** Duke of Valencia. Spanish statesman and general, born 1800, died 1868. In 1844 he formed his first ministry, and received from Queen Isabella the rank of marshal and the title of Duke of Valencia. His Government was overthrown in 1846, but he subsequently formed other ministries.

NARVIK. A seaport of Norway, on the north-west coast. Pop. 6000.

NARWHAL (*Monŏdon monocĕros*). A cetaceous mammal found in the northern seas, averaging from 12 to 20 feet in length. The body colour is whitish or grey spotted with darker patches. There is no dorsal fin. The dentition of the narwhals differs from that of all other members of the dolphin family. In the female both jaws are toothless, but the male narwhal has two incisors in the upper jaw, which are sometimes developed into enormous projecting tusks, though commonly only the one on the left side is so developed, being straight,

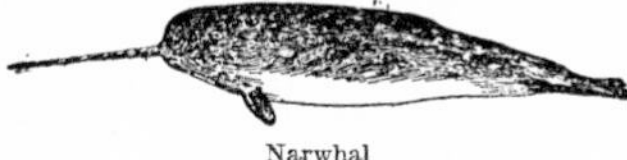

Narwhal

spiral, tapering to a point, and in length from 6 to 10 feet. It makes excellent ivory. From the frequency with which the narwhal appears as having a single horn it has obtained the name of the *Sea-unicorn, Unicorn-fish*, or *Unicorn Whale.* The food of the narwhal appears to consist chiefly of mollusca, and notwithstanding its formidable armature it is said to be inoffensive and peaceable. The Greenlanders obtain oil from its blubber, and manufacture its skin into useful articles.

NASEBY. A village in Northamptonshire, England, 7 miles from Market Harborough. In 1645 Fairfax and Cromwell completely defeated Charles I. in the vicinity.

NASH, Paul. British painter. Born in London, 11th May, 1889, he was educated at S. Paul's School and the Slade School. He held his first exhibition in 1911, but it was not until 1918, when his work as an official war artist (1917-18) was shown, that he attracted attention. He developed charm and individuality as a landscape painter, and held an important exhibition in London in 1924. Later exhibitions were held in the Mayor Gallery (drawings and water-colours), 1925; Redfern Gallery (wood-engravings), 1928; and Leicester Gallery (paintings), 1928. In 1931 he was British representative, Carnegie International Exhibition Jury of Award. He also produced woodcuts, and book illustrations, of which the series of wood-engravings, *Genesis* (1924), are the most important.

NASH, Richard. Known as *Beau Nash*, born at Swansea 1674, died 1761. He was master of the ceremonies at Bath, and for many years was sole arbiter of fashion. He died in comparative indigence.—Cf. Oliver Goldsmith, *Life of Richard Nash.*

NASH, Thomas. English poet, playwright, and pamphleteer, was born in 1567, and died in 1601. He was educated at St. John's College, Cambridge, which he dutifully described as "an university within itself." After graduating B.A. in 1586, he probably visited Italy and Germany.

By 1588 he had settled in London, and adopted the precarious profession of literature. His first work was *The Anatomie of Absurditie* (1589), a kind of comic companion work to Stubbes's *Anatomie of Abuses.* He then became a protagonist in the Martin Marprelate controversy, lashing the Puritans with merciless satire. There is some doubt as to how many of the innumerable anonymous pamphlets were Nash's work, but his *nom de guerre* seems to have been Pasquil, and he almost certainly wrote *Martin's Month's Minde* (1589), *The First Parte of Pasquil's Apologie* (1590), and *An Almond for a Parrat* (1590). On the conclusion of this controversy Nash declared war upon Gabriel Harvey and his brothers, and a series of most amusing pamphlets followed, culminating in *Have with You to Saffron Walden* (1596). Three years later the controversy, which had gone to scandalous lengths, was stopped by the Archbishop of Canterbury.

Other interesting works of Nash are: *The Terrors of the Night* (1594); *Christ's Tears over Jerusalem* (written in 1593, during a temporary fit of repentance); and *Lenten Stuffe* (1599), an encomium of Yarmouth and its red herrings. *The Unfortunate Traveller, or the Life of Jack Wilton* (1594), is the earliest English picaresque novel (q.v.). It attempted a new kind of writing which was not again attempted until the time of Defoe.

As a prose writer Nash stands very high; in fact, his prose is more like that of Shakespeare than is that of any of his contemporaries. He has the same irrepressibility, the same delight in inverted logic, and the same inexhaustible wealth of vocabulary. His two favourite authors and models appear to have been Rabelais and Aretino. As a dramatist Nash does not stand high. His *Isle of Dogs* is lost; but his completion of Marlowe's *Dido, Queen of Carthage* is poor. *Summer's Last Will and Testament*, a satirical masque, is more successful; it contains a charming poem on spring, which is justly given first place in *The Golden Treasury*.—Cf. Sir Walter Raleigh, *The English Novel.*

NASHUA. A city of New Hampshire, United States, the county seat of Hillsborough county, on the Nashua River; served by the Boston & Maine Railway. There is a piscicultural station, a trade in agricultural produce, and varied manufactures. Nashua was settled in 1655, incorporated (as Dunstable) in 1673, and became a city in 1853. The name was changed in 1836. Pop. (1930), 31,463.

NASHVILLE. A city of Tennessee, United States, the second city and capital of the state, and the county seat of Davidson county, on the Cumberland River; served by the Louisville & Nashville, and the Nashville, Chattanooga, & St. Louis Railways. It has four universities, the Nashville, Vanderbilt, Fisk (coloured students), and Roger Williams (Baptist). A great commercial centre, Nashville has an extensive transit trade. In Centennial Park is a replica of the Parthenon at Athens. It was settled in 1780 as Nashborough, and was incorporated (as Nashville) in 1784, being admitted a city in 1806. Pop. (1930), 153,866.

Nashville: University of Nashville

NASIK. A district and town of Bombay province, India. Native cereals are raised in the district. The town is Nasik, on the headwaters of the Godaveri at the foot of the Western Ghâts. It is a place of Hindu pilgrimage, and is on the Bombay-Delhi Railway. Area of district, 5877 sq. miles; pop. 844,000. Pop. of town, 42,756.

NASIRÂBÂD, or **MAIMANSINGH.** A town of Bengal, India, an important centre of the rice trade; connected by railway with Chittagong and Dacca. Pop. 22,000.

NASIRIYA. A town of 'Iraq, on the Euphrates, 110 miles from Basra.

NASMYTH (nā'smith), **Alexander.** A landscape painter, born at Edinburgh in 1758, died in 1840. He went early to London, and studied under Allan Ramsay, painter to George III. He afterwards proceeded to Rome, and on his return to Edinburgh he commenced portrait painting, but soon abandoned it for landscape. His style is remarkable for its simplicity and beauty.

NASMYTH, James. Son of the preceding, born in 1808, died in 1890. He was educated at the School of Arts, Edinburgh, and in engineering under Maudslay in London. He removed in 1834 to Manchester, where he became a successful machine constructor and inventor. The steam-hammer, which has rendered possible the immense forgings now employed, was invented by him in 1839. The steam pile-driver and the safety foundry ladle are among his other inventions. He was also a skilled astronomer.

NASSAU. A district of Germany. *See* HESSE-NASSAU.

NASSAU. A seaport city and capital of New Providence, Bahama Islands (of which it is also the capital). It is defended by forts, and is an export centre for sponges, fruit, salt, and some cotton. There is a wireless station. Nassau was founded by the English in 1629. Pop. 12,975.

NASTUR'TIUM. The genus to which the watercress belongs. Also a popular name for *Tropæŏlum majus*, or Indian cress, an American climbing annual with pungent fruits and showy orange flowers; and for *T. minus*, a much smaller species.

NATAL. A province of the Union of South Africa, bounded by Cape Province, Basutoland, Orange Free State, Transvaal, Swaziland, Portuguese East Africa, and the Indian Ocean. The area is 35,284 sq. miles. The coast-line is little broken, and there is practically only one harbour, which is that of Durban. The surface is finely diversified, rising by successive terraces from the Indian Ocean towards the mountains on the western frontiers, where the chief summits are Champagne Castle, 10,357 feet, and Mont aux Sources, about 11,000 feet. The minerals comprise coal, ironstone, limestone, gold, and marble.

Natal is well watered, but none of its rivers is navigable. The climate is healthy. There are forests in the west and north. Cattle, sheep, and goats are numerous, but rinderpest is prevalent. Maize is by far the chief cereal crop; others are wheat, barley, oats, and all kinds of fruits and vegetables. In the warm coast region cotton, tobacco, bananas, pineapples, sugar-cane, tea, and coffee grow well, sugar being an export of some importance, while some tea is also exported. Wool, gold, hides and skins, and coal are important exports.

The capital is Pietermaritzburg, but Durban is the largest town. There is a whaling industry in Durban, regulated by the Provincial Government. Since 1910 Natal has been a province in the Union of South Africa. Pop. (1921), 1,429,398 (including 1,139,804 natives and 141,649 Asiatics.) The white population in 1931 was 177,424.

History.—Natal was discovered in 1497 by Vasco da Gama. A small English settlement was formed on Port Natal in 1823. Afterwards discontented Boers from the Cape Colony entered the country, and in 1839 set up a republic at Port Natal; but in 1843 Natal, after hostilities with the Boers, was proclaimed British. In 1856 it was separated from Cape Colony and made a separate colony. Zululand was annexed in 1897. The invasion of the colony by the Boers in 1899 was followed by the four months' siege of Ladysmith, and its relief by General Buller's forces.—BIBLIOGRAPHY: A. H. Tatlow, *Natal Province—Descriptive Guide and Official Handbook* (annual); Cullingworth's *Natal Almanac*; R. Russell, *Natal, The Land and its Story*.

NATATO'RES. The name, now obsolete, given by Illiger in 1811 to six families of swimming birds. They are characterized by short legs placed behind the centre of gravity, toes webbed or united by a membrane to a greater or less extent, close oily plumage to protect them from low temperature of the water, in which they mostly live and obtain their food. They include the ducks, geese, swans, flamingoes, the penguins, auks, divers, grebes, gulls, pelicans, cormorants, and gannets.

NATCHEZ. A seaport-city of Mississippi, United States, the county seat of Adams county, on the Mississippi; served by the Mississippi Central Railway. It is a great cotton-shipping centre. Jefferson Military College is here. Settled by the French as a fort, Natchez passed first to Britain (1763) and then to Spain (1779), passing finally to the United States in 1798. It became a city in 1803. Pop. 13,422.

NATION AND NATIONALITY. A nation is usually defined as a people inhabiting a certain extent of territory and united by common political institutions, or an aggregate of persons closely associated with each other by common descent and speaking the same or a cognate language. Nationality, on the other hand, is the term designating the *quality* of being a nation, or the condition and status of belonging to one. Frequently, however, the two terms, nation and nationality, are used interchangeably, and hence a certain confusion in the definition of the two concepts. Thus the Jews are sometimes called a nation, though they had for centuries no national home or government, and were dispersed throughout the world. Nationality, however, besides, being the quality or characteristic of what is national, may be defined as a population or a group *aspiring* to become a political unity on a common territory; it is thus a nation *in posse*.

A nation is to be distinguished both from a race and from a state, as several nationalities may be living under the same government. Scotland is a nation, but not a state. Nor is citizenship synonymous with nationality. With regard to the elements which form a nation, they are various, and opinions of historians and sociologists differ as to their importance. History proves that the same group of factors may produce a nation in one case, but will have no effect in another. Anyhow, it would be wrong to imagine that a nation is merely the result of race, language, religion, common territory, or even common political institutions. The formation of a nation differs almost in every case, depending upon each or some of these unifying principles.

The principal element instrumental in the formation of a nation is a common past—and a common tradition. Renan rightly defined a nation as a social group whose solidarity has been established by the sentiment of the sacrifices made in the past, and of those it is still ready to make in the future. A nation is thus a social group, usually inhabiting a certain territory, conscious of its collective unity, animated by a sense of its solidarity, united by the bonds of common life and labour, suffering and sacrifice, devotion and danger, and inspired by a " will to live " and to co-operate. The collective unity of a nation is, however, the result not so much of common race or language as of a common cultural inheritance, not so much of territory as of tradition. A nation is a psychological phenomenon rather than an ethnical, corresponding to a political fact. It implies a common past, and rests upon the tangible fact of a national home and a close co-operation in the present.

The sense of nationality and the principle of nationalities are modern creations, " the culmination of history," as they have been defined. In the ancient world the political unit was the city or the tribe, whilst in mediæval times states were based upon the principles of feudal law. The Roman Empire was a state and not a nation, although the *Pax Romana* was a sentiment almost akin to what we call in modern times national feeling and national pride.

Christianity tended towards the disintegration of nationality, and St. Paul, who appealed to humanity at large, was the greatest opponent of the principle of nationality. In modern times, however, the principle of nationalities has been advocated by politicians and sociologists. It is argued that nations should be homogeneous in race and reconstructed upon ethnological principles. John Stuart Mill had already maintained (*Representative Government*) that nationality and citizenship should be co-extensive—in other words, that the world should consist of national states, and that empires including a variety of races and nations should be broken up.

But it was in the nineteenth century that the principle of nationality acquired such a preponderating place in the history of nations, in sociology and in politics. The growth of nationalities and the creation of Nation-States were the outstanding features of European history during the nineteenth century; and the problems of National " self-determination " which helped to produce the Great War and were certainly not disposed of by the Peace Treaties have been a source of continuous difficulty since the map of Europe was redrawn.

The exaggerated sense of nationality, of the manifestation of the ego of social or ethnic groups, developed the modern tendency of *nationalism*, which again reached its culmination during the latter half of the nineteenth and the beginning of the twentieth centuries. The object of nationalism is commonly self-government or Home Rule, where a people are under the rule of an alien government. In the majority of cases the feeling of nationalism is fostered and stung into acute self-consciousness by oppression. In modern practical politics nationalism has resulted in the reconstruction of Poland, the creation of Czecho-Slovakia, the independence of Egypt, and in the policy of Zionism.—BIBLIOGRAPHY: A. E. Zimmern, *Nationality and Government*; J. Holland Rose, *Nationality as a Factor in Modern History*; E. Renan, *Qu'est-ce qu'une nation ?*; T. Ruyssen, *What is Nationality ?*; I. Zangwill, *The Principle of Nationalities.*

NATIONAL AIRS. The adoption by a country of a particular song or hymn as its national anthem is a practice dating from comparatively modern times, and one in which Great Britain took the lead with *God save the King*. The origin of this familiar air was long a question of dispute, and there is even yet some difference of opinion on the subject. Once ascribed to the musician Dr. John Bull (1563-1628), it is now generally regarded as the work of Henry Carey (1692-1743), though there are still some who believe it to be an importation from Germany. First printed (1742) in the *Harmonia Anglicana*, it remained unnoticed until three years later, when the Jacobite rising of the " '45 " drew it from obscurity; its rendering at Drury Lane Theatre on Saturday, 28th Sept., in that year was " encored with repeated huzzas." It was reprinted in the *Gentleman's Magazine* of the following month, and has remained the British national anthem since that date.

The *Auld Lang Syne* of Burns is Scotland's national song: Ireland has *The Wearin' of the Green*, an Irish street ditty of 1798, set to an old English air; and Wales appropriates *God bless the Prince of Wales* and the still more stirring *Men of Harlech*. The American *Yankee Doodle*, of somewhat doubtful origin, is generally recognized as being an English air with words by Dr. Schuckburgh, an American army surgeon; it dates from 1755. This song must to some extent share its claim as national representative with *Hail, Columbia! The Star-spangled*

Banner, John Brown's Body, S. F. Smith's *My Country 'tis of Thee,* and Julia Ward Howe's *Battle Hymn of the Republic.* Colonial national songs include *The Maple Leaf for ever* of Canada, written and composed (1871) by Alexander Muir, and New Zealand's *God girt her about with the Surges,* by Reeves.

Chief among European national anthems is the *Marseillaise* of France, written and composed in 1792 by Rouget de Lisle, and named from its having been the popular revolutionary song of the Marseilles volunteers in Paris. More than one national anthem of the Continent was either inspired by, or adapted from, that of Great Britain. *Heil dir im Siegeskranz,* an adaptation of *God save the King,* became the Prussian national hymn in 1793, the English air being used; while Haydn drew from the same source his inspiration to compose (1799) the stately national hymn of Austria, the words finally used, *Gott erhalte Franz den Kaiser,* being written by Baron Zedlitz.

A German translation of the British anthem, set to the original music, was sung at a royal celebration in Denmark in 1790, though the Danish national hymn is now *Kong Christian,* with music by Hartmann. Belgium's *La Brabançonne* is, like the *Marseillaise,* a revolutionary song, and dates from 1830, the words being by Jenneval, set to an air by Campenhout. Of the same date is General Lvoff's magnificent Russian anthem, *God the All-terrible,* composed in 1830 and since included (in H. F. Chorley's version of the words) in many an English hymnal. In Hungary the honour is shared between the poet Vörösmarty's *Be true to the Land of thy Birth,* Erkel's *Bless our Land with Gladness,* and the *Rákóczy March* by an unknown composer of the seventeenth century. Norway has also several national hymns, of which it must suffice to mention Björnson's *Yes, we Love this Land,* to music by Nordraak. Sweden has *King Karl, the Young Hero,* by Tegner, while the Dutch anthem is *Oh, ye within whose burning veins,* by Tollens, dating from 1730. In Southern Europe must be mentioned Greece's *Sons of Greece, Arise!* and Portugal's *Hymno constitucional,* composed by Pedro I., Emperor of Brazil. Finally, a national anthem, *May our Lord (Mikado) for ever reign,* is found as far east as Japan.

NATIONAL DEBT. The national debt of a country is the gross capital sum which the Central Government owes to persons from whom it has borrowed money, mainly for purposes of war. The development of national debts as we know them dates roughly from the beginning of the nineteenth century, and has taken place almost entirely since the middle of the seventeenth century. There are, indeed, innumerable earlier examples of borrowing by kings and republics during emergencies, when revenue fell short of requirements. The first king whose debts are recorded in the history of public finance is Henry III. (1216-1272). It was common in the Middle Ages for kings to accumulate treasures by various methods of extortion, including forced "loans" from their subjects, and repudiation of their debts. The decay of this system is connected with the rise of parliamentary authority and control of the purse; along with the growth of modern capitalism, which increased opportunities for borrowing. It is not without significance that mediæval Venice and Genoa, where banking systems had grown up, are amongst the earliest instances of states with a regular national debt. One of the earliest of the Italian banks was, in fact, an association of the State's creditors, who managed the revenues of the republic (Genoa). The English goldsmith-bankers were also creditors of the State.

The origin of the British national debts was also bound up with the foundation in 1694 of the Bank of England. The Bank of England was, indeed, founded upon a perpetual loan of £1,200,000 to the State. This loan was the first National Debt, in the accepted sense of the term. The Bank was established largely for the purpose of lending money to the Government of William III., whose finances were in a chaotic condition. The debt grew rapidly during the wars of the eighteenth and early nineteenth century, increasing from £21½ million in 1697 to £52 million in 1713, £79¼ million in 1748, £138⅗ at the end of the Seven Years' War in 1763, nearly £250 million at the Peace of Versailles in 1783, and over £742½ million in 1814, when Napoleon was banished to Elba. These are the figures of the funded debt; there was also an enormous floating or unfunded debt, representing in 1816 a total National Debt, funded and unfunded, of £885 million. This was the highest point reached until the recent European War, on the eve of which the debt stood at £711 million. During the war it rose rapidly to no less than £8079 million in Dec., 1919, which was about the maximum reached.

Before the European War the bulk

of the debt (£586 million in 1914) was funded debt. This term originally signified debt the interest of which was charged upon definite taxes, revenues, or funds; but with the improvement of British credit it became customary to charge interest upon the general revenue of the country, and funded debt came to mean the permanent debt in respect of which the State had undertaken to pay interest, but not to repay the capital at any definite date. Since the European War the expression is sometimes used more loosely to include debt which is not permanent, but is not redeemable for a period of years.

The counterpart of funded debt is unfunded or floating debt, which strictly means redeemable debt, but is now sometimes loosely used to designate short maturities—particularly Treasury Bills and Advances on Ways and Means Certificates. There is also a small class of debt intermediate between funded and unfunded debt, consisting of terminable annuities—a favourite form of borrowing in times gone by.

During the European War British Government borrowing was represented entirely by redeemable debt (unfunded debt in the strict sense). The conditions attached to the loans were most diverse, with a view to attracting as much capital as possible, and the periods of maturity varied. Of the total debt of £8079 million in Dec. 1919, about half (£4451 million) was due for repayment within from five to sixty years.

In peace-time the British Government normally aims at reducing the burden of the debt by redemption out of surplus revenue. The first plan for a Sinking Fund was formed by Walpole in 1717 and adopted by his successor Stanhope, by which legislation was required to appropriate the surplus revenues of the Bank and what was then known as the General Fund, to the redemption of debt. Pitt, in 1786, brought forward a Sinking Fund scheme which was designed to liquidate the entire National Debt in a period of forty-five years; but as his scheme actually resulted in the State raising about £330 million at an average cost of rather more than 5 per cent. to pay off a debt carrying interest at 4½ per cent., the fallacy of Pitt's plan was realized in the course of the subsequent half century. From then onwards—1829 to 1914—the Sinking Fund arrangements were based upon the principle of applying to the redemption of debt only the excess of revenue derived from taxation over the expenditure for current needs.

For some years before the war two Sinking Funds existed for the purpose. The Old Sinking Fund consisted of the sum by which Exchequer receipts in any year happened to exceed Exchequer issues in respect of expenditure chargeable against income; and the New Sinking Fund consisted of the balance of a permanent annual charge for the service of the debt after defraying the actual expenditure for such service. During the war the Sinking Funds were, of course, suspended, and the permanent post-war policy in regard to reduction of debt has not yet been settled. The most important post-war measure affecting the Debt was the Government's conversion operation carried out in the autumn of 1932, when about £2000 million of 5 per cent. War Loan were transformed into a 3½ per cent. loan.

The growth of debt among countries engaged in the European War eclipsed all previous records, and left the countries concerned staggering under a burden which some cannot bear. Settlement of these inter-govermental war debts is now a question of serious political and economic significance. (*See* WAR DEBTS.)

Apart from war debts, an increasing amount has been borrowed by an ever-growing number of countries for purposes of economic development. The chief source of capital for investments of this character before the war were Great Britain, France, and Holland; since the war the principal, almost indeed the only, lender of capital abroad has been the United States.

National debt contracted abroad and expressed in foreign currencies is known as external debt, while debt contracted in national currency within the country is known as internal debt. Internal debt, however, may be purchased by foreigners, and external debt may be purchased by nationals; and to the extent to which this is done the importance of the distinction is lessened.

During the war Great Britain contracted a large external debt, mainly to the United States Government, and the European Allies contracted external debts to the British Government and to the United States Government. The service of the debt contracted for purposes of development is rendered easy, because the revenue of the borrowing country is directly increased by the investment of capital; but the service of war debts involving the transfer of money payments which have no connection with the financing of international trade, creates very difficult problems affecting the exchange of currencies and the interchange of goods and services among creditor and debtor countries. These conditions, far more than the impoverishment of the countries involved in the war, have rendered the problem of inter-governmental war debts peculiarly difficult.—BIBLIOGRAPHY: Adam Smith, *Wealth of Nations*; Adam, *Public Debts*; Robert Hamilton, *Inquiry concerning the Rise and Progress, etc., of the National Debt of Great Britain and Ireland*; Andreades, *History of the Bank of England*; C. F. Bastable, *Public Finance, Statistical Abstract of the United Kingdom*; *British Finance during and after the War* (1914-21), edited by A. W. Kirkaldy.

NATIONAL GALLERY, The. The British national picture-gallery. This collection of paintings, situated in Trafalgar Square, London, originated in a collection formed by Angerstein, consisting of 38 pictures, 29 by old masters and 9 by British painters, and purchased with public funds in 1824 for £57,000 as the nucleus of a national gallery. Since that time the collection has been greatly enlarged by purchases out of moneys provided by Parliament, as well as by bequests and gifts. Of the latter the most munificent has been that of Vernon in 1847, a collection of 157 works of English painters. Another highly valuable section is that of the pictures and drawings by Turner bequeathed to the nation at his death in 1851. In 1871 a valuable prize was secured by the purchase for £75,000 of Sir R. Peel's collection, consisting of 77 paintings and 18 drawings. In 1885 Parliament voted £70,000 for the purchase of a single picture, the *Ansidei Raffaelle*, together with £17,500 for another, Vandyck's *Charles I. on Horseback*.

The National Gallery now comprises fully 1200 pictures, and though specially strong in examples of the British school of painting, foreign masters are fully represented. In 1887, by the completion of the new rooms, which had been in progress since 1885, sufficient space was obtained to permit of an orderly arrangement of the pictures. This gallery, while not the largest, is one of the finest in all Europe.

A **National Gallery of British Art** was presented to the nation by Sir Henry Tate, and opened in 1897.

The National Portrait Gallery is distinct from the National Gallery, though adjoining it. Founded in 1856, it now contains about 2000 portraits and busts. The Scottish National Gallery and National Portrait Gallery are accommodated in Edinburgh.

NATIONAL GUARDS. In France, an armed organization of the inhabitants of towns or districts for local defence, differing mainly from the militia and volunteers of Britain in that it was at the disposal of the respective municipalities rather than of the Crown. After the suppression of the communal revolt in Paris (1871) the National Assembly decreed the dissolution of the National Guard.

NATIONAL HEALTH AND UNEMPLOYMENT INSURANCE.—The idea of State responsibility for the distress arising to the individual out of illness (and consequent inability to work), and out of unemployment, grew very gradually in the British public mind. Its beginnings were visible in the Poor Law legislation of the early nineteenth century, but not till after nearly a hundred years was there anything like a general acceptance of this common responsibility and a sense of remedial obligation on the part of the State. The only provision against ill-health and unemployment the workmen could make, apart from personal savings, was through their trade unions, and historically the trade union sickness and unemployment benefits were the forerunners of the State insurance system.

In 1911, however, was passed an Act of Parliament which imposed the necessity of accepting the principle of State responsibility for meeting the individual hardship accruing from sickness and unemployment by a State system of insurance against these evils. This Act was described (in its preamble) as "an Act to provide for insurance against loss of health and for the prevention and cure of sickness, and for insurance against unemployment and for purposes incidental thereto." It became law in Dec., 1911, and was put into force as from 15th July, 1912.

This Act of 1911, though in itself only a beginning, now forms the basis of a much more imposing superstructure of insurance than was then contemplated, and is worthy of some detailed consideration. It was in three parts. Part I. dealt with National Health Insurance, Part II. with Unemployment Insurance, and Part III. with miscellaneous provisions relating to Parts I. and II. Seeing that Health Insurance and Unemployment Insurance, both under this 1911 Act and at the present day (1933), are administered by separate departments of Government, it will be more convenient for the purposes of this article to deal with each subject separately. (*See also* PENSIONS.)

Health Insurance.—Speaking broadly, every working person between the ages of sixteen and seventy receiving wages or salary at a rate amounting to less than £160 a year was insurable under this 1911 Act, and in the case of manual workers insurance was compulsory. There were *exceptions*, such as employees of public authorities and institutions, whose work was of a permanent nature, and also certain *exemptions*, notably persons able to prove that they had private means amounting to not less than £26 a year.

The rates of contribution payable under the original Act in respect of each insured person were: for a man, 7*d*. a week, for a woman, 6*d*. a week; but of this sum the employer paid 3*d*. a week, whether for a man or a woman; so that the ordinary rate of contribution was 4*d*. a week by the male worker and 3*d*. a week by women workers. In the case of employees over twenty-one years of age whose remuneration did not exceed 2*s*. 6*d*. a working day and did not include the provision of board and lodging by the employer. varying rates of contribution were paid. Persons exempt from insurance paid no contributions, but the employer nevertheless paid his 3*d*. per week in respect of each one. To the contribution paid for each fully-insured person the State contributed in effect 2*d*., so that the total sum available for the provision of benefits was 8*d*. in the case of a woman, and 9*d*. in the case of a man, the employer's contribution representing three-ninths of this latter sum, the State's two-ninths, and the worker's four-ninths. The phrase "Ninepence for fourpence" was widely current at the time as representing the workers' insurance "bargain." The standard cash benefits were 10*s*. a week for men and 7*s*. 6*d*. a week for women as sickness benefit; 5*s*. a week for both men and women as disablement benefit; and 30*s*. as maternity benefit.

To obtain the fullest benefits of Health Insurance it was necessary under this 1911 Act (and still is) for the insured person to become a member of what was known as an "approved society." Friendly societies of various types had for many years been giving "sickness benefits" to their members, and it was considered desirable to make use (after establishing suitable safeguards) of the best parts and features of this ready-made machinery for administering benefits under a State scheme of Health Insurance. Most of the leading friendly societies of the country, and a great many trade unions, qualified as approved societies. In addition, some of the large industrial insurance companies established separate sections for administering benefits under the Act, and these sections were recognized as approved societies. Any insurable person who was not a member of an approved society might participate in the State insurance scheme as a "deposit contributor," but with certain limitations as to privileges as compared with a member of an approved society. There were also certain facilities for "voluntary contribututors."

The benefits to the insured person under the 1911 Act were as follows:

1. Medical Benefit. Medical attendance during illness, including the provision of medicine.[1]
2. Sanatorium Benefit. Treatment in sanatoria or similar institutions for sufferers from tuberculosis.
3. Sickness Benefit. Payment, for a period not exceeding twenty-six weeks during incapacitation from work by disease or disablement, of 10*s*. a week in the case of men, and 7*s*. 6*d*. a week in the case of women.
4. Disablement Benefit. Payment of 5*s*. a week for either men or women so long as incapacity for work continued after the twenty-six weeks of "sickness benefit" had terminated.[2]
5. Maternity Benefit. Payment in the case of the confinement of the wife of an insured person or of any other insured woman of a sum of 30*s*.

Many acts amending the 1911 Act have been passed, and they have had very considerable effects on its benefits, scope, and mode of administration, but without any great alteration of underlying principle. Under the 1911 Act Health Insurance was administered by four separate national Commissions, one each for the four kingdoms, and one joint Committee of these four Commissions. Local Insurance Committees in each county and county borough administered "medical benefit," all other benefits, except those of deposit contributors, being administered through the approved societies. But since 1919 England and Wales have come under the Ministry of Health, and Scotland under the Scottish Board of

[1] In Ireland medical benefit was not provided, and the rates of contribution payable in respect of insured persons were correspondingly smaller.

[2] Sickness and disablement benefits ceased when the insured person reached the age of seventy years

Health. In 1922 the Irish Insurance Commission's work passed to the Government of Southern Ireland, except for health services in respect of insured persons resident in Northern Ireland, which were transferred to the Government of Northern Ireland, and placed by them under the Ministry of Labour for Northern Ireland.

9*d*. and 6*d*. Voluntary contributors pay the whole contribution of 1*s*. 6*d*. in the case of men and 1*s*. 1*d*. in the case of women. After the age of sixty-five, employed persons cease to pay contributions and the employer continues to pay 9*d*. (equivalent to his share of the ordinary rate) as long as employment continues after the age-limit is reached. Statutory rates

	Sickness Benefit.		Disablement Benefit.	
	Men.	Women.	Men.	Women.
1913	£3,623,220	£1,770,371	..	..
1914	4,014,187	1,732,327	£124,212	£36,781
1915	3,141,548	1,393,402	514,681	210,573
1916	2,683,782	1,176,181	655,241	308,688
1917	2,495,637	1,163,941	706,050	355,994
1918	2,877,861	1,445,812	729,780	393,891
1919	3,098,263	1,326,998	772,232	430,282
1920	3,667,081	1,678,092	1,104,621	629,890
Total	25,601,579	11,687,124	4,606,817	2,366,099
Average per Annum	3,200,200	1,460,891	658,117	338,014

The various amending Acts, 1913–21, also altered very considerably the rates of contribution and of benefit. Following the lessening of money values and the rise in wages during the European War, an Act was passed in 1919 to bring within the scope of the State Health Insurance scheme workers in receipt of wages and salaries not exceeding £250 a year. From 5th July, 1920, the contribution payable in respect of insured persons was increased and benefits were readjusted.

Other amendments of note to the 1911 Act concerned insured women who married; soldiers, sailors, and airmen who were allowed to continue their insurance membership during service, the contributions payable in respect of them being met by the Admiralty, the Army Council, and the Air Council; and mercantile mariners (masters, seamen, or apprentices), who are subject to special provisions as to Health Insurance. In 1924 the existing legislation relating to Health Insurance was consolidated, and in 1925 the Widows', Orphans', and Old Age contributory Pensions Act was grafted on to the scheme. As from 1926 a combined scheme of Health and Pensions has been in operation; the health insurance age being lowered from seventy to sixty-five in January 1928. Under this combined scheme the ordinary rate of contributions is 1*s*. 6*d*. for men and 1*s*. 1*d*. for women; employers pay 9*d*. in respect of men and 7*d*. in respect of women, the employees' share being respectively

of benefit were altered to 15*s*. a week for men and 12*s*. a week for women (full rates) after two years of insurance and the payment of 104 weekly contributions. The disablement benefit is at the normal rate of 7*s*. 6*d* a week for both men and women. Maternity benefit is now 40*s*. when the claimant can show 42 weeks of insurance and the payment of 42 contributions. Additional benefits are provided by approved societies, the valuation of whose assets and liabilities shows them to be in a position to do so. Some of these benefits are payments in cash, and others "treatment" benefits, or benefits in kind.

The accompanying table of expenditure of approved societies (England and Wales) on sickness and disablement benefits in the years 1913-20 allows of some generalizations as to the incidence of sickness and disablement among the working-classes —the classes to whom the Health Insurance Act applies virtually exclusively.

Allowing for the respective maximum rates of sickness and disablement benefit current during these periods, this expenditure for the eight years represents a yearly average of one week's

Sickness.	*Disablement.*
6,217,048 men	2,699,011 men
3,771,405 women	1,378,536 women
9,988,453	4,077,547

a total of 14,066,000 weeks' work lost on an average every year, or a period of 270,000 years. In 1930 England and Wales lost about 26½ million weeks' work through sickness, the equivalent of the year's work of 510,000 persons, in the insured or working-classes alone.

The number of insured persons entitled to medical benefit in Great Britain and Northern Ireland is now (1933) considerably over 17 millions, of whom nearly 11½ millions are men and more than 5¾ millions are women; there are about 250,000 "deposit contributors." The number of doctors taking part in the Insurance Medical Service is approximately 16,000. They give every year approximately 60 million attendances to insured persons, and about 58 million insurance prescriptions are dispensed. The third valuation of the approved societies in 1931 showed an amount of £167,145,000 standing to their credit, of which nearly £50 million represented outstanding "reserve values," the remainder being accumulated contributions, plus interest.

Unemployment Insurance.—The Unemployment Insurance Section of the 1911 Act came into force on the same date as the Health Insurance Section, viz. 15th July, 1912, and was administered for some years by the Board of Trade.

It applied only to certain trades: (1) building, (2) construction of works, (3) shipbuilding, (4) mechanical engineering, (5) iron-founding, (6) construction of vehicles, (7) sawmilling. About 2¼ million workers (including about 10,000 women) were covered by the original scheme.

The rates of contributions were as follows:

	Per week.
For every workman employed in an insured trade	2½*d*.
For every employer in respect of each workman so insured . . .	2½*d*.

Certain reduced rates applied in the case of workmen below the age of eighteen.

To the money thus raised from employers and employed the Government added an amount equal to one-third.

The rate of unemployment benefit in respect of each week following the first week of unemployment was 7*s*., but no benefit was paid to a worker under seventeen years of age, and to a worker between the ages of seventeen and eighteen benefit was paid at one-half the ordinary rate. Benefit was not paid for more than fifteen weeks in any period of twelve months.

Various amending Acts were passed between 1914 and 1931, the most important legislation affecting the Unemployment Insurance Scheme being the Acts of 1916-1918, covering the munition workers, etc; the 1920 Act, which extended the scheme to all manual workers and non-manual workers earning not more than £250 a year; the three Acts passed in 1921, providing for the payment of "uncovenanted" benefit; the two Acts of 1922, which amalgamated existing rates of contributions and instituted further "special periods" of benefit; the 1924 Acts, which made the payment of benefit continuous and reduced the "waiting period"; the 1925 Act, which amended the provisions as to qualifications for benefit; the 1927 Act, which embodied some of the recommendations of the Blanesborough Committee and altered both the rates of contributions and the scales of benefit; the 1930 Act, which abolished the "genuinely seeking work" clause and again altered the scale of benefits by increasing them; and the Acts of 1931 (including the Economy Act) which gave effect to many of the proposals of the Unemployment Insurance Commission and the May Economy Report.

The Act of 1920, which came into operation on 8th Nov. of that year, extended the principle of compulsory unemployment insurance to all manual workers and to virtually all workers in receipt of less than £250 per annum. The main exceptions were private domestic servants, agricultural workers, established (i.e. permanent) civil servants, teachers, and (subject to a certificate from the Minister of Labour that the employed person was not liable to dismissal except for misconduct, neglect, or unfitness, and that the terms of his employment made unemployment insurance unnecessary) the servants of public authorities and companies. The number of persons brought into unemployment insurance by this extension, which is still in force, was approximately 9,000,000.

The position as regards contributions, benefits, and qualifications for benefit has thus been altered materially on many occasions. Under the Economy Act, 1931, the rates of contribution enforced by the first Order issued, with effect as from 1st Oct. of that year, were as shown in table on opposite page. Provision has been made for reduced rates of contributions to come into force when the "extended period" (which means in effect the period of insolvency of the Fund) comes to an end.

Benefits have also been materially

Class.	Employers' Contribution.	Workers' Contribution.	Exchequer Contribution.	Total.
Men (between 21 and 65) . .	10*d.*	10*d.*	10*d.*	2*s.* 6*d.*
Women (between 21 and 65) . .	9*d.*	9*d.*	9*d.*	2*s.* 3*d.*
Men (between 18 and 21) . .	9*d.*	9*d.*	9*d.*	2*s.* 3*d.*
Women (between 18 and 21) . .	8*d.*	8*d.*	8*d.*	2*s.* 0*d.*
Boys under 18 . .	5*d.*	5*d.*	5*d.*	1*s.* 3*d.*
Girls under 18	4½*d.*	4½*d.*	4½*d.*	1*s.* 1½*d.*

reduced under the Economy Act. The ordinary rates are as follows:

	Weekly Rate.
Men (16 to 65)	15*s.* 3*d.*
Women (16 to 65)	13*s.* 6*d.*
Men (18 to 21)	12*s.* 6*d.*
Women (18 to 21)	10*s.* 9*d.*
Boys (17 to 18)	8*s.* 0*d.*
Girls (17 to 18)	6*s.* 9*d.*
Boys under 17	5*s.* 6*d.*
Girls under 17	4*s.* 6*d.*

Dependants' allowances were fixed at 8*s.* per week for an adult dependant and 2*s.* a week for each child under fourteen (the latter being payable also in respect of a child between fourteen and sixteen receiving instruction in a day school, or unable to receive such instruction on account of physical or mental infirmity). Conditions of a restrictive character are imposed upon the payment of these benefits and payment is subject to fulfilment of strict statutory conditions both in respect of "standard" and "transitional" benefits. The "standard" benefit is now payable only to applicants who satisfy the first statutory condition (i.e. the payment of not less than 30 contributions during the two years preceding the claim), and benefit is payable for no more than 156 days (26 weeks) in the benefit year. Claimants who cannot satisfy this condition and have exhausted their right to benefit may, however, qualify for "transitional" benefit if not less than eight contributions have been paid in respect of them during the preceding two years, if they can prove that they are normally in insurable employment, that they would, but for the 156 days' benefit rule, have been entitled to benefit, and that their circumstances are such that while unemployed they are in need of assistance (i.e. a Means Test). The "waiting period" for benefit is again six days, and there is a "continuity" rule by which spells of unemployment may be linked up to form a continuous period and applied to claims for benefit and "waiting" period. In addition to the first statutory condition (i.e the 30 contributions rule), there are four other statutory conditions which the claimant must satisfy before benefit is payable, and there are certain positive disqualifications for benefit (e.g. refusal of suitable employment, stoppages due to trade dispute, and "misconduct," such as absence from work without leave and other breaches of discipline).

At the time when the Royal Commission was appointed, in 1930, the borrowings of the Insurance Fund amounted to £60 million, and was then increasing at the rate of £43 million a year. Unemployment Insurance was costing £110 million a year (including £4 million of interest on the debt, and £6½ million for administration); whereas the contributions of employers and workpeople totalled no more than £30 million; so that the State was called upon to provide £80 million by direct subventions or out of borrowed money. A limit of £115 million was imposed by Parliament upon borrowing, and money required to balance the Fund must now be provided as a deficiency grant for the Government out of current revenue. The estimated charge on the Exchequer for 1932-33 was £79,000,000.

NATIONALIZATION. Acquisition by the state of land or any other public utility, usually by purchase. The word is commonly used to describe the socialist policy of public ownership. The nationalization of the land has been proposed in Great Britain, and a society exists to forward the idea. Nationalization has been carried to extreme lengths in Russia under the Soviet, but in other countries it has been mainly confined to public utilities, such as telegraphs and telephones, railways, electrical power supply, passenger transport, and the like.

NATIONALISTS. A term applied to a political party in a country, forming part of another country, which demands autonomy or complete independence. In this sense the term was generally applied to the Irish political party whose programme included the more or less complete separation of Ireland from Great Britain. The Irish Nationalist party almost disappeared in 1918 when the Sinn Fein party took its place. There is at present a nationalist movement in Scotland and other countries. The term is also used by ultra-patriotic parties and groups which claim to represent a national resurgence or awakening, such as the Hitler movement in Germany. (*See* GERMANY, HITLER, NAZI MOVEMENT.)

NATROLITE. A zeolite of the Mesotype group, so called on account of the great quantity of soda it contains. It occurs in the cavities of volcanic lavas, or as a direct decomposition-product within soda-lime felspars, and consists of 48 per cent. silica, 26 alumina, 16 soda, and 10 water.

NATRON ($Na_2CO_3 10H_2O$). Native sodium carbonate or mineral alkali, found in the ashes of several marine plants, and abundantly in lakes in Egypt, and in some mineral springs.

NATRON LAKE. A lake of Africa, near Lake Magadi. Both contain enormous deposits of soda.

NATTERJACK, or NATTERJACK TOAD. The *Bufo calamīta*, a species of toad found in various parts of Western Europe, in certain parts of Asia (including Tibet), and not uncommon in England. The general colour is lightish-brown, spotted with patches of a darker hue. A line or streak of yellowish tint passes down the middle line of the back. It does not leap or crawl like the common toad, but rather runs, whence it has the name of walking or running toad. It has a deep and hollow voice, audible at a great distance. It is often found in dry situations.

NATURAL GAS. *See* PETROLEUM.

NATURAL HISTORY. In its widest sense, that department of knowledge which comprehends the sciences of zoology and botany, chemistry, natural philosophy or physics, geology, palæontology, and mineralogy. It is now, however, commonly used to denote collectively the sciences of botany and zoology, and it is sometimes restricted to denote the science of zoology alone.—BIBLIOGRAPHY: Kerner, *The Natural History of Plants*; Ainsworth Davis, *The Natural History of Animals*.

NATURALISM. In philosophy, is the theory which maintains that the cause of events in the universe can be explained by immanent natural principles, and denies the existence of any transcending power. It is a tendency to look upon nature as the fundamental cause of everything that exists and to explain everything in terms of nature. It denies the dualism of matter and mind, mental phenomena being only manifestations of matter. Reducing as it does the principles governing the universe to mechanical laws, naturalism is synonymous with materialism but it differs from it in so far as it is not concerned with the problem of the essence of matter.

Sometimes naturalism admits the existence of a dual principle, matter and mind, but denies the transcendence of the first cause, or God, which is both *natura naturans*, and *natura naturata*. It is thus synonymous with *Pantheism* (q.v.). Naturalism is not, strictly speaking, a philosophical system, as it pervades various philosophical doctrines. The result of, and stimulated by, a scientific awakening, naturalism is a revolt against the supernatural—and an attempt to explain phenomena in scientific terms, reducing everything to the laws of matter, motion, and evolution.

Democritus, Epicurus, and Lucretius were naturalists. The philosophies and doctrines of Aristotle, Spinoza, and Hobbes may be called naturalistic in their tendencies, and modern philosophy, endeavouring as it does to explain experience in terms of natural science, is generally naturalistic. Whilst the older naturalism, however, was frankly atheistic, modern naturalism is agnostic in its tendencies.

In literature, naturalism is the extreme of realism, and even something more than realism. The realist closely imitates nature, whilst the naturalist not only describes the realities of life, but revels in the description of its more repellent aspects. Naturalism is the keynote of the works of many modern French authors, particularly of those of Zola, and of the modern German drama. In English literature we have many realists, but their realism has never been so extreme as to deteriorate into naturalism.—BIBLIOGRAPHY: R. Otto, *Naturalism and Religion*; J. Ward, *Naturalism and Agnosticism*; J. S. Haldane, *Mechanism, Life, and Personality*.

NATURALIZATION. The process by which an alien adopts the status of a subject. In the United Kingdom the conditions of naturalization are governed by the British Nationality and Status of Aliens Acts, 1914 and 1918.

The Home Secretary may grant a certificate of naturalization to any alien who satisfies him (1) that he has resided in His Majesty's dominions or been in the service of the Crown for at least five years out of the preceding eight, at least the last year of residence having been in the United Kingdom; (2) that he is of good character and has an adequate knowledge of the English language; and (3) that he intends to reside in His Majesty's dominions or continue in the service of the Crown. The certificate is not effective until the oath of allegiance has been taken. The power of the Home Secretary to refuse a certificate is absolute. A naturalized alien has all the rights and obligations of a natural-born subject.

NATURAL PHILOSOPHY. *See* PHYSICS.

NATURAL SELECTION. The fundamental idea implied in Charles Darwin's teaching. On 1st July, 1858, the two essays written independently by Darwin and Alfred Wallace were submitted to the Linnæan Society of London as a joint paper "On the Tendency of Species to form Varieties; and on the Perpetuation of Varieties and Species by Natural Means of Selection." In this communication Darwin first made public the phrase "natural selection," and Wallace "the struggle for existence," although the former had given expression to both ideas in his notebooks twenty years before this public announcement.

On 24th Nov., 1859, Darwin's *magnum opus* was published "On the Origin of Species by Means of Natural Selection, or the Preservation of Favoured Races in the Struggle for Life"—a title which clearly defines what is implied in Darwinism. Some years afterwards he wrote, "I have spoken of selection as the paramount power, whether applied by man to the formation of domestic breeds, or by nature to the production of species." In other words, Darwin claimed that, just as men by careful selection of animals or plants showing certain qualities can breed a great variety of horses, dogs, pigeons, or in fact almost any animal or plant, so the varied natural circumstances may prove unfavourable to the living organisms presenting some traits and favourable to these presenting others, and bring about by natural means a selective process in some respects analogous to what the breeder effects by the deliberate choice of animals and plants for mating.

For more than half a century this claim has been assailed by every kind of misrepresentation as well as by serious and honest argument; and at the present time it has become a fashionable pose among certain biologists to scoff at natural selection and erroneously to pretend it was put forward to explain the variability of organisms. But Darwin himself refuted such criticisms in advance when he wrote (*Origin of Species*): "Some have even imagined that natural selection induces variability, whereas it implies the preservation of such variations as arise . . .; unless such occur natural selection can do nothing." This is a clear and explicit statement of unassailable fact, which is not weakened, but immensely strengthened, by the modern developments in the study of heredity and variation. (*See* EVOLUTION.)

A vast literature has grown up as the result of the discussion of the leading principle of Darwin's illuminating generalization. A useful and concise guide to this controversial writing is Professor E. B. Poulton's *Charles Darwin and the Theory of Natural Selection* (1901), and the more recent criticisms are dealt with in Professor Edwin S. Goodrich's excellent little book, *The Evolution of Living Organisms.*

NATURAL THEOLOGY. A branch of theology dealing with the knowledge of God's existence as derived from the observation of nature and through the light of reason, independent of revelation. It is religion derived from nature and reason, by the aid of which, without that of supernatural revelation, it endeavours to prove the existence of God. It treats of the nature, character, and attributes of God; the relation of God to the world and to man, and of man and the world to God.

One of the principal arguments of natural theology is what may be called the *cosmological argument.* Every effect must have a cause, and the laws of natural selection or survival of the fittest must have had a law-giver. The prevalence of order in nature tends to prove that the universe is an event or a generated existence, the work of intelligence. Both organic and inorganic nature alike show clear proofs of harmony and order, presupposing an intelligent cause.

Another argument is based upon design, and is called the *teleological* argument. We notice how nature is constantly acting with a deliberate design, or purpose, how the whole universe is adapted to its environment, and how the different parts of the organism are adjusted in the interests of the whole. It cannot be the result of random disorder, "purposeless change superinduced upon meaningless uniformity," but the work of a transcendental and powerful Being who originated all things with a purpose. Even the laws of evolution and of natural selection cannot, according to natural theology, exclude the argument from design. "Selection," wrote A J. Balfour, "may enable organic species to adapt their powers to their environment, and their environment to their powers, but it cannot produce either the original environment, or the original living matter."

It is further claimed by natural theology that the idea of the existence of a Supernatural, Superior Power is innate in the human mind, and as the human mind is capable of conceiving such a Supernatural Being, it is evidence of the reality of existence of such a Power. Questions of natural theology were discussed by various ancient philosophers, as Socrates, Plato, Aristotle, and Cicero; but the first regular treatise on the subject was the *Theologia Naturalis* of Raymond de Sabunde, who died in 1432. Among modern works on the subject are: Paley's *Natural Theology*, Chalmers's *Natural Theology*, and *The Bridgewater] Treatises*. *See* THEISM.—BIBLIOGRAPHY: A. J. Balfour, *Theism and Humanism*; R. Flint, *Theism*; F. Max Müller, *Natural Religion*.

NATURE PRINTING. A method which has occasionally been used for producing pictures of such objects as ferns and seaweeds. The essential feature of the method is that no drawing is needed, the electro used by the printer being derived from an impression made on a metal plate by the object itself.

NATURE WORSHIP, or NATURISM. The worship of nature as a whole, i.e. of all things in nature, including not only the elements and celestial bodies, but also plants, animals, and man. Nature worship is to be distinguished both from naturalism, which is a system of philosophy, and from natural religion, which endeavours to prove the existence of God without the aid of Revelation.

According to some thinkers, nature worship is the most ancient form of religion. Primitive man, destitute of religion, ignorant but emotional, seized with wonder at the aspect of the world and its constant changes, attributed to the phenomena surrounding him a life and an activity similar to his own. Constantly in touch with nature, dependent upon it for his daily existence, benefiting by its bounties, threatened by its dangers, to him nature was at once awe-inspiring and worshipful, in turn hostile and friendly, and his thoughts became concentrated upon it and upon its striking phenomena. Conceiving nature as animated throughout, attributing to the external objects which surrounded him a motion and life similar to his own, he evolved the idea of supernatural beings dominating the most striking phenomena. "In his anxiety," writes Professor Menzies (*History of Religion*), "for food and warmth, man could not fail to think of the beings who, he had observed, had power to supply him with these comforts." Struck by the activity of the objects of nature, their movements, motions, and powers, he compared them to his own personality, concluded that they were alive, and worshipped them.

It is generally admitted that nature worship is of very ancient date, and that since his earliest existence man always showed a tendency to experience vague religious emotions when coming into contact with nature. But the theory of Max Müller, who maintained that nature worship was the most primitive form of religion, and also the theories of Tylor and Spencer, who endeavoured to prove that ancestor worship was the earliest form of religion, have been discarded by ethnologists. It has been proved that man worshipped other gods even before he turned to nature as a subject of adoration.—BIBLIOGRAPHY: D. G. Brinton, *The Religions of Primitive Peoples*; Sir J. G. Frazer, *The Golden Bough*.

NAU'KRATIS. An ancient Greek city in Egypt, which stood on a navigable canal in the western part of the Delta near the Canopic branch of the Nile. It existed as early as the beginning of the seventh century B.C., and had been a place of great splendour. Excavations on the site of the city by Flinders Petrie have been productive of highly valuable results.—Cf. W. M. Flinders Petrie, *Naukratis*.

NAUMBURG (noum'bu̦rh). A town of Prussian Saxony, in the valley of the Saale. One of the principal buildings is the cathedral, partly Gothic and partly Romanesque, completed in 1249. The manufactures consist of combs, playing-cards, leather, and hosiery. Pop. 26,960.

NAU'PLIUS. A term applied to the earliest stage in the development of the lower Crustacea. The naupliiform larva has an ovate unsegmented body, a median eye, and three pairs of limbs. This form is regarded as the primitive form of all crustaceans.

NAURU, or PLEASANT ISLAND. An island of the Southern Pacific, in 166° E. long., 26 miles S. of the equator. The climate is healthy and malaria is unknown. Six-sevenths of the total area of 5396 acres is phosphate-bearing.

Until 1914 Nauru formed a part of German New Guinea, and was occupied (Nov., 1914) by a detachment from the Australian expedition at Rabaul. By the Peace Treaty (1919) the British Empire became mandatory by League of Nations' mandate dated 17th Dec., 1920, and authority, administrative, legislative, and judicial, is vested in an Administrator, whose expenses are met from local revenue and from the proceeds of the sale of phosphates. The quality of these phosphates is very high, and the total deposits are estimated at 100,000,000 tons, of which 4,000,000 tons have already been removed. There is a wireless station communicating with Tsingtau, and other Pacific islands. The total population of the island in 1932 was 2316 (including 1475 natives, 696 Chinese, 4 other Pacific islanders, and 141 Europeans).

NAU'SEA. The sensation of sickness with an inclination to vomit. It occurs in many functional disorders, as well as in organic disease, of the stomach. It also arises reflexly, as in sea-sickness, as the result of emotions, disgust, and fear, or following irritation and disturbance of almost any part of the abdominal tract.

NAUTILOIDEA. A great group of shell-bearing cephalopods, now represented only by the genus Nautilus, but including genera of various forms throughout Palæozoic times. The shell is chambered, and the partitions are simply curved. The tube running through them is practically central, and the calcareous neck supporting it at each partition is directed backwards. The straight form Orthoceras (q.v.) is an important genus. The genus Nautilus appears in Triassic times.

NAU'TILUS. A genus of cephalopods with many-chambered shells, the only surviving genus of the subclass Tetrabranchiata. The shell of the pearly nautilus (*N. pompilius*) is a spiral with smooth sides. The turns or whorls are contiguous, the outer whorl covering the inner. The chambers of the shell are separated by transverse septa, and one after the other have been the residence of the animal, being successively abandoned as it has grown. The animal thus always resides in the cavity of its outermost or external chamber. A siphuncle connects the body with the air-chambers, passing through each transverse septum till it terminates in the smallest chamber at the inner extremity of the shell. These internal chambers contain only air. By means of the siphuncle the animal is enabled to sink itself or to swim.

Pearly Nautilus (*Nautilus pompilius*) in section

The nautilus is an inhabitant of the tropical seas. Only three or four existing species are known, though the fossil species exceed a hundred. The name is often loosely applied to the shells of different genera of mollusca. The animal which has been said to sail in its shell upon the surface of the water is the paper-nautilus or argonaut. (*See* ARGONAUT.)

NAUVOO. A city of Illinois, United States, in Hancock county, on the Mississippi. It was founded in 1840 by the Mormons, and afterwards occupied between 1850 and 1858 by a company of French Socialists. Pop., in 1846, about 15,000; pop. (1930), 965.

NAVAJO (or NAVAHO) INDIANS (nȧ-vä'hō). A tribe of American Indians numbering about 12,000. They occupy a reservation in the north-west of New Mexico and the north-east of Arizona.

NAVAL CADETS. *See* NAVY.

NAVAL DIVISION, Royal. In modern times naval forces have successfully been employed as land forces. The British Naval Brigade, under Sir Percy Scott, took a prominent part at Ladysmith and Colenso (South African War), and both the French and Germans have used naval forces in previous campaigns, as well as in the European War. The formation of the Royal Naval Division (subsequently known as the 63rd (R.N.) Division or R.N.D.) at the end of Aug., 1914, and the use on land of men trained for sea-service was therefore no new departure.

The three brigades were fully constituted by 24th Aug., 1914, and comprised the 1st Brigade (Benbow, Drake, Hawke, and Collingwood Battalions), 2nd Brigade (Nelson, Howe, Hood, and Anson Battalions), and the Marine Brigade (9th, 10th, 11th, and 12th Battalions). Each of the naval battalions took the name of a famous admiral.

In 1914 they suffered disaster at Antwerp, and during the night of 9th Oct. many men were interned in Holland. As a division they fought in Gallipoli, and, after the evacuation, working parties were reformed at Stavros (Salonica front), the whole division subsequently embarking for France, where they captured Beaucourt (13th to 14th Nov., 1916) during the battle of the Ancre, and took a heavy share in the fighting until the Armistice (11th Nov., 1918), when they were on the Harmignies-Villers-St. Ghislain line, and still advancing.—Cf. Fry and M'Millan, *The Complete History of the Royal Naval Division.*

The official intimation read: "Monday, 7th September, 1914.—After providing for all present and forseeable future needs of the fleets at sea, there remained available a large number of men belonging to the Royal Marines, Royal Naval Volunteer Reserve, Royal Fleet Reserve, and Royal Naval Reserve. A portion of these have been organized into one marine and two naval brigades, the whole comprising one infantry division, to be called the Royal Naval Division." The marine brigade was organized before the war, and at this time had already been in action at Ostend.

NAVAL RESERVE (ROYAL). *See* Navy.

NAV'AN. A town of County Meath, Irish Free State, 30 miles from Dublin, at the junction of the Boyne and Blackwater. It is on the G.S. Railways, and is an agricultural centre. Pop. (1926), 3649.

NAVANAGAR. *See* Nawanagar.

NAVARRE (Sp. *Navarra*). A frontier province of Northern Spain. The southern district lies in the valley of the Ebro; the northern district is rugged and mountainous, lying on the slopes of the eastern spurs and outlying ranges of the Pyrenees and the Cantabrians. All the rivers excepting the Bidassoa drain to the south, where they join the Ebro. The mountains are afforested; wheat, maize, wines, oil, flax, and hemp are produced; cattle and sheep are reared; freshwater fish are abundant. Pamplona is the capital. Area, 4055 sq. miles; pop. 347,483.

NAVARRE. A former kingdom extending over parts of France and Spain, but occupying mainly the region of the modern province. It arose from the emigration of Christian nobles during the Muslim conquest of Spain in the eighth century, and the first-known king was Sancho Iñiguez (905), whose grandson, Sancho III., "the Great" (970-1035), became the most powerful Christian monarch in Spain. The Iñiguez dynasty came to an end by the death in 1234 of Sancho VII., son of Berengaria by Richard I. of England.

Blanche of Navarre, granddaughter of Charles the Bad, married John II. of Aragon, who succeeded in 1458 and died in 1479, when Navarre passed to Catherine of Foix, who married the French Constable, Jean d'Albret. Jeanne d'Albret, daughter of Catherine, was the mother of Henri de Navarre, who succeeded to the French throne in 1589 as Henri IV. His father being Antoine de Bourbon, Henri was thus the first of the Bourbon kings of France. French Navarre was annexed to France in 1620; Spanish Navarre, which had been annexed by Ferdinand of Spain, ceased to exist apart from Spain after 1512.

NAVARRO, Ramon. Film actor. Born at Durango, Mexico, in 1900, he received a thorough education in violin-playing, dancing, and opera-singing, and is noted for his handsome face and pleasant voice.

NAVEL, or UMBILI'CUS. The aperture or passage in the abdomen which in the adult is normally closed, but in the fœtus or embryo gives passage to the umbilical vessels, by means of which the fœtus communicates with the parent through the placenta. The cicatrization or healing of the navel produces the contracted and depressed appearance so familiar in the external aspect of the structure.

NAVEL ILL AND JOINT ILL. In veterinary science, a complaint due to invasion of the umbilical cord or navel-string by septic organisms. Frequently the primary symptoms are not observed. They consist in loss of spirits and a disposition to stand and arch the back more or less. The teat is not sought, and an increasing indifference to surroundings presently ends in the young animal persistently remaining on the ground, stretched out and somnolent. Treatment is generally unsatisfactory, and prevention is merely a matter of tying the umbilical cord close up to the belly of the lamb, calf, or foal as soon as born, and the application to the dependent portion and to the immediate region of the navel of a mixture of 1 part by measure of pure carbolic acid with 11 or 12 measures of collodion or some other germicide.

NAVICULAR DISEASE. A form of lameness in horses in which the small bone known as the navicular or shuttle bone becomes diseased. One of the tendons (" back tendons ") also shares in the disease. In its course inside the foot, this tendon passes under the navicular bone, which acts as a lever, but is separated from actual contact by an oil-sheath, or bursa, supplying oil to reduce the friction. Causes are various, but heredity is the principal one. The disease is found mostly in well-bred horses about five years of age and upwards. It is rare in draught horses. The fore-limbs are always affected, and no case is on record of the hind being affected. Diagnosis is not easy, and demands careful observation.

Treatment is very difficult, and in advanced navicular disease nothing answers but the division of the sensory nerves by a veterinary surgeon, whereby feeling is cut off (neurectomy or neurotomy) and the animal does not go lame, although the destructive work continues in the foot.

NAVIGATION. The science and art of finding a ship's position at sea, and of determining the proper course on which to sail to reach the port of destination. Near land, special methods are available, which come under *seamanship* (q.v.). In mid-ocean, two main methods are used in combination, " dead reckoning " and astronomical observation.

Dead Reckoning.—In this method, which is an important part of the routine of every ship, position is estimated from approximate knowledge of the distance travelled on a known course from a previous known position. The course is kept by the compass (q.v.), and to determine the true geographical course allowance is made for magnetic deviation (q.v.) and variation or declination (q.v.), as well as for leeway, or the effect of winds and currents; the leeway may be estimated by the eye. with the help of a diagram on the taffrail, as the angle between the ship's fore and aft line and her wake.

The course and distance from a given point being known (*see* Log), the change in position has to be translated in terms of latitude and longitude. About latitude there is no difficulty. The speed in a direction inclined at a given constant angle to the (varying) meridian being given, the speed north or south is found simply by multiplying by the cosine of the angle, and the change of latitude is thus found in miles. The speed east or west is found by multiplying by the sine of the same angle; the distance that would be gone at this speed in the given time is the *departure*. The departure, however, does not give the exact change of longitude at once, unless the course is along a parallel (*parallel sailing*), in which case (change of longitude in miles) = (departure in miles) ÷ (cosine of latitude).

In *plane sailing*, which may be used for short runs, change of latitude and departure are alone considered. In *middle latitude sailing*, the change of longitude is found from the departure by supposing the latitude of the above formula to be the latitude midway between the extreme values for the run. In the method called *Mercator sailing*, which is the most accurate method for long distances, the Mercator chart (*see* Maps) is used, actually or in principle. On this chart the course is a straight line beginning at a given point; the end point of the course can be found easily from the change of latitude calculated as explained above; and the new longitude is then read off the chart, or, more usually, calculated from a table of *meridional parts*, a table which embodies the same facts as are expressed graphically by the chart.

Astronomical Methods.—After a day's run the dead reckoning may easily give a result 5 or 10 miles out, and, unless the weather absolutely forbids, the navigator invariably checks and corrects his dead reckoning by the more refined methods of astronomy. His instrument is the *sextant* (q.v.), and what he observes is the *altitude* (q.v.) of sun, moon, or star. In order to get a clear notion of the exact amount of information given by a single observation of the altitude of a heavenly body, say a star, it is very useful to consider the star's *geographical position*, which is the point where the earth's surface is cut by the straight line from the centre of the earth to the star. Fig. 1 represents a section of the earth's surface by the plane through the star, the ship Z, and the centre of the earth C. X is the geo-position of the star, and EZH is its altitude. But since ZE and XF are practically parallel, the altitude EZH is the complement of the zenith distance DZE or ZCX, and ZCX in minutes of angle is the distance in ZX nautical miles. If the Greenwich mean time is known, the geo-position of the observed

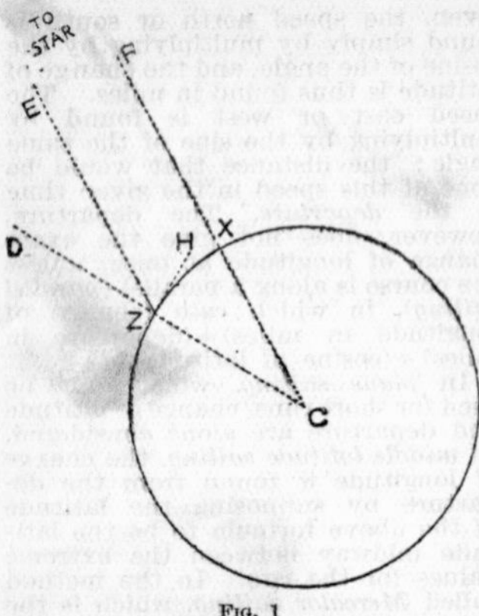

FIG. 1

body may be found from the *Nautical Almanac*. Thus a single observation tells the distance of the ship from a known spot on earth, so that we know that she lies somewhere on a definite small circle of the terrestrial sphere.

Hence if two sights are taken simultaneously, of two stars for instance, we can find two small circles on which the ship must lie, so that her position is fixed as at one or other of two known points, between which we can choose without ambiguity from the dead reckoning. It would hardly ever be practicable to carry this method out on a chart, on account of the great distances involved, but the idea of an observation defining a *position line* on which the ship must lie is of the highest importance, and is continually used in modern practice.

Two special cases are particularly useful. (1) In a meridian sight, the position line, which is always at right angles to the body's bearing, is practically the parallel of latitude, so that a meridian sight gives latitude. (2) When the body is on the prime vertical, i.e. due east or west, the position line is practically a meridian, and the sight gives the longitude. The mathematics of sights on the meridian and on the prime vertical is very simple. Thus, in a meridian sight, even a rough knowledge of Greenwich time gives from the *Almanac* the sun's declination, i.e. the latitude of its geo-position; and the sight gives, as it were, the latitude of the same point relative to the ship, so that the ship's latitude is found by a simple addition or subtraction.

In a morning sight, when the sun is due east, we find the longitude of its geo-position from the exact Greenwich time and the *Almanac*; and we find our own longitude relative to this geo-position from the observed distance between sun and ship, and the rough dead reckoning value of the latitude. The important facts that a noon sight gives latitude from a rough longitude, and that a morning or evening sight gives longitude from a rough latitude, are examples of the simple principle that the perpendicular distance from a point to a line is a *stationary* value, i.e. that a line a little off the perpendicular differs extremely little in length from the perpendicular itself.

When the body observed is neither on the meridian nor on the prime vertical, a little more spherical trigonometry is needed. Thus, in fig. 2, if P be the pole, Z the ship, and X the sun or star (geo-position), the arcs being parts of great circles, we know certain parts of the spherical triangle PZX, the *position triangle*, viz.: (1) ZX ($=z$), the zenith distance of the body, or complement of its observed altitude; (2) PX ($=p$), the polar distance, or co-declination of the body, found from the *Almanac*. We also know approximately (3) ZP ($=c$), the co-latitude, and (4) angle ZPX ($=h$), the *hour-angle* of the body, which is its longitude relative to the ship, or the ship's apparent time by the body regarded as the time-keeper; c being given by the dead reckoning latitude, and h by the dead reckoning longitude combined with information given by the *Almanac* when the Greenwich time is known.

In a morning, or *chronometer*, sight, the rough latitude is sufficient to give a good value of the longitude,

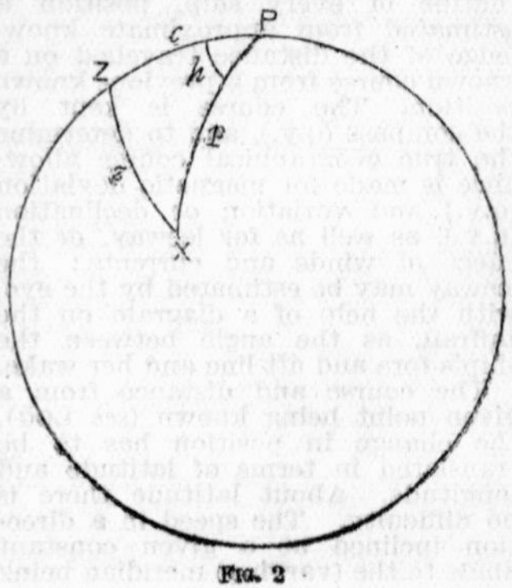

FIG. 2

i.e. we find h from p, z, and c, when the sight is not more than 30° or 40° from the prime vertical. In a sight near noon (*ex-meridian*), the rough longitude gives a good latitude, i.e. we find c from p, z, and h. A morning chronometer sight of the sun is part of the daily routine of a carefully navigated ship. The longitude obtained, combined with the addition due to the run to near noon, as worked out on the chart, is then used to find the latitude by an ex-meridian sight. As a check, an observation may be taken of the sun's meridian altitude.

An interesting method, really old, but not well known till some twenty or thirty years ago, is what is called the *new navigation*. Instead of using the rough dead reckoning latitude to get a fairly exact longitude, or vice versa, we take both latitude and longitude from the dead reckoning, and determine the corresponding distance of the geo-position of the sun by calculation. The true distance is known from the sight. If the calculated distance is, say, 10′ (i.e. 10 minutes of the meridian, or 10 nautical miles) less than the true observed distance, the position line through the dead reckoning position is 10′ too near the sun. The correct position line is therefore the line perpendicular to the sun's bearing, and 10′ farther from the sun than the practically parallel line through the dead reckoning position.

Another sight is taken a few hours later and worked out on the same principle, the first position line being carried forward the proper distance to fit the run between the two sights. We have therefore two position lines at the time of the later sight, and the ship's position is fixed. Two sights taken simultaneously, and worked out by this method, give the *fix* at once. In good weather, with the sun at least occasionally visible, a navigator should find a fix within something like a mile of his position.

The place which navigation holds among the more exact sciences was won at a comparatively recent date. The great difficulty was always longitude. Latitude was easy to get, by pole-star or meridian sun, so that navigation in olden times was sometimes little more than a matter of getting on to the right parallel, and then sailing on due east or west till the destination turned up. The problem of longitude, at least from the astronomical side, is simply the problem of exact time-keeping, and this was not solved till the invention of the chronometer by John Harrison in 1735. (For the intensely interesting story of the prizes offered by the British Government for a solution of the longitude problem, and of Harrison's difficulties in making his claim good, cf. his life in the *Dictionary of National Biography.*)

In spite of the development of wireless communication, it seems unlikely that the chronometer, constructed with the utmost refinement of mechanical skill, will ever cease to be an indispensable aid to scientific navigation. — BIBLIOGRAPHY: W. Hall, *Modern Navigation*; W. R. Martin, *Navigation*; Sir W. Thomson (Lord Kelvin), *Navigation: a Lecture*.

NAVIGATION ACTS. A collective term employed to denote a number of laws protecting British shipping interests and affording them advantageous privileges. By an Act passed in the twelfth year of Charles II., 1660, supplementing and confirming an Act passed by Cromwell in 1651 aimed against Dutch trade, it was enacted that no goods should be imported into England in any other than English ships, save when the goods were the genuine growth or manufacture of the country to which the ship belonged. The 12 Car. II. further provided that the master and three-fourths of the mariners should also be English. Enactments of 1660 and 1663 confined colonial carrying trade to English bottoms, and was at the root of the American War of Independence.

These prohibitions were retained until the adoption of the principle of free-trade, since when they have gradually been relinquished. In 1849 the restrictions on foreign shipping were repealed, except in regard to the coasting trade; the restrictions as to the manning of British ships were repealed in 1853; and in 1854 the coasting trade was thrown open to foreign vessels, subject to the same rules as British vessels.

NAVY. General Definition. — A navy is an organization whereby a varying number of vessels are equipped and armed for war; and manned by specially trained crews of a strength sufficient not merely to handle the ships themselves, but to use the weapons they carry. With the progress of scientific knowledge navies have developed from comparatively simple beginnings into the most highly technical and complex aggregations of fighting force ever known in history, but the above general definition is applicable to all periods.

At the present day all navies in the world are standing organizations composed of vessels which are the State property of their respective countries, and are manned by crews who are State servants while so employed. But up to the end of the sixteenth century, and even somewhat later, a portion of the navy of most maritime powers consisted during a period of hostilities of privately owned trading ships temporarily converted to belligerent purposes, and placed at the disposal of the State either voluntarily or compulsorily.

Sometimes such ships were called upon to undertake all naval duties, including major operations; as, for example, in the case of those which were specially provided under statutory obligation by certain English seaports to assist in defeating the Spanish Armada in 1588. These vessels were included in the composition of the main fleets together with the ships of the Crown, and while so employed were under the direct orders of the Crown officers in command of the fleets in question. But as naval ordnance increased in size it necessitated an increasing specialization in the design of vessels built to carry an artillery armament, and owing to this change the temporary conversion of merchant ships no longer provided useful fighting units. And so it came to pass that during the seventeenth century the temporarily armed merchant ship disappeared from the main war fleets, and all fighting craft thenceforward were State-owned and State-manned, except those known as privateers.

A privateer was a vessel of minor force fitted out at private expense to attack an enemy's trade with the object of private profit, but her status had to be legalized by written authority from the Crown or she was regarded as a pirate. She acted under no orders except from her owner as a general rule, and formed no part of the regular war navy of her flag. In the nineteenth century, however, privateering was abolished by the mutual consent of the principal maritime powers, and thereafter no privately owned vessel was permitted by international custom to carry an armament except for purely defensive purposes.

General Functions.—A navy—like an army—can only conduct operations in its own element, and, as it cannot enter and seize the domestic territory of an enemy, it is only useful for subsidiary purposes in the case of wars in which the opposing sides have practicable access to each other by land. But where they cannot reach each other except by sea routes the operations of the navies assume a first-class importance, and may even comprise the whole conflict.

When a nation is acting purely on the *defensive*, under such circumstances the success of its navy is absolutely decisive; but if its war policy is *offensive* or conquering, victory on the sea has usually to be followed up by operations on the land, for which purpose the passage of its land forces across the water to the enemy's territory can be ensured by naval success alone. A navy therefore—if maintained on an adequate scale—is capable at all times of acting as a complete instrument of defence against the attack of an enemy who can only arrive by water; but it is not capable in itself of acting as an instrument of decisive conquest or aggression except under certain special conditions mentioned below. For example, the complete efficiency of naval defence against attack from oversea was illustrated by the defeat of the Spanish Armada, and the repulse of the many attempts to invade Great Britain that were made from time to time by France, but failed through the victories of Russell, Byng, Hawke, and Nelson.

In some of these instances the invading army was actually embarked and suffered attack *en route*; in others it was assembled in readiness to cross when the fighting fleet had cleared the way. But in every case without exception the success of the defending navy wrecked the whole enterprise.

This power to defend naturally extends to all portions of a State which are only accessible to an enemy by sea. Thus it is that the distant parts of the British Empire such as Australia, New Zealand, Canada, and South Africa are secure against invasion while the British navy remains strong enough to meet any other, except that it cannot defend Canada against the United States. Similarly, the French colonies are safe against attack by any power which cannot first defeat the navy of France.

History has also proved that it is possible under favourable circumstances for a navy, operating defensively, to save the country to which it belongs from final defeat even after occupation by the army of an oversea enemy. The most notable instance of such an occurrence took place when the Japanese sent an army of a quarter of a million to invade Korea towards the close of the sixteenth century. The army crossed the intervening straits without opposition and conquered the whole land, but was cut off from home by the subsequently complete victory of the Korean navy over that of Japan. As Korea had been devastated by the land-war the Japanese troops were dependent on seaborne supplies from home, not only for reinforcements and munitions of war, but for food, and being unable to obtain them were compelled to abandon all the conquered territory and sue for peace, or accept the alternative of perishing by starvation.

As part of the general strategy of attack and defence it is also one of the functions of a navy to maintain intact the maritime routes connecting the various portions of its own State or empire, if these happen to be divided up by the sea, and to break up the corresponding connections of the enemy. If these connections are severed, it prevents concentration of land forces or munitions of war at any threatened point of territory. As comparatively recent examples of this, the defeat of the Spanish navy by that of the United States in 1898 prevented Spain from dispatching reinforcements or supplies to the Spanish garrisons in Cuba, Porto Rico, and the Philippine Islands, and the Spanish Government asked for terms of peace in consequence, and surrendered them all.

Similarly, the rupture of the German sea communications with the German colonies in 1914 left the latter entirely dependent on their own resources for defence. On the other hand, the preservation of the Allied lines of sea communication by the superior power of the British navy enabled large contingents and supplies to reach Europe from the most distant parts of the British Empire, and permitted the French to bring their colonial troops across in safety from Africa. It is this function of the British navy of protecting sea communications that stands as the foundation of the whole system of imperial defence, for even the land frontiers of India, Canada, and the various portions of Africa and Palestine under the flag are dependent for security upon the power of the empire to send its troops by sea routes to their defence.

On the other hand, the inadequacy of a navy in itself to undertake a war of territorial conquest is frequently illustrated in history; for, except in the special circumstances mentioned hereafter, it does not necessarily follow that defeat on the sea brings sufficient pressure to bear on an enemy to compel a general surrender. Thus the British naval victories over the French were usually supplemented by military operations on the land, on a scale of varying importance from the landing of a few companies of troops to seize a West Indian island up to the employment of whole armies at Blenheim and Waterloo.

Similarly, when in the wars with China and Russia the Japanese used their navy with entire success, that success did guarantee the safety of their own domestic territory, but was quite insufficient to attain their object in embarking on hostilities, which was the expulsion of their enemies from Korea and Manchuria. To that end naval victory was no more than a necessary foundation for further effort.

Given certain special conditions, however, a navy can finish an offensive war unaided by land forces; although such circumstances only arise when hostilities are the outcome of a purely maritime subject of dispute, or when the heart of the defending belligerent state is so situated as to be peculiarly vulnerable to naval assault. As examples of the first of these conditions may be quoted the succession of wars fought between Great Britain and Holland in the seventeenth century, which all broke out through a competition to obtain the maritime carrying trade of the world. Victory at sea ensured this in itself.

Examples of the second conditions are afforded by the battle of Copenhagen and the naval attacks that were made from time to time on the sea capitals of the formerly existing Mahommedan states in North Africa, such as Blake's descent on Tunis and Exmouth's on Algiers. Here the main wealth and strength of a defending belligerent lay so immediately contiguous to the water as to be directly within striking distance of naval weapons.

But besides its functions in connection with the defence of its own national territory and the attack on an enemy's, the duties of a navy extend to the attack and defence of property on the sea, a form of operation which may on occasion produce a strong effect on the course and results of a war. In exercising this function a navy conducts hostilities under belligerent rights differing fundamentally from those which are generally recognized by civilized states as permissible in warfare on the land. An army cannot enter any foreign territory except that of an enemy without violating the rights of neutrals, and its sphere of operations is therefore very limited. Nor, as a generally accepted rule among civilized states, may the private property of enemy subjects be seized on the land without compensation.

At sea, however, there are no geographical limits to the area within which a navy may strike its blows, provided that no act of war takes place within 3 miles of a neutral coast; and all enemy property, whether public or private, is legitimately subject to seizure except non-contraband of war carried on neutral ships. A navy may even seize the property of neutrals on the sea—under certain restrictions—if that property is on its way to the enemy's ports or ships.

This universally recognized right to lay hands on all vessels under a hostile flag, whether of State or private ownership, necessarily varies in its power to injure an enemy according to the extent of his dependence on his seaborne trade. In self-contained countries with a very limited mercantile tonnage such as the United States and Russia its effect is necessarily small, and the power of a navy to exercise formidable strategic pressure in that way is proportionately reduced. But if on the other hand a state is largely dependent for national prosperity on its seaborne trade its loss may be serious, and if this dependence is so extensive as to include necessaries of existence its loss may lead to consequences which are absolutely decisive.

For example, the difficulties that beset Germany in the European War through the stoppage of external supplies of food and raw material were undoubtedly contributive to her ultimate downfall; and on the other hand a comparatively small addition to the shipping losses sustained by her enemies through the activities of her submarines would have certainly caused the downfall of Great Britain. The latter eventuality was only averted because the submarines were too few, in face of the measures devised to cope with them.

In a time of war the dispositions of a navy are naturally governed by the strategic situation of the moment, and in times of peace they are generally such as to meet the requirements of war with the least possible delay. In all countries a portion of the navy—usually consisting of the older ships, but sometimes with a proportion of the new—is laid up in home ports, either with partial crews or with no crews at all. On an outbreak of hostilities these are manned from the various naval depôts and categories of the reserve and sent to their war stations. The other portion of the navy is permanently kept in a fully-manned condition, as a precaution against sudden emergency and a means of training for officers and men.

Thus, for example, more than half the ships of the British navy lie at the three great naval headquarters of Portsmouth, Plymouth, and Chatham, either with nucleus crews, in which case they are grouped in squadrons under their own admirals, or unmanned altogether, in which case they belong to no squadron for the time, but remain under the custody of the authorities of the local Government dockyards. The other sections are mostly vessels of the newer types, and these are all fully manned without any reserve elements in their crews.

Of these latter vessels the majority belong to the fleets whose movements, manœuvres, and general exercises and practices are carried out in or near home waters. The remainder are distributed on foreign stations, that is to say the Mediterranean, North America, China, South Africa, and East Indies. In Australia there is a small Colonial-owned squadron. Until the war of 1914 the disposition of the British ships on foreign stations was regulated by the disposition of that of the next strongest European naval powers, so that in the event of a sudden war with such rivals British trade in all seas should receive an immediate measure of protection.

Thus, up till the end of the nineteenth century, the presence of a French or Russian ship in Asiatic, African, or American waters was always balanced by the neighbourhood of a British ship of approximately equal force; but when the German navy began to take rank in the early twentieth century as next to that of England, it was the German dispositions that received attention in a similar fashion. During the European War the whole navy was employed as the changes in the situation necessitated from time to time, and the majority of the ships on distant stations were recalled when the German cruisers had been destroyed, except those engaged in escorting convoys. But with the return of peace some reversion towards the practice of maintaining squadrons on foreign stations took place, although not under strategic necessity.

As a subsidiary or minor function it is the duty of all navies to prevent piracy at sea, although in modern times occasions for the exercise of that function are very rare. At the same time the mere existence of navies provides in itself an almost completely sufficient guarantee against the existence of pirates, and if all navies were abolished it is unquestionable that the present security of the seas would be materially reduced.

To some extent armed ships also assist in protecting life and property in semi-civilized lands where local conditions render these insecure; but their ability to do so is necessarily confined to coastal regions and those bordering on navigable rivers, such as the seaboards of the Central and South American Republics and the main waterways of China.

Material Composition of Navies.—A fighting ship is built to carry the weapons of war of the period to which she belongs, in order to destroy enemy ships or such enemy property on the land as may be within her reach. From the earliest periods of naval history therefore her design has exhibited a parallel development to that of the weapons in question, and reflected the tactical principles of her era.

In the ancient Greek and Roman navies the sword and spear were the chief weapons of combat, and no effective attack was possible until these could come into play by boarding the enemy. To facilitate this manœuvre speed and handiness were the prime qualification of the ancient war galley, which were obtained by a large number of oars and special rudder power.

For the first fourteen centuries of the Christian era the true fighting ship remained a galley, specially designed to close and board the enemy under the motive power of oars; but the details of her construction were modified, and instead of the three tiers or banks of oars used by the Greeks she carried one only, in which each oar was handled by three rowers. Even when gunpowder began to revolutionize all war the mediæval galley only mounted one or two guns in her bow to fire ahead, as it was impossible to mount them on the broadside or beam without seriously reducing the number of oars and losing speed. But by that time the great art of sailing to windward had become known, which revolutionized all navigation by enabling ships to dispense with oars altogether, and thereby to mount guns on the broadside in considerable numbers without interfering in any way with their power of movement.

This sealed the fate of the galley as a fighting type; for when she tried to close and board a vessel so armed, the latter simply manœuvred to cover her approach and then raked her fore and aft. All tactical ideas therefore underwent a complete change, and it was to English seamen that the change was chiefly due; although by the end of the sixteenth century their lead had been followed in all the principal navies, and the broadside artillery armament had become the true standard of offensive and defensive power. At first it was carried on the upper deck level only; but as ordnance increased in size it became necessary to carry it lower, which was rendered possible by the invention of ports permitting the guns to be pointed through the ship's side instead of over it.

To mount a battery thus, however, an interior deck had to be added to the structure of the ship, which with the guns themselves interfered so seriously with the space available for cargo that from that period the temporarily armed merchant ship ceased to be a match for the specially built ship of war, and disappeared by degrees from the main fighting fleets.

For three hundred years from the latter half of the sixteenth century all navies consisted of ships built of wood, moved by the wind, and armed on the broadside; and it was with this embodiment of certain tactical ideas that the British fought their way to the premier maritime position in the world, by defeating the Spaniards in the sixteenth century, the Dutch in the seventeenth, and the French, Dutch, and Spaniards combined in the eighteenth.

The reign of this type was of very great historical importance, coinciding as it did with the making of modern Europe, the populating of America by the white man, and the opening of the East to direct sea trade. But although in its general conception the application of the type was extensive and enduring, considerable differences were to be found in the size and force of the individual ships, not only from one period to another, but in those of contemporary production. This was due in the first place to the varying requirements of war.

For such duties as scouting and the attack and defence of trade, small vessels were quite as efficient as large, and a much greater number could be built at the same cost. Thus in all navies a variety of sizes prevailed in the individual ships from the earliest adoption of artillery mounted on the broadside system.

It was in the seventeenth century that the first notable advances were made in size and in details of design by the introduction of a second battery deck in the larger vessels forming the main battle force, to be followed eventually by a third. But although the three-decker represented the extreme concentration of fighting power in one hull, she had the tactical disadvantage of being as a rule slower and less weatherly than her smaller consorts of two gun-decks only, and the latter type invariably predominated in all navies in a proportion of ten or twelve to one. Both classes were known after the seventeenth century as ships-of-the-line.

Next in size to the ship-of-the-line came the vessels with one tier of guns only below the upper deck, and next to these again the smallest classes which carried all their armament on the upper deck. The former were eventually designated frigates, and the latter corvettes and sloops according to force. The frigates were the fastest sa lers of all, and a certain number nearly always accompanied large battle fleets as scouts. From corvettes up to ships-of-the-line all sizes carried an identically shaped sail plan, on a scale varying with tonnage, which was set on three masts with three yards on each and known as the "ship rig."

In the early nineteenth century a fourth yard on all masts was added. A few of the sloops were similarly rigged, but the majority had only two masts, and were either brigs or schooners. The smallest of all were cutters. With the passage of time the typical ship of every class presented an ever-increasing size. Thus while the earliest three-deckers carried only 90 guns, the last to be launched carried 131. Similarly, the two-decker armaments increased from 60 to 90, and the frigate armaments from 36 to 50. Moreover, the guns increased in size and destructive power as well as in numbers. Until long after the Napoleonic wars the standard line-of-battle weapons were 24- and 32-pounder smooth-bore guns firing solid round-shot, but by 1840 the 68-pounder had been introduced, and a few years later shells had been invented.

Continual improvements in ordnance sealed the doom of the wooden broadside ship-of-the-line in favour of entirely new types of fighting craft, but before that happened a revolutionary change had taken place in her motive power by the introduction of steam machinery. It was first installed as an aid to sails only, but within twenty years, that is to say by 1860, it had been extended to all ships that were classed as effective for war, as their fighting source of movement. Thirty years after its first application to vessels in the British navy it had become the principal instead of the auxiliary moving agency of the whole fleet, and twenty years later again sails had disappeared in all modern ships of every size and force. The transition was thus completed in half a century.

The great era of evolution in weapons which entirely changed the forms of naval architecture began about 1860. Shell-fire had proved so destructive in the Crimean War that some method of mitigating its effects came to be regarded as imperative, and resulted in the application of armour to the sides of a new type of ship. Moreover, as guns increased threefold in weight within a very short period, it was structurally impracticable to build ships capable of carrying the same large numbers as were in use in the older designs, with the added burden of armour. The three-decker and two-decker disappeared therefore to make way for a single-decked class carrying no more than one-fourth as many weapons, but of a vastly more powerful pattern, and protected by armour.

The decisive superiority of this novel design received conclusive demonstration in the American Civil War, and at the Austro-Italian battle of Lissa, the last occasion on which a ship-of-the-line of the old style ever went into action. Armour thenceforward became an invariable feature in every ship built for the battle-fleet duties of the former two- and three-deckers in all navies of importance. But the ever-increasing size of guns still went on, decreasing the number a vessel could carry, even with a great increase in tonnage, and stimulated efforts to find methods of putting them to the utmost use.

In a broadside ship only the weapons on one side could be engaged at one time, unless under very unusual circumstances. Half the armament of such a ship remained idle therefore even in battle. To overcome this grave objection yet another new type of vessel appeared, known as the turret-ship. In this design the original practice of carrying all the armament on the upper deck was revived, but the guns were mounted on the centre line of the deck in revolving armoured turrets so as to be able to fire over either side.

In this way the entire armament could always be brought into action instead of only a half, and a turret-ship with only four weapons could engage a broadside ship with eight on equal terms. The broadside principle of mounting thereupon stood condemned, and after 1878 no broadside ships were added to the navy except in the smaller classes. Some years before that came to pass smooth-bore ordnance had been completely replaced by rifled, although breech-loaders were not adopted till 1880, and muzzle-loaders had not entirely disappeared till near the end of the century.

The centre-mounted armament vessel thus became the successor of the old ship-of-the-line, and received the official designation of battleship. For more than sixty years the development of the type has been continuously progressive in every feature. The displacement of the largest armoured designs has increased from 4000 to 40,000 tons; their speed from 9 to 28 knots; the weight of their heaviest gun from 6½ to 98 tons.

Armour increased in thickness from the original 4 inches to 2 feet within fifteen years, to meet the increasing penetrative power of ordnance; and subsequent improvements in its metallurgical treatment during preparation have more than trebled its resisting strength, so that although its thickness has now receded to a maximum of 13 inches, that gives a protective efficiency equal to 3½ feet of the wrought iron with which the first armoured ships were cased. In 1875 Whitehead torpedoes were included in the armament of all battleships building, and as a protection against under-water attack their internal subdivision was increased till it is now tenfold greater in proportion to tonnage than in the first subdivided vessels.

Another innovation of this period was a structural alteration whereby a ram took the place of the old-fashioned bow in all new types built for the line of battle, and some of the smaller classes also. This idea, whereby the hull of a vessel itself became a weapon, had a temporary success at Lissa owing to the bad gunnery of the rammed ships in defending themselves, which gave the ram an undeserved reputation, for it never again played any part in war, and proved a fruitful source of danger to consorts by aggravating the effects of accidental collision.

Speaking generally, all these great advances in fighting designs were only rendered possible by the radical change in shipbuilding material, first from wood to iron, and then from iron to steel, which began in the British navy from the early 'sixties. The limit of size in wooden hulls had been reached, and only on an iron or steel basis could tonnage be increased and rigidity ensured so as to meet the constantly growing weight of armour and guns. But about ten years after the introduction of iron shipbuilding and armour a more important and far-reaching change than any above mentioned was on the eve of its appearance, in the new science of under-water attack by such entirely novel weapons as the torpedo and the mine.

Before their invention no vessel had anything to fear from any invisible form of danger, and the war value of every craft afloat was measured solely by her guns. After their invention the whole theory of naval warfare based on the undisputed supremacy of heavy ordnance in big ships was seriously and increasingly challenged, and in the great wars which followed vastly more loss was occasioned by under-water weapons than by the gun.

The chief difference between the torpedo and the mine is that the former is a moving weapon and the latter a stationary obstacle. The Whitehead torpedo was invented about the year 1870, originally in the form of a surface boat driven by compressed air, and carrying a charge in the bow to explode on striking a ship's side; but by an important early development the boat was replaced by a cigar-shaped shell of steel, which ran below the surface by a device of horizontal rudders actuated by hydrostatic pressure according to depth. This self-propelled weapon was ejected in its earlier days from a wheeled carriage on deck if used from a ship, but afterwards from an under-water tube, and if used from a boat simply by dropping into the water.

Another form of torpedo which proved effective in the American Civil War and Russo-Turkish operations was simply an explosive charge carried at the end of a long spar projecting from the bows of a steam launch or pinnace; but the introduction of quick-firing guns rendered the close approach of the boat impossible, and the spar torpedo became obsolete. The mine is an anchored explosive charge floating at a set depth under water in an iron or steel case, usually of spherical shape, which explodes on being bumped; but it can only be used in moderately deep water, for otherwise the weight of the mooring cable is too great for its buoyancy.

It can be removed by a sweep, which consists of a wire cable dragged between two small vessels such as trawlers, or by a paravane, which is an apparatus shaped like a Whitehead torpedo with vertical planes, and towed from near a ship's bow. The planes are acted on by the pressure of the water as the ship moves ahead in such a way that the paravane tries to diverge outwards at an angle and tautens the towing line. If the line then strikes the moorings of a mine, it pushes the latter clear of the ship into a cutter fixed to the paravane, which severs the moorings and allows the mine to rise to the surface. All large ships are now fitted with these.

The invention of the Whitehead torpedo produced a weapon whereby the smallest-size ship had a chance to destroy or disable the largest, and brought two new classes into existence specially for its use, namely, the torpedo-boat, which was a very fast small surface craft, and the submarine, which attacks entirely submerged.

To deal with torpedo-boats a larger type on the same general lines was introduced with a combined torpedo and light-gun armament, and designated the torpedo-boat destroyer. Before many years had passed she had rendered the torpedo-boat obsolete and taken her place as a surface torpedo craft. The torpedo-boat destroyer is also one of the most effective enemies of the submarine.

Submarines of a practically useful design were first built in France, and first adopted in the British service at the beginning of the present century. In all submarines the general principle is that of a vessel which can be submerged to any desired depth by the admission of water to compartments known as ballast tanks, and by the downward pressure of horizontal rudders or hydroplanes. To rise again the rudders are turned so as to press upwards, and the water in the tanks blown out by compressed air.

Propulsion when submerged is effected by electric engines to avoid combustion in an enclosed hull, and surface propulsion by petrol or steam. One or more guns are usually carried for surface action in addition to several torpedo-tubes for attack when submerged.

Frigates, corvettes, and sloops, armed on the broadside, and built either entirely or partially of wood, survived the wooden ship-of-the-line by about twenty-five years; but were gradually replaced by iron or steel successors known by the general term of cruisers. Cruisers varied very greatly in size and armament for thirty years after their first appearance, ranging from 1500 to 15,000 tons in displacement; but in all high speed was a special feature. In later types armour was carried, but even the most powerful cruiser was never quite a match for a contemporary battleship. Since 1907 the armoured cruiser has been gradually superseded by a new type designated the battle-cruiser, and is now no longer represented in the British navy.

The battle-cruiser carries the same calibre armament as the contemporary battleship proper, and equals or even exceeds her in tonnage; but her guns are fewer and her armour lighter, which enables her to carry more powerful engines and attain a somewhat higher speed. In dimensions and fighting force she bears much less resemblance to a true battle unit, and on this account she is included in the category of "capital ships," under which term all such units are grouped. The modern unarmoured or light cruiser carries her guns on the centre line instead of the broadside, a great improvement in tactical efficiency.

As compared to the modern capital ship her fighting force presents a good parallel to that of the frigate when compared to the three-decker. One other new class of vessel has been added within a very recent period to the composition of every fully equipped navy, and that is the aircraft carrier, which, as her name implies, is designed to carry the scouting seaplanes playing an important part in modern war. To provide the necessary deck area for the aircraft to alight on, the aircraft carrier is necessarily a large vessel of battleship dimensions.

Space does not permit here of a detailed description of the developments in naval propelling machinery since the introduction of steam, but it corresponds roughly to that in the mercantile marine, from simple to compound reciprocating engines, and thence to direct-acting and geared turbines. Boilers have passed from the rectangular low-pressure pattern to the high-pressure cylindrical, and thence to the water-tube. Oil fuel has completely superseded coal in the British service, after a transition period in which both were used.

The ships in the British navy are all British built and armed, being constructed in the Royal Dockyards at Portsmouth, Plymouth, Chatham, and Sheerness, or by contract; and their repairs and overhaul were formerly carried out under similar arrangements, but are now entirely undertaken in the royal establishments. Here also all equipment, armament, and stores are maintained in stock. Ships on foreign stations are kept in repair in H.M. Dockyards at Malta, Gibraltar, Hong-Kong, Bermuda, and Simon's Bay; those of the Australian navy in the Commonwealth Government yard at Sydney.

An exact statement of the numbers

comprising a modern navy does not convey an accurate impression of its true war value, because a proportion of the whole—which continually varies—consists of ships which are obsolete and comparatively useless except for subsidiary duties. In the era of the wooden broadside type designs changed so slowly, and hulls built of seasoned timber lasted so long, that ships often remained fully efficient for war for half or even three-quarters of a century, and required little attention when lying up in reserve—as they sometimes did for twenty years after being launched, before going to sea at all.

But since 1860 designs have changed so rapidly that in ten or fifteen years a vessel has ceased to count as up-to-date. Being, moreover, very intricate machines, liable to rapid deterioration even when not in use, they get worn out in a third of the time of their more simply constructed wooden predecessors. Taking effective ships only, therefore, the numbers given below represent a fair approximation to the actual war strength of the British navy in 1932 :

(*a*) *15 capital ships.*—These carry armaments varying from eight guns of 13P-inch calibre to eight of 15-inch, and range in size from 29,000 to 42,000 tons, and in speed from 21 to 31 knots. Four are battle-cruisers.

(*b*) *52 cruisers.*—These carry armaments varying from five 6-inch to seven 7P-inch, and range in size from 3750 to 7500 tons, and in speed from 23 to 31 knots.

(*c*) *150 surface torpedo craft.*—These include sixteen flotilla leaders, all the remainder being destroyers. They carry from four to six tubes and a light-gun armament, and vary in size from 880 to 1800 tons, and in speed from 34 to 37 knots. All are fitted with depth charges for destroying submarines. A few are fitted as minelayers and carry no torpedoes or guns.

(*d*) *52 submarines.*—These vary in surface displacement from 420 to 2425 tons, and in surface speed from 15 to 24 knots. They are fitted with from four to eight torpedo-tubes. Three carry a 12-inch gun, but the remainder a light-gun armament only.

In addition to the above four categories there are other classes necessary in war for auxiliary duties ; for certain of which classes a nucleus is maintained permanently for emergencies, and the balance drawn from the mercantile marine as required during hostilities. These consist of armed merchant cruisers, sloops for convoy work, minesweepers, and patrol craft. In 1932 about thirty-four effective sloops and thirty-two minesweepers were on the permanent list. Destroyer and submarine flotillas also have depot ships which are not fighting units. For other special peace duties the Admiralty maintain seventeen river gunboats, thirteen surveying ships, and sundry other vessels. There are eight aircraft ships ; destroyers and submarines in flotillas of eight to twenty. A combination of squadrons and flotillas with auxiliary ships makes up a fully constituted fleet.

Organization of Naval Personnel.—The crew or ship's company of a vessel manned for war differs from that of a vessel employed in trade through the necessity of carrying enough men to use her armament in addition to those required for moving and handling her. In the earliest periods of naval history these two elements were separate. Later they were combined, and later yet separated again. Thus in the days of war galleys the oars were handled by unarmed men, whose duty was confined to moving the vessel into position for the fighting section to attack.

This division of responsibilities lasted right down to the late Middle Ages, only disappearing when the motive agency of oars had been finally abandoned in favour of sails, and broadside artillery fire had become the accepted method of engaging an enemy. Even then in some countries such as Spain the distinction between the fighters and the seamen survived for a time. But in England the seaman was also the fighter from the Tudor period.

This combination of duties lasted for about three centuries, and coincided with the greatest era of British naval history. Then with the advent of steam propulsion the ancient principle of separating the fighting portion of the crew from the portion employed to drive the ship was revived, and remains in force in all navies except that of the United States, in which the same officers do duty in both branches.

In the constitution of the *personnel* of a navy there is necessarily a graded sequence of rank and responsibility just as in any organization maintained for war. A ship is under the immediate command of an officer whose rank corresponds to her importance as a fighting unit, and the aggregations of ships which are known as fleets or squadrons, according to size, are commanded by officers of a higher rank bearing the title of admiral—with a distinctive prefix—and designated collectively as *flag-officers,* because any ship carrying one flies a special flag to denote the fact.

The British navy has four grades of flag rank, known respectively as admiral of the fleet, admiral, vice-admiral, and rear-admiral. Next in order of authority to flag-officers come captains, commanders, lieutenant-commanders, lieutenants, sub-lieutenants, midshipmen, and naval cadets. A temporary rank known as commodore also exists, which comes between rear-admiral and captain, and is held by captains while occupying certain appointments. All above midshipmen are commissioned officers. These constitute the executive branch as distinguished from the engineer, medical, accountant, and Royal Marine branches of the service; and no officer unless of the executive branch is competent, or permitted by the regulations, to command a ship.

To hold commissioned rank in the executive branch an officer must first have qualified by examination in the navigation and handling of a ship, and in all the principal technicalities of the seaman's profession; and must also be trained in the use of naval armaments. In the United States navy the executive branch—or *line branch* as it is called in America—also carries out all the work of the engineers, but in the British service they are only trained in the general theory and practice of engine-room duties.

Entry into the executive branch of the British navy is made by passing first a board of selection and then a qualifying examination. The candidate then becomes a naval cadet, and spends a period of elementary professional instruction in the Royal Naval College at Dartmouth. Thence he is sent to sea, and serves for a term of years as naval cadet and midshipman, to complete his professional training. At the conclusion he is examined in seamanship, and then passed through special finishing courses of instruction at the various naval educational establishments such as the gunnery, torpedo, and pilotage schools, and the Royal Naval College at Greenwich, at each of which he undergoes examination.

If successful he is considered professionally qualified for command, and receives a sub-lieutenant's commission. Thenceforward his future advancement is dependent on selection for each step up to the rank of captain, except that as a lieutenant of eight years seniority he automatically becomes a lieutenant-commander. From captain upwards through each of the first three grades of flag rank all promotion is by seniority, but it becomes selective again for the highest rank of all, that of Admiral of the Fleet.

An officer who reaches the age of 55 before arriving at the top of the captains list is obliged to retire. A rear-admiral must retire at 60, a vice-admiral or an admiral at 65, and an admiral of the fleet at 70. Retirement is also compulsory in all these ranks if an officer remains unemployed for a certain period varying with rank.

In the British service up till the seventeenth century none were permanent servants of the Crown if below captain's rank. A list of so-called king's captains was maintained by the Lord High Admiral, from which all commanding officers were selected. When not actually employed afloat, these officers received a retaining salary known officially as half-pay, in order to compensate them for their disability to undertake other kinds of employment. An officer below the rank of captain was merely engaged for the period in which the ship in which he held rank was in commission, that is to say manned and equipped for State service with a captain in appointed command. At the end of the commission he was discharged with the ship's company, and the Crown had no further call on him unless he voluntarily rejoined.

By degrees, however, the system of a retaining allowance was extended to other ranks, and before the nineteenth century it included all commissioned officers of the executive branch. Under both the old and the new systems, when an officer was or is appointed to a ship his name is inserted on her ledger for full pay, and he is said to be "borne on her books." On full pay he exercises all the authority of his rank as laid down in the regulations, and is himself subject to the provisions of the Naval Discipline Act.

In all navies of importance a certain selected proportion of the executive officers of commander's, lieutenant-commander's, and lieutenant's rank receive an extended training as specialists in separate technical sections of the science of war. In the British navy these are known as gunnery, torpedo, war staff, navigating, and signal officers. War staff officers undergo a comprehensive instruction in naval history, strategy, tactics, and war administration, and carry out war staff duties.

In addition to the executive officers, all navies are provided with other branches of commissioned rank, but of non-seaman character, that is to say, the engineers, surgeons, and paymasters. Of these the most important are the engineers, although in different navies there is a great variety in the status they occupy. In the United States Navy their duties are considered so essentially a part of the war efficiency of a ship that they are entrusted to the executive or "line" branch, and in that navy there are no separate engineer officers, an arrangement which works very well.

In the British navy the engineers are entered as naval cadets with the executives, and the earlier stages of their service is precisely the same. Not till they reach commissioned rank does the separation begin, and after that their duties lie apart, but their ranks correspond up to vice-admiral. In other navies the engineers are quite a separate branch from the start of their career, and the number holding commissioned rank is small.

All navies are supplied with medical officers, who are responsible for the health of the men as their designation implies; and most navies possess an accountant or paymaster branch, who carry out all clerical work connected with payment, victualling, and clothing; keep the records of service of every man borne on the books; and conduct the secretarial duties required in the official correspondence of flag and commanding officers. Large vessels in the British navy also carry a chaplain of the Established Church of England, and a naval instructor for the midshipmen.

The British and United States navies differ from all others by including in their composition a section organized on a military basis and holding military instead of naval titles of rank. These are the Royal Marines and the United States Marine Corps. With officers of the Royal Marines the terms of service, the training, the system of authority and responsibility, and the uniform, are military rather than naval. They are only subject to naval discipline when actually afloat, and at other periods are quartered in barracks under the local military authorities. Unlike naval officers, they are not dependent for full pay on being borne on the books of a ship. But they are trained in naval gunnery, war staff duties, and wireless telegraphy.

Next in authority to the officers who are officers from entry, and eligible for promotion to the highest ranks, are those who rise from the lower deck and are designated collectively as warrant officers. In their case advancement ends at a rank which is equivalent to that of lieutenant.

In the British navy eligibility to become warrant officer on passing the necessary tests has been extended within recent years to all the various sections of the lower-deck personnel, including the engineering, nursing, accountant, victualling, telegraphist, and educational elements, as well as the combatant and shipwright, and the system now prevailing has become too complex for description in a general article; but the warrant officers of most importance to the war efficiency of a navy are the gunners, torpedo gunners, boatswains, shipwrights, and engineers. The duties of these officers are largely concerned with the custody, repair, and maintenance of armament, equipment, and stores.

The officers in general form the supervising body under whom the crew or ship's company of a fighting vessel carry out their various duties. In the British navy those who are not officers are not officially known as holding a "rank" but a "rating." Broadly speaking the ratings forming a ship's company may all be divided into the fighting and engine-room sections, for although a certain proportion are neither seamen nor stokers nor trained to the use of arms, such as the writers, wireless telegraphists, cooks, stewards, sick-berth staff, etc., every one of these has his station in action either to pass up ammunition, attend to telephones, read the fire control instruments, or assist the wounded.

The system of grading a ship's company varies in different navies, but not greatly. In the seaman branch of the British service the sequence of ratings is chief petty officer, petty officer, leading seaman, able seaman, ordinary seaman, and boy; and in the stoker and other branches it is approximately correspondent except that there is no equivalent rating below that of ordinary seaman. In most foreign navies a proportion of the hands are recruited by compulsory service, but in the British and United States navies all are voluntarily recruited except in abnormal times, when the whole male population is subject to conscription, as in the European War.

In the eighteenth and nineteenth centuries the British seafaring population was also liable to seizure by impressment for service in the navy if the requirements of war were not adequately met by voluntary entries. In most navies a proportion of the men who enter voluntarily are allowed to engage for a long period, and from these the petty officers are usually selected; but the remainder, and all those who enter under compulsion, are only required to serve for short terms.

When continuous service was first established in the British navy, however, all ratings entered under this new method were under an equal obligation to serve for ten years, and at a somewhat later period this was raised to twelve. At the expiration thereof smart men of good character were permitted, if they so desired, to re-engage for ten years more; and at the completion of this second term they were discharged on pension. Members of the seaman branch were entered as boys in the royal training ships, where they were prepared for the navy, but all other branches were entered direct for sea service.

In its main features this system has remained in force for about sixty years since its first gradual adoption; but certain modifications have taken place. Early in the present century the advantages of manning a navy in part by entering a percentage of the ratings for short service under the pennant, followed by a term of years in a permanently organized reserve, attracted the attention of the Admiralty, especially after the great success of the partially short-service fleet of Japan in its war with Russia.

A revised arrangement was therefore adopted whereby a proportion of the entries were only required to serve five out of their twelve-years engagement actually afloat, and then passed for the remaining seven into a new organization designated the Royal Fleet Reserve, in which they received a retaining pay and remained liable to be called up for service whenever required. It was on this combination of long and short service that the British navy was manned on the outbreak of war in 1914, and it still stands in force in 1922.

At the close of the war extensive reductions were necessary, and these had brought the total personnel down to approximately 91,410 by 1932, inclusive of Royal Marines. All are divided for administrative purposes among three main divisions, known as port divisions, of which the respective headquarters are the naval depot barracks at Portsmouth, Plymouth, and Chatham. On entering any branch of the navy a recruit is detailed to one of these divisions of the service, and belongs to it permanently until his final discharge, no matter where he may be employed while wearing naval uniform. Having passed the medical and other tests, and been accepted for entry, he is sent to the depot barracks of his division to await drafting to sea, and to these same barracks he returns on each occasion of his ship being paid off, there to await orders as to joining another.

In the seaman branch, however, a boy is not detailed to a port division till he has finished his time in the training ship, nor does his twelve-year period of engagement begin to count till he is an ordinary seaman. At Portsmouth, Plymouth, and Chatham, in addition to the divisional depot barracks, are established a gunnery and a torpedo school for passing men through the necessary training of the combatant branch on first entry, and to re-qualify in the latest improvements after each period of service afloat. At each port are also barracks for the local division of Royal Marines.

When the Admiralty decide that a ship is to be commissioned—that is to say, manned for service either with a full or a partial crew—either on completion as a new vessel, or after lying up in charge of the dockyard authorities for a time, the commander-in-chief at the port where she lies is instructed to detail a ship's company for her from the depot barracks of the local port division on a given date. The captain and officers are appointed to join on the same day by the Admiralty, and the ensign and pennant are hoisted, the latter being the captain's emblem of command.

In a vessel to carry an officer of flag rank, an admiral's flag takes the place of the pennant. When manned and ready for sea in all respects the ship sails to join her squadron, unless she has been commissioned with a partial crew only, in which case she remains at her port in reserve. When commissioned for foreign service a ship usually retains her crew without any change—except in minor details—until she returns home, or until the whole crew is relieved by a fresh crew at the expiration of two years if she is to remain abroad. But if commissioned for service in home waters she usually discharges a proportion of her crew annually to the depot, and receives thence a fresh draft in exchange. By this means the periods of foreign and home service are roughly equalized for all ratings in the port division.

In addition to the Royal Fleet Reserve, the British navy differs from foreign services in having three other categories of reserves, namely the Coast Guard, the Royal Naval Reserve, and the Royal Naval Volunteer Reserve. The Coast Guard is composed of naval ratings who have completed a period of their service with the fleet and been selected for transfer to carry out coast watching, preventive, and life-saving duties.

The Royal Naval Reserve stands on a different footing altogether, inasmuch as neither officers nor men have ever belonged to the regular navy, although they must be professionally competent for seafaring employment either on deck or in the engine-room. As a guarantee of fitness the officers must hold the Board of Trade certificates required in the mercantile marine, and the ratings must be noted in the Registry of Shipping as seamen or stokers by trade. The Royal Naval Reserve has three branches of officers, namely the executive, the engineer, and the paymaster; and two branches of men, the seamen and the engine-room. Entry is subject to special tests, and promotion is by selection. The ratings engage for five-year periods, which can be repeated if character is satisfactory.

To impart a training for war, officers and men have to attend annual or biennial courses of instruction and drill in ships of the navy, and while so employed receive full pay; to which at other times is added a retainer under certain conditions. A separate branch is solely devoted to mine-sweeping, in which the officers must be qualified for trawler command, and are granted a special warrant rank designated skipper, which places them on a list of their own.

The Royal Naval Volunteer Reserve is another body consisting of men who have not served in the navy itself originally; but they differ from the Royal Naval Reserve in receiving no retainer, and being dependent on no professional attainments for entry. Very few are of regular seafaring occupation, but a proportion of the officers are amateur yachtsmen qualified by Board of Trade certificates, and competent to command small craft such as trawlers and motor-launches. These form the auxiliary patrol in war.

The whole control and administration of the British navy is theoretically in the hands of the Lord High Admiral, a great Officer of State, but for more than two centuries his duties have been entrusted to a board known as the Lords Commissioners of the Admiralty. At the head of this board sits a cabinet minister known as the First Lord, who collaborates with six naval officers of senior standing and two civilian members of Parliament.

The responsibility of the board is collective, but by custom the senior of the naval officers—who is known as First Sea Lord—attends to all matters concerned with the peace and war distribution of the navy, assisted by the Fifth and Sixth; the Second attends to all duties connected with personnel; the Third to every matter connected with the building, maintenance, equipment, and armament of ships; and the Fourth to the provision and issue of stores and supplies. One civilian member deals with the financing of the navy in its parliamentary aspects, and the other attends to all questions connected with Admiralty works on land, such as docks, workshops, naval barracks, etc.

The entire authority of the Board of Admiralty and of every officer and petty-officer in the British navy is founded upon the parliamentary statute known as the Naval Discipline Act. This embodies the Articles of War—setting forth the general principles of disciplinary obedience—the legal procedure for courts-martial, and a code of punishments. It empowers the Admiralty to issue all necessary instructions of the administration of the service; and such of these as are of a standing nature are included in an official volume designated the *King's Regulations and Admiralty Instructions*, copies of which are on board every ship in commission.

As the British navy is a constitutional force, the Naval Discipline Act does not require annual parliamentary sanction like the Army Act, but remains on the Statute Book until its entire revision by a fresh Act is considered nationally desirable, with such lesser amendments as changing circumstances may from time to time render expedient.

The existing Act dates from 1869, and except in minor details has undergone little alteration.—BIBLIOGRAPHY: *King's Regulations and Admiralty Instructions*; F. T. Jane's *Fighting Ships*; Sir J. S. Corbett, *Drake and the Tudor Navy*, and *England in the Mediterranean*; Vice Admiral G. A. Ballard, C.B., *Influence of the Sea on Political History of Japan*; H. W. Wilson, *Ironclads in Action*; Captain A. T. Mahan, *Influence of Sea-Power on History*, and *Influence of Sea-Power on French Restoration and Empire*; *Brassey's Naval Annual*; D. Hannay, *A Short History of the Royal Navy* (from 1217 to 1688).

NAVY LEAGUE. A British propagandist society established in 1895 for the purpose of keeping up public interest in the Royal Navy, and for the support of the ideals of British naval supremacy. The headquarters are at Victoria Street, London, S.W.

NAWANAGAR. A native state of Kathiawar, India, in the Gujarat division of Bombay Presidency, with a seaboard on the Gulf and Little Rann of Cutch. The throne of Nawanagar was ascended in March, 1907, by Ranjitsinjhi (q.v.), better known to Britishers as one of the greatest batsmen who ever lived. Cereals are grown. A railway connects Rajkot with Nawanagar, the principal town and seaport on the Gulf of Cutch. It was founded by Jam Rawal in 1540. There is a pearl-fishery, and among other industries is that of cloth-making. The town water-supply is drawn from a 600-acre reservoir, and is led by an aqueduct some 9 miles long. State area, 3791 sq. miles; pop. 345,353. Pop. of town about 50,000.

NAXOS. The largest and most important of the Cyclades group, in the Ægean Sea; area, 175 sq. miles. It is mountainous (culminating points 3294 and 3251 feet altitude respectively), but is also agriculturally productive and is renowned for the quality of its oils, fruits, wines, cereals, and cotton. Marble is also worked, and it is recorded that the sculptors of Naxos formed an important school of early Greek art. Remains of colossal but unfinished statues are still extant in several of the quarries. Emery is an important mineral product. Naxos, a seaport on the north-west coast, is the capital.

Naxos was a member of the Delian League, but was annexed by Athens after a revolt in 417 B.C., and remained under Grecian domination until the disruption of the empire. An old castle located in the town of Naxos is a relic of the daring capture of the island in A.D. 1207, and the foundation of a duchy by a Venetian, Marco Sanudo. The duchy was independent until its extirpation by the Turks, who took Naxos in 1566. The island has formed a part of the kingdom of Greece since the War of Independence. Pop. 15,000.

NAYARIT. A maritime state of Mexico, on the Pacific, lying around the line of 22° N. lat. It is encircled by the Sierra de Nayarita, except where a break is made by the valleys of the Rio Grande de Santiago and its affluent the Guazamota, and others, which traverse the state. Wheat, tobacco, sugar, and coffee are produced; gold, silver, and lead are worked. Tepic is the capital. Area, 10,953 sq. miles; pop. 170,054.

NAZARENES, or NAZARÆANS. A designation given to the early Christians from the town of Nazareth, where Christ dwelt (Matt. ii. 23; Acts xxiv. 5). The name was also applied to a sect which arose at the end of the first century, and existed chiefly in Egypt. They are supposed to have retained a judaizing adherence to the Mosaic law, and to have held heretical views about the divinity of Christ.

NAZARETH. An ancient town of Galilee, the early home of Christ, now called En-Nâsira. It is not mentioned in the Old Testament, and was an obscure place, a mere village, in the time of Christ (John i. 46). Oriental Christians call themselves Nasâra, hence the name of the place is preserved in En-Nâsira. The modern town stands on the slopes of the Jebel-es-Sîkh. There is a Latin monastery, a church (1730), and the house or workshop of Joseph located in an enclosed court. During the European War Nazareth was captured by British troops on 20th Sept., 1918. Pop. 7,424.

NAZ'ARITES, or NAZIRITES. Among the ancient Jews, persons who devoted themselves to the peculiar service of Jehovah for a certain time or for life. The law of the Nazarites (from the Heb. *nazar*, to separate) is contained in Num. vi. 1-21.

NEAGH, Lough (lo*h* nā or nā'*àh*). A lake of Ulster, Ireland, the largest in the British Isles, being 19 miles long by 12 miles broad, and covering an area of 153 sq. miles. It washes the counties of Antrim, Armagh, Tyrone, and Londonderry.

Its greatest depth is 102 feet, and it is 48 feet above the sea-level. The outlet of Lough Neagh is at its north extremity through Lough Beg into the Lower Bann, and it is connected by a canal system with Belfast, Newry, and Lough Erne. Its waters are well known for their petrifying properties.

NEAN'DER, Johann August Wilhelm. Protestant theologian, born of Jewish parents at Göttingen in 1789, died at Berlin 1850. He was early converted to Christianity, and was appointed extraordinary professor of theology at Heidelberg, in 1812. In the same year, however, he accepted an invitation to the University of Berlin, where he spent the remainder of his life in uninterrupted labours for the good of the Church and general learning. His chief works are his *Life of Christ*, in refutation of Strauss; his *General*

History of the Church; and his *History of the Apostolic Church*.

NEANDERTHAL MAN (ne-an'der-tal). The Palæolithic race in the Mousterian stage of culture has been called the Neanderthal, the races of the earlier stages being "pre-Neanderthal." The name Neanderthal was first given because fragments of a human skeleton and the upper part of a skull with distinctive characters were discovered in 1857 in a cave in Neanderthal, near Düsseldorf. Since then a large series of similar skeletal remains have been found. During the third inter-glacial epoch the Neanderthal type of man occupied Europe from Gibraltar to Düsseldorf, and from Southern England to the Carpathians.

A skeleton found in 1908 in a grotto near La Chapelle-aux-Saints in France makes it possible for us to realize what sort of men the Neanderthals were. They were of

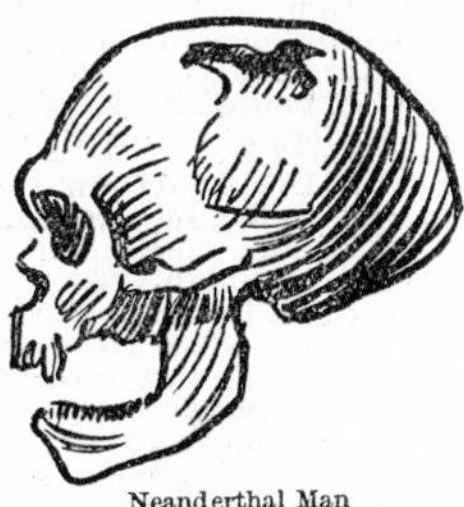

Neanderthal Man

short stature with clumsy and muscular bodies; the body was carried in a half-stooping slouch upon short legs bent at the knees, while the head protruded forward from a short, massive, and stiff neck. The head was very large and flattened, with poor frontal development, the brain being largest in the posterior region, believed to be concerned chiefly with the faculties of memory and observation. Probably the Neanderthal was an ideal tracker. He had heavy and protruding eyebrow ridges, very large eye-sockets, a broad nose, and a receding chin. His body may have been covered with hair. The arms were relatively short, and although the hands were large, they lacked that "delicate play between the thumb and finger characteristic of modern races."

It would appear that the Neanderthals entered Europe from Africa in association with southern fauna, but they remained during the subsequent cold period when northern fauna returned to South-Western Europe. The flint implements manufactured and used by them are those first identified among the relics found at Le Moustier, near the Vézère, and since called Mousterian.

There was a much closer kinship between the Neanderthal Mousterian industry and the industries of the pre-Neanderthal peoples of the earlier Acheulean, Chellean, and pre-Chellean epochs than between the Mousterian industry and that of the Aurignacian, which was introduced by the Cro-Magnon races which belonged to the *Homo sapiens* (modern man) group. *Homo sapiens* replaced, and perhaps displaced, *Homo neanderthalensis* of the Mousterian culture stage. Neanderthal man's Mousterian industry, the highest of its class, was the last industry of the Lower Palæolithic age, during which there were other human types now called *Eoanthropus* and *Palæanthropus*.

Some ethnologists hold that the natives of Australia are direct descendants of Neanderthal man. Others contend that Neanderthal man has no modern representatives, and they argue that the Australians belong to the species *sapiens*. *Homo sapiens* and *Homo neanderthalensis* were descended from the same ancient stock, but became specialized along their distinctive lines. Early ancestors of both stocks retained certain features in common, and among modern men the Australians still retain some in a modified degree. Rhodesian man was of Neanderthal type.

NEATH. A town and river-port of Glamorganshire, South Wales, on the Neath; served by the Great Western Railway, and by canal. Copper-smelting, tin-plates, steel, and chemical manufactures are among the industries. In the heart of a vast coal-mining region, Neath has a profitable transit trade in coal. Near the town are the remains of Neath Castle and Abbey, both founded about 1130-31, when Neath also came under the domain of the Lords of Glamorgan. Pop. (1931), 33,322.

NEBO, or **NABU.** An ancient Assyrian and Babylonian deity, lord of the planet Mercury, and ruler of the hosts of heaven and earth, according to Babylonian inscriptions, especially honoured in Borsippa. Statues of Nebo have been found in Nineveh.

NEBRAS'KA. A west-north-central state of the United States. From an altitude of 5000 feet in the west it slopes eastward to the valley of the Missouri (1000 feet altitude), which forms the Nebraska-Iowa

Nebo

boundary. The Platte (or Nebraska) River traverses the state; the Niobara forms part of the northern boundary; both join the Missouri. The chief towns are Omaha (pop. 1930, 214,006), Lincoln (pop. 1930, 75,933), the state capital, Grand Island (pop. 1930, 18,041), and Hastings (pop. 15,490). Nebraska City (pop. 7230) is a small place, the county seat of Otoe county, occupying the site of Fort Kearney.

Communications, etc.—The Union Pacific, Chicago & North-Western, and other railways converge on Omaha. The railway mileage for 1931 was 6243, and there was an additional 145 miles of electric railway track. Roman Catholicism is the predominant religious faith.

Production and Industry.—Agriculture is of great importance, Nebraska being third wheat-growing state of the United States (24,600,000 bushels in 1932). Other crops are maize (269,293,000 bushels, 1932), oats (74,190,000 bushels), and sugar-beet (832,000 tons). Live-stock raising is progressive; abattoirs and canneries are mainly located at South Omaha. Sheep-farming (wool clip, 2,786,000 lb., 1931), mining, and quarrying are important; the potash industry is the largest in the United States; the slaughtering and meat-packing industry has its centre at South Omaha; printing and publishing, soap and candles, and brick and tile manufactures are extensive.

The Missouri is navigated by vessels plying between Omaha and Sioux City (Iowa). The Federal irrigation district of western Nebraska embraces 532,617 acres. 20,225 acres of land unappropriated and unreserved (1932) are available for settlement.

Education, Religion, etc.—Education is compulsory between the ages of seven and sixteen years, and there are four State normal schools. The State University at Lincoln (founded 1871), the Creighton University (R.C.) at Omaha, the Nebraska Wesleyan University (M.E.), and Hastings College (Presbyterian) at Hastings are the most important academic institutions for higher instruction. There is an Indian Reserve of 12 sq. miles; pop. (1931), 4358. State area, 77,510 sq. miles (of which 702 sq. miles are water); pop. (1930), 1,377,963.

Nebraska was sold to the United States by Napoleon in 1803 (Louisiana purchase). It became a territory in May, 1854, and was made a state on 1st March, 1867. In 1882 and 1908 it annexed small parts of Dakota. There are 93 counties in the state. The present Government comprises a Governor, and a Legislature composed of a Senate (33 members), and a House of Representation (100 members). Legislators are elected for two years. Two Senators and five Representatives are sent to Congress.—Cf. A. E. Sheldon, *History of Nebraska.*

NEBUCHADNEZZAR (in Jeremiah and Ezekiel, **Nebuchadrezzar**). A king of Babylon, celebrated as the conqueror of Judah. He reigned from 604 to 561 B.C. according to the opinion of modern chronologists, or from 606 to 563 B.C. according to that of older chronologists. He was the son of Nabopolassar, by whom the Kingdom of Babylon was definitely made independent of the Assyrian monarchy. In the fourth year of Jehoiakim, King of Judah (605-604 B.C.), he defeated Pharaoh-Necho, King of Egypt, at Carchemish (Circesium), on the Euphrates, and subjugated Syria and Palestine, carrying off with him the sacred vessels of the temple and the chief Jews into captivity.

He destroyed Tyre in 585, and some years later he invaded and ravaged Egypt. During the peaceful years of his reign he rebuilt in a magnificent manner Babylon and many of the other cities of the empire, and constructed vast temples, aqueducts, and palaces—revealed by recent excavations (1899-1911). His insanity and the events preceding are only known to us from the Book of Daniel.

NEB'ULA (pl. **nebulæ**). In astronomy, the name given from their cloud-like appearance to a class of celestial objects mostly visible only in telescopes. One or two of the largest can be faintly discerned by the naked eye under the most favourable circumstances. Many objects formerly reckoned as nebulæ have been resolved into stars under the application of more powerful telescopes, but the spectroscope shows that many others are not stellar.

Nebulæ may be divided into two main groups: (1) the green nebulæ, which give a spectrum of bright lines, and must be composed of glowing gas; (2) the white nebulæ, which give a continuous spectrum, upon which in some cases dark lines can be discerned. The white nebulæ must contain incandescent solid or liquid matter, or else gas at high pressure. They may consist of stars. In practically all cases they appear to have a spiral form, the typical structure being that of a central nuclear mass, from which diverge at opposite sides two spiral arms. The thickness of the spiral is small compared with its areal extension.

Spiral nebulæ present to us different appearances according to their inclination to our line of sight. In their distribution on the celestial sphere the white nebulæ avoid the Milky Way. The largest is the Great Nebula in Andromeda. The green or gaseous nebulæ appear mostly in or near the Milky Way. They include the sub-classes of Irregular and Planetary Nebulæ. Of the former kind is the Great Nebula in Orion. Planetary nebulæ present a roughly circular form, and are named from their resemblance to planetary discs as shown by the telescope.

The green nebulæ contain hydrogen and helium, but the brightest line in their spectrum is unknown terrestrially, and was formerly attributed to a hypothetical chemical element, which was designated *nebulium*. This line, and others characteristic of nebulæ, have now been shown by Bowen to be due to ionized oxygen and nitrogen, and doubly ionized oxygen. Some astronomers think that the spiral nebulæ may be external galaxies of stars, or island universes comparable with our own and at enormous distances from it, but others consider that they are subordinate parts of our universe, being star clusters too closely packed for telescopic resolution.

NEBULAR HYPOTHESIS. A theory proposed by Laplace to account for the features of the solar system. It postulated the former existence of a vastly extended nebula, containing the materials now forming the sun, planets, comets, etc. The nebula was supposed to have a motion of rotation. Owing to loss of heat by radiation it contracted, the rotation increasing, until a ring of matter was detached at its periphery. With further contraction successive rings separated. Each ring subsequently consolidated itself to form a planet, revolving round the final residual central mass, which is our present sun. Satellites were similarly formed to revolve round some of the planets.

There are several formidable, and in fact insuperable, dynamical objections to the theory. Some of these relate to the formation of rings, their aggregation, the orbital inclinations, certain retrograde motions, and the sun's slow rotation. While development from some kind of nebular beginning is generally believed in, it is recognized that the hypothesis must be greatly modified. Chamberlin and Moulton have propounded the *Planetesimal Hypothesis.* It is suggested that another stellar body made a comparatively close approach to the "pre-sun."

Owing to the tidal strains produced the sun was disrupted, and matter was ejected in two arms which extended outwards in convoluted form, the configuration resembling a spiral nebula. In the scattered matter (planetesimals) there were certain larger and denser masses, which acted as centres of aggregation for the finer surrounding material, and thus formed planets. It is claimed that the theory accounts satisfactorily for many of the characteristics of the system, while avoiding the difficulties involved in the Laplacian hypothesis.

NECHO, or **NEKU.** A king of Egypt, mentioned in 2 Kings xxiii. 29 and Jer. xlvi. 2. He belonged to the twenty-sixth dynasty; succeeded his father, Psammeticus I., and reigned from 610 to 594 B.C. He extended his dominions from the south of Syria to the Euphrates; defeated Josiah, King of Judah, at Megiddo, but was ultimately driven back by Nebuchadnezzar.

NECKAR. A river in Germany which rises in Württemberg, in the Black Forest, and flows through Baden into the Rhine at Mannheim after a course of 247 miles. Its tributaries include the Fils, Rems Kocher, and Jagst on the right, and the Ens on the left. On its banks are Heidelberg, Mannheim, Heilbrönn and Tübingen. It is navigable as far as Canstatt.

NECKER, Jacques. French minister of finance, born at Geneva 1732, died 1804. In 1776 he received an appointment to the Treasury, the direction of which he retained for

Neckar River flowing through Heidelberg

five years. His suppression of abuses created him many enemies at court, and shortly after the publication of his famous *Compte Rendu* he resigned and retired to Switzerland, where he published his *Administration of the Finances*, which had an immense circulation.

He was recalled as Comptroller-General in 1788, and supported the convocation of the States-General, but was again dismissed in 1789. No sooner was his removal known than all Paris was in a ferment. The storming of the Bastille followed (14th July), and the king found himself compelled to recall the banished minister. He resigned in Sept., 1790, and passed the rest of his life in Switzerland.—Cf. Mme de Staël, *La Vie privée de M. Necker*.

NEC'ROMANCY (Gr. *nekromantia*, from *nekros*, corpse, *manteia*, divination). The divination of the future by questioning the dead. This superstition originated in the East, and is of the highest antiquity. We find mention made of necromancy in the Scriptures, where it is strongly condemned. In the *Odyssey* Homer has made Odysseus raise the shade of Tiresias from the infernal regions. In many parts of Greece there were oracles of the dead, the origin of which is lost in the obscurity of history. Although this practice has been condemned by the Christian Church from the very first, it has not yet entirely ceased. The term is often extended so as to include the general art of magic.

NECROP'OLIS (literally " city of the dead "). A name originally applied to a suburb of Alexandria devoted to the reception of the dead, and hence extended to the cemeteries of the ancients generally. The name has also been given to some modern cemeteries in or near towns.

NECRO'SIS (literally " mortification "). A medical term signifying the death of the bone substance. It is a condition of the bone substance corresponding to what gangrene is in the soft parts, thus distinguished from *caries*, which corresponds to ulceration in the soft parts. Necrosis is usually a result of inflammation of the bone, and is often attributed to cold, but frequently it is due to constitutional disease.

NECTAR. In Greek mythology, the drink of the gods, which was imagined to contribute much towards their eternal existence. It was said to impart a bloom, a beauty, and a vigour which surpassed all conception, and together with ambrosia (their solid food) repaired all the decays or accidental injuries of the divine constitution.

NEC'TARY. In botany, a gland secreting a sugary solution (nectar), or a spur or other structure serving for the reception of nectar. Most insect-pollinated flowers possess one or more nectaries, the secretion providing the principal attraction for insect-visitors. Any part of the flower may bear nectaries, e.g. the petals in buttercup or columbine, stamens in Cruciferæ, carpels in marsh marigold. Extra-floral nectaries occur on many leaves (e.g. broad bean), and are said to act as decoys, diverting ants and other " unbidden guests " from the flowers.

NECTOCALYX. In some compound jelly-fishes (Siphonophora), the name applied to polypes in the form of swimming bells, which propel the colony by their alternate contraction and expansion.

NECTRIA. A genus of ascomycetous Fungi, group Pyrenomycetes. *N. ditissima* causes a dangerous canker on ash, apple, etc. ; *N. cinnabarina*, the coral-spot, is very common on dead branches, especially those of red currant, and may also behave as a parasite.

NECTURUS. A genus of large Salamanders found in the United States of America. They have four well-developed feet, external gills, and broad tails. There are two species, a northern one with a brown body, spotted with black (*N. maculosis*), and one found in the rice-fields of the Southern States (*N. punctatis*), which is without spots. In winter these Salamanders protect themselves from frost by burrowing deep in the mud.

NEEDLE. A small instrument of steel, pointed at one end, and having an eye or hole in it through which is passed a thread, used for sewing. From very ancient times needles of bone, ivory, wood, and bronze have been used. The manufacture of steel needles was first introduced into England in the reign of Elizabeth. The manufacturing operations that an ordinary sewing-needle goes through are very numerous, and many of the processes are performed by automatic machinery with great saving of time and labour.

Redditch, in Worcestershire, is the chief seat of needle manufacture in Britain, and the best foreign needles are made at Aix-la-Chapelle. An ordinary sewing-needle is made of Sheffield crucible steel drawn to wire of suitable diameter. When cut into lengths, each sufficient to make two needles, the wires are straightened by rolling them in bundles under a heavy iron tool. At one time the points were made by holding the wires to a grinder by hand, but now the wires are fed on to a revolving wheel, to the rim of which they are fixed by rubber bands, and each in turn is brought against a grindstone.

The operation is repeated for the other end. The grooves at the ends are then pressed, the eyes pierced, and the needles separated. They are then hardened and tempered by a suitable heat treatment and oil quenching. Finally the needles are scoured, and the eyes smoothed and polished. Modifications of the ordinary sewing-needle, such as those used in the various forms of sewing-machines, in sail-making, bookbinding, glove-making, and darning are manufactured in the same way.

NEEDLE-ORE (aikinite, or " acicular bismuth "). Native sulphide of bismuth, lead, and copper, occurring in the Urals, embedded in quartz in long, thin, steel-grey orthorhombic prisms. It consists of lead 35·8, copper 11, bismuth 36·7, and sulphur 16·5, and usually accompanies native gold.

NEGAPATAM'. The port of Madras, India. It was an early settlement of the Portuguese, fell to the Dutch (1660), and has been British since 1781. It is an emigrant port for Rangoon and the Federated Malay States. Pop. 54,016.

NEGLIGENCE. In law, the omission to do that which ought to be done. When such want of care results in injury to another, or involves a wrong done to society, it renders the party guilty of negligence liable to either an action for damages or trial for misdemeanour. In law there are recognized three degrees of negligence: *ordinary*, the want of ordinary care or diligence; *slight*, the want of great care or diligence; and *gross*, the want of slight care or diligence. The person charged with negligence must have been under an obligation to exercise care or diligence either assumed by contract or imposed by law.

An alleged act of negligence must always be the proximate cause of the injury sustained; but any injury caused to a person by another who at the time is exercising due care in the commission of a lawful act is not actionable. An error of judgmeut is not negligence. The question of negligence is usually one for a jury, and the onus of proof rests on the plaintiff, except when the thing resulting from the negligence speaks for itself. A master is responsible for the negligence of his servants in the course of their employment, but in no case can redress be had where contributory negligence on the part of the plaintiff is proved.

NEGRILLOS. A pygmy race of tropical Africa, such as the Akoni of the Gabun, the Obongo of the Ogowi, Doko of Abyssinia, Akka, Bambutte, Manbettu of the Congo, and the Vazimba of Madagascar. The Akka have their hair evenly distributed, like the Dravidians of India. They have average heads, and are Mesaticephalic. Their height varies between 4 feet 1 inch and 4 feet 10 inches.

NEGRI-SEMBILAN (literally "nine states "). One of the Federated Malay States, comprising a confederation of the small native states of Sungai-Ujong, Johol, Jelebu, Rembau, and five smaller states. The supreme authority is vested in the State Council, which is composed of the Sultan, the British Resident and his secretary, and some selected Malay chiefs and Chinese merchants.

The Resident is responsible to the Governor of the Straits Settlements, who is, incidentally, the High Commissioner. Negri-Sembilan is traversed by mountain spurs (Mount Ophir, 3840 feet) which are densely afforested in the highest regions. The State railways bifurcate at Gemas, Negri-Sembilan, to form east and west coast routes, joining the Siamese railways on the Perlis-Siam and Kelantan-Siam boundaries respectively. Area, 2550 sq. miles; pop. (1931), 233,799.

NEGRI'TOS. The name given to several small black peoples inhabiting the islands, etc., of South-Eastern Asia, and often confounded with the Papuan race. The chief tribes are the Aëtas, the indigenous people of the Philippine Archipelago, still inhabiting the interior of the Islands of Luzon, Negros, Panay, Mindoro, and Mindanao; the Semangs of Malacca; and the Mincopies inhabiting the Andaman Archipelago.

Negrito

They are dwarfish in stature, averaging from 4 feet 6 inches to 4 feet 8 inches in height; the nose small, flattened or turned up at the apex, and the hair soft and frizzled. The aborigines of Tasmania, now extinct, were of this race. The fusion of the original woolly-haired Negrito with the straight-haired Malay has given rise to the frizzly-haired Melanesian.

NEGROES. A race of mankind probably indigenous to equatorial Africa, but now ranging from the southern margin of the Sahara as far as the territory of the Hottentots and Bushmen, and from the Atlantic to the Indian Ocean. The typical negro is described as having a black skin, woolly or crisp hair, a protuberant mouth with thick lips, nose thick and flat, long narrow skull, hair of the face scanty, thorax compressed, long arms, calves poorly developed, and feet comparatively flat with long heels. The slave system has alienated great numbers of negroes from their native country mostly to America and the West India Islands, where there has been considerable intermixture of races. There are nearly 10,000,000 negroes in the United States.

NEGRO RIO. A river of Latin America, the largest left-bank affluent of the Amazon (q.v.). Its principal tributaries are the Uaupés, Padauiry, Rio Branco, and Parima. Length, about 1350 miles, practically navigable throughout.

NEGROS. *See* PHILIPPINES.

NEHEMI'AH. A Jewish governor who was born in captivity, but was made the cup-bearer of Artaxerxes Longimanus, King of Persia. He was sent, 444 B.C., as governor to Jerusalem, with a commission to rebuild the walls and gates of this city. He accomplished his purpose, but not without difficulties, arising partly from the poverty of the lower classes of the people, and partly from the opposition of the Ammonites and other foreign settlers. The Book of Nehemiah contains Nehemiah's account of his proceedings, with other matter which forms a supplement to the narration contained in the Book of Ezra.

NEISSE (nī'sė). A town and railway junction of Germany, in Upper Silesia, on a river of the same name. The church of St. James was completed in 1430. Neisse was formerly administered by the Bishop of Breslau, and was capital of the principality of Neisse. Pop. 32,604.

NEJD. A sultanate of Central Arabia, inhabited by Wahabis, and formerly part of Jebel Shammar. Since 1901 it has gradually increased in power—Hasa was wrested from the Turks in 1914; Ibn Saud, Sultan of Nejd, annexed Jebel Shammar and made captive the representative of the Ibn Rashid dynasty in 1921; and in 1924 he made war on the Hejaz and captured Mecca, the Sherifian capital. In Dec., 1925, he entered Jidda, and, on the abdication of King Ali in the same month, became King of the Hejaz. A treaty embodying Britain's recognition of his complete independence was signed at Jidda in 1927 (*see* HEJAZ). In 1926 'Asir (*see* YEMEN) came under the protectorate of Ibn Saud. In 1932 the name of the combined kingdom of Hejaz and Nejd, with dependencies, was changed to that of Saudich or Saudi Arabia. The actual sultanate only touches the coast of Hasa, on the Persian Gulf. Riyadh, capital of Nejd, is also one of the capitals of Saudi Arabia, the other being Mecca; the largest town in Nejd is Hufuf.

Nejd produces fruits, dates, wheat, barley, wool, hides, saman, etc. Horses are exported to Bombay, and camels to Syria and Egypt. In 1928 the unit of currency in Nejd and Hejaz became the silver *Riyal*, replacing the Turkish *Mejidieh*. The basis of exchange is the pound sterling (fixed value £1 stg. = 10 *Riyals*). The population is estimated at 3,000,000. In 1925 the boundary with Transjordan was definitely settled. In 1928 Sir Gilber Clayton and 'Iraqi delegates met Ibn Saud at Jidda. Negotiations failed, but Ibn Saud promised to observe all existing truces and treaties. *See* ARABIA; HEJAZ; JIDDA.—Cf. H. St. J. B. Philby, *The Heart of Arabia*.

NELLORE. A town of India, in the Presidency of Madras, capital of district of the same name. It is on the Madras-Calcutta main line, and communicates with Madras by the Buckingham Canal. Pop. 35,863, The district lies on the Coromandel coast; area, 7973 sq. miles. It is famous for its breed of cattle. Pop. 1,400,000.

NELSON, Horatio, Viscount. A younger son of a Norfolk clergyman, was born at his father's rectory of Burnham-Thorpe on 29th Sept., 1758. Through his mother he was a great-grand-nephew of Sir Robert Walpole, and a nephew of Maurice Suckling, a naval officer who became Comptroller of the Navy. Under his uncle's influence he entered the navy in 1770 at the age of twelve, and in 1773 he took part in an expedition to the North Pole.

Suckling was a scientific sailor, and he impressed on the boy the necessity of acquiring an expert knowledge of his profession, and was able to help him to promotion. His first active service was in the War of American Independence, and he attracted the attention of Admiral Lord Hood, who regarded him, in spite of his youth, as an authority on naval tactics. Like Wellington, he found his opportunity in the great French war which broke out in 1793. During the first years of the war he was employed in the Mediterranean, and he lost the sight of his right eye in the reduction of Corsica.

He acquired his first reputation in the battle of Cape St. Vincent (14th Feb., 1797), when his daring and ability contributed much to the completeness of the victory won by Sir John Jervis (Lord St. Vincent) and were recognized by his creation as a Knight of the Bath. In the following July, in an independent operation against Teneriffe, he received a wound which necessitated the amputation of his right arm.

In 1798 he was sent in pursuit of Napoleon's expedition to Egypt, and on 1st Aug. he won the battle of Aboukir or the Nile. He adopted the daring device of sending part of his fleet between the French ships and the shore, and so attacked them on two sides, and his exploit constitutes the most daring and the most complete naval victory of modern times. Out of thirteen ships of the line and four frigates, with which the French began the fight, they had, at the end of the day, only two ships and two frigates. He was made Lord Nelson of the Nile by George III., and Duke of Brontë by the King of Naples, whose dominions had been endangered by Napoleon's Mediterranean expedition.

Nelson was entrusted with the protection of Naples, and this appointment had a disastrous influence upon his private life. He had married in 1787, apparently happily, but at Naples he fell in love with the famous Emma, Lady Hamilton, the wife of the British Minister, with whom he contracted a permanent liaison. In December the French took Naples from the land, and Nelson accompanied the Neapolitan court to Palermo, and organized the blockade of Naples, which was recovered in June, 1799.

As commander-in-chief of the Neapolitan navy he dealt severely with deserters to the French, and his conduct has been attributed to the personal influence of Lady Hamilton. The censure is unjust, but it is not so easy to defend a subsequent refusal to obey the order of his commander-in-chief and to leave Naples; he was, however, suffering from the effects of a head-wound received at the Nile. His health was bad, he imagined that his career was over, and he returned to England in company with the Hamiltons. A separation from his wife immediately followed, and he made her a liberal allowance.

In 1801 Nelson was sent, under the command of Sir Hyde Parker, to break up the Northern Confederation, which had proclaimed an armed neutrality against Great Britain as a protest against the British methods of blockade. He wished to deal a decisive blow by leaving a portion of the expedition to watch the Danish fleet and proceeding into the Baltic to destroy the Russian fleet, but Parker regarded the project as rash, and it was decided to attack Copenhagen. Parker accepted Nelson's scheme of attack, and entrusted the most important part to him.

In the course of the battle (1st April, 1801) Nelson received a signal, "Discontinue the action," and, putting a telescope to his blind eye, remarked, "I do not see the signal"; but he was aware that it was intended only to relieve him of the responsibility if he should deem a withdrawal desirable. Ultimately he suggested a truce to put an end to the slaughter; an armistice was arranged, and the murder of the Emperor Paul, which had taken place a week before the battle, broke up the Northern Confederation.

When the French war was renewed, on the rupture of the Treaty of Amiens in 1803, Nelson was given the command of the fleet in the Mediterranean, and for nearly two years he watched for an opportunity of destroying the French fleet and rendering impossible Napoleon's projected invasion.

In 1805 Napoleon devised a scheme for obtaining a temporary command of the Channel without risking a battle. The French and Spanish fleets were to escape from the harbours in which they were being watched by the British, and, while the British fleet was dispersed in search of them, they were to return and convoy a French army to England. Part of the scheme was successfully accomplished, but in the end Nelson found the enemy near Cadiz and fought the battle of Trafalgar. He had only twenty-six ships against thirty-three of the enemy, but he succeeded in bringing a superior force against the particular portion of the enemy's fleet which he selected for attack at successive stages of the battle.

At the proper time he himself attacked the enemy's centre and pierced their line, but was mortally wounded on the quarter-deck of his flagship, the *Victory*. Before he died he heard of the surrender of fourteen ships—the final number was twenty-two—and his last words were "Thank God, I have done my duty," a reference to the famous signal which he had hoisted at the crisis of the battle, "England expects that every man will do his duty" (21st Oct., 1805).

He had aimed at the annihilation of the enemy's fleet, and his object was practically accomplished, for he had secured his country from the danger of invasion. Nelson was buried in St. Paul's on 9th Jan., 1806, and in 1829 Trafalgar Square was planned as a permanent memorial; the column and statue were completed in 1849, and the bronze lions were added in 1867.—Bibliography: R. Southey, *Life of Nelson*; Captain A. T. Mahan, *Life of Nelson*; J. C. Jeaffreson, *Lady Hamilton and Lord Nelson*.

NELSON. A seaport and chief town of the district of Nelson, New Zealand, on Tasman Bay, South Island; served by railway south-west to Glenhope, with projected extensions to Christchurch. It was settled by the New Zealand Company in 1841, and has a large coasting trade. Pop. (1932), 12,700.

NELSON. A municipal borough in North-East Lancashire, England, on the L.M.S. Railway. There are cotton-factories, confectionery-works and engineering establishments. The town is connected with Burnley (3 miles) and Colne by tram. Nelson is a modern town, and became a borough in 1890. Pop. (1931), 38,306.

NELSON RIVER. A river of Canada, which issues from Lake Winnipeg, and after a tortuous course of about 350 miles falls into Hudson Bay at Port Nelson. The Saskatchewan, which enters Lake Winnipeg, is frequently taken as the Nelson River, and the united length is then about 1700 miles.

NELUM'BIUM. A genus of aquatic plants inhabiting the fresh waters of the temperate parts of the world, type of the nat. ord. Nelumbiaceæ, having large polypetalous flowers with

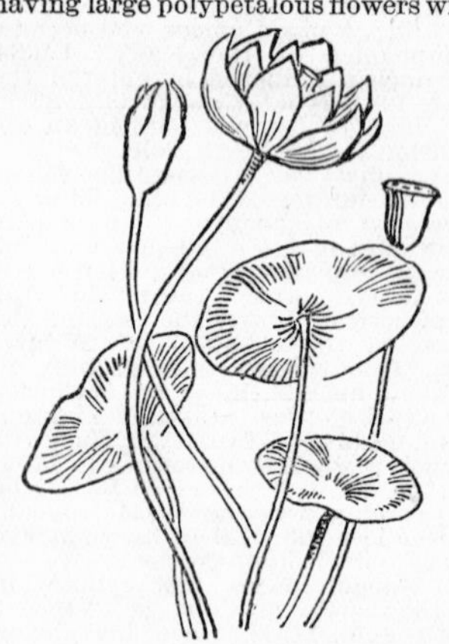

Nelumbium

numerous stamens. The best-known species is *Nelumbium speciōsum*, the Hindu and Chinese lotus, a magnificent water-plant of the rivers and ditches of all the warmer parts of Asia, the Malay Archipelago, Australia, and also found in the Nile (formerly at least). The numerous canals of China are filled with it, its tubers being there used as a culinary vegetable.

It is a most beautiful plant, with peltate leaves and handsome rose-coloured flowers on tall stalks, and is frequently cultivated in hothouses. In Asia it is generally deemed sacred, and figures in religious rites. *N. luteum*, the yellow water-bean of the southern United States, has starchy rhizomes, with tubers like those of the sweet-potato, which are used for food.

NEMATEL'MIA, or **NEMATHELMINTHES.** The invertebrate phylum including those parasitic worms which possess bodies of rounded or cylindrical shape, together with a smaller number of non-parasitic forms. Among the most familiar are the Gordiacĕa, or " Hair-worms." These possess slender hair-like bodies, and are found as parasites in the interior of beetles and other insects, during the first stages in their development. On arriving at sexual maturity they escape from the bodies of their hosts and seek the water of pools, in which the eggs are deposited in the form of lengthened chains.

The embryos produced from these ova are provided with a retractile proboscis and hooks, by means of which they penetrate the bodies of insects, and there develop into the sexually mature worms. Superstition formerly credited horse-hairs, introduced into water, with the remarkable property of becoming transformed into these living creatures.

Another order of the Nematelmia is that of the Nematōda, which includes the following notable forms: round-worm (*Ascaris lumbricoides*), human intestines; horse-worm (*A. megalocephala*), intestines of horse; seat-worm (*Oxyuris vermicularis*), human large intestine; hook-worm (*Dochmius duodenalis*), a dangerous parasite that burrows in the walls of the small intestine of man; gape-worm (*Syngamus trachealis*), of poultry and game-birds; *Trichina spiralis*, a minute species, of which enormous numbers may be found encysted in the muscles of rat, pig, and man; the guinea-worm (*Filaria medinensis*), and its minute ally (*F. sanguinis hominis*) that is a blood parasite in man. Some plant diseases are caused by nematodes, e.g. clover-sickness (*Tylenchus devastatrix*), ear cockle (*T. tritici*) of wheat, and beet-sickness (*Heterodera Schachtii*).

NEMAT'OCYST. | In zoology, a " thread-cell " of the Cœlenterata, that is, a cell or minute sac, in the interior of which is a long filament, often serrated or provided with spines, and capable of being swiftly protruded. It is to their nematocysts that the power of stinging possessed by many of the jelly-fishes, etc., is due.

NEMATODA. *See* NEMATELMIA.

NEME'AN GAMES. Ancient Greek games, held in the valley of Nemea in Argolis, where Hercules is said to have killed the Nemean lion. They recurred ordinarily every second year, and were similar in character to the other Greek games.

NEMER'TINEA. Represented by the marine " ribbon-worms." They possess flat, ribbon-like bodies, which, as in the Borlasia of the British coasts, may attain a length of more than 15 feet. Some of the species of the type-genus Nemertes, attain a length, in their extended state, of 30 or 40 feet, which they can suddenly contract to 3 or 4 feet. There is a curious proboscis, contained in a sheath when at rest, and capable of being protruded from the front end of the body.

NEMESIA. A genus of South African herbs, ord. Scrophulariaceæ. *N. strumosa* is a valuable garden annual, the race introduced by Messrs. Sutton showing an extraordinary range of beautiful colours.

NEM'ESIS. The personification of the righteous anger of the gods, inflexibly severe to the proud and insolent, i.e. retributive justice. In Homer she does not appear as a person, but the word *nemesis* is used as a noun in the sense of righteous anger. In the *Theogony* of Hesiod she is the daughter of Night, the avenging Fate who checks and punishes the favourites of Fortune.

NEMOURS. A town of France, in the department of Seine-et-Marne, on the Loing; served by the Paris-Lyon-Mediterranean Railway. There is a feudal castle, and an old church. In the vicinity there are important quarries of Fontainebleau sand. Many Gallo-Roman remains prove the antiquity of Nemours, which is presumed to have taken its name from the woods (*Nemora*) by which it was once surrounded. In the twelfth century the lordship of Nemours (in Gâtinais) belonged to the House of Villebeon, but was sold to King Philip III. (1274-76), and became a county in 1364. Charles VI. of France erected it into a duchy in 1404, and presented it to Charles III. of Evreux, King of Navarre. The Duchy of Nemours was in the possession of the Orleans family at the time of the Revolution. Pop. 5074.

NENNIUS. The supposed author of a collection of chronicles and genealogies styled *Historia Britonum*, written in Latin, and reaching down to A.D. 655. The author is supposed to have been a monk at Bangor in Wales. The authorship and authenticity of Nennius have been much disputed.

NEOCO′MIAN. In geology, a term applied to the lowest stage of the Lower Cretaceous series, represented in England by the Hastings Sand and Weald Clay.

NE′OGENE. In geology, a name given by some geologists to the Pliocene and Miocene systems, to distinguish them from the older Oligocene and Eocene strata.

NEOLITH′IC. This term was originally applied to the polished and other implements of the latter part of the Stone Age, so as to distinguish them from the earlier implements called Palæolithic. "Neolithic Age" or "Neolithic phase of culture" are, however, terms that must be applied with caution, especially outside Western Europe. During the Neolithic Age, which has not everywhere, even in different areas of Europe, the same chronological significance, stone implements were polished, domesticated animals became common, cereals and fruit-trees were cultivated, pottery made, linen woven, boats were in use, and definite religious beliefs were entertained.

At the same time some stone-polishing peoples had only the dog as a domesticated animal and did not practise agriculture. Louis Siret has found evidence in Spain which points to the intrusion there of Easterners who extracted ores and carried them away to the foundries of their own country, or those of the peoples who purchased ores. They introduced into Spain the fine flint-working called Neolithic, which Siret considers to be of Egyptian origin. Different kinds of flint were used, but no local beds of these can be traced. This new industry spread over the northern maritime area.

Associated with these flints have been found religious objects shaped from ostrich eggs from Africa, and Egyptian ivory, alabaster vases, figurines of the mother-goddess of Mesopotamia, amber from the Baltic, and jet from Whitby in Yorkshire. Of special interest are the green-stone axes, for one of these has been found associated with a "prehistoric canoe" discovered in Clyde silt, at Glasgow, about 25 feet above the present sea-level. One Glasgow canoe had a cork plug, and the cork must have come from Spain or Italy where cork trees grow.

Neolithic polished stone axes are so finely balanced that they revolve on a centre of gravity. The mathematical skill required for their construction cannot be regarded as "primitive." Evidently the Neolithic industry was introduced by a people in a comparatively high stage of civilization. The barley-seeds used were those of cultivated barley which grows wild in Egypt. Siret's view is that the Easterners who introduced the Neolithic industry into Spain visited all the maritime west and north. That Egypt was in touch with the colonies of Easterners in Spain is suggested not only by the ivory, etc., but also by a diadem of gold found in a necropolis in Southern Spain which belongs to the age of polished stone.

These colonies of Easterners in Spain were broken up by a bronze-using people from Central Europe. Siret refers to them as Phœnicians, and suggests that the native Iberians, among whom the imported Neolithic industry spread, had no knowledge of the metals the Easterners had come to collect. It was in the interests of the strangers to keep the natives ignorant. They used flint themselves in their colonies, and the Neolithic industry reached a high state of development in consequence. Among the exports of the colonists were silver-bearing lead, tinstone, copper ore, and gold dust. *See* FLINT IMPLEMENTS.

NEON (symbol, Ne; atomic weight 20·2), an element occurring in minute quantity in the atmosphere. The gas was discovered by Ramsay and Travers in 1898, along with two other new elements, which they called krypton and xenon. The proportions by volume in which the minor gaseous constituents of the atmosphere occur are, in parts per million: argon, 9330; neon, 12·3; helium, 4·0; krypton, 1·0; xenon, 0·05. Chemically, they are all inert elements (*see* PERIODIC TABLE). Next to hydrogen and helium, neon is the least easily condensed of the gases. *See* ISOTOPES.

NE′OPHRON. A genus of birds of the vulture family, one species of which (*N. percnoptĕrus*) inhabits Southern Europe, Egypt, and Asia. It is known as the Alpine or Egyptian vulture, Pharaoh's hen, etc.

NEO-PLATONISM. A philosophical system resting upon a religious basis which arose in the third century of our era, and flourished in the pagan world of Hellas and Rome. It was the direct result of the religious yearning which had taken possession of the Roman world, and an attempt to construct a religious philosophy or theosophy inspired by Greek thought. It was at once the swan-song of Greek philosophy and a last effort of Paganism to stop the living waters of Christianity which were pouring over the world.

Neo-Platonism is idealistic and spiritualistic, with a tendency towards mysticism. Eclectic, according to the fashion of the age, it endeavours to unite Plato's idealism with the religion of the East, to blend Platonic ideas with Oriental mysticism. It arose at Alexandria, where East and West met and commingled, where the contemplative Orient, with its tendency towards the supernatural and miraculous, and Greece with her subtle investigating spirit, in other words, logical analysis and feeling, fused, and produced a new phase of thought, prevalent during the first centuries of our era. Greek philosophers, no longer interested in empirical and rational science, turned their attention to religion, and endeavoured to solve the problems of knowledge and virtue.

Neo-Platonism aimed at the highest knowledge—the knowledge of the absolute, a knowledge which alone would lead to a perfect acquaintance with the universe. The aim of philosophy, taught the Neo-Platonists, should be the knowledge of the *One* which is the cause and essence of all things, the original and primitive light from which everything emanates. This knowledge can be obtained not by thought and reflection, but in a perfect manner by *intuition*, which precedes thought, and by attaining a sort of spiritual ecstasy. Neo-Platonism rests therefore upon the proposition that the *absolute*, that which is above the senses, is the foundation of the world; and that it is knowable by intuition, or ecstatic contemplation.

God is the Alpha and the Omega of everything, the beginning, the middle, and the end (He was, He is, and He shall be), and the real object of man's strivings should be an absorption in God, or a communion with God. This God of the Neo-Platonists is a mystical trinity, consisting of three hypostases or substances, having for its basis unity, which is the universal principle. From the *One* emanates the *Nous*, or pure intelligence, the image of God, and which, like the Logos of Philo, is an agglomeration of ideas. From the *Nous* emanates the world-soul, and from this again emanate the individual souls, which give rise to matter. The whole spiritual world is thus to be considered as one spiritual being. God did not create the world, nor is it an evolution from Him. It is an emanation from God, like the light radiating from the sun, without diminishing the latter.

The sensible world is but an image of the intelligible world; time is an image of eternity, and emanates from it. Evil is either apparent or necessary, but if it is necessary it ceases to be evil. The soul of man, Neo-Platonists taught, is restless until, freed from the world of matter, the world of sense and reason, it returns to God by way of knowledge and is absorbed in Him. Neo-Platonism is thus both theistic and pantheistic. It teaches that God is transcendent, but it conceives everything as an emanation from Him.

There were three schools of Neo-Platonism: the Alexandrinian-Roman, the Syrian, and the Athenian. To the Alexandrinian school belonged Ammonius Saccas (A.D. 175-242), the supposed founder of the system, Longinus, Plotinus, and Porphyry. The Syrian school is represented by Iamblichus (330), who strongly manifested an Anti-Christian tendency, and Proclus (411-85).

As a religion Neo-Platonism could not compete with Christianity, although it influenced the theology of St. Augustine; but as a philosophy it was again studied during the Middle Ages, and especially with the rise of humanism (q.v.). It influenced the philosophical doctrines of Giordano Bruno and Jacob Boehme, and has affinities with the systems of Fichte, Schelling, and Hegel.—BIBLIOGRAPHY: C. Bigg, *Neo-Platonism*; T. Whittaker, *The Neo-Platonists*; R. M. Jones, *Studies in Mystical Religion*; Vacherot, *L'École d'Alexandrie*.

NEOT'TIA. A small genus of Orchidaceæ, readily distinguished by its habit, all the species being leafless brown-stemmed saprophytes, with sheathing scales in place of leaves. One species, the bird's-nest orchis (*N. nidus-avis*), is a native of Britain.

NEPÁL. An independent state on the north-eastern frontier of India, among the Himálaya. Mount Everest is within the state. Kathmandu (pop. about 80,000) is the capital; the surrounding valley has a pop. of 300,000. The people are mainly Gurkhas, mixed with Bhutias, Gurungs, Magars, Murmis, Newars, Kiratis, Limbus, Lepchas, and many other distinct but lesser races. The inhabitants of Sikkim (q.v.) are also Nepálese. Hinduism, the faith of the Gurkhas, has almost obliterated the Buddhism of the more primitive peoples.

The standard of coinage is the silver mohar, equivalent to 6 annas

8 pies, Indian; copper pice are circulated, fifty being the equivalent of a silver mohar; the Indian rupee is accepted.

The valleys are cultivated for rice, tobacco, millet, and oil-seeds, and a good export trade is maintained with British India in hides, skins, cattle, opium, gums, resins, dyes, jute, wheat, pulse, rice and cereals, spice, clarified butter, oil-seeds, tobacco, timber, and saltpetre. There are valuable forests in the south. Imports to Nepal include cattle, sheep, and goats; salt, sugar, tobacco, spices, drugs and dyes, petroleum, leather; brass-, iron, and copper-ware; and piece goods, In 1927 the first railway line (25 miles) into Nepál was opened from Raxaul to Amlekhganj. State area about 54,000 sq. miles; pop. estmated at about 5 to 6 million.

The Gurkhas are a Rajpút race who migrated from Udaipur (Rájputána), settled the province of Gurkha (Nepál), and, during the eighteenth century, overran the whole country. The government is a military oligarchy, and since 1867 supreme power has been vested in the Prime Minister, who is incidentally a general in the British army. Since 1856 the Tibetan Government has paid annual tribute in Rs. 10,000 to Nepál, and receives a representative of Nepál at Lhasa and at other trade-centres for the encouragement of inter-state commerce.

By the Anglo-Nepálese Treaty of Segowlie (2nd Dec., 1815) a British Envoy and a small escort of sepoys live at Kathmandu, but exercise no authority in Nepálese internal affairs. During the European War the Prime Minister of Nepál supplied 20 battalions of infantry, 200,000 recruits to the Indian army, and maintained a training-reserve of 20,000 men. In recognition of Nepálese support the Indian Government makes to Nepál an annual payment of 10 lakhs of rupees.—BIBLIOGRAPHY: P. Brown, *Picturesque Nepál*; I. Massieu, *Népál et pays himálayens.*

NEPH'ELINE, or **NEPH'ELITE.** A mineral silicate of aluminium and sodium, occurring in plutonic or volcanic rocks, in small masses or veins, and in short hexagonal prismatic crystals. It is usually colourless or yellow. Its massive form, as in nephaline-syenites, has a gummy aspect, and has been called *elæolite.* Nepheline occurs abundantly in certain districts in trachyte and basalt, though it is very rare in the British Isles. It is very often altered to sodium-zeolites, and thus disappears from many rocks of great geological age.

NEPHRODIUM. A large and cosmopolitan genus of leptosporangiate Ferns, family Polypodiaceæ. The best known is *N. Filix mas,* the common male or shield fern.

NEPHTHYS. An Egyptian deity, daughter of Seb and Nut, and sister and wife of Seth. Her proper sphere was the nether world, though she occurs in the upper world as the instructress of Horus. She is associated as one of a tetrad with Osiris, Isisi, and Horus.

NE'POMUK, Johann von. The patron saint of Bohemia, born at Pomuk, in Bohemia, about 1330, martyred 1393. In 1378 he became court-preacher to King Wenceslaus (Wenzel), but incurring the displeasure of that monarch, he was cruelly tortured and thrown from the bridge over the Moldau into the river (1393). In the course of the fifteenth, sixteenth, and seventeenth centuries many legends gathered round his name, and in 1729 Benedict XIII. canonized him. The day consecrated to his memory is the 16th of May.

NEPTUNE. The chief sea-god of the ancient Romans. When the Greek mythology was introduced

Neptune, from a statue at Rome

into Rome, he was completely identified with the Greek Poseidōn, all the traditions relating to whom were transferred by the Romans to their own deity. In art he is usually represented as armed with a trident, and the horse and the dolphin are his symbols.

NEPTUNE. In astronomy, the most distant of the known planets, its mean distance from the sun being 2,793,000,000 miles, and its least distance from the earth 2,675,000,000 miles. The eccentricity of its orbit is ·00855; its inclination to the plane of the ecliptic is 1° 47′. Its apparent diameter is about 2·5″. Its real diameter is estimated at about 34,000 miles, and it seems to have very little polar compression.

Its mass is about 17 times that of the earth, and it revolves round the sun in 164·8 years. It has one satellite, whose period is 5 days 21 hours; mean distance from the planet, 222,000 miles; revolution retrograde. Neptune was discovered in 1846 in a position indicated independently by Leverrier and Adams, and deduced from a series of recondite mathematical calculations to find a body which could account for the long-observed perturbations of Urănus.

NEPTUNIAN THEORY. A name given to a geological theory of Werner which referred the formation of all rocks and strata to the agency of water; opposed to the *plutonic, igneous,* or *Huttonian theory.*

NE′REÏDS. In classical mythology, sea-nymphs, daughter of Nereus and Doris, daughter of Oceanus, and constant attendants on Poseidon or Neptune. They are represented as riding on sea-horses, sometimes with the human form entire, and sometimes with the tail of a fish. They were distinguished on the one hand from the Naiads or the nymphs of fresh water, and on the other hand from the Oceanides or nymphs of the ocean.

NE′REÏS. A genus of bristle-worms (Chætopoda) with long segmented bodies, antennæ or feelers, eyes when distinct four in number; mouth usually with horny jaws. Some of the species are found in most seas.

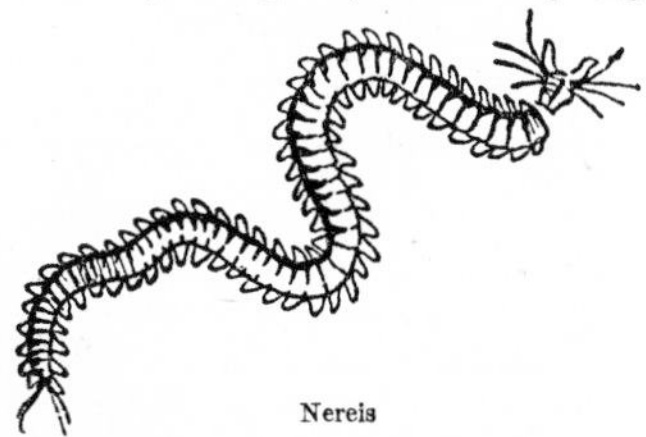

Nereis

NEREOCYS′TIS. A sea-weed of the nat. ord. Laminariaceæ, found on the north-western shores of America and opposite shores of Asia, remarkable for the stems which attain the length of 45 fathoms, swelling at the top into large cysts or bags filled with liquid; these becoming entangled, form large floating islands on which sea-otters rest.

NEREUS (nē′rūs). In classical mythology, a sea-god, the father of the Nereïds. He was the son of Pontus (Sea) and Gæa (Earth). In the ancient works of art, and also by the ancient poets, he is represented as an old man, with a wreath of sedge, sitting upon the waves with a sceptre in his hand.

NERI, St. Filippo de'. The founder of the Congregation of the Oratory in Italy, was born in Florence in 1515, died 1595. He founded the order of "Priests of the Oratory," which was approved by Gregory XIII. in 1595. He was canonized in 1622.

NERO, Lucius Domitius Ahenobarbus (after his adoption by the Emperor Claudius called *Nero*

Nero

Claudius Cæsar Drusus Germanicus). Roman emperor, the son of Gnæus Domitius Ahenobarbus and Agrippina, the daughter of Germanicus. He was born in A.D. 37 at Antium, and after the marriage of his mother (her third marriage), with her uncle, the Emperor Claudius, was adopted by that prince, and married to his daughter Octavia. When Nero was about seventeen years of age his mother poisoned her husband, Claudius, and succeeded in raising to the throne her son, over whom she expected to exercise the most absolute control.

Nero became emperor in 54, and the year following disposed of the rightful heir, Britannicus, by poison. For the first few years his public conduct, under the control of Burrhus and Seneca, was unexceptionable; in private, however, he disgraced himself by the most odious vices, and his mother endeavoured to retain her influence by shamefully complying with his inclinations. In 59 Nero caused this detestable woman to be murdered, and then, fearing no rival in power, gave full scope to the darkest traits of his character. In 62 he repudiated his wife Octavia.

The burning of Rome in 64 has been charged upon Nero himself, who, however, accused the Christians of the act. His debaucheries and cruelties occasioned an almost general conspiracy against him, known as that of Piso, in 65, the discovery of which led to more tortures and bloodshed. The revolt of Vindex was also suppressed. That of Galba in 68 succeeded, and Nero escaped arrest by stabbing himself, being then in the thirty-first year of his age and the fourteenth of his réign. He was a lover of arts and letters, and possessed much taste as a poet and histrionic performer.—BIBLIOGRAPHY: Tacitus, *Annales*; B. W. Henderson, *Life and Principate of the Emperor Nero*.

NERVA. The successor of Domitian, and one of the most virtuous of the Roman emperors. He was born in Umbria A.D. 32, died A.D. 98. He was twice consul, and was elected emperor on the death of Domitian in 96. He adopted Trajan, who succeeded him.

NERVII. An ancient people of Gallia Belgica, famous for the stand they made against Cæsar's advance in 57 and 54 B.C. They submitted to the Romans in 53 B.C. Their territory was co-extensive with the old diocese of Cambrai.

NERVOUS SYSTEM. This is evolved for the purpose of correlating an individual with his surroundings, and of controlling and co-ordinating the various bodily processes essential to health. The actions for example of the heart, of the lungs, and of the various organs concerned in digestion are all correlated to bodily needs by means of the nervous system. Its work, however, is not by any means limited to the governance of these functions, vital though they be. It receives external impressions and enables the individual to work as a whole and to carry out actions of attack, defence, procuring of food, and so on. And the nervous system, in its central part at any rate, is also the seat of the processes that govern conscious existence.

Impressions (or stimuli) conveyed to the central nervous system from the surrounding world give rise to sensations of smell, taste, touch, or sight, etc., and as a result of such sensations emotions are called forth which may be pleasant or painful. Again, the muscular movements which result in walking, writing, speaking, or gesture are to be regarded as expressions of the activities of certain parts of the nervous system.

The nervous system is made up of nerve cells and fibres. The central parts, e.g. the brain, are composed largely of cells. The nerves (e.g. those running to supply the muscles of the limbs) consist entirely of fibres, but every nerve fibre is an offshoot from a cell. Nerve fibres may be very long, of course. Nerve cells are very minute and nerve fibres extremely fine. They can only be discerned and investigated with powerful microscopes. The structural unit of the nervous system is therefore the cell plus its processes, and this unit is usually termed a "neuron." The nervous system, as can readily be understood, contains many myriads of neurons. From the point of view of function neurons may be receptive or conductive, according as they convey external impressions inwards or conduct outwards nervous impulses which give rise to bodily actions.

Nerve cells, when studied microscopically, have many fibres springing off from them. There is, however, a main process (or fibre), an essential conducting one, and this is known as the "axis cylinder" or "axon." Many such go to make up what we ordinarily know as a nerve. There are, in addition to the axons, other offshoots from the cell, called "dendrons." These in comparison with axons are short and never extend any distance from the parent nerve cell: they branch and intertwine, axons do not.

The axons and dendrons bring the different nerve cells into relation with each other, and thus they bring about the co-ordinated action of the different neurons. Fibres, it must be remembered, are solely conducting agents in the nervous system: nerve cells are governing and nutritive.

If a nerve fibre is separated from its nerve cell it speedily degenerates and disappears. The same happens if the cell itself dies or is severely damaged.

Looking at the nervous system from another point of view we may say it is divided into two portions, the cerebro-spinal and the vegetative. The *cerebro-spinal nervous system* consists of the brain enclosed within the bony walls of the skull, the spinal cord occupying a canal in the centre of the vertebral column (spine), and the various nerves that issue from brain or cord. The nerves springing from the brain are called cranial nerves; those issuing from the spinal cord spinal nerves. From the interior of the skull the brain passes down through a large bony aperture at the skull base, and becomes then the spinal cord, which extends down to the lumbar region of the spine.

The *vegetative nervous system* is a complicated system of ganglia (ganglion = a group of nerve cells) and nerve fibres which innervate the muscular fibres that are present in the internal organs, digestive tubes, and glands. It is developed from the cerebro-spinal system, and remains connected with it. It is not under the control of the will and it governs all the important life-sustaining processes such as respiration, circulation, and digestion. To it we owe our general sense of bodily well-being in health and the feelings of distress or pain when vital functions are interfered with.

Within the skull the brain is divided into four main parts, viz.:

1. **The cerebrum** or large brain, which fills the entire cavity of the upper part of the skull and represents about seven-eighths of the whole brain. It is divided into two halves, one on each side, the right and left cerebral hemispheres. Its surface is increased in area by being thrown into folds or convolutions, which form the cerebral cortex or bark. The cortex consists of a thick layer of grey nervous matter made up of nerve cells, whilst the interior of each hemisphere contains white matter made up of conducting nerve fibres.

2. **The cerebellum** or small brain is situated in the back of the skull, below and behind the cerebrum. It is a highly important part, and its surface is very finely convoluted.

3. **The medulla oblongata** or bulb, which is placed far down, lies in front of the cerebellum, and connects the brain with the spinal cord.

4. **The pons varolii**, which is a broad band of nervous tissue lying above the medulla and connecting it with the cerebrum and also with the cerebellum.

The spinal cord is about 18 inches long and one-third to half an inch in diameter. In its passage through the spinal canal it gives off thirty-one pairs of nerves which emerge from each side of the cord by two roots, an anterior (motor) and a posterior (sensory) root. These roots unite and form nerve trunks which contain fibres subserving both motion and sensation, and are therefore usually known as mixed nerve trunks The posterior roots contain chiefly afferent nerve fibres, i.e. fibres conveying impressions (usually of sensation) into the central nervous system; the anterior root fibres are those of a great efferent system and subserve the conduction of motor impulses from the brain and spinal cord outwards to the muscles. The mixed nerve trunk therefore is both afferent and efferent, or motor and sensory.

The *spinal cord* on cross-section shows a central H-shaped collection of grey matter, the points of the H being usually referred to as horns, anterior and posterior on each side. Surrounding the grey matter and forming the outer zone of the cord on section is white matter made up mainly of fibres which run up and down. These fibres connect the brain with the cord and thence with the various mixed nerves of the body and *vice versa*; they also connect different nerve cells in the cord with one another.

We may now consider the various parts of the cerebro-spinal system from the point of view of function, but it is necessary first of all clearly to understand the meaning of *reflex action*. When a stimulus falls on a sensory surface (e.g. skin) or sense organ (called receptor) the stimulus, of whatever nature, gives rise to an impulse which passes along an afferent fibre in a mixed nerve and reaches the spinal cord via one of the posterior roots. In the cord it travels through a number of neurons in the grey matter, becomes modified, and finally leaves the cord via an efferent fibre in an anterior root to reach and throw into action some muscle or gland.

This pathway is called a reflex arc and consists of (1) a receptor; (2) afferent nerve fibre; (3) neurons in spinal cord; (4) efferent nerve fibre; (5) muscle or gland. If the reflex arc is interrupted at any part (by disease or injury of the cord or nerves), then the reflex action dependent on its integrity is abolished. The *spinal cord*, it may now be noted, is a series of centres for reflex actions. It is in addition a conductor conveying impulses which originate in the higher nerve centres in the brain to all the different parts of the body, via the efferent fibres in the spinal mixed nerves.

Impressions from the skin, muscles, etc., painful or otherwise, pass along the afferent fibres to the cord via the posterior roots and thence are conducted upwards to the brain. The *medulla oblongata* also acts as a reflex centre, and serves as a conducting path for impulses passing between the brain and cord. Some most important and vital reflexes are effected through the medulla, e.g. those regulating the heart's action and the calibre of the blood vessels and those regulating the breathing and movements of the stomach (e.g. vomiting).

The *pons varolii* contains centres for certain important cranial nerves (e.g. the facial), which centres are innervated from the cerebral cortex. It connects through certain fibres the cerebrum with the cerebellum and it also contains many fibres subserving upward and downward conduction between brain and cord. The *cerebellum* is intimately concerned in the power of maintaining the equilibrium of the body, and with the capacity of making the co-ordinated bodily movements characteristic of a healthy person. If a bird have its cerebellum removed, attempts to fly only result in chaotic and futile movements of its wings and equally futile are the attempts of a quadruped to walk, under the same circumstances.

The *cerebral cortex* is a recent addition to the nervous system from the evolutionary point of view. Certain lower animals have no cerebral hemispheres worth speaking of, but as we ascend the scale the cerebral cortex becomes more and more prominent, and in man the cerebral hemispheres form the greater part of the brain. The *cerebrum* receives stimuli, and can give effect to them by means of efferent impulses; but it also registers stimuli, producing a permanent record, and so subserves memory. An animal without a cerebral cortex can carry out reflex movements co-ordinately through the cerebellum, etc., but it has no volition, or intelligence. The cerebral grey matter is very rich in cells, and highly differentiated.

Disease in man and experiments in animals have shown that different areas of the cerebral cortex subserve different functions. There is, for example, a special motor area, interference with which produces paralysis, a special visual area, a special speech area, etc. The farthest forward parts of the cerebrum (frontal lobes) are especially concerned with the intellectual processes, and reach their greatest development in the human cerebral cortex.

Diseases of the nervous system are broadly classified as functional and organic. In the latter there are obvious naked-eye or microscopic changes in structure. The former are not characterized by any detectable degenerative change: they include such conditions as neurasthenia, hysteria, shell shock, where the symptoms are mainly nervous though not associated with any known change in brain, spinal cord, or nerves.—BIBLIOGRAPHY: E. A. Schäfer, *Textbook of Physiology*; W. D. Halliburton, *Handbook of Physiology*; J. R. Whitaker, *The Anatomy of the Brain and Spinal Cord*; J. R. Angell, *Psychology*; C. S. Sherrington, *The Integrative Action of the Nervous System*.

NESS, Loch. A lake of Scotland, in Inverness-shire, part of the Caledonian Canal. It is long and narrow, in the valley of Glenmore. Length, about 23 miles; breadth, $1\frac{1}{4}$ to 2 miles; greatest depth, about 130 fathoms. The outlet of the lake is by the River Ness (famous for its salmon-fishing) into the Moray Firth.

NEST. The place where a bird lays its eggs, hatches them, and shelters

Nest of Tailor Bird

its young until they are fledged. The materials used are extremely various, being such as mud or clay, twigs or branches, leaves, grass, moss, wool, feathers, etc. Some birds, for the sake of protection, excavate burrows in banks or sandy cliffs in which to

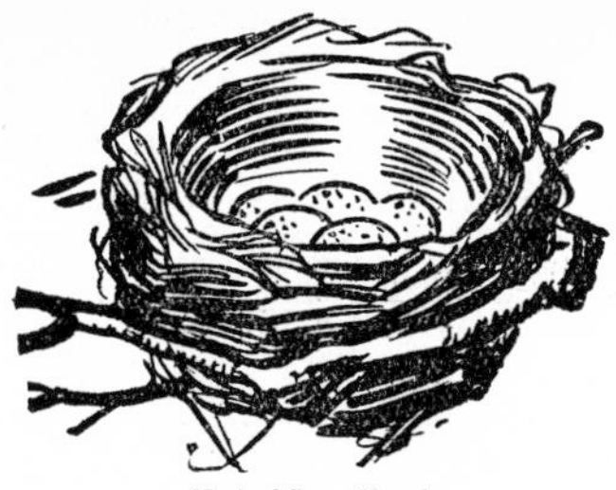

Nest of Song Thrush

make their nests. Many mammals also are nest-builders, notably mice, moles, dormice, squirrels, foxes, weasels, badgers, rabbits, etc.; and nests are also constructed by certain fishes, reptiles, crustaceans, insects, etc.

NESTOR. One of the Greek heroes at Troy, son of Neleus, King of Pylos, who took part in the hunting of the Calydonian boar, and in the Argonautic expedition. He is noted as the wisest adviser of the chiefs before Troy, after the fall of which he retired to Pylos, where he lived to a great age.

NESTOR. Russian historian, born about 1056, was a monk at Kiev, and died in 1114. He wrote a *Chronicle* in his vernacular tongue, which has been the foundation of Slavonic history.

NESTORIANS. A Christian sect of Western Asia, named from their founder Nestorius, formerly of greater importance than they are at present. One portion of them is united with the Roman Catholic Church though using the Greek ritual. They have a patriarch residing at Diarbekr. The larger body of them remains as a distinct sect, in Mesopotamia, Syria, Persia, etc. They recognize only three sacraments, baptism, the Lord's Supper, and ordination; and their priests are allowed to marry. There is a Nestorian body in India called Christians of St. Thomas.

NESTO'RIUS. Heresiarch, was presbyter at Antioch and Bishop of Constantinople from A.D. 428 to 431. He incurred the charge of heresy by maintaining that in the person of Christ the two natures were not so united as to form but one person. Cyril of Alexandria, at the Council of Ephesus in 431, procured the condemnation of the doctrine taught by Nestorius and the deposition of the patriarchs. He was banished to the deserts of Egypt, where he suffered much and died (440).—Cf. A. Harnack, *History of Dogma*.

NET. An open fabric made of thread, twine, or cord, woven into meshes of fixed dimensions, firmly knotted at the intersections. Nets are used for a great variety of purposes, as for protecting fruit-trees, for collecting insects, for hammocks, screens, etc., but chiefly for hunting and fishing. The chief kinds of nets used in fishing are the trawl, the drift, the seine, the kettle or weir, and the trammel or set nets. The trawl is a triangular bag with an arrangement for keeping its mouth open, drawn along the bottom of the water. The drift and seine nets are very long in proportion to their breadth, and differ from each other only in the manner in which they are employed. The seine has a line of corks along one of its long borders, and a line of leaden weights along the other; so that when thrown into the water it assumes a perpendicular position.

It is used near the shore, being dragged to land, with any fish it may enclose, by ropes fastened to the ends. The drift-net also hangs upright, but is used in the open sea, and more especially in herring-fishing, the fishes as they drive against it becoming caught by the gills. Kettle and weir nets are structures fixed on stakes placed along the coast between high and low water. Trammel or set nets are also fixed between stays, but act like drift-nets. Formerly all nets were made by hand, but since 1820, when James Paterson established a machine-net factory at Musselburgh, hand-made nets have been superseded.

NETHERLANDS, The, or **HOLLAND** (in Dutch *Nederland*, or *Koninkrijk der Nederlanden*). A kingdom of Europe lying on the North Sea.

Netherlands. One of the Dutch canals

General Features.—The Netherlands form the most characteristic portion of the great plain of Northern and Western Europe. It is the lowest part of this plain, some portions of it being 16 to 20 feet below the surface of the sea, and nearly all parts too low for natural drainage. The coast-line is very irregular, and the country is protected from the sea by lines of dunes and artificial dikes; the dune-line has been broken through by the sea, and the submerged land behind it forms the Zuider Zee. Following an Act in 1918, the work of draining the Zuider Zee, and thus forming a new province of about 820 sq. miles, was begun in 1924. It is expected that the scheme will be completed in 1939. The fragments of the broken barrier that once kept out the sea remain as the Frisian Islands.

Almost the only heights are the sand-hills, about 100 to 180 feet high, forming a broad sterile band along the coast of South and North Holland; and a chain of low hills, of perhaps similar origin, south-east of the Zuider Zee. The highest elevation, 656 feet, is in the extreme south-east. The general aspect of the country is flat. It comprises eleven provinces, as follows:

Province.	Land Area, Square Miles.	Population, 1931 (est.).
Guelders . .	1,941	843,233
North Brabant	1,921	908,681
Overyssel . .	1,301	528,477
Friesland . .	1,251	402,241
South Holland .	1,130	1,989,946
North Holland.	1,059	1,537,580
Drente . .	1,029	225,591
Groningen. .	886	395,423
Limburg . .	846	566,916
Zealand . .	690	247,938
Utrecht . .	526	415,545
Total . .	12,580	8,061,571

The census of Dec., 1930, showed a population of 7,935,565. Including interior waters, the area (1930) was 13,203 sq. miles, and the total area, inclusive of gulfs and bays, amounted to (1930) 17,771 sq. miles. The principal towns and their populations in 1932 were:

Amsterdam .	766,263	Nimegen .	84,034
Rotterdam .	587,316	Tilburg .	80,890
The Hague .	449,614	Arnhem. .	79,322
Utrecht. .	156,194	Leiden .	71,598
Haarlem .	122,386	Apeldoorn .	62,044
Grongingen .	107,158	Maastricht .	61,763
Eindhoven .	93,234	Hilversum .	59,632

Colonies.—Holland is the third colonial power, and her possessions may be divided as follows: **Dutch East Indies** (area, 733,296 sq. miles; pop. (1930), 60,731,025), comprising Java and Madura, Sumatra, Riau-Lingga Archipelago, Banca, Billiton, Borneo (part of), Celebes, Moluccas, Timor, Bali, and Lombok. **Dutch West Indies,** comprising Surinam or Dutch Guiana (area, 54,291 sq. miles; pop. (1931), 155,888); Curaçao, a colony made up of two groups of islands, viz. Curacao, Aruba, and Bonaire in the first group; St. Martin (southern half), St. Eustatius, and Saba in the second group. Area 403 sq. miles; pop. (1931), 71,769. (All the above colonial figures are approximate.)

Internal Communication. — The total length of rivers and navigable canals is about 4660 miles. The chief rivers of the Netherlands are the Rhine, Maas (or Meuse), Schelde, and Yssel. The navigable canals, having a total extent of 2000 miles, are collectively more important than the rivers. The chief are the North Holland Canal, between Amsterdam and the Helder, length 46 miles; and the more important ship canal, 15 miles long, 28 feet deep, and 200 feet wide, from the North Sea to Amsterdam, and connected by locks with the Zuider Zee, the lock at Ymuiden, the largest in the world, being opened by Queen Wilhelmina in 1930. There are about 3000 miles of roads and (1929) 1916 miles of tramways. Railways are on the 4-foot-11-inch gauge, and the two principal lines had (1931) a length of 2278 miles. All railway concerns, four in number, are private. There is a State railway company, but it is so called merely from the fact that the road is State property. It is now proposed to bring the railway companies under one control. There are regular air services between Amsterdam and London; Amsterdam, Brussels, and Paris; Amsterdam and Hamburg; Rotterdam and Berlin; Amsterdam and Malmo.

Climate.—The mean temperature is not lower than in like latitudes in the British Islands, and the quantity of rain (26 inches) is somewhat less; but the winter is much more severe.

Production: Agriculture.—Wheat, rye, barley, oats, buckwheat, peas, beans, mustard seed (brown and white), carraway seed, flax, tobacco, potatoes, sugar-beets, chicory, onions. In the provinces of Zealand, South Holland, North Holland, and Groningen, large estates predominate; small estates are confined to North Brabant, Limburg, Overyssel, and Guelders. Dairying is progressive, and much cheese, butter, and margarine are produced and exported, notably to the United Kingdom.

Fisheries.—There are herring and

oyster fisheries, employing in 1931, 4895 vessels of all kinds.

Minerals.—Coal is found in the province of Limburg. The total output for the whole country in 1932 was 13,756,447 metric tons. There are three State and four private mining concerns. Lignite, peat, and salt at Boekelo (56,414 tons in 1931) are also worked.

Commerce. — The following are the principal imports, and, in parentheses, the chief sources of supply: coal (Germany, Belgium, United States, Britain); Wheat (Belgium, United States); maize (United States); linseed (Argentine); timber (Germany, Finland, Sweden); copra (Dutch East Indies); cotton yarns (Britain); nitrate of soda (Chile); flour (United States, British India); iron and steel (Germany, Belgium); petrol (United States, Mexico); raw coffee (Brazil, Dutch East Indies); barley (United States, Rumania); rails (Germany, Belgium); motor-cars (Germany, United States); fuel oil (Mexico); boots (Britain).

Currency, etc.—Silver is the money chiefly in circulation. The standard coin is the 10-florin piece (6·048 grammes of fine gold), and the unit of silver coinage is the gulden (florin, 9.45 grammes of fine silver). The gulden (guilder or florin) of 100 cents =**1s.** *8d.*, i.e. 12 =£1 at normal rates of exchange. The rijksdaalder = 2½ guilders. There are gold pieces of 10 guilders and of 5 guilders; coins of ½, ¼, and $\frac{1}{10}$ guilder; 5 cent pieces in nickel; and ½ cent, 1 cent, and 2½ cent pieces in bronze. The metric system of weights and measures is in force.

People.—The stock to which the people belong is the Teutonic, the great majority of the inhabitants being descendants of the old Batavians. They comprise over 70 per cent. of the population, and are chiefly settled in the provinces of North and South Holland, Zealand, Utrecht, and Gelderland. The Flemings of North Brabant and Limburg, and the Frisians, inhabiting Friesland, Groningen, Drente, and Overyssel, form the other groups.

Religion.—In religion the growth of Roman Catholicism is marked. The provinces of North Brabant and of Limburg have always been pre-eminently Roman Catholic, and the Protestant strongholds are the provinces of the north-east Friesland, Groningen, and Drente. In Gelderland, North and South Holland, and Overyssel the Roman Catholic minority is very large and increasing. There is no State Church, but the Budget makes allowances for all the Churches, the proportions being (in 1933): Protestant, 1,721,000 guilders; Roman Catholics, 705,000 guilders; Jansenists, 17,500; and Jews, 16,200 guilders. The adherents of the various bodies (1920 census) are given as:

Dutch Reformed	2,826,633
Other Protestants	832,164
Catholics	2,444,583
Jansenists	10,461
Jews	115,223
Other creeds and Atheists, etc. .	636,240
Unknown	1,010

Political parties are mainly divided on religious lines.

Government.—The Government is a constitutional monarchy on British lines, the succession to the throne being vested in the male line of the Royal House of Orange-Nassau, but passing in default of male heirs to the female issue. The sovereign attains majority at the age of eighteen years. The Crown possesses large executive powers, and is assisted by a Council of State (14 members, nominated by the sovereign).

The States-General (Parliament) consists of a First Chamber (50 members, elected for nine years indirectly by the provincial states, one-third seeking re-election every three years), and a Second Chamber (100 Deputies, elected for four years directly by single-member constituencies, and retiring in a body). Elections are by universal suffrage and proportional representation. Members of the Lower House are paid 5000 guilders (£420) annually.

Amsterdam is the commercial capital of the Netherlands; the seat of government and residence of the sovereign is at The Hague.

Defence.—The navy is maintained for the dual purpose of coastal defence and colonial protection, and includes four coast-defence ships of two 9·4-in. and four 6-in. armament, one of two 11-in. and four 6-in. armament; two cruisers carrying two 5·9-in. and eight 4·7-in. guns, and two others of ten 4·7-in. weapons. There are three armoured gunboats in the East Indies.

Other ships include seventeen small destroyers, twenty-four submarines (the O8, an interned vessel bought from Britain in June, 1917), two submarine depot ships, and twelve mine-layers. The peace strength of the Netherlands army (including "landweers") is about 8370 officers and 349,000 men, with 156 field and 42 heavy guns. An additional 156,000 trained and 250,000 untrained men are available for mobilization. The infantry carries the Mannlicher magazine-rifle, model 95; cavalry and engineers are armed with the Mannlicher carbine; field artillery is armed with a shielded 7·5 cm. quick-firing Krupp gun.

Education.—Secular and sectarian instruction are separate. Education is compulsory between the ages of seven and thirteen years. Private schools and institutions may be endowed by the State or by the community or province. In 1931-32 there were two private and four public universities (Leiden, Utrecht, Groningen, Amsterdam); one technical university; two high schools of commerce, one at Rotterdam, and the other at Tilbury (founded in 1927); twelve navigation schools (in 1928-29); fifty-six public (classical) schools; and other elementary, infant, "middle-class," and "working-class" schools. In addition, the veterinary school at Utrecht and the agricultural school at Wageningen were created universities in 1918.

History.—The southern portion of the Low Countries belonged at the beginning of the Christian era to Belgic Gaul. The northern portion, inhabited by the Batavians and Frisians, formed part of Germany. The southern portion as far as the Rhine was held by Rome up to A.D. 400, after which it came under the rule of the Franks, as did subsequently the rest of the territory also. In the eleventh century the territory comprised in the present kingdoms of Belgium and the Netherlands formed a number of counties, marquessates, and duchies corresponding more or less with the modern provinces.

By the latter part of the fifteenth century all these had been acquired by the Duke of Burgundy, and passed to the House of Habsburg on the marriage of the daughter of Charles the Bold to the son of the Emperor Frederick III. On the abdication of Charles V. in 1556 they passed to his son Philip II. of Spain. In consequence of religious persecution in 1576 Holland and Zeeland openly rebelled, and in 1579 the five northern provinces — Holland, Zeeland, Utrecht, Guelders, and Friesland— concluded the Union of Utrecht, by which they declared themselves independent of Spain. They were joined in 1580 by Overijssel, and in 1594 by Groningen.

After the assassination of William of Orange, 10th July, 1584, Maurice became stadtholder. His victories at Nieuport and in Brabant, the exploits of the Dutch admirals against the navy of Philip II., the wars of France and England against Spain, and the apathy of Philip II. caused in 1609 the Peace of Antwerp. The independence of Holland was fully secured by the Peace of Westphalia. In the middle of the seventeenth century the United Netherlands were the first commercial state and the first maritime power in the world, and for a long time maintained the dominion of the sea. The southern provinces alternated between the rule of Spain and Austria till 1797, when they came under the power of the French Republic.

In 1806 Louis Bonaparte became King of Holland, but in 1810 it was incorporated with the French Empire. In 1815 (Congress of Vienna) all the provinces of modern Holland and Belgium were united by the Treaty of Paris to form the Kingdom of the Netherlands. This arrangement lasted till 1830, when the southern provinces broke away and formed the Kingdom of Belgium. King William I. attempted to reduce the revolted provinces by force; but the Powers intervened, and finally matters were adjusted between the two countries in 1839. *See* BELGIUM.

The king abdicated in 1840, and was succeeded by his son Willem II. (1840-49), he being again succeeded by his son Willem III., who died in 1890, leaving his ten-year-old daughter Wilhelmina as queen under the regency of the queen-mother, Emma. The queen attained her majority on 31st Aug., 1898, and during the South African War Holland was decidedly in sympathy with the Boer cause, affording refuge to the fugitive President Kruger. Queen Wilhelmina married Prince Henry of Mecklenburg-Schwerin on 7th Feb., 1901, and the heir-apparent, Princess Juliana, was born in 1909. During the European War Holland maintained a large army to protect her neutrality, and many British troops were interned at Groningen after the fall of Antwerp. Holland afforded a refuge to the ex-Kaiser and to the Kronprinz Wilhelm on the fall of the German Empire. In 1932 she entered into a tariff union with Belgium and Luxembourg.

Language and Literature.—The literary language of the Kingdom of the Netherlands is in English called *Dutch*, but by the people themselves is called *Hollandsch* or *Nederduitsch*, that is, Low Dutch. This name it receives in opposition to the *Hochdeutsch* or High Dutch, the literary language of modern Germany. Closely allied to the Dutch is the Flemish language. Both languages belong to the Low German group of the Teutonic or Germanic branch of the Indo-European family of languages. The two languages, or rather dialects, are in fact in their early history identical. What may strictly be called Dutch literature, as distinguished from Flemish, dates from the last quarter of the sixteenth century.

The chief names of this period are those of Coornhert, von Marnix, Spiegel, and Visscher, who did much to polish and regulate the language and to produce correct models both of prose and verse. Pieter Cornelis-zoon Hooft (1581-1647) brought the prose style to a high degree of excellence; and Joost van den Vondel (1587-1679), the greatest of Dutch dramatists, performed the same service for the language of poetry.

Jacob Cats, familiarly known in Holland as "Father Cats" (1577-1660), on the other hand, confined himself to the sphere of everyday life. He was distinctively the poet of the people, and his writings are still popular. Among other leading names in pure literature are those of Constantyn Huygens (1596-1686), a satirist, epigrammatist, and didactic poet; Jacob van Westerbaan (died 1670) and Jan van Hemskerk (died 1656), both erotic poets; and Dirk Kamphuisen (died 1626), a celebrated hymn-writer.

Among dramatists were Brandt (died 1685), who was also an historian and epigrammatist; Oudaan (died 1692), a political writer and lyrist; and Antonides van der Goes (died 1684), celebrated also as a lyrist. The principal writer of comedies was Bredero (1585-1618). Dutch poetry declined towards the end of the seventeenth century partly through French influence, but a revival set in with Jacob Bellamy (1757-86). Willem Bilderdijk (1756-1831) shone in all departments of poetry. J. F. Helmers (1767-1813) won great applause by the descriptive poem *De HollandscheNatie.* Hendrik Tollens (1780-1856) was as a lyrist the avowed favourite of his country, and his *Overwintering der Hollanders op Nova-Zembla* is regarded as the best descriptive poem in the Dutch language.

An important service was rendered to the literature of his country by Jacob van Lennep (1802-68), who, incited by the example of Scott and Byron, introduced romanticism, and successfully repressed French classicism by his masterly treatment of native tales and historical subjects in narrative poems. The novelists who rank next to van Lennep are Oltmans, Mrs. Bosboom-Toussaint, and Douwes Dekker (Multatuli).

The list of later Dutch prose writers also includes Schimmel, N. Beets, W. A. van Rees, Weitzel, Lange, J. ten Brink, Opzoomer, Limburg-Brouwer, and the historians Fruin (called the Dutch Motley) and Hofdijk, the dramatist H. Heijermans, the poets Boutens, H. Gorter, Leopold, and others. Dutch names famous in classical learning include those of Erasmus, Lipsius, Grotius, Gronovius, etc.; in science, Huygens, Leeuwenhoek, etc.; in philosophy, Spinoza; and in medicine, Boerhaave.

BIBLIOGRAPHY: *The Netherlands* (in *Peace Handbooks*, vol. v.; H. M. Stationery Office, with a bibliography); Dr. A. Heringa, *Free Trade and Protection in Holland*; G. W. Edwards, *Holland of To-day*; W. E. Griffs, *Young People's History of Holland*; D. C. Boulger, *Holland and the Dutch*; J. C. A. Everwijn, *Beschrijving van Handel en Nijverheid in Nederland* (an abstract is published in English entitled, *A General View of Trade and Industry in the Netherlands*).

NETLEY. A village of England, in Hampshire, on Southampton Water; served by the London & South-Western Railway. The Royal Victoria Hospital was erected at

Netley Abbey

Netley in 1857 as a military hospital, and has accommodation for 1000 patients. Candidates for the Army Medical Service are partially trained in this hospital. There are ruins in the vicinity of a Cistercian monastery founded in 1239-40.

NETTLE. A genus of plants (Urtica) belonging to the nat. ord. Urticaceæ, and consisting chiefly of neglected weeds, having opposite or alternate leaves, and inconspicuous flowers, which are disposed in axillary racemes. The species are mostly herbaceous, and are usually covered with extremely fine, sharp, tubular hairs, placed upon minute vesicles filled with an acrid and caustic fluid, which by pressure is injected into the wounds caused by the sharp-pointed hairs. Hence arises the well-known stinging sensation when these plants are incautiously handled.

Many species of nettle are known, of which three are found in Britain—the Roman nettle (*U. pilulifera*), the small nettle (*U. urens*), and the great nettle (*U. dioica*). Nettles yield a tough fibre which may be used as a substitute for hemp. Nettle-porridge and nettle-broth are dishes made from young and tender nettles cut in March or April.

NETTLE-RASH, or **URTICARIA** (Lat. *urtīca*, a nettle). A common disease of the skin, an eruption closely resembling nettle-stings both as to appearance and as to the sensations it originates. It consists of small wheals, either red or white, sometimes both, having the centres white and the margins red. The disease may be either acute or chronic When it is acute, generally more or less of fever accompanies it. In almost all cases it arises from a disordered condition of the digestive organs, produced either by indigestible food, or in some persons by particular kinds of food which others eat with complete impunity.

NETTLE TREE (Celtis), nat. ord. Urticaceæ. A deciduous tree, with simple and generally serrated leaves, much resembling those of the common nettle, but not stinging. It has a sweet, fleshy, drupaceous fruit. The common or European nettle tree (*C. austrālis*) grows to the height of 30 or 40 feet, and is frequently planted for ornament in the south of France and north of Italy. The wood is useful for various purposes. *C. occidentālis*, sometimes called the sugar-berry, is a much larger tree, often attaining a height of from 60 to 80 feet. It is a native of North America from Canada to Carolina. A variety, *C. crassifolia*, is often called hackberry. *See* HACKBERRY.

NEUCHÂTEL (Ger. *Neuenburg*). A Swiss canton, bounded by France, Vaud, the Lake of Neuchâtel, and Bern. Neuchâtel was an independent principality as early as 1034. After various vicissitudes it came into the hands of the King of Prussia, as heir of the House of Orange. In 1814 it was received into the Swiss Confederacy, and was the only canton with a monarchical government, which it preserved till 1848. After threatened war in May, 1857, the King of Prussia renounced all his rights in Neuchâtel.

The Lake of Neuchatel, 23½ miles long by 3½ to 5 miles broad, communicates through the Aar with the Rhine. Grazing and dairy-farming are extensively carried on in the canton; wine, fruits, hemp, and flax are produced. The chief manufactures are lace, cotton, watches, and clocks (Chaux de Fonds and Locle). The people are mainly French-speaking Protestants. Area 305 sq. miles; pop. (1930), 124,324.,

The capital, which has the same name, stands on Lake Neuchatel west of Bern. It has a castle, formerly the residence of the Princes of Neuchâtel, and now occupied by the Government offices; an old Gothic church of the twelfth century, and a gymnasium or college, containing a valuable natural history collection founded by L. J. R. Agassiz a native of the town. Pop. 22,668.

NEUILLY-SUR-SEINE. A suburb of Paris.

NEUILLY, Treaty of. *See* BULGARIA.

NEUMÜNSTER (noi′mün-stėr). A town of Germany in the Prussian province of Schleswig-Holstein, on the Schwale and on the Altona-Kiel Railway. It is the centre of the railway system of Holstein. The original name was Wipendorp. Pop. 39,895.

NEUNKIRCHEN (noin′kir*h*-ėn), or **OBER-NEUNKIRCHEN.** A town of Prussia, in the district of Trèves, Saarbrucken. It lies in a great coal-basin, and has a large iron-foundry. In Feb., 1933, the explosion of a gasometer devastated a large part of the town. Pop. 41,031.

NEUQUÉN. A mountainous territory of the Argentine, traversed by the Neuquén, an affluent of the Rio Negro. Lake Nahuel-Huapi (q.v.) is in the territory. Large numbers of cattle, sheep, horses, etc., are reared. Area, 37,245 sq. miles; pop. (1932), 40,895.

NEURAL′GIA. The name given to that species of morbid pains which occur only in the course of one or more distinct nerves, and by this locality are distinguished from other pains. In neuralgia of the fifth nerve the pain is in one half of the face, and if the central branch is affected the pain is confined to the upper jaw; neuralgia of the chief nerve of the thigh (*sciatic nerve*) extends along the buttocks and back of the thigh down to the knee, and is called *sciatica*. It also affects the front, back, and outside of the leg, and the whole foot except its inner border; while neuralgia of the intercostal nerves manifests itself in a belt or circle of pain around the breast. The presence of neuralgia almost invariably indicates a weak state of the general system.

The most common and best ascertained of the neuralgias are those of the nerves of the skin (*dermalgia*); but nerve pains occur also in other parts, as in the joints, muscles, and in the bowels (*enteralgia*). Many of the internal parts may be the seat of similar local affections; such, for example, are nervous affections of the heart and respiratory organs, which, however, do not usually manifest themselves by acute pain, but by special symptoms. The primary causes of the injury to the nerve producing neuralgia may be very various. It may be inflammation of the nerve itself, a swelling in or upon it, irritation of it produced by an ulcer or suppuration or swelling of the adjacent parts, especially the cavities of the bones, etc.

Thin-blooded persons and those of weak nerves are most liable to be affected by neuralgia, which varies much both in degree and duration. It is often chronic, and often suddenly occurs during the progress of other acute diseases, as in typhus or intermittent fevers. The treatment also of course varies with the nature of the different cases, some admitting of easy cure by the administration of nourishing food, and by the use of iron and quinine, and other tonics, while for others the aid of surgery has to be called in.

NEUROP'TERA. An order of insects which undergo an incomplete

Neuroptera (Dragon-Fly)

metamorphosis, distinguished by the possession of four well-developed membranous wings, which are generally of equal or nearly equal size. The name Neuroptera ("nerve-winged") is applied to the group in allusion to the large size of the nervures or supporting "ribs" of the wings, which are very conspicuous and give to the wings a reticulated or network-like appearance. The mouth is generally masticatory, the head large and distinctly separable from the thorax, the antennæ usually slender. The tarsi possess from two to five joints. No sting exists.

In some Neuroptera the metamorphosis may approach very nearly to the holometabolic or "complete" variety. In general the larvæ are aquatic, the pupa in the majority of cases closely resembling the perfect insect. The chief families included in the order comprise the Libellulidæ or dragon-flies; the caddis-flies (Phryganeidæ); the may-fly family (Ephemeridæ); the Myrmeleontidæ, or "ant-lions"; the Hemerobiidæ, or "lace-winged flies"; and the Termitidæ, represented by the celebrated "white-ants" or termites of tropical regions. See the different articles.

NEURO'SIS. *See* NERVOUS SYSTEM.

NEUROT'IC. A term introduced into medicine to indicate some relationship to the nervous system. Thus a neurotic disease is a nervous disease. So medicines that affect the nervous system, as opium, strychnine, etc., are called *neurotics*.

NEUSATZ (noi'zàts), or **NOVI SAD** (Ujvidek). A town of Yugoslavia, formerly in Hungary, on the Danube, opposite Petervarad, on the main line to Belgrade. Pop. (1931) 63,966.

NEUSIEDLER SEE (noi'zēd-lėr zā), or **LAKE NEUSIEDL.** A lake on the Austro-Hungarian readjusted frontier. It is salt and shallow, and water has several times disappeared from it entirely. The last occasion was between 1865 and 1870, when crops were grown on its bed and the remains of lake dwellings were made visible.

NEU-STRELITZ. A town of Germany, capital of Mecklenburg-Strelitz, between Lakes Zierk and Glambeck. It is regularly built in the form of a star, the eight rays of which converge on a spacious market-place, and there is a palace, which formed the residence of the reigning grand-dukes until 1918. It contains a collection of over 100,000 books. Pop. 12,260.

NEU'STRIA. In the geography of the Middle Ages, the western kingdom of the Franks, in the north of France, so called in opposition to *Austrasia* (Austria, Oestreich), the eastern kingdom of the same. On the death of Clovis (511) his sons divided his territories into two parts, which received these names. Neustria lay between the Meuse, the Loire, and the ocean.

NEUTER. In zoology, a term applied to indicate those insect forms—represented chiefly among the ants, bees, and wasps—in which the characteristics of sex are either present in a rudimentary condition or may not be developed at all. Thus among the ants the community consists of males, females, and neuters, or "workers" as they are also termed. These ant-neuters are simply (sexually) undeveloped females, and upon these forms the performance of all the laborious duties of the ant-colony devolves. In the bees the neuters, or workers, are similarly sterile females.

The differences between the fertile females and neuters—both of which are developed from fertilized ova—appear to be produced through differences in the food upon which the respective larvæ are fed, and through similar and surrounding circumstances which affect the nutritive development of the larvæ. Plenty of food is thus said to produce females, and a scantier or different dietary males or neuters. *See* PARTHENOGENESIS ; ANT ; BEE ; WASP.

NEUTRAL'ITY. In international law, that state of a nation in which it does not take part, directly or indirectly, in a war between other nations. The term *neutral*, or *neutrales*, dates from the fifteenth century, *medii*, or *medii amici*, being its equivalent in classical Latin. To maintain itself in a state of neutrality a nation is often obliged to assume a threatening position, to be able to repel, in case of necessity, every aggression on the part of either of the belligerents. Such neutrality is termed an *armed neutrality*.

In maritime wars the treatment of effects of the enemy on board neutral vessels, or neutral effects on board a hostile vessel, gives rise to very important questions. In former times the principle was pretty generally admitted that the ownership of the goods on board of the vessels was the only point to be considered, and not the property of the vessels themselves. The belligerents, therefore, seized merchandise belonging to the enemy on board of neutral vessels ; but they restored neutral property seized under the enemy's flag. But the endless investigations which this system caused, since a consequence of it was the searching of neutral vessels, produced by degrees a new and totally contrary principle, that the flag protects the cargo.

The plenipotentiaries of Great Britain, Austria, France, Prussia, Russia, Sardinia, and Turkey, assembled at Paris in April, 1856, agreed that the neutral flag should cover an enemy's goods, with the exception of contraband of war ; and that neutral goods, with the exception of contraband of war, are not liable to capture under the enemy's flag. In the arbitration (in 1872) at Geneva of the *Alabama* claims of the United States against Great Britain, three rules were agreed to by the parties, to the effect that a neutral Government is bound to use due diligence to prevent the fitting out in, or departure from, any of its ports of a vessel which it has reasonable ground to believe is intended to carry on war with a power with which it is at peace ; that it is bound not to permit a belligerent to make use of its ports as a basis of naval operations, or a source of recruitment of men or military supplies ; that it is bound to exercise due diligence in its own ports or waters, and as to all persons within its jurisdiction, to prevent any violation of these duties and obligations.

Certain states, such as Belgium and Switzerland, have been made permanently neutral, i.e. have been neutralized. They are bound to observe neutrality, and as long as they observe it, the guaranteeing powers undertake to protect them from attack. The immediate cause of Britain's entry into the European War was the invasion of Belgium by Germany, one of the guaranteeing powers.—BIBLIOGRAPHY : W. E. Hall, *Rights and Duties of Neutrals* ; C. F. Wicker, *Neutralization* ; J. Westlake, *International Law* ; Sir T. E. Holland, *Studies in International Law*.

NEUVE CHAPELLE. A village of France, in the department of Nord, seized by the Germans and retaken by Indian troops during Oct., 1914. It was practically destroyed during the European War, and was "adopted" by Blackpool. For the battle of Neuve Chapelle, 10th to 12th March, 1915, *see* EUROPEAN WAR.

NEUWIED (noi'vēt). A town of Germany in Rhenish Prussia, 7 miles below Coblenz, on the right bank of the Rhine. It contains a palace, and has an establishment of the Moravian Brethren, who amount to 500 or 600 individuals, and have excellent schools, which are attended by many English pupils. Pop. 20,322.

NEVA. A river of Russia, which issues from Lake Ladoga, and flows into the Gulf of Finland below Leningrad by several mouths. It is generally frozen over from October to April. Its commercial importance is enhanced by canals.

NEVA'DA. A state in the mountain division of the United States, lying wholly within the Great Basin at a mean altitude of 5500 feet. The surface is rugged ; mountain spurs and isolated ranges traverse the state, which is drained mainly by the Humboldt, falling into Humboldt Lake. The Colorado River forms the south-eastern boundary. Carson City (pop. 1930, 1596) is the state capital; Reno (pop. 18,529) is the largest town.

Communications, etc.—Three main lines traverse the state from east to west, the Southern Pacific and the Western Pacific in the north, and the San Pedro, Los Angeles, & Salt Lake system in the south. In 1932 there were 2131 miles of steam railway. Roman Catholicism is the predominant religious faith.

Production and Industry.—Nevada has some agriculture: corn, wheat, barley, and potatoes being produced; stock-raising and sheep-farming are important; there were 2,434,400 acres of national forest-land in 1932. An irrigation scheme embraces 160,000 acres, but agricultural development is retarded by bad communications. In 1932, 51,221,934 acres were unappropriated and unreserved and available for settlement. Manufactures are unimportant, and are chiefly allied with agriculture; but the state is exceptionally rich in minerals, gold (output, 1931, 139,194 ounces), silver (1931, 2,368,624 ounces), copper, lead, zinc, graphite, iron, mercury, tungsten, sulphur, gypsum, and stone being worked.

Education, etc.—Education is compulsory between the ages of seven and eighteen years; there is a State university at Reno (founded 1886). The Indian Reserve has an area of 1300 sq. miles; pop. (1931), 4975. State area, 110,690 sq. miles (869 sq. miles being water); pop. (1930), 91,058.

Nevada was admitted to the Union as a state on 31st Oct., 1864. The state is divided into seventeen counties. The present Government comprises a Governor, and a Legislature consisting of a Senate (17 members, elected for four years, one-half seeking re-election biennially) and a House of Representatives (37 members, elected for two years). Two Senators and one Representative are sent to Congress.—Cf. S. Davis, *History of Nevada.*

NEVERS (nè-vār). A town of France, capital of the department of Nièvre, on the right bank of the Loire, 153 miles S.S.E. of Paris. It is the see of a bishop, and has a cathedral (in part dating from the eleventh century, restored 1883) and a *hôtel de ville.* Nevers has potteries and porcelain-works, producing ware which has long been famed. The navy cannon-foundry, the largest ordnance foundry in France, was in 1881 turned into a practical school for boiler-making and engine-fitting. Pop. 27,700.

Nevers: Porte du Croute

NEVIS. An island of the British West Indies, one of the Leeward group, forming with St. Kitts and Anguilla the Presidency of St. Kitts and Nevis. Cotton, sugar, cocoa, limes, oranges, etc., are produced. Charlestown is the port and capital. Area, 50 sq. miles; pop. 11,569.

NEW ALBANY. A city of Indiana, United States, county seat of Floyd county, on the Ohio; served by the Chicago, Indianapolis, & Louisville Railway. Automobiles and iron goods are manufactured. There are abattoirs, canneries, etc. New Albany became a city in 1893. Pop. 25,819.

NEWARK. A city and port of entry of New Jersey, United States, county seat of Essex county, on the Passaic; served by the Pennsylvania Railway and by an elaborate electric-traction system, and steamers. It is a great manufacturing city, and originated in Milford (1666), a colonial offshoot of Connecticut. It became a city in 1836. Pop. (1930), 442,337.

NEWARK. A municipal borough of Nottinghamshire, England, on the Devon; served by the L.M.S. and L.N.E. Railways. The corn-market is one of the largest in the kingdom. Iron-founding, brass-founding, brewing, and the manufacture of boilers and agricultural implements are carried on. The ruined castle was the scene of King John's death in 1216, was thrice besieged as a stronghold of the king during the Civil War, and was the scene of the surrender of Charles I. to the Scots army. Pop. (1391), 18,058.

NEW BEDFORD. A city and port of entry of Massachusetts, United States, the county seat of Bristol county, on the Acushnet River; served by the New York, New Haven, & Hartford Railway. It is a cotton-centre, and was at one time the centre of the American whale-fishery. The city was incorporated in 1812, and became a city in 1847. Pop. (1930), 112,597.

NEWBERN. A city of North Carolina, United States, the port of entry for Pamlico district, on the estuary of the Neuse. It has a large trade in lumber, tobacco, cotton, and naval stores. Newbern was founded by Swiss settlers in 1710. Pop. (1931), 18,055.

NEW BRIGHTON. A watering-place of Cheshire, England, part of Wallasey, at the north-east corner of the Wirral Peninsula; it has steamer connection with Liverpool and elsewhere. There is excellent bathing, a fine promenade, and a landing-pier. It is part of the borough of Wallasey.

NEW BRIGHTON. Since 1898 a part of Richmond borough, New York City (q.v.), on Staten Island, 6 miles S.W. of Manhattan.

NEW BRITAIN (formerly the German colony of Neu Pommern or New Pomerania, Bismarck Archipelago). A Pacific island in the Australian territory of New Guinea, administered by the Commonwealth under League of Nations' mandate dated 17th Dec., 1920. The capital is now Rabaul; but until 1910 it was located at Kokopo (Ger. *Herbertshöhe*), on the Gazelle Peninsula; the principal harbour is Blanche Bay. There are European coco-nut plantations (42,848 acres in 1918).

The island is traversed by a range of hills (The Father, 7500 feet) with several active volcanoes. It is afforested in parts, and has a warm, humid climate with a heavy annual rainfall. The indigenous population is of Melanesian origin and generally of good physique, excepting in the Gazelle Peninsula, where there is much disease. Bêche-de-mer (" pidgin English ") is the *lingua franca* of the coast. The area is about 10,000 sq. miles, but if Duke of York Island and other adjacent islands are included it is 14,600 sq. miles. The native population *in the explored areas* in 1931 was 88,000.

NEW BRUNSWICK. A maritime province of the Dominion of Canada, extending between the Bay of Fundy (south) and the province of Quebec (north), and connected with Nova Scotia by a narrow isthmus. The deeply indented coastal regions are flat; elsewhere the surface is undulating, rising to central and northern highlands among spurs of the Appalachians. The state capital is Fredericton (pop. 1931, 8828); St. John (46,640, 1931) and Moncton (20,617) are export seaports.

Communications, etc.—There were in 1929, 1934 miles of railway track in the province, which is traversed by the Canadian Pacific, Canadian National (Grand Trunk), and the Maine Central Railways. The predominant religious beliefs are Roman Catholic and Baptist.

Production and Industry.—Agriculture, mining, and fisheries are extensive; New Brunswick is of no importance in manufactures. Barley (1931, 285,000 bushels), wheat (142,000 bushels), oats (6,718,000 bushels), mixed grains (56,000 bushels), potatoes (6,341,000 cwt.), turnips (2,589,000 cwt.), hay and clover (760,000 tons), are produced. Butter and cheese are made; dairying and stock-raising are widely practised. The value of fruit produced in 1931 amounted to 206,050 dollars. The production of apples was 40,000 barrels. A few manufactures are connected with agriculture and forestry (paper pulp). There are 10,600 sq. miles of forests in the state, consisting mainly of spruce used for paper pulp. These forests abound in moose and caribou.

The fisheries (herring, salmon, lobster, and cod) employ about 17,000 hands, and the canneries, etc., another 7000. Coal and gypsum are widely worked; other minerals are stone, iron, manganese, copper, antimony, natural gas and oil (the latter near Moncton).

Education, etc.—Education is free and undenominational. The provincial university (founded 1800) is at Fredericton. There is also Mount Allison University at Sackville, and the University of St. Joseph's College at Memramcook. Area, 27,985 sq. miles (74 sq. miles being water); pop. (1931), 408,255.

Constitution and Government.—New Brunswick was discovered by Jacques Cartier (1534), and was settled by the English in 1761, but the province actually dates from 1784, when it was separated from Nova Scotia. It entered the Federation of 1867. The Government consists of a Lieutenant-Governor and a Legislative Assembly (38 members, elected for five years), with a responsible ministry headed by a Premier. Ten Senators and eleven members of Parliament are sent to the Dominion Parliament at Ottawa.

NEW BRUNSWICK. A city of New Jersey, United States, county seat of Middlesex county, on the Raritan; served by the Pennsylvania Railway and Delaware-Raritan Canal. The Dutch Reformed Church maintains Rutger's College and a theological seminary at New Brunswick. There are manufactures of india-rubber goods, paper-hangings, and machinery. It was settled in 1681, incorporated in 1736, and became a city in 1784, taking its name in 1714 to commemorate the accession of a member of the House of Brunswick to the throne of Great Britain. Pop. (1931), 34,555.

NEWBURN. Urban district of Northumberland. A colliery centre, it is 5½ miles west of Newcastle, and 276 miles from London by the L.N.E. Railway. The town stands on the Tyne, and has metal works and some manufactures. Pop. (1931) 19,539.

NEW'BURY. A municipal borough in Berkshire, England, giving name to a parliamentary division, on the Kennet, which is made navigable to Reading and joins the Thames. There are maltings and corn-mills, and a considerable traffic is carried on by the Kennet and Avon Canal. During the Civil War two battles were fought in the vicinity, both resulting in victory for the Royalists. The borough includes Speenhamland. Pop. (1931), 13,336.

NEW'BURYPORT. A city and port of entry of Massachusetts, United States, the county seat of Essex county, on the Merrimac; served by the Boston & Maine Railway. It was settled in 1635, incorporated in 1764, and became a city in 1851. Pop. (1920), 15,609.

NEW CALEDONIA. A French island of Oceania, in the Melanesia division of the Australasian festoon. It is about 250 miles long and 31 miles broad, and is crossed by two parallel ranges of mountains (Mount Humboldt, 5570 feet). Nouméa, the capital (pop. 10,708), is connected by a narrow-gauge railway (20 miles) with Paita, and has a harbour. Some of the inhabitants are of convict origin, but the majority are mixed Melanesian and Polynesian, with some Japanese, Tonkingese, Malays, and Javanese. No convicts have been sent to New Caledonia since 1896, and the convict element is gradually decreasing; the local penal settlement is on Nou Island. The average rainfall is about 40 inches.

Production.—About 500 sq. miles of the island are afforested; the cultivable land produces coffee, copra, cotton, cassava, maize, tobacco, bananas, and pineapple; sheep and cattle are raised. New Caledonia is one of the world's store-houses of nickel, other exports being chrome ore and manganese, coffee, copra, rubber, guano, and preserved meats (canned).

Imports are mainly coal, flour, rice, and wine. Public instruction is provided in public and private (municipal assisted) elementary schools; classical and technical education is given by the Collège la Pérouse at Nouméa. A cable runs from New Caledonia to Burnet Heads near Bundaberg, Queensland. There is a monthly steamer service with Sydney, New South Wales. Area 6275 sq. miles; pop. 47,505 (16,794 whites; 3611 Asiatic immigrants).

Dependencies.—Isle of Pines (area, 58 sq. miles; pop. about 600); Wallis Archipelago (area, 40 sq. miles; pop. 4500), governed by a French resident; Loyalty Islands (q.v.; area, 800 sq. miles); Huon Islands, a barren group; Futuna and Alofi, south of the Wallis Archipelago (pop. about 1500). *See* OCEANIA.—BIBLIOGRAPHY: D. Vallet, *La Colonisation française en Nouvelle-Calédonie*; R. H. Compton, *New Caledonia and the Isle of Pines* (*Geographical Journal*, Feb., 1917).

NEWCASTLE, William Cavendish, Duke of. Born in 1592, died 1676. Son of Sir Charles Cavendish, he was made Earl of Newcastle by Charles I. On the approach of hostilities between the Crown and Parliament he embraced the royal cause, and was invested with a commission constituting him general of all His Majesty's forces raised north of the Trent, with very ample powers. Through great exertions and the expenditure of large sums from his private fortune he levied a considerable army, with which, for some time, he maintained the king's cause in the north.

When the royal cause became hopeless he retired to Holland. He returned after an absence of eighteen years, and was rewarded for his services and sufferings with the dignity of duke. He was the author of several mediocre poems and plays, and a treatise on horsemanship

NEWCASTLE. A watering-place in County Down, Northern Ireland, on Dundrum Bay. It is famed for bathing and golf. Pop. (1926), 2119.

NEWCASTLE. A town of Natal, South Africa, 160 N.W. of Durban. It is a great coal-mining and iron-and steel-manufacturing centre. Pop. 4274 (2017 white).

NEWCASTLE. A town of New South Wales, Australia, on the Hunter River, and connected with Sydney by rail. It stands in the largest of the Australian coal-fields to which it owes its existence as a town. Pop. (1931), 103,700.

NEWCASTLE-UNDER-LYME. A municipal borough of Staffordshire, England, on Lyme Brook; served by the L.M.S. Railway. Coal- and iron-mines and potteries are carried on in the neighbourhood. In the town itself there are brewing, malting, tanning, and paper-making. The district near was once the forest of Lyme. Pop. (1931), 23,246.

NEWCASTLE - UPON - TYNE. A city, county-city, and river-port of Northumberland, England, on the Tyne; served by various main lines of the London, Midland, and Scottish and London and North-Eastern

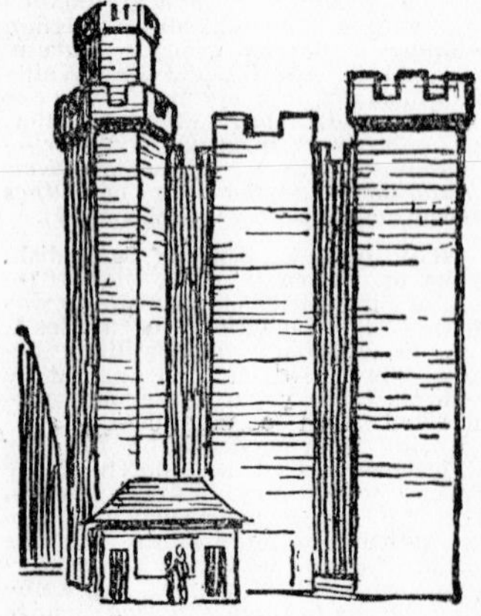

Newcastle: The Norman Keep

Railways. Among the public buildings are the cathedral of St. Nicholas rebuilt (1172-78) on the site of a foundation of 1091; the Roman Catholic cathedral of St. Mary; the Moot Hall, in which the assizes for the county are held; the keep and black gate or entrance to the castle, built by Henry II. between 1172 and 1177, but founded originally in 1080 and rebuilt by William Rufus; Royal Infirmary (1906); and Armstrong College and the College of Medicine, which form part of the University of Durham. There is a series of fine bridges across the Tyne to Gateshead; one of these is the famous High Level Bridge of Robert Stephenson (length, 1375 feet, upper part 112 feet above high water); others are the Scotswood Suspension, (Swing (1876), King Edward VII. (Railway), and Redheugh.

A new high-level bridge was opened by King George V. in 1928. Newcastle, owing to the rich mineral products of the neighbourhood, has attained a first position among the great centres of British enterprise. Some of the more important of its industries are shipbuilding and allied trades, the manufacture of locomotives and general engineering, electrical power distribution, and many manufactures. There are markets for cattle, fish, vegetables, and grain. Situated in the midst of one of the largest coal-fields in England, it exports immense quantities of coal. Newcastle is one of the Tyne ports (which include also North and South Shields).

Newcastle is situated at the eastern termination of the wall of Hadrian (A.D. 120). The castle or fortress was built by Robert, son of William the Conqueror, about 1080, about which time it received its present name. Newcastle was a frequent object of attack in the wars between England and Scotland. It was taken by the Scottish Covenanting army in 1640 and in 1644, and in 1647 Charles I. was delivered here by the Scottish army to the parliamentary commissioners. After the European War Newcastle "adopted" Arras (1920). It has a broadcasting station (288·5 M., 1 kW.). Pop. (1931), 283,145.

NEWCHWANG. A city and treaty port of Fengtien province, China, on the Liaoho; served by the South Manchuria and the Peiping-Mukden Railways. The port is ice-bound for three months annually. Pop. (1930), 106,040.

NEW COLLEGE. One of the colleges of Oxford University, founded in 1379 by William of Wykeham, Bishop of Winchester and Lord Chancellor of England.

NEWCOMB, Simon. American astronomer, born in Nova Scotia in 1835, died in 1909. He settled in the United States in 1853, and graduated in science at Harvard in 1858. In 1861 he became professor of mathematics in the United States navy, and later on occupied a high position at the Washington Observatory. In 1877 he was made director of the *American Nautical Almanac*, and in 1894 became professor of mathematics and astronomy in the Johns Hopkins University. Among his numerous publications are: *The Recurrence of Lunar Eclipses*, *Popular Astronomy*, and

Compendium of Spherical Astronomy (with G. S. Holden).

NEW'COMEN, Thomas. A locksmith at Dartmouth, in Devonshire, born in 1663, died in 1729, one of the inventors of the steam-engine. The engine associated with his name used steam under pressure to raise the piston. The fall of the piston was caused by the pressure of the atmosphere above, and a partial vacuum below the piston. The vacuum was produced by the condensation of the steam by injected cold water. The merit of first applying the steam-engine to practical purposes is due to Newcomen, who worked in association with Captain Savery and John Calley.

NEW ENGLAND. The north-east division of the United States, comprising the states of Maine, New Hampshire, Vermont, Massachusetts, Rhode Island, and Connecticut. The inhabitants are styled "Yankees." Originally called North Virginia when granted by James I. to the Plymouth Company in 1606, it received the name of New England from Captain John Smith, who explored and made a map of the coast in 1614. Area, 66,176 sq. miles; pop. (1930), 8,166,341. (*See* articles on the six component states.)

NEW FOREST. A large tract in England, in the south-west of Hampshire, forming one of the royal forests, about 144 sq. miles (93,000 acres) in area, which is commonly said to have been laid waste and turned into a forest by William the Conqueror. There are several villages within the forest area, including Brockenhurst and Lyndhurst (the forest capital), both served by London & South-Western Railway. Oak and beech are the principal trees. (*See* HAMPSHIRE.)

NEWFOUNDLAND. An island in the North Atlantic, separated from the mainland of Canada by the Straits of Belle Isle, and forming, with its dependency Labrador, a dominion of the British Empire. Newfoundland does not form a part of the Dominion of Canada. It is the tenth largest island in the world, and is roughly one-third larger than Ireland. The coast (about 2000 miles) is irregular and deeply indented; low ranges of hills (Mount St. Gregory, 2226 feet) sweep down almost to the sea from summits only a few miles inland, the hinterland being generally undulating, interspersed with numerous lakes, rivers, and marshes.

The population, therefore, is confined principally to the outposts on the coast, and the most densely inhabited area is in the south-east part of the island around St. John's (pop. 1931, 42,645), the capital city which alone accounts for about one-eighth of the total insular population. Other towns are Harbour Grace, Bonavista, Carbonear, Twilingate, and Grand Falls. The total area is 42,734 sq. miles; pop. (1931), 277,285. Newfoundland possesses in Labrador an area of 110,000 sq. miles (pop. (1931), 4,264). This possession was confirmed by the Privy Council in 1927.

Communications.—In 1926 there were 907 miles of Government railway line (3-foot-6-inch gauge) and 56 miles of private line. The main line is from St. John's to Port-aux-Basques (545 miles); branch lines connect with terminals at Bonavista, Lewisporte, Heart's Content, Grate's Cove, Trepassey and Placentia, Millertown, Bonne Bay (projected), and Fortune (projected). Other communication is effected by steamer either to points along the coast or to the mainland, a fleet of seventeen steamers bening maintained for the purpose.

Social Conditions.—Amongst the Newfoundlanders there are practically no rich people and comparatively few poor, the love of home and of home life being a pronounced national characteristic. In religion Roman Catholics as a sect are predominant, but Protestants (mainly Anglican, Methodist, and Salvation Army) form about two-thirds of the population. The religious element enters largely into the life of the community, and the population of many of the outposts frequently consists of a group of persons of the same creed or denomination.

Liquor prohibition has been adopted, but, owing to the close proximity of the French islands of St. Pierre and Miquelon, a considerable amount of smuggling is carried on. Education is on the denominational system, and there are Church of England, Roman Catholic, and Methodist colleges. The legal coin of the Dominion is the gold dollar of 4*s.* 1½*d.* (normal) British.

Production.—Newfoundland generally is not climatically suitable for cereal-raising, opposed as it is to the frigid currents that flow down the west coast of Greenland, but the climate is not quite so bad as is generally represented, and there are no extremes as on the mainland. There is a long, cold winter and a considerable amount of rain, but farming is carried on extensively, and parts of the island are well adapted for stock-raising. Through the comparative shallowness of the soil the ordinary farm implements, such as spades, are unsuitable, and specially shaped ones are used.

The chief agricultural products are hay, potatoes, cabbage, turnips, and some oats; sheep, swine, and cattle are raised, with some ponies for use in mines. Forests of the interior are utilized for the manufacture of paper pulp (at Grand Falls, Bishop's Falls, Lomond in Bonne Bay, etc.), which is sent to England for use in newspaper production. Mineral resources are extensive, coal, oil-shale, iron (on Wabana property, Bell Island, the third greatest hematite deposit in the world; at Bay St. George, a highly titaniferous magnetite of about 50 to 60 per cent. iron and 2 to 12 per cent. titanium), copper, lead ore, pyrites, chromite ores, manganese, molybdenite, gold, silver (all lead ores of Newfoundland are argentiferous), platinum, and many non-metallic minerals being found.

Fishing is the oldest industry, and the governing factor which regulates the life and business of the community. Cod-fish is the principal catch, and is exported chiefly to Spain, Portugal, Brazil, Greece, Italy, and the United Kingdom. Seal-fishing is important in spring; lobsters are caught, and there is some whaling.

Newfoundland was discovered by John Cabot on 24th June, 1497, and was annexed in the name of Henry VII., who presented Cabot with the sum of £10 as a reward for his labours. In 1809 the government of Labrador was transferred from Canada to Newfoundland. During the European War Newfoundland provided nearly 15,000 men for the empire's service, a unit known as the Royal Newfoundland Regiment taking part in the Gallipoli, Egyptian, and Western Front campaigns, and being especially distinguished at Beaumont Hamel (1916) during the battle of the Somme.

An additional body of about 3000 seamen (Royal Naval Reserve) was attached to the naval services. —BIBLIOGRAPHY: Captain E. J. Edwards, *Report on Trade and Industrial Resources of Newfoundland*, 1922 (H.M. Stationery Office); D. W. Prowse, *A History of Newfoundland*; Lord Birkenhead, *The Story of Newfoundland*.

NEWFOUNDLAND DOG. A breed originally peculiar to Newfoundland, now common in this country. In appearance it is large and handsome,

Newfoundland Dog

with thick curly hair, either black or black-and-white in colour. The black-and-white variety is known as the "Landseer," after that painter's well-known picture, and is probably a cross from the original breed, which was entirely black. The Newfoundland is a good retriever and a fine swimmer, and displays great courage and fidelity.

NEWGATE. The celebrated jail of the city of London, mentioned as a prison early in the thirteenth century. In the fifteenth century Sir Richard Whittington in his will

Newgate Gaol

left funds to rebuild it; it was rebuilt a second time after the great fire of 1666, and a third time in 1778-80, but required much restoration after the No Popery or Gordon Riots of 1780. It was demolished in 1902-3, and the Central Criminal Court (Old Bailey) now stands on its site.

NEW GUINEA. An island of Oceania, in the Melanesia division of the Australasian festoon, and, excluding Australia, from which it is separated by Torres Strait, the largest island in the world. Physically it lies wholly within the tropics, and is traversed by enormous mountain masses, except in the south-westernmost area, which is generally low and swampy. Politically the island is partitioned between the Dutch and the British Empire, everything west of the 141st meridian of longitude (area, 160,692 sq. miles) belonging to the former, the eastern portion being in British possession. The south-eastern division, Papua (q.v.), is an Australian territory, and the north-eastern division (formerly German) is the "mainland" of the territory of New Guinea, for which Australia is mandatory power.

The Dutch colony formed part of the residency of Ternate (Moluccas), but was created a province in 1920, and is neither greatly developed nor exhaustively explored, although several mountains and the lower courses of rivers have been named and mapped. Much of the hinterland is covered with dense primeval forests. Rice, maize, yams, and sugar-cane are raised by the natives (Melanesians). Area of the island (estimated), 312,000 sq. miles (greatest length, 1490 miles; greatest breadth, 480 miles).

The island was sighted by Abreus in A.D. 1511; was visited by the Portuguese Don Jorge de Menesis (1526) and by the Spaniard Alvaro de Saavedra (1528); and in 1606 Torres, on his way to the Philippines, sailed through the strait that now bears his name. In 1793 New Guinea was annexed by two commanders in the service of the East India Company, and the three colonizing powers (British Empire, Germany, Netherlands) agreed to partition, each having suzerainty over islands adjoining its own territory.

In Sept., 1914 (European War), German New Guinea was seized and occupied by Australian troops. The territory is now administered by Australia under mandate from the League of Nations dated 17th Dec., 1920.—Cf. E. V. Hesse-Wartegg, *Samoa, Bismarckarchipel und Neu Guinea.*

NEW GUINEA, Territory of. That portion of the German New Guinea Protectorate which lay south of the equator (excepting only the Island of Nauru, q.v.), and which was known in German times as the "Old Protectorate." The total area is 93,430 sq. miles. The principal islands (with their German names) and their approximate areas are:

Division.	Area in Sq. Miles.	Population (Native). 1931.
North-East New Guinea (Kaiser Wilhelm Land)	69,700	207,000
Bismarck Archipelago—		
New Britain (Neu Pommern)	14,600	143,000
New Ireland (Neu Mecklenburg)	2,800	41,000
Lavongai (Neu Hannover)	460	6,790
Admiralty Islands	6,630	14,500
Other Islands	1,115	
Solomon Islands—		
Bougainville	3,880	} 30,400
Buka	190	} 7,550
Totals	91,000	251,017

Many of these figures are mere estimates. Almost every division includes a number of small adjacent islands. The part of North-East New Guinea not under Government influence is excluded.

The mainland of New Guinea is the northern section of Eastern New Guinea, and was formerly known as Kaiser Wilhelm Land. Mountain ranges sweep down to the coast, leaving only a narrow but very fertile strip near sea-level. The hinterland is rugged and mountainous, with heights reaching to over 11,000 feet, and as all trade and communication are by sea along the coast, the interior is left almost wholly to the native population and is little known. In Astrolabe Bay are some sheltered harbours, including Konstantinhafen, Friedrich Wilhelm Hafen, and Alexishafen, the best on the coast.

Rivers.—Of the many rivers the most important are the Sepik (Kaiserin Augusta) and the Ramu (or Ottilien). The Bismarck Archipelago and the Solomons are in general mountainous, and flat only near their coasts. In all the islands the streams are rapid and unnavigable. Among harbours are Blanche Bay (New Britain), Mioko (Duke of York Island), Nares Harbour (Admiralty Island), and Queen Carola Harbour (Buka Island). Rabaul is the capital.

Climate, etc. — Throughout the territory, except in the mountains, the climate is hot and moist all the year round. The mean temperature on the mainland is 80° F., with high humidity. There is no cool season, and rain falls in all months, the (coast) average rainfall being between 100 and 150 inches. In the Bismarck Archipelago there is a comparatively dry season from May to September. The islands are outside the typhoon area. Dysentery is prevalent among the natives, with some Tokelau ringworm and elephantiasis; malaria, dysentery, and blackwater fever exact a heavy toll among the whites. Apart from disease, the climate is enervating for Europeans.

Production.—Maize, rice, arrowroot, taro, coco-nut and oil palm, rubber (ficus, hevea, and kastilloa), cotton, sisal hemp, cocoa, coffee, lemon, and citronella grass. Some birds of Paradise and feathers are exported.

Inhabitants, etc.—The natives of the mainland are mainly mixed Papuans and Melanesians, split up into many tribes. The islanders are chiefly Melanesians, the Admiralty Islanders showing a Papuan and perhaps Polynesian admixture; in the extreme west of the archipelago they have Malay and Chinese affinities. Many languages are used, but bêche-de-mer is the *lingua franca* of the territory. The approximate population of the territory (enumerated and estimated) is 394,362, exclusive of the unexplored mainland, but including 2139 British, 1214 Chinese, 209 Dutch, 399 Germans, 33 Japanese, and 152 Americans (1932).—BIBLIOGRAPHY: *German Foreign Possessions in the Pacific* (*Foreign Office Handbook*); *Official Year-Book of the Commonwealth of Australia. No.* 14 (1901-20); H. Schnee (editor), *Deutsches Kolonial Lexikon.*

NEW HAMPSHIRE. A state in the New England division of the United States, with a short coast-line on the Atlantic. It is mountainous in the north-central portion and is generally interspersed with mountain, lake, and stream. The state capital is Concord (pop. 1930, 25,228); the largest city is Manchester (pop. 1930, 76,834). Railways are owned or operated by the Boston & Maine system, excepting a Canadian National (Grand Trunk) line in the north. There were 1163 miles of steam track in 1932 and also 151 miles of electric railway. 63 per cent. of the total population are Roman Catholics, and about one-fifth are foreign-born, being mainly Swedes, Russians, Irish, and Canadians.

Agriculture is important, hay, corn, potatoes (1,320,000 bushels, 1932), and oats being produced. Fruit-growing is extensive; sheep-raising for wool-production, dairying, and cattle-breeding are progressive. Mineral deposits are undeveloped, some granite, mica, mineral waters, and scythe-stones being produced. Manufactures are mainly confined to the southern region of the state, and include boots and shoes, and cotton and woollen goods. Education is compulsory between the ages of eight and fourteen years, extensile to sixteen years if the elementary grades are not completed.

Roman Catholic parochial schools are maintained in all cities, and in several of the larger towns; elsewhere religious instruction is not given. The principal non-sectarian colleges are Dartmouth College at Hanover (founded 1769) and the New Hampshire University at Durham (founded 1866). State area, 9041 sq. miles (10 sq. miles are water). pop. (1930), 465,293.

New Hampshire was the first of the original thirteen states of the Union. The state is divided into ten counties. Modern Government comprises a Governor and a Legislature composed of a Senate (24 members, elected for two years) and a House of Representatives (from 418 to 427 members, according to population, to which representation is proportional). Two Senators and two Representatives are sent to Congress. —BIBLIOGRAPHY: J. G. Palfrey, *History of New England*; J. N. M'Clintock, *History of New Hampshire.*

NEW HANOVER, now **LAVONGAI.** An island in the Australian territory of New Guinea, administered by the Commonwealth under mandate of the League of Nations. It was formerly Neu Hannover, of the German Bismarck Archipelago, and was occupied by the British in 1914. It is mountainous and heavily timbered, and produces coco-nuts, rubber, coffee, and cotton. The natives are of Melanesian extraction; the *lingua franca* of the coast is bêche-de-mer ("pidgin English"). The area is uncertain but is probably about 460 sq. miles. The pop. (1931), 6790.

NEW HAVEN. The principal city and seaport of Connecticut, United States, the county seat of New Haven county, on New Haven Bay; served by the New York, New Haven, & Hartford Railway. The city is widely known as the seat of Yale University, which was transferred from Saybrook in 1716. It is a great transport city, and has an enormous coastal trade. Munitions, iron- and steel-ware, hardware and cutlery, canned meats, and rubber goods are manufactured. New Haven became a city in 1784. From 1701 to 1703 it was joint capital of the state. Pop. (1930), 162,655.

NEWHAVEN. A seaport of Sussex, England, on the Ouse; served by the London, Brighton, & South Coast Railway. It is the starting-point of the Newhaven-Dieppe cross-Channel service, and has a good coastal trade and some shipbuilding. All civilian steamboat services were suspended during the European War, when Newhaven became a base for the delivery of war material. Pop. (1931), 6790.—**Newhaven** is also the name of a fishing-port of Midlothian, Scotland, on the Firth of Forth; now included in Edinburgh, and served by the L.M. & S. Railway.

NEW HEBRIDES. A volcanic island chain of Oceania, in the Australasian festoon, comprising the main islands of Tanna, Espiritu Santo, Malekula, Epi, Ambrym, Efate or Sandwich, Erromanga, and Aneityúm. They are under joint Anglo-French administration. Coconuts (for copra), maize, millet, coffee, cotton, sandal-wood, cocoa, and bananas are produced, and kauri pine

New Hebrides : Native House

is exported from Aneityúm. Trade is chiefly with Sydney and New Caledonia (Nouméa). Importation or distillation of spirits is prohibited. The natives are of Melanesian origin. Quiros discovered the islands (1606), but Captain Cook revisited and named them in 1774. Area, 5700 sq. miles; pop. native, 50,000, with 219 British, 931 French, and 5081 foreigners.—Bibliography: *Convention between the United Kingdom and France concerning the New Hebrides* (London, 1907); G. Bourge, *Les Nouvelles Hébrides*, 1606-1906.

NEW IRELAND. An island in the Australian territory of New Guinea, administered by the Commonwealth under mandate of the League of Nations dated 17th Dec., 1920. It was formerly New Mecklenburg, second in size and importance of the German Bismarck Archipelago, and was occupied by the British in the island. Kavieng has a good harbour (Nusa) and is the chief town (European pop. 179); Namatanai (European pop. 15) is the only other town. Coco-nut plantations occupy (1931) 55,800 acres. The natives are of Melanesian extraction; the *lingua franca* of the coast is bêche-de-mer ("pidgin English"). Area, between 3000 and 3500 sq. miles; pop. (1931), 41,000; European, 422.

NEW JERSEY. A maritime state in the middle Atlantic division of the United States. It is mainly a lowland region, comprising a vast coastal plain covering more than a half of the state area, and is traversed in the north-west by the Appalachians. The state capital is Trenton (pop. 1930, 123,356); other cities are Newark (442,337), Jersey City (316,715), Paterson (138,513), Camden (118,700), Elizabeth (114,589), Bayonne (88,979), Passaic (62,959), East Orange (68,020), Atlantic City (66,198), Hoboken (59,261).

Communications.—In 1932, 2284 miles of steam and 1093 miles of electric railway track traversed the state. Practically all the great trunk lines and subsidiaries converging on New York from the south or west, or on Philadelphia from the south, must pass through New Jersey on account of its geographical position.

Religion, etc.—There were 174 miles of canals in 1932. 51·5 per cent. of the church-going inhabitants are Roman Catholics, and more than half of the total population are foreign-born, coming principally from Italy, Germany, and Ireland.

Production and Industry.—Agriculture, horticulture, fruit-growing, forestry, and market-gardening are practised, maize (6,930,000 bushels in 1932) and hay (318,000 tons, 1932) being the principal agricultural products. Fruit and vegetables are canned in forty-four factories.

Fisheries yield trout, perch, bass, black bass, etc., in lakes and streams; shad, menhaden, and sturgeon fisheries exist on the Delaware River and Bay and in the New Hampshire littoral. Mineral deposits include magnetic iron, talc, zinc, manganese and graphite, limestone and trap rock, sand, gravel, and clay. Mineral waters, Portland cement, peat, and greensand marl (from which potash salts are made) are minor products. The principal manufactures are in oil-refining, high explosives, foundries and machinery, silk goods, wire and wire-cloth, and chemicals.

Education, etc.—Education is free and compulsory between the ages of seven and sixteen years. The nonsectarian universities include Princeton (founded 1746) and New Brunswick and Stevens Institute of Technology at Hoboken (founded 1870). State area, 8224 sq. miles (710 sq. miles are water); pop. (1915), 2,844,342 (including 95,281 coloured), (1930), 4,041,334.

Constitution and Government.—New Jersey was one of thirteen original states of the Union. The state is divided into twenty-one counties for local government. The central authority comprises a Governor, Senate (21 members, elected by counties for three years, one-third seeking re-election annually), and a General Assembly (60 members, elected annually by counties on a basis proportional to population). Two Senators and fourteen Representatives are sent to Congress.—BIBLIOGRAPHY: E. J. Fisher, *New Jersey as a Royal Province*; E. P. Tanner, *The Province of New Jersey.*

NEW LEON. A state of Mexico known as Nuevo Leon.

NEW LONDON. A city and port of entry of Connecticut, United States, the county seat of New London county, on the Thames; served by the New York, New Haven, & Hartford Railway, and by steamers. It is a naval station, with construction and repair depots. Woollens, silks, and machinery are manufactured, and there are foundries and engine-works. Pop. 29,640.

NEWLYN. A watering-place of Cornwall, England, 2 miles from Penzance.

NEWMAN, Francis William. Younger brother of Cardinal Newman, was born in London, 1805, died in 1897. He was educated at Ealing and at Worcester College, Oxford, graduating double first (1826). From 1826 to 1830 he was Fellow of Balliol, but resigned in consequence of his conscientious scruples about signing the Thirty-nine Articles. He was appointed classical tutor at Bristol College (1834), professor of classics at Manchester New College (1840), and professor of Latin at University College, London, 1846-63, from which time he gave himself to literature. His writings exhibit great scholarship and versatility. Among them are: *The Soul: its Sorrows and Aspirations* (1849); *Phases of Faith* (1850); and *Theism* (1858).

NEWMAN, John Henry. Cardinal, born at London 1801, died in 1890. He was educated at Ealing and Trinity College, Oxford, where he graduated with third-class honours (1820), and was elected Fellow of Oriel College. He was vice-principal of St. Alban's Hall (1825-26) under Dr. (afterwards Archbishop) Whately, and was incumbent of St. Mary's, Oxford, and chaplain of Littlemore (1828-43). During this last period he took part with Keble and Pusey in originating the Oxford movement; was a leader in the propaganda of High Church doctrines, and contributed largely to the celebrated *Tracts for the Times.* The last of these, on the elasticity of the Thirty-nine Articles, was censured by the University authorities, and was followed by Newman's resignation of his livings (1843) and secession to the Church of Rome (1845).

Ordained a priest of that Church, he was successively head of the Oratory of St. Philip Neri at Birmingham, rector of the Roman Catholic University of Dublin (1854-58), and principal of the Roman

Cardinal Newman

Catholic School at Edgbaston. In 1879 he was created a cardinal. He wrote some remarkable works sustaining the doctrines of the Church of Rome, particularly the *Apologia pro Vitâ suâ* (1864), and the *Reply to Mr. Gladstone* (1875) on the Vatican Decrees.—BIBLIOGRAPHY: R. H. Hutton, *Cardinal Newman* (English Leaders of Religion Series); W. Barry, *Newman*; W. Ward, *Life of John Henry, Cardinal Newman*; E. A. Abbott, *The Anglican Career of Cardinal Newman.*

NEWMARKET. A town of West Suffolk, England, on the L. & N.E. Railway. It is the headquarters of the Jockey Club and of English racing, and the racecourse (Newmarket Heath) has ten courses, including one of 4 miles in length. Eight race-meetings are held annually, the chief races being the Two Thousand Guineas (April) and the Cesarewitch (October). Newmarket was made a racing-centre by James I. and by Charles II. The heath is crossed by a trench known as the Devil's Dyke. The Astley Institute and the King Edward VII. Memorial Hall are notable. The rural district of Newmarket is in Cambridgeshire. Pop. (1931), 9753.

NEW MEXICO. A state in the mountain division of the United States, on the Mexican frontier, traversed by the Rio Grande del Norte and by parallel mountain ranges (Truchas, 13,156 feet; Baldy, 12,660 feet; Costello, 12,635 feet) running roughly north and south. Generally it is one enormous, sloping plateau cut up in the north by the Rockies. To the east of the state is the plateau Llano Estacado.

Towns, Populations, etc.—The state capital is Santa Fé (pop. 1930, 11,176); other towns are Albuquerque (1930, 26,570), Raton (6090), Las Vegas (9113), and Roswell (11,173). Indian Reserves have an area of 5524 sq. miles, and a pop. (1930) of 28,113, mainly of the Apache, Navaho, and Pueblo tribes. The population includes a large number of Mexicans (Spanish-Americans), Austrians, Italians, and Germans. Roman Catholicism is the predominant faith.

Communications.—2284 miles of steam (1932) and 11 miles of electric railway track traverse the state, through which run two transcontinental lines (Atchison, Topeka, & Santa Fé—Chicago to San Francisco; and the Southern Pacific —New Orleans to San Francisco) and their ramifications; the northern districts are served also by a branch of the Denver & Rio Grande system.

Production and Industry.—Maize (3,267,000 bushels, 1932), wheat (1,320,000 bushels, 1932) and potatoes are produced by the help of an irrigation scheme which, on the completion of existing schemes, will embrace 945,000 acres. Horses, cattle, sheep, and pigs are largely raised; the wool clip yielded 16,362,000 lb. of wool in 1931. 4,172,000 acres of afforested land are State-owned, and another 40,00,000 acres are under private control (1932). Mineral resources are valuable, granite, sandstone, limestone, marble, gold, silver, copper, lead, zinc, turquoise, and gypsum and mica in small quantities being produced. Manufactures are mainly allied to forestry and agriculture, but there is a large railway rolling-stock repair and construction industry.

Education.—Education is free and compulsory between the ages of six and sixteen years, and the use of English is enforced. Religious instruction in schools is prohibited, except in schools specially provided for that purpose and conducted outside of normal school hours. There are twenty-six Indian schools maintained by the Federal Government, and three normal schools. The principal colleges are that of agriculture and mechanics at Las Cruces (founded 1890), a school of mines at Socorro (founded 1895), a military institute, and the University of New Mexico at Albuquerque (founded 1892).

Constitution and Government.—New Mexico was for long in association with Mexico proper, but after the Mexican War (11th May, 1846, to 2nd Feb., 1848) New Mexico passed to the United States. The territorial boundaries included part of Texas, all Utah, a part of Colorado, and all Arizona, but the region was subsequently disrupted, and in Nov., 1911, New Mexico was admitted to the Union as a state. The state is divided into thirty-one counties. The modern Government consists of a Governor and a Legislature, comprising a Senate (24 members) and a House of Representatives (49 members). Two Senators and one Representative are sent to Congress.—Cf. M. Frost and A. F. Walker, *The Land of Sunshine.*

NEWNHAM COLLEGE. An English college for the higher education of women at Cambridge, founded in 1871, and incorporated in 1880. Women are not admitted under eighteen years of age, and the course of study corresponds with that of Cambridge University, the members of the college being expected to prepare for a Tripos examination at the end of their third year.

NEW ORLEANS. The largest city and commercial capital of Louisiana, United States, on the Mississippi; served by the Louisville & Nashville, Southern Pacific, Illinois Central, Texas & Pacific, and seven other railway systems. It is built on an alluvial flat, and is saved from inundation by *levees* or embankments built along the city front and along the river. The city covers an area of 200 sq. miles. Public buildings are architecturally uninteresting excepting the cathedral of St. Louis (1794) and the archbishop's palace (1737). The city is called the "Crescent City" from its form as a crescent on a bend of the river.

Industry.—Sugar-refining is an important industry; machinery, cotton goods, shoes, cigars, and furniture are produced. New Orleans is second only to Liverpool as the foremost cotton port of the world; it is an outlet for the produce of the southern country drained by the Mississippi, such as sugar, molasses, rice, tobacco, maize, wheat, oats, and flour, in addition to the main export, cotton.

On account of the wetness of the surrounding country the dead are not buried at New Orleans, and corpses (except Jewish) are stored in tiers within large vaults, at a height of 12 feet above the ground. Tulane University (law, arts and sciences, medicine, and technology), universities for coloured students, the Orleans University, and the Jesuit College (1847) are of educational importance. Pop. (1930), 458,762.

New Orleans was founded by the Sieur de Bienville (1718), and is named in honour of the duc d'Orleans, then Regent of France. It was long the administrative centre of French Louisiana, was ceded to Spain (1763), returned to France (1800), and was bought by the United States (1803). It became a city in 1813, and was unsuccessfully attacked by the British in 1815.

NEW PLYMOUTH. A town of North Island, New Zealand; capital of the Taranaki district. It is in a dairying and stock-raising district, and exports butter, cheese, and bacon. Pop. (1932), 18,650.

NEWPORT. A borough, market-town, and the capital of the Isle of Wight, on the Medina, and the headquarters of the insular railway system. The principal building is the church of St. Thomas (1854-56). Near by are the ruins of Carisbrooke Castle. Newport replaced Carisbrooke as capital of the island. Pop. (1931), 11,313.

NEWPORT. A burgh of Fifeshire, Scotland, on the Firth of Tay near Dundee. Pop. (1931), 3275.

NEWPORT. A county borough, seaport, and market-town of Monmouthshire, England, on the Usk; served mainly by the Great Western and London Midland & Scottish Railways. It has a large shipping trade in coal and iron, and has manufactures in steelwork, nails, glass, pottery, railway plant, boilers, and chemicals. There is some shipbuilding. A transporter bridge crosses the Usk. Newport is an outlet of the South Wales coal-field. Pop. (1931), 89,198.

NEWPORT. Urban district and market town of Shropshire. It is 140 miles from London and 18½ from Shrewsbury, on a joint line of the G.W. and L.M.S. Railways. The town is an agricultural, centre, and here is the Harper Adams Agricultural College. Pop. (1931), 3439.

NEWPORT. A city and port of entry of Rhode Island, United States, the county seat of Newport County, on Narragansett Bay; served by the New York, New Haven, & Hartford Railway. It is a former state capital, and is a summer-resort. Newport became a city in 1853. Pop. (1930), 27,612.

NEWPORT NEWS. A city and port of entry of Warwick county, Virginia, United States, on Hampton Roads, at the mouth of James River. It has an enormous sea-going and coasting trade, and some shipbuilding and manufactures. Pop. (1930), 34,417.

NEW PROVIDENCE. An island of the Bahamas (q.v.), British West Indies. Nassau, the capital, is also capital of the Bahamas. Pop. (1931), 19,756.

NEWQUAY. A watering-place on the north coast of Cornwall, England. Pop. (1931), 5958.

NEWRY. A seaport of County Down, Northern Ireland, on the Newry; served by the Great Northern Railway, by electric railway, and by a line to Greenore. The river is canalized to afford access to Newry Harbour by sea-going vessels. There are large flax-spinning mills; milling, distilling, tanning, brewing, and the manufacture of bricks, etc., are staple industries. Agricultural produce is exported. Newry is an ancient town, and is mentioned in the *Annals of* 1162: "the monastery . . . of Newry was burnt and also the yew tree which St. Patrick himself had planted." The name is derived from *Iubhar-cinn-tragha* (the Yew at the head of the Strand), which, shortened to *Iubhar*, was eventually corrupted to Newry. The newer part is called Ballybot. Pop. (1926), 12,159.

NEW SIBERIA. The collective name for three uninhabited island-groups of the Arctic Ocean, viz. Anjou, Laiakhov, and De Long, which are nominally administered by the Russian government of Yakutsk. They contain a wealth of fossilized mammoth bones. Area, about 9650 sq. miles.

NEW SOUTH WALES. The oldest state of the Commonwealth of Australia. An outstanding orographical feature is the various mountain ranges of the Australian Cordillera or Divide, which, under various names, traverse the coastal area from north to south, the culminating point being Mount Kosciusko (7310 feet). Towards the west the highlands descend to the Great Plains, which is drained by the Darling, Murrumbidgee, and Murray, originally independent rivers discharging separately into a sea that once occupied the basin of the Lower Murray. The emergence of the land has engrafted these three rivers to one trunk, the Lower Murray, on the western borders of New South Wales.

The 255,000 sq. miles of the Great Plains, beside the Darling, the Murray, and the Lower Murray, give no contribution to the river except that which may arise from springs in their beds. On the east the rivers are short and powerful. New South Wales has a coast-line of 700 miles (or 443 sq. miles of territory to 1 mile of coast-line), extending between Point Danger (north) and Cape Howe (south). The main waters of the Murray form the southern boundary-line. State area, exclusive of Federal capital territory (Canberra and Jervis Bay), but including the dependency of Lord Howe Island (q.v.), 309,432 sq. miles; pop. (1932), 2,529,734, of which 1,283,068 were males.

Towns.—Sydney (pop. 1931, 1,256,230) is the capital; other towns and their populations (1931) are: Newcastle (103,700), Broken Hill (22,950), Lithgow (15,050), Holroyd (14,990), Cessnock (13,860), East and West Maitland (11,940), and Lismore (10,514).

Communications.—The State railways are mainly of 4-foot-8½-inch gauge, and (1931), 6044 miles were open for traffic. There are also 109 miles of privately owned railways, mainly colliery lines.

There is no uniformity in gauge throughout Australia, each state having different standards, and varied standards prevailing in each state, e.g. New South Wales has an additional 45 miles of 5-foot-3-inch gauge, 79 to 80 miles of 3-foot-6-inch gauge, and 36½ miles of 5-foot-0-inch gauge. There are only 19·53 miles of railway to each 1000 sq. miles of New South Wales territory.

Tramways, with the exception of one short line, are Government property, and are controlled by the Railway Commissioners. Steam tramways operate at Newcastle, Broken Hill, Parramatta, between East and West Maitland, and from Sutherland to Cronulla. Other systems are mainly electric. The standard Government gauge is 4 feet 8½ inches. There are 118,341 miles of roads, 27,471 miles of which are metalled. The largesta rch bridge in the world, namely that over Sydney Harbour, was opened in 1932. (*See* SYDNEY.)

Social Conditions.—The aboriginal population of New South Wales was never large. Immigrant races consist mainly of the three divisions of the United Kingdom and their descendants. Non-Europeans comprise half-caste aboriginals and Asiatics, with some Africans, Polynesians, and Americans, the whole comprising 10·72 per 1000 of total population.

About 83 per cent. of the population are Australian born, 13 per cent. of the remainder being natives of the United Kingdom, and 0·72 per cent. natives of New Zealand, that is, about 96 to 97 per cent. of the total population are either Australasian or belong to the United Kingdom.

The population of New South Wales, as is general throughout Australia, are transplanted Britons, with all the essential characteristics of their British forbears, the desire for freedom from restraint being perhaps somewhat accentuated through the greater opportunity for open-air existence and the absence of the restrictions of older civilizations.

Religion.—The principal religions are: the Church of England, with an overwhelming majority; the next in importance being Roman Catholic, Presbyterian, and Methodist. Religion and State are separate; the Church of England is under the guidance of the Archbishop of Sydney, who is Metropolitan of New South Wales and Primate of Australia and Tasmania; a Roman Catholic Archbishop of Sydney controls the bishops of the eight State dioceses.

Education.—Education is free and compulsory between the ages of seven and fourteen years, and is under State control. Arrangement is made for the teaching of Japanese in selected high schools, of which there are thirty-eight in the state. There is a State school of aviation at Richmond. A college of practical agriculture (Hurlstone, near Sydney) prepares students for the Hawkesbury Agricultural College. The University of Sydney is the largest and best-equipped in the Commonwealth; the Technical College and Technological Museum is also located at Sydney, and there are other technical colleges at Maitland, Newcastle, Bathurst, Broken Hill, Albury, and Goulburn. State school children are medically inspected once every three years.

Commerce.—The principal exports are gold, silver, copper, lead, tin, coal, wool, metal manufactures, wool tops, butter, wheat, flour, fruit, jam, timber, meat (frozen and tinned), rabbits, hides and skins, leather, tallow, pearl-shell, and coco-nut oil.

Production and Industry.—New South Wales produces about seven-eighths of Australian coal, and is the mining state of the Commonwealth. Iron, gold, silver and lead, copper, tin, wolfram, zinc, and shale are worked. Agriculturally New

South Wales is wealthy, and is the principal sheep-rearing and wool-producing state (about 305,613,000 lb. of wool as in the grease in 1918-19, and 497,200,000 lb. in 1931-32). Cattle, horses, and pigs are also raised; oranges, lemons, mandarines, and other citron fruit are grown; wheat, maize, barley, oats, potatoes, and tobacco are cultivated.

There is some vine-growing, and a considerable industry in dried raisins and currants, as well as in table grapes and wines. Sugar-cane is cultivated. An extensive irrigation and artesian boring scheme anticipates the conservation of the water-supply on the Murray drainage system of the Great Plains. State forests, under the administration of a Commission, cover an area of 5,152,462 acres, and 1,523,715 acres have been set apart as timber reserves; in 1931, 372 sawmills had an output estimated at £1,131,000. Among manufactures are those of butter and cheese, brewing, tobacco, ore-smelting, jam and fruit packing, and bacon- and ham-curing. There is one sugar-refinery; the sugar-mills have an annual output of raw sugar weighing 297,335 tons.

History.—New South Wales was discovered by Captain Cook in 1770, and founded as a penal settlement (at Botany Bay) in 1788. One of its early Governors was the notorious Captain Bligh, who was deposed by the colonists in 1808. The most important events in its history since convict immigration ceased in 1840 are the establishment of representative institutions in 1843; the erection of Victoria into a separate colony in 1850; the important discovery in May, 1851, of extensive auriferous tracts, with a consequent increase in population and prosperity. The first railway, from Sydney to Parramatta, was opened in 1855.

An international exhibition was held at Sydney in 1879. The Intercolonial Conference held at Sydney in 1883 was the first practical step towards the federation of the colonies, which was finally effected by the Australian Commonwealth Act passed through the Imperial Parliament in 1900. On 1st Jan., 1901, New South Wales joined the federated "colonies" as a state of the Australian Commonwealth. The state is subdivided into 141 counties.

Modern Government.—Legislative power is vested in a Parliament comprising a Legislative Council of not less than 21 members (123 in September, 1932) appointed by the Crown for life, and an elected Legislative Assembly, 90 members. Executive power is in the hands of a Governor appointed by the Imperial Government.—BIBLIOGRAPHY: *Official Year Book of New South Wales* (annual); J. W. Edgeworth, *New South Wales: Historical, Physiographical, and Economic.*

NEWSPAPERS. Early History of the Newspaper.—The newspaper, as distinguished from other periodicals, is a daily or weekly publication which exists to report and comment upon current events.

The origin of the newspaper is usually sought in such productions as the Roman *Acta Diurna* or the Chinese *Peking Gazette*. But the *Acta Diurna* were no more than short public announcements posted in the Forum, and the *Peking Gazette* has little in common with our present day ideas of a newspaper. The newspaper, as we understand it, dates from the time when the invention of printing made possible the production of a number of copies of the same issue, and even after the invention of printing it was nearly two hundred years before regularly published newspapers were produced.

The immediate forerunners of the newspaper in Britain were weekly news-letters compiled in the sixteenth century by writers at Court to inform their masters of important events while they were themselves away on travel. Examples are the Paston Letters and the Sydney Papers. Printed news-pamphlets and news-books date on the Continent from 1609, the German publication, *Avisa Relation oder Zeitung*, followed in 1616 by the *Nieuwe Tijdingen*, printed in Antwerp. The first English newspaper was the *Weekly Newes*, published in London from 1622 by Bourne and Archer. *Newes from Most Parts of Christendom* was produced by Nathaniel Butter in opposition, and the two publications later combined under the title of *Newes of the Present Week*. The first regularly illustrated periodical was the *Mercurius Civicus*, begun in 1643.

During the seventeenth century the printing of newspapers—though it was encouraged by the eager desire for news and the wish to spread political propaganda during the Civil War—was held up by a variety of causes, including the Star Chamber edict against the printing of news from foreign parts, and a government suppression of the press from Oct. 1649 to June 1650. But the main barrier was provided by the Licensing Laws, which forbade the setting up of manuscript in type without a licence from the Archbishop of

Canterbury or the Bishop of London, and not until 1695 was the Licensing Act finally abolished.

In Nov., 1665, appeared the *Oxford Gazette* as the official organ of government, the Court being at Oxford at the time. This became, in 1666, the *London Gazette*, and it has continued to appear twice a week ever since. Thirty years later, in 1696, Edward Lloyd started *Lloyd's News*, which was discontinued after a time, and later revived as *Lloyd's List*. The successful *Daily Courant* appeared in 1702, and was soon followed by the *Country Gentleman's Courant*. On the 19th of Feb., 1704, the greatest of all journalists, Daniel Defoe, began the issue from Newgate Prison of his famous paper, *The Review*. In 1709 came Steele's *Tatler*, and in 1711 Steele and Addison's *Spectator*.

Other factors were to limit the development of newspapers in Britain for nearly another century and a half—after a most hopeful beginning—for this was the moment selected by the Government to impose a Stamp Tax, which as shown in Swift's *Journal to Stella*, killed off the reputable journals almost overnight. Even the *Spectator* lasted only for a few months. The more scurrilous and venal, however, maintained their ground, being secretly subsidized by political factions, as well as by the Government out of public funds.

In the middle of the century the Stamp Act was made more exacting, but in 1753 the total annual sales of newspapers in England already amounted to nearly 7½ millions. By 1760 this had grown to nearly 9½ millions, which increased again to nearly 11½ millions by 1767. "Taxes on knowledge" continued to be multiplied, and by 1804 the Stamp Tax amounted to no less than 3½*d.* per copy.

Constant efforts to escape payment were made, resulting in incessant prosecutions. Many of the so-called newspapers which were forced to struggle on underground were grossly indecent, blasphemous, and revolutionary sheets. Reputable papers which paid the tax honestly were at prohibitive prices, and even a popular writer, such as Cobbett, could not produce his *Political Register* for less than 9*d.* a copy. Notable papers of this period were *The Rambler*, Dr. Johnson's 2*d.* bi-weekly, started in 1751, and his weekly *Idler*, started in 1758. In 1761 John Wilkes' *North Briton* was produced—a paper which had much to do with securing the liberties of the press, and the *Public Advertiser*—which contained the famous "Letters of Junius." In 1794 two important daily newspapers which still exist, *The Times* and the *Morning Post*, were founded, as well as the *Morning Advertiser*.

But it was not until 1836 that—thanks to the efforts of Bulwer Lytton, Richard Cobden, and others—the Stamp Tax was reduced to a penny, and in 1855 it was finally abolished.

This of itself was enough to secure an enormous increase in the number of newspapers published. Local newspapers, professional and trade papers appeared; and at the same time began those enormous scientific and mechanical developments which made possible the immediate collection of news from all over the world, and the prodigious output which are characteristic of newspapers to-day.

The Nineteenth Century: Developments in the Printing Press.—From 1450 to 1811 improvements in the printing press were scarcely worth recording. The introduction of the new Stanhope Press to *The Times* offices in 1800 made possible the production of only 150 completed copies in an hour, and at this date no paper enjoyed a circulation of more than 4500 copies. This was the circulation of the *Morning Post* in 1802, when Coleridge, Moore, Wordsworth, and Mackworth Praed were writing for the paper—eight years earlier its circulation had averaged a meagre 350.

In 1811 Koenig patented the world's first cylinder press. In 1814 two of his improved machines were installed in *The Times* office, giving, each of them, a production of 500 copies per hour. In 1845 the first rotary newspaper printing press was produced, embodying the principle of a central cylinder on to which the formes of type were locked. Improved versions of such machines—the Hoe and the Applegarth—would produce as many as 20,000 papers in an hour, printed upon one side.

In 1861 Hoe & Co. adapted their machines to take stereo plates instead of type, a tremendous gain to newspaper publishers, as it now became possible to run numerous machines by casting a stereo plate for each from the original type. In the same year the paper duty was abolished. The price of paper also fell enormously over the next twenty-five years. During all this time, up till 1870, newspapers were printed flat and roughly folded by street-sellers, but now the automatic folder was introduced. Meantime the output of machines had enormously increased, and by 1901 it was possible for a machine to produce 24,000 twelve-page papers in an hour.

Similarly the developments, first of the railway, then of the telegraph and telephone, had brought world news within the range of the daily paper, and the spread of popular education had made possible far wider circulations than had been dreamed of fifty years before.

A large number of newspapers was founded during this century, The *Daily News* was launched in 1846 under the editorship of Charles Dickens. The *Daily Telegraph* was first published in 1855, the *Daily Chronicle* in 1877, the *Daily Mail* in 1896, and the *Daily Express* in 1900. Meantime, provincial newspapers were springing up in every town, Sunday papers—notably the *Observer*, the *Sunday Times*, the *News of the World*, and *The People*—were founded. In addition, magazines, journals, and papers devoted to every trade, pursuit, sport, and hobby made their appearance by the hundred.

This period, from 1850 to 1900, was a period of the ownership of newspapers by great private families, who took, in the main, a high view of their responsibilities, appointed able and trustworthy men as editors, and left control of policy to them. Financial interests came second to public policy and intellectual dignity.

But about 1890 the rapid development of displayed advertising enormously increased the possibility of making money out of newspapers. The chief interest of the advertiser lay in a vast circulation, for which he was prepared to pay large sums. If a newspaper was to achieve a huge circulation, clearly it had to be very different from the staid, closely packed newspapers of 1890.

The Newspaper of To-day.—In 1888 the *Star*, a newspaper of a new popular type, was launched as a London evening paper. The *Star* took for its columns whatever contained "human interest"—politics, crime, fashion, art, music, serial stories, books. But the first man fully to realize and exploit the possibilities awaiting the new type of paper was Alfred Harmsworth (Lord Northcliffe), the effect of whose work has been to change entirely not merely the newspapers, but the reading habits of a nation. Harmsworth in 1896 launched a halfpenny morning newspaper—the *Daily Mail*—the market for popular journals having been previously tested not only by the *Star*, but by such weekly papers as *Tit-Bits*, *Answers*, and *Pearson's Weekly*.

With the success of the *Daily Mail* began a shifting of interest from the mainly political to the popular—and simultaneously a growth of importance in the managerial side of newspapers, which had hitherto been entirely subject to the editorial. At the same time there started the great change from the system of private proprietorship to that of ownership by big limited liability companies.

Changes in contents followed the changes in control. News, and information on any matter of human interest, became of greater importance than the measured comment of newspapers thirty years earlier. The interests covered by a newspaper widened to include all its readers' activities. Home pages, sports pages, as well as special features for women and children were introduced, and the publication of serials, stories, and life-histories became a regular feature of newspaper work.

An important element in popularizing the daily newspaper was the introduction of the half-tone illustration. Illustrations previously had been mainly line engravings, which lacked the authenticity and "news-interest" of the half-tone. The success of the half-tone was responsible for the growth of the "picture paper"—of which the first was the *Daily Mirror*, launched originally by Lord Northcliffe as a serious paper for women interested in public affairs. The *Daily Mirror* was followed by the *Daily Sketch* and the *Daily Graphic*, which had been in existence for some time as a penny illustrated paper. All newspapers then began to include a page of half-tone pictures and to publish pictures in the news columns also—*The Times* and *Daily Telegraph* being the last to do so.

As popular newspapers increased in number and popularity—the ½*d. Daily Express* appeared in 1900, the *Daily Mirror* in 1904, the *Daily News* was reduced to a ½*d.* in 1904, as was also the *Daily Chronicle*—competition between them became keener. New inducements were offered to the public to become readers. The offer of free insurance was first made in *Answers* and in *Tit-Bits*. Sir Charles Starmer applied the idea to daily newspapers, and was rapidly followed by Lord Northcliffe.

During the last twenty years the number of national daily newspapers has been considerably reduced, while the number of London evening newspapers has been reduced from nine to three. Circulations of the remaining newspapers have tended to increase, the most astonishing rise in circulation being that of the *Daily Herald*. The *Daily Herald* was taken over by Odhams Press and first issued in its new form in March, 1930. The circulation sprang from about 300,000 to over 1,000,000 overnight, and has continued to increase ever since. In July, 1933, a certified net paid circulation of over 2,000,000 was published.

The chief factor in newspaper progress during this period has been the increase in advertising, which has made of the daily newspaper an important part of the machinery of buying and selling, and has borne by far the larger part of the enormous cost involved in producing the modern huge-circulation newspaper.

A few years ago it was estimated that the annual revenue from advertising in London newspapers alone amounted to £13,000,000, of which £9,000,000 went to the morning and £4,000,000 to the Sunday and evening newspapers.

The Production of a Modern Newspaper.—A fair estimate of the combined circulations of the morning and evening journals of Great Britain and Ireland is 15,000,000, or considerably more than an average of one newspaper to every home. The total number of newspaper workers is about 60,000, of whom roughly 6000 are journalists.

The staff of a newspaper consists generally of an editor-in-chief, an assistant editor, a day editor, a night editor, a news editor with his staff of reporters, a foreign editor with a staff of sub-editors, a chief sub-editor with a staff of sub-editors; in addition to literary editor, sporting editor, leader writers, critics, experts on all technical subjects, and correspondents all over the country and in every foreign capital.

News is received through the correspondents, through the reporters, and *via* the news agencies. The most famous of the news agencies—Reuters—was founded in Paris in 1849. This was followed in 1863 by the Central Press, in 1865 by the Press Association, and in 1870 by the Central News and the Exchange Telegraph. The news agencies maintain staffs throughout the world, whose whole business is the collection and dissemination of news. News is transmitted by post, telephone, telegraph, by wireless, beam-wireless, and by aeroplane. Photographs are carried by land, sea, and air, and transmitted by telepicture.

The news as it flows into the newspaper offices is examined, reworded where necessary, and passed on by the sub-editors to the chief sub-editor, who passes it on to the composing-room to be set up in type. In addition, the feature articles, criticisms of plays, music, art, etc., have to be written and approved, and throughout the day conferences of the editorial staff take place to decide on the importance of the various " news stories," and the general arrangement of the paper.

On reaching the composing-room the " copy," as it is called, is distributed to the operators of the Linotype machines.

The Linotype machine, which was introduced towards the end of the nineteenth century, supersedes the old method of type-setting by hand, and abolishes all the work of " distributing " type again after it has been used. Headings and matter for advertisements are often set up by the Ludlow machine, in which the matrices from which the type is cast are simply set by hand in a metal box. This is placed in the machine, which casts automatically.

The lines of type being set are boxed in " galleys " and placed in an electric press, from which proofs are pulled. The proofs are distributed to the editorial departments for revision, and to expert readers to be examined for corrections. The " make-up " of the page is then arranged. When this has been done, blocks for the illustrations made and mounted, and advertisements placed in position, the page is ready in a form in which it might be printed on a flat press.

But modern newspapers are printed on rotary machines from huge rolls of " newsprint." It is necessary therefore for the flat page to be made round; this is done by covering the type with a sheet of papier-maché-like material from which a mould of it is taken. From these moulds semi-circular metal plates are cast—giving an exact replica of the type—and from these the newspaper is printed.

A modern newspaper printing machine will print from four rolls of paper simultaneously, and uses up about a hundred miles of paper every day. The finished newspapers, printed, folded, and cut, pour out at a rate of 50,000 in an hour. Finally, the " fudge-box "—invented by Mr. Mark Smith and first used in the *Manchester Evening News*—is used to print the latest news in the stop-press space after the stereo plates are on the machine. Fleets of motor-vans, special newspaper trains, steamboats, and aeroplanes then distribute the editions throughout the country.

BIBLIOGRAPHY: J. Grant, *The Newspaper Press: its Origin, Progress, and Present Position*; J. D. Symon, *The Press and its Story*; A. Baker, *The Newspaper World*; G. B. Dibblee, *The Newspaper*; *The British Press*, ed. Herbert Tracey; J. E. Rogers, *The American Newspaper*; L. E. Hatin, *Histoire politique et littéraire de la presse en France*; Lord Northcliffe, *Newspapers and their Millionaires*. For technical information, *The Story of the Newspaper Printing Press*, by George A. Isaacs, J.P., M.P.

NEWT, or **EFT**. The popular name applied to various genera of amphibians included in the ord. Urodela ("tailed") of that class. Water-newts, or "water-salamanders" as they are sometimes termed, possess a compressed tail, adapted for swimming. These forms are oviparous, and though aquatic in their habits they are yet strict air-breathers.

The larval gills are cast off on maturity being reached, or about the third month of existence. The larval tail is retained throughout life. The male animals are distinguished by the possession of a crest or fleshy ridge borne on the back. The food consists chiefly of aquatic insects, larvæ, etc. The great water-newt (*Triton cristātus*) is about 6 inches in length; the spotted newt (*T. vulgaris*) averages about 3 inches; and both are common in freshwater pools and ponds in Britain.

NEWTON, Sir Isaac. English mathematician and natural philosopher, the foremost scientist of this if not of any country, was born at Woolsthorpe, Lincolnshire, in 1642, and died at Kensington in 1727. He was educated at Grantham Grammar School and Trinity College, Cambridge, where he commenced residence in 1661. In 1664 he was elected scholar, and in 1667 Fellow of his college. In 1665, at the time of the plague, Newton went to stay at Woolsthorpe, and, if a favourite story may be believed, it was the fall of an apple in the garden there which gave the first start to the train of thought which ultimately led him to the discovery of the law of gravitation.

The hypothesis that the moon is held in its orbit by the same force of attraction to the earth as causes the fall of the apple, and that the intensity of this force diminishes inversely as the square of the distance from the centre of attraction, can easily be tested arithmetically, and Newton actually made the calculation, with a result, however, which was adverse to the theory, owing, as it turned out, to the erroneous value accepted at that time for the length of the earth's radius. In 1670, with the better value for the radius which had been obtained by Picard, the moon calculation came out quite satisfactorily, and by 1684 Newton had worked out a great part of the theory in its application to the motions of the planets and their satellites.

His great work on dynamics and astronomy, *Philosophiæ Naturalis Principia Mathematica*, usually referred to simply as the *Principia*, was composed in the years 1685 and

Sir Isaac Newton

1686. The appearance of its pages is in strong contrast to that of modern treatises on the subject, Newton casting his demonstrations into purely geometrical form where a writer of the present day would invariably use the calculus. Newton succeeded Isaac Barrow (q.v.) as Lucasian professor of mathematics in 1669, and was elected a Fellow of the Royal Society in 1671.

In 1689 he was elected to Parliament as one of the members for the University of Cambridge. In 1694 he was appointed to the Wardenship of the Mint, and in 1697 to the Mastership. In 1703 he became president of the Royal Society, and was re-elected annually during the remainder of his life.

Newton's discoveries in pure mathematics and in optics are almost as celebrated as those he made in astronomical theory and in dynamics. In optics his great achievement was the discovery of the relation between colour and refrangibility, and his investigations on the prismatic spectrum are classical (*see* LIGHT; REFRACTION; SPECTRUM). He invented a reflecting telescope, and investigated the theory of the colours of thin films (Newton's rings). He had difficulties about accepting a wave theory of light, and gave dynamical explanations of reflection and refraction on the basis of the corpuscular theory.

In mathematics we have Newton to thank for many methods and results. The *Binomial Theorem* (*see* MACLAURIN'S THEOREM), *Newton's Interpolation Formula* (*see* DIFFERENCES, FINITE), and *Newton's Triangle*, the last a method of fundamental utility for expanding an implicit algebraic function, are a few of the subjects associated with his name, but it is as the inventor of the method of *fluxions* (q.v.), the direct and immediate forerunner of the modern infinitesimal calculus, that he has made the deepest mark on the history of mathematics.

His controversy with Leibnitz as to which of them was the first discoverer of the principle of the calculus was settled entirely in Newton's favour; some competent people, indeed, who had considered the evidence, were inclined to the view that Leibnitz really stole the original idea from Newton. Opinion now gives Leibnitz rather more credit as at least a partially independent discoverer; and as a historical fact the immensely superior notation introduced by Leibnitz must be given a large share of the credit for the rapid development of mathematical science on the Continent during the eighteenth century, at a time when slavish adherence to Newton's methods of expression was paralysing English mathematics (*see* MACLAURIN, COLIN). (*See* DYNAMICS; KINETICS; NEWTON'S LAWS OF MOTION; KEPLER'S LAWS; GRAVITATION; GRAVITY; INTERFERENCE.)

Apart from the *Principia*, the chief works of Newton which were published in separate form are: *Optics*, *Tractatus de Quadratura Curvarum*, and *Enumeratio Linearum Tertii Ordinis*. An important paper is that entitled *Analysis per Equationes Numero Terminorum Infinitas*. A complete collection of Newton's works was published in 1779-85 by Dr. S. Horsley.—BIBLIOGRAPHY: Sir D. Brewster, *Memoirs of the Life, Writings, and Discoveries of Sir Isaac Newton*; W. W. R. Ball, *A Short History of Mathematics*.

NEWTON. A city of Massachusetts, United States, in Middlesex county; served by the Boston & Albany Railway. There are woollen, cord, and other manufactures. Newton was settled in 1631, and became a city in 1873. It was formerly called Cambridge, the name being changed in 1692. Pop. (1930), 65,276.

NEWTON ABBOT. A town and railway junction of Devonshire, England, at the head of the Teign estuary; served by the Great Western Railway. There are railway workshops, and pottery is made. The tower of the church of St. Leonard's is interesting, and on a pedestal before it William of Orange was proclaimed king (1688). Pop. (1931), 15,003.

NEWTON-IN-MAKERFELD, or **NEWTON-LE-WILLOWS.** A town of Lancashire, England, served by, and a junction on, the London Midland & Scottish Railway. There are paper- and glass-works, railway workshops, and iron-foundries. Pop. (1931), 20,150.

NEWTON'S LAWS OF MOTION. These laws form the basis of the science of dynamics (q.v.). The ancients, while acquainted with the principles of statics, made little or no progress in kinetics. Their astronomers (Hipparchus, Ptolemy, and others) studied deeply and successfully the motions of the heavenly bodies, but left untouched the problem of accounting for those motions by the action of forces. The kinetics of terrestrial bodies was also beyond the scope of the science of the ancients.

Not till the time of Galileo Galilei (1564-1642) was a correct foundation laid for the modern science of kinetics. Galileo established by experiment and observation the laws of falling bodies, which contradicted the dictum of Aristotle that the velocities of bodies are proportional to their weights. By his famous experiment of dropping bodies of various weights from the top of the leaning tower of Pisa, he showed that (allowing for the effects of air resistance) all bodies tend to fall at the same rate. Again, while the ancients looked upon motion in a circle ("the perfect motion") as the fundamental type, Galileo propounded as the first law of motion, "that a body left to itself would move uniformly in a straight line."

From the time of Galileo to that of Newton advances in kinetic science were made by several natural philosophers, and specially by C. Huygens, who gave the kinetic theory of the pendulum. In the introductory part of the *Philosophiæ Naturalis*

Principia Mathematica, which may be described as a treatise on dynamics with applications to astronomy, Sir Isaac Newton gave in his three Laws of Motion a statement of the fundamental principles of dynamics (q.v.), such as were (he says) already generally accepted by mathematicians, and amply confirmed by experiment and observation.

The logical completeness of Newton's account of the theory, as well as the experimental evidence for it, has given rise to much discussion. (*See* the treatise of Mach, which gives a very comprehensive survey of the historical development of dynamical theory up till about 1880.) It has been pointed out that the definitions of *mass, motion, force, time-measurement*, and *absolute rest* are so interconnected that the fundamental postulates are not made clear, and certainly not explicitly stated. The phrase " uniform rectilinear motion," for example, has no meaning unless we have a *frame of reference*, for positions, and a means of defining equal intervals of time.

Newton's view as to absolute rest and motion may be indicated by this quotation: " The effects by which absolute motion is distinguished from relative are the centrifugal forces of rotation. For merely relative rotation these forces are zero; in true rotation they exist in a greater or less degree." Then follows the well-known experiment of the rotating bucket of water, which shows the effects of centrifugal force, though the water may be at rest relatively to the bucket.

It is easy to show that if two bodies, or rigid frames, have relative to each other a uniform motion of pure translation, then *both*, or *neither*, would satisfy the condition that all other motions relative to it as base could be accounted for by forces obeying the third law, so that absolute rest is undefinable on Newton's own principles. The recent theory of relativity (q.v.) opens up a new point of view for the whole subject. *See* KINETICS.—BIBLIOGRAPHY: E. Mach, *The Science of Mechanics*; J. Clerk Maxwell, *Matter and Motion*; P. G. Tait, *The Laws of Motion*.

NEWTON STEWART. A town and police burgh of Scotland, in Wigtownshire (one suburb in Kirkcudbrightshire), on the Cree; served by the L.M.S. Railway. The textile industry is carried on, and the town is a tourist centre. Pop. (1931), 1914.

NEWTOWN (W. *Drefnewydd*). A town of Montgomeryshire, North Wales, on the Severn; served by the G.W. Railway and the Montgomeryshire Canal. It is the chief seat of Welsh flannel manufacture. Pop. (Newton and Llanllwchaiarn, 1931), 5152.

NEWTOWNARDS. A town of County Down, Northern Ireland, near the head of Strangford Lough. It is 14 miles from Belfast by rail. The chief industries are flax-spinning and linen and muslin manufacturing Pop. (1926), 10,150.

NEW ULM. A city of Minnesota, United States, the county seat of Brown county, on the Minnesota; served by the Minneapolis & St. Louis and the Chicago & North-Western Railways. There are grain-elevators and manufactures of cigars, machine tools, shirts, bricks, and flour. Settled in 1854, New Ulm was incorporated in 1876. Pop. 7308.

NEW WESTMINSTER. A town of British Columbia, Canada, on the Fraser River; served by the Canadian Pacific and local railways. Salmon-canning and sawmilling are the main industries. New Westminster was founded in 1858, and was formerly capital of the mainland. Pop. 18,000.

NEW YEAR'S DAY. The first day of the year, from the earliest times observed with religious ceremonies or festive rejoicing. New Year's Day, being the eighth day after Christmas, is the festival of Christ's circumcision. The day is a holiday, celebrated with religious service all over the European continent, though not generally in Britain nor in the United States. The Anglo-Saxon year used to begin on 25th Dec., but at the Conquest it was changed to 1st Jan. Later, England, however, like all Christian countries, began the year with the 25th of March. With the introduction of the Gregorian Calendar (in 1582) the 1st of January was restored in the majority of Christian countries as New Year's Day, but in England only in 1751. In Scotland the new year began on 1st Jan. from 1599.

NEW YORK. A state in the Middle Atlantic division of the United States, the thirtieth in area but the first in wealth and population, and called, therefore, the " empire state." It has a considerable seaboard on the Atlantic, mainly on Long Island, and has coast-lines of 75 miles on Lake Erie and of 200 miles on Lake Ontario, by which, with the St. Lawrence River, it is bounded from east to north. In the north-east rise the well-timbered Adirondack Mountains (Mount Marcy, 5377 feet); the Catskills

(Slide Mountain, 4205 feet), also densely wooded, traverse the east-central regions. There are large State forest-reserves in both areas.

The region extending from the Adirondacks to Pennsylvania (in the south) is a flat, well-watered, temperate plateau. Albany (pop. 1930), 127,412) is the state capital, but New York (q.v.) is by far the most important city; others are Buffalo (pop. 573,076), Rochester (pop. 328,132), Syracuse (pop. 209,326), Utica (pop. 101,740), Albany (127,412), and Yonkers (pop. 134,646), and there are fifteen other towns of over 30,000 inhabitants. Indian Reserves have an area (1930) of 137 sq. miles; pop. 4959.

Communications.—New York State had (1931) 8226 miles of railway track and also 936 miles of single-track electric railway, the principal railways being the Long Island (on Long Island); Lehigh Valley; Erie; New York, Central, & Hudson River (operating also the West Shore Railway); Delaware Lackawanna, & Western; Pennsylvania; Mohawk & Hudson; and the Delaware & Hudson systems. State commercial canals include the Erie Canal (339 miles—Lake Erie to Lake Champlain), the Oswego Canal (Lake Erie to Lake Ontario), and the State Barge Canal (New York City to Buffalo). The total length of canals used for commercial purposes in 1931 was 525 miles.

People.—About a quarter of the population is foreign-born, and includes chiefly German, Irish, English, and Scots, Italian, Russian, Austrian, Canadian-English and -French, French, and Swiss elements.

Production and Industry. — The state, of great manufacturing importance, has also an extensive agricultural industry, corn (20,790,000 bushels, 1932), wheat (3,916,000 bushels, 1932), oats (27,032,000 bushels), roots and hay, tobacco, and sugar-beet being the principal crops. Fruit and vegetable production are also important. Dairying is progressive, the production of milk in 1931 being 7,367,235,000 lb., and sheep-farming is extensive (1932, 2,732,000 lb. of wool). Mining and quarrying yield iron, talc, crude petroleum (3,363,000 barrels, 1931), natural gas, granite, trap-rock, sandstone, marble, limestone, and salt. Infusorial earth, garnet, emery. and crystalline quartz are also produced. Manufactures and exports are widely varied. (*See* NEW YORK CITY.)

Publications and Languages.—In 1931 there were 2115 newspapers, of which 192 were dailies and 861 weeklies, published in English. There were in addition 17 in Spanish, 31 in Italian, 19 in German, and 4 in Yiddish. Other representative and important languages are Hungarian, Polish, French, Bohemian, Arabic, Greek, Portuguese, Swedish, Lithuanian, Chinese, Croatian, Finnish, Serbian, Albanian, Hebrew, Judæo-Spanish, Welsh, Persian, and Ukrainian.

Education.—Education is compulsory between the ages of seven and sixteen; physical training is compulsory; and military training between the ages of sixteen and nineteen for pupils of colleges and public or private schools is rigorously enforced. There are 163 universities and professional schools, including Columbia University (founded 1754) and Cornell University at Ithaca (founded 1857); Five are devoted entirely to women; the University of Rochester (1846) and ten others have students of both sexes, and the others are exclusively devoted to men.

Area and Population.—Area, 49,204 sq. miles (1550 sq. miles water; technically an additional 3140 sq. miles of water on Lakes Ontario and Erie are within the state); pop. (1930), 12,588, 066.

Constitution and Government.—New York was one of the original thirteen states of the Union, which she joined in 1788. For local government purposes there are 62 counties. The modern Government consists of a Governor and a Legislative, comprising a Senate (51 members, sitting for two years) and an Assembly (150 members, elected annually). Two Senators and 45 Representatives are sent to Congress.—BIBLIOGRAPHY: H. A. Stebbins, *A Political History of the State of New York*, 1865-69; E. H. Roberts. *The Planting and Growth of the Empire State*; D. C. Sowers, *The Financial History of the New York State from* 1789 *to* 1912.

NEW YORK CITY. The metropolis of the American continent, the principal seaport, and the second largest city in the world, situated at the confluence of the Hudson and East Rivers, and on New York Bay, an extensive natural harbour. The bay is divided into an outer harbour (Lower Bay), separated from the Atlantic by Sandy Hook Bar, and an inner harbour (Upper Bay), in which stands the Bartholdi Statue of Liberty (on Bedloe's or Liberty Island). In the bay are several islands, including Ellis Island, the United States immigration station.

The chief portion of the city is situated on Manhattan Island, 13½ miles long and generally about 1¾ miles broad, and separated by the narrow channel of Harlem River from the mainland; while on the opposite shores of the East River are Brooklyn and Long Island City, and on those of the Hudson, Jersey City, Hoboken, etc. Since Jan., 1898, Brooklyn, Long Island City, Staten Island, etc., have been incorporated in New York.

Street Plan.—The plan upon which the newer portion of the city is laid out consists of parallel *avenues* (seven to the mile) named numerically, and running from south to north. Avenues are intersected at right angles by *streets* (twenty to the mile), also numerically named, and running from east to west. Fifth Avenue (7 miles long, 100 feet wide) is the great central avenue, and all the streets running east from it have the prefix *east*, and those running west the prefix *west*, and the houses are numbered accordingly. Fifth Avenue was the fashionable and aristocratic street, but has become more and more devoted to business, although many of the older families still reside there, particularly the millionaires, whose mansions overlook the Central Park.

The main business district centres round Broadway, with the Metropolitan Opera House (intimately associated with Enrico Caruso), the enormous department stores, and the theatres. Madison Avenue, next east of Fifth Avenue, is a street of costly private houses and beautiful churches. Central Park extends between 59th and 110th Street and between Fifth and Eighth Avenue. More than a dozen other small public parks and squares are scattered over the city, the finest of the latter being Union Square on the east side of Broadway, and Madison Square on the east side of Fifth Avenue.

Buildings and Institutions.—The circumstance that the city is hemmed in by water, the high price of ground, and the improvement in the construction of elevators or lifts, early stimulated an upward instead of a lateral expansion in building construction, and accounts for the now famous "sky-line," broken by skyscrapers, many of which rear massive towers to a height of well over 300 feet. Among these are the Empire State Building, the highest building in the world, 1248 feet above street level; the Woolworth Building (55 storeys, 750 feet); the Singer Building (612 feet); Metropolitan Life Assurance Company (693 feet); Commercial Cable (317 feet); and the *New York Times* Building (363 feet) at 42nd Street and Broadway.

The buildings most worthy of notice, in an architectural aspect, are the Sub-Treasury; the City Hall, attractively set in the centre of an ornamental park; the post office, at the south end of City Hall Park; the Academy of Design; and Columbia University. The churches of all denominations number about 500, and include St. Patrick's (R.C.) Cathedral, built of white marble in the decorated style of the thirteenth century, and the Collegiate Church, dating from 1628. The principal religious faith is the Dutch Reformed. New York is generously provided with hospitals, asylums, and institutions of all kinds. The most important seat of learning in the city is Columbia University, founded by charter of George II. in 1754. New York University was founded in 1831. There are also a number of medical schools and theological colleges and seminaries, besides the Cooper Union.

New York is the terminal station of the three great trunk lines of the New York Central; the New York, New Haven, & Hartford (both Grand Central Terminal); and the Pennsylvania Railway systems.

Trade, etc.—New York is primarily a commercial city and a centre of distribution of domestic and foreign products, but it is also the centre of a vast manufacturing interest. The industries, however, are more of a varied character than individually important, the chief being connected with clothing, meat-packing, printing and publishing, and brewing. The water-supply is partly furnished from Croton Lake, an artificial reservoir supplied by Croton River, from which the water is conveyed by an aqueduct of stone masonry of a capacity of 115,000,000 gallons per day a distance of 40 miles to New York. A further enlargement brings water from the Askokan Reservoir (86 miles).

By the Act of 1897, under which Greater New York was constituted, the whole city is under a mayor, elected for four years, who appoints heads of departments; a president of the council, elected for four years also, who acts as deputy-mayor; and a council and board of aldermen. Each of the five constituent boroughs, Manhattan, Bronx (mainland), Queens (Long Island), Brooklyn (Long Island), and Richmond (Staten Island), has its own president and borough board.

History.—New York Bay and the Hudson River were first visited by Verrazano (1524), followed in 1609 by Henry Hudson. It was first settled three years after on the southern extremity. The Dutch

NEW YORK: EQUITABLE BUILDING OFFICES OF THE AMERICAN SURETY CO. AND TRINITY CHURCH

settlement of Nieuw Amsterdam (founded 1621) had 1000 inhabitants in 1649. In 1664 it surrendered to the British, and took its new name from the Duke of York (afterwards James II.). New York was taken from the Americans by the British at the beginning of the War of Independence (26th Aug., 1776), and held as the British headquarters till its close (evacuated 25th Nov., 1783). From 1785 to 1790 it was the seat of the Federal Government, and at New York Washington was inaugurated to the presidency in 1789.

During the war of 1812-15 its foreign commerce was almost annihilated. The first regular line of packet ships to Liverpool was started in 1817. The opening of the Erie Canal in 1825 gave a great stimulus to internal commerce. Since that date the progress of New York has been wonderful. It has two broadcasting stations, Brooklyn (54·52 M.) and Richmond Hill (49·02 M., 0·5 kW.) Pop. in 1830, 202,589; in 1850, 515,547; in 1870, 942,292; in 1880, 1,206,600; in 1890, 1,513,501; in 1910 (as extended), 4,766,883; on 1st April, 1930:

Manhattan	1,867,312
Bronx	1,265,258
Brooklyn	2,560,401
Queens	1,079,129
Richmond	158,346
Total New York	6,930,446

BIBLIOGRAPHY: Mrs. S. van Rensselaer, *History of the City of New York* (2 vols.); R. R. Wilson, *New York, Old and New*; Theodore Roosevelt, *New York.*

NEW ZEALAND, Dominion of. A British dominion consisting of an archipelago in the South Pacific Ocean. The dominion proper comprises North Island (44,281 sq. miles), South Island (58,092 sq. miles), Stewart Island (670 sq. miles), and the Chatham Islands (372 sq. miles); total area, 103,265 sq. miles; pop. (1926), 1,344,384 (including 63,670 Marois); estimated pop. in 1932, 1,455,167 (excluding Maoris). In addition there are the outlying islands (area, 307 sq. miles; the dependencies—the Auckland, Cook, and Kermadec Islands, Niue, and the Ross Dependency; and the mandated territory of Western Samoa. There are nine provincial districts, four in North Island (Auckland, Taranaki, Wellington, and Hawke's Bay) and five in South Island (Nelson, Marlborough, Canterbury, Otago, and Westland). These districts are subdivided into seventy-seven counties. The census of New Zealand is quinquennial, but as an act of national economy, that due in 1931 was postponed.

Physiography.—The islands are long and narrow, and occur on a ridge which separates the Southern Pacific on the east from the Southern Ocean on the west. The three islands are connected by a submarine ridge, no part of which is more than 100 fathoms deep, while the line marking the 500 fathoms has a long extension to the north-west, and in that direction the New Zealand ridge is connected with Melanesia and Queensland by a platform never more than 2000 fathoms deep.

New Zealand: Typical scene, North Island

Across this formerly continuous land New Zealand received most of its present animals and plants by migration.

The geographical backbone of New Zealand consists of a system of fold mountains running south-west to north-east nearly the whole length of South Island, and continued in North Island up to East Cape. The chief volcanic mountains are found in the Taupo volcanic area—wide plains of lava and volcanic ash. The hollows in those plains are filled by lakes, such as Lakes Taupo and Rotorua. Above these plains lie many hills formed by volcanoes, including Ruapehu (9175 feet), Ngauruhoe (7515 feet), and Tongariro (6485 feet). The other chief volcanic mountains occur along the coasts and on the edges of foundered areas. Such is Mount Egmont, rising as a snow-capped cone from the coast of Taranaki (8250 feet).

The chief rivers of New Zealand rise in the Southern Alps. On the west rivers are short and powerful; on the east the distance to the sea is longer, and rivers flow across the wide Canterbury Plains. Lakes of the North Island occur in basins on the volcanic plains, such as Lake Taupo, drained by the Waikato, New Zealand's longest river. The Cold Lakes of the South Island lie in deep fiord-like valleys, the floors of which sink below the level of the sea; thus Manapouri, 597 feet above sea-level (at the surface), is 1462 feet deep.

Climate.—The climate is typical of a maritime country, the influence of the adjacent seas rendering it uniformly equable and healthy. In North Island the climate is of the Mediterranean type with winter rains; in South Island the climate is similar to but much warmer than that of England. The rainfall on the west coast of South Island ranges from 100 to 200 inches per annum.

Social Conditions: Aborigines.—The original natives of New Zealand, called Maoris, a people of Polynesian origin, are supposed to have emigrated from the Navigators' or the Sandwich Islands some centuries ago. The Treaty of Waitangi was signed on 6th Feb., 1840, at the Bay of Islands, and New Zealand became a British colony through the cession to Queen Victoria by the Maori chiefs, of their rights as rulers in return for Queen Victoria's personal assurance of protection and recognition of their rights as British subjects.

With few exceptions the Maoris have kept the treaty in letter and in spirit, and the New Zealand administration has always planned and legislated for the protection of the aboriginal population against exploitation by land-dealers and speculators, and towards their firm establishment upon the soil. The unravelling of a tangled skein of "land titles" was rendered even more complicated by the Maori laws of succession, which vest interest in a dead man's property in all his family and relatives equally, irrespective of the degree of relationship, presumably upon the reasoning that all are descended from a common ancestor. This "common ancestor" generally gained his title to the property by eating the former owner.

Religion.—There is no State religion. The Anglican Church has six dioceses; an archbishop resident at Wellington assisted by an archbishop coadjutor and three bishops control Roman Catholic affairs. The Anglican faith has an overwhelming majority (42·21 per cent.), and Presbyterianism follows (24·60 per cent.), with Roman Catholics (12·89 per cent.), and Methodists (9·02 per cent.) in addition. Other faiths are insignificant.

Education.—Elementary education is free, secular, and compulsory between the ages of seven and fourteen. Secondary education is provided for in numerous high schools, grammar schools, colleges, etc. At the head of the higher education is the University of New Zealand, an examining body empowered to grant honours, degrees, and scholarships. Affiliated to it are Otago University, at Dunedin, Canterbury College (Christchurch), Auckland University College, and Victoria College (Wellington). There are also many special schools, native schools, etc.

Towns. — Wellington, on Cook Strait is the capital of the Dominion (pop. 1921, 88,876, or including the entire metropolitan area, 107,428); other towns are Christchurch (1921, 67,292), Auckland (1921, 81,718), Dunedin (1921, 59,198), Wanganui (1921, 164,92), Palmerston North (1921, 15,648), and Invercargil (1921, 15,204).

Towns.—Wellington, on Cook Strait, is the capital of the Dominion (est. pop. 1932, 144,800); other towns and their estimated populations (1932) are Christchurch (128,900), Auckland (218,400), Dunedin (87,400), Wanganui (27,800), Palmerston North (23,200), Invercargill (24,350), Napier (19,300), Timaru (18,650), New Plymouth (18,650), Hamilton (18,250) and Gisborne (16,400).

Communications.—In 1932 there were 3315 miles of Government railways and 117 miles of private lines. All the principal towns have tramway systems. The telegraph system is controlled by the Government.

Production.—The chief economic products of New Zealand are dairy produce, frozen meat, and wool. In North Island the conditions for dairy farming are exceptionally good, owing to the almost perpetual natural feed and the extraordinary mild climate. About two-thirds of the total land surface is suitable for agriculture; wheat, oats, and barley being the principal products.

Forests.—About 12,500,000 acres are afforested.

Minerals.—Gold, tungsten, silver, and coal are found.

Manufactures. — Meat - preserving, etc.; butter and cheese; ham- and bacon-curing; grain-milling; soap and candles; wood and timber; engineering; printing and bookbinding; motors and cycles; tanning, etc.; boots and shoes; clothing, etc. The largest output is in meat, butter and cheese, leather, and grain-milling.

Commerce.—There is a large trade with India and Burma, and with Ceylon; rice, coffee, tea in bulk, hessian, jute bagging and sacking, corn-bags, etc., being imported from the former, and desiccated coconut, cocoa-beans (uncrushed), tea in bulk, fibres and yarns (coir, jute, hemp, and flax) coming from the latter. Chief exports and values in 1931 were:

Commodity.	Value 1.
Butter . . .	£10,649,527
Frozen meat. .	8,892,555
Wool . . .	5,515,376
Cheese . . .	4,461,293

1 The value is shown in New Zealand currency.

History.—New Zealand was first discovered by Tasman in 1642, but little was known of it till it was circumnavigated by Cook in 1769 and 1774. The first permanent settlement was made by missionaries in 1815, but no regular authority was established by the British Government till 1833, when a resident was appointed, with limited powers, and subordinate to the Government of New South Wales. In 1840 New Zealand was erected into a colony; in 1841 it was formally separated from New South Wales and placed under its own independent governor; and in 1852 it received a constitution and responsible government.

Troubles with the natives of the North Island about land have given rise to frequent Maori wars, and so late as 1886 a disturbance about land arose. In 1865 the seat of government was removed from Auckland to Wellington. In 1873 the Public Works Policy was inaugurated, and large loans were raised for immigration, harbours, railways, roads, etc. In 1876 the colony was divided into counties. Commercial depression prevailed from 1880 to 1890. Much recent legislation has been in favour of the working man, for promoting land and ex-soldier settlement, etc. The colony became a "Dominion" in 1907. In 1923 the Ross Dependency in the Antarctic was declared to be a British settlement attached to New Zealand. In Feb., 1931, a destructive earthquake devastated the Hawke's Bay area in North Island.

See NORTH ISLAND; SOUTH ISLAND; STEWART ISLAND.

BIBLIOGRAPHY: *New Zealand Official Year Book: Report on Commercial Conditions in the Dominion of New Zealand* (1921) (H.M. Stationery Office Publication); G. W. Russell, *New Zealand To-day*; John White, *Ancient History of the Maori*; G. H. Scholefield, *New Zealand in Evolution, Industrial, Economic and Political*; P. Marshall, *The Geography of New Zealand*; R. P. Thomson, *A National History*.

NEY (nā), **Michel.** Duke of Elchingen, Prince of the Moskwa,

Michel Ney

Marshal and Peer of France, born in 1769 at Sarre-Louis, executed 7th Dec., 1815. He entered the military service in 1788, rose to the rank of general of division in 1798, and as such distinguished himself in the Rhine campaign. Appointed marshal of the empire by Napoleon in 1805, he achieved victory over the Austrians at Elchingen, and took part in the battle of Jena. During the Russian campaign he commanded the 3rd Division at the battle of the Moskwa, and conducted the rearguard in the disastrous retreat.

When Napoleon abdicated and the Bourbon dynasty was established, Ney took the oath of allegiance to the king and received a command; but when the emperor landed from Elba, his old general joined him at Lyons and opened the way to Paris. In the campaign which followed it was Ney who led the attack on the British centre at Waterloo, and after five horses had been killed under him he only retired from the field at nightfall. When the Allies entered Paris, he escaped in disguise to the provinces, but was finally arrested, brought back to Paris, tried for treason, and condemned to death.—Cf. H. Welschinger, *Le Maréchal Ney*.

NGAMI. A South African lake in the Bechuanaland Protectorate. During the rainy season the water is fresh, but in the dry season it becomes brackish and almost disappears. Ngami was first visited by Livingstone and Oswell in 1849.

NGANHWEI, or **ANHWEI.** An inland province of China, west of the maritime province of Kiang-Su, drained by the Yangtze Kiang, etc. It is level country, excepting in the south and west-central districts, and tea (Keemun) is extensively produced. North of the Yangtze Kiang lies the most prolific rice-producing belt of all China. The capital is Anking. Area of province, 54,826 sq. miles; pop. (estimated), 20,198,840.

NIAG'ARA. A river of North America, separating Ontario from the state of New York, and conveying the waters of Lake Erie into Lake Ontario. It is 33½ miles long, and varies in breadth from 1 to 4 miles, being about the former where it issues from Lake Erie, near the city of Buffalo. It is occasionally interspersed with low wooded islands, the largest of which, Grand Island, has an area of 17,000 acres. The total descent in the river's course between the two lakes is 331 feet.

About 15 miles from Lake Erie a sudden narrowing and descent in the channel causes what are called the Rapids, below which the river, here divided by Goat Island, is precipitated over the celebrated falls. The rush of the river is such that the water is shot a clear 40 yards from the cliff, leaving a narrow pathway for a short distance below for the adventurous. The cataract on the south side of the island, called the American Fall, is 165 feet high, width 1400 feet; that on the Canadian side, called the Great or Horse-shoe Fall, is 158 feet high, width 2600 feet.

Below the falls the river rushes with great velocity down the sloping bottom of a narrow chasm for a distance of 7 miles. About 3 miles below the falls a sudden turn in the channel causes the water to whirl in a vast circular basin before renewing its journey. Logs and other floating material sometimes continue whirling here for many days. The water is gradually wearing away the rock, so that the falls are moving slowly backwards at the rate of 5 feet a year. About a furlong below the falls is a steel arch bridge (main span, 840 feet) for an electric tramway and other traffic; lower down are a cantilever bridge and a steel arch bridge carrying railway lines. Special areas are reserved as public parks on both sides. The falls now supply a great amount of water-power, and electricity is generated on a great scale. On the American side is the city of Niagara Falls (pop 1930, 75,460), and opposite is the Canadian city of the same name.

NIAM-NIAM (properly **A-ZANDEH**). A negroid people in Central Africa, on the watershed north of the Welle (Uele) River, South-Eastern Sudan. The name Niam-Niam is a Dinka word for great eaters. The Niam-Niam are a hunting people, and are of a compact and powerful build, with long nose, small mouth, broad lips, and reddish-brown or copper-coloured skin. Apparently at a comparatively recent period they wandered from the west to their present habitation, and made themselves masters of the country. They have a well-founded reputation for cannibalism.

NIAS. A Dutch island in the Malay Archipelago, lying west of Sumatra. The people are of Malay extraction. Rice, sugar, and pepper are grown extensively. Area 1800 sq. miles; pop. estimated at 200,000.

NIBELUNGENLIED (nē'bė-lung-ėn-lēt; "Lay of the Nibelungen"). German epic written in the Middle High German dialect, and dating from about the twelfth century. It is divided into thirty-nine sections, contains some 6000 lines, and is constructed in four-lined rhymed stanzas.

The tale, briefly told, is this: Kriemhild lives with her brother Gunther, King of Burgundy, at Worms. To his court comes Siegfried, son of Siegemund, King of the Netherlands. This Siegfried is possessed of the Nibelungen gold hoard, a magic sword, a cloak of darkness, besides great strength and courage. Thus equipped he comes to the court and wins the love of Kriemhild.

In gratitude for his success Siegfried undertakes to assist Gunther, the brother of his bride, in his efforts to win the hand of Brunhild, an Icelandic princess. Together they sail for the far north, and there Gunther succeeds, with the help of Siegfried's cloak of darkness, in winning the three test games of skill which the lady played with him. Still on the bridal night the princess mocked at Gunther her husband, wrestled with him, bound him, and hung him up scornfully against the wall. But the next night Gunther, with the invisible help of his friend Siegfried, overcomes the bride, and the latter carries away her girdle and ring. Siegfried and his wife Kriemhild next appear on a visit to the Burgundian court at Worms, where Gunther the king now resides with his wife Brunhild.

While there the two ladies quarrel, and in her rage Kriemhild taunts Brunhild with having had dealings with her husband Siegfried, and in proof thereof she produces the ring and girdle which he took from her chamber on the bridal night. Brunhild bitterly resents this calumny and meditates vengeance. This she accomplishes by the hand of Hagen, one of her husband's warriors, who slays Siegfried in his sleep. With rage and grief in her heart the widowed Kriemhild broods over the possibility of revenge.

Thirteen years pass, and then Kriemhild marries Etzel, King of the Huns. Again thirteen years pass, and then at her instigation Etzel invites Gunther and Hagen with 10,000 warriors to visit the capital of the Huns. This they accept, and while they are seated at a great feast the Burgundians are all massacred by the Huns, with the exception of Gunther and Hagen.

These two are delivered up to Kriemhild, who completes her vengeance by slaying them both, while she in her turn is killed by a Hunnish warrior who is enraged at her cruelty. This epic has been produced in modern German by Simrock, Bartsch, and Gerlach, and translated into English by Lettsom, Birch and Needler, while a resumé will be found in one of Carlyle's miscellanies.—Cf. F. E. Sandbach, *The Nibelungenlied and Gudrun in England and America.*

NICÆ'A (modern **ISNIK**). An ancient city of Asia Minor, the capital of Bithynia, founded by Antigonus, and renowned as the seat of the second Œcumenical Council assembled by Constantine in A.D. 325. At this council the nucleus of the Nicene creed was promulgated. After the foundation of the Latin Empire in Constantinople (1204), Theodorus Lascaris made Nicæa the capital of his empire, but it gave place to Constantinople on the recovery of that city by the Greek emperors (1261), and fell finally to the Turks in 1333.

NICARAG'UA. A republic of Central America, between Honduras (north) and Costa Rica (south), having coast-lines on both the Atlantic (Caribbean Sea, 300 miles) and the Pacific (200 miles).

General.—Most of Northern Nicaragua is from 2000 to 3000 feet above sea-level, and on it rises a series of volcanoes, of which Consequina, on the Gulf of Fonseca, is famous for its tremendous eruption of 1835. There is a wide eastern coastal plain known as the Mosquito Coast (q.v.). The uplands of Nicaragua end to the south and southwest on the edge of a depression which begins on the Pacific side in the Gulf of Fonseca, and is continued by the valleys of Lakes Managua and Nicaragua and the Rio San Juan de Nicaragua to the Caribbean. This depression forms the lowest valley across America.

The Cordillera de los Andes rises to the east of the depression and flanks the plateaux which slope gradually from the main Cordillera to the Caribbean. Among rivers are the Segovia, forming part of the Honduras-Nicaragua frontier, the Hueso, Rio Grande, Bluefield, and Rama, but the San Juan from Lake Nicaragua is the only one of any importance for navigation.

Towns.—Managua, on the southern shores of Lake Managua is the capital and seat of government pop. 1926, 32,536); it was damaged by earthquake in 1931 but is being rebuilt; other towns are León, a former capital (23,565); Granada (18,066); and Matagalpa (10,271). Corinto and S. Juan del Sur are the two seaports of Western Nicaragua, and through them pass 86 per cent. of the exports. Bluefields is the principal Atlantic port.

Communications.—Roads are few and bad. There are 150 miles of motor roads and 200 miles of cart roads. The chief railway (159 miles) is the Pacific Railroad of Nicaragua, from Corinto to León, Managua, Granada, and Diriamba (pop. 6151), with branches to El Viejo and Monotombo; a further 55 miles are under construction from León to El Sauce, and from San Jorge to San Juan del Sur. This line is owned partly by the United States Government, who hold 49 per cent. of the stock. The Pan-American Airways have a bi-weekly service connecting Managua with the United States and the Central America republics. The Tropical Radio Telegraph Company have stations at Managua, Bluefields, and Cabo Gracias. There are also stations at Bragman's Bluff, El Crallo, and Rio Grande.

Social Conditions.—The people of Western Nicaragua are of mixed Spanish-Indian extraction, with a proportion of full-blood in both classes. In the eastern half the inhabitants are mainly Mosquito and Lambo Indians, West Indian negroes, and Americans. Spanish is the principal language. Roman Catholicism is predominant, but all religions are tolerated, and none are State-aided. There is an archbishopric of Nicaragua with see at Managua, and three bishoprics of León, Granada, and Matagalpa, the Bishop of Matagalpa being coadjutor to the Archbishop at Managua. The army was disbanded in 1927, all arms being handed over to a National Guard of about 2000 men.

Education.—Elementary education is free and compulsory. About 60 per cent. of the population are illiterate. All secondary schools are private, and secondary education is neither compulsory nor free. The schools were closed after the earthquake of 1931, and are being opened (1933) as the finances of the Republic allow. There are universities at Managua, León, and Granada, also a number of State normal schools.

Currency.—The monetary unit is nominally the gold *cordoba* ; other coins are the silver *cordoba*, 10 cent, 5 cent (copper-nickel), 1 cent (copper-zinc), and ½ cent pieces, and paper *cordobas*. The metric system of weights and measures is in use.

Climate.—The altitude of Nicaragua ensures a fairly mild, healthy climate. In the tropical coastal belt there are wet seasons between May and November on the Pacific side, and from June to December on the Atlantic.

Production.—Farming, timber, and mining are the chief sources of wealth, and the republic is divided into two productive regions, east and west.

Agriculture.—Bananas, coco-nuts, plantains, oranges, pineapples, yucca, rice and wheat (Nueva Segovia district), tobacco (Masaya), coffee, sugar-cane, cacao, corn, beans, dairy-farming, butter and cheese.

Forestry.—Mahogany, cedar, dyewoods, and gums.

Minerals.—Gold, silver, copper, and precious stones.

Forests are infested with jaguar, puma, and ocelot. Alligators swim in lake and river ; a kind of fresh-water shark inhabits Lake Nicaragua ; vultures, toucans, and humming-birds are abundant. Among snakes are the python, rattlesnake, and coral.

Government.—The present Constitution of Nicaragua came into operation in April 1913, and invests the executive power with a President appointed for four years. Legislative power is vested in a Congress, comprising 43 Deputies, elected by universal suffrage for four years (Lower House), and 24 Senators, elected for six years (Upper House). The President exercises his functions through a Council, comprising Ministers for Foreign Affairs and Public Instruction, Finance, Interior, Justice and Police, War and Marine, and Public Works. For local government the republic is divided into 13 departments and 2 comarcas, each under its own political and military administrator. In 1924 a new electoral law was devised and was applied to the presidential election of that year, when a Conservative-Republican President (Sr. Carlos Solorzano) was elected.

Since becoming independent of Spain in 1821 Nicaragua has had a stormy history. There was a revolution in 1926, and civil war continued throughout 1927, the U.S.A. taking an active part in the conflict. For 20 years (1912-32), save for a brief interval in 1925-6, Nicaragua was under the virtual control of the United States, whose intervention kept a Conservative government in power there until 1925. Under this regime U.S. controlled the customs, the railways, and the bank, and was given (in 1914) the right to construct the Nicaraguan Canal (q.v.). America's intervention ceased in 1932 following the election of that year. Area of republic, 51,660 sq. miles ; pop. by 1920 census, 638,119 (of which 75 per cent. are located on the western side). The estimated pop. in 1930 was 750,000. *See* MOSQUITO TERRITORY. — BIBLIOGRAPHY : F. Palmer, *Central America and its Problems* ; S. J. Bernardo Portas, *Compendio de la historia de Nicaragua.*

NICARAGUA. A lake of Nicaragua, Central America ; length, 100 miles ; breadth, 45 miles ; depth, 15 to 250 feet ; altitude, 118 feet. It discharges through the Rio San Juan to the Caribbean. At its north-western extremity it is connected by the Rio Penaloya with Lake Managua (length, 30 miles ; area, about 600 sq. miles), whose waters it receives, and which once formed a part of Lake Nicaragua. On the Island of Ometepe (Lake Niçaragua) are the twin-peaks Ometepe (5643 feet) and Madera.

NICARAGUA CANAL. A proposed Nicaraguan ship-canal between the Caribbean and the Pacific Ocean. The proposal was first mooted in 1849, but disputes with Great Britain, who then owned the proposed Caribbean entry (on the Mosquito Coast), hindered practical progress, and the Panama route was decided upon by an International Congress at Paris in 1879. The route was purchased by the U.S.A. in 1916 (the Canal route being alienated to them for a cash payment of 3,000.000 dollars) along with the Pacific naval base in the Bay of Fonseca and Corn Island on the Atlantic. The canal scheme is not likely to materialize because of the Panama Canal.

NICCOLITE. *See* COPPER NICKEL.

NICE (nēs ; It. *Nizza* ; ancient **Nicæa**). A Riviera city and seaport of France, on the Baie des Anges, an arm of the Mediterranean, capital of the department of Alpes Maritimes. The original town was clustered round a hill near the shore, crowned by a strong castle. The new city lies to the west and north of this, on the right bank of the Paillon.

Nice is much resorted to as a health resort during winter. The climate is mild, the mean temperature being 60° F. ; but the changes of wind are sudden, especially in spring. There is an annual carnival in April, and also an aviation meeting. Nice is the Greek Nicæa, founded by Phocæans from Marseilles in the fourth century B.C. It belonged to Sardinia from 1814 to 1860, when it was ceded to France. Both Garibaldi and Masséna were natives of the district. Pop. (1931), 219,549.

NICE, Councils of. Ecclesiastical councils held at Nice or Nicæa, in Asia Minor, in A.D. 325 and 787. The object of the first Council of Nice, which was convened by Constantine, was to settle the controversies which had arisen in regard to the doctrine of the Trinity. The session lasted about two months. A creed was adopted by the council in its later form known as the Nicene Creed (q.v.). The council of 787 was summoned by the Empress Irene, with the concurrence of the Pope, and it decreed that images were to be used as aids to devotion.

NICENE CREED. A summary of Christian faith adopted by the Council of Nice against Arianism A.D. 325, altered and confirmed by the Council of Constantinople A.D. 381. Its characteristics are the insertion of the term " of one substance with the Father," directed against the Arian heresy ; the insertion of the words " and the Son " ; and the omission of the clause " He descended into Hell." It is recited both in the Roman Catholic and in the Anglican Church liturgies. The " Filioque " clause, which stated that the Holy Ghost proceeded from the Father and the Son, was the chief cause of disagreement between the Eastern and the Western Churches.

NICHOL, John Pringle. Astronomer, born 1804 in Brechin, Forfarshire, died 1859. Licensed for the Scottish Church, he turned his attention to astronomy, and acquired so much reputation that in 1836 he was appointed professor of astronomy in Glasgow University. Among Dr, Nichol's literary works may be mentioned : *The Architecture of the Heavens* (1838), *Contemplations on the Solar System* (1838), *The Stellar Universe* (1848), and the *Planetary System* (1851). He likewise edited a *Cyclopædia of Physical Sciences*, published in 1857.

NICHOLAS, St. Bishop of Myra, in Lycia, is believed to have lived under Diocletian and Constantine, and to have suffered persecution under the former ; but little is known of his life. His feast-day in the Roman calendar is 6th Dec. ; he is the patron saint of poor maidens, sailors, travellers, merchants, and children (Santa Klaus), and is one of the most popular saints in the Greek Church.

NICHOLAS I. (Nikolai Pavlovitsh). Tsar of Russia, third son of Paul I., born 1796, died 1855. He ascended the throne in 1825. He made war with Persia in 1827-28 ; joined in the Treaty of London, which secured the independence of Greece ; and made one of the allied powers who destroyed the Turkish fleet at Navarino in 1827. This affair led to war between Russia and Turkey, in which the latter was defeated, paid indemnity, and signed the treaty of peace at Adrianople in 1829. Nicholas suppressed the Polish insurrection which broke out in the following year with relentless severity.

In 1848 he assisted Austria with an army corps in putting down the rising in Hungary. Early in 1852 began the Russian effort to take over the holy places and assume the protectorate of the Christians in Palestine. This led to the Crimean War, and Nicholas is said to have boasted that he had two generals who would conquer the world—General January and General

February. However, he fell a victim to his own officers, and died of a chill ere he reached the scene of operations.

NICHOLAS II. Tsar of Russia and the last of the Romanovs, was born on 6th May, 1868, the son of Alexander III. by Maria Feodorovna. His early education was supervised by an English tutor, and his military training was undertaken by General Danilovitsh. Upon the death of his elder brother George, he automatically became Tsarevitsh, but neither his capabilities nor his education were such as to fit him for the assumption of supreme power in the vast empire of Holy Russia, to which he succeeded on 1st Nov., 1894.

On 26th Nov., 1894, he married Princess Alix of Hesse, of German descent on her father's side, and of English descent on the side of her mother, Princess Alice, the daughter of Queen Victoria; the empress embracing Orthodoxy, and assuming the title of Alexandra Feodorovna. She was undoubtedly the evil genius of the Russian Empire, and although she never betrayed imperial secrets to Germany, as has frequently been suggested, and was in fact a rabid anti-Hohenzollern, her hysterical nature and nervous temperament threw her into the arms of the false prophet Rasputin, who obtained a vast influence on the Tsarevitsh Alexis, and who sought to make and to depose ministers and counsellors, and actually became the hidden ruler of all Russia.

On the outbreak of the European War the Tsăr's disposition towards fatalistic mysticism, his apathy towards social reforms demanded by the progressive spirit of the times, and his feeble grasp upon foreign politics and the trend of home affairs, daily became more evident. Russia at this crisis demanded a firm and resolute leader for the working out of her political salvation, but unfortunately the Tsar Nicholas was weak. He offered little resistance to the Revolution of 1917, and in March, when he received a telegram at his army headquarters outlining the state of affairs at Petrograd and demanding his abdication, he resigned the throne with composure to the Grand Duke Mikhail rather than expose the Tsarevitsh Alexis to the storm of revolutionary politics.

The Grand Duke Mikhail refused to accept the Tsardom, and the emperor was transferred, a prisoner, from Tsarskoe Selo to Tobolsk in company with the empress, the Tsarevitsh, the Grand Duchess Tatiana, to whom rumour had already promised a place on the Royal House of Windsor, and her three sisters. In 1918 they were removed to Ekaterinburg by the Bolsheviki, and were jailed in a three-roomed house under the guardianship of one Yurkovsky, a Jew inspired by all the fanaticism of a downtrodden race against the Romanovs, to whom he attributed the oppression which for many years indelibly stamped the peasant and the artisan of Imperial Russia.

The advance of Koltchak caused the greatest anxiety to the Moscow Soviet, who anticipated a strong "White" effort to release the imperial family. In July the Ekaterinburg Soviet placed their signatures to the order for the execution of the prisoners, and entrusted the task to Yurkovsky. On the night of 16th July, 1918, the imperial family were awakened, huddled into a cellar, and by torchlight the sentence was read; all the members of the unhappy family were killed by rifle-fire, the ex-Tsar himself, it is alleged, by Youkovsky, who fired a revolver. A few days later, it is stated, the bodies were removed outside Ekaterinburg and destroyed by fire.

NICHOLAS I. King of Montenegro, was born in 1841, educated at Paris and Trieste, and succeeded his uncle Danilo II. in 1860. He belonged to the House of Petrovitsh-Njegosh, in which family the prince-bishopric had been hereditary since 1696, and was handed down from uncle to nephew. As a member of the "Black Clergy" celibacy was an essential condition of the *vladika* or prince-bishop, but this was ignored by Danilo II., who married and declared his principality hereditary by direct descent in the male line. Nicholas I. was the son of Mirko Petrovitsh, brother of Danilo II., and his father resigned all claims to the throne in his favour.

As ruler he was an ardent reformer in matters civil, military, and educational, and (in 1878) he obtained from the Powers recognition of Montenegrin independence. In 1910 he assumed the title of king, much against the wishes of his subjects, and his unsuccessful wars entirely alienated the sympathy of Montenegro from the Royal House. During the European War Nicholas threw in his lot with the Allies, was forced to abandon his country, and was eventually deposed, Montenegro being merged in the Serb-Croat-Slovene Kingdom (Yugo-Slavia). Even before his deposition the aged monarch was sarcastically apostrophised as "Nicholas the first and Petrovitsh the last." He died at Antibes on 1st March, 1921, and is buried at San Remo. *See* MONTENEGRO.

NICHOLAS (Nikolai Nikolaivitsh). Russian Grand-Duke, was born in 1856, the grandson of Tsar Nicholas I., and a first cousin of the Tsar Alexander III. He served in the Russo-Turkish War (1877), and subsequently was appointed to important cavalry commands, becoming Inspector-General of Russian Cavalry in 1895. In this capacity his skill as a soldier and his ability as an organizer were constantly demonstrated. He made a clean sweep of everything, good or bad, and brought the Russian cavalry up to a standard of efficiency that made it, as a body, one of the finest in the world.

During the Revolution of 1905 he joined the newly created Council of National Defence, and was appointed to command the Imperial Guards and the St. Petersburg (Petrograd) military district. On the outbreak of the European War, the Grand-Duke Nicholas was hastily summoned to supreme command on the Eastern Front, and although handicapped by the deployment of the army before his arrival, and the co-operation of generals of whom he knew but little and who knew but little themselves, his strategy was the one factor that saved the Russian armies from a Waterloo or a Sedan in the retirement from the Narew-Vistula-San-Carpathians salient of 1915.

His new positions were maintained throughout 1916 and 1917 by the Tsar, who assumed command in Aug., 1915, the Grand-Duke Nicholas becoming Governor-General and Commander-in-Chief in the Caucasus. Here, in co-operation with Yudenitsh, he achieved considerable success in advances against Trebizond and Erzerum, thus relieving, incidentally, the pressure on the British forces in the East. On the collapse of the empire (1917) he retired to the Crimea, but emigrated (1918) and went to live near Paris (1919). He died in 1929.

NI'CIAS. Athenian statesman and general, who displayed much skill and activity in the time of the Peloponnesian War. He was put to death after the ill-success of his expedition to Sicily (414 B.C.).

NICKEL. A lustrous silver-white metal of great hardness, taking a very fine polish, magnetic, and when perfectly pure, malleable and ductile; symbol, Ni; atomic weight, 58·68. It can be rolled into sheets and drawn into wire, and melts at 1452° C. It is chiefly found in the United States, Canada (Sudbury district of Ontario), New Caledonia, and Germany.

Nickel has become an object of considerable importance, and is extracted by several processes, including smelting, wet methods, and a process in which gaseous nickel carbonyl is produced, known as the Mond process. The salts of nickel are mostly of a grass-green colour, and the ammoniacal solution of its oxide is deep blue. Nickel mixed with brass in varying proportions is now well known and largely used as German silver or nickel silver. (*See* GERMAN SILVER.)

Another important use of the metal is for coating articles by the electroplate process. (*See* ELECTRO-PLATING.) Nickel is also largely used in the manufacture of special steels, such as nickel steel and nickel-chrome steel, which have properties very valuable for certain engineering purposes.

NICKEL-GLANCE, or GERSDORFFITE. A greyish-white, massive, and granular ore of nickel, on the average consisting of 35·5 nickel, 45·2 arsenic, and 19·3 sulphur, part of the nickel being sometimes replaced by iron or cobalt. In crystalline form it resembles pyrite.

NICKEL-PLATING. The process by which a coating of nickel is placed upon another metal, and the essentials of the process, as in electroplating, are a proper solution of the metal and a suitable electric current. *See* ELECTRO-PLATING.

NICOBAR ISLANDS. A British archipelago of twelve inhabited and nine uninhabited islands in the Bay of Bengal, lying between Sumatra and the Andamans, and extending over a length of 163 miles. They are of volcanic origin. Total area, 635 sq. miles. In 1931 there were 9481 Nicobarese. The islands are divided into three groups, Northern, Central, and Southern, the main islands in each being Car Nicobar, Camorta with Nankauri, and Great Nicobar.

The central group of four islands forms the magnificent natural harbour of Nankauri. Coco-nuts are the stable commodity in which the Nicobarese have traded for upwards of 1500 years. The production is estimated at from 6 to 15 million nuts per annum, one-half coming from Car Nicobar. Much copra is made and exported. There is no money as such, the coco-nut being the standard of currency.

The climate is tropical and generally unhealthy for Europeans. English and Hindustani are fairly well understood. The Nicobarese are as light-skinned as the Burmese, and are very intelligent, with a great facility for figures and a *penchant* for languages, and they present a curious example of semi-civilization of an effective type which has been evolved without undergoing much influence from more highly civilized races.

The Nicobars are mentioned by writers from Ptolemy onwards, and there is a persistent legend of the natives having tails. The Danes and Austrians occupied the group, but it lay abandoned until the British formally took possession in 1869, and it is now under the Chief Commissioner of the Andamans and Nicobars. Two Agencies are maintained, one at Car Nicobar and the other at Camorta (Nankauri).—Cf. H. S. Montgomerie, *Nicobar Islands* (in the *Geographical Journal* for Jan., 1922).

NICOLA'ITANS. A sect in the early Christian Church, mentioned in Rev. ii. 6. They are characterized as inclining to licentious and pagan practices, and their tenets and practices have been compared to the teaching of Balaam. The sect is supposed to have been founded by Nicolas, the proselyte of Antioch, one of the seven deacons, but this theory has been refuted.

NICOSI'A. A city of Sicily, in the province of Catania. It is the see of

Street in Nicosia

a bishop, and has a Norman cathedral. There are sulphur-springs and salt-mines in the neighbourhood. Pop. 16,000.

NICOSI'A, or LEFKOSI'A. The capital of Cyprus, situated in the centre of the island. Its lofty walls and bastions still present an imposing appearance, and it has a number of mosques and Greek churches, and the residence of the High Commissioner. It has manufactures of silk, cotton, leather. Nicosia was one of the centres of disturbance in the Cypriot rebellion of 1931. Pop. (1931), 23,677.

NIC'OTINE. An alkaloid occurring in the tobacco plant, *Nicotiana Tabacum.* Tobacco contains from 1 to 8 per cent. of nicotine in the form of salts of malic and citric acid, obtainable from an aqueous extract of the tobacco by heating with an alkali and steam-distilling. It is a colourless, hygroscopic, highly poisonous liquid with an unpleasant odour, and oxidizes in air, acquiring a brown colour. An impure nicotine extract is sometimes used as an insecticide.

NICTHEROY. A city of Brazil, capital of the state of Rio de Janeiro, on the north shore of the Bay of Rio de Janeiro. Icaratry, a suburb, is a popular sea-bathing resort. Praia Grande is the commercial quarter. Flannels, tobacco, soaps, and spirits are manufactured. Pop. (1930), 108,233.

NICTITATING MEMBRANE, or **"THIRD EYELID."** A thin membrane by which the process of winking is performed in certain animals, and which covers and protects the eyes from dust or from too much light. It is chiefly found in birds and fishes, and is represented in a rudimentary condition in man, and higher mammals generally, by the "semilunar folds," situated at the inner or nasal angle of the eye.

NIEBUHR (nē'bör), **Barthold Georg.** Historian, born at Copenhagen 1776, died at Bonn 1831. He studied law at Göttingen, and philosophy at the University of Kiel; became in 1796 private secretary to the Danish Minister of Finance, and soon after under-librarian in the royal library of Copenhagen. In 1798 he visited England and attended the University of Edinburgh for one session. Having been appointed historiographer-royal, he delivered lectures on Roman history in the University of Berlin, and in 1811 published them in two volumes.

In 1816 he was appointed Prussian minister to the Papal court at Rome, and there he resided until 1822, chiefly occupied in historical research. At the latter date he returned to Bonn and became adjunct professor of ancient history at the university. Here he continued his *Roman History*, the third volume of which appeared after his death. He also superintended the *Corpus Scriptorum Byzantinorum*, and published various archæological and philological treatises. His *Roman History* covered only the period down to the first Punic War, but introduced a new era in the study of Roman antiquity.

NIEL (ni-el), **Adolphe.** French marshal, born 1802, died 1869. He was educated at the École Polytechnique, Paris, and the Military School, Metz; took part in the expedition against Constantine in Algeria; assisted as head of the staff of engineers at the siege of Rome in 1849 during the revolutionary movement under Garibaldi; commanded the engineers and planned the operations against Sebastopol in 1854-55; distinguished himself in the Italian campaign of 1859, and was thereafter made a marshal of France by Napoleon III.

NIEMEN, or **MEMEL.** A large river in Russia, Lithuania, and East Prussia. It rises in the government of Minsk, flows at first west past the town of Grodno, where it becomes navigable; then north; then again west, separating Kovno and Poland; and finally enters East Prussia, passes Tilsit, and falls into the Kurisches Haff. It is 640 miles in length, and is navigable as far as Grodno, 400 miles. The Niemen is of considerable commercial importance, and was a strategic point during the European War, the Russians having retreated to this river in 1914 and in 1915.

NIETZSCHE, Friedrich. German philosopher and poet, born at Röcken, near Lützen, in Prussian Saxony, 15th Oct., 1844, died insane at Weimar, 25th Aug., 1900. He was of remote Polish descent, he himself always emphasizing the fact that he was a noble Pole and not a German. The son of a pastor, he was educated at Naumburg and Pforta, and afterwards studied at the Universities of Bonn and Leipzig. Through the influence of his teacher Ritschl he was appointed professor of classical philology at Basel in 1869. Here he lectured for ten years, until he was compelled to resign his lectureship on account of ill-health.

A pension granted him by the university, together with a small private income, enabled him to wander about Europe and to live in places most suitable for his health. He spent his time mostly in the Engadine and the Piviera. In Jan., 1889, at Turin, he became suddenly insane, and thus remained until his death. Nietzsche never elaborated a system of philosophy, although he intended to do so in his book *The Will to Power*, which remained fragmentary. Essentially a poet, he considered philosophy to be a constant criticism of life and thought. Divested of the paradoxical tone which his writings assume, his main ideas may be stated to be as follows: the impulse dominating all living beings, including man, is the will to live, that is to obtain power and domination, and to overcome all obstacles which make life difficult.

The endeavour of the human race should be to rise still higher above the lower races of animals, from which it had emerged. Just as man had evolved from the ape, so the man of the future, the super-man, will evolve from the ape-man of the present, humanity being only a transition and not a goal. He imagined the super-man as a complete man in whom beauty and strength, intellectuality and nobility of character, will-power and profundity are united, a man possessed of a big heart and a high spirit. The code of morality of these master-men will differ from the morality of the herd, the slave-morality, for morality is only an expedient which a race in its struggle for life found useful, and which can and should be modified by the super-men.

Intensely interested in morality and ethics, he attacked the traditional moral standards, and, without actually condemning love, pity, and sympathy, as is erroneously supposed, he suggested an innovation of moral conceptions. This innovation he called *The Transvaluation of Values*. Nietzsche thus preached an intense individualism, an affirmation of life and a love of life. He sang a hymn in praise of the creative faculty, the joy of life, and the healthy sense of existence. He admired the Greek ideal and conception of life. The Greeks, he said, loved not only beauty, but also strength and power, and among them there was a harmony between body and soul, a Dionysian exuberance and enthusiasm.

This conception of the Greek genius, with which his artistic soul was intoxicated, the distinction between the Dionysian and the Apollonian elements, he elaborated in his book *The Birth of Tragedy* (1872). Captivated by Darwinism, by the theories of evolution, of natural selection, and of struggle and survival of the fittest, he built upon these his theory of the new race, the new aristocracy of the future, the complete men, the masters and rulers.

The teaching of Nietzsche exercised an immense influence upon the literature of the last decade of the nineteenth and the beginning of the twentieth century. It can be traced in the works of Ibsen and Gorky, of Strindberg and Przybyszewski, of Sudermann and D'Annunzio, as well as in those of G. B. Shaw. Nietzsche's works include: *The Birth of Tragedy* (1872); *Human, All Too Human* (1878); *The Dawn of Day* (1881); *The Joyous Wisdom* (1882); *Thus Spake Zarathustra* (1883-84); *Beyond Good and Evil* (1886); *The Genealogy of Morals* (1887); *The Twilight of the Idols* (1889); and *Ecce Homo*, published in 1908.—BIBLIOGRAPHY: *Works*, English translation, edited by Oscar Levy (18 vols.); H. L. Mencken, *The Philosophy of Nietzsche*; Chatterton-Hill, *The Philosophy of Nietzsche*; A. Fouillée, *Nietzsche et l'Immoralisme*; H. Lichtenberger, *La Philosophie de Nietzsche*; A. Ludovici, *Who is to be Master of the World?*

NIEUPORT (Fl. *Nieuwpoort*). A town of Belgium, province of Flanders, on the Yser. It is connected by canal with Furnes. Nieuport played an important part during the European War (battle of the Yser). In 1920 it was awarded the Croix de Guerre. Pop. 4000.

NIÈVRE (nyāvr). A department of Central France, watered by the Loire, Nièvre, Allier, Cure, Yonne, and Aron; area, 2658 sq. miles. It is generally hilly, produces some good wine, and has nearly a third of its surface afforested. Minerals include iron and coal. Nevers is the capital; other towns are Château Chinon, Clamency, and Fourchambault. Nièvre forms a part of pre-Revolutionary Nivernais. Pop. (1931), 255,195.

NIGELLA. Fennel-flower, or love-in-a-mist, a genus of annual plants, nat. ord. Ranunculaceæ, comprising some twenty species, with finely-cut leaves resembling those of fennel. The seeds of *N. sativa*, a native of Southern Europe and the Levant, are pungent and aromatic, and are used as seasoning in Eastern countries, sometimes also in Europe. Some species are cultivated for their flowers, such as *N. damascena*, whose flowers are pale blue.

NIGER. A river of West Africa, and the third of that continent, rises on the inside of the coastal rampart in the Futa Jallon Hills (French Guinea), flows as far as Timbuktu, and then, instead of following its ancient course through the Sahara to the Gulf of Gabes, turns completely round, breaks through the rampart at Bussa, and reaches the sea (Gulf of Guinea) on the coast it started from after a course of 2600 miles. It is of considerable value as a commercial highway, for its main fall from 2764 feet at its source to 1000 feet above sea-level, where it receives the Tankisso tributary, takes place in the first 260 miles of its course. Baro is at the head of ocean navigation.

Below Segu, the Niger enters an old lake floor, over which it spreads in the form of a delta, the branches of which collect in the Debo Swamp. Formerly this lake extended far into the Sahara, and had, at an earlier date, an exit through the Sahara to Algeria and the Mediterranean. At Kabara, the port of Timbuktu, the river comes up against the Saharan plateau, and flows due east at the foot of it for 250 miles, contracting to a stream hardly 100 yards across.

From here the Niger flows southeast to the granite-bar of Bussa that it has worn down so much that this impediment no longer guards the inland water from the encroachment of the coastal streams. Between Bussa and Rabba there are several rapids but no tributaries of any size enter the river from Kabara to Rabba, and as a result of loss by evaporation and soakage the Niger is not as big as its tributary, the Benue, at their confluence.

The delta commences at Abo, 80 miles from the sea, and although the Niger discharges a larger volume of water than the Nile it reaches the Atlantic by so many outlets, scattered along 250 miles of coast; that its true mouth was uncertain until the brothers Lander (1830) descended the river from Bussa to the Sea. Mungo Park lost his life in the rapids at Bussa (1805).

NIGER COLONY. A colony of French West Africa comprising that part of the French Sudan which from 1912 to 1920 was a military territory, and which lies east of Upper Volta and north of Dahomey and Nigeria. The Niger, on which stands Zinder, the capital, is the western boundary. The colony is desolate in the north, wooded in the centre, and has rich pasture-lands in the south. Water is scarce everywhere. In 1920 a civil administration was set up, and in 1922 it was erected into a colony. Area, 455,405 sq. miles; pop. (1931), 1,542,714.

NIGERIA. A British West African colony and protectorate bounded by the Gulf of Guinea, the Cameroons (the British mandated part of which is, for administrative purposes, attached to Nigeria), French West

1 Most of the great African rivers have been diverted from their original courses.

Africa, and Dahomey. Area, c. 372,674 sq. miles; pop. (1931), 19,928,171. The chief town and port and the seat of government is Lagos, and other ports are Forcados, Akassa, Brass, Bonny, Port Harcourt, and Calabar.

In the Southern Provinces the chief inland places are Abbeokuta, Ibadan, and Benin, and in the Northern Provinces the chief places are Kaduna (the administrative centre), Bussa, Lokoja, Kano, and Yola. The coasts are low, swampy, and mangrove-fringed, with numerous creeks (many of them mouths of the Niger) and rivers. Behind the coastal strip is a broad densely-forested belt which opens into a zone of hills and park-lands. The extreme north, beyond the Niger and the Benue, the two great rivers, consists of a great plateau on which the desert is slowly encroaching.

Lagos, Nigeria

Religion and Education.—In the Northern Provinces Mahommedanism is the prevailing religion, with Kano (q.v.) as its centre, and embraces the Hausa, Fulani, and other tribes. Paganism predominates in parts, but both Protestant and Roman Catholic missions are established. Education follows the principles adopted for the Anglo-Egyptian Sudan and is strictly secular, religious teaching being entirely optional. The principal schools are located at Kano. In the Southern Provinces there are four British Protestant societies, and two French Roman Catholic societies who have established churches and stations. Education is progressive, and there is an elementary and secondary school system with a residential school at Bonny, a mission grammar-school at Lagos, and a high school at Calabar.

Justice.—The Supreme Court for both provinces is under a Chief Justice of Nigeria; each province has a court comprising the Resident and his assistant, and there are Mahommedan courts and Judicial Councils for the pagans. Cantonments, with Station Magistrates, are located at Kano, Kaduna, Lokoja, Port Harcourt, and Zaria. No child born after 1st Jan., 1900, may be a slave, and no free person may be enslaved, but slavery still exists in the Northern Provinces, although it has been shorn of most of its abuses and has practically died a natural death.

Great Britain entered Nigeria solely on the question of the manumission of slaves. A fixed policy of liberation of slaves was pursued and the evil has slowly but steadily been banished from Nigeria (though there are still slaves in some inaccessible parts).

Products.—The chief products are palm-oil and kernels, rubber, ground-nuts, shea-butter, cotton-lint, ivory, cocoa, kola-nuts, drugs, mahogany, etc. Tin, iron, silver, manganese, lead, coal (Udi coal-field,) etc., are the chief minerals.

Communication.—There is a western railway line from Lagos to Kano (704½ miles), with various branch lines; the extension from Kano to N'Guni was opened in 1930. This line is joined at Kaduna by the eastern line from Port Harcourt (569 miles). The eastern line was completed in 1926, except for the bridge across the Benue, on which work started in 1928. The rivers and creeks form excellent means of transport, and there are some splendid roads. There is a wireless station at Lagos.

Commerce.—In the north there is a great caravan trade with Kano as the emporium. In 1931 the total value of exports was £10,644,519, and of imports £6,744,199. The chief exports were palm kernels, palm-oil, tin ore, cocoa, hides and skins, cotton-lint, and ground-nuts. Liverpool has a large West African trade.

Currency.—Since 1913 West African silver coinage of 2*s*., 1*s*., 6*d*., and 3*d*. pieces has been in circulation, but there is also a nickel coinage of 1*d*., ½*d*., and $\frac{1}{10}$ of a penny pieces. Currency is controlled by the West African Currency Board which sits in London.

History.—The history of Nigeria revolves round slavery and the slave trade. At one time a number of "creeks," now known as mouths of the Niger, but then supposed to be independent rivers, became the "Oil Rivers," and upon their banks were established "factories" or trading-stations where palm-oil, shea-butter, ivory, and hardwoods were exported. In 1886 the Royal Niger Company was chartered and took over the administration of the country. At that time Nigeria was in the hands of the Fulah kingdom of Sokoto, established by the Sultan Othman Dan Fodio, a contemporary of Napoleon and equally successful in war. Independent kingdoms existed in Bornu (near Lake Chad) and Ilorin (in the Yoruba country, north of Lagos).

By 1851 Lagos was the centre of the West African slave trade, and the hinterland was devastated by terrible raids. Two of the Fulani states bordering on the Niger were subdued by the Company in 1897, and raiding in these territories at once ceased. During 1851 the King of Lagos appealed to the British against a usurper, and British naval forces restored him to the throne on condition that he suppressed the slave trade. He did so, but his son and successor was unable to control the activities of the slave dealers, and ceded his kingdom to Britain in 1861. By this means the greatest stronghold of slavery became a British colony in which individual liberty was free to all.

In 1899 the Company surrendered its charter, and on 1st Jan., 1900, its territories became the two protectorates of Northern and Southern Nigeria, the latter absorbing the Niger Coast Protectorate formed in 1893 from the Oil Rivers Protectorate (1885). The main task of Britain was the subjugation of the Hausa states in Northern Nigeria, which includes the negro state of Bornu (q.v.) and part of Borgu (q.v.). In 1906 the colony and protectorate of Lagos (q.v.) were added to Southern Nigeria, which became the colony and protectorate of Southern Nigeria, and in 1914 this was united to Northern Nigeria, the whole becoming the colony and protectorate of Nigeria.

The boundaries of the colony were readjusted, and the protectorate was divided into the Northern and Southern Provinces. There is a Governor and an Executive Council acting for colony and protectorate, and a Legislative Council for the colony and the Southern Provinces. The Governor legislates for the Northern Provinces. The Northern and the Southern Provinces have Lieutenant-Governors. Sir Donald C. Cameron has been Governor of the Colony and Protectorate since 1931, when he replaced Sir Graeme Thomson. *See* West Africa.

Bibliography: G. T. Basden, *Among the Ibos of Nigeria*; A. Schultze, *The Sultanate of Bornu* (translated by P. A. Bonton); A. H. Unwin, *West African Forests and Forestry*; *Handbook of Nigeria* (1924); Sir F. D. Lugard, *Report on the Amalgamation of Northern and Southern Nigeria*; E. H. L. Schwarz, *A South-African Geography*.

NIGHT-HAWK, or BULL-BAT. A species of goat-sucker or night-jar (*Chordiles virginiānus*), a bird universally known in the United States, 9½ inches in length and 23 inches in extent of wing. It flies in the morning and afternoon rather than at night. The general colour is mottled blackish brown and yellow above with brown bars below. It is a bird

Night-Hawk

of strong and vigorous flight, and its prey mostly consists of beetles and other large insects. Other American species are the "chuckwill's widow" (*Antrostomus carolinensis*) and the "whip-poor-will" (*A. vocifĕrus*), both of which, like the night-hawk, arrive in May, and leave the States in September or October.

NIGHT-HERON. A name given to several species of wading birds belonging to the genus Nycticorax and family Ardeidæ (herons). The species occur in Europe, Asia, Africa, and America, and the name is derived from their nocturnal habits, which, however, are less pronounced during the breeding season. The common European night-heron is the *Nycticŏrax griseus*, a bird well known in many parts of Southern Europe, especially in the region of the Lower Danube, but only occasionally seen in Britain. It is about 20 inches in length, and has three long narrow feathers proceeding from the nape of the neck, and hanging backwards, pure white in colour. The prevailing colours of the upper parts are blackish green and ashy grey, of the under parts straw colour. The food consists of worms, insects, molluscs, frogs, small fishes, etc.

NIGHTINGALE, Florence. Daughter of William Shore Nightingale, Embley Park, Hampshire, born at Florence 1820, died in 1910. At an early age she manifested a keen interest in suffering humanity, and from philanthropic motives she visited the chief military hospitals in Europe, and studied the chief nursing systems. During the Crimean War (1854) the hospital accommodation was found to be very defective, and Miss Nightingale promptly volunteered to organize a select band of nurses at Scutari.

The offer was accepted by the War Office, and within a week Miss Nightingale was on her way to the East, where she rendered invaluable service to the sick and wounded by her incessant labours in nursing and hospital reform. The strain, both mental and physical, which this work demanded permanently injured her health to a serious extent. A sum of £50,000 was raised by public

Florence Nightingale

subscription in recognition of her services, and this she devoted to the founding of an institution for training nurses, attached to St. Thomas's Hospital, London. The Order of Merit was conferred upon her in 1907. Her works include: *Notes on Hospitals* (1859), *Notes on Nursing* (1860), *On the Sanitary State of the Army in India* (1863), *Notes on Lying-in Institutions* (1871), and *Life or Death in India* (1873).—Cf. L. Strachey, *Eminent Victorians.*

NIGHTINGALE. A well-known perching bird (*Daulias luscinia*) of the thrush family. The nightingale sings at night, and its famed chant is the love-song of the male, which ceases when the female has hatched her brood. It is a native of many parts of Europe and Asia, and of the north of Africa. It is migratory, extending its summer migrations as far north as the south of Sweden. In England, where it appears about the middle of April, it is rather a local bird, some parts appearing to be quite unsuited to its habits; the northern counties are seldom visited, and in Scotland and Ireland it is unknown.

Nightingale (*Daulias luscinia*)

It feeds on caterpillars and other larvæ, frequents hedges and thickets, and builds its nest on the ground or near it, laying four or five eggs of a blue colour. The young are hatched in June, and are prepared to accompany their parents in their southward migration in August. It is solitary in its habits, and its colouring is very inconspicuous. Another species (*D. philomela*) is native to Europe east of the Rhine; and a third species (*D. hafizi*) ranges from the Caucasus through Persia and Turkestan.

NIGHTMARE. A state of oppression or feeling of suffocation which sometimes comes on during sleep, and is accompanied by a feeling of intense anxiety, fear, or horror, the sufferer feeling an enormous weight on his breast, and imagining that he is pursued by a phantom, monster, or wild beast, or threatened by some other danger from which he can make no exertion to escape. The sufferer wakens after a short time in a state of great terror, the body often covered with sweat. It is the result of the revival during sleep of some intensely emotional experience the memory of which is repressed during waking hours.

NIGHTSHADE. The English name of various species of plants, chiefly of the genus Solānum (to which the potato belongs). The woody nightshade or bittersweet (*S. dulcamāra*) and common or garden nightshade (*S. nigrum*) are British plants, the former growing in hedges and among bushes, and the latter in gardens, fields, and waste places. The roots and leaves of *S. Dulcamāra* are narcotic, and have been applied to various medicinal uses. The berries, if not absolutely poisonous, are dangerous. *S. nigrum* is fetid and narcotic, and has also been employed medicinally. *Deadly Nightshade* is *Atrŏpa Belladonna*. (*See* BELLADONNA.) For "Enchanter's Nightshade," *see* that article.

NIGRINE. A variety of rutile (mineral titanium dioxide), slightly more ferriferous than rutile, found in black grains or rolled pieces. Its ally *ilmenorutile* may contain 10 per cent. of iron peroxide.

NIHILISM (Lat. *nihil*, nothing). A term applied in metaphysics to the doctrine that nothing exists, and that consequently no knowledge is possible. It denies the objective reality of either truth or morality. The term Nihilism is, however, generally applied to the doctrine of the Russian revolutionary Socialists during the latter half of the nineteenth century. In the beginning, Russian Nihilism was merely an intellectual current of thought, a cult of extreme individualism concentrating all its efforts upon the emancipation of man from the factors of social life. It was concerned not so much with the people as a social collectivity as with man as an individual, man oppressed and fettered by intellectual, moral, and social shackles.

As a theory Nihilism criticized religion, family and marriage relations, all the prejudices created by custom and tradition, and aimed at the abolition of all social and political institutions. The term was first used by Turgeniev in 1862, who drew a perfect type of a nihilist in his novel *Fathers and Sons*. J. de Maistre, however, had already spoken of *rienism* in his correspondence. Nihilism was negation, because it denied and was anxious to abolish the existing order of things; it was destructive because it tended to destroy the whole social structure, but it preached destruction with a view to the pleasure of building up. To confuse Nihilism with Terrorism is, however, as wrong as (in Kropotkin's words) "to confuse a philosophical movement like Stoicism or Positivism with a political movement such as, for example, republicanism."

"La joie de détruire," wrote Bakunin, "est en même temps la joie de créer." The first Nihilists were philosophers, mystics, and altruists. Their aim was the deliverance of the sufferers from the chains of tradition, and the deliverance of the Russians from the oppression of autocracy. Their leaders, such as Tshernyshevski, Mikhailov, Lavrov, and others, were intellectuals, and their propaganda was peaceful. But Tsardom retaliated with prison, exile, and penal servitude, and peaceful propaganda having proved a failure, the Nihilists resorted to terrorist methods.

Nihilism in the seventies became, despite the efforts of the organized circles to prevent the adoption of a physical force policy, synonymous with bombs and dynamite, terror and assassination. Vera Sassaulitsh shot General Trepov, the Chief of the Police, in St. Petersburg in Jan., 1879, and on the 13th March, 1881, Alexander II. was assassinated by a bomb thrown by Grinetzky. Reaction and severe measures against political criminals followed, and the Nihilist party was crushed. New revolutionary organizations arose, and their struggle for freedom culminated in the Russian Revolution (q.v.) of 1917.—BIBLIOGRAPHY: S. Stepnaik, *Underground Russia*; Kropotkin, *Memoirs of a Revolutionary*; A.S. Rappoport, *Pioneers of the Russian Revolution* (Bibliography).

NIIGATA (nē-i-gä'tȧ). The chief town of the province of Echigo, Japan, situated on the west coast of Honshu and on the left bank of the Shinanogawa. This port was opened to foreign trade in 1858 as one of the five treaty ports; but the obstructed state of the river, the open anchorage, and the severe winter have hitherto prevented the development of trade apart from traffic with Vladivostok and Siberian ports. The town is well built, the streets are traversed by canals; there is a hospital and a college, and a considerable coasting trade. Pop. (1930), 125,108.

NIJMWEGEN, NYMEGEN (nī'mā-gen), or **NIMEGUEN** (nim'e-gen). A city in the Dutch province of Gelderland, delightfully situated on the slopes of several hills, reaching down to the Waal. It has a fine old church (St. Stephen's), and a Renaissance town hall of the sixteenth century. The industrial occupations include tanning, brewing, metal goods, cotton manufactures, etc. The town is celebrated for the treaty of peace concluded in 1678 between France, and Holland, and Spain, and for that of 1679 between the German Empire,

France, and Sweden. It was formerly a strong fortress, but the fortifications have been changed into promenades. Pop. (1932), 84,034

NIJNI-NOVGOROD. A government in Central Russia; area, 19,797 sq. miles; pop. about 2,000,000. The surface forms a plain, occasionally broken and diversified by low undulating hills. It is drained by the Volga. The soil is poor, and the crops, chiefly hemp and flax, not very abundant. A large part is covered with forests.

NIJNE - TAGILSK (nizh - nē - tá - gilsk'). A town of Russia amid the Ural Mountains, in the government of Perm, and 150 miles east of the town of Perm, in the midst of a district very rich in minerals. Pop. about 45,000.

NIJNI-NOVGOROD, now **GORKY.** Capital of the government of the same name, at the junction of the Oka and Volga, 255 miles east of Moscow. The town forms three parts: the upper district, including the citadel; the lower portion, called the Nijni Bazaar; and the suburb, occupied by the great annual fair, and containing 6500 booths, besides other structures for its accommodation. This fair, begun in 1816, was held annually between 25th July and 10th Sept., old style. Here there was gathered together an immense multitude of people from all parts of Russia and many parts of Asia, and the annual value of the merchandise sold before the European War was estimated at about £40,000,000. The chief products sold are cotton, woollen, and linen goods, tea, silk and silk goods, metal wares, furs, leather, porcelain, earthenware, glass, coffee, and wine. A university was opened here in 1918. It has two broadcasting stations (761·4 M., 1·8 kW., and 500·8 M.). Pop. (1926), 350,300.

NI'KĒ. In Greek mythology, the goddess of victory, the daughter of Styx and the giant Pallas. She was rewarded by Zeus with the permission to live in Olympus, for the readiness with which she came to his assistance in the war with the Titans. There is a temple to her on the Acropolis of Athens still in excellent preservation.

NIKOPOLIS (Gr. "City of Victory"). The name of several ancient cities, of which the principal are:—

Asia.—(1) A town of Bithynia, on the coast of the Bosporus, a few miles north of Chalcedon. (2) A town of Cappadocia, founded by Pompey on the spot where he gained a decisive victory over Mithridates.

Africa.—A town of Ægypt, founded by Augustus Cæsar in 24 B.C. on the place where he defeated M. Antonius, and in commemoration of the surrender of Alexandria.

Europe.—(1) A city of Epeirus, erected by Augustus, now represented by the town of Préviso. It commemorated the victory of Actium (31 B.C.). (2) A town of Thrace, near the mouth of the Nessus, presumably founded by Trajan. (3) A town of Thrace, erected by Trajan in memory of his victory over the Dacians.

NILE (Gr. *Neilos*, Lat. *Nilus*). A historic river, the largest of Africa, and the longest in the world except the Missouri-Mississippi. Its main stream, known as the *Bahr-el-Abiad*, or White Nile, has its chief source in the equatorial lake Victoria (Nyanza). It actually rises, however, near to the

The Nile Valley

parallel of 4° S. lat. as the Shimiyu, coming from the direction of Lake Manjaro. What is known as the *Bahr-el-Azrek*, or Blue Nile, a much smaller stream, joins the White Nile at Khartoum, lat. 15° 40′ N.

The source of the Blue Nile was discovered in the Abyssinian Highlands (Lake Tsana) by Bruce in 1770, while the actual source of the other, or true Nile, was for long the subject of speculation and exploration. The Nile, near where it flows out of Lake Victoria (altitude, 3867 feet), forms the Ripon Falls, and discharges into Chioga Lake (altitude, 3318 feet). It then traverses a steep gorge, passes the Murchison Falls, and enters the Albert (Nyanza) (altitude, 2229 feet), falling, therefore, through 1438 feet in 242 miles (6 feet fall in 1 mile).

From Albert Nyanza the Nile flows north as the *Bahr-al-Jebel*, or mountain river, to Lake No (altitude, 1350 feet), a distance of 720 miles, and a fall of 1 foot to the mile. Lake No is on the *Bahr-al-Ghazal*, a part of the Nile that is practically stagnant, and covered with floating reeds and papyrus, called "sudd."

From its junction with the Sobat, the Nile becomes the *Bahr-al-Abiad*, and is joined at Khartoum by its most considerable affluent, the *Bahr-al-Azrek*, or Blue Nile. Without the Blue Nile the river would be unable to reach Lower Egypt, and the Bahr-al-Ghazal would be a drainless area similar to Lake Chad. Its last tributary, the Atbara, comes from the hills around Lake Tsana, and for the rest of its course (1500 miles) the Nile receives no contributory stream. From Khartoum to Aswan is the Nubian Nile, embracing all the cataracts, and at Aswan begins the Egyptian Nile, without which the history of Egypt could never have been written, and her natural wealth would have remained for ever obscure.

In Egypt, at the head of the Delta, 13 miles N. of Cairo, it divides into two main branches, leading down respectively to Rosetta and Damietta, where they enter the Mediterranean. As rain scarcely ever falls in the greater part of the valley of the Nile, the river owes its supplies to the copious rains and the vast lake areas of the tropical regions in which it takes its rise, and its volume thus depends upon the season.

It begins to increase in June, attains its greatest height about September, and then subsides. (*See* SUDAN.) The ordinary rise at Cairo is about 25 feet. During the flood a great portion of the Delta, and of the valley higher up, is inundated. This annual inundation, now controlled by the great Aswan Dam, the Sennar Dam (*see* GEZIRA), and other works (*see* EGYPT), in ancient times caused the Nile to be worshipped as a god by Egyptians, Greeks, and Romans. Its length is about 4194 miles.—Cf. W. S. Churchill, *The River War*, which contains excellent maps and matter descriptive of the two Niles.

NILGIRIS. A district of India, in Madras Presidency, comprising entirely the area of the Nilgiri Hills. It produces little save native food-grains and coco-nuts. Area, 1009 sq. miles; pop. 118,600.

NILSSON, Christine. Born at Hassaby, near Wexiö, in Sweden, 1843. Accompanied by her brother, she used to sing at village fairs and places of public resort, where she also played on the violin. In 1857 her talent attracted the attention of a wealthy gentleman, who had her educated as a singer at Stockholm, and afterwards at Paris.

In 1864 she made her first appearance as Violetta in *La Traviata* at the Théâtre Lyrique, Paris, and she appeared in 1867 for the first time at Her Majesty's Theatre, London. Among her most famous impersonations were Ophelia in Thomas's *Hamlet*, and Margaret in Gounod's *Faust*. In 1872 she married M. Auguste Rouzaud, who died in 1882; in 1886 she married Count A. de Miranda. She died in 1921.

NIMACH, or NEEMUCH. A town and cantonment of Gwalior, Central India, 1613 feet in altitude. It is on the railway between Indore and Ajmer Merwara. Pop. 12,000.

NIMBUS. A term applied in art, especially in sacred art, to a kind of halo or disc surrounding the heads of sacred persons, of Christ, the angels, or saints; as also to a disc or circle sometimes depicted round the heads of emperors and other great men. The nimbus in representations of God the Father is of a triangular form, with rays diverging from it all round; in representations of Christ it contains a cross more or less enriched; that of the Virgin Mary consists of a circlet of small stars, and that of angels and saints is a circle of small rays. When the nimbus is depicted of a square form, it indicates that the person was alive at the time of delineation. Nimbus is frequently confounded with *aureola* and *glory*.

NÎMES, or NISMES (nēm; ancient **Nemausus**). A city of Southern France, capital of the department of Gard. It is an episcopal see. Its manufactures are chiefly of silk and cotton goods; it has a considerable commerce, and is the great entrepôt of Southern France for raw silk; it is also an important market for wine and brandy. Among the buildings is the cathedral of S. Castor; but Nîmes is chiefly remarkable for its Roman remains, including an ancient temple, with thirty beautiful Corinthian columns, now serving as a museum and known as the *Maison Carrée*; the amphitheatre, a circus capable of seating 20,000 persons; the temple of Diana; the ancient Tour Magne, on a hill (Mont Cavalier) outside of the city, supposed to have been a mausoleum; and two Roman gateways.

Nîmes was, for about 500 years, in the possession of the Romans. In the sixteenth century it became a stronghold of Calvinism, and suffered much during the civil wars, as also by the revocation of the Edict of Nantes, and during the Revolution. It has a broadcasting station (237·2 M., 1 kW.). Pop. (1931), 89,213.

NIMROD. Described in Gen. x. 8-12 as a descendant of Ham, a son of Cush, a mighty hunter before the Lord, and the beginning of whose kingdom was Babel, Erech, Accad, and Calneh in the land of Shinar.

NIN'EVEH. An ancient ruined city, formerly capital of the Assyrian Empire, in Mesopotamia, on the Tigris, along which, and opposite to the town of Mosul, it occupied an extended site. The first recorded notice of Nineveh is in Gen. x. Again it is spoken of in the book of Jonah as a "great city." It remained the capital of Assyria till about 606 B.C., when it was taken and burned by the Babylonian Nabopolassar and the Median Cyaxares.

It was maintained as a local tradition that this ancient capital of Assyria lay buried on the left bank of the Tigris opposite Mosul; but the fact was not definitely settled until in 1841 M. Botta began excavations in the vast mounds which there existed. He was followed in this by A. H. (afterwards Sir Henry) Layard, who explored a great portion of the large angle formed by the Tigris and the Zab. In the mounds of Kuyunjik, opposite Mosul, he excavated the palaces of Sennacherib, Assurbanipal, and Esarhaddon. The walls of the city, which the inscriptions describe as Ninua, stretch along the Tigris for 2½ miles, and the elaborate outworks, moats, and defences can still be traced.

The important discoveries made by Layard were continued by Loftus, Hormuzd Rassam, and G. Smith, and in still more recent years (1923-28) by Dr. Campbell Thomson and Mr. R. W. Hutchinson, and the result of their labours deposited in the British Museum.—Cf. Sir A. H. Layard, *Nineveh and its Remains.*

NING-PO. A city of China, in the province of Chê-kiang, and on the Takia or Ning-po River, about 16 miles from its mouth. It is surrounded by a wall 25 feet high, 15 feet wide, and 5 miles in circuit, built in A.D. 870. The site of the former city of Ning-po, which existed 2200 B.C., is near the modern city. Ning-po was declared a treaty port in 1842. Pop. (1931), 218,774.

NINIAN, St. A missionary preacher who spread Christianity among the Picts in the beginning of the fifth century. He was ordained bishop of the Southern Picts by Pope Siricius in 394. Ninian selected Candida Casa, or Whithorn (Wigtownshire), as his chief seat, but prosecuted his labours in all parts of Southern Scotland, and even as far north as the Grampians. He died in 432. His festival is the 16th Sept.

NINUS. The fabulous founder of the Assyrian Empire, and of its capital Nineveh. He married Semiramis, wife of Onnes, but was afterwards murdered by his wife, who ruled as regent for her son Ninyas. His temple-tomb near Babylon is referred to by Thisbe in *A Midsummer Night's Dream* as "Ninny's tomb."

NI'OBĒ. In Greek mythology, the daughter of Tantalus, King of Lydia, married to Amphion, King of Thebes. Proud of her numerous progeny, she provoked the anger of Apollo and Artemis (Diana) by boasting over

Niobe

their mother Leto (Latona), who had no other children but those two. She was punished by having all her children put to death by those two deities. She herself was metamorphosed by Zeus (Jupiter) into a stone (on Mount Sipylus, Asia Minor) which shed tears during the summer. This fable has afforded a subject for art, and has given rise to the beautiful group in the Uffizi Gallery at Florence, known by the name of *Niobē and her Children.*

NIO'BIUM, or **COLUMBIUM** (chemical symbol, Cb; atomic weight, 93·1). A rare metal discovered in 1801 in the black mineral *columbite* from North America. The element is comparatively rare, but exists in minute quantity as the pentoxide in a considerable number of minerals. It is almost invariably associated with tantalum. It is a steel-grey metal of specific gravity 12·75, and melting-point 1950° C., and is only slightly attacked by acids. Like tantalum it has a marked influence on the properties of steel when associated with it.

NIORT (ni-ōr). A city of France, capital of the department of Deux-Sèvres, on two hills washed by the Sèvre-Niortaise. Its town house and the keep of the old castle are interesting buildings. The staple manufactures are leather and gloves, and the trade, particularly in claret, is extensive. Pop. 25,935.

NIPA. A genus of palms of which there is but one species, *N. fruticans,* a native of the East Indies, Philippines, etc., growing on marshy coasts. It has no stem, fronds about 20 feet long, and edible fruits.

NIP'IGON, or **NEP'IGON.** A lake of Canada, in Ontario, about 30 miles N.W. of Lake Superior. It is about 70 miles long and 40 miles broad; area, 1590 sq. miles. It is connected with Lake Superior by the Nipigon River, a famous trout-stream.

NIPIS'SING, Lake. A lake of Canada, in Ontario, north-east of Lake Huron, irregular in coast-line; length, 48 miles; breadth, 20 miles; area, 330 sq. miles. It contains numerous islands, and finds its only outlet by French River (55 miles) into Lake Huron. The lake will form a part of the Georgian Bay Canal.

NIPPLEWORT. A plant of the genus Lapsăna (*L. communis*), nat. ord. Compositæ, growing commonly as a weed by the sides of ditches and in waste places.

NIPPON. *See* JAPAN.

NIRVANA (Skt. *nirvāna,* blowing out or extinction, i.e. of sin; from *vā,* to blow). Nirvana or Nigban is the Tibetan Nyangan. In Buddhism it is a state of spiritual satisfaction, an "earthly paradise," to live in which the passions must be conquered; there must be absence of desire in this life, an inward peace. Nirvana is synonymous neither with the Christian ideal of a future state, nor yet with annihilation; it is attained in this world and in this life. Death—or transmigration, as the Buddhist doctrine teaches—is the reward of Nirvana.

Such a doctrine is prognosticated in the deep melancholy of Ecclesiastes, in the choruses of Sophocles, in the despair of Job and Jeremiah, the *Apologia* of Plato, and in the soliloquy of Hamlet; yet this has nowhere led to suicide as the path to Nirvana, but to fasting, prayer, alms-giving, and self-sacrifice. The life of self-sacrifice that so distinguishes Gautama Buddha, his voluntary acceptance of poverty, his proclamation of a universal brotherhood, and his war on the caste system are remarkable features of his career. But after him Brahmanism rose triumphant, and drove Buddhism into other lands, and the region of Sakya Muni's birth and labours became a place of pilgrimage to peoples from distant lands. According to the *Rajguru* of Assam the Nirvana of Sakya Muni occurred 196 years before Chandragupta, in the eighteenth year of Ajatra Satru.

NISÂMI, Abu Mahomet Ben Yusef, Sheikh Nisâm-ed-Dîn. One of the great poets of Persia, and the founder of the romantic epic, born about A.D. 1100, died in 1180. He was a special favourite of the Seljuk princes, who then ruled in Persia. Besides a *Divan,* or collection of lyrics, he wrote five larger poems, which have been extensively circulated in Persia and India.

NI'SAN. A month of the Jewish calendar, the first month of the sacred year and seventh of the civil year, answering nearly to our March. It was originally called Abib, but began to be called Nisan after the captivity.

NISH, NICH, or **NISSA** (ancient **Naissus**). A town of Yugoslavia, in Serbia, on the Nishava, 150 miles S.E. of Belgrade. It is the seat of a Greek bishop, and has celebrated hot springs and baths. It was the native place of the Emperor Constantine the Great. Nish, which became the temporary seat of the Serbian Government on the outbreak of the European War, was captured by the Bulgarians on 5th Nov., 1915, and retaken by the Serbians on 12th Oct., 1918. Pop. (1931), 35,384.

NISH'APUR. An ancient city of Persia, in the province of Khorasan. Turquoises of excellent quality have long been found in its vicinity. Omar Khayyám was born (1123) and is buried there. Pop. 14,500.

NIS'IBIS, or **ANTIOCHIA MYGDONIÆ.** The modern *Nisbin,* an ancient city of Mesopotamia, on the Mygdonius. During the European War it was a strategic point as the eastern terminus of the Bagdad Railway.

NITELLA. A genus of stoneworts or Charophyta, differing from Chara by the internodes being naked, and in the detailed structure and arrangement of the sexual organs.

NITRATE. A salt of nitric acid. The nitrates are generally soluble in water, and are readily decomposed at high temperatures. Deposits of nitrates of calcium and certain alkali metals are present in small quantities in almost all soils. Potassium nitrate or nitre (q.v.) occurs thus in commercial quantities in the plains of Northern India, and enormous accumulations of sodium nitrate exist in Northern Chile. These latter deposits, which are known as Chile saltpetre, cubic nitre, or soda nitre, are found on an arid plateau above the coast. The great value of this nitrate lies in its application to agriculture as a fertilizer on impoverished soil.

All crops require nitrogen in order to build up the complex organic nitrogen compounds found in their tissues. The most economic form in which this nitrogen can be supplied is as sodium nitrate, potassium nitrate being taken up by the trade in explosives. The effect of a nitrate as a manure is enormous, in certain cases giving a crop three times as heavy as when no nitrogen is supplied. Nitrates are formed in the soil from ammonium salts by certain species of bacteria, the nitric acid ultimately produced combining mostly with lime derived from calcium carbonate in the soil. Nitrates should not be used as fertilizers on light porous soils where the rain will sink the manure below the range of the roots. For the manufacture of nitrates from atmospheric nitrogen, *see* NITRIC ACID.

NITRATE OF SILVER, or **LUNAR CAUSTIC** ($AgNO_3$). A white crystalline salt obtained by dissolving silver in nitric acid and allowing the solution to crystallize. It forms tabular crystals which are soluble in water and melt at 218° C. The fused product, cast in the form of sticks, is known as lunar caustic, and is used in medicine as a cautery. It is also used in photography and in silvering mirrors for optical instruments. It forms the basis of "marking-inks," as it is readily reduced to metallic silver on coming in contact with organic matter.

NITRE, also called **SALTPETRE.** The name by which potassium nitrate (KNO_3) is commonly known. It is produced by the action of nitrifying bacteria in soils containing potash and nitrogenous organic matter, and forms an efflorescence upon the surface of the soil in tropical countries, notably India. In some parts of Europe it is obtained by mixing animal matter and loose earth in heaps, which are allowed to stand for several years to oxidize (nitrify), after which the nitre may be extracted by lixiviation. It is chiefly prepared, however, from Chile saltpetre by treatment with potassium chloride.

It is a colourless salt which crystallizes in six-sided prisms and possesses a cooling salty taste. Nitre is an essential constituent of gunpowder and of certain blasting-powders and fireworks. It is also used for the preservation of meat, as a diuretic and febrifuge in medicine, and as a flux in metallurgy.

NITRIC ACID (HNO_3). One of the most important compounds of nitrogen. In the pure state it is a colourless, strongly fuming, and corrosive liquid, which boils at 86° C. and has a specific gravity of 1·52. On exposure to light it becomes yellow, due to partial decomposition into nitrogen peroxide, oxygen, and water. The ordinary commercial acid contains about 70 per cent. of the pure substance, and is known in the arts as *aqua fortis*.

It is commonly obtained by heating Chile saltpetre (sodium nitrate) with concentrated sulphuric acid, when the following reaction takes place: $H_2SO_4 + NaNO_3 = HNO_3 + NaHSO_4$. The operation is carried out in cast-iron or earthenware retorts, the nitric acid vapours being condensed in a series of water-cooled earthenware spirals. The residue in the retorts, known as "nitre-cake," which consists mainly of sodium bisulphate, is run out in the liquid state into iron trays and allowed to solidify.

Nitric acid is a strong acid, forming with metallic bases a series of salts, the nitrates. It contains about 75 per cent. of oxygen, a great part of which it readily yields to other substances, acting in this manner as a powerful oxidizing agent. Thus starch, sugar, and other organic substances, when treated with the moderately dilute acid, are oxidized at its expense with the production of lower oxides of nitrogen.

When the concentrated acid is used, nitro-compounds are frequently formed, containing the group $-NO_2$ in place of part of the hydrogen of the original substance. In this manner nitro-cellulose (gun-cotton), nitro-glycerine, and tri-nitro-toluene (the high explosive known as T.N.T.) are produced. A mixture of concentrated nitric and hydrochloric acids, known as *aqua regia*, or nitro-muriatic acid, is used as a solvent for gold and platinum. Nitric acid is employed in etching on steel and copper; in metallurgy and assaying; and also in chemical industry, mainly in the manufacture of intermediate products for dyes and drugs.

Until a few years ago the only method of practical importance for the manufacture of nitric acid was the one in which Chile saltpetre is used. The supply of this material though large is not inexhaustible; at the present rate of consumption it is estimated to last for not more than fifty years. During the last two decades a vast amount of research has been carried out with a view to obtaining nitric acid and other nitrogenous compounds from nitrogen, which forms four-fifths of the volume of the air.

When air is subjected to a high-tension electrical discharge, a small proportion is converted into nitric oxide (NO), by direct combination between the elements, at the very high temperature produced by the arc. This gas can be readily converted into nitric acid, which is now manufactured by the above method on a commercial scale.

The principal processes at present in successful technical operation are the Birkeland-Eyde, the Schönherr, and the Pauling. The only essential difference between them lies in the construction of the electric furnaces used. In the Birkeland-Eyde process this consists of a sheet-steel chamber in the form of a low wide cylinder resting on its side. It is lined internally with fire-brick so as to leave a narrow disc-shaped space in the centre, into which project the electrodes, consisting of water-cooled copper tubes, the ends of which are placed about ¼ inch apart in the centre of the furnace. Perpendicular to these are the two poles of an electro-magnet.

The electrodes are supplied with alternating current at about 5000 volts, whilst direct current is fed to the coils of the electro-magnet, which has the effect of deflecting the arc so that it presents the appearance of a circular sheet of flame. A current of air is driven through the furnace, remaining in contact with the arc, which has a temperature of about 3200° C., for a very short time. The hot gases leaving the furnace contain up to 1·5 per cent. of nitric oxide; they are cooled and passed into large oxidation chambers, and then to absorption towers filled with fragments of quartz, down which trickles an absorbing liquid.

If water is used, a solution of nitric acid is obtained; with caustic soda solution, sodium nitrate or nitrite is formed, according to whether oxidation of the gases has been complete or partial. Owing to the large amount of power required, these processes are mainly in operation in Scandinavia and other countries where an abundant supply of cheap water-power is available.

A process, known as the Ostwald process, for the manufacture of nitric acid by the catalytic oxidation of ammonia by atmospheric oxygen has also been used with considerable success. The ammonia used is obtained either as a by-product from the manufacture of coal-gas (*see* COAL-TAR; GAS MANUFACTURE), or from calcium cyanamide (*see* CYANAMIDE), which is itself prepared by the action of atmospheric nitrogen on calcium carbide (q.v.). A process for the direct synthesis of ammonia from its elements nitrogen and hydrogen, which promises to become of great importance, has been devised by Haber and recently improved by Claude.—BIBLIOGRAPHY: G. Martin and W. Barbour, *Industrial Nitrogen Compounds and Explosives*; Sir Edward Thorpe, *Dictionary of Applied Chemistry: Physical and Chemical Data of Nitrogen Fixation* (Ministry of Munitions, Nitrogen Products Committee).

NITRIDES. A name given to the compounds of nitrogen with other elements, e.g. phosphorus, boron, silicon, and the metals. Magnesium nitride is formed when nitrogen is passed over heated magnesium.

NITRIFICATION. A bio-chemical process carried on in soil—and also in sea-water—by certain bacteria, particularly species of Nitrobacter and Nitrosomonas, consisting in the oxidation of ammonia—produced by putrefaction and decay—to nitrates. It is of the very greatest importance in the economy of nature, because nitrates form the normal source of nitrogenous food for green plants, and thus also for the animal kingdom.

NITRO-BENZOL, or **NITRO-BENZENE** ($C_6H_5NO_2$). Prepared by adding gradually, with stirring, a mixture of 12 parts concentrated nitric acid and 16 parts concentrated sulphuric acid to 10 parts benzene contained in an iron or earthenware vessel. The temperature is kept below 30° C. until all the acid has been added; the mixture is then heated to 75° C. for a short time to complete the reaction. The nitro-benzol, which floats on the surface of the waste acids, is separated and distilled.

It is a pale yellow, highly refracting liquid; boiling-point, 211° C.; specific gravity, 1·2. It has a strong odour of bitter almonds and is poisonous, but in spite of this it is used in perfumery under the name of "oil of mirbane." It is manufactured on a large scale, since on reduction it yields aniline, the parent substance of many dyes and drugs.

NITRO-COMPOUNDS. Compound derived from hydrocarbons and other organic compounds by the substitution of the univalent nitro-radical NO_2 for hydrogen.

NITROGEN (chemical symbol, N; atomic weight, 14·008). An element occurring in the free state in the atmosphere, of which it forms 78·06 per cent. by volume. It also occurs in small quantity in the gases of volcanoes, and in some mineral springs. In the combined state the element is very common both in the animal and in the vegetable kingdom; e.g., proteins, albumens, alkaloids, etc., contain nitrogen combined with carbon, hydrogen, and oxygen. Large quantities occur combined with sodium or potassium and oxygen in Chile saltpetre ($NaNO_3$) and saltpetre (KNO_3), and united with hydrogen in ammonia and ammonium salts.

Nitrogen is a colourless, tasteless gas which may be liquefied at low temperature and high pressure, the boiling-point at 760 mm. pressure being −196° C. Chemically it is an inert substance, and does not readily combine with oxygen nor hydrogen nor with the metals at ordinary temperatures. At high temperatures it unites with metals, forming *nitrides*. It forms five oxides, which are prepared indirectly from the nitrates.

These are: *nitrous oxide* or laughing gas, N_2O (q.v.); *nitric oxide*, NO, prepared by the action of metallic copper on nitric acid, a colourless gas which becomes brown on exposure to air, forming nitrogen peroxide; *nitrogen peroxide*, NO_2, formed by heating dry lead nitrate, a deep-brown gas with an unpleasant odour; it dissolves in cold water, giving an acid solution containing a mixture of nitric and nitrous acids; *nitrogen trioxide*, or *nitrous anhydride*, N_2O_3, formed by reducing nitric acid with arsenious oxide; it is a brown gas which when cooled to −21° C. is a deep-blue liquid; it dissolves in water, giving a solution of *nitrous acid*.

Nitric anhydride or *nitrogen pentoxide*, N_2O_5, obtained by dehydrating nitric acid with phosphorous pentoxide, is a white solid melting at 30° C.; dissolved in water it yields a solution of nitric acid. Nitrogen forms compounds with hydrogen, the most important being ammonia. The nitrates and nitric acid are the most important compounds of nitrogen. Recently an active form of nitrogen has been prepared by subjecting the gas to electric discharge; in this form it readily transforms yellow phosphorus into red phosphorus, and reacts with nitric oxide to form nitrogen peroxide.

Nitrogen may be prepared by the decomposition of ammonium nitrite,

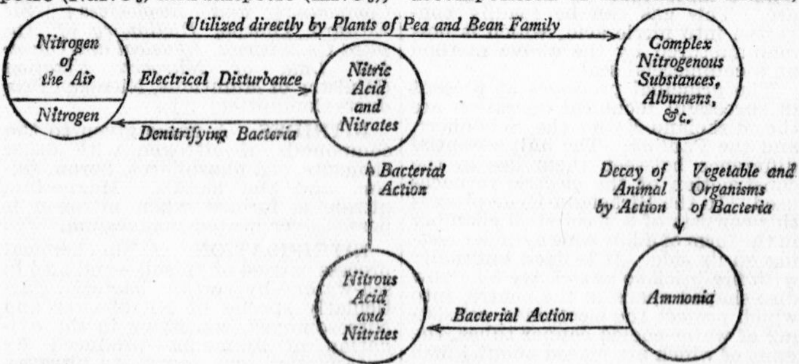

$NH_4NO_2 = N_2 + 2H_2O$; or by the decomposition of ammonium dichromate, $(NH_4)_2Cr_2O_7 = N_2 + Cr_2O_3 + 4H_2O$; or by passing air over heated metallic copper to remove oxygen and collecting the residual gas. Commercially the substance is prepared from liquid air by fractional distillation; liquid nitrogen, being more volatile than liquid oxygen, distils over first.

Nitrogen is an essential constituent of plant and animal tissues. It is therefore an important fact of nature that large supplies of it are available for building up plants. Plants cannot generally utilize nitrogen as such with the exception of the leguminosæ; these are able to absorb nitrogen from the atmosphere by means of bacteria which are present in the roots; these bacteria utilize atmospheric nitrogen, and thereby supply the plant. All other plants absorb nitrogen by their roots in the form of nitrates.

There is a complete nitrogen cycle in nature. Nitrogen of the atmosphere is transformed in small quantity into *nitric acid* by means of electrical disturbances. This nitric acid dissolves and finds its way by means of rain into the soil, where it is transformed into *nitrates* and absorbed by the plant roots. As vegetable and animal matter decays, it is attacked by bacteria which transform the nitrogenous substances into *ammonia*; the ammonia so produced is carried into the soil, and there it is attacked by bacteria which transform it into *nitrites*, the salts of *nitrous acid*.

These nitrites are in turn attacked by bacteria and transformed into *nitrates*, and these are absorbed by the plant and transformed into complex nitrogenous bodies. Nitrogen is thus continuously absorbed from the air and transformed into compounds to be used again in building up fresh supplies of nitrogen compounds.

Synthetic methods have recently been introduced, whereby both nitric acid (q.v.) and ammonia may be produced from atmospheric nitrogen, directly or indirectly. It is calculated that there are about 20,000,000 tons of nitrogen in the air over every square mile of the earth's surface, so that the amount of raw material for the synthetic production of important nitrogen compounds is practically unlimited. The inertness of nitrogen to chemical reagents at moderate temperatures has rendered this supply useless until recent years. *See* NITRIC ACID; AMMONIA; CYANAMIDE.

NITRO-GLYCERINE. *See* EXPLOSIVES.

NITROLIM, or NITROLIME. The trade name for calcium cyanamide. At the great works at Odda, in Norway, the cyanamide is ground to a fine powder, and sent out in bags with a double lining as *nitrolim*. *See* CYANAMIDE; NITRIC ACID; NITROGEN.

NITROUS ETHER, $(C_2H_5)NO_2$. The nitrite of the organic radical ethyl. It is a yellowish liquid, and when mixed with about four times its volume of rectified spirit forms the *nitrous ether*, *nitric ether*, *spirit of nitrous ether*, or *sweet spirit of nitre* of the Pharmacopœia. This mixture is often employed to increase the flow of urine, and to counteract feverishness.

NIUE, INIUE, or SAVAGE ISLAND. A Pacific island in the Micronesian division of Oceania (18° 5′ s. lat., 169° 52′ w. long.), attached to New Zealand since June, 1901. It is composed of two coral terraces, 90 feet and 220 feet respectively in altitude, but only the lower terrace is inhabited. Bananas and coco-nuts are exported. The circumference is 40 miles; area, about 100 sq. miles; pop. (1926), 3795 (30 white).

NIVELLES (Fl. *Nyvel*). A town of Belgium, in the province of Brabant, on the Thines. The church of St. Gertrude was founded in 1048. It is a railway junction and has railway workshops. Paper is manufactured. Pop. 12,794.

NIVÔSE (literally "snow-month"). The fourth month of the French Revolutionary Calendar, beginning on 21st Dec., and ending on 19th Jan.

NIZAM' (Urdu, *nizām*; Ar. *nidam*, order, administration, arrangement). In India, the title of the ruler of Hyderabad in the Deccan, derived from *nizam-ul-mulk*, governor or regulator of the empire, a name adopted by Azof Jah in 1719, and since that time adopted by his successors.

NOAH. One of the patriarchs of the Old Testament, son of Lamech, is described in the book of Genesis as being chosen by God for his piety to be the father of the new race of men which should people the earth after the deluge. Having been warned by God of the coming flood, he built a vessel (the *ark*) by His direction, and entered it with his family and all kinds of animals.

After the waters had subsided the ark rested on Mount Ararat, where Noah offered a thank-offering to God, and was assured that the earth should never again be destroyed by a flood, as sign whereof God set the rainbow in the clouds. While modern accounts place Mount Ararat in Armenia, older traditions locate it in the mountains of the Kurds, east of the Tigris.

NOAILLES (no-āy), **Adrien Maurice, Duc de.** French soldier, was born 1678, and died 1766. During the minority of Louis XV. he was President of the Council of Finance and member of the Council of Regency, which he left, however, in 1721, rather than concede the presidency to Cardinal Dubois. Exiled by the influence of Dubois, he was, on his death, recalled and reinstated in his former offices. During the Austrian War of Succession he held a command on the Rhine; and in 1743, through the impetuosity of his nephew, the Count of Grammont, he lost the battle of Dettingen. He served under Marshal Saxe at Fontenoy.

NOBEL, Alfred. Swedish engineer and inventor of dynamite, born at Stockholm in 1833, died 1896. His father established a nitro-glycerine business at St. Petersburg (Petrograd) about 1860, and some seven years later the son accidentally discovered a method of lessening the danger of explosion attending the use of that substance. Subsequently he made other important inventions relating to blasting materials, smokeless powder, armour-plates, etc., and established large works at Brefors in his native country.

NOBEL PRIZES. Annual prizes awarded from a fund established under the will of Alfred Nobel. By his will Nobel devoted the bulk of his fortune of over £2,000,000 to the foundation of five annual prizes, each worth about £8000, to be awarded for the most important inventions or discoveries of the year in (1) physical science, (2) chemistry, and (3) medical science or physiology; (4) for the most important literary work of an idealistic character; and (5) for the greatest effort in the cause of international brotherhood and peace.

There is no distinction of nationality in the awards, but each candidate must be proposed by a recognized representative of science, literature, etc., before the 1st of Feb. in the year at the end of which the awards are made. There is an English Nobel Prize Committee, while the foundation is administered by a Board of Control at Stockholm. There are also Nobel Institutes, established for the study of physical chemistry and for the advancement of matters connected with literature and peace.

The first distribution of the Nobel prizes took place in 1901, the recipients being: W. Röntgen, J. H. van't Hoff, E. von Behring, Sully Prudhomme, H. Dunant, and F. Passy. Among British recipients of the prize have been: physics, Lord Rayleigh, J. J. Thomson, Sir W. H. Bragg and W. L. Bragg, C. G. Barkla; chemistry, Lord Ramsay, Sir E. Rutherford, F. Soddy, F. W. Aston; medicine, Sir Ronald Ross, Sir Charles Sherrington (1932, jointly with Professor E. D. Adrian); literature, Rudyard Kipling, M. Maeterlinck, W. B. Yeats, John Galsworthy (1932), G. B. Shaw; peace, Sir W. R. Cremer, Sir Austen Chamberlain; and among women recipients, Madame Curie.

NOBILE. *See* NORTH POLAR EXPEDITIONS.

NOBILITY. A rank or class of society which possesses hereditary honours and privileges above the rest of the citizens. Such a class is found in the infancy of almost every nation. Its origin may be attributed to military supremacy, to the honours paid to superior ability, or to the guardians of the mysteries of religion. Among the ancient Romans the patricians originally formed the nobility; but a new order of nobility arose out of the plebeians, consisting of those who had held curule magistracies and their descendants, enjoying the right of having images of their distinguished ancestors.

Among the ancient German tribes only obscure traces of hereditary nobility are found. The dignities of the counts of the Franks, the aldermen and great *thanes* of England, as also of the *jarls* (in England *eorlas*) of Denmark, were accessible to every one distinguished by merit and favoured by fortune. In Venice a civic nobility grew up consisting of a series of families who gradually acquired all political power and kept it to themselves and their descendants.

In England hereditary nobility, the nobility belonging to the titles of duke, marquess, earl, viscount, and baron, is now entirely personal, though formerly, as a result of the Norman Conquest, it was connected with the holding of lands. In Spain and Italy still, the same rank depends in greater measure upon property; and in France and Germany the *de* and *von* of titles points to the same fact. In France and Germany nobility is common to all the members of the noble family, and the German nobility formed a very exclusive caste.

In France and Germany the nobles long formed a class of sovereigns within their own domains. The French Revolution first deprived the nobles of that country of their privileges and exclusive rights, as that of jurisdiction, etc.; and the decree of 19th June, 1790, abolished hereditary rank entirely. Under Napoleon I. arose a new hereditary nobility, with the titles of princes, dukes, counts, barons, and chevaliers, which descended to the eldest son. After the restoration of the Bourbons (1814) the ancient nobility reclaimed their former rights and privileges.

Nobility was again abolished in 1848, but was restored during the reign of Napoleon III. In Norway the Parliament abolished nobility by the three successive decrees of 1815, 1818, and 1821. In Great Britain titles of nobility can only be conferred by the sovereign, and that by patent, in virtue of which they become hereditary. Life peerages, however, are also conferred. The nobility, as the term is commonly used, consists of those holding the titles already mentioned (or all above the rank of baronet) and their more immediate connections; but if the term were to be used as generally in Europe the gentry would also be included, or all families entitled to bear coat-armour.

Those of the nobility who are peers of England, of Great Britain, or of the United Kingdom, have a hereditary seat in the House of Lords, while the Scottish peers elect sixteen of their number to represent their order, and until 1922 the Irish peers used to elect twenty-eight representatives for the same purpose.

NOBLE, Sir Andrew. British physicist, artillerist, and engineer, born 1831, died 1915. He was educated at Edinburgh Academy and the Royal Military Academy, Woolwich, and entered the Royal Artillery in 1849. He did valuable work as secretary to the Select Committee on Rifled Cannon in 1858, and was the next year appointed Assistant Inspector of Artillery.

He joined the firm of Sir W. G. Armstrong & Co. in 1860, and his successful work as an administrator and organizer was soon recognized, and he was elected chairman of the company. His experimental work on guns and explosive actions was the basis of the great improvements found in modern artillery. He was created a baronet in 1902, and received many British and foreign orders.

NOBLE. An ancient English gold coin, value six shillings and eightpence, first struck in the reign of Edward III., 1344. The noble having increased in value to 10 shillings, a

Obverse Reverse

Gold Noble of Edward III., 1344, from an example in the British Museum

coin of the former value of a noble was issued by Henry VI. and Edward IV., and called an *Angel.* Half-nobles and quarter-nobles were also in circulation at the same period.

NODDY (*Anous stolidus*). A seabird of the family Laridæ (gulls), widely diffused through the northern and southern hemispheres, and well known to sailors for its fearlessness or stupidity, allowing itself even to be captured by hand; hence its name. The noddy is a rare visitant to the British shores; but is very abundant in warmer climates, as in the West Indies. There are several other species.

NODE. In astronomy, one of the points in which two great circles of the celestial sphere, such as the

Noddy

ecliptic and equator, the orbit of a planet and the ecliptic, intersect each other; and also one of the points in which the orbit of a satellite intersects the plane of the orbit of its primary. The node at which a heavenly body passes to the north of the plane of reference is called the *ascending node*; that where it passes to the south is called the *descending node.* The straight line joining the nodes is called the *line of nodes.*

NODE. In botany, the point of insertion of one or more leaves on a

Node

stem. The piece of stem between two nodes is an internode.

NODE. In physics, a point in a vibrating body where there is no motion. A string fixed at its ends, e.g. vibrates so that these ends are nodes (*see* HARMONICS). If a plate of glass or metal is supported, and a bow is drawn across the edge, particles of fine sand, strewn over the plate, will arrange themselves in lines, along which it is evident no vibration has taken place. These lines are called *nodal lines.*

NODE. In geometry, a point at which a curve intersects itself, so that it has two distinct tangents at the point. A *cusp* (q.v.) is the limiting case of a node at which the two tangents are coincident. If the tangents are imaginary, the node is called a *conjugate point.*

NOGI, Maresuke, Count. Japanese general, was born in Choshu, of Samurai parentage, in 1849, and committed *hara-kiri* in 1912. In his early career he saw service during the Civil War of 1877, and commanded a brigade at the battle of Kinchow (1894), and at the taking of Port Arthur from the Chinese. From 1896 to 1900 he was Governor of Taiwan (Formosa).

Nogi became celebrated during the Russo-Japanese War of 1904-05, when he commanded the Third Army, which besieged Port Arthur, and eventually brought about the surrender of the city. His famous flanking movement decided the sanguinary battle of Mukden. At the conclusion of the campaign he received the Orders of the Rising Sun and Golden Kite. While the State funeral of the Emperor Mitsu Hito was in progress, the Count and Countess Nogi committed suicide in order to rejoin the master whom, throughout their lives, they had so faithfully served. With the death of the general the male line became extinct, his two sons having been killed before Port Arthur.

NOISSEVILLE (nwȧs-vēl). A village of France, in Lorraine, to the east of Metz, the scene of a fiercely contested battle during the Franco-German War, 31st Aug. and 1st Sept., 1870, between the forces of Prince Frederick Charles and those of Marshal Bazaine. The Germans were victorious.

NOLA. A town of Campania, Italy, in the province of Caserta, on the railway to Bajano. Bells are said to have been first made here. It occupies the site of an Etruscan city, captured by the Romans in 313 B.C., in which the Emperor Augustus died. Pop. 17,000.

NOMADS. Tribes without fixed habitations, generally engaged in the tending and raising of cattle, and changing their abode as necessity requires or inclination prompts. North Africa and the northern and middle parts of Asia are still inhabited by nomadic tribes.

NOME. A town of Alaska, U.S.A., situated on Norton Sound. On the discovery of gold in 1899 it became the centre of a famous mining area, but its population, which in 1900 was 12,500, had decreased in 1930 to 1213.

NOMINALISM. A term in scholastic philosophy designating the theory that only individual objects have real existence, whilst *universals* are nothing but names. In other words, individual concrete objects alone are real, while the genus is only a symbol, or a word. Nominalism thus meant that no interest could be taken in a world of abstractions. It was a reaction against neo-Platonism, limiting as it did man's study to what he could observe, to a world of concrete, individual objects. To a certain extent nominalism is the forerunner of positivism (q.v.).

Nominalism is opposed to realism, which maintains that general ideas are not formed by the understanding, but have a real existence independent of the mind, and apart from the individual object—that, for example, beauty in the abstract has a real existence, apart from a beautiful thing. The problem, already discussed by Boethius, was revived by John Roscellinus, Canon of Compiègne, in the eleventh century. It was condemned at Soissons in 1092, and the realists became the predominating school.

A reconciliation between the two opposing theories was attempted by Abelard, who taught that although ideas are not found actually existing in the objects themselves, they can yet be conceived by the mind as existing independently and apart from any concrete embodiment of them, and that accordingly they are not mere words. This doctrine was called *conceptualism.* In the beginning of the fourteenth century the dispute was again revived by the English Franciscan William of Occam, a disciple of Duns Scotus. The nominalists, although often persecuted, gradually gained the ascendancy in France as well as in Germany. *See* SCHOLASTICISM.

NOMOGRAPHY. A graphical method of evaluating formulæ and solving equations. Suppose that a number x is determined when the values of two other numbers a and b are given; we may have, e.g. $x = a^3b^2$, or $x^2 + ax + b = 0$. Then two straight lines A and B are graduated, not necessarily to the same scale, and, as a rule, placed parallel to each other; and a curve X is drawn and so graduated that the straight line joining the graduation a on the scale A to the graduation b on the scale B cuts the curve X at the graduation x, corresponding to the number x which is required. The illustration is a nomogram which gives the solutions between 0 and 10 of any equation of the quadratic type $x^2+ax+b=0$, for values of a and b from -10 to 10. If the scale on the right (b) is taken as the axis of Y, and the origin at the point 0 on that scale, the equation of the curve is $Y = -X^2/(X+1)$, the second scale (a) being placed along the line $X = -1$.

To find, e.g. the positive root of the equation $x^2+5x-3=0$, lay a ruler across the page from $+5$ on the a scale to -3 on the b scale; the ruler will cut the curve at the graduation 0·54, which is the root required. In numerical evaluations it is often useful to have several straight scales, graduated in various ways, and perhaps not parallel to each other; in these cases several applications of the ruler are made to the diagram, according to a definite plan, and the final answer is read off one of the scales.

Nomography is coming to be used rather extensively, especially in routine engineering calculations. The preliminary process of constructing a suitable nomogram may take some time, but if the number of calculations all of one type is large, it may be time well spent. The recent development of the method is chiefly due to P. M. D'Ocagne, whose *Traité de Nomographie* is the standard work on the subject.—Cf. S. Brodetsky, *A First Course in Nomography.*

NONCONFORMITY. Nonconformity is a general term for dissent from an Established Church. It is specially associated with English history after the Reformation, and it acquired a new and definite significance after the Restoration of 1660. The earliest Nonconformists were the "Separatists" of the reign of Elizabeth, who met together for private worship, though many of them did not repudiate connection with the English Church. Some of these, like the Anabaptists, exercised no permanent influence upon English history; the most important were the holders of what was afterwards known as Presbyterianism, and there were also advocates of Independency, now described as Congregationalism.

The word "Puritan" was used to cover the whole movement, but it included men who would now be regarded as Low Churchmen. The refusal of James I. to accept the Millenary Petition in 1603, and the failure of the Hampton Court Conference in 1604, made a permanent breach between the more extreme Puritanism and the Church of England, and the king's policy of repressing Puritanism led both to the growth of Puritan congregations in England and to Puritan emigration to the New World (*see* PILGRIM FATHERS).

In the reign of Charles I. the religious policy of Laud drove not only Low Churchmen but also moderate Churchmen to support the Puritans, and the Presbyterians were in a majority in the House of Commons in the Long Parliament. Their influence in Parliament was, however, out of proportion to their numbers and influence throughout the country, and after the defeat of the Royalists by Cromwell and the New Model Army the Independents came into power, and by Pride's Purge (1648) expelled the Presbyterian majority of the House of Commons. Under the Commonwealth and Protectorate what had been Nonconformity became the Established Church, Presbyterians and Independents being alike eligible to hold livings.

After the Restoration an attempt was made to compel conformity with the Church of England, by a series of measures known as the Clarendon Code. The Corporation Act restricted office in a municipal corporation to men who took the sacrament annually in accordance with the rites of the Church of England. The effect of these measures was to create a large number of Nonconformist congregations, and in 1664 Parliament passed a Conventicle Act to prohibit any exercise of public worship outside the Church.

In 1665 this was followed by the Five Mile Act, which forbade a Nonconformist minister to come within 5 miles of any market town or of any parish where he had held the living, or to teach in a school. Charles II., in 1672, issued a Declaration of Indulgence, suspending the operation of these Acts and also of the penal laws against Roman Catholics, but the Anglican Parliament forced him to withdraw the Declaration and to assent to the Test Act (1673), which, though aimed primarily against Roman Catholics, included Protestant Nonconformists in its provision that any one who held office under the Crown should take the sacrament in the Church of England.

Nonconformists had welcomed Charles's Declaration of Indulgence, but the policy of his successor, James II., alarmed them, and they joined with the Church in protesting against his Declarations of Indulgence and supported the Revolution. William III. was anxious to bring about a comprehension of Nonconformists within the Church, but efforts in this direction were unsuccessful, and they had to be content with the measure of relief given by the Toleration Act (1689), which relieved them from the fines inflicted for non-attendance at their parish churches, and allowed them to worship in licensed and registered chapels. During the Tory reaction in the end of Anne's reign an Occasional Conformity Act was passed to prevent Nonconformists from qualifying for office by taking the sacrament on rare occasions, and a Schism Act to deprive them of the opportunity of educating their children in their own doctrines.

Both these Acts were repealed in the reign of George I., but Walpole did not dare to propose to repeal the Corporation Act or to relieve his Nonconformist supporters from the disabilities of the Test Act. He did, however, pass in 1727 an Act which was interpreted as exempting Protestant Nonconformists from the penalty for holding office without taking the sacrament, and this Indemnity Act was passed annually until the repeal of the Test and Corporation Acts in 1828. An Act of 1836 permitted Nonconformists to solemnize marriages in chapels registered for that purpose, and in 1871 the Universities Test Acts gave them admission to the Universities of Oxford, Cambridge, and Durham.—BIBLIOGRAPHY: D. Neal, *History of the Puritans*; J. Heron, *A Short History of Puritanism*; E. Dowden, *Puritan and Anglican*.

NONJURORS. Clergy and laymen who, though not Romanists, refused to take the oath of allegiance to the Government and Crown of England at the Revolution, when James II. abandoned the throne. The Nonjurors numbered upward of 400 clergy, and included the Archbishop of Canterbury, William Sancroft, and several bishops. *See* ENGLAND (ECCLESIASTICAL HISTORY).

NONNUS, or NONNOS. A later Greek poet, born at Panopolis, in Egypt, who lived about the beginning of the fifth century A.D. He is the author of a poem entitled *Dionysiaca*, in forty-eight books, in which the expedition of Bacchus (Dionysus) to India is described; also of a paraphrase, in Greek hexameters, of the Gospel of St. John.

NORBITON. An urban district of Surrey and a residential suburb of London, on the Southern Railway (London and South-Western Railway section), 12 miles from London. Pop. (1931), 12,652.

NORBURY. A district of Surrey and a residential suburb of London, on the Southern Railway and the Metropolitan tramway system, 7 miles from London.

NORD. A department in the north-east of France, bordering with Belgium; area, 2228 sq. miles. The coast, marked by a long chain of sandy hillocks, furnishes the two harbours of Dunkirk and Gravelines. The interior is a fertile alluvial flat, intersected by sluggish streams and canals. The principal minerals are coal and iron, which were extensively wrought, the occupations connected with or depending on them rendering this department among the most important in France prior to the European War. The capital is Lille. The mineral industry was totally destroyed during the war, and the greater part of Nord was occupied and devastated by the Germans. Pop. (1931), 2,029,449.

NORDENSKIÖLD (nor'den-sheuld), **Nils Adolf Erik, Baron.** A Swedish naturalist and explorer, born at Helsingfors 18th Nov., 1832, died at Stockholm 12th Aug., 1901. He devoted himself to science, and was appointed to some important posts, but becoming obnoxious to the Russian authorities he settled in Sweden. He made geological discoveries in Spitzbergen, and took part in all Arctic expeditions sent out by the Swedish Government. On a North Polar expedition in 1868 he reached the high latitude of 81° 42′.

Having turned his attention to Siberia, after making two successful voyages through the Kara Sea to the Yenissei, he decided to attempt the accomplishment of the north-east passage, or passage by sea round Northern Asia to the Pacific. Aided by the King of Sweden and others, Nordenskiöld was enabled, July, 1878, to sail in the *Vega*, which was the first vessel to double the most northern point of the Old World, Cape Tchelyuskin, and after passing through Behring's Straits reached Japan, 2nd Sept., 1879.

NORDERNEY. A small island belonging to Prussia, province of Hanover, on the coast of East Friesland; area, about 8 sq. miles; pop. 4060, chiefly fishermen of the old Frisian stock.

NORDHAUSEN (nord'hou-zn). A town of Germany, in the Prussian province of Saxony, on the Zorge and on the slopes of the Harz Mountains. It has a Roman Catholic cathedral and an old town house. It manufactures lacquerware, chemicals, etc.; and has extensive distilleries and breweries. Pop. 35,056.

NÖRDLINGEN (neurd'ling-ėn). A walled town of Germany, in the

Republic of Bavaria, on the Eger, near the Württemberg frontier, with well-preserved wall and towers, and a Gothic church (St. George) surmounted by a tower 345 feet high. It has manufactures of carpets, woollen and linen goods, leather, etc. In the Thirty Years War the Swedes were defeated here, 6th Sept., 1634, by the Imperialists, and on 3rd Aug., 1645, the French under Condé and Turenne defeated the Imperialists under Franz von Mercy. Pop. 9380.

NORDSTRAND. An island of Germany, on the west coast of Schleswig; area, 21 sq. miles. The greater part of it was swept away in 1634 by a flood, which drowned 15,000 persons. Pop. about 2500 Frisians by origin.

NORE. (1) A part of the estuary of the Thames, about 50 miles below London, and east of Sheerness, encumbered with sandbanks. On the eastern side the Nore lightship has

Nore Lightship

been anchored since 1792.—(2) A river of Ireland, rising in the Slieve Bloom Mountains, on the borders of Tipperary and Leix, and joining the Barrow about 2 miles above New Ross; length, 70 miles. It admits vessels of considerable size as far as Inistioge (10 miles), and barges to Thomastown.

NORFOLK (nor'fok). A maritime county of Eastern England, with 90 miles of seaboard to the North Sea; area, 1,315,064 acres, or about 2054 sq. miles. The surface is generally flat, with some slight swells and depressions in the north part. The coast consists principally of cliffs, partly chalk and partly alternate strata of clay, gravel, loam, and sand. These are gradually being undermined by the sea, which is in many places making inroads on the land. The principal rivers are the Yare, in the east, with its affluents the Bure, the Wensum, and the Waveney; and the Ouse, in the west, with its feeders the Little Ouse, the Wissey, etc. The Yare and its tributaries expand near the sea into meres or *broads*, which, largely covered with bulrushes and sedges, are the resort of a great variety of water-fowl.

The county is served by the L.N.E. Railway. It is noted for agricultural progressiveness, barley (mainly for malting), wheat, and oats being raised, and dairying and fruit-growing practised. The manufactures consist chiefly of woven goods. Norfolk has extensive fisheries of both herrings and mackerel. Oil-shale is worked in the King's Lynn district. Five members are returned to Parliament. The county town is Norwich; the chief seaport is Yarmouth. Pop. (1931), 504,846.

Norfolk was occupied in early times by the Iceni, and several stations were founded by the Romans. It became part of East Anglia, and eventually became one of the richest areas of England through its wool-producing industry.—Cf. W. Rye, *History of Norfolk*; E. W. Priest, *Vanishing Local Traditions of Norfolk*.

NORFOLK. A city and port of entry of Norfolk county, Virginia, United States, on the Elizabeth River (an arm of Chesapeake Bay), and served by the Chesapeake & Ohio, the Southern, the Norfolk & Western, the Virginian, and other railways, and by many steamship lines. It is an important United States naval station, with constructive and repairing establishments, and is the second largest city of Virginia state. Much cotton is exported, with peanuts, coal, grain, fruit, and oysters. Norfolk was founded in 1682, incorporated in 1736, and became a city in 1845. Pop. (1930), 129,710.

NORFOLK ISLAND. An island of the Southern Pacific, in 29° 3′ 4″ S. lat., 167° 58′ 6″ E. long., described as "the Madeira of the Pacific." It is 900 miles distant from Sydney (New South Wales); the coast-line is 20 miles; except on the south-west, inaccessible cliffs rise from the sea. The climate is equable, ranging from 56° to 82°, with a mean of 68°.

Produce.—Bananas and (in parts) coffee, oranges, lemons, guavas, pineapples, and passion fruit are raised. Butter is produced. Cattle, horses, sheep, pigs, and poultry are reared. Schools of whales (sperm and hump-backed) visit Norfolk Island annually, and edible fish abound in the surrounding waters. Exports are mainly lemon-peel, lemon-juice, and hides.

The "All-Red" cable from Great Britain, via Vancouver, Fanning Island, and Fiji, bifurcates at Norfolk for New Zealand and Brisbane respectively. Education is free and compulsory up to fifteen years. Area, 13 sq. miles (5 miles long by 3 miles wide); pop. (1931), 992, 545 being males.

Norfolk Island was first colonized in 1788 by H.M.S. *Sirius*, a small penal settlement being established at Port Jackson. The descendants of the *Bounty* mutineers became too numerous to subsist on Pitcairn Island, and were removed thence to Norfolk Island (1856). In 1856 the island was severed from Tasmania, and is now administered (since 1st July, 1914) from Melbourne through an Administrator and Chief Magistrate.

NORHAM. Village of Northumberland. It is 8 miles from Berwick-on-Tweed, and 340 miles from London by the L.N.E. Railway. It is visited for its castle, which, mentioned in *Marmion*, was a border fortress belonging to the Bishop of Durham. It is the centre of a small district called Norhamshire, which was part of the county of Durham until 1844. Pop. 697.

NORIA. *See* PERSIAN WHEEL.

NOR'ICUM. A province of the Roman Empire, south of the Danube, and corresponding generally to modern Carinthia and Styria, with parts of Bavaria and Austria. The original inhabitants were Celtic, and were subdued by the Romans in 14-16 B.C.

NORMAN ARCHITECTURE. The round-arched style of architecture, a variety of the Romanesque, introduced at the Norman Conquest from France into Britain, where it prevailed till the end of the twelfth century. In its earlier stages it is plain and massive with but few mouldings, and those principally confined to small features; as the style advanced greater lightness and enrichment were introduced, and some of the later examples are highly enriched. The chevron, billet, nail-head, and lozenge mouldings are distinctively characteristic of this style. The more specific characteristics of churches in this style are: cruciform plan with apse and apsidal chapels, the tower rising from the intersection of nave and transept; semi-cylindrical vaulting; the doorways, deeply recessed, with highly decorated mouldings; the windows small, round-headed, placed high in the wall, and opening with a wide splay inside; piers massive, generall cylindrical or octagonal, and sometimes enriched with shafts; capitals cushion-shaped, sometimes plain, more frequently enriched; buttresses broad, with but small projection; walls frequently decorated by bands of arcades with single or interlacing arches.

Norman Doorway: Castle Rising, Norfolk

In course of time the arches began to assume the pointed character; the piers, walls, etc., to be less massive; short pyramidal spires crown the towers; and altogether the style assumes a more delicate and refined character, passing gradually into the Early English. Besides ecclesiastical buildings, the Normans reared many castellated structures, the best remaining specimen of which is the Keep of the Tower of London. The walls of Norman buildings were of great thickness, and the piers supporting their arches were usually of immense girth, yet notwithstanding this massiveness the buildings frequently gave way.

The Abbaye aux Hommes and the Abbaye aux Dames at Caen, Normandy, afford excellent examples of this style; as also parts of the cathedrals of Durham, Peterborough, Norwich, and Canterbury, as well as many smaller churches.—Cf. E. G. Browne, *Norman Architecture*.

NORMAN CONQUEST. The battle of Hastings (or Senlac), by which William of Normandy became an English king in 1066, was the culmination, not the beginning, of a process of Normanization. Edward the Confessor, the last monarch of the House of Wessex, was the son of Emma of Normandy, and had been brought up by his mother's kinsfolk while Canute (Emma's second husband) was reigning in England. After his accession, in

NORMAN ARCHITECTURE: ABBAYE AUX DAMES, CAEN

1042, Edward set himself to introduce Norman manners and customs into England; he was surrounded by Norman courtiers and ecclesiastics, and he wished his cousin, William, Duke of Normandy, to succeed him. The king had to face the powerful opposition of Godwin, Earl of Kent, and, after his (Godwin's) death in 1053, of his son Harold, both leaders of an English party.

In the year preceding Edward's death, Harold was shipwrecked on the Norman coast, and was compelled to take an oath to acknowledge William's claim, but when the Confessor died, the Witan, or Great Council, chose Harold as his successor, and he was crowned on 6th Jan., 1066. William at once began to prepare to invade England, and Harold had also to meet a Danish invasion, assisted by one of his own brothers. He defeated the Danes at Stamford Bridge on 25th Sept., but the Norman attack immediately followed, and Harold had to lead a tired army from Northumbria to Sussex to fight the new enemy. The battle (14th Oct.), fought on a hill then known as Senlac, about 8 miles from Hastings, was fiercely contested, but resulted in a complete Norman victory, and Harold was killed.

The city of London at first was opposed to the Conqueror, but he devastated and laid waste all south-eastern England until the Londoners were convinced of the hopelessness of the English cause, and they submitted in December. William the Claimant (as he described himself) was crowned in Westminster Abbey on Christmas Day, 1066, as the lawful successor of the old English kings, and he promised to retain the law of England. None the less, the Norman Conquest marked a great turning-point in English history. and was followed by fundamental changes in law and in organization.

As different parts of the country fell successively under his power, William distributed the land among his own followers, and English society became divided into a ruling class of Norman land-owners and a subject class of English, a distinction which, within about a century, was obliterated by inter-marriage. Anglo-Saxon England had been developing in the direction of feudalism, and the process was accelerated by the introduction of Continental feudalism, with, however, some important limitations to the power of the feudal barons.

The most important results of the Conquest were the unification of England under a strong absolute monarchy, and the introduction of Norman financial and legal methods and institutions—among them the jury, first employed as a financial expedient, and used for the compilation of *Domesday Book,* William's famous survey of the land and live-stock of the country. *Domesday Book* was regarded as a great grievance by the English, as were also the forests which the Norman kings created for their hunting. From 1066 until the reign of John, England was closely associated with the Duchy of Normandy, and one portion of the old duchy—the Channel Islands—still belongs to the English Crown.

NORMANDY. District of France, formerly a province. In the north of the country, Normandy is now divided into the departments of Seine Inférieure, Eure, Orne, Calvados, and Manche. It was taken by Rollo and his Norsemen in 912, and was an English possession from 1066, but was lost finally in 1449. The chief towns are Rouen, the capital, Dieppe, Havre, Caen, Bayeux, Cherbourg, and Mont-St.-Michel.

The ground is fertile, producing corn, hemp, flax, and fruit (chiefly cider-apples). There is iron near Caen. It has large fisheries, and sheep and dairy-farming in the interior.

NOR'MANTON. A town in the West Riding of Yorkshire, on the Calder, and an important railway junction of the L.M.S. and L.N.E. Railways. Pop. (1931), 15,684.

NORNS. In Scandinavian mythology, the three Fates, representing the *past*, the *present*, and the *future*, whose decrees were irrevocable. They were represented as three young women, named respectively Urd, Verdandi, and Skuld.

NORRISTOWN. A borough and city of Pennsylvania, United States, county seat of Montgomery county, on the Schuylkill; served by the Pennsylvania and other railways, by electric railway to Philadelphia, and by the Schuylkill Canal. Norristown was founded in 1785, and was incorporated as a borough in 1812. It has extensive woollen- and cotton-factories, rolling-mills, foundries, etc. Pop. (1930), 35,853.

NORRKÖPING (nor-cheup'ing). A town of Sweden (founded in 1384), at the mouth of the Motala Elf in the Bravik, a gulf of the Baltic. The Motala Elf flows through the town, making several falls within it, and is crossed by several bridges. It has manufactures of woollens, cottons, etc., and has sugar-refineries and shipbuilding yards. Pop. (1932), 61,799.

NORMANDY: OLD HOUSES, ROUEN

NORTE (nor'tā), **Rio Grande del.** A river of North America, forming for a long distance the boundary between Mexico and the United States, a d falling into the Gulf of Mexico. Length, about 2000 miles.

NORTH, Frederick, Lord. Earl of Guilford, the eldest son of Francis, first Earl of Guilford, born in 1732, died 1792. He is best known as having been the chief of the administration during the American War of Independence. In 1770 he succeeded the Duke of Grafton as minister, when his retention of the tea-duty, imposed upon the American colonists, led to the rising in America, and to the declaration of independence, 4th July, 1776. Lord North resigned on the 20th of March, 1782. He became Earl of Guilford by the death of his father in 1790.

NORTH. One of the cardinal points, being that point of the compass which is exactly in the direction of the North Pole. In the case of the celestial sphere, north means the direction towards the North Pole of the heavens. *See* POLE.

NORTHALLERTON. A town of England, capital of the North Riding of Yorkshire; served by the L.N.E. Railway. The industries include some tanning and currying, brewing, malting, engineering, and saddlery-making. Three miles outside the town, on the north, was fought the battle of the Standard (1138). Pop. (1931), 4787.

NORTH AMERICA. The northern half of the Western Continent or New World, extending northwards from Mexico, which it includes, and embracing also the United States, Canada, and Alaska. The total area is about 8,700,000 sq. miles, and the pop. approximately 170,000,000. *See* GEOGRAPHY (under "Land Forms"); AMERICA; and articles under various countries.

NORTHAMPTON. A county and municipal borough of England, county town of Northamptonshire, on the Nene; served by the London, Midland, and Scottish Railway. Northampton has four noteworthy parish churches, viz. St. Giles, St. Peter's, All Saints, and St. Sepulchre's, one of the three round churches of England. There is a Roman Catholic cathedral. The staple manufacture is boots and shoes for home and export trade. There are also iron- and brass-foundries, breweries, corn-mills, etc. Ironstone is found in the neighbourhood, and smelting-furnaces are at work. Northampton sends one member to Parliament. Pop. (1931), 92,314.

NORTHAMPTON. An inland county of Eastern England; area, 638,612 acres. It includes the Soke of Peterborough. The county is pleasantly diversified by low hills, extensive woodlands watered by numerous rivers and streams, the chief of them being the Welland, Nene, Avon, and Cherwell. The county is traversed by the London, Midland, and Scottish, and London and North-Eastern Railways, and by the Grand Union and other canals. The principal grain crops are wheat, barley, and oats. The rearing of sheep and cattle is a principal object with the Northamptonshire farmers. Northamptonshire is a famous hunting county. Northamptonshire sends four members to Parliament. Pop. (1931), 309,428.

NORTHAMPTON. A city of Massachusetts, United States, the county seat of Hampshire county, on Connecticut River; served by various important railways. Cutlery, brushes, paper, cotton, and woollen goods are manufactured. Pop. 24,381.

NORTH AUSTRALIA. *See* NORTHERN TERRITORY.

NORTH BERWICK. A royal burgh and watering-place of East Lothian, Scotland, at the entrance to the Firth of Forth. It is a famous golfing centre, and here is Tantallon Castle. Pop. (1931), 3473.

NORTHBROOK, Thomas George Baring, Earl of. English statesman, son of the first Baron Northbrook, born in 1826, died in 1904. After holding various important offices, he became Viceroy of India in 1872. This office he resigned in 1876, and was created Earl of Northbrook. From 1880 to 1885 Lord Northbrook was First Lord of the Admiralty under Gladstone; but in 1886 he opposed the Home Rule policy of the Premier.

NORTHCOTE, James. Born in Plymouth in 1746, died 1831. He studied art under Sir Joshua Reynolds, became highly successful as a portrait-painter, and won both wealth and reputation. Two of his best works were for the Shakespeare Gallery—the *Murder of the Two Princes in the Tower* and *Hubert and Arthur.* He published *Memoirs of Sir Joshua Reynolds*, comprising *Anecdotes of his Contemporaries* (1813), and a *Supplement* (in 1815); and *Memoirs of Titian* (1830), in which he was assisted by Hazlitt.

NORTH-EAST PASSAGE. A passage for ships along the northern coasts of Europe and Asia to the Pacific Ocean, formerly supposed likely to be of commercial value. The first to make the complete voyage by this passage was the Swedish explorer Nordenskiöld (in 1878-79), after it had been attempted in vain for upwards of three centuries. *See* NORTH POLAR EXPEDITIONS.

NORTHERN IRELAND. The smaller of the two political divisions of Ireland, situated in the N.E. of the island and comprising the major part of Ulster; area, 3,351,444 sq. miles; pop. (1926), 1,256,561. The chief towns and seaports are Belfast (the capital) and Londonderry, and other places are Enniskillen, Coleraine, Newry, Lisburn, and Carrickfergus.

James Northcote

Religion, Education, etc. — The principal religious denominations are Presbyterian (393,374), Episcopalian (338,724), Methodist (49,554), and Roman Catholic (420,428). In accordance with the Education Act (Northern Ireland), 1923, a system of local control of education has been set up, with the Minister of Education as the supreme authority. In Belfast is Queen's University. The Royal Ulster Constabulary has a strength of 3000. For constituent counties, physical features, history, etc., *see* IRELAND.

Production and Industry.—Northern Ireland is mainly agricultural, 952,183 acres being under crops in 1931. The chief corn crop is oats, and the chief green crop is potatoes. In 1931, 7440 acres were devoted to flax. Dairying and stock-rearing are important industries, there being, in 1931, 680,649 cattle and 793,834 sheep. Mining and quarrying are carried on to a certain extent, the chief products being igneous rock, chalk, granite, clay, and sandstone, with some iron ore. Belfast is the centre of important linen and ship-building industries, which employ 85,000 and 11,000 people respectively. In 1931 the value of linens exported from the United Kingdom was £5,431,515, almost all of which came from Northern Ireland. Other manufactures are ropes and twines, tobacco, soap, aerated waters, biscuits, etc.

Communications.—There are in Northern Ireland 754 miles of railway track and 180 miles of canals (Newry Canal and Ulster Canal).

Constitution.—The Government of Ireland Act, 1920, which provided for separate Parliaments in Northern and Southern Ireland, was accepted by the Ulster Unionists, and the Parliament which was duly elected in 1921 was opened by the King in person. By this Act, as amended by the Irish Free State (Consequential Provisions) Act, 1922, Northern Ireland has also a separate Executive Government. Parliament consists of a Senate and a House of Commons (both elective), who have power to legislate for Northern Ireland except in regard to (1) matters of Imperial concern (the Crown, combatant forces, war, peace, external trade, etc.); and (2) certain matters reserved to the Imperial Parliament (such as the postal service). In the event of a disagreement between the two Houses, a joint sitting is to be held and a decision arrived at by an absolute majority. The ministry (of 26 members) advises the Governor (representing the King), in whom the executive power is vested. Northern Ireland is represented in the Imperial Parliament by thirteen members. The usual channel of communication between the Government of Northern Ireland and the Imperial Government is the Home Office. After the settlement of Irish problems in 1922, boundary disputes between Northern Ireland and the Irish Free State still continued. A Commission to inquire into the question was set up in 1924, but in 1925 Mr. Baldwin intervened, and a settlement was arrived at whereby no boundary alteration was made (*see* IRISH FREE STATE.)

NORTHERN TERRITORIES (Gold Coast). Bounded west and north by French territories, and east by Togoland. They are administered by a Chief Commissioner (subject to the Governor), with headquarters at Tamale, and are divided into the Southern Province (chief town, Tamale), and the Northern Province (chief town, Navoro); area, 30,486 sq. miles, with an additional 13,041 sq. miles of mandated territory; pop. (1931), 717,275 (107 non-Africans). Agriculture and stock-breeding are the industries. They became a British Protectorate in 1901. Part of Togoland (q.v.) is administered with the Northern Territories.

NORTHERN TERRITORY. A region of Australia, comprising all land lying between the meridians of 129° and 138° E. long., and north of the line of 26° S. lat., which divides it from South Australia. The area is 523,620 sq. miles, almost entirely in the Torrid Zone. The Australian aborigines located in the territory numbered, in 1931, 21,242. A Protector of Aboriginals, resident at Darwin (the chief town and port), is entrusted with their care. Aboriginal Reserves cover an area of 33,000 sq. miles. The population, in 1931, exclusive of aboriginals, was 4193.

Herds of wild buffaloes are found on the mainland and on Melville Island. There are Government cattle stations, and an extensive meat-packing factory exists near Darwin. A great dairying industry could be developed. Agriculture is undeveloped, but rice, maize, sugar-cane, and many tropical products can be raised. Gold, tin, copper, wolfram, and salt are found. Bêche-de-mer is also exported, and the territorial waters abound in marketable fish.

In 1827 the Northern Territory became part of New South Wales, but in 1863 was annexed to the province of South Australia. On 1st Jan., 1911, it was transferred, with adjacent islands, to the Commonwealth. By the North Australia Act (1926), the Northern Territory was divided at lat. 20° S. into North Australia (capital, Darwin) and Central Australia (capital, Alice Springs). This Act was repealed in 1931.—BIBLIOGRAPHY: *Official Year Book of the Commonwealth of Australia*; B. Spencer, *The Native Tribes of the Northern Territory of Australia.*

NORTHFLEET. An urban district of Kent, England, on the Thames, adjoining Gravesend; served by the Southern Railway. Shipbuilding and the manufacture of paper and chemicals are the main industries. Pop. (1931), 16,429.

NORTH ISLAND. The northernmost island of the Dominion of New Zealand. It contains the largest cities, Wellington (city pop. 1932, 144,800) and Auckland (city pop. 1932, 218,400). In 1932, 1533 miles of State railway traversed the state, connecting Wellington with Auckland, Napier, New Plymouth, and other towns. The east and south-east of North Island is devoted to sheep-raising, and the south-west specializes in dairying. The northern division has a progressive fruit-farming industry. There are four provincial districts, viz. Auckland, Wellington, Hawke's Bay, and Taranaki. Area, 44,281 sq. miles; pop (1932), 984,277. *See* NEW ZEALAND.

NORTHMEN. The inhabitants of ancient Scandinavia, or Norway, Sweden, and Denmark, who in England were also called *Danes.* They were fierce and warlike tribes, who as early as the eighth century made piratical expeditions to all parts of the European seas, these piratical robbers being known among themselves as *vikings.*

In A.D. 795 the Scandinavians established themselves in the Faröe Isles and in Orkney; towards the middle of the ninth century they founded the governments of Novgorod and of Kiev, in Russia; and after the discovery of Iceland certain powerful Norwegian families, taking refuge from the persecutions of Harold, King of Denmark, settled in that island (in 870).

In the ninth century they made repeated incursions into France, and it became necessary to purchase their withdrawal with gold. Bands of them settled permanently in France, and Charles the Simple was obliged (912) to cede to them the province afterwards called *Normandy,* and to give his daughter in marriage to Rollo, their chief. Rollo embraced the Christian religion and became the first Duke of Normandy.

The course of events was somewhat similar in England. Egbert, in the beginning of the ninth century, had no sooner made some approaches towards a regular government than the Danes made their appearance. Under Alfred (871-901) they overran great parts of England, but were finally defeated, and those of them who remained in the country had to acknowledge his sway. But they returned, under his successors, in greater force, obtained possession of the northern and eastern part of the country, and in the beginning of the eleventh century three Scandinavian princes (Canute, Harold, and Hardicanute) ruled successively over England. The Saxon line was then restored; but in 1066 William, Duke of Normandy, a descendant of Rollo, obtained the English throne, an event known as the Norman Conquest.

According to the Saga narratives the Northmen were the first discoverers of America. The coasts of Spain, Italy, Greece, and Asia Minor were ravaged by them, and in Byzantium the bodyguard of the emperors long consisted of Northmen known as Varangians.

NORTH POLAR EXPEDITIONS. Expeditions of discovery in the Arctic regions. In 1517 Sebastian Cabot was commissioned by Henry VIII. to search for a North-West Passage round America to India; and from that time onwards the discovery of such a passage became a favourite project with explorers. Frobisher, Davis, Hudson, Bylot, and Baffin successively engaged in this enterprise.

Then after a lapse of nearly two centuries the record of Arctic research was taken up by such men as Ross and Parry (1818), who were followed by Sir John Franklin. Franklin set sail in command of the *Erebus* and *Terror* in May, 1845, and by the month of July reached Whalefish Islands in Davis' Strait. On the 26th of that month the ships were seen in lat. 74° 48′ N., long. 66° 13′ W.; after which no further intelligence concerning them was received. It was not, however, till the beginning of 1847 that serious apprehensions were entertained regarding the expedition. The most strenuous efforts were then made by both the English and the Americans to obtain tidings of Franklin. Among the numerous expeditions sent out by sea and land in search of the missing navigator and his company were those of Richardson and Rae (by land, 1847), of Moore (1848-52), of Kellet (1848-50), of Shedden (1848-50), of Sir James Ross (1848-49), of Saunders (1849-50), of Austin and Ommaney (1850-51), and of Penny (1850-51).

In 1850 MacClure set out by Behring Strait on a search expedition, and to him is due the honour of having ascertained the existence of the long-sought-for North-West Passage. Other expeditions between 1850 and 1855 were: Collinson's, Rae's, Kennedy's, Maguire's, Belcher's, MacClintock's, and Inglefield's. In 1853 Rae, proceeding to the east side of King William Sound, obtained the first tidings of the destruction of Franklin's ships. In 1855 Anderson, proceeding up the Great Fish River, also discovered relics of the *Erebus* and *Terror*. At length MacClintock (1857-59) set all

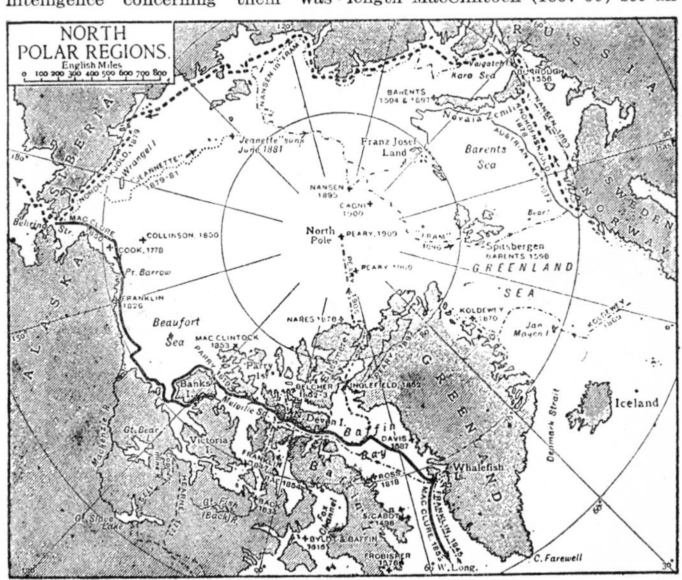

Map of the North Polar Regions, showing the Routes of the Chief Expeditions of Discovery

doubts at rest regarding the fate of Sir John Franklin and his companions by establishing the fact that they had died in 1847.

Dr. Kane made some important observations during the progress of his Arctic explorations, 1853-55. Then followed the expeditions of Dr. Isaac Hayes in 1860 and 1869, and those of Captain Charles Hall in 1860 and 1864.

Similarly efforts were also made to discover a North-East Passage to the Pacific Ocean. In 1553 Willoughby rounded North Cape; in 1556 Burrough reached the south point of Novaya Zemlia and Waigatch Island; in 1580 Pet and Jackman penetrated into the Sea of Kara; in 1594-96 Barents discovered Bear Island and Spitzbergen, and rounded the east point of Novaya Zemlia.

Dashnef in 1648 discovered Behring Strait, which was rediscovered in 1728 by Behring, whose name it bears. A more correct idea of the configuration of the coast on either side of Behring Sea was first obtained by Cook in 1778; but with the exception of this, to the Russians is due nearly all the credit, until recently, of the explorations on the North Asiatic coasts. The North-East Passage was at last accomplished by Professor Nordenskiöld (q.v.), of Sweden, who in 1878 sailed eastward along the whole of the north coast of Europe and Asia, emerging through Behring Strait early in 1879.

The northern portion of the American continent, in the region of the Coppermine River, was first explored by Hearne in 1771. In 1789 Mackenzie discovered the great river called after him. The north coast eastwards to the Great Fish River was explored by Franklin, Richardson, and Back in two expeditions by land, the first from 1819 to 1821, and the second from 1825 to 1826, while in 1834-35 Back, in company with King, proceeded down the Back or Great Fish River. Since then much has been done in exploring Northern Canada, though much still remains undone.

The Germans sent out their first expedition to the Polar regions in 1868 under Captain Koldewey, and a second in 1869 under the same captain. An Austrian expedition under the conduct of Lieutenants Payer and Weyprecht, dispatched in June, 1872, discovered Franz-Joseph Land, to the north of Novaya Zemlia. In 1875 Britain sent out an expedition under Captain Nares. Among later expeditions were that of the unfortunate *Jeannette* (1879), sent out under the command of Lieutenant De Long, to explore the Arctic Sea through Behring Strait; and the expedition sent out by the United States under Lieutenant Greely (1881-84). Dr. Nansen, starting in 1893, reached 86° 14′ N. lat., surpassing all previous explorers.

Commander Peary did splendid work in North Greenland and elsewhere, and in 1909 reached the Pole. An American impostor, Dr. Cook, claimed to have reached it in 1908. With Peary's success the Pole ceased to be the main objective, and expeditions took a more scientific turn. The chief names in this period are Knud Rasmussen (1910, 1912, 1916), de Koch (1913), Koch (1920), and Stefansson in the *Karluk* (1913-18).

Roald Amundsen (1918-20) completed the North-East Passage, and left his ship to make a drift in the Polar Sea. He himself made an attempt to reach the Pole by aeroplane in 1925, but did not succeed. In 1926, however, he crossed the Pole in the airship *Norge* on a voyage from Spitzbergen to Alaska. A few days previously two Americans crossed the Pole in an aeroplane. There were Oxford University expeditions to Spitzbergen and North-East Land in 1921 and 1924. There have been numerous Russian, Dutch, etc., expeditions. In 1928 the Italian airship *Italia*, commanded by General Nobile, crossed the North Pole but was wrecked in the Arctic. Nobile and a few others were rescued, and Amundsen lost his life in attempting to give help.

NORTH SEA. A large branch of the Atlantic Ocean lying between Great Britain and the continent of Europe. The area is 190,000 sq. miles. The North Sea is deepest on the Norwegian side, where the soundings give over 190 fathoms; but its mean depth is no more than 31 fathoms. The bed of this sea is traversed by several submarine ridges, such as the Dogger, Jutland, and Great Fisher Banks. The fisheries, especially of herring, cod, ling, haddock, flat-fish, etc., are exceedingly valuable.

NORTH STAR. The north polar star, the star α of the constellation Ursa Minor, which is close to the true pole. As its altitude above the horizon, when certain corrections are applied, gives the latitude of a place, it is of great importance to navigators in the northern hemisphere.

NORTHUM′BERLAND. A northern maritime county of England, bounded south and south-west by the counties of Durham and Cumberland; east by the North Sea; and north and north-west by Scotland. Area, 1,291,978 acres, of which about 717,000 acres are arable, meadow, and pasture. The highest hills, the Cheviots, on the north-west border, towards Scotland, are admirably suited for pasture-lands. The county is watered by the Tyne, Wansbeck, Blyth, Coquet, Aln, and Till.

Coal-measures occupy an area of 180 sq. miles, and yield immense quantities of coal; lead, iron, limestone, and freestone are also wrought. Arable and stock husbandry are both prosecuted with success, and the short-horned cattle mostly reared are much prized. The chief industries include ship-building and rope-making; forges, foundries, iron-, hardware-, and machine-works, chemical-works, potteries, glassworks, etc. The coast abounds in cod, ling, haddock, and a variety of other fishes. Northumberland returns three members to Parliament. Principal towns: Newcastle, Tynemouth, Shields, Morpeth, and Alnwick. Pop. (1931), 756,723. —Cf. J. E. Morris, *Northumberland*.

NORTHUMBERLAND, Duke of. English title held by the family of Percy. In 1377 Henry Percy was made Earl of Northumberland, and the title was held by his descendants until 1670, when it became extinct. Concurrently from 1551 to 1553 John Dudley was Duke of Northumberland. In 1683 George, a natural son of Charles II., was made Duke of Northumberland, but he died without heirs in 1716.

In 1749 Algernon Seymour, 7th Duke of Somerset, who had married the heiress of the Percies, was made the Earl of Northumberland. His son-in-law, Sir Hugh Smithson, succeeded, by special arrangement, to his titles, taking the name Percy. In 1766 he was made a duke, and the present duke is his descendant. Alan Ian, the 8th duke, who died in 1930, was one of the proprietors of *The Morning Post*. The duke's chief seat is Alnwick Castle and his estates are in Northumberland. His eldest son is called Earl Percy.

NORTHUM'BRIA. One of the seven Saxon kingdoms of Britain, which extended from the Humber to the Forth, and was bounded on the west by the Kingdoms of Strathclyde and Cumbria. It was founded by Ida, an Anglian chief, in A.D. 547, and at first extended only from the Tyne to the Forth, and was known by the name of Bernicia. In 560 the Kingdom of Deira, the district between the Tees and the Humber, was added to Northumbria. During the eighth century it was the home of Cædmon, Bede, Alcuin, Egbert, and other great men of letters. In 792 it was ravaged by the Danes, and again in 844 and 867. It was the scene of important events in English history till the grant of the Lothians to the King of Scots, and the final conquest of Northumbria by William I.

NORTH WALSHAM. A market town of Norfolk, England, on the Ant; served by the L.N.E. Railway and a joint line. Lord Nelson was educated at the grammar school (founded 1606) at Paston, 3½ miles distant. Pop. (1931), 4137.

NORTH-WEST FRONTIER OF INDIA. The North-West Frontier is roughly an area based on a chord 900 miles long from the Killick Pass to Karachi. Along this frontier of about 1000 miles in extent we have for neighbours Afghanistan and the various independent tribes, and behind these the vast territories of Russia—the highways leading towards India are not very numerous.

Passes.—The majority of the passes are of high altitude, very difficult, and snow-bound for the greater part of the year. Even when crossed they only admit to a region of few inhabitants, scanty supplies, and more mountain ranges. From the north the Khyber Pass is perhaps the best known and most used; then the Kurram, the scene of Lord Roberts's advance into Afghanistan in 1878; the Tochi and Gomal routes come next; and lastly the various routes from Kandahar towards Quetta.

The Durand line fixes British responsibility with Afghanistan, and behind this there is the administrative frontier of India, which lies chiefly at the foot of the hills; between these two frontiers is a strip of tribal territory averaging perhaps about 60 miles in width, inhabited by independent tribes, an area where almost constant fighting is taking place, and where the lessons of mountain warfare are being repeatedly brought to notice.

Physical Features.—This tract of country, which the Indian Government protects and occupies in certain areas, is a tangled mass of mountains, intersected with confusing defiles and ravines, the few roads there are being generally near British posts. Otherwise it is a mass of paths and tracks, all of which the inhabitants know intimately; the villages are generally tactically sited, and nearly all defended. Water is scarce, but where obtainable the soil is fertile. There are few large rivers. The smaller ones in winter are often dry, but in the summer after a thaw become raging torrents, which go down almost as rapidly as they rise, but are a serious obstacle to military operations. The climate varies according to the height. In winter it is very cold and bracing, but very hot and oppressive in summer, especially in the valleys. It is a bare, inhospitable region, producing little food-stuff, and perhaps for this reason has few attractions for annexation.

Inhabitants.—The inhabitants of this area have from time immemorial raided all who have passed through their land, and have joined when they have felt so inclined the armies of the invaders of India. Almost every conqueror of India has hired their services; many of them have been enlisted in the Indian army, where they make excellent soldiers. They are known as Pathans, speak a language called Pashtu, are very democratic, ignorant, and fanatical, responding readily to the demand for a religious war. They are ideal skirmishers, and are hampered by no supply-columns, each man as a rule carrying ten days' rations on his person.

The Pathan form of tribal government enables official relations of a sort to be maintained with British political officers; but the Councils of the Elders of the Tribe cannot always restrain the younger bloods, especially among the more democratic tribes.

NORTH-WEST FRONTIER PROVINCE. A province of North-Western India formed in 1901, comprising the British districts of Dera Ismail Khan, Bannu, Peshawar, Hazara and Kobat, and the agencies of North Waziristan, South Waziristan, Chitral, Swat and Dir, the Khyber, and the Kurram. It became a governor's province in 1932. The people are largely Pathans. Peshawar is the seat of administration. Only about one-third of the territory lying along the Punjab border is actually British territory. Between this and the Afghan frontier is the tribal area. The agencies and tribal lands have an area of about 25,472 sq. miles. The districts and administered territories have an area of 13,518 sq. miles, and a pop. (1931) of 2,425,076.

NORTH-WEST PASSAGE. A passage for ships from the Atlantic Ocean into the Pacific by the northern coasts of the American continent, long sought for, and at last discovered in 1850-51 by Sir R. MacClure. It is of course valueless as a trade route. In 1903-5 Amundsen made the entire voyage in his vessel the *Gjoa*.

NORTH-WEST PROVINCES. *See* UNITED PROVINCES OF AGRA AND OUDH.

NORTH-WEST TERRITORIES. A northern region of the Dominion of Canada, subdivided (since 1st Jan., 1920) into the districts of Mackenzie, Keewatin, and Franklin. They include all Canada above the parallel of 60° N. lat., excepting Yukon, which was formerly known as Rupert's Land and the North-Western Territories. A Commissioner directs the government by a Council of five members. The Royal Canadian Mounted Police patrol the territories. Area, 1,309,682 sq. miles (34,298 sq. miles being water); pop. (estimated), 12,000. *See* CANADA; MACKENZIE; etc.

NORTHWICH. A town of Cheshire, England, at the confluence of the Dane and Weaver; served by the L.M.S. Railway and the Cheshire lines. There are extensive mines of rock-salt, alkali-works, and breweries. Pop. (1931), 18,728.

NORTON, Caroline. An English poet and novelist, grand-daughter of R. Brinsley Sheridan, born in 1808, died 1877. Her poems nearly all belong to the earlier part of her literary career. Her best novels are *Stuart of Dunleath* and *Old Sir Douglas*.

NORWAY (Norw. *Norge*). A maritime country on the western and northern sides of the Scandinavian Peninsula, bounded on the north-east by Russian Lapland, and east by Sweden, and washed on all other sides by the sea—by the Arctic Ocean on the north, the Atlantic and the North Sea on the north-west and west, and the Skagerrak on the south. It is about 1080 miles in length, and its greatest breadth is about 275 miles, but towards the north it narrows so much as to be in places not more than 10 miles wide; area, 124,588 sq. miles, or rather more than the British Isles. The total population by the 1930 census was returned at 2,814,194. The country is divided into twenty prefectures, or *fylker*, of which the capital, Oslo (pop. 1930, 253,124), forms one, and the city of Bergen (pop. 1930, 98,303) another. Other important towns and their populations are Trondhjem (pop. 54,458), Stavanger 46,780), and Drammen (25,493).

Physical Features.—Norway consists largely of a plateau of great geographical antiquity. Its rocks are chiefly composed of crystalline schists which had been worn down and the material redeposited as Sandstones, like those of the Scottish Highlands, at the earliest times known to geology. There is a steep slope to the Atlantic, and the highest mountains, many of which are snow-covered and support large glaciers, rise in the Norwegian side of Scandinavia, so that the rivers are generally short torrents rushing into the Atlantic, and are utilized for hydro-electric power-producing and for timber-floating.

The principal lake is the Miösen.

An important feature in the 2110 miles' length of coast-line is the occurrence of the deep fiords, which attract so many tourists to Norway. They are deep rifts which run far back into the land. Their walls are steep; their course very angular; they frequently divide, reunite, and enclose mountain-blocks, which are cut off as islands when the valleys between are flooded by the sea.

Communications.—The country is so high that internal communications are difficult, and farming is only possible on the small flats deposited by rivers at the head of the fiords, or at the mouths of tributary streams that plunge over the edge of the plateau into the fiord. Hence the dwellers along the Norwegian fiords depend on boats for intercommunication. There were 2178 miles of State railways in 1931, and another 229 miles of line were under private control. The gauges are widely varied. 121 miles of State and 26 miles of private railways are electrified. There are thirty wireless stations throughout Norway, and one at Spitsbergen.

Production and Industry. The chief mineral products are silver, copper ore, pyrites (the most important mineral for both its sulphur and copper content), felspar, iron ore, and nickel ore. The forests are estimated to cover an area of about 28,956 sq. miles, and form, with the fisheries, the most important source of national wealth. 70 per cent. of the forests are under pine trees. Fishing employs upwards of 90,000 hands. In 1930, 73,830 persons were engaged in the cod fisheries; in 1929, 28,315 in summer herring fishery, and 4938 in mackerel fishery. Whale, walrus, and seal fisheries are also followed, 2,317,000 barrels of whale-oil being produced in 1931. Agriculture is not a lucrative business, and large tracts fit for cultivation are non-existent. Some oats, barley, hay, wheat, and rye are produced (all in order of importance). Dairying, however, is more or less progressive.

Norway possesses much potential power in her innumerable torrents and waterfalls, and as she lacks coal this power is being developed to the utmost possible extent. This power is used chiefly in the production of electro-chemical products (ammonium nitrate, calcium nitrate, nutrium nitrate, sodium nitrate, calcium carbide, and ferro-silicon), the most important manufacturing industry of Norway. Other manufactures include clothing, food-stuffs, leather and rubber, machinery, paper, tobacco, matches, wood pulp, condensed milk, and oil. Imports include food-stuffs, minerals (unwrought and manufactured), carriages, machinery, dye-stuffs, and vegetable produce.

Social Conditions.—The Norwegian fiord-dwellers are fishermen and farmers, and the Norwegians in general, in proportion to the size of their country, are one of the most nautical nations of Europe. The Evangelical Lutheran religion is endowed by the State and is the national Church, the king being supreme head and nominating the clergy. All other religions are tolerated (excepting Jesuits), but their number is very small, and includes only Roman Catholics (3000), Methodists (11,000), Baptists (8000), Mormons (500), and Quakers (100). Education is compulsory between the ages of six to

Norway : The Naerö Fiord

seven and fourteen years. There is one university (founded 1811) at Olso. It is State subsidized, as is also the Technical High School at Trondhjem.

Currency.—The Norwegian monetary unit is the gold *krone* of 100 *öre*; at par it equals 1*s*. 1½*d*. or 18·16 *kroner* to the £1 sterling. Weights and measures conform to the metric system.

Government.—Norway is a limited hereditary monarchy, with a Constitution (*Grundlov*) dated 17th May, 1814. On a new succession the sovereign must be crowned at Trondhjem. The members of the Legislative Assembly or *Storting* are elected every three years by voters who have themselves been elected by the citizens possessing a certain qualification. It subdivides itself into two chambers—one, the *Lagting*, consisting of one-fourth of the members; the other, the *Odelsting*, has the remaining three-fourths. Every Bill must originate in the *Odelsting*. When carried in that body it is sent to the *Lagting*, and thence to the king, whose assent makes it a law. The king has a double veto, but should a Bill be passed by three successive *Stortings* formed by separate and subsequent elections, it becomes law automatically without reference to the king. Titles of nobility were abolished early in the nineteenth century. Government offices are open only to members of the Established Church.

Defence.—The army is a national militia, service being universal and compulsory between the ages of eighteen and fifty-five. Levies are called at the age of twenty-one years; they serve twelve years in the line, twelve years in the *landvärn* (national defence), and twelve years in the *landstorm* (local defence). There are 6 divisions of all arms, a flying-corps of 5 battalions, and the garrison artillery. Divisional strength is dependent upon the population of the recruiting area. In 1932 the strength of the permanent forces was 893 officers and 4573 other ranks. In that year about 10,000 men were trained. Armament comprises Krag-Jörgensen 6·5-mm. rifles and Erhardt quick-firing guns of 7·5 cm. The navy has 4 ironclads, 17 torpedo-boats, 1 gunboat, 3 destroyers, 9 submarines, and 3 (and a fourth nearing completion) mine-layers—all for coast defence. Personnel comprises about 900 officers, warrant-officers, and men, and 700 men conscripted annually. All seafaring Norwegians between the ages of twenty and forty-four years are liable to maritime conscription.

History.—In the earliest times Norway was divided among petty kings or chiefs (*jarls*), and its people were notorious for their piratical habits. Harald Haarfager (who ruled from A.D. 863 to 933) succeeded in bringing the whole country under his sway, and was succeeded by his son Erick. He was ultimately driven from the throne, which was seized in 938 by his brother, Hako I., who had embraced Christianity in England.

Magnus the Good, the son of St. Olaf and Alfhild, an English lady of noble birth, was called to the throne in 1036; and having in 1042 succeeded also to the throne of Denmark, united both under one monarchy. (*See* DENMARK.) After his death the crowns of Norway and Denmark again passed to different individuals.

In 1319 the crowns of Norway and Sweden became for a short time united in the person of Magnus V. Erick of Pomerania succeeded, by separate titles, to Norway, Sweden, and Denmark; and in 1397 was crowned king of the three kingdoms. Sweden then for a time became a separate kingdom; but the union between Denmark and Norway was drawn closer and closer, and the latter ultimately became a mere dependency of the former.

After the defeat of Napoleon by the Allies in 1813, it was arranged by the Treaty of Vienna in 1814 that Denmark must give up Norway, and the result was the union of the two countries under the Swedish crown, each remaining practically independent. The union was not unaccompanied by friction, partly owing to the democratic character of the Constitution of Norway.

In 1905 Norway demanded a separate consular service, and, this being refused, the *Storting* declared the union with Sweden at an end. Sweden acquiesced on certain conditions, and Norway having (by plebiscite) decided to remain a monarchy, Prince Charles of Denmark, the husband of Princess Maud, daughter of King Edward VII., was invited to be king—now reigning as Haakon (or Hako) VII. By a treaty of 1920 the sovereignty of Norway over Spitsbergen and adjacent islands was recognized. In 1921, serious labour troubles arose within the country, culminating in the National Strike of May. Prohibition, introduced about the same time by the Conservative Party, remained in force until 1927. Meanwhile, the Labour Party had grown in power, and in 1928 was for a short time in office. An event of 1929 was the marriage at Oslo of the Crown Prince Olav to Princess Martha of Sweden. In 1930, Norway was elected to the Council of the League of Nations.—BIBLIOGRAPHY: C. L. Paus, C.B.E., *Industrial and Economic Conditions in Norway* (H.M. Stationery Office); T. B. Willson, *History of the Church and State in Norway*; R. N. Bain, *Scandinavia*; E. C. Otté, *Scandinavian History*.

Language.—Danish is employed by the higher classes and in the literature of Norway as a direct consequence of the former political union, but Norwegian exists side by side with Danish and Swedish as an independent language. In the written language two idioms exist, "rigsmaal" and "landsmaal," both being officially used. The Norwegian language is in most popular use in the country districts.

Literature.—The oldest Norwegian literary monuments are the runic inscriptions, dating from the third century. In the ninth century Bragi composed poetry in the Old Norse language, and his poem *Ragnars Drapa* is incorporated in the *Snorra Edda* of Snorri Sturluson. In 1380 Norway was united to Denmark, and for over four centuries the country lost her national characteristics. Her literature, just as her history, is Danish.

It is only since 1814, when by the Peace of Kiel Norway was ceded to Sweden, that a purely national Norwegian literature begins. The great poets of the early nineteenth century were H. A. Wergeland (1808-45) and J. Welhaven. The former first achieved success in 1829 with his lyrics, and one of his best poems is *Den Engelske Lods* (The English Pilot). A. Munch wrote *The Maid of Norway*, and Peter Christian Asbjörnsen (1812-85) utilized the folk-tales and popular poetry preserved among the Norwegian peasants, and in 1841 published, jointly with Jörgen Moe (1813-82), *Norske Folke Eventyr* (Norwegian Popular Tales).

A new era of Norwegian literature was inaugurated by the works of Björnson and Henrik Ibsen (q.v.). No longer confined to Scandinavia, Norwegian literature has become known abroad and entered the arena of world literature. Among other modern Norwegian writers may be mentioned: the poet Herman Wildenvey (1885-); the dramatist G. Heiberg; and the novelists Jonas Lie, Alexander Kjelland (1849-96), and Knut Hamsun (1860-). A powerful writer of historical novels is Madame Sigrid Undset (*b.* 1882). Kinck, who is also a novelist, is still more noteworthy as a master of the short story. A writer in the Landsmaal or "New Norwegian" tongue (the old language of the people), is Kristofer Uppdal (*b.* 1878), navvy and Socialist, whose works breathe the spirit of the Labour movement. Among Norwegian writers of accounts of polar explorations are Roald Amundsen (q.v.) and Fridtjof Nansen (q.v.).—BIBLIOGRAPHY: E. W. Gosse, *Dano-Norwegian Literature*, 1815-65; P. Botten-Hansen, *La Norvège littéraire*.

Music.—The outstanding and characteristic figure in the history of Norwegian music is, of course, that of Eduard Grieg (1843-1907), and a sketch of Norwegian music must centre on him. Born at Bergen in 1843, he received his first music lessons from his mother, who was an excellent pianist. It is interesting to note that his great-grandfather, Alexander Greig, was an Aberdeen merchant, who fled to Bergen in 1745, having taken a part in the Jacobite rising of that year. Grieg's school days over, he proceeded to the Leipzig Conservatoire, where, among others, he had as fellow-students Arthur Sullivan, Edward Dannreuther, Franklin Taylor, and Carl Rosa.

Having completed his student period at Leipzig, he selected Copenhagen as a centre to work in, and here he came under the influence of Gade and Nordraak. Soon after, he transferred his energies to Christiania, where he married his cousin, Nina Hagerup, in 1867. At this time he was greatly encouraged and helped by Liszt, and as a result of his interest and commendation, the Norwegian Government granted the composer a pension. He was now able to give up teaching, and to devote all his time to composition, and from this period onward we have some of the most original and personal work of the composer.

Leaving Christiania, he settled at Bergen, where he at once set to work on the composition of music to Ibsen's play *Peer Gynt*, which brought him a world-wide reputation. His position as a composer was now assured and established, and dating from the production of his *Peer Gynt* music to his death at Bergen in 1907, his career was a steady record of success. The outstanding qualities of Grieg's music are its poetry, refinement, originality, and harmonic freshness. His most notable works are the music to *Peer Gynt*, the Piano Concerto, the three Sonatas for Violin and Piano, and many beautiful songs and piano pieces.

Apart from Grieg, the most distinguished names in the history of Norwegian music are Ole Bull (1810-80), a romantic figure, who, though remembered chiefly as a violinist, did much to establish a Norwegian school of music, and was one of the first to encourage the young Grieg; Kjerulf (1815-63) is best known by some charming songs and short piano pieces; Svendsen (1840-1911), whose well-known *Romance* for violin, and brilliant and effective orchestral pieces, particularly the four Norwegian Rhapsodies, and *Carnival at Paris*, have made his name familiar in all the concert-rooms of Europe; Richard Nordraak (1842-66), whose untimely death at the early age of twenty-four cut short a life of great promise; Christian Sinding (born 1856), who, with Grieg, is generally regarded as the most original and characteristic composer of the Norwegian school; his best works are a fine Symphony in D minor, some excellent chamber music, and many attractive piano pieces which have become very popular.

NORWAY-MAPLE. A tree of the genus Acer, the *A. platanoides*, which grows to a great size and has large handsome leaves resembling in shape those of the vine. It grows in Norway, Germany, Switzerland, etc. Its wood is held in great estimation, and its juice yields sugar.

NORWAY-SPRUCE. A valuable tree of Norway and Northern Europe, the common spruce of Britain—*Picea* (less correctly *Abies*) *excelsa*. *See* SPRUCE.

NORWICH (nor'ich). A city of England, the county town of Norfolk, on the Wensum near its confluence with the Yare, and served by the L.N.E. Railway. It is a picturesque old town, and with its gardens and orchards covers a large area. The Cathedral of Holy Trinity, founded in 1096 and completed about 1500, exhibits varying styles of architecture. It has extensive cloisters,

Norwich : The Cow Tower

and a lofty tower and spire 315 feet high. There is also a modern Roman Catholic cathedral. The castle, a noble feudal relic, reputed to have been built by Uffa about 1066, is practically a ruin; part is used as a museum and art gallery. St. Andrew's Hall, originally the nave of the Blackfriars' Church, the Guildhall, and the bishop's palace, also deserve mention.

The industries comprise boot- and shoe-making; the spinning of woollen, worsted, and mohair yarns; the making of mustard, starch, and blue; iron-working, brewing, etc.

History.—The town was founded in the fifty century, rose to be capital of the Kingdom of East Anglia, and, by the middle of the tenth century, was a large and wealthy town; but in 1002 it was laid in ashes by the Danes. Shortly after rebuilding by the Danes, it had become (eleventh century) a large and populous place, and its prosperity kept steadily increasing, till in 1328 Edward III. made it a staple town for Norfolk and Suffolk. He induced Flemish weavers to settle in it, and others arrived during the reign of Elizabeth. Its worsted goods were long famous. Since 1298 it has had separate representation in Parliament. Pop. (1931), 126,207.

NORWICH. A city of Connecticut, United States, the county seat of New London county, on the Thames; served by the New York, New Haven & Hartford, and the Central Vermont Railways, and by steamers. Hydro-electric power is derived from the local falls of the Thames. Norwich was settled in 1659, and became a city in 1784. Pop. (1930), 36,019.

NORWICH CRAG. In geology, an English formation belonging to the later Pliocene, resting on the Chalk and London Clay. It consists of irregular beds of ferruginous sand and clay, and at the base a bed with remains of Mastodon, Elephas, Hippopotamus, Equus, and other mammals, associated with marine shells.

NORWOOD. A residential district of South-East London, in the south of the borough of Lambeth. It represents the site of a seventeenth-century oak forest. The buildings include the Royal Normal College of Music for the Blind. There is a large cemetery at Norwood, and on Beulah Hill there was a spa.

NORWOOD. A city of Ohio, United States, in Hamilton county; served by the Cincinnati, Lebanon & Northern, and the Baltimore & Ohio S.W. Railways. It is a north-eastern suburb of Cincinnati, was settled in 1789, incorporated in 1888, and became a city in 1902. Pop. (1930), 33,411.

NORWOOD, Cyril. English educationist. The son of a clergyman, he was born 15th Sept., 1875, and was educated at the Merchant Taylors' School and St. John's College, Oxford. After a brilliant career, he passed first into the civil service, and for two years was a clerk at the Admiralty. In 1901 he left the Service and became a master at Leeds Grammar School; in 1906 he was elected headmaster of Bristol Grammar School; and in 1916 he went to Marlborough where he introduced some rather drastic reforms. In 1926 he was appointed headmaster of Harrow. Dr. Norwood has written on educational subjects.

NOSE. The organ in man and the higher animals exercising the sense of smell, and concerned through its apertures or passages in the function of respiration and in the production of voice. The bones of the nose comprise the boundaries of the nasal *fossæ* or cavities, which open in front in the nasal apertures, and behind into the pharynx or back part of the mouth. The front nostrils, or openings of the nose, are in the skeleton of an oval or heart shape, while the openings of the posterior nostrils are of a quadrilateral form. The bones which enter into the entire structure of the nose number fourteen.

In addition there are certain cartilaginous pieces which assist in forming the structure of the nose, lateral cartilages on either side, and a cartilaginous septum in the middle between the two nostrils. There is also a bony septum which unites with the cartilaginous septum to form the complete partition of the nose. Several special muscles give a certain mobility to the softer parts of the organ.

The nostrils and nasal cavities are lined by the mucous membrane, richly furnished with arteries and veins and covered with a copious mucous secretion which keeps it in the moistened state favourable to the due exercise of the function of smell. The proper nerves of smell, the *olfactory* nerves, form the first pair of cranial nerves or those which are connected with the brain; while the nerves of common sensibility of the nose belong to the fifth pair of cranial nerves. The olfactory nerves are distributed in the mucous membrane of either side in the form of a sort of thick brush of small nerve-fibres. The study of the comparative anatomy of the nasal organs shows us that man possesses a sense of smell greatly inferior in many instances to that of the lower animals. The distribution of the olfactory nerves in man is of a very limited nature when compared with what obtains in such animals as the dog, sheep, etc.

All Vertebrates above fishes generally resemble man in the essential type of their olfactory apparatus. In most fishes the nostrils are simply shut or closed sacs, and do not communicate posteriorly with the mouth. The proboscis of the elephant exemplifies a singular elongation of the nose, in which the organ becomes modified for tactile purposes. In the seals and other diving animals the nostrils can be closed at will by sphincter muscles or valves. The most frequent diseases or abnormal conditions which affect the nose comprise congenital defects, and tumours or polypi.

NOSTOC. A genus of blue-green Algæ. The plants consist of rounded or lobed masses of jelly, in which is embedded a tangle of necklace-like filaments composed of minute spherical cells. Some species are edible, and others are constituents of various lichens (e.g. Collema).

NOSTRADA'MUS, true name **MICHEL DE NOSTREDAME.** A French physician and astrologer of Jewish extraction, born 1503, died 1566. He studied first at Avignon, and afterwards at the medical school of Montpellier. After taking his degree he acted for some time as a professor, but eventually settled as a medical practitioner at Agen, and finally, after travelling in Italy, at Salon, near Aix, about 1544, where he wrote his famous *Prophéties* or astrological predictions written in rhymed quatrains. They obtained great success, although many condemned their author as a quack.

Catherine de' Medici invited him to court to cast the horoscope of her sons; the Duke of Savoy travelled to Salon for the express purpose of visiting him, and on the accession of Charles IX. he was appointed royal physician. In 1550 he published an *Almanac* containing predictions about the weather, the first of a numerous family of such productions.

NOSY-BÉ. A French island off the north-west coast of Madagascar, of which it is a dependency. It is about 14 miles long by 8 miles broad, has a mountainous surface, and appears to be of volcanic origin. Rice, maize, tapioca, and bananas are the principal products. The chief town is Hellville (named after Governor de Hell, who occupied the island in 1841). The harbour is good. Area, 130 sq. miles (including adjacent islands); pop. (1931), 12,000.

NOTABLES. In French history, a body consisting of noblemen, archbishops, high legal functionaries, and magistrates of cities, appointed and convoked from time to time by the king, as being a more pliant instrument than the States-General. The first assembly of Notables of any importance was in 1558. From 1626 there had been no meeting, but the troubles preceding the Revolution led to the Notables being assembled in 1787. A second meeting was held in Nov., 1788, to consult on the manner of assembling the States-General; but soon after everything was overturned by the Revolution.

NOTO. A town of Sicily, in the province of Syracuse. *Old Noto* (ancient *Netum*) was destroyed by earthquake in 1693, and the present city was built ten years later. Pop. 32,000.

NOTTINGHAM. A city of England, the county town of Nottinghamshire, near the Trent; served by the L.M.S. and L.N.E. Railways. It occupies a site overlooking the Vale of Trent, and has one of the finest and largest market-places in the kingdom. The castle, which crowns the summit of a rock, was originally built by William the Conqueror as a means of overawing the outlaws frequenting the recesses of Sherwood Forest. Dismantled by Cromwell, it subsequently became the property of the Duke of Newcastle, who in 1674 erected a large mansion on part of the site. This, after being partly burned in riots connected with the

Nottingham Castle

reform movement in 1831, now contains the Midland Counties Art Museum, free library, etc.

The principal educational and literary institutions are the University College and Technical School, High School for boys, the Blue-coat School, the School of Art, the People's Hall, and the Mechanics' Institute. A new university building was opened in 1928, and the new Civic Hall in 1929. An arboretum covering 18 acres is a feature of the town. The staple manufactures are hosiery and lace, the latter being a sort of speciality. There are also manufactures of cotton, woollen, and silk goods, and of articles in malleable and cast iron. The borough sends four members to Parliament.

History.—Nottingham was a place of importance in Anglo-Saxon times, and was twice or thrice taken by the Danes. Charles I. raised his standard here in 1642, and next year the town and castle were taken by the Parliamentarians. Serious riots, occasioned by the introduction of machinery, took place in 1811-12 and 1816-17. On the rejection of the reform bill by the House of Lords in 1831 there was again repeated rioting. It became a city in 1897. Pop. (1931), 268,801.

NOTTINGHAM, or **NOTTS.** An inland county of England. Area, 540,015 acres, of which about 454,000 are arable, meadow, and pasture. The general surface, with exception of the Vale of Trent, is undulating. The principal river is the Trent, with its affluents the Soar and Idle. The greater portion of its area is composed of rocks of the Permian and New Red Sandstone systems. The chief mineral is coal. The soil is generally extremely fertile. The crops usually cultivated are wheat, rye, barley, oats, beans, and pease. The manufactures include lace, hosiery, machinery, silk- and cotton-spinning, bleaching, coal-mining, iron- and brass-founding, glove-making, etc. The county returns five members to Parliament. Pop. (1931), 712,681.

Under the Saxons Nottinghamshire was a part of Mercia, and eventually passed to the Danes. There are scattered remains of antiquarian interest.

NOUMEA. The chief town and port of New Caledonia (q.v.). It contains the Collège la Pérouse. Pop. (1931), 10,708.

NOU'MENON (plural, *Noumena*). In Kant's philosophy, an object conceived by the understanding or thought of by the reason, as opposed to a *phenomenon*, or an object such as we represent it to ourselves by the impression which it makes on our senses. The *noumenon* is an object in itself, not relatively to us.

NOVARA. A province of Piedmont, Italy, on the Swiss frontier. Area, 1391 sq. miles; pop. (1931), 389,352.

NOVARA. A city of Italy in and capital of the province of Novara, situated between the Agogna and Terdoppia Rivers, and a railway junction for Milan (31 miles) and Turin. Pop. (1931), 63,211.

NOVA SCOTIA. A maritime province of Canada. It is divided into two parts, a southern or mainland division forming a peninsula connected with New Brunswick by the narrow Isthmus of Chignecto, and a northern or island division (Cape Breton Island) separated from the peninsula by the Strait of Canso. Halifax is the capital, principal seaport, and largest city (pop. 1931, 59,275); other towns are Sydney (pop. 23,089), Glace Bay (20,706), Dartmouth (9100), New Glasgow (8858), Sydney Mines (7769), Amherst (7450), Yarmouth (7055), and Truro (7901).

Communications.—Nova Scotia is covered by an intricate railway system, and transportation facilities are highly developed. There are 1420 miles of steam railway track, including the systems of the Canadian Government and of the Canadian Pacific. The roads of the province are excellent, and there are 14,682 miles of highways. A regular subsidized coasting service is maintained by steamboats plying between all ports.

Social Conditions.—As a single body Roman Catholicism is the predominant religious belief, Protestants —Baptists, Anglicans, Methodists, and Congregationalists—following in order of importance. Other faiths are practically non-existent. Education is free and compulsory, and is undenominational. The Provincial Agricultural College and a Teachers' Training College are located at Truro, and there is a Provincial Technical College granting degrees in mining, chemical, electrical, and civil engineering. There is no direct Government taxation, and revenue accrues chiefly from the Dominion subsidy, royalties on coal and minerals, and from special taxes on motor-cars, theatres, marriage licences, banks, and incorporated companies.

Production : *Agriculture.*—Fruit is cultivated, apples being the principal crop. The province is suitable for and is largely devoted to dairy-farming. The wool-clip yielded 1,638,000 lb. in 1931, and there are pigs innumerable. Wheat, oats, roots, hay and clover, and potatoes are raised. *Forests.*—Over 12,000 sq. miles of Nova Scotia are afforested, and include spruce, fir, hemlock, oak, maple, and birch trees. *Fisheries.*—Cod, lobster, herring, mackerel, and haddock are caught in the Nova Scotia fisheries—the most extensive in Canada. *Minerals.*—Coal, iron, gold, copper, silica, gypsum, antimony, lead, silver, limestone, manganese, tungsten, and diatomaceous earths are found. The present coal-fields cover an area of 1000 sq. miles, and the gold-fields about 10,250 sq. miles. Steel and iron are also produced.

Area, etc.—The area of Nova Scotia is 21,428 sq. miles (360 sq. miles being water surface). Pop. (1931), 512,027.

History, etc.—Nova Scotia was settled by the French as Acadia (q.v.). It was one of the original provinces of the Dominion, and under the British North America Act of 1867 it is empowered to make laws and to exercise control generally over purely local affairs. The Legislature comprises a Lieutenant-Governor appointed and paid by the Federal Government, a Legislative Council (21 members, nominated for life by the Crown), and a House of Assembly (38 members, chosen by popular vote and sitting for five years). Ten Senators and 14 members of Parliament are sent to Ottawa. *See* CAPE BRETON.—Cf. P. H. Smith, *Acadia*.

NOVAYA ZEMLIA. A Russian archipelago in the northern littoral of European Russia. It represents, physically, the continuation of the Ural Mountains into the Arctic Ocean. There are two main islands, which have a combined length of about 600 miles, and separate the Kara Sea on the east from Bahrent's Sea on the west. It is very mountainous. Novaya Zemlia was discovered by Richard Chancellor in 1553, and Stephen Borough landed on the southern island in 1556. Many expeditions have included the group in the itinerary of their polar voyages.—Cf. A. P. Engelhardt, *A Russian Province of the North* (translated by H. Cooke).

NOVEL. The modern novel and the mediæval romance of love and prowess have, each taken at its best, much in common, and that in things essential, character and character-revealing incident, yet, both for practical purposes and in reality, they are distinguishable by the difference of setting. The fact that while the world of romantic happenings lies east of the sun and west of the moon in the days of brave King Arthur or good Haroun Al-Raschid, the world of the novel is that of real life, primarily and preferably "actual, ordinary" contemporary life; in the historical novel the life of the past reproduced so as to give the illusion of this vivid contemporaneity.

The novel adds to the interest of incident, character, and sentiment that of vividly portrayed manners and environment. It is thus naturally a product of the time in which, after the revival of learning, men's minds were turning away more and more from romance to the ever closer study of the realities of life and character. The way was prepared by such reactions against romance as the picaresque story and the parody of romance, both the product of Spain, the last home of chivalrous romance;

and the greatest of these, *Don Quixote,* caught at once and to perfection the atmosphere of everyday, open-air, genial life and humanity. In England the picaresque story received masterly handling from Defoe in *Robinson Crusoe* (1719-20), *Moll Flanders* (1722). Bunyan's allegory clothed itself in the garb of everyday life as naturally as Spenser's in the splendours of romance and poetry. Swift related impossible and grotesque adventures with an air of sober reality.

Early Novelists. — Comedy and satire all tended in the same direction, but the immediate precursor of the novel was the periodical essay, *The Tatler* and *The Spectator,* the delighted interest they aroused in the little details of life and manners, and their didactic but fresh handling of problems of conduct and sentiment. Samuel Richardson (1689-1761) completed the work in his *Pamela* (1740), *Clarissa* (1748), and *Sir Charles Grandison* (1753). *Clarissa,* the greatest of these, with a picture of certain aspects of English life presents in letter-form the dramatic and tragic history of a fatal conflict of wills, in the heroine the revealing conflict of inclination and principle in a high and heroic but intensely human soul.

Beginning with a parody of *Pamela* and its too prudential ethics, but taking the line of construction indicated by the picaresque story and *Don Quixote,* Henry Fielding (1707-54) in *Joseph Andrews* (1742), *Tom Jones* (1749), and *Amelia* (1751) gave in flowing and buoyant prose a genial yet ironical and penetrating picture of English life, higher and lower, in country and city.

The irritable Scotsman Tobias Smollett (1720-71), following the picaresque line of violent and sordid incident more closely, and drawing considerably on his personal experience in *Roderick Random* (1748) and *Peregrine Pickle* (1751), presented in angry and lurid colours a picture of lower London life and drew some notable professional types. In *Humphry Clinker* (1771), in the letter fashion of Richardson, he gave a delightful picture of Bath and Clifton, London and Scotland, and of the adventures of an admirable group of realistic characters touched with the exaggeration of the humourist.

The Irishman Laurence Sterne (1713-68), a virtuoso of the first water, the Harry Lauder of the English novel, able to delight and hold us by gesture and grimace, showed in *Tristram Shandy* (1759-67) and *A Sentimental Journey* (1768) that the novel could dispense with plot, almost with incident, so long as it preserved the realistic setting, character, humour, and sentiment.

Oliver Goldsmith's *The Vicar of Wakefield* (1766) adds no new feature, but bears the impress of a charming fancy, sentiment, and humour.

These great creators of the modern novel of contemporary life and manners, humorous, sentimental, realistic, had many contemporaries and successors, of whom, passing over eccentric divagations, as Thomas Amory's *John Buncle* (1756), Robert Paltock's *Life and Adventures of Peter Wilkins* (1751), and Eric Raspe's *Baron Munchausen's Narrative* (1785), the legitimate continuers are Frances Burney, whose *Evelina* (1778) delighted readers by its picture of London society, its impression of life studied freshly and directly "*from* the life, disguised and adulterated as little as possible by *exceptional* interests and incidents," which is the soul of the novel; and, at the beginning of the next century, Maria Edgeworth, whose vivid pictures of Irish manners in *Castle Rackrent* (1800), *Ormond* (1817), *The Absentee* (1809) helped to direct Scott to similar work, and Jane Austen, whose earliest works, *Northanger Abbey, Pride and Prejudice, Sense and Sensibility,* were written long before publication. In these and the later *Mansfield Park* (1814), *Emma* (1815), and *Persuasion* (1818), Miss Austen, working within the narrow limits of her experience and in a spirit of gentle and amused but penetrating satire, drew life with entire veracity and impeccable art if limited sympathy.

Romantic Movement.—Meantime the sphere of the novel had been invaded by the spirit of romance, inaugurated by Horace Walpole's *Castle of Otranto* (1764), and revolution, which produced a flood of pseudo-romantic, pseudo-historical, and Rousseau-ish didactic novels, which include Beckford's brilliant extravaganza *Vathek* (1786), Mat Lewis's *The Monk,* Mrs. Radcliffe's *The Mysteries of Udolpho* (1794-95) and *The Italian* (1797), William Godwin's *Caleb Williams* (1794), Thomas Day's *Sandford and Merton* (1783-89). Most of them are but names now, but the effort to combine with the actuality of the novel the romantic effects of mystery, the charm of scenery, and the "sense of the past" enlarged the scope of fiction. To it we owe not alone the historic novel of Scott and his followers, but such occasional real achievements in the element of spiritual and psychological mystery as Lytton's *Haunted and the Haunters* (1859), Dickens's *Edwin Drood* (had that been completed).

Stevenson's *Doctor Jekyll and Mr. Hyde* (1866), and Oscar Wilde's *Dorian Gray*.

What was legitimate in the craving for a more imaginative picture of life in the Romantic Movement was satisfied in the main by Sir Walter Scott (1771-1832), who combined the solid and satisfying portrayal of character and manners of his great eighteenth-century predecessors with a vivid rendering of past ages, romantic scenery, and heroic figures. What has proved most enduring in the *Waverley Novels* (1814-32), of which the greatest are the distinctively Scottish novels, is the truthful and humorous portrayal of bourgeois and peasant character presented as in essentials the same in all ages.

Realism.—Scott's successors in the Victorian Age swung back from romance to realism, but the social interest, which the novel had manifested from its outset and which the reforming spirit of the Revolution had made more impatient for practical remedies, gave an obvious purpose to the satire of Thackeray, the satire and sentiment of Dickens, the high seriousness of George Eliot, the impulsive sympathy of Kingsley. The range of life too which the novel reflected was enlarged: politics in Disraeli and others, the life and mind of children, provincial life and slum life, asylums, prisons, convict-establishments (as in Charles Reade's *It is Never too Late to Mend*)—nothing is outside the compass of the modern novel.

Of the Victorians the supreme creator is Charles Dickens. From *Sketches by Boz* (1833) to *Edwin Drood* (1870) he painted the life and character he knew, that of the lower middle and upper lower classes of London and English towns, with representative types from other spheres, with vividness and with a touch of the fanciful and the grotesque which it is difficult to assign aright to his imagination or his penetrating vision. He combines some of Shakespeare's creativeness with Ben Jonson's close observation of manners and oddities.

William Makepeace Thackeray (1811-63) excelled in the portrayal of just those classes which Dickens drew with least understanding. In *Vanity Fair* (1847-48), *Pendennis* (1849), *The Newcomes* (1854-55) he showed himself the brilliant satirical painter of English upper-class snobbery in a period of its most devastating ravages. Both Dickens in *Barnaby Rudge* and *A Tale of Two Cities*, and Thackeray in *Henry Esmond* and *The Virginians*, diverged from their main trail into the historical novel, but with little shifting of the centre of interest in the work of each—vivid if grotesque portrayal of character in the one, a flowing comment full of irony and sensibility on life, its beauties and its follies, in the other. Charles Kingsley's *Alton Locke* (1850) and *Yeast* (1851) are studies with a purpose of modern society, as are most of Charles Reade's novels, but Kingsley's *Hypatia* (1853) and *Westward Ho!* (1855) and Reade's *The Cloister and the Hearth* (1861) are brilliant essays in the historical romance coloured by a modern didactic reference. George Eliot's serious and heavily charged novels are at their best in their pictures of provincial manners, *Scenes from Clerical Life*, *Adam Bede*. In *Romola*, an historical novel, she failed. Disraeli's novels combine a strain of commonplace sentimental fiction with a brilliant portrayal of the political and social setting in which the events are presented.

A less brilliant and thoughtful writer than Thackeray, nearer to Jane Austen but with a stronger vein of sentiment, Anthony Trollope (1815-82) proved himself, especially in the Barsetshire novels, *The Warden* (1855) and others, an even finer, more good-humoured portrayer of the amenities and snobbery of English life in clerical and county circles.

The Brontës, Charlotte and Emily, in *Jane Eyre* (1847), *Villette* (1853), *Wuthering Heights* (1847), brought into the novel a new strain of passion with its power to transfigure ordinary persons, happenings, and surroundings. Of Mrs. Gaskell, a real artist, Lytton, Wilkie Collins, Blackmore, William Black, and others—all popular Victorian novelists—no more than mention is possible.

The dominating figures in English fiction as the reign of Queen Victoria drew to a close were George Meredith and Thomas Hardy, and of younger men Rudyard Kipling and Robert Louis Stevenson, and the influence of the older men is stronger to-day than that of the younger. The younger men rather extended the sphere of the novel, or played new varieties on older themes than essentially modified its tone.

Kipling is the novelist of Anglo-Indian and soldier life, with a rare command of colloquial and poetic idiom. *Kim* (1901) is his greatest single achievement. Stevenson went back to the theme of the romantic novel of Scott in *Kidnapped*, *Catriona*, and *The Master of Ballantrae*, and explored fresh romantic fields in the South Sea Isles, all in a style of elaborate beauty and melody and rhythm, which raised the level of literary technique in the novel.

Meredith and Hardy are the realists of a new age which had parted with the Christian tradition which from Richardson to Dickens had provided a spiritual relief from the tension of tragic or sordid story. They contemplate life in the disillusioning light of Darwinian science, blending comedy and tragedy—Meredith in a style of overstrained subtlety and brilliance, Hardy in language of simple and beautiful clarity. Meredith's favourite *milieu* is aristocratic and wealthy society, *Richard Feverel*, *Evan Harrington*, *The Egoist*, etc.; Hardy's greatest achievements, *Far from the Madding Crowd* (1873), *The Mayor of Casterbridge* (1886), *The Woodlanders* (1887), *Tess of the d'Urbervilles* (1891), delineate middle-class and peasant types from the south-west of England. Their influence has been felt in a more sombre, unrelieved realism in the work of George Gissing, *Demos* (1886), *New Grub Street* (1891), *The Odd Women* (1893); of Hale White, *Mark Rutherford*, *Catherine Furze*, and others; in Arnold Bennett's *The Old Wives' Tale*; and John Galsworthy's studies of the injustice of social conditions and moral conventions, *The Forsyte Saga*.

But romance has never lost its charm for English readers, and Stevenson has been followed in the romance of character and incident as in beauty of style by Joseph Conrad, *Youth*, *Lord Jim*, *Chance*, *The Typhoon*, and others. Nor has pure comedy been banished; witness the lighter work of Bennett and the riverside yarns of W. W. Jacobs, *Many Cargoes*, *At Sunwich Port*.

The provincial and regional novel of John Galt, Sir Walter Scott, Maria Edgeworth, has been carried on by J. M. Barrie, *Auld Licht Idylls*; James Stephens, *A Crock of Gold*; and many others; while the pure fairy tale has taken from the novel the vivid realistic setting: Lewis Carroll's *Alice in Wonderland*, Stevenson's *New Arabian Nights*, and G. K. Chesterton's extravaganzas *The Napoleon of Notting Hill*, *The Man who was Thursday*, *The Ball and the Cross*. The interest of H. G. Wells's scientific romances, *The War of the Worlds*, *The Invisible Man*, etc., is the exhibition of human nature, English suburban humanity as the same in all circumstances. His latest stories enrol him with the social reformers.

Of all sciences psychology has most allured the novelist, and the greatest of recent novelists, the American-Englishman Henry James, enriched the craft of the novelist by the subtlety with which he portrayed the inner conflict of mind and heart so much richer than the external drama: *The American*, *What Maisie Knew*, *The Awkward Age*, *The Golden Bowl*, *On the Wings of a Dove*. Recent theories of psychology are reflected vividly in the works of D. H. Lawrence (*The Lost Girl*), May Sinclair, James Joyce, and others; and in *The Midget* Walter de La Mare has suggested with delicacy of feeling and imagination the mind and heart of a dwarf.

The works of Aldous Huxley (*Antic Hay*, *Point Counterpoint*, *Brief Candles*, *Music at Night*) are good examples of a particular type of English post-War novel, brilliant, witty, philosophical, decadent in a negative rather than in a positive way. Hugh Walpole has written many novels since he published *The Wooden Horse* in 1909; the latest, *The Fortress*, appeared in 1932. J. B. Priestley's *Good Companions*, *Angel Pavement*, and *Faraway* have achieved considerable popularity. John Buchan, whose first novel was published so long ago as 1898, has found a wide public for his tales of romantic adventure, of which *Greenmantle*, *Salute to Adventurers*, and *The Courts of the Morning* are felicitous examples.

Among women writers are May Sinclair, Rose Macaulay (the witty author of *Potterism*, *Dangerous Ages*, *Told by an Idiot*, *Staying with Relations*), and Sheila Kaye-Smith, whose novels of Sussex life, *Sussex Gorse*, *Tamarisk Town*, *Saints in Sussex*, are among her most popular works.

NOVELLO, Vincent. English musician and publisher. Born in London 6th Sept., 1781, the son of an Italian father and an English mother, he was a chorister at the Sardinian Chapel, where he learnt the organ. He was organist in several chapels in London and was a founder of the Philharmonic Society in 1813. He wrote much sacred music, and introduced into England many unknown compositions by the great masters. His first work in 1811, a collection of sacred music, marked the founding of the publishing house of Novello. He died 9th Aug., 1861.

NOV'GOROD, or **VELIKI-NOVGOROD** ("Great Novgorod"). A town of Russia, capital of the government of the same name, on the Volkhov, near the point where it issues from Lake Ilmen, 103 miles S.S.E. of Leningrad. It was during the Middle Ages the largest and most important town of Northern Europe.

It is divided into two parts by the river, the Kremlin or citadel and the trading town. The former contains the cathedral of St. Sophia, built after the model of St. Sophia at Istanbul; besides which there are numerous churches and several monasteries. A monument was erected in 1864 to commemorate the thousandth anniversary of the foundation of the Russian state by Rurik. Pop. 28,400.

NOVI, or **NOVI LIGURE.** A town of Piedmont, Italy, in the province of Alessandria. At Novi on 15th Aug., 1799, the French under Joubert (who was killed) were defeated by the Russians and Austrians. Pop. 18,000.

NOVI-BAZAR′, NOVI-PASAR′, or **YENIPASAR.** A town of Yugoslavia, formerly in Turkey, and assigned to Serbia in 1913. It is situated on the Rashka, 130 miles S.E. of Bosna-Serai. From 1878 to 1908 it was held by Austria. Taken by the Austrians in 1915, it was recaptured by the Serbians in Oct., 1918. Pop. 13,434.

NOVO - CHERKASSK′ (" New Tcherkask "). The capital of the Don Cossack Territory, in South Russia, on a tributary of the Don, 40 miles from the Sea of Azov, founded in 1805 by the inhabitants of Old Tcherkask. It has a considerable trade, but the manufactures are unimportant. Pop. 62,274.

NOVOROSSISK. A seaport of Caucasia, on the Black Sea, near the western extremity of the Caucasus, with large petroleum-shipping trade and exports of cereals. Pop. 67,955.

NOYADES (nwâ-yăd; Fr., from *noyer*, to drown). The name given to the execution of political prisoners by drowning them, practised during the French Revolution, especially by Carrier at Nantes. One method adopted was crowding the victims into a boat, withdrawing a plug in the bottom, and casting them adrift.

NOYES, Alfred. English poet. Born in Staffordshire, 16th Sept., 1880, his first volume of poems was *The Loom of Years* (1902), but his *Forty Singing Seamen* (1907) and *Drake* (1908) established his fame as a poet of the sea. He lectured in America in 1913 on *The Sea in English Poetry*, and from 1914 to 1923 he was Professor of English Literature at Princeton. Amongst his other publications are *A Salute from the Fleet* (1915), *Walking Shadows* (1917), *Robin Hood* (1927), *The Immortal Legions* (set to music by Sir Edward Elgar), the *Last Voyage* (1930), and *The Torch-bearers* (1931).

NUBIA. A name popularly given, in a more or less restricted sense, to the region of North-East Africa lying south of Egypt and forming the northern portion of the Anglo-Egyptian Sudan (q.v.). Remains of ancient edifices are numerous, chiefly below Dongola. The Nubians belong to the Arabian and Ethiopian races, who converge in the Nile basin; they are a handsome race, of dark-brown complexion, bold, frank, cheerful, and more simple and incorrupt in manners than their neighbours either up or down the river. Their language is a variety of the negro speech of Kordofan. Pop. estimated at 1,000,000 or 1,500,000.

NUBLE. An inland province of Chile, watered by the Nuble and other streams, and sloping from the Andes to Concepción. Wheat and stock are raised in the west; vine-growing is progressive. Chillán is the capital. Area, 5462 sq. miles; pop. (1930), 231,890.

NUCELLUS. The central solid portion of the ovule, internal to the integuments, constituting, in flowering plants, the megasporangium in the strict sense. *See* OVULE.

NUDIBRANCHIATA. The sea-slugs, a group of marine gastropod molluscs. They have no shells in their adult state, and there are no true gills. Breathing is effected by the skin, or by variously shaped projections from the body. The sea-lemons (Doris) are a common example.

NUEVA ESPARTA. An insular state of Northern Venezuela, on the Caribbean Sea. Margarita (q.v.) is the main island. La Asunción is the capital. It lies on the east shore of Margarita, but the harbour and many of the buildings are tumble-down and generally dilapidated. Panamá hats, linen, hammocks, and bricks are made. State pop., 69,392. Capital (estimated), 3000. *See* VENEZUELA.

NUL′LIPORE. A name given to certain red Algæ (species of Lithothamnion, etc.) common on coral islands. From secreting lime on their surface, and forming reefs like coral, they were formerly supposed to be a kind of zoophytes.

NUMANTIA. An ancient town of the Arevaci in Spain, on the Douro, and near the town of Soria in Old Castile. It had great natural strength, and is celebrated for its desperate resistance to the Roman power, especially in the siege by Scipio Africanus in 134-133 B.C., when it had to surrender, though most of its defenders then surviving put themselves to a voluntary death. The town was destroyed by the conqueror.

NUMA POMPILIUS. The second king of Rome, who is said to have reigned from 714 to 672 B.C. He was of Sabine origin, and was distinguished as a philosopher and legislator, though, like the other early kings, he has more a legendary than an historical existence. He was regarded as the founder of the most important religious institutions of the Romans, and left writings explanatory of his system, which were burnt by order of the Senate when accidentally discovered 400 years after his time.

NUMBER. In the simplest sense of the word, it is synonymous with *positive integer*; in this sense a number is one of the series 1, 2, 3, 4, etc. With these numbers addition and multiplication are possible always, subtraction and division in certain cases only; we cannot take 5 from 3, nor divide 12 by 7. All restrictions on the generality of the operations of subtraction and division are removed when we introduce negative and fractional numbers. The numbers thus placed at our disposal have the form $\pm p/q$, where p and q are positive integers. Such numbers constitute the field of *real and rational* number. If a and b are integers we can now solve the equations $x + a = b$, $ay = b$ in all cases.

There still remain some arithmetical problems, however, for which rational numbers do not suffice. To find the side of a square whose area is 2 sq. feet is the same thing as to find a number whose square is 2, and it was proved by the Greek geometers, in effect, that no rational x gives $x^2 = 2$. This defect is remedied by the introduction of *irrational*, or *incommensurable*, numbers. Arithmeticians have been in the habit of treating these in somewhat rough and ready fashion, solving $x^2 = 2$, e.g. by writing $x = \sqrt{2}$, and then assuming that this $\sqrt{2}$ can be manipulated in every way like an ordinary rational number.

Modern mathematicians, especially Dedekind, Weierstrass, and Cantor, have put the theory of the irrational number on a sound logical basis. The methods of Dedekind and of Cantor may be illustrated by the example of $\sqrt{2}$. Dedekind divides all rational numbers into two classes: (a) those whose squares are less than 2, (b) those whose squares are greater than 2. This mode of division satisfies the conditions: (1) every rational number belongs to one class or the other; (2) every number belonging to the lower class is smaller than every number belonging to the upper; (3) the lower class has no maximum, and the upper class has no minimum. A division, or *section*, of the rational numbers, fulfilling these conditions, defines an irrational number, and Dedekind shows that the ordinary operations of arithmetic can be extended so as to apply to the numbers thus defined. In Cantor's method two *sequences* of rational numbers are considered, e.g.

$$1,\ 1{\cdot}4,\ 1{\cdot}41,\ 1{\cdot}414,\ 1{\cdot}4141,\ \ldots$$
$$2,\ 1{\cdot}5,\ 1{\cdot}42,\ 1{\cdot}415,\ 1{\cdot}4142,\ \ldots$$

The numbers in the upper row have squares less than 2, those in the lower row have squares greater than 2, and the difference between corresponding numbers in the two rows becomes as small as we please by going far enough with the sequences. The two sequences define $\sqrt{2}$. It may be shown that one of the sequences by itself is sufficient for the purpose.

Another useful way of viewing an irrational number is to consider its expression as a decimal fraction. We know that the decimal which expresses any rational number either terminates or recurs. A decimal which does neither one nor the other represents an irrational number, and every irrational number can be represented by such a decimal. Whichever definition we take, the results are easily proved to be equivalent. The whole field of numbers definable in any of the three ways is called the arithmetical continuum. It is the domain of the real variable in mathematics.

Irrational numbers originated in problems of geometry, and one of the best ways of obtaining a clear view of their nature is to bring them into relation with the lengths of segments of a line. On a line OX mark off a unit segment OU, and take any point P on the line. The ratio OP/OU may be a rational number, or it may not. If we imagine *all* the points taken, such as P, for which OP/OU is rational, there are still points of the line left out. Any one of these omitted points corresponds to an irrational number, and the whole system of points on the line may be regarded as in exact correspondence with the arithmetical continuum. For imaginary or complex numbers, *see* THEORY OF FUNCTIONS OF A COMPLEX VARIABLE. *See* ARITHMETIC; COMMENSURABLE.—BIBLIOGRAPHY: G. Chrystal, *Algebra*; H. S. Carslaw, *Fourier Series and Integrals*; E. H. Hobson, *Theory of Functions of a Real Variable.*

NUMBER, Atomic. It was proved by Moseley (q.v.) that the frequencies of the X-ray spectra of a large number of elements could be represented by the formula $a(N-b)^2$, where a and b are the same for all the elements, and N is an integer which changes by 1 as we pass from any element to its neighbour in a table of the elements arranged in a certain order, practically the order of their increasing atomic weights. Moseley called N the atomic number of the element. Hydrogen has the atomic number 1, helium 2, lithium 3, and so on, up to uranium, the atomic number of which is 92.

It is now generally believed by physicists that the atomic number represents the net number of unit positive charges in the nucleus of the atom. In a neutral atom this is the same as the number of free or planetary electrons outside the nucleus. Helium, e.g., being of atomic weight 4, has four unit positive charges (protons) in its nucleus, but these are combined with two cementing electrons, so that the atomic number is $4-2=2$; and there are two planetary electrons, the loss of which changes the helium atom into an α-particle. *See* ELECTRON; ISOTOPES; MATTER; RADIO-ACTIVITY; RAYS, ELECTRIC; SPECTRA, THEORY OF; X-RAY SPECTRA; PERIODIC TABLE.

NUMBERS, Theory of. A branch of pure mathematics which deals with the properties of positive integers. It is a subject which has been cultivated by some of the greatest mathematicians, more especially by those of the school to which practical application makes little appeal. Some of the chief names are Diophantus, Fermat, Gauss, Legendre, Kummer, Dirichlet, Riemann, Jacobi, Hermite, Cayley.

The theory has been carried very far; only a few elementary points can be referred to here. The most important classification of the natural numbers is into primes and composite numbers. The number of primes is infinite. It has been shown that the ratio of the number of primes less than x to $x/\log x$ tends to 1 as x increases indefinitely. The idea of congruence, and of residue, with respect to a modulus (m) is fundamental. If $a-b$ is divisible by m, a and b are congruent; if there is a remainder p, less than m, when a is divided by m, a is said to have the residue p, and we write $a \equiv p \pmod{m}$. If m is a prime, and a prime to m, then $a^{m-1} \equiv 1 \pmod{m}$, (*Fermat's Theorem*). If m is a prime, $(m-1)! \equiv -1 \pmod{m}$, (*Wilson's Theorem*). There is a theory of congruences, very similar to the theory of algebraic equations. The congruence $ax \equiv b \pmod{m}$ is equivalent to the ordinary *Diophantine* equation $ax-my=b$, where x and y have to be integers.

The great master of Diophantine analysis was the French mathematician Fermat (1601-65), whose re-edited works were published at Paris, 1891-94. His famous *Last Theorem* (*see* INDETERMINATE ANALYSIS) is still unproved, but if there is any value of n, greater than 2, for which $x^n+y^n=z^n$ is soluble in integers, that value must be greater than 7000; so much has been established by the work of innumerable mathematicians. Fermat himself left a marginal note in one of his books distinctly asserting that he had a proof of the theorem, and he has never been convicted of a false assertion, though he once made a wrong conjecture, viz. that 2^m+1 is a prime when m is a power of 2; Euler proved that this is wrong when $m=2^5$.—BIBLIOGRAPHY: G. Chrystal, *Algebra*; L. E. Dickson, *History of the Theory of Numbers*; G. H. Hardy, *Some Famous Problems of the Theory of Numbers*.

NUMBERS, Book of. The fourth of the books of the Pentateuch. It takes its name from the records which it contains of the two enumerations of the Israelites, the first given in chaps. i.-iv., and the second in chap. xxvi. It contains a narrative of the journeyings of the Israelites from the time of their leaving Sinai to their arrival at the Plains of Moab, and portions of the Mosaic Law. Formerly the authorship was implicitly attributed to Moses, but some modern scholars resolve the book into various parts, to each of which is assigned a separate author. *See* PENTATEUCH.

NUMIDIA. A Roman province of North Africa, between Mauretania and Africa, corresponding to the modern Eastern Anglia. The indigenous wandering people were called Nomades by the Greeks, and, Latinized, the name became Numidæ, hence Numidia. They were subdued by the Carthaginians, reunited under Masinissa in 201 B.C., and remained under a native monarchy until 46 B.C., when Juba I. allied himself with Pompey, and his country was annexed as a Roman province by Julius Cæsar. The Numidians formed light cavalry in both the Carthaginian and the Roman armies.

NUMISMATICS (Lat. *numisma*, a coin). The study of coins and medals, a branch of archæology, the importance of which is being increasingly recognized by the student of history. The distinction between coins—pieces struck for currency—and medals—purely commemorative pieces—is comparatively modern. The medal as we know it goes back to the fifteenth century; but it is not till a much later date that the word acquired its present specialized meaning. On the other hand, ancient coinages were not so stereotyped as modern ones, and their great value lies in many cases in the commemorative nature of their types.

Coins are of use to the student in various ways, though their value must not be exaggerated. Firstly, they tell us that certain towns or rulers issued money. In the majority of cases we are well informed regarding these from other sources. On the other hand, whole dynasties are known only from their coins. The best-known examples are the long series of coins of the Greek kings of India and Bactria who succeeded Alexander the Great. They are quite unknown to history, and but for their coins we should never have known that Alexander's conquest had such a permanent effect in the East. To come nearer home, many kings of the ancient Britons are known only from their coins.

A certain amount of geographical information is also obtained; an examination of the find-spots of the coins of a dynasty enables us to get some idea of the extent of its territory. In a few cases we often know of ancient towns from their coins. A good deal of information regarding ancient leagues and alliances has been deduced from coins. Dated series of coins, unfortunately not common in ancient times, are of great value for chronological purposes. In this lies the great value of Mahommedan coins for example. The analysis of finds of coins, by reasoning from the known to the unknown, has yielded much information of real chronological value.

Greek and Roman coins have been of immense value for the study of mythology, as they give much information about local cults and myths, of which we know nothing from other sources. The importance to the student of art and sculpture of a series of works of art like coins is also very great, because they can be dated and located more accurately than statues. This enables us to classify schools and periods of art. In addition, they preserve representations of statues and buildings now lost. Coins are the most durable of all antiquities, and to them we owe a series of portraits of many great men, whose features would otherwise have remained unknown to us.

Coinage was invented by the Greeks in the eighth century B.C., and independently about the same time by the Chinese. The designs or "types" of the earliest Greek coins were heraldic in their nature. They were uninscribed, and the type—the seal (*phoce*) at Phocæa, for example—served to identify it. With the development and multiplication of coinages and the use of inscriptions, greater variety of types became possible. Local myths and legends were illustrated, and divine emblems began to appear. Athens early evolved the type of the head of Athena on one side, and her emblem, the owl, on the other. The idea was soon copied, and we have such combinations as Zeus and his thunderbolt, Hercules and his club, etc.

By the fourth century B.C. it was the convention to have a deity's head on one side. After the death of Alexander the Great, his deified head was placed on coins by his successors. Soon the rulers of the various dynasties to whom his empire fell deified themselves in their lifetime and put their portraits on their coins, and thus before the beginning of the Christian era a portrait of the reigning monarch had become the natural obverse type of a coin. The first portrait of a living Roman to appear on coins is that of Julius Cæsar. The period of civil war following his death gives many interesting portraits—Brutus, Antony, Cleopatra, etc.—and when Augustus gained the empire he put his portrait on the coins, and the practice henceforth became the regular one. The reverse types gradually become more and more conventional as we approach modern times. It is interesting to note that the penny of George V. still shows directly the influence of the Athenian moneyers of the sixth century B.C.—BIBLIOGRAPHY: G. F. Hill, *Handbook of Greek and Roman Coins*; Th. Reinach, *L'Histoire par les monnaies*; G. Macdonald, *Coin Types: their Origin and Development*; B. V. Head, *Historia Nummorum*; S. Lane-Poole, *Coins and Medals*; H. A. Grueber, *Handbook of Coins of Great Britain and Ireland*; E. Burns, *Coinage of Scotland*; J. S. Dye, *Coin Encyclopædia*; G. D. Mathews, *Coinages of the World*.

NUMMULITE (Lat. *nummus*, money; Gr. *lithos*, stone). A name common to the members of an extensive class of fossil perforate and many-chambered foraminifera, having externally somewhat the appearance of a piece of money (hence their name), and internally a spiral cavity divided by partitions into numerous chambers communicating with each other by means of small openings. They vary in size from less than ⅛ inch to 1½ inches or more in diameter.

Nummulites occupy an important place in geology, on account of the prodigious extent to which they are accumulated in Eocene strata. They are often piled on each other nearly in as close contact as the grains in a heap of corn. They occur so abundantly in some beds that the name of *nummulitic* limestone is given to the strata so characterized. The "Nummulitic series" is characteristic of the Old World, often

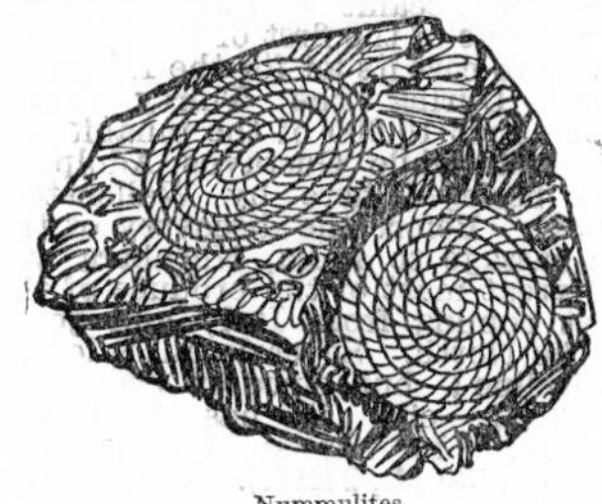

Nummulites

attains a thickness of many thousand feet, and extends from the western shores of Europe and Africa through Asia to the east of China. The pyramids of Egypt are constructed of a stone largely composed of nummulites. After a time of great abundance in the Eocene, nummulites sink rapidly in importance, though a small form occurs in modern seas.

NUNC DIMITTIS ("now lettest thou depart"). The first two words of the Latin version of the canticle of Simeon given in Luke ii. 29-32, and used as the designation of the whole canticle, which forms parts of the evening service in the *Book of Common Prayer*.

NUN'CIO (Lat. *nuntius*, messenger). An ambassador of the first rank (not a cardinal) representing the Pope at the court of a sovereign entitled to that distinction. A Papal ambassador of the first rank, who is at the same time a cardinal, is called a legate. The title of *internuncio* is given to an ambassador of inferior rank, who represents the Pope at minor courts. Formerly the Papal nuncios exercised the supreme spiritual jurisdiction in their respective districts. But now, in those Catholic kingdoms and states which hold themselves independent of the court of Rome in matters of discipline, the nuncio is simply an ambassador.

NUNEATON. A town of Warwickshire, England, on the Anker; served by the L.M.S. Railway, and by a canal. Coal-mining is conducted in the vicinity. Cotton, woollen, and woven worsted goods, hats, bricks, tools, and tiles are manufactured. There are ironworks. Nuneaton was formerly a great ribbon-manufacturing town. It originated in a Benedictine house founded in 1150. Here was born the novelist whose pen-name was George Eliot. Pop. (1931), 46,305.

NUPE. A province of Nigeria, on the north of the Niger; area, 6400 sq. miles; pop. (estimated), 200,000. Bida is the capital. Formerly a powerful native state, Nupe came into conflict with the Royal Niger Company in 1897, and the company's troops captured Bidd. In 1903 the region came under the direct administrative control of the British Government, but remains under the nominal rule of an Emir.

NURAGHI (nụ-rä'gē). The name given to certain ancient structures peculiar to Sardinia, resembling in some respects the "burghs" or "brochs" (q.v.) found in some of the northern parts of Scotland. They are conical structures with truncated summits, 30 to 60 feet high and 35 to 100 feet diameter at the base, built of unhewn blocks of stone without mortar. They generally contain two or three conically vaulted chambers one above the other, connected by a spiral staircase in the thickness of the wall, and are built either on natural or artificial eminences. Their purpose is not known, but they are probably prehistoric monumental tombs. Diodorus Siculus, relating the traditions of his time, says that these buildings dated from the time of Iolaus, nephew to Heracles.

NÜREMBERG (nur'ember*h*). A city in the Republic of Bavaria, on the small River Pegnitz, belonging to the Main basin. It is surrounded by well-preserved ancient walls, which have, however, been breached in several places to afford access from the extensive and rapidly increasing suburbs.

Within the walls it is one of the best-preserved specimens of a mediæval town in existence. The

Pegnitz, traversing the town from east to west, divided it into two nearly equal parts—the north and the south, which communicate by numerous bridges. It contains a large market-place and several interesting churches, among the finest of which are the Gothic churches of St. Lawrence and St. Sebaldus, both dating from the thirteenth century. The former among other treasures of art contains an elaborate and delicately carved ciborium of stone in the form of a Gothic spire, 65 feet high, by Adam Krafft; the latter, St. Sebald's monument, the masterpiece of Peter Vischer, consisting of a rich late-Gothic altar shrine and canopy in bronze adorned with numerous statues and reliefs. Other places of

Nüremberg

worship are the fourteenth-century Marienkirche (Roman Catholic), and the Jewish synagogue in Oriental style (1867-74).

The castle dates from the reign of Friedrich Barbarossa (1158); part of the interior was fitted up in Gothic style (1854-56) as a royal residence. The town hall is adorned with frescoes by Albert Dürer, and a relief in stucco by Kern. The Germanic National Museum, founded in 1852 in a suppressed Carthusian monastery, a Gothic building of the fourteenth century with extensive cloisters, and greatly extended by the addition of the Augustinian monastery rebuilt adjoining, now ranks among the first in Germany, and is exceedingly rich in works illustrative of the arts and industries of the Middle Ages. It has also a library and a collection of charters.

There are several fountains, the chief of which is the Schöne Brunnen, erected between 1385 and 1396, and restored between 1821 and 1824, in the form of a graceful Gothic cross, 63 feet in height, adorned with numerous figures. There are modern statues of Dürer, Hans Sachs, Melanchthon, and other celebrities. The town library contains 80,000 volumes, and educational institutions are numerous.

Nürnberg has extensive breweries, railway-carriage and lead-pencil manufactories, and produces fancy articles in metal, carved wood, ivory, etc., toys, chemicals, clocks and watches, cigars, playing-cards, etc. Printing and bookbinding are also extensively carried on, and the hop-market is the most important on the Continent. The town is celebrated, in connection with its industry, for the invention of watches.

History.—Nürnberg was an independent imperial town down to 1806, when it became a Bavarian city. It was one of the first of the imperial towns to cast its lot for the Reformation. During the Thirty Years War about 10,000 of the inhabitants perished, while Gustavus Adolphus was besieged here by Wallenstein (1632). Before the discovery of the sea-passage to India, Nürnberg was the great mart of the produce of the East coming from Italy and going to the North. Several causes led to a decline; but since it became a Bavarian city it has prospered greatly. It has a broadcasting station (239 M., 2 kW.). Pop. (1925), 392,494.

NURSERY. In its application to gardening and forestry the term nursery means an establishment or place for the propagation of plants by means of seeds, cuttings, grafts, etc. Commercially a nursery is a plant emporium, often of considerable importance, and the term nurseryman is synonymous with plant dealer or trader. In all civilized countries there are nursery gardens where plants likely to be in demand are stocked for sale, and the proprietors often render valuable service by introducing and propagating for subsequent distribution plants from other countries which may prove useful either decoratively or economically. In its more limited meaning, the term is used for any portion of a garden or forest that is set apart for the rearing of plants. Many large private gardens have a nursery in this sense.

The art of raising plants from seeds and by the various artificial methods in use in gardening and arboriculture is a special one. A man may be a good cultivator without possessing a knowledge of this art. Consequently when he needs fresh stock he applies to a nurseryman, in the belief that he can supply it in the right condition for becoming established and a success. It is the business of the nurseryman therefore to discover by experiment whether a new introduction will thrive best on its own roots, or as a grafted plant. There are numerous cases in which climatic or other obstacles have been surmounted by grafting, and others in which layering has to be resorted to for success. All this is the work of the propagator, who is indispensable to the nurseryman; in fact, the nursery business is based on skilful propagation, and the horticulture of a country is very largely dependent on the quality of the productions of the nursery.

But a nursery in its modern development is more than a garden for the raising of young stock. In his position as an introducer and dealer the nurseryman has extended his operations to those of a cultivator of well-grown examples of his wares, and a nursery may contain superb specimens of many kinds of plants which equal and often surpass the best to be found in other establishments. Thus a well-appointed nursery is an excellent school of gardening in its various phases. It is in a position to supply not only young plants properly prepared for growing on in the garden, but also well-developed specimens, ready made as it were, together with experts trained in all the arts of cultivation. Modern horticulture is greatly indebted to the enterprise and skill of the nursery proprietor.

NURSERY SCHOOL. Institution which provides for the healthy development of children between the ages of two and five, thus bridging the gap (in England) between the Infant Welfare Centre and the Elementary School. The establishment of state Nursery Schools in 1929 was due largely to the pioneer work of Miss Margaret M'Millan at Deptford. In them great stress is laid on the value of open-air, sunlight, play, rest, and cleanliness.

NUT. In botany, a one-celled fruit containing, when mature, only one seed, and enveloped by a pericarp of a hard, woody, or leathery texture, rarely opening spontaneously when ripe. Among the best-known edible nuts are the hazel-nut, the Brazil-nut, the walnut, chestnut, and coconut. Valonia-nuts, gall-nuts, and myrobalan-nuts are used in tanning and dyeing, the last two also in ink-making; betel-nuts in making tooth-powder and tooth-paste; and coquilla-nuts and vegetable-ivory (the kernel of the nut of the ivory palm, q.v.), being very hard and capable of taking on a fine polish, are used in making various small articles. Of the examples mentioned several, such as the walnut and coconut, are not nuts in a botanical sense.

NUTATION. In astronomy, a small subordinate gyratory movement of the earth's axis, due mainly to the attraction of the moon. There is also an extremely small annual nutation, due to the sun. The lunar nutation has a period of about nineteen years, depending on the revolution of the lunar nodes, and in virtue of it the pole would describe among the stars, in a period of about nineteen years, a minute ellipse, having its longer axis directed towards the pole of the ecliptic. The consequence of this real motion of the pole is an apparent approach and recession of all the stars in the heavens with reference to the pole in the same period; and the same cause gives rise to a small alternate advance and recession of the equinoctial points, by which, in the same period, both the longitudes and right ascensions of the stars are also alternately increased and diminished.

Nutation, however, operates only as a modification of a much larger and progressive motion of the pole, viz. the precession of the equinoxes, and in virtue of the two motions the path which the pole describes is a gently undulating curve, the undulations constituting a nutation or "nodding" of the earth's axis. Both these motions arise from actions of the sun and moon upon the equatorial protuberance of the earth. *See* PRECESSION.

NUT'CRACKER. The name of a perching bird rarely seen in Britain. It belongs to the crow family (Corvidæ). The *Nucifrăga caryocatactes*, or European nutcracker, is about the size of the jackdaw, but with a longer tail. It combines to a considerable extent the habits of the woodpeckers and those of the omnivorous birds. It has received the name of nutcracker from its feeding upon nuts. The allied form, *Picicorvus columbianus*, noted for the diversified beauty of its plumage, frequents rivers and seashores in America.

NUT'HATCH. The common name of birds of the family Sittidæ. The common European nuthatch (*Sitta cæsia*) is a climbing bird, of shy and solitary habits, frequenting woods, and feeding on insects chiefly. It also eats the kernel of the hazel-nut, breaking the shell with great

Nuthatch (*Sitta cæsia*)

dexterity. The female lays her eggs in holes of trees, and hisses like a snake when disturbed.

NUTMEG. The kernel of the fruit of *Myristica moschāta* or *fragrans*. This fruit is a nearly spherical drupe of the size and somewhat of the shape of a small pear. The fleshy part is of a yellowish colour without, almost white within, and four or five lines in thickness, and opens into two nearly equal longitudinal valves, presenting to view the nut surrounded by its arillus, known to us as *mace*. The nut is oval, the shell very hard and dark brown. This immediately envelops the kernel, which is the nutmeg as commonly sold in the shops.

The tree producing this fruit grows principally in the Islands of Banda in the East Indies, and has been introduced into Sumatra, India, Brazil, and the West Indies. It reaches the height of 20 or 30 feet, producing numerous branches. The colour of the bark of the trunk is a reddish-brown; that of the young branches a bright green. The nutmeg is an aromatic, stimulating in its nature, and possessing narcotic properties. It is much used in cookery. Nutmegs yield by distillation with water about 6 per cent. of a transparent oil consisting chiefly of myristicene ($C_{10}H_{16}$), and having an odour of nutmeg, and a burning, aromatic taste.

NUTRITION. The act or process by which organisms, whether vegetable or animal, are able to absorb into their system their proper food, thus promoting their growth or repairing the waste of their tissues. It is the function by which the nutritive matter already elaborated by the various organic actions loses its own nature, and assumes that of the different living tissues, i.e. is assimilated—a process by which the various parts of an organism either increase in size from additions made to already formed parts, or by which the various parts are maintained in the same general conditions of form, size, and composition which they have already by development and growth attained. It involves and comprehends all those acts and processes which are devoted to the repair of bodily waste, and to the maintenance of the growth and vigour of all living tissues. *See* ALIMENT; FOODS AND FOOD VALUES.

NUX-VOMICA. The fruit of a species of Strychnos (*S. nux-vomica*), ord. Loganiaceæ, growing in various places in the East Indies. It is about the size and shape of a small orange, and has a very bitter, acrid taste. It is known as a very virulent poison, and is remarkable for containing the alkaloid, strychnine.

NYASA, Lake. The third largest lake of Africa, long and narrow, occupying a depression in the floor of the Great Rift Valley; length, about 350 miles; breadth, from 15 to 60 miles; altitude, 1565 feet. It is drained by the Shiré River flowing to the Zambezi, and is fed by the Bua, Rukuru, Songwe, and other rivers. The water is fresh, and the level is variable. Fort Johnston, at the extreme southern end, and Karonga, are the principal ports.

NYASALAND. Formerly British Central Africa, a British Protectorate, forming a narrow strip of territory, 520 miles long and from 50 to 100 miles broad, lying along the southern and western shores of Lake Nyasa.

Area, etc.—Land area, 37,596 sq. miles, divided into 2 provinces, each under a Provincial Commissioner, and 19 districts, each under a District Commissioner and his assistant. Pop. (1931), 1,498,836 natives, 1537 Asiatics, and 1910 Europeans (residing mainly in the Shiré Highlands).

Physiography.—Running from N. to S. is one of the southern extensions of the Rift Valley (which extends from Palestine to Beira). Between the eastern edge of the Angoni Plateau and the western shore of the lake there is a narrow coastal strip, from 10 to 20 miles wide, carrying an normous native population. This strip varies from 1565 feet (the level of Lake Nyasa) to 2000 feet in altiutde. The Angoni Plateau varies in altitude between 4000 feet and 8597 feet. To the west of the lake, Nyasaland is mountainous. The white population is located on the Shiré, Highlands Plateau, about

80 miles long by 25 miles wide, most of which is above 3000 feet in altitude (Zomba, 6647 feet). South of Lake Nyasa is Lake Shirwa, without an outlet, of varying area and entirely unnavigable. South of this lake is the Mlanje tableland (culminating point, 9846 feet), in the valleys of which is found the Mlanje cedar.

Transport.—Shiré River is the most important river of Nyasaland. It emerges from Lake Nyasa, flows in a southerly direction to the Zambezi, which it joins below Chindio; length, 275 miles, the lower 50 miles being in Mozambique (Portuguese). The central part of the river is interrupted by the Murchison cataracts, but until the Lower Shiré became unnavigable it formed practically the only approach to Nyasaland from the outside world. Roads are classified as wagon roads, main roads, or carrier roads. There are 450 miles of main, and *c.* 3000 miles of other roads. A railway runs from Blantyre to Chindio on the Zambezi (174 miles), and in 1922 a railway from Murraca (opposite Chindio) to Beira in Portuguese East Africa was opened (175 miles). A road from Salisbury in Southern Rhodesia to Blantyre in Portuguese East Africa is now open for motor traffic. A bridge across the Zambezi to join these two lines is under consideration.

Towns.—Trade ports are: Port Herald (Lower Shiré), Kota-Kota, Karonga, and Fort Johnston on Lake Nyasa. Chinde, at the mouth of the Zambezi, is held by Nyasaland on a ninety-nine years' lease (dating from 1892), and is exempt from Portuguese taxes, etc., but the Trans-Zambezia Railway (*see* ZAMBEZIA) has practically killed the harbour and trade of Chinde. Zomba is the seat of government; Blantyre (Shiré Highlands) is the chief settlement; other towns are: Mlanje and Limbe, and (on Lake Nyasa) Bandawe, Chintechi, Nkata, and Likoma.

Social Conditions.—The indigenous population is of Bantu-Negro stock, divided into ten groups. Among languages are Swahili, Chinyanja, and Yao. Native education is in the hands of missionaries. Education is controlled by the Education Department. There are three elementary schools for European children. They are not Government owned but receive grants from the Government.

Production: Agriculture.—Nyasaland is devoted almost entirely to agriculture, cotton, tobacco, and tea, being the principal products. Coffee, hemp, and rubber are subsidiaries, all in order of importance. Both mauritius- and sisal-hemp are grown. Wild landolphia rubber was formerly one of the staple exports, but has now been replaced by planted rubber (Ceara and Para). Rice is cultivated by the natives along the lake shore; oranges, lemons, pineapple, bananas, mangoes, paw-paws, loquats, guavas, and grenadillas, flourish over the major portion of the Protectorate; apples, peaches, pears, and strawberries do well in the highlands. The climate is not suitable for horses, and cattle-rearing is not extensive through the menacing *tse-tse* fly.

Forestry.—The cypress forests of Mount Mlanje are the only important forest resources, although there are sporadic growths of African mahogany (*Khaya Senegalensis*), or *Mbawa*.

Minerals.—Nyasaland is not rich in minerals, although mica has been exported from the Dedza region. Coal has been located near the Shiré River, and the existence is reported of graphite, plumbago, garnets, copper, mercury, gold, asbestos, and iron ore, but not in paying quantities.

History.—In 1859 David Livingstone discovered Lake Nyasa, and two years later missionaries settled at Zomba. By the Anglo-German Treaty of 1st July, 1890, respective German and British spheres were fixed, and a British Protectorate was proclaimed on 14th May, 1891. In 1893 the territory became the British Central Africa Protectorate, but the present nomenclature (Nyasaland Protectorate) was introduced in 1907.

On the outbreak of the European War both British and German forces rapidly mobilized, and each endeavoured to strike the first blow. On 22nd Aug. the British force was concentrated at Karonga, equipped and ready for action. On Lake Nyasa the Germans placed an armed steamer (*Hermann von Wissmann*), which the British steamer *Gwendolen* dismantled in harbour at Sphinxhaven (13th Aug., 1914), thus opening the campaign and ensuring to the British the command of the lake. By land the Germans concentrated at New Langenburg, advanced (20th Aug.) across the Songwe River, seized Kapora, and on 8th and 9th Sept. were completely routed at Karonga. In May, 1915, a naval detachment captured Sphinxhaven.

Government.—Nyasaland is administered for the Colonial Office by a Governor and Commander-in-Chief, assisted by nominated Executive and Legislative Councils.

BIBLIOGRAPHY: E. Dane, *British Campaigns in Africa and the Pacific, 1914-18*; D. J. Rankin, *The Zambezi*

Basin and Nyasaland; Sir H. H. Johnston, *British Central Africa.*

NYBORG. A seaport on the east of the Island of Fünen, Denmark, connected by rail with Odense, and by steamer with Korsör, on Zeeland. It was founded in 1170, and was one of the foremost Danish towns of the Middle Ages. Pop. 9470.

NYCTAGINA'CEÆ, or **NYCTAGIN'EÆ.** A natural order of plants inhabiting the warmer parts of the world, typical genera of which are the Mirabilis or marvel of Peru (*see* MIRABILIS), Abronia, and Pisonia. The roots of many of the species are fleshy, purgative, and emetic.

NYCTALOPIA. *See* NIGHT-BLINDNESS.

NYCTANTHES. A genus of shrubs or small trees, ord. Oleaceæ. *N. Arbor tristis* is the night-flowering jasmine or sad tree of India, the sweet-scented flowers of which open in the evening and fall off about sunrise.

NYIREGYHAZA (nyi-red'yė-hä-zȧ). A town and railway junction of Hungary. There are mineral springs in the neighbourhood, and it has salt, soda, and saltpetre manufactories. Pop. (1930), 51,308.

NYKÖPING (nü-cheup'ing). A seaport town of Sweden, capital of the län of Södermanlän, and at the mouth of the River Nyköping, on the Baltic. It has shipbuilding and several minor industries. Pop. (1932), 11,900.

NYLGHAU. The *Boselaphus tragocamēlus*, a species of antelope as large as or larger than a stag, inhabiting the forests of Northern India, Persia, etc. The horns are short and bent forward; there is a beard under the middle of the neck; the hair is greyish-blue. The female has no horns. The nylghau is much hunted as one of the noblest beasts of the chase, the skin of the bull being in demand for the manufacture of native shields. The name nylghau literally means "blue ox," and has, doubtless, been applied to this animal from the ox-like proportions of its body. They are known to breed freely in confinement.

NYMPH. A larval insect differing from the adult only as regards size and absence of wings.

NYMPHÆA'CEÆ. A natural order of aquatic plants containing the water-lilies of various parts of the world. They are polypetalous hypogenous exogens, with the sides of the cells of the fruit covered with numerous seeds. The leaves are peltate or cordate and fleshy; the stalks both of flowers and leaves vary according to the depth of the water on the top of which the leaves float. The stems are bitter and astringent, and the seeds, which taste like those of the poppy, may be used as food, and hence the *Victoria Regia* is called water-maize in South America.

Species.—The species are mostly prized for the beauty of their flowers; as the *Nymphœa alba*, or white water-lily, which grows in pools, lakes, and slow rivers in Britain; the *N. cœrulea*, or blue lotus of the Nile, often cultivated in gardens; the *N. Lotus*, or white lotus of the Nile; the *Nuphar lutĕum*, or yellow water-lily; and the *Victoria Regia.*

NYMPHS. In mythology, a numerous class of inferior divinities, imagined as beautiful maidens, not immortal, but always young, who were considered as tutelary spirits not only of certain localities, but also of certain races and families. They occur generally in connection with some other divinity of higher rank, and they were believed to be possessed of the gift of prophecy and of poetical inspiration. Those who presided over rivers, brooks, and springs were called *Naiads*; those over mountains, *Oreads*; those over woods and trees, *Dryads* and *Hamadryads*; those over the sea, *Nereids.*

NYSTAD (Fin. *Uusikaupunki*). A town and seaport of Finland, on the Gulf of Bothnia. A peace was concluded there between Russia and Sweden in 1721, and gave Russia large Baltic territories, her "window to Europe." Pop. 5000.

O

O. The fifteenth letter and the fourth vowel in the English alphabet. In English O represents six or seven sounds and shades of sound: (1) as in *note, go,* etc. (2) The similar short sound as in *tobacco.* (3) The sound heard in *not, gone.* (4) The same sound lengthened as in *mortal.* (5) The sound in *move, do, tomb, prove.* (6) The same sound but shorter as in *wolf, woman.* (7) The sound of *u* in *tub,* as in *come, done, love.* It is also a common element in digraphs, as *oo, oa, ou.*

OAK. The general name of the trees and shrubs belonging to the genus Quercus, nat. ord. Cupuliferæ, having monœcious flowers, those of the males forming pendulous catkins, those of the females solitary or in clusters, and having an involucre which forms the well-known "cup" of the fruit—the acorn. The oak from the remotest antiquity has obtained a pre-eminence among trees, and has not unjustly been styled the "monarch of the woods." In the traditions of Europe and a great part of Asia the oak appears as a most important element in religious and civil ceremonies. It was held sacred by the Greeks and Romans, and no less so by the ancient Gauls and Britons.

Species.—The species of oak are very numerous, generally natives of the more temperate parts of the northern hemisphere, but found also in Java, Mexico, and South America. They have alternate simple leaves, which are entire in some, but in the greater number variously lobed and sinuated or cut; evergreen in some, but more generally deciduous. The British oak (*Q. Robur*) is found in two forms or varieties, by some regarded as distinct species—*Q. sessiliflōra* and *Q. pedunculāta*; the wood of the former is heaviest and toughest, that of the latter being in favour with cabinet-makers for ornamental work. (*See* DURMAST.) For more than a thousand years British ships were mainly built of common oak (*Q. Robur*). The common oak attains a height of from 50 to 100 feet or even 150 feet, with a diameter of trunk of from 4 to 8 feet. Noble specimens of oak trees, and some of them historically celebrated, exist in almost all parts of Britain, but are much more frequent in England than in Scotland. The oak serves a great number of useful purposes, the wood being hard, tough, tolerably flexible, strong without being too heavy, and not readily penetrated by water.

Among the other chief species are the black American oak (*Q. nigra*); the white or Quebec oak (*Q. alba*); dyer's oak (*Q. tinctoria*), the bark of which is used for tanning and dyeing leather; red oak (*Q. rubra*); the cork oak (*Q. Suber*); live oak (*Q. virens*); the Turkey oak (*Q. Cerris*), furnishing a valuable timber; the valonia oak (*Q. Ægilops*), whose acorn-cups are largely used in tanning; the kermes oak (*Q. coccifĕra*); the edible oak (*Q. æscŭlus*), yielding edible acorns; and evergreen oak (*Q. Ilex*).

British Oak

1, *Quercus pedunculāta*, acorns scattered and on obvious peduncle. 2, *Quercus sessiliflōra*, acorns sub-sessile, crowded, and on a condensed peduncle.

The bark of the common oak tree and of several others is preferred to all other substances for the purpose of tanning, on account of the amount of tannic and gallic acid it contains. Oak galls, morbid growths caused by insects (*see* GALLS), are also much used in tanning, especially those of *Q. infectoria.* Oak bark is also used medicinally as an astringent. The name oak is sometimes popularly applied to timber of very different genera of trees; thus African teak is often called *African oak*; while in Australia the term oak is applied to some species of Casuarina. What is known as *green oak* is a condition of oak-wood caused by its being coloured with the spawn of *Pezīza æruginōsa*, a species of fungus.

OAK-BEAUTY. The popular name of a British moth (*Amphydasis prodromaria*), whose caterpillar feeds on the oak.

OAKHAM. The county town of Rutland, England, situated in the Vale of Catmos, and served by the L.M.S. and L.N.E. Railways. It has a fine old church, a castle built in the twelfth century, and a grammar school. Pop. (1931), 3191.

OAKLAND. A city of California, United States, the county seat of Alameda county, opposite San Francisco and on the east side of San Francisco Bay; served by the Atchison, Topeka, and Sante Fé, the Ogden branch of the Southern Pacific, and other railways. It is a residential city, but has some shipbuilding, fruit-canning, flour-milling, and other industries. Oakland was incorporated in 1852, and became a city in 1854. Pop. (1930), 284,063.

OAKUM. The name given to vegetable fibre which is obtained by the disintegration of old tarred or untarred ropes, the fibre from the latter being known as white oakum. A considerable quantity of oakum picking is done in prisons, and the resulting teased fibre is used for caulking the seams of ships, bolt-holes, joints of various kinds, and, in general, for preventing leaks.

OA'MARU. A seaport of South Island, New Zealand, on the railway from Dunedin. Grain and wool are exported and meat is chilled. Limestone of exceptional building utility from the vicinity was used in erecting the town. Pop. 7510.

OAR-FISH ((*Regalĕcus banksii*). One of the ribbon-fishes, a peculiar deep-sea fish, 12 to 20 feet or more in

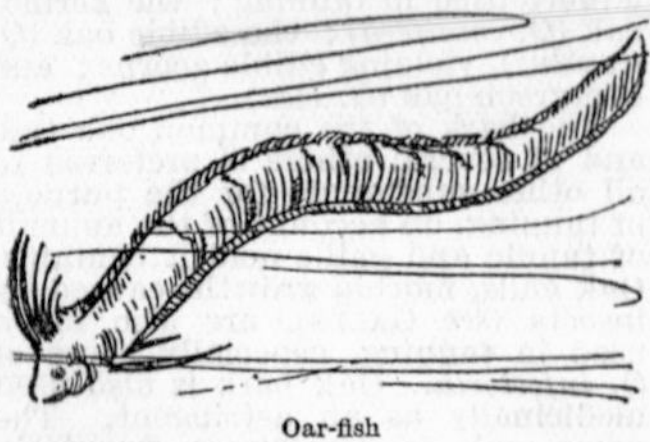

Oar-fish

length, but having a narrow and extremely compressed body. It is of a silvery colour, and is only rarely met with, usually in a dying condition. A much smaller Indian species (*R. russelli*) possesses a narrow rod-shaped body.

OA'SIS. A fertile place in a desert. The oases of Northern Africa are generally river valleys, the waters of which are for the most part underground, or depressions surrounded by short ranges of hills, from which small brooks descend, sometimes forming a lake in the centre. In ancient times the most celebrated oasis was that to the west of Egypt, containing the temple of Jupiter Ammon, now called the Oasis of Siwah. Oases have been formed by sinking artesian wells (q.v.)

OAT, or OATS (Avēna). A genus of edible grasses cultivated extensively in all temperate climates, and, though principally grown as food for horses, largely used when ground into meal as human food. There are about sixty species, the principal of which are: *A. sатīva* (the common oat); *A. nuda* (naked oat, pilcorn, or peelcorn); *A. orientālis* (Tartarian or Hungarian oat); *A. brevis* (short oat); *A. strigōsa* (bristle-pointed oat); *A. chinensis* (Chinese oat); etc.

The cultivated species of oats are subdivided into a large number of varieties, which are distinguished from each other by colour, size, form of seeds, quality of straw, period of ripening, adaptation to particular soils and climates, and other characteristics. The yield of oats varies from 20 bushels to 80 bushels per acre according to soil, etc. The weight per bushel varies from 35 to 45 lb., and the meal product is about half the weight of the oats. Oatmeal is a cheap and valuable article of food, and its value seems to be becoming more appreciated among the wealthier classes as it is being neglected by the poorer. The wild oat (*A. fatua*) is supposed to be the original of all the species, but its native country is unknown.

OATES, Lawrence Edward Grace. English explorer. Born in 1880, he was educated at Eton and became a soldier. He served with the cavalry in South Africa (1901-2) and later wars in India and Egypt. In 1910 he went with Scott on the expedition to reach the South Pole. On 17th March, 1912, when they were returning and in dire straits, Captain Oates, who was crippled with frost, walked out into the open and met his death in order to make the task of his comrades easier. His epitaph is "a very gallant gentleman." A district in Antarctica is named after him.

OATES (ōts), **Titus.** British perjurer and conspirator, born in London about 1649, died 1705. He took orders in the Church of England, became a chaplain in the navy, and was discharged for misconduct. In 1677 he turned Roman Catholic, and resided for some time at the Jesuit Colleges of Valladolid and of St. Omer, but was dismissed for repeated misdemeanours in 1678.

He returned to England and concocted the story of the famous "Popish Plot." He revealed fictitious details of the plot to Sir Edmund Berry Godfrey, and for some time was lodged handsomely in Whitehall, and received a pension of £900 from Parliament. The effects of this perjury continued for two years until, after the execution of Stafford, there was a revulsion of public opinion. Convicted of perjury, he was sentenced to be pilloried five times a year, whipped from Aldgate to Newgate, and imprisoned for life. On the accession of William and Mary he was liberated, and lived to a bad old age, enjoying an ill-deserved pension of £300 a year. Oates is introduced by Sir Walter Scott into *Peveril of the Peak*, where he is made to speak a peculiar dialect.

OATH. A solemn assertion or promise, with the invocation of God to be a witness of the truth of what we say, hence at the end of the judicial oath, "So help me God." Various forms have been associated with oath-taking. Thus, men have proclaimed and symbolized their promise by chopping a fowl in two, by standing within a circle of rope, by placing the hand under another's thigh, by dipping weapons into or drinking blood, or by stretching the hand upwards in the direction of the sky.

Amongst the early Christians the question of oath-taking was a matter of much controversy, objection to it being founded upon Christ's command of "Swear not at all" (Matt. v. 34); but this injunction was held by Athanasius and others only to prohibit colloquial as distinct from judicial swearing. This objection is still maintained, however, by Mennonites, Quakers, and Anabaptists; and the Secularists in England, upon other grounds, refuse the judicial oaths. Roman Catholics believe that the Pope has authority to release a person from any obligation into which he has entered, even when he has bound himself by an oath.

By the law of England (applying also to Scotland) an oath of allegiance must be taken by the chief officers of State, judges, justices, members of Parliament, etc. Since 1888, however, members of Parliament are allowed to affirm. The chief officers of State are required to take in addition an official oath well and truly to serve the sovereign in the office upon which they are entering, and judges to take a judicial oath. Jurors are required to take an oath that they will perform their functions honestly; and witnesses were formerly required to take an oath, but now, in all cases where the party objects on the ground that he has no religious belief or that the taking of the oath is contrary to his religious belief, an affirmation is permitted.

Until 1909 the English practice in judicial oath-taking was to kiss the New Testament, but by the Oaths Act of that year the party taking the oath now holds the book in his uplifted hand. The administering of unlawful oaths in Britain is an offence punishable by penal servitude.

OAXACA, or **OAJACA.** A maritime state of Southern Mexico, traversed by spurs of the Sierra Madre. Cocoa, coffee, sugar, and tobacco are raised. Oaxaca is the capital. Area, 35,689 sq. miles; pop. (1930), 1,070,852.

OAXACA, or **OAJACA.** A town of Mexico, capital of the state of Oaxaca, and on the railway to Mexico City. It has a cathedral and some museums and institutes. In the vicinity was Naxyaca, anciently the capital of the Zapotecas. Pop. (1930), 24,000.

OBADI'AH. One of the twelve minor prophets, who foretells the speedy ruin of the Edomites. The prophecy was probably uttered during the period which elapsed between the fall of Jerusalem (586 B.C.) and the conquest of Edom by Nebuchadnezzar (583 B.C.).

O'BAN. A municipal burgh, seaport, and watering-place of Argyllshire, Scotland; served by the L.M.S. and L.N.E. Railways. It is the tourist headquarters of the Western Highlands, the terminus of the railways, and the starting-point of the steamers. There is a Roman Catholic cathedral. Dunstaffnage and Dunolly Castles (ruined) are in the vicinity. It is a yachting centre and here the Argyllshire gathering is held in September. Pop. (1931), 5759.

O'BE, or **O'BI.** A river of Siberia, U.S.S.R., rising in the Altai Mountains. It pursues a circuitous course north-west to Samarova, where it bifurcates, both branches falling into the Gulf of Obi; length, 2500 miles. Its chief tributaries are the Irtish, Tobol, Tom, and Tchulim—all, like the main river, important waterways.

OBE'AH, or **OBI.** A species of witchcraft practised among negroes of the West Indies. The practiser of this form of superstition is called an Obeah-man or -woman, and possesses great influence.

OBEÏD, El-. The capital of Kordofan, Sudan, on a plain (about

2000 feet altitude) to the north of the Jebel Kordofan. It is a place of transit on the Darfur-Egyptian trade route, and is the centre of the *Bedeira*, one of the most important tribes of Kordofan. A railway, built 1909-11, connects it with Khartoum.

El-Obeïd was taken by the Mahdi (from the Egyptians) in 1883 after a year's siege, and was razed during the Dervish Empire. In 1899, during the advance of Kitchener, and the riverain armies, El-Obeïd fell to the Sirdar's forces, and was subsequently rebuilt. —Cf. W. S. Churchill, *The River War*.

OB'ELISK (Gr. *obeliskos*, diminutive of *obelos*, a spit). A term applied to stone monuments of a rectangular form, diminishing towards the top, generally terminating in a low pyramid. The proportion of the thickness to the height is nearly the same in all obelisks, that is, between one-ninth and one-tenth ; and the thickness at the top is never less than half, nor greater than three-quarters of the thickness at the bottom.

Structures resembling obelisks have been discovered in Assyria, in the ruined cities of Nineveh and Nimrud, but the obelisks proper were peculiar to Egypt, and the country abounded with them. They were all monoliths, and varied in height. Many of these obelisks have been removed thence to Rome and other places. They seem to have been erected to record the honours or triumphs of the monarchs. The two largest obelisks were erected by Sesostris in Heliopolis ; the height of these was 180 feet. They were removed to Rome by Augustus. A fine obelisk of Rameses II. was brought from Luxor to Paris in 1833, and the two known as Cleopatra's Needles are now in London and New York. The obelisks which were common to Rome, Florence, etc., had all been removed from Egypt during its domination by the Roman emperors. —Cf. H. H. Gorringe, *Egyptian Obelisks*.

Cleopatra's Needle, London

OBERAM'MERGAU. A village of Upper Bavaria, in the valley of the Ammer ; served by electric railway from Munich. It is famous as the home of the Passion Play, which took place periodically from 1634 until 1910. It was usually performed at intervals of ten years, but was performed in 1922 instead of 1920 owing to the aftermath of the European War ; it took place again in 1930. The village was once an important trade centre, but is now devoted entirely to agriculture and wood-carving. There is a Benedictine monastery (of Ettal), founded in 1338, dissolved in 1803, and rebuilt in 1884. Pop. nominally about 1600.

Oberammergau

OBERHAUSEN. A town of Germany, in Prussian Rhineland, on the Rhine, and a junction on the Wesel-Emmerich and Köln-Hamburg Railways. It is a centre of the iron industry, the Gutehoffnungs-Hütte iron- and steel-works employing over 24,000 hands. There are also coal-mines, and glass-, porcelain-, and chemical factories. Pop. 89,900.

O'BERON. In folklore, the king of the elves or fairies, and husband of Titania. He appears first in the old French poem, *Huon de Bordeaux*, but is best known from Shakespeare (*Midsummer Night's Dream*) and from Weber's opera, *Oberon*. Oberon is also the subject of an epic by Wieland, and of a masque by Ben Jonson (*Oberon, the Faery Prince*).

OBLA'TI, or OBLATES. A name given from an early period in the

Roman Catholic Church to children dedicated to the Church, and now applied to such persons as associate themselves like monks or nuns but without taking vows. Under the name of Oblati of St. Ambrose a congregation of secular priests was established at Milan in 1578 by St. Charles Borromeo. The Oblates of Mary Immaculate, or of the Immaculate Conception, were founded in 1815, at Aix, by the Abbé Mazenod. Their duties were to consecrate themselves to spiritual ministrations, especially to the young, to the poor, and to prisoners. The order has houses or missionary establishments in France, England, Scotland, and the United States.

OBOE (ō'bō). A musical wind-instrument resembling a clarionet in shape, and sounded through a double reed. It consists of three joints besides the mouthpiece, and its compass is generally from B below the treble clef to F in alt, with the intermediate semitones, being a compass of two octaves and one fifth. The name oboe is from the Italian; the French form, *hautboy* (*hautbois*), was formerly more frequently used.

OBOK (Fr., *Obock*). A port on the Red Sea, opposite Jibuti, included in the French Somali Coast Protectorate. It was formerly an independent sultanate, but was acquired by the French in 1856, officially annexed in 1862, and occupied in 1884.

OB'OLUS. An ancient Greek silver coin, the sixth part of an Attic drachma, equal to 1¼*d.*; multiples

Brass Obolus of Metapontum
Actual diameter of coin, 1⅛ inches

and sub-multiples of this coin were also used, and pieces of the value of 5, 4, 3, 2, 1½ oboli, and ½, ⅓, ¼th of an obolus respectively are to be found in collections.

OBREGON, Alvaro. Mexican president. Born in 1880, with Villa and Gonzalez he took a leading part in Carranza's revolution, 1913. As, head of the constitutional forces, he entered Mexico City, 15th Aug., 1914. When, in 1915, Villa turned against Carranza, Obregon led the campaign against Villa. Chosen President in Sept., 1920, he held that office till 1924. Succeeded then by Calles, he was again elected President four years later to follow Calles, but was assassinated on 17th July, 1928.

O'BRIEN, William Smith. Irish Nationalist, born 1803, died 1864. Entering Parliament in 1826, he joined the Young Ireland group of politicians, and advocated the use of physical force. In an endeavour (1848) to effect a rising in Tipperary, he was surrounded in a cabbage-garden, arrested, tried by special commission at Clonmel, and sentenced to death, but in the end this was commuted to transportation. He was set at liberty in 1854, and fully pardoned in 1856.

OBSCUR'ANTISTS. A word originally used at the time of the Revival of Learning, and applied to the opponents of progress and enlightenment. The term is derived from Ulrich von Hutten's famous satire, entitled *Epistolæ obscurorum virorum*, directed against the monks of Cologne.

OBSERVATORY. An institution or building supplied with the necessary scientific instruments and devoted to the observation of natural phenomena, astronomic, magnetic, or meteorological. The astronomical observatory is the one of most general interest. Astronomical observation began at an early date in China; the pyramids in Egypt seem in some way to have been associated with stellar observation; and the first historical observatory was founded in Alexandria 300 B.C. Its work was begun by Aristillus, and continued by Timocharis, Hipparchus, Aristarchus, and others.

The first European observatory was built at Nürnberg by Bernhard Walther in 1472, and this was followed in the sixteenth century by Tycho Brahe's famous observatory on the Island of Hveen, near Copenhagen, while another was erected by the Landgrave of Hesse at Cassel in 1561. Through the labours of Tycho practical astronomy became associated with the universities, so that Leyden and Copenhagen founded observatories. These were followed by the construction of the Royal Observatory at Paris (1667); the Greenwich Royal Observatory (1675); the Tusculan Observatory, near Copenhagen (1704); Berlin (1705; new observatory 1835); Vienna (1756); Dublin (1785); Königsberg (1813); Sydney (1820); Cape of Good Hope (1820); Edinburgh (1825); Pulkova, near Petrograd (1839); Cambridge, United States (1839); Washington, United States (1845); Melbourne (1853); Lick

Observatory, California (1888); Lowell Observatory, Arizona (1894); Yerkes Observatory, Wisconsin (1896); Mount Wilson Observatory, California (1905); and the Einstein Observatory at Potsdam (1921).

The director of the Royal Observatory at Greenwich is the Astronomer Royal, and the director of that at Edinburgh is the Astronomer Royal for Scotland. The chief observatory instruments are the telescope, equatorial, transit circle, and transit instrument, together with the sidereal and the solar clock. In the larger observatories the application of spectrum analysis, photography, photometry, etc., has greatly increased the number and variety of observations. The observatory building must be constructed in a very stable manner, and as the instruments must be out of contact with the walls and flooring, they are supported on stone pillars having foundations separate from the rest of the building.

OBSID'IAN. Vitreous lava, or volcanic glass, lava which has become glassy by rapid cooling. The chemical composition of the rhyolites and trachytes allows most readily of the formation of obsidian in association with their flows. In Hungary and the Yellowstone Park thick masses of this volcanic glass occur.

Obsidian was anciently used both for implements and for religious purposes. The early Cretans found it on the Island of Melos, and imported and used it at the very dawn of their history. Obsidian was carried into Egypt, Troy, Cyprus, Greece, and Malta. The Jews used obsidian as well as flint in religious ceremonies. Obsidian implements have been found in Neolithic strata near Nineveh. In ancient Egypt, during the Pyramid age, the copper statues of Pharaoh Pepi I. and of his son were given eyes of obsidian. As shells were used for mummy eyes, it would appear that obsidian was likewise regarded by the Egyptians as a " life-giving " substance.

Obsidian was an important article in the trade of ancient times. There are extensive obsidian-mines at Hidalgo, in Mexico, and the Aztecs and the Maya peoples of Central America made their sharpest weapons and their most serviceable implements of obsidian, their copper not being hardened sufficiently to be kept sharp when edged. The Aztec god, Tezcatlipoca, had an obsidian mirror which appears to have served a double purpose as a religious object. It revealed " the will of the gods," and was used, as was a crystal by the Greeks and Romans, for lighting sacred fires. The Orphic poem on precious stones (verses 177 *et seq.*) describes the Greek method. Crystals were used for lighting sacred fires by the Siamese and the Chinese.

In Peru, obsidian mirrors, which were polished and had concave surfaces, were used, as were crystals elsewhere, to kindle holy fires, being held so as to concentrate the rays of the sun. In Peru, as in Rome, the sacred fire was guarded by vestal virgins. The Peruvian virgins were brides of the sun, as the Roman virgins were brides of the fire. In Peru, mirrors were used by women, and it was " a disgrace if not ignominy " to men to look in mirrors.

Evidently obsidian was in the New World closely associated with women, fire, and the sun when used for religious purposes. The god Tezcatlipoca, who was especially connected with obsidian, resembles in certain of his aspects the black god Krishna of India. His statue in Mexico was of black obsidian. Black stones were kept by the Maya peoples in their temples to reveal " the will of the gods," and these may have been of obsidian. There are references in the Chinese texts to mirrors and screens of jade and stone which had a religious value. In Peru the tombs of the Incas have yielded mirrors of burnished silver and of obsidian, as well as vases and ornaments of gold and silver.

It would appear that obsidian, like pearl-shell, crystals, jade, gold, and silver, acquired at an early period, and retained for many centuries, a religious value, and that it was connected with the sun, the " eye " of heaven, and therefore with fire and the " vital spark."

OBSTETRICS, or **MIDWIFERY.** The branch of the practice of medicine concerned with the welfare of women during childbirth; but it also includes within its scope the ailments to which a mother is subject during the periods of gestation and lactation, and is also closely related to gynæcology or the treatment of the diseases peculiar to women, many of which are the result directly or indirectly of child-bearing.

Among primitive peoples it is not uncommon for a woman to give birth to a child without help from attendants of any sort; but it is perhaps more usual for a woman to attend her and to care for the child when born. Such an attendant may be merely a relative or friend, or a woman who practises as a midwife. Even in this country at the present time a considerable number of women are attended in child-birth merely by midwives; and two centuries ago it was the exception rather than the rule for a lying-in woman to be attended by an obstetric surgeon or man-midwife, as he was then called. Thus, when he was called in by George III. to attend his young queen's confinement, Dr. William Hunter merely waited in an ante-room in case the midwife needed his assistance.

In the middle of the eighteenth century the art of midwifery was passing through a severe struggle. For the practice was almost exclusively in the hands of the midwives, and even when men practitioners devoted themselves to obstetric practice it was merely as advisors to the midwives, who tried to preserve the art as a monopoly for their sex and only called in men's help when they got into difficulties—a phase of history that is now being repeated when qualified medical practitioners of the female sex attempt to make the same claims as the midwives made two centuries ago.

The establishment of the position of the man-midwife in London and England was largely the work of two Lanarkshire practitioners, Dr. William Smellie and Dr. William Hunter. Smellie came to London in 1739 and bore the brunt of the fierce conflict for supremacy with Mrs. Nihell, the champion of the midwives; but his predecessor Sir R. Manningham had already founded the first maternity institution. William Hunter turned his attention chiefly to midwifery, and his knowledge of anatomy, his professional skill and polished manners, contributed very materially to the establishment of obstetric surgery and the rôle of the male practitioner, as well as to the development of the science and art of obstetrics. Hunter was appointed man-midwife to the Middlesex Hospital in 1748, and Surgeon Accoucheur to the British Lying-In Hospital next year.

When Smellie came to London the art of midwifery was in its infancy, and he was mainly responsible for the introduction of the use of forceps to assist the extraction of the child in cases of difficult labour. The obstetric forceps had been recently invented by the Chamberlens in France, but it was a most dangerous if not positively destructive instrument; and Smellie set himself the task of finding better methods which in cases of difficult labour would subject the child's life to less risk. He laid down the rules for the safe application of the forceps, and rendered an incalculable service to medical practice and mankind.

But the opposition of Hunter, who regarded the instrument as a dangerous invention, brought it into disfavour towards the end of the eighteenth century, until the French surgeon, Baudelocque, restored it to its rightful place as an indispensable aid in the obstetric surgeon's work. Although William Hunter delayed reform in this matter, in other ways he was responsible for the introduction of wiser methods into midwifery. In particular he taught obstetric surgeons and midwives to leave it to nature to get rid of the after-birth and not to attempt to remove it forcibly unless there were very definite reasons for adopting such a procedure.

The birth of a child is a natural act which in the majority of cases takes place without any artificial assistance; and it is a wise rule in the case of normal and healthy women to interfere with the physiological process of parturition as little as possible. But it not infrequently happens, especially under the conditions incidental to life in large industrial centres, that the mother's pelvis may be contracted or distorted or her muscular powers inadequate for the expulsion of the child. In the latter case the use of an instrument, the forceps, to assist the extraction of the child from the mother's womb may be necessary. In the former case the disproportion between the size of the baby's head and the outlet from the mother's body may be so great that it is impossible for the child to be born in the normal way, even with the help of forceps. In such cases the surgeon may be compelled to open the abdominal cavity and, after cutting into the womb, remove the infant through the front of the mother's body. This operation is known as Cæsarian Section, because of the tradition that Julius Cæsar was brought into the world in this way.

In other cases difficulties arise from the fact that the infant may occupy some unusual position in the mother's womb. Normally the head is placed below and is born first; as the head of the new-born child has a bigger diameter than its body, if the head dilates the passage of exit the birth of the child's body and limbs is a simple matter. But if some other part of the body tends to emerge first, difficulty and delay are likely to result. To prevent this the obstetric surgeon often resorts to the operation of *turning*, that is, altering the position of the child in the womb so that it will be more favourably placed for parturition.

Before the birth of the child the membranous sac (or caul), in which the child is contained within the womb, bursts and allows the water (amniotic fluid) to escape; then the child is born, and later on the after-birth (or placenta), by which the navel string (umbilical cord) is attached to the lining of the womb, comes away and so completes the last stage of labour. Some of the most awkward complications of labour are due to a malposition of the placenta; others result from a faulty or incomplete removal of the after-birth.

One of the great triumphs of preventive medicine is the discovery that by means of thorough cleanliness and adoption of aseptic methods such ailments as puerperal fever and "white leg" can be prevented. In former times these results of infection were responsible for a vast number of deaths in child-birth or of serious disability in those whose lives were spared. The training of midwives in asceptic methods has been the means of reducing the risks of child-bearing very materially, and of sparing the lives of vast numbers of mothers and children.

In addition to being an art that aims at assisting women in child-birth, minimizing the risks both to mother and child, and preventing unnecessary suffering, midwifery can also be regarded as the branch of medical science concerned with the study of all the conditions to which a woman and her offspring are exposed as the result of pregnancy and during the period of lactation.

Many of the gynæcological ailments, such as misplacements of the womb, the development of cysts of the ovary or tumours of the womb, or interference with the tubes that carry the ova to the womb, directly affect the diagnosis and treatment of the conditions found among pregnant women. In some cases the fœtus which has developed from a fertilized ovum may be prevented from reaching the womb, being retained within the tube or oviduct or even in the ovary itself. These cases are described as extra-uterine pregnancies (tubal or ovarian respectively), and call for surgical interference to prevent more serious consequences. Thus the growth of the fœtus will eventually lead to a rupture of the tube or ovary, with serious hæmorrhage, and the escape of the fœtus itself into the mother's body cavity, from which it has to be removed by surgical operation.

Within recent years there has been considerable legislation dealing with obstetrics, and during the past twenty years four important Acts relating to the subject have been passed. (1) The Midwives Act (1902, amended 1918) deals with the training of midwives and lays down certain regulations in regard to their practice. (2) Notification of Births Act (1907) requires that every birth (live or dead) be notified to the Medical Officer of Health of the district in which it has occurred. (3) The Maternity Benefits of National Insurance Act (modified 1913) provides a sum of money for the insured woman, or wife of an insured person at the time of confinement. (4) The Maternity and Child Welfare Act (1918) gives power to local authorities to make arrangements for the provision of ante-natal clinics for mothers, and home-visiting of mothers; to ensure that the mother has skilled attendance during her confinement, and hospital accommodation in abnormal cases; also for the establishment of post-natal clinics for systematic advice and treatment of infants, with hospital accommodation when serious complications arise.

Midwifery as a Career.—Midwifery offers scope to the woman who takes up nursing too late in life to obtain a general hospital training, though here as elsewhere such a training would stand her in very good stead. The status of the midwife is much improved since the passing of the Midwives' Acts in 1902 and 1918, enforcing compulsory registration and training. The course is a twelve-months' one (or six months for a general nurse), and a certificate is given by the Central Midwives' Board, Queen Anne's Gate Buildings, Westminster, London. Training can be had at any Maternity or Lying-in Hospital recognized by the Board, to whom application for particulars should be made.

OCARI'NA. A musical wind-instrument of clay or metal, of torpedo shape, pierced with a number of small holes, and giving a sweet tone.

OCCAM, or OCKHAM, William of. Mediæval monk and scholar, known as *Venerabilis Inceptor* and *Doctor Invincibilis*, born about the end of the thirteenth century, probably at Ockham, in Surrey, died at Munich in 1349. Educated at Oxford and at the University of Paris, he became a Franciscan, and his attitude on the question of evangelical poverty led to controversy with Pope John XXII. Seized and imprisoned at Avignon, he escaped in 1328, and was cordially received by Louis the Bavarian in Italy. He was excommunicated, and spent the rest of his life at Louis's court, engaged in constant polemical warfare against the Papal authority. In 1342 he became general of the Franciscans. Occam is regarded as the second founder of nominalism (q.v.), for which he secured a final victory over realism, and he was a forerunner of the Reformation. Several Latin works by him are extant.

OCCASIONALISM. The doctrine of occasional causes, the theory evolved by the Cartesians, which maintains that mind and matter act upon each other not directly but upon the occasion of certain changes in the one or the other. It explains the reciprocal action upon each other of the soul and the body. As the soul and body, according to Descartes, are two entities with entirely different properties, the essence of the former being thought and that of the latter extension, a difficulty naturally arose as to how the one can act upon the other.

Descartes, therefore, assumed that the intercommunication between soul and body was the result of divine interference. The suggestion was taken up by several of his disciples, who taught that on the *occasion* of the determinations of the mind God himself excites in the body the sensations corresponding to them, and on the *occasion* of the motions of the body He excites in the mind the sensations and passions which correspond to them. The doctrine was subsequently developed by Geulincx (1624-69), who may be considered as the real founder of occasionalism, and Malebranche (1638-1715). Occasionalism has much in common with Leibnitz's doctrine of *pre-established harmony*, from which, however, it must be distinguished.

OCCLUSION. In chemistry, the absorption of a gas by a metal, as of hydrogen by palladium. Thus, in the process of decomposing water, a strip of palladium, if used as the negative electrode, will absorb or "occlude" from 800 to 900 times its volume of hydrogen, swelling during the process. Other examples of occlusion are the absorption of hydrogen by red-hot platinum, of carbonic oxide by red-hot cast-iron, and of oxygen by melted silver. Palladium, even when cold or slightly warm, will take up a very considerable quantity of hydrogen.

OCCULTATION. The term used in astronomy for the hiding of a star or planet from our sight through the interposition of another nearer celestial body, and specifically applied to the concealing of a star or planet by the moon.

OCEA'NIA. The collective term for the islands of the Pacific Ocean, but particularly applied only to those in the South Sea. These islands may be divided into lines or festoons as indicated in the map, the course of the lines being dependent on the geological structure of the adjacent continents. The principal groups are the Australasian Festoon, the Micronesian Festoon, and the South Pacific Chain (including Polynesia, q.v.).

Australasian Festoon.—This consists of a line of islands east of Australia, formed of continental rocks. The festoon begins on the south with the archipelago of New Zealand, and continues northward through Norfolk Island, New Caledonia, New Hebrides, the Solomons, and ends in New Guinea. *Melanesia.*—The northern islands are peopled by Melanesians, a branch of the negro race, having the woolly hair, short heads, dark skins, thick lips, and broad noses of the negro. The islands from New Guinea to New Caledonia form Melanesia, and they rest upon the submarine Melanesian plateau. These islands are related to Australia both geologically and by the characteristics of their flora and fauna, and are the remains of a formerly continuous land connecting New Zealand with both New Guinea and Australia.

Micronesian Festoon.—This festoon is roughly concentric with the Australasian Festoon, and includes the islands known as Micronesia and some of the islands included in Polynesia. It begins to the east of the Philippines, with the Caroline and Marshall Islands, and extends south-eastwards through the Gilbert and Ellice groups to the Fiji and Tonga Islands. These groups all occur on the edge of a submerged plateau which extends south-westward to Australia, and they would appear to have been connected with that continent.

South Pacific Chain.—The chain comprises a long line of islands branching from the Micronesian Festoon at the Samoan group and extending eastward across the Southern Pacific. Its islands may be the last survivors of a land which once connected South America and Australasia, and enabled the marsupials and land-tortoises found in both regions to migrate from one to the other. The South Pacific Chain includes the Low Archipelago or Paumotus, the Society Islands, the Cook Islands, and the Marquesas

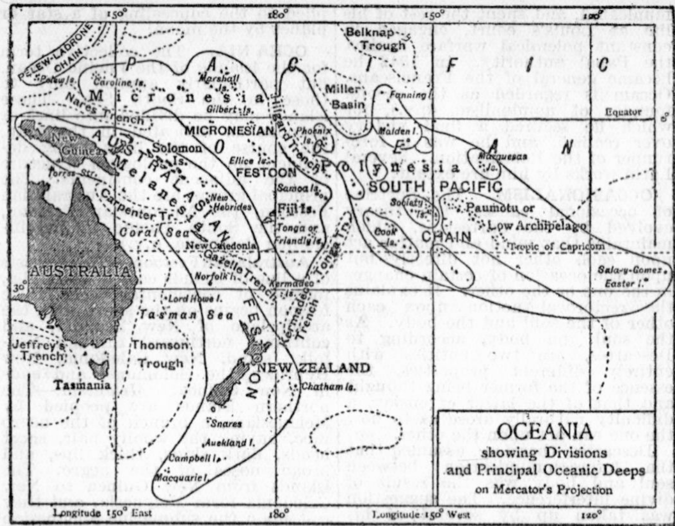

OCEANIA
showing Divisions
and Principal Oceanic Deeps
on Mercator's Projection

Islands, Easter Island, and Sala-y-Gomez.

OCEAN ISLAND. *See* GILBERT ISLANDS.

OCEANOGRAPHY. The branch of geography which deals with the seas and oceans. The province of the oceanographer is the investigation of the physical properties of sea water, the distribution of temperature and salinity, the movements of sea water, the deposits on the floor of the ocean, the origin of ocean basins, and the physical conditions of marine life. The science has considerable practical importance in relation to marine food fisheries, problems of navigation, questions of coastal erosion, and the laying and maintenance of deep-sea cables. As a science it is closely related to physics, chemistry, and geology. Its foundations were laid by the voyage of H.M.S. *Challenger* (1872-76). For a sketch of its history, *see* DEEP-SEA EXPLORATION.

Oceans and seas cover 70·8 per cent. of the surface of the globe. The distribution is most irregular: in the northern hemisphere 60·7 per cent. of the surface is water, and in the southern hemisphere 80·9 per cent. The globe can be divided into hemispheres of which one has 52·7 per cent. of water surface, and the other 90·5 per cent.

There are actually only three great oceans, Atlantic, Pacific, and Indian, all of which are connected by the so-called Southern or Antarctic Ocean. For the sake of convenience the term Southern Ocean is generally applied to the waters south of a line joining the southern extremities of Africa, Tasmania, New Zealand, and South America. The Arctic Ocean is really an enclosed sea of too small an extent to merit the name of ocean.

Seas are of two forms: those narrowly connected with the ocean, such as the Mediterranean Sea, Baltic Sea, Red Sea, or Arctic Ocean; and those with wide connection with the ocean, such as the North Sea, Barent's Sea, or Weddell Sea. Enclosed seas show great differences in temperature, salinity, and circulation compared with oceans in the same latitudes.

The floor of the oceans consists essentially of three areas: the continental shelf between the shore and the 100-fathom line; the steep continental slope between 100 and about 1700 fathoms; and the abyssal area, a more or less undulating plain below 1700 fathoms on an average. From the abyssal area there rose not infrequently volcanic cones that often appear above the ocean waters as lofty, isolated islands. The weight of evidence tends to support the view that the great ocean basins are permanent features of the surface of the globe, but the problem is far from settled. One of the great obstacles in the way of its solution is the lack of information regarding the solid rocks, below the accumulated deposits on the ocean floor. On the other hand, there is no doubt that the form and depth of many seas have materially changed even in recent geological times. *See* DEEP-SEA EXPLORATION; HYDROGRAPHY; GEOGRAPHY.

OCE'ANUS. In classical mythology, the eldest of the Titans, regarded as the god of the ocean or the river surrounding the earth. Oceanus and Tethys were regarded as the parents of rivers, and of the Oceanides or ocean nymphs. The Greeks considered the earth as a flat circle surrounded by a river (Oceanus), and the term ocean was thus applied especially to the Atlantic, in contradistinction to the Mediterranean Sea.

OCEL'LUS. One of the minute simple eyes of insects, many echinoderms, spiders, myriapods, crustaceans, molluscs, annelids, etc. In insects these ocelli or stemmata are usually situated on the crown of the head between the great compound eyes, whose simple elements they resemble in structure, and in rare cases may be the sole organs of vision. They are probably used for distant vision, and the compound eyes for near vision.

O'CELOT (*Felis pardalis*). A well-known carnivorous mammal of the cat kind ranging from Arkansas to Paraguay. It attains a length of

Ocelot (*Felis pardalis*)

about 3 feet, while the tail measures some 18 inches more. The ocelot inhabits great forests; its food consists mainly of birds and rodents; and it is timid but bloodthirsty.

OCHIL HILLS (ō'hil). A hill range of Scotland, on the borders of Perth, Clackmannan, Kinross, and Fifeshire; length, about 25 miles; average breadth, about 12 miles; highest summit, Ben Cleuch, 2363 feet.

OCHRE. The name given to naturally-occurring hydrated oxide of iron. It is found in the form of an earth mixed with silica and alumina, and varies in colour from light yellow to reddish brown. It is employed as a pigment in the manufacture of paints, and also for colouring paper, linoleum, and other substances. It is prepared for use by grinding and washing to remove sand, etc. Incrustations of the oxides of other metals such as nickel, antimony, and bismuth are also termed ochres, but are of less importance.

O'CONNELL, Daniel. Irish agitator, born in Kerry in 1775, died at Genoa in 1847. He was educated at a school in Cork and the Catholic colleges of St. Omer and Douai, studied for the Irish Bar, and soon became distinguished for legal skill and oratory. Turning his energy to Irish politics, he advocated Catholic Emancipation; skilfully kept the agitation within constitutional lines; became member for Clare in 1828; and attained his triumph in the following year when the Government of the Duke of Wellington granted the Catholic claims.

After the Reform Bill he became conspicuous as the head of a parliamentary body called "O'Connell's Tail." In 1841 he called together enormous meetings throughout Ireland, and loudly raised a cry for the Repeal of the Union. The Government determined to put down the agitation, and O'Connell was arrested, convicted, and sentenced to twelve months' imprisonment with a fine of £2000. In a few months the House of Lords quashed this judgment. Meanwhile, however, a new and more advanced party had sprung up in the Repeal Association, and the health of O'Connell was broken down. He made his last speech in Parliament in April, 1847.

OC'TANT. In astronomy, that position or aspect of a heavenly body, as a planet or satellite, when halfway between conjunction or opposition and quadrature, or distant from another point or body the eighth part of a circle or 45°. The word is also applied to an older form of instrument for measuring angles, on the same principle as the sextant, but having an arc of only 45°. Owing to the doubling of the angle by reflection, it measured angles up to 90°, and was commonly called a quadrant.

OCTAVE. In music, an interval of eight notes, as from C to C′, or B_1 to B (*see* ACOUSTICS). When two notes an octave apart are sounded together, their mental effect is almost the same as that of a consonance. The physical explanation is simple. Whatever the frequency, i.e. number of vibrations per second, of a note may be, the frequency of its octave is just double. But if we represent the frequency of a note by 1, the frequencies of its harmonics (q.v.) will be 2, 3, 4, etc.; and the note an octave higher with its harmonics will have frequencies 2, 4, 6, 8, etc. Thus, as Helmholtz puts it, when a higher voice executes the same melody an octave higher, we hear again a part of what we heard before, and at the same time we hear nothing that we had not previously heard.

OCTA'VIA. Daughter of Gaius Octavius and of Atia, and sister to the Emperor Augustus, illustrious for her virtues, her beauty, and her accomplishments. She was the widow of Claudius Marcellus, by whom she had a son and two daughters, when she was married, at the instance of her brother, to the triumvir Mark Antony. The latter neglected her for Cleopatra, Queen of Egypt, an insult which Octavianus greatly resented, and which helped to bring about the war between himself and Antony. Octavia died in 11 B.C.

OCTA'VO. The size of one leaf of a sheet of paper folded so as to make eight leaves: usually written *8vo*; hence, a book having eight leaves to the sheet. There are different sizes of octavo, arising from the different sizes of paper employed; as, *foolscap 8vo*, *demy 8vo*, *imperial 8vo*.

OCTOBER (from the Lat. *octo*, eight). Originally the eighth month in the Roman calendar, whence its name, which it still retained after the beginning of the year had been changed from March to January.

OC'TOPUS. A genus of dibranchiate Cephalopoda, familiarly known as poulpes. They have eight arms, each with two rows of suckers, which are sessile or unstalked. The prominent head is joined to the body by a distinct neck, and the body itself is short, generally more or less rounded in shape, and unprovided with side or lateral fins. They have attained a notoriety from tales circulated concerning their ferocity and the existence of gigantic members of the genus, though the largest cephalopods that have been met with have belonged to other genera.

Octopus

The *O. vulgāris*, or common poulpe, is found on the British shores, but is more common in the Mediterranean. It is said to reach a length of 9 feet and a weight of 68 lb., the arms being long and slender. A related form (*Eledone moschata*), which possesses but one row of suckers on each arm, is eaten by natives of the Mediterranean littoral.

OCTROI (ok-trwȧ). An old French term signifying a grant, privilege, or monopoly from Government to a person or to a company. Octroi also signifies a tax levied at the gates of French cities, towns, etc., on produce brought in for use. Abolished in 1791, it was again introduced in 1799.

OCU'BA-WAX. A vegetable wax obtained from the fruit of *Myristica ocūba*, *officinālis*, or *sebifĕra*, a plant of the nutmeg genus growing abundantly in the marshy grounds on the shores of the Amazon and its tributaries. It is easily bleached, and is used extensively in Brazil for the manufacture of candles.

ODDFELLOWS, Independent Order of. A large and extensively ramified friendly society, having its headquarters in Manchester. It was originally an association of a convivial kind, modelled on freemasonry, and still retains passwords and secret signs. It assumed its present form at a convention in Manchester (1813), and has spread widely in Britain and elsewhere. The organization was introduced into the United States in 1819, and severed its connection with the British Union in 1842. Branch societies exist in most countries. *See* FRIENDLY SOCIETIES.

ODE (Gr. *ōdē*, song). Originally a poem intended to be sung; a lyric poem written in an elaborate form, and usually dignified in subject and style. There were two kinds of ode in ancient Greece, one the personal utterance of the poet, the other the choric song of the poet's trained band of dancers. Both kinds of composition have been imitated in modern times, so that the word "ode" is loosely applied to any elaborate lyric poem.

The personal ode reached perfection in the hands of Alcæus, Anacreon, and Sappho; in Roman times Catullus imitated Sappho with complete success, and Horace took Alcæus and Anacreon for his models. These two great Latin poets gave the personal ode or lyric a popularity which it would not otherwise have enjoyed.

The choral ode developed upon different lines, and eventually became the ode proper. Alcman first gave it a strophic arrangement, which became one of its essential features. Stesichorus, Ibycus, and the greater Simonides developed it until it culminated in the work of Bacchylides and Pindar.

In modern times the ode was revived by Ronsard and the members of the Pléiade. Its popularity in France was not long-lived. In England Spenser wrote two fine odes, his *Epithalamium* and *Prothalamium*. Ben Jonson and some of his "sons" wrote elaborate poems which they called edes; and Milton wrote several lofty odes.

Abraham Cowley, however, was the first to elaborate the "Pindaric Ode" in English, his idea of Pindar was that he wrote a kind of *vers libre*, a theory which made the Greek model an easy one for those poets who found their genius cramped by the exigencies of rhyme and rhythm. It is only comparatively recently that it has been recognized that Pindar's verse obeys the most exacting laws. Dryden and Congreve may be mentioned as writers of odes. The latter wrote a *Discourse on the Pindarique Ode* (1705). Gray's odes approach more nearly to the Pindaric model; those of Collins are of the lyric kind. Wordsworth, Coleridge, Tennyson, Shelley, Keats, Swinburne, and Victor Hugo have all written odes, some entirely irregular, some merely elaborate lyrics, and some conforming more closely to the Greek type.—Cf. E. Gosse, *English Odes.*

ODENBURG (Magyar *Sopron*). The chief town in Western Hungary, 35 miles S. of Vienna. Pop. *c.* 40,000.

ODENSE. A seaport-city, the third largest of Denmark, capital of the Island of Fünen, on the River Odense, and served by ship-canal to Odense Fjord. There are manufactures of cloth, tobacco, and chemicals, and exports of dairy-produce and hides. Hans Andersen was born at Odense. Pop. (1930), 56,759.

ODENWALD (ō'den-vält). An afforested mountain area (Katzenbuckel, 2057 feet) of Hesse-Darmstadt, Germany, between the Neckar and the Main. It is about 50 miles in length, presents charming scenery, and is rich in legend.

ODER (Lat. *Viadus*). A river of Germany, which rises in the Moravian tableland, Czecho-Slovakia. It flows through Moravia, Silesia, and Brandenburg, widens into the Stettiner Haff, and enters the Baltic by three channels; length, 560 miles. The traffic on this river and connected canals is important. It has been canalized between Ratibor and Swinemünde (480 miles). On its banks are Breslau, Glogau, Frankfort, Küstrin, Stettin, and Kosel.

ODES'SA (Rom. *Istrianorum portus*). Seaport of the Ukraine. On the Black Sea, about 25 miles from

Odessa : The Law Courts

the mouth of the Dniester and 90 miles south-west of Kherson, in the government of that name. Odessa is in the midst of a grain district. When the Dardanelles were closed by Turkey, in 1914, Odessa was cut off from the allies, and was bombarded by the Turks. Captured by German forces in March, 1918, it was taken by the Bolshevists in 1920. It has a broadcasting station (450·4 M., 4 kW.). Pop. 475,500.

ODIN. The chief god of Scandinavian mythology, the omniscient ruler of heaven and earth, having his seat in Valaskjalf, where he receives through his two ravens, *Hugin* and *Munin*, tidings of all that takes place in the world. As war-god he holds his court in Valhalla, where all brave warriors arrive after death and enjoy the tumultuous pleasures they delighted in while on earth. His wife is Frigga. The fourth day of the week, Wednesday, derived its name from this deity. *See* NORTHERN MYTHOLOGY.

ODOA'CER, or ODOVACAR. Ruler of Italy after the fall of the Western Empire, A.D. 476 to 493. He was of German origin, the son of Edico or Idico, hereditary head of the Scyrri tribe, and received his early training in the camp of Attila, King of the Huns. He joined the imperial guard of the Roman army, was chosen head of the barbarian confederates, and having overthrown Romulus Augustulus, the last of the Roman emperors, he assumed the title of king in 476. Out of policy he paid court to the Byzantine Emperor Zeno, from whom he received the title of *Patricius* or Patrician.

In 489 Italy was invaded by the Ostrogoths under Theodoric, and Odoacer was defeated in a series of battles. Besieged in Ravenna, he capitulated, and was at first well treated by Theodoric, who shared the kingdom with him. In March, 493, however, Odoacer was treacherously killed by the Gothic king.

ODONTOGLOS'SUM. An extensive genus of orchids, natives of Central America, much prized by cultivators for their magnificent flowers, which are remarkable both

Odontoglossum luteo-purpureum

for their size and the beauty of their colours. A considerable number of species have been introduced into Europe, and grow well in a moderate temperature. *O. crispum* or *O. Alexandræ* is a superb flower, named after the late Queen Alexandra.

ODONTOPTERYX. An Eocene fossil bird from the London Clay of the Isle of Sheppey. It was probably a web-footed fish-eating bird, most nearly allied to the ducks and geese. It had a bill with saw-like bony projections resembling teeth.

ODONTORNI'THES. A name for certain fossil birds characterized by having teeth, as Hesperornis and Ichthyornis (q.v.).

ŒCUMEN'ICAL (Gr. *oikoumenikos* pertaining to the whole inhabited world), universal, an epithet applied to the general councils of the Church. From the time of the Council of Chalcedon (A.D. 451) the patriarchs of Constantinople took the title of œcumenical, in the same sense as the epithet Catholic is used in the Western Church. *See* COUNCIL.

ŒDEMA. The effusion of fluid into the subcutaneous tissues of the body. It may be either general or local. The most common forms of general œdema are cardiac œdema, due to weakness of the heart's action, and seen first in the most dependent parts remote from the heart; renal œdema, due to disease of the kidneys and usually seen under the eyes, in the lower part of the back, in the genitals, and in the legs; hepatic œdema, due to disease of the liver, and seen in the legs with accumulation of fluid in the abdominal cavity.

Slight œdema often occurs in anæmia, and may be considerable in pernicious anæmia. Œdema may arise in the wasting diseases of infants and children, and is often present in the later stages of tuberculosis and cancer. Local œdema is seen in wounds and infected areas along with other signs of inflammation, and it occurs when there is obstruction to the flow of blood in the veins of any part.

Œ'DIPUS. In ancient Greek legend, son of the Theban King Laius and his queen Jocasta. He was exposed as an infant—on account of an oracle saying that Laius would be killed by his son—and was brought up at the court of Corinth. He left his foster-parents, however, the Delphic oracle having advised him to avoid the soil of his country. In a narrow road in Phocis he met King Laius and unknowingly killed him. Having solved the riddle of the Sphinx, he became King of Thebes, and married his mother Jocasta—a fate foretold by the Delphic oracle. On realizing what had been done Jocasta hanged herself, and Œdipus put out his own eyes. The *Œdipus* of Æschylus and that of Euripides are lost, but the *Œdipus Tyrannus* and *Œdipus Coloneus* of Sophocles remain. The story has also been made the subject of tragedies by Corneille, Voltaire, Chénier, Dryden, and Lee.

OEHLENSCHLAGER (*eu'*lĕn-shlā-gĕr), **Adam Gottlob.** Danish poet and dramatist, born at Vesterbro, Copenhagen, 1779, died 1850. After an irregular education he tried the stage, but failed in the profession of actor. He then studied law, but after 1802 devoted himself to literature, and in 1803 published his first volume of poems.

Recognized as the chief Danish poet, he received a Government grant which enabled him to visit Germany, France, Switzerland, and Italy (where he met Goethe, Fichte, and Madame de Staël). His finest works, such as *Baldur hin Gode, Palnatoke, Axel og Valborg*, and the tragedy of *Hakon Jarl*, were written at this period. Returning to Denmark in 1810, he was appointed professor of æsthetics in the University of Copenhagen. His chief works, besides those above-mentioned, are: *Helge, Hroars Saga, Nordens Guder, Erik og Abel, Dronning Margrethe*, and *Dina*.

OELSNITZ (eulz'nits). A town of Germany, in Saxony, on the White Elster, with manufactures of cottons, yarn, and wool, and industries in brewing and pearl-fishing. Pop. 14,000.

OERSTED, or **ORSTED** (eur'sted), **Hans Christian.** Danish physicist, born in 1777, died at Copenhagen 1851. He studied at the University of Copenhagen; spent several years at the expense of Government in Holland, Germany, and Paris; was in 1806 appointed extraordinary professor of physics at Copenhagen; and in 1812-13, while on a second tour in Germany, he drew up his views of the chemical laws of Nature, which he afterwards published in Paris under the title of *Recherches sur l'identité des forces électriques et chimiques*. His fame rests on his discovery (in 1819) of the fundamental principles of electro-magnetism.

OESEL (Esthonian *Saaremaa*). An island of Estonia, at the entrance to the Gulf of Riga, formerly in the government of Livonia, Russia. The coast-line is bold, but the surface is generally low and level. Stock-raising, agriculture (flax, hemp, and corn), and fishing are the staple industries. Arensburg (Estonian *Kuresaare*) is the chief town. The people are Estonians, and the island forms one of nine districts of Estonia Area, about 1000 sq. miles; pop. 51,500.

ŒSOPH'AGUS, or **GULLET.** The muscular tube which leads from the pharynx or back part of the mouth to the stomach. In man the length of the gullet is from 9 to 10 inches. It begins at the fifth cervical or neck vertebra, at a point corresponding with the cricoid cartilage of the larynx, and it runs in a slightly deviating course downwards to the stomach. Thus in the neck it lies close behind the windpipe; whilst in the chest it bends to the right side and then to the left before it pierces the midriff or diaphragm—which forms the floor of the chest—by a special aperture existing in that structure.

Internally the gullet is lined with mucous membrane, and between the mucous and muscular layers cellular tissue exists. The mucous or lining membrane is thick and of pale colour, and is arranged in longitudinal furrows or folds. In the lower animals the modifications of the œsophagus are various. In birds, for instance, it presents the expansion known as the *crop*.

OFFA. A king of Mercia, who attained the throne after Ethelbald, on defeating the usurper Beornred, A.D. 757. He brought Kent under his sway, and reduced the power of Wessex by a defeat inflicted in 777. He also defeated the Welsh, took from them part of their border lands, and to keep them within their new limits erected here the rampart known as Offa's Dyke. He founded the Abbey of St. Albans, was a liberal patron to the Church, and promoted trade with the Continent. He died in 796.

OFFALY. The modern name of King's County (q.v.).

OFFA'S DYKE. A rampart along the English and Welsh border from the vicinity of Newmarket, in Flintshire, to Beachley, at the mouth of the Wye; length, about 100 miles. Its erection is ascribed to King Offa of Mercia.

OFFENBACH, Jacques. French composer, born of Jewish parents at Cologne 1819, died 1880. He entered the Paris Conservatoire in 1835; became proficient on the violoncello, and for some time played on this instrument in the orchestra of the Théâtre Comique.

In 1847 he became conductor at the Théâtre Français, and subsequently opened the "Bouffes Parisiens," where he enjoyed immense popularity as the composer of such operas as *Orphée aux Enfers, La Grande Duchesse, La Belle Hélène, Madame Favart, La Barbe Bleue, Geneviève de Brabant*, and *La Prin-*

cesse de Trébizonde. His last opera, *Les Contes d'Hoffmann,* was produced at the Opéra Comique in the February following his death.

OFFENBACH (of'en-bȧ*h*). A town of Germany, in Hesse, on the Main, and on the electric railway to Frankfort. It has an old castle, and is an important commercial and manufacturing centre, its industries embracing various chemical products, as aniline, white lead, vaseline, celluloid, metal goods, leather and leather goods. Offenbach was founded in the tenth century, and in 1685 it became the residence of the Counts of Isenburg-Birstein, being annexed to Hesse in 1816. Pop. (1925), 79,362.

OFFENBURG. A town of Baden, Germany, on the Kinzig. It possesses a statue of Sir Francis Drake commemorating the introduction of the potato into Europe, and a castle destroyed in 1689 and rebuilt about 1834-35. Manufactures include tobacco, cotton, machines, stained glass, and dyes. Pop. (1925), 16,613.

OFFICERS (MILITARY). The commissioned officers of the army as distinct from the warrant and non-commissioned ranks. The word is derived from the Latin *officium,* through the French, and in its original meaning implies " one who holds an office." In the army its meaning is exclusively as above, the prefix " commissioned " being understood. In earlier times—the seventeenth century—the word commissioned was used in its substantive form, i.e. " commission officer," and the prefix was in more general use than it is now ; but, whether used with prefix or without, the word officer implies that he who is entitled to the description becomes so in virtue of the fact that he holds the King's Commission.

The Army Act defines the word as follows : " The expression officer means an officer commissioned or in pay as an officer in His Majesty's Forces, or any arm, branch, or part thereof ; it also includes a person who, by virtue of his Commission, is appointed to any department or corps of His Majesty's service, or of any arm, branch, or part thereof ; it also includes a person, whether retired or not, who, by virtue of his Commission or otherwise, is legally entitled to the style and rank of an officer of His Majesty's said forces."

Every officer on first appointment is given a parchment document known as a " Commission," which is signed by the Secretary of State for War and countersigned by the Sovereign. This commission appoints the recipient to be " an officer in our (Land) Forces . . . in the rank of second-lieutenant, or in such higher rank as we may from time to time hereafter be pleased to promote you." Then after reciting the duty of an officer to " exercise and well discipline in arms both the inferior officers and men serving under you . . .," it continues, " and we do hereby command them to obey you as their superior officer, and you to observe and follow such orders and directions as from time to time you shall receive from us or any superior officer according to the Rules and Discipline of War . . ."

The different grades or ranks of military officers in the British army are: second-lieutenant, colonel, brigadier (colonel-commandant, 1920-28), major-general, lieutenant-general, general, field-marshal. That of brigadier (known between 1920 and 1928 as colonel on the staff or colonel-commandant) is perhaps more in the nature of an appointment than a rank, but as this designation replaces the old rank of brigadier-general, and as officers holding that rank wear a special badge consisting of a " crown above three stars, the two lower stars side by side," it is included here. Of the other ranks that of captain is the oldest, followed by lieutenant (holding the place of *locum tenens*). The rank of major was originally " sergeant-major," and colonel is derived probably from Italian or Spanish. In the seventeenth and early eighteenth century the highest rank in the army was that of the " captain-general," that of field-marshal being of more modern origin.

OFFICERS (NAVAL). The principles governing appointments to commissions in the Royal Navy are similar to those which apply peculiarly to the Army, but the mode of procedure is somewhat different, and the vast amount of both general and specialized knowledge required of the average naval officer makes it necessary for him to begin his apprenticeship to the sea at a very early age.

Naval officers are divided into two great classes, executive and administrative. The former are directly concerned with navigation and with offensive or defensive action ; the latter class includes paymasters, surgeons, and engineers. Formerly the executive ranks alone had the privilege of wearing what is known as the " executive curl," i.e. a curl over the topmost gold-braided ring indicating rank, while the administrative officers wore plain gold-braided bands with colours

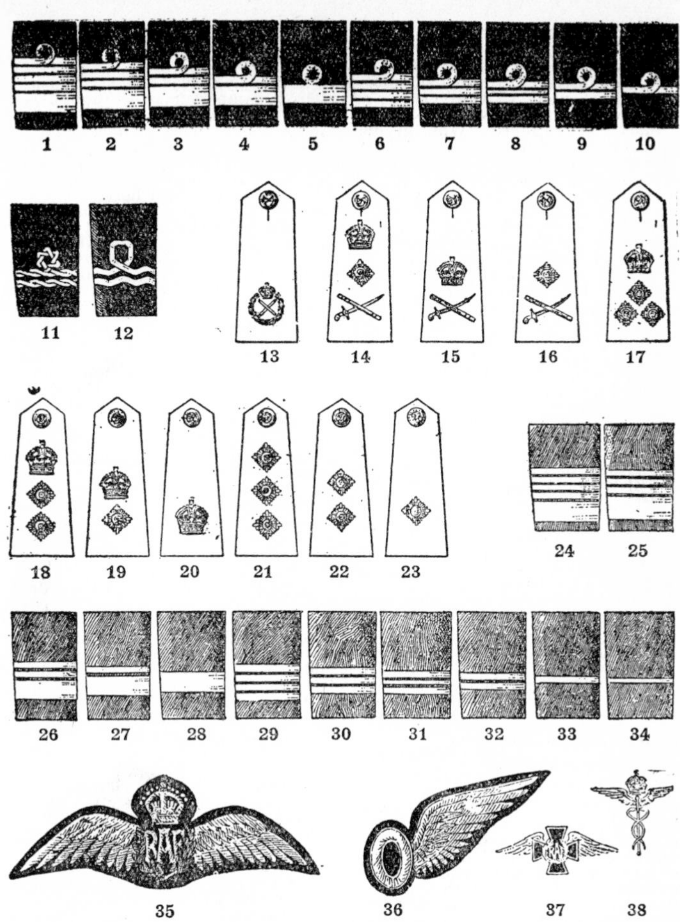

OFFICERS : MARKS OF RANK

Navy.—Navy-blue with gold sleeve lace. 1, Admiral of the Fleet. 2, Admiral. 3, Vice-Admiral. 4, Rear-Admiral and Commodore (1st class). 5, Commodore (2nd class). 6, Captain. 7, Commander. 8, Lieutenant-Commander. 9, Lieutenant. 10, Sub-Lieutenant and Mate.

Royal Naval Reserve.—11, Lieutenant (other ranks vary as in the Navy).

Royal Naval Volunteer Reserve.—12, Lieutenant (other ranks vary as in the Navy).

Navy, Civil Branch.—Engineer Officers wear purple cloth between the gold stripes of their rank ; Medical Officers wear red cloth between the stripes : Dental Officers, orange cloth ; Paymasters, white ; Instructors, light-blue. The ordinary naval nomenclature is used to describe all ranks, as "Surgeon Admiral," "Engineer Vice-Admiral," "Instructor Captain," etc.

Army.—Khaki-coloured cloth ; shoulder-straps with badges in embroidery or metal. 13, Field-Marshal. 14, General. 15, Lieutenant-General. 16, Major-General. 17, Colonel Commandant. 18, Colonel. 19, Lieutenant-Colonel, 20, Major. 21, Captain. 22, Lieutenant. 23, Second-Lieutenant.

Royal Air Force.—Grey-blue, gold lace for full dress, black and blue lace for service dress. 24, Marshal of the Air. 25, Air Chief Marshal. 26, Air Marshal. 27, Air Vice-Marshal. 28, Air Commodore. 29, Group Captain. 30, Wing Commander. 31, Squadron Leader. 32, Flight Lieutenant. 33, Flying Officer or Observer Officer. 34, Pilot Officer. Breast Badges : 35, Pilot. 36, Observer. Cap Badge : 37, Chaplain. Collar Badge : 38, Medical Officer.

between, indicative of their branch. The administrative ranks had also a distinctive nomenclature, such as fleet-paymaster or fleet-surgeon.

Since the European War all distinction between both classes has been eliminated, excepting as regards the colour-band, which, in a reddish colour, indicates a surgeon, in white a paymaster, and in purple an engineer. During battles at sea the paymaster's department performs definite duties in carrying wounded, etc. Naturally, the administrative ranks are highly specialized as apart from the Royal Navy. For executive rank a naval cadet enters a recognized training college at from twelve to thirteen years of age, and eventually becomes a midshipman (q.v.); known in naval parlance as a "snotty." As a midshipman he takes part in all shipboard routine, and eventually attains the rank of sub-lieutenant.

The executive ranks, with their Army and Air Force equivalents, are as follows:

Royal Navy.[1]	Army.
1. Admiral of the Fleet.	1. Field-Marshal.
2. Admiral.	2. General.
3. Vice-Admiral.	3. Lieutenant-General.
4. Rear-Admiral.	4. Major-General.
5. Commodore.	5. Colonel-Commandant.
6. Captain.	6. Colonel.
7. Commander.	7. Lieutenant-Colonel.
8. Lieutenant-Commander.	8. Major.
	9. Captain.
9. Lieutenant.	10. Lieutenant.
10. Sub-Lieutenant.	11. Second-Lieutenant.
11. Midshipman.	

Royal Air Force.

1. Marshal of the Air.	7. Wing-Commander.
2. Air Chief Marshal.	8. Squadron Leader.
3. Air-Marshal.	9. Flight-Lieutenant.
4. Air Vice-Marshal.	10. Flying Officer (or Observer).
5. Air-Commodore.	11. Pilot Officer.
6. Group Captain.	

See Warrant Officer.

OFFICIAL RECEIVER. In England, a public official who performs certain duties in the bankruptcies of individuals and the winding-up of companies. He investigates the circumstances of a bankruptcy, and reports to the court with a view to a prosecution in the event of any misdemeanour under the Bankruptcy Acts, takes charge of the estate until a trustee is appointed, and generally supervises the trustee when appointed, or himself acts as trustee in small bankruptcies, etc. His duties in the winding-up of a company are similar. *See* Liquidator.

OFFICIAL SECRETS. It is a felony for any person, for a purpose prejudicial to the State, to enter or be near a prohibited place (dockyard, factory, camp, defence-work, etc.), or make or communicate any such sketch, model, note, or document, or give any such information as is likely to be useful to an enemy. It is a misdemeanour for any person to communicate to an unauthorized person any secret official code or password, or any information relating to a prohibited place, that may have been entrusted to him or obtained by virtue of his office, or to retain any document, etc., relating to a prohibited place, or any official document, after his right or duty therewith has ceased; or for any person finding or otherwise coming into possession of any official document not to restore it to the person by whom it was issued or to a police constable. (See the Official Secrets Acts, 1911 and 1920.)

OG. King of Bashan at the time of the conquest of Canaan by the Israelites, by whom he and his people were destroyed. He has been transformed by rabbinical fables into one of the giants who lived before the flood, and escaped the general inundation by taking refuge on the roof of Noah's ark.

OGDEN. A city of Utah, United States, the county seat of Weber county, at the confluence of the Weber and Ogden Rivers, and served by the Union Pacific, Southern Pacific, and Denver & Rio Grande Railways. It stands at an altitude of 4338 feet in the Wahsatch range, and in an agricultural and mining area. It was laid out by Brigham Young in 1850, and became a city in 1851. Pop. (1931), 40,272.

OGDENSBURG. A city and port of entry of New York, United States, in St. Lawrence county. It stands at the confluence of the Oswegatchie with the St. Lawrence River, and is served by the Rutland and the New York Central & Hudson Railways, and by lake and river steamers. The city became the see of a Roman Catholic bishop in 1872. Ogdensburg was settled in 1749 as the Indian settlement of La Presentation (founded by Abbé Piquet, 1708-81, for converted Iroquois), and became a city in 1851. Pop. (1930), 16,915.

OGEE (ō-jē′). In architecture, a moulding consisting of two members,

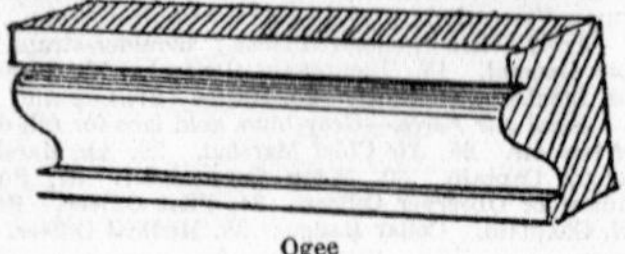

Ogee

[1] In bygone times there was a Master who performed navigating duties under the Captain. A Paymaster equivalent in rank to a Commander is a Paymaster-Commander. Similarly, other administrative ranks are addressed as Surgeon-Commanders, Engineer-Commanders, and so on upwards or downwards in grade as the case may be.

the one concave, the other convex, or of a round and a hollow; otherwise called a *cyma reversa*. (*See* CYMA.) An *ogee arch* is an arch with a similar curve.

OG'HAM, or **OGAM.** A particular system of writing formerly practised by the Celtic peoples of Ireland, Scotland, and Wales. It is chiefly found in inscriptions on stone, but also, though more rarely, in books. The Ogham characters (also called *oghams*) consist principally of lines or groups of lines deriving their significance from their position on a horizontal or chief line; under, over, or through which they are drawn either perpendicular or oblique; curves rarely occur. Authorities differ as to the total number of letters represented in the alphabet, some making sixteen, others twenty-five. Regarding the age of this form of writing, it is now supposed that it was used not only in prehistoric times, but also so late as the ninth and tenth centuries. Stones with ogham inscriptions are found in Leinster and Connaught, also in some parts of Wales.

OGLIO (ol'yō). A river of North Italy, which rises in the Alps, drains Lake Iseo, and falls into the Po; length, 150 miles.

OGPU. *See* TCHEKA.

O'HIGGINS, Ambrosia (1720-1801). An Irishman, was Captain-General of Chile and Marquis of Osorno (1788), and became Viceroy of Peru in 1796. His son, Bernardo O'Higgins (1778-1842) became Dictator of Chile (1817) and declared its independence of Spain (1818), driving out the Spanish troops. He resigned in 1823, and retired to Lima. The province commemorates the O'Higgins family.

O'HIGGINS, Kevin Christopher. Irish statesman. Born in 1892, after the Easter rebellion of 1916 he joined the Sinn Fein Movement, and was interned. While in gaol, he was elected member for Queen's County. In 1922 he became Minister of Justice in the New Free State Government, and established the Civic Guard, which put down disorder firmly. While the controversy with de Valera on the taking of the Oath in the Dail was proceeding, O'Higgins was assassinated by unknown men, 10th July, 1927.

OHI'O. A river of the United States, formed by the union of the Alleghany and Monongahela at Pittsburg, Pennsylvania. It flows W.S.W., separating the states of Western Virginia and Kentucky on the south from Ohio, Indiana, and Illinois on the north, and enters the Mississippi at Cairo. Its length from Pittsburgh to its junction with the Mississippi is 975 miles; area of basin, 214,000 sq. miles. Its principal affluents are the Miami, Kentucky, Wabash, Cumberland, and Tennessee, and on its banks are Pittsburgh, Cairo, Cincinnati, Louisville, Evansville, and Mount Vernon. It is the most important commercial tributary of the Mississippi, and the largest after the Missouri.

OHIO. A state in the east-north-central division of the United States; extending north to south between Lake Erie and the state of Michigan and the Ohio River, and partaking of the nature of a rolling plain sloping to the south and to the east. The state capital is Columbus (pop. 1930 290,564); other cities are: Cleveland (pop. 1930, 900,429), Cincinnati (451,160), Toledo (290,718), Akron 255,040), Dayton (200,982), Youngstown (170,002), and Canton (104,906).

Communication.—There are no important navigable inland waterways, and transport is dependent primarily upon the railways, which include the Missouri; Kansas & Texas; the St. Louis & San Francisco; the Atchison, Topeka, & Santa Fé; the Chicago; and the Rock Island & Pacific Railways. The railway mileage for 1931 was 8732, besides 2049 miles of electric track.

Industries.—Agriculture is the principal industry, producing corn (121,872,000 bushels in 1932), oats 45,344,000 bushels), wheat, tobacco, hay, fruits and vegetables, and sugar-beet. Dairy-farming, and horse-, sheep-, and cattle-breeding are important. There are extensive manufactures of butter and cheese, and also a meat-packing trade. Ohio ranks fourth in mineral production of the United States, coal and clay being the chief products. Petroleum, sandstone, limestone, salt, grindstones, and mineral-waters are also found.

Education, etc.—Education is compulsory between the ages of six and eighteen years. There are thirty-eight teachers' training institutions and forty universities and colleges, among which are the State University at Columbus (founded 1872), Cincinnati University (1874), State universities at Athens (1804) and Oxford (1809), and a School of Applied Science at Cleveland, established in 1880. Area, 41,040 sq. miles (300 sq. miles being water), exclusive of 3443 sq. miles on Lake Erie. Pop. (1930), 6,646,697.

Government.—Ohio was admitted to the Union in 1803. There are eighty-eight counties. Modern government comprises a Governor and a Legislature, consisting of a Senate

(35 members, elected for two years) and a House of Representatives (130 members, elected for two years). Two Senators and 24 Representatives are sent to Congress.—BIBLIOGRAPHY: E. O. Randall and D. J. Ryan, *History of Ohio* (5 vols.); E. L. Bogart, *Financial History of Ohio*; R. King, *Ohio* (in American Commonwealth Series.)

OHLAU. A town of Upper Silesia, at the confluence of the Ohlau and Oder, near Breslau, and on the railway to Cracow. It was a residence of the Sobieski family, and became a town in 1290. In 1919 it was included in the Silesian plebiscite area after belonging to Prussia since the annexation of Silesia in 1742. Pop. 9320.

OHLIGS. A town of Prussian Rheinland, with foundries, mills, and manufactures of cutlery and steel products. It is a railway junction on the line to Cologne. Pop. 24,300.

OHM (ōm), **Georg Simon.** German physicist, born 1787, died 1854. He became successively professor of physics at Cologne, director of the Polytechnic at Nürnberg, and professor of physics at the University of Munich. Ohm was the discoverer of what is known as "Ohm's Law" in electricity; and among his scientific works were *Die Galvanische Kette* and *Grundzuge der Physik*.

OHM. The unit of resistance to the passage of electricity defined at the International Conference on Electrical Units held in London, Oct., 1908, and established as the legal standard in Britain by Order in Council in 1910. The ohm is defined as the resistance to an unvarying electric current by a column of mercury of constant cross-section which has a mass of 14·4521 grammes and a length of 106·300 centimetres. The mercury must be kept at the temperature of melting ice during the observation.

OHMMETER. A direct-reading instrument used to measure resistance; commonly resistances of great magnitude such as those of insulation. The instrument has two coils with the same number of turns of wire and with their axes at right angles. The needle suspended in these coils is deflected by an amount depending on their resultant action. One coil is connected to a known resistance, and the other to the unknown resistance. With a fixed voltage-supply the deflection will depend on the value of the unknown resistance, and the scale is graduated to give its magnitude in megohms. In Evershed's megger, which is the type generally used, a permanent magnet frame is used, and the two coils at 45° to each other are used as the moving system. The two circuits are connected in parallel to the brushes of a hand-driven generator, which provides an electrical supply at 500 volts.

OHM'S LAW. An important law in electricity, deduced by Georg Simon Ohm, to the effect that *the intensity of the electric current is directly proportional to the whole electromotive force in operation, and inversely proportional to the sum of the resistances in the circuit.* *See* ELECTRICITY.

OHNET (ō-nā), **Georges.** French novelist and dramatist, born at Paris in 1848, died 1918. He entered the legal profession, but soon abandoned it for journalism. In 1875 his play, *Regina Sarpi*, was produced with great success in Paris, and shortly afterwards he began his series of social novels entitled *Les Batailles de la vie*. He also wrote others, and successfully dramatized several of his novels. Among his best-known novels are: *Le Maître de forges* (1882), *Le Brasseur d'affaires* (1901), *La Grande Marnière, Le Revenant* (1913).

OÏD'IUM. A genus of microscopic Fungi. *O. Tuckeri* is the conidial stage of *Uncinula spiralis*, the vine mildew, parasitical, in the form of a white and very delicate layer, upon the leaves and green parts of vines, and destroying the functions of the skin of the part it attacks. Powdered sulphur and a spray of sulphide of potash are effective remedies.

OIL-BEETLE. The name given to beetles belonging to the genus Meloë, and the family Cantharidæ, from the oily-like matter which they exude. The perfect insects have swollen bodies, with shortish elytra, which more or less overlap each other, and have not a straight suture, as in most coleopterous insects.

OIL-CAKE. A cake or mass of compressed linseed or rape, poppy, mustard, cotton, and other seeds from which oil has been extracted. Linseed-cake is much used as a food for cattle, its value as a fattening substance being greater than that of any kind of grain or pulse. Rape-cake is used as a fattening food for sheep. These and other oil-cakes are also valuable as manures.

OIL CITY. A city of Pennsylvania, United States, in Venango county, on the Alleghany; served by the Pennsylvania, the Erie, and the Lake Shore & Michigan Southern Railways. It is the centre of the West Pennsylvania oil-fields (discovered in 1859), and has large refineries. Oil City was settled in 1825, and became a city in 1871. Pop. 22,075.

OIL-ENGINE. *See* INTERNAL-COMBUSTION ENGINE; MOTOR-CAR ENGINE.

OIL-GAS. The inflammable gas obtained by allowing oils, such as shale-oil or petroleum, to drop into hot metal retorts. The oils actually employed are those too heavy to use for burning purposes, e.g. shale-oil with a specific gravity 0·840. It is used as a substitute for coal-gas in lighting railway-carriages, since it has a higher illuminating power, is free from sulphur, is readily compressed, and is inexpensive.

OIL OF BEN, *See* HORSE-RADISH TREE.

OIL-PALM (*Elæis guineensis*). An African tree abounding on the west coast, whose fruit yields palm-oil (q.v.).

OILS. Consist either of hydrocarbons, as in the mineral oils, or of glyceryl esters of the fatty acids, as in animal and vegetable oils. They are colourless or yellow, lighter than water, and immiscible with it.

Greases and fats are oils that are solid at ordinary temperatures but otherwise of similar composition. The so-called essential oils (q.v.), such as oil of cloves, lemon, eucalyptus, etc., are not true oils, but are related to a class of compounds known as the terpenes.

1. **Hydrocarbon oils** are obtained from the oil shales of Scotland and elsewhere, and also from the petroleum of America, Russia, Burma, and other countries. The shale oils consist mainly of paraffins and olefines. Russian petroleum is composed chiefly of napthenes, whilst American petroleum contains paraffins mixed with olefines and napthenes.

For commercial purposes the crude product is distilled and separated into the following lighter and heavier oils:

(*a*) The most volatile and inflammable fractions (specific gravity, 0·66-0·77; boiling-point, 80°-150° C.), consisting of benzene, petrol, and naphtha (q.v.), are used in extracting fats, for the dry cleaning of garments, in the preparation of paints as a substitute for oil of turpentine, and as a fuel for internal-combustion engines.

(*b*) Illuminating oils, such as so-called paraffin oil, petroleum, and kerosene (specific gravity, 0·78-0·88; boiling-point, 150°-300° C.). These oils are used for burning in lamps, for cleaning machinery, and in the preparation of oil colours.

(*c*) Lubricating oils (specific gravity, 0·89-0·92; boiling-point, over 300° C.). These are yellow-coloured oils more or less viscid in character, and are extensively used for lubricating machinery. Both these and the illuminating oils undergo a process of refining in order to remove deleterious impurities and to improve the colour.

(*d*) Viscous or buttery products, amber to dark-brown in colour, which are mainly used for lubricating the cylinders of steam, gas, and internal-combustion engines. Vaseline also belongs to this class of oils.

All the above fractions consist of more or less complex mixtures of hydrocarbons, and are chemically neutral and inert. At ordinary temperatures the strongest acids and alkalies have no action on them. The residue left in the distilling retorts is used as a source of fuel for the distillation of the crude oil.

2. **Animal and vegetable oils** are obtained from animal fats and the seeds of various plants by pressing, or by extraction with volatile solvents. These fats and oils consist mainly of tristearin, tripalmitin, and triolein and can be readily decomposed by means of superheated steam into glycerine and a fatty acid (stearic, palmitic, oleic acid, etc.). On boiling with caustic alkalies, soap (q.v.) and glycerine are produced. These oils are insoluble in water, only slightly soluble in alcohol, but dissolve readily in ether, benzene, chloroform, carbon bisulphide, and petroleum spirit. Their specific gravity varies from 0·88-0·96. They cannot be distilled unchanged, but on heating they are partially decomposed.

The fatty oils may be divided into three groups:

(*a*) Drying oils, which absorb oxygen and harden when exposed to the air. These are largely used in the preparation of paints, varnishes, etc., and comprise linseed, hemp, poppy-seed, fir-seed, and Chinese-wood oils.

(*b*) Semi-drying oils, e.g. rape, colza, cotton-seed, castor, sesame, croton, and grape-seed olis. These become thicker on exposure to air, but do not completely harden.

(*c*) Non-drying oils, such as olive, almond, sperm, cod-liver, seal, whale, neatsfoot, coco-nut, palm, and also tallow, lard, and butter. Palm-oil and tallow are largely used in the manufacture of margarine, soaps and candles. Sperm and colza oils are mainly used for burning in lamps; butter and lard and the purest forms of olive, cotton-seed, coco-nut, and sesame oils are used almost exclusively for purposes of food, whilst castor, almond, coco-nut, and coco-butter oils are used medicinally. See PARAFFIN; PETROLEUM.

OIRATSK. An autonomous region of Soviet Russia, consisting of part of the former Altai Province. *See* Russia.

OISE (wäz). A river in France, which rises in the Belgian Ardennes, flows south-west across the department of Oise, and joins the Seine on its right bank about 6 miles below Pontoise; total course, 186 miles, 60 miles of which are canalized.

OISE. A northern department of France, drained by the Oise, Aisne, Nonette, Ourcq, and Brèche; area, 2272 sq. miles. A considerable part of it is devoted to wheat, and dairying is extensively practised. Barley, oats, and rye are also raised. The vine is not much cultivated but fruits are abundant, and much cider is made. The manufactures are unimportant. Beauvais is the chief town; others are Compiègne, Chantilly, Noyon, Clermont, and Senlis. The department was partly invaded by the Germans in Aug.-Sept., 1914, and again, during their last drive, in the summer of 1918. Pop. (1931), 407,432.

OKA. A river of Central Russia, which rises in the government of Orel, and after a course of 800 miles, navigable from Orel, joins the Volga at Nijni-Novgorod.

OKA'PI (*Ocapia Johnstoni*). An African ruminant closely related to the giraffe, discovered, though not actually seen alive, in Uganda by Sir H. H. Johnston in 1899-1900. It

Okapi (*Ocapia Johnstoni*)

lives in the densest parts of the forests bordering the Semliki River, on the frontier of Uganda and the Congo Free State, and is of the size of a large antelope or mule, without horns or other similar appendages. The ears are larger than those of the giraffe, and the bony cores of the latter species are represented in the okapi by mere bumps. The legs and the hinter part of the body are striped in a zebra-like fashion. These animals generally go about in pairs, male and female, and live chiefly on leaves

OKAYAMA. A town of Honshiu, Japan, on the Lower Asahi River, and served by railways to Shimonoseki, Tatai, Uno (for Shikoku), and Tsuyama. Rice, cottons, silks, and yarns are produced. Pop. (1930), 139,222.

OKEECHO'BEE LAKE ("Big Water"). A shallow lake in Southern Florida; 40 miles long, 25 miles broad; maximum depth, 12 feet; now partially drained by a canal to the Caloosahatchee River, thus giving a waterway to the interior.

OKEHAMPTON. A borough of Devonshire, England; served by the Southern Railway. It was a borough in 1086, and had a castle. There are remains of the chapel, etc., of a fifteenth-century castle. Pop. (1931), 3352.

OKHOTSK, Sea of. An arm of the Northern Pacific, enclosed by Kamchatka, the Kuriles, Yezo, and Sakhalin. On the north shore is Okhotsk, a town of U.S.S.R. There is extensive whaling.

OKI ISLANDS. A Japanese four-island archipelago in the Japan Sea, due north of Izumo province. The largest island is Dogo, containing the capital, Saigo, which maintains a regular cross-channel service with Sakai on the mainland (44 miles). Area, about 131 sq. miles.

OKLAHOMA. A city of Oklahoma, United States, the state capital and the county seat of Oklahoma county, on the Canadian River (North Fork); served by the Missouri, Kansas & Texas; the Atchison, Topeka, & Santa Fé; and by other railways. It is the seat of Epsworth University (founded 1901), and has a large trade. Settled in 1889, it became a city in 1891. Pop. (1930), 185,389.

OKLAHOMA. A state in the west-south-central division of the United States, part of the great basin of the Mississippi, traversed by the Arkansas, Cimarron, Red, and Canadian Rivers, which frequently dry up during the summer. Oklahoma City is the state capital (pop. 1930, 185,389); other cities are Muskogee (32,026), Tulsa (141,258), Enid (26,399), and Okmulgee (17,097).

Communications.—In 1932 6778 miles of steam and 217 miles of electric railway traversed the state, including the Atchison, Topeka, & Santa Fé; the Chicago, Rock Island, & Pacific; the Missouri, Kansas, & Texas; the St. Louis & San Francisco; and the Santa Fé Pacific Railways.

Production and Industry.—Oklahoma is an agricultural state, producing corn (65,760,000 bushels in 1932), wheat 43,626,000 bushels), oats (24,012,000 bushels), sorghum, potatoes, flax, fruit, and cotton (3,187,000 acres produced 1,080,000 bales, 1932). Dairying is progressive, and the western part of the state is devoted to stock-raising. Petroleum, oil and natural gas, coal, zinc, and lead are found. Manufacturing industries include cotton-ginning, cotton-seed products (oil and cake), and flour-milling.

Education, etc. Whites and negroes are separated for educational purposes, all colours other than negro being classified officially as white. There is a State system of education, embracing all grades from elementary to professional instruction. The State University at Norman was founded in 1892; there is an Agricultural and Mechanical College at Stillwater (founded 1891), and an Agricultural and Normal University at Langston (founded 1897) for negroes. Indian Reservations occupy an area (1932) of 60 sq. miles; pop. 92,725. Area, 70,057 sq. miles (643 sq. miles being water); pop. (1930), 2,396,040.

Government.—The state of Oklahoma was constituted on 16th Nov., 1907, and comprises the former Indian Territory and the Territory of Oklahoma. Government consists of a Governor and a Legislature, comprising a Senate (44 members, elected for four years) and a House of Representatives (from 115 to 120 members, elected for two years). Two Senators and 9 Representatives are sent to Congress.

OLAF II., or **ST. OLAF.** One of the most celebrated of the Norwegian kings, great-great-grandson of Harald Haarfagr, and son of Harald, chief of the district of Gränland, was born about 995, died in 1030. He was a friend of the Normans, and fought as an ally of Ethelred's in England. He afterwards established himself on the throne of Norway, and was a zealous supporter of Christianity. Canute the Great having landed in Norway with an army, Olaf fled to Russia, and in attempting to recover his dominions he was defeated and slain at the battle of Stiklestad. Since 1164 he has been honoured as the patron saint of Norway. The Order of St. Olaf, a Norwegian order given in reward for services rendered to king and country or to art and science, was founded in 1847 by King Oscar I.

OLD AGE PENSIONS. Notwithstanding long advocacy by social reformers, it was not until 1909 that the first statute (The Old Age Pensions Act, 1908) providing for State grants to aged persons came into force. The maximum pension under that Act was 5*s.* per week, and the limit of income for receipt, of any pension, £31, 10*s.* per annum, but from time to time the rates have been increased and under the various Acts are now as follows: 10*s.* per week when the yearly income does not exceed £26, 5*s.*; 8*s.* when it exceeds £26, 5*s.* but not £31, 10*s.*; 6*s.* when it exceeds £31, 10*s.* but not £36, 15*s.*; 4*s.* when it exceeds £36, 15*s.* but not £42; 2*s.* when it exceeds £42 but not £47, 5*s.*; and 1*s.* when it exceeds £47, 5*s.* but not £49, 17*s.* 6*d.* If the income exceeds £49, 17*s.* 6*d.*, no pension is payable.

The claimant must have attained seventy years of age, have been a British subject for the preceding ten years, and have resided in the United Kingdom for twelve years since attaining age fifty if he is a natural-born British subject, and for twenty years in all if he is not natural-born; but any temporary absences not exceeding three months in each case, any residence abroad in Crown service or while maintaining or assisting to maintain a dependent in the United Kingdom, and any periods of absence in service on board any vessel registered in the United Kingdom of a person who before such absence was residing in the United Kingdom, as well as absence in the Isle of Man or Channel Islands, if the person was born in the United Kingdom, and any period of residence in Southern Ireland before the establishment of the Irish Free State, may count as residence in the United Kingdom.

For the purposes of the Acts the income of a claimant may be (1) income from investments or property; (2) other income reasonably expected to be received in cash during the succeeding year (except sickness benefit under a medical certificate during three months in any year); and (3) the yearly value of any benefit or privilege enjoyed by the claimant, e.g. free board and lodging, or the advantage accruing from the use of property personally enjoyed by him except furniture and personal effects. Income under head (1) is not the actual yield from the investments but is a percentage of the capital value. The first £25 of capital value is disregarded; the income from the next £375 is taken as 5 per cent. and from the balance 10 per cent. A deduction of £39 a year, or £78 a year in the case of a married couple living together in the same house, is allowed from any means not derived from earnings. The income of each of a married couple living together in the same house is taken to be one-half of the total income of the couple.

By the Blind Persons Act, 1920, a person unable to follow an employment through blindness may obtain a pension at age fifty on similar conditions.

By the Widows', Orphans', and Old Age Contributory Pensions Act, 1925-31, persons who have paid a specified number of contributions under the Insurance Acts are entitled to a pension of 10*s*. per week on attaining the age of sixty-five, and are not affected by income conditions. A married woman is entitled to pension at the age of sixty-five if, when she attains that age, her husband is alive, and is himself sixty-five or over, and entitled to old age pension in right of insurance. The pension is in right of the husband's insurance, and the wife does not require to be an insured person. If an insured person married after 29th April, 1925, and was sixty years of age when he married, his wife will not be entitled to an old age pension in right of his insurance, even if otherwise qualified, before the expiration of three years from the marriage, unless immediately before the marriage she was in receipt of a widow's pension under the Acts.

OLD BAILEY. The sessions-house, in London, in which the Central Criminal Court holds its monthly sittings for the trial of offences committed within the city and county of London, the county of Middlesex, and some parts of the counties of Surrey, Kent, and Essex. It is situated in a street of the same name, running from Ludgate Hill to Smithfield. The Old Bailey is described by Dickens in *A Tale of Two Cities.* It was destroyed by fire in 1780 (during the Gordon Riots), but was rebuilt, and is now officially known as the Central Criminal Court.

OLDBURY. A town of England, in the county of Worcestershire, in the heart of a mining district; served by the L.M.S. Railway. It has manufactures of chemicals, iron- and steel-works, edge-tool and nail-works, brick- and tile-works, limestone-quarries, and extensive iron- and coal-mines. Pop. (1931), 35,918.

OLDCASTLE, Sir John, Lord Cobham. Born in the fourteenth century, in the reign of Edward III., died in Dec., 1417. He obtained his peerage by marrying the daughter of Lord Cobham. He was one of the most prominent of the Lollards, and under Henry V. was accused of heresy; but the king, with whom he was a favourite, delayed the prosecutions against him, and tried to convince him of his alleged errors, but in vain. He was then cited before the Archbishop of Canterbury (1413), condemned as a heretic, and sent to the Tower, whence he escaped into Wales. Four years afterwards he was retaken and burned alive. He wrote *Twelve Conclusions*, addressed to the Parliament of England. When Shakespeare's *Henry IV.* first appeared, the name given to the fat knight was Oldcastle, but there is not the faintest resemblance between the characters of Falstaff and the Lollard leader.

OLD CATHOLICS. Religious communities, found chiefly in Germany, Holland, and Switzerland, who have separated from the Church of Rome. The name was first assumed by a party in the Church of Rome who, led by Dr. Döllinger, professor of ecclesiastical history at Munich, refused to accept the decree of the Vatican Council of 1870, teaching and defining the universal jurisdiction and personal infallibility of the Pope. Though united in protesting against the new dogma, the Old Catholics claim to be faithful to the ancient traditional constitution of the Church; have never seceded from it; and still hold they have a joint interest in its possessions. The chief centres of the Old Catholic movement are the universities of Germany; but the movement spread also in Switzerland.

At the first Old Catholic congress, held at Munich, Sept., 1871, it was determined to form separate congregations for the body, and to enter into a close connection with the Church of Utrecht (the so-called Dutch Jansenists). After this the Old Catholic movement spread more rapidly. At their second congress, held at Gürzenich, 1872, the Old Catholics resolved to elect Dr. Joseph Reinkens as their first bishop. At the third congress, held in 1873 at Constance, a synodal constitution was adopted.

The Old Catholic movement in Germany was greatly aided from the first by the position taken up by the Imperial Government, and still more by the Governments of some of the separate states. The Imperial Government declared the right of Old Catholics to retain what offices they held, and the emoluments of these offices, in spite of any sentence of excommunication passed on them by their bishops. The Old Catholic movement has had a similar course in Switzerland. There also the bishops unanimously supported the new dogma, and excommunicated the priests who rejected it; but there also the State intervened, and zealously protected the latter. The Jansenist Church in Holland is affiliated with the movement.—BIBLIOGRAPHY: C. J. Loyson, *Catholic Reform*; A. M. E. Scarth, *The Story of the Old Catholic and Kindred Movements.*

OLDENBURG. A free state in the north of Germany, consisting of three separate and distinct territories, viz. Oldenburg, Lübeck, and Birkenfeld; total area, 2480 sq. miles. (1) The first of these divisions, Oldenburg, is bounded on three sides by Hanover and Bremen. The country is flat; the soil marshy and sandy, with little cultivation and large tracts of heath and forest; there are no hills or lakes; the principal river is the Weser, and the internal navigation is facilitated by a large canal, which connects the Hunte and the Ems. The chief crops are wheat, oats, rye, hemp, and rape. Stock-raising and apiculture are extensive, and there are industries connected with cotton, wool, jute, etc. Pop. (1925), 442,029.

(2) Lübeck, situated in East Holstein, north of the town of Lübeck, is bounded partly by the Baltic; area, 210 sq. miles, of which the greater part is cultivated. Chief town, Eutin. Pop. (1925), 47,494.

(3) Birkenfeld, situated in Rhenish Prussia, is a hilly country with fertile valleys; area, 194 miles; pop. (1925), 55,649; the chief towns, Birkenfeld and Oberstein. Oldenburg was raised to the dignity of a grand-duchy by the Congress of Vienna in 1815, and the greater part of the two principalities was added to its territory. The state became a republic in 1918, the grand duke having abdicated. The republic is now governed by a Landtag consisting of forty-six members, elected for three years.

OLDENBURG. A town of Germany, capital of the free state of Oldenburg, on the Hunte. It has fine promenades on the site of the old fortifications, public library of 150,000 volumes, picture-gallery, gymnasium; manufactures of glass, leather, and earthenware. Pop. 52,723.

OLDHAM. A municipal and county borough of Lancashire, England, on the Medlock; served by the L.M.S. Railway and by canal. The town hall is a copy of the Temple of Demeter (near Athens). There are a museum, an art gallery, and a lyceum with observatory. Spinning and weaving of cotton are the staple industries. Pop. (1931), 140,309.

OLDHA'MIA. A fossil organism first found in Cambrian shales in County Wicklow, and now known from Cambrian and Ordovician strata elsewhere. It consists of radial or fan-like impressions of rods or tentacles, and has been variously regarded as a plant, a tentaculate worm, and a hydrozoan.

OLD RED SANDSTONE. A geological term made popular by the writings of Hugh Miller, and applied by him to the red sandstone which underlies the Carboniferous system, in contradistinction to the New Red Sandstone, which overlies the latter. It is the freshwater and terrestrial representative of the Devonian system. *See* GEOLOGY.

OLEA'CEÆ. A natural order of gamopetalous dicotyledons, chiefly inhabiting temperate climates. They are shrubs or trees, with opposite simple or compound leaves and small flowers. The species best known are the olive, the lilac, the privet, and the ash.

OLEAN'DER. A plant of the nat. ord. Apocynaceæ, genus Nerium, the *N. Oleander*, known also by the name of rose-bay, a beautiful evergreen shrub, with flowers in clusters, of a fine rose or white colour but of an indifferent smell. The plant, especially the bark of the root, is medicinal and poisonous.

OLEAS'TER (*Elæagnus hortensis*, ord. Elæagnaceæ). Also called wild olive tree, a small tree of the south of Europe and west of Asia, often cultivated in English gardens and shrubberies especially for its blossoms, which are very fragrant. It flowers in May.

OLE'IC ACID ($C_{18}H_{34}O_2$). Exists in many fats and oils as olein. It may be obtained by saponifying olive-oil with caustic soda. Its sodium salt is present in hard soap, and its potassium salt in soft soap.

OLENEK'. A river of Northern Siberia which rises under the polar circle, and enters the Arctic Ocean to the west of the Lena delta; length, about 900 miles.

OLÉRON (ō-lā-rōn̦). An island of Western France, about 1 mile from the coast of the department of Charente-Inférieure, to which it belongs. Greatest length, 18 miles; greatest breadth, 7 miles; area, 66 sq. miles. With the exception of the west side the surface is generally fertile, producing good corn and wine. It has two towns, Château and St. Pierre, the former fortified. The population is about 17,250.

OLFAC'TORY NERVES. The nerves of smell, the first pair of cranial nerves or nerves connected with the brain. They arise from olfactory cells placed in the lining membrane of the upper part of the nasal cavity.

OLHÃO (ol-yä'ųņ). A seaport of Portugal, in the province of Faro, noted for its sardine fisheries. Pop. 10,000.

OLIGARCHY (Gr. *oligos*, small number, and *archē*, government). In politics, a term applied to that form of government in which the supreme power is placed in the hands of a small exclusive class, or of a few individuals. It is the antithesis of *ochlocracy*, or the rule of the crowd.

Aristotle distinguishes between the monarchic, aristocratic, and republican (commonwealth) governments, on the one hand, and tyranny, oligarchy, and democracy, the perverted forms of government, on the other. The first three forms of government are in the interest of the public, whilst the latter are selfish, allowing their personal interests to predominate. According to Aristotle, an oligarchy is a government in which the political influence of the wealthy predominates. Thus, according to him, as well as Plato (*Republic*), an oligarchy is really a limited aristocracy. Hobbes (*Leviathan*) maintained that oligarchy is really synonymous with aristocracy, being a term of opprobrium used by opponents of that form of government.

In reality, however, there is a vast difference between the rule of an aristocracy and that of an oligarchy. The government of the former is one in which the supreme power is in the hands of an exclusive class, who are, or are considered to be, the élite of the community, whilst the rule of an oligarchy is the perverted form of such a government, the power having been usurped by a few members of the class to the exclusion of their colleagues.

The meaning of the term oligarchy has certainly changed since the times of Plato and Aristotle, and an oligarchy need not be based on either birth, blood, wealth, or social position. No oligarchies existed in Asia, where the despotic rule of one individual was prevalent, although the governments of several Phœnician cities were oligarchic. All Greek cities had either aristocratic or oligarchic governments, such as the rule of the thirty tyrants in Athens; and in Rome the rule of the decemvirs and of the triumvirs were also oligarchies. Both in Greece and in Rome aristocratic and oligarchic governments formed the transition between the monarchy and the democracy.

During the Middle Ages oligarchies existed in the republics of Genoa, Florence, and Venice. The Grimaldis and Fieschis, the Dorias and Spinolas were the rulers. In Venice the oligarchic rule continued for a considerable time, and was abolished only in 1797.

OLI'GOCENE. A geological system marked out by Beyrich in 1854, and including strata previously assigned to the upper part of Lyell's Eocene system. The European beds are best developed in the Paris basin and Germany; but J. W. Judd showed that in England the system is represented by the "fluviomarine" series of Hampshire and the Isle of Wight.

OL'IGOCLASE. A soda-lime felspar, the soda predominating; it occurs in granite, diorite, and other igneous rocks.

OLIN'DA. A seaport-city of Brazil, in the state of Pernambuco, on the Atlantic, once (for 200 years) the capital of Pernambuco province. It was founded in 1535, and is the seat of a bishopric. There is a wireless station. Pop. 10,000.

OL'IPHANT, Laurence. Son of Sir Anthony Oliphant, Chief Justice of Ceylon, was born at Cape Town 1829, died in 1888. He studied law at the University of Edinburgh; travelled extensively in Southern Russia and the Crimea; became private secretary to Lord Elgin when he was Governor-General of Canada, and subsequently accompanied him (1857) on his mission to China and Japan. Returning to Europe, he became Paris correspondent to *The Times*; entered Parliament for the Stirling Burghs in 1865, but retired in 1868. After being connected with a socialistic religious community in the United States, he founded himself a religious community in Palestine, near Mount Carmel.

Besides frequent contributions to periodical literature, he published: *Journey to Khatmandu*, *The Russian Shores of the Black Sea*, *Minnesota and the Far West*, *The Transcaucasian Campaign of Omer Pasha*, *Masollam* (a novel), *Sympneumata*, and *Scientific Religion*, the last works exhibiting his peculiar mysticism and tendency to spiritualism.

OLIPHANT, Margaret (maiden name, **Wilson**). Novelist, born near Musselburgh, Scotland, 1828, died 1897. Her first novel, published in 1849 under the title of *Passages in the Life of Mrs. Margaret Maitland*, won instant attention, and was followed thereafter by more than a hundred books, by which the author maintained a high place as a novelist.

Among her best books are: *Squire Arden*, *Lilliesleaf*, *Salem*

Chapel, The Minister's Wife, Kirsteen, and *The Marriage of Elinor.* Besides this fictional work she wrote a *Life of Edward Irving,* lives or memoirs of Francis of Assisi, Count Montalembert, Molière, Cervantes, Sheridan, Laurence Oliphant, etc., *Historical Sketches of the Reign of George II., The Makers of Florence, The Makers of Venice, The Makers of Modern Rome,* a *Literary History of England in the Nineteenth Century,* etc.

OLIVA'REZ, Gaspar de Guzman, Count of. Spanish statesman, born in 1587, died 1645. Educated at the University of Salamanca, he was appointed gentleman of the bedchamber to the Prince of Asturias, and when his royal master succeeded to the throne as Philip IV., Olivarez was appointed Prime Minister. For twenty-two years (1621-43) his power was almost unlimited, but the severity of his administration ultimately caused revolt in Catalonia and Andalusia, while the Portuguese threw off the Spanish yoke. The end of his policy was public discontent and his own private disgrace. He was confined by the king at Toro, where he died.

OLIVE. A fruit tree of which there are several species, the most important being the common olive (*Olea europœa,* nat. ord. Oleaceæ). It is a low-branching evergreen tree, in height from 20 to 30 feet, with stiff, narrow, dusky-green or bluish leaves. The flowers are small and white, and are produced in axillary racemes, and appear in June, July, and August. The fruit is a seeded drupe of an oblong spheroidal form, with a thin, smooth, and usually blackish skin, containing a greenish soft pulp adherent to a rough, oblong, and very hard stone. It is bitter and nauseous, but replete with a bland oil.

The olive is a native of Syria and other Asiatic countries, and flourishes only in warm and comparatively dry parts of the world. It grows slowly, and is very long-lived. The olive tree has in all ages been held in peculiar estimation. It was anciently sacred to Athene. Olive wreaths were used by the Greeks and Romans to crown the brows of victors, and it is still universally regarded as an emblem of peace.

The wood of the olive tree is beautifully veined, and has an agreeable smell. It is in great esteem with cabinet-makers on account of the fine polish of which it is susceptible. But the olive tree is principally cultivated for the sake of its oil, which is contained in the pericarp or pulp. (*See* OLIVE-OIL.) It is cultivated for this purpose in Italy, France, Spain, Malta, European and Asiatic Turkey, the Ionian Islands, etc., and is easily propagated either by seed, grafting, or slips. It is very tenacious of life. The fruits are also used at table, not in the natural state, but generally pickled, the green unripe fruits being deprived of part of their bitterness by soaking them in water, and then preserved in an aromatized solution of salt.

Another species of olive, the *O. fragrans,* inhabits China, Japan, and Cochin-China. The flowers are used by the Chinese to mix with and perfume their tea, and also, together with the leaves, for adulterating tea. The only American species (*O. americāna*) is in some districts called *devil-wood* on account of the excessive hardness of the wood and the extreme difficulty of splitting it.

OLIVE-OIL. A well-known fixed, non-drying oil obtained by expression from the pulp of the ripe fruit of the olive (*Olea europæa*). It is an insipid, inodorous, pale yellow or greenish-yellow, viscid fluid, unctuous to the feel, inflammable, insoluble in water, and nearly insoluble in alcohol. It is one of the lightest of the fixed oils. Olive-oil is much used as an article of food in the countries in which it is produced, and to a smaller extent in other countries, to which it is exported also for medicinal and manufacturing purposes.

The best olive-oil is said to be made in the vicinity of Aix, in France; the kind known by the name of Florence is also of a superior quality, and is mostly used for culinary purposes. By far the largest proportion of the oil brought to England is imported from Italy. Spain also sends a large quantity. The oil is also known as *Sweet-oil.* It is sometimes adulterated with other oils such as cotton-seed, earthnut, lard, poppy, rape, or sesame.

OLIVES, Mount of, or **MOUNT OLIVET** (known by the Moslems as *Jebel et-Tûr*). A mountain situated on the east side of Jerusalem, from which it is separated by the Valley of Jehoshaphat and the brook Kedron. It is closely associated with the life of Christ. The principal summit has the name of Mount of Ascension, and here stands the modern Armenian chapel of that name. But, according to the Scriptures, the scene of the Ascension was near to Bethany (Luke xxiv. 50), which is on the farther side of the hill from Jerusalem.

OLIV'ETANS. A branch of the

Benedictine order, founded in 1313 by Tolomei of Siena, in Italy, and named from Monte Oliveto Maggiore near that city, where their first monastery was erected.

OL'IVINE, called also **CHRYSOLITE.** A mineral, olive-green in colour, occurring in basic igneous rocks, such as gabbro and basalt, and in certain meteorites. It is an orthosilicate of iron and magnesium. $(Mg{\cdot}Fe)_2SiO_4$, and readily decomposes into the much softer hydrous silicate serpentine. In its fresh form it is used as a gem, having a suitable hardness, above that of felspar. Olivine may arise in dolomitic limestone from contact-action by igneous rocks, when hydration produces beautiful serpentinous marbles. Almost pure olivine-rocks are known, usually containing chromite, as at the Dun Mountain in New Zealand, and the serpentinous matter filling the famous diamond-pipes of South Africa is derived from olivine-rock.

OLMÜTZ, or **OLOMOUC.** A city of Czechoslovakia, in Moravia, on the March, which almost encircles it. It has a cathedral, erected by King Wenzel III., who was murdered there in 1306; and its manufactures are chiefly of linen and woollen cloth. In 1886 its fortifications were turned into pleasure-grounds. The Convention of Olmütz, between Austria and Prussia, was signed on 29th Nov., 1850. Pop. (1930), 65,989.

OLNEY. A small market-town of England, in the north of Buckinghamshire, near the Ouse. In the market-place is the house in which the poet Cowper resided (1767-86), his friend the Rev. John Newton occupying the rectory; and it was from this place that the *Olney Hymns*, their joint production, received their name. Pop. 2651.

OLONETZ'. A northern government of Russia, now part of the Karelian Republic; area, about 49,000 sq. miles. The most marked physical feature is its lakes (including Onega and Ladoga), streams, and morasses (occupying one-fifth of the total area). The climate is rigorous in the extreme. Timber constitutes almost the whole wealth of the government. The chief means of support of the inhabitants are forestry, hunting, and fishing. The capital is Petrozavodsk.

OLSTFOLD, or **OSTFOLD.** A county or *fylke* of Norway, at the north-east of Christiania Fiord; traversed by the Glommen and by the Christiania-Sweden Railway. Fredrikstad, Sarpsborg, and Fredrickshald are the principal towns. Area, 1613·4 sq. miles; pop. (1930), 167,030.

OLYM'PIA. A locality in Greece, the scene of the famous Olympic games, a beautiful valley or plain lying in the middle portion of the ancient district of Elis, in the western part of the Peloponnesus (Morea). Here were collected thousands of statues of the gods and of victors in the games, treasure-houses full of votive offerings, temples, altars, tombs, and in a word the most precious treasures of Grecian art.

Among the buildings were the Olympiēum or great temple of Zeus, containing the colossal statue of the god by Phidias; the Heræum or temple of Hera; the Metroum or temple of the mother of the gods; the twelve treasure-houses; the Prytanēum, in which the Olympic victors dined after the contests; the Bouleuterion, in which all the regulations regarding the games were made; and these were all surrounded with walls, having a length of about 1800 feet and a breadth of 1500 feet. Excavations made in the course of last century, in 1829, and from 1875 to 1881, have brought to light numerous valuable works of art, besides remains of ancient buildings, etc.

OLYM'PIADS. The periods of four years between each celebration of the Olympic games, by which the Greeks computed time from 776 B.C., the first year of the first Olympiad, till A.D. 394, the second year of the 293rd Olympiad.

OLYM'PIAS. The wife of Philip II., King of Macedonia, and the mother of Alexander the Great. Her haughtiness, and more probably her infidelity, led Philip to repudiate her, and to marry Cleopatra, the niece of King Attalus. The murder of Philip, which soon followed this disgrace (336 B.C.), some have attributed to the intrigues of Olympias. After the death of her son and his successor Antipater, she was besieged by Cassander in Pydna, and, having to surrender, she was put to death after a mock trial (316 B.C.).

OLYMPIC GAMES. The great national athletic festivals of the ancient Greeks were so called from being held at Olympia, near Elis, in Peloponnesus. Their origin is lost in a remote antiquity; the generally received opinion was that they were established by Heracles, in celebration of a victory, 1222 B.C. Strabo objects to this that Homer would have mentioned them had this been so. Their history is only clearly recorded from 776 B.C., when they were revived and reorganized. From that date onwards they were held every fifth year, or rather in the first month after the lapse of four years, from the previous celebration.

The principal sites connected with the games were the wooded Sacred Grove, or Altis, about 200 yards square, in which were placed the sanctuaries; the Gymnasium and Palæstra, lying to the west of this; with the Stadium and the Hippodrome, the actual scenes of contest, on the east. It is most probable that in its early days the festival was one of local interest only, organized and taken part in by the Peloponnesians; later other Greek states were attracted to the games, and the assembly became pan-Hellenic; while, after the Roman conquest, the victors themselves took part in the festival, in which both Tiberius and Nero distinguished themselves.

Women were excluded, even from being present, upon pain of death, though it is clear that this rule was not always strictly observed, for women are known to have taken part on some occasions, and to have received the victor's crown. For a long time there was but a single superintendent of the games; later two, then twelve, eight, and finally ten officials were appointed.

The opening of the games was preceded by a proclamation of universal peace throughout the land. Previous to this all intending competitors had spent ten months of severe training in the gymnasium. The first day of the festival appears to have been devoted to the offering of sacrifices, and to the classing and arranging of the competitors by the judges, previously sworn to strict impartiality and to the rejection of a bribe. On this day there were also contests for the trumpeters.

The second day was allotted to boys, who contested in wrestling, boxing, and foot- and horse-racing. Their place was taken on the third day by the men, who engaged in similar "events," and whose foot-races were of several kinds, as once, twice, and several times over the course. There were, too, races for men clad in heavy armour. On the fourth day took place the *pentathlon*, or five-fold contest, the events of which included running, leaping, wrestling, throwing the discus, and throwing the spear. These were followed by horse- and chariot-races, with contests for the heralds.

The proceedings terminated on the fifth day with further sacrifices, processions, banquets to the victors, and the presentation of the crowns. These last, the sole rewards, were of no intrinsic value, being merely wreaths of twigs gathered from the sacred olive tree—believed to have been planted by Heracles—which grew in the Altis. Nevertheless these simple prizes were greatly coveted, and carried with them much honour to their possessors.

The victors were received in their native towns with the greatest acclamation; songs—among them fourteen of Pindar's extant lyrics—were composed in their honour; statues were raised to them; they were allotted a prominent position on all public occasions, and were largely exempted from taxation. In 364 B.C. the control of the games was taken over by the Pisæans, and they were finally prohibited and suppressed in A.D. 994 by Theodosius I.

The site of Olympia was explored and excavated by German scholars between 1874 and 1881, when, among many other valuable treasures of antiquity, the Hermes of Praxiteles was brought to light. (*See* Botticher's *Olympia*; also various German works.)

The *Olympiad*, or period of four years between the celebration of the games, furnished a mode of reckoning time which was first introduced by Timæus, an historian of the third century B.C. The calculation of an olympiad is from 776 B.C., and the date of any olympiad according to the Christian era is found by subtracting one from the olympiad's number, multiplying by four, and, if the result is less than 776, subtracting it from that number, when the date B.C. will be found. If the number is greater than 776, the difference will be the date A.D.

OLYMPIC GAMES, Modern. In 1894, representatives of several countries met in Paris on the initiative of the Baron de Coubertin to consider the question of reviving the ancient Olympic Games. As a result of this step the first modern meeting took place in 1896 at Athens, the ancient Stadium being rebuilt with a seating capacity of 45,000. The events included the usual track and other sports, with many modern introductions, such as tennis, cycling, fencing, rifle- and revolver-shooting, and swimming competitions.

Among competitors from foreign countries Great Britain was meagrely represented, while the United States achieved a marked success, nine of their athletes securing prizes in every event for which they entered. A striking feature was the Marathon race, commemorative of the bringing to Athens news of the Greek victory at Marathon; the distance was about 26 miles. The two following meetings were held in Paris (1900) and St. Louis (1904).

At the latter city a greatly extended programme included numerous competitions for native races, in which American Indians, Africans, Ainus, Filipinos, and others engaged. The results disappointed the expectations of many, for the coloured men proved in most cases far inferior to their white opponents. The Greeks, desiring a meeting of more marked Hellenic stamp, held one at Athens in 1906, the royal families of Greece and England, including the late King Edward VII., being among the spectators. Here the Marathon race was won by Sherring, a Canadian.

Two years later the games were held in London, in connection with the Franco-British Exhibition. The prize for the Marathon race from Windsor Castle to Olympia, went to Hayes, an American; Dorando Pietri, an Italian, who first actually passed the post, collapsed and was helped for the last few yards. He received a special prize from Queen Alexandra. Subsequent meetings were held at Stockholm (1912), Antwerp (1920), Paris (1924), Amsterdam (1928), and Los Angeles (1932).

OLYM'PUS. The name given to several mountain ranges by the ancients. The most celebrated of them was situated in Thessaly, at the eastern extremity of the range called the Cambunian Mountains, and now called by the Greeks Elymbos or Olymbos. It rises to the height of 9700 feet above the level of the sea, and was the highest mountain in ancient Greece. The earliest Greeks looked upon it as the highest of all mountains, as the central point of the earth's surface, and as the place where the gods dwelt.

In aftertimes Olympus became the synonym for heaven. The other most important elevation bearing this name was the Mysian Olympus, a range of lofty mountains in the north-west of Asia Minor, now called Kheshish Dagh, Ala Dagh, Ishik Dagh, and Kush Dagh. Olympus in Cyprus may also be mentioned.

OMAGH (ō'-mä). The county town of Tyrone, Irish Free State, on the Strule; served by the Great Northern Railway. There are a Roman Catholic cathedral, and a Protestant church, and the remains of a castle. Linen and milling are the industries. Pop. (1926), 5124.

O'MAHA. The largest city of Nebraska, United States, county seat of Douglas county, on the Missouri; served by the Chicago, Milwaukee, and St. Paul, the Illinois Central, the Union Pacific, and six other railway systems. It is the seat of the State and of Creighton Universities, and has also two medical colleges. There are large railway workshops of the Union Pacific, and large silver-, gold-, lead-, and other smelting-works. Omaha was settled in 1854, and became a city in 1857. Pop. (1930), 214,006.

OMÁN. An independent state of South-Eastern Arabia, on the Gulf of Oman and the Arabian Sea, extending from the borders of El Hasa to Ras Sajir, with a coastline of 900 miles. Muscat is the capital, and trade is carried on through the ports of Muscat and Matrah. The people are Arabs, although there is a strong infusion of negro blood along the coast, Muscat (pop. 4300) and Matrah (pop. 8200) being almost entirely peopled by negroes and Baluchis.

The Maria Theresa dollar is in general use, and on the coast the Indian rupee circulates. An Ománese copper coin is the *muhammadi* of 20 *gaj* (11½ muhammadi = 1 dollar). Trade is brisk in dates, fruit, fish, limes, cotton goods, and hides and skins, which are exported mainly to India, the majority of the trade being in the hands of British Indians. Camels are bred in the interior, where the authority of the Sultan is nominal. Area, 82,000 sq. miles; pop. about 500,000.

Ahmed bin Sa'eed founded the dynasty of Yemenite Imams (1741) to which the present Sultans belong. In the nineteenth century the Imam of Omán reigned over a large slice of Arabia, a strip of the Persian coast, and a coastal area south of Cape Guardafui in Africa, which included both Sokotra and Zanzibar.

Sultan Sa'eed died in 1856, and by the arbitration of Lord Canning, Viceroy of India, his dominions were divided among the two claimants as the Sultanates of Zanzibar and Omán respectively. Omán has been under British protection since 1918. *See* MUSCAT.

OMAN, Sir Charles William Chadwick. English historian, born at Mozufferpore on 12th Jan., 1860. After a distinguished academic progress he was appointed Chichele Professor of Modern History at the University of Oxford. A member of the British Academy, he has been associated with many learned societies, among them the Royal Historical Society (president, 1917-21); the Royal Numismatic Society (president, 1919-30); and the Royal

Archæological Institute (president, 1927). From 1919 he represented Oxford University in Parliament. He was knighted in 1920. His publications include *A History of Greece*, 1888; *A Short History of England*, 1895; *A History of the Art of War in the Middle Ages*, 1898; *A History of the Peninsular War*, 1902-30; *Castles*, 1926; *Napoleonic Studies*, 1929.

OMAR I. Successor of Abu-bekr, and second Caliph of the Moslems after Mahomet. He was born about A.D. 582, became a follower of Mahomet about 615, and succeeded Abu-bekr in 634. His caliphate is celebrated for the great extension of Mahommedanism which took place while it lasted.

He extended his dominion over Egypt, Syria, and Palestine, whilst his generals invaded Persia, defeated the army of Yezdegerd, and conquered the capital and kingdom. He died in 644 at Medina, mortally wounded by a Persian slave. Omar was the first Caliph to bear the title of Commander of the Faithful, and he also established the custom of dating from the Hijra.

OMAR KHAYYÀM'. Persian poet, astronomer, and mathematician, born at Nishapur in Khorasan, died there A.D. 1123. His scientific works, which were of high value in their day, have been eclipsed by his *Rubaiyat*, a collection of about 500 epigrams in praise of wine, love, and pleasure, and at the same time depressingly pessimistic. There is an admirable poetic translation of the *Rubaiyat* or *Quatrains* by Edward Fitzgerald (1859).

Omar Khayyàm

OMDURMAN. A city in the Anglo-Egyptian Sudan, on the White Nile, opposite Khartoum, and the former capital of the Mahdi's empire. It is the native trading-place of the Sudan. Pop. 103,669.—**The battle of Omdurman** was fought on 2nd Sept., 1898, between the combined British and Egyptian troops and the forces of the Khalifa. The dervishes were completely overwhelmed and defeated by Lord Kitchener.—Cf. Winston S. Churchill, *The River War.*

OM'EGA (Gr., signifying "great *o*"). The name for the Greek long *o*. It was the last letter in the Greek alphabet, as alpha was the first; and from the expression in Rev. (chap. i. 8), "I am Alpha and Omega, the beginning and the ending," the signs Α Ω became with the Christians symbolical hieroglyphics. Inscriptions on tombstones, public documents, etc., very often began with these two letters, meaning "In the name of God."

OMMIADES, or **OMMEYADES** (om-i-ads). The second dynasty which held the Arabian caliphate until they in turn were superseded by the Abbasides. The founder of the dynasty was Moawiyah, who claimed the throne after the death of Othman, his cousin, and became fully recognized as Caliph after the death of Ali his rival and Hussein his son. *See* CALIPH.

OMNIBUS. A Latin word signifying "for all," and now applied in several languages to the well-known vehicle used for the conveyance of passengers at a cheap rate. The first conveyances of the kind were those which came into use in Paris (March, 1662) in consequence of an edict of Louis XIV., but they soon fell into disuse, and were not again reintroduced until 1827.

Shillibeer started the first omnibus in London on 4th July, 1829, and they were introduced into New York in 1830, and Amsterdam in 1839. The abbreviation "'bus," originally somewhat colloquial, is now a recognized word. Shillibeer's 'bus was drawn by three horses abreast, but the later type was usually drawn by two horses, and provided accommodation for passengers on the roof. Later developments were a winding stairway and comfortable seats on top. The introduction of motors has completely revolutionized the capabilities and the construction of the 'bus. *See* MOTOR VEHICLES.

OMSK. A town of Siberia, province of Akmolinsk, at the junction of the Om with the Irtish, and on the

Omsk: The City and Mosque

Trans-Siberian Railway. It contains a cathedral and various other churches, Governor's palace, and military institutions. Pop. (1926), 178,300.

ON'AGER, or GHOR-KAR. A species of wild ass (*Equus onager*), originally inhabiting the great deserts of West and West-Central Asia, and also of North-West India. *See* ASS.

Onager

ONAGRA'CEÆ. A natural order of polypetalous dicotyledons, herbs, trees, and shrubs, with opposite or alternate simple leaves, and often handsome flowers. They have an inferior ovary, and all the parts of the flower are four or a constant multiple of that number. The species chiefly inhabit the more temperate parts of the world, and have white, yellow, or red flowers; such as the great American genus Œnothēra or evening-primroses, the common wild willow-herbs (Epilobium), and the fuchsias of our gardens.

ONE'GA. A river of Russia. Issuing from Lake Latcha, government of Olonetz, it flows first north-east, then north-west, and after a course of 240 miles falls into the White Sea at the south-east extremity of the Gulf of Onega.

ONE'GA. A lake of Russia, near the centre of the government of Olonetz, and, after Lake Ladoga, the largest lake in Europe, covering an area of 3765 sq. miles. There are numerous islands and an abundant supply of fish. It discharges into Lake Ladoga by the Svir. The southern shores have been canalized to assist navigation, and Onega is connected by the Vytegra with the Mariinskaya canal-system. *See* MURMAN.

ONEIDA (o-nī'da). A lake in the state of New York, United States, the western and lower end of which is about 18 miles S.E. of Lake Ontario. It is 20 miles long, 4 miles broad, and its waters find a vent by Oneida River into Lake Ontario at its south-east corner, after they have united with the Seneca and formed the Oswego River.

ONEIDAS. Once a North American Indian tribe or nation belonging to the confederacy of the Hurons, and inhabiting Central New York. A remnant of them now inhabit a reservation in Wisconsin.

O'NEILL, Eugene Gladstone. American dramatist. Born in New York, 16th Oct., 1888, he tried commerce, the sea, and other callings before he began to write. He went to Harvard University, 1914-15, and in 1916 spent the summer at Provincetown, where he met the group who produced nearly all his short plays. He rapidly became the most famous of the younger American dramatists. He has written *Beyond the Horizon* (1920), *Anna Christie* (1922), *Emperor Jones* (1922), *The Hairy Ape* (1922), *The Great God Brown* (1926), and *Strange Interlude* (1928), amongst others.

ONION. A well-known liliaceous plant of the genus Allium, the *A. Cepa*, the bulbous root of which is much used as an article of food. It is a biennial herbaceous plant with long tubulated leaves, and a swelling, pithy stalk. The peculiar flavour varies much according to the size of the bulb, the small reddish onions having much more pungency than the larger ones. The onion may be grown from the tropics to the coldest verge of the temperate zone. There are at least twenty varieties, the Strasbourg, Spanish, and Portuguese being among the best.

ONOMAC'RITOS. A Greek poet and mystic, who lived at Athens, arranged and explained the so-called oracles of Musæus, and having been detected making an interpolation in one of these, was banished from Athens by Hipparchus about 516 B.C. He is supposed to have been the author of the *Orphic* hymns.

ONTA'RIO (formerly **Upper Canada, or Canada West**). The most populous province of the Dominion of Canada. It is bounded north by the James and Hudson Bays; west by Manitoba; south by the St. Lawrence River, the Great Lakes, and the Rainy River; and east by the Ottawa River, separating it from Quebec. Area, 412,262 sq. miles, of which 41,382 acres are water. The district of Patricia, in the north of the province, was added in 1912. Ontario has many lakes, such as Nipigon, Lake of the Woods, etc.

The chief rivers are boundary rivers: the Ottawa, Niagara, and Albany, the last entering James Bay, part of Hudson Bay. The Falls of Niagara in part belong to the province. Ontario consists of two chief divisions, the peninsula between the great lakes and the Ottawa, and the much larger portion to the north-west. The country has no hills of importance. The drainage in eastern Ontario is to the St. Lawrence, that of the north-west is mainly to Hudson Bay.

This part is rich in forest and mineral wealth, and has also great stretches of wheat land. Here the climate shows great extremes, while in the south-eastern and peninsular portion it is agreeably tempered by the proximity of the lakes. In this part the crops raised are chiefly wheat, barley, oats, peas, and potatoes, while fruit-growing is successfully carried on. The farmer here also engages in stock-raising and dairy-farming with a success largely due to the easy accessibility of markets by rail, or by lake, river, and canal navigation. About one-half of the milk, cheese, and butter of Canada is produced in Ontario.

Immense quantities of pine and pulp-wood are taken from the northern forests. Minerals include the silver of Cobalt, the nickel of Sudbury, copper, iron, lead, gypsum, mica, petroleum, salt, and marble. An important gold discovery was made at Red Lake in 1926. Chief among manufactures are lumber, paper pulp, paper, furniture, hardware, leather, agricultural implements, steam-engines, etc.

Education in the common schools is free, and there is liberal Government provision for high schools and colleges, technical institutions, and the universities. The capital is Toronto, and government is under a Lieutenant-Governor, a Cabinet, and a Legislative Assembly or Parliament of 112 members. Ontario sends 82 members to the House of Commons of Canada, and 24 members to the Senate. The Dominion capital, Ottawa, is in the province, also Hamilton, London, and Kingston. Pop. (1931), 3,426,488, of whom about 26,000 are Indians.

ONTARIO, Lake. The smallest and most easterly of the great Lakes of North America, lying along the north-east side of the state of New York, and forming part of the boundary between the United States and Canada; greatest length, 190 miles; greatest breadth, about 55 miles; area, 7540 sq. miles. It receives the waters of Lake Erie by the Niagara, and discharges its waters by the St. Lawrence into the Atlantic, 1000 miles distant.

The Hudson, and the Oswego and Erie Canals, form a connection through the United States between it and the Atlantic. It is navigable throughout its whole extent, but shore ice impedes winter navigation. The most important places on its shores are Toronto, Hamilton, Kingston, and Coburg, in Canada, and Oswego in the United States.

ONTOL'OGY. The science of being, dealing with the ultimate principles of material and spiritual phenomena, and investigating reality in its ultimate nature. Aristotle employed the term first philosophy but not ontology, which is sometimes used as synonymous with metaphysics.

The term was first introduced by Christian Wolff (1679-1754), who divided metaphysics into ontology or philosophy of being, psychology or philosophy of mind, cosmology or philosophy of nature, and theology, which deal respectively with being as being, and with the soul, the world, and God. Kant, however, maintained that in dealing with being independently of its representation in consciousness, ontology was attempting a vain and impossible task. He directed his criticism especially against the so-called *ontological proof* of the Divine existence, i.e. the conclusion of the existence of a Supreme Being from the fact that the idea of such a Being is innate. *See* METAPHYSICS.

ONYCHIA. Inflammation of the nails. It may be due to injury, pressure, or exposure to X-rays—traumatic onychia—or it may be due to a small abscess at the edge of the nail—septic onychia. The condition is also seen in general diseases with manifestations elsewhere, as in ringworm, favus, and syphilis.

ONYGENA. A genus of Ascomycetous Fungi, group Plectascineæ. They are saprophytes growing on decaying horns, hoofs, feathers, etc. *O. equina* is not uncommon on sheep's horns in the Scottish Highlands and other hilly districts.

ONYX. A banded agate, in which dark layers are contrasted with white or milky-grey layers between them.

OODNADATTA. A township of South Australia, on the transcontinental railway to Darwin, Northern Territory (q.v.), of which it has been the railhead since 1891. Work on the extension to Darwin began in 1927, and the first train reached Alice Springs in 1929. Mica is brought to Oodnadatta by camel from Mount Brassey in the Macdonell ranges, 500 miles distant.

OOGONIUM. The female organ in Thallophytes (Algæ and Fungi), a cell containing one or more female gametes or ova.

OÖLITE (ō'o-lit). A species of limestone composed of globules clustered together, commonly cemented by calcium carbonate. The granules vary in size from that of small pinheads to that of peas. When the grains are very distinct and well rounded, it is called roe-stone; when they are large and pea-like, the rock is known as pisolite, pea-grit, or peastone.

In modern tropical waters, and in desiccating lakes like that of Utah, oölitic grains are formed by the concentric deposition of aragonite round minute organic or inorganic nuclei, under the drying influences of a shore-region and the rolling action of the waves. Oölitic limestones of ancient date are often associated with corals and marine shells, but the aragonite has passed into calcite.

Oölitic structure often occurs in ironstones from a form of concretionary deposition. What is known as the *Oölite* or *Oölitic series* of rocks in geology consists of a series of strata comprehending a number of oölitic limestones, calcareous sandstones, marls, etc., which underlie the Cretaceous strata and rest on the Lias. *See* JURASSIC.

OÖMYCETES. One of the main subdivisions of the Phycomycetes or Lower Fungi, characterized by the possession of distinct male (antheridia) and female (oögonia) sexual organs. *See* ZYGOMYCETES.

OÖSPORE. In botany, the name given to the ovum after it has been fertilized by the male gamete; the zygote of an oögamous plant.

OOST (ōst), **Jacob van, the Elder.** One of the best Flemish painters, born at Bruges in 1600, died 1671. He proceeded to Rome, where he became the pupil chiefly of Annibale Caracci. In his youth he was so successful a copyist of Rubens and Vandyck that his copies still deceive connoisseurs.

OOST, Jacob van, the Younger. son of the preceding, born in 1637, studied at Paris and Rome, lived about forty years at Lille, and died at Bruges in 1713. His style is more marked, and his pencil is freer than that of his father.

OOSTERHOUT (ō'stėr-hout). A town of the Netherlands, in the province of North Brabant, 5 miles N.E. of Breda. It has potteries, breweries, tanneries, corn-mills, beet-sugar factory, and some trade in grain, cloth, and timber. Pop. 15,107

OOTACAMUND, or UTAKAMAND. A hill station of Madras Presidency, India, and the summer headquarters of the Madras Government, situated in the Nilghiri Hills on a branch line from Podanur. It is 7228 feet above sea-level, and lies in an amphitheatre surrounded by hills overlooking an artificial lake nearly 1½ miles long. Pop. 19,500.

OO'TRUM. A soft, white, silky, and strong Indian fibre, derived from the stem of *Dæmia extensa*, a plant of the nat. ord. Asclepiadaceæ, abundant in many parts of India.

OOZE. A white unctuous mud, consisting almost entirely of carbonate of lime, and occurring at a depth sometimes of 2500 fathoms, on the bed of the Atlantic and Pacific Oceans, where material from the shore-zones cannot mingle with the truly oceanic types of deposit.

It is formed chiefly by the accumulation of the dead shells (tests) of foraminifera, commonly mingled, of course, with the remains of other marine creatures. The deposit bears an interesting resemblance to the beds familiar to the geologist as chalk, this formation also being made up largely of foraminiferal shells, and the most prominent genus, Globigerina, being especially characteristic of both.

OPAH, or KING-FISH. A large and beautiful sea-fish (*Lampris luna*), constituting a distinct family (Lamprididæ) related to the sticklebacks. It is a native of the Eastern seas, but found in the Atlantic and Arctic Oceans, and sometimes, though more

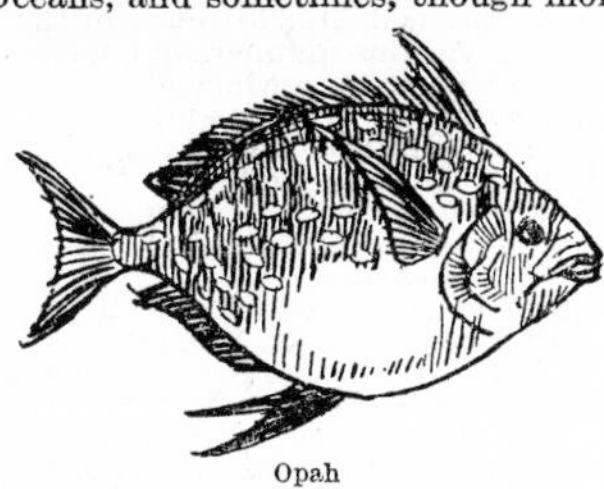

Opah

rarely, on the British coasts. It is about 4½ feet long and weighs 140 to 150 lb. Its colours are very rich, the upper part of the back and sides being green, reflecting both purple and gold, and passing into yellowish-green below, the fins bright vermilion. The flesh is highly esteemed.

OPAL. A mineral commonly milky-white by reflected light; its iridescent varieties come under the class of pellucid gems. It consists of uncrystallized silica with about 10 per cent. of water, and is very brittle. The iridescence of the varieties used as gems is due to layers of various refractive powers. The gem-varieties are found in many parts of Europe, especially in Hungary, in Mexico, Queensland, the East Indies, etc. The substances in which it is most frequently found are rhyolite and a ferruginous sandstone.

In the course of geological time it passes into chalcedony, by crystallization and yielding up its absorbed water. There are many varieties or species, the chief of which are: (*a*) *precious* or *noble opal*, which exhibits brilliant and changeable reflections of green, blue, yellow, and red; (*b*) *fire opal*, which simply affords a red reflection; (*c*) *common opal*, whose colours are white, green, yellow, and red, but without the play of colours; (*d*) *semi-opal*, the varieties of which are more opaque than common opal; (*e*) *hydrophane*, which assumes a transparency only when thrown into water; (*f*) *hyalite*, which occurs in small transparent colourless globular and botryoidal forms, with a vitreous lustre; (*g*) *menilite*, which occurs in irregular or reniform masses, and is opaque or slightly translucent. Formerly the opal was believed to possess magical virtues.

OPAVA. *See* Troppau.

OPEN-BILL (*Anastŏmus lamelligĕrus*). An African bird of the stork family, so named from the odd formation of the beak, which at the anterior

Open-Bill

end exhibits a gap between the mandibles as if part of them were worn away though they meet at the points. The chief food is molluscs, and perhaps this formation of bill has something to do with the opening of the shells. Another species (*A. oscitans*) inhabits India and Indo-China.

OPENHEARTH PROCESS. *See* Steel.

OPERA. Opera may be defined as drama set to music and performed upon a stage, and the history of opera is the story of man's attempts to bring drama and music into an ever closer union. During the closing years of the sixteenth century the advanced musical spirits had been growing more and more discontented with the limited range of expression offered by the contemporary music. This was ideally suited to the utterance of religious emotions, but from its very nature was quite unable to take on any dramatic significance.

So strongly was the need for a wider musical expression felt that attempts had been made to write dramatic music on the contrapuntal model, but the results were not distinguishable from the music of the Church excepting as regards the text alone. An example of this is offered by *L'Amfiparnasso,* a so-called comic drama which was produced at Modena in 1594. It contained five characters, and the music, of which there was a plentiful supply, consisted of a series of madrigals in five parts written inevitably in purely contrapuntal style and sung unaccompanied.

There was therefore no orchestra and no overture ; all five voices were always singing, and when the drama required that only one or two of the characters should be on the stage, the remainder of the little company continued singing from the "wings," as is conclusively proved from woodcuts contained in the published score of the work.

The growing discontent with things musical would seem to have focused itself in a little band of Florentines—aristocrats, men of letters, and musicians, all glowing with the spirit of the Renaissance. They met in the house of one of their number with the avowed intention of reviving musical declamation as it was practised in the early Greek tragedies.

For various reasons, some of them technical, this was not possible, but in their endeavour after it this band of pioneers lighted on the idea of solo-song, and in doing so accomplished, no doubt unwittingly, one of the most sweeping revolutions in the history of art.

Among the musicians of this little company (there were three in all) was one Vincenzio Galilei, father of the astronomer, and a musician trained in the contrapuntal school. His orthodox musical upbringing, however, did not in any way damp his pioneer zeal, and he was the first to compose music for a solo voice to a secular text and with accompaniment for a single instrument.

These early works were called cantatas, and the development from this simple but all-important essay in the writing of dramatic music to the composing of the first opera was rapid and direct. In 1597 Jacopo Peri, another musician of the commany, set music to *Dafne*, a play written by a poet member, and the work was privately performed in Florence at the palace of one of the noble members.

So much success attended this production that Peri was asked in 1600 to write something similar for production as a part of some high wedding festivities. He did so, and the result was *Eurydice*, the first real Italian opera to be given in public, and the ultimate ancestor of all operas.

It is significant of the strong desire that existed for the development of music on dramatic lines that this first opera achieved a remarkable success and brought European fame to its composer.

In a preface to his opera, Peri says that in studying the drama of the ancients he felt convinced that they had adopted a tone of expression other than everyday speech, which though never rising into song was nevertheless musically coloured.

This induced him to observe carefully the various manners of speaking in daily life, and these he endeavoured to reproduce in music as faithfully as he could. He was thus probably the first man to write *recitative.*

The progress which opera made in its early years was remarkably rapid, and it would seem as if the whole musical world had been waiting for it. Florence was its birthplace, but it spread quickly to the other important towns of Italy, Mantua being the first of them to have opera. In 1607, only seven years after the production of Peri's *Eurydice* in Florence, Monteverdi, the first great name in the history of opera, a man of undoubted genius and a musical pioneer, produced a work called *Arianna*, which was so successful that the reigning duke at once commanded a second opera, which appeared in the following year.

It was on the same subject as Peri's work, but while Peri had been satisfied with a very moderate orchestra consisting only of one harpsichord (fore-runner of our pianoforte), three instruments of the lute family, and three flutes, or seven instruments in all, Monteverdi, writing only eight years later, had increased the orchestra to thirty-three, and had introduced stringed instruments and wind instruments.

In the earliest years we read of the enormous expense which attached to the mounting and producing of operas, and it was only reigning princes who could afford the luxury, and then only on occasions of great public rejoicing. To Venice belongs the honour of opening the first public opera-house, and thus transferring opera from the exclusive patronage of the nobility to the wider and more vivifying patronage of the people.

This was in 1637. By the close of the century there were eleven opera-houses in Venice alone. The other Italian cities showed operatic activities in varying degree, but for long Florence and Venice were the two great nurseries of the new art.

Opera, which had originated in

Italy as, to some extent, a derivative of the classical drama, was quickly taken up in other European countries, but in the lands of its adoption took on distinctive national qualities. French opera was directly derived from the ballet, which had always been a favourite form of entertainment with the French kings. The chief glory of its early years was G. B. Lulli, an Italian who spent his life in Paris. In England, opera was the direct outcome of the masque, and Henry Purcell its greatest exponent.

As a young lad he may have heard Milton's *Comus* performed, with music by Henry Lawes, and would no doubt be inspired by it to try his pen on really dramatic music, which that of Henry Lawes was not. However that may be, he wrote at the age of seventeen an opera on the subject of *Dido and Æneas* which may be regarded as the first English opera. It is a work with lasting powers of appeal, and has been produced in London in recent times. Its distinctive characteristics are the rhetorical perfection of its recitatives and the natural beauty of its melodies.

Germany's first operas were imported direct from Italy and were sung in Italian. They did not appear till about fifty years after their beginning in Italy, so that the country which was destined to go farthest in opera was very slow in taking it up. Not till 1681 did a really German work meet with any success. In that year a *singspiel* called *Adam and Eve* was publicly performed in Hamburg in the German language, and its first performance marked the beginning of German opera.

The high aims which distinguished the Florentine pioneers were unfortunately lacking in the operatic outlook of some of their followers, and Italian opera for a time sank to a very low level of artistic merit. Up to about the year 1850 its history might roughly be divided into three stages, in which the dramatist, the composer, and, finally, the vocalist held sway.

Verdi, the greatest opera-composer that Italy has produced, provided in his life-work examples of the conventional style in his early operas, but with ripening experience had the rare faculty of outgrowing his early methods, and gave to the world in *Aïda, Othello,* and *Falstaff* works of remarkable power and beauty, written in the modern idiom. Other notable Italians were Leoncavallo (1858-1919), whose best-known work is the opera *Pagliacci,* and Puccini, composer of *La Bohème, La Tosca, Madame Butterfly,* and *The Girl of the Golden West.* Puccini's last opera, *Turandot,* was produced in 1926, two years after his death.

A powerful and universal influence was exerted in the operatic world by Richard Wagner, who may be called the latest of the operatic reformers. He had been preceded in this rôle by Gluck and Weber, the former of whom, in his later works, had abandoned the conventionalities and aimed solely at truth of dramatic expression, with such success that his *Orfeo, Alceste,* etc., are still among the most beautiful numbers of the operatic repertoire.

Weber was the chief among the pioneers of the Romantic opera, his best-known work being *Der Freischutz,* unfortunately only familiar to the public of this country by its overture. Wagner, profiting by the labours of both Gluck and Weber, and adding still more of his own, has taken his place as the greatest of all opera composers. His method of composition, in which the orchestral score is compounded of *leitmotiven* or representative themes, has found many followers, and the possibilities of interest which are inherent in such a system of, so to speak, running orchestral commentary are not likely soon to be exhausted.

Among Russian operatic writers may be mentioned Rimsky-Korsakoff (whose *Coq d'Or* was produced in 1910) and Moussovgsky, composer of *Boris Godounoff.*

British composers of opera at the present time include among others: Dame Ethel Smyth (*The Boatswain's Mate*), Gustav Holst (*The Perfect Fool,* produced in 1922), and Frederick Delius (*Koanga,* produced in 1932). Opera in Britain owes a great deal to Sir Thomas Beecham, the famous conductor and founder of the British National Opera Company.—BIBLIOGRAPHY: Grove's *Dictionary of Music and Musicians,* article *Opera* (vol. iii.); E. Markham Lee, *The Story of Opera*; A. Elson, *A Critical History of Opera* (giving an account of the rise and progress of the different schools, with a description of the master-works in each); W. J. Henderson, *Some Forerunners of Italian Opera*; H. E. Krehbiel, *A Book of Operas: their Histories, Plots, and Music.*

OPER'CULUM. Literally a lid or cover, and specifically applied to a horny or shelly plate developed in certain univalve Mollusca upon the hinder part of the foot, and serving to close the aperture of the shell when the animal is retracted within it. It is also applied to part of the gill-cover of fishes; and to a sort of stopper with which some tube-making annelids (Serpulidæ) close the entrance to their dwellings.

OPHICLEIDE (of'i-klīd). A brass wind-instrument of music invented to supersede the serpent, and now superseded by the euphonium. It generally consists of a wide conical tube, terminating in a bell like that of a horn, with a mouthpiece and ten holes or ventages which are stopped by keys. Ophicleides are of two kinds, the bass and the alto; the former has a compass of three octaves and one note, ranging from B on the third space below the bass-staff to C on the third space of the treble-staff, including all the intermediate semitones. The alto ophicleide (an inferior instrument) has the same extent of compass, but starts an octave higher.

OPHIOCEPH'ALUS. A genus of tropical fresh-water fishes, native to Africa and Asia, allied to the climbing perch, and like it able to live a long time out of water.

O'PHIR. A region to which the ships of Solomon and of Hiram, King of Tyre, made voyages, bringing back gold, almug-wood, and precious stones. Some identify it with the Ophir mentioned in Gen. x. 29, which was apparently situated in Arabia; while others place it in India, or in Africa.

OPH'ITE. Green porphyry or serpentine, an altered igneous rock of a dusky-green colour of different shades, sprinkled with spots of a lighter green. It is coloured by chlorite or serpentine. Called also *Ophiolite.*

OPH'ITES. A Gnostic sect of the second century, so called because they held that the serpent by which Eve was tempted was sacred. Like most Gnostics, they advocated the emancipation of man from the control of the demiurgos. The serpent, therefore, who had tempted Eve and introduced an element of revolt against the demiurgos, was, according to their belief, a benefactor of humanity. The sect existed as late as the sixth century.

OPHIUCHUS (of-i-ö'kus). The Serpent-bearer, called also *Serpentarius*; one of the ancient northern constellations, representing a man holding a serpent, which is twined about him. The moderns, however, make a separate constellation of the Serpent.

OPHIUROI'DEA. A class of the Echinodermata, comprising star-fishes known as brittle-stars and sand-stars. These animals have long, slender-jointed arms, which may either be branched or simple. Creeping is effected by a wriggling movement of the arms.

OPHTHALMIA, or **CONJUNCTIVITIS.** Inflammation of the conjunctiva of the eye, and all the forms are marked by redness and swelling of the white part of the eye, varying according to the severity of the infection, and by a muco-purulent discharge which glues the edges of the eyelids together at night.

The patient complains of considerable irritation and itching, and of a sensation of sand in the eyes, but there is no pain or intolerance to light in ordinary uncomplicated conjunctivitis.

The condition may be acute or chronic, and commonest types of the acute form are catarrhal; purulent, which is an extremely dangerous and contagious type; membranous, which is diphtheria affecting the eye; and phlyctenular.

In chronic conjunctivitis the signs and symptoms are similar, but less severe, and the condition may last for a long time. Granular conjunctivitis, or trachoma, is a type which has appeared in this country with the increased number of aliens, especially Russian Jews. It is a subacute condition and very persistent, and is characterized by the appearance of gelatinous granulations, like sago grains, scattered over the conjunctiva. Since the introduction of careful supervision of the eyes of aliens at the port of arrival, the spread of trachoma has been considerably lessened.

OPHTHALMOSCOPE. An instrument for observing the internal structure of the eye. It consists of a mirror by which light, from an artificial source, is directed into the eye of the patient, and a double-convex lens, by which the illumined parts of the structure of the eye are magnified. The observer looks through a hole in the centre of the mirror with the light to the side of, and slightly behind, the patient's head.

OPIE, John. English painter, the son of a carpenter, born in the village of St. Agnes, near Truro, Cornwall, 1761, died 1807. His talent was accidentally discovered by Dr. Wolcot (Peter Pindar), who took the boy to London. When his portrait-painting ceased to be fashionable, he devoted himself to historical and Scriptural subjects with such success that he became a Royal Academician in 1788, and was elected professor of painting to the Royal Academy in 1805.

He was the author of a biography of Sir Joshua Reynolds in Pilkington's *Dictionary of Painters*, and his four lectures on painting, with a memoir, were published by his wife, Amelia Opie (1769-1853), who acquired considerable fame as a writer of tales and poetry. Opie is well represented in the National Gallery and in the National Portrait Gallery. His remains were interred in St. Paul's Cathedral near those of Sir Joshua Reynolds.

OPIUM. The inspissated juice of a species of poppy (*Papăver somniférum*), cultivated on a large scale principally in Hindustan and in Asiatic Turkey, but well known in many places as a garden plant, being an annual with white, red, or violet flowers and glaucous leaves.

The opium is the juice that flows from incisions made in the green heads or seed-capsules of the plant after the fall or removal of the petals, and the best flows from the first incision. The juice is at first a milky liquid, but soon solidifies and turns black, and is then scraped off and collected.

It is one of the most energetic of narcotics, and at the same time one of the most precious of all medicines, and is employed in a great variety of cases, but most commonly for the purpose of procuring sleep and relief from pain.

In medicine it is very commonly used in the form of *laudanum*, which is a simple tincture or extract in spirits of wine; it is also an ingredient in various patent and other remedies. Another opium preparation is *morphine* (q.v.).

In its natural state opium is heavy, of a dense texture, of a brownish-yellow colour, not perfectly dry, but easily receiving an impression from the finger; it has a faint smell, and its taste is bitter and acrid. The principal part of our supply of opium is brought from Turkey, whence it is imported in flat pieces or cakes, covered with leaves.

In the case of many temperaments opium produces such agreeable effects, whether a delightful dreamy calm, a state of pleasant exhilaration, or beatific visions, that numbers of persons are led to use it habitually, as others use alcohol in some form, though over-indulgence in it is attended with at least as evil effects as over-indulgence in the latter. But like tobacco it is taken by vast numbers without any apparent result one way or other.

Some habitual takers of opium can take as much in a day as would kill ten or twenty persons unaccustomed to it. It is taken in two ways, known as opium-eating and opium-smoking. The habitual use of opium is most common in China, the south-east of Asia, and the Malay Archipelago, where it is chiefly smoked in a special pipe.

The pipe, or rather the stem of the pipe, is about the length and size of an ordinary flute; the bowl is generally made of earthenware. The smoker, who is always lying, or at least reclining, takes a small portion of opium about the size of a pea on the end of a spoon-headed needle, heats it at a lamp, and then places it in the bowl of the pipe, the pellet of opium having previously been perforated with the needle. He then brings the opium to the flame of the lamp, inhales the smoke in several inspirations, and is then ready to repeat the process with a fresh quantity of opium until the desired intoxication ensues.

Large quantities of opium used to be consumed in China, a great part of which came from India, though much was produced in China itself. The use of opium in China was put down between 1906 and 1916. In 1917 the importation of Indian opium into China ceased.

OPON. A town of the Philippines, on Mactan Island, Cebú, opposite Cebú City. Maguey cultivation is the staple industry. Magellan was killed at Opon in 1521. Pop. 22,250.

OPOP'ONAX. The inspissated juice of an umbelliferous plant (*Opoponax Chironium*), a fetid gum-resin imported from Turkey, and now and again used as an antispasmodic in nervous complaints. There is a compound perfume which also receives this name.

OPOR'TO (ancient **Portus Cale** or **Gaia**; Rom. *Castrum Novum*; Port. *O Porto*, the port). A city and seaport of Portugal, the second largest in the republic, capital of the province of Entre Douro e Minho, on the Douro, about 2 miles from its mouth, and along which it extends for 2 miles. The river is crossed by two bridges, one of them the railway bridge, and the other carrying two roadways.

Among the chief buildings are the granite cathedral on the site of an ancient castle of the Suevi; the church of S. Francisco (built 1404); the bishop's palace, an enormous building; and the Torre dos Clerigos (Tower of the Clergy), a granite tower, 210 feet high.

The principal trade is in wine,

white and red, but chiefly the latter (*port* wine, so named from this town), which is principally exported to Britain through Leixões, the port of the city. There are some manufactories of hats, silks, cotton, woollen, and linen stuffs, pottery, lace, glass, leather, and paper. Pop. (1930), 232,380.

Oporto, with its opposite suburb of Cale, gave its name to Portugal (i.e. Portus Cale), and existed as a trading-town before the Roman conquest. The Alani founded *Castrum Novum* on the north bank. During the Moorish occupation it was razed to the ground by Almansor of Cordova in A.D. 820, but was rebuilt and repeopled by Gascons and French as *Portus Gallorum* (999), a name from which some authorities derive the word Portugal. "Leal e invicta cidade" (the loyal and unconquered city) is the official title of Oporto.

The great event in the history of Oporto was the siege of 1832 and 1833, when Dom Pedro IV. landed at Arnosa on 8th July, 1832, and was shut up in Oporto with 7000 men. The town was besieged by Dom Miguel. Wellington effected the passage of the Douro on 11th May, 1809, and forced the French under Soult to beat a precipitate retreat from Oporto.

OPOS'SUM. The name of several species of well-known American marsupial mammals, usually possessing a long prehensile tail. The type-genus is Didelphys. They are nocturnal and, in most cases, arboreal in their habits, living constantly on trees, and there pursuing birds, insects, etc., although they do not despise fruit. The females of certain species have an abdominal pouch into which the teats project, and within which the young can be sheltered.

The best-known species of opossum

Yellow Woolly Opossum

is the *Didelphys virginiana*, very common in the United States. It is almost the size of a large cat, the general colour whitish-grey, and the whole hair of a wool-like softness. On the ground the motions of the opossum are awkward and clumsy, but on the branches of a tree it moves with great celerity and ease, using the prehensile tail to assist its motions.

When caught or threatened with danger the opossum counterfeits death, and "playing 'possum" has on this account passed into a proverb as used to indicate any deceitful proceeding. The female has from ten to fifteen young, which are for a long time nourished in the pouch, to which they resort when alarmed.

In pouchless species the young, when old enough to leave the teats, are carried on the back, and in some cases hold on by their prehensile tails to the forwardly bent tail of their mother. The water opossum or yapock (Chironectes), native to tropical America, lives in streams and feeds on fish and crustaceans. It has webbed hind-feet, and is about the size of a large rat.

OPOSSUM-SHRIMP. The popular name of several species of Mysis, a genus of small crustaceans. They receive their name from the females carrying their eggs and young in a pouch between the thoracic legs.

OPPELN. A town of Silesia, on the Oder. It has an old royal castle, and the oldest church of Upper Silesia (St. Adalbert), founded A.D. 995. Pop. 41,507.

OPPENHEIM (-hīm). A town of Germany, in Hesse-Darmstadt, on the Rhine. It is of considerable importance; was taken by the Swedes (1631) and French (1689, 1792, and 1794). There is a trade in wine. Pop. 3750.

OPPIAN. The name of two Greek authors, one of whom wrote a poem entitled *Halieutica* (Fishing), and the other a poem on *Cynegetica* (Hunting). The author of the *Halieutica* flourished about A.D. 170. The author of the *Cynegetica* was born at Apamea or Pella, in Syria, and flourished about A.D. 210. There is also a prose paraphrase of a poem on bird-catching, attributed to Oppian; but it is doubtful to which of the two it belongs.

OPPOSITION. In astronomy, the situation of two heavenly bodies when diametrically opposed to each other, or when their longitudes differ by 180°. The moon when in opposition to the sun appears as full moon; a planet in the same position is at its nearest and brightest, and on the meridian at midnight. *See* CONJUNCTION.

OPPY. A village of France, in the department of Pas-de-Calais. It was the scene of severe fighting during the European War (battle of Arras) between April and May, 1917, and was a strong place on the Hindenburg line.

OPTICAL ILLUSIONS. In early times devices operated by physical forces, the properties of which were little known by the ordinary people, were in use, not only in the shows of reputed wizards, but also as a necessary part of some forms of religious services. Hero describes, in his *Pneumatica,* a small temple which opened its doors to allow the invisible god to come out among his people whenever an offering was burned on the altar. The operating mechanism was out of sight, and the motive power was the heat, which caused the expansion of the air in the hollow altar. When the offering cooled, the air contracted, the temple doors closed, and the period of religious exultation was over.

Spectral pictures, reflections of moving objects, and "visions" on smoke were sufficiently common in the fourteenth to sixteenth centuries to be referred to in the works of the authors of that period. In later times we find the same old tricks performed, but considerably improved by the use of appliances of much better construction. Boxes and cabinets provided with mirror-backed partitions, to give them the appearance of being empty, have been much used by Tobin, Pepper, Maskelyne, and other illusionists. Assistants were made to appear in and disappear from these boxes in the most remarkable way.

In 1858 Henry Dircks introduced the use of an inclined sheet of plate-glass to the stock-in-trade of the stage illusionist. The actors performed, partly behind the glass and partly in a well below but in front of the stage, from which positions they produced reflections on the glass which could be observed by the audience. The formation of these reflections could be stopped at any instant to make the "ghosts" disappear. The device was described by Dircks at the meeting of the British Association in 1858. John Henry Pepper joined Dircks in patenting and demonstrating the apparatus, which was always spoken of as "Pepper's Ghost."

OPTICAL LANTERN, or MAGIC LANTERN. An apparatus which is capable of producing, on a screen, enlarged images of small suitable objects. The apparatus comprises a source of light enclosed within the lantern body, a condenser lens system, the object to be exhibited (such as a photograph in the form of a lantern slide, or a cinematograph film), an objective lens system, and the screen on which the image is formed.

The condenser consists of two large plano-convex lenses placed with their plane surfaces outermost. The light collected by the condenser converges to pass into the objective; on its way it passes through the lantern slide situated immediately in front of the condenser in a frame called the slide stage.

The objective consists of a converging system of lenses similar to a photographic objective; it is corrected for spherical and chromatic aberration, and is provided with a

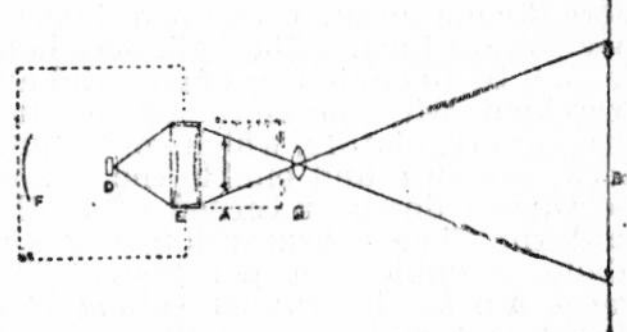

Diagram of an Optical Lantern

D, Lamp. *E,* Condenser. *A,* Slide. *C,* Objective. *B,* Screen. *F,* Reflector.

rack and pinion for varying the distance from the slide in order to focus the image on the screen. The screen is preferably a flat wall with a smooth white surface of plaster of Paris; a linen sheet forms a portable screen.

When electric current can be obtained from a public or private source, the illumination is generally done by means of an electric arc. The current is led through two carbon rods; it enters the upper or positive carbon, and, bridging the air-gap between the carbons, sets up an intensely luminous flame or arc. (*See* ELECTRIC LIGHT: ARC LIGHT.) With a "direct current" supply, the upper carbon burns faster, and is therefore made thicker than the lower carbon.

The carbon holder has a convenient mechanism for causing the ends of the rods to touch or separate, and for adjusting the position of the arc laterally or vertically. The arc is set up by applying the voltage to the carbons, which are first made to touch, then immediately separated to such a distance that the arc does not hiss.

One effect of the arc is to form a crater at the end of the upper carbon; this crater is the most luminous part of the arc, and it is utilized by sloping the carbons backwards at an angle of about 30°. A rheostat or regulating resistance is included in the circuit for the purpose of adjusting the strength of the current.

The voltage, which depends on that of the supply mains, may be from 50 to 500, but a low voltage is more economical as a pressure of 50 volts is all that is required to pass the requisite current through the arc. In a "hand-feed" arc, the carbons are adjusted by hand from time to time as required.

Lime light is produced by projecting against a cylinder of lime a very hot flame obtained by burning the gases oxygen and coal gas together. The lime is raised to a white heat, and becomes a source of great luminosity. The lime cylinder on its holder takes the place of the electric arc within the lantern body.

The gases are carried in steel cylinders at a maximum pressure of 1800 lb. per square inch. The cylinders hold from 6 to 40 cubic feet of gas, and are provided with pressure gauges and pressure regulators, which ensure uniform pressure and enable the jets to be turned down or turned off at the lantern. The consumption of gas is about 3 cubic feet per hour. The gases are led by rubber tubing to a double jet which when lit plays on the lime cylinder. The coal gas may be taken direct from gas mains, or hydrogen gas may be used instead.

Lime-light lanterns have been employed in theatres for illuminating purposes, and hence has arisen the use of the phrase "in the lime light"; but the more convenient electric illuminant has displaced this method of lighting almost entirely. The optical lantern is also employed to project images of opaque objects (episcopic projection). This is done by means of the light reflected from the object; the latter requires very strong illumination, and the rays from it are passed through the objective as in the previously described (diascopic) method.

When combined with the microscope, the optical lantern forms a projection microscope which enables a number of spectators to see simultaneously a microscopic section or other small object. The lantern may also be adapted for exhibiting the working of various physical and chemical experiments in the lecture room. (*See also* CINEMATOGRAPH.)—BIBLIOGRAPHY: Lewis Wright, *Optical Projection*; Colin N. Bennett and others, *Handbook of Kinematography.*

OPTICS. The science of light and vision. The subject is treated under such headings as LIGHT and LENS, where other references are given. The present article contains some theoretical matter which may be usefully read in connection with LENS.

An *optical system* is a combination of lenses or mirrors or both, made for the purpose of obtaining images of objects. In a perfect optical system the first condition to be fulfilled is that every object point shall have one definite corresponding image point; or, in other words, that a system of rays diverging from, or converging to, a point before entering the system, shall diverge from, or converge to, another point after passing through the system. In actual combinations of lenses, this condition is sometimes satisfied to a high degree of approximation, but never rigorously.

The process of image formation may be illustrated by the example of a single-bi-convex lens of glass. Let the lens be bounded by two spherical

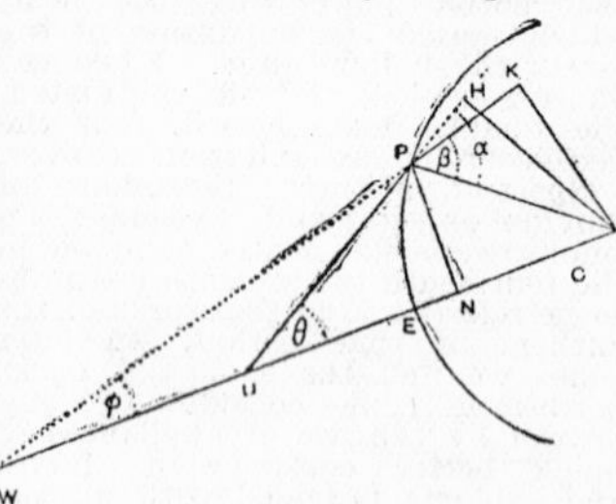

FIG. 1

surfaces, (1) with centre C and radius r, (2) with centre D and radius s. Let a ray starting from an object point U meet the surface (1) at P. According to the law of refraction (q.v.) the ray will be bent towards the normal PC, and if PK is the line which it takes in the glass, we shall have $\sin\alpha = \mu \sin\beta$, where μ is the index refraction from air to glass.

If CH is perpendicular to UP, CK to PK, and PN to UC, this gives $UC \sin\theta = \mu \cdot WC \sin\varphi$, or $UC \cdot PN/UP = \mu \cdot WC \cdot PN/WP$, or $UC/UP = \mu \cdot WC/WP$. Let us now suppose that the pencil of rays of which UP is one is very thin, so that the angle PUC is not more than 2° or 3°. Then, very approximately, UP = UE, and WP = WE. We thus have $UC/UE = \mu \cdot WC/WE$. Let $UE = u$, $WE = w$; then $(u+r)/u = \mu(w+r)/w$, or $1/u - \mu/w = (\mu-1)/r$ . . . (A). Every ray such as UP therefore very approximately passes after refraction through the point W in CU, given by (A).

We have next to consider in the

same way what happens to the pencil through W, after refraction at the surface (2). If the ray WP after refraction at (2) takes a line meeting WD at V, then, by the method already used, $VD/VG = \mu \cdot WD/WG$. If $VG = v$, $WG = w'$, this gives $\mu/w' - 1/v = (\mu - 1)/s$ . . . (B). A small pencil of rays through W therefore passes through V after refraction. Hence the original pencil through U becomes a pencil through V after passing through the lens.

If the lens is very small we may take $w' = w$. By adding (A) and (B) we then get:

$1/u - 1/v = (\mu - 1)\ (1/r + 1/s)$ . . . (C).

Denote the reciprocal of the expression on the right of (C) by f; then $1/f = (\mu - 1\ (1/r + 1/s)$ . . . (D), and $1/u - 1/v = 1/f$ . . . (E). We see from (E) that when v is infinite, $u = f$;

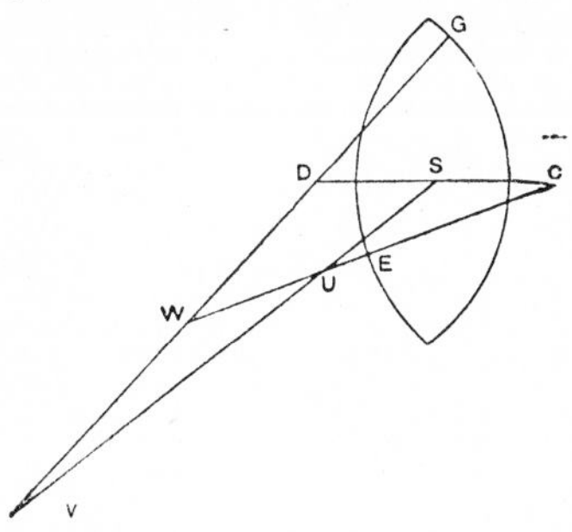

FIG. 2

hence rays proceeding from a point at distance f from the lens become parallel. Similarly when u is infinite $v = -f$; hence a parallel beam converges to a point at distance f on the other side of the lens; the *focal length* of the lens is therefore f as given by (D). *Any* ray through U passes through V after its two refractions.

Take as a special case a ray in the line VU. After the refractions this ray continues to pass through V, and therefore proceeds, according to our approximation, on its original line. Now it can be shown by geometry that a ray, which after emergence from the lens continues in a line parallel to its original line, must pass through a centre of similitude of the two spherical surfaces, which here is a point dividing DC in the ratio of the radii. This point S is the *optical centre* of the lens; for a thin lens it is the point where the axis DC cuts the lens. Hence V is found when U is given from the two conditions that V is the line US, and that VS ($=v$) and US ($=u$) are connected by the relation (E). These are the facts which are assumed for the construction of the diagrams in the article LENS.

OPTIMISM. The antithesis of pessimism; the tendency to look upon everything in the most favourable light. Emotional optimism, to be distinguished from philosophical or systematic optimism, is instinctive, and depends greatly upon temperament.

A man is an optimist, and always inclined to look upon the hopeful, bright side of life, because he is organically so constituted, i.e. is born with an optimistic disposition. Such an emotional optimist is not free from a certain amount of egoism, as the fact of the endless suffering of numerous beings does not disturb his equanimity and happy disposition.

In philosophy, optimism is the doctrine which maintains that the universe, in spite of the apparent imperfections and the evil in it, is the best, and could not be otherwise than it is. In his *Théodicée* Leibnitz, referring to the objections of Bayle, endeavoured to show that among the possible worlds which presented themselves to His infinite intelligence, God has chosen and created the one which He considered to be the best.

What appears imperfect in the world when considered by itself, is by no means so when considered with regard to the whole. If this world were not the best then either the omnipotence or the perfect benevolence of God would have to be denied. Leibnitz's theory was developed and even exaggerated by Pope in his famous *Essay on Man*, and severely criticized and ridiculed by Voltaire in his philosophical novel *Candide*.

Among ancient philosophers, Democritus was a decided optimist, Heraclitus a pessimist. Plato and Plotinus were optimists. The latter went so far as to maintain that prisons, wars, epidemics, and death were all very good and useful for humanity. Socrates, and to a certain extent Aristotle, were optimists. Among modern philosophers, Descartes, Spinoza, and above all Leibnitz, were optimists.—BIBLIOGRAPHY: Sir L. Stephen, *History of English Thought in the 18th Century*; Guttmacher, *Optimism and Pessimism in the Old and New Testaments*; J. Sully, *Pessimism*.

OPTOPHONE. An instrument the purpose of which is to enable the blind to read ordinary printed matter, such as books or newspapers. This is accomplished by producing in a telephone receiver a series of musical notes forming what one may call musical motifs representing the various letters as these are passed over by the instrument in traversing a line of printing. The sense of hearing is thus used instead of the sense of sight.

FIG. 1.—Optophone in use

The instrument is the invention of Dr. E. E. Fournier d'Albe, and has been developed by Messrs. Barr & Stroud, Limited, Glasgow. It depends for its action upon a very remarkable property of selenium, a chemical element (discovered in 1817 by the Swedish chemist Berzelius) which, in its grey crystalline form, varies greatly in electrical conductivity in accordance with the amount of light to which it is exposed, though the resistance is always high.

The full effect of light on the conductivity of grey selenium is not attained instantaneously by any means. But, though it takes a comparatively long time (some minutes) for the light to produce its maximum effect, a measurable and useful variation in the conductivity takes place in periods of exposure and eclipse as short as $\frac{1}{1000}$th or even $\frac{1}{10000}$th of a second.

Instruments can therefore be constructed that can detect pulsations of light of periods corresponding to those of the vibrations in audible sounds. A properly prepared selenium bridge connected in series with a battery and a telephone receiver, and exposed to illumination and eclipse alternating some hundreds of times per second, causes corresponding pulsations of current through the telephone, and produces audible sound of corresponding pitch and quality.

In the optophone the printed page to be read is placed face downwards on a glass plate supported on a suitable stand (*see* figs. 1 and 2, general view and diagram). Beneath the plate is placed a tablet of porcelain pierced with an aperture to permit the passage of a small pencil of light upwards, and so through the glass on to the paper. The upper surface of the tablet, around the aperture, is prepared as a sensitive selenium bridge, and connected to a battery and a telephone.

The bridge receives only light reflected from the page. The illumination of the bridge is thus much greater when the pulsating light falls on a white part of the page than it is when the light falls on a black part, i.e. on a portion of a letter.

The light used in the optophone is obtained from a small straight-filament electric lamp (an ordinary "festoon" lamp). Through the intervention of a perforated disc kept in rapid rotation by a tiny magneto-electric motor, the light that falls on the printed matter forms five bright spots, forming what is called the "scala." Each spot is pulsating at a rate corresponding to the number of holes in the circle of perforations to which it belongs, multiplied by the number of revolutions per second of the disc.

Thus, if there be 18 holes in the innermost circle, 24, 27, 30, and 36 in the other circles respectively, and the disc makes 540 divided by 24—about 22—revolutions per second, the second circle of holes will produce 540 pulsations of light—corresponding to the note C′. The numbers of holes given above are in proportion to the vibrations in the notes G, C′, D′, E′, G′ (soh, doh, ray, me, soh).

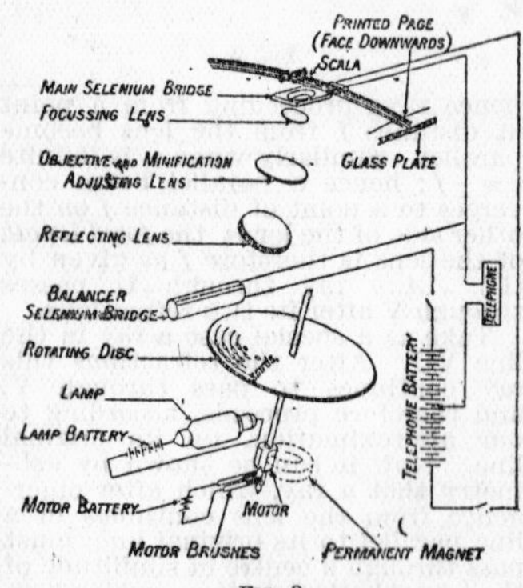

FIG. 2

A change in the speed of rotation of the disc of course alters the pitch of the notes, but the intervals remain unaltered. A faster or slower rotation of the disc than that supposed only alters the key. Too high or too low a pitch lessens the audibility of the note for a given intensity of light.

OPUN'TIA. A genus of plants of the Cactus order, having stems consisting of flat joints, broader above than below, but ultimately in process of growth losing this appearance. Their native country is South America. Many have handsome flowers, and some of them yield a pleasant subacid fruit. *O. Tuna* and *O. coccinellifera* are cultivated for the cochineal insect. *O. vulgaris* is the prickly-pear, and *O. Ficus indica* the Indian fig. *See* INDIAN FIG ; PRICKLY-PEAR.

ORACH, or **ORACHE** (or'ach). The popular name of several British plants of the genus Atriplex, ord. Chenopodiaceæ, plants with mealy foliage, generally growing near the sea. A cultivated species (*A. hortensis*) is known as garden or mountain spinach, being used like spinach.

OR'ACLES (Lat. *orare,* to pray). The places where the gods of the Greeks, Romans, and Egyptians gave responses to the inquiries of worshippers. The term was also applied to the answers themselves which the gods were supposed to give, by words uttered or otherwise, to those who consulted them upon any occasion. The credit of oracles was so great that vast numbers flocked to them for advice. Scarcely any war was waged, or peace concluded, or new form of government instituted, or new laws enacted, without the advice and approbation of some oracle.

The Greek oracles were the most celebrated, the earliest being that of Zeus (Jupiter) at Dodona. Of the other gods Apollo had many oracles, but that at Delphi held the first place, and it was often applied to for explaining obscure answers obtained at Dodona. Another famous oracle of Apollo was in the Island of Delos.

The Romans had no important oracles of their own, but had recourse to those of Greece and Egypt. The early Christians ascribed the oracles in general to the operation of the devil and his agents ; but the practices of the priests, the manner and circumstances of delivering the oracles, the ambiguity of their answers, and the art of accommodating them to all events, amply demonstrate their human origin ; yet they long maintained their standing, and sunk only with the freedom and independence of Greece. Under the reign of Theodosius the temples of the prophetic deities were shut up or demolished.

ORADIA MARE. The modern name of the Rumanian city formerly known as Grosswardein (q.v.).

ORAN (Ar. *Wahran,* a ravine). A fortified seaport and French naval torpedo-station, the second city of Algeria, on the Gulf of Oran ; capital of the department of Oran, and served by railway (250 miles) from Algiers. Esparto grass, wine, cattle, cereals, hides, and minerals are exported. Oran was built by the Moors, taken by Spain (1509), and held by them until 1792. France took possession in 1830. Pop. (1931), 163,743.

ORAN. A maritime department of Algeria, on the Mediterranean ; area, 23,500 sq. miles ; pop. (1931), 1,436,661.

ORANG', or **ORANG-UTAN** (*Simia satyrus*). One of the anthropoid or

Orang-Utans (*Simia satyrus*)

man-like apes or monkeys. This animal seems to be largely confined to Borneo and Sumatra. It is one of those animals which approach most nearly to man, being in this respect only inferior to the chimpanzee and gorilla. It is utterly incapable of walking in a perfectly erect posture.

Its body is covered with coarse hair of a brownish-red colour ; in some places on its back it is 6 inches long, and on its arms 5 inches. The face is destitute of hair save at the sides. It attains the height of from 4 to 5 feet, measured in a straight line from the vertex to the heel. The arms reach to the ankle-joint. The hind-legs are short and stunted, the nails of the fingers and toes flattened.

They swing themselves along from tree to tree by the aid of their long arms, but their gait on the ground is awkward and unsteady. At birth the head of the orang resembles that of the young child. These apes are remarkable for strength and intelligence, and capable of being highly domesticated if captured young. They feed chiefly on fruits, and sleep on trees. *See* MAN; APES; MONKEYS.

ORANGE. The fruit of the *Citrus Aurantium*, and the shrub or tree itself, nat. ord. Rutaceæ. The orange is indigenous in China, India, and other Asiatic countries, and was first introduced into Portugal about 1520. It is now extensively cultivated in Southern Europe. In Portugal and Spain the fruit forms an important article of commerce. Large quantities are also produced in the Azores, in Africa, America (especially in Florida), and the West Indies, in Australia, and the Pacific Islands.

The tree is a middle-sized evergreen, with a greenish-brown bark. The leaves are ovate, acute, pointed, and at the base of the petiole are winged. The white flower exhibits a calyx with five divisions, a corolla with five imbricate petals, stamens equal in number to the petals or a multiple of them, and along with the petals inserted on a hypogynous disc, the filaments being united in several bundles.

The fruit is globose, bright-yellow, and contains a pulp which consists of a collection of oblong vesicles filled with a sugary and refreshing juice; it is divided into eight or ten compartments, each usually containing several seeds. The principal varieties are the common sweet or China orange, the bitter or Seville, the Maltese or red-pulped, the Tangerine, the Mandarin or clove, and the St. Michael's. The leaves, flowers, and rind yield fragrant oils much used in perfumery and for flavouring essences. The wood is fine-grained, compact, susceptible of a high polish, and is employed in the arts. The citron and lemon are allied fruits.

ORANGE (ancient **Arausio**). A town of South-Eastern France, in the department of Vaucluse, and on the Meyne; served by the Paris-Lyons-Mediterranean line from Lyons to Marseilles. It is celebrated for its Roman remains, including a triumphal arch erected in honour of Tiberius, and a theatre of the period of Hadrian, restored in 1894.

Arausio was the capital of the Cavari, and here the Cimbri and Teutones defeated a Roman army in 105 B.C. In the eleventh century it became the capital of a countship, and passed as the Principality of Orange to the House of Nassau (sixteenth century), giving name to the Orange family who were subsequently rulers of the Netherlands and of England. By the death of William III. the principality passed to France, through Prussia (Treaty of Utrecht, 1713). Pop. 11,080.

ORANGE. A city of New Jersey, United States, in Essex county, a terminal station of the Orange branch of the Erie Railroad, and served also by a branch of the Delaware, Lackawanna, & Western Railroad, and by electric lines to South Orange and Newark. It is within easy distance (14 miles west) of New York City, and contains the mansions of many business men. The local hats are celebrated. Orange was settled in 1670, and became a city in 1872. Pop. (1930), 35,399.

East Orange is a residential city formed from part of Orange in 1863. It became a city in 1899. Pop. 54,000.—**West Orange** is 12 miles from New York on the Erie Railroad, and is also a residential town formed from Orange proper in 1862. Thomas Alva Edison's laboratories are at West Orange. Pop. about 16,000.

ORANGE-BIRD (*Spindalis nigricephala*), a Jamaican bird, one of the tanagers, so called from its orange-coloured breast.

ORANGE FREE STATE. An inland province of the Union of South Africa, lying between the Vaal and Orange Rivers, and, like the Transvaal, forming a part of the South African Plateau. It is a great grass-covered plain traversed by stark rivers and hills of dolerite or ironstone. The rivers are tributaries of the Vaal for the most part, and they run in a north-westerly direction.

From the north they are the Klip, Wilge, Rhenoster, Valsh, Zand or Vet, Modder, Riet, and the Orange itself, from Aliwal North. Parallel to the watershed there is the Caledon, and on the north-west there is the Vaal, parallel to the Caledon. Bloemfontein is the capital (pop. 1921, 39,034); Eur. pop. 1931, 28,496.

Social Conditions.—The climate is healthy. The Dutch Reformed Church is the predominant religious body, and an equivalent number of coloured persons have no religion. Lower and secondary education is controlled by the Province, higher instruction by the Union. Fees are charged at all schools, and except where parents object instruction is bilingual (English and Dutch).

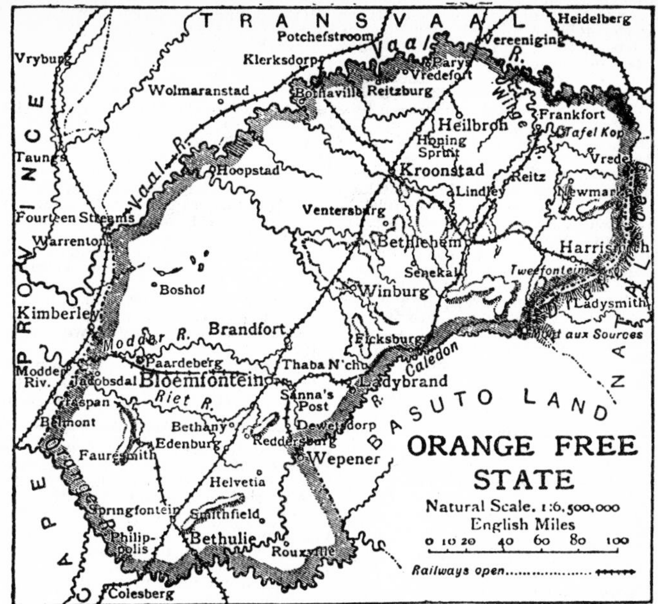

There are secondary schools in all towns, and a Normal College and a Polytechnic College in addition.

Production.—A great, rolling plain with an annual rainfall of 22 inches, the Orange Free State is suitable for dry farming, and large areas are covered with mealie fields and (in the Basuto borderland) with wheat. Terrible droughts occur, when the entire country is denuded of vegetation. The main industry is stock-raising, cattle and horses doing well, and sheep fairly in the flats towards the Orange River.

The mineral wealth of the province consists mainly of diamonds; these are either in "dry diggings" (i.e. mines working volcanic pipes, such as Jagersfontein and Koffeefontein) or "river diggings" (i.e. alluvial claims along the Vaal River, chiefly round Christiania in the Boshof country). The coal area lies north of Kroonstad.

Currency, etc.—The coinage is British, as are the weights and measures; the land measure is the Morgen, equal to $2\frac{1}{10}$ acres approximately.

Area, etc.—The area is 49,647 sq. miles. The pop. in 1921 was 628,827, of whom 188,758 were white, representing an intercensal increase of more than 13,000 on the white population of 1911. Political leadership in the State was in the hands of General Hertzog ('96), the leader of the Dutch Nationalists, forming an overwhelming proportion of the inhabitants. White pop. by 1931 census was 205,324.

See SOUTH AFRICA; BOERS; TRANSVAAL; DE WET.

BIBLIOGRAPHY: A. H. Keene, *Africa* (vol. ii.); Chr. de Wet, *Three Years' War* (1899-1902).

ORANGE-LILY (*Lilium bulbiferum*), a species of lily having a scaly bulb, a leafy stem $2\frac{1}{2}$ feet high, small dark-brown bulbs in the axils of the leaves, and large orange-coloured flowers.

ORANGEMEN. Members of the Orange Institution deriving their name from William III. (the Prince of Orange). This Institution is composed of Irish Protestants, united to support and defend the rightful sovereign, the Protestant religion, the laws of the Realm, the Legislative Union, and the succession to the throne in the House of Windsor being Protestant; and united further for the defence of their own persons and properties, and the maintenance of the public peace.

It is exclusively an association of those who are attached to the Protestant religion, but is essentially a political organization, its object being primarily to maintain the Protestant ascendancy in Ulster.

The Orange Institution was formed on the evening of the day on which the battle of the Diamond was fought, 21st Sept., 1795. It grew rapidly, and continued to grow during the period of intense political excitement aroused by the introduction of the Home Rule scheme for Ireland. Its home was in Ulster, and it has always been strongest there in proportion to the number of inhabitants, but it has spread all over Great Britain and the colonies, being especially active in Canada.

Mr. Asquith's proposals for Home Rule had the effect of greatly increasing the membership of the order, and naturally the division of the country into two parts, under separate governments, has not tended to weaken its influence in the six counties (Ulster) or to endear it to the Irish Free State (q.v.). The order now admits women. The Orange Institution is organized upon a basis somewhat similar to that of freemasonry. Every member must belong to a private lodge, which must meet once a month. Higher branches of the organization are the District Lodge, meeting once a quarter; the County Grand Lodge, meeting twice a year; the Grand Lodge of Ireland, meeting twice a year; and the Imperial Grand Lodge.

Candidates for admission to the order must be over eighteen years of age, must be loyal to the king, must be Protestants and, if married, married to Protestant wives, and must promise to defend the Constitution, support the civil power, and be faithful to other Orangemen. Six months after his admission (twelve months after his admission if he be under twenty years of age) an Orangeman may be admitted to the higher degree of Purple.

The Institution of Royal Black Knights of Ireland forms in effect a higher branch of the Orange Institution, though the two organizations are independent of one another and controlled by totally different officials. Every candidate for admission as a Black Knight must be a Purpleman of at least six months' standing. There are twelve degrees in the Black order, the highest of them all being that of Red Cross. Black Knights sit in Preceptories, not Lodges, and their secretary is called a Registrar.

Every Orangeman is bound to wear regalia when sitting in his Lodge, and when attending an Orange procession or the funeral of a brother Orangeman. It is customary to wear a collar when in the Lodge, and a sash on other occasions. The anniversaries kept by the Institution are the 5th Nov., the day both of the Gunpowder Plot and of the landing of William III. at Torbay, and the 12th July.

The 12th July is actually the anniversary of the battle of Aughrim, but, by a confusion between the old and new styles, it is sometimes regarded as the anniversary of the battle of the Boyne, which was fought on 1st July, old style.

ORANGE RIVER, or **GARIEP.** The largest river of South Africa, rising in the Drakensberg, forming part of the north boundary of Cape Province and the Orange Free State, and falling after a total course of about 650 miles into the Atlantic. Its tributary, the Vaal, forms the southern boundary of the Transvaal.

ORANGE ROOT (*Hydrastis canadensis*), a plant of the ord. Ranunculaceæ, found in Canada and the northern United States, with a thick underground perennial stem yielding a yellow dye.

ORATO'RIO. An oratorio is a musical setting for voices and orchestra of a sacred story, and includes recitatives, arias, duets, trios, etc., and choruses, with orchestral introduction or overture and possibly occasional interludes. A certain measure of the dramatic element is implied in its general plan, but the most typical examples of oratorio contain a large proportion of numbers of a purely contemplative nature.

A stage representation is not intended, though it has been tried at least once, when Mendelssohn's *Elijah* was produced as a sacred opera. The enterprise was rewarded with only a qualified success. In its origin, however, oratorio had been associated with the stage, for it was originally the outcome of plays on Biblical subjects which, in combination with simple incidental music, had been introduced by Filippo Neri towards the close of the sixteenth century as a means of deepening the power and effect of religious instruction.

These sacred performances were given in the Oratory of Santa Maria at Rome, of which Filippo Neri was the founder, hence the name oratorio.

The term was not immediately adopted, the earliest of these sacred works being generally referred to as "sacred dramas with music."

As in the case of opera, the Italians, though they had originated the oratorio, were not able to carry it to its fullest development. This great work was reserved for Germany. Early in the seventeenth century Heinrich Schütz went from Saxony to Venice to study music, and imbibing there all the latest tendencies, returned to his native land and applied them, with all the sincerity of a deeply religious nature, to the composition of settings of the Resurrection and the Passion.

Nearly a hundred years later Johann Sebastian Bach perfected the work by producing among many other fine examples of sacred music his wonderful setting of the Passion according to St. Matthew, universally acknowledged as the greatest oratorio which has ever been written.

In this immortal work the story is related by various solo voices, with the chorus taking the part of the crowd, while reflections on the various incidents of the story are beautifully conveyed by solos, duets, choruses, and especially by chorales, harmonized with consummate art and intended in performance to be taken part in by the congregation.

The people of this country have always had a strong affection for the oratorio form, and when Handel, after a long career as a purveyor of Italian opera, turned his attention to it, he found a speedy recognition for what was generally felt to be his true *métier*. Most of his oratorios have a preponderating amount of the dramatic element, but it is noteworthy that the *Messiah*, which is the most universally popular musical work in this country, is entirely contemplative in character.

Many oratorios have been written by British composers and also by foreign composers for British festivals. In the latter class the outstanding example is Mendelssohn's *Elijah*, written for the Birmingham Festival in 1846. Among native works first place must certainly be given to the sacred choral works of Sir Edward Elgar. *The Dream of Gerontius*, *The Apostles*, etc., are works of which any nation may well be proud.—BIBLIOGRAPHY: Grove's *Dictionary of Music and Musicians*, article "Oratorio" (vol. iii.); A. W. Patterson, *The Story of Oratorio*; Robert Turnbull, *Musical Genius and Religion*.

ORBICULI'NA. A genus of minute foraminifers, found alive in tropical seas, as also fossil in the tertiaries. They have their name from their flattened globular shape.

ORBIT. In astronomy, the path of a planet or comet; the curve-line which a planet describes in its periodical revolution round its central body. The orbits of the planets are elliptical, having the sun in one of the foci; and the planets all move in these ellipses by this law, that a straight line drawn from the centre of the sun to the centre of any one of them, termed the *radius vector*, always describes equal areas in equal times. Also, the squares of the times of the planetary revolutions are as the cubes of their mean distances from the sun.

The satellites also move in elliptical orbits, having their respective primaries in one of the foci. The *elements of an orbit* are those quantities by which its position, form, and magnitude, for the time, are determined; such as the major axis and eccentricity, the longitude of the node, the inclination of the plane to the ecliptic, and the longitude of the perihelion.

ORCAGNA (or-kán'yá), **Andrea di Cione.** One of the greatest of the early Florentine artists after Giotto, born in 1308, supposed to have died in 1368. He was the son of a goldsmith, who instructed the boy in the rudiments of his art. Painting, sculpture, architecture, and mosaic work were all within the sphere of his artistic genius; and his productions compare favourably with the best of a period so rich and distinguished in the art of Italy.

As a painter he executed the beautiful frescoes in the Strozzi chapel in Santa Maria Novella at Florence; the chapel San Michele and its magnificent tabernacle in the same city are grand memorials of his architectural and sculptural talent. His style is remarkable for exquisite design, graceful pose, and delicate execution. Boccaccio has perpetuated his name in his *Decamerone*. His *Coronation of the Virgin* is in the National Gallery, London.

ORCHARDSON, Sir William Quiller. British painter, born in Edinburgh in 1835, died in 1910. He exhibited in the Royal Scottish Academy till 1862, and then removed to London. He became A.R.A. in 1868, full Academician in 1879, and was knighted in 1907. He was among the first painters of his day, a fine colourist, and most of his works are skilfully dramatic and picturesque. Among his more notable pictures are: *The Challenge*, *Christopher Sly*, *The Queen of the Swords*, *Napoleon on Board the*

"*Bellerophon*," *Un Mariage de convenance*, *Salon of Mme. Récamier*, *The First Cloud*, and *The Young Duke*.

ORCHELLA (or-kel'á). Name of several species of Roccella, a genus of lichens, originally brought from the Levant, and employed from very early times as a dye agent. Large quantities are gathered in the maritime rocks of the Canary and Cape Verde Islands. A purple and a red dye, known as orchil or archil, are prepared from them.

ORCHESTRA. Of all man's achievements in music the modern full orchestra is from some points of view the most wonderful, summing up in the various instruments which compose it so much of mechanical ingenuity, and offering to the thoroughly equipped composer possibilities in the way of colour combination and consequently of musical eloquence which are almost without limit.

Like all similar achievements it is the result of a long process of evolution, the earlier stages of which may be briefly traced. The first attempts at constituting an orchestra in the modern sense are coeval with the beginning of dramatic music, and date, therefore, from the early years of the seventeenth century.

Monteverdi, the outstanding operatic composer of that time, by greatly increasing the number of instruments in his accompaniments, and especially by introducing for the first time so large a proportion of stringed instruments played with a bow, must be regarded as the chief among the pioneers. But neither he nor his contemporaries had any fixed idea regarding the instruments most appropriate to be used, nor the relative proportions of the various tone-families which would give the desired results.

These all-important matters could only be decided by time and experience, and it is possible to trace with fair completeness the gradual evolution from a heterogeneous collection of instruments to that ordered and stable arrangement which Haydn and Mozart always employed, and which is the essential part of the huge orchestras of to-day.

The full modern orchestra is made up of four distinct sections, comprising respectively the stringed instruments, the wood-wind instruments, the brass instruments, and the percussion instruments. The first three of these sections or families contain within themselves instruments of high, medium, and low pitch approximating in general to the soprano, contralto, tenor, and bass of an ordinary choir, and so are able at any time to stand alone and render a complete account of the musical scheme.

In the string section the four voices are represented roughly by first violins, second violins, violas, and 'cellos and double basses, and among them they include a range of about six octaves. They are always present in considerable numbers in an orchestra of symphonic proportions, and the four parts which they normally represent are frequently multiplied by subdivision, especially in modern scores.

Further, they are capable of greater technical execution than any other instruments, and for these various reasons are always regarded as the fundamental section of the orchestra. In the wood-wind department the four "voices" are represented roughly by flutes, oboes, clarinets, and bassoons, while in the brass-wind section the instruments are trumpets, horns, trombones, and tubas; but it should be understood that in all three departments the analogy with the four voices of a chorus is only partial.

All instruments have a wider range than any voice, and in many cases there are very striking and important differences of tone-quality in different parts of the compass, and the qualified composers know how to use these in giving the fullest possible expression to their musical ideas. Thus the topmost range of the 'cello is admirably suited for certain types of melody, and will frequently be found sounding above the violas, or even the violins. This overlapping of the various instruments for purposes of colour-effect is specially prevalent in writing for the wood-wind group.

The percussion instruments include the drums, cymbals, triangle, bells, gong, etc., and are mainly used to emphasize the rhythm. Only the timpani, or kettledrums, and the bells give sounds of definite pitch.

Such instruments as the piccolo, sounding an octave higher than the flute, the cor-anglais, sounding a fifth lower than the oboe, the bass-clarinet and the double bassoon, sounding an octave lower than their prototypes, and the tubas, the lowest of the brass instruments, are not always written for, but their use is quickly becoming universal, as is already the custom of writing for three each of the wood-wind group and four of trumpets and horns. The harp is also a regular constituent of the modern orchestra.

Notable British orchestras are the Hallé Orchestra, Manchester, the London Symphony Orchestra, the

B.B.C. Orchestra, and the Scottish Orchestra.—BIBLIOGRAPHY: Grove's *Dictionary of Music and Musicians*, article "Orchestra" (vol. iii.), also "Instrumentation" (vol.ii.); Hamilton Clarke, *A Manual of Orchestration* (popular); W. H. Daly, *The Concert-Goer: a Handbook of the Orchestra and Orchestral Music*; Cecil Forsyth, *Orchestration* (the best and most up-to-date work on the subject); Prout, *The Orchestra* (2 vols.).

ORCHHA (orch-hă'), or **URCHHA.** A native state of Central India. It lies to the south of the British district of Jhansi, between that district and Chhatarpur; area, 2079 sq. miles; pop. 284,948. The chief towns are Tehri, the present capital, and Orchha, the old capital. Pop. of latter, 4000.

ORCHIDACEÆ (or-ki-dā'sē-ē), or **ORCHIDS.** An extensive order of monocotyledons (nearly 2000 species being known), consisting of herbaceous plants or shrubs, with fibrous or tuberous roots; a short stem or a pseudo-bulb; entire, often sheathing leaves; and showy flowers, with a perianth of six segments in two rows, mostly coloured, one, the lowest, generally differing in form from the rest, and known as the *labellum*. The essential organs are combined into a central *column*, which is the most characteristic feature of the flower.

Normally only one stamen is fertile (two in Cypripedium), and the pollen is aggregated into a pair (rarely two or four pairs) of club-shaped pollen-

Orchid

Orchis: Bee Orchis

masses (*pollinia*). The unilocular inferior ovary contains an immense number of ovules attached to three parietal placentæ.

The pollination arrangements of orchids are very extraordinary (cf. Darwin, *Fertilization of Orchids*). They are natives of all countries, but very cold and dry climates produce but few species; some of them grow in the ground, but a large number are epiphytes, growing upon trees; and it is above all in the great virgin forests of South America and of the East Indies that the orchids abound.

The orchids attract much attention, and are cultivated with zeal on account of the beauty or curious shapes of the flowers (which often assume the forms of reptiles, insects, and other denizens of the animal kingdom), or for their not unfrequently fragrant smells.

The cultivation of orchids has of recent years become very fashionable, large sums being often paid for new or rare varieties. The nutritive substance called salep is prepared from the roots and tubers of several species; the fragrant vanilla is obtained from two species of a genus of that name.

ORCHIS. The typical genus of the ord. Orchidaceæ, comprising hardy perennials with tuberous fleshy roots, containing much starch;

natives of Europe, temperate Asia, and a few of North America. There are several British species with showy reddish-purple or pale-pink flowers. *O. mascŭla* yields salep. See ORCHIDACEÆ.

ORCIN, ORCINOL, or DIHYDROXYTOLUENE ($C_7H_8O_2$). A substance obtained from certain lichens, e.g. orchella weed, etc., by boiling with lime and water and extracting with ether. Orcin is a colourless crystalline compound soluble in water; its ammoniacal solution readily absorbs oxygen from the air and becomes purple in colour, and on the addition of acetic acid to this solution a red colouring-matter, *orcein*, is precipitated, which is one of the colouring-matters of the dyes prepared from lichens.

ORCZY, Baroness Emmusca. Pen name of Mrs. Montagu Barstow, novelist and playwright. Born at Tarnaörs in Hungary, she was educated at Brussels and Paris, and began writing in 1900 with *The Old Man in the Corner*, a series of detective stories. In 1905 she wrote *The Scarlet Pimpernel.* Two other plays appeared in 1910 and 1918, *Beau Brocade* and *The Legion of Honour*. She is the author of numerous novels, several being sequels to *The Scarlet Pimpernel*, which has been dramatized.

ORDEAL TREE. A name of two poisonous trees: *Erythrophlœum guineense* of Guinea and *Tanghinia venenōsa* of Madagascar. See ERYTHROPHLŒUM; TANGHIN.

ORDER. In zoology and botany, a subdivision of a class or large division of animals or plants, which, although agreeing in the characters common to the whole class, yet are more closely allied by some special features. Thus in the class Mammalia we have the order of the Primates, including lemurs, monkeys, apes, and men; in the class of Insecta we have the order of Lepidoptera, moths, and butterflies; in the class of Monocotyledonous Plants the order Liliaceæ; etc. An order of flowering plants is divided into tribes, which may be grouped in suborders; while an animal order is made up of families.

ORDERI'CUS VITA'LIS. An Anglo-Norman chronicler, born in the neighbourhood of Shrewsbury in 1075, his mother being English, his father a French priest. He received his education in the Abbey of St. Evroul (Normandy), where the name Vitalis was conferred on him, and in due time he became a priest. He wrote in Latin an ecclesiastical history in thirteen books, from the birth of Christ down to his own time. The later books are a valuable contribution to history, as they offer a good description of the life and times of William the Conqueror, of William II., and of the first of the Crusades. He died after 1143.

ORDER OF MERIT. A very exclusive British order instituted by King Edward VII. on 26th June, 1902. The order carries with it no special title or precedence, but those who have received it have the right to put the letters O.M. after their names. The badge consists of a red enamel gold cross, patée convexed, with the words "For Merit" in gold letters within a laurel wreath on a blue enamel centre. On the reverse side is the imperial and royal cipher on a blue ground.

The badge is surmounted by an imperial crown, and is suspended by a parti-coloured ribbon, half blue and half crimson. Naval or military recipients of the order have two silver crossed swords with gold hilts, placed saltirewise between the angles of the cross. The badge is not worn in miniature, neither is the ribbon sewn on the coat, for the regulations lay down that officers in uniform are to wear the badge round the neck on all occasions.

ORDERS, Military. Fraternities or societies of men banded together in former times for military and partly for patriotic or Christian purposes. Free birth and an irreproachable life were the conditions of admission. The chief were the Templars, the Teutonic Knights, and the Order of St. John of Jerusalem.

ORDERS OF ARCHITECTURE. The chief styles or varieties exhibited in the architecture of the Greeks and Romans. Technically the chief feature of the order is the column—including base, shaft, and capital—and its superincumbent entablature (consisting of architrave, frieze, and cornice).

The character of the order, however, is displayed not only in its column, but in its general forms and detail, of which the column is, as it were, the regulator. There are five classic orders, namely, Grecian:—Doric, Ionic, and Corinthian; Roman:—Tuscan, and Roman or Composite. See ARCHITECTURE; COLUMN.

ORDINAL. The prescribed form of service used at the ordination of clergy, as in the English, Roman Catholic, and Eastern Churches. The ordinal of the English Church was originally drawn up in the time of Edward VI. It was altered to some extent in the reign of Queen Elizabeth, and again revised in 1661.

ORDINARY. In English law, a bishop, or other person having peculiar or original ecclesiastical jurisdiction in a diocese, in contradistinction to extraordinary or delegated jurisdiction. In Scotland the epithet *ordinary* is applied to all the judges in the outer house of the Court of Session, such judges being termed *lords ordinary*; and the sheriff of a county is called the *judge ordinary*. As a nautical term an *ordinary* seaman is one not qualified to take the helm or sail the ship, and is thus distinguished from an *able* seaman.

ORDINATION. The initiating of a Christian minister or priest into his office. The English Church considers ordination as a real consecration; the High Church party maintaining the dogma of the regular transmission of the episcopal office from the apostles down to the bishops of the present day. For ordination in the English Church, subscription to the Thirty-nine Articles is requisite.

The ceremony of ordination is performed by the bishop by the imposition of hands on the person to be ordained. In most Protestant countries with a State Church, ordination is a requisite to preaching; but in some sects it is not held necessary. In the Presbyterian and Congregational Churches ordination means the act of settling a licensed preacher over a congregation, or conferring on him general powers to officiate wherever he may be called.

ORDNANCE DEPARTMENT. In modern times this term is not used in connection with any one branch of the army, but may still be applied conveniently to include a variety of organizations dealing with munitions of war, and all being complementary to each other.

(*a*) The Department of the Master-General of the Ordnance. The fourth military member of the Army Council is known as the Master-General of the Ordnance, and is responsible to the Secretary of State for War for the entire work of his department of the War Office. The department consists of three main divisions, each under its own director, and dealing with (1) artillery, (2) fortification and works, (3) factories.

(*b*) The Ordnance Committee, presided over by an admiral with a senior military officer as vice-president, and having equal numbers of naval and military officers as members. This committee is subject to the Master-General.

(*c*) The Ordnance Factories.

(*d*) The Royal Army Ordnance Corps, comprising the personnel of the corps and organized in sections for home and companies for foreign service. The officers of the corps have the usual military rank, but are classed for departmental purposes as ordnance officers first to fourth class, according to the appointment held.

(*e*) The Royal Army Ordnance Corps establishments include "ordnance central depots," "ammunition depots," and the "Royal Army Clothing Department and Factory," and it is in this last only that the Royal Army Ordnance Corps appears in the rôle of manufacturer. The "ordnance factories" proper, as in (*c*), are to all intents and purposes civil departments, and the R.A.O.C. deals only with the finished products much as does the wholesale firm in civil life.

In the case of the clothing department, however, it is both manufacturing and distributive, all articles of clothing for the troops being manufactured at Pimlico and issued to units on demand. For purposes of supply of ordnance stores in peace-time the country is divided up into areas, each in charge of an officer known as a Deputy Assistant Director of Ordnance Services; in war the same official superintends the work of ordnance depots in the field, and issues ordnance stores and clothing to units.

With regard to the title of the Master-General of the Ordnance, the following extract from Grose's *Military Antiquities* may be of interest as showing that—comparatively at any rate—the duties of the Master-General are on much the same lines now in the days of heavy guns as they were in the time of King Richard III., when the office first originated, and when the principal items of supply were no doubt bows and arrows, battle-axes, and lances. As quoted by Grose, the "Master of the Ordonnance" is to see that the troops "lacke no kynde of municion or such other necessaries which apperteine to the said Mr. of th' Ordonnance."

ORDNANCE SURVEY. The official survey of Great Britain and Ireland, originally instituted under the direction of the Master-General of the Ordnance. The name is also applied to the department of the Civil Service which carries out the work. The first step towards the production of a topographical map of any part of the United Kingdom was taken shortly after the rebellion of 1745, during the course of which the want of a reliable map of the Highlands had been much felt by the Government forces.

A map was made of the Highlands, and one of the rest of Scotland followed. With a view to the production of an accurate map of the whole kingdom, General Roy, in 1783, measured a base on Hounslow Heath, and in 1791 the Ordnance Survey Department came into official existence. When the Board of Ordnance was abolished in 1855, the survey was placed under the War Office.

In 1870 it was transferred to the Board of Works, and in 1890 to the Board (now the Ministry) of Agriculture and Fisheries. The staff consists mainly of officers and men of the Royal Engineers, controlled by a Director-General, with headquarters at Southampton. The survey for the 1-inch map was begun in 1794, and the first sheet was published in 1801. In 1824 the work was transferred to Ireland, where the scale adopted was 6 inches to the mile, a large-scale map being needed for the purposes of land valuation.

The Irish survey was completed in 1840, and in the same year a survey of Great Britain for a map on the 6-inch scale was begun. Work on the scale of 1/2500, or approximately 25 inches to the mile, was commenced in 1854, and sheets to this scale are now available for all cultivated parishes. The 1/2500 map is periodically revised, no sheet being allowed to go more than twenty years out of date.

In England and Scotland the second revision is now going on. A survey for a map of Ireland to the same scale was begun in 1887. The 6-inch map is a reduced copy of the 25-inch, and is itself used as the basis for the 1-inch and smaller scales. The 1-inch map is revised every fifteen years. The smaller maps, with scales ½-inch, ¼-inch, $\frac{1}{10}$-inch, and 1/1,000,000 are made by reduction from the 1-inch. For towns of 4000 or more inhabitants, maps are provided on the scale 1/500.

Scientific surveys have been carried out by the State in nearly all civilized countries. Worthy of special mention are the Coast and Geodetic Survey of the United States, which dates from 1817, and the Trigonometrical Survey of India, which occupied the years from 1832 to 1881. The Geological Survey of the United Kingdom began operations in 1832. Its results are published on the 1-inch Ordnance Survey maps. For practical details *see* SURVEYING.

ORDONNANCES. The name given in France, before the Revolution of 1789, to decrees, edicts, declarations, and regulations issued by the king for regent. From 1789 until the Restoration in 1814 the ordonnances were replaced by decrees of the executive. Since 1848 the term ordonnances has disappeared, and is replaced by *decrees.*

ORDOVICIAN. A name substituted by C. Lapworth, in 1879, for the geological system and period that were previously called Lower Silurian or Upper Cambrian. The Ordovices were a tribe inhabiting North Wales.

ORE. A naturally occurring body which contains a metal or metals in the mineral form, in sufficient quantity and in such a condition as to make its extraction a profitable undertaking on a commercial scale at a given time and place. The commonest are metallic sulphides, e.g. galena and iron pyrites. Oxides and carbonates are also frequently met with.

If the metal occurs in the free state in nature, it is said to be *native.* Metals are commonly obtained from their ores by smelting. Ores are commonly found in veins or lodes. *See* MINING, and the articles on the different metals.

ÖREBRO (*eu'*re-brų). A town of Sweden, capital of the län or county of the same name, at the western extremity of the Hjälmar Lake. It has an old royal castle, now used as a museum, and a considerable trade with Stockholm by the Hjälmar and Maelar Lakes and the Arboga Canal. Örebro is the seat of the principal State Railway workshops, and is an important railway junction. It was once the residence of Gustavus Vasa and of Charles IX. Pop. (1932), 37,968.

OR'EGON. A maritime state in the Pacific division of the United States. It is traversed by the Cascade range (Mount Hood, 11,760 feet). There is a low coast range, and between it and the Cascade range is the valley of the Willamette, which joins the valley of the Columbia River (the northern boundary of the state). Excepting for these two valleys Oregon is everywhere mountainous. The state capital is Salem (pop. 1930, 26,266); other cities are Portland (301,815), Eugene (18,901), Klamath Falls (16,093), Astoria (10,349), and Medford (11,007).

Communications.—There is a railway mileage of 5150, and an additional 540 miles of electric track, the principal systems being the Oregon Railroad and Navigation Company (owned by Union Pacific), the Southern Pacific, and the Astoria & Columbia River. The Columbia and Snake Rivers are open to navigation up to 570 miles from the sea by means of the Dalles and Celilo Canal (opened 1915). Portland is at the head of sea-borne navigation on the Columbia River.

People.—About one-seventh of the population is foreign born. Indian Reservations occupy (1931) 1756 sq. miles ; pop. 4260, but there are 4776 other Indians within the state. The principal religious bodies are Catholic, Methodist, and Presbyterian.

Production and Industry.—In the Willamette Valley the rainfall is good, and all the crops of a temperate zone are raised. East of the Cascade range the land is semi-arid, but will be considerably improved by irrigation. One-fifth of the standing timber of the United States is found in the Oregon afforested areas, which occupy (1932), 11,939,400 acres. Wheat, oats, barley, root crops, sugar-beet, plums, apples, pears, and, in places, loganberries and strawberries are raised. Fish are abundant, and include the halibut, oyster, salmon, and sturgeon. There is some mineral wealth in gold, silver, and copper, and in coal, granite, lead, gypsum, platinum, and occasional precious stones.

Education, Area, etc.—Education is compulsory between the ages of eight and sixteen years. There is an agricultural college at Corvallis (founded 1870), a university at Eugene (founded 1876), and several denominational colleges. Area, 96,699 sq. miles (1092 sq. miles being water) ; pop. (1930), 953,786.

Government.—Oregon joined the Union on 14th Feb., 1859. There are 36 counties. Modern government consists of a Governor and a Legislative Assembly, comprising a Senate (30 members, elected for four years, one half retiring biennially) and a House of Representatives (60 members, elected for two years). The referendum principle has been adopted with modifications. Two Senators and three Representatives are sent to Congress.—Cf. J. B. Horner, *Oregon: her History, Great Men, and Literature.*

OREL (Russian pron. or-yol′). A province of Russia, south of the Tula and Kaluga ; area, 18,042 sq. miles. Grain, hemp, hops, and tobacco are raised, and live-stock, particularly horses, are extensively reared. Manufactures are chiefly confined to the distillation of spirits. The principal rivers are the Oka, the Desna, and the Sosna. Pop. 2,816,000.

OREL. A town of Central Russia, capital of the province of Orel, at the junction of the Oka and Orlik Rivers ; served by four converging lines of railways, and by canals connecting with the Caspian, the Black Sea, and the Baltic. Pop. 77,895.

O′RENBURG. A province of Russia, partly in Europe and partly in Asia ; area, 73,254 sq. miles ; pop. 2,272,000. A very large part of the surface consists of steppes, but the agricultural districts in the northwest supply large quantities of grain for export. Gold abounds along the whole Ural chain, and there are also copper-, iron-, and salt-mines. The population consists chiefly of the Finnish Votiaks and Tepyaks, and Tartar Bashkirs.

ORENBURG. A town of Eastern Russia, capital of the province of Orenburg, on the Ural ; served by the Orenburg-Tashkent Railway. Soap, candles, and hardware are manufactured, and there is a large trade with Khiva and Bukhàra. Pop. (1926), 129,160.

ORENSE. A mountainous inland province of North-West Spain, traversed by the Minho. Fruit is extensively grown in the temperate valleys, cattle are raised, and iron is mined. It forms the southern portion of the old Kingdom of Galicia. Area, 2694 sq. miles ; pop. (1931), 427,831.

OREN′SE (ancient **Aurium**). **A** city of Spain, capital of the province of Orense, on the Minho, which is crossed by a bridge built in 1230 by Bishop Lorenzo. It is about 1300 feet long and 130 feet high. The cathedral was founded in 1220. Near by are the hot (sulphur) springs of Las Burgos, and the baths of Caldas de Orense, which are known to the Romans. Pop. 21,581.

OREODAPH′NE, or **MOUNTAIN-LAUREL.** A genus of plants of the nat. ord. Lauraceæ. The fruit of *O. opifĕra*, a native of Northern Brazil, yields a volatile oil, which is used as a liniment, and when kept for a short time deposits a quantity of camphor. *O. bullata*, found at the Cape of Good Hope, is called *stinkwood* on account of the disagreeable odour of its wood, which, however, is hard, durable, and takes an excellent polish.

OREODOXA. A genus of tropical American palms. *O. regia* is the royal palm or palmiste, one of the noblest of the tribe; *O. oleracea* is the cabbage palm.

ORES'TES. In Greek mythology, the son of Agamemnon and of Clytemnestra. When his father was murdered, he was saved from a similar fate by his sister Electra. He was sent to Phocis, where he formed an intimate friendship with Pylades, the son of King Strophius. He was then called upon by the Delphian oracle to avenge his father, and hastened to Mycenæ, where he slew Clytemnestra and Ægisthus.

For this murder he was relentlessly pursued by the Eumenides or Furies, and only succeeded in appeasing those terrible goddesses by carrying out the instructions of the Delphian oracle to bring back the statue of Artemis from Tauris to Argos. Married to Hermione, daughter of Menelaus, Orestes ruled over his paternal kingdom of Mycenæ, and over Argos, upon the death of its king. Orestes is the hero of several Greek tragedies, notably the *Choëphori* and the *Eumenides* of Æschylus, the *Electra* of Sophocles, and the *Orestes* and *Iphigenia in Tauris* of Euripides.

ORGAN. In the fourth chapter of Genesis Jubal is called " the father of all such as handle the harp and organ," but it need scarcely be said that the organ there spoken of bore no striking resemblance to the mechanical marvel so often referred to at the present day as the " King of Instruments." No doubt the fact was early discovered that sound could be made by the passing of air across the end of a tube, and that the pitch of the sound depended upon the length of the tube; and a collection of graduated tubes such as the Punch-and-Judy showmen frequently uses to-day is probably much nearer in essence to Jubal's " organ " than is our modern instrument.

Nevertheless we of to-day in building our organs are linked with Jubal and his period by means of a common method of tone-production, which brings sound from pipes by means of air pressure. The history of the progress from Jubal's " Pan's-pipe " to the modern organ is largely conjectural until about the eleventh century of the Christian Era, but it can be shown that some of the most important ideas in connection with the instrument had been discovered in pre-Christian times, though the power to take full advantage of them, depending entirely on mechanical invention, had to await the slow development of man's mechanical ingenuity.

It will suffice here to say that the early organs were of a very primitive type indeed, and called for severe exertion on the part of the performer. The keys were at least three inches wide and had to be moved with a blow from the clenched fist. Hence the name *pulsator organorum* frequently given to organists of that period.

From about the second half of the fifteenth century progress became gradually more rapid, and it has been maintained up to the present day, when organ-builders vie with each other in the elaborating of mechanical contrivances and of mechanical means of bringing them under the control of the player.

The modern organ of large dimensions generally has four manuals, or keyboards (though some have five), and a set of keys placed under the player's feet and called the pedals. The pedals have a range of $2\frac{1}{2}$ octaves and the manuals a range of 5 octaves. The number of " stops " may be from 60 to 70 or even more, and there are, further, many mechanical devices for coupling up the various manuals with each other or with the pedals and for performing other useful functions.

By means of wind pressure electrically applied the manipulation of the keys produces the various notes, while the quality, timbre, and loudness or softness of the sound produced are controlled by the same means through the stops and the several manuals. The actual device employed to convey the wind pressure to the pipes is the *wind-chest,* a wooden box divided into compartments for various stops (not more than nine to each chest), and carrying the organ pipes on the upperboards above its top surface.

The *console,* or visible keyboard-arrangement, is connected by electric cables, with the *relay machine,* where the electrical impulse is transformed into a pneumatic action, maintaining the requisite air-pressure in the key-channels, and when the key is pressed allowing the *pallet* at the foot of each pipe to fall and admit an inflow of air. Key, stop, and manual action work on this principle, which does away with the old " slider " stop-action.

The wind is supplied to the modern organ by an electrically-driven rotary fan, conveyed by a *wind-trunk* to a *junction-box,* and thence distributed to each wind-chest by separate ducts.

Organ pipes are made either of metal or wood, and as regards their manner of producing sound are divided into two classes, flue pipes and reed pipes. The great majority are of the flue class, and produce their tone through the resonance of the enclosed column of air, which is set in vibration by the current of compressed air forced through a slit at the foot of the pipe.

In reed pipes the reed is the sound generator. This thin strip of metal is so placed at the base of the pipe as to come in contact with the stream of compressed air as it enters, and so is set in vibration. Flue pipes are either open or are closed at the top. In the latter case the pitch of the note is an octave lower than that given by an open pipe of the same length. The quality of the tone is also changed, due to the removing of half of the upper harmonics (*see* OCTAVE).

On the *Great* manual most of the foundation stops such as the Diapasons are to be found; on the *Swell* manual the chief reed stops are generally placed, perhaps because they are specially effective for that increasing and decreasing of the tone amount which is made possible on this manual by means of the shutters. They form one side of the swell box, which encloses all the pipes on this manual, and which can be opened or closed at will by means of a foot lever.

On the *Choir* organ are to be found soft stops suited for accompaniment purposes, and on the *Solo* organ the various "fancy stops" are placed. Mechanical contrivances called couplers enable the player to join any two manuals together or any manual to the pedal board, and so have the resources of both made available from one.—BIBLIOGRAPHY: Grove's *Dictionary of Music and Musicians*, article "Organ" (vol. iii.); Hopkins and Rimbault, *The Organ: its History and Construction*; A. Eaglefield Hull, *Organ Playing: its Technique and Expression*; H. Hiles, *Catechism of the Organ: an Introduction to the Study of Modern Organ Building.*

ORGAN, Organization. In biology, the term *organ* is applied to all the definite parts with special functions, forming as a whole the structure of a living body, whether animal or vegetable. The dissimilarity between the organs of which a living being is composed forms a very striking contrast to the structure of lifeless bodies. A lifeless body—such as a mineral—exhibits generally a sameness or homogeneity of structure. Its intimate parts or particles are usually of a similar kind or nature.

Hence this broad and patent distinction has resulted in the employment of the terms *organic* and *organized* to express the characteristics of living beings; whilst to the lifeless part of creation the opposing term *inorganic* is applied. *Organization* thus means the possession of definite organs, structures, or parts, which have definite relations to each other; and an *organism* is a whole, an animal or plant, possessing such organs.

ORGANIC CHEMISTRY. The chemistry of the compounds of carbon. (Compare the section on "Organic Chemistry" in the article CHEMISTRY.) Until comparatively recent times the number of carbon compounds known was small, and these were derived from animal or vegetable sources, hence the belief that they could not be prepared in the laboratory, but required some "vital force."

In 1828 Wöhler succeeded in producing urea, an animal product, from the substance ammonium cyanate; thus urea was built up without the aid of a vital force. This was at first regarded as an isolated case, but it marked the turning-point in organic chemistry, and from that time we may date the beginning of synthetic chemistry of the carbon compounds, and the overthrow of the idea of organic origin for all carbon compounds.

At the present day many thousands of carbon compounds are known, and the number is being increased yearly by the synthesis of new compounds. The number of carbon compounds exceeds the number of compounds of all the other elements put together. The carbon atom can unite with other carbon atoms to an extraordinary degree. A few of the other elements show a tendency to unite with each other, but the chains are never long, whereas in carbon compounds exceedingly complex substances are built up owing to the special combining power of the carbon atom.

Carbon in the majority of its compounds is tetravalent, and the recognition of fixed valency (q.v.) and the tetravalent nature of the carbon atom, due to Couper and Kekulé (q.v.), has done much to elucidate the structure of carbon compounds and to develop organic chemistry.

Organic or carbon compounds are divided broadly into the *aliphatic* or open-chain compounds, or methane derivatives; the *aromatic*, closed-chain, or homo-cyclic compounds, or benzene derivatives; and the *heterocyclic* compounds, in which the ring is not completely built up of carbon atoms, but may contain nitrogen or sulphur, etc. Classification of the compounds is greatly simplified by arranging the compounds in homologous series (*see* CHEMISTRY).

A type member of each series may be used to show the general properties and general methods of preparation of any other member. Thus amongst the hydrocarbons (q.v.) there are the *paraffin series*, methane (CH_4), ethane (C_2H_6), etc.; the *olefine series*, ethylene (C_2H_4), propylene (C_3H_6), etc.; the *acetylene series*, acetylene (C_2H_2), etc.; the *benzene series*, benzene (C_6H_6), toluene (C_7H_8), etc.

Certain groups of atoms are typical of different classes of compounds; thus, *alcohols* all contain one or more hydroxyl groups (OH) united to carbon, *ketones* contain the carbonyl (CO) group united to carbon, *aldehydes* the group (CHO), acids the carboxyl group (COOH), and so on, the particular group conferring certain characteristics on the compound.

In organic chemistry the arrangement of the atoms in the molecule is taken into consideration, and until the use of structural formulæ in organic compounds had developed very little progress was made. In inorganic chemistry it is sufficient to know the molecular formula for a substance; e.g. Na_2CO_3 represents sodium carbonate and only sodium carbonate.

On the other hand, the formulae C_2H_6O represents not merely ethyl alcohol but also methyl ether, and these substances are totally different in chemical properties; hence in organic chemistry some knowledge of the structure of the molecule must be obtained.

Kekulé did much to develop structural formulæ. He introduced the idea that the carbon atom may be regarded as being situated at the centre of a tetrahedron with the valencies directed to the apices, and from this he developed for many substances structural formulæ which were afterwards proved correct by building up the compound from its elements, using these formulæ.

By ascertaining the structure of a substance it became possible to synthesize the substance, and theoretically there is no organic compound, no matter how complex, which cannot be built up from its elements if the constitution is known. The making of structural formulæ marks the first great stage in the advance of organic chemistry. When the structure is understood it becomes only a question of time, and the finding of correct conditions, to synthesize the compound required.

One of the best known examples of this is the substance *indigo*, a dye obtained from the indigo plant. The dye is a valuable one, and research was started to find the chemical composition of the substance. When that was found, the substance was synthesized, although it took some time before this "artificial" or synthetic indigo could be manufactured sufficiently cheaply to compete with the natural product. Many instances of this kind could be cited.

Sixty years ago few organic compounds were known, and these, in many cases, were not pure, and their constitution was not known. Since that time development has been rapid; Kekulé with his ring structure for benzene paved the way, and results quickly followed. The wonderful range of synthetic colouring matters in use at the present day shows how much organic chemistry has advanced.

Before the time of Perkin (q.v.) dyes were prepared from natural colouring matters, such as the madder root from which alizarine was prepared. Perkin investigated the tarry residue from the manufacture of coal-gas, and from that abstracted by fractional distillation numerous substances, amongst these the compound anthracene; from anthracene he prepared alizarine, and so succeeded in synthesizing the natural colouring matter of the madder root.

Alizarine and its derivatives form a series of adjective dyes. Coal-tar yields also hydrocarbons, phenols, cresols, naphthalene, etc., all organic substances which are the starting-points in the preparation of synthetic dyes, drugs, and explosives.

Modern *explosives* (q.v.) are the result of much research in organic chemistry. The high explosive "T.N.T.," trinitrotoluene, is prepared by nitration of toluene obtained from coal-tar. Picric acid, another substance used in the preparation of explosives, is obtained by nitrating phenol. Nitroglycerine, one of the ingredients of dynamite, is obtained by forming the nitric ester of glycerine, a by-product in the manufacture of soap.

The process of *fermentation* (q.v.) has been known for a long period, but only in recent years have fermentation processes been studied. To Pasteur is due the advance in this branch of chemistry. Pasteur proved fermentation to be a chemical process brought about by chemical agents known as enzymes. These enzymes are present in certain bacteria, and by means of these large amounts of material may be caused to undergo profound chemical change. Thus, sugars may be broken down to ethyl alcohol and carbon dioxide by an enzyme present in yeast cells; alcohol may be caused to oxidize rapidly in air to acetic acid by means of an enzyme present in the micro-organism *mycoderma aceti*. Many fermentation processes of this kind are now in use.

Many *alkaloids* have been synthesized, and several which we regarded as simple substances have been proved to be mixtures of sub-

Oriel College

stances. Great advance has been made in the synthesis of drugs. Drugs were originally obtained from natural sources by expressing the juice of roots and leaves of plants; synthetic drugs have now largely superseded these. Such substances as antifebrine or acetanilide, phenacetine, antipyrine, aspirin, and many other antipyretics are made from derivatives of benzene.

Hypnotics such as chloral, paraldehyde, and sulphonal are prepared from derivatives of methane. Local anæsthetics such as novocaine, β-eucaine, substances less harmful than cocaine, are also derivatives of methane. Salvarsan and atoxyl are synthetic organic compounds containing arsenic.

Industry owes a large debt to the development of structural organic chemistry, and almost every substance in use at the present day is manufactured pure and in quantity as a result of careful research into chemical constitution and synthetic methods. In the plant, complex organic substances are built up from simple substances such as carbon dioxide, water, and alkali nitrates; from these, colouring matters, starch, cellulose, sugars, and acids are formed.

By examining these substances the organic chemist has learned much, and has been able to synthesize many of them, but how they are formed continuously and apparently easily in the plant is not yet fully understood. Recently research on photosynthesis has made it clear that light of a particular wavelength plays an important part in building up these complex substances. We have in the plant a very perfect factory for the manufacture of organic compounds. For "Bibliography," *see* CHEMISTRY.

ORGANIC RADICALS. In organic chemistry, groups of atoms such as the methyl radical CH_3 and the nitroradical NO_2, which exist in whole series of compounds.

ORIEL COLLEGE, Oxford. A college founded in 1326 by Edward II. on the suggestion of Adam de Brome, his almoner, for a provost and ten fellows. St. Mary's Hall, founded 1325, has since 1902 been united with Oriel College. Among those connected with Oriel College were William Langland (author of *Piers Plowman*), Sir Walter Raleigh, Bishop Butler, Matthew Arnold, and Cecil Rhodes, who left a large sum of money to the college.

ORIEL WINDOW. A window projecting from the outer face of a wall, in plan semi-hexagonal, semioctagonal, or rectangular, thus having three or more sides, divided by mullions and transoms into different bays and other projections, and supported by brackets or corbels. A projecting window rising from the ground is sometimes called an oriel, but is more properly a bay-window.

ORIENTE. An inland territory of Ecuador, South America, roughly triangular in shape, and forming a

Oriflamme

wedge between Colombia (north) and Peru (south). It consists of the two provinces, Napo Pastaza and Santiago Zamora, formed in 1925. In area it occupies about half the state, and lies almost wholly in the valley of the Marañon (Upper Amazon). Towards the west the land rises to form a formidable western boundary in the Cordillera Oriental of the Andes, which has done much to hinder development, although the western areas of Oriente are eminently suitable for cotton-growing. Archidona is the territorial capital. Area 219,095 sq. miles, mostly uninhabited. Pop. (1931), 186,000.

ORIFLAMME (Lat. *aurum*, gold, and *flamma*, flame). Until Charles VII.'s reign, the sacred royal standard of France. The earliest military standard of the Frankish monarchy was the blue banner of St. Martin, but from the time of Louis VI. it was replaced by the oriflamme of the abbey of St. Denis, which was presented to the comte de Vexin, lord-protector of the convent.

When Philip I. united Vexin to the possessions of the Crown, it fell to him to bear the banner as protector of the abbey. It was a piece of red taffeta fixed on a golden spear, in the form of a banner, and cut into three points, each of which was adorned with a tassel of green silk.

ORIGEN (Origenes, surnamed **Adamantius**). One of the greatest and most influential of the Greek

Origen

Fathers, born probably at Alexandria A.D. 185-186, died at Tyre 253 or 254. His father suffered marytrdom at Alexandria in 202 under the Emperor Severus. A pupil of Pantænus and Clement, Origen lectured with much success in Alexandria, and gained the patronage of Bishop Demetrius.

His own studies were pursued with extraordinary zeal; he lived an ascetic life, and is said to have become a eunuch in order to be free from the lusts of the flesh. A journey to Rome during the episcopate of Zephyrinus greatly increased his reputation, and Christian communities in various countries vied with each other in securing his services.

About 228 he visited Palestine on his way to Greece, and at Cæsarea was ordained a presbyter. Apparently Demetrius disapproved of Origen's admission to the priesthood; at any rate, he forced Origen to leave Alexandria in 231, afterwards excommunicating him. Origen settled at Cæsarea, which became thenceforth the centre of his labours.

In a new persecution, under the Emperor Decius, Origen, who was viewed as a pillar of the Church, was thrown into prison at Tyre, and subjected to the most cruel sufferings, ultimately resulting in his death. He was a great speculative theologian, and wielded a determining influence upon subsequent Christian thought, and, in particular, upon the doctrines of the Trinity and the Person of Christ. He was credited with some 6000 works, doubtless the exaggeration of popular report.

Of his extant works perhaps the best known are the *Peri Archōn* (*De Principiis*) and the *Contra Celsum.* This last is considered as the most complete and convincing defence of Christianity of which antiquity can boast. *See* HEXAPLA. — BIBLIOGRAPHY: Adolf Harnack, *History of Dogma*; W. Fairweather, *Origen and Greek Patristic Theology.*

ORIHUELA. A town of Alicante, Spain, on the Segura, and in a plain known as the Garden of Spain. It is on the Murcia-Elche Railway. Orihuela has been a bishopric since 1265. It was the Auriwelah of the Moors, who occupied it from 713 until its recapture by Don Jaime I. of Aragon in 1265. Pop. 37,500.

ORINO'CO. A river of South America, one of the largest in the world, rising in the Sierra Parima, in Venezuela. After a circuitous course it falls into the Atlantic opposite Trinidad, its principal mouth being 20 miles wide; length, about 1600 miles. The Orinoco is connected with the Rio Negro, a tributary of the Amazon, by the Cassiquiari, a natural canal joining the two rivers, and it receives the waters of many large rivers. During the rainy season it inundates the immense plains through which it flows, presenting to the eye a boundless expanse of waters. The scenery on its banks is magnificent beyond description. Two remarkable rapids occur in the upper part of the Orinoco, and from these the river is navigable to its mouth (about 780 miles).

O'RIOLE. A name popularly applied to two families of perching birds. The American orioles constiture the family Icteridæ, closely allied to finches. The Baltimore-bird (q.v.), oriole, or golden robin (*Ictĕrus baltimore*) is a familiar species of this family. Here too belong the bobolink (*Dolichonyx oryzivorus*), the crow-blackbird (*Quiscalus versicolor*), and the curious cow-birds (Molobrus), most of which have cuckoo-like habits.

The orioles proper, or those of the Old World, are included in the family

Baltimore Oriole (*Ictĕrus Baltimore*) : Golden Oriole (*Oriŏlus galbŭla*) in flight

Oriolidæ. They are found in Asia, Africa, the islands of the Indian Archipelago, and Southern and Eastern Europe. The golden oriole (*Oriŏlus galbŭla*) is the typical form, and the only European member of the group.

The wings and tail of the males are black, and contrast powerfully with the golden colour of the body. In size it resembles a common thrush or blackbird. It chiefly inhabits Southern Europe, but is occasionally found in Britain. The song is loud and resembles the sound of the flute. The Indian mango-bird (*O. Kundoo*) is very similar in appearance.

ORI'ON. In Greek mythology, a giant hunter. According to Homer, he was a beautiful youth, of whose charms Eōs (Aurora) became enamoured. The gods were jealous of her love, and Artemis slew him with her arrows. According to other writers, he died of the sting of a scorpion. The hero after his death was placed with his hounds in the heavens as a constellation, which bears his name.

ORION. A constellation situated south of the ecliptic, but almost bisected by the equinoctial. It is considered to represent the figure of a man with a sword hanging from his belt. The principal stars are four, forming a large quadrilateral, representing the right and left shoulders, right knee, and left foot, and three in a slanting line representing the belt.

The three stars forming the sword are beneath the belt. The middle star in the sword is a multiple star, surrounded by the Great Nebula (*see* NEBULA). Orion is considered to be the grandest of the constellations. It is referred to by Homer, and also in Job and Amos.

ORISSA. A former Hindu kingdom, now forming the southern portion of the province of Bihar and Orissa (q.v.), and comprising the division of Orissa (area, 13,743 sq. miles ; pop. 5,300,398) and the tributary states (all Oriya-speaking ; area, 28,046 sq. miles ; pop. 3,250,000). The tributary states do not form a part of British India, and are self-controlling under the guidance of a Resident. *See* BENGAL ; INDIA.

ORISTANO. A city of Sardinia, on the west coast (Gulf of Oristano), with a steamer and railway service to other points on the coast, and a trade in fish, wheat, and wine. Pop. 7000.

ORIZABA. A city of Mexico, state of Vera Cruz, on the railway to Mexico City. It stands in a valley at an altitude of 3975 feet, and is one of the most important Mexican cotton-mill cities. There are breweries and a large jute factory. Pop. 50,000.

ORIZABA, Pico de. An extinct volcanic mountain peak of Mexico, known to the Aztecs as Citlaltepetl or Star Mountain, lying within 26 miles north of Orizaba City. It was first ascended in 1848, and last erupted in 1566. Altitude, 18,204 feet.

ORKNEY ISLANDS (the ancient **Orcădes**). A group lying off the northern coast of Scotland, and separated from it by a channel called the Pentland Firth, about 6 to 8 miles broad ; aggregate area, 376 sq. miles. There are about ninety islands and islets, but only twenty-nine are inhabited. Pomona or Mainland is the largest of the group ; others of considerable size are : Hoy, South and North Ronaldshay, Westray, San-day, Eday, Stronsay, Rousay, and Shapinshay.

Scapa Flow, the base of the Imperial Grand Fleet during the European War (1914-18), is bounded by Pomona, Hoy, and South Ronaldshay. Excepting Hoy, none of the islands have hills of any height; there are no large streams, but many lakes and springs. Trees scarcely exist. The rocks belong to the Old Red Sandstone formation, and clay and peat-moss abound.

The climate is moist but not cold, being remarkably mild in winter. Agriculture, pasturing, and fishing are the supports of the inhabitants, manufactures being restricted to hosiery, chiefly hand-made by women. The fisheries are vigorously prosecuted. Agriculture is not in a flourishing condition, and the crofters of the islands were included in the Crofters' Act of 1886. The chief town is Kirkwall.

An Orkney Farmhouse

It is probable that the Picts originally possessed the islands, but in the eighth century and subsequently they were occupied by the Northmen. In the ninth century Harold Haarfager attached them to Norway, and for several centuries they were ruled by jarls or earls, who sometimes owned allegiance to Norway, sometimes to Scotland. About the middle of the thirteenth century they were transferred to Alexander III., King of Scotland; but the Norwegians continued to assert their sovereignty.

James III. of Scotland received the islands as a dowry with Margaret of Norway in 1468, and ever since they have belonged to Scotland. Many Norse customs and Scandinavian expressions of speech still persist in the Orkneys, and there is a tradition that the islands will one day be reunited to Norway. The Orkney Islands form together one county, but for parliamentary purposes unite with Shetland to return one member to the House of Commons. Pop. (1931), 22,075.

ORLANDO, Vittorio Emmanuele. Italian diplomat and jurist, was born at Palermo in 1860. In 1883 he became a professor of constitutional law in his native city, and eventually he entered the Italian Parliament (1898) as Deputy for Partinico, Sicily. He accepted the portfolio of Public Instruction in the Giolitti-Tittoni Cabinet (1903-5), and that of Justice under Giolitti (1907-9) and Salandra (March, 1914).

In 1916, when Salandra resigned and Boselli became Prime Minister, Orlando retained the ministry of the Interior, and by his weakness and indecision was largely to blame for the shambles of Caporetto. In Oct., 1917, he succeeded Boselli as Prime Minister, and to him was largely due the *moral* of Italy during a time of acute distress and danger.

Orlando was one of the "Big Four" at the Peace Conference of Versailles (1919), but his ministry fell in June of that year on account of the Fiume crisis. In 1919 he was elected President of the Chamber. He at first supported Fascism, but was alienated over the Matteotti affair, and in 1925 retired from Parliament.

ORLÉANAIS (or-lā-á-nā). One of the pre-Revolutionary provinces of France. It now forms the departments of Loir-et-Cher and Loiret, and parts of Eure-et-Loir, Nièvre, Seine-et-Oise, Sarthe, Indre-et-Loire, and Cher. Orléans was the capital.

ORLÉANS, House of. French royal family, two branches of which, the Valois-Orléans and the Bourbon-Orléans, occupied the throne of France. The first duc d'Orléans was Philip, fourth son of Philip VI. (1344-75), and the second was Louis I. (1372-1407), comte de Valois, and a brother of Charles VI. In 1498, on the death of Charles VIII., Louis, duc d'Orléans, a son of the poet Charles of Orléans, became king under the title of Louis XII. The last sovereign of this branch, the Valois-Orléans, was Henri III. (died 1589).

The second branch of the House of Orléans, that of Bourbon-Orléans, is descended from Philip, duc d'Orléans, son of Louis XIII., and a younger brother of Louis XIV. His son Philip, duc d'Orléans, was Regent of France during the minority of Louis XV. The title passed to the descendants of the duke, one of whom, Louis Philippe, duc de Chartres, became King of France in 1830. The grandson of Louis de

Philippe (q.v.), the comte de Paris (1838-94), became head of the royal house and royalist party, leaving a son, the duc d'Orléans (1869-1926) to inherit his claims.

ORLÉANS, Jean Baptiste Gaston, Duc d'. Third son of Henry IV. of France and Mary of Medici, born 1608, died at Blois 1660. Louis XIII. was jealous of the duke, who was constantly intriguing against the King and the Government of Richelieu. By his first marriage, with Mary of Bourbon, heiress of the House of Montpensier, he had a daughter, the author of some interesting memoirs. During the disturbances of the Fronde he joined De Retz, the soul of the Fronde, who, however, soon saw through the character of his fickle and feeble confederate. After the termination of the troubles (1648) the duke was banished to Blois.

ORLÉANS, Louis Philippe Joseph, Duc d'. Better known as *Philippe Égalité*, a cousin of Louis XVI. and great-grandson of the Regent Philippe. He was born at St. Cloud 13th April, 1747, and died 6th Nov., 1793. In 1769 he married the daughter of the duc de Penthièvre. He was notorious for his dissoluteness of manners, and the extreme, though vacillating political conduct by which he courted popularity. His opposition to the court began in 1771, and he became the rallying-point of its enemies.

In 1787 he was exiled for the part he took in the Assembly of Notables; in 1789 he was one of the nobles who joined the Tiers État (Third Estate); in 1792 he went over to the revolutionary party without reserve, took the name of *Philippe Égalité* ("Philip Equality"), and voted for the death of Louis XVI. It did not save him from being arrested as a Bourbon, condemned, and beheaded.

ORLÉANS, Philippe, Duc d'. Son of Louis XIII. and of Anne of Austria, and the only brother of Louis XIV. of France, was born in 1640, and died in 1701. He was the founder of the House of Bourbon-Orléans, which for a short time held the throne of France. In his twenty-first year he married Henrietta of England, sister of Charles II. The great esteem which the king showed for this princess excited the jealousy of his brother, and her sudden death was attributed to poison, to the administration of which the duke was suspected of being accessory.

The second marriage of the duke, with the Princess Elizabeth of Bavaria (1671), was arranged by Louis to secure the neutrality of the Elector Palatine in the approaching war against Holland. In this war the duke distinguished himself in spite of his effeminacy.

ORLÉANS, Philippe, Duc d'. Regent of France, son of Philippe, duc d'Orléans, and the Princess Palatine Elizabeth, born 1674, died 1723. He fell early under the influence of the clever and unscrupulous Abbé (afterwards Cardinal) Dubois, who continued his confidant and adviser through life. He made his military début at the siege of Mons (1691), and in 1693 distinguished himself at Neerwinden, but only to arouse the jealousy of Louis XIV., his uncle, who compelled him to retire from the army. In 1692 he married Mlle de Blois, the legitimated daughter of Louis.

Philippe Duc d'Orléans

In 1707 he was appointed to succeed the Duke of Berwick in Spain, and completed the subjugation of that country. He was recalled, however, being suspected of intriguing for the crown of Spain, and again forced into retirement. On the death of the king (1st Sept., 1715) he was appointed regent. On acceding to power the regent found the finances in extreme disorder, and endeavoured to improve matters by retrenchment and peace; but his reckless introduction of a vast paper currency brought the nation to the verge of bankruptcy. He resigned the government to Louis XV. on 13th Feb., 1723.

ORLÉANS (ancient **Genabum, Lat.** *Civitas Aureliani*). A city of France, formerly capital of Orléanais, now of the department of the Loiret, on the Loire. It has a Gothic cathedral, destroyed by the Huguenots in 1567, and rebuilt from 1601 onwards; two hôtels de ville, a palais de justice, and other notable buildings. The manufactures include cotton, linen goods, pottery, refined sugar, and vinegar.

Philip of Valois erected Orléans into a duchy and peerage in favour of his son, and Orléans has since continued to give the title of duke to a prince of the blood royal. In 1428 the city sustained a siege against the English, and was relieved by the Maid of Orléans (*Joan of Arc*), whose statue in bronze, erected in 1855, stands in the Place du Martroi. The city was taken and retaken more than once in the Franco-German War in the latter part of 1780. Pop. (1926), 70,611.

ORMER (Fr. *oreille de mer*, "sea-ear"). The ear-shell, a large marine univalve shell-fish belonging to the

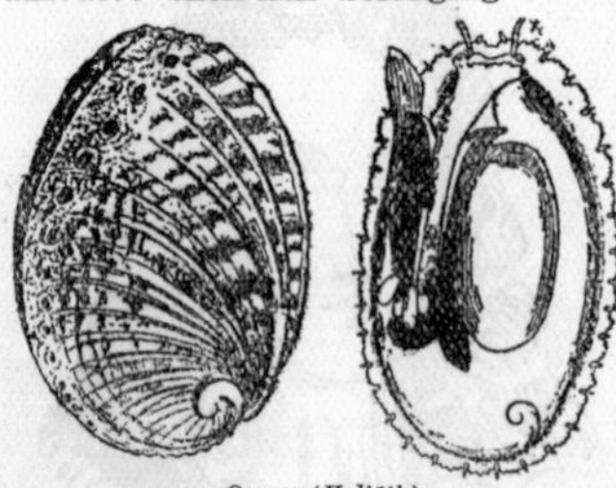

Ormer (*Haliōtis*)
Exterior of shell and diagrammatic view of interior.

genus Haliōtis, common on the shores of the Channel Islands, where it is cooked after being well beaten to make it tender. The shell is common as a mantelpiece ornament on account of its pearly interior.

ORME'S HEAD, Great. A bold, flat-topped headland of Carnarvonshire, North Wales, at the mouth of the River Conway, reached by a funicular railway. The fashionable watering-place of Llandudno is situated between the Great and Little Orme's Heads.

OR'MOLU (Fr. *or moulu*, literally, "ground gold"). In English frequently applied to a metal compounded of copper and zinc (mosaic gold), nearly resembling brass, but having a colour more like that of gold. In French *or moulu* signifies a paste of gold and mercury used for gilding, and the colour imparted to a surface by that paste.

ORMSKIRK. An urban district and town of Lancashire, England; served by the L.M.S. Railway. Its chief occupations are brewing and rope-making, and there are large collieries. Ormskirk is noted for its gingerbread. Pop. (1931), 17,121.

ORMUZ. An island opposite Bandar 'Abbās, on the Strait of Ormuz, connecting the Persian Gulf with the Gulf of Oman. It was the site of one of the wealthiest commercial cities of the East, which was founded in the third century, and occupied originally the mainland on the north side of the strait. In A.D. 1300 a new city was built on the Island of Ormuz on account of Mongol depredations.

This was taken by the Portuguese in 1507, and was held by them until besieged and captured by the British in 1622, when Bandar 'Abbās and Gombroon were founded, and the city was allowed thenceforth to fall into decay. In the island there are large deposits of red ochre, thousands of tons of which are exported annually to the United Kingdom. The climate is hot; the wet season begins in January and ends in March.

ORMUZD, or **ORMAZD** (*Ahura-mazda*, the Oromasdes of the Greeks and Romans). The Supreme Being in the Zoroastrian religion. He is represented in the *Avesta* as the sovereign of the realm of good, light, and truth, the lord of the universe, and the creator of earthly and spiritual life. He rewards the good and punishes the wicked. As the principle of good Ormuzd is opposed to Ahriman, the lord of the bad creation.

Ormuzd is not self-existent, but has sprung from Zazvan-Akarana (infinite and uncreated time). He contains within himself the opposite principles of good and evil, which were afterwards separated by the Magi into distinct individualities. As a deity Ormuzd approaches the Judæo-Christian conception of Jehovah; and like the latter is omniscient and omnipotent, the One Who was, Who is, and Who shall be. —Cf. J. H. Moulton, *Early Zoroastrianism*.

ORNE. An inland department of North-Western France, drained by the Orne, Eure, Sarthe, and other rivers, and traversed generally by ridges of low hills. It is noted for horses and for dairy produce (including Camembert cheese). Cattle are raised; cereals include wheat and barley; the hills are afforested; much fruit is grown. Alençon, the capital, and the towns of Laigle, Argentan, Flers, and Domfront are all served by the Western Railways. About a half of Orne belonged to pre-Revolutionary Normandy—the rest to the Duchy of Alençon and to

Perche. Area, 2371 sq. miles; pop. (1931), 273,717.

ORNE. A river of France, rising near Sées, in the department of Orne, passing through Calvados, and falling into the English Channel; length, 95 miles. It is canalized from Caen to its mouth.

ORNITHOLOGY (Gr. *ornis, ornithos*, a bird; *logos*, a discourse). The study of birds. These vertebrate animals constitute a sharply defined class (Aves), and can be briefly defined as feathered bipeds with the fore-limbs converted into wings, which are usually but not always employed for flight. They are undoubtedly of reptilian stock, and the term Sauropsida is often applied to birds and reptiles collectively.

The form and structure of birds have been evolved in relation to flight. The bony skeleton, for example, though firm is light, being largely traversed by air-spaces. The framework of the compact trunk is rigid, but as a compensation the neck is extremely flexible, and the head can be moved about with great freedom, for there is only a single occipital condyle articulating with the first vertebra.

The back of the head is large and rounded, for the brain is well developed, a character correlated with marked intelligence. The mouth is bounded by a *beak* or *bill*, devoid of teeth (except in some extinct types), but covered by a firm horny sheath. The shape of the beak is related to the habits, and presents a great range of variation, it being, e.g., hooked in a bird of prey, elongated and slender in the woodcock which probes for its food, and a short firm cone in the seed-eating finches. The *nostrils* are usually at the base of the beak, and are sometimes associated with a bare swollen patch of skin, the *cere*. The eyes are large, and provided with translucent third eyelids or nictitating membranes, which can be moved with great rapidity. There are no external ears.

The wings possess the same regions as ordinary fore-limbs, i.e. upper arm, forearm, and hand, but there are only three digits, one of these being the thumb. Since the chief use of the wing is to support the *wing-quills* or *rowing feathers* (remiges), its skeleton is firm, as the result of the fusion of certain bones. The remiges are divided into primaries and secondaries, attached respectively to hand and forearm. Their bases are overlapped by *wing coverts*.

The thumb ends in a small claw and bears a tuft of feathers, the *bastard wing* (ala spuria), that probably helps in turning movements. The tail is reduced to a sort of stump, and its vertebræ are usually fused into a laterally flattened *ploughshare bone* (pygostyle), for supporting the *tail-quills* or *steering feathers* (rectrices), the bases of which are overlapped by *tail coverts*. An *oil-gland* usually opens on the upper side of the tail, its secretion being used for preening feathers.

The hind-limbs are set on far forwards, each consisting of thigh, shank, tarsus, and foot. The shank is equivalent to a lower leg fused with the upper part of the ankle, while the "tarsus" consists of the lower part of the ankle fused with three of the instep bones (metatarsals). It follows that the ankle-joint at the junction of shank and tarsus is *intertarsal*, i.e. in the middle of the ankle region.

The bird is digitigrade, walking on its toes, of which the normal number is four, a backwardly directed great toe (hallux), and forwardly directed second, third, and fourth toes. Tarsus and foot are covered with scales, a reptilian feature, and the toes are clawed. The length of the hind-limb and the nature of the foot vary greatly with the habits. Birds of prey, for example, possess powerful grasping feet armed with talons; climbing forms, such as parrots, commonly have the fourth toe directed backwards like the hallux; aquatic birds are mostly web-footed.

The *external skeleton* consists of the horny sheaths covering the jaws, the claws, the scales above-mentioned, and various kinds of feathers, all being of epidermal origin. A typical *feather* consists of a basal hollow *quill* continued into an elastic *rachis*, the axis of the expanded *vane*, and bearing flattened *barbs*. These last bear smaller branches, *barbules*, connected by minute hooks, so as to form a firm light expansion for beating on the air. There may be a second, usually smaller, vane at the base of the first; the barbules of this "after shaft" do not bear hooks.

In addition to quill-feathers and coverts there are numerous *contour-feathers*, of similar structure, which determine the general outline of the body. They do not cover the entire surface, but are arranged in definite tracts (pterylæ), which vary in different species and are some aid to classification. The intervening patches (apteria) are to some extent bare, but imperfect *down-feathers* and also hair-like *filo-plumes* may be found growing upon them. This characteristic covering of feathers entangles air and helps to prevent loss of heat from the surface of the body.

Feathers are of a great variety of colours, mostly due to the presence of pigments, but the metallic iridescent appearance seen in such forms as humming-birds is of physical character, and depends on the presence of microscopic ridges that act like prisms. Male birds are as a rule more brilliantly coloured than their mates, and may possess other secondary sexual characters.

Female birds are usually coloured and marked so as to harmonize with their surroundings, a measure of protection from foes being thus gained. Feathers are shed or moulted once or twice in the year, and there may be a marked contrast between summer and winter plumage.

Digestive Organs.—Not only the beak but also the *tongue* exhibits many variations in form. When used for securing insects, as in woodpeckers, it is often rendered sticky by the secretion of special glands. The gullet commonly dilates into a *crop* for storing food, especially in plant-eaters, and the *stomach* consists of a glandular *proventriculus*, in which gastric juice is secreted, followed by a muscular *gizzard* with a horny lining. This serves as a grinding apparatus, and small hard bodies, such as stones, are swallowed for the purpose of increasing its efficiency. The intestine opens into a cloaca.

Blood System.—The blood is hotter than in Mammals, varying from 103° F. to 110° F. The red corpuscles are oval nucleated discs. The heart consists of two auricles and two ventricles, and the arch of the aorta turns to the right, whereas in Mammals it turns to the left.

Respiratory Organs.—The immobile *lungs* are firmly attached to the dorsal wall of the thorax, and are connected with numerous *air sacs*, that communicate with air-spaces in the bones. This greatly reduces the specific gravity of the body. The organ of voice (syrinx) is situated where the trachea divides into bronchi.

Urinogenital Organs.—These communicate with a cloaca, which also receives the intestine. There is no urinary bladder, and the urine is semisolid. The organs of generation are internal: only one ovary and oviduct are present; the large eggs are invested in firm calcareous shells.

Muscular System.—In a flying bird the flesh of the well-developed breast is made up of muscles that depress and raise the wings in flight. These are attached to a large plate or *keel* that projects from the breast-bone (sternum). In running birds, such as ostriches, that do not fly though they possess small wings, the breast-bone is a broad curved plate devoid of keel.

Birds that live and roost among trees or shrubs possess a *perching mechanism*, an arrangement by which the toes can be all brought together at the same time by a pull exerted upon a single tendon connected with two muscles of the legs. When the bird is roosting, the weight of the body bends the limb in such a way as to pull on this tendon and bring all the toes firmly against the branch or other supporting object, the danger of falling off during sleep being thus averted.

Nervous System and Sense Organs.—The cerebral hemispheres of the brain are large, in relation to the possession of considerable intelligence, and the sense organs are well developed. Part of the internal ear (membranous labyrinth) consists of a slightly curved tube (lagena) that has to do with the appreciation of musical sounds.

Habits.—Nesting and migration are the two most interesting. A few birds, such as the Megapodes of New Guinea and North-East Australia simply lay their eggs in hot sand or decaying vegetation, where they hatch out without any further attention. But incubation takes place in the vast majority of cases, the necessary heat being supplied by the body of the parent or parents.

Some birds, such as guillemots, do not construct nests, but usually some sort of receptacle is made for the reception of the eggs, and this may be of very elaborate character. When eggs are exposed to view they are generally coloured and marked to harmonize with surroundings, and this is commonly true of newly hatched young in cases where these run from the nest and are not helpless nestlings. Cuckoos and a few other forms deposit their eggs in the nests of other species.

Nesting habits are undoubtedly instinctive; this is also true for the habit of migration, regarding which a vast number of facts are known. In this country four cases can be distinguished: (1) *winter visitors* which fly north in spring to their breeding quarters; (2) *summer visitors* that come from the south to breed here; (3) *birds of passage* that appear for a short time in spring and autumn, resting on their way to and from their breeding quarters in the north; (4) *gipsy migrants*, that wander from one part of the country to another, apparently in search of food. Migrating birds are known to take definite routes, some of which correspond to vanished land surfaces, but how they find their way is an unsolved problem.

Classification.—This is a matter of extreme difficulty, and a large number of systems have been advanced. The following embodies the views most generally favoured.

Sub-class I.: Archæornithes. Includes only the extinct Archæopteryx, a Jurassic toothed form about the size of a rook. The tail was long and bore pairs of quill-feathers.

Sub-class II.: Neornithes. Tail abbreviated. Division A: Ratitæ. Flightless running birds, with no keel to the sternum and reduced wings. Here are included ostriches, rheas or South American ostriches, cassowaries, emeus, and the little New Zealand kiwi (Apteryx): also extinct types—some gigantic—the New Zealand moas (Dinornis, etc.), and the roc (Æpyornis) of Madagascar. Division B: Odontolcæ. A few extinct toothed birds from the Cretaceous (Hesperornis, etc.), with reduced wings and keelless sternum. Division C: Carinatæ. Wings usually well developed, and sternum with keel for attachment of muscles of flight. Most birds belong to this division, which is divided into fourteen orders of very unequal size.

1. **Ichthyornithes.**—Small extinct birds (Ichthyornis, etc.) of the Cretaceous period, possessing teeth in sockets, and well-marked powers of flight.

2. **Colymbiformes.**—Aquatic birds with webbed or lobed toes, the hallux being very small. The divers (Colymbidæ) have webbed feet, and the grebes (Podicipedidæ) lobed toes.

3. **Sphenisciformes.** — Penguins (Spheniscidæ), with webbed feet, and wings converted into paddles.

4. **Procellariiformes.** Oceanic birds with great powers of flight, webbed feet, hooked beak, and nostrils drawn out into a pair of bony tubes. Albatross, fulmars, shearwaters, and petrels (Procellariidæ).

5. **Ciconiiformes.**—A large assemblage of birds that are for the most part aquatic. Four sub-orders: (*a*) Steganopodes. Marine web-footed forms with the hallux turned forwards, and united by a membrane with the other toes. Tropic birds (Phæthontidæ), gannets and boobies (Sulidæ), cormorants and snake-birds (Phalacrocoracidæ), frigate-birds (Fregatidæ), pelicans (Pelicanidæ). (*b*) Ardeæ. Long sharp beak, elongated legs, web between bases of middle and outer toe. Herons and bitterns (Ardeidæ), hammer-heads (Scopideæ). (*c*) Ciconeæ Long necks and legs, feet partially webbed, beak stout. Storks (Ciconiidæ), ibises and spoonbills (Ibididæ). (*d*) Phœnicopteri. Much elongated neck and legs, webbed feet, beak very large and sharply bent downwards. Flamingoes (Phœnicopteridæ).

6. **Anseriformes.** — Aquatic birds mostly feeding on plants. Horned screamers, etc. (Palamedeidæ) of South America; feet not webbed. Swans, geese, and ducks (Anatidæ), with webbed feet.

7. **Falconiformes.**—Diurnal birds of prey. Strong hooked beak with cere at base; carnivorous; strong flyers. Vultures, carrion feeders, with head and neck more or less bare of feathers; American vultures (Cathartidæ), including the gigantic condor (*Sarcorhamphus gryphus*); Old World vultures (Vulturidæ); secretary birds (Serpentariidæ) of Africa; eagles, hawks, falcons, buzzards, kites, etc. (Falconidæ); ospreys (Pandionidæ).

8. **Tinamiformes.**—The tinamous, of South America, resembling game-birds in appearance, but of more primitive character.

9. **Galliformes.** Game-birds. Mostly ground forms with stout beak and short strong legs with blunt claws, adapted for scratching. Hemipodes or button-quails (Turnicidæ); megapodes or mound-builders (Megapodiidæ); curassows and guans (Cracidæ); Guinea-fowl, turkeys, pheasants, partridges, grouse, pea-fowl, jungle fowl, etc. (Phasianidæ); hoatzins of South America (Opisthocomidæ).

10. **Gruiformes.** — Marsh-dwelling crane-like birds; hind toe raised well above the ground. Rails (Rallidæ); cranes (Gruidæ); trumpeters (Psophidæ); crested screamers, etc. (Cariamidæ); bustard (Otididæ).

11. **Charadriiformes.** — (*a*) Limicolæ. Plovers, stilts, phalaropes, sand-pipers, curlews, woodcock, and snipe (Charadriidæ); pratincoles and coursers (Glareolidæ); stone curlews (Œdicnemidæ); jaçanas (Parridæ). (*b*) Lari. Gulls, terns, and skuas (Laridæ). (*c*) Alcæ. Auks (Alcidæ). (*d*) Pterocles. Sand grouse (Pteroclidæ). (*e*) Columbæ. Extinct dodo and solitaire (Dididæ); tooth-billed pigeons (Didunculidæ); pigeons and doves (Columbidæ).

12. **Cuculiformes.** — Two toes turned backwards. (*a*) Cuculi. Cuckoos (Cuculidæ); plantain-eaters (Musophagidæ). (*b*) Psittaci. Parrots, parakeets, macaws, and cockatoos (Psittacidæ); lories, kaka and kea parrots of New Zealand (Trichoglossidæ).

13. **Coraciiformes.** — (*a*) Coraciæ. Rollers (Coraciidæ), motmots and todies (Momotidæ), kingfishers (Al-

cedinidæ), bee-eaters (Meropidæ), hornbills (Bucerotidæ), hoopoes (Upupidæ). (*b*) Striges. Owls (Strigidæ). (*c*) Caprimulgi. Night-jars or goatsuckers (Caprimulgidæ), frog-mouths (Podargidæ), oil-birds (Steatornithidæ). (*d*) Cypseli. Swifts (Cypselidæ), humming-birds (Trochilidæ). (*e*) Colii. Colies or mouse-birds (Coliidæ). (*f*) Trogones. Trogons (Trogonidæ). (*g*) Pici. Jacamars and puff-birds (Galbulidæ), barbets and honey-guides (Capitonidæ), toucans (Rhamphastidæ), woodpeckers and wrynecks (Picidæ).

14. **Passeriformes.**—Here are included the perching or insessorial birds, some 5500 species, more than half the number of known forms. They embrace all the small singing birds, among others. Classification is difficult, depending as it does on anatomical details, especially those concerning the small muscles attached to the organ of voice (syrinx).

Over fifty families are recognized, of which the following are among the more familiar : larks (Alaudidæ), wagtails and pipits (Motacillidæ), thrushes and warblers (Turdidæ), swallows and martins (Hirundinidæ), tits (Paridæ), birds-of-paradise (Paradiseidæ), crows and their allies (Corvidæ), finches and buntings (Fringillidæ).

See numerous articles on groups and individual species contained in this work.

BIBLIOGRAPHY : A. H. Evans, *Birds* (Cambridge Natural History) ; R. Lydekker, *Royal Natural History* (vols. iii. and iv.) ; J. R. Ainsworth-Davis, *Natural History of Animals* ; Alfred Newton, *A Dictionary of Birds*; Hans Gadow, *A Classification of Vertebrata*; F. G. Aflalo, *Natural History* (Vertebrates) *of the British Isles* ; Elliott Coues, *Field and General Ornithology*.

ORNITHORHYNCHUS (*Ornithorhynchus anatinus*), the duck-bill or duck-billed platypus of Southern and Eastern Australia and Tasmania. With the echidnas or porcupine ant-eaters of Australia and New Guinea it forms the order Monotremata—the lowest division of the mammalia. This curious animal has the shape and size of a small otter covered with short brown fur ; a horny flat bill like a duck ; a short flat tail ; short legs with five-toed and webbed feet, terminated by claws. The eyes are small ; external ear wholly wanting. The skull is bird-like in conformation ; brain of low type ; coracoid bones as in reptiles well developed. Small grinding teeth are at first present, but are ultimately replaced by horny plates. Its young are produced from eggs, are born blind and hairless, and suckled from milk-glands destitute of nipples, which open into a temporary pouch. It forms large burrows in river and lake banks, rising from near the surface of the water to a height of perhaps twenty feet above it, the nest being at the higher end. It swims for its food, which consists of bivalve molluscs, insects, worms, larvæ, etc.

OROBANCHACEÆ (-ban-kā′si-ē). The broom-rape family of plants. They are herbaceous parasites, with scales in place of leaves, and attach themselves to the roots of different plants, as the *Orobanche major* to broom and furze, *O. ramōsa* to hemp, *O. rubra* to thyme, and *O. hedĕræ* to ivy.

OROTA′VA. A town of the Canary Islands, in the north-west of the Island of Teneriffe. It exports quantities of fruit, wine, and cochineal, and is a health-resort. Pop. about 10,000.

ORPEN, Sir William. British artist. Born in County Dublin, 27th Nov., 1878, he was educated at Dublin Metropolitan School of Art and the Slade School. He was President of the International Society and several other Art Societies. During the Great War he was appointed an official artist, and in 1918 he held a great exhibition of his war pictures, many of which he presented to the nation. Elected A.RA. in 1910 and R.A. in 1919, he was perhaps best known as a portrait painter. He wrote *An Onlooker in France* (1921) and *Stories of Old Ireland and Myself* (1924). He died 29th Sept., 1931.

ORPHEUS (or′fūs). In Greek mythology, one of the most famous of Greek legendary singers, the chief representative of the art of song. He is also represented as the founder of a religious sect. He is not mentioned in Homer and Hesiod, but appears in the lyric period, and becomes surrounded by a multitude of celebrated legends. According to a later development of the story of Orpheus, he was the son of Œagrus and the Muse Calliope.

To him is attributed the application of music to the worship of the gods. Apollo presented him with his lyre, and the Muses instructed him to use it, so that he moved not the beasts only, but the woods and rocks with its melody. Having lost his wife Eurydice by the bite of a serpent, he descended to Hades to try and get her back. His music so moved the infernal deities Pluto and Persephone that they allowed her to return to earth, on condition that her husband, whom she was to follow, would not look back till they had reached the upper world. This condition the impatient Orpheus violated and lost his wife for ever.

He is said to have met his death at the hands of a band of furious Thracian women engaged in the mystic rites of Bacchus, and whose advances he had rejected. He is represented as one of the Argonauts, and to him is ascribed the origin of the so-called Orphic mysteries connected with the worship of Bacchus. —BIBLIOGRAPHY: J. E. Harrison, *Prolegomena to the Study of Greek Religion*; C. A. Lobeck, *Aglaophamus*.

ORPHISM. From the sixth century a mass of religious literature was attributed to Orpheus, and Orphic sects or societies were formed all over Greece.

These societies practised a mystical worship, attached to no particular temple, and promulgated their views in literary works. Their devotions were addressed to Dionysus Zagreus, in whom they idealized the conception of intense sorrow for human misery. He was a lower-world deity, who was to purify the soul and make it immortal. Instead of indulging in the enthusiasm and orgies of the Bacchic worship, the members of the Orphic societies practised an ascetic purity of life and conduct.

The sacrificial rite consisted in partaking of raw flesh torn from the bull of Dionysus, and those who had participated in it afterwards ate no other animal food. The earliest authors who expounded their doctrines were Pherecydes and Onomacritus. One sect of them held a doctrine curiously like that of indulgences. They offered by sacrifices and songs to procure for the rich pardon for their own sins and for those of their ancestors.

The soul, according to Orphic teaching, was immortal. After death it passed to Hades, where it was either rewarded or punished, and reborn again in man or animal. The transmigration of the soul was, however, not eternal, as through pure living a soul would safely pass through the danger of the Nether World. When it had been acquitted of guilt three times, it was free and then passed to the Islands of the Blest.

The bulk of the poems attributed to Orpheus have been proved to be forgeries of Christian grammarians, of the Alexandrian school. A portion of them, however, belong to the time of Onomacritus, or earlier, and include hymns, a theogony, a poem called *Minyas*, or the *Descent into Hades*; oracles and songs for initiation, and sacred legends.—BIBLIOGRAPHY: C. A. Lobeck, *Aglaophamus*; S. Reinach, *Cultes, Mythes et Religions*.

OR'PIMENT. A mineral consisting of arsenic and sulphur (As_2S_3), of a bright-yellow colour, passing into golden; specific gravity, 3·5. It occurs in laminated or lamellar masses, monoclinic in concretions, and more rarely in crystals.

ORPINGTON FOWL. *See* POULTRY.

ORRELL. Urban district of Lancashire. A centre of the cotton industry, it is 3 miles from Wigan and 199 from London, by the L.M.S. Railway. Pop. (1931), 6957.

ORRIS ROOT, or IRIS ROOT. The root of several species of Iris, especially of the *I. florentina,* which on account of its violet-like smell is employed in perfumery and in the manufacture of tooth powder. It is also used in pharmacy as a pectoral.

ORSI'NI. One of the most illustrious and powerful families of Italy. It became known about the eleventh century, and had already acquired high rank and extensive possessions in the Papal States when one of its members, Giovanni Gaetano, was raised to the pontificate under the title of Nicholas III. (1277-80). The feud between the Orsini and Colonna families, celebrated in history, commenced towards the close of the thirteenth century.

It is distinguished for bitterness, unscrupulousness, and violence, assassination being not unfrequently resorted to. Many of the Orsini became famous military chiefs. Vincenzo Marco Orsini (Benedict XIII.) succeeded Innocent XIII. as Pope in 1724. The Orsini family is now divided into two branches, the Orsini-Gravina at Rome and the Orsini of Piedmont.

OR'THITE. A hydrous silicate of aluminium containing the rare metals cerium, lanthanum, didymium, and yttrium, occurring in granite and other rocks in Sweden, Greenland, the Urals, etc. It is a species of the epidote series, and is also known as *allanite*.

ORTHO'CERAS. A genus of fossil cephalopods, having straight or slightly curved chambered shells, allied to the nautilus, and occurring from the Cambrian to the Trias.

OR'THOCLASE. A silicate of aluminium and potassium, the common felspar of granites, rhyolites, and trachytes. It crystallizes in the monoclinic system, commonly in twinned forms. Transparent crystals are styled *adularia* and *sanidine.* The colour varies from white to yellowish or red; it is opaque, transparent, or translucent; specific gravity, 2·56; hardness, 6, that is, it cannot be scratched by a knife when fresh. Orthoclase breaks down on weathering into kaolin (q.v.).

OR'THODOXY. A term signifying purity of faith, correctness of belief, and a conformity to the rules determined by an ecclesiastical organization. It is the antithesis of heterodoxy. The term, however, is necessarily a relative one, as there are as many different conceptions of orthodoxy as there are Churches. Every Church is apt to consider its doctrines as orthodox, and those of other denominations as heterodox.

The standard by which the orthodoxy of religious beliefs is tested is found by Protestants in the Scriptures, whilst Roman Catholics find it in the infallibility of the Pope and the Catholic Church. The Eastern Church, called also the Greek Church, is officially styled The Holy Orthodox Apostolic Eastern Church, just as the Roman is the Catholic Church, the one asserting its orthodoxy, the other its catholicity.

On account of its universality and antiquity the Eastern Church indeed claims the exclusive privilege of orthodoxy. It excludes all the additions to the definitions of the first seven œcumenical councils which alone represented the entire Catholic Church. The term orthodoxy may also be applied to opinions and doctrines in general which are currently accepted as correct, whether in the domains of law and literature, art or morality, history, politics, or economics.

ORTHOGRAPHIC PROJECTION. That projection used by geographers in the construction of maps in which the eye is supposed to be at an infinite distance from the sphere, so that the rays of light coming from every point of the hemisphere may be considered as parallel to one another. This method of projection is convenient enough for areas not too far from the centre of the picture. *See* MAP.

ORTHOPÆ'DIA. *See* SURGERY (ORTHOPÆDIC).

ORTHOP'TERA (Gr. *orthos,* straight, *pteron,* a wing). An order of insects in which the metamorphosis is incomplete. They have four wings, the anterior pair being semi-coriaceous or leathery, usually with numerous nervures, the wings sometimes overlapping and sometimes meeting like the roof of a house. The feelers are generally straight, filiform organs.

The limbs vary in conformation according to their methods of movement. There is no resting or pupa stage, and the young insects differ from the adults only in size and the absence of wings. These insects are divided into running (Cursorial) and leaping (Saltatorial) Orthoptera. Of the former division the cockroaches, earwigs, mantis insects, walking-stick insects, and walking leaves form the chief families. The Saltatoria are represented by the locusts, some of which want wings entirely, crickets, and grasshoppers. *See also* ENTOMOLOGY.

ORTLER-SPITZE, or ORTLER. A mountain of the Alps, in the Trentino, North Italy, the highest peak of the Eastern Alps; height, 12,802 feet. The group to which this mountain belongs is known as the Ortler Alps, in the chain of the Rhætian Alps. It was first ascended in 1804.

OR'TOLAN (*Emberīza hortulāna*). A bird of the bunting sub-family, a

Ortolan

native of North Africa and Southern Europe. The colours are yellow on the throat and around the eyes, the breast and belly being of reddish hue, whilst the upper part of the body is brown varied with black. Its delicate flesh is much esteemed by epicures, and large quantities are annually caught and fattened for the table in the south of France, Italy, and Cyprus.

ORTO'NA. A town of Chieti, South Italy, on the Adriatic. It was destroyed by the Turks in 1566. It has a cathedral and a ruined castle. Pop. 19,895.

ORTYX. An American genus of gallinaceous birds allied to the quails and partridges. *See* QUAIL.

ORU'RO. A western department of Bolivia, on the Chilian, Tacna-Arica frontier, among the Andes, at an average altitude of from 12,000 to

13,000 feet. It contains Lake Poopo. Tin is produced, and llama-wool is exported. Oruro is the capital. Area, 20,657 sq. miles; pop. about 142,366.

ORURO. A town of Bolivia, capital of the department of Oruro, the railway and mining centre of the republic, and the Bolivian terminus of the Antofagasta Railway. There is a School of Mines; boots and alcohol are manufactured. Pop. 40,700.

ORVIE'TO (ancient **Volsinii ; Urbibentos** ; Lat. *Urbs Vetus*). A city of Perugia, Italy, on an isolated rock near the confluence of the Paglia and the Chiana, ascended by funicular railway. It is noted for a cathedral founded in 1285, and a museum (in the Palazzo dei Papi) dating from 1296, which contains Etruscan antiquities and mediæval works of art. Wine is made and traded. Pop. 19,409.

Orvieto occupies the site of Etruscan *Volsinii*, destroyed by the Romans in 280 B.C. Procopius mentions the city as *Urbibentos*, but it was known as *Urbs Vetus* after his time. It was taken by Belisarius (539), by the Lombards (606), and by Charlemagne, and for long enjoyed possession of a large territory, providing also a safe harbourage for oppressed Popes. The city became a part of Italy in 1860.

ORYCTER'OPUS. The generic name of the aardvark or Cape anteater (*O. capensis*) of South Africa, an insectivorous edentate mammal.

ORYX. The name of the genus of antelopes represented by the addax (*Oryx nasomaculata*) and by other species, found in large herds chiefly in the northern portions of the African continent, but also in Arabia and Syria. The horns are very long, annulated, and curved backwards. The gemsbok (*Oryx gazella*) of Southern Africa is another species included in this genus.

Oryx

OSAGE. A river of the United States, which rises in Kansas, flows through Missouri, and after a winding course of 500 miles joins the Missouri 10 miles below Jefferson City. Drainage area, 15,000 sq. miles.

OSAGE ORANGE (*Maclūra aurantiăca*). A tree of the nat. ord. Moraceæ (mulberry), indigenous to North America, where it is frequently used as a hedge-plant. It produces a large yellow fruit of a woody texture, somewhat resembling an orange, but not edible.

OSA'KA, or **OZAKA** (ancient **Naniwa**). An industrial city of Honshiu, Japan, on a plain opening to Osaka Bay, and at the mouth of the Aji (Yodogawa). The city is traversed by canals and river branches, and has a harbour for ocean-going steamships, also an electric railway service.

There is a mint (opened 1871), and a castle (founded 1583), within which is an arsenal. Shipyards, cotton-mills, sugar-refineries, and ironworks are representative commercial concerns, and there are markets for rice and cereals, and a stock exchange, etc. Pop. (1930), 2,453,573.

The name Osaka dates from 1492, when it was altered from *Naniwa*. In 1583 the Emperor Hideyoshi made the city his capital, and devoted himself to its improvement. The port was opened to foreign trade in 1868, and the University of Osaka established in 1880. The city's boundaries were extended in 1915.

OSBORNE HOUSE. A favourite residence of Queen Victoria, in the Isle of Wight, 1 mile from East Cowes. The grounds were bought by Queen Victoria in 1845, and the house built by Cubitt. Other residences on the estate are Barton Manor and Osborne Cottage. The estate and house were presented to the nation by Edward VII. in 1902, and were turned into a convalescent home for army and navy officers.—**Osborne College,** an institution for training naval cadets, built in the grounds of Osborne House. Opened in Aug., 1903, the college was closed in 1924, the cadets being transferred to the Royal Naval College at Dartmouth.

OSBORNE JUDGMENT. Judicial decision of the House of Lords. It was given on 21st Dec., 1909, in the case of W. V. Osborne against the Amalgamated Society of Railway Servants, after the decision of the

King's Bench had been reversed in the Court of Appeal. The judgment declared void a Trades Union rule which provided for an enforced levy from its members towards the payment of M.P.'s salaries, and dealt a blow at the political activities of the Trade Unions.

OSCANS (Lat. *Osci*). An Italian people, the earliest-known occupants of Central Italy, subdued by the Sabines. Their language was closely allied to the Latin. Some wall-inscriptions in it have been found in Pompeii. There are no remains of it except on coins and inscriptions.

OSCAR I., Joseph François Bernadotte. King of Sweden and Norway, son of Bernadotte (Charles XIV.), born at Paris in 1799, died 1859. In 1823 he married Joséphine, eldest daughter of Prince Eugène Beauharnais. During the reign of his father he was three times (in 1824, 1828, and 1833) Viceroy of Norway, where he made himself popular by his good administration. He acceded to the throne in 1844, and encouraged education, agriculture, railways, telegraphs, etc. He resigned in favour of his eldest son, Charles XV., in 1857.

OSCAR II. King of Sweden (and for many years also of Norway), born 21st Jan., 1829, died 8th Dec., 1907. He succeeded his brother, Charles XV., in 1872. He showed much sense and dignity in the movement resulting in the separation of Norway from Sweden. Under the pen-name of Oscar Fredrik he wrote historic works of value, and was noted among Swedish lyric poets.

OSCHERSLE'BEN. A town of Prussia, in Saxony. A junction of the Magdeburg-Halberstadt Railway, it has manufactures of sugar, spirits, and manures. Pop. 13,545.

OSCILLATORIA. A genus of filamentous blue-green Algæ. Several species are common on the margins of pools, on damp walls, in greenhouses, etc. The filaments carry out slow swinging or writhing movements, hence the generic name.

OSH. A town of Turkistan, in the Turcoman Republic, commanding the entrance of the valley leading to the Alai Highlands. There are two towns, native and Russian. Near by is the *Takht-i-Suleiman*, or "Throne of Solomon," a mountain of pilgrimage for Mahommedan pilgrims of Central Asia. Trade is with China. Altitude, 4000 feet ; pop., 29,088.

OSHKOSH. A city of Wisconsin, United States, the county seat of Winnebago county, on Lake Winnebago ; and served by the Chicago, Milwaukee, & St. Paul, the Chicago & North-Western, and other railways, and by river- and lake-steamers and electric-traction lines. There is an extensive lumber trade ; carriages, wagons, and general wooden goods are manufactured. Oshkosh was settled in 1836, and became a city in 1853. Pop. (1930), 40,108.

OSI'RIS (Egyptian *As-ar*). Supposed by some to have been pronounced "Usir(i)." The view has been urged that this god was of Libyan origin, and that his name originally signified "the Old One." In pre-Dynastic times he was connected with the Delta city of Dedu,

Osiris

which the Greeks called Busiris ; and after the Osirian faith spread southward, he was connected also with Abydos, where he was known as "first of the Westerners."

As the invention of the potter's wheel was credited to Ptah, god of Memphis, during the Pyramid Age, the introduction of the agricultural mode of life was credited to Osiris ; he was also regarded as the introducer of good laws, and as one who visited peoples outside Egypt as a missionary.

In the earliest Egyptian texts Osiris is regarded as a dangerous god, and he and his Underground Paradise in the west are greatly dreaded. The souls of the dead are adjured to go east, but at least one Pyramid text favours the west. Ultimately the Osirian cult of the west and the solar cult of the east were fused, while the local pantheons became solarized and Osirianized.

At an early period Osiris was connected with the Nile. In one of his phases he controls that river ; in another he is the Nile itself. The drama of the Nile must therefore be considered so that the " nature of Osiris," declared to be " more secret than that of all gods," may be investigated. In the days before this river was harnessed it fell so low that in parts it scarcely seemed to flow. The period of the " Low Nile " was hazy, hot, and sterile. For fifty days the *Hamseen*, or " sand-wind," swept from the south, coating every green thing with dust, and reducing the vitality of human beings and animals.

In June the cool and refreshing north wind (the Etesian wind of the Greeks) began to blow, clearing away the dust from vegetation. Then the Nile commenced to rise. For a few days the river ran green, coloured by the green scum of stagnant pools which was pushed down by the fresh water from the distant tropical lakes suddenly swollen by heavy rain. This was the " Green Nile," or " water of greenness."

Afterwards the rising Nile was tinged with red clay until it looked like blood. This was the " Red Nile." Then it acquired a yellowish tint from the mud before it ultimately assumed a sky-blue colour. As soon as the sand was moistened by the " Green Nile " it became alive with insect and other life, while grass and flowers appeared.

That Osiris was regarded as the personification of the " Green Nile " and as the vitalizing principle is made evident in the Pyramid Text (589), which reads, " Horus comes ! He beholds his father in thee, *renpt* (greenness) in thy name of *Mu renpu* (water of greenness)." Rameses IV. recognized this aspect of Osiris in his hymn which declares: " Thou (Osiris) art indeed the Nile, great on the fields at the beginning of the season ; gods and men live by the moisture that is in thee." The " Green Osiris, as the " Green Nile," was supposed to make vegetation green.

When the Egyptians puzzled themselves to discover what particular life-giving substance coloured the Green Nile, they concluded that it was malachite. As they believed that the river had its source in the sky, they then imagined " malachite pools " and " malachite lakes " situated beyond the horizon. In the pools the gods dwelt as birds and these birds were the " Imperishable Stars " (Pyramid Texts, 1748, etc.). Pyramid Text 567 refers to the stars as a source of malachite powder (dew).

Malachite was ground and mixed with fat to be used as an antiseptic for wounds, and for eye-paint for human beings and for gods. This paint was used " to make them healthy " (to ensure longevity). When it was found that copper could be extracted from malachite, Horus was depicted as a red god, and associated with the *mesniu* (coppersmiths).

At Edfu Horus forged in his " foundry " (temple) the copper sun which was drawn from the green (malachite) sun of the Underworld, where the " Green Osiris " judged the dead. Men prayed for " copper souls," and copper statues were made for kings. The Black Osiris was identified with the black mud of the " low Nile," and when gold could be separated from the silver of natural electrum, with the black powder to which quicksilver was reduced in the process. Maspero notes that green powder and black powder formed part of the offerings to the dead in the Pyramid Age.

The striking coincidence that a red metal came from green malachite, as a " Red Nile " came after a " Green Nile," appears to have left its impress on Egyptian religious ideas and myths. The new doctrines connected with metal symbolism were superimposed on the old doctrines connected with the god who was slain by his brother, and whose blood tinged the Nile. Other doctrines and myths were fused.

The conflict between Horus and Set had originally a solar significance. It was introduced into the Osirian myth, Horus being identified with the son of Osiris, and Set with the slayer of Osiris. More myths and doctrines were added or created, Hathor, mother of Horus, figuring as Isis. Osiris was connected with the sun, moon, and stars, and the calendar, with the goat-god, the bull-god, etc., while he still retained his connection with the ancient pig-god, Set becoming the black pig.

In the Greek period Osiris, as *Asar-hapi*, was the " Serapis " bull-god. He never, however, lost his original character as the first man who opened or discovered the path to Paradise, where he became king and judge of the head. In the Osirian Paradise the souls sowed and reaped barley and cultivated fruit-trees. Moral worthiness qualified souls to enter this paradise.

OSLO. Port, the capital of Norway, formerly Christiania, province of Aggershuus or Oslo, at the head of the long narrow inlet called Oslo Fjord, about 60 miles from the open sea or Skaggerack. The houses are mostly of brick and stone, and are generally plain buildings. Important public buildings are the royal palace, the House of Representatives or *Storthing*, the Governor's palace, and the cathedral. An interesting building is the fine old castle of Aggershuus, with its church and citadel crowning a point jutting out into the fjord. Attached to the university—the only one in Norway, opened in 1813, and attended by over 1500 students—is a museum, containing a fine collection of antiquities. The manufactures of the city consist of woollen cloth, ironware, tobacco, paper, leather, soap, spirits, glass, etc., and there are extensive breweries. The exports are principally timber and iron. The environs are exceedingly beautiful. Census pop. (1930), 253,124.

OS'MIUM (symbol, Os; atomic weight, 190·9). One of the platinum metals; it is bluish-white and lustrous. It has a specific gravity of 22·5, being thus the heaviest of all bodies. It may also be obtained in crystals, or as a black amorphous powder, which is readily oxidized. Osmium is the most infusible of all the metals. It combines with chlorine in different proportions, also with sulphur, and forms alloys with some other metals. The oxide OsO_4 forms colourless crystals, is very volatile, and highly poisonous; it is an acidic oxide, and is also an oxidizing agent.

OSMO'SIS and **OSMOTIC PRESSURE.** *See* SOLUTION.

OSMUN'DA. The type-genus of Osmundaceæ (q.v.). *Osmunda regālis*, the flowering or royal fern, which grows to the height sometimes of 10 feet, is a native of Britain and other parts of the Old World, as well as of North America. It is often cultivated as an ornamental plant on account of its striking appearance, the fructification forming a fine panicle somewhat resembling that of a flowering plant.

OSMUNDACEÆ. A small family of ferns, in many respects intermediate between the Eusporangiate and the Leptosporangiate divisions. The living genera are Osmunda and Todea. They are an ancient family, many species being known from the Mesozoic rocks.

OSNABRÜCK, or **OSNABURG.** An ancient town of Prussia, in Hanover, on the Hase. It possesses many interesting buildings, and was formerly an important seat of linen manufacture, giving name to the coarse linen known as Osnaburg. The Treaty of Westphalia (1648) was discussed in the town hall of Osnabrück. Its chief manufactures are chemicals, iron and steel, paper, cotton, and tobacco.

Osnabrück : The Alsladter Hof

Erected into a see in 888, the town was surrounded by walls in 1082. It entered the Hanseatic League, but never rose to be a free imperial city. (Pop. (1919), 85,079.

OSORREI, or **OSORHEI.** A town of Rumania, formerly in Hungary, and known as Maros Vasarhely. It is situated 80 miles by rail from Cluj (Kolozsvar). Pop. 25,000.

OSPREY ((*Pandīon haliaëtus*). A well-known raptorial bird, called also *fishing-hawk*, *fishing-eagle*, and *sea-eagle*. It occurs both in the Old and New World, near the shores of the sea, or great rivers and lakes, and builds its nest in high trees and cliffs. It lives on fish, and pounces with great rapidity on its prey, as it happens to come near the surface of the water, the toes being armed with strong curved nails.

The general body-colour is a rich brown, the tail being banded with light and dark (in the old birds the tail is pure white), head and neck whitish on their upper portions, and a brown stripe extends from the bill down each side of the neck; under parts of the body whitish, legs of a bluish tint. In length the osprey averages about 2 feet, the wings measuring over 4 feet from tip to tip. The female lays three or four eggs.

The American bald-eagle (*Haliaëtus leucocephălus*) pursues the osprey, who drops his prey with the view of

Osprey (*Pandion haliaëtus*)

escaping, when the eagle immediately pounces after the descending fish, and seizes it ere it touches the water.

OSSETES (os-sēts'). One of the numerous tribes or peoples inhabiting the Caucasus, belonging to the Indo-European family, and to the Iranic branch of it. They are at a lower stage of civilization than some of the neighbouring peoples. Their religion consists of a strange mixture of Christianity, Mahommedanism, and Paganism. They number about 170,000.

OSSETT. A municipal borough of England, West Riding of Yorkshire, near the Calder; served by the L.M.S. & L.N.E. Railways. It has woollen manufactures, and there are coal-mines in the neighbourhood. Pop. (1931), 14,838.

OSSIAN. A real or mythical Irish poet, to whom are attributed certain poems, the subject of a great literary controversy of the latter half of the eighteenth century and the commencement of the nineteenth. It originated by the publication of two epics, *Fingal* (1762) and *Temora* (1763), by James Macpherson (q.v.). Both are a record of the deeds of a great Celtic hero, Fingal. In the first of these poems he is assumed to war with the Danes, leading to their ultimate expulsion; but in *Temora* he is placed farther back, and his struggles are with the Romans.

These and some minor poems Macpherson attributed to Ossian, the son of Fingal, and alleged that his version was a literal translation of works which had been transmitted orally in the Gaelic language from bard to bard until the introduction of writing permitted them to be committed to manuscript. Immediately on the publication of *Fingal* it attained an immense popularity. It was translated within a year into all the principal languages of Europe, and numbered among its admirers the ripest scholars and the most distinguished men of genius of the age.

The question of authenticity, which was raised immediately on the publication of *Fingal*, was noticed with somewhat lofty disdain by Macpherson in his preface to *Temora*, and although he then professed to be able to meet it by the production of the originals, he generally maintained throughout the controversy an angry silence.

At first the judgment of Dr. Blair, who wrote an elaborate critical dissertation in favour of the authenticity of the poems, was regarded as of paramount authority throughout Europe; and notwithstanding the emphatic denunciation of Dr. Johnson, and objections of other critics, the believers in the genuineness of Ossian continued to hold their ground until Malcolm Laing's unsparing criticism, first in the introduction to his *History of Scotland* (1800), and afterwards in an annotated edition of the poems themselves (1805), gave a death-blow to the position of those who maintained the integrity of the Ossianic epics.

In 1797 the Highland Society chose a committee to inquire into the authenticity of the poems. The report published in 1805 states that the committee had not been able to obtain any one poem the same in title and tenor with the poems published by Macpherson; that it was inclined to believe that he was in the habit of supplying chasms, and of giving connection by inserting passages which he did not find, and to add what he conceived to be dignity and delicacy to the original, by striking out passages, by softening incidents, by refining the language, etc., but that it was impossible to determine to what degree he exercised these liberties.

In 1807, after the death of Macpherson, and in accordance with his will, appeared the Gaelic originals of his poems, with a Latin translation, and accompanied by a new dissertation on their authenticity by Sir John Sinclair. Hence arose a new and singular controversy.

It was asserted that these originals, the manuscripts of which were all in the handwriting of Macpherson, were translated by himself from the English, and this charge seems to be about as well substantiated as that of the original fabrication. What appears really to have been decided is that Ossian was a real or mythical Irish bard of the second or third century, of whom there are probably no authentic remains, although some brief poems, which cannot be traced farther back than the eleventh century, are attributed to him.

There are numerous traditions regarding him both in Scotland and Ireland. That Macpherson possessed considerable, and often conflicting, material, collected in the Highlands, which he worked up into a continuous whole, in epic form, and that he himself produced the connecting links, seems beyond doubt.—BIBLIOGRAPHY: G. Eyre-Todd, *Introduction to Macpherson's Poems of Ossian*; A. T. Nutt, *Ossian and the Ossianic Literature*; J. F. Campbell, *Popular Tales of the West Highlands, Orally Collected with a Translation.*

OSSOLI, Margaret Sarah Fuller. American author, was born in 1810 and died 1850. She edited *The Dial* and contributed to *The New York Tribune*. She married the Marchese Ossoli, and both perished in a shipwreck off Long Island.

OSSOVETZ, or **OSOWIEC.** A fortress town of Poland, on the Bobr. It was of enormous strategic importance during the European War. The Bobr is a small stream of no great breadth, but over 12 feet deep. It traverses a valley of impassable swamps, across which the high road and railway lines run by the only practicable crossing. This crossing was defended by Ossovetz, then a Russian third-class fortress, with solid-concrete forts, and modern heavy guns made in the Putilov foundries.

On 25th Sept., 1914, the German assault began, and the Russians opened the sluices of the Bobr. The town was bombarded for four days (27th Sept. to a.m. 1st Oct.) with little effect, and the swamp and the narrow causeway beat the Germans, whose infantry lines were deployed at a distance of four miles. A sortie by the garrison accounted for three German guns, and forced the besieging force to withdraw. As the offensive on the Niemen had also failed, the Russians resumed their onward march a fortnight later.

In February and April, 1915, renewed attempts were made to take the town, but were of little avail. On 19th Aug., 1915, the entire front from Ossovetz to Vladimir Volynsky was evacuated, and on 22nd Aug. the forts of Ossovetz were definitely abandoned, and the Russians withdrew to the Brest-Litovsk line.

It is a peculiar point about Ossovetz that before the continuous bombardment of the heaviest siege artillery of Europe it could not be reduced, whereas infinitely more powerful and better-equipped fortresses on all fronts had readily succumbed. *See* maps under EUROPEAN WAR.

OSTEITIS. Inflammation of the substance of bone. In its chronic forms it may result in suppuration; in caries, a decay of the bone in particles; or in necrosis, a decay of the bone in slices. In acute cases low diet, aperients, etc., are employed; but in chronic cases tonics, good air, and possibly removal of the diseased bone may be required.

OSTEND'. A seaport and principal sea-bathing resort of Belgium, province of West Flanders, on the North Sea, 77 miles N.W. of Brussels. It is situated on a sandy plain, and is protected against the sea by a solid wall of granite. The entrance to the port is narrow, and dangerous in bad weather, but the basins within are very extensive. The cod- and herring-fishing and the cultivation of oysters are considerable industries, and the export of butter, eggs, poultry, and rabbits is extensive.

It is a station for Dover and London steamers, and a terminus for branch railway lines connecting the town with various Continental systems. There is a Kursaal. Ostend dates from 1072, and sustained a memorable siege by the Spaniards from 4th July, 1601, to 28th Sept., 1604, when it capitulated. During the European War (q.v.) it was taken by the Germans on 14th Oct., 1914. A lighthouse, replacing the one destroyed in 1916, was completed in 1924. Pop. (1931), 47,313.

Under German occupation the digue at Ostend became a fortress, a veritable city of block-houses, concrete-works, gun-platforms, and dug-outs, and the Tirpitz battery of heavy guns, with a range of 30,000 yards, was placed in position alongside, the guns being protected by cupolas of special thick armour.

In the early months of the occupation the German High Command realized the value of Ostend as a base for harassing operations with torpedo-craft, and indeed for aggressive naval effort of whatever description. The narrow and tortuous channel to the town was carefully dredged, and the canal from Bruges to Ostend thoroughly surveyed.

Towards the end of 1916, German "raids" from Ostend and Zeebrugge became so frequent that it was urged upon the authorities that the only method of stopping these raids was to destroy the Flanders ports. Tons of high explosives had already been dropped by air-craft, but the damage, however great, had always been more or less repaired.

In Nov., 1917, the Plans Division of the Admiralty, at the head of which was a young flag-officer named Roger Keyes, conceived and elaborated a programme for the permanent disablement of Zeebrugge and Ostend by sealing them up with concrete-filled block-ships. On the morning of 23rd April, 1918 (St. George's Day), the Zeebrugge-Ostend block-ships moved off, the Ostend operations being under the direction of Commodore Hubert Lynes, R.N. A change of wind rendered the scheme practically abortive, and the flares, carried by motor-launches to show the ends of the wooden piers leading to the harbour, were extinguished by gun-fire, with the result that the block-ships ran aground and were blown up outside the entrance.

The *Vindictive*, still seaworthy, but badly battered, was chosen for a second attempt, and set out again on 9th May. Commodore Lynes was again in chief command, Commander A. E. Godsal taking command of the *Vindictive*. The Germans were completely surprised, and two motor-boats had torpedoed the pier ends, and seaplanes and monitors were already bombarding the shore batteries, before a return fire was opened. Under a hail of projectiles the *Vindictive* steamed in with controls demolished, Commander Godsal in the conning-tower.

As she laid her nose to the eastern pier, and prepared to swing her 320 feet of length across the channel, the conning-tower was struck by a shell from the shore batteries, and Commander Godsal was blown to pieces. Lieutenant V. A. C. Crutchley, V.C., took command, but the *Vindictive* was lying at an angle of about 40° to the pier, hard and fast. The commander gave the order to clear the engine-room and abandon ship.

Engineer - Lieutenant - Commander Bury was last man off, and he blew the main charges by the switch installed aft. Lieutenant Crutchley blew the auxiliary charges in the forward 6-inch magazine, and the old ship sank and lay on the bottom of the channel. For all practical purposes Ostend was immobilized, and Bruges was deprived of importance as a torpedo base. The losses were slight, and were chiefly incurred by the *Vindictive* company when abandoning ship. *See* EUROPEAN WAR.

OSTEOPATHY. A system of medical treatment founded in 1874 by an American physician, Dr. A. T. Still. The leading idea of the system is that structural derangement of the body is the chief cause of disease. All the tissues of the body are subject to such derangements, or "lesions." For the treatment of these, osteopathists hold that drugs are useless. Their method is to adjust the affected parts by finger manipulation, and to leave the rest to nature.

OSTERODE (os'te-rō-dė), (1) A town of Prussia, in Hanover, at the foot of the Harz Mountains. It manufactures woollen, cotton, and linen goods, white lead, leather, oil, machinery, etc. Among its buildings are St. Giles's Church (724) and the Rathaus (1552). Pop. 7500. (2) A town of East Prussia, on a small lake (Drewenz), with manufactures of machinery, distilleries, etc. Pop. 16,482.

OS'TIA. An ancient city of Italy, at the mouth of the Tiber. It was of great importance as the port of Rome and as a naval station, and for a long period it engrossed the whole trade of Rome by sea. The port, however, was never good, and owing to the gradual accumulation of the mud and other deposits brought down by the river it ultimately became inaccessible to ships of large tonnage.

Many efforts were made by various Roman emperors to improve the port, but without much success. It was destroyed by the Saracens in the ninth century. Excavations were begun under Pope Pius VII., again in 1854, and in 1880, disclosing three temples, a theatre, the forum, etc. The modern Ostia (founded by Gregory IV. in 830) is a village connected by tramway with Rome and the sea-beach.

OSTRA'CION. The type genus of the trunk-fishes (Ostraciontidæ), included in the division Plectognathi, which forms a sub-order of the Teleostei or bony fishes. The body is enclosed in a literal armour-casing of strong bony plates or scales of the ganoid variety, which are immovably united, and invest every part of the body save the fins, of which the dorsal and anal are the chief agents of locomotion, while the pectorals draw currents of water over the gills. The caudal fin is used as a rudder, or for propulsion. These fishes do not attain a large size, and are common in tropical seas.

OS'TRACISM (Gr. *ostrakon*, a shell). A political measure practised among the ancient Athenians by which persons considered dangerous to the State were banished by public vote for a term of years (generally ten), with leave to return to the enjoyment of their estates at the end of the period. It takes this name from the shell or tablet on which each person recorded his vote.

The votes were counted by the archons, and in the event of there being 6000 votes against a statesman he was obliged to leave the city within ten days. Among the distinguished persons ostracized were Themistocles, Aristides, and Cimon, son of Miltiades, who were afterwards recalled. Ostracism was introduced at Athens, 508-507 B.C., and was abolished in about 417 B.C.

OSTRAVA, or OSTRAU. A town of Czechoslovakia, in Moravia, on the Ostrawitza. It has coal-mines, iron-works, and candle-factories. Pop. (1930), 125,347.—**Polish Ostrava,** which adjoins this town, formerly in Austrian Silesia, is engaged in the same industries. Pop. 22,890.

OSTRICH (*Struthio camēlus*). A running bird, of the family Struthionidæ, of which it is the type. It

Ostrich (*Struthio camēlus*)

inhabits the sandy plains of Africa, Arabia, and Mesopotamia, and is the largest bird existing, attaining a height of from 6 to 8 feet. The head and neck are nearly naked; the general body plumage is black, the wing and tail feathers white, occasionally with black markings; the quill feathers of the wings and tail have their barbs wholly disconnected, hence their graceful appearance.

The legs are extremely strong, the thighs naked. There are only two toes, the hallux or hind toe being wanting. The pubic bones are united, a conformation occurring in no other bird. The wings are of small size and are incapable of being used as organs of flight, but the birds can run with extraordinary speed, outdistancing the fleetest horse. The bill is broad and of a triangular depressed shape.

The food consists of grass, grain, etc., and substances of a vegetable nature, and to aid in the trituration of this food the ostrich swallows large stones, bits of iron and glass, or other hard materials that come in the way. Ostriches are polygamous, each male consorting with several females, and they generally keep together in flocks. The eggs average 3 lb. in weight, and several hens often lay from ten to twelve each in the same nest, which is merely a hole scraped in the sand.

The eggs appear to be incubated mainly by the cock-bird, assisted by his hens in the daytime, but also partly by the heat of the sun. The South African ostrich is often considered as a distinct species under the name of *S. australis.* Three South American birds of an allied family (Rheidæ), of the genus *Rhea,* are popularly known as the American ostriches, differing chiefly from the African form in having the head feathered and three-toed feet, each toe armed with a claw. (*See* RHEA.)

The ostrich has been hunted from the earliest ages for its feathers, which have always been valued as a dress decoration. The feathers of the back are those most valued, the wing and tail feathers rank next. The black plumes are obtained by dyeing. The finest white feathers are exported from Tripoli, Egypt, Tunis, and Algiers, and the bulk of these find their way to Paris. Great Britain imports most of its ostrich feathers from Cape Colony. Ostriches having become scarce in that country, an attempt was made about 1858 to domesticate them, and with such success that ostrich-farming forms an important source of wealth. The market value of the feathers naturally varies with their quality, the prevailing fashion, and the supply.

OSTROG. A town of Poland, in the old Russian government of Volhynia. It is the place where the Bible was first printed in Slavonic (1581). Pop. 17,000.

OSTWALD, Wilhelm. German chemist, born at Riga in 1853, and educated at Dorpat. He was professor of chemistry at the polytechnic in Riga from 1882 to 1887, when he was appointed professor of physical chemistry at Leipzig. This post he held until 1906. He made important discoveries in physical chemistry, including the Dilution Law which bears his name and which shows the relationship between molecular conductivity and dilution.

His work on catalysis, especially in the manufacture of nitric acid by the catalytic oxidization of ammonia, was the foundation of industries important both from the standpoint of economic production and in making the explosive manufacturers of his country independent of the imported supplies of nitrates.

During the European War, when importation was impossible, the synthetic production of nitrates was a factor of considerable importance to Germany. Ostwald was honoured by many British and foreign universities and learned societies. He was the founder of a number of German scientific periodicals, and is the author of many works on chemistry, most of which have been translated into English. He died in 1932.

OSTYAKS, or **OSTIAKS.** Three different tribes of Finnish origin inhabiting the north-west of Siberia. They are known as the Ugrian Ostyaks, the Samoyedic Ostyaks, and the Yenisei Ostyaks. They inhabit the banks of the Irtysh and the Ob and the Yenisei, between the Upper and Lower Tunguska. The first two tribes are both linguistically and racially akin, whilst the Yenisei Ostyaks differ linguistically and to some extent physically from all the tribes living in Siberia.

All the three tribes number now about 25,000. Their religion is mostly Shamanism, although the Yeniseian Ostyaks, are officially reckoned as members of the Russian Orthodox Church.—Cf. article in Hastings's *Encyclopædia of Ethics and Religion*.

OSU'NA (ancient **Urso,** later **Orsona**). A town of Southern Spain, in the province of Seville. It has a church built in 1534 on the site of a Moorish mosque. Manufactures include iron, linen, soap, articles in esparto, etc., and there is a large trade in oil, grain, etc., with Seville and Malaga. Osuna was taken from the Moors in 1240. Pop. 15,650.

OSWALDTWISTLE. An urban district of Lancashire, England, served by the L.M.S. Railway. There are cotton-factories, print-works, coal-mines, and stone-quarries in the district. Pop. (1931), 14,221.

OSWE'GO. A city and port of entry of New York, United States, the county seat of Oswego county, on the Oswego River, where it falls into Lake Ontario. It is served by the New York, Central, & Hudson River; the New York, Ontario, & Western; and the Delaware, Lackawana, & Western Railways; by steamboat, and by the Oswego Canal (Lake Ontario-Erie Canal). The city has a fine modern harbour, miles of quays, and extensive accommodation for its gigantic trade in grain and lumber with Canada and elsewhere. It is famous for its vast starch-factory, and has extensive mills, tanneries, foundries, machine-shops, and shipyards. The river supplies ample water-power. Founded in 1724, it became a city in 1848. Pop. (1930), 22,652.

OSWESTRY (os'es-tri). A rural district and municipal borough of Shropshire, England; served by the Great Western Railway. It is of great antiquity, deriving its name from Oswald, King of Northumbria, slain here in 642, and makes some figure in early English history.

Coal and limestone are worked in the neighbourhood. There are railway workshops, agricultural implement works, and breweries. In the neighbourhood are Oswald's Well and Old Oswestry. Pop. (1931), 9754. The rural district has a pop. of 16,603.

OSYMAN'DYAS. An ancient king of Egypt, mentioned by Diodorus Siculus, who reports that he invaded Asia with a vast army, and penetrated as far as Bactria, and that on his return he erected at Thebes a monument to himself of unparalleled magnificence, with a sitting colossal statue of enormous size. The Memnonium at Thebes has been represented as his monument.

OTA'GO. A provincial district of New Zealand, in the South Island, till 1876 one of the original six provinces. It is situated south of the provincial districts of Canterbury and Westland; area, 25,220 sq. miles. The interior is mountainous; many peaks attain the height of from 3000 to 9000 feet, but there is much pastoral land; the north-east consists of extensive plains. Otago, although it possesses valuable gold-fields, is chiefly a pastoral and agricultural district, second only to Canterbury in wheat production.

The climate is similar to that of Britain, but warmer and more equable. The largest river is the Clutha or Clyde, the largest of New Zealand. There are also extensive lakes, as the Te Anau, 132 sq. miles; the Wakatipu, 112 sq. miles in area.

Coal has been found in abundance. Otago was founded in 1848 by the

Scottish Free Church Association; it is now the most populous division of the Dominion. The capital is Dunedin; the next town in importance is Oamaru. Pop. (est. 1932), 222,600.

OTAL'GIA. A painful affection of the ear. It may be due to inflammation of the ear; it may be a symptom of other diseases; or it may be a species of neuralgia. It is often associated with other nervous ailments such as toothache, and neuralgic pains in the face; and as its intensity and duration generally depend upon the condition of the latter, otalgia is probably only a local symptom of the other troubles. Children, especially during their fast-growing period, are frequently subjected to otalgic pains. The treatment is the same as for neuralgic affections.

OTARU. A seaport of Hokkaido, Japan, on the main railway to Sapporo. Pop. (1930), 144,887.

OTIDIDÆ. A family of carinate birds comprising the bustards, and usually included in the ord. Gruiformes.

OTI'TIS. Inflammation of the ear, accompanied with intense pain. Within the tympanum it is called middle-ear disease; and like all other inflammations it may be acute or chronic. It often follows the simple exanthemata of childhood. Tubercular and syphilitic subjects are particularly liable to this disease. Otitis is often a serious malady, producing fever and delirium, and ending in suppuration, and generally in the rupture of the tympanum and more or less deafness.

It may, and usually does, spread backward into the mastoid process, causing a mastoid abscess. The peculiar seriousness of middle-ear disease is due to the risk of the spread of the inflammatory process to the brain or its large venous sinuses, causing abscess of the brain or clotting of the blood in the sinuses, either of which may lead to fatal results.

OTLEY. An urban district and town of Yorkshire (West Riding), England, on the Wharfe; served by the L.M.S. & L.N.E. Railways. It has a grammar-school, founded 1602; a Norman church (All Saints), containing relics of the Fairfax family; and a mechanics institute (1869). Machine-making is the principal industry. Pop. (1931), 11,020.

O'TOLITHS. Small calcareous bodies contained in the membranous labyrinths or internal ears of vertebrates; and also in the sense-organs concerned with maintenance of balance (stato-cysts) that occur in molluscs, crustacea, some annelids, and certain jelly-fishes. In some crustacea, as prawns, the stato-cysts open externally, and foreign particles (sand-grains, etc.) introduced from the exterior play the part of otoliths.

OTORRHŒA. A purulent or muco-purulent discharge from the ears following middle-ear disease.

OTRAN'TO (ancient **Hydruntum**). A city of Apulia, Southern Italy, in the province of Lecce, and on the south-east coast of the Strait of Otranto. It is joined by railway to Brindisi (45 miles), and is the starting-point of submarine cables to Valona and Corfu. Otranto was taken from the Byzantine emperors in 1068 by Robert Guiscard, and was razed by the Turks in 1480. Prior to that time it was of great commercial importance, but the modern city is dormant commercially. Pop. 3022.

OT'TAWA. The ninth river of Canada and the principal tributary of the St. Lawrence, rising in the Laurentian Plateau (Quebec Province), and forming for some distance the boundary between Ontario and Quebec. It discharges into the St. Lawrence above Montreal, after a course of about 685 miles. The Chaudière Falls above the city of Ottawa are 200 feet wide and 40 feet high, and provide hydro-electric power. The city of Ottawa consumed 54,000 h.p. of electric energy so generated in 1921. Lumber is sent down-stream by the main river and by the tributaries Rideau, Madawaska, Lièvre, Coulogne, and Gatineau.

OTTAWA. A city of Ontario, Canada, in Carleton county, the capital and administrative centre of the Dominion. It stands on the Ottawa, where it receives the Rideau, and is served by all Canadian trans-continental lines, by the New York Central Railway, and by electric tramways. River-steamers connect with Montreal and Kingston on the St. Lawrence (via the Rideau Canal) during the summer season.

On 3rd Feb., 1916, the Dominion Parliament buildings, excepting the Senate House and library, were destroyed, and have been reconstructed, the main front being 470 feet long and 100 feet high, surmounted by a tower of 300 feet. Other notable buildings are the National Museum, the Observatory, the Dominion Mint, Rideau Hall (the Governor-General's official residence), and the Château Laurier, an enormous hotel in Major's

Hill Park (facing Parliament buildings), owned and controlled by the Grand Trunk Railway. There are Anglican and Roman Catholic cathedrals, and a Catholic university.

Ottawa is a centre of the Canadian lumber trade, and immense quantities of timber pass through the city's innumerable sawmills. Other industries are mainly dependent upon the hydro-electric power generated by the Chaudière and Rideau Falls, and include iron-works and foundries and factories for the production of cement, candles, paper and paper-pulp, agricultural implements, and tents. In 1920 there were 388 industrial establishments of all classes. Pop. (1931), 124,988.

Ottawa: Cathedral of Notre Dame

Ottawa was founded in 1827 by Colonel By of the Royal Engineers, who built a canal from the Chaudière Falls to Kingston on Lake Ontario, but the site and falls were described by Champlain in his *Voyages* of 1613. The canal was the precursor of Bytown, which in 1854 became a city as Ottawa, and in 1858 Ottawa became the Canadian capital.

In 1932 the conference of representatives of the governments of the British Commonwealth was held at Ottawa. The Ottawa Conference (q.v.) marked a material departure in Economic policy within the Commonwealth and brought to an end the Free Trade policy pursued by the U.K. for three generations.

Ottawa Conference, The.—The Imperial Economic Conference which met at Ottawa in July-Aug., 1932, marked an important departure in British trade policy. It was decided to hold this conference to consider economic questions which could not be dealt with at the Imperial Conference of 1930, and Ottawa was chosen as its seat on the invitation of the Canadian Government. Representatives attended from all the self-governing dominions and from India. The subjects proposed for discussion included questions of monetary policy, the distribution of industries within the British Commonwealth of nations, trade policy, and machinery for continuous consultation on economic matters affecting the Commonwealth. Its chief economic result was to confirm and extend Britain's departure from the historic Free Trade policy pursued by this country for three generations. (See Free Trade.)

The principal declaration of policy adopted by the Ottawa Conference stated that the nations of the British Commonwealth were entering into certain agreements with one another for the extension of mutual trade by means of reciprocal preferential tariffs, in the conviction that "by the lowering or removal of barriers among themselves provided for in those agreements, the flow of trade between the various countries of the Empire will be facilitated, and that by the consequent increase of purchasing power of their peoples the trade of the world will also be stimulated and increase; further, that this Conference regards the conclusion of these agreements as a step forward which should in the future lead to further progress in the same direction, and which will utilise protective duties to ensure that the resources and industries of the Empire are developed on sound economic lines." The agreements referred to in this resolution chiefly affected the trade policy of Great Britain, but there were also reciprocal concessions made by the dominions with the object of facilitating imports from Great Britain.

Among the undertakings given to the dominions by the British Government were (1) continuation of the provision as to free entry of Empire produce contained in the Import Duties Act and Horticultural Products Act, 1932, which Acts marked the first breach in the British free trade system; at Ottawa the British Government undertook to prolong free entry for the duty-free products specified in these Acts for the period covered by the Ottawa agreements (viz. five years, with certain exceptions in the case of India); but for eggs, butter, poultry, cheese, and other milk products imported from Australia, Canada, New Zealand,

South Africa, Southern Rhodesia, and Newfoundland, free entry was guaranteed for no more than three years certain, at the end of which period the British Government reserved the right to review the basis of preference; (2) imposition of fresh duties on foreign imports, either new or in addition to those imposed under the two Acts; (3) maintenance for five years (except with consent of the Dominion Governments concerned) of the general 10 per cent. **ad valorem** duty imposed by the two Acts on a wide range of foreign imports (including wheat-flour and grain, tinned meat, canned salmon, dried fruits, peas, potatoes, fresh and frozen fish; and a variety of raw materials); (4) regulations respecting meat imports, chilled and frozen beef, mutton, and lamb and (after further consideration) bacon and ham, with the object of raising wholesale prices in the United Kingdom, and the stimulation of home production and empire imports; (5) various other undertakings with respect to the importation of live cattle, preference for tobacco, Indian coffee and cotton, and similar matters.

Great Britain also undertook, in its agreement with Canada, that if either of the two Governments were satisfied, the preferences granted were likely to be frustrated by "the creation or maintenance" of prices through State action on the part of any foreign country, powers were to be taken by the Government concerned to prohibit entirely, in whole or part, the import of any products from that foreign country calculated to make the Anglo-Canadian agreement effective. This article was directed mainly at the "dumping" policy attributed to Soviet Russia.

Reciprocal concessions made by the Dominion Governments included, in the case of Australia, the standardisation of the preference given to British goods. In the case of Canada, Britain's preferential position in Canadian markets was improved in respect of some 215 items, covering about 40 per cent. of this country's trade with Canada; many of the goods itemized being placed on Canada's free list, or the duty against British goods being lowered or duties on foreign goods increased. In the agreement with New Zealand, existing preferences to British exports were standardized, in respect of four items lowered, and the surtax abolished on all British goods. Existing preferences in the South African market were guaranteed in the agreement with South Africa and improved in certain cases. India undertook to give a 10 per cent. preference on existing "revenue" duties and also a 10 per cent. preference on protective duties unless it was decided (by the Tariff Board) that the full measure of protection is required against British exports to India. Newfoundland and Southern Rhodesia also granted preferences on a short list of items.

As far as British trade is concerned, the broad effect of the Ottawa agreements was to impose duties on about 60 per cent. of our total imports, leaving about 40 per cent. on the "free list." With regard to the "value" of the Dominion Governments' concessions to this country, it was calculated at the time of the Ottawa Conference that about £25,000,000 to £30,000,000 of British trade was affected out of a total British export trade of £700,000,000.

Among the general declarations concerning trade policy within the British Commonwealth contained in the agreements with Australia and Canada was one affirming as a general principle that "protection by tariffs shall be afforded against United Kingdom products only to those industries which are reasonably assured of sound opportunities of success." It was also agreed by Canada that during the currency of the Ottawa agreements tariffs should be based on the principle "that protective duties shall not exceed such a level as will give United Kingdom producers full opportunity of reasonable competition on the basis of the relative cost of economical and efficient production."

In accordance with a decision of the Ottawa Conference a committee, composed of two representatives of each of the participating Governments, was set up to consider means of facilitating economic consultation and co-operation between the several Governments of the Commonwealth and to make a survey of various agencies already existing, e.g. the Imperial Economic Committee (q.v.), Empire Marketing Board (q.v.), Imperial Institute (q.v.), etc. It was subsequently agreed that this Committee should include representatives of the "Colonial Empire" and of Southern Rhodesia. A joint secretariat was also appointed. In addition to a series of recommendations respecting existing agencies, this Committee rpoposed that it should itself continue in existence as an Imperial Committee on Economic Consultation and Co-operation.

OTTAWA. A city of Illinois, United States, the county seat of La Salle county, on the Illinois; served by the Chicago, Rock Island, & Pacific, and the Chicago, Burlington, & Quincy Railways, and by the Illinois and Michigan Canal. It is the seat of a college, and has manufactures of agricultural implements, carriages, and wagons, musical instruments, and tobacco. In the vicinity is a medicinal spring; coal, glass-sand, and clay are found near by. Ottawa was founded in 1830, and became a city in 1853. Pop. 15,094.

OTTER. A carnivorous mammal, family Mustelidæ or weasels, genus Lutra. There are several species, differing chiefly in size and fur. They all have large flattish heads, short ears, webbed toes, crooked nails, and tails slightly flattened horizontally. The common river-otter, the *Lutra vulgāris* of Europe and Asia, inhabits the banks of rivers, feeds principally on fish, and is often very destructive, particularly to salmon.

The under fur is short and woolly, the outer is composed of longer and coarser hairs of dark brown hue. They burrow near the water's edge, line their nest with grass and leaves, and produce from four to five young. The weight of a full-grown male is from 20 to 24 lb.; length from nose to tail 2 feet, tail 15 to 16 inches. Otter-hunting in Great Britain is now limited to a few districts. The American or Canadian otter (*Lutra canadensis*) averages about 4 feet in length inclusive of the tail. It is plentiful in Canada, and furnishes a valuable fur, which is a deep reddish-brown in winter, and blackish in summer. Other species are found in South America, Africa (South and West), India, and Malaya.

The sea-otters (Enhydris), represented typically by the great sea-otter (*E. lutris*), inhabit the coasts of the North Pacific Ocean, but are of comparatively rare occurrence. The tail is short, measuring about 7 inches only; weight 60 to 70 lb. The fur is soft, and of a deep lustrous black, or of a dark maroon colour when dressed, and is much prized. In general appearance the sea-otter somewhat resembles a small seal.

OTTO I., the Great. Emperor of Germany, son of Henry I., born 912, died 973. He was crowned King of Germany at Aix-la-Chapelle in 936. His reign of thirty-six years was an almost uninterrupted succession of wars. After a fourteen years' struggle he subdued Boleslas, Duke of Bohemia; he wrested the Duchies of Suabia, Bavaria, and Lorraine from the Dukes of Bavaria and Franconia, and gave them (in 949) to his sons Ludolf and Henry, and to his son-in-law Conrad, Count of Worms, respectively.

He delivered the Italians from the oppressions of Berengar II., married the widow of their last king, and was crowned King of Lombardy (951). In 961 he was crowned King of Italy, and in the following year emperor by Pope John XII., who took the oath of allegiance, but soon repented and took to arms. Otto deposed him and placed Leo VIII. in the Papal chair; he also punished the Romans for replacing John after his departure.

The Byzantine court refused to acknowledge Otto's claim to the imperial dignity; but he defeated the Greek forces in Lower Italy, and the Eastern emperor, John Zimisces, gave the Greek Princess Theophania to his son Otto in marriage.

OTTO II. Youngest son of Otto I., was born in 955, died at Rome 983. His elder brothers had all died before their father, who caused him to be crowned King of Rome—the first instance of the kind in German history. He subdued the revolt of several powerful vassals, including his cousin, Henry II., Duke of Bavaria.

In Italy he suppressed a rising under Crescentius, and then attempted to drive the Greeks from Lower Italy; but they called in the aid of the Saracens from Sicily (981), and Otto suffered a total defeat (982). He escaped by leaping into the sea, was picked up by a Greek ship, from which he afterwards escaped by a ruse, and died soon after at Rome.

OTTO III. Son of the preceding, and the last of the male branch of the Saxon Imperial House, born 980, died 1002. He was only three years old when he succeeded his father. At the age of fifteen he marched into Italy and crushed a fresh insurrection fomented by Crescentius. He was consecrated emperor in 996 by Gregory V., a near relative of his own. He next suppressed a second rebellion under Crescentius, whom he caused to be beheaded. John XVI., the Pope installed by the latter, was also captured, cruelly mutilated, and killed by the populace.

On the death of Gregory, Otto raised his old tutor, Gerbert, to the pontificate under the title Sylvester II. Peace in Rome was, however, only temporary, and until his death Otto was mostly employed in quelling disturbances in various parts of Italy. Some historians assert that his death was due to poisoning—an act of revenge on the part of the widow of Crescentius.

OTTO I. King of Greece, second son of King Ludwig I. of Bavaria, born 1st June, 1815, died 26th July, 1867. Educated at Munich, he travelled in Germany and Italy for the purpose of completing his education. Nominated King of Greece by the Conference of London on 7th May, 1832, he was recognized by the Greeks on 8th Aug., 1832, and

Otto I.

ascended the throne on 6th Feb., 1833. Married to Princess Amelia of Oldenburg he had no children and founded no dynasty. When the Revolution of 1862 drove him from the throne he returned to Bamberg in Bavaria, where he died.

OTTOMAN. *See* TURKEY.

OT'TUMWA. A city of Iowa, United States, the county seat of Wapello county, on the Des Moines; served by the Chicago, Milwaukee, & St. Paul, the Wabash, and the Chicago, Rock Island, & Pacific Railways. It is a centre of coal-mining, and has industries of pork-packing and iron and steel manufactures. It was founded in 1843, and became a city in 1857. Pop. (1930), 28,075.

OTWAY, Thomas. English dramatist, was born in 1652, and died in 1685. He was educated at Winchester and Christ Church, but left Oxford without a degree. He was always interested in the stage, and after a highly unsuccessful appearance as an actor in Mrs. Behn's *Forc'd Marriage,* he began to write plays.

His earliest play, a feeble tragedy, *Alcibiades,* was produced in 1675, and saved from complete failure by the acting of Betterton and Mrs. Barry, who acted in all Otway's plays. His next play, *Don Carlos* (1676), was a better play, and won great popularity in spite of the wholesale slaughter at the end of it. Otway adapted Racine's *Bérénice* and Molière's *Les Fourberies de Scapin,* the latter retaining the stage until last century.

His original comedies, *Friendship in Fashion* (1678), *The Soldier's Fortune* (1681), and *The Atheist* (1684) are undistinguished by any merit. Nor can much be said in favour of his tragedy, *The History and Fall of Caius Marius,* a curious hybrid in which part of *Romeo and Juliet* is grafted on to Plutarch's *Life of Marius.*

The two works which keep the fame of Otway alive are *The Orphan* (1680), a most pathetic play, and his masterpiece, *Venice Preserved* (1682), which is easily the greatest of all Restoration tragedies, in spite of its witless comic scenes which satirize the first Earl of Shaftesbury under the name of Antonio.

Otway lived in extreme poverty, and the usually accepted story of his death is that he choked when ravenously eating some bread after a long period of inanition. He was madly in love with Mrs. Barry, the principal actress in his plays, and though this unrequited affection made his life unhappy, it probably made him a better tragic poet. *The Orphan* and *Venice Preserved* tower high above the bombast and the banalities of the restoration stage.—Cf. E. Gosse, *Seventeenth Century Studies.*

OUDENARDE (ö-dn-ärd), or **AUDENARDE.** A town of Belgium, province of East Flanders, on the Scheldt. The Hôtel de Ville, dating from the sixteenth century, is one of the finest town halls in Belgium. The town has sustained several sieges, but is best known in history by the memorable victory gained over the French on the 11th of July, 1708, by Prince Eugene and the Duke of Marlborough. Pop. 6950.

OUDH, or **OUDE** (oud). The eastern portion of the United Provinces of Agra and Oudh, bounded on the north by Nepál, and on the other sides by the province of Agra; area, 24,158 sq. miles. Oudh, formerly a Mogul province (subsequently kingdom, 1819), became subordinate to the British after the battle of Kalpee, in 1765. The king was deposed for misgovernment in 1856, and his territory was amalgamated with the North-Western Provinces. Since 1902 Oudh has been joined to these to form the

United Provinces of Agra and Oudh. Lucknow is the capital. Pop. 12,794,979 (mostly Hindus).

OUDINOT (ö-di-nō), **Charles Nicolas.** Duc de Reggio, peer and marshal of France, born at Bar-le-Duc in 1767, died in 1847. In 1791 he was elected commandant of a volunteer battalion, and gave many striking proofs of valour, which gained him speedy promotion. In 1792 he was colonel of the regiment of Picardy, in 1793 brigadier-general, and in 1799 general of division. Masséna made him chief of the general staff, and under his command he decided the battle of the Mincio.

In 1804 Napoleon gave him the command of a grenadier corps of 10,000 men, at the head of which troops he performed many exploits, winning the battle of Ostrolenka, and deciding the fate of three great battles—Austerlitz, Friedland, and Wagram. He was severely wounded in the Russian campaign of 1812. In the campaign of 1814 he took an active part and was wounded for the twenty-third time.

After Napoleon's abdication he gave his adhesion to the Bourbons, to whom he ever afterwards remained faithful, and who heaped upon him every honour.—His eldest son, Nicolas Charles Victor, born in 1791, died in 1863, commanded the troops which effected the capture of Rome from Garibaldi in 1849.

OUDTSHOORN. A town of Cape Province, South Africa, 40 miles N.N.E. of Mossel Bay. It has many educational establishments. Pop. (1921), 10,698 (white pop. 1931, 5649).

OUNCE (*Felis Uncia*). One of the digitigrade carnivora found in Northern Africa, Arabia, Persia, India, and China. The length of the body is about 3½ feet, the tail measuring about 2 feet. It is a large cat, resembling the leopard and panther, but with a longer and more hairy tail and a thicker fur, somewhat less in size, and not so fierce and dangerous. In some places it is trained to hunt, like the cheetah.

Ounce (*Felis Uncia*)

OUNDLE SCHOOL. Founded by Sir William Laxton (died 1556), who was Lord Mayor of London in 1544, and a prominent member of the Grocers' Company. The school is still maintained by the Worshipful Company of Grocers. The new schools were built in 1883, and have been greatly enlarged since. There are nine boarding-houses as well as a preparatory house. A large block, including a great hall, library, art museum, and class-rooms, was opened in 1910. A new science block was built in 1914.

The five laboratories are splendidly equipped. The school chapel is a war memorial. There are 540 boys at the school, which owes much of its success to F. W. Sanderson, who was headmaster from 1892 until his death in 1922, and who introduced highly original and effective methods of education.

OU'REBI (*Nanotragus scoparia*). An antelope of South Africa, found in great numbers in the open plains, and much hunted for its flesh. It is from 2 to 3 feet high, of a pale dun colour, and the male has sharp, strong, and deeply ringed horns.

OURO-PRETO (ō'ro-prā'to). A city of Brazil, in Minas-Geraes, on the railway from Rio de Janeiro. Founded in 1711 as Villa Rica, it was the capital of the state till 1897, when it was superseded by Bello Horizonte, or Minas. It was once one of the great mining centres of Brazil, but the gold-mines are now exhausted. Pop. about 15,000.

OUSE (öz). A river of Yorkshire, formed by the junction of the Swale with the Ure near Boroughbridge; it flows tortuously south-east past York, Selby, and Goole, 8 miles east of which it unites with the Trent to form the estuary of the Humber. Its total course is 60 miles, for the last 45 of which (or to York) it is navigable.

OUSE. River of Sussex. It rises near Horsham and flows to the English Channel at Newhaven, 30 miles long. It passes Lewes, to which town it is navigable by small vessels.

OUSE (öz), **Great.** A river of England, rises near Brackley, in the county of Northampton, flows in a general north-easterly direction, traverses the counties of Buckingham, Bedford, Huntingdon, Cambridge, and Norfolk, and falls into the Wash at King's Lynn, after a course of about 160 miles, for the latter two-thirds of which it is navigable.

OUSELEY, Rev. Sir Frederick Arthur Gore, Bart. English composer, born 1825, died in 1889, only son of Sir Gore Ouseley, at one time British Ambassador to Persia and Russia. His works include treatises on harmony, on counterpoint and fugue, and on musical form and general composition, and he wrote much church music.

OUTCROP. In geology, the exposure of any rock at the surface of the ground. An inclined stratum will produce an outcrop running practically in the direction of the strike.

OUTRAM (ou'tram), **Sir James.** British soldier, born at Butterley Hall, Derbyshire, 1803, died 1863. In 1819 he joined the East India Company, and in 1828 he was selected to undertake a mission to the wild hill tribes of the Bombay Presidency, a task in which he acquitted himself with credit. As adjutant to Lord Keane he took part in the Afghan War in 1839, and distinguished himself at the capture of Khelat, and by his dangerous ride disguised as a native devotee through the enemy's country to Kurrachee (1840).

After the capture of Ghuznee he performed the duties of British Resident at Hyderabad, Sattara, and Lucknow. Nominated Chief Commissioner of Oudh in 1856, he commanded the Persian expedition in 1856-57. During the Mutiny he joined Havelock at Cawnpore in Sept., 1857, and fought under him until Lucknow was relieved by Sir Colin Campbell. He was created a baronet, and received the thanks of Parliament. He died at Pau, and was buried in Westminster Abbey.

OUT'RIGGER. An iron bracket fixed on the side of a boat, with a rowlock at its extremity, so as to give an increased leverage to the oar without widening the boat; hence, a light boat for river matches provided with such apparatus. The name is also applied to a contrivance in certain foreign boats and canoes, consisting of a projecting framework or arrangement of timbers for counterbalancing the heeling-over effect of the sails, which are large compared with the vessel's breadth.

OUZEL, or OUSEL (ou'zl). Small perching birds closely related to the thrushes. The common or ring ouzel (*Turdus torquātus*) is a summer visitant of Britain, and its specific

Ouzel: Ring Ouzel

name is derived from the presence of a broad semilunar patch or stripe of white extending across its breast. The water ouzel (*Cinclus aquaticus*) belongs to a different family. (*See* DIPPER.) Ouzel is also an old or poetical name for the blackbird.

OVAHERERO. A Bantu people of the South-West Africa Protectorate, related to the Ovambo. The name is applied collectively to the Herero people. They are the "Damaras" or "Cattle Damaras" described by early explorers.

OVAMBO, or OVAMPO. A negroid people of the South-West Africa Protectorate, inhabiting the country known as Ovamboland, south of the Kunene River and north of Damaraland. Ovambo is the Herero name of these tribes who call themselves Aajamba. With the Ovaherero they constitute the south-western division of the Bantu family, but the Ovambos are the cultivators and the Hereros the cattle-men of a race different from the ordinary Bantu.

They have more of the Hamitic element within them, whereas in the ordinary Bantu the Arab or Semitic element predominates. The two Ovambo dialects, Kwanyama and Ndonga, are common also to South Angola, where some Ovambos are found.—Cf. E. H. L. Schwartz, *A South African Geography*.

OVAR'. A town of Portugal, district of Beira, near the Atlantic, on the north shore of the Bay of Aveiro. It has valuable fisheries and considerable trade. Pop. 10,500.

OVA'RIAN TUMOUR. A morbid growth in the ovary of a woman, sometimes weighing as much as 30, 50, or upwards of 100 lb. or more, consisting of a cyst containing a thin or thick ropy fluid, causing the disease known as *ovarian cyst*, which is now generally cured by the operation of ovariotomy.

OVARIOT'OMY. The operation of removing the ovary, or a tumour in the ovary (*see* above); a surgical operation first performed in 1809, and long considered exceedingly dangerous, but now performed with great and increasing success, especially since the adoption of the antiseptic treatment inaugurated by Lister.

O'VARY, or **OVARIUM.** The essential part of the female generative apparatus in which the ova or eggs are developed. The ovary in the female corresponds to the *testis* of the male. In adult women the ovaries exist as two bodies of somewhat elliptical shape, and compressed from side to side, of whitish colour and uneven surface. They are situated one on each side of the womb, and are attached to the hinder portion of the body of the womb by two thin cord-like bands—the *ovarian ligaments*—and by a lesser fibrous cord to the fringed edge of the Fallopian tube.

Each ovary is about 1½ inches in length, and about 1½ drachms in weight, and contains a number of vesicles known as ovisacs or Graafian follicles, in which the ova are developed. The functions of the ovary, which only become active on the approach of puberty, are, first, the formation of ova, their maturation, and their final discharge at periodic menstrual epochs into the uterus or womb; and, secondly, the secretion of certain chemical materials or hormones which are distributed by the blood-stream throughout the body, and determine the development of the secondary sexual characters distinctive of the adult women.

The ovum may be impregnated and detained in the uterus, or pass from the body with the menstrual flow. The ovaries are subject to diseased conditions, chief among which are cancer and the occurrence of tumours and cysts.

O'VARY. In botany, is a hollow case enclosing ovules or young seeds, containing one or more cells, and ultimately becoming the fruit. Together with the style and stigma it constitutes the female system of the vegetable kingdom. When sunk in and united to the floral receptacle, it is called inferior; when separate, superior.

OVEN BIRDS. Perching birds belonging to the family Dendrocolaptidæ, found in South America; typical genus, Furnarius. They are all of small size, and feed upon seeds, fruits, and insects. Their popular name is derived from the form of their nest, which is dome-shaped, and built of tough clay or mud with a winding entrance.

OVER. A district of Cheshire, on the Weaver, and served by the L.M.S. and Cheshire Lines Railways. It forms part of the urban district of Winsford and Over, has sheep and cattle fairs, and is the centre of a salt-manufacturing industry.

OVERBURY, Sir Thomas. English poet and essayist, and victim of one of the most infamous crimes in history, was born in 1581, and poisoned in 1613. He was educated at Queen's College, Oxford, and was a member of the Middle Temple. In 1601 he met Robert Carr, afterwards King James's favourite, and struck up a firm friendship with him. When Carr rose to prominence, Overbury advised him in all his affairs, so that the queen nicknamed him Carr's "governor" or tutor.

In about 1611 Carr fell in love with Frances Howard, who had married the third Earl of Essex in 1606. Lady Essex sought to annul her marriage in order that she might marry Carr, and Overbury used all his influence to oppose the match. The countess contrived to get Overbury imprisoned in the Tower, and, not satisfied with that, got poison served with his food. The poison was so unskilfully administered that it caused only excruciating agony, not death.

After being imprisoned three months and seventeen days, Overbury was fatally poisoned by a clyster of corrosive sublimate on 14th Sept., 1613. Ten days later the Countess of Essex's marriage was annulled, and on the following Boxing Day she was married to Carr, now Earl of Somerset. She was not accused of the murder of Overbury until 1615; she pleaded guilty and received a pardon, but her less guilty husband was imprisoned for six years, and four of her humbler accomplices were hanged.

Overbury's sensational death gave an adventitious fame to his writings, which were all posthumously published. His poem, *The Wife*, is a smooth but undistinguished didactic poem. The *Characters*, which were first printed in the second edition of this poem, are well written, but only in part the work of Overbury.—Cf. A. Amos, *The Great Oyer of Poisoning*.

OVERLAND ROUTE. The quickest way from Great Britain to India. The route runs via Dover, Calais, Paris, Maçon, the Mont Cenis Tunnel, and Bologna, to Brindisi, thence by steamer to Alexandria, from there by railway to Suez, thence by steamer to the destined Indian port. The average time is from eighteen to twenty days. Alternative routes are from Marseilles or Venice by steamer to Alexandria, and thence by rail to Suez.

OVERREACH. In horses, an injury to the heel of the fore foot caused by the inside rim of the toe of the hind shoe. If fore shoes are too long in the branches they are frequently wrenched off. Overreach is most common in hunters and thoroughbreds, and invariably happens when galloping. On examination, the skin will be found detached from before, backwards, showing that the inside of the shoe of the hind toe causes the cut in its backward action. The remedy consists in hammering down the inside rim of the hind toe, so that it is quite smooth and bevelled off.

OVERSEA SETTLEMENT COMMITTEE. British Government committee appointed in 1909 to bring the Government into closer touch with the settlement of British subjects in the Dominions and elsewhere. It is non-political and widely representative, and advises on land development, settlement schemes, assisted passages, training, etc. The Government's contribution in any one year is limited to three million pounds.

OVERSEAS POSSESSIONS, Government of. Our colonial organization is based on the principle that each of our colonies should be gradually educated in self-government, and should be admitted progressively to an ever larger exercise of powers within its own borders until it eventually reaches the status of a dominion. Thus the colonies stand in an infinite variety of relations to the mother country. Excluding protectorates like Uganda or Zanzibar, where the native chiefs have a considerable share in the administration, and mandatory colonies assigned to Britain under the scheme of the League of Nations, colonies may be classified according to the degree of self-government which they possess.

1. *Colonies* not completely self-governing. Within this group there are various subdivisions, according to the degree of representative government attained. (*a*) Crown colonies proper, where the legislative and executive powers are vested in a Governor representing the Crown, e.g. Gibraltar. (*b*) Colonies where the administration is carried on by the Governor, assisted by an executive and a legislative council both nominated by the Crown, e.g. Ceylon, Falkland Islands. (*c*) Colonies possessing a legislative council wholly or partly elected, and an executive council nominated by the Crown, e.g. Jamaica.

2. *Dominions* possessing complete domestic self-government with legislative powers which, though legally controllable by the Imperial Parliament, are unrestricted within their own territories. In the dominions there is a Governor-General appointed by the Crown, and there are generally two legislative chambers and a ministry selected as under the English party system.

Legislature.—The only restrictions on the legislative autonomy of the dominions are these. (1) They are subject to any Act of the Imperial Parliament whose provisions are declared in the Act to be applicable to them. (2) Any provision in a statute passed by the legislature of any colony which is repugnant to any imperial statute applying to the colony is void in terms of the Colonial Laws Validity Act, 1865. (3) The measures of all colonial legislatures are subject to veto by the Crown which may on the advice of the Colonial Secretary be exercised by an Order in Council within a period of two years, and that even although the Governor has given his assent. All measures passed by colonial legislatures must receive the Governor's assent.

In general this is not refused, but if the interests of the mother country are involved and may sustain detriment, it is his duty to exercise his veto even in opposition to his ministers. Again, in the case of certain Bills, he is required to reserve them for consideration of the Crown, or, while assenting, to suspend their operation pending their approval by the Crown.

Administration.—While in Crown colonies executive power is exercised by the Governor subject only to the control of the Colonial Office, self-governing colonies have virtually full autonomy in internal affairs. The position of the Governor in these approximates to that of a constitutional sovereign, as he acts with the advice of local ministers, and personally interferes but little except when imperial interests are involved.

In law, however, the legislative and executive powers of dominions do not extend to external relations. They cannot conclude treaties without the consent of the Imperial Government, though in the case of Canadian treaties with the United States this rule was not observed, as Canadian interests only were involved.

Judiciary.—The appointment of judges in colonies which are not self-governing is vested in the Crown. The sole remaining judicial link between the dominions and the mother country is provided in the Judicial Committee of the Privy Council, which still exercises the royal prerogative of hearing appeals from all courts, superior as well as inferior, in the British colonies.

Where no appeal lies as of right, a petition must first be presented to the Crown for leave to appeal, and this will not in general be granted in civil cases unless such leave is in accord with the rules in force in the colony, and in criminal cases unless there has been *prima facie* a gross miscarriage of justice in the colonial courts.

Even before 1914 the progressive principle on which the relation of the mother country to the colonies was based made a sharp contrast between the formal legal tie, which tended to become theoretical, and the virtual independence which the dominions in fact exercised. The necessities of the European War accelerated tendencies already long at work. The sense of imperial solidarity has been quickened, and with it the consciousness that the British Empire is a union of independent nations whose interrelation can no longer be served by the old machinery devised to meet the case of colonies which had not developed into dominions.

The march of events has seemed to point the way for a permanent constitutional machinery which would at once preserve the unity of the empire and, while maintaining the independence of the dominion in matters of purely local interest, would admit them to a real participation as equal members in an imperial commonwealth in the control of policy which affected all its parts.

A decisive step in this direction was the summons of representatives from the dominions to attend an Imperial Cabinet in London in 1917, and in the same year the meeting of an Imperial War Conference at the Colonial Office. The vital part played by the dominions in the European War, and the sacrifices which they had voluntarily undertaken in the cause of international freedom, conferred on them an equitable if not a strictly legal right to be consulted in the final settlement.

Thus the dominions were accorded full status with regard to representation at the Peace Conference, and became signatories of, and ratified, the Treaty of Versailles on the authority of their own Parliaments. Finally, they have been admitted to full membership in the League of Nations.

The system of representative government in the colonies was first applied in Canada in 1867, and was successively extended to New Zealand, New South Wales, Victoria, Tasmania, Newfoundland, Queensland, Cape Colony, West Australia, Natal, the Transvaal, and Orange River Colony. A new era was opened in 1900, when the first step towards *intercolonial federation* was taken in the formation of the Commonwealth of Australia, followed in 1909 by the Union of South Africa.

It may be instructive, as illustrating the extent to which the principle of self-government has been realized in the British Empire, to summarize the main features in the constitutional position of some of the dominions. In the Commonwealth of Australia the legislative power is vested in the king and a Federal Parliament consisting of a Senate and a House of Representatives.

The Senate, on the principle of equality, is composed of six members from each of the states, elected for six years, while the members of the Lower House are elected according to the electoral laws of the various states. If a Bill introduced in the Lower House has been twice rejected in the Senate, the Government may dissolve both Houses of Parliament, and if, after an election, the new Senate again reject the measure, both Houses sit together as one Assembly, and a decision is reached by a simple majority.

If any measure proposing to amend the Constitution is twice rejected by the Senate, it is submitted to a referendum in which a majority of votes in a majority of states is decisive. The executive power is vested in the Governor-General, assisted by a Cabinet composed of the heads of the administrative departments, who must all be members of the legislature. The supreme judicial power is vested in a federal court called the High Court of Australia.

This court is the guardian of the Constitution, and the arbiter of the limits under the Constitution of the powers of the Commonwealth and the several states, and it may certify that certain questions ought to be referred to the King in Council.

In the Union of South Africa the executive power is vested in the king in person or his representative the Governor-General, appointed by the Imperial Government to hold office during the royal pleasure, and assisted by an executive council of ministers. The legislative power is exercised by the king, a Senate, and a representative House of Assembly.

The Senate consists of 40 members, 8 being nominated by the Crown and 8 by each of the four provinces, holding office for ten years. The House of Assembly contains 121 members, elected for five years, coloured subjects being barred from membership. A measure rejected by the Senate in two successive sessions is submitted to a joint session of the Upper and Lower Houses for final decision. Parliament has full powers to make laws for the peace, order, and good government of the Union. The veto of the Governor on its legislation is in practice virtually obsolete.

The provinces are provided with councils which resemble English county councils, and exercise certain limited legislative powers delegated to them by the Union Parliament. The supreme judicial power is exercised by the Supreme Court of South Africa, appointed by the Governor-General in Council, with original and appellate jurisdiction.

There is in general no appeal, as of right, from the Supreme Court of South Africa to the King in Council, but the South Africa Act, 1909, reserves right to the King in Council to grant "special leave to appeal from the Appellate Division of the Supreme Court to the King in Council." A somewhat similar position obtains in regard to the Irish Free State. There is there a Supreme Court—whose decisions are final and conclusive—a High Court, a Court of Criminal Appeal, a Circuit Court, and a District Court. The Supreme Court (Saorstat Eireann) has appellate jurisdiction for all decisions of the High Court; but under the Constitution of the Irish Free State the right of any person to petition the King for special leave to appeal from the Supreme Court to His Majesty in Council is safeguarded.

The status of the dominions was completely altered by the findings of the Imperial Conference of 1926, which defined them as autonomous communities in every way equal in status to Great Britain. This definition was given legal form by the Statute of Westminster in 1931, and the dominions are now completely autonomous.

OVERSEAS TRADE. Name given to a department of the British Government that exists to promote trade with foreign countries. It was set up in 1917 and is under the joint control of the Board of Trade and the Foreign Office. The offices are at 35 Old Queen Street, London, S.W.1, and 73 Basinghall Street, London, E.C.2.

OVERSEERS. Public officers appointed annually in every parish of England and Wales, whose primary duty it is to assess the inhabitants for the poor-rate, collect the same, and apply it to the relief of the poor. The office, instituted in 1601, is compulsory, and entirely gratuitous; but several classes of persons, such as peers, members of Parliament, clergymen, Dissenting ministers, barristers, attorneys, doctors, military and naval officers, and others whose avocations require continual personal attendance, are exempt from serving. Numerous miscellaneous duties, other than their original duty of relieving the poor, are now imposed, by statute, on overseers. Thus they have to draw up the lists of all those entitled to vote for members of Parliament, of those qualified to serve as jurors and as parish constables, etc. In the larger parishes it is customary for the inhabitants to appoint assistant overseers, salaried officials who relieve the annual overseers to some extent of their duties.—Cf. Sir G. Nicholls, *History of the English Poor Law.*

O'VERTURE. In music, an introductory symphony, chiefly used to precede great musical compositions, as oratorios and operas, and intended to prepare the hearer for the following composition, properly by concentrating its chief musical ideas so as to give a sort of outline of it in instrumental music. This mode of composing overtures was first conceived by the French. Overtures are, however, frequently written as independent pieces for the concert-room.

OVERYSSEL (ō'vėr-ī-sėl), or **OVERIJSSEL.** A province of the Netherlands; area, 1301 sq. miles. It is watered by the Ijssel, which separates it from Gelderland, and by the Vecht and its affluents. Except a strip along the Ijssel, presenting good arable and meadow land, the surface is mostly a sandy flat relieved by hillocks, and the principal industries are stock-raising and dairy-farming. Chief towns, Zwolle (capital), Deventer, Almelo, and Kampen. Pop. (1931), 528,477.

OVID (Publius Ovidius Naso). Roman poet, was born 43 B.C., and died A.D. 17. He belonged to a wealthy equestrian family of Upper

Italy, and received the education which was usual in the case of men of that class. He studied rhetoric at Rome and qualified as a barrister, but was more noted for his eloquence than for being learned in the law. He held several minor public appointments, but his love of ease was stronger than his ambition, and as he was well-to-do he soon gave up law for poetry.

From his earliest days he had a fatal facility in verse-writing; as he says himself, "Whatever I endeavoured to say was verse." He became the unofficial Poet Laureate of the dissolute and heartless court circle. In spite of his wonderful fecundity he was thirty years old before he published his first book, the *Amores*. This is a collection of love-poems, many of which are addressed to a lady named Corinna, probably a courtesan. There is no passion in these poems, but there is plenty of ease and graceful writing. The *Medicamina formæ*, a poem upon cosmetics, does not rise above the banality of its subject.

The *Heroides*, letters from heroines of poetry and legend to their husbands or lovers, is a much better piece of work. In it Ovid displays not merely his usual gifts of ease and excellent style, but in a deep knowledge of women's hearts. It is believed that the last six of these epistles are not genuine.

Ovid's most famous or infamous work is his *Ars Amatoria* (Love-making as a Fine Art), a kind of handbook to the art of seduction. This has been described as the most immoral though not the most demoralizing poem in the world. It is entirely free from all morbid sentiment, and is full of worldly wisdom and a not at all unkindly humour. Its nearest counterpart in English is *Don Juan*. The *Remedia Amoris* was intended to be a kind of antidote to the *Ars Amatoria*. It is no better in its morality than its predecessor, and is very decidedly less interesting.

Ovid intended the *Metamorphoses* to be his *magnum opus*, though he did not give it its final polish. It is a long poem in fifteen books, and relates all the mythological tales which have to do with transformations. It begins with the transformation of Chaos into Cosmos, and ends with the metamorphosis of Julius Cæsar into a star. It is a formidable task to read this poem through, but it has passages of great beauty, and as a storehouse of mythology was drawn upon more freely than any other Latin poem.

The *Fasti*, in six books, is an account of the Roman calendar and festivals. It was to have been in twelve books, but was not completed. Ovid makes the best of his somewhat intractable material, and the poem has good passages; but it is on the whole more valuable for the antiquarian information it conveys than for its poetical qualities.

After being the fashionable poet of the smart set at Rome for thirty years, in A.D. 8 Ovid was suddenly banished to Tomi, on the Black Sea, by a mandate of the emperor. Much speculation has been made as to the exact cause of his banishment, but in spite of many ingenious and not a few absurd conjectures, it is safe to say that the true story will never be known, save in the unlikely eventuality of more evidence being discovered.

The alleged reason for his disgrace was the publication of the *Ars Amatoria*, which had taken place ten years previously; he may also have had some share in abetting or in failing to check the misconduct of the younger Julia. Tomi was on the outskirts of the Roman Empire, and Ovid found life there unendurable. He was cut off from books, friends, and all the decencies of life. He lived in hope of being recalled to Rome, but this was not to be. After the death of Augustus, Tiberius was equally opposed to his return, and he died heartbroken after nearly ten years of exile.

Ovid wearied for Rome when at Tomi, and has succeeded in handing on some of his weariness to those who read the poems which he wrote there, the *Tristia* and *Epistulæ ex Ponto*. They are monotonous reiterations of complaints, and are mainly inspired by home-sickness. Ovid had all Horace's egoism without Horace's saving grace of humour. His other works include the *Ibis*, an elegiac invective, and the *Halieutica*, a didactic poem on the natural history of fishes. Among his lost works are a *Medea*, which is praised by Quintilian, and an encomium upon Augustus written in Gothic, which would have been of the greatest philosophical interest if it had been preserved.

As a poet Ovid occupies a peculiar position. He wrote with a fluency that was detrimental to his work, and was, as Quintilian says, too indulgent as a self-critic. As an elegiac poet his work ranks below that of Propertius and Tibullus; but as a writer of narrative verse he stands not only far above them, but above almost everyone save only Homer.

His poetry has been immensely influential, far more so than that of the other elegiac poets, more so than even that of Horace and Virgil. He has, perhaps, always been more popular with poets than with scholars. Tasso, Ariosto, Chaucer, Spenser, and Milton—these are but a few of those who are followers of Ovid. Very noticeable is his influence upon Shakespeare, of whom Francis Meres wrote in 1598: "The sweete wittie soule of Ovid lives in mellifluous and hony-tongued Shakespeare."

He cannot be ranked with the world's greatest poets, but he must stand in a prominent place on account of his great narrative gifts, and his influence upon poets more highly endowed than himself.—BIBLIOGRAPHY: W. Y. Sellar, *Roman Poets of the Augustan Age*; G. Boissier, *L'Opposition sous les Césars*; Nageotte, *Ovide, sa vie, ses œuvres*; A. Church, *Ovid* (Ancient Classics for English Readers Series).

OVIEDO. A maritime province of Northern Spain, on the Bay of Biscay, co-extensive with the ancient Kingdom of Asturias. It is cut up by spurs of the Cantabrian Mountains, and is drained by the Navia and the Nalon (with the Narcea). The eastern districts are served by a coastal railway from Santander to Villaviciosa and Gijon; the line from Valladolid runs to Oviedo and the coast, and has branch systems serving the central districts. The Nalon Valley coal-field is the first in Spain. Sardines and tunny are exported. Horses are raised. Oviedo is traversed by the famous Madrid-Gijon *Camino Real*, built by Charles V. Area, 4205 sq. miles; pop. (1931), 796,667.

OVIEDO (ō-vi-ā'dō). A city of Spain, capital of the province of same name. Oviedo was founded by King Fruela I. (756-768). It has a cathedral (rebuilt between 1388 and 1528), a church built by Ramiro I. (1035-63), and a university dating from 1604. Its manufactures include hats, arms, textiles, and leather goods. Pop. (1931), 76,071.

OVIPOS'ITOR. An appendage attached to the abdominal segments of certain insects, and used for placing the eggs in situations favourable to their due development, this being sometimes in bark or leaves, or even in the bodies of other animals. The sting of bees, wasps, etc., is a modification of an ovipositor or homologous structure.

OV'OLO. In architecture, a convex moulding, generally a quarter of a circle; but in classic architecture there is usually a departure from the exact circular form to that of an egg: hence the name (Lat. *ovum*, an egg).

OV'ULE. The megasporangium of flowering plants, which ripens into the seed. A typical ovule consists of a solid central portion, the *nucellus*—the megasporangium proper, enclosing the *embryo-sac* (megaspore)—invested by one or more often two coats, the *integuments*, which do not completely cover it, but leave a narrow channel (*micropyle*) open at the apex for the entrance of the pollen-tube.

The ovule is attached to the placenta of the carpel by a stalk, the *funicle*, the point of junction of which with the nucellus is termed the *chalaza*. Ovules are rarely straight (orthotropous), most often doubled back on the funicle (anatropous), sometimes curved around the middle (campylotropous), or with their long axis at right angles to the funicle (amphitropous).

OVUM. The "egg" or female germ-cell, which, after being fertilized by fusion with it of a minute male germ-cell (sperm), is capable of developing into a new and independent being. The essential parts to be recognized in the structure of every true ovum consist, first, of an outer membrane known as the *vitelline membrane*. Within this are the *vitellus* or *yolk* (cytoplasm), and the *germinal vesicle* (nucleus) containing the *germinal spot* (nucleolus). *See* OVARY; REPRODUCTION.

OWEN, John. Welsh writer of Latin epigrams, was born about 1563, and died in 1622. He was educated at Winchester and New College, Oxford. He became eventually headmaster of King Henry VIII.'s School, Warwick. His Latin epigrams are divided into twelve books, the first four of which were published in 1606, and the rest at four different times. They became immensely popular in England and Scotland, and won an even wider fame on the Continent.

Owen was commonly considered the equal, if not the superior, of Martial. His epigrams were translated into English, French, German, and Spanish. They are extremely clever epigrams, and contain much of Martial's wit, though they have none of his poetry.

Owen was a stalwart Protestant, and one of his epigrams is said to have lost him an inheritance from a Catholic uncle, and to have caused his works to be placed on the *Index Prohibitorius*. It is as follows:

An Petrus fuerit Romæ, sub iudice lis est;
Simonem Romæ nemo fuisse negat.

Another very famous line was popularized though not written by Owen, who adapted it from a line of Matthew Borbonius. It is:

Tempora mutantur, nos et mutamur in illis,

and is often erroneously ascribed to Virgil or Ovid.

OWEN, Sir Richard. British scientist, born at Lancaster 1804, died in 1892. Educated at Lancaster Grammar School and the medical schools of Edinburgh, Paris, and London, he became assistant curator of the Hunterian Museum. In 1834 he was appointed professor of comparative anatomy at St. Bartholomew's Hospital; in 1836 professor in anatomy and physiology at the Royal College of Surgeons; and in 1856 superintendent of the natural history department in the British Museum, from which last post he retired in 1883.

Owen was the greatest palæontologist since Cuvier, and as a comparative anatomist was a worthy successor to Hunter. He was a voluminous writer on his special subjects, and an honorary Fellow of nearly every learned society of Europe and America. Among his works are: *Lectures on the Comparative Anatomy of the Invertebrate Animals, Lectures on the Comparative Anatomy of the Vertebrate Animals, History of British Fossil Mammals and Birds, History of British Fossil Reptiles, Principles of Comparative Osteology, On the Anatomy of Vertebrates, The Fossil Reptiles of South Africa*, and *The Fossil Mammals of Australia*.

OWENSBORO'. A city of Kentucky, United States, the county seat of Daviess county, on the Ohio; served by the Louisville & Nashville, the Illinois Central, and the Louisville, Henderson, & St. Louis Railways. It is a tobacco centre, with a large river trade and manufactures of wood and flour. Oil is found, and cattle are raised in the vicinity. Owensboro' was founded in 1798 as Yellow Banks, and became Rossborough in 1816. Pop. (1930), 22,675.

OWEN SOUND. A port of Ontario, Canada, on Lake Huron. It is served by both the transcontinental lines and lake steamers. There is a good harbour, and the industries include flour mills and lumber mills. Pop. 12,839.

OWL PARROT (*Stringops habroptilus*). The type and only known representative of a peculiar group of the parrot family, is a large bird, a native of the South Pacific Islands, and especially of New Zealand. In aspect and in nocturnal habits it resembles the owl. It feeds on roots, which it digs out of the earth with its hooked beak. It seldom flies; it is generally to be seen resting in hollow stumps and logs, and is said to hibernate in caves.

OWLS. A group of birds forming a well-defined family (Strigidæ), including nocturnal birds of prey. The head is large and well covered with feathers, part of which are generally arranged around the eyes in circular discs, and in some species form horn-like tufts on the upper surface of the head. The beak is short, strongly curved, and hooked. The ears are generally of large size, prominent, and in many cases provided with a kind of fleshy valve or lid, and their sense of hearing is exceedingly acute.

The eyes are very prominent and full, and project forwards, the pupils being especially well developed—a structure enabling the owls to see well at dusk or in the dark. The plumage is of soft downy character, rendering their flight almost noiseless. The tarsi are feathered, generally to the very base of the claws, but some forms, especially those of fish-catching habits, have the toes and even the tarsi bare.

Barn Owl (*Strix flammĕa*)

The toes are arranged three forwards and one backwards; but the outer toe can be turned backwards at will, and the feet thus converted into hand-like or prehensile organs.

In habits most species of owls are nocturnal, flying about during the night, and preying upon the smaller quadrupeds, nocturnal insects, and upon the smaller birds. Mice in particular form a large part of their food.

During the day they inhabit the crevices of rocks, the nooks and crannies of old or ruined buildings, or the hollows of trees; and in these situations the nests are constructed. Owls vary greatly in size, the smallest not being larger than a thrush.

In their distribution they occur very generally over the habitable globe, both worlds possessing typical representatives of the group. The common white or barn owl (*Strix flammĕa*) is the owl which has the greatest geographical range, inhabiting almost every country in the world. The tawny brown or wood owl (*Syrnium aluco*) is the largest of the species indigenous to Britain, and is strictly a woodland bird, building its nest in holes of trees. The genus *Asio* contains the so-called horned owls, distinguished by elongated horn-like tufts of feathers on the head.

The long-eared owl (*Asio otus*) appears to be common to both Europe and America. It inhabits woods.

Long-eared Owl (*Asio otus*)

The short-eared owl (*Asio accipitrīnus*) frequents heaths, moors, and the open country generally to the exclusion of woods. It has an enormous geographical range. The eagle owl (*Bubo ignāvus*) is rare in Britain, but occurs in Norway, Sweden, and Lapland, and over the continent of Europe to the Mediterranean.

A similar species (*B. virginianus*) extends over the whole of North America. Owls of diurnal habits are the hawk owl (Surnia) and the snowy owl (Nyctea). The hawk owl mostly inhabits the Arctic regions, but migrates southwards in winter, as does the snowy owl, which is remarkable for its large size and snowy plumage. The little owl (*Carine noctua*), the bird of Pallas Athena, is spread throughout the greater part of Europe, and has been introduced into Britain.

One of the most remarkable of owls is the burrowing owl (*Speotyto cunicularia*) of America and the West Indies, which inhabits the burrows of the marmots (q.v.) or prairie-dogs — the owls possessing themselves of these burrows and breeding therein, much to the discomfort of the original possessors of the abodes.

OX. The general name of certain well-known ruminant mammals, family Bovidæ (Cavicornia). The characters are: the horns are hollow, supported on a bony core, and curved outward in the form of crescents; there are six incisor teeth in the under jaw and two canines of similar shape, but no incisors nor canines in the upper; the naked muffle is broad.

Typical species are *Bos taurus*, or common ox; *B. bonasus*, aurochs, or bison of Europe; *B. americanus*, or buffalo of North America; *B. bubalus*, or proper buffalo of the eastern continent; *B. caffer*, or Cape buffalo; *B. grunniens*, or yak of Tibet, etc. The name ox is used also in a more restricted sense to signify the male of the bovine (*Bos taurus*) castrated, and full-grown, or nearly so.

The young castrated male is called a *steer*. He is called an *ox-calf* or *bull-calf* until he is a year old, and a *steer* until he is four years old. The same animal not castrated is called a *bull*. Besides the European ox there are several other varieties, as the Indian or zebu, with a hump on its back, the Abyssinian, Madagascar, and South African. *See* CATTLE, BISON, BUFFALO, YAK, etc.

OXALIC ACID ($H_2C_2O_4$). A dibasic acid which occurs in a few plants in the free state, but more generally as the acid potassium salt, e.g. in wood-sorrel, rhubarb, etc., or as calcium salt in certain lichens. The pure acid may be prepared by oxidizing cane-sugar with nitric acid; various other complex compounds, like starch and cellulose, also yield the acid on oxidation.

It is manufactured mostly from potassium formate, which on heating decomposes, yielding potassium oxalate and hydrogen. It crystallizes in large transparent four-sided prisms of composition $H_2C_2O_4.2H_2O$. The water of crystallization is readily removed when the crystals are heated to 60°-70° C., giving anhydrous oxalic acid. It is soluble in water, and forms a series of salts with the metals known as the oxalates, some of which are of industrial importance.

Binoxalate of potassium, KHC_2O_4, familiarly known as "salts of sorrel" or "salts of lemon," is used in the removal of iron mould from wood and linen; ferric oxalate, $Fe_2(C_2O_4)_3$, is used in photography; and oxalic acid is used in certain types of calico-printing and for whitening leather, etc. Both the acid and its salts are violent poisons.

OXALIDA'CEÆ. A natural order of polypetalous dicotyledons, of which the genus Oxălis or wood-sorrel is the type, comprising herbs, shrubs, and trees, remarkable, some of them, for the quantity of oxalic acid they contain. Some American species have tuberous edible roots. For two species *see* BLIMBING and CARAMBOLA.

OXENSTJERNA, Axel, Count. Swedish statesman, born 1583, died in 1654. He studied theology at Rostock, Wittenberg, and Jena; and in 1602 returned to Sweden and entered the service of Charles IX. On the accession of Gustavus Adolphus, in 1611, he was made Chancellor.

He accompanied his king during his campaigns in Germany, taking charge of all diplomatic affairs; and on the fall of his master at Lützen (1632) he was recognized, at a congress assembled at Heilbronn, as the head of the Protestant League.

In 1645 he assisted in the negotiations with Denmark at Bromsebro, and on his return was created count by Queen Christina, whose determination to abdicate the crown he strongly but unsuccessfully opposed.

OXFORD. A city and county town of England, capital of Oxfordshire, and seat of one of the most celebrated universities in the world. It is situated on a gentle acclivity between the Cherwell and the Thames, here called the Isis, and is served by the Great Western and the L.M.S. Railways from London and Reading.

Oxford, as a city of towers and spires, of fine collegiate buildings old and new, of gardens, groves, and avenues of trees, is unique in England. The oldest building is the castle keep, built in the time of William the Conqueror and still all but entire.

Of the numerous churches the first is the Norman cathedral, begun about 1160. It not only serves as the cathedral of Oxford diocese, but also forms part of the collegiate buildings of Wolsey's foundation of Christ Church, of which the head is dean of the diocese. Other churches are St. Mary's, used as the University Church, with a tower and spire (dating about 1400); All Saints', the city church (eighteenth century), with a Græco-Gothic spire; St. Giles's (twelfth and thirteenth century); and St. Barnabas, a modern building.

Of the university buildings the most remarkable are Christ Church, the largest and grandest of all the colleges, with a fine quadrangle and other buildings, a noble avenue of trees (the Broad Walk), the cathedral serving as its chapel; Magdalen College, considered to be the most beautiful and complete of all; Balliol College, with a modern front (1867-69) and a modern Gothic chapel; Brasenose College; and New College (more than 500 years old), largely consisting of the original buildings, and especially noted for its gardens and cloisters; besides the Sheldonian Theatre, a public hall of the university; the new examination schools, new museum, Bodleian Library, Radcliffe Library, and other buildings belonging to the university. (*See* OXFORD UNIVERSITY.)

Oxford depends mostly on the university, and on its attractions as a place of residence. The establishment of the Morris Motor Works at Cowley, however, has made it an important industrial centre.

The history of the town of Oxford begins in 912, when it was occupied by Edward the Elder, King of the West Saxons. The town received a charter from King Henry II., granting the citizens the same privileges and exemptions as those enjoyed by the capital. During the seventeenth century Parliaments were often held at Oxford, and in the seventeenth century it was again prominent in history as the headquarters of the Royalist party. It sends one member to the House of Commons. Pop. (1931) 80,540.

OXFORD, Earl of. *See* ASQUITH.

OXFORD CLAY. In geology, a bed of dark-blue or blackish clay, interposed between the Bath and Coralline, so called from its being well developed in Oxfordshire.

OXFORD GROUP. Religious movement in the Church of England. Founded by the Rev. Frank Buchman, an American Methodist minister, it first took root in England at Oxford and represents an attempt to revive the spirit of first-century Christianity. Stress is laid upon confession, self-dedication, and guidance. The movement has spread rapidly over the British Isles and in America, and has been extended to Germany, France, and other continental countries.

OXFORD HOUSE. Settlement in Bethnal Green, London, E.C. It was founded in 1884 by members of the University of Oxford to carry on religious and social work among the poor under the auspices of the Church of England. The original building is in Mape Street, but the settlement includes several others, among them St. Margaret's House, a centre for work among women.

OXFORD MOVEMENT, The. Has been described as a revival of that conservative, patristic, sacramental form of Anglican piety and theology of which Laud was the precursor and Andrewes the typical representative. Its immediate cause was the supposed menace to religion of the contemporary religious and political "liberalism." For the movement took shape in an age when the spirit of freedom was at once asserting itself within the Church of England, and setting itself against it—the age, namely, both of the "Broad Church" theology and of the Catholic Emancipation Act and the Reform Bill.

In a sermon preached from the university pulpit at Oxford on 14th July, 1833, John Keble sought to arouse the Church to the danger of the situation. That sermon, according to John Henry Newman, marks the beginning of the Oxford Movement. But the real, as distinguished from the formal, beginning was largely due to Newman himself, and took place in Sept., 1833, when there appeared the first of the *Tracts for the Times by Members of the University of Oxford.* Of the ninety tracts issued between 1833 and 1841 a large proportion came from Newman's own pen.

During those years Newman was the most influential leader of the movement. Edward B. Pusey was second to him in prominence among the "Tractarians," and on his withdrawal from participation in the movement succeeded him in the leadership. The "Tractarians" and their followers became known indeed as "Puseyites." Newman's withdrawal was occasioned by the storm of indignation and controversy that greeted the appearance in 1841 of his famous *Tract No.* 90, in which he showed pronounced sympathy with Romanism as against Protestantism.

His secession to Rome in 1845 may be said to mark the end of one phase of the movement. But the influence of the movement upon the Church of England, and upon the Anglican Church generally, has been deep and lasting. It has not only served to revive the Anglo-Catholicism of the days of Bishop Andrewes on the side of doctrine, it has revived it also on the side of worship, by its restoration of ritual and stately ceremonial. The centenary of the movement was celebrated in 1933.—BIBLIOGRAPHY: R. W. Church, *The Oxford Movement*, 1833-45; J. H. Newman, *Apologia pro Vita Sua*; J. A. Froude, *The Oxford Counter-Reformation* in *Short Studies on Great Subjects*; S. L. Ollard, *Short History of the Oxford Movement.*

OXFORDSHIRE. A south-midland county of England. It is bounded by Northampton, Warwick, Gloucester, Berks, and Buckingham; area, 479,224 acres. The southern part of the county presents alternations of hill and dale, the former, particularly the Chiltern Hills, being beautifully varied with fine woods, tracts of arable land, and open sheep downs. The central parts are more level, and are also adorned by numerous woods.

The Great Western, L.N.E., and L.M.S. Railways serve the county, which is intersected by the Oxford Canal. Dairy-farming is largely practised, and great quantities of butter are made. Manufactures are of little importance. The principal rivers are the Thames or Isis, Thame, Evenlode, Cherwell, and Windrush. The abbreviated title for Oxfordshire is Oxon. Pop. (1931), 209,599.

OXFORD UNIVERSITY. One of the two great English universities, established in the Middle Ages, and situated in the city of Oxford (q.v.). Like Cambridge it embraces a number of colleges forming distinct corporations, of which the oldest is believed to be University College, dating from 1253, though Merton College was the first to adopt the collegiate system proper. The following list contains the name of the colleges, with the date at which each was founded:

1.	University College	1253
2.	Balliol College	1268
3.	Merton College	1274
4.	Exeter College	1314
5.	Oriel College	1326
6.	Queen's College	1340
7.	New College	1379
8.	Lincoln College	1427
9.	All Souls' College	1437
10.	Magdalen College	1458
11.	Brasenose College	1509
12.	Corpus Christi College	1516
13.	Christ Church	1546
14.	Trinity College	1554
15.	St. John's College	1555
16.	Jesus College	1571
17.	Wadham College	1612
18.	Pembroke College	1624
19.	Worcester College	1714
20.	Keble College	1870
21.	Hertford College	1874

Of the so-called "Halls," which were similar institutions, but differing from the colleges in not being corporate bodies, only St. Edmund Hall now remains.

Oxford University is an institution of quite the same character as that of Cambridge. Most of the students belong to and reside in some college (or hall), but since 1869 a certain number have been admitted without belonging to any of these institutions. The students receive most of their instruction from tutors attached to the individual colleges, and those of each college dine together in the college hall and attend the college chapel. The ordinary students are called "commoners." The style or title by which the corporation is known is The Chancellor, Masters, and Scholars of the University of Oxford. The head of the university is the Chancellor.

The chief governing bodies are the House of Convocation, the Congregation of the University, and the Hebdomadal Council. The House of Convocation, which includes all Doctors and Masters whose names are on the register, elects to nearly all the offices in the gift of the university; gives the final sanction to all new statutes; transacts nearly all the formal business of the university as a corporate body; and elects the parliamentary representatives.

The Congregation of the University, which includes professors and other officials and all resident members of Convocation, can amend, confirm, or reject legislative proposals laid before it, but all these must originate with the Hebdomadal Council, which consists of about twenty members, partly official, but mostly elected, and which meets every week in term time.

The office of Chancellor is almost purely honorary; the Vice-Chancellor is in fact the supreme executive and judicial authority of the university. Two proctors are chosen yearly to maintain the discipline of the university.

The university is open, without respect of birth, age, or creed, to all who have passed the necessary examinations or other tests. Students enter as commoners or as "scholars" or "exhibitioners," according as they obtain some of the numerous scholarships or exhibitions which may be competed for.

The university possesses faculties in Law, Theology, Medicine, Literæ Humaniores, Modern History, English Language and Literature, Mediæval and Modern Languages, Oriental Languages, Sciences (including Mathematics), Physics, and Biological Science. There are also boards of studies for Music, Philosophy, Politics, and Economics, as well as a University Extension Board.

Candidates for the degree of B.A. must pass three distinct examinations: Responsions (known among under-graduates by the designation "Smalls") before the masters of the schools; first public examination before the moderators ("Moderations"); and the second public examination before the public examiners ("Schools"). If the student wishes to take his degree with "honours," a residence of four years is usually necessary.

Honours may be taken in *literæ humaniores* (classics), English language and literature, mathematics, jurisprudence, modern history, theology, natural science, and Oriental studies. Any B.A. may proceed to the degree of M.A., without further examination or exercise, in the twenty-seventh term from his matriculation, provided he has kept his name on the books of some college or hall, or upon the register of unattached students for a period of twenty-six terms. In the case of all other degrees (except honorary ones) some examination or exercise is necessary.

Women were admitted to the examinations in 1884, and were first given degrees in 1920. Four colleges for women have been established: Somerville Hall, Lady Margaret Hall, St. Hilda's Hall, and St. Hugh's Hall. These are four independent theological foundations: Pusey House and Wycliffe Hall (Anglican), and Mansfield College and Manchester College (Nonconformist). The Oxford Union Society is the chief debating society, and there is a well-known dramatic society, the O.U.D.S. The university has a famous press, the Clarendon Press, with offices in Oxford and London.

The total number of students, 1932–33, was 4711. The total number of professorships, etc., in the university was 450. The total annual revenues are between £400,000 and £500,000. The institutions connected with the university include: the Bodleian Library (the second in the kingdom), the Ashmolean Museum, Botanic Gardens, Taylor Institution for modern languages, University Museum, Radcliffe Library, Observatory, and Indian Institute. Since 1604 the University has sent two members to Parliament.—BIBLIOGRAPHY: H. C. Maxwell-Lyte, *History of the University of Oxford*; G. C. Brodrick, *History of the Uni-*

versity of Oxford; J. Wells, *Oxford and Oxford Life*; Hastings Rashdall, *History of Universities in the Middle Ages*.

OXIDES. The compounds of oxygen with other elements. The elements, with the exception of fluorine, bromine, and the gases of the argon group, all unite with oxygen directly or indirectly to form oxides. The oxides may be classified into *basic oxides, acidic oxides, neutral oxides*, and *peroxides*. The basic oxides contain metal united with oxygen, e.g. calcium oxide or quicklime (CaO), sodium oxide (Na_2O), etc. These react with acids, forming a salt of the metal and water. Acidic oxides contain non-metals united with oxygen, e.g. sulphur dioxide (SO_2), phosphorus pentoxide (P_2O_5); these unite with a base to form a salt and water.

Certain of the metals form both basic and acidic oxides; thus chromium forms a basic oxide (Cr_2O_3), chromic oxide, and an acidic oxide (CrO_3), chromium trioxide; and again some metals form oxides which have both basic and acidic properties, e.g. zinc oxide (ZnO) reacts with acids to form a salt and water; it also dissolves in alkalis, forming a salt and water. Neutral oxides show no reaction with either acid or base, e.g. hydrogen oxide or water (H_2O), nitrous oxide (N_2O), carbon monoxide (CO).

Peroxides contain an excess of oxygen which is easily liberated, e.g. hydrogen peroxide (H_2O_2), sodium peroxide (Na_2O_2), barium peroxide (BaO_2). *See* also articles on individual chemical elements.

OXLIP (*Primŭla elatior*). A kind of primrose growing wild in East Anglia, intermediate between the primrose and cowslip, but distinct from the hybrids between these two.

OXUS, AMU, AMU DARYĀ, or **JAIHŪN.** A large river of Central Asia, which has its sources between the Thian Shan and Hindu Kush ranges in the Pamir, flows west through a broad valley, receiving many affluents, and north-west through the deserts of Western Turkestan, bordering on or belonging to Bukhāra and Khiva, to the southern extremity of the Sea of Aral, where it forms an extensive marshy delta.

It is generally held that the lower part of the course of the Oxus was at one time different from what it is now, and that the river entered the Caspian Sea. The principal headstream of the Oxus is by some considered to be the Panja River, which rises in a lake of the great Pamir, at a height of 13,900 feet. The Oxus for a considerable distance forms the boundary between Afghanistan and Bukhāra. Total course, 1300 miles.

OXYCHLORIDE. The chloride of a metal or non-metal where part of the chlorine is replaced by oxygen, as in phosphorus oxychloride ($POCl_3$), bismuth oxychloride (BiOCl), etc.

OXYCOC'CUS. A genus of plants of the nat. ord. Vacciniaceæ, commonly known as the cranberry (q.v.).

OXYGEN (chemical symbol, O; atomic weight, 16·00). The most widely distributed of all the elements, $\frac{8}{9}$ by weight of water, $\frac{1}{4}$ by weight of air, and about $\frac{1}{2}$ of silica, chalk, and alumina consisting of oxygen. It exists in the atmosphere in the free state mixed with nitrogen; it enters into the constitution of most minerals and rocks; it exists in the tissues and blood of animals; it is essential to life, and all decay of organic vegetable and animal matter is carried on through its agency.

Oxygen was first isolated in 1774 by Joseph Priestley, who gave the new gas the name of *dephlogisticated air*. Lavoisier the year following put forward the opinion that the new gas was identical with the substance which exists in the air, and gave it the name oxygen (from Gr. *oxys*, acid, and root *gen*, to produce) because he supposed it was present as the active constituent of all acids.

Oxygen is a colourless inodorous gas; it is rather heavier than air. It is slightly soluble in water at ordinary temperature—a fact which is of importance, as the dissolved gas is the source of oxygen supply for fish and other aquatic life.

Oxygen was first liquefied by Pictet in 1877 by the application of intense cold and pressure. Liquid oxygen is a bluish transparent liquid which boils at $-182{\cdot}9°$ C. at 760 mm.; when the pressure is reduced evaporation takes place so rapidly that part of the oxygen is obtained as a hard blue solid. Chemically oxygen is very reactive, and readily unites with all the elements with a few exceptions.

The union of oxygen with the elements is known as oxidation, and the compounds formed are the oxides (*see* OXIDES; CHEMISTRY). Some elements when brought in contact with oxygen at ordinary temperature unite with it so violently as to produce light and heat; in other cases oxidation is much slower, e.g. the rusting of iron. All phenomena of ordinary combustion or burning of substances are cases of oxidation, the substance in burning uniting with the oxygen of the air. A combustible substance is one which readily unites with oxygen.

Oxygen plays an important part in nature. In inspiring, animals receive into the lungs a supply of oxygen; this oxygen is carried by the blood to various parts of the body, and there aids in tissue-building, etc.; the deoxygenated blood returns to the lungs and again receives a supply of oxygen.

Trees and green plants evolve oxygen, which is formed during decomposition of carbon dioxide absorbed from the atmosphere by the green parts of the plant. Oxygen is manufactured in considerable quantity for industrial purposes.

It was formerly obtained by electrolysis of water or from barium dioxide in Brin's process, but of recent years practically all oxygen has been prepared by Linde's liquid-air process, in which oxygen is separated from liquid air by fractional distillation.

Oxygen is used in medicine and industrially for maintaining a supply of fresh air in enclosed spaces; for the production of high temperatures, oxygen mixed with hydrogen in the oxy-hydrogen flame giving a temperature sufficient to melt platinum; in oxy-acetylene welding and metal cutting; and for thickening oils.

OXYR'IA. A genus of plants of the nat. ord. Polygonaceæ. The only species native to Great Britain is *O. reniformis* (mountain-sorrel), which is found on some of the highest mountains.

OXYU'RIS. A genus of internal parasitic thread-worms, which rapidly multiply and pass from the intestine to other organs. *O. vermiculāris*, often found in the human rectum, is usually about a quarter of an inch long.

OYSTER. An edible bivalve mollusc, and a near ally of the mussels, etc. It belongs to the genus Ostrea, family Ostreidæ, the members of which are distinguished by the possession of an inequivalve shell, the one half or valve being larger than the other. The shell may be free, or attached to fixed objects, or may be simply embedded in the mud. The foot is wanting. A single (adductor) muscle for closing the shell is developed.

The common oyster (*Ostrea edūlis*) is the most familiar member of the genus. The fry or fertilized ova of the oyster are termed "spat," and enormous numbers of ova are produced by each individual from May or June to September—the spawning season. The spat being discharged, each embryo is found to consist of a little body enclosed within a minute but perfectly formed shell, and possessing vibratile filaments or cilia, by which the young animal at first swims freely about, and then attaches itself to some object.

In about three years it attains its full growth. The oysters congregate together in their attached state to form large submarine tracts or "oyster-beds," as they are termed.

Oysters are found all over the world, and are commercially the most important fishery product.

The United States and France are the chief seats of the oyster industry. In the United States the natural oyster-beds are still a source of great wealth, while in Europe the native beds have long since been practically destroyed. Large quantities of American oysters are now sent to Europe; and the American are generally larger than the European. In Europe the oyster industry has practically ceased to be oyster fishery and is now oyster culture.

In Great Britain the chief centre of the industry is in the Thames estuary. In Scotland the oyster has hitherto been left pretty much to itself and to nature; hence the depopulation of the once famous beds of the Firth of Forth, and the fact that the "Pandores" of Prestonpans are things of the past.

In England, and especially in the Thames estuary, brood oysters are laid down in fattening beds, where they obtain food which gives them a peculiar thinness of shell and delicacy of flavour, and that green colour which is so much esteemed by epicures. The oysters thus laid down and bred in these situations are known as "natives," and fetch the highest price in the market.

Oyster culture is prosecuted on various parts of the coast, chiefly by private companies. The most ancient of these is the Whitstable company, which has worked its present ground on the south side of the entrance to the Thames from time immemorial. In Britain oyster-beds, being below the medium line of the tides, belong by right to the crown, and can only be claimed as private property in virtue of a royal grant.

In order to prevent the total extirpation or great diminution of the supply of oysters a close season has been fixed, by a convention between England and France, applying to the seas between the two countries. The close season lasts from the 1st of May to the 31st of Aug. The pearl oyster (*Meleagrīna margaritifera*), of the Indian and Pacific Oceans, belongs to a different family.

OYSTER-CATCHER (*Hæmatŏpus ostralĕgus*). A bird belonging to the well-known plover family (Charadriidæ), and popularly known as the

Oyster-catcher

"sea-pie." It is distinguished by its long, thin, wedge-shaped, orange-coloured bill, and its black and white plumage. It is a permanent resident in Britain, and frequents the sea-coast, where it feeds on mollusca.

O'ZARK MOUNTAINS. A chain of the United States, intersecting in a south-westerly direction the states of Missouri and Arkansas; height, about 2300 feet.

OZOKE'RITE. A greenish or yellowish solid mineral hydrocarbon of a pleasantly aromatic odour, existing in the bituminous beds of the coal-measures, and occurring chiefly in Galicia (Poland) and in Roumania. Small quantities of it have been found at Uphall, in Linlithgowshire, and at Urpeth Colliery, Newcastle-on-Tyne, and various other places. It contains 85 per cent. of carbon and 14 per cent. of hydrogen. When purified it forms a hard paraffin, from which excellent candles are manufactured. It is used to some extent as an adulterant of beeswax. *See* PARAFFIN.

OZONE (Gr. *ozō*, I smell). The element oxygen in a modified or allotropic form. When heated it yields pure oxygen, and it has been shown that 2 volumes of ozone yield 3 of oxygen, and hence the formula O_3. It is a colourless gas with a characteristic odour, and may be condensed to a blue liquid at low temperatures. It is an extremely powerful oxidizing agent, readily converting copper, mercury, and silver into their oxides in the presence of moisture. When an electric machine is set in operation, a peculiar smell may be perceived; after a discharge of lightning the same smell is perceptible. The substance which manifests this odour is ozone. In industry it is used for refining palm and linseed oils, for cleansing brewers' casks, and for other purposes where an oxidizing gas is useful. It bleaches numerous substances, such as indigo and natural fibres.

P

P. The sixteenth letter and twelfth consonant in the English alphabet. It is one of the mutes and labials, and represents a sound produced by closely compressing the lips till the breath is collected, and then letting it issue. In English words beginning with *pn*, *ps*, and *pt*, *p* is silent.

PAARL, The. A town of Cape Province, South Africa, 36 miles from Cape Town, on the Berg River. Pop. 12,407 (7783 white in 1931).

PABNA'. A district and town of the Rájsháhi division, Bengal, near the Ganges; contains a large indigo factory. Area (district), 1678 sq. miles; pop. 1,500,000; (town), 19,300.

PACA, or **SPOTTED CAVY** (Cœlogenys). A genus of rodents allied to the agoutis, family Dacyproctidæ. The common paca (*C. paca*) is one of the largest of the rodents, being about 2 feet long and about 1 foot high. In form it is thick and clumsy, and the tail is rudimentary. In habits the pacas are chiefly nocturnal and herbivorous. They excavate burrows, run swiftly, and swim and dive with facility. They are found in the eastern portion of South America, from Paraguay to Surinam. The flesh is said to be savoury.

PACHIRA (pa-kī'ra). A genus of tropical American trees allied to the baobab tree. The largest flowered species, *P. macrantha*, found in Brazil, attains a height of 100 feet, and has flowers 15 inches long. The plants are familiar in our hothouses under the name of *Carolinea*.

PACHMANN, Vladimir de. The world-famous pianist, was born at Odessa in 1848. His father, who was a noted musical amateur, was his first teacher, and Pachmann followed up this early instruction by a course of study at the Conservatorium of Vienna. He made his first public appearance as a pianist in Russia in 1869, and although meeting with much success he retired for a further period of hard study, which lasted for eight years.

After a short spell of public playing he again retired for two more years of study, and on reappearing was at last satisfied with his achievements. His first appearance in Britain was at London in 1882. As an interpreter he was unequal, but his renderings of Chopin, especially the more delicate works, were unrivalled, and offered memorable examples of piano-playing at its highest. He died in Rome on 7th Jan., 1933.

PACHO'MIUS. A scholar of St. Antony, born about A.D. 292. He is said to have been the first who introduced, instead of the free hermit life, the regular association of monks living in cloisters. He founded one of the first monastic institutions on Tabenna, an island of the Nile, in 318. He was also the founder of the first nunnery, and at his death is said to have had the oversight of above 7000 monks and nuns.

PACHUCA, or **HIDALGO.** A city of Mexico, capital of the state of Hidalgo, in a rich silver-mining region, about 8200 feet above the sea. Pop. (1931), 40,293.

PACHYDER'MATA. The name formerly applied to an artificial assemblage of mammals, including the elephants, tapirs, hippopotamus, rhinoceros, swine, and hyrax—all of which forms were distinguished by their thick skin, by their non-ruminant habits, and by their possessing more than one hoof on each extremity. The group is now divided among the various sub-orders of the Ungulata. *See* UNGULATA.

PACHYGLOSSÆ. A section of saurian reptiles having a thick fleshy tongue, convex, with a slight nick at the end. It includes the iguanas and agamas.

PACHYRHIZUS (pak-i-rī'zus). A genus of tropical leguminous plants common to both hemispheres. *P. angulatus* has fleshy roots of great length and thickness, which are used in times of scarcity as an article of diet.

PACIFIC OCEAN (formerly called also the **South Sea**). The largest of the oceans of the globe, extending between America and Asia-Australia. It exceeds in compass the whole of the four continents taken together, and occupies more than a fourth part of the earth's area, and fully one-half of its water surface. On the west it extends to the Indian Ocean, and has several more or less distinct seas connected with it—the China Sea, Yellow Sea, Sea of Japan, Sea of Okhotsk, etc.; on the north it communicates with the Arctic Ocean by Bering Strait, on the south it is bounded by the Antarctic Ocean, and on the east it joins the Atlantic at Cape Horn.

Within this enormous circumference it includes the numerous islands composing the groups of Australasia and Polynesia, and those adjoining America and Asia. The average depth of the Pacific is greater than that of the Atlantic, and its bed is more uniform. The deepest sounding obtained in the Philippines gave a depth of nearly 5350 fathoms.

The trade-winds of the Pacific are not so regular in their limits as those of the Atlantic, and this irregularity extends over a much wider region in the case of the south-east trade-wind than in the case of the north-east. The cause of this is the greater number of islands in the South Pacific Ocean, which, especially in the hot season, disturb the uniformity of atmospheric pressure by local condensations.

The north-east trade-wind remains the whole year through within the northern hemisphere. The south-east trade-wind, on the other hand, advances beyond the equator, both in summer and winter, still preserving its original direction.

In the region stretching from New Guinea and the Solomon Islands south-eastwards there are no regular winds. The zones of the two trade-winds are separated by regions of calms and of light winds, the limits of which vary, of course, with the varying limits of these zones. In the China seas the terrible typhoon occasionally rages, and may occur at any season of the year.

The Portuguese were the first Europeans who entered the Pacific, which they did from the east. Balboa, in 1513, discovered it from the summit of the mountains which traverse the Isthmus of Darien. Magellan sailed across it from east to west in 1520–21. Drake, Tasman, Behring, Anson, Byron, Bougainville, Cook, Vancouver, La Pérouse, and others traversed it in different directions in the seventeenth and eighteenth centuries. The principal Pacific powers are United States, Japan, and Great Britain, and the question of the control of the Pacific was discussed at Washington in 1921. In addition to the numerous trade routes a submarine telegraph cable runs from Vancouver, by way of Norfolk Island, to New Zealand and Australia.

PACINIAN CORPUSCLES. In anatomy, minute oval bodies appended to the extremities of certain nerves, especially those of the hands and feet. The function of the Pacinian corpuscles (named after Pacini, an Italian anatomist, who first described them in 1835) is probably connected with the sense of touch, but is not certainly known.

PACK'FONG. A Chinese alloy of a silver-white colour, consisting (though different accounts are given of its composition) of copper, zinc, nickel, and iron. It was formerly used by watch-makers, mathematical instrument makers, and others for a variety of purposes for which nickel alloys are now employed.

PACTUM ILLICITUM. In Scots law, an unlawful contract, whether it be directly illegal, *contra bonos mores*, or inconsistent with the principles of sound policy.

PACU'VIUS, Marcus. Ancient Roman tragic poet, born at Brundusium in 219 B.C., passed the greater part of his life at Rome, where he became famous both for his poetry and his paintings, retired to Tarentum during his last years, and died at the age of ninety in 129 B.C. Only fragments of his tragedies exist.

PADANG'. A seaport of Sumatra, the coastal terminus of the railway to the hinterland. It is the chief market in Sumatra for coffee and gold. Coffee, tobacco, copra, and hides are exported. The harbour is at Emmahaven. Pop. 51,976.

PADDINGTON. A north-western parliamentary borough of the county of London, wedged between Marylebone and Kensington, and including such districts as Maida Vale and Bayswater. It is largely residential, and has many mansions and flats around Hyde Park, in Bayswater, and near Kensington Gardens.

The terminus of the Great Western Railway, familiarly known as "Paddington," is in Praed Street. Harrow Road intersects the borough; Edgware Road forms the eastern and Bayswater Road a part of the southern boundaries of Paddington. Paddington is not mentioned in *Domesday Book*, and was probably attached at that time to the manor of Tyburn. It was given by Edward VI. to the see of London. Pop. (1931), 144,950.

PADDLE-FISH, or SPOON-BILL. The *Polyŏdon folium*, a large fish allied to the sturgeons, so named from the elongated broad snout with which it stirs up the soft muddy bottom in search of food. It often reaches a length of from 5 to 6 feet. The paddle-fishes are exclusively North

Paddle-Fish

American in their distribution, being found in the Mississippi, Ohio, and other great rivers of that continent.

PADDLE-WHEELS. In steamships, the wheels (generally two in number, one placed on each side of the vessel) provided with boards, vanes, or floats on their circumferences, and driven by the engine for the ship's propulsion through the water. The vanes are usually of the "feathering" type. This system of propulsion is an efficient one, but necessitates the use of very slow-running engines. Where rivers are very shallow or liable to obstruction by floating timber or growing vegetation, a single stern wheel of the paddle type is used for propulsion.

PA'DERBORN. A town of Prussia, in the province of Westphalia. It is the see of a Roman Catholic bishop, and has a fine old cathedral, part of which dates from the eleventh century. The manufactures are unimportant, but there is a considerable trade. A Hanseatic town in the eleventh century, it became Prussian in 1859. Pop. 33,719.

PADEREWSKI (pă - de - ref'skē), **Ignace Jan.** Polish pianist and composer, born in 1860. He could play the piano when he was three years old, and in 1872 went to Warsaw to study, soon afterwards touring through Russia, Siberia, and Roumania. In 1878 he became professor at the Warsaw Conservatoire, and in 1884 at the Strasbourg Conservatoire. He appeared in public at Vienna in 1887, subsequently in Paris in 1889, and in London in 1890, with universal admiration.

Paddle-wheel (Paddle Steamer)

His first visit to America took place in 1891. He composed a number of pieces for piano, orchestra, and voice, including an opera entitled *Mauru.* In 1899 he married the Baroness de Rosen. In 1919 he became Premier of the new Polish Republic, but resigned the premiership in December of the same year. In 1921 he abandoned Politics, and returned to music as a career. During the World War he organized a relief fund for Polish sufferers and formed a corps of Polish volunteers.

Paderewski

He also represented Poland at Washington in 1917–18, and took the lead in the establishment of Polish Republic. In 1919 he was made first Premier of Poland and was a delegate for his country to the League of Nations in 1920.

PAD'IHAM. A town and urban district of Lancashire, England, on the Calder; served by the L.M.S. Railway. St. Leonard's Church dates from the fifteenth (rebuilt nineteenth) century. The town is largely industrial, and is a centre of quarrying and coal-mining. Pop. (1931), 11,632.

PADILLA (pá-*d*ēl'yá), **Juan Lopez de.** A Spanish hero, born in 1484, died 24th April, 1521. In 1518 he became the leader in the insurrection of the Castilian towns (the so-called Communidades) against the arbitrary policy and Flemish advisers of Charles V. The fate of the insurrection was decided by the battle of Villalar, in which Padilla was wounded and taken prisoner. He was executed on the following day. His wife, Maria Pacheco, defended Toledo for some time after his death, and on its fall fled to Portugal. The names of Padilla and his wife are still household words among the Castilians.

PADINA. A genus of brown algæ, family Dictoytaceæ. *P. Pavonia*, the peacock's tail, is one of the most beautiful of British seaweeds. The fronds are fan- or sometimes cup-shaped, and marked with concentric rows of iridescent hairs, which give a characteristic mother-of-pearl-like appearance to the plant.

PADISHAH′. A title of the Sultan of Turkey and of the Shah of Persia. The word is derived from *pad* (ruler or king), and *shah* (king, prince). The title may be literally interpreted as "king of kings," cognate with Negus-negusti.

PAD′STOW. An urban district, town, and seaport of Cornwall, England, on the estuary of the Camel; served by the Southern Railway. It is a very ancient place, and furnished ships for the siege of Calais in 1346. Pop. (1931), 1929.

PADUA. A province of Venetia, North Italy, on the Venetian Plain, traversed by the Bacchiglione, Adige, and Brenta. Wheat, wine, and rice are produced; sericulture is extensive. Area, 826 sq. miles; pop. (1931), 632,160.

PAD′UA (ancient **Patavium**; It. *Padŏva*). A city of Italy, capital of the province of the same name, on the Bacchiglione, which traverses it in several branches; served by, and a junction on the railway from Venice. Several streets are lined with mediæval arcades.

The principal buildings are the Palazzo della Ragione (1172-1219); the church of S. Antonio of Padua (who was an associate of St. Francis of Assisi), founded in 1231, and restored in 1749; the cathedral (1550), with an adjoining baptistery adorned with frescoes of date 1380; and the university, which, founded in 1222, was one of the principal seats of learning in the Middle Ages. Many names famous in learning and art are connected with Padua, such as Galileo, Scaliger, Tasso, Giotto, Lippo Lippi, and Donatello. Pop. (1931), 131,066.

Padua traces its origin to Antenor, the mythical King of Troy, brother of Priam, and under Augustus was the wealthiest town of Upper Italy. All ancient monuments were destroyed by the barbarians on the decline and fall of the Roman Empire. The city was annexed to Venetia in 1405, and passed to Italy in 1866.

PADUCAH. A city of Kentucky, United States, the county seat of M'Cracken county, at the confluence of the Tennessee and Ohio Rivers. It is served by the Illinois Central Railway, and is the terminus of a branch of the Chattanooga & St. Louis Railway. Steamers run to Tennessee River ports. There is a trade in agricultural produce, implements, minerals, and tobacco, and there are large railway repair shops. Paducah was settled in 1821, and is named after a local Indian chief. It became a city in 1856. Pop. (1930), 33,541.

PÆAN. In Greek, a hymn to Apollo or to other deities, or a song in praise of heroes. A pæan was sung, previous to battle, in honour of Ares (Mars), and after a victory, in praise of Apollo. The word is derived from Pæan, an ancient Greek god of healing, afterwards identified with Apollo. In the hymns to Apollo the phrase *Io pæan* was frequently repeated, and hence these hymns were also called *pæans*.

PÆSTUM (Gr. *Posidonia*). An ancient Greek city of Lower Italy, on the Gulf of Salerno. It is celebrated by the Latin poets for the fragrance of its twice-blowing roses, and its mild and balmy air. Little now remains of it but some fragments of its walls and the well-preserved ruins of two Doric temples of extreme interest, which were discovered

Pæstum: Temple of Jupiter

in the middle of the eighteenth century. The city was settled by a Greek colony from Sybaris 524 B.C.

PAEZ (pá-eth'), **José Antonio.** One of the founders of South American independence, born of Indian parents near Acarigua, Venezuela, in 1790, died at New York in 1873. He entered the patriot army in 1810, rose to general of division in 1819, and took a leading part in the battle of Carabobo, which secured the independence of Colombia in 1821. At first he acted in concert with Bolivar, but in 1829 he placed himself at the head of the Revolution which culminated in the independence of Venezuela, of which he was the first President.

PAGAN. A town of the Myingyan district of Upper Burma, on the Irrawaddy. It was founded in A.D. 847 by King Pyinbya, and was capital until the fall of his dynasty in 1298. Pagan is full of decaying Buddhist temples and pagodas. Pop. (estimated), 7000.

PAGANI'NI, Niccolo. Italian violinist, born at Genoa 27th Oct., 1782, died at Nice 27th May, 1840. His father, who had some knowledge of music, and discerned the talents of his son, put him at a very early age under the best masters (Costa, Rolla, Paer) to learn music, and particularly the violin. With this instrument his progress was so rapid that at the age of nine he was able to perform in public at Genoa. His first engagement was in 1805, at Lucca, where he found a patroness in Princess Eliza, Bonaparte's sister. In 1813 he left Lucca for Milan, and in 1828 visited Vienna.

From this period his fame was world-wide. The wonder which he excited was caused not merely by the charm of his execution and his extraordinary skill, but also by his external appearance, which had something weird and even demoniacal in it. After visiting almost all the great towns of Germany he made a musical tour through France and Great Britain, realizing immense gains. His last years were spent at a villa near Parma.—Cf. S. S. Stratton, *Niccolo Paganini: his Life and Work.*

PAGANS. A term applied to the worshippers of many gods, the heathens, or to any one who professes no religion whatever. The term is found for the first time in an edict of Valentinian (368), and is applied to the dwellers in villages (*pagani*). It appears that at that period polytheism had been abandoned, and Christianity became predominant in the towns, whilst the ancient polytheistic faith still continued to linger in the villages (*pagi*) and country districts.

The *pagani* of the Latin races corresponded to the "men of the heath" among the Teutonic races. Another explanation is that according to which *paganus* was originally employed in opposition to *milites*, professional soldiers. The Christians being considered as the soldiers of faith, all non-Christians were termed pagans. In the Middle Ages the name of pagans was given to all heathens and Mahommedans, i.e. all those who were neither Jews nor Christians, theirs being considered the only true religions.

In modern times, however, Mahommedans, who worship the one Supreme God of the Jews and the Christians, are not called pagans. Paganism has never been really and thoroughly eradicated, in spite of the triumph of monotheism and Christianity. Numerous are the pagan practices which have gained entrance into the religions both of Christianity and Judaism.

PAGO'DA. A name given to a tower-like structure in the East (India, China, and Japan), connected with a temple or serving as a shrine. The temple proper is generally of pyramidal form, and of a number of stories, of great size and height, and embellished with extraordinary splendour. Connected with it may be various other structures, open courts, etc., the whole forming architecturally a very imposing group. Pagodas are numerous not only in Hindustan but also in Burmah, Siam, and China. The statues in the temples, which are also called *pagodas*, are often of a colossal size.

PAHANG'. The largest of the Federated Malay States, on the east coast of British Malaya. In the east it is mountainous, but towards the coast it is low and swampy. The principal river is the Pahang, to the drainage basin of which, with its tributaries, the state exclusively belongs. Rubber, timber, tin, and other minerals, coco-nuts, and copra are produced. The eastern railway system runs to Kuala Lipis. Area, 14,000 sq. miles; pop. (1931), 180,111.

Pekan is the seat of the Sultan; Kuala Lipis is the administrative centre, and is connected by motor-road with Kuala Kubu, in Selangor. Pahang voluntarily surrendered the control of foreign affairs to a British Resident in 1887, and the Raja (now Sultan) agreed to a British Protectorate in 1888. *See* MALAYA.

PAIGNTON. An urban district and seaside-resort of Devonshire, England, on Tor Bay; served by the Great Western Railway. It contains the ruined palace of the Bishops of Exeter, and a Bible Tower, where Miles Coverdale resided while translating the Bible. There is a pleasure-pier, also a considerable production of cider. Pop. (1931), 18,405.

PAINE, Thomas. Political and deistical writer, born in 1737 at Thetford, in Norfolk, died at New York in 1809. The son of a staymaker, he tried many ways of making a living in his earlier years, and in 1774 emigrated to America, with a letter of introduction from Benjamin Franklin. Paine threw himself heart and soul into the cause of the colonists, and his pamphlet entitled *Common Sense*, written to recommend the separation of the colonies from Great Britain, and his subsequent periodical called *The Crisis*, gave him a title to be considered one of the founders of American independence. In 1787 he returned to England, and in answer to Burke's *Reflections on the French Revolution* wrote his *Rights of Man*.

A prosecution was commenced against him as the author of that work, but while the trial was pending he escaped to France, where he was chosen member of the National Convention for the department of Calais. On the trial of Louis XVI. he voted against the sentence of death, proposing his imprisonment during the war and his banishment afterwards.

This conduct offended the Jacobins, and towards the close of 1793 he was excluded from the Convention, arrested, and committed to prison, where he lay for ten months, escaping the guillotine by an accident. Just before his confinement he had finished the first part of his work against revelation, entitled *The Age of Reason*, which was published in London and Paris in 1794. He remained in France till Aug., 1802, when he returned to America.

PAINESVILLE. A city of Ohio, United States, the county seat of Lake county, on Grand River; served by the Lake Shore & Michigan Southern, the Baltimore & Ohio, and the New York, Chicago, & St. Louis Railways, and by electric-traction lines. It is the seat of Lake Erie College (for women), and is a farming and horticultural centre. Founded in 1800, it became a city in 1902. Pop. (1930), 10,944.

PAINLEVÉ, Paul. French politician. Born in Paris, 5th Dec., 1863, he became a professor of mathematics at the Sorbonne, and in 1906 was elected an independent Socialist deputy for Paris, but it was not until he became a member of M. Briand's cabinet in 1915 that he became important. He was Minister of War in March, 1917, in Ribot's cabinet, and formed his own cabinet in Sept., 1917. He met Lloyd George and Orlando at Rapallo, and their discussions resulted in the foundation of the Supreme Allied Court of Versailles. He was defeated by Clemenceau in Nov., and was not again Premier until 1925, since when he has been War Minister in several cabinets. In 1932 he joined the government of M. Herriot, and became Minister of Air, as he had been in 1930–31. He is the author of several scientific works and political studies.

PAINTING. The representation of objects by the application of colour to a surface is among the oldest of the arts, though the number of early examples which survive is small. Important among these are the vigorous and realistic palæolithic paintings of animals on the walls of the cave of Altamira in Spain, executed in black, red, and yellow.

In Ancient Egypt a wide range of colour was used, including a famous blue made from copper, with a medium of gum or glue, for the decoration of walls, coffins, and papyrus manuscripts. Similar methods were employed in Mesopotamia; and in Crete (*c.* 2000-1500 B.C.) true fresco painting (*see* FRESCO) was also widely used, of which fine examples exist at Knossos.

In all this painting, the emphasis is on profile and contour, and there is no serious attempt to express solid form or space; though certain Cretan examples foreshadow later developments by suggesting landscape or architectural backgrounds, and by representing figures in crowds. Of the mural paintings and panel pictures produced in large numbers in Greece, very few authentic examples survive; but the vase paintings and literary sources indicate their character.

In the sixth century B.C. there is a transition from simple outline to the use of inner markings to express form; and in the fifth century foreshortening is attempted, and space is expressed by placing figures on different levels, and the use of rudimentary landscape backgrounds.

In the fourth century, Greek painting, as represented by Apelles, Zeuxis, and Protogenes, reached its highest development, in which foreshortening difficulties were overcome, but problems of space only inadequately solved. This appears from the wall paintings of Pompeii, the majority of which are copies of Greek pictures, though a few may be originals. The Romans were content to repeat Greek motives, and use Greek methods.

In both countries a range of colour was employed almost as wide as in modern painting. On panels, the medium was wax (*see* ENCAUSTIC PAINTING) and another of unknown composition; for wall decoration, the Romans used a species of true fresco extensively, as well as the tempera methods (*see* DISTEMPER) preferred by the Greeks.

After the barbarian invasions and the disruption of the Roman Empire, painting found its chief home in Byzantium (Constantinople), whose artists employed the classic methods of fresco and tempera in an art mingling Hellenic and Eastern elements, and marked by conventional, non-realistic treatment of the figure and by rich decorative quality. More important, however, were the Byzantine mosaics (*see* MOSAIC), which mainly contributed to the revival of painting in Italy in the thirteenth century.

Of this, Siena was among the most important centres; and here developed an art Byzantine in type, but with a lyrical quality of linear design of its own. Duccio, followed by Pietro and Ambrogio Lorenzetti, and Simone Martine were the leaders of the school, whose influence, however, steadily waned before that of the Florentines.

Among these, the first great figure was Giotto, whose feeling for solid sculpturesque form and monumental design, combined with power of individual characterization and a sense of drama, make him one of the most potent influences in Italian art. After his death, however, Florence for a time was dominated by the decorative linear painters such as Lorenzo Monaco, until the rise of Masaccio.

The famous fourteenth-century treatise of painting by Cennino Cennini tells us that these early painters mainly used egg-tempera as their medium on panels, and either this or true fresco on walls, developing the method, which subsequently became universal, of covering with a layer of thin new plaster the portion of the wall to be painted each day.

With Masaccio begins the great age of Italian painting. He was the first satisfactorily to express space, and to use light and shade to give both unity and greater plastic quality. Later fifteenth-century painters hardly rivalled his achievement in these respects; but the restless spirit of scientific inquiry which marked Florentine art is exemplified by the researches of Paolo Uccello into perspective, and by a severe realism which is combined in Fra Filippo Lippi and Botticelli with a lyric decorative quality, in Fra Angelico with a tender mysticism, and in Pollaiulo and Andrea del Castagno with a passionate austerity.

Florentine influence soon dominated Siena; bred in North Italy (mainly through the work in Padua of the sculptor Donatello) a great school of which Andrea Mantegna is the chief figure; and extended even to Venice.

Meanwhile, in the fifteenth century an important school of painting had developed in Flanders, in which the brothers Hubert and John Van Eyck and Roger Van der Weyden were prominent, whose work is marked by intense realism, fine colour, and great technical skill. Its influence was felt in France, Spain, Germany, and extended to Italy, where the Flemish method of painting (in which transparent coloured varnishes were used over a tempera ground on which the picture had previously been painted in monochrome) led to the development of modern methods of oil painting, which put into artists' hands a medium of unrivalled range and flexibility.

The earlier masters first *laid in* their work in monochrome, with full light and shade, and then applied colour by means of *glazes* (thin coats of transparent paint) and *scumbles* (thin and therefore semi-transparent coats of opaque paint). These methods persisted until the nineteenth century; but in the seventeenth the direct painting characteristic of modern work appears.

At the end of the fifteenth and the beginning of the sixteenth century Italian painting reached its culminating point in the art of the High Renaissance. Leonardo da Vinci and Michelangelo achieved unrivalled grandeur in design, richness of chiaroscuro, and plastic quality; while Raphael adds a Florentine sense of form to an Umbrian feeling for space, derived largely from his master Perugino.

This period also saw the rise of the Venetian school, which was so profoundly to influence seventeenth and eighteenth century art. Developed in a society of which wealth, stability, and material splendour were the characteristics, the art of Giovanni Bellini and his followers struck a note of delight in external display and rich opulent colour, to which Giorgione and the young Titian join the spirit of pagan poesy which underlies the Renaissance in Venice.

Titian in his later years, however, and Tintoretto reflect the disillusionment expressed by the Counter-Reformation, and show a rejection of the older use of definite form and positive colour in favour of atmospheric envelopment and strong contrasts of light and shade. A temporary challenge to Italian supremacy in the sixteenth century came from Germany in the art of Holbein and Dürer; but in the seventeenth century the centre of gravity in painting definitely passed to Northern Europe.

The traditions of the High Renaissance were, however, in some measure maintained in the mannered and skilful art of the Bolognese and Roman eclectics, while a realistic revival of widespread influence centred round the personality of Caravaggio; and in the eighteenth century there arose an important group of topographical painters such as Canaletto and Guardi, and of decorative painters such as Tiepolo, whose work and influence were of real importance.

Outside Italy, the genius of Rubens once more brought the school of Flanders into prominence, after a period of eclipse. He combined the qualities of his Flemish predecessors with designs inspired by the Venetians, into an art unrivalled in its expression of dynamic energy; and his pupil Vandyck, still more strongly influenced by Italy, developed a style in portraiture of singular dignity and refinement, if sometimes mannered and sentimental, which was to become an abiding force in English art.

In the seventeenth century also developed the Dutch School, in its realism, colour, and craftsmanship akin to the Flemish, but with distinct character due to the tastes of the wealthy burghers who dominated society in Holland. Their demands helped the rise of the Dutch portrait painters, represented by the brilliant though superficial Frans Hals; of the genre painters, such as Vermeer and De Hooch; of the still-life painters; and of the landscape painters such as Hobbema, Cuyp, and Ruisdael, who prepared the way for the English landscape school.

Supreme above all his contemporaries in his insight into character and his imaginative power was Rembrandt, who developed a powerful and individual use of chiaroscuro, based on the introduction of light into luminous darkness to emphasize and reveal the forms it shrouded. Contemporary Spanish painters found the realistic tendencies of the age and the use of strong light and shade well suited to their temperament. El Greco, a Cretan trained in Venice, stands by himself in his use of colour and bold distortion of form as a means of emotional expression; but he paves the way for the dramatic, sombre, and realistic art of Ribera and Zurburan.

In the developed art of Velasquez, however, realism is united to dignity and reticence, and light and shade are used to obtain a series of silhouettes from which a linear design is woven. This in some measure anticipates the work of Manet and his followers, and with other qualities makes Velasquez one of the fathers of modern painting.

Murillo's considerable talent was obscured by sentimentality, and an unhappy compromise between the use of light and shade and of positive colour. He is the last great personality in Spanish painting, save for the isolated figure of Goya, whose savagely satiric and technically accomplished art of the late eighteenth and early nineteenth century powerfully influenced French painting. But the real successor to the artistic supremacy of Italy was France.

In the sixteenth century a group of realistic portrait painters, typified by Jean Clouet and his son François, and a group of decorative painters, represent respectively the naturalistic instinct and the passion for close-knit logical design which in combination have produced the finest and most characteristic French art.

In the seventeenth century appear the powerful and dignified art of Nicolas Poussin, which is a living force in landscape and figure painting; the poetic landscapes of Claude Lorrain, full of golden light; the sincere and well-characterized portraits by Philippe de Champaigne; and the realistic peasant groups of the brothers Le Nain. There follows the group of portrait painters and decorators, headed by Charles Le Brun, whose chief employment centred round the personality and palaces of Louis XIV., and produced an art characteristic of the age in its pompous and somewhat empty splendour.

Similarly, eighteenth-century tastes and manners are reflected in the painters of *fêtes galantes*, among whom Watteau showed incomparable imaginative power and beauty of handling; in the decorative paintings of Boucher, and the exquisitely delicate work of his greater pupil Fragonard; in the sentimental genre work of Greuze and others; and in the sincere and accomplished still-life and genre of Chardin.

With the Revolution and the rise of the neo-classic movement, of which David is the central figure, this gay, sensuous, and often whimsical and fantastic art was succeeded by one to which sombre colour, sculpturesque form, and severe design gave its character.

Meanwhile in England, where great artistic activity in the Middle Ages had been followed by two centuries of domination by foreign artists, there came in the eighteenth century a revival of a native art in which Hogarth plays a great part. His fondness for anecdote, his realism pushed to the point of caricature, and his use of rich colour are characteristic of English painting.

Best known by his genre work, he is also an important member of the group of portrait painters headed by Reynolds, Romney, and Gainsborough, the rise of which was assisted so much by the sense of individual importance which marked life in eighteenth-century England.

At the same time the topographical painters prepared the way for the landscape school, wherein Gainsborough, Wilson, and John Crome are the chief personalities, followed by Constable and Turner. Constable's naturalism and handling of colour deeply influenced the French Romantics, while from Turner the Impressionists learnt their chief lessons.

Otherwise, the history of nineteenth-century painting centres round France, where a bewildering succession of personalities and movements appear, only to be compared to those seen in Italy from 1430 to 1530. The tradition of neo-classicism was vigorously maintained in the work of Ingres, an incomparable draughtsman; but its supremacy was challenged by the Romantics, headed by Delacroix, who stood for a passionate subjective art in which colour played a great part. A similar outlook appears in the landscapes of the Barbizon school, led by Corot and Rousseau; and their devotion to the French countryside has a counterpart in the poetic art of Millet, wherein the French peasant is the main theme.

A tendency towards mannerisms and academic coldness in the middle of the century was checked by the rise of the Realists, prominent among whom was Courbet, and of the two types of impressionism (q.v.) represented respectively by Manet's early work, and by Claude Monet. To-day, the doctrines and practice of the impressionists largely inspire painting in all Western countries; but recently a movement in revolt has developed in which Cézanne is the leading figure (*see* POST-IMPRESSIONISM).—BIBLIOGRAPHY: A. P. Laurie, *Materials of the Painter's Craft*; A. H. Church, *The Chemistry of Paints and Painting*; G. Moreau-Vautier, *The Technique of Painting*; C. J. Holmes, *The Science of Picture Making*; A. Michel, *Histoire de l'Art*; Woltman and Woermann, *History of Painting*; R. Muther, *History of Modern Painting*; J. A. Crowe and G. B. Cavalcaselle, *History of Painting in Italy*; D. S. MacColl, *Painting in the 19th Century*.

PAINTS AND PIGMENTS. Paints and pigments are closely related to one another, the latter being the dry coloured powders which form the bases of the paints.

Paints.—The various constituents of an oil paint are known as the *base*, the *vehicle*, the *solvent*, and the *driers*. As an example, the base may consist of a pigment such as white lead, red lead, oxide of iron, etc., which is mixed into a thin paste with linseed oil (the vehicle) and turpentine (the solvent or "thinner"). "Driers" such as litharge, sulphate of zinc, or borate of manganese may be added to hasten the drying and hardening of the paint.

The linseed oil is usually rendered siccative by heating it with driers before mixing it with the other ingredients of the paint, causing it to absorb oxygen from the air more readily and form a tough elastic coating round the particles of pigment. The turpentine, which soon evaporates, enables the paint to be spread in a thin even coat.

In place of linseed oil other drying oils such as hemp, poppy seed, and nut oils are sometimes employed in the cheaper kinds of paints; whilst petroleum is also used in place of turpentine.

For *enamel paints* the vehicle consists of a varnish composed of resin dissolved in turpentine and methylated spirit, the desired colour being obtained by the incorporation of suitable pigments. Of late years cellulose paints have come much into favour, especially for houses and furniture partly owing to the rapidity of their drying.

Artists' oil colours are very similar to ordinary paints, but more care is bestowed on their preparation, especially in the choice of pigments, which must be unaffected by atmospheric influences and light. The pigment is made into a paste with the oil or oil varnish mixture, and then put through a mill furnished with granite rollers, after which it is squeezed into tubes ready for use.

Water colours differ in principle from oil and enamel colours in that the vehicle consists of a solution of gum arabic, dextrine, or isinglass, etc. These paints are sold either in dry cakes, which are rubbed down with water for use, or as a paste which also needs thinning with water. The pigments employed in the preparation of water colours are as a rule similar to those used in oil paints.

Casein colours are made by incorporating a pigment with a mixture of casein and powdered quicklime, water being added until a thick paste is obtained which is then finally ground in a mill and packed in sealed cans. These colours are much used for distempering walls, and have the advantage of being washable. Various paints, such as those possessing damp-proof, fire-proof, anti-fouling, or luminous properties are used for special purposes.

Pigments. — Pigments are the coloured substances which are mixed with suitable vehicles to form paints. They differ from dyes in being insoluble. They should be unaffected by air, water, and sunlight, or by gases with which they come in contact. Pigments are chiefly of mineral origin and may consist of the oxide, carbonate, silicate, sulphate, chromate, etc., of various metals such as lead, zinc, mercury, cadmium, iron, chromium, and barium. Other pigments of animal or vegetable origin are also used, but to a less extent, as they are usually somewhat fugitive.

In the case of paints and artists' colours compounded with linseed oil, a certain amount of reaction takes place between the pigment and the vehicle. Linseed oil consists of the glyceryl esters of various fatty acids which react chemically with metallic compounds to form salts which may be regarded as metallic soaps. Oxides of iron and chromium form compounds of this nature which dry readily on exposure to air. The lead soaps dry more slowly with the formation of a somewhat elastic compound, whilst those formed from zinc are hard and brittle.

Chemical Composition of Pigments : Elementary Substances.—These consist chiefly of finely-powdered metals such as gold, aluminium, silver, and platinum, which are used when a metallic effect is required. Carbon is the chief constituent of black pigments such as ivory, lamp, and charcoal blacks, graphite (black lead), and Indian ink. The purest form of black pigment, known as carbon black, is permanent, and of great intensity and covering power. It is largely manufactured by the incomplete combustion of the gases naturally occurring in Alberta and elsewhere.

Oxides.—Zinc white, chromium green, red lead, cobalt black, manganese brown, and antimony white are all oxides of their respective metals. Iron oxide is the main constituent of the ochres, burnt sienna, Venetian red, and Indian red. Many pigments consist of mixtures of the oxides of various metals such as burnt umber (iron and manganese), cobalt blue (cobalt and aluminium), and cobalt green (cobalt and zinc). Prussian brown is an oxide of iron prepared by heating Prussian blue to a red heat ; it is of a nut-brown colour, and is perfectly permanent. Many of these pigments, especially the ochres (q.v.) and siennas are found in the natural state ; they are prepared for use by grinding and washing.

Red lead is formed when litharge or white lead is heated to a gentle red heat in the presence of air. It is much used as a pigment for decorative work, but is not suitable for use in artists' colours. Zinc white is prepared by heating metallic zinc to its boiling-point and mixing the vapour with a large supply of air, when oxidation takes place.

Carbonates.—White lead consists of a basic lead carbonate, and is manufactured by the action of carbonic acid gas (CO_2) on basic acetate of lead, which is formed by treating the metal with vinegar (acetic acid). As a source of CO_2, fermenting dung or waste furnace gases are used. White lead forms the basis of many white or light-coloured paints used for decorative purposes. It possesses good covering power, but darkens in the air (owing to the presence of sulphuretted hydrogen), and is poisonous. Calcium carbonate (chalk or whitening) is used as an adulterant in common pigments, but is of little use for paint-making.

Sulphides.—Vermilion is a sulphide of mercury (HgS) which is found native, but is also prepared from its elements by fusion and sublimation. Cadmium yellow consists of the sulphide, likewise antimony red. King's yellow and realgar or red orpiment are sulphides of arsenic, which are found native and also prepared artificially. They are both poisonous, but notwithstanding this the former is used in oil painting. Griffith's zinc white (lithopone) is an oxysulphide which has largely replaced white lead, on account of its greater permanence.

Sulphates.—Permanent white or *blanc fixe* consists of artificially prepared barium sulphate ($BaSO_4$); it is perfectly permanent, has good covering powers, and has largely replaced white lead. Freeman's white lead contains a large proportion of lead sulphate, and is less objectionable than ordinary white lead as a pigment.

Chromates.—Chrome yellow is lead chromate ($PbCrO_4$), obtained by the action of sodium chromate on a solution of a lead salt, preferably the acetate (sugar of lead). Chrome red is the basic chromate prepared in a similar manner from the basic acetate, or by treating chrome yellow with an alkaline solution. Chrome orange is a mixture of the above-mentioned pigments. Lemon chrome consists of barium chromate and is a very stable colour; zinc and strontium chromates are also used as yellow pigments.

Silicates.—Terre-verte, a natural green ochreous earth, consists of iron, magnesium, and potassium silicates, and is fairly permanent. Smalt (royal blue or Saxon blue) is a silicate of potash and cobalt, made by fusing their respective oxides with sand. Ultramarine blue is prepared by fusing together clay and sulphur with soda and finally grinding the product; it is fairly permanent except in the presence of acids.

Miscellaneous Compounds.—Brunswick green is an oxychloride of copper. Scheele's green is a copper arsenite, whilst Schweinfurt green is a basic form of the same compound. Both these pigments are exceedingly poisonous, and their use should be prohibited. Nürnberg violet consists of manganese metaphosphate. Prussian blue is composed of ferric ferrocyanide (*see* CYANIDES). Cobalt yellow or aureolin is potassium cobaltinitrite. Naples yellow consists of lead antimonate; it is not permanent.

Animal and Vegetable Pigments.—Sepia, a dark-brown colouring matter obtained from the ink-sac of the cuttle-fish, is a permanent pigment much used for water colours, but not suited for oil colours. Cochineal lakes are made in various shades of crimson, purple, and carmine, but the colours fade in sunlight and in contact with oxidizing bodies. Yellow lakes are made by precipitating an extract of Persian berries with alumina; the colours are fugitive. Indigo blue, gamboge, and the red madder lakes are more permanent.

Asphaltum, or mineral pitch, possesses a dark-brown colour, but is sensitive to light and should never be used for oil painting. The various lakes prepared from aniline dyes are not very permanent, but are, nevertheless, used for certain purposes. Bituminous paints with waterproof properties are used for steel, for steel ships, house-roofs, etc., and where damp-proofing is desired. *See* BITUMEN.

General Remarks on the Choice of Pigments.—In the compounding of a paint it is of great importance to choose pigments which do not react chemically with one another, or with the vehicle, in such a way as to produce alteration of the colour on exposure to air or light. All compounds of lead, copper, and silver readily combine with sulphuretted hydrogen, which is present in air, especially near towns, with the formation of a black sulphide. For this reason alone such pigments should be avoided in all artists' colours or other paints where permanence is required. Further, if such pigments are mixed with others containing sulphides, a similar reaction will take place, although this may be retarded to a certain extent by using a vehicle of a resinous or varnish-like nature.

Other pigments possessing oxidizing properties, such as chromates, tend to become green by the formation of chromium green. They also have an oxidizing action on sulphides and pigments of an animal or vegetable origin; but this is also less marked when a resinous vehicle is used. Other influences also tend to destroy the colour of a pigment, such as strong sunlight and air, especially in the presence of moisture.

In this respect pigments of an animal or vegetable nature are as a rule inferior to those of mineral origin. For artists' colours the pigments which should be avoided, above all others, are lead compounds, especially red and white lead; also chromates, asphaltum, and animal and vegetable pigments of a fugitive nature.

The *adulteration* of paints and pigments is often practised, but is not always easy to detect. Carbon black is sometimes found to be ivory black mixed with indigo. Antimony red is adulterated with red lead; white lead or zinc white are found mixed with china clay or whitening. These adulterations can only be detected by chemical tests after removal of the vehicle by means of a solvent, and recovery of the pigments in the dry powder form.

Fuller information on many of the pigments mentioned above is given in separate articles.

BIBLIOGRAPHY: J. N. Friend, *Introduction to the Chemistry of Paints*;

A. P. Laurie, *Facts about Processes, Pigments, and Vehicles* (for art students); G. Zerr and R. Rubencamp, *Treatise on Colour Manufacture.*

PAISIELLO (pà-i-si-el'lō), **Giovanni.** Italian composer, born at Taranto, 9th May, 1741, died at Naples 5th June, 1816. His first opera, *La Pupilla*, was performed at Bologna in 1763. From this period commenced a long career of success, which attended him at Modena, Parma, Venice, Rome, Milan, Naples, and Florence. In 1776 he was induced to enter the service of Catherine II. of Russia, as musical tutor to the grand duchess.

Here during eight years' residence he composed his best productions, *La Serva Padrona* and *Il Barbiere di Seviglia.* He then visited Vienna, where he composed *Il Rè Teodoro*, another of his best operas, and twelve symphonies for the Emperor Joseph II. He returned to Naples in 1785, and, with the exception of three years spent in Paris, he remained there the rest of his life.

PAISLEY (ancient **Vanduara**). A municipal burgh and manufacturing town of Scotland, in the county of Renfrew. It stands on the White Cart, near its confluence with the Clyde, and is served by the L.M.S. Railway. It consists of an old town on the west or left, and a new town on the east or right bank of the river, communicating by three handsome bridges.

The Abbey Church, belonging to a Cluniac monastery founded in 1163 by Walter, son of Alan, High Steward of Scotland, the first of the Royal House of Stewart, was dedicated to (among others) St. Mirren (Mirinu), the patron saint of Paisley, and to St. Milburgha of Much Wenlock (Shropshire), the home of the original monks. Since 1860 the main body of the church, consisting of a nave and two aisles, the latter separated from the nave by five massive clustered columns on each side, has been the parish church. In 1889 a monument was erected by Queen Victoria over the burial-place of Robert III.

In St. Mirren's Chapel or the Sounding Aisle, on the south side, stands a tomb supposed to have been built in honour of Bruce's daughter Marjory. An imposing modern Baptist church, the Coats Memorial, is one of the finest church edifices in Scotland, and was erected by the Coats family. Nearby is Crookston Castle, a twelfth-century structure, which was a possession of the Stewart family until 1567, and eventually passed to the family of Montrose. It now belongs to the Maxwells of Pollok.

Paisley has been long noted for its manufactures, especially of textile goods. The shawl manufacture, introduced about the beginning of the nineteenth century, and long a flourishing industry, is not now a staple, but the textile manufacture is still large, though the chief industry is that of cotton thread, for which Paisley is celebrated throughout the world. The factories of the firm of Coats are within the town.

Among the other manufactures are tapestry, embroidery, tartans, and carpets. There are also dye- and print-works, engineering-works, soap-works, manufactories of starch, cornflour, mustard, and chemicals; distilleries, breweries, and shipbuilding yards, chiefly for river steamers. The River Cart was widened and deepened in 1894, and a harbour was constructed. Wilson, the ornithologist, the poet Tannahill, and Professor Wilson (Christopher North) were natives of Paisley.

Paisley was the site of *Vanduara*, a Roman fort built on Oakshaw Hill about A.D. 84. As Passeleth the town is mentioned in 1157, and was granted to Walter, son of Alan (i.e. Fitzalan), who built the Abbey around which the town gradually extended. It became a barony in 1488, and as such returned a member to the Scots Parliament. Pop. (1931), 86,441.

PAL'ADIN. A term originally applied to the *Comes palatii*, Count of the Palace, or Count Palatine, the official who superintended the household of the Carlovingian sovereigns, and then to the companions in arms of Charlemagne, who belonged to his court. In the romances of chivalry the word was applied to the semi-fabulous companions of Charlemagne and to the Knights of the Round Table. The word was afterwards used by the romantic poets of Italy for a knight-errant generally.

PALÆARCTIC REGION. In zoology, one of six divisions of the world based upon their characteristic faunæ. It embraces Europe, Asia (except South Arabia and the area south of the Himálaya and their continuations), and Africa north of the Tropic of Cancer.

PALÆOLITHIC AGE. Lord Avebury (when Sir John Lubbock) divided the "Stone Age" of archæology into two parts, (1) the Palæolithic or "Old Stone" Age, and (2) the Neolithic or "New Stone" age. The former term was applied to the older roughly chipped flint imple-

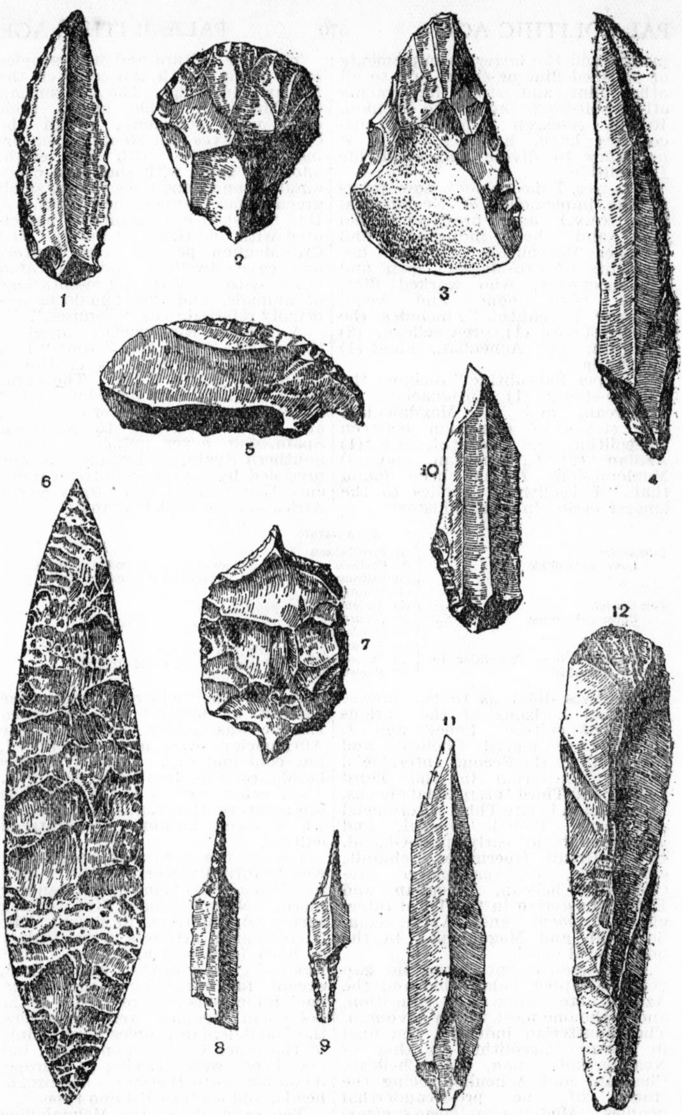

UPPER PALÆOLITHIC IMPLEMENTS

1, Aurignacian (Chatelperron point). 2, 3, Aurignacian (keeled scrapers). 4, Aurignacian point. 5, Magdalenian (" parrot-beak " graving-tool). 6, Solutrean (" laurel-leaf " point). 7, Solutrean (drill or borer). 8, 9, Solutrean (awl and " shouldered " point). 10, 11, 12, Magdalenian (industrial and art implements).

ments, and the latter to implements of polished flint or stone, and to all other flint and stone implements after polishing came into fashion. Recent research work and discoveries have, however, made it necessary to divide and subdivide Palæolithic.

"Lower Palæolithic" now refers to the implements of Neanderthal man (q.v.) and pre-Neanderthal man and their industries, and "Upper Palæolithic" to the implements of Cro-Magnon man and his successors, who worked flint, stone, horn, bone, and wood. "Lower Palæolithic" includes the culture-stages (1) pre-Chellean, (2) Chellean, (3) Acheulian, and (4) Mousterian.

"Upper Palæolithic" includes the culture-stages (1) Aurignacian, (2) Solutrean, and (3) Magdalenian. The stages of transition between Palæolithic and Neolithic are (1) Azilian, (2) Tardenoisian, and (3) Maglemosian. It has been found that "Palæolithic" applies to the longest period in human history.

The new culture and new peoples came from North Africa over the Italian land-bridge. The Aurignacian (Cro-Magnon) people buried their dead with ceremony, as in the Grimaldi caves near Mentone, smearing the bodies with red earth, adorning them with shell and other amulets, and sometimes placing small green stones between their teeth. A Red Sea shell has beenfound associated with one Grimaldi burial. The Cro-Magnon peoples were hunters and cave-dwellers, and decorated caves with realistic representations of animals, and with female figures usually referred to as "Venuses."

A typical Aurignacian burial is that of the "Red Man" (not "Red Lady") of Paviland cave, Gower Peninsula, South Wales. The Solutrean industry was introduced at a later period from Eastern Europe, and swept westward to Northern Spain, but never influenced Italy, Southern Spain, or Britain. It was preceded by a proto-Solutrean influence that entered Italy from North Africa and reached England.

PALÆOLITHIC

Interglacial. Lower Palæolithic	(1) Pre-Chellean (2) Chellean (3) Acheulian (4) Mousterian	Pre-Neanderthal and Neanderthal races (Warm and cold epochs and fauna.)
Post-Glacial. Upper Palæolithic	(1) Aurignacian (2) Solutrean (3) Magdalenian	Reindeer Age. (Cro-Magnon and other races.)
Transition from Palæolithic to Neolithic	(1) Azilian (2) Tardenoisian (3) Maglemosian	Early Red Deer Age. (Iberian, Northern, and other races.)

Scientists differ as to the precise geological horizons of the various stages of culture. Penck and J. Geikie have placed Chellean and Acheulian in the Second Interglacial epoch, Mousterian in the Third Glacial and Third Interglacial epochs, Aurignacian in late Third Interglacial and early Fourth Glacial, and Magdalenian in early post-Glacial. Boule, Breuil, Obermaier, Schmidt, etc., have, however, placed pre-Chellean, Chellean, Acheulian, and Early Mousterian in the Third Interglacial epoch, and Aurignacian, Solutrean and Magdalenian in the post-glacial epoch.

This arrangement leaves no gap between Upper Palæolithic and the Azilian, etc., stages of transition, and is the one most widely favoured. The Mousterian industry, the final in Lower Palæolithic, is that of Neanderthal man, pre-Chellean, Chellean, and Acheulian being the stages of the pre-Neanderthal peoples. Modern man (*homo sapiens*) represented by the Cro-Magnon races in Western Europe, inaugurated the Upper Palæolithic culture-stages, beginning with Aurignacian.

During the Solutrean epoch the climate of Central and Western Europe was milder than when the Aurignacian was first introduced, but cold and dry. Open-air camps beside rock-shelters were favoured. Then came, with a lowering of the temperature, the Magdalenian epoch, which owed nothing to Solutrean culture.

During the Solutrean epoch flint was beautifully worked, the laurel-leaf lance-heads being of outstanding merit. No subsequent flint-working surpassed Solutrean in finish. The Magdalenian artifacts were mainly of horn (reindeer) and bone. Flint was not greatly used or well worked, except for engraving; the Aurignacian methods were revived. If the Solutrean peoples were intruders, the Magdalenian peoples were mainly of the older Cro-Magnon stock, but new types were arriving in Europe, including proto-Iberians, some broad-heads, and a proto-Eskimo type.

The cave art of the Magdalenian stage reached a high standard of excellence, so high, indeed, that it is comparable with modern art. Animals were engraved and painted in caves, probably for magico-religious purposes. The art of sculpture in low relief was practised, while bone and ivory were finely carved, occasionally "in the round." Female human figures were favoured as in Aurignacian times. The Solutrean figures were mainly male.

Magdalenian culture reached Britain, and its influence has been traced by the Abbé Breuil as far north as Argyllshire. Aurignacian, Solutrean, and Magdalenian are included in the "Reindeer Age." As the climate grew milder the reindeer migrated northward, and the red deer arrived, inaugurating a "Red Deer Age" during the early part of which Magdalenian civilization was broken up, and the cave art ceased.

Following the red deer, the wild cow, boar, and other animals came the Azilian peoples. They imitated Magdalenian reindeer-horn harpoons in red deer horn, and introduced bows and arrows. On cliff-shelters in Eastern Spain they painted and engraved scenes of daily life and the chase. Like the Magdalenians, the females wore skirts and head-dresses, necklaces, armlets, and anklets. Sometimes women hunted like the men. Great animal drives were favoured. The art became conventionalized until animals and hunters were represented by symbols and alphabetical signs.

The Azilians met and mingled with a people who entered Europe through Italy, where the Aurignacian culture still prevailed. Tardenoisian implements included microliths (pygmy flints), which were apparently used for fishing. The Azilian-Tardenoisian culture entered Britain and reached Scotland, a typical station being the MacArthur cave, Oban.

Meanwhile an intruding people from Siberia passed down both sides of the Baltic. They were probably the ancestors of the fair Northern race. Their culture is called Maglemosian. It shows Magdalenian influence, but the harpoons were mainly one-sided, and chiefly of bone. Maglemosian artifacts have been found in North-East England, and Maglemosian influence has been traced in Scotland.

The Maglemosians may have crossed to Britain by the North Sea land-bridge, especially when the rivers were frozen. Before the Neolithic industry was introduced in Northern Europe, the English Channel and North Sea land-bridges were severed. *See* NEOLITHIC.

PALÆONTOL'OGY (Gr. *palaios*, ancient *onta*, beings). The scientific study and description of fossil organic remains, that is, of the relics of plants and animals that preceded those prevalent at the present day. In the articles on FOSSILS and GEOLOGY some idea has been given of the various modes of preservation of these remains, and of their philosophic interest as a basis for the reconstruction of the history of life upon the globe.

The palæontologist, though he relies very largely on the researches of the zoologist and the botanist, utilizes their results to form pictures of successive faunas and floras, whether he deals with limited areas like the British Isles, or surveys, from period to period, the progress of life in contemporaneous continents and seas. The imperfections of the material with which he deals necessitate some knowledge of the possibilities of mineral change. The more he appreciates the physical characters of strata in the field, the more sure will be his reading of earth-history. If he has been so fortunate as to preside in the open country at the extraction of the fossils with which he deals, he will experience all the joy of the archæologist who breaks for the first time into the frescoed chambers of a tomb.

The true zoologist or botanist has seen his subjects as they lived; the true palæontologist has at any rate seen them as they died. The excavation of a slab of Old Red Sandstone, with its fishes caught in some shallow of a shrinking estuary, or overwhelmed by a sudden run of sand, gives a vivid meaning to the details of fins and scales that are worked out later in the cabinets of museums.

In a block of clay, the age of which must be measured in millions of years, molluscan shells may lie heaped together as on the floor of a modern sea, and the mass brings the requisite touch of natural history into the description of characters by which species are defined.

Palæontology is essentially a progressive science. Fossils must often be named in the first instance from very imperfect material, and subsequent discoveries may furnish warning corrections or welcome confirmations of conjecture. The elongation of a finger in the pterosaurs showed that these reptiles were endowed with powers of flight; but now the impression of the wings of Rhamphorhynchus are known from the fine-grained limestone of Eichstätt, in Bavaria. The downward bend of the termination of the vertebral column in the well-known marine reptile Ichthyosaurus was long ascribed to fracture; but slabs from Württemberg have revealed to us that the column was continued as the support of the lower half of a bilobed tail.

In some cases new discoveries have led to the transfer of a genus from one order, or even from one class, to another. In fossil botany, particularly, the assignment of a specimen in the first instance is often fraught with doubt, since much depends on the mode of reproduction of the plant, or on the structure of a stem that has been flattened down to a mere carbonaceous film.

Whole groups of soft-bodied animals may have left mere tracks and burrows in the rocks, and it is difficult to reconstruct from footprints the forms of massive vertebrates. On the other hand, surprising specimens come to light which help to fill in the growing record. Moulds of jelly-fish occur at Eichstätt, and even in the earliest Cambrian strata of North America.

The famous fossil bird Archæopteryx was first known by the impress of a feather ; then by a headless skeleton showing both wings and tail. But these remains are now surpassed by a second skeleton, which reveals the skull with its toothed jaws. These specimens lead the palæontologist to comparisons with reptiles of the same geological age, and he is rewarded by the unique skeleton of a small and doubtless arboreal dinosaur, Compsognathus, the bones of which contain air-cavities like those of birds.

The amplification of knowledge in regard to forms already recognized may be further illustrated from the trilobites. Though these creatures were known to British palæontology in 1698, they gave no evidence of limbs.

Hermann Burmeister, in his detailed studies of 1846, concluded that these flexible parts were so perishable as to have left no traces in the rocks. Recent researches, however, by C. D. Walcott, C. E. Beecher, and others have revealed the limbs in a remarkable series of American specimens. These observations have been greatly developed by P. E. Raymond in 1921, and indicate trilobites as the primitive stock from which all other crustacean lines diverge.

The restoration of mammalian skeletons from a mass of mixed material, such as that in the Lower Pliocene river-bed of Pikermi, requires the utmost knowledge of the osteology of modern forms. Such knowledge made the names of Georges Cuvier and Richard Owen famous ; yet even in such cases the fortunate isolation of a complete skeleton may do much to aid us in appreciating the animals as they lived.

The dry lands of the central states of North America have furnished a wealth of material, both reptilian and mammalian, and it is pleasant to remember that Owen lived to realize the fascination of the dinosaurs and ungulates disentombed by C. D. Cope and O. C. Marsh. Such specimens as the skeleton of Stenomylus, a gazelle-shaped ancestor of the camels, from the Lower Miocene of Nebraska, in which very little is due to restoration, mark the great enrichment of palæontological material since Cuvier published his *Recherches sur les ossemens fossiles de quadrupèdes* in 1812.

Gideon Mantell discovered the remains of Iguanodon near Maidstone in 1825, and established the genus as reptilian ; but more than fifty years elapsed before the full structure of the animal was elucidated by the unearthing of complete skeletons at Bernissart, near Mons, in Belgium.

The study of minute differences between allied organic forms has naturally led palæontologists, in common with botanists and zoologists, to multiply both genera and species, and to subdivide many genera that seemed at one time well defined. This is notably the case with the well-known group of the Ammonites. The study of these cephalopods was immensely extended by the discovery of a host of Triassic forms in the Eastern Alps, and Ammonites as a genus have long ceased to appear in classifications.

We may become impatient of the laborious revisions that prevent our museum-labels from being ever precisely up-to-date ; but the close scrutiny of details has a far-reaching result in indicating lines of descent and variation. The accumulated lists of names that meant so little to the early workers, who could only wonder at the infinite variety of creation, now represent to the palæontologist the basis of a wide philosophy.

Problems of climate as well as of life-habit are raised by the tracing of closely similar or identical species on a given geological horizon over wide spaces of the globe. Equally interesting is the study of the parallel succession of genera, and even of species, in areas now separated by continental blocks or oceanic depths. Some species, in unfailing sequence, like the graptolites studied by C. Lapworth, mark out zones for the stratigrapher with a detailed precision that would have delighted William Smith.

Though the pioneers in geology were tempted to hang back, and to exclude human origins from their domain, the " organized fossils " of man himself have now become a matter of palæontology. The proofs of the existence of past races, such as that named from the Neanderthal, which have been gathered from caves and prehistoric tombs, have been supplemented by casually deposited bones, such as the skull of *Eoanthropus Dawsoni* found in Sussex in 1911, and the massive jaw-bone, with its simian suggestions, dug out from under 75 feet of glacial strata at Mauer, near Heidelberg, in 1907.

Already on the European continent there are schools of "Human Palæontology," and the popular notion that the study of fossils is utterly dry and uninspiring will probably receive its death-blow from the anthropological aspects of the science.

Illustrations of the matters touched on above, and of many in the previous article on FOSSILS, will be found in the plates accompanying the present article.

BIBLIOGRAPHY: K. von Zittel, *History of Geology and Palæontology* (English translation); *Handbuch der Palæontologie*, and a smaller work, *Palæozoologie* (English version of the last by Eastman and others); A. M. Davies, *Introduction to Palæontology*; F. A. Bather, *Guide to the Fossil Invertebrate Animals in the British Museum*; A. S. Woodward, *Outlines of Vertebrate Palæontology*; also British Museum guides to fossil vertebrates; A. C. Seward, *Fossil Plants*.

PALÆOTHE'RIUM. An extinct genus of Ungulate or hoofed quadrupeds in the line of the horse, but with three toes, which all reach the ground. These animals resembled tapirs, and varied in size from a sheep to a horse. They had, in all probability, a short mobile snout or proboscis. This genus forms the type of the family Palæotheriidæ, which occur as fossils in Eocene and Miocene strata.

PALÆOZOIC. The name of the geological era that includes the periods from the beginning of the Cambrian to the end of the Permian. In this "old-life" era, all the classes and an immense number of the orders of invertebrate life are represented, and many now require to be traced to ancestors in Proterozoic times. At the close of the era, however, the vertebrates have not advanced beyond primitive types of reptiles. *See* GEOLOGY.

PALAIS-ROYAL (pȧ-lā-rwȧ-yȧl). A popular resort of the Parisians. The original palace, designed by Jacques Lemercier, was built (1629-36), by Richelieu, and by him presented to Louis XIII. It originally bore the name of Palais Cardinal, but after the death of Louis XIII. (1643) the queen regent and the royal family established themselves in the palace, which from that time bore the name of Palais-Royal.

It was confiscated by the Republicans in 1793, and the Tribunal sat in the palace during the Reign of Terror. At the Restoration it was repurchased by the duc d'Orléans, but in the Revolution of 1848 it was again appropriated to the State. In 1871 it was set on fire by the Communists, but has since been restored. The Théâtre Français, the Théâtre du Palais-Royal, and several shops form parts of the buildings of the Palais-Royal.

PALANPUR. A native state and town of India, in Gujerat, Bombay province; area, 1750 sq. miles: pop. (state), 236,694; (town), *c.* 17,250.

PALAP'TERYX (the "ancient apteryx"). A genus of large struthious birds, whose remains are found in New Zealand.

PAL'ATE. The name applied to the roof of the mouth. It consists of two portions, the *hard* palate in front, the *soft* palate behind. The former is bounded above by the palatal bones, in front and at the sides by the alveolar arches and gums, being lined by mucous membrane; behind it is continuous with the soft palate. It supports the tongue in eating, speaking, and swallowing.

The *soft palate* is a movable fold suspended from the posterior border of the hard palate. It consists of mucous membranes, nerves, and muscles, and forms a sort of partition between the mouth and the hinder nostrils. Its upper border is attached to the posterior margin of the hard palate; its lower border is free. The *uvula* hangs from the middle of its lower border, and on each side are two curved folds of mucous membrane called the *arches* or *pillars* of the *soft* palate. Between these on either side of the pharynx are the two glandular bodies known as *tonsils*.

The upper surface of the soft palate is convex, the lower surface is concave with a median ridge, the latter pointing to the early or embryo stage of its formation, when it consists of two distinct parts. Non-union of these halves and of those of the hard palate constitutes the deformity known as *cleft palate*, often associated with hare-lip. Glands are abundant in the soft palate, secreting the mucus which serves to lubricate the throat during the passage of food.

The soft palate comes into action in swallowing, and also in speaking, being of great importance in the utterance of certain sounds. The special use of the uvula is not well known. It is often relaxed or enlarged, causing a troublesome cough.

PALAT'INATE (Ger. *Pfalz*). A district of Germany which, before the Revolution of 1918, was under the rule of counts-palatine (Pfalzgrafen), and consists of two separate portions distinguished as the Upper and Lower Palatinate. *See* BAVARIA.

PALAT'KA. A city and port of entry of Florida, United States, the county seat of Putnam county, on the St. John's River, and served by the Atlantic Coast line, Florida East Coast & Georgia Southern, and Florida Railways. It is a terminal station of the latter. At the head of ocean navigation on the St. John's River, it has a coastal shipping trade with New York and other ports. There is a large trade in agricultural produce. Pop. about 5000.

PALAU. *See* PELEW.

PALAZZO'LO ACREIDE. A town of Sicily, 28 miles west of Syracuse. Here are the remains of the ancient city of Acrae, founded by Syracuse 663 B.C. Pop. 15,140.

PALE, The, or **THE ENGLISH PALE.** A name formerly given to that part of Ireland, in Dublin, Kildare, Meath, and Louth, which was completely under English rule, in distinction to the parts where the old Irish laws and customs prevailed.

PALEÆ (pā'lē-ē). In botany, the bracts or pales enclosing the individual flowers of grass.

PALEMBANG'. A town of Sumatra, capital of the Residency of same name, on the Moosi, here called the Palembang. There is a population of 109,069, partly inhabiting houses raised on piles, and partly living on rafts moored in the river. Its port is one of the best in the Malay Archipelago. The Residency has an area of 33,173 sq. miles ; pop. 872,552.

PALENCIA. A province of Spain. It is fertile and watered by the Carrion and Pisuerga. The manufactures include paper, porcelain, and leather. Area, 3256 sq. miles ; pop. (1931) 209,128.

PALEN'CIA. A town of Northern Spain, capital of the province of same name, situated on the Carrion, an affluent of the Pisuerga. It is a bishop's see, and has a fine Gothic cathedral dating from the fourteenth century. The manufactures include shawls, blankets, agricultural machinery, etc. Palencia is the ancient Pallantia, capital of the Vaccaei. It became the seat of the Castilian kings in the twelfth century. The University of Palencia, founded in 1208, was transferred to Salamanca in 1239. Pop. 23,936.

PALER'MO (ancient **Panormus**). A seaport, capital of Sicily, beautifully situated on the north coast. It is built in the form of an amphitheatre facing the sea, and is divided into four quarters by two main streets. It has a fine sea-front, public gardens and fountains, electric tramways, etc.

Its public edifices include a cathedral of the tenth century which contains monuments of the Emperor Frederick II. and King Roger the Norman. Other notable buildings are several churches ; a royal palace of Saracenic origin, amid beautiful gardens, containing the chapel of King Roger, called Cappella Palatina (Palatine Chapel), built in a mixed Saracenic and Norman style, and dating prior to 1132, having the walls entirely covered with rich Byzantine mosaics on a golden ground.

The National Museum and picture gallery, containing some of the oldest monuments of Greek plastic art to which a definite date can be assigned (sixth century B.C.) ; the archiepiscopal palace, the custom house, the university, three theatres, and numerous other structures of architectural interest. The port is enclosed by a mole 1300 feet in length.

Palermo is the residence of the military commandant of the island, and has an arsenal and shipbuilding yards. The manufactures consist chiefly of silks, cottons, oil-cloth, leather, glass, and gloves. The principal exports are sumach, wine and spirits, fruits, sulphur, skins and hides, olive-oil, essences, cream of tartar, asphalt, etc.; imports, colonial produce, woollen, cotton, and silk tissues, hardware, earthenware, etc. The fisheries are very productive, and give employment to nearly 40,000 hands.

Founded by the Phœnicians, Palermo afterwards became the capital of the Carthaginian possessions in Sicily. It was called by the Romans Panormus, and taken by them in 254 B.C. The Saracens held it for a time, and in 1072 it fell to the Normans. The German emperors and the French subsequently held it, and since the Sicilian Vespers (1282) it has shared the fortunes of the Sicilian Kingdom. The court of Naples resided here from 1806 to 1815. Garibaldi captured the town in 1860. Pop. (1931), 389,699.

PALERMO. A mountainous maritime province of Northern Sicily, traversed by railways along the coastal fringe. Citrus-growing is extensive ; sulphur and wines are produced. Area, 1927 sq. miles ; pop. (1931), 843,742.

PAL'ESTINE. A maritime country of the Mediterranean administered by Great Britain, under mandate from the League of Nations, as a Jewish national home. It is a small, oblong piece of territory, bounded by the Mediterranean on the west, the Syrian Desert on the east, by a line running from west of Rafa to east of Taba, at the head of the Gulf of Akaba (i.e. along the Hejaz-Egyptian frontiers), and on the south and north by a line not yet entirely delimited, but settled by the Franco-British Convention of 23rd December 1920.

Physiography. — Concentrated in the narrow strip between sea and desert there are three distinct natural regions. Along the low, unbroken coast is the maritime plain of Philistia and Sharon. Separating the maritime plain and the Rift Valley are the highlands of Judea and Samaria. In the east is the Rift Valley, drained by the Jordan (q.v.), linking the series of lakes. Beyond the Rift Valley is an eastern range, which fronts the wide wastes of the deserts beyond.

Jordan Valley.—The Jordan Valley forms one of the most extraordinary features in the world. It marks the end of a great line of faulting that can be traced from the flanks of the Lebanon Mountains, south through the Gulf of Akaba to the great lakes of Africa. It forms a great depression, which falls from sea-level to 1273 feet below sea-level in the Dead Sea, and the bottom of the Dead Sea is probably another 1300 feet deeper.

Three principal streams, viz. the Nahr-el-Leddan, the Nahr Baniyas, and the Nahr Hasbani, unite in the Plain of Hule (150 feet altitude) to form the headwaters of the Jordan, which winds through the morass of the Hule and falls by a series of cataracts and waterfalls (at the rate of 65 feet to the mile) to the Lake of Galilee (Tiberias), which lies in a great rock basin 682 feet below sea-level. Leaving the Lake of Galilee, the waters become turbid and eventually fall into the Dead Sea.

The salinity of the Dead Sea is its remarkable feature. In consequence of extraordinary evaporation the water is impregnated with 26 per cent. of mineral salts, and is extremely buoyant.

Highlands. — The highlands, of porous limestone, vary in height between 1500 and 2000 feet, and fall precipitately to the Jordan Valley. The Pass of Shechem marks a break where the mountains are continued seaward by the ridge of Carmel (1810 feet altitude), north of which lies the Plain of Esdraelon, which forms the natural link between the interior valley and the sea, and separates the mountains of the north from the highlands of the south. The highest points are Tell 'Asur (3318 feet altitude), near Beth-el, and Ebal (3077 feet altitude).

Climate.—The wide differences in altitude which are experienced in such a confined area lead to a corresponding range of climatic conditions, but broadly there are only two seasons—a dry, hot summer, and a rainy but comparatively warm winter. Three climatic zones may be distinguished: the humid, subtropical coastal belt; the mountains with a temperate and drier climate; and the unhealthy tropical depression of the Ghor. There are very great daily variations in temperature. Frost seldom occurs on the coast, and never in the Jordan Valley, but in the mountains snow falls and frost is not infrequent from December to February.

About the end of November the rainy season begins, but about five-ninths of the total fall occurs in January and February, and one-third from mid-March to the end of April. The sirocco sets in in May and again in October, the thermometer rising to 100° F. or more. A light sea-wind arises almost every morning and blows till sundown, when the cooler land-breeze begins.

Social Conditions: Races.—The predominant race is Mussulman-Arabs, but the Jews are rapidly increasing, mainly by immigration from Russia and Rumania. There are also some Christians, Druses, and Samaritans.

Languages.—Official languages are English, Hebrew, and Arabic.

Education.—There were, in 1931, 308 State-maintained schools, and several in part State-owned. Agricultural schools (Jewish) are located at Mikweh-Israel and Petach-Tikvah; a high school (Jewish) at Jaffa, and Jewish agricultural experiment stations at Atlit and Zichron-Jacob. At Jerusalem two Government training colleges for men and women, a school of pharmacy, a law school, and a technical college are maintained. The Jewish and Christian communities provide almost entirely for the education of their own children, and the Zionist Organization has a very complete Education Department. The Hebrew University at Jerusalem, inaugurated in 1925, has 171 students. The new museum for antiquities, presented by John D. Rockefeller, jun., is almost completed.

Currency, Weights and Measures.—The currency unit (introduced in 1927) is the Palestine pound or dinar, which is based on the pound sterling. The Palestine pound is divided into one thousand mils. There are special local systems of length and area, weights, and capacity, but the metric system is followed by the Government.

Communications: Railways.—The following principal railways are in operation:

1. Kantara—Al-Arish—Rafa—Ludd—Tulkeram—Haifa, 257 miles.
2. Jaffa—Lydda—Jerusalem, 54 miles.
3. Raphaih—Beersheba (Bir-es-Seba), 37 miles.
4. Haifa—Al-Afuleh—Al-Hamme, 60 miles.
5. Haifa—Acre, 11 miles.
6. Afule—Jenin—Nablus (Shechem)—Tulkeram, 61 miles.

There are 529 kilometres of track. During 1922 the Kantara-Raphaih section was operated by the Palestine Railways under War Office authority, and was known as the "Sinai Military Railway." In 1928 this section (125 m.) was being worked by the Palestine Railways for the Air Ministry. On 26th Sept., 1892, the Japha (Jaffa)-Jerusalem Railway was opened. The Haifa-Damascus route was opened in 1905. It crosses the Great Plain of Esdraelon, and traverses the Ghor to Semarh (Sea of Galilee), where it swings round and follows the valley of the Yarmur to join the Syrian Railway at Edrei (Ed Dra'a), with extensions to Mecca and Medina.

Roads, etc.—There are 445 miles of metalled roads throughout Palestine, in addition to many hundreds of miles of ordinary tracks. Imperial Airways Ltd. have an aerodrome at Lamakh. There is also a service between Egypt and Ramleh.

Shipping.— Jaffa and Haifa are the principal ports, but Acre and Gaza are also important. By the autumn of 1933 the modern harbour at Haifa will be open to shipping. About thirty shipping lines maintain an international and inter-Palestinian coastal service. The British *Prince* line runs a weekly steamer; others are the Khedivial Mail, Lloyd Triestino, Affréteurs Réunis (weekly), Messageries Maritimes, Dutch Oriental, and Maritimi Italiani (bimonthly).

Production: Agriculture.—The full development of Palestine is largely potential. It is essentially an agricultural country. Ezekiel the prophet referred to the export of wheat from Tyre, and this wheat came from the land of Judah, but from the name "wheat of Minnith," by which nomenclature it was distinguished, it must originally have been raised to the east of Jordan, where Minnith is located. This simply means that Minnith wheat was imported wheat, and it probably came from the Haurán (the ancient land of Bashan, now known as the Nukrah).

In the time of Ezekiel the east Jordan lands were the granary of Palestine, but Palestine under British mandate lies only west of Jordan, and the wheat-yield of these lands, although not comparable economically with that of Transjordania, is nevertheless astounding when consideration is given to the poorness of the soil and the conditions under which crops are raised.

The principal farm crops are wheat, barley, millet, tobacco, olives, melons, and lentils. Sheep, goats, and camels are raised. Before the European War cotton was gradually being introduced into the Jewish agricultural colonies. Where the translators of the Authorized Version of the Bible have set down "linen" or "flax," "cotton" might well be read, and is more probably correct. The "tree-linen" with which Rahab covered the two spies is undoubtedly cotton. Yakut, the Arab geographer, mentions the plant (A.D. 1225), and Abu'l-Fida says (A.D. 1321) that cotton was exported from Palestine to Ceuta (Morocco).

Forestry.—Reafforestation is being undertaken by the Government, about three million trees being planted in 1929.

Minerals.—Palestine is rich in limestone; sandstone is found in the coastal regions; rock-salt is abundant in the Ghor; and gypsum is found in parts. Sulphur is worked in the Dead Sea littoral, for the exploitation of which a concession was made in 1929. Near Tiberias and at El Harume there are mineral springs.

Industries.—Soap for export is the chief manufacture of Jerusalem, and is also made in Nablus and Haifa. Olive-oil is manufactured at Nablus and elsewhere, and wine-making is virtually a monopoly of the Jewish colonies.[1]

Commerce.—Exports include, oil soap, peas, melons, wine, and oranges (from the Jaffa district). The latter are exceptionally thick-skinned, and are more suitable for transport than any other competitive oranges on the market. The best are sent to Liverpool, which receives some two-thirds of the crop. Egypt and Turkey take the remainder. Each orange crop is worth over £2,000,000. Imports are confined mainly to rice, sugar, petroleum, and cottons.

Towns.—The growing towns of the interior are situated at advantageous points on the railways and trade routes, e.g. Nablus, Jerusalem, Beth-el, and Hebron—old strongholds in the Judæan highlands. Jerusalem is of vast strategic importance, and marks the point where the highway from the Levant makes for the Rift Valley.[2]

[1] It could not be otherwise, when it is remembered that wine is prohibited by the *Koran*, and the Muslim element can neither make it nor trade in it if they follow the precepts of the Prophet with any faith.

[2] Strategically, Palestine is the most vitally important section of the "highway out of Egypt to Assyria," and its possession is of paramount value to the control of the Suez route to the East. Hence the Palestinian operations during the European War (q.v.).

PALESTINE

The Church of the Holy Sepulchre, Jerusalem.

Haifa is the natural outlet for the rich wheat-lands of the Haurán, but will depend, for its future importance, upon a vast improvement in railway and harbour works. Other towns are Jaffa, Tel-Aviv, and Gaza.

Government.—The ostensible aim of the British Government, in accordance with the Balfour Declaration (*see* " History "—this article), is to make Palestine the Jewish national home, without prejudicing the non-Jewish communities within the mandatory area, who will be entitled to claim equal religious and political rights. In Palestine the task of forming this Jewish Home is in the hands of the Palestine Zionist Executive, a branch of the World Zionist Organization, formed by Theodore Herzl in 1897, which is officially recognized by the British Empire and by the Palestinian administration. A National Committee, elected by an elected assembly convened by the Jews of Palestine, acts as an intermediary between the Jewish peoples and the administration.

The Moslems have a Supreme Council of their own. A new Constitution was promulgated in 1922. This provides for a High Commissioner, a Legislative Council (consisting of 10 official and 12 elected unofficial members), and an Executive Council. As large numbers of the Arab inhabitants refused to vote, no legislative council was elected, but its place was taken by an Advisory Council appointed by the High Commissioner in terms of the Palestine (Amendment) Order in Council of 1923. The central problem of policy is to reconcile the obligation to establish Palestine as a National Home for the Jews, with the rights of non-Jewish communities already settled there. (*See* HISTORY.)

Area and Population.—The mandatory region has an area of 9000 sq. miles approximately, and lies entirely west of Jordan. Pop. (census 1922), 757,182 (590,890 of Mahommedan belief, 83,794 Jews, 73,024 Christians, 7028 Druses, and 163 Samaritans). The county is divided into two districts (Jaffa and Haifa) and the Jerusalem division. The official languages are English, Arabic, and Hebrew.

See ZIONISM ; JERUSALEM ; JORDAN ; DEAD SEA ; SYRIA ; LEBANON, and other articles.

History.—The name Palestine, from the Hebrew *Pelescheth*, means the land of the Philistines. It is properly only applicable to the south-west part of the country. The ancient name of the country was Canaan, and when thus named, in the time of the patriarchs, it was parcelled out among a number of independent tribes, all probably Semitic. In the time of Moses the district east of the Jordan was taken and divided among the tribes of Reuben and Gad, and the half-tribe of Manasseh ; and latterly the whole territory was apportioned among the twelve Jewish tribes (*see* JEWS).

In the time of Christ Palestine was held by the Romans, and was divided into the four provinces of Galilee, Samaria, Judea, and Perea. In A.D. 636 the battle of Ajnadain was followed by the capitulation of Jerusalem and the surrender of Palestine to Islam. Cæsarea was the last to hold out, and was taken by storm in 638. The severities exercised towards Christians gave rise to the Crusades, and the eastern shores of the Mediterranean passed from the domination of the Mahommedans after the taking of Jerusalem by the Crusaders in 1099.

At this time a Christian kingdom was established, but when Saladin won the battle of Hittin (1187), the collapse of the Christian power was so complete that within three years only Antioch, Tripolis, and Tyre remained in Christian hands. Despite their almost superhuman efforts to recover the Holy Land, the treaty of 1192 left the Crusaders little territory beyond the seaboard from Acre to Jaffa.

Saladin died in 1195, and his empire, which then extended from the Euphrates to the Nile, was partitioned among his family, although the actual rulers of Egypt would appear always to have had first claim on Syria in general. Under the Mamelukes, who supplanted the dynasty of Saladin, Egypt and all Syria formed for 267 years (1250-1517) one united kingdom, and was unsuccessfully attacked during that period by the Crusaders, by the Mongols under Hualagu, the grandson of Genghis Khan (1260), and by Timour the Lame (Tamerlane), who took Syria in 1402. Palestine and Egypt both fell to the Osmanli Turks in 1517, in whose hands they remained for 400 years.

Palestine was conquered by British Empire forces in Allenby's campaign of 1917-18, Jerusalem surrendering to General Allenby on 9th Dec., 1917. Until 1st July, 1920, Palestine was under a military administration, and was handed over on that date to a civil administrator (Sir Herbert Samuel). The Treaties of Sèvres (1920) and Lausanne (1923) provided for the abandonment by the Ottoman Empire of all sovereign rights over the Holy Land. This caused much political controversy between officials of the British Empire at home and abroad, and was incidentally responsible for the non-co-operation and *swaraj* movements in India during 1921-22.[1]

Palestine was conquered partly by the assistance of Mahommedan troops including Indian soldiers of the Muslim faith. Before entertaining war with Turkey, and before agreeing to serve in arms, not only against co-religionists but against the "Caliph of Islam," i.e. the Sultan of Turkey, who is always mentioned in Friday prayers and in the Friday Sermon, these Muslim soldiers had to be assured that there was no question of a religious issue in the contemplated war, and they demanded British guarantees for the integrity of the Sultanate and for the preservation of the holy places of Islam to the recognized Caliph.

These guarantees were given in good faith by Mr. Lloyd George, who was subsequently a party to the partition of Turkey which has raised a storm of dissent throughout the Mahommedan world. To the Muslim, Palestine is sacred ground, second only in importance to Mecca and Medina, or, in the case of Persian Shiites, to that of Kerbala. According to Mahommedan tradition, Mahomet made his ascent into Paradise from the Aksa Mosque at Jerusalem, to which he had been transported from Mecca in a single night.

Despite Muslim protest, a draft mandate was submitted to the League of Nations in Dec., 1920, and was entrusted provisionally to the British Empire, as agreed upon by the Supreme Allied Council at San Remo (25th April, 1920). The Balfour Declaration of 2nd Nov., 1917,[2] had as its object the provision of a Jewish national home in Palestine, and this was embodied in the Treaty of Sèvres.

A Mandate incorporating it was entrusted to Great Britain by the Allied Conference at San Remo in 1920, approved by the League of Nations in 1922, and recognized by the United States in the Palestine Convention of 1924. The Mandate clearly recognized that the establishment of Jewish National Homes in Palestine was not to prejudice the civil and religious rights of existing non-Jewish communities in Palestine. Trouble arose between the Jewish immigrants and the Arab population, culminating in 1929 in disturbances amounting almost to massacre. A Commission of Inquiry was appointed which reported to the Mandatory Powers, the report also being considered by the Mandates Commission of the League of Nations.

Racial animosities were intensified by Jewish dissatisfaction with the slow progress made in developing the policy of the Jewish National Home, and, on the other hand, by Arab opposition to Jewish land settlement. In 1930 considerable controversy was aroused by the publication of a White Paper by the Labour Government, in which the Dominions Secretary (Lord Passfield) (q.v.) seemed to present a modified view of the Jewish National Home policy. Later the Government (in Feb., 1931) restated its policy with regard to Palestine in a letter from the Prime Minister to Dr. Chaim Weizmann, denying that the terms of the White Paper meant a prohibition upon the acquisition of additional land by Jews, but expressing also the Government's intention to facilitate the settlement of "landless Arabs" on the land.

The Future of Palestine.—Much has been said about the development of Palestine, its future prospects, and the probable effects of concentrating a small number of Jews in a territory that is overwhelmingly Muslim. In its whole history Palestine has never formed a politically independent state, excepting in name. Three distinct faiths, Christian, Jew, and Mahommedan, have direct claims upon the country. Of these, the Christian has treated the country with least respect; he has sought to wax rich by exploiting the pious pilgrims, and he ranks third in respect of religious toleration.

To the Jew Palestine is less sacred than it is to the Christian, whose Founder and Saviour lived, suffered, and was martyred within its confines, but the Jew's claim is the oldest historically, and he at least believes that

[1] The connection between these two happenings may not be intelligible from a superficial examination of them. The Pan-Islamic movement in days before the European War was actively propagated by Abdul Hamid II. and by the Young Turk Committee of Union and Progress, and found some considerable support among the Mahommedans of Northern India. Although politically disunited, the common possession of one Sacred Book, and of a more or less common political ambition, and the recollection of the glorious early history of all-conquering Islam, unites them more or less in thought, and Muslim states are always ready, therefore, to sympathize both actively and passively in the misfortunes of their brethren and to rejoice whole-heartedly in their successes. The growing fear of European domination has tended, as it always will, towards a grudging moral support of the only powerful Mahommedan nation that remains in existence. And this despite the fact that statistics prove the more rapid spread of Muslim faith and thought in countries under European protection than in independent Mussulman states. *See* PAN-ISLAMISM.

[2] The Declaration reads: "His Britannic Majesty's Government view with favour the establishment in Palestine of a national home for the Jewish people, and will use their best endeavour to facilitate the achievement of that object, it being clearly understood that nothing shall be done which may prejudice the civil and religious rights and political status enjoyed by Jews in any other country."

his progenitors, Abraham, Isaac, and Jacob, lie buried under the floor of the mosque in Hebron. The cradle of the Jewish race was either Mesopotamia or Egypt, and not Palestine, in which the founder of the Jewish faith never even set foot.

Apart from the Muslim belief in the translation of Mahomet to Paradise from Jerusalem, the Arab as well as the Jew claims descent from Abraham, and has a profound belief in all the Jewish prophets. Again, the mosque of Omar, which stands on the site of the Hebrew temple, is especially sacred to all three contending faiths.

The Jew accepts Moses but rejects Christ and Mahomet; the Christian accepts both Moses and Christ but not Mahomet; and the Mahommedan accepts all the three, Mahomet, Christ, and Moses, as prophets, and in virtue of such recognition he would appear to have a paramount right to the custody of the holy place of civilization.

Despite the prolonged period of Turkification endured by Palestine, which was especially intensified by the doctrine of Pan-Islamism (q.v.) under the reign of Abdul Hamid II. and under the Young Turk Committee of Union and Progress, the three powerful religions are still in existence side by side, and the future of Palestine will only be definitely settled by an adjustment of their differences. *See* ZIONISM; TURKEY.

BIBLIOGRAPHY: A. R. Hope Moncrieff, *New World of To-day* (with economic data); *Foreign Office Handbook* (with bibliography); Baedeker's *Palestine and Syria* (1911 edition, with chief routes through Palestine and Syria); J. Ball, *Geography and Geology of West Central Sinai*; E. Grant, *The People of Palestine*; O. H. Lock, *The Conquerors of Palestine*; N. Wiltushewitz, *The Industrial Development of Palestine.*

PALESTINE EXPLORATION FUND. A British archæological research organization, with headquarters in London, founded in 1864 for the promotion of excavation work in Palestine and Syria. Many expeditions have been organized, including 1865-66, preliminary survey led by Captain Wilson; 1867-70, survey led by Lieutenant Warren; 1872-77, survey of Western Palestine and Cyprus; 1881, survey of Eastern Palestine; and 1890-1903, excavations at the buried cities of Tel-al-Hesi, associated with the name of Flinders Petrie. During 1920 operations were resumed.

PALESTRI'NA, Giovanni Pierluigi (or **PIETRO ALOISIO**) **da.** Italian musical composer, born at Palestrina, from which he took his name, in 1524, died in 1594. In 1551 he was appointed by Pope Julius III. master of a choir of boys in the Julian Chapel, and was the first to receive the title of chapel-master. In 1554 he published a first collection of Masses, and Julius admitted him into the college of choristers of the Pope's chapel. He was dismissed by Pope Paul IV. in 1555, but in the same year he was appointed chapel-master of San Giovanni in Laterano.

In the meantime the Council of Trent, on reassembling in 1562, pointed out the necessity of a reform in church music, which had become vulgar and profane. A commission was appointed, and Palestrina composed three beautiful Masses which created quite a revolution in sacred composition. One of them, the *Missa Papæ Marcelli*, is still celebrated. In 1571 Palestrina was appointed chapel-master of the Basilica San Pietro in Rome. A complete edition of his works was published in Leipzig between 1885 and 1893 (33 vols.).

PALESTRI'NA (ancient **Præneste**). A city of Central Italy, province of Rome. It is of Greek origin, and had become important long before Rome existed. Under the Roman Empire the town attained great magnificence, and was often the residence of the emperors. Palestrina has numerous ancient remains, noteworthy among which are those of an immense Temple of Fortune. Among modern buildings the most noteworthy is the Barberini Palace. Pop. 7467.

PALEY, Frederick Apthorp. Grandson of the following, was born in 1816. Educated at Shrewsbury, he went afterwards to St. John's College, Cambridge, and took his degree in 1838. In 1846 he became a Roman Catholic, and in 1874 accepted the post of professor of classical literature in the Catholic College at Kensington. He died in 1888. His best title to fame rests on the valuable work he did as editor and annotator of classical texts, especially Æschylus and Euripides.

PALEY, William. British theologian, born at Peterborough in 1743, died 1805. Educated at Christ's College, Cambridge, he graduated B.A. as Senior Wrangler in 1763, and M.A. in 1766, and subsequently became a Fellow and tutor of his college. At the age of twenty-four he was ordained. In 1780 he became prebendary of Carlisle, and in 1785 chancellor of the diocese. In 1794 he was made prebendary of St. Paul's and sub-dean of Lincoln; and in

1795 he received the rectory of Bishop-Wearmouth. He also received in this year the degree of D.D. from Cambridge University. His chief works are: *The Principles of Moral and Political Philosophy* (1785); *A View of the Evidences of Christianity* (1794); *Natural Theology, or Evidences of the Existence and Attributes of the Deity collected from the Appearance of Nature* (1802), founded on a work by Nieuwentyt, a Dutch philosopher. Paley's system of moral philosophy is founded purely on utilitarianism. He was a strenuous supporter of Wilberforce and Clarkson in their efforts to abolish the slave-trade.

PALGRAVE, Francis Turner. British poet and critic, was born in London in 1824, and died in 1897. Educated at Charterhouse and Balliol College, Oxford, he became a Fellow of Exeter College. For some years he held a post in the Education Department, and from 1885 to 1895 was professor of poetry at Oxford. His literary works include: *Idylls and Songs* (1854), *Golden Treasury of the Best Songs and Lyrical Poems* (1861), *Sonnets and Songs of Shakespeare* (1865), *Essays on Art* (1866), and *Selected Lyrical Poems of Herrick* (1877).

PÂLI. The sacred language of the Buddhists. It is the language in which the oldest religious, philosophical, and historical literature of Buddhism is written, and is especially the language of the sacred books of the Buddhists of Ceylon, Burmah, and Siam; but it is no longer spoken anywhere, though a corrupt form of it is to some extent used for literary purposes. The language appears to have been derived immediately from Sanskrit, to which it is as closely related as Italian is to Latin. Like Prakrit, however, Pâli, as compared with classical Sanskrit, shows a marked decadence

The study of Pâli was introduced into Europe by Lassen and Burnouf. One of the most interesting portions of the Pâli literature is the collection of folklore known as the *Iatakas*. Pâli works of a non-sacred character are: the *Dipavamsa*, a history of Ceylon to A.D. 300; the *Mahavamsa*, another history of Ceylon, written about the end of the fifth century A.D.; and the *Rasavahini*, a collection of fables and legends.—Cf. *Journal of the Pâli Text Society*.

PALICOUREA (pā-li-kö'rē-a). A genus of plants, nat. ord Rubiaceæ, tropical American shrubs, with flowers of various sizes in compound thyrses or corymbs. *P. officinalis* is reported to be a powerful diuretic, and *P. tinctoria* forms a fine red dye, much valued in Peru. *P. densiflōra* yields coto bark.

PAL'IMPSEST (from Gr. *palin*, again, *psēstos*, rubbed), a manuscript prepared by erasure for being written on again, especially a parchment so prepared by washing or scraping. This custom was brought about by the costliness of writing materials, and was practised both by the Greeks and Romans, and in the monasteries, especially from the seventh to the thirteenth centuries. It was in the seventh century, when the conquests of the Caliph Omar had cut off from Europe the supply of papyrus furnished by Egypt, that a great deficiency in the supply of parchment began to be felt. The scarcity continued until the general use of parchment was superseded by paper. That which replaced the ancient manuscripts was nearly always some writing of an ecclesiastical character. The parchments which have been scraped are nearly indecipherable.

At the Renaissance attempts were made to decipher the ancient and underlying writing, but for want of chemical appliances the attempts were generally unsuccessful. It was only in the eighteenth century that decided progress was made. Those which have been washed have often been revived by chemical processes. Fragments of the *Iliad* and extensive portions of many Greek and Roman writers have been recovered by these means.—Cf. Sir E. M. Thompson, *An Introduction to Greek and Latin Palæography*.

PALISSY, Bernard. A French artist and philosopher, born about 1510, died in 1590. He was appren-

Palissy Ware Jug

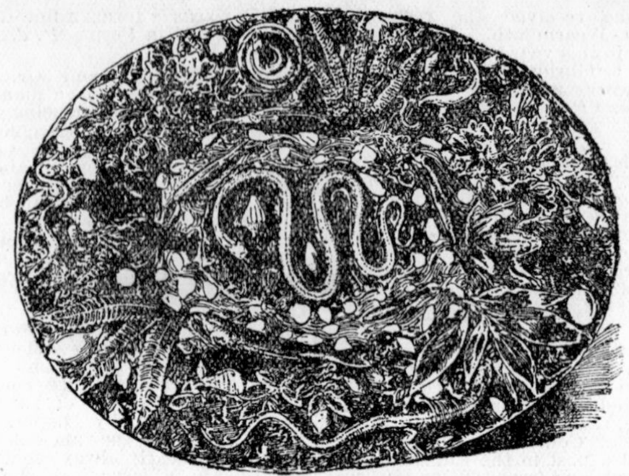

Palissy Ware Dish

ticed in a glass-works at Agen, where he learned the art of painting on glass. He then travelled in Germany, returning to France in 1535. At Saintes, where he settled, he started to make experiments, resolved to discover the mode of producing white enamel. After sixteen years of unremunerated labour (1538-54), he at last obtained a pure white enamel, affording a perfect ground for the application of decorative art.

He was now able to produce works in which he represented natural objects grouped and portrayed with consummate skill, and his enamelled pottery and sculptures in clay became recognized as works of art. In 1562 he went to establish himself at Paris, where he continued to work at his art, and also delivered scientific lectures, which were attended by the most distinguished men in Paris, and contained views far ahead of his time. Palissy suffered persecution as a Huguenot, was arrested in 1589, and thrown into the Bastille, where he died. His *Œuvres complètes* were edited by Anatole France in 1880.—Cf. Henry Morley, *Palissy the Potter*.

PALITANA. A native state of Kathiawar Peninsula, Bombay Province, India. It contains Satrunjaya, a holy mountain covered with Jain temples, and overlooking Palitan (pop. 14,000). the state capital. A railway runs to Ahmadabad, with connections to Bhavnagar and Mehsana. Sugar, cereals, and cotton are produced. Area, 290 sq. miles; pop. 52,860.

PALIU'RUS. A genus of deciduous shrubs, natives of the south of Europe and Asia Minor, and belonging to the nat. ord. Rhamnaceæ. *See* CHRIST'S-THORN.

PALK STRAIT. A channel between the mainland of India (Deccan) and the north part of Ceylon, abounding in shoals, currents, sunken rocks, and sand-banks. It is called after Palk, who was Governor of Madras in 1764.

PALL. A covering of black velvet thrown over a coffin while being borne to burial, the ends of which in a walking procession are held by the friends of the deceased. In another sense the pall or *pallium* is an ecclesiastical vestment sent by the sovereign pontiff on their accession to patriarchs, primates, and metropolitans, and sometimes, as a mark of honour, to bishops. It is made of white lambs' wool, and consists of a narrow strip of cloth encircling the neck and shoulders, with two narrow pieces hanging down, all embroidered with crosses.

PALLADIAN ARCHITECTURE. A species of Italian architecture due to Palladio, founded upon the Roman antique as interpreted by the writings of Vitruvius, but rather upon the secular buildings of the Romans than upon their temples. It is consequently more applicable to palaces and civic buildings than to churches.

A characteristic feature of the style is the use of engaged columns in façades, a single range of these often running through the two principal stories. It was introduced into England by Inigo Jones, a follower of the Venetian school of Palladio.

PALLA'DIO, Andrea. One of the greatest classical architects of modern Italy, was born at Vicenza in 1518, died at Venice in 1580. He studied at Rome, came under the influence of the work of Vitruvius and of Alberti, and on his return to Vicenza he established his fame by his designs for many noble buildings both there and in other parts of Italy, notably among them being the Palazzo della Ragione. From 1560 he erected many buildings at Venice, among them the churches of S. Giorzio Maggiore and of the Capuchins, and some of the palaces on the Grand Canal. He also designed many country villas in different parts of North Italy. He was the author of a *Treatise on Architecture.*

PALLA'DIUM. A wooden image of Pallas Athene which is said to have fallen from heaven, and to have been preserved in Troy. The Trojans believed that their city would be invincible so long as it contained the Palladium. The Romans pretended that it was brought to Italy by Æneas, and preserved in the temple of Vesta at Rome, but several Greek cities claimed to possess it.

PALLA'DIUM. A metal discovered by Wollaston in 1803, and found in small quantity associated with native gold and platinum. It closely resembles platinum, but is harder, lighter (specific gravity, 11·4), and more easily oxidized; symbol, Pd; atomic weight, 106·7. It has been used for dental purposes, for making scientific instruments, and for absorbing hydrogen. At the ordinary temperature it absorbs many times its own volume of hydrogen.

PALLAS. One of the minor planets revolving round the sun between Mars and Jupiter. Its orbit is inclined 35° to the ecliptic. It was discovered in 1802 by Olbers at Bremen, being the second minor planet to be found. It revolves round the sun in 4·61 years. Professor Barnard estimated its diameter at about 300 miles.

PALL-MALL. An ancient game, in which a round boxwood ball was, with a mallet or club, struck through a ring elevated upon a pole, standing at either end of an alley, the person who could do so with fewest blows, or with a number agreed on, being the winner. The game, introduced during the reign of Charles I., was formerly practised in St. James's Park, London, and gave its name to the street called Pall Mall.

PALMA. An episcopal city of Spain, capital of the Island of Majorca and of the Spanish province of Baleares. It is built in the form of an amphitheatre, and enjoys an extremely mild and salubrious climate. The principal public buildings are the cathedral, dating from the thirteenth century, the exchange, the Governor's palace, and the town house. There are normal and nautical schools, a school of fine arts, two public libraries, and a museum. Shipbuilding-yards employ numerous hands. Pop. 81,602.

PALMA, or **SAN MIGUEL DE LA PALMA.** The most north-westerly of the Canary Islands; area, 280 sq. miles; capital, Santa Cruz de la Palma, the principal port. It consists for the most part of elevated mountains, and in the north the coast is high and precipitous. The climate is agreeable and healthy, and the soil fertile. Besides a small quantity of grain, La Palma produces wine, fruits, sugar, honey, wax, and silk. Pop. 53,000.

PALMA DI MONTECHIARO (montā-kyä'rō). A town of Sicily, in the province of Girgenti. The castle of Montechiaro crowns the summit of a hill to the west of the town. Pop. 15,500.

PALMATE. In botany, formed like a hand. A palmate or digitate leaf is a compound or lobed leaf in which the leaflets or lobes diverge like the fingers of a hand, as in horse-chesnut or castor-oil plant.

PALM BEACH. A famous winter resort of the U.S.A., in Florida.

PALMER, Edward Henry. English Oriental scholar, born at Cambridge, 1840. He was a member of the survey expedition to Sinai (1868-69) and to Moab (1869-70), and on his return became professor of Arabic at Cambridge (1871). In 1882 he was killed by the Arabs in the Sinaitic Peninsula. Among his numerous works are: *Oriental Mysticism* (1867), *The Desert of the Exodus* (1871), and *A Persian-English Dictionary* (1876).

PALMERSTON (pä'mėr-stun), **Henry John Temple, Viscount.** English statesman, was born in Westminster 1784, died 1865. Educated at Harrow, Edinburgh University, and St. John's College, Cambridge, he succeeded his father in the title (an Irish one) in 1802. In 1807 he was returned as member for Newport, Isle of Wight, and became Junior Lord of the Admiralty in the Duke of Portland's administration.

In 1809 he became Secretary for War, and two years later he was elected member for Cambridge University. He was a supporter of Catholic emancipation, and retired from office in the Wellington ministry in 1828 with others of the Canning party. He had already made a reputation for his command of foreign policy, and in 1830 he was made Foreign Secretary in the Whig ministry of Earl Grey. From this time he continued to be a member and leader of the Liberal party.

In 1831 he was returned for Bletchingley, and after the Reform Bill (1832) for South Hants. He retired from office in Dec., 1834, but in April, 1835, he resumed his former appointment under Lord Melbourne. He continued in office as Foreign Secretary until 1841.

It was during this period that he gained his great reputation for vigilance and energy in the conduct of foreign affairs. In 1845 he supported the repeal of the corn-laws, and in 1846 he was Foreign Secretary in the Russell ministry. Several causes of dissatisfaction, the chief being his recognition of Louis Napoleon without consulting his colleagues, led to Palmerston's resignation in Dec., 1851.

In Feb., 1852, he became Home Secretary in the coalition ministry of Lord Aberdeen. On the resignation of this ministry he became Prime Minister in 1855, remaining so, with a brief interruption, for the remainder of his life. He was made D.C.L. of Oxford in 1862, and elected Rector of Glasgow University in 1863.—BIBLIOGRAPHY.: Walter Bagehot, *Biographical Studies*; L. C. Sanders, *Life of Viscount Palmerston*; Sir E. Ashley, *Life and Correspondence of Henry John Temple, Viscount Palmerston.*

PALMERSTON, now **DARWIN.** The chief settlement of the Northern Territory of South Australia, on Port Darwin, accessible to ocean-going steamers of the largest draught. Pop. 1000.

PALMERSTON NORTH. A town of North Island, New Zealand. Pop. (1932), 23,200.

PALMET'TO PALM. A common name of several palms, especially of the *Sabal Palmetto*, the cabbage-palm. It attains the height of 40 or 50 feet, and is crowned with a tuft of large leaves.

PALMISTRY. The popular name for the art, or according to its professors the science, of chiromancy (Gr. *cheir*, the hand, *manteia*, divination), by which it is claimed that not only the character of a person, but also the events, both past and future, of his life, may be discovered on examination of the palm of the hand. The practice of palmistry is of considerable antiquity. It was known to the ancient Greeks, and is alluded to by Pliny and Aristotle; was in vogue to some extent among the Romans; and has been employed in India since a remote period, chiefly by a special caste of Brahmins known as the Joshi, who, though still pursuing the calling, show little of the skill displayed by their ancestors.

Palmistry was widely prevalent during the Middle Ages, a leading work of that period on the subject being Johann Hartlieb's *Die Kunst Ciromantia* (Augsburg, 1475). A famous palmist of more recent times was the well-known Frenchwoman Marie Anne Lenormand, who was in great request by the Parisian fashionable world of her day (1772-1843), and was frequently consulted by the leading ladies of Napoleon's court.

Authorities of the nineteenth century were the French writers D'Arpentigny and Desbarrolles, who published respectively *La Chirognomie* (Paris, 1843) and *Les Mystères de la main* (1859). D'Arpentigny deals chiefly with chirognomy, an allied art which confines its study to the general form of the hand and fingers. The palmist proper confines his attention rather to the "mounts" of the hand, those elevations, namely, which occur at the bases of the fingers and thumb, and also on that portion of the hand extending from the base of the fourth finger to the wrist; to the "lines" with which the palm itself is freely marked; and to the "bracelets" seen upon the wrists. The mounts are seven in number, one upon the base of every finger, with two others on the palm. They are named after the planets. Marked development of the mount of Venus at the base of the thumb implies a loving character; on the first finger (Jupiter), ambition and pride; the second (Saturn), fatality; the third (Apollo), art or riches; the fourth (Mercury), science or wit; while the two on the palm itself are those of Mars, denoting courage or cruelty, and of the Moon, implying folly or imagination. Of the lines, that of "life," if long, will promise length of days; it lies around the base of the thumb.

Crossing the palm somewhat diagonally is the line of "head," which should be clearly marked and long. That of "heart," parallel with it but nearer the finger-bases, denotes a loving and devoted character. Other lines, not found in every hand, are all supposed to possess a special signification. The bracelets, or *racette*, on the wrists add value to the " line of life."

Palmistry is still fashionable at the present day, though, if practised for gain and with intent to deceive, is a punishable offence. Modern works dealing with the subject include: Oxenford's *Modern Palmistry* (1900); Frith and Allen's *Chiromancy* (1901); Phanos's *Hand-reading* (1903); and Stephenson's *Practical Palmistry* (1904).

PALMIT'IC ACID ($C_{16}H_{32}O_2$). A fatty acid occurring in many fats, whether of the animal or vegetable kingdom, such as palm-oil, butter, tallow, lard, etc., and existing partly in a free state but generally in combination with glycerine as the glyceride *palmitin*. It is a colourless, crystalline substance, which melts at 62·6° C. The sodium salt of the acid is a soap (q.v.).

PALM-KALE. A variety of the cabbage extensively cultivated in the Channel Islands. It grows to the height of 10 or 12 feet, and has much the aspect of a palm.

PALM-NUT CAKE. An artificial feeding-stuff produced from the kernel of the palm-nut (*Elæis guineensis*) after the extraction of the oil.

PALM-OIL. The product of the oil palm (*Elæis guineensis*) indigenous to West Africa. This palm grows to a height of 30 feet, and is surmounted by a feathered group of 15-feet leaves. The industry maintained by the products of the oil palm is one of the most important in Nigeria (West Africa), where the tree grows wild and where the product forms the staple export.

Palm-oil is obtained from the large, oval-headed, red-coloured fruits by boiling in water the fleshy pulp which surrounds them, and skimming the orange-coloured fat from the surface. The fat has then the appearance of butter-fat, and is used largely in Europe in the preparation of soap and candles. The kernels themselves are pressed for oil, which is utilized for lubricants and margarine.

Hitherto the industry has been dependent upon the wild oil palms of West Africa for supply, but the trees have successfully been raised in plantations in parts of Malaya and in Sumatra, and the oil palm may be a potential source of wealth as a plantation crop in the Eastern tropics, and may become more of an economic proposition as regards yield than even the indigenous palms of Nigeria. Palm-wine, a cheap fermented liquor of doubtful quality, is distilled by the natives of Nigeria to replace the cheap spirits whose importation has been prohibited.

PALMS. The Palmaceæ, a natural order of arborescent monocotyledons, chiefly inhabiting the tropics, distinguished by their fleshy, colourless, six-parted flowers, enclosed within spathes; their minute embryo lying in the midst of albumen, and remote from the hilum and their large, rigid, plaited or pinnated leaves.

The palms are among the most interesting plants in the vegetable kingdom, from their beauty, variety, and associations, as well as from their great value to mankind. While some, as *Kunthia montāna*, *Oreodoxa frigida*, have trunks as slender as the reed, or about as long as a ship's cable (*Calămus rudentum* being 500 feet), others, as *Jubæa spectabilis* and *Cocos butyracea*, have stems 3 feet and even 5 feet thick; while some are of low growth, as *Attalēa amygdalina*, others exhibit a stem towering from 160 to 190 feet high, as *Ceroxylon andicŏla* or wax-palm of South America. Also, while they generally have a cylindrical undivided stem, *Hyphæne thebaica* (the doum palm of Upper Egypt) and *Hyphæne coriacea* are remarkable for their repeatedly divided trunk. About 1100 species are known, but it is probable that many are still undescribed.

Wine, oil, wax, flour, sugar, sago, etc., are the produce of palms; to which may be added thread, utensils, weapons, and materials for building houses, boats, etc. There is scarcely a single species in which some useful property is not found. The coco-nut, the date, and others are valued for their fruit; the cabbage-palm for its edible terminal buds; the fan-palm and many more are valued for their foliage, whose hardness and durability render it an excellent material for thatching.

The sweet juice of the Palmyra and others, when fermented, yields wine; the centre of the sago-palm abounds in nutritive starch; the trunk of the wax-palm exudes a valuable wax; oil is expressed in abundance from the oil-palm; many of the species contain so hard a kind of fibrous matter that it is used instead of needles, or so tough that it is manufactured into cordage; and, finally, their trunks are in some cases valued for their strength, and used as timber, or for their elasticity or flexibility. There is only one European species, the *Chamærops humilis*. *See* ARECA; BETEL-NUT; CABBAGE-PALM; COCO-NUT; DATE;

DOUM PALM; FAN-PALM; PALM-OIL; PALMYRA PALM; etc.

PALM SUNDAY. The last Sunday before Easter, on which Christ's entry into Jerusalem, when palm branches were strewed before him, is celebrated. Palm Sunday, also called *Pascha Floridum* and Flower Sunday, is still celebrated with much solemnity by the Roman Catholics; branches are strewed in the churches, and a procession takes place. Formerly a wooden ass, with the figure of Christ on it, was drawn on rollers in procession. The state of Florida, discovered on Palm Sunday, 1512, received its name from this day.

PALMY'RA (Heb. *Tadmor*, City of Palms). An ancient city of Syria, now in ruins, situated in an oasis 140 miles E.N.E. of Damascus. Founded or enlarged by Solomon in the tenth century B.C., it was an entrepôt for the trade between Damascus and the Mediterranean, and during the wars between the Romans and the Parthians it acquired great importance.

It became the faithful ally of Rome, and during the reign of Gallienus (260-268) Odenathus, the ruler of Palmyra, established an independent Palmyrene kingdom. Odenathus was succeeded by his widow Zenobia, to whom Palmyra chiefly owes its fame, and who took the title of Queen of the East. She was besieged in Palmyra by Aurelian, and compelled to surrender.

On his departure the inhabitants revolted, on which Aurelian returned and destroyed the city (A.D. 273). He permitted the inhabitants to rebuild it, but it never recovered its importance. In 1400 Tamerlane completely destroyed it. There are remains of ancient buildings, chiefly of the Corinthian order, with the exception of the Temple of the Sun, which is Ionic.—Cf. Wood-Dawkins, *Ruins of Palmyra and Baalbeck.*

PALMY'RA PALM (*Borassus flabelliformis*). The common Indian palm, a tree ranging from the north-eastern parts of Arabia through India to the Bay of Bengal. In India and other parts of Asia it forms the chief support of 6,000,000 or 7,000,000 of population. Its fruit is a valuable food, its timber is excellent, and it furnishes thatch, cordage, and material for hats, fans, umbrellas, etc. It produces sugar and arrack, and its leaves are used for writing-tablets.

The young shoots are boiled and eaten, the seeds are edible, and the fruit yields a useful oil. A full-grown palmyra is from 60 to 70 feet high, and its leaves are very large. The name palmyra-wood is frequently given to other woods of a similar nature.

PALO'LO, or **PALOLO WORM.** A marine annelid (*P. viridis*) found in great abundance near the coral reefs in the South Sea Islands. They are taken in large numbers in nets by the islanders, who esteem them, alive or roasted, as a great delicacy.

PALÜDAN - MÜLLER, Frederik. Danish poet, born in 1809, died in 1876. Educated at Copenhagen University, he began his career as a poet in 1832. His works include: *Adam Homo*, a humorous didactic poem; *Kalanus*, an Indian tragedy; *Adonis*, a poetic romance; *Amor and Psyche*, a lyrical drama; etc.

PAMIERS (på-mi-ā). A city of Southern France, capital of an arrondissement, in the department of Ariège. It has a seventeenth-century cathedral, and manufactures woollens, paper, bricks, and flour. Roger II., comte de Foix, built a castle in the twelfth century, around which the town grew up. Pop. 12,131.

PAMIR, or **PAMIRS** (the "Roof of the World"). An elevated mountain region of Central Asia, regarded as formed by the meeting of the Himalaya and Tien Shan mountain systems. It consists of plateaus having a general elevation of more than 13,000 feet, dominated by still loftier ridges and summits (25,000 feet) clothed with eternal snow.

There are several small lakes here, and the sources of the Oxus take their rise in the Pamir. The atmosphere is exceedingly dry, the extremes of heat and cold are very great, and a great part of the surface is barren. The Kirghiz, however, find a certain amount of pasture for their cattle in summer, and in favoured localities there is a little cultivation.

PAM'LICO SOUND. A shallow lagoon of the United States, on the south-east coast of North Carolina. It is 80 miles long, from 8 to 30 miles wide, and separated from the ocean by long, narrow, sandy islands.

PAMPAS (Peru. *bamba* or *pampa*, a steppe). A name given to the vast treeless plains of Latin America. Shallow lakes or swamps occur in some parts, and the pampas have sometimes the character of a salt steppe. Enormous quantities of wheat are raised, and cattle are widely reared on the pampas.

PAMPAS-GRASS (*Gynerium argentěum*). A grass which grows in the pampas in the southern parts of South America. It has been introduced into Europe as an ornamental plant. It has panicles of silvery flowers on stalks more than 10 feet high, and its leaves are from 6 to 8 feet long. The male and female flowers are on separate stalks.

PAMPE'RO. A violent wind from the west or south-west which sweeps over the pampas of Argentina and Uruguay.

PAMPHYL'IA. An ancient province of Asia Minor, extending along the Mediterranean from Cilicia on the east to Lycia on the west. It was inhabited by a mixed race, partly Greek and partly Semitic. Pamphylia never attained any political importance. It was subject successively to Persia, Macedonia, and Syria, to the Pergamene dominions, and eventually (133 B.C.) to Rome, although some Greek colonies for a time maintained their independence.

PAMPLO'NA (ancient **Pompelo** or **Pompeiopolis**). A city of Spain, and capital of the province of Navarre or Pamplona, and of the ancient kingdom of Navarre, on the Arga, a tributary of the Aragon. The town has a cathedral, founded in 1100 and rebuilt in 1397, and a bull-ring capable of seating 8000 persons. It was built by Pompey in 68 B.C., and was once known as Pampeluna. The Plaza de Castillo is one of the finest squares in Spain. Pop. (1931), 43,221.

PAN. A rural divinity of ancient Greece, the god of shepherds, represented as old, with two horns, pointed ears, a goat's beard, goat's tail, and goat's feet. The worship of Pan originally existed in Arcadia, and was first introduced into Athens after the battle of Marathon, in which it was asserted that he had assisted the Athenians.

His festivals were called by the Greeks *Lycœa*, and were known at Rome as the *Lupercalia*. This shepherd god was afterwards regarded by some philosophers, especially the Stoics, as the All-supporting God of nature, and personified the universe (Gr. *To Pan*, The All). Pan invented the syrinx or *pandean* pipes. From him comes the expression *panic fear*, because he was believed to cause sudden and often inexplicable terror.

PANAMÁ. Capital of the Republic of Panamá on the Gulf of Panamá, and on the Pacific coast of the Isthmus of Panamá. The city lies on a tongue of land, across which its streets stretch from sea to sea. It has a university, and is to be the site of the Bolivarian University. Panamá is chiefly im-

Pan : from a statue in the British Museum

portant as the Pacific terminus of the interoceanic railway and also of the Panamá Canal. The railway, which has been in operation since 1855, runs across the isthmus from Panamá to Colón (Aspinwall) on the Atlantic. Pop. (1930), 114,103.

PANAMÁ. A republic of Central America, co-extensive with the Isthmus of Panamá, bounded northwards by the Caribbean, and on the south by the Pacific Ocean. The eastern and western frontiers merge respectively with the Republics of Colombia and Costa Rica. The republic has an extreme length of about 480 miles; breadth between 30 and 120 miles; and a total area of 32,380 sq. miles. Pop. (1930), excluding the Canal Zone, 467,459.

Physiography : Orography.—Panamá is generally mountainous. In the east it is traversed by the Serrania del Darien, an Andean range, partly in Colombia; in the west there are two ranges, the Sierra de Chiriqui and a part of the Cordillera of Talamanca, which extends over the Costa Rican frontier. Upon these latter ranges rise a series of volcanoes, attaining in the Chiriqui volcano an altitude of 11,265 feet. The mountains are in places broken by low passes, averaging 300 feet above sea-level.

Rivers and Lakes.—None of the 480 rivers of Panamá are navigable, and, although some are of considerable length, they are all torrential in the wet season. The principal one is the Chagres, rising near the Pacific and flowing first south-west and then north to the Caribbean. A ten-mile strip of territory running from the Caribbean to the Pacific is traversed by the Panamá Canal (q.v.), and is completely under the authority of the United States, who purchased their rights for 10,000,000 dollars, and pay an additional 250,000 dollars yearly. There are two artificial lakes, Gatun and Sosa (Miraflores), both in the Canal Zone.

Climate.—The climate is tropical, and the Caribbean coast is slightly warmer than on the Pacific side. At Panamá the temperature varies from 68° to 95° F. Between January and the end of March is the dry season, when a north-easterly wind prevails ; the wet season lasts from April to December.

Social Conditions : People.—The Panamanians are of mixed Spanish, Indian, and negro extraction, and, like all mongrels, they have few redeeming qualities. There are some temporary immigrant Americans and Europeans, with about 3000 Chinese and over 40,000 British West Indian subjects.

Religion.—Roman Catholicism predominates, excepting in the Canal Zone, which is overwhelmingly Protestant.

Education.—Nominally education is free and compulsory between the ages of seven and fifteen years, and there is a university at Panamá. In 1926 it was decided to erect at Panamá the Bolivarian University, as an expression of pan-American solidarity. Many young people of both sexes are trained in Europe and the United States at the expense of the State.

Defence.—There is neither army nor navy, but a police contingent of 60 officers and 630 men is maintained.

Currency.—The unit of currency is the balboa, equivalent in value to the United States silver dollar. Other silver coins are the ½ balboa piece (12·5 grammes, ·900 fine), and ¼ and $\frac{1}{10}$ balboa pieces ; and nickel coins of 5 and 2½ cents. There is no paper money.

Weights and Measures. — Both English and metric systems are used.

Transport and Communication : Railways.—The Colón-Panamá Railway (47·61 miles) operates through the Canal Zone Territory. It is the property of the Panamá Railroad Company, which is in turn owned by the United States. The only other railways are (1) those operated by the United Fruit Company on their banana plantations in Bocas del Toro, and (2) a narrow-gauge line between Pedregal and Boquete (province of Chiriqui), with branches from David to La Concepcion, now extended to the Port of Puerto Armuelles, and from Dolega to Potrerillos.

Shipping.—This is dependent entirely upon the Panamá Canal.

Roads.—Road communication between Panamá City and Costa Rica is under construction. That between Panamá City and David, the capital of Chiriqui province, was completed in 1931 (315 miles).

Telegraphs. — Wireless communications are maintained by the Canal Zone radio stations. Submarine cables run between Jamaica and Panamá, from Colón to the United States and Europe, and from Panamá to North and South American ports. The Jamaica-Panamá route is British ; the others belong to the " All America Cables." There is also an extensive inland telegraphy system of thirty-seven offices.

Production.—Bananas are the staple export, and all trade in this commodity is in the hands of the United Fruit Company. The trade has suffered much, as in Jamaica, from uncontrollable outbreaks of Panamá disease. Coco-nuts, copaiba, sarsaparilla, ipecachuanha, and mahogany are also important. Coffee is produced near the Costa Rican frontier, in the province of Chiriqui, and much caoutchouc is collected wild from the Cordilleras, or is cultivated on the coasts.

On the Atlantic side (province of Coclé) there is a large co-operative agricultural undertaking which produces coca, coffee, and caoutchouc. Sugar and tobacco are also grown ; cattle, horses, pigs, mules, and goats are raised ; and hides form a valuable item in the Panamánian export list. There is much land available and suitable for settlement by immigrants. Pearl-fishing is practised off Coiba Island, and off the Perlas (q.v.) in the Gulf of Panamá. Nearly every common mineral exists excepting coal, but none of the deposits have hitherto been worked.

Divisions. — For administrative purposes Panamá is divided into nine provinces, which with their capitals are as follows :

Bocas del Toro (Bocas del Toro).	Los Santos (Las Tablas).
	Colón (Colón).
Coclé (Penonomé).	Herrera (Chitré).
Chiriqui (David).	Veraguas (Santiago).
Panamá (Panamá City).	Darien (La Palma).

The capital is Panamá City, on the Pacific. Colón is on the Atlantic coast. Smaller ports are : (Atlantic) Bocas del Toro, Portobello, Mandinga (opened Sept., 1916); (Pacific) Aguadulce, Pedregal, Montijo, Puerto Armuelles, and Puerto Mutis.

Government.—The executive is in the hands of a President, elected by direct vote for four years and not eligible for re-election. A National Assembly of 32 members (one per 15,000 electors) is elected every four years, and meets biennially on 1st Sept. There are also 3 Vice-Presidents and a Cabinet of 5 ministers. Each of the provinces is under a Governor.

History.—Panamá was formerly a department of the Republic of Colombia, and asserted its independence on 4th Dec., 1903, being recognized shortly afterwards by the United States and by other Powers. On 6th April, 1914, the United States and Colombia completed a treaty at Bogotá whereby the latter agreed to recognize Panamánian independence in return for the sum of 25,000,000 dollars and certain rights in the Canal Zone, but this agreement (Treaty of Bogotá) was not ratified by the United States Senate until 20th April, 1921. It was ratified by the Colombian Congress on 24th Dec., 1921.

A frontier dispute with Costa Rica was submitted to United States arbitration, who pronounced against Panamá, and the Costa Ricans have now occupied (since Sept., 1921) the disputed region, although their possession is not officially recognized by Panamá.

BIBLIOGRAPHY: Constantine Graham, *Report on the Economic and Commercial Situation in Panamá* (H.M. Stationery Office); H. A. Franck, *Things as they are in Panamá*; J. Streitberg, *La République de Panamá*.

PANAMÁ, Isthmus of (formerly called the **Isthmus of Darien**). Has a breadth of from 30 to 70 miles, connects North with South America, and separates the Pacific from the Atlantic. The coast is rocky and lofty along the Caribbean Sea, but low and swampy along the Pacific. From the heights of the isthmus Balboa was the first European to see the Pacific Ocean.

PANAMÁ CANAL. Almost from the time of the discovery of the two Americas the advantages of a waterway between them have been apparent. Columbus, indeed, believed an opening to exist; and on a globe made by John Schoner in 1520, preserved in the town library of Nürnberg, a cutting across the Isthmus of Darien is shown.

Spanish geographers and sailors urged the making of a canal, but all such ideas were discouraged by Philip II. In the eighteenth century plans were completed by the Dutch, but were never put into actual operation.

It was not until 1880 that the French, fired by the success of the Suez Canal, decided to finance de Lesseps in a similar undertaking in Panamá. Lesseps estimated that the scheme would cost £24,000,000 and could be completed in eight years. But his calculations were made from insufficient data and without regard to climate and other conditions. From the first his workmen suffered cruelly from fever and disease, which were attributed, wrongly enough, to the clouds continually hanging over the Cordilleras.

Also, the phenomenally rapid rise of the River Chagres in the rainy season was not allowed for. In itself the design of Lesseps for a sea-level canal is not unsound, and the work done by his labourers was all good; but to cut a canal through a ridge of the Cordilleras (there only 500 feet high) and to cope with the waters of the Chagres and other mountain streams was a colossal enterprise.

Too late, Lesseps changed his plans, and began making locks to lessen the amount of excavation. Unfortunately the financial side of the scheme had been grossly mismanaged, and between neglect and dishonesty large sums had melted away. In 1889 the Company was obliged to go into liquidation, having spent £66,000,000 since the time of its inception. From being a national hero, Lesseps became an object of execration, for thousands of small families had entrusted him with their savings.

A new Panamá Company was formed upon the failure of the old one, and continued the work of excavation for another eight years, and in 1904 the United States Government stepped in and took over the whole responsibility. From that time onwards the history of the canal is the history of a struggle between nature and science. Instead of taking armies of workpeople to Panamá to die, the United States sent them there to live healthily.

Under the leadership of Major Ronald Ross and General Gorgas, an organized attack upon the disease-carriers of the district—the mosquitoes—was begun. Every ditch and pool which might harbour mosquitoes was treated with oil, and special houses having doors and windows covered with copper-wire gauze were put up wherever houses were needed. Every possible precaution was taken to safeguard the health of the workmen and their

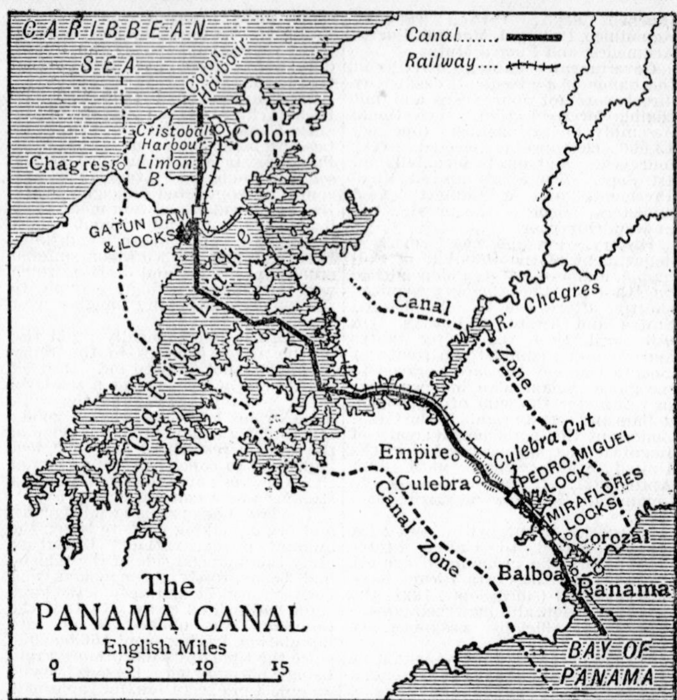

families, the result being that Panamá is now one of the healthiest places in the world.

The work did not, however, proceed without interruption. Although a certain amount of excavation had been done, a vast amount remained undone, for modern vessels require deep draught and plenty of room for manœuvring. The total length of the canal is a little over 50 miles, and its minimum depth 41 feet. The position which has given most trouble is that known as the Culebra Cut, a stretch of 9 miles through the ridge. Here the excavators were continually hindered by landslides, the soil being of a soft, sticky nature, so that it slipped in great layers. At one time it was said that a million cubic yards of earth were in motion. Eventually the sides of the cut will find their own angle of repose, and the slides, in any serious proportions, will come to an end.

At each end of the canal, at Gatun and Miraflores, are locks for raising ships to the high level. These locks are so big as to form one of the greatest engineering triumphs of the world. At Gatun it was necessary to build an enormous dam. The effect of this dam has been to turn the Chagres Valley into a great lake, where the Chagres and other streams can rise or fall as rapidly as they please without doing any damage.

This dam, made very largely of material excavated from the Culebra, now Gaillard, Cut, is the largest ever attempted, being 3¼ miles long. Its width at sea-level is 1900 feet, the reason for such extraordinary solidity being found in the fact that many engineers refused to believe that a dam at Gatun could be built with safety.

The canal, though not entirely finished, was opened for traffic on 14th Aug., 1914. Obviously the moment was an anxious one for those interested in the railways of the continents. Railway rates are necessarily greatly in advance of canal rates, and in the case of the American trans-continental railways haulage is particularly costly on account of the great chains of mountains which they have to traverse.

In practice it has been found cheaper to send goods from New York to the west coast by sea and canal than by rail over the Rocky Mountains. But the length of time occupied by the water route precludes the possibility of the railway being superseded for many kinds of traffic.

The fact that the opening years of the canal's existence were spent under conditions of war has prevented the formation of really instructive and significant statistics; moreover, the aforesaid "angles of repose" in the banks of the Culebra Cut not having been reached, stoppages to traffic occurred several times until 1917 by reason of the landslides; since that time, however, the channel has been kept clear. The official opening was on June 12th, 1920.

In spite of these circumstances, however, the canal has proved itself an important factor in the world's trade. Japan, naturally, has been in the forefront of the foreign nations making use of it, while cargoes from the East Indies, notably rubber, are accounting for more and more of the tonnage passing through.

On 18th Nov., 1903, a treaty between the United States and Panamá was signed which provided facilities for the construction and maintenance of the canal, and granted to the United States in perpetuity the use of a zone (Canal Zone) of 5 miles in width on either side of the canal, within which the United States exercises sovereign rights. The proposal to cede part of Colon to the Canal Zone, and to compel Panamá to join with the United States in time of war, was rejected by the National Assembly in 1927, but the matter has again been brought up for discussion. The area of the zone is 552·8 sq. miles. Pop. (1932), 30,980.

PANATHENÆ'A. Festivals celebrated at Athens in honour of Athena, tutelary deity of the city. The festivals were of two kinds: the *great Panathenœa*, held every fifth year, and the *lesser Panathenœa*, observed annually. They consisted of athletic and musical contests, followed by sacrifices and feasts.

After the *great Panathenœa* there was a solemn procession, in which the *peplos*, a sacred woollen garment woven by young virgins, was carried and placed on the statue of the goddess. The festival was so holy that criminals were released from the prisons on the occasion of its celebration.

PANAY. An island of the Philippines, the westernmost of the Visayan group, between Mindoro and Negros. It is of triangular form, about 100 miles broad and 100 miles long. It ranks fifth in size among the Philippine Islands, is mountainous but very fertile, yielding much sugar, tobacco, etc. The chief occupation of the inhabitants is agriculture, and staple products are sugar, rice, and copra. Capital, Iloilo. Area, 4448 sq. miles; pop. *c.* 800,000.

PANCHATANTRA (Skt. *Five Books*). A famous collection of Indian stories and apologues attributed to Vishnu-Sarma, better known as Pilpai or Bidpai. The original Sanskrit, of ancient but uncertain date, consists of five books which form so many sections, each preceded by a preface. It is one of the Indian books of knowledge, and was written by a Brahman for the edification and instruction of the three sons of a King of Dekkan.

The *Panchatantra* was translated into Pehlevi in the sixth century A.D. under the title *Kalilah and Dimnah*, into Hebrew by Rabbi Joel, and into Latin in 1262. The narratives are throughout interspersed with sentences, extracts from legal codes, maxims, thoughts, etc. The *Panchatantra* is one of the sources of the *Hitopadesa* (q.v.).

PANCRAS. The patron saint of children, traditionally reputed to have been a native of Synnada, in Phrygia. He was at Rome during the persecutions of Diocletian, refused to give up Christianity, and was beheaded at the age of fourteen years. In art he is represented with a palm in one hand and a sword in the other.

PAN'CREAS. The sweet-bread of animals; one of the viscera of the abdomen. In man it lies behind the stomach in front of the first and second lumbar vertebræ. The pancreas is an oblong gland about 8 inches long, 1½ inches broad, and from ½ to 1 inch thick. Its right extremity, called the *head*, lies in a bend of the duodenum. The *tail* or left extremity extends to the spleen.

The structure of the pancreas is similar to that of the salivary glands. It is composed of lobules throughout. The secretion of this gland is conveyed to the intestine by the *pancreatic duct*. This duct runs from right to left, and is of the size of a quill at its intestinal end. The *pancreatic juice* is a clear, ropy fluid. The functions of the pancreatic juice in digestion are devoted to the conversion of starchy elements into sugar and to the assimilation of fatty matters. It also acts upon proteid matters.

PANDA, or WAH (*Ailurus fulgens*). A mammal constituting a special family allied to the bears, found in the woody parts of the mountains of Northern India, about equal to a large cat in size. It is chestnut-brown in colour, and dwells chiefly in trees, feeding mostly on vegetable food, but also devouring insects and eggs.

Panda (*Ailurus fulgens*)

PANDANA'CEÆ. The Screw-pine family of plants, monocotyledonous trees or shrubs, with flowers unisexual or polygamous; perianth wanting, or consisting only of a few scales. The fruit is either in parcels of fibrous drupes or in berries. The leaves are long, imbricated, and amplexicaul. Aerial roots are a feature of many. They are tropical plants, and furnish edible and other useful products. The typical genus is Pandănus. *See* SCREW-PINE.

PANDECTS. A collection of laws, systematically arranged, from the works of Roman writers on jurisprudence, to which the Emperor Justinian gave the force of law, A.D. 533. The collection is also known as the *Digest*. The Justinian Code had been previously compiled by the order of the emperor, and the *Digest*, or *Pandects*, were designed to supplement it. The *Pandects* are divided into fifty books.

PANDO'RA. In Greek mythology, the first woman on earth, made from clay by Hephæstus, and sent by Zeus to mankind in vengeance for Prometheus's theft of heavenly fire. Each of the gods gave her some gift fatal to man. According to later accounts, the gods gave her a box full of blessings for mankind, but on her opening the box they all flew away, except hope. Epimetheus, brother of Prometheus, married her.

PANGANI. A maritime district of Tanganyika Territory, East Africa, comprising a low coastal belt which rises to western highlands, and is traversed by the Pangani River in the north, which forms a part of the boundaries with Wilhelmstal and Tanga. A branch of the Tanga railway line extends to Handeni. Pangani, the capital, is a coast town at the mouth of the Pangani River, and has a large trade. Pangani district was occupied by the British in Aug., 1916.

PAN-GERMANISM (Ger. *All-Deutschtum*). A German political movement which, from a psychological point of view, is the idea of German unity carried to its logical conclusion. Like Pan-Slavism, it is the expression of national pride, the aim of the Teutonic race, believing in its own supremacy over others, to unite the scattered members into one powerful organization, political, social, and economic. The foundations of Pan-Germanism were laid in 1813, when German nationalism was being fostered during the struggle against Napoleon, and the poets Arndt and Koerner sang of German unity and of a greater Germany. Metternich, who had only the prosperity of Austria at heart, was afraid of allowing the sentiment of nationalism to develop in the then loose confederation of German states, and for a time he succeeded in crushing it. When, however, Austria's splendour came to an end on the battlefield of Sadowa, and Prussia's power increased, and especially after the foundation of the new German Empire in 1871, the idea of Pan-Germanism developed more rapidly.

The Pan-German Union (*All-Deutscher Verband*) was established in 1891, and under the hegemony of Prussia an endeavour was made not only to extend German rule over the German-speaking populations in Austria, the Baltic provinces, Switzerland, and Bohemia, but also to propagate German racial solidarity in Scandinavia and Holland, and to carry German culture to Africa and Brazil. A policy of naval and colonial expansion was preached, emigration of Germans was encouraged, and German literature was systematically spread. The Revolution of 1918 has not abated the zeal of the Pan-Germans.

PAN'GOLIN. The name applied to the Scaly Ant-eaters (Manidæ),

Pangolin, or Manis

forming a family of the Edentate order of mammals. They occur in Southern Asia and Africa; have the body invested by a covering of imbricated scales of horny material; vary from 3 to 4 feet in length; and defend themselves by assuming the form of a ball. The tail is long, and the feet are provided with strong curved claws, which assist the animals in burrowing. The jaws are destitute of teeth, and the tongue is of great length. The food consists of insects. The four-toed pangolin (*Manis tetradactyla*) inhabits Western Africa.

PANICLE. A form of inflorescence differing from a raceme in having a branched instead of a simple axis. *See* INFLORESCENCE.

PAN-ISLAMISM. An Ottoman political ideal having as its basis the reunion of the scattered religious sects and political divisions of Islam under one head, for the resistance of further encroachment on Mahommedan territories by European powers, and for the ousting of European rulers from Asia and Africa. This ideal finds expression in Arabic by a phrase *Ittihad al-Islam*, meaning "Islamic Union" or Pan-Islamism, and was first mentioned in English in *The Times* of 19th Jan., 1882.

The Ottoman interpretation of the movement was simply a confederation of Muslim peoples on German lines and under Turkish hegemony, but was represented in the religious light as "a unification of the Islamic Empire under the spiritual power of the Sultan, as Caliph." In support of this policy the theory that there could be only one legitimate successor to the Prophet was widely canvassed, and it was emphasized that, while on the disruption of the Islamic Empire, the area of religious influence still continued to expand, so also did the political subdivisions continue to multiply.

Dissension was the true cause of Islamic weakness, but given solidarity, the consolidation of widely scattered sects and peoples under Ottoman hegemony, Islam might once again become politically formidable. The Sultan Selim I. (A.D. 1512-20) by his conquests (notably of Egypt) was successful in a partial enforcement of Pan-Islamic ideals, and Abdul Hamid II. made use of the movement politically to preserve the integrity of his dominions, and to secure freedom from European interference in purely internal matters, by representing himself and his nation, then the strongest Islamic power, as the natural champions of weak and oppressed Muslims throughout the world.

By this move he became a formidable enemy, and was much applauded by Germany, who had few Mahommedan subjects by comparison with Great Britain or France, and who naturally regarded the policy of Abdul Hamid as working out indirectly the salvation of Prussian as opposed to foreign interests in the Near East.

In 1903 a Pan-Islamic Society was established in London, and by 1911 (Salonika Congress) the Young Turk Committee of Union and Progress had repudiated their policy of 1909, and were canvassing all Muslim states under European control on behalf of the Pan-Islamic doctrine, urging all good Mahommedans to acknowledge the Sultan of Turkey as their legitimate sovereign, and emphasizing the Oriental fact, "religion first, nationality last."

Sectarian difficulties beset the reformers. Turkey had always maintained the questionable right to interfere in Persian affairs, "for Persia is a Muslim state." The great majority of Persians are of the Shiite sect of Mahommedanism, and are violently opposed to the Sunnite, or Ottoman creed. These sects are the most powerful in Islam, but the Shiite is the weaker of the two, and the Persian was urged by the Young Turk propagandist to "remember he was a Muslim and to forget he was a Shiite."

Under a similar scheme the smaller sects of Islam (Isma'ilis, Zeidis, etc.), which rendered any scheme of unification impracticable, were to be wiped out and their adherents incorporated with the great bulk of Muslims.

With the advent of the European War affairs moved rapidly. Turkey subordinated her foreign policy to that of a European power (Germany) and went to war, proclaiming a *jihad* that nobody would either countenance or join. The Keeper of the Holy Places, the Sherif of Mecca, entered on the British side in 1916, and in so doing he damned for ever the Turkish cause in the eyes of the already disgusted and Turk-ridden Arabs.

At the end of the war the formation of the Kingdom of the Hejaz, the disruption of Turkey in Europe, the occupation of Constantinople by foreign troops, and the general shrinking of Turkish power, extent, and prestige gave Pan-Islamism a blow from which in all probability it will never sufficiently recover to resume its place as a powerful, formidable problem in European politics.—BIBLIOGRAPHY: *Foreign Office Handbook No.* 57; G. Wyman-Bury, *Pan-Islam v. Arabia Infelix*. The subject is followed in the Cairene monthly, *Al-Manar*, published in Arabic, from 1899 onwards, and also in the *Revue du Monde Musulman* (1911-19).

PANKHURST, Emmeline. British suffragist. Born 14th July, 1858, she was the daughter of Robert Goulden of Manchester, and married, 1879, R. M. Pankhurst, barrister and advocate of woman's suffrage (died 1898). She helped to found the Woman's Franchise League (1889). In 1903 she was instrumental, with her daughter Christabel, in founding the Women's Social and Political Union.

Arrested in 1908 for breaches of the peace, she was imprisoned, but was released on grounds of health. Imprisoned in 1912, she went on hunger-strike, and was released. In 1913 she was sentenced to three years' penal servitude, but again refused food and was released. During the Great War she lent her organization to the cause of recruiting and munitions. With the extension of the suffrage to women in 1918, she joined the Conservative Party. She died 14th June, 1928.

PANNO'NIA. A province of the ancient Roman Empire, between the Danube and the Alps, and thus comprising Hungary, Yugo-Slavia, and present Austria. The Pannonians, an Illyrian race, were finally subdued by Tiberius, A.D. 8, and Pannonia became a Roman province. It had numerous towns, of which Vindobona (Vienna) was the chief.

PAN-SLAVISM. A name given to the efforts of the Slavonic races in Europe to promote union and co-operation. The efforts comprise a literary, a sentimental, and a political movement.

Patriotism and idealism gave birth to the movement, and it was strengthened by the feeling of the weaker nationalities that union was necessary. The Pan-Slavonic idea has existed for centuries, but it took shape only in the nineteenth century, fostered by Russia's defeat of Napoleon, and receiving a stimulus for the nationalistic tendencies of the century.

The poet Kollar summed up Pan-Slavism as follows: "The head of the dear goddess Slava (Glory) is Russia, the Czechs constitute her arms and hands, the Serbs are her two feet, whilst the other Slavonic populations are her weapons."

An important effort to promote Pan-Slavism, and to bring about a political union of the Slavs, was made in 1848, stimulated by the rival efforts at union made by the German nations. A Pan-Slavonic Congress met at Prague (June, 1848), and another at Moscow in 1867. In 1869 Danilevsky, one of the apostles of Pan-Slavism, published his famous work, *Russia and Europe*, wherein he outlined Russia's mission and advocated Pan-Slavism under the leadership of that country —the greatest Slav power, and therefore the natural protector of the weaker Slavs. "Russia," he wrote, "had a mission not only to civilize the Orient, but also to breathe the healthy spirit of the Slav into Europe."

Pobiedonoszev, the procurator of the Holy Synod, was another ardent advocate of Pan-Slavism, and the movement received a new stimulus during the European War, when all the Slav peoples united against Teutonic aggression. In reality, however, Pan-Slavism never possessed a reasonable chance of realization. The fact that the Slavonic race comprises nations so bitterly hostile as Russia and Poland, and the diversities of the religious creeds, as Greek Orthodoxy and Roman Catholicism, have made and will make all attempts to unite the scattered elements of such a race impracticable.

PANTELLARIA. A volcanic island of the Mediterranean, 70 miles south-west of Sicily, of which it is a dependency, included in the province of Trapani; length, north to south, 9 miles; breadth, 6 miles. It produces wine, olives, etc. Pop. 8873.

PAN'THEISM (Gr. *pan*, all; *theos*, God). The doctrine which teaches the unity of God and the world in the sense that God is synonymous with all-comprehensive Being, whilst the universe consists in modifications of Being. Goethe once remarked that he had never yet met anybody who knew exactly what Pantheism really meant. This was to a certain extent just, and the definition of Pantheism is somewhat difficult, as it has been conceived in so many ways by different philosophers.

Generally speaking, the fundamental principle of Pantheism is that there is only one Being, absolute, eternal, and infinite beneath the apparent diversity of things. As the etymology of the term indicates, Pantheism teaches that God is everything and that everything is God.

It deprives God of all human attributes, and identifies Him with the universe. He is the ever-creative, ever-active force of nature, the cause and design, the spirit, whose thoughts and nature are reality. He is present in every atom of the universe, in every grain of sand in the desert, and in every blade of grass in the field.

"He most gloriously," writes Heine (*Religion and Philosophy in Germany*), "manifests Himself in man, who both feels and thinks. In man God reaches self-consciousness, and through man He reveals this self-consciousness."

According to the different conceptions of pantheistic philosophers, Pantheism either denies any real existence to the world as distinct from the one absolute Being, or it considers the world as part of the Deity, flowing out from it, or again it teaches that God is lost *in* the world.

Pantheism is thus both a system of philosophy and of religion, and is either theistic or atheistic. The pantheism of the Brahmans, and especially that of Spinoza, who had "drunk divinity in deep draughts from the brimming goblet of nature," was theistic, whilst the pantheistic doctrine of Haeckel was atheistic.

In contradistinction to Deism, which teaches *transcendence*, the principal tenet of Pantheism is *immanence*. There is no personal, extramundane God, as anthropomorphic Theism maintains.

> What God would *outwardly* alone control,
> And on His finger whirl the mighty whole?
> He loves the *inner* world to move, to view,
> Nature in Him, and He in Nature, too.

The term Pantheism was first made use of by Toland in 1705, but pantheistic creeds existed long before. The earliest school of Greek philosophy, the Ionian, was pantheistic. Epicurus and Lucretius in ancient, and Giordano Bruno in modern times, were pantheists. St. Paul may be said to be teaching Pantheism when he says: "In Him we live, and move, and have our being." Pantheism has been taught in the *Upanishads* and the *Vedanta*, and Virgil clearly teaches Pantheism in the sixth *Æneid* (724-732).

The pantheistic doctrine has been especially elaborated by Spinoza (q.v.), who is considered as the father of modern Pantheism. Schiller and Goethe, Lessing, and Herder were Pantheists, or Spinozists, and Shelley clearly proclaims a pantheistic creed in the following lines:

> Yet not the lightest leaf,
> That quivers to the passing breeze,
> Is less instinct with Thee;
> Yet not the meanest worm,
> That lurks in graves and fattens on the dead
> Less shares Thy eternal breath.

—BIBLIOGRAPHY: G. C. Plumptre, *General Sketch of the History of Pantheism*; J. A. Picton, *Pantheism*; F. M. Cornford, *From Religion to Philosophy*; A. M. Fairbairn, *Studies in the Philosophy of History and Religion*; R. Flint, *Antitheistic Theories*.

PAN'THEON (or pan-thē'on; Gr. *pan*, all, *theos*, god). A celebrated temple at Rome, built in 27 B.C. by Marcus Agrippa. It is a large edifice of brick, built in circular form, with a portico of lofty columns. It has the finest dome (q.v.) in the world (142½ feet internal diameter, 143 feet internal height), and its portico is almost equally celebrated. Pope Boniface IV. transformed it into a Christian church, dedicated to St. Mary of the Martyrs (607). It is now known in Rome as La Rotonda. Raffael, Victor Emmanuel II., and other famous men are buried within its walls.

The Pantheon in Paris, for some time the church of Ste Geneviève, is a noble edifice with a lofty dome. Designed by Jacques Germain Soufflot, and constructed between 1764 and 1789, it is devoted to the interment of illustrious men. Among the great Frenchmen whose remains lie in the Pantheon are Voltaire, Rousseau, Victor Hugo, and President Carnot. The heart of Gambetta was buried in the Pantheon in 1919.

PANTHER (*Felis pardus*). One of the Felidæ or cat family, of a tawny colour, diversified with rosettes of black spots, a native of Asia and Africa. It is identical with the leopard (q.v.). The name panther (in vulgar language *painter*) is given to the puma in America.

PAN'TOGRAPH, also called **PANTAGRAPH** (from Gr. *pan*, all, and *graphein*, to write or delineate). An instrument consisting of four limbs joined together by movable joints, and so constructed that by means of it maps and plans may be copied mechanically either on the scale on which they are drawn or on an enlarged or reduced scale. In calico printing a pantograph machine, making use of this action, is employed to a considerable extent to reduce the proposed design to a suitable scale, and transfer it to a varnish-covered copper roll. While the stylus is moved over the design on the pattern plate a number of points cut out a series of reduced facsimiles in the varnish coating. The number of points can be varied to suit the number of repetitions of the pattern in the length of roller. Separate rolls are used for each colour. Afterwards the rolls are etched with nitric acid through the cuts in the varnish.

PAN-TURANIANISM.[1] An Ottoman political movement which first appeared as such after the disastrous Balkan Wars of 1912-13.[2] It originated in the dreamy ideals of a few "intellectuals" of Turkey, who desired the expurgation of exotic features, mainly Arabic and Persian, from the Turkish literary language, and the consolidation of the Turanian peoples as a purely Turkish state,

[1] The word "Turanian" was appropriated by European philologists to describe the languages or agglutinative tongues of Asia and North-Eastern Europe. The Persian word, *Turan*, is used in Persian mediæval poetry to indicate the steppes and deserts of Central Asia, in opposition to *Iran*, the peaceful, cultivated, and enclosed lands of Persia.

[2] The article, TURANIAN, should be consulted. A map showing the enormous range of the Turanian peoples accompanies that article. It may be remarked that only the Finns, Magyars, and Osmanli Turks, or those branches which have been in close contact with the Aryan groups of Europe, have been raised from their primitive state to a comparatively advanced degree of civilization.

inhabited by Turks, and healthily fostered by the old Turkish traditions. The scheme was advanced by peaceful propaganda, and the notion found favour with many progressive Turks, who were fired with the spirit of nationalism and had discovered their affinities with other Turkish-speaking peoples.

The Balkan Wars of 1912-13 raised Pan-Turanianism from an obscure ideal to a political reality, the essential principles being incorporated in the programme of the Committee of Union and Progress. At this time, also, was the focus of Turkish domination removed from Europe to Anatolia; Turkey abandoned her position and traditional dominance as a great European power, and began a new scheme of Anatolian regeneration and Turkification, in which many non-Turk and non-Muslim communities were either assimilated or else completely wiped out. During 1916 Turkish was made the compulsory language for every-day affairs, and, since that time, the break-up of Russia has rendered the unification of the Turanian peoples not only possible but intensely practicable.

It is impossible to think of Pan-Turanianism without considering the policy of Pan-Islamism. The two are diametrically opposed, but they are synonymous in their penultimate and final objectives, which are respectively (*a*) the regeneration of purely Turkish traditions and ideals, and the formation of a militaristic state on the German model; and (*b*) the aggrandizement of Turkey at the expense of European and non-Turkish powers. Recent religious (Muslim) revivalism has been decidedly anti-Ottoman, and Pan-Islamism, despite the Turkish masquerade, is anything but a religious movement. When the objectives are considered, the doctrine which finds most favour with the modern Turkish Government is self-evident, for these objectives can be attained more surely on the certain basis of a common language than on a doubtful uniformity of religion. Naturally, however, the Pan-Islamic doctrine has been maintained in the political programme, partly because the policy of Abdul Hamid has faithfully been followed by more recent administrators, and partly because it cannot, for obvious reasons, be scrapped.[1]

Turkish Pan-Turanianism is a modified form of Irredentism, and is the only ideal by which the Ottoman Empire may expect to expand and find some compensation for the vast territorial losses she has sustained within recent times. *See* PAN-ISLAMISM; TURANIAN; TURKEY; PALESTINE.

PA'OLI, Pasquale de. Corsican patriot, born in 1726, died in 1807. In 1755 he was appointed captain-general by his countrymen, who were struggling for their independence against Genoa. He organized the government and military resources of the island, and maintained a protracted and generally successful struggle with the Genoese. The latter being unable to subdue the island, sold it to France in 1768. Paoli resisted for a time, but was ultimately compelled to yield, and took refuge in England.

After the Revolution of 1789 he was recalled by the National Assembly, and made lieutenant-general of Corsica. Disagreements with the Democratic party in France soon led him to throw himself into the arms of England, and through his influence the crown was offered to George III. Subsequently he withdrew to England, and received a pension from the British Government.—Cf. James Boswell, *Account of Corsica and Memoirs of P. Paoli.*

PAPACY. The office and authority of the Pope or Bishop of Rome, which, it is claimed, extends over the whole Catholic Church, depends upon an interpretation of the words of Our Lord, "Thou art Peter, and upon this rock I build my Church" (St. Matt. xvi. 18), and upon the belief that St. Peter was Bishop of Rome, and that his supreme authority has descended to his successors. Recent research has tended to confirm the tradition that St. Peter visited, and suffered martyrdom in Rome, and the connection of the imperial city with the two great apostles, St. Peter and St. Paul, tended, after the destruction of Jerusalem, to make Rome the natural centre of the Christian Church.

The Bishops of Rome, at all events from the time of Victor in the end of the second century (*see* list under heading POPE), claimed the right of intervention in the affairs of other Churches. This claim was not readily admitted; it was entirely

[1] Despite this, the comprehensive notion of uniting the Turkish-speaking peoples, the scrapping of the word "Turk," and the introduction of the title "Turanian" have been widely canvassed. The Nationalists also favour the introduction of pagan pre-Islamic heroes like Jenghiz Khan and Hualagu to oust the Prophet and the Four Pious Caliphs, and Turkish Boy Scouts are permitted and encouraged to carry flags bearing the pre-Islamic Turkish wolf, although animal reproductions of any sort are prohibited by Muslim tradition. The translation of the *Koran* from the sacred language into Turkish has also raised a storm of indignation against Turkey throughout the Muslim world.

repudiated by the Eastern Church after the transference of the Empire to Constantinople, and the spread of Christianity in Western Europe led to the rise of national Churches (in Spain and Gaul, and among the British and the Irish) which had only a very loose connection with Rome. Even in Italy the barbarian invasions restricted the bounds of Papal authority.

The founder of the greatness of the Papacy was Gregory the Great, who began the missionary enterprises which resulted in the establishment among the English and the Germans of Churches bound to Rome by the closest ties, and acknowledging the complete Roman supremacy. These influences ultimately affected France, and, from the time of Charlemagne, the new Western Empire acknowledged the spiritual authority of the Papacy. The Papal claims were assisted by the forgeries known as the False Decretals, and especially by the invention of a story that the Emperor Constantine had conferred upon the see of Rome not only spiritual, but also temporal, authority in Italy and the west of Europe.

The rising influence of the Papacy in the seventh and eighth centuries was checked by fresh barbarian invasions and by the disrepute into which the see of Rome itself fell. From this condition it was rescued by the Emperor Otto I. towards the end of the tenth century, and for nearly a hundred years Papacy and Empire acted in harmony, the latter being the predominant force.

The second founder of the greatness of the Papacy was Gregory VII., who, after making important internal reforms in the Church, challenged the right of the emperor and other temporal princes to invest bishops with their insignia of office (*see* INVESTITURES). The conflict ultimately resulted in a compromise known as the Concordat of Worms, but it greatly increased the prestige of the Papacy. In the course of the struggle the Countess Matilda of Tuscany bequeathed to the see of Rome large territories in Italy, and Papal influence was farther extended by the circumstance that the Pope represented the feeling of Christian Europe in the Crusading movement.

The struggle between Papacy and Empire continued throughout the twelfth and thirteenth centuries, and brought about the fall of the imperial House of Hohenstaufen and an interregnum in the Empire. The greatest Pope of the period was Innocent III. (1198-1216), who made the influence of the see of Rome felt all over Europe, and also began the consolidation of the Italian territories of the Church into a great Papal State, which ranked as one of the powers of Europe.

A decline in Papal authority began in the latter half of the thirteenth century, and successive Popes fell under the domination of the growing power of France. This tendency, after a check in the time of Boniface VIII. (1294-1303), culminated in the transference of the Papacy from Rome to Avignon, which was the residence of successive Popes from 1305 to 1377. This "Babylonish exile" was followed by a series of elections of rival Popes, known as the Great Schism to distinguish it from a similar series of schisms which had occurred during the struggle between Papacy and Empire. It began in 1378, largely through a desire of many of the elect ing body, the College of Cardinals, to return to Avignon, and it was brought to an end in 1415 by the Council of Constance. A period of comparative peace followed, but the position of the Papacy as an Italian state gave rise to difficulties, and, in the end of the fifteenth century, a succession of Renaissance Popes were rather temporal princes than heads of the Church, and some of them, like Alexander VI., were men of notoriously bad character.

The shock of the Reformation seemed likely, at first, to destroy the Papacy altogether, but it was followed by internal reforms, and by the counter-Reformation which re-established the Roman Church in many parts of Europe and especially in Southern Germany. The decisions of the Council of Trent (which closed in 1563) gave a new unity to the Church, and the Society of Jesus proved a great missionary force, while the Inquisition crushed out Protestantism in Spain, the Huguenots ceased to be aggressive in France, and the growth of European colonies in South, and afterwards in North, America extended the sway of Papacy into the New World.

In the process of recovery from the first and most formidable effects of the Reformation, the Papacy, under Pius V., Gregory XIII., and Sixtus V., played a remarkable part, and the course of events in the first quarter of the seventeenth century seemed likely to restore to their successors the old authority in continental Europe. But the rise of the power of Sweden and Holland, and the aggrandizement of France, were inimical to the Papal authority, and Gallicanism produced a serious breach between Rome and Paris. In the great European crisis of 1688–89 the sympathy of Innocent XI. was with Austria and William of Orange rather than with Louis XIV. and the House of Stewart.

In the eighteenth century the political prestige of the Papacy declined, its moral influence was attacked by the philosophic movements of the time, and the general unpopularity of the Jesuits led to the suppression of the order from 1773 to 1814. The misgovernment of the states of the Church was notorious, and the French Revolution led to the loss of the temporal power and to the captivity of Pius VI., who died in exile. His successor, Pius VII., made in 1801 a Concordat with Napoleon, and three years later anointed him as emperor, but in 1809 Napoleon annexed the Papal States, and the Pope was a prisoner in France until 1814.

After the fall of Napoleon the Papal States were restored, but successive Popes had to depend on foreign military aid to maintain control of them. In 1848 Pius IX., who had been elected two years earlier as a Pope of liberal tendencies, was driven from Rome by a republican outbreak, and when he was restored by the French in 1850, he adopted a repressive policy. Nine years later the greater part of the Papal States was forcibly incorporated in the Kingdom of Italy, and the retention of Rome was possible only with French help, the withdrawal of which in 1870 brought about the capture of Rome by the Italians.

Meanwhile, Pius IX. had been asserting and extending the spiritual claims of the Papacy. In 1864 he issued a *Syllabus* condemning the tendencies of contemporary thought, and in 1870 his influence over the Vatican Council procured the promulgation, as an article of faith, of the dogma of Papal infallibility—that the Pope, when speaking *ex cathedra*, is divinely endowed with infallibility in defining any doctrine touching faith or morality, and that any such doctrine is binding on the Church. Pius IX. refused to come to terms with the Italian Government, and declared himself " the prisoner of the Vatican." Between 1870 and 1929 no Pope left the grounds of the Vatican.

In 1929 the Roman Question was settled by the signature of the Lateran Treaty between the Vatican and Italy. This treaty was in three parts: (1) a Political Treaty recognizing the full and independent sovereignty of the Holy See in the City of the Vatican ; (2) a Concordat regulating the condition of religion and of the Church in Italy ; (3) a Financial Convention, by which the Holy See received 750,000,000 lire in cash (about £8,000,000) and 1,000,000,000 lire in Italian 5-per-cent. State bonds, this being a full and final settlement of all the financial claims of the Holy See against Italy. Since the ratification of this treaty the Pope has, therefore, resumed his temporal power, and has even made a ceremonial exit from his retirement. The Vatican City is now an independent state, and passports to enter it must bear a special visé.—BIBLIOGRAPHY : M. J. M. Bell, *A Short History of the Papacy* ; M. Creighton, *History of the Papacy* (Renaissance Period) ; A. R. Pennington, *Epochs of the Papacy* ; F. Nippold, *History of the Papacy in the Nineteenth Century.*

PAPAL STATES. The name given to that portion of Central Italy of which the Pope was sovereign by virtue of his position. The territory extended irregularly from the Adriatic to the Mediterranean, and subsequently comprised an area of 15,289 sq. miles with 3,126,000 inhabitants. Rome was the capital.

The foundation of the Papal States was laid in A.D. 754, when Pepin le Bref presented the exarchate of Ravenna to Stephen II., Bishop of Rome. Benevento was added in 1053, and in 1102 Matilda of Tuscany left Parma, Modena, and Tuscany to the Pope. In 1201 the Papal States were formally constituted an independent monarchy.

During the Middle Ages various territories were added to or subtracted from the Pope's possessions, which were incorporated with France by Napoleon in 1809, but restored to the Pope in 1814. A revolution broke out in Rome in 1848, and the Pope fled to Gaeta, but he was reinstated by French troops, and Rome was garrisoned by French soldiers unto 1870. In the meantime one state after another threw off its allegiance to the Pope and joined the Kingdom of Italy, and when the French left Rome in Aug., 1870, King Victor Emmanuel took possession of the city, declared it the capital of Italy, and thus abolished the temporal power of the Pope.—Cf. H. E. Manning, *Temporal Power of the Pope.*

PAPAVERA'CEÆ. The poppy family of plants, an order belonging to the polypetalous dicotyledons. It contains about 160 species, mostly members of the northern temperate regions. They are smooth herbs, rarely shrubs, with alternate, often cut leaves, and solitary handsome flowers. The poppies are the most familiar members.

PAPAW' (*Carica Papăya*, nat. ord. Papayaceæ), a tree indigenous to Latin America, now widely cultivated in tropical countries. It grows to the height of 18 or 20 feet, with a soft herbaceous stem, naked nearly to the top, where the leaves issue on every side on long footstalks. Between the leaves grow the flower and the fruit, which is of the size of a melon. The juice of the tree is acrid and milky, but the fruit when boiled is eaten with meat, like other vegetables. The juice of the unripe fruit is a powerful vermifuge; the powder of the seed is manufactured as *papain*, a proteid ferment answering the same purpose. The juice of the tree or its fruit, or an infusion of it, has the singular property of rendering the toughest meat tender, and this is even said to be effected by hanging the meat among the branches.

PAPEETE. The capital and seaport of the Society Islands, in Tahiti. Pop. (1931), 7061.

PAPER. Consists of sheets of material prepared by the felting of fine fibres derived from various plants.

Historical Survey.—The art of paper-making dates from very early times. It appears that in the second century the Chinese and Japanese used bark and tow for this purpose. In earlier times written communications and records were inscribed on clay tablets and the waxed surfaces of wood or metal. The Egyptians used the unravelled stem of the papyrus reed and the dried skins of animals in the form of vellum or parchment. During the eighth century the Arabs were using linen and cotton rags for the manufacture of pulp for paper-making, but it was not until about three hundred years later that the art was introduced into Spain by the Moors. From Spain the craft spread to Italy at the end of the thirteenth century, and to France and Germany about a hundred years later.

The first record of paper manufacture in England occurs in Wynkyn de Worde's *De Proprietatibus Rerum*, printed in 1495 at Caxton's Press, wherein mention is made of a mill at Stevenage, in Hertfordshire, belonging to one John Tate. In 1588 Spielman obtained a licence from Queen Elizabeth to make paper at Dartford, in Kent, where some of the finest paper is still made. It was not until about 1685 that the industry was firmly established in England. The first paper-mill in America was erected near Philadelphia in 1690.

The method of manufacture was practically the same as that in use at the present day for the production of *hand-made* paper, such as is used for bank-notes, drawing-paper, etc. The rags were thoroughly cleansed, boiled, and beaten into a pulp with water to the consistency of cream. A finely woven wire sieve was dipped into the vat, and sufficient pulp removed to form a sheet of paper. A horizontal shaking motion was given to the sieve, which caused the fibres to felt or interlock, the water draining away through the fine holes in the sieve. The sheet or "water-leaf" was then placed between felt and subjected to pressure. After drying, the paper was dipped in size (to render it non-porous), and finally dried and smoothed by passing it through rollers under pressure.

Up to the beginning of the nineteenth century every sheet had to be laboriously made by hand, but at this time the first machine for producing paper in bulk in this country was set up by Fourdrinier at a mill at Frogmore, in Hertfordshire. During the last century the paper-making industry developed rapidly, partly as a consequence of the repeal of the paper duty in 1860, but mainly owing to the increased demand for printing surfaces.

Manufacture. — The supply of "rags" and waste from the textile looms soon proved insufficient for the needs of the rapidly growing industry, and other sources of supply had to be sought. Routledge's experiments with the esparto grasses of Spain and North Africa led to a new source of raw material for paper manufacture—the grasses, after passing through the necessary boiling, beating, and bleaching processes, giving about 50 per cent. of their weight of fine fibre. The straw of cereals and the fibre obtained by disintegrating coniferous and other woods are now also largely used in paper-making. The highest grades of paper are still made from rags; flax and hemp produce the most durable papers, followed by cotton, and finally by a mixture of wool and linen.

When rags are used, the first process consists in sorting them into different grades. Linens are separated from cottons and are sub-divided into various qualities. They are freed from dust by placing them into a revolving wire cage, and then cut into small pieces. In the next process the material is treated in high-pressure spherical rotating boilers with an alkaline solution for a period varying with the quality of the rags. The alkalies employed are either soda or caustic soda, and especially lime. This process serves to destroy colouring-matters and to decompose materials of a fatty and albuminous nature. When the boiling is completed, the liquor is drained off and the rags thoroughly washed. The boiled rags are then placed in a machine in which rotating discs studded with knives reduce them to small pieces. By continued application of this process, sometimes in another machine, the rags are finally reduced to a pulp, which after bleaching and further purification is ready to be made into paper.

Other materials, such as esparto and straw, require more drastic treatment. The boiling is carried out in stationary vessels under a greater pressure and with a strong solution of caustic soda, the liquor being circulated by means of steam. The excess of caustic soda is recovered by evaporation of the waste liquors and used again.

Wood is treated by two different methods. In the first the dressed logs are disintegrated and torn into fibres by pressing them, sideways on, against a large grindstone revolving about 200 times per minute. The shredded material is then sieved; the coarser fibres are ground in a mill and mixed in the wet state with the fine siftings. This mechanical wood-pulp is only used for very inferior papers, as the fibres are short and the paper soon becomes discoloured. The other method is of a chemical nature. The sliced wood is boiled under considerable pressure with a solution of either caustic soda or calcium bisulphite; this treatment dissolves the non-cellulose constituents of the wood, leaving the cellulose in a suitable state to break up into pulp by further mechanical means. This so-called chemical wood-pulp is of a lighter colour, and produces a better quality paper than mechanical wood-pulp.

White Paper.—For the production of white paper all pulps, except those prepared from white rags, require bleaching. This is carried out by treating the pulp, in a machine called a potcher, with a solution of bleaching-powder (calcium hypochlorite). Great care must be taken to remove all excess of this material after the process is completed, or the strength of the paper will deteriorate on keeping. The usual method is to add a solution of a salt, known as an antichlor, such as sodium hyposulphite or sodium sulphite, to decompose all traces of the bleaching-material which remain. The pulp, from whatever source it is derived, is then further purified by thinning it with water and passing it slowly through long troughs, called sand tables, where any heavy particles fall to the bottom. It is then strained by sucking it through a diaphragm containing narrow slits, which allow the water and fine fibres to pass—pieces of woody matter, and of rags which have escaped pulping, remaining on the upper side. The pulp is then allowed to flow on to a travelling wire cloth, which allows the water to pass through, the mass of fine fibres remaining being removed on a travelling band of felt. This material, which is known as "half-stuff," resembles thick blotting-paper, and is stored on reels or in bins ready for the final process.

In this operation the half-stuff is beaten up with a quantity of pure water until it is of a thoroughly uniform and milky consistency. Colouring-matters are added at this stage, and also filling or loading materials, such as China clay, barium sulphate, or plaster of Paris, in a pure and very finely divided condition. These serve to fill up the pores of the paper and to give it a more solid texture.

In order to render the fibres of a paper more or less impervious to water, and thus enable it to be used for writing purposes, it is "sized." This is performed by adding to the beaten and loaded pulp a solution of resin soap, followed by the addition of a solution of aluminium sulphate. This has the effect of covering the individual fibres with a more or less waterproof medium. The treated pulp is now run into a storage-tank containing agitators, which keep the material thoroughly mixed. From this vessel it flows in a regulated stream on to the endless wire cloth of the paper-making machine, which is of similar construction to that used in the preparation of the half-stuff, but has a finer mesh, and has also imparted to it a lateral motion or "shake" for the purpose of inducing the fibres to felt in all directions. Most of the water flows through the meshes as the wire cloth moves on. Suction-boxes remove a further quantity of water and assist in consolidating the fibres. If a watermark is to be given to the paper, it is impressed at this stage by means of a "dandy roller" consisting of wire gauze, and having woven upon it in wire the design of the watermark. The moist paper and the endless wire cloth then pass between felt-covered press-rollers, after which the paper is conveyed by an endless travelling felt between further press-rollers. The paper is then led over a number of steam-heated drying-cylinders, and finally passed between iron rollers in order to compress it and impart a smooth surface to it. Finally, the edges of the paper are cut, and the endless sheet is either wound upon a reel or cut up into sheets as occasion demands.

Hand-made papers are still used for certain purposes; the method of their preparation, which has been already described, has not altered materially during the last century. Such papers are often sized after the sheets are made, animal size being generally used for this purpose.

Blotting-papers and **filter-papers** are made in the same way as ordinary paper, but the pulp is left unsized and unloaded, and for this reason it is absorbent.

Cardboard is manufactured by laying freshly made sheets of paper upon one another, and firmly pressing them together while still damp.

Pasteboard, a similar material, is made by pasting dried and finished sheets of paper one over another till the requisite thickness is obtained.

Papier-mâché is chiefly made from old paper by boiling and beating it to a pulp with water, and mixing the pressed pulp with glue, starch, paste, or other adhesives, and forcing it into a mould. After drying, the articles are treated with linseed oil and again dried at a higher temperature, and finally gilded, painted, or lacquered. Papier-mâché is also made by pasting several sheets of paper on metal cores; the articles are finally polished with pumice-stone and decorated. It is largely used for making bowls, trays, boxes, and other articles where lightness and strength are needed, and also for the production of the mould or "flong" for casting the curved plates used on the printing-cylinders of modern rotary presses.

Carton pierre and **ceramic mâché** are similar compositions used in decorative work in place of stucco and plaster.

During the last few decades the output of paper in this country and in America has increased enormously. The raw material chiefly used for the production of newspapers consists of wood-pulp, prepared in America and Scandinavia, where wood is plentiful and the water-supply abundant. In England, Lancashire is the largest paper-making centre; some of the finest papers are made near Dartford, in Kent. Scotland possesses mills in the valley of the North Esk. In America the mills are mostly situated in the eastern states. Massachusetts produces a large quantity of high-quality paper, commoner varieties being made in the state of Maine. Recently large mills have been started in Newfoundland for the production of paper for the requirements of the modern press. The imports of paper and paper-making materials into the United Kingdom amount to several millions sterling annually. An enormous variety of papers is now made to satisfy the demands of the modern printer and publisher. In addition, large quantities of pulp are used for the manufacture of brown paper for wrapping purposes, and for wall-papers.—BIBLIOGRAPHY: H. A. Bromley, *Paper and its Constituents*; T. W. Chalmers, *Paper Making and its Machinery*; C. F. Cross and E. J. Bevan, *A Text-book of Paper Making*; R. W. Sindall, *Paper Technology*.

PAPHLAGO'NIA. In ancient geography, a mountainous district in the north of Asia Minor, between Bithynia on the west and Pontus on the east, separated from the latter by the Halys. On the coast was the Greek city Sinope. Paphlagonia was first subdued by Crœsus, King of Lydia, and afterwards formed part of the Persian Empire, until its satraps made themselves independent. It was ruled by native princes from 316 B.C. until subdued by Mithridates (63 B.C.), on whose overthrow the district was incorporated with the Roman Empire.

PA'PHOS. Two ancient cities in Cyprus—Old Paphos, a little more than a mile distant from the south-western coast, upon a height; and New Paphos (modern *Baffa*), 7 or 8 miles to the north-west of Old Paphos, situated on the seashore. The first was famous in antiquity for the worship of Aphroditē (Venus). At New Paphos St. Paul preached before the proconsul Sergius.

PA'PIAS. One of the Apostolic Fathers, Bishop of Hierapolis. He is described by Irenæus as a "hearer of John and a companion of Polycarp," and was martyred at Pergamus in A.D. 163. He was the author of five books on the *Sayings of our Lord*, all lost, except a few valuable fragments, which give important information as to the early traditions regarding the New Testament: e.g. that Matthew's Gospel was believed to have been written in Hebrew, and that the evangelist Mark was the interpreter (*hermeneutēs*) of Peter, and wrote to his dictation.

PAPIL'IO. A genus of butterflies (Lepidoptera), the type of a family (Papilionidæ) including a large number of species native to most parts of the world, especially South America. One of them, the swallow-tailed butterfly (*Papilio machāon*), is found in the English fens.

PAPILIONA'CEÆ. A division of plants, forming a sub-order of the Leguminosæ (q.v.), distinguished by the resemblance of the superior petals of their flowers to the extended wings of a butterfly (Lat. *papilio*). The best-known examples are the pea and bean, which are the typical plants of this division.

PAPILLÆ. The name applied in physiology to small or minute processes protruding from the surface of the skin, or of membranes generally, and which may possess either a secretory or other function. The papillæ of the skin are largely tactile, while those of the tongue produce the sense of taste. Papillæ, modified in structure, are found in internal organs, and possess secretory or other functions.

PAPIN (på-paṇ), **Denys.** French physicist, born in Blois, in France, in 1647, died in 1712. Having visited England, he was in 1681 admitted a Fellow of the Royal Society. The revocation of the Edict of Nantes preventing him from returning to his native country, he settled at Marburg, in Germany, in 1687 as professor of mathematics, retaining this charge till 1707. He is best known for the invention denominated Papin's Digester.

PAPINIA'NUS, Æmilius (Papinian). Roman lawyer, born under Antoninus Pius, about A.D. 140. His learning and integrity won him the first offices of state, and he was ultimately chosen prefect of the prætorian guards under the Emperor Septimius Severus, whom he accompanied to Britain. The Emperor Caracalla caused him to be executed in 212. In the *Pandects* are 595 excerpts from his works.

PA'PION (*Cynocephālus hamadryas*. A species of dog-headed baboon, akin to the mandril. It was held in great reverence in Egypt, selected individuals being kept near the temples, in the caves of which their mummied forms have been often found.

PAPPUS, Alexandrinus. Mathematician, flourished at Alexandria in the fourth century after Christ. All his works appear to have perished, except portions of his *Mathematical Collections*, which are of great value. They include geometrical problems and theorems, a treatise on mechanics, etc.

Pappus's Theorem is a fundamental result in projective geometry; it is the special case of Pascal's Theorem (*see* GEOMETRY) which arises when the conic degenerates into two straight lines.

PAPPUS. In botany, the feathery appendage that crowns many single-seeded seed-vessels, for example, the down of the dandelion.

PAPU'A. An Australian dependency in the south-eastern part of the Island of New Guinea, including the adjacent islands of the Trobriand, Woodlark, Louisiade, and d'Entrecasteaux groups. Papua lies wholly within the tropics; the northernmost point touches 5° S. lat., and the southernmost portion (comprising Sudest and Rossel Islands) lies between 11° and 12° S. lat. It is separated from Australia by Torres Strait, and has a length from east to west of 800 miles; area, 90,540 sq. miles. The coast-line has a total length of 3664 miles, of which 1728 are on the mainland and 1936 on the islands.

A mountain-chain rises in the eastern end of the territory, forms a great central ridge, and extends westwards as the Owen Stanley range (Mount Victoria, 13,200 feet). On the western side the coastal territory is low and swampy for a distance of nearly 300 miles. The mountains and much of the lowlands are afforested, and streams are many, the largest draining to the Gulf of Papua. The Fly River drains a large area of Dutch territory. It has a length of 620 miles within the Australian dependency, and is navigable by steam-launch for over 500 miles. Other rivers are the Turama and Purari.

Communications.—There are many good harbours and five ports of entry, viz. Port Moresby, Daru, Kulumadau, Woodlark Island, and Samarai. Communication is purely maritime—by large steamers every three weeks from Sydney to Port Moresby, thence by coasting-vessels to convenient ports. Port Moresby and Samarai have wireless installations.

Social Conditions: People.—The native Papuans are a people whose ethnological affinities have never been properly settled. As the interior of the country is unexplored, their number is only guessed at about (1932) 275,000. Their languages and dialects are widely varied. Some tribes have settled down to peaceful habits, and five missionary bodies are at work among them. The European population consists mainly of Government officials, planters, store-keepers, clerks, and miners. There were 1144 Europeans in 1932.

Currency.—Commonwealth notes are legal tender, and the currency is identical with that of Australia and the Motherland.

Education.—A number of missionary schools is scattered throughout the territory, and the attendance of native children is compulsory where English is taught.

Production : Agriculture.—In 1931 there were 256 plantations, with 61,219 acres planted, the principal crops being coco-nuts, rubber, and sisal-hemp. Secondary products are bowstring hemp, kapok, coffee, tobacco, vanilla, cocoa, tapioca, cinnamon, tea, rice, and maize. Natives are compelled by law to plant coco-nuts for home consumption.

Forestry.—120 varieties of timber have been catalogued. Sandal-wood is indigenous, and sandal-oil is distilled from its roots. Ebony is produced for export.

Indigenous Products.—These include native rubber (*Ficus Rigo*), sugar-cane, cotton plants, nutmegs, ginger, bamboos, palms, bananas, bread-fruit, edible nuts, sago-palms, and species of vegetables and fruits. Mangrove bark is exported for tanning purposes.

Fisheries.—Pearl-shell fishing is important; bêche-de-mer and trochus shell are found.

Minerals.—To date the following minerals have been discovered: gold (alluvial and river-dredged), copper, tin, lead, zinc, cinnabar, osmiridium, iron, gypsum, manganese, sulphur, graphite, chromite, lignite, and petroleum. Topaz and beryl are the only gems. Large beds of good coal are supposed to exist.

History.—Surveys of the east coast of New Guinea demonstrated to Queensland, and to Australia generally, the danger to her commerce which would be consequent upon foreign possession of the islands and coasts opposite to Cape York, and of the entrance to the splendid waterway inside the Barrier Reef. Queensland accordingly annexed the mainland opposite her shores east of the 141st meridian, but her action was discountenanced by the Imperial Government, and it was not until 1884 that the Protectorate was proclaimed. It was subsidized by Queensland, New South Wales, and Victoria until 30th Sept., 1888, when it was declared a Crown colony of the empire. On 1st Sept., 1906, Papua was placed under the authority of the Commonwealth of Australia, by whom it is now divided into eight magisterial districts. It is not an integral part of the Commonwealth.

—BIBLIOGRAPHY: *Stewart's Handbook of the Pacific Islands*; J. H. P. Murray, *Papua, or British New Guinea*; W. N. Beaver, *Unexplored New Guinea*; R. W. Williamson, *The Mafulu Mountain People of British New Guinea*; *Official Year Book* (Commonwealth of Australia, No. 14, 1901-20).

END OF VOLUME VII.